Christin is All

Christ is All

No Sanctification by the Law

Christ is all and in all (Col. 3:11)

David H.J.Gay

BRACHUS

BRACHUS
8 Ivy Lane
Wilstead
BEDFORD
MK45 3DN
e-mail: davidhjgay@googlemail.com

BRACHUS 2013

In the main text, Scripture quotations, unless otherwise stated, are from the New King James Version (NKJV). Other versions are not usually noted in the extracts. Abbreviations are as follows:

Authorised King James Version (AV)
New American Standard Version (1977) (NASB)
New International Version (NIV)
Today's New International Version (TNIV)
New English Bible (NEB)

OTHER BOOKS BY THE SAME AUTHOR

UNDER DAVID GAY
Voyage to Freedom
Dutch: Reis naar de vrijheid
Christians Grow Old
Italian: I credenti invecchiano
Battle for the Church (First Edition)

UNDER DAVID H.J.GAY
*The Gospel Offer **is** Free (First and Second Editions)*
Particular Redemption and the Free Offer
Infant Baptism Tested
Septimus Sears: A Victorian Injustice and Its Aftermath
Baptist Sacramentalism: A Warning to Baptists
Battle for the Church (Second Edition)
The Priesthood of All Believers
John Colet: A Preacher to be Reckoned With
The Pastor: Does He Exist?

[In Colossians 3:11] the apostle was arguing for holiness. He was earnestly contending against sin, and for the maintenance of Christian graces, but he did not, as some, who would like to be thought preachers of the gospel, resort to reasons inconsistent with the gospel of free grace. He did not bring forward a single legal argument... He knew that he was writing to believers, who were not under the law but under grace, and he therefore fetched his arguments from grace, and suitable to the character and condition of 'the elect of God, holy and beloved'. He fed the flame of their love with suitable fuel, and fanned their zeal with appropriate appliances... He... goes on to declare that the believer's life is in Christ, 'for you are dead, and your life is hid with Christ in God'. He infers holiness from this also... He then brings forward... that in the... church, Christ is the only distinguishing mark... Now, as the only distinction which marks the Christian from other men, and the only essential distinction in the new world of grace, is Christ, we are led to see beneath this fact a great underlying doctrine. In the realm of grace, things are what they seem. Christ is apparently all, because he is actually all. The fact of men possessing Christ is all in all in the church, because in very deed Christ is all in all. All that is real in the Christian, all that is holy, heavenly, pure, abiding and saving, is of the Lord Jesus. This great granite fact lies at the basis of the whole Christian system; Christ is really and truly all in all in his church, and in each individual member of it... This little text is yet one of the greatest in the whole Bible... It would not be in the compass of arithmetic to set down the value of this sapphire text. I might as soon hope to carry the world in my hand as to grasp all that is contained in these few words... Who can compress 'all things' into a sermon [or a book!]? I will warrant you that my discourse this morning will be more remarkable for its omissions than for what it contains, and I hope that every Christian here will be remarking on what I do not say; for then I shall have done much good in exciting meditations and reflections. If I were to try to tell you of all the meaning of this boundless text, I should require all time and eternity, and even then all tongues, human and angelic, could not avail me to compass the whole... How this... rebukes the coldness of saints. If Christ be all in all, then how is it we love him so little? If he be so precious, how is it we prize him so little?... Christ is all, my brethren, yet look how little we offer to him... God stir us to holy fervency, that if Christ be all for us, we may be all for Christ... Christ is all in all; therefore, 'put on, as the elect of God, holy and beloved, put on tender mercies, kindness, humility, meekness, longsuffering'. The exhibition of the Christ-life in the saints is the legitimate inference from the fact that Christ is all to them. If Christ is all, and yet I being a Christian am not like Christ, my Christianity is a transparent sham, I am nothing but a base pretender, and my outward religiousness is a pompous pageantry for my soul to be carried to hell in – nothing more. It is a gilded coffin for a lifeless spirit... Without Christ you are nothing, though you be baptised, though you be members of churches, though you be highly esteemed as deacons, elders, pastors. Oh, then, have Christ everywhere in all things, and yet constrain men to say: 'To that man, Christ is all in all; I have marked him; he has been with Jesus, and has learned of him, for he acts as Jesus did'.

C.H.Spurgeon

Contents

Note to the Reader

Several people have helped me in the writing of this book, especially by a critical reading of the manuscript. I thank them for all their comments, stimulating conversations and helpful suggestions. The mistakes which remain, of course, as well as the arguments and conclusion, are mine, and I bear sole responsibility for them.

I have continued with the procedure I have recently adopted, and put most of the extracts in a section all of their own at the end of the book – 'Extracts with Comments'. This, I think, has the advantage of making the book itself more 'streamlined', and easier to read. Alas, to my mind, it tends to diminish the force of what I want to say at the time of saying it. But there it is. May I ask, reader, that as you work your way through the following pages, you don't run away with the idea that I have grabbed what I assert out of thin air. Far from it. Where I have used the writings of others, I have documented my sources and given plenty of extracts; naturally enough, in the section with that heading! I have noted the relevant page number for the extracts for each particular chapter, and a book-mark left in the appropriate part should keep things flowing fairly easily. Of course, just because I cite many other writers, it must not be taken to mean that I overvalue the scholarship, ideas and views of men. I certainly do not take them as my authority – that is solely and entirely Scripture – but I want you to know, reader, what other men have said, both wise and otherwise.

To save repeating arguments and examples I have already set out elsewhere, in previous books I have referred to my other works. Since this annoys some readers, in this volume I have severely curtailed the habit, virtually dropping it in the main body of the text. Unfortunately, this may sometimes leave the impression that I have merely asserted a point without justification, and it also fails to let the reader know where he can find more on the matter in hand. Bit of a catch-22! So let me say it just this once: for the complete picture of my position, this book should be read in conjunction with my other works.

Sometimes when looking at a painting, you can tell that the artist has enjoyed himself. Although I have passed through difficult times with this book – writing it from time to time over several years – the Lord has blessed me very much in the labour, and I hope it shows. Of all my works thus far, this volume, I think, gets closest to something that A.W.Tozer wrote:

The only book that should ever be written is one that flows up from the heart, forced out by inward pressure. When such a work has gestated within a man, it is almost certain that it will be written. The man who is thus charged... will not be turned back by any blasé considerations. His book will be to him not only an imperative; it will be inevitable... The book... has to be written if for no other reason than to relieve an unbearable burden.[1]

My prayer is that God will bless those who read my book. Above all, may he help us all, by his Spirit, to live it out. May Christ be all – for all of us. If this book does anything towards making him such, then he must receive all the praise.

---

[1] Tozer: *Divine* pp11-12.

An Important Clarification

The word 'sanctification' will appear repeatedly throughout this book. Let me say how I am using it. And there is need!

I fully accept that the elect, immediately they are brought into Christ by faith, are fully, absolutely, perfectly, utterly, completely, irreversibly and permanently sanctified (have I stopped every loophole?) by the application of Christ's work to them by the Holy Spirit (see, for instance, 1 Cor. 1:2,30; 6:11; 2 Thess. 2:13; Heb. 2:11; 10:10,14, 29; 13:12; 1 Pet. 1:2; Jude 1). In this book, however, I am not talking about that. I do not question it in the least, but *that* sanctification is not the issue which concerns me here.

Not in any way undermining what I have just said – but, nevertheless, with equal vehemence in stating it – Scripture teaches that believers are new creatures in Christ, and that this new life will show itself – must show itself – by their growth in grace and in the knowledge of their Lord and Saviour, Christ Jesus. Indeed, this new life, and its development, is the cardinal evidence of their saved condition; without it, their profession is false (see, for instance, 2 Cor. 5:17; 7:1; Phil. 3:12-16; Col. 3:10; 1 Thess. 4:3; 2 Pet. 1:5-11). In other words, believers must be sanctified!

To distinguish this latter 'sanctification' from the former, let me make use of the phrase that has been commonly used for centuries, even though, I admit, it cannot be found in Scripture; namely, 'progressive sanctification'. In this book, however, I usually drop the 'progressive', and talk about 'sanctification'. Even so, I am confident that no well-meaning reader can misunderstand my meaning in any particular context.

I realise that what I have said will be a red rag to some. Nevertheless, I am unrepentant. I am convinced that when Scripture speaks of 'holiness, without which no one will see the Lord' (Heb. 12:14), it is not referring to that absolute sanctification which the elect have upon believing, but to 'progressive sanctification', to personal godliness; the context of Hebrews 12:14 is invincible proof that it is so. Of course, I am not suggesting that the believer can make progress in holiness by his own power, nor that his progressive sanctification will ever be perfect in this life – it must always be 'progressive', literally work in progress! – even so, I do say that Scripture calls upon the saved sinner to work out his salvation by God's grace in the power of the Holy Spirit (Phil. 2:12-13). Furthermore, while it is the believer's duty and privilege to obey God in this command – he is responsible for the 'perfecting [of his] holiness in the fear of God' (2 Cor. 7:1) – he has the assurance that, under the terms of the new covenant, the Spirit will inevitably move him to it, and enable him to do it, so that he can join the apostle in declaring: 'By the grace of God I am what I am'. Again, whatever good is accomplished by, through, and in the believer, he with Paul can only say it was 'yet not I, but the grace of God which was with me' that did it (1 Cor. 15:10). Finally, with the writer to the Hebrews, all believers must pray: 'Now may the God of peace who brought up our Lord Jesus from the dead, that great shepherd of the sheep, through the blood of the everlasting covenant, make [us] complete in every good work to do his will, working in [us] what is well pleasing in his sight, through Jesus Christ, to whom be glory for ever and ever. Amen' (Heb.13:20-21).

Introduction

As I have explained, in this book I am concerned with the believer and progressive sanctification. In particular, how can this sanctification be measured? What is the rule? Above all, the great question is: *How* is the believer to be sanctified? *That* is what I want to get at.

Before I go any further, however, I need to make one thing clear. Although I will say a great deal about sanctification, sanctification itself is not the goal for the believer. I hope my book does not give the impression that it is. Glorification through sanctification is the believer's objective (John 17:22-24; Rom. 8:21,29-30; 9:23; Eph. 2:7-10, for instance), and this to the eternal glory of God. True, sanctification is designed to prepare the believer for the glory to come, and to lead him to it, all in fulfilment of the everlasting purpose of God, but glorification is the believer's end. And what is this 'glorification'? When Christ returns, God will sanctify his elect completely, having 'predestined' them 'to be conformed to the image of his Son, that he might be the firstborn among many brethren' (Rom. 8:29; see also 1 Cor. 15:49; Phil. 3:21; Col. 1:18; 2 Thess. 2:14; 1 Pet. 5:10; 1 John 3:2). Meanwhile, sanctification is the process by which believers 'are being transformed into the same image from glory to glory' (2 Cor. 3:18). 'Everyone who has this hope in [Christ] purifies himself, just as he is pure' (1 John 3:3). Thus the way to glory is through holiness, but glory, not sanctification, is the end for the believer. Having made that important point, let us now move on to the topic in hand: the believer and his sanctification.

John Calvin set out what he called three uses of the law, the third of which is the one which applies here. He taught that the believer is sanctified by the law. The law is the believer's rule. The Reformed, following Calvin, have incorporated his third use of the law into their Confessions, they have written about it extensively, and they have frequently castigated any who dare to disagree. They do it to this day.

Well, I, for one, disagree. And I want to take the issue back to those who advance the law as the believer's rule. I want to show, from Scripture, that they are mistaken. I want to do more. I want to set out the biblical way of sanctification.

I am not only concerned with the Reformed. Many evangelicals, whether they know it or not, are following Calvin, to argue that progressive sanctification is produced by the application of the law to the believer, the law being his perfect rule of life. Then again, as always, there is the incipient form of all this – in that much contemporary evangelical preaching amounts to sanctification by the law, though such a phrase might not be used. Calls for sanctification are too often made in terms of external conformity, this being a consequence of (knowingly or unknowingly) making the law the believer's rule of life. I call this 'recipe preaching'; follow the instructions, tick the boxes, conform to the rules, and you will be sanctified.[2] Not so!

---

[2] To avoid cumbersome circumlocution, when I refer to 'the Reformed', it should be clear when I am including evangelicals more generally.

The fact is, whether overt or incipient (and the latter is more insidious than the former), *legal* preaching is far more common than many realise. There is not enough *gospel* preaching today. And, as a result, believers are impoverished. No, it is not a printing mistake. *Believers* suffer when the gospel is not preached.

By now, it must be obvious that I am not crossing swords with the Reformed and others over some trivial or arcane issue, a concern for the few. Far from it! If any professing believer is not concerned to know how he can 'grow up in all things into him who is the head – Christ', is not concerned to know how he can 'walk worthy of the Lord, fully pleasing him, being fruitful in every good work and increasing in the knowledge of God', and is not concerned to know how he can fulfil the apostle's demand and 'grow in the grace and knowledge of our Lord and Saviour Jesus Christ' (Eph. 4:15; Col. 1:10; 2 Pet. 3:18), then I doubt his profession. No! Progressive sanctification – what it is, the motive for it, and the way to produce it – is an issue of the utmost seriousness, and one which has far-reaching consequences, not least the glory of God. Surely, *that* must make it a matter of vital interest to all believers!

The Reformed and others say this sanctification is by the law. I disagree. Hence this book.

The believer and the law is a vitally important subject, about which many people are thinking and writing today, expressing opinions which vary immensely. Feelings run high. It is, speaking colloquially, at one and the same time 'a hot potato' and 'a thorny issue'.[3]

'Just a minute! You've gone off the rails before you start! What problem? There is no problem about the law. In Matthew 5:17-20, Jesus is categorical. He did not come to destroy the law. As long as time shall be, not one jot or tittle of the law will pass away. To break even the least of the commandments, and to teach others to do so, is the road to disaster. End of story!'

Well, if that really is all there is to it, then, indeed, that *is* the end of the story. Except... Except what? The overwhelming majority of us believers will have to change our ways – and pretty radically, at that! We will light no fire on the sabbath (indeed, we will precisely keep all the sabbath rules) – and that sabbath being from Friday sunset to Saturday sunset – otherwise... We will cancel all debts every seven years. We will stone to death every rebellious son. We will sacrifice, keep the feasts, observe the new moon, and so on, and on... Moreover, we shall have to try to work out what to do with all those passages in the New Testament – and there are plenty of them – that assert that believers are not under the law. Hmm! Food for thought. Back to the drawing board? Let's start again.

The believer and the law is a vitally important subject, about which many people are thinking and writing today, expressing opinions which vary immensely. Feelings run high. It is, speaking colloquially, at one and the same time 'a hot potato' and 'a thorny issue'. This is hardly surprising since, in the New Testament, we are confronted by a tension over the believer and the law. Everyone who has looked into the subject has found it so. But this is nothing strange. There is a tension, or seeming paradox, for

---

[3] The extracts for this chapter begin on p333.

14

instance, over God's decree to save the elect and his expressed desire to save all men. It is just one of a long list of antinomies in Scripture. We live by faith with such things. We have to go as far as Scripture warrants in resolving the paradoxes, but in the end we go on by faith.

Although the believer and the law is a contentious and complicated topic, it is, nevertheless, a rewarding study. More, it is an essential study because it impinges on many biblical and theological issues – the interpretation of Scripture, the continuity/discontinuity of the two Testaments, the interpretation of prophecy, salvation history – and, above all, the person and work of Christ. And, ultimately, this last, reader, is what my book is about. I hope you find Christ written large in these pages, and find *him* as the climax of all I say. I have chosen the title deliberately: *Christ is All*.

Moses himself told us: 'The LORD your God will raise up for you a prophet like me... Him you shall hear' (Deut. 18:15). We know that 'the law was given through Moses, but grace and truth came through Jesus Christ' (John 1:17). God the Father directed us to him: 'This is my beloved Son, in whom I am well pleased. Hear him!' (Matt. 17:5). Christ declared himself to be 'the good shepherd', drawing on the practice of a shepherd in his day – 'the sheep hear his voice... for they know his voice'. Thus it is with my sheep, said Christ: 'They will hear my voice... My sheep hear my voice... and they follow me' (John 10:3-4,16,27). At the transfiguration, 'they saw no one but Jesus only' (Matt. 17:8). And we have the command: 'Fix your thoughts on Jesus' (Heb. 3:1, NIV). So I say again, reader, make this request of me as you read my book: 'Sir, we wish to see Jesus' (John 12:21). My desire is to exalt Christ so that as many as possible might 'see' him. If you do not, I have failed miserably. *Or you have!*

As I argue for what I see as the biblical position on the law, and especially its place in the life of the believer, inevitably I have to paint the background. Consequently, my book has a negative element. I need to show what, in my opinion, is *wrong* before I try to set out what is *right*. After all, we know that Paul himself usually wrote about the law because he was moved to deal with trouble over it. Judaisers were attacking many churches in New Testament times, trying to get believers under the law; their teaching was the main source of error in those days. Paul confronted it. And how relieved and pleased we should be that God granted him the courage, the wisdom and the grace to do it! Above all, how thankful we should be that by the Holy Spirit he won the day. Or, at least, he established the truth in the New Testament.[4] Sadly, every generation has to fight the battle all over again. But this is to anticipate! The fact is, the apostle was affected by the background.

And the background for me, for many years, has been the Reformed view of the law; namely, that the law is the believer's rule of life. This was my position for many years, but it was severely challenged when I was preaching through Hebrews. Further reading and study clarified my understanding, and, preaching through Galatians, and enjoying iron-sharpening discourse with some fellow-believers, and, now, the writing of this book, have brought it even more sharply into focus. So much so, I am convinced the Reformed view on the law is wrong. And this, primarily, is the background against which I set out my view on the law. In saying this, I do not mean to ignore what I

---

[4] Some modern-day Judaisers, of which there is no lack, take a very different view of Paul and his letters (see, for instance, revelations.org.za/Passion).

might call the dispensational approach to the law, but that is not the background for me. I will, however, mention it in passing. Also, in recent years, I have had to face Judaisers who want to take believers under the law for both justification and sanctification; indeed, for everything, full stop.[5] Even so, as I say, I concentrate mainly on the Reformed view of the law, particularly as formulated by John Calvin, and especially his third use; namely, that believers are under the law for sanctification.

But, having already mentioned the Judaisers' attack upon the churches of the New Testament, and Paul's response to it, and since, because of that, it must play a significant part in what follows, let me say a few words about it. I will only flag up the salient points at this stage, but it is essential that we get off on the right foot. Truth to tell, there is a great deal of confusion about this issue, not to say slipshod exegesis, or even smoke and mirrors, in what has been said about it. Now it is not surprising to find that carelessness – not to attribute any worse motive – at the start, leads to all sorts of trouble down the road. As a hill-walker, I know by painful experience that to take the wrong path when setting out can have a considerable bearing on the rest of the day, not to mention one's feet. The fact is, Reformed teachers are not averse to saying that the Judaisers' attack on the New Testament churches was over the ceremonial law (I will have much more to say on this unwarranted gloss), especially circumcision. Furthermore, the Judaisers, so it is said, were thinking only about justification. In other words, their attack has no relevance for my book, it has nothing to do with the Reformed uses of the law, especially with Calvin's third use of it concerning believers and their sanctification. In this way, the Reformed can neatly dispose of the Judaisers and their doctrine, shunting it all into a distant siding and forgetting all about it.

Very convenient, but very wrong. In apostolic days, the Judaisers, it is true, *were* majoring on circumcision. But that was only the tip of the iceberg; or, to change the figure, the point of their particular needle. The Judaisers, if I may anticipate the Puritan dictum by 1500 years, certainly pierced with the needle of circumcision, but they had a much larger and longer thread to draw. True, the mantra of the Judaisers was 'unless you are circumcised according to the custom of Moses, you cannot be saved' (Acts 15:1), but this must not be taken to mean that they were addressing only the unconverted, or even that they were addressing the unconverted at all. The fact is, on hearing the report of the conversion of the Gentiles (Acts 15:3-4), some believing Pharisees demanded *their* circumcision (Acts 15:5). Further, consider the highly significant statement found in the letter which 'the apostles, the elders, and the brethren' wrote 'to the *brethren* who are of the Gentiles' (Acts 15:23-29). The writers deplored the fact that 'some who went out from us have troubled *you* with words, unsettling *your* souls'. What had those false teachers, those Judaisers done? They had told the Gentile *believers*: '*You* must be circumcised and keep the law' (Acts 15:23-24). Moreover, they had categorically instructed the *church* at Antioch: 'It is necessary to circumcise [the Gentile converts], and to command *them* to keep the law of Moses' (Acts 15:5). Putting all this together, we learn that in Antioch the false teachers taught

---

[5] To my certain knowledge, those who are once bitten by the teaching of the Judaisers find themselves on a treadmill of exploring, arguing about, and trying to practice laws, rules and regulations in ever-increasing minute and precise detail. What is more, it might start with sanctification by law, but it quickly morphs into justification by law.

the *brethren* to keep the law (Acts 15:1), and in Jerusalem the Pharisees demanded that Gentile *believers* keep it (Acts 15:5). Not the unconverted at all.

We must be clear about this. The New Testament churches knew nothing of an unregenerate church-membership. If any member was living inconsistently with a profession of regeneration, and would not respond to discipline, he was expelled (Matt. 18:15-19; Acts 5:1-11; 8:18-23; 1 Cor. 5:1-13; 2 Thess. 3:6-15; 1 Tim. 1:19-20). As the New Testament drew to a close, Christ rebuked churches that were beginning to anticipate what was to come in the years which followed – that is, grow lax and sinfully tolerant – and warned of direct intervention (Rev. 2:1 – 3:22). Indeed, even before that, he had taken a direct hand in discipline where the church had failed (1 Cor. 11:17-22,27-32). The notion of a mixed church-membership, 'in it to win it', 'a good pool to fish in', and so on, is nothing but the ruinous outcome of Christendom, utterly foreign to the New Testament. This being so, we must not read Christendom back into the New Testament. It is too easy to do it! Indeed, it is frequently done, and many hare-brained schemes have been devised to cope with the diabolical consequences. All this is totally wrong. It must not be allowed to colour our thinking here! In short, when the false teachers slipped into the churches (Gal. 2:4; Jude 4), they were attacking *believers*. The Judaisers wanted *believers* to go under the law. We must not shuffle this off to unbelievers. I say it again: the early church was plagued with false teachers who wanted to bring believers under the law.

What did 'the apostles, the elders, and the brethren' think about the problem? Peter said it was wrong to put a yoke on the neck of these 'disciples' (Acts 15:10), and James argued similarly, describing those to whom he was referring as 'Gentiles who are turning to God' (Acts 15:19). He was convinced 'that [the Jerusalem meeting] should not trouble' Gentile *converts* (Acts 15:19), as the law-teachers were doing by their emphasis upon Moses, agreeing with Peter who had described Moses' law as 'a yoke... which' they, as Jews, could not 'bear'. So why ever would they think of putting it 'on the neck of the [Gentile] *disciples*' (Acts 15:10)? As a result, 'the apostles, the elders, and the brethren' wrote to the Gentile believers, in plain and unmistakeable terms, dissociating themselves from these false teachers, 'to whom we gave no such commandment' (Acts 15:24). And, in the letter they wrote, they addressed their words to the Gentile '*brethren*' (Acts 15:23) concerning *their* behaviour – not the way they should address unbelievers. Paul and Silas read the letter to the *brethren* at Antioch (Acts 15:30-33), and decided to travel to the *churches* which had been planted and, among other things, read this letter to *them* (Acts 16:4-5). Finally, years later, James would recall that the letter had been written to, and had 'concerned the Gentiles who *believe*' (Acts 21:25).

The point is, it will not do to argue that the false teachers, and therefore the apostles in their response, were speaking only about justification. Justification is, primarily, a matter for unbelievers. When the false teachers declared: 'Unless you are circumcised according to the custom of Moses, you cannot be saved', they were addressing *converts*, *believers*, *disciples*, *churches*. And salvation cannot be confined to 'justification'.

Nor will it do to say that the Judaisers were talking only about circumcision, part of what the Reformed like to call 'the ceremonial law'. Read the verses quoted above – 'keep the law', 'keep the law of Moses'. The apostles, knowing the Judaisers were talking about the whole law, the law of God, the law of Moses, pulled off the wraps which the Judaisers had so conveniently draped over their arguments. Anticipating what Paul would later say to the Galatians: 'Every man who becomes circumcised... is a debtor to keep the whole law' (Gal. 5:3). The *whole* law!

Another thing. The Judaisers had a theology behind them. First, they knew that God had revealed himself to Abraham and to Moses, and that the Abrahamic covenant was a covenant of promise, and the Mosaic covenant was a covenant of law. Their theology was this: these two covenants are one and the same. That is what they claimed. They argued for the oneness of these two covenants. How do we know this? Although the apostle does not quote them, and therefore we do not have their actual words, we can argue back from the way Paul dealt with the Judaisers. The evidence is plain to see. Paul would not have spent the time he did refuting the notion of the oneness of the covenants if the Judaisers were not advocating it. And, make no mistake, that is precisely what the apostle did; he devoted considerable time and energy in taking the idea of the oneness of the two covenants, and showing how wrong it was. See, for instance, the last four chapters of Galatians. When we come to look at the verses in detail, I will show how vigorously Paul argued for the distinction in the two covenants; more, we shall see how cogently, how invincibly, he set out the contrast between the two covenants; further, we shall see how he made it as plain as noonday that believers, whether Jew or Gentile, are members of the new covenant – that is, they are the spiritual children of Abraham – and that without the law. And not only in Galatians. The same can be found in Romans, 2 Corinthians, Philippians, and so on. In short, in dealing with the Judaisers, Paul knew he had to take their faulty theology of the oneness of the covenants, and prove it false. And that is what he did. No! Well... he did – but that's not all he did. Let me spell it out: he took a firm grip of their theology of the covenants, and *demolished* it! Those who are *au fait* with what is to come, will know how relevant all this is in dealing with Reformed theology today – in particular, the Reformed insistence on Calvin's third use of the law.

In addition, as I have noted in passing, 'genuine' Judaisers have not died out. Quite the reverse! With the rise of the internet, their pernicious influence is on the increase, and, as I know only too well, they are succeeding in their efforts to entice professing believers into bondage – *and worse*! For all these reasons, the Judaisers in the New Testament continue to play a significant part in the background to the present discussion. So much, for now, regarding the Judaisers.

In the main, however, the Reformed view of the law is the background against which my book is set. Nevertheless, the end product is not entirely negative, since – while I do not pretend to have untied every knot – I bring my book to a close by making the clearest statement I can of the believer's rule of life. In all this I have set out to be practical and down-to-earth. I want my book to be *useful*.

Reader, although I have openly acknowledged my book's negative aspect, please do not misunderstand me. Although I say some strong things against Reformed teaching on the law, I do not intend to cast the slightest aspersion on the character, motive, intention, or practical godliness of those many believers who hold that view. Though I criticise their views, I hold such believers in the highest regard in Christ. We disagree on the law, yes, but I am one with them in the Lord in their call for practical godliness in the life of the believer. The fact is, as I will show, although Reformed teachers speak in glowing terms about the power of the law to sanctify the believer, when they come to exhort believers to practical godliness they almost always do as the New Testament does – *which is to preach Christ*. You see my point: Christ *is* all!

And, coming from the other direction, just because I agree with a man on any particular aspect of the law, it does not mean I endorse everything he has written on the subject, let alone every other subject!

I have said there are a variety of opinions on the law. At one end of the spectrum we have the reconstructionist; that is, one who thinks the entire law of Moses is binding in every detail upon believers today. At the other extreme we have the libertine, commonly called the antinomian. This is a difficult word, meaning different things to different people, and is often used as a theological swear word. It is a handy label to fix on somebody whose views you don't like! Nearly always the word is used loosely, with little or no definition. As with Humpty Dumpty, the word means just what its user intends it to mean! The truth is, an antinomian is, literally, one who is against law; he is lawless; he does what he wants. The law of Moses? Well... whether it is the law of Moses or any other law, the real antinomian has no regard for it whatsoever.

So here we have the two extremes in this debate on the law; the reconstructionist and the antinomian. And in between we find a host of different views on the subject.

I realise, of course, almost certainly I myself will be (falsely) called an antinomian. Of course, as I have hinted, I would not be the first man to find himself in this position of being mislabelled thus. I would be in honourable company, including Paul himself. But some may well pile on the abuse to label me a dispensational antinomian. With all the strength I can muster, I deny the charges before they are made, even though I know they will continue to be levelled against me, whatever I say. I wish, however, I could clear my name of the charge of antinomianism, and for this reason: I want my argument over the law to be given a fair hearing. It would be sad if my book were to be rejected merely because some critic had slapped a nasty sticker on the cover. Indeed it would be *wrong* to dismiss what I say by branding me with a pejorative term – which in any case is false. I am not a dispensationalist. I am not an antinomian. I deplore antinomianism.

I will do more than deny the charge of antinomianism, however. Reader, I will do what I can to reassure you that I am not anti-law. So much so, I have been actually accused of legalism![6] This shows how confused is this debate. But I will go further, taking the issue back to where it more properly belongs; namely, to Reformed believers themselves. To spell it out: while some of my Reformed friends will probably accuse me of playing fast and loose with God's law, I think they should get rid of the plank in their own eye. It is the Reformed who often play pick-and-mix with the law.

Strong words. I will justify them.

There is another possible outcome of my book. Instead of being dismissed as an antinomian, I might be labelled a neonomian. I flatly deny it. I do not believe that God has changed his mind, that he has established an easier law in the gospel, that men keep this new law in order to be justified. I strongly deny a consequence of neonomianism;

---

[6] This word – another elastic word – will occur again, and is yet one more of those handy words with which to abuse an opponent. It does not occur in the Bible, but I will use it to speak of a system of rules and regulations for salvation; in particular, for sanctification – or rather, for conformity to certain cultural or sociological *mores*.

namely, preparationism.[7] In fact, preparationism is a consequence not only of neonomianism. It has also reared its head among hyper-Calvinists, and plagued mainstream Reformed teaching. In fact, preparationism is more properly laid, as I will prove, at the door of the Reformed. Calvin – and many of his followers since – by their view of the law, and what underpins it, have taught preparationism to a greater or lesser degree. In light of this, may I suggest that any Reformed critic of my work, who is tempted to dismiss it as just another form of neonomianism, should bear in mind the proverb – those who live in (Reformed) glass-houses had better not throw stones!

Since name-calling, name-fixing, or whatever, seems to be endemic, let me say that my position might be reasonably pigeonholed as 'new-covenant theology' – though I have no wish to classify myself by such terminology. I will explain further as we go on, but, in brief, I maintain that while there is some continuity between the two Testaments, there is an even greater discontinuity between them. While I do not in any way dismiss the Old Testament – please read my book, and let me prove it! – I am convinced that we must read and interpret the Old Testament in light of the New – *and not the other way round*. I am convinced that the epochal watershed of salvation history occurred when Christ abolished the old covenant, and established the new. It follows, therefore, that the biblical contrast between the 'old' covenant and the 'new' must be given its full weight. There must be no talk of an 'old' covenant being 'renewed'.[8] Nor must talk of 'different administrations of one covenant of grace' mask – obliterate – the radical newness of the new covenant compared with the old.

The consequences are immense. These include entrance into the Christian life. *That* is no trivial matter! Another consequence is the one in hand. How and why is the believer to grow in grace? *That*, likewise, is no trivial matter! Reformed theology (covenant theology) has one answer. New-covenant theology has another. The great question is, of course, what do the Scriptures say?

Now for my book. In Part 1, I look at the basic terms involved in the debate. In Part 2, I examine Reformed teaching on the law. Part 3 is an examination of every major New Testament passage on the subject.[9] In Part 4, I set out what I see as the believer's rule of life, and tackle seven objections to it. After which, I give a 'Conclusion'. There then follows the large selection of extracts with comments. Finally, I list my sources.

Reader, as I have admitted, I do not pretend that this book is easy, but if it helps – without intending in any way to patronise – may I suggest that you will lose little, if, on first reading, you skim chapters 3 and 6, and the extracts? I ask that you give my book a fair perusal. More – do not fail to be a Berean (Acts 17:11). If you find what I have written contradicts Scripture, reject my words. Would you also write to me and show

---

[7] I will explain this word more fully as we go on; I have more to say on the matter, but for now let me say that I am talking about the insistence on preaching the law to sinners in order to give them an experience to prepare or make them 'fit' for faith in Christ.
[8] We must stick to Scripture, and speak of the '*old* covenant' and the '*new* covenant'. Speaking and thinking in terms of an '*older* covenant' leads to all sorts of damage. Yes, the new covenant is a *better* covenant than the old covenant (Heb. 7:22), but the Bible never says it is a *newer* covenant. Nor should we! These are not trivialities.
[9] But what about Matt. 5 – 7 (especially 5:17-18)? I have already raised this key passage. True, I have not given it a separate chapter, since I think it better to have a detailed look at Matt. 5:17-18 when dealing with the Sermon on the Mount in chapter 16 p236; see also 'Extracts' p498.

me the right way? I would appreciate it very much. But if you find any profit in these pages, give God the praise.

Finally, I realise that in writing this book I leave myself a hostage to fortune. 'Physician, heal yourself!' But I do not send this book out into the world because I have attained to the standard I spell out. I make no pretence of that! I do not boast about it, but it is the sad fact. I am a sinner. I fall short. The best closing prayer I ever heard was: 'Lord, make us as good as others think we are'. Even so, remember, reader, every sermon you have ever heard, every prayer you have said 'Amen' to, every hymn you have ever sung, and every book you have ever read, was produced by a sinner – a sinner, like yourself!

Part One

The Basics

Chapter 1

What Is the Law?

Before I plunge into the deep, I must define my terms, and give a brief summary of the various biblical meanings of 'the law'.[1] And there is need! Most evangelicals think of 'the law' as a moral system encapsulated in the ten commandments. This is a bad, bad mistake, and the source of much misunderstanding and trouble. True, 'the ten commandments' *is* a biblical phrase, but its use in Scripture is very rare, and the law is never defined in this way, never! The phrase 'ten commandments' occurs only three times in the entire Bible (Ex. 34:28; Deut. 4:13; 10:4), never once in the New Testament. Of course, the 'tablets of stone', and 'the ministry... written and engraved on stones' are mentioned in the New Testament (2 Cor. 3:3,7), but whether these are references exclusively to the ten commandments or to the entire Sinai covenant is debatable. So where did the idea – that 'the law' means 'the ten commandments' – come from? It originated with Thomas Aquinas in the 13th century, was developed by the Reformers, and reached its zenith in the following hundred years under the Puritans. It is still with us. And it confuses – and worse than confuses – the debate right at the start.

How does the Bible speak of 'the law'?

The two main words are *torah* (instruction)[2] in the Old Testament, and *nomos* in the New. Sometimes 'the law' refers to the entire Scriptures;[3] sometimes the Old Testament;[4] sometimes the Pentateuch,[5] or Moses' teaching;[6] sometimes the ten commandments (but whether just the ten commandments is open to question);[7] sometimes a system or universal principle;[8] sometimes the Mosaic covenant;[9] sometimes several of these concepts coalesce.[10]

Take Romans 3:19 as a particular example: 'Now we know that whatever the law says, it says to those who are under the law, that every mouth may be stopped, and all the world may become guilty before God'. The context tells us what 'the law' is here.

---

[1] The extracts for this chapter begin on p336.

[2] The meaning of *torah* is 'teaching', 'doctrine', or 'instruction'; the commonly accepted 'law' gives a wrong impression. We should, perhaps, think in terms of 'custom, theory, guidance or system' (see Wikipedia).

[3] Ps. 19:7, for instance.

[4] John 10:34 quoting Ps. 82:6; John 12:34 alluding to Dan. 7:14; John 15:25 quoting Ps. 35:19 and 69:4; 1 Cor. 14:21 quoting Isa. 28:11-12, for instance.

[5] John 1:45; Luke 16:16; 24:44; Gal. 4:21, for instance.

[6] Josh. 1:7-8; 2 Kings 14:6; John 5:46; 1 Cor. 9:9, for instance. 1 Cor. 9:9 is the only place where Paul used the phrase, 'the law of Moses', probably meaning the five books of Moses.

[7] Rom. 7:7,14, for instance.

[8] Rom. 7:21,23; 8:2a, for instance. 'The law of faith' (Rom. 3:27) clearly means the *principle* of faith. See chapter 16 p214.

[9] Deut. 5:1-3,5-22; 6:1; 9:9,11,15; 10:4-5,8, for instance. (I admit 'the law' does not appear in these verses – as a phrase – but they are clearly talking about it).

[10] Matt. 11:13; 12:5; John 1:17; 12:34, for instance.

It must refer to more than the ten commandments, and more than the Pentateuch. After all, in Romans 3:10-18, Paul quotes extensively from the Psalms, and from Ecclesiastes and Isaiah, all the while talking about 'the law'. Some, however, limit 'the law' of Romans 3:19 to what they call 'the moral law', the ten commandments. This is wrong. 'The law' here refers to the entire Old Testament, especially the Mosaic law.

To summarise: In Scripture, the word 'law' is capable of several meanings. It certainly is not always(!) the ten commandments. In fact, it overwhelmingly refers to *all* the Mosaic legislation. Let me give some evidence for what I say.

Moses spoke 'every *precept* [*commandment*, NASB and NIV]... according to the *law*... saying: "This is the blood of the *covenant* which God has *commanded* you"... According to the *law* almost all things are purified with blood' (Heb. 9:19-22). 'Moses came and told the people all the *words* of the LORD and all the *judgements*... And Moses wrote all the *words* of the LORD... He took the book of the *covenant* and read [it]... And Moses took the blood, sprinkled it on the people, and said: "This is the blood of the *covenant* which the LORD has made with you according to all these *words*"' (Ex. 24:3-8). What were these *words*, these *judgements*, this *covenant*, this *law*? Everything which God made known to the Hebrews leaving Egypt (Ex. 12 – 13), in the wilderness of Sinai (Ex. 15 – 16; 19:1 – 24:8, and far beyond), the covenant (Ex. 19:5), the words the LORD commanded (Ex. 19:7), the ten commandments (Ex. 20), the judgements (Ex. 21 – 23). Clearly, law, commandments, precepts, statutes, words of the LORD, judgements and covenant are all encompassed in the one word 'law'. Indeed, 'law' includes virtually everything from Exodus 12 to the end of Deuteronomy (the renewal of the law in Moab), including Leviticus and Numbers.

In particular, when Paul spoke of 'the law', he almost always meant the Jewish law, the law of God given to Israel through Moses as recorded in the first five books of the Bible.

There is another point: Paul frequently used the word 'law' without the definite article – a fact which many readers of the English New Testament may not be aware of, since the translators have often introduced the definite article to make the text read 'the law', instead of what Paul actually wrote; that is, 'law'. But the lack of the article, contrary to how it might seem, is Paul's way of stressing his concept of law, not the opposite.

In short, 'the law' in Scripture really amounts to the revelation of God to Israel, principally through Moses on Sinai, including (but far from being restricted to) the ten commandments engraved on the two stone tablets. And this is the overriding meaning I will attach to 'the law'.[11] With this in mind, I now turn to a more detailed examination of the Scriptures. I will show, first of all, that not only was the law given to the Jews, it was given *only* to them, and to *them* only.

---

[11] In saying this, I except biblical prophecies of the new covenant. As for which 'law' it is that fulfils such prophecies, see chapter 18.

Chapter 2

To Whom Did God Give the Law?

With regard to the law, Paul divides the human race into two.[1] All are sinners, but some have sinned 'without law'; the rest have sinned 'in the law' (Rom. 2:12). This is the biblical divide – those 'under the law', and those 'without law' (1 Cor. 9:20-21). Those 'in the law' have the law of God; those 'without law' do not. Clearly, therefore, the law could not have been given to all men. If it had, Paul's division would have been utterly meaningless; indeed, nonsensical.

Those 'in' or 'under' the law are the Jews, God having made known his entire law to Israel (Rom. 3:1-2; 9:4); those 'without law' are, therefore, non-Jews, Gentiles. We are specifically and repeatedly told that God did not reveal his law to any other nation but Israel.[2] He did not deal in this way with any other people (Deut. 4:6-45; 5:26; 7:6-11; Ps. 147:19-20; Rom. 9:4). The principle underlies Romans 9:30-32. We are told expressly that the Gentiles do not have the law (Rom. 2:12-14), but that it was given to the Jews, being 'the statutes and judgements and laws which the LORD made between himself and *the children of Israel* on Mount Sinai by the hand of Moses' (Lev. 26:46), God immediately reiterating the point with the closing verse of Leviticus: 'These are the commandments which the LORD commanded Moses *for the children of Israel* on Mount Sinai' (Lev. 27:34).[3] Right from the start, while the people were camped in the wilderness of Sinai, even as Moses was called up to the mountain to receive the law,

---

[1] The extracts for this chapter begin on p337.

[2] Israel became a nation in Egypt (Gen. 46:3; Deut. 26:5), particularly at the exodus leading to Sinai (Gen. 12:1-2; 17:2-14; 46:3,26-27; Ex. 1:5,7; 2:24-25; 3:6-8,10,15-18; 4:5,22-23; 6:2-8; 7:4,16; 8:1; 9:1; 12:2,17; 13:3-10; 15:11-18,26; 16:22-30; 18:1; 19:3-6; 31:13-17; 32:11-14; 33:13; Deut. 4:20,34; 16:1; 27:9; 28:9; Ps. 114:1-2; Ezek. 20:5-12,20; Acts 7:14,17), and confirmed at the giving of the covenant just before entering Canaan (Deut. 26:18; 27:9). This is when God distinguished them from all other nations by starting their calendar, giving them the feasts and the sabbath as an integral part of his law. 'What great nation is there that has such statutes and righteous judgements as are in all this law which I set before you this day?' (Deut. 4:8). Deut. 4:7 shows the same in his nearness to Israel and his willingness to hear their prayers. In short, Deut. 4:32-38. Israel's position was *unique*, not merely *special*. Now these things are clearly contrasted to the creation-gift of beasts, birds, fish, planets and the like 'which the LORD your God has given to all the peoples under the whole heaven as a heritage' (Deut. 4:17-19). The contrast is enforced further: 'But the LORD has taken you and brought you out of the iron furnace, out of Egypt, to be his people, an inheritance' (Deut. 4:20). And, as I say, one of the greatest distinctions God made between Israel and all other nations was to give his law to Israel – and to no others. The law divided, separated, Israel from all other people. See Ps. 103:7.

[3] This is not to be confined to the so-called 'ceremonial law' – see chapter 7. For now, notice how this blanket description in the closing verse of Leviticus includes at least the second, third, fourth, fifth, seventh, eighth and ninth commands (Lev. 19:3,4,11-13,16,30; 20:9,10; 23:3; 24:10-23; 26:1,2) of the so-called 'moral law'. As for the rest, the first commandment is implied throughout Leviticus – see in particular Lev. 26:1, the sixth in Lev. 19:16-18, and transgression of the tenth is pervasive – Paul found it so (Rom. 7:7), since the Jews thought it summed up the law, and to break it to be the root of all sins.

God prefaced it all: 'Thus you shall say to *the house of Jacob*, and tell *the children of Israel...*' (Ex. 19:3-6). God opened the ten commandments thus: 'I am the LORD your God, who brought *you* out of the land of Egypt...' (Ex. 20:2). And after the re-giving of the law, God could declare to Moses: 'According to the tenor of these words I have made a covenant with you and with *Israel*' (Ex. 34:27). (See also 2 Kings 17:13; 2 Chron. 5:10; 6:11; Neh. 9:1,13-14; *etc.*).

Nor was it the last time Israel was reminded of the fact. Solomon called Israel to 'take care to fulfil the statutes and judgements with which the LORD charged Moses *concerning Israel*' (1 Chron. 22:13). When Israel was removed from the land and taken into captivity, the king of Assyria replaced the children of Israel in Samaria with foreigners. These foreigners, it is recorded, brought their own gods, and their own 'rituals'. Rejecting the law of the Hebrews, they did not 'follow *their* statutes or *their* ordinances, or the law and commandment which the LORD had commanded *the children of Jacob*, whom he named *Israel*' (2 Kings 17:34). Addressing Israel, God could speak of 'the statutes, the ordinances, the law, and the commandment which he wrote for *you*' (2 Kings 17:37), promising Israel they would not 'wander any more from the land which I gave *their* fathers – [but] only if *they* are careful to do according to all that I have commanded *them*, and according to all the law that my servant Moses commanded *them*' (2 Kings 21:8). As with the land, so with the law – both had been given to Israel, and no others. When God revealed his law to Israel, he expressly commanded them not to do as the pagans did, but to 'observe my judgements and keep my ordinances... [to] keep my statutes and my judgements' (Lev. 18:1-5,26-30). Centuries after Sinai, God had to complain that Israel had not done this: 'You have not walked in my statutes nor executed my judgements, but have done according to the customs of the Gentiles which are all around you' (Ezek. 11:12), they had 'conformed to the standards of the nations around' them (NIV), breaking God's law (Deut. 12:29-32).[4] This makes sense if, and only if, God's (and Israel's) laws were different to the laws, principles, statutes, norms, judgements and standards of the pagans.

Asaph reminded Israel that the LORD 'established a testimony in *Jacob*, and appointed a law in *Israel*, which he commanded *our* fathers' (Ps. 78:5). Daniel, when praying for the children of Israel, could speak of God's 'laws, which he set before *us* by his servants the prophets' (Dan. 9:10-13). God reminded Hosea, concerning Israel: 'I have written *for him* the great things of my law' (Hos. 8:12). And 'God, the one of Sinai... God, the God of *Israel*' (Ps. 68:8, NIV), commanded Israel to 'remember the law of Moses, my servant, which I commanded him in Horeb *for all Israel*, with the statutes and judgements' (Mal. 4:4). In Numbers 15, God said the law applied to the Jews, and those who would be reckoned Jews – proselytes and sojourners.

To say that the law applies to the entire human race, is to render these statements and demands utterly superfluous and meaningless. What is more – and a glance at the passages quoted above will confirm it – we are talking about the law, the law of God, the law of Moses, the whole law, the law in its entirety. The law was given to Israel, for Israel, to distinguish Israel from all others.

Nor was this a mere quirk of history. As I have noted, God treated the Jews as special, showing special regard for them in giving them his law. This was his *purpose*. He gave

---

[4] If Ezek. 5:5-7 is right – but see footnote – Israel was worse than the pagans (Ezek. 16:47).

his law to the Jews *in order to* distinguish them from all others. Division was God's intention in giving the law to the Jews. Division! Separation! Distinction was God's great concern for Israel (Lev. 20:24,26).[5] And it was the law that especially marked the Jews out from the Gentiles, serving as a dividing wall, a partition, a demarcation between them and the pagans (Gal. 3:23-25 – note the 'we' and 'our'; Eph. 2:11-16). The law regulated their national and personal life in every respect. Finally, it was a temporary measure confining Israel until the coming of Christ (Gal. 3:19-24).

Moses, when repeating God's law in Moab, made it plain to whom it was given, declaring: 'Hear, O *Israel...* The LORD our God made a covenant with *us* in Horeb... He said: "I am the LORD your God who brought you out of the land of Egypt, out of the house of bondage"' (Deut. 5:1-2,5-6). God said 'Israel', and he meant Israel, and only Israel. It was only Israel whom he had delivered from Egypt.[6] But not only was the preface to the ten commandments peculiar to Israel. The fourth commandment concerned the sabbath which was a special sign for Israel (Ex. 31:13,16-17; Ezek. 20:12,20), and the fifth commandment referred to the land promised to Israel. In addition, the overwhelming bulk of the hundreds of other commandments contained in the law were spelled out in terms which belonged only to Israel. In short, Gentiles were not brought out of Egypt – in fact many of them (that is, the Egyptians) perished in Egypt or the Red Sea.[7] Gentiles were not given the sabbath as a special sign that they were the people of God. Gentiles were not given the pillar of cloud and fire. Gentiles were not given the manna. Gentiles were not given the promised land – the truth is, they had to be removed from it. Gentiles were not given the ordinances of the tabernacle. And so on. As just one example of how these things are linked, take Nehemiah 9:5-15.

Sadly, all this has too often been forgotten, and the law which was given uniquely to Israel, and applied only to them, has been mistakenly applied to Gentiles in the gospel age, to the confusion of both law and gospel.[8]

What is more, not only did God at Sinai give his law to Israel, and only to Israel, but prior to Sinai, nobody had the law – not even the patriarchs (Deut. 5:3; Rom. 5:13).[9] Notice how explicit Moses was at the repetition of the law in Moab, when reminding the Israelites of the first giving (and its re-giving) of the law at Horeb (Sinai): God did not make the covenant 'with our fathers, but with us' (Deut. 5:3). Who were these 'fathers'? and who were the 'us'? The 'fathers' were the patriarchs and their descendants who had died before the giving of the law at Sinai; God did not give his law to them. The 'us' were the Israelites – the people (with their children) who, having been delivered from Egypt, were gathered as the nation of Israel at Sinai – it was to them that God originally gave the law, and it was to their children that he was now renewing it in Moab. That generation of Hebrews at Sinai, therefore, was the first to receive the law. The patriarchs – the 'fathers' – who lived before the children of Jacob

---

[5] God's presence also distinguished them from all other people (Ex. 33:16).

[6] The exodus from Egypt continued to preface references to the law. See 2 Kings 17:36, for instance.

[7] Some pagans had joined the Israelites as proselytes (Ex. 12:38,48-49; see Neh. 10:28; Est. 8:17; Isa. 56:3).

[8] See chapter 7.

[9] As I have said, Israel *as a nation* did not exist before the exodus and the giving of the law. The giving of the law was a vital aspect of *making* them into a nation.

even entered Egypt, let alone left it – did not have the law. The song of Moses, when he 'blessed the children of Israel before his death', is plain: 'The LORD came from Sinai, and dawned on them from Seir... from his right hand came a fiery law for them... Moses commanded a law for us, a heritage of the congregation of Jacob... Levi... shall teach Jacob your judgements, and Israel your law' (Deut. 33:1-4,8,10).[10] (See also Deut. 11:1-7; 29:9-15).[11]

That nobody had the law before Sinai is clear – since Paul expressly pointed out that the law came – 'was added' – 430 years after God's covenant with Abraham (Gal. 3:16-17,19). It was *revealed* at Sinai; it was not *renewed*. How can it be claimed that God gave the law to Adam at creation, or to the patriarchs? Yet many do say it! No! As Christ said, when replying to the Pharisees' question over the divorce-certificate regulation introduced by Moses (Deut. 24:1-4): 'From the beginning [Adam] it was not so' (Matt. 19:7-8). The law was given to Moses 430 years *after* the promise to Abraham, not given to Adam hundreds of years *before* Abraham. In stressing this, I am not straining out arithmetical or historical gnats. To say that Adam was given the Mosaic law is to miss a point of major consequence, contradicting Paul's argument in Romans 5 and Galatians 3, to which I shall return.[12] The law was given to Moses long after God had revealed his saving purpose in and to Abraham.

This is a point of such importance, I must take a few moments to explain what I am talking about.

The eschatological importance of the epoch of the law

This point – the place of the law in salvation history, the eschatological importance of the epoch of the law – cannot be over-stressed. This word 'eschatological' will come again and again in these pages. Let me explain how I am using it. I am thinking of the way in which God, in time, works out his eternal decree to save his elect, and thus exalt his Son in their final glorification. I have in mind the way God arranges everything to bring about his purpose, the place every last thing has in that great plan. 'Salvation history' is one of the great themes (the *greatest* theme?) of the Bible. It permeates Romans 3 – 11 and Galatians 3 – 4, for example. So what is this 'salvation history' that I am talking about? The 'salvation' aspect is God's redemption of his elect, culminating in their eternal glorification in the image of Christ. But what of the 'history'? This needs nuancing. God decreed the redemption of his elect – the purpose, means and ends of their redemption – in eternity, but he is accomplishing it in time, as a part of history. Adam, the promise to Abraham, the law at Sinai, the coming, life, death, resurrection and ascension of Christ, Pentecost, the return of Christ, and so on, are 'milestones' in this historical process which is divided into two great ages, two

---

[10] Not only did the law have a beginning on Sinai; it had an end-point also, and that by God's intention. Paul said the law 'entered' the Jewish world at the time of the exodus (Rom. 5:20; Gal. 3:17,19), as a temporary system for the Jews, to last only until Christ came (Gal. 3:19), when he fulfilled it, thus bringing it to the end God had designed for it (Matt. 5:17-18; Rom. 10:4; 2 Cor. 3:7,11; Heb. 7:18; 8:13; 9:8-9). Right from the start, it was 'fading away' (2 Cor. 3:11,13, NIV). I will return to this vital point.

[11] The words, 'him who is not here with us today' (Deut. 29:14-15), refer to the descendants of the Israelites, not to all the rest of the human race.

[12] Adam, of course, was given his own commandment which he broke (Rom. 5:14).

great eras, two great dispensations or epochs – before Christ and after Christ.[13] Everything centres on Christ and his work. He (in his death, burial and resurrection) is the watershed of the two ages, the climax of all history, including and especially salvation history.

The two ages in question are very different. Adam is the head, the founder, of one age; Christ, of the other (Rom. 5:12-19). Adam's age is characterised by flesh, sin, law and death.[14] Christ's age is characterised by the Spirit, righteousness, grace and life. All humanity is by birth united to Adam, and comes under the regime of the first age through Adam's sin. All the elect are united to Christ (from eternity, by God's decree; in experience, through faith in Christ), and come under the regime of the new age in, by and through Christ's death, burial and resurrection.

It is at this point that the time element of the word 'history' needs nuancing. The truth is, the two ages are running alongside each other, and have done so since the beginning of salvation history. It is not that Adam's age lasted until Christ's resurrection; Adam's age is still with us. That is why I am using the present tense: Adam's age *is* characterised by flesh, sin and law. All humanity *is* by birth united to Adam and *comes* under the regime of the first age through Adam's sin – *is* not *was*. So when I speak about salvation history, I am thinking of two ages, yes, but not merely in the sense of time. Rather, I am thinking more particularly in terms of their characteristics. I am thinking of two realms, two regimes. The old, Adamic, age or realm is the age or realm of the flesh, sin, law and death. The new, Christian, age or realm is the age or realm of the Spirit, righteousness, grace and life. The work of Christ took place in time, in history, and was the historical break-point or watershed for these two ages or realms, certainly, but for any particular individual the transformation comes at the point of saving faith. Conversion brings a change of regime, a change of age, a change of covenant. 'If anyone is in Christ, he is a new creation; old things have passed away; behold, all things have become new' (2 Cor. 5:17). Speaking to believers, Paul could declare: 'The Father... has delivered us from the power of darkness and conveyed [transferred] us into the kingdom of the Son of his love' (Col. 1:12-13). Peter: 'You are a chosen generation, a royal priesthood, a holy nation, his own special people, that you may proclaim the praises of him who called you out of darkness into his marvellous light; who once were not a people but are now the people of God, who had not obtained mercy but now have obtained mercy' (1 Pet. 2:9-10).

And when and what will be the culmination of salvation history? That, too, centres on Christ. The culmination will be when Christ 'delivers the kingdom to God the Father... that God may be all in all' (1 Cor. 15:24-28).

So when I talk of the 'eschatological significance of the epoch of the law in salvation history', I mean the status of the law in this scheme of salvation, how it fits into God's accomplishment of salvation – that is, its place both in time and characteristics. The law was given at a particular time and lasted for a limited time and for a specified purpose. What was its role? What is its role today? In other words, I am

---

[13] I am leaving aside the eternal age following the second coming of Christ – which lies outside history – to concentrate on 'this present time' (Rom. 8:18) in contrast to the age preceding it.
[14] I am not contradicting myself – see below; law characterised Adam's age even though he was not given the law of Moses. I will explain.

speaking about the law in two senses – historical and experiential – historical, for humanity; experiential, for the individual.

Having explained what I mean by the place of the law in salvation history, let me take up my main theme once again. The law, the whole law, was given to the Jews, for the Jews, at Sinai. How fitting, therefore, for Paul to call it 'our fathers' law', 'the law of the Jews' (Acts 22:3; 25:8).[15] When addressing Felix, Paul could easily link his 'worship [of] the God of my fathers' with 'the law and... the prophets' (Acts 24:14). How apt, therefore, was his reminder to the Jews – as distinct from the Gentiles – that they had the law (Rom. 2:27). How pointless if all men had it!

Think of the way in which Paul preached to the Gentiles.[16] Think of his experience at Lystra (Acts 14:11-18). The Gentiles were about to worship him and Barnabas. How did the brothers stop the pagans? What arguments did they use? Did they cite the first and second commandments? They did not! Instead, from nature they challenged pagan folly in trying to worship them. In effect, they asked: 'Does not nature teach you?'[17] If the Gentiles had been given the law, why did Paul not quote it against them? The fact is, since the Gentiles did not have the law, Paul could not use it in his approach to them, and he made no attempt to do so. The same goes for his preaching to the Athenians in the Areopagus (Acts 17:18-34). Paul used what the pagans were familiar with.[18]

Compare this approach with Christ addressing the rich young Jew (Matt. 19:16-22).[19] Think of Peter preaching to 'Jews and proselytes' (Acts 2:10); he was able to quote freely from the Old Testament (Acts 2:16-21,25-31,34-35). Again, when preaching to the Jews in the temple (Acts 3:11-26), he referred to Moses and 'all the prophets, from Samuel and those who follow, as many as have spoken'. In particular, he pointed them to 'the covenant which God made with our fathers' (Acts 3:18,22-26), and later quoted the Psalms (Acts 4:11). Think of Stephen's approach when he was preaching to the Jews: 'You... who have received the law', he said (Acts 7:52-53). Likewise, Paul used the law when preaching to the Jews (Acts 13:39; 22:3,12; 23:3,5; 28:23, for instance) – as in his defence against the Jews (Acts 24:14; 25:7-8), speaking of 'our people' and 'the customs of our fathers' (Acts 28:17). *But never once did he use*

---

[15] Peter called it 'our law' (that is, of the Jews, as opposed to belonging to you) when speaking to a Gentile (Acts 10:28, NIV).

[16] In chapters 4 and 9, I will more fully question and probe the Reformed claim that the preaching of the law must precede the preaching of the gospel to Gentile sinners.

[17] Compare 1 Cor. 11:14.

[18] I do not say there are no Old Testament echoes whatsoever in these addresses. After all, Paul, a converted Jew, was steeped in those Scriptures, including the law. Naturally, he thought and spoke in such terms. Compare, for instance, Acts 14:15 with Ex. 20:11. But although he *thought* like this, never once in these addresses did Paul explicitly quote the Old Testament – which the pagans did not know – yet he quoted a Greek poet (Acts 17:28) – which they did know. See also Tit. 1:12. Paul's *arguments*, of course, were Christian, not pagan. Here is the lesson. A preacher must use terms which his hearers can understand – or else explain them. He has to adjust his language to suit his hearers, not the other way around. See chapter 9.

[19] Incidentally, as I will show, the Reformed like to think preaching what they like to call 'the moral law' (the ten commandments) prepares sinners for Christ. But when addressing the rich young Jew, Christ used all the law, not just sixteen verses of it! Note his use of Lev. 19:18.

the law when addressing Gentile unbelievers. Why not? Because he only used the law when he could say: 'I speak to those who know the law' (Rom. 7:1).

None of this was an accident. The preachers of the New Testament knew where their unconverted hearers were coming from. They knew that the Jews had the law, and therefore the gospel preachers were able to use it. The Gentiles did not have the law, so they did not refer them to it. In this, they were following Amos who, addressing the nations, Damascus, Gaza, Tyre, Edom, Ammon, Moab, Judah and Israel, reproved them for their sins (Amos 1:1 – 2:16).[20] Not once did the prophet mention the law when speaking to pagans, but on turning to Judah he immediately complained that 'they have despised the law of the LORD, and have not kept his commandments' (Amos 2:4).[21]

The overtones of James' statement in Acts 15 are unmistakeable: 'Moses has had throughout many generations those who preach him in every city, being read in the synagogues every sabbath', he declared (Acts 15:21). 'Synagogues' and 'sabbath' are not Gentiles terms![22] Years later, when Paul arrived at Jerusalem, James told him about the believing Jews in Jerusalem who 'have been informed about you that you teach all the Jews who are among the Gentiles to forsake Moses' (Acts 21:21-25). Paul did not deny it.[23] The implication is clear. The Jews were under Moses; the Gentiles were not.[24] Note further the contrast between Paul's actions (as a Jew) and the requirements laid upon Gentiles, as recorded in Acts 21:21-25. As the apostle explained: 'To the Jews I became as a Jew... to those who are under the law, as under the law... to those who are without law, as without law'. Why? In order to 'win the more... I do [this] for the gospel's sake' (1 Cor. 9:19-23).

Acts 2:23 is very interesting in this connection. Peter, preaching Christ, told the Jewish crowd on the day of Pentecost: 'You have taken [him] by lawless hands, have crucified [him], and put [him] to death'. The Jews were responsible for crucifying Christ but, to do the dirty work, they used Roman hands, Gentile hands, 'lawless hands'. The NASB, translating the phrase, 'by the hands of godless men', has a

---

[20] See also Ezek. 25 – 30, for instance.

[21] I admit Amos did not explicitly refer to the law when addressing Israel at this time, although he alluded to it. The point is, however, the prophets often reproved Israel, but never pagan nations, for breaking the law. When Isaiah spoke to the 'rulers of Sodom' and told them to 'give ear to the law of our God', and to the 'people of Gomorrah' concerning sacrifices (Isa. 1:10-11), he was being ironical. He was in fact addressing Judah, calling Judah a virtual Sodom and Gomorrah – as the context makes plain. 'They declare their sin *as* Sodom' (Isa. 3:9). As God, through Jeremiah, said of Jerusalem: 'All of them are *like* Sodom to me, and her inhabitants *like* Gomorrah' (Jer. 23:14). See Deut. 29:23; Amos 9:7; Rev. 11:8. Returning to Amos, while it is true the prophet did not reprove Israel specifically for breaking the law, he did speak of them as distinct from the nations in having the prophets (Amos 2:11; 3:7-8), being chosen (Amos 3:2); having the feasts (Amos 5:21-22,25), being the chief nation (Amos 6:1).

[22] See Acts 22:12,19; 26:11; *etc*.

[23] A week later, catching sight of Paul in the temple, the (unbelieving) Jews from Asia stirred up the crowd, vociferously complaining that 'this is the man who teaches all men everywhere against the people, the law, and this place' (Acts 21:28).

[24] To develop this: Would Paul tell Jews to forsake Moses, and yet – allowing for sake of argument that they were under Moses – tell Gentiles to stay under his law? Even worse: would Paul tell believing Jews to leave Moses, yet make believing Gentiles come under Moses? This is the nub of the question I am addressing in this book.

marginal note: 'Lawless hands, or, men without the law; that is, heathen'. The NIV correctly notes: 'Of those not having the law (that is, Gentiles)'. Christ had already foretold this is what would happen: 'The Son of Man... will be delivered to the Gentiles and will be mocked and insulted and spit upon. They will scourge him and kill him' (Luke 18:31-33). Peter, steeped in Jewish thought, was using the phrase, 'lawless men', in the Jewish sense. The men he was talking about were 'men without the law'. That is to say, they were law-less, outside the law of God, Gentiles. The Jews boasted of their having the law. They were the only people to have it. All the rest were 'law-less'. So, as Peter said, Christ was crucified by the Jews (who had the law) making use of the Gentiles (who did not have the law, the without-the-law people) to do the work. See also Matthew 20:18-19; and Galatians 2:15, where 'Jews by nature' are contrasted with 'sinners of the Gentiles' or 'Gentile sinners' (NIV). 'Sinners' and 'Gentiles', in such a context, means those who are law-less, outside the law, beyond the pale.

When the Jews wanted Christ put to death, they could tell Pilate: '*We* have a law, and according to *our* law he ought to die' (John 19:7; see Lev. 24:16), but the Roman governor had already told them: '*You* take him and judge him according to *your* law' (John 18:31). When the Jews of Corinth brought Paul to court before Gallio, accusing him of persuading 'men to worship God contrary to the law' (Acts 18:11-16),[25] Gallio refused to entertain the case, on the grounds that it was none of his business. He roundly told them he would not get involved in 'a question of words and names and your own law'; '*your own* law', I emphasise. With a dismissive, 'Look to it yourselves; for I do not want to be a judge of such matters', he cleared the court. Claudius Lysias spoke in a similar way when writing to Felix, calling the accusation laid against Paul by the Jews, 'questions of *their* law' (Acts 23:29), no concern of his, something outside his jurisdiction, comprehension and competence. The Jews confirmed this by telling Felix they had 'wanted to judge [Paul] according to *our* law' (Acts 24:6). Festus was in the same quandary as Felix. While he was familiar with 'the custom of the Romans', he was 'uncertain of such questions' as he was now being asked, 'questions... about *their own* religion' (Acts 25:16,19-20). Paul, standing before Agrippa, was happy to think his judge was an 'expert in all customs and questions which have to do with the Jews', including the words of the prophets. '*Our* religion', he called it (Acts 26:1-5,26-27) – with the clear implication that Gentiles generally speaking had at best only a limited knowledge of God's revelation to the Jews, and their customs, religion and *law*. All this is strange, to put it mildly, *if these Gentiles had been as much under the law as the Jews*. I realise these Gentiles were politicians as well as magistrates, soldiers or kings, and I would not treat their words as the final authority on biblical principles, but they do nothing to contradict the claim that the law was given only to the Jews.[26]

And what of Hebrews 7:11? We are told that 'under [the levitical priesthood] the people received the law'. While it is not easy to determine precisely what the writer meant, at the very least we may speak of a link between the levitical priesthood, the Israelites and the law. In fact, it is much stronger than this. It was *under* the levitical priesthood that Israel received the law. The NIV and the NASB use the word *basis*; Israel received the law *on the basis* of the levitical priesthood. Now who received the

---

[25] The law of Moses, they meant, not the law of Corinth.

[26] In chapter 7, I will deal with the objection that such passages are concerned with the ceremonial or judicial law. They are not! As I keep saying, we are talking about the whole law.

levitical priesthood? The Jews. The Jews and no others. No Gentiles had the levitical priesthood. Consequently, only the Jews could have received the law, since no people could have the law without the levitical priesthood, and *vice-versa*. The two were inextricably linked (Heb. 7:11-12,14,18-19,22,28). The two stood or fell together: 'The priesthood being changed, of necessity there is also a change of the law' (Heb. 7:12). Under this system – unique to the Jews – the law required Levi to collect the tithe from his brothers – not all men (Heb. 7:5). And so on.

Therefore, of all nations, Israel alone received the law.

But what about Romans 3:19?

What about Romans 3:19?

The verse reads: 'Now we know that whatever the law says, it says to those who are under the law, that every mouth may be stopped, and all the world may become guilty before God'. Surely this teaches that all men – Jews and Gentiles – are under the law? But, no, it does not, even though at first glance it seems like it.

As I have shown, the context proves that 'the law' here includes at least the ten commandments, but more; it is the Old Testament as a whole. It is the law, the law in its entirety. Furthermore, note how Paul said that the law speaks to those who are under it. This ought to give pause for thought. If all men are under the law, then Paul wrote what amounts to a truism. The fact that he made such an observation at all – the law speaks to those who are under it – indicates there is something to be taken notice of. To whom was he referring? Who were those who were 'under the law', those to whom the law speaks? The context from Romans 2:1 and on is conclusive. He was clearly referring to the Jews. *They* were under it. It was given to *them*. The law certainly stopped their mouths. They had the law, they were under it, but since they failed to keep it, it condemned them. It took away all their excuse. Pharisees might think that *knowing* the law, *having* the law, was all that counted (John 5:39,45; 7:49; 9:28; Rom. 2:17-29), but, far from being justified by possession of the law, they would 'be judged by the law', 'for', as the apostle explained, 'not the hearers of the law are just in the sight of God, but the doers of the law will be justified' (Rom. 2:12-13).

But what of the Gentiles in Romans 3:19? The words, 'to those who are under the law', imply there are others who are *not* under the law. The Gentiles, Paul explained, did not have the Jews' advantage – they were not given the law, they were not under it (Rom. 2:12-15). Even so, some of them, at least, were living up to the light they had – and 'by nature do the things in the law... who show the work of the law written in their hearts' – and in this respect did better than the Jews.[27] This does not mean that some Gentiles by their works were free of sin and so avoided God's wrath. No! The point is, God is impartial. The Jews who had the law will be judged, and the Gentiles who did not have the law will also be judged, and both will be judged fairly by God (Rom. 1:18 – 3:20). What is more, if the Gentiles, who never had the advantage of receiving the law, were unable to voice any excuse for their sin, how much more guilty were the Jews – who had the law, and boasted about it (Rom. 2:17-24)! The Jews had the light of God's word (Ps. 119:130). The Gentiles did not. But even so, all sinned and were

---

[27] See the next chapter for a thorough examination of Rom. 2:14-15.

'guilty before God' (Rom. 3:19,23); the Jews against the law, and the Gentiles against some sort[28] of moral consciousness. And both were responsible. The principle is clear: more light, more responsibility!

This is Paul's argument. Whether or not men had the law, Paul had already 'charged both Jews and Greeks that they are all under sin' (Rom. 3:9). As he said, quoting and citing the Old Testament (the law): 'There is none righteous, no, not one... none... none... none... For there is no difference; for all have sinned and fall short of the glory of God' (Rom. 3:9-23). And as with sin, so with salvation, there is no difference between Jew and Gentile (Rom. 3:28-31; 10:12-13). God is impartial between them. In short: 'Now we know that whatsoever the law says, it says to those who are under the law, that every mouth may be stopped, and all the world may become guilty before God' (Rom. 3:19). The Jews – who had the law – were silenced by it. The Gentiles – who did not have the law – had no excuse in any case. Hence, all the world is guilty before God. 'God has bound all men over to disobedience' (Rom. 11:32, NIV). 'The Scripture has confined all under sin' (Gal. 3:22) – all men, 'all things' (Gal. 3:22, NASB margin), 'the creation... the creation... the creation... the whole creation' (Rom. 8:19-22). In short: 'Both Jews and Greeks... are all under sin... For all have sinned and fall short of the glory of God' (Rom. 3:9,23).

In other words, Romans 3:19 supports the claim that the law was given to the Jews, and not to the Gentiles.

Many Reformed teachers will have none of it. The law was given to all men in Adam, they say; it was reinstated to all men through Moses; and all men are under the law today. Some go further. Men will be under it in eternity.[29]

These statements are wrong on several counts. Although it is claimed that men know the law of God by nature, and have done so from Adam, it is significant that such teachers never include the sabbath in trying to justify their claim. Let us think about this for a minute. Are we really to believe that pagans know they must rest from Friday sunset to Saturday sunset? Can anybody tell us of a pagan people, completely without Scripture, which keeps the sabbath? or feels guilty for not keeping it? Can anyone point to any man – including the patriarchs — before Exodus 16, who kept the sabbath?

Furthermore, the notion that the moral law was *reinstituted* or *reinstated* or *restated* on Sinai because it had fallen into obscurity, is without a shred of evidence. Romans 5:20 disproves it: the law – the whole law – *entered* at Sinai; it was not *restated* because it had fallen into obscurity! It entered the world at that time. More of this anon. Much more!

---

[28] I admit my expression is (deliberately) vague. I will go into it further in the next chapter.

[29] A staggering – not to say, ridiculous – claim. The law is 'made', 'not... for a righteous person, but for the lawless and insubordinate' (1 Tim. 1:9-12). Will the eternal glory be populated by men and women who need a law against murder, sodomy and 'any other thing that is contrary to sound doctrine', and glory in it? Reformed writers refer to 'the permanence and glory of the moral law'. This book is my attempt to write on the permanence and the glory of the *gospel*. The glory of the law was fading and passing away even as it was given (2 Cor. 3:7-18). As the New Testament expressly states, it was a temporary measure, 'added' until the Christ's fulfilment of his Father's will in his first coming, and has no glory now in comparison to the gospel since Christ fulfilled and thus abolished it (Gal. 3:19; Eph. 2:15; Heb. 7:18; 8:7-13; 9:5-10). I will go into all these matters.

But the simple point I wish to make in this chapter is that the law was given to the Jews at Sinai. It was not given to the Gentiles, either at Sinai or at creation. It was not given to the Gentiles, full stop.

But what of those places in the New Testament where Paul addresses believers as those no longer under the law? Since he must have been including Gentiles in at least some of the passages, does this not mean that the Gentiles *were* under the law, after all? The answer is, No! As I come to the passages, I will deal with the question in detail, but for now I simply state that on several occasions, Paul was speaking either of his own personal experience as a Jew, or else he was speaking of the Jews and not Gentiles. And even when he was clearly addressing Gentiles, he was often rebuking them for seeking to go under the law, allowing themselves to be put under it by false teachers, Judaisers, or going back to the slavery of pagan principles – this last, having nothing to do with the law of Moses at all! Christ has redeemed his people from all bondage.

Even so, reader, there are some passages where such explanations still do not satisfy. Romans 2:14-15 is the explanation of all such. I now turn to these very important verses.

Chapter 3

Romans 2:14-15

Let me quote the verses:

For when Gentiles, who do not have the law, by nature do the things in the law, these, although not having the law, are a law to themselves, who show the work of the law written in their hearts, their conscience also bearing witness, and between themselves their thoughts accusing or else excusing them.

I wish to deal with two main views of the passage. First things first, however.[1]

What is the context?

As always, this is vital. The context always holds the key to the interpretation. The passage opens (verse 12) with 'for', linking it with what has gone before, arguing from what has gone before. As I explained in the previous chapter, Paul is here showing the impartiality of God's judgement of all sinners, whether Jew or Gentile; 'there is no partiality with God' (Rom. 2:11). Judgement is the context, and the context is judgement. Paul is not trying to praise Gentiles in Romans 2:14-15. In fact, he is not speaking to Gentiles at all. Rather, he is reminding Jews that God is fair in his judgement. In particular, he says, although the Jews have received the law (given to them by God) and the Gentiles have not, the truth is, some Gentiles (though without the law) live to a standard which puts the Jews (who have the law) to shame. *And God notes the fact!* Jews might think they get special treatment because they received the law, but they are mistaken. God looks at the life, the actions, the works of a man, *not his advantages.* God looks at what a man does with his opportunities and advantages. He does not accept the man just because he gave him those opportunities and advantages. Romans 2 teaches it plainly. As for the Jews bragging about having the law, the boot is on the other foot; more light brings more responsibility (John 9:39-41; 15:22,24). This is the context.

Now for Romans 2:14-15. The word 'law' appears several times in the two verses. With the exception of the clause, 'are a law to themselves', the law in question is the law of Moses. And when Paul spoke of 'Gentiles, who do not have the law', he did not mean that some Gentiles have the law and others do not. The comma is very important.[2] Gentiles, Gentiles as Gentiles, Gentiles as a whole, do not have the law. Although there is no article before Gentiles – it is Gentiles, not *the* Gentiles – it makes no difference. As I pointed out in the first chapter, the frequent lack of the definite article before 'law' only serves to strengthen the notion of 'the law'. 'The Gentiles' or 'Gentiles' – it is all the same. Gentiles do not have the law. This is part and parcel of being a Gentile! As I showed in the previous chapter, the law was given to the Jews

---

[1] The extracts for this chapter begin on p342.
[2] There is no punctuation in the original. This always has to be supplied. Over this first comma, there is no debate, and it is, as I say, of the utmost importance to take full account of it.

and not to the Gentiles. In Romans 2:14-15, Paul takes this point for granted, and builds on it. Contrasting Jew and Gentile (Rom. 2:9-10), the apostle speaks, on the one hand, of those who 'have sinned without law' – Gentiles – and on the other, of those who 'sinned in the law' – Jews (Rom. 2:12). Only the Jews were given the revelation of God's 'knowledge and truth in the law' (Rom. 2:20). The Gentiles were not. They were 'in darkness' (Rom. 2:19). They did not have the law.

So far, so good. The Gentiles do not have the law. We have seen this much before. But, even so, Reformed writers, as I have explained, do not always accept this obvious point, so clearly revealed in Scripture. They often claim that the ten commandments were given to all men, and that they were written on the hearts of the pagans. Romans 2:14-15 says nothing of the sort. Quite the reverse! It expressly says that Gentiles did not have the law! If this fact is ignored or explained away, Paul's point is lost.

What about the punctuation of Romans 2:14-15?

This, as I have noted, has to be supplied. No manuscript gives us the definitive punctuation. This is simply a fact. Whatever version we use, the translators have supplied the punctuation. Now then, should the second comma come just after 'by nature', or just before? In other words, there are two possibilities:

1: 'When Gentiles, **who do not have the law by nature,** do the things in the law'
2: 'When Gentiles, who do not have the law, **by nature do the things in the law**'

Which is it? The overwhelming majority of scholars and translators opt for the second.

The placing of the comma is no quibble. If the comma is placed as in the first possibility, 'by nature' qualifies the 'having' of the law: Gentiles do not have the law, and it is by nature that they do not have it. If the comma is placed as in the second possibility, 'by nature' qualifies the 'doing' of the law: Gentiles do not have the law, but some of them by nature do the things in the law.

Let me take the first; that is, 'by nature' qualifies the fact that the Gentiles do not have the law. Is this right? Was Paul saying that Gentiles do not have the law by nature? Now *phusei* (by nature), it is true, can mean 'by birth, by physical origin', and such a use would be in keeping with other scriptures (Rom. 2:27; Gal. 2:15, for instance).[3] Consequently, if, in Romans 2:14-15, the comma comes after 'by nature', the passage reads: 'When Gentiles, *who do not have the law by reason of birth*, do the things in the law'.

As I say, this makes excellent sense. But it may not be the right position for the comma!

The alternative – and the most common – version, which puts the comma before 'by nature', simply says that Gentiles do not have the law; whether by reason of birth, or otherwise, is not specified.

To sum up thus far: Jews had the law; Gentiles did not. But whether or not this is by reason of birth depends on the comma coming before or after 'by nature'. Whichever it

---

[3] Rom. 2:27 also confirms the earlier point; namely, Jews have the law whereas Gentiles do not. The original is 'you who with letter'. The NKJV supplied the word 'your' in 'you... with *your* [letter or] written code'. The NASB put it as 'you who though having the letter of the law'. In other words, Paul is contrasting Gentiles, who do not have the law, with Jews, who do.

is, it makes no difference to the overall argument concerning the possession of the law. Gentiles do not have the law. Whether or not they do not have it 'by nature' does not alter the fact that they do not have it in the first place.[4]

But this, of course, leads to a second point – one with far-reaching consequences. Granted that Gentiles do not have the law, when it says they 'do the things in the law', how do they do these things? Do they do them 'by nature' or what? Once again, it depends on the comma.

There are two main possibilities

1. If the comma comes *after* 'by nature', in what I will call the minority version, Romans 2:14-15 reads: 'When Gentiles, who do not have the law by nature, do the things in the law, these, although not having the law, are a law to themselves, who show the work of the law written in their hearts, their conscience also bearing witness, and between themselves their thoughts accusing or else excusing them'. This means, *some* say, that even though Gentiles by virtue of birth do not have the law, in some cases they keep it. And, although it is not specified here, since no sinner can keep the law by his own power, this must mean they keep the law by grace. In other words, the verses are speaking about Gentiles who are in the new covenant;[5] that is, they are Gentile believers.

2. If the comma comes *before* 'by nature', in what I will call the majority version, Romans 2:14-15 reads: 'When Gentiles, who do not have the law, by nature do the things in the law, these, although not having the law, are a law to themselves, who show the work of the law written in their hearts, their conscience also bearing witness, and between themselves their thoughts accusing or else excusing them'. According to the majority version, this means that even though Gentiles do not have the law, by nature some of them have a measure of the law ('the work of the law') written on their hearts, and this, coupled with an active conscience, enables them to live out – to a certain degree – the things the law demands ('the things in the law') even though they do not have the law as such. That is to say, all Gentiles, even though they do not have the law, have a rudimentary knowledge of it written in their hearts, and some of them live up fairly well to the light they have.

These are the two possibilities I wish to consider.[6] I will give my reasons for rejecting the first, and accepting the second, the majority view. In short, Romans 2:14-15 is speaking of unbelieving Gentiles who do not have the law – whereas the Jews do – yet

---

[4] Of course, the Jews after Sinai had the law by virtue of birth. But Rom. 2:14-15 is concerned with Gentiles, not Jews.

[5] See chapter 18 for the new covenant, and, especially, what 'the law' is in that covenant. It is one of the major issues in this debate.

[6] We can dismiss the Pelagian view that some Gentiles keep the law by their own natural ability. Original sin and human depravity rule it out (Job 14:4; Ps. 51:5; Rom. 1:18-32; 3:9-20,23; 8:7; 1 Cor. 2:14; Gal. 3:22; Eph. 2:1-3; 4:17-19). Far from being within the power of *nature*, it takes the *supernatural* work of the Spirit to make a dead sinner live, and give him heart-delight in God and his law (John 3:1-8; Jer. 31:33-34; Heb. 8:6-13). See also Matt. 23:37; John 5:40; 6:44-45; 12:37-40; Acts 26:18; Rom. 5:10; 1 Cor. 1:21; Gal. 4:8; Eph. 5:8; Col. 1:21. As I have said, I will return to the question of which law is the law of the new covenant.

in some cases Gentiles more nearly keep the law than do the Jews. But let me consider the two possibilities before I show why I plump for the second.

Possibility 1. The minority view: Does Romans 2:14-15 teach that some Gentiles are believers, and therefore keep the law by the provisions of the new covenant?

As I have said, if the comma comes after 'by nature', as in the minority version, Romans 2:14-15 states that even though Gentiles by reason of birth do not have the law, some of them keep it. Although it is not here specified, these Gentiles keep the law because they are in the new covenant. In other words, they are Gentile believers who keep the law by grace (with an implied contrast, perhaps, with 'by nature'). In short, although Paul does not say so, the passage refers to believing Gentiles in the new covenant (Jer. 31:33; Heb. 8:10; 10:16). Romans 2:6-11 is cited in support.[7]

But this claim simply does not fit the overall context of Romans 1:18 – 3:20; namely, man's sin, and the consequent wrath of God on all mankind. The context is king, remember! And, as we have seen, judgement is the context. Above all, Paul is here considering God's justice, his judgement, his fairness in executing wrath on all the human race, both Jew and Gentile. Consequently, to introduce at Romans 2:14-15 the thought that some Gentiles are converted and possess the blessings of the new covenant (the law written on the heart) without so much as a whisper of an explanation, seems forced. Very much so. Something jars. By this stage in the letter, Paul has not sufficiently set out the gospel to be able to introduce the concept of the new covenant and its provisions. Yet, we are asked to believe, Paul did it, and did it without any reference to Jeremiah (or Ezekiel or any other prophet), and with no comparison to the old covenant. He did it, apparently, as an aside.[8] Contrast the way the writer to the Hebrews brought in the new covenant (Heb. 8:1-13; 10:15-18), having built his case solidly over several chapters, and the way Paul himself spoke of it in 2 Corinthians 3. Are we to think Paul could mention such a momentous matter *in passing* in Romans 2? Surely not! Paul was not speaking of the new covenant in Romans 2:15. The context is judgement!

But what of Romans 2:7,10? Here Paul does speak of believers who by their attitude and works show their inward experience of grace; at least, this is how I understand the verses.[9] If this is so, does Romans 2:7,10 not support the view that

---

[7] It is almost always taken for granted that the law written in the heart in the new covenant is the law of Moses. But this is to beg the question – a big question, at that! Perhaps the biggest question of them all. See chapter 18. As I have already said, it is one of the major issues in this debate.

[8] Moreover, he did it as an aside within an aside; Rom. 2:13-15 is in brackets, which have to be supplied, of course. The argument runs from Rom. 2:12 directly to Rom. 2:16, missing out the verses in between: 'For as many as have sinned without law will also perish without law, and as many as have sinned in the law will be judged by the law... in the day when God will judge the secrets of men by Jesus Christ, according to my gospel'.

[9] Some think Paul is speaking of the hypothetical case – if a man could keep the law perfectly, he would be justified. While I think this is a truth (see below, and chapters 6 and 10), I do not think it is what Paul is saying in Rom. 2:7,10. In brief, this is because the contrast in Rom. 2:6-11 is not between those who keep the law *perfectly* – and are justified – and those who keep

Romans 2:14-15 speaks of Gentiles in the new covenant? I think not. The two passages, Romans 2:4-11 and 2:12-24, deal with different things. Up to the end of Romans 2:3, Paul has been setting out a massive indictment of the human race, and God's impartial judgement of sinners on the basis of their works, and he has yet more to say about it. But he does not develop his argument in the verses which immediately follow. It is in Romans 2:12-24 where he does that. What is his argument? Just this: God's impartial judgement of sinners is according to their works; *having the law of Moses makes no difference.* Jew (or Gentile, for that matter) may condemn others, but 'do you think this, O man, you who judge those practicing such things, and doing the same, that you will escape the judgement of God?' (Rom. 2:3). The fact is, 'there is no partiality with God. For as many as have sinned without law will also perish without law, and as many as have sinned in the law will be judged by the law' (Rom. 2:11-12). As far as Paul's argument goes, it is verses 11-12, not 4-11, which follow on from Romans 2:3. 'Do you think this, O man, you who judge those practicing such things, and doing the same, that you will escape the judgement of God?... For there is no partiality with God. For as many as have sinned without law will also perish without law, and as many as have sinned in the law will be judged by the law'.

What I am saying is, Romans 2:4-11 is *not* a development of Paul's main argument; *rather, it is an aside – a passionate aside at that.* As I read it, Paul the preacher cannot help himself. Overwhelmed by what he has just written – about the wrath for God – in the verses leading up to Romans 2:3, he is moved with compassion for sinners, and he shows it.[10] The harrowing thought of the terrible consequences of God's wrath, in the judgement and condemnation of hardened and impenitent sinners, which the apostle has just set out in Romans 1:18 – 2:3, moves him – compels him – to interrupt his argument for a moment. He must get his passionate thoughts down 'on paper'! Running ahead of himself, almost breaking out into the positive aspect of the gospel, his feelings compel him to address ignorant sinners, those who 'despise the riches of [God's] goodness, forbearance, and longsuffering, not knowing that the goodness of God leads [them] to repentance', and who in consequence 'are treasuring up... wrath' for themselves (Rom. 2:4-5). He has to let his main argument go by the board for a moment. He must inject a note of hope into the thunderous cataract of warning and doom. This is why he declaims on the two sorts of men – the godly and the ungodly – the two classes being shown for what they are by their works. Wanting no sinner – Jew or Gentile – to come to 'indignation and wrath, tribulation and anguish' (Rom. 2:8-9), Paul, by means of a searching question (Rom. 2:4), tries to bring sinners to repentance.

But this white-hot discussion is a digression from his main theme, which he left at the end of Romans 2:3; namely, God's impartial judgement based on works. It is, as I say, as he moves from Romans 2:10 to 2:11, and especially as he opens verse 12, that

---

90% of it (well, the ten commandments – see Jas. 2:10-11) – and are condemned – but between those who seek after God and godliness, and those who do not; the latter are 'self-seeking'. The law does not come into it. Paul does not even mention it. But what of Rom. 2:13? In this verse, Paul *does* state the hypothetical case – perfect obedience to the law would bring justification. Yes. But the difference lies in the fact that Paul has now introduced the idea of law. Even so, in Rom. 2:13 Paul is not merely stating a hypothetical case. He is driving home the point that *having* the law is not enough – it is *doing* the law which counts. God's judgement is according to works, as before.
[10] Compare Rom. 9:1-5; 10:1.

Paul lets go of his impassioned plea to sinners,[11] and gets back on course – God's impartial judgement – *but now he develops his case by introducing the notion of 'law'.* I stress this. Paul has not mentioned 'law' up to this point. This is why I say Romans 2:7,10 and 2:14,15 are not dealing with the same issues.[12] Whereas there is no mention of 'law' in Romans 1:1 – 2:11, 'law' is the dominant note of Romans 2:12-24.[13] Romans 2:4-11 and 2:12-16, therefore, deal with different things. Consequently Romans 2:7,10 and 2:14-15 do not describe the same people, or speak about the same issues.

Nor do I think Paul's later statement in Romans 2:28-29 militates against what I am saying. In Romans 2:25-29, Paul is moving on to yet another aspect of God's impartial judgement based on works; namely, it does not matter if a man is circumcised in the flesh or not. What matters is his heart, and the consequent effect on his life. Once again, this is not the issue in Romans 2:14-15.[14]

And what about the verses themselves (Rom. 2:14-15)? They cannot be speaking of the fulfilment of the promise of the new covenant. Romans 2:14-15 does not say that Gentiles have *the law* written on their hearts. Rather, they have *the work of the law* written on their hearts. Nor does Romans 2:14-15 say that Gentiles keep the law; it says 'when' they 'do the things in the law'. What is more, the words in Romans 2:14-15, 'who do not have the law', cannot apply to the regenerate since, according to God's promise in Jeremiah 31:33, the regenerate *do* have the law – written on their hearts: 'I will put my law in their minds, and write it on their hearts'. In addition, those spoken of in Romans 2:14 have only a *knowledge* of the law, whereas those in the new covenant *delight* in it. What is more, how can the regenerate be said to be 'a law to themselves'? They are under the law to Christ (1 Cor. 9:21; Gal. 6:2). Finally, it is significant that there is no mention whatsoever of the Holy Spirit in Romans 2:14-15 or its context.[15] For all these reasons, Romans 2:14-15 cannot be referring to regenerate Gentiles in the new covenant.[16]

---

[11] As I have indicated, the 'for' in Rom. 2:12 builds on the fact that 'there is no partiality with God' (Rom. 2:11), not on the impassioned aside of Rom. 2:4-11.

[12] As above, Rom. 2:13-15 is in brackets. The main argument goes from Rom. 2:3 directly to Rom. 2:11, and from Rom. 2:12 directly to Rom. 2:16, missing out the verses in between. 'Do you think... that you will escape the judgement of God?... As many as have sinned in the law will be judged by the law... in the day when God will judge the secrets of men by Jesus Christ'.

[13] In Rom. 1:1 – 2:11 'law' is not mentioned; in Rom. 2:12-24 it comes 16 times; in Rom. 2:25-29, it comes another 5 times – plus 'written code' and 'letter'. I do not say 'law' always means the Mosaic law here, but overwhelmingly it does.

[14] See below for a note on Rom. 2:25-27. See also Rom. 4 where Paul deals with the way the two issues impinge, not on condemnation, but on justification. There he does it in the opposite order; circumcision (Rom. 4:9-12), then law (Rom. 4:13-16).

[15] When Paul raised the new covenant in 2 Cor. 3, he mentioned 'the Spirit' 6 times.

[16] Furthermore, if Rom. 2:14-15 does describe regenerate Gentiles, and if 'the work of the law' must be understood as 'the law', then it means that the law which is written on the heart in the new covenant must be the law of Moses (the law Paul was mainly speaking of in Rom. 2). And this needs proof. As I have said, I will return to 'the law' in the new covenant in chapter 18. It is, as I keep pointing out, one of the major issues in this debate.

None of this is quibbling. 'The work of the law'[17] is equivalent to 'a life which in some measure corresponds to the law', a long way short of saying that Romans 2:14-15 is concerned with Gentiles in the new covenant.

So much for the minority view of the passage. I do not think it holds up. If however the minority version *is* right, and the passage does refer to the new covenant, then it could be properly quoted as a verification of what I will have to say on that subject throughout my book. But it does not ring true, at least for me.[18] As a result, I am left with the second possibility.

Possibility 2. The majority view: Does Romans 2:14-15 teach that some unbelieving Gentiles live a life which shows a rudimentary knowledge of the law?

If the comma comes before 'by nature', Romans 2:14-15 states that even though Gentiles do not have the law, some of them, by the light of nature, coupled with an active conscience, live out to a certain degree the things the law demands – 'the things in the law' – thus showing some measure of the law – 'the work of the law' – written in their hearts. In other words, Gentiles, even though they do not have *the* law, have *a* law, a vague, rudimentary knowledge of law written in their hearts; they have a conscience, some sense of right and wrong. And some of them instinctively live up fairly well to the light they have.[19]

In addition, Romans 1:19-20,32 speaks of precisely the same thing as Romans 2:14-15.[20] Compare: 'Gentiles... show the work of the law written in their hearts' (Rom. 2:14-15), with the reference to all men in Romans 1:19-20: 'What may be known of God is manifest in them, for God has shown it to them. For since the creation of the world his invisible attributes are clearly seen, being understood by the things that are

---

[17] It is not the same as 'the works of the law' (Rom. 9:32; Gal. 3:10). Rom. 2:15 is concerned with Gentiles. The other verses are to do with the Jews – who had the law – and who were trying to keep it for justification. In Rom. 9:30-32, the contrast is drawn between Gentiles – 'who did not pursue righteousness' – and Israel – who did pursue 'the law of righteousness', but failed 'because they did not seek it by faith, but as it were, by the works of the law'. 'The works of the law' means the carrying out of *all* that the law requires. But this is not what Paul was saying in Rom. 2:14-15. Here we are told, not that the law is written in Gentile hearts, and that they keep it, but: 'Gentiles... do *the things in the law*... who show the *work of the law* written in their hearts'. Nothing here, I suggest, about earning justification by keeping the Mosaic law. The Gentiles do not even have the law.

[18] Paul wrote 'Gentiles'. The context does not favour – to put it mildly – the notion of *believing* Gentiles. It is not convincing to say that Paul deliberately left 'the Gentiles' unspecific at this stage so that he could slowly build up his case! And it runs completely contrary to the idea that he introduced the new covenant here, since – if he did – he did so in a most abrupt manner, and dropped it just as abruptly – and all without any mention of 'the Spirit'.

[19] Generally this was the view of the Puritans, and many others. I understand Rom. 2:25-27 in this light also. The man with the 'written code and circumcision' (Rom. 2:27) is a Jew, whereas an 'uncircumcised man' (Rom. 2:26) is a Gentile. Paul proposes the case of a Gentile who, though not having the law or circumcision, to a measure 'keeps the righteous requirements of the law' (Rom. 2:26).

[20] Note the *phusikēn* (natural) and *phusin* (nature) in Rom. 1:26-27, and *phusei* (by nature) in Rom. 2:14.

made, even his eternal power and Godhead, so that they are without excuse', 'that which is known about God is evident within them; for God made it evident to them' (NASB), 'what may be known about God is plain to them, because God has made it plain to them' (NIV). And according to Romans 1:32, all men know 'the righteous judgement of God', 'the ordinance of God' (NASB), 'God's righteous decree' (NIV). Surely this lies behind Peter's words in Acts 10:35: 'In every nation whoever fears him and works righteousness', 'does what is right' (NASB). While Cornelius was not a converted man at the time, he had a measure of light and he lived up to it. All this comes under Genesis 1:26-27: 'God created man in his own image'. God created man a moral creature, a rational creature. Man was given a conscience, he could weigh his actions and thoughts, he had been given a sense of right (and wrong, after sin entered the world). God 'has put eternity in their hearts' (Eccl. 3:11). This marks man out from the animal, and this is the meaning of Romans 2:14-15.

To sum up: the comma should come as in all the leading English versions;[21] that is: 'When Gentiles, who do not have the law, by nature do the things in the law'. In other words, Romans 2:14-15 speaks of unbelieving Gentiles[22] who, though they do not have the law, show by their lives that they have a rudimentary knowledge of right and wrong, and by an active conscience they live up to that standard according to the light they have. The NIV footnote of John 1:9 is relevant: Christ 'gives light to every man who comes into the world'; or 'enlightens every man coming into the world' (NASB, margin). Every man has a conscience enlightened by a rudimentary knowledge of right and wrong.

We have a test-bed to hand. 'The law was given through Moses' (John 1:17), yes, but the people who lived before Moses were judged for their wickedness. Why? Because all are sinners (Rom. 3:9,23), whether before or after Moses, whether under the law or not, and because the sinners in question knew they were doing wrong. How did they know that? God explains: he does not judge sinners for breaking a law they were never under, but for suppressing the truth that is *in them* (Rom. 1:18-19).

Let me explore this a little. God gave his law to Israel on Mount Sinai through Moses. Also, 'by the law is the knowledge of sin' (Rom. 3:20), 'sin is lawlessness' (1 John 3:4), 'where there is no law there is no transgression' (Rom. 4:15), and 'sin is not imputed when there is no law' (Rom. 5:13). Yet even before Sinai 'death spread to all men, because all sinned... Death reigned from Adam to Moses, even over those who had not sinned according to the likeness of the transgression of Adam'. This was because through Adam 'sin entered the world, and death through sin, and thus death spread to all men, because all sinned' (Rom. 5:12-14). They sinned in Adam, and they sinned in their own right. They had no excuse. By creation they had known 'the truth', but, as a consequence of the fall, they had stifled this knowledge, and given God up. Therefore God gave them up to a life of sin and misery, including sexual perversion, envy, murder, the breakdown of family life, and the glorying in wickedness (Rom. 1:18-32). All this dates from Adam's fall, is with us yet, and will be with us until Christ shall come again. Not that things are as bad as they might be. This is earth, after

---

[21] But see NASB.

[22] If the correct punctuation is 'by nature do the things', it means that the Gentiles in question cannot be regenerate. Do the regenerate *by nature* keep the law? They do it *by grace*, do they not?

all, and not hell! There is still a rudimentary knowledge of right and wrong in men. Conscience has not been entirely seared, let alone obliterated. This is the point of Romans 2:12-14. Nevertheless, 'the whole world lies under the sway of the wicked one' (1 John 5:19).

What evidence is there for it? Evidence in abundance. For the present day, the calling of witnesses would be superfluous. Virtually every news bulletin and newspaper is full of violence and wretchedness. As for the start of the misery, and its development among men, the Bible tells us plainly about that. Even though the law had not been given, the variety of sins men committed, as recorded in the book of Genesis and the early chapters of Exodus, is legion. Murder, anger, hatred, war, plunder, idolatry, ill-treatment, slavery, adultery, drunkenness, lying, sexual abuse and depravity of almost every hue – including homosexuality, prostitution and rape, polygamy and incest – jealousy and envy, deceit, cheating, blasphemy, hypocrisy, and so on, all defiled humanity. And yet the law had not been given! After God's covenant with Noah (Gen. 9:1-7), men knew by direct revelation that murder was wrong, but, of course, they had instinctively known that long before Noah's time. I have already referred to: 'Does not nature teach you?'[23] In short, with the exception of the sabbath,[24] all the other commands of the ten were broken *before the ten commandments had been given*.[25]

But, and of far greater significance, reader, notice that whatever sin was committed as recorded in the book of Genesis, God never once referred to any of the ten commandments. Of course not! They were not yet given to Israel. Israel, as a nation, did not yet exist. Yet the concept of wickedness and sin on the one hand, and righteousness on the other, is written plainly in the book (Gen. 6:5,9,11-12; 8:21; 13:13; 15:16; 17:23; 18:20,23-32; 20:4,6; 31:36; 34:7; 38:26; 39:9; 44:5; 50:17), as is the concept of obedience to commands (Gen. 6:14,22; 7:1-5,16; 8:15-18; 26:5). On occasion, God gave men direct revelation concerning sin (Gen. 9:1-7; 17:23; 20:3-7; 31:7-13,24,29), but generally not. Though there was some sense of God, some fear of God, in the human race (Gen. 20:11; 21:22-23), yet in this regard Jacob and his family stood out from pagans (Gen. 34:7; 39:9). Furthermore, changes in morality occurred as time passed. In truth, some things which had been commanded by God, and practiced by men *before* Sinai, were regarded as sins *after* Sinai; altar building, for instance (Gen. 26:25; 35:1). The theme continues when we come to the early chapters of Exodus; God commands or instructs men (Ex. 7:6; 12:50; 15:26; 16:4,16,23,28,32,34; 17:1; 18:16,20,23); his ordinances are set up (Ex. 15:25; 17:15, plus several before that); and men go on sinning (Ex. 9:27,34; 10:16-17), disobeying (Ex. 16:17-20). Yet the first appearances in the Bible of the word 'law' (apart from 'in-laws') come at Genesis 26:5; 47:26 (and this not *torah*); 49:10; Exodus 12:49; 13:9; 16:4,28 and 18:16,20, and how rare they are at that stage![26]

---

[23] Compare 1 Cor. 11:14.

[24] In Ezek. 20:18,21,24, God complained of sabbath-breaking by the Jews in the wilderness but not in Egypt, yet they sinned by idolatry before that (Ezek. 20:7-9). It is, of course, dangerous to argue from silence, but in Ps. 106:7, although the Jews in Egypt forgot God's many mercies, no mention is made of neglect of the sabbath.

[25] The sabbath was a special case. God gave it to the Jews in the wilderness, as recorded in Ex. 16. They immediately broke it!

[26] And they do not all refer to a law from God.

What is the explanation of all this? As I have said, Reformed teachers nearly always claim it was because the law of Sinai had been given to all men in Adam. There is no biblical warrant for it. In fact, it flies in the face of Scripture. The only explanation lies in Romans 2:14-15. A rudimentary knowledge of the work of the law is inscribed on all men's hearts since Adam's fall. This is what Romans 2:14-15 teaches. This is what the record of the days before Sinai declares. Men sinned in those days. Some had some commands from God, which some obeyed and others did not. But the sense of right and wrong, even though somewhat hazy, existed in men, and did so *before the Jews received a written law from God*. Indeed, even before the giving of the law to Israel, some pagans had a more finely-tuned sense of right and wrong than some of the godly. Take the episode of Abraham (and Sarah) lying to Abimelech king of Gerar, the latter's reaction, and his reproof of the father of the faithful (Gen. 20). Abimelech certainly showed a greater sense of morality than Abraham. The same can be said for Abimelech king of the Philistines and Isaac (and Rebekah) (Gen. 26). Hamor the Hivite, though he certainly had his faults, showed more integrity than Jacob's sons (Gen. 34). Where did pagans get their sense of right and wrong, their sense of injustice? Romans 2:14-15 is the clear biblical explanation.[27]

A notorious child-murderer is given what most people consider to be a lenient sentence, and there is a public outcry: 'It's not right! It's not fair! It's unjust! Something ought to be done about it!' I agree – but where did it come from, this sense of rightness and wrongness, fairness and unfairness? Two men are overheard having a quarrel: 'I helped you when you were in trouble, and now you won't do the same for me! It's not fair! You won't catch me twice!' Again, I ask, where does this talk of right and wrong, fair and unfair come from? Why do we speak to ourselves – sometimes to rebuke ourselves for an action or a word, but more often than not to excuse ourselves? Two children are playing on the mat: 'No! You went first last time. It's my turn now'. How do children know *instinctively* (whether or not the parents have taught them) that they should take turns? 'If there's a God, why does he allow war or famine or pestilence or earthquakes or whatever? Why do the innocent have to suffer as well as the guilty? If he's God, can't he stop it?' Where does this sense of good and bad, innocence and guilt, come from? How do we know that pain, misery and death are bad? Where does kindness come from? How do we know that kindness is good, and cruelty bad? I ask again: Where does all this 'morality' come from? Why is it universal in the human race? The explanation is Romans 2:14-15.

This is a point of far greater significance than at first appears, as I will now explain.

What bearing does this have on the rest of my book?

Just this: as I explained at the close of the previous chapter, since the Gentiles do not have the law of Moses, care must be taken in the exegesis of those New Testament passages which speak of sinners who were once under the law, but have by Christ been delivered from it. Those passages which were written to converted Jews or proselytes present no problem. But what of those passages which were written to converted Gentiles? One explanation is that those believing Gentiles needed to be taught the Old

---

[27] Interestingly, Moses, in recording these things, never tries to read the law back into the history.

Testament background to their faith, especially with regard to the law. Why? Because often they were being attacked by Judaisers who wanted them to submit to the law. Paul wrote to teach believers some basic facts about the law, in order to highlight the stupidity, the wrongness, of converted Gentiles going under the old, fulfilled and abolished Jewish system. And since they, as Gentiles, before conversion, were never under the law, why on earth would they think to put themselves under the very law from which Christ, by his death, released believing Jews? Paul would have none of it!

Having said that, there are a few remaining passages where it does appear that believing Gentiles had also in some sense been under the law in their unregenerate days, and were now delivered from it in Christ. I will bring such to your attention, reader, as we go on. The question is, how can these passages be explained? How were these Gentiles under the law before conversion? The answer is Romans 2:14-15.

Let me give but one illustration. Take Romans 7:4. Assuming that the recipients of the letter were *not* converted Jews or proselytes – and is that certain?[28] – then we have to face the fact that Paul told rank-Gentile believers that they have 'become dead to the law', they had 'died to the law' (NIV).[29] How can this be – since they were never under the law?

I make the following suggestion: Israel, having the law from Sinai, served as a model – a paradigm – to show how God deals with people under law. The Gentiles, while not under the law of Moses, are nevertheless under some sort of law (Rom. 2:14-15). While Romans 7:4, then, is strictly applicable only to Jewish believers, the principle applies equally to Gentile converts and 'their' law.

This has large consequences. Anticipating further developments, as we shall see, the history of the Jews shows the utter uselessness of sinners attempting justification by works. Since the Jews could not find salvation through the law, even the law given them by God, then no system of works will enable sinners to earn salvation. This leaves the human race in total, helpless bondage – a bondage from which only Christ can deliver.

This very important corollary comes directly from this look at Romans 2:14-15. Paul's teaching here is of far greater significance than it seems at first glance. From time to time throughout the book, therefore, I shall refer back to this passage, and the explanation of it which I have put forward in this chapter.

---

[28] My best 'guess' is that the church in Rome contained a mixture of Jews, proselytes and Gentiles, all converted to Christ.
[29] The apostle declared: 'I... died to the law' (Gal. 2:19).

Part Two

The Reformed Case

Chapter 4

Calvin's First and Second Uses of the Law

The Reformers, retaining the fundamental view of the law as promulgated by the medieval Church, but reacting against Romish legalism,[1] and the (largely imagined) antinomianism of the Anabaptists, produced their own threefold use of the law.[2] In particular, Calvin's three uses of the so-called 'moral law' became standard Reformed teaching.[3] Large claims have been made for this system – 'well-developed', 'well-known', 'a consistent doctrine', and such like. We shall see! The big question, however, is, *is it scriptural?*

Before I examine Calvin's third use – which is the most significant for my book, as it was in his own writings and system – I glance at his first and second uses. *First*, Calvin claimed, the law prepares sinners for Christ, and leads them to him. *Secondly*, he said, the law restrains sin in the unregenerate.

Let me briefly examine these claims.

Does the law prepare sinners for Christ?

By preparationism, I mean the preaching of the law to sinners in order to give them an experience to make them 'fit' for faith in Christ. Some argue that although men preach the law, the preparation is all of God's Spirit. Others argue for degrees of self-preparation.[4] Even though Calvin was confusing and ambiguous, if not contradictory, he did teach preparationism. Calvin, of course, did not teach *self*-preparation. Nor did he think preparation *merits* pardon. A law work, he argued, is the *way* to Christ, not the *warrant* for coming.

Let me prove that Calvin did indeed sow the seed of preparationism – that the law does prepare sinners for Christ. The first work of the law, he said, is to convict the (elect) sinner of his sin, his spiritual impotence and his condemnation, and so drive him to seek for mercy in Christ alone. Sinners, Calvin claimed, fall into two camps. Citing – but misunderstanding and misapplying (see chapter 9) – 'the law was our tutor to bring us to Christ' (Gal. 3:24),[5] he argued that some sinners are not fit to receive Christ, but need to be made sensible of their misery, and to be completely humbled, while other sinners need a bridle to restrain them, to induce fear – *terror* – and despair until they turn to Christ. But both cases, according to Calvin, are met by the law, which brings sinners to Christ, and prepares them to receive him. That word 'prepares' casts a long shadow!

---

[1] But Calvin himself has been justifiably accused of legalism. See chapter 5.
[2] The extracts for this chapter begin on p348.
[3] Calvin was not unique in this business, but he was the principal player.
[4] See below and chapter 9.
[5] As I will explain, 'to bring us' is a misleading insertion into the text, which reads: 'The law was our tutor to Christ'. In addition, 'tutor' is not the best translation, with its overtone of 'educator'.

Although Calvin was not alone in sowing the seed from which preparationism grew, it was *his* system which played the major part. And grow it did! Not only have immense powers been ascribed to the law, Calvin's system has led to far-reaching consequences for sinners and for preaching.

In his *Institutes*,[6] Calvin offered no scripture to support his claim that the law keeps some sinners in fear until they are regenerated. In trying to justify this lack of scripture support, Calvin was patronising, arguing there is no need to provide proof since the case, he claimed, is so obvious. Furthermore, as I mentioned above, Calvin also misunderstood and misapplied Galatians 3:24, the key verse for his first use of the law. I will not stop to analyse this now, leaving it until chapter 9. At this point, I want to deal as briefly as I can with the outworking of Calvin's view of the law as far as it concerns the preparation of sinners for Christ.

But why am I doing this? It is not central to my main theme – that is, the believer and the law. So why am I going off on this tangent? In the first place, it involves a misinterpretation of Galatians 3:24, and since Galatians plays a vital role in the biblical understanding of the relationship of the believer and the law, with Galatians 3 at the centre of its argument, it is vital not to misinterpret the verse. In addition, a look at the grim effects of the misapplication of the law in the preaching of the gospel to *sinners* will afford a salutary warning about the dangers of misapplying the law to the *believer*. And, as we proceed, I will indicate where preparationism can produce lasting damage in the life of believers. No, it is not a printing mistake. I said preparationism can damage *believers*, and I meant it. It is for these reasons that I spend just a little time on this aspect of Calvin's view of the law, and give a thumb-nail sketch of what it has given rise to.

Although Calvin laid out the principles of preparationism, it was the Puritans who followed and developed his view of a law work before faith, with large consequences. First, the early Puritans began by breaking down a sinner's conversion into legal stages. But this was not enough. The next generation of Puritans took one of these stages, and broke this down into sub-stages. The result was that Calvin's initial system was stretched far beyond what he could have imagined.

William Perkins, for instance, ended up with four necessary works of preparation, to be followed by four stages of grace, capping it all by specifying five steps in the receiving of Christ, all of these stages being 'precise'. David Clarkson specified fifteen steps, with many subdivisions within his list. Joseph Alleine's 'infallible prescription' for a sinner's conversion involved sixteen steps, all of which were spelled out once again in precise detail. And so it has gone on in one form or another. New England, too, felt the icy grip of preparationism.

Such an approach led to an emphasis upon the 'sensible sinner'. 'Sensible' sinners are the regenerate who, conscious of their sin and need of salvation, repent, and desire Christ. They are, therefore, demonstrating that they must be elect. Such sinners, some have claimed, may be invited to trust Christ, but no others. Some Puritans, and others since, have even asserted that the gospel invitation is to be governed by this precise way and order in which, they assert, the Spirit brings sinners to Christ. All such conclusions are grievously unbiblical, and have produced much damage and misery in the lives of countless men and women.

---

[6] Calvin, it is important to remember, said he had set out his views most fully in his *Institutes*.

The precise distinctions drawn in describing and specifying the nature of 'sensibility' have proved too subtle for many. The notion has erected daunting barriers, with the result that sinners have not always felt able to come directly to Christ without first spending time with Moses at Mount Sinai, and without being able to speak of an experience of a detailed law work preparing them for the Redeemer. Under such a system, sinners are taught to concentrate on whether or not they are sensible, on their sense of the law and its effects in their hearts, and this has effectively kept many from the Lord Jesus, hindering them from trusting the Saviour, sometimes imprisoning them in a harrowing anxiety for a considerable period of time, even for years. Not only so. It can also keep believers from a sense of assurance. In fact, under this system, a lack of assurance, in the end, becomes the best assurance, while the clearest pointer to damnation is a sense of security. Legalism was bound to follow the introduction of such teaching. And this legal system of preparation leading to perpetual doubt, stemming principally from Perkins, became the standard Christian experience for three hundred years.

To preach the gospel properly, so the theory goes, the preacher must begin with the law. A thorough law work is essential – essential before a sinner can be invited to trust Christ or has any warrant to trust Christ.

Is this right? Certainly not! Leaving to one side (until chapter 9) consideration of the all-important textual argument (Gal. 3:10 – 4:7), let me in a more general way expose the unscripturalness of preparationism. No such preaching-distinctions concerning a law work can be found in the biblical records of gospel addresses to Gentiles, or in the doctrinal explanations in the New Testament. True, the sinner needs to be convicted of his sin before he will trust Christ. Yes. And the Spirit, said Christ, will do the work: 'He will convict the world of sin... of sin, because they do not believe in me' (John 16:8-9). But this, according to preparationism, is not enough. The sinner needs to be convinced that he is convicted of sin, and this is by the law. He needs to know he has had 'a law work', a *thorough* law work. He needs to be convinced he is prepared, convinced that he is truly convicted. Otherwise he cannot believe, he is not 'fit for Christ', he has no warrant to expect pardon from Christ; indeed, he has no warrant or encouragement to trust Christ. In short, until a sinner knows he is truly 'sensible', he cannot trust Christ. The fact is, some have gone so far as to claim he is not even invited or commanded to trust Christ! This means, of course, that the Spirit must convict a sinner that he is 'sensible', otherwise no sinner will ever be saved. But where in Scripture do we come across a promise that the Spirit will convict of conviction? Or, to put it another way, where do we find a promise that the Spirit will assure the sinner that he has led him through all these stages? And, do not forget, all this must be so for every sinner.

The truth is, when men prescribe specified steps of conviction the sinner must take or experience before he is warranted to come to Christ, before he is warranted to feel he is invited to trust Christ, they contradict the frequent call such preachers make – or ought to make – to the sinner not to look to himself but to Christ. The preparationist teaches the very opposite. He demands that the sinner be assured he has taken the legally specified steps, many of which are highly spiritual, and has taken them before conversion!

Efforts have been made, of course, to mitigate this. But some of these efforts have been bizarre. So much so, they have compounded the problem. Let me make myself clear. In saying this, I am talking about the strange advice which has come (and still comes) from Reformed teachers, including Puritans, not excepting some of the greatest Puritan preachers, (Reformed) household-names, published by top Reformed publishing houses. For instance, sinners have been urged to wait for God to have mercy upon them, meanwhile to cultivate 'civility and religion'. Other ways out of the impasse have involved tortuous, even contradictory, twists of logic, with sinners being told to distinguish between that which is a typical conversion experience, and that which is exceptional. God, they are informed, usually brings the sinner to Christ through a law work; usually, but there are exceptions. So, in order to get himself out of the quagmire of preparationism,[7] the trembling sinner has to believe he is an exception to the rule! The sinner who lacks 'legal terrors' – that is, lacks clear preparatory evidences – nevertheless need not worry, so he is told, if he sees he has 'a minimum of conviction of sin', and he trusts Christ. Ah! but *herein* lies the crunch. Anxious sinners who have been reared under such teaching, *do* doubt, they cannot see *clear* evidences, they cannot see that they truly trust Christ, and when they are told legal preparations do not *always* go before faith, once again they have to believe they are the exception to the rule. It is like a physician trying to reassure his anxious patient: 'Your symptoms indicate cancer, but there are exceptions and you may be one, but usually the conclusion is inevitable; not always, but usually'. Would it be any wonder if the patient thought he had cancer, and that his doctor was in a muddle? Similarly, whatever qualifications are invoked to guard the preacher's words, the anxious sinner listening to the twists and turns of preparationism would be almost certain to come away thinking: I, at any rate, need the evidences of legal preparations, *just to make sure*.[8]

For the fact is, many have been more definite. A law work is essential, they have declared, before conversion. A sinner *must* be prepared for the Lord Jesus, before he can receive him. Advocates of this system are adamant. Until a sinner, by the law, has been awakened, convicted and made to feel distress for his sin, he must not be invited to Christ or given the gospel offer. As I have already remarked, such a detailed, specified process can be drawn out – even over many years. This is not at all surprising. Instead of being concerned with trusting Christ, the sinner is trying to measure his evidences of preparation. Repentance, for example. Am I repentant? Am I sincerely repentant? Am I repentant enough? Have I spent long enough at Sinai? Can I come to Christ yet? Am I sufficiently prepared to come? Such questions are bound to arise in the sinner's mind when reared on a diet of preparationism. And what is the outcome? The sinner probes the law and its work in his heart, when all the time he should have been trusting Christ. What is more, if the sinner does need these qualifications, then he must know precisely how much of them he needs, and how to measure them. What suggestions, reader, do such teachers have for advising the sinner how to measure the amount of repentance he has experienced, and whether or not he has the minimum required? Where can he obtain the necessary dip-stick?

Reader, I agree that much contemporary preaching is feeble. But the remedy is not, as is claimed, to preach the law. We need to preach Christ and him crucified, with all

---

[7] And I mean 'quagmire' – Pilgrim went through Bunyan's Slough of Despond *before* he found forgiveness, remember. And do not forget Bunyan's years of harrowing doubt after his conversion. The extracts will verify my claims in this paragraph.
[8] Do not miss the point. The *unconverted* are advised and expected to be able to make such fine spiritual distinctions – and about themselves, to boot!

the power the sovereign Spirit will give us (1 Cor. 2:2). Leaving aside the question of the law, I do not for a moment deny that all who come to Christ must and will have been taught of God before they come (John 6:45); in other words, they must and will have been prepared. In addressing sinners, however, we must not confuse the gospel invitation – which is unfettered – with God's secret working within the elect. God's secret decree does not limit the invitation, any more than God's general invitation and command to all sinners governs his decree.

Let me explain. God will effectually work only in the elect, but he desires and demands that unbelievers be given the gospel invitation and command, universally and promiscuously. We must not try to play God's sovereign decree against his revealed desire to see sinners saved. Nor must we eliminate one to leave the other, and so, we think, preserve our rational credentials. Let us, with the utmost confidence, drive this locomotive at full speed along two parallel rails, rails which meet only at infinity.

Furthermore, the encouragements God adds to the invitation – addressing the weary, hungry, thirsty, and so on – must not be preached as barriers for the sinner to climb over, but rather as they are intended; namely, encouragements to ease the sinner's doubts, and clear the way to Christ.

In particular, consider this emphasis upon the law as a preparative for Christ. If the preparationists are right, and a thorough law work is essential before conversion, as a warrant for the issuing of the gospel invitation to sinners, why do we not read at least one example of it in the New Testament? I admit that Christ and the apostles used the law when addressing Jews – but when did they do the same when addressing Gentiles? There is no evidence whatsoever that the apostles thought they had to preach to give such sinners a thorough law work before commanding them to trust Christ. In fact, *never once did any apostle use the law when addressing Gentile unbelievers.* Why not?

Consider the apostle's words to the church at Corinth. Just as an aside – but what an aside! – in a passage dealing with the abuse of gifts, Paul writes thus: 'If the whole church comes together and everyone speaks in [languages], and some who do not understand or some unbelievers come in, will they not say that you are out of your mind? But if an unbeliever or someone who does not understand comes in while everybody is prophesying, he will be convinced by all that he is a sinner and will be judged by all, and the secrets of his heart will be laid bare. So he will fall down and worship God, exclaiming: "God is really among you!"' (1 Cor. 14:23-25, NIV). Leaving to one side the issue of gifts, the point I wish to bring out is this: An unbeliever comes into the meeting. If he finds a babble – everybody speaking, nobody listening, nobody even understanding what anybody else is saying – what will he think? It's a madhouse! And he's right; too right! If, on the other hand, he finds orderly, clear teaching and instruction, it might well be, by God's grace, that he is convicted of his sin, that he is cut to the heart, and his innermost thoughts are revealed to him. It might be that he gets a real sense of God's presence. It might even be that he is converted. But, at the very least, he is convicted of his sin. Very well. My question is this: Are we to understand that what Paul wanted at Corinth was for the entire church to meet and instruct each other in an orderly manner – yes, that's what he wanted! – but that the subject matter should be the law, specifically the ten commandments? Strange he did not specify it here. Ah well! Even so, preparationists must think it to be so. How else, according to their theory, could any sinner be convicted of his sin? It wouldn't be any use speaking on Christ and his cross, would it? That wouldn't do the job! It has to be the law![9] Hmm! If any preparationist thinks that the subject matter at Corinth was the law (and that at every meeting), then, with apologies to Lewis Carroll, and borrowing Alice's expostulation to the Queen of Hearts: 'What a strange world they must live in'!

Where is the evidence that the Samaritans (Acts 8:12), the Ethiopian eunuch (Acts 8:27-38), Cornelius (Acts 10:34-45), the people of Lystra, Iconium and Antioch (Acts 14:21-22), the Philippian jailer (Acts 16:30-31), the people of Athens (Acts 17:16-34), to name but a few non-Jews (and the Samaritans were a special case, and it is probable that the eunuch and Cornelius were proselytes), had 'the moral law' preached to them? Where do we read of Christ or the apostles preaching the law to Gentiles? Since the establishment of the new covenant, preaching the law had been the work of Judaisers (Acts 15:1,5), not the apostles.[10] Let me draw on something I said in chapter 2. Think of the apostle's experience at Lystra (Acts 14:11-18). The Gentiles were about to worship him and Barnabas. How did the brothers stop the pagans? What arguments did they use? Did they cite the first and second commandments? They did not! Instead, from nature they challenged pagan folly in trying to worship them. In effect, they asked: 'Does not nature teach you?' If the Gentiles had been given the law, why did Paul not quote it against them? The fact is, since the Gentiles did not have the law, Paul could not use it in his approach to them, and he made no attempt to do so. The same goes for his preaching to the Athenians in the Areopagus (Acts 17:18-34). Paul, confronting the Greeks over their superstitious idolatry, did not apply the law to them. The fact is, his words had a very different ring. He used what the pagans were familiar with, quoting a Greek poet! He told them God had 'overlooked' 'these times of ignorance' in the past, 'but now commands all men everywhere to repent' (Acts 17:30). I do not say these passages contain no allusions whatever to the Old Testament. Certainly, Paul *thought* in such terms – and *argued* from it – his sermons are full of it – but he did not explicitly quote the law to pagans who had no knowledge of it.

In case there should be any doubt, Paul was *not* preaching the law to Gentile sinners in the opening chapters of Romans. As I have already remarked,[11] 'law' does not make an appearance in Romans until we reach chapter 2 and verse 12. What is more, the apostle's different approach to Gentiles and Jews in Romans 1:18 – 3:20 stands out a mile. When addressing Gentiles, observe how he tackles them on their inward 'light' (conscience) (Rom. 1:19),[12] which they suppress; the works of nature ('creation') (Rom. 1:20), which they see and enjoy; the obvious deductions (Rom. 1:19-21,23,25,28), which they stifle; and their 'natural' appetites (Rom. 1:26-27), which they pervert. But he does not use the law!

Finally, to make the eschatological point once again, note the 'now' of Acts 17:30.

---

[9] 'Unless we are prepared by the law, we have no experience at all, the cross is just a quaint story, the gospel offers men nobody knows what, and makes little sense to modern men'. And so on. I am not making it up. Such things are said by contemporary Reformed-teachers. See 'Extracts' p426; see also pp348,420.

[10] As we have seen, when the apostles addressed Jews, they used the law, but, even so, they did not preach it to them. There is vast difference between the two.

[11] See chapter 3.

[12] According to Rom. 2:14-15. See chapter 3.

Despite this clear evidence, when the Reformed lay out what is required of preachers when attempting to bring sinners to Christ, they are not averse to making large claims for the law. They even put the law on a par with the gospel itself. If truth be told, they sometimes give it a more important role! Law and grace – the pair of them – are described as the two principal weapons in the Spirit's armoury, with the law always – always – at the very core of the sinner's conviction, regeneration, repentance and faith. It is no use preaching mercy through Christ, so it is said, unless it is preached with the law. As for the cross, it is but a 'quaint story', one which incites curiosity and promotes miserable feelings in the sinner, but really does precious little good to modern man.[13] To preach the gospel without the law is to offer the sinner nobody knows what! What is the great need? How will sinners find Christ? Preach the law! This is the panacea. Only when the law has had its effect, then and then only will Christ's attractiveness and justifying righteousness make any sense to sinners today. All this is claimed for the law.[14]

Reader, this is breath-taking! If we adopt this programme, we must, I suppose, tell sinners that Christ is hard to understand, unattractive, but never fear, Moses will prepare you, and Moses will show you the way. Simply to preach Christ is not enough, however. Moses must come first. If this is so, then we may expect a new version of the Bible to appear – which version will tell us, I suppose: 'I determined not to know anything among you except [*Moses and*] Jesus Christ and him crucified', and in that order: 'I am determined to preach Christ – but only after preaching Moses'. Again, we shall have to listen to the apostle stating: 'We preach Christ crucified – *but only after we have fully set out the law*'. Away with this! Let us stay with what Paul actually wrote in 1 Corinthians 2:2 and 1:23. The same goes for John 14:6. 'I am the way', said Christ, 'no one comes to the Father except through me'. Apparently, so we are told, it is through Christ, *first having gone through Moses and been prepared by his good offices*. How all this can be made to fit with the signal lack of law in the following passage, one which deals specifically with gospel addresses, I am at a loss to comprehend:

Now all things are of God, who has reconciled us to himself through Jesus Christ, and has given us the ministry of reconciliation; that is, that God was in Christ reconciling the world to himself, not imputing their trespasses to them, and has committed to us the word of reconciliation. Now then, we are ambassadors for Christ, as though God were pleading through us: we implore you on Christ's behalf, be reconciled to God. For he made him who knew no sin to be sin for us, that we might become the righteousness of God in him. We then, as workers together with him also plead with you not to receive the grace of God in vain. For he says: 'In an acceptable time I have heard you, and in the day of salvation I have helped you'. Behold, now is the accepted time; behold, now is the day of salvation (2 Cor. 5:18 – 6:2).

Do not miss the apostle's passionate stress on grace, going hand in hand with the conspicuous absence of any talk of the law.

---

[13] As I have shown, in accordance with his firmly established principles (1 Cor. 9:21), Paul did not think it right or necessary to use the law when addressing the 'modern men' of his day at Lystra and Athens.

[14] As I keep saying, see the extracts!

These are vital considerations. All talk of the law preparing sinners for Christ is wide of the mark. As I will show, Galatians 3:24-25 certainly does not teach it. What is more, John 16:8-11 teaches that the Spirit convicts men of sin on the grounds of their attitude to Christ, not on the basis of the law, and John 3:18; 8:24 teaches that ultimately sinners are condemned for not trusting Christ, not for breaking the law. The law does not open sinners' eyes to their sins and Christ. Christ alone does that. It is his preciousness that shows our worthlessness; his holiness, our sin; his grace, our pride; his love, our hatred; his submission to the Father's will, our inbred, habitual rebellion and self-seeking; his sweetness, our bitterness. And so on.

As John Berridge put it:

> *The law provokes men oft to ill,*
> *And churlish hearts makes harder still;*
> *But gospel acts a kinder part,*
> *And melts a most obdurate heart.*[15]

And what about John Newton? What was it that convicted that hardened slaver of his sin? Was it the threatenings of the law? Let him tell us in his own words:

> *In evil long I took delight,*
> *Unawed by shame or fear;*
> *Till a new object struck my sight,*
> *And stopped my wild career.*
>
> *I saw one hanging on a tree,*
> *In agony and blood,*
> *Who fixed his languid eyes on me,*
> *As near his cross I stood.*
>
> *Sure, never till my latest breath,*
> *Can I forget that look;*
> *It seemed to charge me with his death,*
> *Though not a word he spoke.*
>
> *My conscience felt and owned the guilt,*
> *And plunged me in despair;*
> *I saw my sins his blood had spilt,*
> *And helped to nail him there.*
>
> *A second look he gave, which said,*
> *'I freely all forgive;*
> *This blood is for thy ransom paid;*
> *I die that thou may'st live'.*
>
> *Thus, while his death my sin displays*
> *In all its blackest hue,*
> *Such is the mystery of grace,*
> *It seals my pardon too.*[16]

And, of course, we have the well known hymn by Joseph Hart:

---

[15] Berridge: *Sion's* number 150; Gadsby: *Hymns* number 49.
[16] *Gospel Hymns* number 701.

Come, ye sinners, poor and wretched,
Weak and wounded, sick and sore;
Jesus, ready, stands to save you,
Full of pity, joined with power.
He is able, he is able;
He is willing; doubt no more.

Come ye needy, come, and welcome,
God's free bounty glorify;
True belief and true repentance,
Every grace that brings you nigh.
Without money, without money
Come to Jesus Christ and buy.

Let not conscience make you linger,
Nor of fitness fondly dream;
All the fitness he requireth
Is to feel your need of him.
This he gives you, this he gives you,
'Tis the Spirit's rising beam.

Come, ye weary, heavy laden,
Bruised and mangled by the fall;
If you tarry till you're better,
You will never come at all.
Not the righteous, not the righteous;
Sinners Jesus came to call.[17]

Of all the many excellent things in Hart's hymn, do not miss: 'All the fitness he requireth/ Is to feel your need of him'. 'Just so', say the Reformed, 'just so. And he gives it by the law'. Oh? Where did Hart say that? Hart ascribed conviction of sin – as Christ did – to Christ by his Spirit: 'This he gives you, this he gives you,/ 'Tis the Spirit's rising beam'. I see no mention of Moses or the law whatever.

The consequences of all this legal preparationism, however, do not fall only upon the unconverted sinner; as I have indicated, the believer, too, can suffer. And how! And it is this which impinges on my main discussion in this book; namely, the believer and the law. Note the word 'legalism' I used a few moments ago. How can the notion that the law prepares sinners for Christ, that it makes them fit to receive him, affect the believer? By storing up years of harrowing gloom and torment for him! Even though he has come to Christ, preparation-by-law can play havoc with the believer's sense of assurance. Written history records many examples of those who suffered under it. What is more frightening, unwritten history must obscure a much larger number of damaged souls.

Take Jonathan Edwards. He suffered under it. At one stage, he doubted his conversion. As he recorded in his diary for December 18th, 1722, he could not testify to having had a preparatory work, nor to having been regenerated, precisely as the Puritans had specified. On November 6th, 1724, he felt some relief concerning his doubts as to whether or not he trusted Christ. Yet on May 28th, 1725, he was still doubting if he was truly converted. For help, he vowed to turn back to those very Puritans who had led him into the doubt in the first place! Richard Baxter had trudged

---

[17] *Gospel Hymns* number 402. Hart: *Hymns* number 100, p133.

precisely the same depressing path a hundred years before. His doubts over many years arose because he could not detect evidences in his life that he had taken the steps of preparation delineated by earlier Puritans. As a result, he was for ever poring over his sins and deficiencies, or doubting his sincerity. Baxter eventually got release by seeing that all the time his eyes should have been on Christ and not his own heart. Thomas Goodwin said similar things. These men, in the first place, should have been sent to Christ and not to the law. And when they found they were in trouble, they should have gone to Christ and not to the law.

The preparation men ought to have listened to John Wheelwright, John Cotton's only ministerial supporter in the 1636-1637 New England crisis over antinomianism. Wheelwright, Anne Hutchinson's brother-in-law, had spelled it out: 'To preach the gospel, is to preach Christ... and nothing but Christ'.[18] But the preparationism of Thomas Hooker and Thomas Shepard won the day, and, as a result, preparationism-for-conversion became the hallmark of New England theology, with severe consequences. Nathaniel Ward warned the arch-preparationist Hooker he had gone too far: 'You make as good Christians before men are in Christ, as ever they are after... Would I were but as good a Christian now, as you make men while they are but preparing for Christ'.

Spurgeon in his sermon, 'The Warrant of Faith', which he preached in 1863 on 1 John 3:23, strongly criticised some of the Puritans for their emphasis upon preparationism. As he argued, we should tell a sinner that, whatever his condition, he requires no preparation or qualification, but he must at once trust Christ and take him to be his all in all. The sinner does not need 'months of law work'. Spurgeon was blunt with his hearers. If they were trusting in the fact that they had felt the terrors of the law, they were mistaken. They must trust Christ and not their feelings. Preparationists, in their delineation of what a sinner *must* be and experience before he may come to Christ, actually describe what a saint *is*, after he has come to Christ. Preparationists, with their talk of the law, discourage sinners from going straight to Christ.

As the Particular Baptist Confession of 1644, expressly denying Calvin's position, put it:

The tenders of the gospel to the conversion of sinners is absolutely free, no way requiring, as absolutely necessary, any qualifications, preparations, terrors of the law, or preceding ministry of the law.

Sadly, not all the spiritual descendants of the 1644 Particular Baptists have kept to this biblical position. Not only were there differences in the 1677 (1689) Particular Baptist Confession – when the Particular Baptists, in part for political reasons, adopted the Reformed stance on the law – but some Particular Baptists developed the disastrous doctrine that a sinner must be sensible before he can be invited to Christ. As a consequence of the views of John Gill, J.C.Philpot, William and John Gadsby, crippling limitations were imposed upon the preaching of the gospel – as can be seen in the Gospel Standard Articles.[19] Notice 'can be seen'. I am talking about that which is going on today.

Not all the Reformed have adopted a full-blown preparationism, of course, but many have. In any case, the seeds of it are there in their system of law. They must not

[18] The root of the 'antinomian' controversy in New England was preparationism. In fact, I suspect at bottom it was hyper-Calvinism.
[19] See Articles numbers 24,32,33 and certain aspects of 34.

be surprised that from time to time those seeds germinate, grow and bear fruit, and when they do, the cost paid by the souls of men and women is frightening. Furthermore, many Reformed teachers are calling for the preaching of the law today. It may sound 'biblical', but 'biblical' is precisely what it is not![20] As I said, right at the beginning, we suffer too often from legal preaching these days – both overt and incipient. We need *gospel* preaching. We must have Christ! Who was it advised a would-be preacher: 'Whatever you do, young man, preach Christ!' And what of the man who complained of a sermon he had sat under: 'Not enough of Christ in it for me!' Above all, we know what Paul would have said in response to law-preachers today: 'I determined not to know anything among you except Jesus Christ and him crucified' (1 Cor. 2:2). Christ, and him preached, both convicts and converts the sinner!

So much for Calvin's first use of the law. Now for the second.

Does the law restrain sin in the unregenerate?

Calvin, in his second use of the law, said it does. Stressing the part played by fear – even terror – Calvin declared that the law restrains the unregenerate, even though they 'rage and boil' and are 'inflamed' by this restraint. And not only the unregenerate. The children of God also benefit from this legal regime, even though they gain little from it. So, ambiguously, asserted Calvin.

There is not much to say on this. Since Calvin quoted only one scripture to 'support' his case, 1 Timothy 1:9-10, which says nothing – *nothing* – about restraining sin, and because, reader, I am not able to deal with human philosophy, I leave his statement as it stands. It is without scriptural foundation.

Even so, Calvin has been followed by many who have tried harder than he to prove it from Scripture, but have fared no better. Yet some have gone as far as to assert that the *main* end of the law is to restrain transgression. The 'supporting' passages cited (Rom. 2:8-9; 5:13-14; Gal. 3:19; 2 Tim. 3:16), say no such thing. Take Galatians 3:19. It says nothing to support the claim. Let me remind you of what it *does* say about the law: 'It was added because of transgressions'. This, of course, is a fact. But it certainly does not say: 'It was added to *restrain* transgressions'. The law *revealed* and *aroused* sins, reader, but it did not *restrain* them. And this is admitted, even by some who quote the verse! In any case, all this misses the point entirely. Paul was speaking of the historical role of the law, and its temporary nature – 'it was added because of transgressions, till the Seed should come to whom the promise was made' – not of its supposed role in restraining sin in the unregenerate. The idea that the law exists today to do something which was ended nearly 2000 years ago by the coming of the Christ, is remarkable, to say the least. Coming from the other direction, if the law *was* given to deter men from sin, to bring them to Christ, and so on, why was it limited to the time that the Seed should come? Surely Calvin, and those who follow him, argue that the law restrains sin and brings men to Christ *nowadays*, do they not?

Above all, of course, Romans 7:5,7-12 destroys the case for the law restraining sin in the unregenerate. Leaving detailed comment on it until chapter 10, for now I let

---

[20] If Rom. 3:20; 4:15; 5:13,20 does support the practice, why is there no New Testament example of law-preaching to Gentile unbelievers? Do not forget the context of such verses. Do not forget the eschatological!

Paul's words – recording his own experience of the law before he was regenerate – speak for themselves:

For when we were in the flesh, the sinful passions which were aroused by the law were at work in our members to bear fruit to death... I would not have known sin except through the law... But sin, taking opportunity by the commandment, produced in me all manner of evil desire. For apart from the law sin was dead. I was alive once without the law, but when the commandment came, sin revived and I died. And the commandment, which was to bring life, I found to bring death. For sin, taking occasion by the commandment, deceived me, and by it killed me.

That the law does not restrain sin, is perfectly clear. The law certainly did not restrain Paul's sin. The fact is, the law revealed and, above all, aroused it. The law does not make a man stop sinning. Only Christ does that. Only Christ can make a sinner holy. He *is* all! Anticipating just a little, as we shall see, there is a link between Romans 4:14; 5:20; 7:8 and Galatians 3:15-25. The pedagogue (child-custodian) disciplined a minor (see chapter 9), but his instruction could actually goad the minor to do the very thing he was forbidden. Forbidden fruit fascinates! Adam and Eve found it so. Doesn't every parent know the natural reaction of a child to a command not to do something? And not only a child![21]

Even Calvin himself destroyed his own doctrine. The law makes the sin problem worse in the unregenerate, he said. It certainly does not restrain it. The philosophers, as Calvin said, might teach that the law restrains sin; the Scriptures do not. Again, as Calvin said, until a man is regenerate, and has the law written on his heart,[22] the law actually tends to increase transgression and not restrain it.

This, I realise, will sound preposterous to many. Could Calvin be this self-contradicting? After all he was explicit – the second use of the law is to restrain sin in the unregenerate! As I say, what a self-contradiction! But I am not making it up.[23]

Thus Calvin enunciated his first two uses of the law – to prepare sinners for Christ, and restrain sin in the unregenerate. He was sadly mistaken on both counts. Even so, he has been followed by many.

What can the law do for a sinner? Let me conclude with a biblical summary. Unlike Calvin's first and second uses, it is all negative. The law does not restrain sin in a natural man. On the contrary! It excites it in him (Rom. 7:5,7-11). The law cannot regenerate a sinner dead in sin (Gal. 3:2-5). A sinner cannot receive the Spirit by the works of the law, but only by the hearing of faith (Gal. 3:2,5). The law cannot justify a sinner (Rom. 3:21ff; 4:13ff; 10:4ff; Gal. 2:15-21; 3:10ff).[24] The law cannot restrain sin

---

[21] For more on the law's impotence to make a believer forsake sin, see chapter 16 p261ff.

[22] Once again, this begs a very important question. See chapter 18 for which law is written on the heart in the new covenant.

[23] Please see 'Extracts' p358.

[24] Salvation comes only through grace – which specifically excludes law-works (Rom. 11:6; Eph. 2:8-9). If the law could produce salvation – *if* – it would nullify both faith and the promise (Rom. 4:14; Gal. 3:18). Of course, it would bring salvation *if a man could keep it perfectly* (Lev. 18:5; Rom. 7:10; 10:5; Gal. 3:12). See chapter 6. But this has to be nuanced. Man is born a sinner in Adam, and Adam's fall pre-dates the law (Rom. 5:12-20; 1 Cor. 15:22). Even if a sinner did keep the law perfectly, therefore, he is still a sinner. Every man sins because he is a sinner – he does not become a sinner by sinning. This is why it is essential to maintain the virgin birth of Christ.

in the sinner, nor does it prepare the sinner for Christ. Calvin was wrong on both counts.

So much for Calvin's first and second uses of the law. Now for his third use. Will he do any better with that?

Chapter 5

Calvin's Third Use of the Law

Having glanced at Calvin's first and second uses of the law, in which he focussed on the unregenerate, I now turn to his third use, the 'main' use.[1] Even though Calvin himself was not always consistent about it being the 'main' use, it is usually regarded as such by the Reformed. For them, this third purpose is the law's principal function. As a consequence, it plays a dominating role in the rest of my book.

The law of Moses, so Calvin claimed, is the best means for a believer to discover God's will, and, by meditating on it, be moved to sanctification. In other words, progressive sanctification is by the law. The law, which Calvin called a perpetual, inflexible and perfect rule of life, he likened to a whip rousing a lazy ass, driving the believer to godliness. The law is at once the *motive*, *means* and *standard* of sanctification, teaching the believer what God requires of him, and acting as a whip, thrashing him into obedience, beating down his laziness. Thus the law is both behind the believer – whipping him, compelling him, pricking him – and ahead of him, forever setting an unattainable standard, demanding absolute obedience.

How Calvin reconciled this with what he said elsewhere, I know not. After all, he was clear that God is not pleased with works which are produced through fear, or slavish observance of the law. Notwithstanding this contradiction at its core, and even though Calvin left himself open to the justifiable charge of legalism, the overwhelming majority of Reformed teachers have followed him in his system. The believer is under the binding law of Moses for sanctification; the law is the best rule of godliness in all the Scriptures, its 'chief dish',[2] the perfect rule; the law is a whip, spur or goad for lazy asses who have depraved hearts; those who will not have the law to rule them shall never be saved by the gospel; not to be under the law of Moses is to be both law-less and lawless; the law, not the gospel, is the believer's rule; those who teach the opposite are to be avoided as poisonous snakes. These are the sort of claims which are made by those who take the law as the believer's rule.[3]

Reformed teachers, it seems, have an exceedingly low view of believers. In addition to being 'lazy asses', believers, so it is said, have 'depraved hearts' and are a 'putrid organism', and the law produces slavish fear and resentment in them, stirring up their depravity. It reminds me of the Cretan pagans, 'lazy gluttons' (Tit. 1:12). I admit, of course, that believers can and do 'become dull of hearing' and 'sluggish [lazy]' (the same Greek word is used in both verses), and we are warned against it (Heb. 5:11; 6:12). But is this the way to think of believers in general? For instance, we are warned against sexual immorality (Eph. 5:3), and some believers fall into it, but is our

---

[1] The extracts for this chapter begin on p360.
[2] The law of Moses is not the *chief dish* of Scripture; *Christ* is!
[3] As before, see the extracts.

approach to sanctification to be based upon the assumption that all saints are sexually immoral? Is this the way to describe all believers?[4]

Moving on to the main issue, as my American friends say, 'here's where the rubber hits the road!' Is Calvin right? Does the Bible say that the believer goes to the law to be sanctified? Certainly not! Scripture does *not* teach that believers are under the law as a rule for life. Indeed, it says the very opposite. It says that deliverance from the law is the only way a man can be sanctified. I will prove my assertions. For now I ask you, reader, to consider the following. If the law *is* the rule for believers, they will be in dire trouble, and on two counts.

Two problems for believers if the Reformed view is right

First, if the believer *is* under the law, then any sin – any breaking of the commandments – will bring condemnation. This must be faced. It cannot be baulked or shrugged off. One offence brings guilt and condemnation for all (Jas. 2:10). If believers are under the law, any and every offence must condemn them. There is no evading this by Reformed semantics: 'For as many as are of the works of the law are under the curse; for it is written: "Cursed is everyone who does not continue in all things which are written in the book of the law, to do them"' (Gal. 3:10, quoting Deut. 27:26), and the curses are severe (Deut. 28:15-68; 29:1-29). The law has always condemned every offender. It always will. It can do no other, since it is 'the letter [which] kills... the ministry of death... the ministry of condemnation' (2 Cor. 3:6-9). This includes the believer. If the believer is under the law, he will be condemned by it; he must be. The law does not know whether the person is under it for justification or sanctification, whether the person is a believer or an unbeliever. The law has no mind! It stands inflexible. This is precisely the point about 'law'.[5] It demands obedience in all points. It curses every disobedience. Sadly, every believer sins. The consequence is clear. If the believer is under the law, he is bound to be condemned by it, since he is never free from sin in this life. And yet we are told expressly that 'there is therefore now no condemnation to those who are in Christ Jesus' (Rom. 8:1). Reader, do not limit this verse to the initial experience of justification. The believer is *not* condemned, he is never condemned in any circumstance whatever. Romans 8 comes after Romans 6 and 7. I know commentators disagree about the precise meaning of the 'therefore', but at the very least it must mean 'since a believer is justified, consequently'. Accordingly, since a believer cannot be condemned, even though he still sins, he cannot be under that law which can do nothing but curse and condemn him for the least offence. There is no condemnation to a believer – whether speaking of his sin before or after coming to faith. Yet if he is under the law, he *must* be condemned, something utterly contrary to the gospel. This is the first reason why the law cannot be the believer's rule. I will, of course, face up to the Reformed claim that the condemning power of the law is removed for believers even though it is over them as a perfect rule of life – and show that it is wrong. The fact is, all who are under the law are condemned by that law; unless, of course, they keep it perfectly.

---

[4] I will have something to say on the 'wretched man' of Rom. 7:24. I simply state here that I do not see this as a description of the spiritual man 'at his best'.

[5] As I have indicated, I will show that the *law* of Christ is a very different entity.

Secondly, if the believer is under the law, he is under *the law* – he cannot pick and choose which bits he will obey – which is precisely what Reformed teachers nearly always do.[6] They are wrong. Those under the law have to do as the law demands, do all of it, and do it in the way the law demands. I acknowledge that God wrote the ten commandments on stone 'and he added no more' (Deut. 5:22), but this must not be taken to mean – as Reformed teachers like to assume – that these ten commandments, and these only, are the law which forms the rule of sanctification. There is absolutely no biblical justification whatever for this assumption. I will return to the point, but, as I have already shown, the law is far wider than the ten commandments.[7] In any case, the ten commandments make their appearance, not only on the two stone tablets, but scattered throughout the law, alongside all kinds of regulations on all sorts of subjects. The Old Testament never divides the law into bits. Rather, a host of laws, regulations, ordinances and commands on a variety of matters, all of them, are amalgamated and denominated as 'the law'.

Take just one example. In Leviticus 19, the second, fourth, fifth, eighth and ninth commandments are mixed up with sundry laws on sacrifices, harvest, wages, how to treat the disabled, judgement, gossip, revenge, farm regulations, clothing, sexual relations, how to manage fruit trees for the first five years after planting, the eating of blood, shaving, tattoos, prostitution, the occult, respect for the aged, immigration, and weights and measures. The chapter concludes: 'Therefore you shall observe *all* my statutes and *all* my judgements, and perform them: I am the LORD' (Lev. 19:37). And how many times this, or similar, is repeated throughout Scripture (see Ex. 34:11; Lev. 20:22; Deut. 12:28; 24:8; 2 Chron. 7:17; Neh. 1:5; Ps. 105:45; Ezek. 37:24; and so on)! I will give more examples of the way Scripture mixes up various laws which the Reformed like to keep separate.[8]

Thus, if the law is the perfect rule for sanctification, then it is all the law. Are Reformed teachers willing for this? Take one example. The law *commands* those under it to exact revenge for personal offence: 'Your eye shall not pity: life shall be for life, eye for eye, tooth for tooth, hand for hand, foot for foot' (Deut. 19:21; Ex. 21:23-25; Lev. 24:19-20). In doing this, those under the law, while they have to avoid 'vengeance... against the children of your people' (Lev. 19:18), have to be determined not to forget their mistreatment at the hand of their enemies (Deut. 23:3-4; 25:17-19).

Again, is it acceptable for a Christian to buy a slave? If he is under the law as a perfect rule of obedience he can (Ex. 21:2-9,20). Is a believer able to take a second wife, and having done so, is he duty-bound to have sexual relations with her? If he is under the law, it is so (Ex. 21:10-11). Is it acceptable for a believer, if he has sexual intercourse with a virgin who is not engaged to be married, to settle the matter by paying the right dowry? If he is under the law, it is (Ex. 22:16-17). Presumably, a believing bank manager (or a believing depositor with the bank) should not impose interest on a loan to a fellow-believer (Ex. 22:25). And so on and on and on...

I know the Reformed have their escape routes ready, and I will look at them, but they do not stand scrutiny. If the law is the rule, then it is the law, and it is all the law which is the rule. But, for instance, is this law I have just cited – concerning revenge –

---

[6] See chapter 7.
[7] See chapter 1.
[8] See chapter 7.

the rule for the believer? Is *this* the law for the followers of Christ? If the believer is under the law as the perfect rule of life, it must be so. But what does Christ say? 'You have heard that it was said: "An eye for an eye and a tooth for a tooth". But I tell you not to resist an evil person... You have heard that it was said: "You shall love your neighbour and hate your enemy". But I say to you, love your enemies, bless those who curse you, do good to those who hate you, and pray for those who spitefully use you and persecute you, that you may be sons of your Father in heaven' (Matt. 5:38-45). What does Paul say? 'Repay no one evil for evil... Beloved, do not avenge yourself, but rather give place to wrath; for it is written: "Vengeance is mine, I will repay", says the Lord. Therefore: "If your enemy is hungry, feed him; if he is thirsty, give him a drink; for in so doing you will heap coals of fire on his head"' (Rom. 12:17-20).[9]

So much for the two problems I spoke of.

A glance at the Reformed argument based on the giving of the law to Israel after the exodus from Egypt

Some Reformed writers argue their case like this: the law was given to Israel to show them the way to live because they had been redeemed from Egypt. Similarly, since believers are redeemed from sin, they are, therefore, under that same law for sanctification. Is this right? Certainly not! The argument is fundamentally flawed, and patently so. Israel's redemption from Egypt by the Passover typified the elect's redemption from sin by the blood of Christ, yes. Slavery in Egypt represented the dominion of sin, yes. The blood of the lamb represented the blood of Christ, yes. Canaan represented the redeemed's rest in Christ, yes.[10] But what in the new covenant corresponds to the giving of the law by Moses on Sinai? The believer, like Israel, has had his exodus from his Egypt. He too has come to a mountain and received a law. He too is in a covenant. And he too has entered his promised land. But his exodus is a *new* exodus, he has come to a *new* mountain, he has been put into a *new* covenant, and entered a *new* realm. The two covenants and two sets of events are chalk and cheese. They must not be cobbled together. To find 'spiritual equivalents' for Egypt, the exodus, the mountains and the Passover, *but not the law*, is at best inconsistent. Yet this is the very thing that many do. While they rightly speak of the blood of Christ 'replacing' the Passover, redemption from sin 'replacing' deliverance from Egypt, and so on, they nevertheless try to argue the law of Sinai passes over virtually unchanged into the new covenant. It will not do. Something has 'replaced' the giving of the law to Israel through Moses, just as the realm of sin is the spiritual equivalent of Egypt, the realm of grace is the spiritual Canaan, and the blood of Christ has fulfilled the typical blood of the Passover lamb.

Reformed writers like to find a spiritual equivalent for one part of a passage or an episode (the exodus, as above, or Jeremiah 31, or the rules for circumcision, for instance) but not the other. I say it again. It will not do! What is more, the 'new' must

---

[9] In chapter 17, I will return to Rom. 12:17-20 to illustrate the way the new covenant uses the law.

[10] This is not to be limited to heaven. See chapter 18. Nor is it to be transferred to the keeping the first day of the week – for which there is not the slightest biblical warrant. Matt. 11:28-30 is the rest in question.

be stressed. The old covenant was a shadow; the new, the reality. These two covenants must not be muddled up. In particular, the law of the new covenant is not the law of the old.[11]

Even so, Reformed teachers maintain that believers, like Israel, are under the law, and by 'the law' they mean the very law God spoke on Sinai. If so, they must bite the bullet. The argument runs from Exodus 19:1. What if any believer cannot say – or fails to carry out – this vow in response to the law: '*All* that the LORD has spoken we will do' (Ex. 19:8)? What do Reformed writers suggest this means for the believer? What about the law's curses for disobedience? They are legion (Ex. 21:12,14,23-25; 22:22-24; *etc.*). Does the promise of the presence of the Angel (Ex. 23:20) apply to believers? If so, what of the curse: 'Beware of him and obey his voice; do not provoke him, for he will not pardon your transgressions' (Ex. 23:21)? Are we to understand that believers come under the blessings and curses of Deuteronomy 7:12-15; 28:1-68? What about the terror, limits, darkness and death associated with the law (Ex. 19:12-13,16-24; 20:18-21)? Remember, reader, we are speaking of believers in Christ, a *redeemed* people. Are we not expressly told in the New Testament that believers are far removed from all this, that we have not come to Sinai (Heb. 12:18-24)? How, therefore, can the law be their perfect rule of conduct? Note the negative tone, the fear associated with the law. Is this really the motive and rule for the sanctification of believers?

In any case, far from God giving the law to *sanctify* Israel, the fact is, as Moses told them: 'God has come to *test* you, and that his fear may be before you, so that you may not sin' (Ex. 20:20). Furthermore, the giving of the law is all of a piece with the rest of Israel's experience at the time – God was *testing* the people (Ex. 15:25; Deut. 8:2,16; 13:3). Is this the way of sanctification? There is no textual support to say, as is said, that the Israelites were to keep the commandments *in gratitude* for what the Lord had already done for them in that he had redeemed them. They were being tested!

What is more, it is wrong to assume the law stops at the end of Exodus 20. This is totally artificial and unwarranted, a gross imposition on the text. In any case, take Exodus 23:13: 'In *all* that I have said to you, be circumspect'. Notice how the sabbath law (the fourth commandment of the ten) is included in the *all,* along with *all* the other laws (Ex. 23:1-13). God spoke them *all;* the redeemed, so it is said, must keep them *all*. If not...! After all, they promised: '*All* that the LORD has spoken we will do' (Ex. 19:8). Reader, take your concordance (in book form or on line) and check how often the phrase, '*all* that I have commanded you', or its equivalent, appears in the law. It has to be faced. If believers are under the law because they are redeemed, as Reformed teachers maintain, then it is *all* or nothing. It is all the law. And all its curses.

Am I decrying the ten commandments by saying this? Certainly not! In fact, the boot is on the other foot. The law *is* perfect (Ps. 19:7), a perfect rule to all who are under it – it is, after all, God's law! – *and that without the slightest alteration*. To take any of the Reformed escape routes,[12] is to make void the law. This must be faced by those who claim the law is the rule for believers.

The law cannot justify the sinner. All the Reformed and evangelical are agreed about that. My contention is, neither can it sanctify the saint. The law is neither the motive nor the means of sanctification. As with justification, so for sanctification:

---

[11] See chapters 14 and 16.
[12] See chapter 7.

Christ – and only Christ – is all (1 Cor. 1:30; Col. 3:11). The law cannot make a saved sinner holy; it cannot sanctify (Rom. 6:14ff; 7:1ff; 8:1ff; Gal. 5:16ff; Col. 2:11ff); the New Testament always makes Christ and his grace – never the law – the basis, motive and power for sanctification and godliness of life (Rom. 6:1ff; Gal. 1:3-5; Col. 1:9-18; 2:6-10,20-23; 3:1ff; Tit. 2:11-14; 3:1-8; 1 Pet. 2:9ff; and many others). Reformed writers admit the fact, but fail to draw the inevitable and proper conclusion.[13]

I invite you, reader, to consider the logic of saying that the believer is not under the law, and yet is under the law, at one and the same time – which is precisely what the Reformed do say.

A glance at Reformed logic

Take Thomas Boston. He tried to solve the conundrum by defining two laws. First, the law of works, which has to be done if one is to be saved, and, secondly, the law of Christ, which is the law of the Saviour, binding on his saved people. So far, so good. Here we have two laws. Very different laws, too, one would think. One, the law to be kept by sinners in order to be saved; the other, the law by which Christ governs his people. Two different laws, did I say? Oh no! These two laws, Boston claimed, are one and the same law, the ten commandments. Pause a moment! Two very different laws, one for justification by obedience to the commandments – which the believer is *not* under – and the other for sanctification – which the believer *is* under – yet these two laws are one and the same law, comprising precisely the same commandments? One, the law of Moses; the other, the law of Christ; yet both laws being exactly the same? How can this be? How can this law be both an insupportable burden (Acts 15:10; Gal. 5:1; see also Matt. 23:4), and an easy yoke (Matt. 11:30; 1 John 5:3)?

Consider Boston's explanation. First of all, he limited 'the law' to the ten commandments. That was his first mistake. Having got off to such a bad start, he started to dig himself into a hole. There is, he said, a difference between the ten commandments 'coming from an absolute God out of Christ to sinners', and the same ten commandments 'coming from God in Christ to them'. The law of works and the law of Christ, according to this, are identical, the only difference[14] is that the ten commandments as the law of works come 'from... God... out of Christ', while the ten commandments as the law of Christ come 'from God in Christ'. Oh? Boston continued digging. The law of the ten commandments, he said, remaining the same throughout, issued by the same God, was first the natural law written on Adam's heart at creation, then it became the law of works, then it became the law of Christ. Now that natural law, it is said, can never die; it applies to all men for ever. Even so, for the believer, although the law lives on as the natural law, it dies as the law of works, yet lives on as the law of Christ. And in all three states – in two of which it lives, and in the third it does not – it is precisely the same law.

All this poses a problem, reader, at least to me. Picture the scene. Here stand the ten commandments. As part of the law of God through Moses, they are unchanging. They are inflexible. They say the same thing as they have always said. They demand the same obedience. They administer the same curse as they have always done for the

---

[13] See also chapter 16.

[14] Sorry for the contradiction, reader; it is not mine.

same disobedience. Now, according to Boston, the sinner is under this law by nature, and he also finds himself under this law for his salvation. In both conditions it condemns him absolutely. So he runs to Christ for refuge and relief. And what does he immediately discover? Having been justified by faith in Christ, and released from the law, the first thing he notices is... guess what? He finds himself, without delay, back under the same set of commandments as he was under before, the only difference being the label on the package has changed! This reminds me of a document which was circulated in a government office. On reading the document, the civil servant had to initial it. One man got the document back after a few days with a note attached: 'You were not supposed to read this document. Please erase your initials, and initial your erasure'!

Now the ten commandments condemn those under it who are under it as the law of works. So said Boston. What about the law of Christ? After all, the two laws, according to the claim, consist of precisely the same commandments with exactly the same curses attached. Ah, when the ten commandments are the law of Christ, the curse is removed. Or so we are told. What is more, the conditions of the law which were attached to it as the law of works no longer apply. In other words, all men are always under the law, the same law which demands the same obedience, and warns of the same punishments, as ever it did, since it has not changed in one iota, nor indeed can it change, but, apparently, when dealing with any particular man, the law asks itself which sort of man it is dealing with. If the man is under the law as the law of works it punishes him when he transgresses. If he is under it as the law of Christ, it pardons him. Yet, all the time, all men are under it as the natural law dating from Adam.

So now you understand, believer. At one time, when you were an unbeliever, you were under the law – the ten commandments – by nature. Then you were awakened and came under the law for a second time – for justification. Failing to keep the law for justification, you went to Christ in repentant faith, and were saved by grace. Having become a saved sinner by grace through faith, you were delivered from the law, but Christ immediately put you – where? Under the ten commandments, under the law! But with this difference. In your first two states you were under the ten commandments as the law of works. Now you are under them as the law of Christ. In your first two states, the law pronounced a curse on you, but now it does not, even though you cannot detect the slightest difference in the wording of the commands. You cannot detect any change, because there is none. Not one jot or tittle of the law has been changed. It is still the same law. It all depends whether you are under the law as a law of works or the law of Christ.

I know this sounds incredible, not to say mad. *But I have not been making it up.* Not at all! Here are Boston's actual words:

The law of works is the law [which is to] be done, that one may be saved [whereas]... the law of Christ is the law of the Saviour, binding his saved people to all the duties of obedience... [Yet] the law of works, and the law of Christ, are in substance but one law, even the ten commandments... [There is] a difference [however]... between the ten commandments as coming from an absolute God out of Christ to sinners, and the same ten commandments as coming from God in Christ to them. [But it is] utterly groundless [to say] that the original indispensable obligation of the law of the ten commandments is in any measure weakened by the believer's taking it as the law of Christ, and not as the law of works. [The ten commandments as the law of works come] from... God... out of Christ, [while the ten commandments as the law of Christ come] from God in Christ. The law of the ten commandments, [remaining the same throughout, issued by the same God, was first] the natural law... written on Adam's heart on his creation, while as yet it was neither the law of works nor the law of Christ... Then it became the law of works... The natural law of the ten commandments (which can never expire... but is obligatory in all possible states of the creature...) is, from the moment the law of works expires as to believers, issued forth to them [again]... in the channel of the covenant of grace... Thus it [now] becomes the law of Christ to them; of which law also the same ten commandments are likewise the [substance]... In the threatening of this law [the law of Christ, that is] there is no revenging wrath; and in the promises of it no proper conditionality of works; but here is the order of the covenant of grace... Thus the ten commandments stand, both in the law of works and in the law of Christ at the same time... but as they are the [substance]... of the law of works, they are actually a part of the law of works; howbeit, as they are the [substance]... of the law of Christ, they are actually a part, not of the law of works, but the law of Christ. And as they stand in the law of Christ... they ought to be a rule of life to a believer... they ought [not, however] to be a rule of life to a believer, as they stand in the law of works.[15]

A theological Alice in Wonderland! It makes no sense. It is worse. It strikes at the very root of law as law. Whatever else law is, it is impartial, inflexible – Calvin's very word! When passing sentence, the law does not look at the man in the dock. It looks at the evidence. It requires a verdict. If it has been broken, the law demands and exacts punishment on the offender. It is rigidly applied. It can only act within its own parameters. But within those parameters, it must act.

As I write, the Crown Prosecution Service is being attacked for failing to prosecute a driver for an offence which calls for the stiffest sentence. Rather, it pursued the driver for a lesser offence – when patently the driver was guilty of the worse offence – as even the presiding judge declared. The Crown Prosecution Service responds by saying it can only prosecute on the basis of the law as it stands at present. If the public (and the judge) want justice as they see it, Parliament must change the law. Law is law! Quite right! Examples of this sort are legion.

If guilty of transgression, an offender must be punished. If innocent, he must be acquitted. This is the principle of law.

But what if a man says it is a matter of conscience? He has wasted his breath! There is no place for conscience when it comes to law. Law is inexorable and pays no regard to the conscience of those it controls. Imagine a member of the public pleading conscience, or likes and dislikes, when stopped by a traffic policeman for driving at 50mph in a 30mph zone. The offence will bring a speeding ticket, conscience or no conscience! If not, there would be an outcry – and rightly so. Law is law! Quite right! If the police and the public start to treat the law as 'adjustable', 'pick and choose', chaos will quickly ensue.

I say it again, if guilty of transgression, an offender must be punished. If innocent, he must be acquitted. This is the principle of law. Take the aforementioned policeman. He pulls the driver over, walks up to the car, bends his head and peers through the open window. He discovers that the offender is his friend, one he knows to be a good man. What now? Will the policeman walk away?[16]

---

[15] Fisher pp24-27,155-171. Incidentally, Boston made a mistake which is all too common. The believer has died to the law; the law has not died or, to use his word, 'expired', to the believer.

[16] A policeman did that very thing when he found that he had pulled over his Chief Constable. The next morning, the Chief Constable rightly sacked the policeman. Law is no respecter of persons. Nobody is above the law.

If I may be permitted to push the motoring illustration just a little further in order to make my point: imagine two drivers caught speeding at exactly the same place, at exactly the same time, and by exactly the same margin of excess. Would one driver come away unpunished because his car was the 'sanctification' model, whereas the other man had to suffer the due penalty of the law because he was driving a 'justification' model?

Law is law! It is the principle of God in his word (Deut. 25:1; Prov. 17:15; Nah. 1:3). But not, it seems, the principle of those who advocate Calvin's third use of the law. The ten commandments form both the law of works and the law of Christ at the same time, but in the one state – the law of works – they are not the believer's rule, but in the law of Christ, they are. So it is said. The same law treats men differently. Oh?

Boston's madcap way out of the maze is not the only course adopted by the Reformed. Some have delineated a difference arising out of the two givings of the law at Sinai. After the first giving of the law, when Moses came down the mountain and saw the wickedness of the people, he broke the two tablets (Ex. 32:19). Calling Moses back to the top of Sinai, God then re-issued the two tablets of the law (Ex. 34:4). Yes, this is true. But, without any biblical support, it is claimed that the first issuing of the law was as a covenant of works, whereas the second was as the believer's rule. And thus a believer is both free of the law and under it at the same time. In other words, the second giving of the law at Sinai, after the breaking of the tablets by Moses – but not the first giving – is the believer's rule, although what the difference is between the two givings, I am unable to see. *Nor can anybody else see!*

Yes, when God first gave the law he did so with signs of terror and darkness (Ex. 19:9-25; Heb. 12:18-21), and when he gave it the second time, he caused all his goodness to pass before Moses (Ex. 34:6-8). This, however, does not seem sufficient to bear the weight which has been placed upon it. No biblical writer ever draws attention to it or draws the suggested inference. In showing his mercy to Moses, was God not reassuring him after the judgement following the debacle with the golden calf?

Besides, it was the same law in each case, and the second pair of tablets was an exact replica of the first. What is more, when Paul spoke of the giving of the law (2 Cor. 3), he made no distinction whatsoever between the two givings. And when, referring to the radiance of Moses' face and the need for a veil (the second giving – Ex. 34:29-35), he used terms such as 'the letter [which] kills... the ministry of death written and engraved on stones... the ministry of condemnation' and, by implication called it the old covenant (2 Cor. 3:6-17), he was, as I say, talking about the second giving of the law. How, therefore, this (second) giving of the law can be the believer's rule, I cannot fathom. After all, since 2 Corinthians 3 does refer to the second giving of the law – and so, it is claimed, is the law for the believer's sanctification – why is it expressly called 'the ministry of condemnation'?

How can a believer be free of the law as it is a law of works, and yet be under the very same law as the law of Christ? How can a believer be free from the law when it is given one label, yet under the very same law when given another? How can a believer be not under the law as it was first given, but under it in its second giving?

But if anyone dares to dispute Reformed thinking, he had better know what to expect. Is it right – or fair – to assert that the man who does not accept such crazy reasoning, such distinctions and divisions of the law, and the various roles of the ten commandments, knows neither God nor himself? This is claimed! Now this is what I call 'raising the stakes', reader. So now you know! Risky business, this challenging of Reformed writers, their logic and their view of the law!

The question has been asked, by a Reformed writer: If the law could have justified, what need would there have been for Christ to die to earn salvation? Quite! So when this same writer declared that the law, though it cannot save, does sanctify, may I reply in kind? If the moral law can sanctify, what need is there of the Holy Spirit and the New Testament?

Before I bring this chapter to a close, let me return to Calvin. I do so because he is the fountain-head of this Reformed third use of the law to sanctify the believer. If I held Calvin's view, I would expect – I would hope – to find clarity in his writings. I would demand it. After all, the subject is of major – massive – importance. But what do we find? Confusion. For instance, did Calvin really believe the law is the perfect rule for the believer? Paul said 'you are not under the law' (Gal. 5:18), but Calvin said, oh yes, you are – but in the sense that the law will be 'a kind adviser', but it will no longer restrain your conscience. Now, this is a most interesting statement. Calvin was in effect destroying his own doctrine of the law, particularly his third use. 'Destroying', I said, and 'destroying', I meant. Is the law a perfect *rule* or not? If a ruler does no more than act 'as a kind adviser', I do not see how his advice can fairly be called a *rule*. An adviser merely advises, makes a recommendation. The recipient is at liberty to take it or reject it. Not so with a ruler. He rules, and the subject must obey. No law can be treated as merely advisory. 'Law' and 'advice' are a contradiction in terms. Law is always compulsory. I ask again, therefore, according to Calvin, is the law the believer's rule, or is it his kind adviser? If the law does not restrain the conscience, what does it do? Again, did Calvin believe the law – a source of instruction and a whip to drive the believer – curses failure or not? On the one hand, he could say the law can only exhort the believer, not bind the conscience. On the other hand, the law, the rule of life, not only teaches, it makes 'imperious demands', and thunders with its curse for the slightest failure. The severity which God showed to Israel of old he will show to believers today. So it is claimed. I remind you, reader, of Boston's words. It is 'utterly groundless [to say] that the original indispensable obligation of the law of the ten commandments is in any measure weakened by the believer's taking it as the law of Christ, and not as the law of works'. As with obligation, so with consequence.

Which of these statements do the followers of Calvin believe? They cannot believe them all! As you can see, reader, the law, Calvin tried to argue, though it does not bind the conscience of a believer nor curse him, yet it always condemns and curses for the slightest failure, and punishes as severely as ever it did. Oh? It will not do to say the curse applies to those under the law for justification, but not to those under it for sanctification. The law does not recognise the difference.

Consider the highly significant statement found in the letter which 'the apostles, the elders, and the brethren' wrote 'to the brethren who are of the Gentiles' (Acts 15:23-29). The writers deplored the fact that 'some who went out from us have troubled you with words, unsettling your souls'. What had they done? These false teachers had told the Gentile believers: 'You must be circumcised and keep the law' (Acts 15:24). Indeed, even when Paul and Barnabas reached Jerusalem, some Pharisees were uncompromising: 'It is necessary to circumcise [the Gentile converts], and to command them to keep the law of Moses' (Acts 15:5). Note this, reader. In the church at Antioch, the false teachers taught the *brethren* to keep the law (Acts 15:1), and in Jerusalem the Pharisees *demanded* that Gentile *believers* keep it (Acts 15:5). This sails very close to Calvin's third use of the law, does it not?

How did 'the apostles, the elders, and the brethren' deal with the problem? Did they set out what would come to be known as Calvin's third use of the law? They did not! Why, oh why, if they believed it, did 'the apostles, the elders, and the brethren' not issue a simple but definitive statement along such lines as these: 'Although believers must not keep the law of Moses for justification, they must, even so, keep it for sanctification'? If they had done this simple thing, it would have saved a world of trouble, and once and for all established the Reformed third use of the law; namely, that it is the perfect rule of life for believers. This, of all places – Acts 15 – was *the* place to do it. But they did not! And what eloquence there is in their silence. And when I ask why those believers did not say it – why did the Holy Spirit not put it into their minds to say it?

James was convinced 'that we should not trouble' Gentile converts (Acts 15:19), as the law-teachers were doing by their emphasis upon Moses. Moses' law was, he declared, 'a yoke... which' they as Jews could not 'bear', so why ever would they think of putting it 'on the neck of the [Gentile] disciples' (Acts 15:10)? As a result, 'the apostles, the elders, and the brethren' wrote to the Gentile believers, in plain and unmistakeable terms, dissociating themselves from these false teachers, 'to whom we gave no such commandment'. Having cleared this matter up, and given sundry commands of a temporary nature in order to smooth relations between Jew and Gentile believers in those early, transitional days of the gospel, they then told the Gentiles: 'It seemed good to the Holy Spirit, and to us, to lay upon you no greater burden' (Acts 15:23-28).

It will not do to argue that the false teachers, and therefore the apostles, were speaking only about justification. When the Judaisers declared: 'Unless you are circumcised according to the custom of Moses you cannot be saved', they were addressing *converts*. In any case, sanctification is an essential accompaniment of justification, and an essential constituent of salvation. This point will come up again and again. While Reformed writers often speak of the law's inadequacy to save, too often they limit this to justification. They are wrong!

Reformed teachers may, by their logical niceties and quibbles, try to skirt round the obvious deductions to be drawn from Acts 15, but the chapter stands as a clear indictment of any attempt to impose the Jewish law upon Gentile believers – the apostles would have none of it. There is only one conclusion. The law is gone, grace has come, and consequently all distinction between believing Jews and Gentiles is removed. Law brought slavery; grace brings liberty. Believers are free. And they must not get entangled all over again.

Calvin's third use of the law does not stand scrutiny.

Chapter 6

The Buttress of the Reformed Case: Covenant Theology

As I have explained, the law, say Reformed teachers, is binding on all men, and has been so since God gave it to Adam.[1] In particular, it is binding on believers now; not for justification, of course, but as the perfect rule of their sanctification. The Reformed go further. It is the motive, the spur, the force, the driving power behind that sanctification. That is the Reformed claim. What is the buttress for it? What underpins their position on the law? It is something they call covenant theology. What is this? And what underpins covenant theology?

As I set out to answer these questions, reader, let me offer both an explanation and an apology. You will find what follows complicated, muddled, confused, even contradictory – even more so than Calvin's threefold use of the law. I apologise for this, but there is little I can do about it. No matter how hard I try to make the Reformed theology for their claims on the law easy to follow, I am faced with an impossible task, and this because of the very nature of the arguments which they use. The confusion and contradiction is not of my making; it is theirs. And this will be even more apparent if you read their original works. See, for instance, the quote from Boston in the previous chapter. In light of this complicated Reformed logic, may I remind you of something I said at the start? Without in any way intending to patronise, if you find this chapter too much, on a first reading you will sustain little loss by skipping to the next.

The fact is, since they themselves are unable to sort it out, no wonder I cannot unravel the Reformed tangle! But I fear that this might well make some readers give up, and put my book down. I trust not! Having got this far, may I hope, reader, your interest having been sufficiently aroused, you might be prepared to grapple with the human *illogic* you find in this chapter, and stay with me long enough to move on from the foggy speculations of men into the clear light of Scripture? But, taking Paul as our example, just as he knew that he had to tackle the faulty theology of the Judaisers of his day, we have no choice. We, too, have to expose the fault lines in Reformed covenant-theology today. Even so, since that theology is so complicated, it will inevitably prove rather a tortuous experience. You have been warned!

So, to start at the end and work backwards, covenant theology is the buttress of the Reformed view of the law, but what underpins covenant theology? This can be discovered by answering another question, a question of immense importance: Are the two Testaments continuous or discontinuous? To put it another way: Is every part of the Bible of equal weight and importance? Reader, do not be frightened by such questions. I am not for a moment suggesting that the Bible – all of it – is not equally inspired. It is! The entire Bible is the word of God – from Genesis to Revelation, including both! Nevertheless, the question must be asked, and answered: Does every verse of Scripture have the same weight in the life of the believer today?

---

[1] The extracts for this chapter begin on p369.

Are the two Testaments continuous or discontinuous?

God did not reveal his word all at once. Not only did he spread that revelation over hundreds of years, but he gave us his word in two Testaments. How are these Testaments related to one another? How should believers use them in formulating doctrine and practice? Do they draw principles equally from both, or from the New Testament only? Or... what? This is what I mean by asking if the Testaments are continuous or discontinuous.

It is dangerously simplistic, of course, to polarise such an important debate in this way – as though it must be one or the other. The Testaments are neither continuous nor discontinuous; they are both. The proper way to read the Testaments is to grasp their unity in their discontinuity. Christ is that unity. The Old pointed to him, revealing him in prophecies and shadows. The New reveals him as the fulfiller of those prophecies, the reality of the shadows (Luke 24:27; John 5:46; 1 Pet. 1:10-12; *etc.*). As a consequence, when we read the Bible, we should be looking for Christ, and reading everything through Christ, whose person and work is the unifying factor of Scripture. Granting that, the debate, therefore, really hinges on where the *emphasis* should fall. Should it be on the continuity or the discontinuity?

There is no doubt – or shouldn't be! Discontinuity! We have abundant scriptural evidence for emphasising the discontinuity of the Testaments. For now, take just one place, just one – Romans 3:20-22; note the vital *but now*. The passage reads:

Therefore by the deeds of the law no flesh will be justified in his sight, for by the law is the knowledge of sin. *But now* the righteousness of God apart from the law is revealed, being witnessed by the law and the prophets, even the righteousness of God, through faith in Jesus Christ, to all and on all who believe.

These verses show at once the difference between the two Testaments – that is, the discontinuity between them – but at the same time they show their continuity. As for the discontinuity, nothing could be plainer. The ages of law and grace are very different ages because law and grace are very different systems. As for the continuity, grace was foretold and prefigured by the law and the prophets, but the emphasis of this passage in particular – and the New Testament in general – comes down firmly on the side of the discontinuity. I am not, of course, for a moment suggesting that there was no grace in the Old Testament, and that no sinner was saved in those days. But the fact remains, there is a discontinuity between the Testaments, and *that* is where the weight falls.

Note the contrast. Note the time factor: *now* Christ has come, *now* we are not under the law. The coming of Christ, and our coming to him in repentance and faith, has altered everything – in the former case, historically speaking; in the latter, in a personal sense. Because of the *but now*, all things are new. The coming of Christ is the great turning point, the momentous watershed of history, and the contrast between this age and the old age is written large across the pages of Scripture. And this discontinuity *must* be emphasised. While Paul in Romans 3:20-22 was safeguarding the continuity between the two Testaments, *this was not his primary purpose*. Far from it! Rather, he was setting out the discontinuity between the two. And it is this discontinuity which is of far greater importance than the continuity. Believers ought to recognise – and rejoice in – the differences between the two Testaments, the changes brought about by the eschatological 'but now'. After all, their hope depends – absolutely – on the differences (1 Pet. 2:10)! In speaking of the discontinuity of the two Testaments, I have, in fact, been speaking of the differences between two ages, two systems, two covenants – especially this last; the discontinuity between the old and new covenants.

Scripture puts the weight on the new-ness of the new covenant – and when it says 'new' it does not mean something which was 'old' but is now renewed or amended. It really does mean a *new* covenant, accentuating the distinction between the age of the law and the age of the Spirit. Although it is an over-simplification to put it like this, in moving from the age of the Old Testament to the age of the New there was a fundamental change of covenant; the old gave way to the new (Heb. 7:11-12,18-22; 8:13; 9:15; 10:9; 12:18-24).[2] This, as I have said, is an over-simplification. We know that some people in the Old Testament belonged to the new covenant, and that the believers under the old covenant were looking forward to Christ (John 8:56; 1 Pet. 1:10-12). Some sinners were justified in the Old Testament (see Rom. 4; Gal. 3:6-9), but the doctrine itself was not written so clearly as in the New. This would seem to be stating the obvious. If not, why do we have the New Testament? The position of Old Testament believers was anomalous. They were in the new covenant and therefore delighted in God's law (Ps. 119), but at the same time they were under its burden in the old covenant. But the basic truth stands. There was a fundamental change of covenant with the change of Testament. It did not take place at the first verse of Matthew, of course. It came into effect with the death of Christ; or, more particularly, with the glorification of Christ in his resurrection, and the gift of the Spirit (John 7:39; 12:16,23; 13:31-32; 16:7; 1 Pet. 1:10-12,21). A definite and irreversible change of covenant took place through Christ.

And here is the nub of the debate. Many Reformed people do not accept this discontinuity, or at least its emphasis. They read their Bibles through very different spectacles. Very different!

This was a (the?) bone of contention between the Anabaptists and the Reformers, at the very heart of their disagreements. The Anabaptists rightly put the differences between the old and the new covenants, and the consequent distinction between the Testaments, at the centre of the debate. The Reformers, on the other hand, stressing the continuity of the two Testaments, were confused over the two great biblical covenants, often arguing for their one-ness, and much of their practical theology flowed from it.[3]

Rejecting human logic, the Anabaptists' rule of faith and practice was the Bible alone, especially the New Testament. God has revealed himself in the Bible in a progressive way, they said; the Old Testament is not on a parity with the New; the new covenant is supreme; believers are not the children of the Old Testament or covenant, but of the New; the weapons of their warfare are of the New, not the Old. Arguing out these principles, they stressed the differences in the two ages. Believers, they argued, are under the authority of the Old Testament, but only as far as it testifies of Christ, only insofar as he did not abolish it, and only insofar as it serves the purpose of Christian living. In short, believers are under the authority of the law insofar as it does not contradict the gospel. In this way they distinguished between the Testaments. In about 1544, for instance, Pilgram Marpeck produced a massive book of more than 800

---

[2] Melchizedek collected the tithe from Levi, and this showed his superiority over Levi (Heb. 7:4-10). Similarly, Christ and his law are superior to Moses and his law. For more on Hebrews, see chapter 14.

[3] Although Michael Servetus was not an Anabaptist, in some respects he was close – and Calvin lumped him with them. See p523 for extracts from Servetus' letters to Calvin.

pages contrasting the two Testaments on many topics including forgiveness, rest, faith, sword, offerings, *etc.* The Old Testament, the Anabaptists argued, was temporary; the New, abiding. The Old is symbol; the New, fulfilment. The Old was preparatory and partial; the New is final and complete. The Old speaks of Adam, sin, death and law; the New speaks of Christ and redemption through him. All Scripture must be interpreted Christologically; that is, it must be seen in and through him and his work. If the Old Testament is given the wrong place or status in church and theology, all sorts of dire consequences follow, as could be seen in both Münster and Geneva. Yes, both! Such were the views of most Anabaptists. A few did not see it entirely this way, however; some were sabbatarians who sought to apply Old Testament laws to believers.

The Reformers, on the other hand, propounding a continuous history encompassing one age since the covenant with Abraham, saw only minor differences between the two Testaments – arising out of their time sequence. The Reformers saw no difference in substance between the Testaments. As a result, they responded bitterly to the Anabaptists. Not giving sufficient weight to the relevant passages in Romans, Galatians and Hebrews, they made the mistake of saying (when it suited them) that the Testaments were continuous and not discontinuous, and viewed the Bible as a flat revelation, with every passage having the same authority, regardless of its place in the Bible. Thus Israel and the church became one, and the government of Israel was made to serve as a guide for the State Church in the 16th century.

Here were two distinct approaches to Scripture, still with us. Not all go as far as those reconstructionists who talk of the *Older* and not the *Old* Testament, but those who come down on the continuity side talk about the *Jewish* church as the infant form of the *gospel* church. Further, they base infant baptism on Jewish circumcision, *etc.* All this has large and dire consequences. Reader, to cope with it you will need to be nimble in sorting out the logic and language of covenant theology – the double covenant, the external and the internal covenant, the elect and the church seed, the visible godly, federal faithfulness, and so on. Having done that you will have to come to terms with church members who are acknowledged to be profane and chaffy hypocrites, but, nevertheless, remain glass-eyed ornaments to the church.[4] And so on.

So, how do the Reformed cope with the biblical evidence? As I have said, here we reach the heart of the debate. Many Reformed people do not accept the clear discontinuity; or, at least, deny its emphasis. When they read their Bibles, they look down the wrong end of the telescope, viewing the New Testament through the Old. All sorts of troubles follow. In particular, how does it affect their interpretation of Romans 3:21-22? Some think that the words 'but now' signal a mere change of paragraph, or simply a small matter of timing. They do not! To enfeeble the 'but now' in such a way is tragic. The 'but' and the 'now' must be emphasised, the 'but' as a contrast, and the 'now' in its historical sense. And it is far more than mere history, as I have said. Paul was speaking of the great eschatological 'now', the time of the new epoch, the 'but now' of the new era – the time of the gospel instead of the law, the age of the gospel contrasted with the age of the law, the age and realm of the Spirit and not law, the age

---

[4] Words used by men like John Cotton and Thomas Shepard in 17th-century New England. See 'Extracts' p377.

of faith and not works.[5] No wonder these two words 'but now' have been justly called the most wonderful words in the entire Bible. Lloyd-Jones, for one, did. Quite right, too! As Paul thundered elsewhere: 'Behold, *now* is the accepted time; behold, *now* is the day of salvation' (2 Cor. 6:2). Now! But now!

If anybody should try to dismiss this by saying I am making a mountain out of the mole-hill of one passage, in addition to Romans 3:21, he ought to weigh Romans 5:9,11; 6:22; 7:6; 8:1; 11:30; 11:31 (second 'now' in NIV, NASB); 16:26; along with John 15:22,24; Acts 17:30; 1 Corinthians 15:20; Galatians 4:9; Ephesians 2:12-13; 5:8; Colossians 1:26; Hebrews 8:6; 9:26; 12:26; 1 Peter 2:10.

Note the contrast between the two ages, the two systems, in Romans 4:13-17. The promise to Abraham 'was not... through the *law*, but through... *faith*. For if those who are of the *law* are heirs, *faith* is made void and the promise made of no effect, because the *law* brings about wrath; for where there is no *law* there is no transgression. Therefore it is of *faith* that it might be according to *grace*... not only to those who are of the *law*, but also to those who are of the *faith* of Abraham'. Paul's argument collapses if law is not contrasted with grace and faith. This would seem to be obvious. Sadly, not all can see it. On justification, the Reformers were clear about the distinction between law and gospel, but otherwise they were confused about the two. While they rightly forsook the legal ground for justification, they kept to it for sanctification. And where we find this muddle, we find believers who are virtual 'Mosesians' instead of Christians. In their covenant theology, over-emphasising the *continuity* as they do, they fail to do justice to the revealed *discontinuity* of the two covenants.[6] This I will prove, first by glancing at the biblical teaching on the covenants, and then trying to set out the arguments used by Reformed covenant-theologians.

In all this, a nice point of translation from the Greek arises – should we be talking about *covenant* or *testament*? Almost certainly, the former. The Testaments should have been called the Old and New *Covenants*. And in the text itself, *covenant* should have almost always have been used instead of *testament*, since it would have more truly conveyed the (almost-universal) meaning of the word to readers of the English Bible.[7] And this in itself might well have prevented much of the trouble addressed in this chapter.

Biblical teaching on the covenants: 1. The covenant within the Godhead

Let me start with Scripture, and let me begin at the beginning, where I and Reformed writers are agreed. In eternity past, the triune God determined and decreed to save the elect. This is written large in Scripture. For instance, Paul said he was 'a bondservant of God and an apostle of Jesus Christ, according to the faith of God's elect and the

---

[5] I repeat: I am not saying there was no grace or faith in the Old Testament. I am, I say again, talking about emphasis, overwhelming emphasis.

[6] Dispensationalists err the other way.

[7] Heb. 9:16-17 is the *only* place where *testament* is the right translation; the NIV happily uses *will*. In 2 Cor. 3:14, I disagree with NKJV and AV; see NIV, NASB. Gal. 3:15 could be either – but 'covenant' is the better. Speaking historically, the original use of 'new testament' was for the new covenant. It was only in the 3rd century that 'New Testament', as we now use it, became widespread. Indeed, my AV consistently uses small case for both 'old testament' and 'new testament'.

acknowledgement of the truth which accords with godliness, in hope of eternal life which God, who cannot lie, promised before time began, but has in due time manifested his word through preaching, which was committed to me according to the commandment of God our Saviour' (Tit. 1:1-3). Since God 'promised before time began', he could not have promised to any created being. Therefore he must have promised to himself, within the Godhead. In other words, because of his sovereign grace, love and will, all within himself, God agreed, within the Godhead, to save his elect through his Son, Jesus Christ, by the effectual working of his Holy Spirit. I am willing to call this a covenant – the covenant of grace, no less, except this term is not used in Scripture, but is an invention of covenant theologians. Not only that, their use of the term is far more complicated than the way in which I would want to use it. Leaving that aside, as I say, throughout the word of God there is abundant evidence of this agreement within the Godhead, but since I and Reformed writers are of one mind on this – except on the use of the phrase 'the covenant of grace' – I will say little more on it.[8] This determination, compact, agreement, or promise within the Godhead is not at issue here. It has nothing to do with man. It is an agreement, a decree, a promise within the Godhead. It has nothing to do with the question of the believer and the law. If this was all that covenant theology amounted to, I would have no quarrel with it. But it isn't, and I do.

To move on: the need for salvation arose out of Adam's fall. Through Adam, sin entered the world, and in Adam all the human race sinned and fell. In accordance with God's own determination within the Godhead, at the right time Christ came into the world and earned salvation for all his elect. All in Adam die, and all in Christ live (Rom. 5:12-21; 1 Cor. 15:21-23,45-49). In all this I am sure there is no difference between me and the Reformed.[9]

Biblical teaching on the covenants: 2. God's covenants with men

Down the ages, God has made various covenants with men. He made a covenant with Noah, with Abraham, with Isaac, with Jacob, with Israel at Sinai, with Phinehas, with David, and so on. He also made a covenant which he calls the new covenant.

Biblical teaching on the covenants: 3. The two great covenants with men

The two great covenants which God has made with men are the Mosaic covenant and the new covenant (Gal. 4:21-31; Heb. 7:18-22; 8:6-13; 9:11-28; 10:1-10; *etc.*). In saying this, I do not dismiss the Abrahamic covenant. Certainly not! The fact is, that covenant had two strands to it. One concerned Abraham's physical seed, Israel; the other, his spiritual seed, the church. The first strand was encompassed in the Mosaic covenant; the second in the new covenant. So, as I say, the two great scriptural covenants are the Mosaic covenant and the new covenant.

---

[8] From the plethora of other passages which could be cited, see Ps. 2:8; 40:6-8; 89:3; John 17:6; Eph. 1:11; 3:11; 2 Tim. 1:9; Heb. 13:20. See below for a 'little more'.

[9] Having said that, many Reformed writers push the comparison between Christ and Adam too far. Other Reformed teachers have dissented (see, for instance, Murray: *Collected* Vol.2 pp49-50,58).

The Mosaic law is called the old or first covenant. This includes, but is not confined to, the ten commandments (Ex. 19:5; Deut. 4:13; Jer. 31:31-33; Heb. 8:7-9) – those ten commandments being delineated as the 'words of the covenant': 'And [God] wrote on the tablets the words of the covenant, the ten commandments' (Ex. 34:28). 'So [God] declared to you his covenant which he commanded you to perform, the ten commandments; and he wrote them on two tablets of stone' (Deut. 4:13). The ten commandments constituted God's covenant given on Sinai.[10] But the fact is, the old covenant was *all* the law, and not merely the ten commandments.[11] To despise any of God's statutes, to abhor any of his judgements, to fail to perform all his commandments, was to break his covenant (Lev. 26:15). The 'book of the covenant' contained '*all* the words of the LORD', all his judgements or ordinances, commandments, testimonies and statutes (Ex. 24:3-7; 2 Kings 23:2-3; 2 Chron. 34:30-32; see also, for instance, 1 Kings 2:3; 6:12; 8:58,61; 9:4; 11:11,33-38; 2 Kings 17:13-16,19,34-38; 18:6,12). So the first or old covenant is the law, the law of Moses.

What is the second or new covenant? It is grace in Christ, the gospel (Heb. 7:18-19,22,28; 8:6-13; 9:15; 10:1,8-9,16-17,28; 12:22-24).

Now we are expressly told that Christ removed the old covenant that he might set up the new. He brought in 'the time of reformation' (Heb. 9:10), 'the time of the new order' (NIV). 'He takes away the first that he may establish the second' (Heb. 10:9), 'having abolished in his flesh the enmity; that is the law of commandments contained in ordinances' (Eph. 2:15), 'having wiped out the handwriting of requirements that was against us, which was contrary to us. And he has taken it out of the way, having nailed it to the cross' (Col. 2:14). Having annulled 'the former commandment because of its weakness and unprofitableness', he brought in 'a better hope, through which we draw near to God' (Heb. 7:18-19). Christ is 'mediator of a better covenant, which was established on better promises... He has made the first obsolete' (Heb. 8:6-7,13). 'The law was given through Moses, but grace and truth came through Jesus Christ' (John 1:17).

These are the two covenants which lie at the heart of this debate. While there is some continuity between the old covenant and the new,[12] the Bible speaks of vast differences between them. The old was temporary,[13] it was a ministry of death and condemnation (Rom. 7:7-11; 2 Cor. 3:6-11; Gal. 3:17,19,23-25; 4:1-7,21-31; Heb. 7:18-22; 8:6-13), and was introduced with 'blackness and darkness and tempest... [so that] they could not endure what was commanded... And so terrifying was the sight that

---

[10] As I have said, 'the ten commandments' – as a phrase – comes only three times in all the Bible, but is synonymous with the law on 'the tablets of stone' (Ex. 24:12; Deut. 4:13; 9:10; 1 Kings 8:9; 2 Cor. 3:3), 'the tablets of the testimony' (Ex. 31:18; 34:29), 'the testimony' (Ex. 25:15-16; 40:20), 'the words of the covenant' (Ex. 34:28) and 'the tablets of the covenant' (Deut. 9:9-11; Heb. 9:4). Whether this synonymity is strictly true in every case, is debatable – see chapter 1.
[11] The 'even' of Deut. 4:13 (AV) is in italics; the translators added it because they thought it made the meaning clear. I am not saying they were wrong to do it, but just pointing out the fact. The NKJV translators did the same with 'that is' in Eph. 2:15, which I quote below.
[12] God wrote both; love for God, love for neighbour, honour for parents, faithfulness in marriage, truthfulness, and so on, are common to both.
[13] This must not be glossed. The law, the old covenant, was temporary. God always intended it to be so. See below on Rom. 7; 2 Cor. 3; Gal. 3; Hebrews.

Moses said: "I am exceedingly afraid and trembling'" (Heb. 12:18-21). The new covenant, however, is permanent, the ministry of life, of the Spirit, of righteousness (2 Cor. 3:6-11). 'But you have come to... Jesus the mediator of the new covenant, and to the blood of sprinkling that speaks better things than that of Abel' (Heb. 12:22-24). In short, the old required man's obedience; the new is God's promise. The old was external ritual and ceremonial; the new, inward and spiritual. The old was ruled by fear; the new, by love. The old was bondage, slavery to law and works; the new, freedom, liberty in Christ. The old was for the Jew; the new, for the elect throughout the world. The old said: 'Stay away'; the new says: 'Come'. The old was breakable – and was broken by every man under it except Christ; the new is unbreakable.

This, in brief, is the biblical doctrine on the covenants. As I have noted, some Reformed teachers disagree with what I have said about the two great covenants, but this is only the tip of the iceberg. Covenant theology, I contend, diverges markedly from Scripture, being a logical system[14] invented by men,[15] and imposed on Scripture. But since it underpins the Reformed view of the law, we must look at it, and try to get to grips with it. A word of warning, however! It is like wrestling in a fog with an octopus which has been liberally smeared in Vaseline!

Covenant theology: 1. The covenant of works and the covenant of grace

What is the Reformed idea of a covenant? They say it is an agreement between two or more parties, whether or not the parties are equal.

Covenant theologians say God made a covenant with Adam. But where are we told this in Scripture? They go on to say God made a covenant with all men in Adam. Where are we told this in Scripture? Further, they give this so-called covenant a name, a name which looms large in their writings; namely, 'the covenant of works'. But you will not find this in Scripture.[16] I am not being silly or pedantic, reader. I am well aware that the word 'trinity' does not appear in the Bible. For the moment, I am simply stating a fact. 'The covenant of works' does not appear in Scripture as a term. My contention is, of course, neither does it appear as a concept.[17]

As I have already mentioned, the Reformed have also invented another covenant – 'the covenant of grace' – which is far more complicated than the covenant of works

---

[14] The Reformers and the Puritans, depending far too much on human logic, were not always *biblical* in their reasoning. In too many cases they became Reformed schoolmen, where logical distinctions and terms drawn from rationalism and philosophy, based on Aristotle's logical system, came to be regarded as authoritative as Scripture. This led to scholasticism among the Puritans and their followers. It was a sad mistake.

[15] Although Johann Heinrich Bullinger (1504-1575) was probably the first to publish a work containing the concept of federal salvation, Kaspar Olevianus (1536-1587) was its inventor, in Germany, when he and Zacharias Ursinus (1534-1583) drafted the final version of the Heidelberg Catechism (1562). William Ames (1576-1633) was the leading British exponent of covenant theology, which dominated the Westminster Confession of the Presbyterians (1643-1646) and the Savoy Declaration of the Independents (1661).

[16] Nor will you find it in Calvin, most Reformed creeds, the 39 Articles or the Heidelberg Catechism. This may surprise some Reformed readers.

[17] To try to justify this by reference to 'trinity' is fruitless. The difference is patent. The Bible does not use the word 'trinity', so we have to invent it. But the Bible does use the word 'covenant', and we should not stray from the way it uses it.

(which is problematical enough), so I will leave further explanation of it until we come across it. Just to say, this covenant of grace – as covenant theologians have developed it – does not appear in Scripture either – either in name or concept. What is more, it is impossible to speak of '*the* Reformed idea of the covenant of grace'. The simple fact is, covenant theologians do not see eye to eye with each other on what this so-called covenant of grace is.

Let me summarise so far. Most Reformed writers argue on the basis of a logical system they have invented ('covenant theology'), and in the process they have coined two phrases,[18] 'the covenant of works' and 'the covenant of grace'. These phrases – and the principles behind them – are fundamental, pivotal to covenant theology, and are, so it is said, the heart of Calvinism.[19]

Sadly, this logical contrivance – the covenant of works, and the covenant of grace – invented by Reformed theologians, dominating their theology, has greatly complicated the simplicity of the Bible, and muddied the waters dreadfully.[20] Things have got worse in the past five hundred years as covenant theologians have continued to elaborate and embellish their system, piling confusion upon confusion.

I remind you, reader, the Bible speaks of two covenants – the Mosaic and the new. Notice how the Bible and covenant theology are beginning to diverge already. They sound similar – both are based on two covenants – but they are very different covenants!

Covenant theology: 2. The covenant of grace

Since it is the so-called covenant of works which has most bearing on my book, I will say only a few words about the so-called covenant of grace. As I hinted, Reformed teachers are themselves far from clear about it – which some will admit to. They are not sure, for instance, about who is in the covenant of grace – some think even the unregenerate may be in it. Some think there is not one, but two covenants of grace – one called 'the covenant of redemption' to distinguish it from 'the covenant of grace'. It makes one wonder – as one of their most influential teachers recognised in print – why ever the notion of the covenant of grace caught on. Other problems exist. In addition to who is the second party of the covenant, is the covenant conditional or unconditional? Is it internal or external? What about the difference between the essence and the administration of the covenant? Is it an absolute covenant? Is it a legal question or does it involve life? These are not my questions, I hasten to add. I have culled them from Louis Berkhof's *Systematic Theology*, widely distributed over several decades by the Banner of Truth Trust. All such questions have perplexed Reformed theologians for centuries, and still do. But they are of their own making.

---

[18] 'Coining' does not mean, as so often it is assumed to mean, 'copying'. It means, 'inventing'. Inevitably, therefore, they are unbiblical phrases, even though they have a biblical air about them.

[19] Calvin was not a covenant theologian – he died before the notion had been invented. Apparently, therefore, Calvin would have failed his examination paper on Calvinism!

[20] And not only in a doctrinal sense. The antinomian controversy in New England in the 1630s arose out of it, and preparationism came from it. Antinomianism and preparationism were linked in the New England crisis. See 'Introduction' and chapters 4 and 9.

And what about the covenant of redemption which I mentioned in passing a moment ago? What is this? What about the problems Reformed logicians love to invent and try to solve concerning *this* covenant? Problems such as: On what basis do some Reformed theologians speak of a covenant between the Father and the Son, with no place for the Holy Spirit? Is this non-trinitarian covenant a threat to the doctrine of the trinity or not? Or is it a trinitarian covenant after all – even though it doesn't look like it? What is the connection between the covenant of redemption and the covenant of grace? Are they different or one and the same? These, too, are questions of their own making. Reformed teachers might try to say that their terminology need not confuse us, but the fact is they are themselves confused and divided. They may say it all can be 'put simply', but experience proves otherwise. Leading Reformed theologians disagree among themselves, saying they cannot understand each other's scheme – so what hopes for the average believer under Reformed teachers? The truth is, covenant theology solves nothing. Although those who started it wanted to avoid scholastic definitions, that's where it has ended up, openly ambiguous.[21]

The supreme problem for covenant theologians, however, does not concern the so-called covenant of grace. No! The main problem is with what they call 'the covenant of works'. The great question is, was the Mosaic covenant (the one I am concerned with in this book) the covenant of grace or the covenant of works? Opinions are sharply divided, self-contradictory and, at best, muddled among Reformed teachers. They might wonder why covenant theology has not caught on outside their own circle, but the answer would seem self-evident.

Covenant theology: 3. The biblical covenants, covenant theologians claim, are one and the same covenant

It is at this point that we run into massive trouble. As I said, Reformed teachers say that the various covenants in Scripture are really one and the same – just different administrations of the one covenant of grace. In particular, the Mosaic covenant was essentially the same as that covenant which was established with Abraham.

Judged by Scripture, the suggestion – that all the covenants are one and the same – is incredible. For one thing, the word 'covenant' really speaks of discontinuity, a change, something different, so whatever covenant theology deals with, it must deal with change. 'For the priesthood being changed, of necessity there is also a change of the law' (Heb. 7:12). Do not miss the 'of necessity'!

Take the covenants Reformed teachers try to synthesise. Genesis 3:15 was a promise, not a covenant at all; the covenant with Noah was a covenant with all mankind; the covenant with Abraham, as I have explained, had two aspects, one applicable to his physical descendants, and the other to his spiritual descendants; the Mosaic covenant at Sinai was a covenant of law-works which concerned Israel; the new covenant concerns believers. And there were other covenants down the ages besides these. One would think, judging by Reformed writers, that Paul spoke of the *covenant* (singular) in both Romans 9:4 and Ephesians 2:12. He did not! Take the

---

[21] See below for more on the idea of one covenant, but different *administrations*.

latter. He spoke of 'the *covenants* of promise'![22] Note the plural! The Bible makes much of an 's' on the end of a word (Gal. 3:16).

But many Reformed writers claim that the Abrahamic covenant, the Mosaic covenant and the new covenant are virtually one and the same, and all are covenants of grace and not works. This is staggering. If the covenant of Sinai did not demand law-works, what did it demand? I will have much more to say about this. There again, how can references to the Abrahamic covenant, the Mosaic covenant and the new covenant all apply to *the* covenant? After all, the Jeremiah passage could not be plainer. The new covenant is the *new* covenant, and is expressly said to be 'not according to' the Mosaic covenant (Jer. 31:32). These two, at least, cannot be the same covenant, can they? Let me stress once again the new-ness of the new covenant. Christians are under the new covenant, that covenant which is expressly said to be unlike the Mosaic covenant, the old covenant. Yet Calvin accused the Anabaptists of madness for what he dismissed as the 'pestilential error' of questioning the one-ness of the covenants!

Are we not plainly told that the old covenant has been abolished and the new has come? that believers are not under the law? (See Rom. 6:14-15; 7:1-6; 8:2-11; 2 Cor. 3:7-11; Heb. 7:11-19; 8:6-13; 9:15;[23] 10:16-20). We know the Mosaic covenant has been abolished (2 Cor. 3:7-11). What is more, as the old covenant was abolished and the new covenant came in, a comparison, even a stark contrast, was drawn between the two. Far from being altogether one and the same covenant, they are very, very different. How different can be easily seen in Paul's words:

God... made us... ministers of the new covenant, not of the letter but of the Spirit; for the letter kills, but the Spirit gives life. But if the ministry of death, written and engraved on stones, was glorious... which glory was passing away, how will the ministry of the Spirit not be more glorious? For if the ministry of condemnation had glory, the ministry of righteousness exceeds much more in glory. For even what was made glorious had no glory in this respect, because of the glory that excels. For if what is passing away was glorious, what remains is much more glorious (2 Cor. 3:5-11).

This is vital. The Bible contrasts the two covenants, the old and the new, and contrasts them very sharply indeed. In the following quotations, please observe the use of the words *but*, *yet* and *on the other hand*. These are words of contrast. Powerful words! Words which must not be glossed! Nor should we miss the apostle's hyperbole: 'glorious... glory... more glorious... glory... exceeds much more in glory... glorious... glory... the glory that excels... glorious... more glorious'. And on which covenant does the weight of glory resoundingly fall?

The two covenants are clearly contrasted in the following passages:

---

[22] It is not unknown for covenant theologians, and Baptists who wish to go as far as they can with covenant theology, to misquote Eph. 2:12 as 'the covenant of promise'. As for such Baptists, they should recall the bad and far-reaching effect covenant theology will have on church life. Sadly, some of them, even though they admit differences in the covenants – especially the greatest of all – namely, that the new covenant is new! – attribute panic and some sort of dispensationalism to those of us who will not take the same route as they; that is, we will not opt for covenant theology.

[23] Christ 'is the mediator of the new covenant, by means of death, for the redemption of the transgressions under the first covenant' (Heb. 9:15). Brown thought that these were the sins which were not expiated under the old covenant (Brown: *Hebrews* p413).

For the law was given through Moses, *but* grace and truth came through Jesus Christ (John 1:17).

You are not under law *but* under grace (Rom. 6:14).

For Christ is the end of the law for righteousness to everyone who believes. For Moses writes about the righteousness which is of the law: 'The man who does those things shall live by them'. *But* the righteousness of faith speaks in this way... If you confess with your mouth the Lord Jesus and believe in your heart that God has raised him from the dead, you will be saved (Rom. 10:4-9).

For as many as are of the works of the law are under the curse; for it is written: 'Cursed is everyone who does not continue in all things which are written in the book of the law, to do them'. *But* that no one is justified by the law in the sight of God is evident, for 'the just shall live by faith'. *Yet* the law is not of faith, *but* 'the man who does them shall live by them'. Christ has redeemed us from the curse of the law, having become a curse for us... that the blessing of Abraham might come upon the Gentiles in Christ Jesus, that we might receive the promise of the Spirit through faith (Gal. 3:10-14).

For these are the two covenants: the one from Mount Sinai which gives birth to bondage, which is Hagar – for this Hagar is Mount Sinai in Arabia, and corresponds to Jerusalem which now is, and is in bondage with her children – *but* the Jerusalem above is free... (Gal. 4:24-26).

For on the one hand there is an annulling of the former commandment because of its weakness and unprofitableness, for the law made nothing perfect; *on the other hand*, there is the bringing in of a better hope, through which we draw near to God (Heb. 7:18-19).

But now[24] he has obtained a more excellent ministry, inasmuch as he is also mediator of a better covenant, which was established on better promises. For if that first covenant had been faultless, then no place would have been sought for a second (Heb. 8:6-7).

Are these quotations not sufficient to prove that the old and new covenants are very different? Do they not show that the new is far superior to the old, and plainly so? How can they be the same? If they are, how could Paul say: 'For the law of the Spirit of life in Christ Jesus has made me free from the law of sin and death. For what the law could not do in that it was weak through the flesh, God did by sending his own Son in the likeness of sinful flesh' (Rom. 8:2-3)? Here we have it; two laws, two systems, two economies, two covenants. The old, the law of sin and death; the new, the law of the Spirit of life in Christ Jesus. The contrast, I say again, could not be greater. The old was a covenant of death, the new is a covenant of life. There is no greater contrast than between death and life! No wonder we are told: 'In that [God] says: "A new covenant", he has made the first obsolete' (Heb. 8:13), and that Christ has taken 'away the first that he may establish the second' (Heb. 10:9). Some Reformed teachers censure those of us who dare assert that the old covenant is abolished. But the letter to the Hebrews says it is!

Christ draws a very clear contrast between the old and the new covenants (Mark 2:18-22), illustrating this in two ways: it is futile both to sew a piece of new cloth on to an old garment, and to put new wine into old wineskins. The two covenants are very different. They cannot be cobbled together. Although covenant theologians claim the covenants (the Abrahamic, the Mosaic, and the new, the last two in particular) are one covenant, they are mistaken.

---

[24] Note the 'now'. It is the eschatological key to all this argument.

Covenant theology: 4. The covenant of works

But what of the Reformed covenant of works? Though its advocates have to admit its development is 'something of a mystery', those of us who reject the concept are dismissed as thinking unbiblically. This, of course, needs proof, not mere assertion. Advocates of the covenant of works, aware of the need to be clear about its biblical basis, have to admit its name cannot be found in the first three chapters of Genesis. But why worry about the non-mention of its name? There are bigger problems with it than that! Neither the name – *nor the concept itself* – is found in the entire Bible! Even so, the lack of the term – while this, I freely concede, is not conclusive – should give pause for thought. Yes, if the principle can be found in Scripture, the absence of its name is not important. But is the principle in Scripture? This *is* the question!

Romans 5:12-21, so it seems, is the only passage which, at first glance, can be used to establish the covenant of works, the covenant said to be made with all the human race in Adam. If this is right, and Romans 5:12-21 does speak of the covenant of works, it can only mean that the law is not this covenant of works – since John 1:17, Romans 5:13-14 and Galatians 3:10-29 teach that the law was not given to men until Sinai, 430 years after Abraham, let alone Adam! It could not, therefore, have been given to Adam and the patriarchs.[25] This, in turn, can only mean that the law is the covenant of grace – which, as I will show, is nonsense.

So what about Romans 5:12-21? Reader, as I have made clear, I fully accept – I am convinced, biblically – that in eternity past the triune Godhead agreed to save the elect in Christ. I am also convinced that in Adam all the human race fell into sin. Both Adam and Christ acted as representative heads, acting for all their descendants – that is, in Adam, all the human race; in Christ, all the elect. Adam fell; all the human race fell in and with him. Christ was born under the law, kept the law, died under the law, and was raised from the dead; all the elect are constituted and accounted righteous by God in him, they receiving all the benefits he earned for them by his life, sufferings and resurrection. I find these truths unmistakably taught in Romans 5:12-21 and 1 Corinthians 15:21-23,45-49.

But this is a far cry from the covenant theology invented by Reformed scholars. If truth be told, not all of them accept the usual deductions made by covenant theologians from the passages.

Romans 7:10 is another passage which is sometimes called on to justify the covenant of works. But this verse, according to the immediate context, clearly speaks of the ten commandments (in truth, the law) which, on Sinai, had been addressed to Jews, all of whom, naturally, were sinners. Even so, some Reformed writers claim that, in Romans 7:10, Paul was speaking of the covenant of works given to Adam before he fell. In other words, the law was given to a man who had not sinned. Allowing it to be so for the moment, what Adam made of prohibitions against murder and adultery, and so on, *before he had sinned*, I simply cannot comprehend. And what of 1 Timothy 1:9? 'The law is not made for a righteous person, but for the lawless and insubordinate, for the ungodly and for sinners, for the unholy and profane, for murderers of fathers and murderers of mothers, for manslayers, for fornicators, for sodomites, for kidnappers,

---

[25] See chapter 9.

for liars, for perjurers...'. In which of these categories did Adam find himself *before he fell?*

The main confusion concerning the Reformed covenant of works, as can be seen, arises over the Mosaic covenant. Was the Mosaic covenant the covenant of works or was it the covenant of grace? I mean, of course, in Reformed terms. The Bible knows nothing of either. But this is a fundamental question for covenant theology. Was Sinai a works covenant or a grace covenant? Covenant theologians ought to be able to give us a clear, unequivocal answer to that question. Can they? Will they? The Bible does. Let me prove it.

Covenant theology: 5. Sinai – was it a works covenant or a grace covenant?

Take Galatians 4:21-31. In the allegory of Sarah and Hagar,[26] we are expressly told that the law on Mount Sinai was a covenant of bondage, in contrast to another covenant (Gal. 4:21,24-27), the two women representing these two covenants. What covenant did Sarah represent? The answer is patent. The Abrahamic covenant fulfilled in the new covenant. How do we know? Well, how would the Galatians have understood Paul's allusion? Not having the benefit of 2 Corinthians 3 or Hebrews 8, and limited to what they knew from the apostle's letter they were reading (or having read to them), nevertheless their minds would have leapt to the covenant with Abraham, and for two reasons. First, Paul had already stressed the Abrahamic covenant of promise (Gal. 3:6-9,14-19,29). Secondly, the allegory itself contains the explicit reference to Abraham, Hagar and Isaac, and the implied reference to Sarah (Gal. 4:21-31). Paul, in referring to Sarah, was speaking of the Abrahamic covenant fulfilled in the new. *That* is how the Galatians would have read the apostle. That is how we must read him.

Now whatever view is taken of the covenant represented by Sarah, the covenant represented by Hagar is the law, the Mosaic covenant. Paul was writing to those who desired 'to be under the law'. The allegory spoke of 'two covenants: the one from Mount Sinai which gives birth to bondage, which is Hagar – for this Hagar is [represents] Mount Sinai... and corresponds to... bondage' (Gal. 4:21-25). And this covenant is expressly called a covenant of bondage. In other words, it was a works covenant which no sinner could keep, but which enslaved those under it. Note further, *contrast* was Paul's theme; contrast between law, bondage and flesh, in the one covenant – and promise, freedom and the Spirit, in the other. Paul's argument was directed against the Judaisers who wanted believers to go under the Mosaic covenant. Indeed, as I have shown, they argued that the Abrahamic and the Mosaic covenants were one and the same. Not for a moment would he countenance the thought! The Mosaic covenant, being a covenant of bondage, Paul would have none of it. This puts covenant theologians on the side of the Judaisers, and, therefore, against Paul.

Let me prove it. Many Reformed writers, as I have said, will not have it at any price. In one respect, they have the same faulty theology as the Judaisers. Flying in the face of Scripture, they say there are not two covenants here in Galatians 4, but one; the two women do not represent two covenants, but two *aspects* of one covenant; the

---

[26] 'Allegory' (AV), 'allegorically speaking' (NASB), 'are symbolic' (NKJV), 'taken figuratively' (NIV). From *allēgoreō*, 'to speak allegorically or in a figure' (Thayer).

slavery of the Mosaic covenant was not really a part of that covenant at all; it was all a misunderstanding, a Jewish misinterpretation of the covenant. So it is claimed. But Paul said no such thing. He said it was the covenant itself which enslaved! It was no misunderstanding! The Mosaic covenant was based on a slavish principle, 'do and live' – with its corollary, 'fail and die'. Those under it, the Jews, 'were held prisoners by the law, locked up' by it (Gal. 3:23, NIV).

The law could bring life (Lev. 18:5; Ezek. 18:19; 20:11-25; Matt. 19:17; Luke 10:28; 18:18-20; Rom. 7:10; 10:5), yes, but the obedience had to be perfect (Gal. 3:10; Jas. 2:10). Now, since all men (apart from Christ) are sinners (Rom. 3:23; 1 John 1:8; 3:4-5), no man can be saved by law (Acts 13:39; Gal. 2:16; 3:11). If he could, 'if righteousness comes through the law' – that is, through a sinner keeping the law – 'then Christ died in vain' (Gal. 2:21)! But no sinner can be saved by law. The fault, however, is not with the law, for the law is 'perfect' (Ps. 19:7), 'good' (1 Tim. 1:8), 'holy and just and good' (Rom. 7:12). The fault is with man (Rom. 7:14; 8:3; Heb. 8:7-8). 'If there had been a law given which could have given life, truly righteousness would have been by the law [of God]' (Gal. 3:21).

The law *itself* was a works covenant. It was not a case of the Jews turning a grace covenant into a works covenant! Even so, many Reformed teachers continue to insist the law *was* a (indeed, the) covenant of grace. To confuse the Mosaic covenant with the covenant of works – to deny it is the covenant of grace – is, so it is alleged, the most common error in interpreting the allegory! The 'first covenant' and 'old covenant' are said to refer, not to the Mosaic covenant, but to the whole age between Adam's fall and Christ's [first] coming; the Mosaic covenant and Abrahamic covenant being one and the same.

This is quite wrong. In Galatians 4:21-25, Paul was speaking of two covenants – the old and the new (within the Abrahamic covenant). Those under the law are slaves, those under grace are saints. The two covenants, and those under them, are chalk and cheese. These two covenants cannot be the same covenant. 2 Corinthians 3:6-17, Galatians 3:10-29 and many other places, utterly refute it.

In fact, Reformed theologians themselves deep down – despite their seemingly confident assertions – have a real problem, a massive problem, an intractable problem, with the Mosaic covenant, and are guilty of double-speak. Some admit the Mosaic covenant certainly looks as though it is the covenant of works, but even so, they claim, it is, after all, the covenant of grace. But, reader, the law did not merely look like the law – it *was* the law; the word of God says so! Other Reformed teachers say the law was the covenant of grace 'more legally defined' at Sinai. But how can *grace* be 'legally defined', let alone '*more* legally defined'? Another writer wants it both ways. The law was the covenant of works – a 'modified' version of the Abrahamic covenant – but also a 'renewal' of the single covenant of grace spanning all time from Adam to the eternal state to come. Grace, law, gospel and curse all jumbled together, it seems! Some grace! Some muddle! There have been many versions of the theme. As I have shown, some argue the point from the two givings of the law. The first, so they say, was a works covenant, whereas the second was as a rule to those who are in Christ. In the previous chapter, I demonstrated the schizophrenic nonsense this is.

But what about Hebrews 8:13 and 9:15? Do these passages have any bearing on the so-called covenant of works said to be given to Adam? Certainly not! When God says he has made 'a new covenant', and thus, as the writer immediately adds by way of deduction and explanation, 'he has made the first obsolete' (Heb. 8:13), it does not mean that after Adam fell, God instituted a 'new covenant of grace' with him. The writer to the Hebrews was not talking about Adam at all! There is not the remotest possibility of it! Why, he does not even mention Adam in his entire letter! And in Hebrews 8:13, he was not saying that an old covenant with Adam was replaced by a new covenant with Adam. Nor was he declaring that an old covenant with Adam was replaced by a new covenant with Moses. Nor was he saying that an old covenant of grace was replaced by a new covenant of grace. When the writer to the Hebrews spoke of the old covenant, the first covenant which was made old and replaced, he was referring not to Adam and Eden, but to Moses and Sinai. And when speaking of the new covenant, that altogether different covenant, he was not referring to Moses and Sinai, but to Christ and Calvary. He was asserting that the old covenant of Moses – the law – given at Sinai, has been replaced by the new covenant – a grace covenant – made by Christ on Calvary. This is the simple, undeniable and stubborn (and glorious) fact about Hebrews 8:13. The entire context of Hebrews is incontestable proof of it.

The Puritans, the masters of (or mastered by) covenant theology, certainly showed confusion over all this. They simply could not agree as to what the New Testament means when it refers to the first and second covenants, the old and new covenants. They could not agree as to, in their terms, how many covenants of grace there are. In particular, some said the Mosaic covenant was the covenant of works. Others thought it subservient to the covenant of grace. Others, a mixed covenant of works and grace.[27] Yet others, the majority, thought it was the covenant of grace. And since the Puritans played (and are still playing) such an important role in this debate on the law in general, and covenant theology in particular, this obvious flaw and glaring confusion which lies at the very foundation of their case should give their earnest advocates pause for thought. As covenant theologians have to admit, such divisions and differences of interpretation are 'discouraging'; and so they must be – for those who want to follow the Puritans in their views on the law. Perhaps the edifice Reformed teachers have erected, though outwardly very impressive, might in fact be totally unstable right from the start? Shaky foundations, it seems to me.

Covenant theology is confused – right at its heart. Is the Mosaic covenant the covenant of grace or works, neither or both, or one looking like the other? Is it all to do with the two givings of the law? Is it all a Jewish misunderstanding? Or what? This much is clear: Reformed theologians are able, apparently, to live with this tangle of illogicality, and they seem more-than happy to castigate those (the Jews in their time, and now, me and others like me) who cannot. The truth is, of course, their logic, and its conundrums, are not found in the covenant of Sinai, and have nothing to do with the Jews, but are entirely the province of covenant theologians themselves.[28]

Let me give just one example of the sort of thing I am talking about. Listen to this Reformed writer:

The unbelieving Israelites were under the covenant of grace made with their father Abraham externally... but under the covenant of works made with their father Adam

---

[27] How that can be reconciled with the apostle's declaration baffles me: 'And if by grace, then it is no longer of works; otherwise grace is no longer grace. But if it is of works, it is no longer grace; otherwise work is no longer work' (Rom. 11:6).
[28] See chapter 5.

internally... Further, as to believers among them, they were internally... as well as externally, under the covenant of grace; and only externally under the covenant of works, and that, not as a covenant coordinate with, but subordinate and subservient to, the covenant of grace.[29]

So said Boston. Did you get it, reader? Did you get it when you re-read it? Do you think you will ever really get it? I wonder if Boston got it?

The consequences did not stop with Israel, of course. Every adherent of covenant theology today has to sort out such matters – that is, if they want to be sure about how they and their offspring stand. Are their infant children in the covenant of grace or works? If they are in the covenant of grace, are they in it externally? Or internally? I know from sad experience how an unbeliever can rebuff the call of the gospel, and push aside its warnings, by saying he is (or his father was) 'in the covenant'. I wonder, however, does such an unbeliever know which covenant he is talking about?

The question remains, according to Reformed theologians, was the Mosaic covenant the covenant of grace, or of works, or of grace looking like works, or... what? Since it is fundamental to covenant theology, we have a right to know, surely! Reader, I think I have provided evidence[30] enough to justify my claim: Reformed theologians are divided and confused over the Mosaic covenant. Some think it was the covenant of grace. Some think it was the covenant of works. Some think it was both. Some think it was the covenant of grace looking like the covenant of works. In short, there is no such thing as *the* Reformed view of the Mosaic covenant. They simply cannot tell. As I have observed, this would not matter so much, but according to their own statements, the covenant of works is pivotal to their system. If so, and if *they* cannot decide whether or not the law is the covenant of works, what confidence should others place in their arguments on the believer and the law?

Of far greater importance, what does Scripture say about the Mosaic covenant? Was the law a works covenant? Note, I did not say 'the covenant of works'. I hope I have said enough to make it plain that it was nothing to do with Adam and the Reformed notion of *the* covenant of works. The answer is, of course, the law *was* a works covenant. After all, the Bible speaks of 'the works [or deeds] of the law' (Rom. 3:20; Gal. 2:16; 3:2,5). But there are two principal passages which prove the point. I refer to Romans 10:5-6, and Galatians 4:4-5. This last I regard as the clinching argument.

Proof that the law was a works covenant: 1. Romans 10:5-6

Let me quote the verses: 'Moses writes about the righteousness which is of the law: "The man who does those things shall live by them". But the righteousness of faith speaks in this way...'.

Paul speaks of two ways of attaining righteousness – 'the righteousness which is of *the law*', and 'the righteousness of *faith*'. But the apostle more than *speaks* of two ways. He *contrasts* them: 'The righteousness which is of the law... *but* the righteousness of faith'. Moreover, Paul contrasts them very strongly. In truth, he

---

[29] Fisher p54.
[30] As always, see the actual statements in the extracts. As before, some readers may well be astonished to read what men, with (Reformed) household names, published by top Reformed publishing houses, have been prepared to write.

opposes them. Justification by law, by works, he sets against justification by grace, through faith. Thus it is clear, the law is a works covenant, opposed to grace.

All this is to do with justification. I quite accept the fact. I go further. It is essential for what I want to say. On the question of justification, law and faith (grace) are contrasted. I stress this once again, even though it is obvious, and for the same reason as before; namely, some teachers want us to believe that law and grace go hand in hand. As a matter of fact, some of them, it seems to me, see hardly any difference between the two; and some say they are one and the same. Clearly they are not!

But there is an even bigger point to be made. To which law was Paul referring? The passage, of course, has very close links with Galatians 3:12. Paul quoted Leviticus 18:5 in both places. 'The law' in question, therefore, is the Mosaic law.[31] The upshot? The law of Moses was a works covenant. The law of Moses, I stress. All of it.

This is not the only place where justification is linked with obedience to the law: 'The doers of the law will be justified' (Rom. 2:13). True, because of sin, 'the commandment, which was to bring life', brought 'death' (Rom. 7:10),[32] cursing those under it (Gal. 3:10,13), and 'therefore by the deeds of the law no flesh will be justified' (Rom. 3:20). Consequently, 'a man is not justified by the works of the law but by faith in Jesus Christ... No one is justified by the law... the law is not of faith' (Gal. 2:16; 3:11-12).[33] Yes, all this is true. *But the fact that Paul needed to say it shows that perfect obedience would have earned salvation.* Paul would never have needed to make such statements, nor written Romans 4:1-5, Ephesians 2:8-10 or Philippians 3:9, if law and justification had not been linked.[34] The law required works, which if accomplished, would have earned salvation. Note the connection between the law, the doing of the law – note the various 'doing' words, such as *practice, do, obey, deeds, works, keep* – and life, eternal life, in Leviticus 18:5; Ezekiel 20:11,13; Matthew 19:16-17; Luke 10:25-28; 18:18-20; Romans 2:13,17-25; 10:5-10, for instance.

The law, if kept perfectly, would have merited salvation. Indeed, in one case, the law *was* kept and justification *was* earned – by Christ for his people (Gal. 4:4-5). If perfect law-keeping could not have brought righteousness, then Christ could never have earned salvation for his people through the law (Gal. 4:4-5). This is the 'bigger point' I noted a moment ago. The man Christ Jesus, and only the man Christ Jesus, has attained life by keeping the law. *This* is the point. Perfect obedience to the law brought the reward, because the law demanded works, and promised righteousness for obedience. It is the core of Paul's argument in Romans 4:4; 11:6. The principle applies

---

[31] See chapter 9, where I return to this.

[32] And the law was made only for sinners (1 Tim. 1:9) – sinners before and after their receiving the law. Israel certainly proved it (Deut. 4:1 – 6:25; Neh. 9:13-37; Ezek. 20:11-44; Rom. 9:30 – 10:5).

[33] See Ps. 143:2; Gal. 3:21. But the fact that no sinner could keep the law has no bearing on the issue. The fact remains: perfect obedience would have brought righteousness. Indeed, if Reformed teachers push the point, I would observe how once again they destroy their case by inadvertently exposing yet another difference between law and grace. The law could not bring salvation for any sinner without exception, but grace brings salvation for all the elect without exception! And, of course, the way of salvation has *always* been by faith: 'The just shall live by faith' was first stated in the Old Testament, and thereafter quoted in the New (Hab. 2:4; Rom. 1:17; Gal. 3:11; Heb. 10:38).

[34] I admit the principle is of wider application than the law, but Rom. 4 comes immediately after Rom. 2 and 3; Eph. 2:11-18 after Eph. 2:8-10; Phil. 3:9 is explicit; as is Rom. 4:13-16.

precisely in Christ's case (Gal. 4:4-5). Christ coming under the law amounts to far more than saying Jesus was a Jew. Of course, 'born under the law' does mean that Jesus was a Jew, but it means far more than that. When combined with the following verse, the purpose of Christ's coming, and his being under the law, is spelled out: Christ came to set elect Jews (and Gentiles)[35] free from being confined and condemned under the law, 'to redeem those who were under the law' (Gal. 4:5). Nor must we forget, Paul has already told us that Christ bore the curse of the law in his death (Gal. 3:13). The curse of the law, I repeat, the curse of the entire Mosaic law!

In short, Romans 10:5-6 proves that the law was a works covenant.

Reference to Galatians 4 leads me on to what I have called 'the clinching passage' to prove that the law was a works covenant. Before I come to that, however, let me repeat what I said at the start of this chapter. I realise this section of my book is involved and difficult. At the risk of being wearisome, let me pause to explain, once again, what I am trying to do. In face of Reformed opposition, I am trying to show that the law was a works covenant. It was not the gospel. To this end, I am providing evidence to support my claim that the law promised the Jews justification for perfect obedience. And it really did promise justification. It was not a figment of Jewish imagination (though, of course, justification by the law was in practice not possible to fallen man – no sinner can keep the law perfectly).[36] Perfect obedience to the law would merit justification. That is what the Bible teaches. And this establishes that the law was a works covenant. It was not the gospel. All this has considerable bearing on the way Reformed theology speaks of 'the covenant of works', and what part the law plays in that covenant, itself a pillar of covenant theology, which in turn leads to the idea that sanctification is by the law. And this is why I am tackling it here. Many Puritans, however, were in a muddle over this. Even though they could argue that Christ earned and merited and worked righteousness for his people by keeping the law and dying under the curse of God, they also argued that justification could not come by the law. This is true, of course, in the sense that nobody, but Christ, could or did keep it, but the fact is, *perfect obedience to the law would have brought justification.* Indeed, Christ's perfect obedience *did* earn righteousness for all his people. Not all Reformed writers give Romans 7:10 its proper weight. Indeed, not all Reformed writers refer to the verse or even quote it in their books on the law. This is very odd, or worse, since at first glance it has something to say in contradiction of the Reformed claim that the law was a grace covenant.[37]

Now for 'the clinching passage'.

Proof that the law was a works covenant: 2. Galatians 4:4-5

Let me quote the verses:

When the fullness of the time had come, God sent forth his Son, born of a woman, born under the law, to redeem those who were under the law.

---

[35] See chapters 3 and 9.

[36] Nor is it a figment of (some) Reformed imagination, contrary to advocates of the New Perspective. Perfect obedience to the law would merit justification.

[37] I will return to this in chapter 10.

Let us begin by reminding ourselves that a sinner is justified by faith without the works of the law:

Now the righteousness of God apart from the law is revealed... even the righteousness of God, through faith in Jesus Christ... Therefore we conclude that a man is justified by faith apart from the deeds of the law (Rom. 3:21-22,28).

As I have shown above, however, perfect obedience to the law would bring justification; but it would have to be perfect! If a man offends in one point, he brings the entire system crashing about his ears (Jas. 2:10-11). Paul felt the sting of his breaking the tenth commandment – but in the breaking of the tenth, he broke all the law (Rom. 7:7-12). Perfect obedience, in all points, at every turn, is required!

A sinner, therefore, who seeks justification 'by the works of the law' (Rom. 9:32), is attempting an utter impossibility. *But Jesus Christ, the sinless one, could and did keep the law, and thus establish righteousness for the elect!* As a consequence, justifying righteousness, accomplished by the works of Christ, is imputed to the sinner through faith without his works:

To him who does not work but believes on him who justifies the ungodly, his faith is accounted for righteousness... There is therefore now no condemnation to those who are in Christ Jesus, who do not walk according to the flesh, but according to the Spirit. For the law of the Spirit of life in Christ Jesus has made me free from the law of sin and death. For what the law could not do in that it was weak through the flesh, God did by sending his own Son in the likeness of sinful flesh, on account of sin: he condemned sin in the flesh, that the righteous requirement of the law might be fulfilled in us who do not walk according to the flesh but according to the Spirit (Rom. 4:5; 8:1-4).

God's law demanded works; Christ provided them. The law demanded perfection; Christ provided it. The law demanded atonement by blood (Heb. 9:22); Christ died as a sin offering under the law, shedding his blood on the cross (Rom. 3:25; 4:25; 8:3; 2 Cor. 5:21; Gal. 3:13). 'By one man's obedience many will be made righteous' (Rom. 5:19). This is what enabled Paul to exclaim: 'We establish the law' (Rom. 3:31).[38] And this is the teaching of Galatians 4:4-5.

God sent Christ his Son into the world to redeem those who were under the law. Consequently, the Lord Jesus came as a man (John 1:14), to redeem men (Heb. 2:14). But not only did the Son of God become human. He became a Jew – which meant he was born under the law – born, 'taking the form of a bondservant, and coming in the likeness of men' so that he might be 'obedient to... death, even the death of the cross' (Phil. 2:6-8), 'having become a curse for us', cursed by the law, so that he might redeem us from it (Gal. 3:13). What law is this? The same law as throughout Galatians 3, of course. I will deal with this in chapter 9, but for now I summarise the position: Christ was born under the very law which the Jews were under prior to the coming of Christ; that is, the Mosaic law. And Christ, by keeping that law, and suffering the curse of that law, redeemed the elect who were under it. In other words, Christ accomplished salvation by works. By the works of the law, he earned it.

---

[38] What is more, as I will show, the grace of God in the gospel inevitably moves the believer to sanctification; that is, obedience to all God's revelation – thus honouring God in his entire word, including the law.

This can only mean that the law was a works covenant. If not, how did Christ redeem those under the law by going under the law? Would Reformed teachers say Christ was born under what they call the covenant of grace? Was he cursed by the covenant of grace? Some try to avoid this by saying the curse is to do only with the ceremonial law. This distinction is without biblical warrant, as I will show. But allowing the distinction for sake of argument, is the curse attached to this so-called ceremonial law, or to the law itself? Was Christ made under, and cursed under, the ceremonial law only? Of course not!

Christ came into the world, born a Jew under the law, a works covenant, in order to earn, work, deserve and merit salvation for his people. Did he *earn* it by *works* under a *grace* covenant? The answer is self-evident. The believer's righteousness is an earned righteousness, earned by Christ, earned by keeping the law, earned by suffering under the law, *but only if the law is a works covenant.* Which it is! Of course, no sinner could keep the law and so earn salvation.

As Horatius Bonar put it:

> *Not what these hands have done*
> *Can save this guilty soul;*
> *Not what this toiling flesh has borne*
> *Can make my spirit whole.*

> *Not what I feel or do*
> *Can give me peace with God;*
> *Not all my prayers, and sighs, and tears*
> *Can bear my awful load.*

But Christ could and did, and there the believer rests his soul for ever:

> *On merit not my own I stand;*
> *On doings which I have not done,*
> *Merit beyond what I can claim,*
> *Doings more[39] perfect than my own.*

> *Upon a life I have not lived,*
> *Upon a death I did not die,*
> *Another's life, another's death,*
> *I stake my whole eternity.[40]*

Believers are justified by resting on this finished work of Christ (John 19:30), the one who did all the doing which the holy God required under his law. As a result: 'Christ is the end of the law for righteousness to everyone who believes' (Rom. 10:4).

'What must I do to be saved?' is the question. As we have seen: 'Work', the law thunders. 'Keep me perfectly'. What does the gospel say? 'Believe on the Lord Jesus Christ, and you will be saved' (Acts 16:30-31). 'Trust the Redeemer, who, under the

---

[39] I take this to be poetic licence. Nothing can be *more* perfect! In this matter, how could God accept anything less than *perfect* obedience under the law? What commandment did Christ not keep? What shadow of himself did he not fulfil? What penalty did he not suffer?

[40] Both hymns by Horatius Bonar (*Gospel Hymns* number 536; Bonar pp101,229). Some versions have: 'Upon a life I did not live'. Horatius Bonar entitled the hymn: 'Christ for us'. As he put it in his hymn, 'Complete in him': 'He [Christ] did the work!' (Bonar p224).

law, by his works, earned salvation (see Gal. 4:4)'. If the law was not a works covenant... bang goes our salvation!

Think of the precious promise John gives to all believers: 'If we confess our sins, [God] is faithful and just to forgive us our sins and to cleanse us from all unrighteousness' (1 John 1:9). It is, I say, precious. But it is more. It is truly amazing, staggering. One would expect John to have said something like: 'If we confess our sins, [God] is kind, merciful, loving to forgive us our sins'. But he did not say that! Rather, he spoke of God's faithfulness and justice. Why did he say that God is *'faithful and just* to forgive us our sins'? Faithful? Just? The answer is, of course, God *is* faithful and just to forgive us; he is not only *kind* to forgive us. It is his faithfulness and justice which *demand and ensure* forgiveness. Why? Because Christ has earned it, because Christ has merited it. In that great, eternal agreement, of which I spoke at the beginning of this chapter, God demanded obedience, promising life for that perfect obedience. 'Do and live' was the essence of God's commandment and promise (Lev. 18:5; Rom. 7:10; 10:4-6; Gal. 3:12). It is impossible for God to affirm black is white. He cannot acquit the wicked: 'I will not justify the wicked' (Ex. 23:7; Nah. 1:3). To do so would be to break his own law: 'He who justifies the wicked... [is] an abomination to the LORD' (Prov. 17:15). *But he must justify the righteous!* Just as he cannot justify the wicked, so he must justify the righteous. He can only justify on the basis of righteousness, however, on the basis of work, on the basis of merit, on the basis of perfect obedience. And all this Christ freely accepted in that agreement made within the Godhead in eternity past. And so, in time, at the appointed time, having come into the world, having been made under the law, Christ died under the law in order to accomplish this eternal purpose of God.

Christ said: 'Do not think that I came to destroy the law or the prophets. I did not come to destroy but to fulfil. For assuredly, I say to you, till heaven and earth pass away, one jot or one tittle will by no means pass from the law till all is fulfilled' (Matt. 5:17-18). Let me emphasise this. Christ did not come to destroy the law or the prophets; that is, 'to invalidate, to represent as of no authority, or of diminished authority, those former revelations of the divine will'. In addition to not 'invalidating' the law, Christ did not destroy it, demolish it, dismantle it, or repeal it for, as I will show in chapter 17, the law now plays the role of a paradigm in the believer's sanctification.[41] Rather, speaking of the law in particular, Christ came to fulfil it; that is, he came in order to obey it to the full, and complete it.[42] This he did to the letter, to the jot and to the tittle! And in keeping this works covenant in its entirety, he merited the everlasting salvation of all his people.

---

[41] Note that Christ fulfilled both the law and the prophets, which means, of course, that we must now regard the law in the same way as we regard the prophecies of Christ's first coming.

[42] It will not do (see chapter 7) to try to limit Matt. 5:17-18 to 'the moral law'. Christ came to fulfil and abrogate the law of Moses – the law of Moses entirely – not some artificially designated subsection of the law. The law was both temporary and typical. From Gal. 3:19,25; Eph. 2:14-15; Col. 2:14, it is clear that the law, having served its purpose, ceased. The word 'fulfil' means 'complete', 'fill up', 'perfect'. Christ came to complete divine revelation, carry it forward. So much so, the law, the entire law, having served its purpose, ceased to be of obligation. As a system, it passed away in its entirety. That 'middle wall of partition' was completely taken down. Christ brought the law to its maturity as it found its realisation in him. For more on Matt. 5:17-18, see pp170,236; see also 'Extracts' p498.

'Wait a moment', says an objector. 'Look at Romans 4:5: "[God] who justifies the ungodly". How can this be reconciled with what you have just said? You have been arguing that justification under the law comes by works. How, then, can God justify the ungodly, since no ungodly person can produce the necessary law-works?' What is the answer, the explanation? Just this: Romans 4:5 is speaking about justification under the gospel, not the law. And *this* is the gospel: Christ came under the old covenant, and kept the law (Gal. 4:4-5), thus earning the salvation of the elect, earning it by his works. This is the principle that Christ came under: 'Now to him who works, the wages are not counted as [according to] grace but as debt' (Rom. 4:4). Christ obtained redemption for the elect, earning it, not by grace ('earn' and 'grace' are a contradiction in terms, Rom. 4:4; 11:6), but by his law-works, in order to grant it, by grace, to the elect upon their believing, that they might be 'justified freely by [God's] grace through the redemption that is in Christ Jesus, whom God set forth as a propitiation by his blood, through faith, to demonstrate his righteousness... that he might be just and the justifier of the one who has faith in Jesus' (Rom. 3:24-26). In this way God 'justifies the ungodly'; that is, justifies 'him who does not work but believes on him who justifies the ungodly' (Rom. 4:5). He did this 'that he might be just and the justifier of the one who has faith in Jesus' (Rom. 3:26). But this justification had to be earned by law work. Under the gospel, God justifies the sinner, who does not do the work, who cannot do the work, when the sinner trusts the Christ who, under the law, did the work.

Christ did all this in perfect obedience to the will of his Father. Christ came into the world with the express purpose of saving sinners (1 Tim. 1:15), in order to complete the work given him by the Father: 'My food is to do the will of him who sent me, and to finish his work' (John 4:34). To the Jews, he said: 'I do not seek my own will but the will of the Father who sent me... I have come down from heaven, not to do my own will, but the will of him who sent me' (John 5:30; 6:38). He could speak of 'the works which the Father has given me to finish – the very works that I do' (John 5:36). These works included the miracles, yes, but, above all, they included the work of salvation. The Lord Jesus could say to the Father: 'I have finished the work which you have given me to do' (John 17:4). And, above all, his final shout of triumph on the cross: 'It is finished' (John 19:30); it is accomplished. This is the gospel – God's 'eternal purpose which he accomplished in Christ Jesus our Lord' (Eph. 3:11). In the person and work of Christ, God can declare: 'It pleased the LORD for the sake of his righteousness to make his law great and glorious' (Isa. 42:21, NIV). Christ was born a Jew and lived under the Mosaic law (Luke 2:21-24,27,39; Gal. 4:4). He obeyed the Mosaic law (Matt. 8:4; 19:17-19). He was cursed under the law (Gal. 3:13). In all this, Christ established and magnified the law (Rom. 3:31). He honoured his Father in the law, and in so doing merited the salvation of his people. 'Amazing grace', indeed!

Thus, while forgiveness is an act of God's grace towards the sinner, it is based entirely and only upon the merit, the work, the obedience of Christ. God, therefore, *is* faithful and just to forgive the one who believes and confesses his sin. Why? Because if God did not, he would be unjust, he would be unfaithful. He would fail to keep his promise. Unthinkable! Impossible! Under the law, he promised life upon obedience. It was the will of God that Christ should come under the law, obey it, keep it and fulfil it (Matt. 5:17-18). This demand Christ met. As a consequence, when the sinner cries out to God through faith in Christ, trusting the person, merit and work of Christ, God *must* forgive. Do not misunderstand me, reader, when I say *must*. Very near the start of this chapter, I reminded you that 'God, who cannot lie, promised before time began' (Tit. 1:2), promised the Son that he would justify all the elect on the basis of the Son's obedience. And since God has promised, he has tied himself to his word. And because he has tied himself to his promised word, God must keep his promise. 'He remains faithful; he cannot deny himself' (2 Tim. 2:13). This is the *must*. Under the law, he said: 'Do this and live'. Christ did the doing, and God keeps his promise.

All this proves that the law was a works covenant, a very different covenant to the new covenant. Not only that. It means that the two Testaments, though having a certain continuity, are discontinuous. In short, not only are Calvin's second and third uses of the law wrong, but so is the covenant theology on which those uses are defended and argued.

A few Reformed theologians have seen this. That covenant theology needs correction, modification, and explanation, even recasting, has been admitted by some Reformed teachers, John Murray for one. I would go further. Recasting? Rejecting, more like. Sadly, however, most Reformed theologians do not seem willing even to rethink or recast their covenant theology but have, instead, developed a system of escape routes to get round awkward passages of Scripture. To these escape routes I now turn.

Chapter 7

Reformed Escape Routes

Time and again I will refer to what I call 'Reformed glosses', 'escape routes', or 'waste-paper baskets'.[1] Let me explain. We all meet awkward biblical statements on the law, texts which are hard to fit into our system. We all do, I say. The temptation is to trim the text, pare off awkward corners, insert words, and such like, and thus leave our system pristine. The right way, however, is to trim our system, not Scripture. 'Let God be true but every man a liar' (Rom. 3:4). Running the undoubted risk of being accused in terms of pots and kettles, I contend that the Reformed are particularly subject to this glossing, escape-route, waste-paper basket approach. Let me say at once, if any reader feels I have done it, I would appreciate it very much if he would write to me and give me a chance to examine the accusation and, if necessary, take steps to put it right. All I say is, we must always take full account of the context, and do all we can to avoid imposing our template on Scripture. I contend that the Reformed fail badly in this area.

Let me summarise these Reformed escape routes:

1. The Reformed are not averse to ignoring context to conflate passages which use 'the law' in different ways, treating them as though 'the law' means the same throughout.

2. They say the law is divided into three parts – moral, ceremonial and social or civil. Having divided the law into these three, they say the last two are abrogated for believers, but not the first.

3. They say that certain biblical statements, which do not fit their system, do not refer to the law itself, but to Jewish misunderstandings of the law, or to Jewish glosses on the law, or to legalism.

4. They say that the law must be viewed either as a covenant or as a rule. When it suits them, they play one against the other.

5. They gloss certain biblical statements by wrongly limiting them to justification.

6. Failing all else, they mitigate the severity of the law by pulling its teeth. The believer is under the commandments of the law, they say, but not its curse. In any case, God accepts a sincere effort, even though the believer inevitably fails to keep the law.

Reformed escape routes: 1. Conflate texts which speak of 'the law' in different ways

At best, this is slipshod exegesis. Some writers and teachers cite biblical verses which contain the word 'law', and treat these verses as though they are talking about precisely the same thing. *This must not be assumed.* I raised this point in the very first chapter.

---

[1] The extracts for this chapter begin on p392.

Attention must always be paid to the context, and we must always try to do all we can to make sure that the verses we have conflated really do address the same issue, and really do use 'law' in the same way. I realise I live in this particular glass-house, and if I have failed to keep my own rubric, I am truly sorry. More, if it is pointed out to me, I will rectify it in any subsequent edition. But I am, at least, conscious of the danger.

Let me cite an example of what I am talking about. In chapter 9, I will give an extract from Peter Masters, commenting on Galatians 5:18. He quotes Romans 7:22. Now, for a start, the latter verse appears in a very difficult context (Rom. 7:7 – 8:4), as all must admit. That should make us pause. Masters, however, did not even draw breath. What is more, 'law' is used even in that context in a variety of ways, as I will explain when we come to look at Romans. And then there is the new-covenant use of 'law' – about which I will say more in chapter 16. Finally, as I will show, Romans 7 and Galatians 5 are speaking about very different matters – though, superficially, they appear to be speaking about the same thing. All I am saying here is that if a writer or teacher does not take sufficient care, but uses 'law' with cavalier disregard to the context, it really amounts to the pulling of a conjuring – not to say, confidence – trick. So while not strictly an escape route, this slipshod exegesis is a very effective way of making Scripture say what anybody wants it to say. Watch out for it!

Reformed escape routes: 2. Break the law into three parts

Almost all[2] Reformed teachers divide the law into three parts – the moral law, the ceremonial law and the judicial (or social or civil) law.[3] It is an axiom[4] with them; and it is a catastrophe.[5]

What is the *scriptural* warrant for it? None. The Bible never makes such a division. Certainly the Jews never did. So where did it come from? It is a traditional assumption[6]

---

[2] A.W.Pink proposed an idiosyncratic division of the law, which does not stand scrutiny.

[3] Reformed teachers have a predilection for adjectives to qualify biblical words and so bolster their inventions. For example, *visible/invisible* church, *Jewish/gospel* church, *infant* baptism. The words *moral, ceremonial, judicial, social* and *civil* are not in the Bible. See the previous chapter.

[4] I use the word in the sense of 'a widely accepted principle', 'self-evident' (see *Concise*); in other words, something taken for granted, incapable of proof, but upon which everything which follows is built.

[5] The Reformed threefold division of the law is not merely 'misleading'; it is wrong. Nor will it do to engage in damage limitation by talking of three *dimensions* instead of three *kinds* of law. Whether or not some Reformed teachers talk of three dimensions rather than three divisions, the effect is the same. It reminds me, I am afraid, of the Roman Catholic attempt to explain away the adoration of images by talk of three kinds of worship. Interestingly, this, too, owes much to Aquinas: '*Latria* is sacrificial in character, and may be offered only to God. Catholics offer other degrees of reverence to... Mary and to the Saints; these non-sacrificial types of reverence are called *hyperdulia* and *dulia*, respectively... *Hyperdulia* is essentially a heightened degree of *dulia* provided only to the Blessed Virgin. This distinction, written about as early as Augustine... and... Jerome, was detailed more explicitly by... Aquinas in his *Summa Theologiae*, AD 1270... "The reverence which we pay to God, and which belongs to *latria*, differs from the reverence which we pay to certain excellent creatures; this belongs to *dulia*..."' (Wikipedia). Whether or not the average Romanist can distinguish these three, I have my doubts!

[6] See my 'axiom' above.

taken over from an invention of the medieval Church.[7] In particular, it came from that 'prince of schoolmen', Aquinas, the orthodox theologian *par excellence* of the Roman Catholic Church, whose influence even today in Protestantism, let alone Romanism, is greater than ever. Forming his views by drawing upon Aristotle, Augustine, Paul, classical antiquity, Arabs and medieval Jews – what a combination! – Aquinas devised a system which, though sophisticated, was vague and obscure. It is his labelling of the ten commandments as 'the moral law' which has come to play such an important role in Reformed theology. Sensitive to Papist accusations over antinomianism,[8] the Reformers countered by using Aquinas' tripartite division of the law, claiming that believers are under the moral law for sanctification.

Thus the Reformers, following Aquinas – certainly not Paul – divided the law into three bits – moral, ceremonial and judicial law – calling the last two mere temporary appendages or appendices of the permanent moral law (which they limited to the ten commandments). These appendages were abrogated by Christ, they said, leaving the first part to govern believers as their rule of life. In this way, most believers began to speak about 'the law', when they were actually talking of a minute portion of it – less than 1% – the ten commandments taking up just thirty-two verses of the Bible, counting the repeat! – this tiny fraction of the Mosaic law, now being called 'the moral law', the perfect rule of life![9] All this is said to be 'clear'. History, tradition, creeds, pastors, teachers are said to support the system, while those who question it are labelled and then dismissed as legalists, antinomians, quibblers and lazy-minded.[10] But the fact is, Reformed teachers have their doubts, make vague claims, usually adducing precious little scripture in support, and manifestly misapply references or arbitrarily adjust the meaning of the word 'law' where necessary!

This Aquinas-logic does not stand up. The law is not a menu, a list from which theologians can pick and choose. The law must be used properly: 'We know that the law is good *if one uses it lawfully*' (1 Tim. 1:8). Otherwise, the consequences will be dire. Even so, right from the earliest days of the church, men have been trying to treat the law as a list from which they may select one or two favoured bits; circumcision being a prime example (Acts 15:1,5,24; Gal. 5:2-6; 6:12-13). The same could be said of the sabbath, and other days. But the law must be taken as a whole. It is all or nothing (Gal. 5:3). Scripture speaks of the law as an entity.

Let me remind you, reader, of the ground we have already covered. How did the Old Testament speak of 'the law'? Did it divide it into three parts? Certainly not! Let

---

[7] The Reformed seem shy at owning the source of this major aspect of their thesis on the law. Why?

[8] Compare the way Calvin allowed his reaction to the Anabaptists to colour his view of baptism, the way the Reformers in general allowed their reaction to Rome to colour their view of the priesthood of all believers, and the way the Westminster Assembly's hatred of antinomianism moved them to produce statements skewed by a heavy emphasis upon law.

[9] All advocates of the system say the ceremonial law is now abrogated. As for the judicial law, according to some Reformed teachers, some parts of it have ceased, but some parts remain, while others say all the judicial law came to end in AD70.

[10] This raises a point of massive importance. When will the Reformed put the Bible before their creeds and Confessions? If any take offence at my question, let them answer this: How many Reformed men preach the Confession or the Catechism – Heidelberg, Westminster, 1689 or...? Every man that has done it makes one too many!

me demonstrate this from two places – Leviticus and Numbers. At the end of Leviticus, after God had given Israel a whole host of laws on all sorts of matters, including idolatry, adultery, disrespect for parents, the weekly sabbath, harvest, resting the land every seven years, the year of jubilee with all its regulations for redemption, and so on, Moses recorded: 'These are the statutes and judgements and laws which the LORD made between himself and the children of Israel on Mount Sinai by the hand of Moses... These are the commandments which the LORD commanded Moses for the children of Israel on Mount Sinai' (Lev. 26:46; 27:34). It did not matter whether or not any particular law was found in the ten commandments or the regulations for the tabernacle or the statutes for the ordering of Jewish society. No Jew ever asked which part of the law any commandment came from. It simply would not have crossed his mind. It was all the law of God, all the law of God given for Israel on Sinai. Compare Exodus 20 – 23. Note how the later 'laws' amplify what is given in the ten commandments. These passages demonstrate that the giving of the laws and commandments at Sinai is all of a piece. Together, they form 'the law'.

Take Numbers 15. The stoning of the man for transgressing the law of the sabbath (Num. 15:32-36) is sandwiched between – on the one hand, the laws of sacrifice and offering for sin (Num. 15:1-31) – and on the other, the sewing of tassels on the corners of garments (Num. 15:37-40), this last to remind the Israelites to 'remember all the commandments of the LORD and do them' (Num. 15:39-40). And the chapter concludes with words remarkably similar to the preface to the ten commandments (Num. 15:41; Ex. 20:2; Deut. 5:6). My point is that *it is impossible to detect any biblical difference in the designation of any of these laws.* Sacrifices, offerings, sabbath and tassels all – *all* – come under the one umbrella: 'Ordinance... law... custom... all these commandments... all that the LORD has commanded you by the hand of Moses... the LORD gave commandment... law... the word of the LORD... his commandment... So, as the LORD commanded Moses, all the congregation [obeyed]... Remember all the commandments of the LORD and do them... remember and do all my commandments' (Num. 15:15-16,22-23,29,31,36,39-40). Similar biblical evidence is abundant. Take Deuteronomy 4 – 6; 26 – 30, and so on. Is it not significant that when Israel was about to enter Canaan, and God told them to write and repeat the law's blessings and the curses, and do so in a very public way (Deut. 27), he did not adopt the Reformed view – and stress or stick to the ten commandments?

Centuries later, Jehoshaphat did not seem to be fazed by the Reformed notion. He felt free to instruct the judges to deal faithfully with all cases which came before them, 'whether of bloodshed or offences against law or commandment, against statutes or ordinances', including murder – the sixth commandment (2 Chron. 19:8-11). Once again, the laws, commandments, regulations, ordinances and statutes constituted one law, the law of God given to Israel through Moses. The Jews never divided the law into three. Never!

Nor did Christ! And neither did Paul. If he had introduced such a root-and-branch change to the meaning of 'the law', such a radical break-up of 'the law', it is unthinkable that he would not have spelled it out, giving his reasons very fully. It is such an important issue! At a stroke, the tripartite division of the law virtually solves the New Testament conundrum over the law, and breaks its tension. The apostle's silence speaks volumes. The thought never entered his mind! The tripartite division is neat; it is convenient; but it is wrong!

Indeed, as for 'the law' in the New Testament, its very frequent use is almost indiscriminate. For proof, I refer you, reader, to chapter 1, to what follows below and throughout the rest of my book, and to any concordance. Check for yourself how interchangeably 'the law' is used in the Bible. Reformed teachers might like to have everything neatly sewn up into three little packets so that they can dispose of awkward verses and passages, but when Paul uses the word 'law', he overwhelmingly means the entire Jewish law, the law given to Israel by God through Moses, as recorded in the first five books of the Bible.

Some, who insist on the law as the believer's rule, are prepared to admit that believers have to do what the Jews (or Christ or Paul, I would add) never did; namely, divide the law into three parts. This is honest, but devastating to the Reformed position! And why *have* the Reformed *had* to divide the law? What biblical imperative can they produce? Their system demands it, but what of Scripture? What biblical warrant can they produce? Is there any possibility that such divisions of the law might fall foul of Malachi 2:9? that is, is there any inherent risk of showing 'partiality in the law'? I am well aware that this 'partiality' takes in far more than picking and choosing which bits one will keep and which one will ignore. But the principle stands. And it carries a heavy price. God is not 'partial' (Deut. 10:17-18). And Christ had some strong things to say on the subject (Matt. 23:23; Luke 11:42).

The Reformed way of dividing the law does not pass muster. It is artificial from start to finish. And that's the best to be said for it. Simplistic, it is demeaning to Paul (the main New Testament writer on the law). The apostle simply will not allow himself to be explained away by cramming his doctrine into neat watertight packages. Speaking bluntly, these artificial, simplistic, divisions are an imposition on the text, and are illogical. How are we to know whether or not any particular commandment, statute, law or regulation is moral, ceremonial or social? Take the sabbath. Is the fourth commandment moral, ceremonial or social? Or is it a combination of all three? Reader, what did Calvin think? Those who do not know, may well be surprised – staggered – to discover his view. He certainly would fall foul of Reformed teachers today![11]

---

[11] In brief, while Calvin was (as so often) ambiguous and somewhat self-contradictory, he rightly asserted 'that the substance of the sabbath [is]... in Christ', referring to Heb. 4:10. 'Christ... abrogated the sabbath... The sabbath, although its external observation is not now in use, still remains eternal in its reality'. In other words, the sabbath is fulfilled in Christ – and the rest it typified is now the possession of believers – they are at peace with God through our Lord Jesus Christ (Rom. 5:1ff). Calvin went on: 'The stability of [the sabbath] was best confirmed by [its] abrogation; since, if God now required the same of Christians, it would be putting a veil over the death and resurrection of his Son... The Jews... calumniate us falsely, as if we disregarded the sabbath; because there is nothing which more completely confirms its reality and substance than the abolition of its external use' (Calvin: *Commentaries* Vol.2 pp435,443-444). Again, when concluding his argument on the sabbath, as found in his *Institutes* – he spoke of getting 'quit of the trifling of the false prophets, who in later times instilled Jewish ideas into the people'. He explained what those teachers with their trifling Jewish ideas were doing. They were 'alleging that nothing was abrogated but what was ceremonial in the commandment... while the moral part remains – *viz*. the observance of one day in seven. But this is nothing else than to insult the Jews [and, above all, God himself!], by changing the day, and yet mentally attributing to it the same sanctity; thus retaining the same typical distinction of days as had place among the Jews. And of a truth, we see what profit they have made by such a doctrine. Those who cling to

Notwithstanding these fatal flaws in Reformed teaching, I am afraid it is almost impossible to cite a Reformed work on the law which does not make liberal use of the terms moral, ceremonial and judicial law, even though they are foreign to the Bible, and ambiguous. A term ambiguous among theologians and non-existent in the Bible! Hardly a recommendation! But almost universally assumed!

Lest I be misunderstood, just because I do not talk about the *moral* law, and just because I point out that the Bible does not use the phrase, it does not mean I advocate immorality! A man is not an antinomian just because he does not use Reformed jargon! After all, no biblical writer ever used the phrase. Indeed, if the biblical writers came back and heard somebody extolling 'the moral law', they wouldn't have a clue what the speaker was talking about. Nor am I arguing over mere words. Reformed teachers do not divide the law into three parts for the fun of it. Oh no! A very serious objective is at the back of this. The threefold division of the law is a very effective escape route when the Reformed are confronted by scriptures which will not fit their system. They simply dispose of unpalatable texts by dropping them into the appropriate waste-paper basket! As a result, Reformed teachers can put forward an unbiblical view of the believer and the law. And this has large consequences.

Reformed escape routes: 3. Blame Jewish misunderstanding

Another Reformed escape route is to argue that when Paul says something that clashes with their claim that the law is the perfect rule for believers, he is actually doing no such thing. Rather, he is dealing with a Jewish misunderstanding. The law and the gospel only *seem* to be opposed. It is not so, really. Wherever did the confusion arise, then? It was all the fault of Jewish teachers. Paul was writing against those who use the law *amiss*. Paul, when seeming to speak against the law, was actually writing against the nonsense introduced by false apostles. So it is claimed.

Let me give a few instances. It has been alleged that Romans 4:13-15 and Galatians 3:17 speak of the law's function within the Mosaic covenant, and even then only as the Jews misunderstood it. Reader, notice the glosses here introduced. The passages refer to the law, full stop.

Take Romans 4:13-15: 'For the promise.. was not to Abraham or to his seed through the law, but through the righteousness of faith. For if those who are of the law are heirs, faith is made void... because the law brings about wrath; for where there is no law there is no transgression'. Paul is speaking of the law, not the law qualified by this or that. And notice what he says: 'The law brings about wrath; for where there is no law there is no transgression'. It will not do to say he is talking about some supposed Jewish misunderstanding. Was it *Jewish misunderstanding of the function of the law* which brought about wrath? Are we to believe that where there is no *Jewish misunderstanding of the function of the law* there is no transgression? Are we really to believe that Christ came into the world and died in order to set his people free from *a Jewish misunderstanding of the law*? Christ came to set his people free from the law, not some supposed misunderstanding of it!

---

their constitutions go thrice as far as the Jews in their gross and carnal superstition of sabbatism' (Calvin: *Institutes* Vol.1 pp343-344). *Touché* the Reformed!

As for Galatians 3:17, Paul is saying that the law came 430 years after the promise to Abraham. He is not remotely thinking of any Jewish misunderstanding of the law!

Take 2 Corinthians 3:7 as another example. When Paul speaks of 'the ministry of death, written and engraved on stones', he is referring to (at the least) the ten commandments – not the ten commandments as misinterpreted by Jews. The apostle's words in 2 Corinthians 3:11 are clear enough.

Nor will it do to say that when Paul has strong things to say about 'law' he really means 'legalism'; that is, it is not 'the law' itself that the apostle is concerned with, but the *abuse* of the law. Now, it is true that Paul does address legalism, but when he does so, he uses appropriate phrases (see Rom. 9:31-32; Gal. 2:16; Phil. 3:9; *etc.*). Consequently, this does not in any way justify the shunting of 'awkward' texts into limbo, writing them off as Jewish misunderstanding! Law and legalism are not the same thing at all.

Once again, reader, a serious issue is at stake in all this. Labelling passages – which they find awkward – as a Jewish misunderstanding, or Rabbinism, or legalism, or some such dismissive term, allows Reformed teachers to put forward an unbiblical view of the believer and the law. It is yet another handy waste-paper basket for any tricky passage!

Reformed escape routes: 4. Distinguish between the law as a covenant and a rule

Many Reformed writers argue that believers are delivered from the law in its covenant form, but not as a rule of life. And in this way, the law is said to be binding on believers, with all that that entails!

May I ask Reformed theologians: Christ came under the law (Gal. 4:4). Did Christ come under the law as a covenant, but not as the moral law? Or did he come under the law in both forms? Again, the believer has become dead to the law (Rom. 7:4). Dead to the law as a covenant, but not as a rule? How can a believer be dead to the law as a covenant, yet alive to it as a perfect rule? The fact is, *the Scripture never distinguishes between the law as a covenant and a rule*. The law does not wear different hats. It must be taken as a whole, all or nothing, as it is, a covenant and a rule, and all its regulations must be kept. If one commandment, rule or regulation is broken, the entire law is broken. This is the biblical position. And it is the way we work, for example, in buying and selling a house. If a man agrees to buy a house, he has to keep the rules of the covenant under which he secures the purchase, the rules and the covenant forming but one document. The purchaser, signing the deed, accepts, and has to abide by, all the regulations and stipulations about mineral rights, fences, trading, and so on, as spelled out in the deed of covenant. The covenant and the rule are one.

And thus it is with the law of God. The Israelites were under the law – under the law both as a covenant and a rule, in every one of its stipulations. Where, in Scripture, can the Reformed find the teaching that states that, unlike the Jews, believers are under the law as a rule but not a covenant? In fact, it expressly states that believers are not under the law at all! Take Romans 6:14; 7:4,6; 8:2; Galatians 2:19; 4:31; 5:1,18, for instance.

In any case, it is a tragic mis-exegesis to distinguish between a rule and a covenant when speaking about the law. It will not stand up. Take the experience of the Jews when they discovered the book of the law in the time of Josiah. This book was spoken of as law, *covenant, commandments*, testimonies and statutes, and these terms were used interchangeably (2 Kings 22:8,11; 23:2-3,21,24-25). Again, take these terms: the ark of the *covenant*, the ark of the *covenant* of the LORD, the ark of the LORD's *covenant*. These terms are used repeatedly. What was in the ark? 'Nothing was in the ark except the two tablets of stone which Moses put there at Horeb, when the LORD made a *covenant* with the children of Israel, when they came out of the land of Egypt' (1 Kings 8:9; see also 2 Chron. 5:10). In other words, the ten *commandments* constituted the *covenant*, and this was reinforced when the commandments were placed in the ark of the covenant. The commandments and the covenant were one and the same. Joshua warned the Israelites that when they 'transgressed the covenant of the LORD your God, which he commanded you... then the anger of the LORD will burn against you' (Josh. 23:16). In other words, when they sinned he would punish them. But what is sin? It is the breaking of God's law: 'Where there is no law there is no transgression' (Rom. 4:15). Does this not show that the covenant was the law, and that the law was the covenant? And so it was that Joshua 'made a covenant with the people that day, and made for them a statute and an ordinance in Shechem. Then Joshua wrote these words in the book of the law of God' (Josh. 24:25-26). Law, covenant, commandment – all one and the same.

In short, the distinction in the law drawn by Reformed writers between covenant and commandment is a distinction without a difference or meaning. It is high time it was dropped. Many passages could be cited to show that the covenant stands for laws commanded by God (Ex. 24:4,7; 34:27-28; Num. 15:31; Deut. 29:1-9; Josh. 23:16; Judges 2:19-20; 2 Kings 17:15; Hos. 6:7; 8:1, for instance). So much for the Jews.

Many Reformed, however, want to accept their teachers' assurance that the believer is under the law, not as a covenant, but as a rule. The Reformed wedge between the law as a covenant and a rule is bolstered by tortuous logic, not by Scripture. I ask again, may we be given the plain scripture to assure us of this 'fact'? Moreover, when is the law a covenant but not a rule, and *vice-versa*? How can we tell? And when the law is a covenant, which of their covenants is it – grace or works? As I have shown, covenant theologians cannot come to a consensus about it – after more than 400 years! Even so, Reformed teachers are prepared to take difficult texts and slap one of two labels on them; one marked 'covenant', the other 'rule' – one to which the believer is dead, the other to which he is very much alive. It is, of course, yet another convenient escape route, even though the distinction cannot be justified.

Reformed escape routes: 5. Gloss statements on the law by wrongly limiting them to justification

Of course, there are many statements in Scripture which plainly teach that by the law no sinner will be justified (Rom. 3:20-22; 10:5-6; Gal. 2:16; 3:11-12; 5:4, for instance). But, equally, there are many statements in Scripture which teach that a believer is not sanctified by the law (Rom. 6 – 7, for example). I will not stop to look at these passages now – doing so at the appropriate places as I examine the Scriptures – but it is wrong of Reformed teachers to gloss these by saying they refer to justification – when clearly they refer to sanctification. It will not do. But, yet again, it proves a handy waste-paper basket when any passage proves difficult. Slap the sticker 'justification' on to it, and carry on regardless. It will not do!

Reformed escape routes: 6. Pull the law's teeth

When all else fails, Reformed teachers say believers are under the law, but God will never exact its sanctions upon them. He will accept a good try, doing one's best, a sincere effort, even though, obviously, it must fall short of the standard required. Once again, human logic or philosophy bolster this far-reaching claim, but Scripture justification for it is noticeable by its absence.[12]

And what if the law has *not* lost its teeth?

*The law, of course, has **not** lost its teeth!* It always demands perfect obedience, and curses the smallest breach. Thus it has always done, and it is still the same today. Let me clear the decks: 'You shall not add to the word which I command you, nor take from it, that you may keep the commandments of the LORD your God which I command you... Whatever I command you, be careful to observe it; you shall not add to it nor take away from it' (Deut. 4:2; 12:32). So runs the command of God when declaring his law through Moses. These are very serious stipulations.

What is more, curses are an integral part of that law. 'For as many as are of the works of the law are under the curse; for it is written: "Cursed is everyone who does not continue in all things which are written in the book of the law, to do them"' (Gal. 3:10). This, of course, comes from Deuteronomy 27:26. (See also Deut. 11:26-28; 27:15-26; 28:15-68; 2 Chron. 34:24). As a consequence, 'the law brings about wrath' (Rom. 4:15). There is no getting round these plain statements.

Even so, the Reformed claim, all such dreadful sanctions are abolished under the gospel. In Moses' hands, yes, the law is severe; but not in Christ's. And when Paul contrasts the law and the gospel, he is referring, not to the law, but to its threats, nothing else. So it is claimed. If so, what remains? Not much, I should say. What is a law without punishment? What is a commandment without penalties? The law less severe in Christ's hands? Where are we told this? How does it fit in with Luke 16:17? 'It is easier for heaven and earth to pass away than for one tittle of the law to fail'. What about Matthew 5:17-20? Scripture never tells us the law is in force as the rule of life for believers, but conveniently shorn of its sanctions. Never in Scripture is there any hint that the *claims* of the law can be separated from its *curses*. In the Bible, the law's *precepts* are never separated from its *penalties*.[13] In the Bible, I reiterate, never! The mere suggestion is appalling. I use the word advisedly. Yet, flying in the face of such biblical facts, it is said that even though no believer can keep the law, which demands perfection, God relaxes his law for his children. What an utterly unbiblical notion! For the Reformed to accuse others of antinomianism is nothing but a classic case of beams and motes. I would ask every person who holds to the Reformed uses of the law to find one place in Scripture where the inspired writer states that the law remains a rule for believers but shorn of its sanctions. If a law is deprived of its

---

[12] See chapters 5 and 6. Once again, I can only appeal to readers who doubt my claims to read the extracts – and the entire original Reformed works.

[13] The law stands absolute in its entirety, curses and all. And as a paradigm – see chapter 17 p289 – its curses may be used to illustrate the glories of the gospel.

sanctions, surely it ceases to be worthy of the name *law*! It might be a *recommendation*, but hardly a *rule*.[14]

Yet, Reformed teachers want it both ways. In contradiction of the above, some insist that not only is the unchanging and unchangeable law of God the rule which every man, and this includes the redeemed, lies under for time and eternity, but that its authority – far from being curtailed – is stronger for the believer than the sinner. The obligation to the law is said to be *more intense* for the saved man. Now what can be more intense than the curse and eternal perdition for breaking the law? After all, as is admitted, the law, though broken, never lowers its terms.

So which is it? Are the redeemed under the law as much as they were before conversion – more so, we are told – yet that same law has its penalties reduced, even removed, for them? Or is their obligation to the law, as believers, more intense than it was before? Which is it? More intense or not? When is 'more intense' more intense or less intense? The argument defies reason.

Though Reformed teachers like to think a believer can be under the law but avoid its penalties, it is an impossibility. This truly is to 'make void the law' (Rom. 3:31). Though they might like to accuse others of doing it, the truth is they themselves are guilty of that very thing! *All* who are under the law must keep *all* the law, or else they will suffer *all* its curse. Moses always accuses all those under him. So said Christ: 'There is one who accuses you – Moses' (John 5:45). Can we be shown a man whom Moses does *not* accuse – apart from Christ? Moses could not accuse Christ, because Christ kept the law perfectly. But Moses accuses every sinner, because every sinner has broken his law. And this includes the saints!

To say that the law has lost its teeth is not only wrong. It carries important and heavy consequences. It bolsters the mistaken Reformed view on the believer and the law. It is the last but not least of the Reformed waste-paper baskets.

Reformed escape routes: Summary

Let me gather together the six main escape routes. In order to maintain their system, Reformed teachers are not averse to conflating two or more passages, disregarding the way the original writers used 'law' in those passages. Or, if a verse or passage does not fit their system, they neatly dispose of the difficulty by means of one or other of their waste-paper baskets. Instead of facing up to the teaching of the passage in question, they say it speaks against the ceremonial law, Jewish glosses or misunderstanding, legalism, or the law as a covenant, or the inability of the law to justify. If all else fails, they say that the law still stands but shorn of its sanctions and punishments.

Reader, there is not the slightest justification for the Reformed to 'modify' the law in such ways.[15] The law is not a lump of plasticine to be pulled and twisted to fit into

---

[14] Is Calvin's whip for sluggish asses cordless after all? See chapter 5 on Calvin's 'kind adviser'.

[15] I admit, of course, that there is 'modification' and 'modification'. In chapters 16 and 17, I will show that whereas the Reformed want to modify the law by dividing it into bits, or cutting out its punishment – for which there is no biblical warrant – the believer must read and apply the entire law, but do so through Christ, interpreting the Old Testament in the light of the New. He must do so because he has New Testament warrant for it. That is what Christ and the apostles did. We may, we must, *nuance* the law in accordance with the new covenant. But neither Christ nor any apostle ever spoke of a toothless 'moral law'.

our system. We cannot cut bits off, and stick them back on in any way we choose. To put it no stronger, the Reformed give the impression that that is what they are prone to do. It is quite wrong. Nor should they pick-and-mix. God has always insisted on total obedience to all his commandments, to all his law. I remind you of his demands through Moses: 'You shall not add to the word which I command you, nor take from it, that you may keep the commandments of the LORD your God which I command you... Whatever I command you, be careful to observe it; you shall not add to it nor take away from it' (Deut. 4:2; 12:32). God never allowed Israel to divide his law into various bits, and so set in train the process of rejecting the majority of his law. Reformed theologians should not play word-games with the law of God. They should not make inexplicable changes to Scripture, thereby rewriting 'the law' in Bible texts as 'the moral law' or 'the ceremonial law' or 'the social law', 'the Mosaic economy', and so on when it suits them. I call these changes 'inexplicable', but this is not strictly accurate. These changes are perfectly understandable – if Scripture has to be trimmed or adjusted to fit a logical system invented by men. It is perfectly *understandable*, I say, but *totally unacceptable*. With respect, I say to them, as Christ said to the Pharisees and the scribes, you are 'making the word of God of no effect through your tradition' (Mark 7:13). The truth is, by saying on the one hand the law is permanent and unchanging, but saying on the other the law has been changed, and teaching believers to keep this different law, you expose a fundamental contradiction at the very heart of your system. Indeed, to speak frankly, you make a mockery of the law.

Strong words, I know. I can only repeat the sentiment I expressed when I began this chapter. If any reader feels I have done what I have criticised in others, I would appreciate it very much if he would write to me and give me a chance to examine the accusation and, if necessary, take steps to put it right.

Let me illustrate the consequences of these glosses, by considering passages which have nothing to do with the law. Would Reformed writers apply their gloss technique in these passages? Believers have 'died with Christ from [to, NIV] the basic principles of the world' (Col. 2:20). This is what Paul said. If we used the Reformed glosses, I suppose we should think that believers have died to *certain aspects* of the basic principles of the world, or to *a part of* the basic principles of the world, or to the basic principles of the world *as understood by false teachers*, or to the basic principles of the world, yes, but *only in regard to certain ends*. Paul told us that saints have died to the basic principles of the world, full stop! Again, what about Galatians 6:14? Should the believer say that by the Lord Jesus Christ 'the world has been crucified to me, and I to the world' *in part* or *in regard to certain ends*? Should the same be said of Galatians 2:20? Perish the thought! The believer has been 'crucified with Christ', not crucified with Christ *in part* or *to certain ends*. It would be utterly wrong to trim Scripture to fit it into a human system. The same goes for passages on the law.

Enough of this! 'To the law and to the testimony! If they do not speak according to this word, it is because there is no light in them' (Isa. 8:20).[16] Let us 'give ear to the law of our God' (Isa. 1:10). We 'have Moses and the prophets; let [us] hear them'

---

[16] As far as we stray from Scripture, we move into darkness. As for Reformed believers, I am confining my remarks to these escape clauses on the law. As I said in my 'Introduction', while I do not agree with their system of handling the law, and am prepared to say so in no uncertain terms, I have nothing but the highest regard for their persons and their spirituality.

(Luke 16:29). Let us 'search the Scriptures' (John 5:39). For it is not the theories of theologians, but the word of God which counts, and, in the end, it is only the word of God which counts (2 Tim. 3:16 – 4:4).[17]

But a word of explanation is called for. God has nowhere set out for us a treatise on 'the law'. The only way we can discover his mind on the matter is by studying the law in its context where it appears in the New Testament; in the main, Paul's writings. This, therefore, is the approach I will adopt. I will try to set out what I understand about the law as it is revealed in Paul's letters. But before reaching Paul's letters, a glance at John.

---

[17] The sharp-eyed reader will have noticed that I have urged that we should go to the law (Isa. 8:20) for instruction – and then immediately explained my understanding of 'the law' in this context. This seemingly small detail admirably makes the point I am trying to press home. Who would think that, in order to gain instruction on this vital topic, we should confine our studies to the ten commandments? In this context, 'the law' is the entire word of God, especially the New Testament. See chapter 16 p222.

Part Three

The Biblical Case

What Does the New Testament Say About the Believer and the Law?

Chapter 8

John 1:17

The law was given through Moses, but grace and truth came through Jesus Christ.[1]

God gave the Jews the law through Moses (John 7:19); and we know why: 'The law entered that the offence might abound' (Rom. 5:20). But God has also sent grace into the world by his Son, Jesus Christ (John 1:14; Tit. 2:11-14); and we know why: 'But where sin abounded, grace abounded much more, so that as sin reigned in death, even so grace might reign through righteousness to eternal life through Jesus Christ our Lord' (Rom. 5:20-21). And what a contrast, law and grace! How wonderfully John shines the spotlight on the contrast: 'The law was given through Moses, but grace and truth came through Jesus Christ' (John 1:17)! The translators did not use the word *but* for nothing in John 1:17. The apostle points to a very definite, clear, unmistakeable contrast between law and grace.

Yet Reformed writers seldom give John 1:17 proper consideration in their works on the law. Indeed, the verse's contrast between law and grace has been denied. There is no contradiction between law and grace, so it is said. Even the *but* in John 1:17 has been dismissed as a delusion – a 'will o'the wisp'.[2] True, there is no 'but' in the Greek,[3] but this is far from conclusive. It is certainly there in spirit and by implication. In fact, the lack of the stated 'but' makes its presence even more felt. Its absence speaks louder than its (obvious) inclusion; the finesse in John's turn of phrase would have been blunted by the inclusion of the 'but'. Therefore, although precisely catching the spirit of John's words, our translators, in trying to help us more readily understand the apostle, by introducing the 'but', have, in fact, taken some of the subtlety out of what he wrote. But whether in print, or in our head, the 'but' has to be understood.

Let me prove it. Take: 'God be thanked that *though* you were the slaves of sin, yet you obeyed from the heart that form of doctrine to which you were delivered' (Rom. 6:17). To omit the *though* would be tantamount to making Paul say he was glad his readers had been the slaves of sin, when, in fact, he was thankful that *even though* they had been the slaves of sin, they had nevertheless obeyed the gospel. His argument hinges entirely on the *though*. If anybody dismisses the *though* as an English will o'the wisp, a mere technicality of the language, he virtually destroys what Paul actually said. Yet there is no 'though' in the Greek text! As with the 'but' in John 1:17, its absence speaks volumes.

Similarly: 'Though he was a Son, *yet* he learned obedience by the things which he suffered' (Heb. 5:8). The *yet* is supplied, it is not in the original Greek, but by no stretch of the imagination can it be dismissed as trivial. In fact, its inclusion emphasises the amazing nature of what is being said. It is the most important word in the verse, even though the writer did not use it. Though Jesus was the Son of God, *even so,*

---

[1] The extracts for this chapter begin on p409.
[2] Are 2 Cor. 3:11; Heb. 7:18; 8:13 more of these 'will o'the wisps'?
[3] The NIV, strictly correct here, left it out.

staggeringly, even he, yet he – he of all people – learned obedience by the things which he suffered.

A few more examples must suffice: 'Beloved, do not avenge yourselves, but *rather* give place to wrath' (Rom. 12:19). The *rather* gives the proper emphasis, but it is not in the original. Again, try leaving out the second *must* in John 3:30, *his* in John 6:52 (*his* is vital – any butcher can provide meat, but how could Jesus provide *his* own flesh for them to eat?), *as for* in John 9:29, *that is* in Ephesians 2:15, *rather* in 1 Timothy 4:7 (AV), *and escape* in 2 Timothy 2:26 (the verse becomes nonsense otherwise), *because* in 2 Timothy 4:3; and so on. None of these words are in the Greek!

Returning to John 1:17 – as I said, the *but* being left out, the verse is even more starkly powerful and blunt: 'The law was given through Moses; grace and truth came through Jesus Christ'. In fact, we could – maybe, we should – use a full stop: 'The law was given through Moses. Grace and truth came through Jesus Christ'.

Clearly, however, a word or phrase is implied in the text, and has to be supplied. Reader, you may use *but*, or *whereas*, or *on the other hand,* or *in contrast*. You choose!

In addition, the context of John 1:17 demands the contrast. Read John 1:8,11-13,20. Above all, read John 1:18. There is no *but*, literally, in between the two sentences: 'No one has seen God at any time. The only begotten Son, who is in the bosom of the Father, he has declared him'. Notwithstanding the lack of 'but', who would not agree that John here draws a remarkable contrast? In the past age – the age of law – God did not show his glory as now he has in the age of the gospel. Do not miss the eschatological 'but now' of Romans 3:21 once again (see chapter 6).

Let me take another passage of Scripture to underline the point. I refer to Hebrews 9. The inspired writer, opening the chapter with an exposition of the first or old covenant, soon sounds the note of its uselessness to cleanse the conscience (Heb. 9:1-10). 'It was symbolic... imposed until the time of reformation' (Heb. 9:9-10), 'an illustration... applying until the time of the new order' (NIV). What was this new order, this 'reformation'? It was the coming of Christ, the gospel. How does the writer to the Hebrews state this fact? 'But Christ came', he said (Heb. 9:11), 'when Christ came' (NIV). These words should not be mumbled. They should be thundered: **'But Christ came'!** 'When Christ came'! And the NIV caught the dramatic, stupendous sense of change at this watershed of the ages, exquisitely grasping the point of the 'now' in Hebrews 9:15: 'Christ is the mediator of a new covenant, that those who are called may receive the promised eternal inheritance – *now* that he has died as a ransom to set them free from the sins committed under the first covenant'. Once again, it is the eschatological 'but now', the great turning point of the ages. The shadow has gone, the reality has come. The external is finished, the inward is established. The weak is displaced by the mighty. The useless has been abolished by the effectual. It is John 1:17.

It is wrong to say that the gospel is a *clearer* way of salvation than the law. It is a *different* way, chalk and cheese! It will not do to say that John 1:17 *seems* to speak of the inferiority of the law when compared to the gospel. It does no such thing. The verse teaches that law and grace are very different things, two ages which are strongly contrasted. There is a distinction – more, an antithesis, an opposition, a contradiction – between the two, even as some Reformed writers admit, on occasion at great length.

Many Reformed commentators, however, are weak on the verse, or use their escape routes to say John was speaking about justification only, or about the ceremonial law.

Furthermore, they are not averse to trying to uphold their system – that is, an excessive emphasis upon the continuity of the Testaments – by qualifying John, adding the proviso that, while, of course, the law *was* given through Moses, and grace and truth on the other hand *did come* by Jesus Christ, nevertheless, Moses brought some grace, and, in any case, believers are still under the moral law as a perfect rule of life.

John, of course, said nothing of the sort. What he said was: 'The law was given through Moses, but grace and truth came through Jesus Christ'. And the verse says what it means, and means what it says to the reader of plain English. And it is full of contrast.

As I have said, by leaving out the 'but' John makes his point even stronger: 'The law was given through Moses. Grace and truth came through Jesus Christ'. Leaving out the 'but' actually lays more stress on the *grace*, and emphasises the contrast between that and *law*. It lays more stress on the *came*, and emphasises the contrast between that and the *given*. It lays more stress on *Jesus Christ*, and emphasises the contrast between him and *Moses*:

The **law** was **given** through **Moses**
Grace and truth **came** through **Jesus Christ**

What is more, from John 1:17 we learn that whereas the law *was given through* Moses, Christ *brought* grace. Note the passive/active contrast. Note the contrast between *given* and *brought*. Above all, it is not simply that Moses *received* one thing, and Christ *brought* something else. Both Moses and Christ are associated with covenants, but the difference between their covenants is vast. Moses was given *the law*; Christ brought *grace*. Moses was given *God's* law; Christ brought *his own* grace. Moses was given the old covenant; Christ brought the new. Moses' covenant was written on stone; Christ's is written in the heart. It is not just that Christ gives his people the gospel, and Moses gave the Jews the law. Christ gives his people *grace*, he gives his people a *heart* to love his gospel, but Moses could offer no power to keep the law. This contrast of covenants is a major aspect of the debate on the believer, the law and sanctification, one which I will develop as we go on.

Small as John 1:17 may appear to be, it plays a vital role in the question of the believer and the law. Any work which fails to take proper account of what it teaches, can hardly be considered a serious attempt to get to grips with the biblical evidence on the subject.

Chapter 9

Galatians

Because of its importance in the debate on the believer and the law, I am taking Galatians out of biblical order.[1] The fact is, Paul's argument in this letter, coming so early in the New Testament age, is crucial; it is the 'benchmark' for the doctrine of the law.[2] Before we start, however, just a word or two on 'the law' as used by the apostle in this short letter. It is sometimes claimed that Paul started with one meaning, then switched – without any explanation or hint of it – to a new meaning for a few paragraphs, and then switched back again. Or else, as I will show, Reformed writers frequently add one or other of their usual glosses. This, of course, proves useful in their efforts to fit certain Galatian passages into their system – passages which they would otherwise find worse than awkward. The fact is, however, throughout Galatians (thirty-two times), with only three (obvious) exceptions,[3] when Paul used 'the law', he meant 'the law', the entire law, the law of Moses (including the ten commandments), as at least some Reformed writers recognise. Let us proceed, reader, on this basis. And let us stick to it! Let us allow Paul to tell us what he meant!

Why did Paul write the letter?

Paul, having established his apostolic credentials, spoke of 'the grace of Christ... the gospel of Christ... the gospel' (Gal. 1:1-17). He then referred to a painful experience through which he had passed: Judaisers, 'false brethren... came in by stealth to spy out our liberty which we have in Christ Jesus, that they might bring us into bondage' (Gal. 2:4-5). Paul met the attack more than once – at Antioch (Acts 15:1-2) and Jerusalem (Acts 15:4-29), and in various other churches. Precisely where Galatians 2 fits in the chronology is open to debate, but this is of no relevance to the present issue.

These false teachers, it is to be noted, came into the *church*, and came in with the intention of spying out '*our* liberty', '*our* liberty which *we* have in Christ Jesus, that they might bring *us* into bondage'. I emphasise this. The false teachers were not going out into the world, trying to persuade unbelievers to seek salvation by the law. Far from it! This very important point must not be forgotten when we tackle Paul's arguments later on. The agitators had infiltrated the ranks of *believers*, to attack one of the most treasured possessions of *believers*. Nor had their onslaught been confined, on a limited scale. Not forgetting the letter to the Hebrews, the problem was raising its head in

---

[1] The extracts for this chapter begin on p412.

[2] The precise dating of the letter has no bearing on what follows, although I take it to be by the early 50s, at the latest.

[3] Two of the exceptions are: 'For if there had been a law [legal system] given' (Gal. 3:21), and 'against such there is no law [principle or legal system]' (Gal. 5:23); and in both the closest analogy is the law of Moses. The third and main exception is: 'The law of Christ' (Gal. 6:2). This 'law' (obviously, once again – but see below and chapters 16 – 18) is *not* the law of *Moses*. It is the law of *Christ*.

nearly all the churches – at Antioch, in Galatia, at Rome, Ephesus, Philippi, Colosse... among *converted* Jews and Gentiles. The false teachers were not only talking about the way to be saved, but the implications of being saved. Spiritual *liberty* was at stake. And it was '*our* liberty which *we* have in Christ Jesus' which was under attack. Of course there were implications for unbelievers, but the agitators did not have the unconverted principally in their sights. The infiltrators wanted to bring *believers* into bondage (Gal. 2:4), robbing *them* of their liberty in Christ.

Observe, further, how they went about their task. They were 'smuggled in', 'sneaked in', 'slipped in', intending 'to spy out' or 'inspect, view closely, in order to plot against' believers – especially, as I have said, against one of the most treasured privileges believers have. Note how the apostle stressed the point, saying these 'false brethren' were '*secretly* brought in (who came in by *stealth* to spy out our liberty)' (Gal. 2:4). In addition to the 'false' and 'spy out', do not miss his double use of the same Greek word, *pareiserchomai*. Compare Jude 4 with the word *pareisduō*. It was not an open appeal to unbelievers which concerned Paul. He was alarmed by the Judaisers' secret attack on believers, by their subtle efforts to take *them* under the law.

I will not repeat what I said about these Judaisers in the 'Introduction', but there are three things which must be remembered as we launch out into Galatians; evidence for them will come up time and time again. *First*, do not forget the covenant theology behind their demands. They argued that the Abrahamic and the Mosaic covenants were one and the same. *Secondly*, the question must not be limited to circumcision; it was the entire law (Gal. 5:3). To point out the obvious: circumcision, the principal point of the attack, was not part of the ten commandments, nor was it strictly speaking part of the Mosaic law. See John 7:22. This illustrates the point I have already made; it is quite wrong to limit 'the law' to the ten commandments. And, *thirdly*, although the question concerning the law may have had a bearing on addresses to unbelievers, it was its effect on *believers* which was the real concern here. *As it is mine.*

Why was Paul telling the Galatians about this? Why was he rehearsing his own experience at the hands of the Judaisers? Because the Galatians too were being attacked in precisely the same way. Indeed, said Paul, the attack has been successful to a certain extent, in that you are 'turning away so soon from him who called you in the grace of Christ, to a different gospel', you are listening to, and giving yourselves to, the doctrine of those who 'pervert the gospel of Christ' (Gal. 1:6,7). In other words, the Galatians were giving up their liberty in Christ, and going (back) into bondage. Hence Paul's letter. By spelling out his own experience of the Judaisers, Paul was able to lay down, right at the start, the great marker for the letter; namely, the believer's liberty in Christ Jesus. As we shall see, Paul did a similar thing when writing to several other churches. In God's providence, the apostle's bitter experience had prepared him to be of immense service to other believers – both then and down the centuries. If I may accommodate his words to the Corinthians: 'Blessed be the God and Father of our Lord Jesus Christ... who [delivers] us in all our [spiritual battles], that we may able to [help] those who are [being attacked] with the [defence] with which we ourselves are [delivered] by God' (2 Cor. 1:3-4).

What is this liberty which believers enjoy and might so easily lose? It includes freedom from sin; freedom from its condemnation (now), its power (progressively) and its presence (in glory). It includes freedom from death; spiritual (now), physical (in the resurrection) and eternal. But it also includes freedom from the law. And it was this particular freedom which was under attack by the Judaisers who, if they had managed to get their way, would have brought Paul and his believing friends back into the bondage of subjection to the law. How had he reacted to those who attacked his liberty as a believer? 'We did not give in to them for a moment', he said (Gal. 2:5, NIV). And that was his settled conviction. The protection and cultivation of the believer's liberty (Gal. 2:4; 5:1,13) – with its corollary, the shunning of bondage (Gal. 2:4; 4:3,9,22-25,31; 5:1) – is a major theme of Galatians. In short, Paul was rightly concerned, not only for himself and the immediate church context in which he found himself, but he was thinking of the Galatian believers, 'that the truth of the gospel might continue with *you*' (Gal. 2:5). The fact is, by God's Spirit, he was defending the gospel – especially the liberty it brings – for all the saints of all ages. He was doing it for us! 'Freedom', our freedom in Christ, is the great word, the key word, the heart of Paul's message in Galatians.

The New Testament makes much of this liberty to which the saints have been called, and which Christ accomplished for his people. No wonder! It is one of salvation's greatest glories – liberty in Christ is a joyful, triumphant fact, true for all believers without exception. Believers are free! Since sin is at the root of all bondage, freedom means freedom from sin. Inevitably, therefore, by 'freedom', the apostle meant *freedom from the law since 'the strength of sin is the law'* (1 Cor. 15:56). Paul never tired of the theme; freedom from the law, that yoke of bondage or slavery; freedom from what the Jerusalem meeting called 'the law of Moses... a yoke on the neck... the law' (Acts 15:5,10,24). Of course, the believer's freedom extends much wider than freedom from the law, but it certainly includes it. The believer is not under the law.

Let the apostle spell it out. In addition to the law, the believer has freedom from slavery to 'those which by nature are not gods', 'bondage under the elements of the world... weak and beggarly elements', the observation of 'days and months and seasons and years' (Gal. 4:3,8-10);[4] freedom from 'philosophy and empty deceit, according to the tradition of men, according to the basic principles of the world, and not according to Christ'; freedom from 'the basic principles of the world... regulations' such as 'do not touch, do not taste, do not handle', 'the commandments and doctrines of men' (Col. 2:8,20-22); freedom from being 'slaves of sin' (Rom. 6:6-7); freedom from 'serving' – being 'enslaved to' (NASB) – 'various lusts and pleasures, living in malice and envy, hateful and hating one another' (Tit. 3:3). Freedom is Paul's theme! And it is always connected with the Spirit and not with the law. Without doubt, it is freedom from the law which constitutes a principal part of the believer's liberty. 'Now the Lord is the Spirit; and where the Spirit of the Lord is, there is liberty' (2 Cor. 3:17), the significance of which lies in the context; namely, the 'passing away' of the old covenant, the law, and the sharp contrast between that and the new covenant in Christ, all of which Paul so emphatically stresses (2 Cor. 3:6-17).[5] And liberty is the core, the essence, of the letter to the Galatians.

---

[4] Edgar H.Andrews: Paul's question in Gal. 4:9 does not mean, 'of course', that they were 'reverting to their former idols, but rather seeking to embrace the law of Moses' (see the extracts).

[5] See chapters 11 and 15.

Having sketched in the background of the letter, now let us look at the particular paragraphs which are most relevant for understanding the relationship between the believer and the law. I begin with that attack upon the believer's liberty.

Galatians 2:4-5

False brethren secretly brought in (who came in by stealth to spy out our liberty which we have in Christ Jesus, that they might bring us into bondage), to whom we did not yield submission even for an hour [for a moment (NIV)], that the truth of the gospel might continue with you.

Some very important issues are raised in this account of the apostle's experience, but I will leave a full examination of them until they surface in his major doctrinal statements later in the letter. After all, these verses are simply a statement of what happened to Paul, the doctrinal and practical implications of which he will later work out in close detail. It is as we meet such passages that we will get to grips with his teaching. For now, I simply flag up some of these important topics.

As I have already said, the believer's liberty includes, at least, freedom from the law, and it was this freedom which was under attack by the Judaisers. But what, primarily, was the focus of that attack? What law was it that the agitators were seeking to bring believers under? And, consequently, what was the freedom which Paul stressed so vehemently? Some argue that Paul was defending the believer's freedom from the curse of the law, or freedom from trying to earn justification by the law, or freedom from the ceremonial observances of the law. Is this right? Or is it wider, much wider?

I will not spell out all my reasons here, leaving them until I reach the major passages on the subject, but these suggestions fall woefully short of the facts. Why? Take the first – freedom from the curse of the law. Does anybody think the infiltrators wanted to bring the Galatians under the *curse* of the law? What believer would have allowed himself to be bought into *that*! 'Dear friends, you must come under the law's curse'. 'Is that so? Put my name down'. The suggestion is ludicrous.

Take the second suggestion – freedom from trying to earn justification by the law. Although, of course, believers can get into trouble by thinking in terms of the law for justification – indeed, Paul will tackle this very point (Gal. 5:1-12) – is it their only danger? In this area, is it their greatest danger? Certainly not! The truth is, believers are not seeking to be justified in the first place. They *are* justified. It is accomplished! But they *are* seeking to be sanctified – and herein lies the great threat to their liberty.

As for the third suggestion – that the law in question might be the ceremonial law – notice how Paul, in order to escape from the Judaisers' clutches, did not take the Reformed route of the tripartite division of the law. Neither the infiltrators nor Paul thought or talked in such a way about the law, so the third suggestion is out of the question. As I showed in chapter 7, Scripture simply does not allow such glosses to be imposed upon 'the law'. No! The attack was over 'the law'. True, while circumcision was probably uppermost in the false teachers' minds (Gal. 2:3),[6] as I have already pointed out, and as Paul would later explain, 'every man who becomes circumcised... is a debtor to keep the whole law' (Gal. 5:3). 'The law' is 'the whole law'. There can be

---

[6] But dietary laws were not far below the surface (Gal. 2:11-14).

no picking and choosing. It is the relationship between the believer and the law, the whole law, which Paul was dealing with. In particular, Paul was defending – asserting – the believer's freedom from the law, the whole law.

What happened to Titus at Jerusalem (Gal. 2:1-5) illustrates the point. Because he was a Gentile, the Judaisers wanted him circumcised. Paul refused. He realised it was not a matter of circumcision only – in itself, the key point for the Judaisers – but the whole law (Gal. 5:3). *The believer is free from the rite of circumcision because he is free from the law.* If Paul had given ground when the infiltrators demanded Titus' circumcision, it would have placed in jeopardy this larger, this vital, principle. As a consequence, the apostle would not budge an inch! He knew that obedience to the law meant obedience to the entire law; 90% obedience to the ten commandments is no obedience at all (Jas 2:10-11). To concede obedience on the one point of the entire law, therefore, was to concede obedience to all.

In short, 'the law' is the entire law, and what the apostle says about justification and the law, he says about sanctification and the law. These are such important points, let me show how Paul went on almost immediately to make them in another way.

Galatians 2:15-21

We who are Jews by nature, and not sinners of the Gentiles, knowing that a man is not justified by the works of the law but by faith in Jesus Christ, even we have believed in Christ Jesus, that we might be justified by faith in Christ and not by the works of the law; for by the works of the law no flesh shall be justified... I through the law died to the law that I might live to God. I have been crucified with Christ... I do not set aside the grace of God; for if righteousness comes through the law, then Christ died in vain [for nothing].

I have said 'the law' throughout Galatians 2 means 'the law', 'the whole law'. It does not mean 'the ceremonial law' as opposed to 'the moral law'. Let me prove it. As always, the context is king. The mistake in trying to impose the gloss of 'the ceremonial law' on the freedom of Galatians 2:4 can be seen at a glance. The same goes for this passage. Reader, in the extract just taken from Galatians 2:15-21, try replacing 'the law' with 'the ceremonial law' (as distinct from 'the moral law'). Is it right to say that no man is justified by the works of the *ceremonial* law, and so leave the way open for the suggestion that he is justified by the works of the *moral* law? Of course not! Is it bondage to seek justification by the *ceremonial* law, but freedom to seek it by the *moral* law? Of course not! Again, did Paul, through the *ceremonial* law, die to the *ceremonial* law that he might live to God? Of course not! Believers are justified by faith in Christ and not by the works of the law. And through the law they have died to the law that they might live to God. Righteousness does not come by the law. No glosses, no qualifications, no quibbles. Paul was not speaking of social markers for the Jews. He was not speaking of the so-called ceremonial law in contradistinction to the so-called moral law. He said 'the law', and he meant 'the law', the whole law, and nothing but the law. The fact is, 'the law' in Galatians 2:15-21, is general, any law, but especially the Mosaic law, the Old Testament law, the law of God, the entire law. And since this is the way Paul was using 'the law' in Galatians 2, we must keep to it when thinking about the attack spoken of in Galatians 2:4. Galatians 2:15-21 constitutes part of Paul's rebuttal of the principles of the false teachers. The attack on liberty spoken of in Galatians 2:4,11-15, therefore, was to do with the same law as in Galatians 2:15-21. 'The law' in Galatians 2 means 'the law'.[7]

Now for the second point; namely, that what Paul says about the law and justification he says about the law and sanctification. In this passage, not only was Paul *not* limiting 'the law' to the so-called ceremonial law, neither was he limiting the believer's liberty to justification. When speaking about the wide-sweeping and all-embracing liberty believers have in Christ, he was speaking of freedom from the law, both for justification *and sanctification*. And the believer – since he has liberty – must not go back to bondage by allowing himself to be put under the law – and doing so for whatever reason!

Let me prove it. Notice how Paul, in dealing with the foolish Galatians, wisely started at the beginning; that is, by reminding them of the way of his – and their – justification, which is by grace through faith, not by the works of the law. Not only did Paul remind the Galatians of this, but, it would be more accurate to say, he stressed it, and stressed it both by his use of the negative and by repetition: It is 'not... by the works of the law... not by the works of the law, for by the works of the law no flesh shall be justified' (Gal. 2:16).[8]

But there is more to it. This was, I repeat, only the beginning. As he was setting out the truth concerning justification, Paul took the question of the law further. When he said: 'I through the law died to the law that I might live to God' (Gal. 2:19), he was moving from justification into sanctification – 'that I might live to God'. 'Living to God' is, without question, speaking of the sanctified life of a believer. What is more, the apostle categorically stated that he died to the law 'that' – in order that – 'I might live to God'. *I cannot overstate the importance of this assertion.* Paul died to the law *in order that* he might live to God. In other words, he was asserting that the law neither justifies nor sanctifies, that the believer is not under the law, either for justification or sanctification. The truth is, as I say, he was making the point that to live to God a sinner must die to the law. In short, the law is part of the problem, not the solution! I am not saying a word against the law – the fault lies with the sinner, not the law. But the believer has to be dead to the law in order to live to God. This vital point will come up time and again. As it ought! As we shall see, the apostle later made the same point in Romans 7:4. And since this was true for Paul, as a Jewish believer (Gal. 2:14-15), one who before his conversion was under the law, since *he* had died to the law – indeed *had* to die to the law – in order to live for God, why ever would Gentile believers think of going under the law!

May I reiterate the point I have just made? It is vital. The law is a part of the believer's problem, not the solution. The sinner has to die to the law *in order to* live to God. In Christ, the believer *has* died to the law so that he might bring forth fruit to God.

---

[7] As, with the three exceptions already noted, it does throughout the letter.

[8] As I have explained, this 'traditional view' is questioned by advocates of the New Perspective, but I do not agree that 'the works of the law' denotes primarily circumcision and other social markers. Paul was dealing with attempted justification by merit through law-keeping. See chapter 6.

The main thrust of Galatians 2:11-21, I agree, is justification. But more than that is involved. Practical godliness, daily living, living to God, sanctification, is also bound up in the bundle. As Paul demanded of Peter:

If you, being a Jew, live in the manner of Gentiles and not as the Jews, why do you compel Gentiles to live as Jews? We who are Jews by nature, and not sinners of the Gentiles, knowing that a man is not justified by the works of the law... even we have believed in Christ Jesus, that we might be justified by faith in Christ and not by the works of the law... I through the law died to the law that I might live to God. I have been crucified with Christ; it is no longer I who live, but Christ lives in me; and the life which I now[9] live in the flesh I live by faith in the Son of God... If righteousness comes through the law, then Christ died in vain (Gal. 2:11-21).

Here we have justification and sanctification cheek by jowl. 'Live in the manner of... live as... I might live... I who live... the life which I now live in the flesh I live by faith' – sanctification – is linked with justification – 'justified... justified by faith in Christ'. And both are 'not... by the works of the law... not by the works of the law'.

Thus, it is clear, as far as justification is concerned, the law has nothing to do with the believer.[10] But this is not all. Freedom from the law does not stop at justification. It goes on to sanctification, and includes it. Freedom from the law is essential if the believer is to live a godly life. Essential? Yes, indeed. Remember the 'in order that' which is so clearly stated in the passage: 'I... died to the law that' – in order that – 'I might live to God' (Gal. 2:19). The law produces pride, bondage, mere external conformity to rules, and so on.[11] It is no friend of sanctification.[12] To go to the law after coming to Christ would be a dreadful, retrograde move. It would display a woeful misunderstanding of the grace of God. In truth, it would make void the grace of God. Such a step ought to be out of the question. It would be the exact opposite of Paul's argument! Peter was in danger of doing it, and so were the Galatians, and Paul dealt with them both. That is why he spoke so bluntly and openly to Peter, and wrote the letter to the Galatians. Praise God, he had the courage, the wisdom and the grace to do it! Death to the law is essential for living unto God. And, as before, it will not do to say that Paul was talking about the ceremonial law. He was talking about the law; about the law, I say. Just as a dead man cannot return to his old way of life, neither can a believer go under the law. Just as a widow cannot live with, and submit to, her dead husband (Rom. 7:1-6), neither can a believer live under the rule of the law. In Galatians 2:15-21, Paul, of course, is leading up to Galatians 3:1. See also Galatians 4:4-5. To go back to the law would be to 'build again those things which [Paul, in setting out the gospel] destroyed', making himself 'a transgressor' (Gal. 2:18), 'a law-breaker' (NIV). Weighty arguments here against all who advocate putting believers under the law for sanctification!

This, reader, will sound startling to many. And so it is. But it is what Paul was saying, and kept on saying. Above all, it must not be forgotten – rather, it must be

---

[9] Note the 'now'. Do not forget the 'but now'.

[10] Of course, Christ under the law earned justification for the elect (see chapter 6 and below), but the believer receives this justification entirely apart from the law.

[11] Compare Matt. 15:1-20; Mark 7:1-23.

[12] The law of Christ is a very different entity to the law of Moses – as I will show. I will also explain Paul's use of 'law' in 'the law of Christ'.

stressed – in Galatians, Paul is arguing with believers, not about how they became believers, but how they, as believers, go on in Christ. Sadly, many try to limit Galatians to the law and justification. Nothing could be further from the truth! Believers have not become Christians by the law. They do not remain Christians by the law. They do not grow and make progress by the law. Above all, and this is *the* point of Galatians, they are not sanctified by the law. Indeed, it is only because they have died to the law that believers can be sanctified! To be sanctified, a man must die to the law. No Reformed semantics must be allowed to dull the force of this. And it means that Calvin's third use of the law cannot possibly be right.

This in turn raises other and important issues. Such as: Does the law still have a place in the age of the gospel? Is faith in Christ enough? Or should obedience to the law be added to faith in Christ? What is the role, if any, of the law in the life of a believer? How can a believer be sanctified? I will return to these questions. But not only I! I will return to them because they are the very issues Paul himself raises and deals with. This, in itself, shows that we are on the right track, walking in step with the apostle. So let us calmly proceed, keeping a firm grip on what we have been taught thus far. The law does not justify the sinner. The law does not sanctify the believer.

What does Paul say next?

Galatians 3:1-5

O foolish Galatians! Who has bewitched you...?... Did you receive the Spirit by the works of the law, or by the hearing of faith? Are you so foolish? Having begun in the Spirit, are you now[13] being made perfect by the flesh?

Paul, having raised the question of sanctification,[14] wanted to get the Galatians to think more deeply about it, and especially its connection with the law. He did this by the device of a linguistic explosion closely followed by a series of rapid-fire bullets in the form of sharp questions,[15] six in all. Consider the fourth of these: 'Having begun in the Spirit, are you now being made perfect by the flesh?'

Paul reminded his readers that they had not only 'begun in the Spirit', but they had actually received 'the Spirit', not 'by the works of the law', but 'by the hearing of faith' (Gal. 3:2-3). Begun what? Begun their Christian experience – that is, they had been regenerated, they had been justified by grace through faith in Christ – by the work of the Spirit, and not by the works of the law.

So far, so good. All Reformed and evangelical people will agree. Except, as so often, their usual qualifications and glosses appear. Paul was not asking, for instance, if the Galatians had received the Spirit by 'rigorous' bondage to the 'ceremonial' law. He was referring to obedience to the Mosaic law in its entirety. 'Did the law bring you the Spirit?' The law, I stress!

But the point of Paul's question was not justification. It was sanctification: 'Having begun in the Spirit', he asked, 'are you now being made perfect by the flesh?' (Gal.

---

[13] Note the 'now'.

[14] In Gal. 2:19. Remember, there are no chapter divisions in the original.

[15] Questions are always far more potent than a statement of facts, and a very common way of teaching in Scripture. It is God's own way. See Job 38:1 – 42:1-6, especially Job 38:3; 42:4. Paul used it very often.

3:3). When Paul spoke of 'now being made perfect' (fully accomplished, fully complete), he was speaking about sanctification, was he not? This is the force of his use of 'now being' when he moved on from their initial experience, to ask the Galatians, having been justified, 'are you *now being* made perfect by the flesh?' This is of such importance, I must say it again. When the apostle asked: 'Are you now being made perfect?', what was he talking about? Justification? There is no 'being made' about justification! It is instantaneous. No! The 'now being made perfect' clearly refers to progressive sanctification.

Justification – a once-for-all act of God – precedes, and inevitably leads to, sanctification – a life-long process: 'And you, who once were alienated and enemies in your mind by wicked works, yet now[16] he has reconciled in the body of his flesh through death, to present you holy, and blameless, and above reproach in his sight' – that is, justification – 'if indeed you continue in the faith, grounded and steadfast, and are not moved away from the hope of the gospel' – that is, sanctification (Col. 1:21-23). The link between the two is unbreakable. 'For by grace you have been saved, through faith, and that not of yourselves; it is the gift of God, not of works, lest anyone should boast. For we are his workmanship, created in Christ Jesus for good works, which God prepared beforehand that we should walk in them' (Eph. 2:8-10).[17] The way to glory is through holiness. And that is what Paul is concerned about in this letter to the Galatians – especially the way to produce holiness. And that is not by the law!

This means, of course, that it is a very serious mistake to suggest that Paul's great concern in this letter is justification, though, as I have observed, it is commonly believed and said. No! The apostle was speaking to believers (who were, therefore, already justified!) about *advancing* in Christian experience, not *entering* it. He was speaking not only of the basis of faith, but progress in it – not the ground of salvation, but the way to grow in it. Paul's use of the present continuous tense, 'now being made perfect' (Gal. 3:3), must not be overlooked. He was speaking of the process and progress of sanctification. More precisely, it was not the *ground* or *standard* of the believer's sanctification which concerned him. Rather, *it was the way the believer is to be sanctified*. The Reformed want to concentrate on the 'what' of sanctification. The

---

[16] Note the 'now'.

[17] The link between justification and sanctification was another bone of contention between the Anabaptists and the Reformers. The latter taught the inevitable link between the two, but practice did not always go hand in hand with theory. Luther, for instance, though he rightly emphasised justification by faith, failed to give enough weight to sanctification as essential evidence of it. Hence his attitude to the letter of James, dismissing it as so much hay or straw. In general, Anabaptists rightly demanded sanctification as evidence of justification – so much so, the Reformers falsely labelled them with the stigma of perfectionism; Calvin, repeatedly so. As for the Anabaptists, there is abundant testimony as to their godliness of life. They insisted on it. Although the Reformers tried to dismiss the Anabaptists, they longed that their own churches might be as spiritual. Luther, envying the Anabaptists' godliness, admitted his followers lived as badly as Papists. He coped with it by saying doctrine (light) and life have to be distinguished, thus providing a pragmatic excuse for his followers – with dire consequences. Although I have introduced this historical note, the issue cannot be relegated to the mists of history; it is with us today. I will return to this question of separating justification and sanctification, 'light' and 'life'. Reformed teachers rightly argue they cannot be separated, but when it comes to the believer and the law they often break their rubric.

real question is the 'how'. What is more, of even greater importance is the 'who' will be sanctified, and 'why'.[18]

And this is the very issue I am addressing in this book. So how, according to Paul, are believers sanctified? How does he argue his case? He presses his case by asking these bullet-like questions, not issuing a series of bland statements. As always, he is making his readers *think*. Building on their experience of justification, Paul calls on the Galatians to think, and to think clearly, about *how* they were justified, and, now, *how* they are being sanctified: 'Having begun [justification] in the Spirit', demands Paul, 'are you *now being made* perfect [sanctification] by the flesh?' And when he dismisses the possibility of being 'made perfect *by the flesh*', is he referring to natural powers and abilities? Certainly! He is denying any hope of sanctification by human effort, yes. But Paul is saying far more than that. In the context, the expressions 'by the flesh' and 'in the flesh' are virtually one and the same with 'under the law' and 'by the works of the law'. A reading of Galatians 3:2-3 will prove it. In addition, these verses show that to be 'living by the flesh', 'in the flesh', 'under the law' and 'by the works of the law', is diametrically opposed to 'living, walking in [or by] the Spirit'. So important is this point, Paul returns to it (more than once) and drives it home:

Walk in the Spirit, and you shall not fulfil the lust of the flesh... If you are led by the Spirit, you are not under the law. Now the works of the flesh are... But the fruit of the Spirit is... Against such there is no law. And those who are Christ's have crucified the flesh... If we live in the Spirit, let us also walk in [or by] the Spirit... He who sows to his flesh will of the flesh reap corruption, but he who sows to the Spirit will of the Spirit reap everlasting life (Gal. 5:16-25; 6:8. See also Rom. 8:1-17; 13:14; Gal. 4:5-6).

Finally, Paul's question in Galatians 3:3 – 'Having begun in the Spirit, are you now being made perfect by the flesh?' – is rhetorical. There is no doubt about the answer. The expected answer, the obvious answer, is a resounding: 'No! Of course not!' Sanctification most decidedly is not by the flesh, is not by works of the law. Just as justification is not by the works of the law,[19] but by the work of the Spirit, *so it is with sanctification*. In asking them about their experience of the Spirit, Paul's purpose is not to shine the spotlight on how the Galatians received the Spirit, but rather to get them to grasp the Spirit's role in their ongoing life as believers. They had started the Christian life without the works of the law, he reminds them. Well, then, so they must go on, and go on to the end. There is no more place for the works of the law in the continuance of the believer's experience than there was at its start. In other words, the law could not justify; it cannot sanctify. And just as the unbeliever should not go to the law for justification, neither should the believer go to the law for sanctification. Both should go to Christ! Christ is all! As Paul declared to the Corinthians: 'What I received I passed on to you as of first importance'. What was that? Strictly speaking, it was not 'what'; it was 'whom' – 'Christ', his death, burial and resurrection, all according to the Scriptures (1 Cor. 15:3-4); in other words, the scriptural Christ (1 Cor. 3:11; 2 Cor. 11:4; Gal. 1:6-12; Col. 1:28).

Paul's point about sanctification is *not* secondary compared to the primary thrust of justification, as is claimed. In any case, even if it is, it does not alter the fact:

---

[18] I will enlarge on this in chapter 18 when I deal with the new covenant.

[19] Note the emphasis in the Greek upon 'works of the law' (Gal. 3:2). Controversy over this is what prompted this letter.

sanctification is not by the law. But secondary, this is not! From Paul's sixth rhetorical question – 'Therefore he who supplies the Spirit to you and works miracles among you, does he do it by the works of the law, or by the hearing of faith?' (Gal. 3:5) – we can see that faith, not the works of the law, is the vital element in the ongoing Christian life. Galatians 3:3 demands detailed exposition since it strikes at the heart of the Reformed thesis. Unfortunately, it does not always get it. Indeed, it is sometimes made to say the opposite of what the apostle actually did say! Paul was *not* saying that the law is the way God gives his Spirit to his people when they are justified. Far from it! The fact is, the law cannot justify, nor does it enable the believer to reach that standard of life which must accompany justification. In short, the law can neither justify nor sanctify.

There are two dangers if we get the connection between justification and sanctification wrong. *First*, if we mistakenly put them into separate compartments, forgetting that sanctification can only come after and from the same source as justification – that is, by the power of Christ – we shall become legalists, trying to be holy by our own power, by obeying the law (or man-made rules). The *second* danger occurs when justification and sanctification are treated as one and the same. This leads us to ignore our responsibility to obey God in his word, and thus to work out that which he has worked in us. 'Let go and let God', or 'God does it all', is a tragic misunderstanding of the way to attain a godly life. The believer does not become holy by 'taking it by faith'. He is under the law of Christ. See chapter 16.

As we have seen, and will continue to see, and see even more clearly, the law is to do with sin. It has nothing to do with grace. Indeed, it stands in striking contrast to it (John 1:17; Rom. 3:19-22; 4:15-16; 5:20; Gal. 3:19-25). The law cannot save. It cannot bring grace. While 'grace and truth came through Jesus Christ' (John 1:17), 'the law brings about wrath' (Rom. 4:15). Of course it does, since 'the carnal [fleshly] mind is enmity against God; for it is not subject to the law of God, nor indeed can be. So then, those who are in the flesh cannot please God' (Rom. 8:7-8). So much for the natural man, the sinner outside of Christ. This is what being 'in the flesh' means. This is Paul's way of speaking of those outside of Christ. They cannot, they do not, they will not, submit to God's law. And they are in this state because they do not have the Spirit. So, as Paul reminded the Galatians (and, later, the Romans), justification is not by the flesh, not by the law, but by the hearing of faith, by the work of Christ through the power of the Spirit. No sinner can be justified by the law; he hates it, he will not be subject to it (Rom. 8:7)! The law arouses 'the sinful passions' (Rom. 7:5), it makes sin live (Rom. 7:8-9), and kills the sinner (Rom. 7:10-11). Justification can only be by grace through the Spirit. There is no middle way between 'the works of the law' and 'the hearing of faith'. It is one or the other (Gal. 3:2). And justification is not by the law. So much for justification.

But in Galatians 3:2-3, I reiterate, *Paul was going further than this.* 'How stupid, how wrong of you believers', he was saying, 'to imagine for a moment that, having begun in the Spirit, you might now go to the flesh – that is, to the law – to sanctify you! The law could not save you; nor can it sanctify you'. *This* is what the apostle was teaching. As before, as with justification, so with *growth in the Christian life* – neither is by the works of the law.

To conclude: the believer began his spiritual experience – he has been justified – in the Spirit, not by the law, and just as he began, so he continues – by the Spirit, and not the law. In short, as with justification, so with sanctification. Both are by the Spirit, and not the law. This simple though crucial point, if firmly grasped and fully worked out, would go a long way to sorting out the issue of the believer and the law. The law does not sanctify. The law cannot possibly be the believer's perfect rule of life. Paul's rhetorical questions have ruled it out once and for all.

We now come to a section of massive importance in this discussion, one which goes right to its very heart. Reader, gird up your loins! It is not too much to say that if we get this following section right, the rest of the debate over the believer and the law will largely fall into place. And while there is an abundance of detail in what now follows, do not, I urge you, get lost in it. *Do not miss the big picture!*

Galatians 3:10 – 4:7

For as many as are of the works of the law are under the [better, a] curse; for it is written: 'Cursed is everyone who does not continue in all things which are written in the book of the law, to do them'. But that no one is justified by the law in the sight of God is evident, for 'the just shall live by faith'. Yet the law is not of faith, but 'the man who does them shall live by them'. Christ has redeemed us from the curse of the law, having become a curse for us... that the blessing of Abraham might come upon the Gentiles in Christ Jesus, that we might receive the promise of the Spirit through faith... Now to Abraham and his Seed were the promises made. He does not say: 'And to seeds', as of many, but as of one: 'And to your Seed', who is Christ. And this I say, that the law which was four hundred and thirty years later, cannot annul the covenant that was confirmed before by God in Christ, that it should make the promise of no effect. For if the inheritance is of the law, it is no longer of promise; but God gave it to Abraham by promise. What purpose then does the law serve? It was added because of transgressions, till the Seed should come to whom the promise was made; and it was appointed through angels by the hand of a mediator... Is the law then against the promises of God? Certainly not! For if there had been a law given which could have given life, truly righteousness would have been by the law. But the Scripture has confined all under sin, that the promise by faith in Jesus Christ might be given to those who believe. But before [the] faith came, we were kept under guard by the law, kept for [better, shut up to, confined for] the faith which would afterwards be revealed. Therefore the law was our tutor [better, child-custodian] to bring us [these last three words are not in the original] to Christ, that we might be justified by faith. But after [the] faith has come, we are no longer under a tutor [child-custodian]... Now I say that the heir, as long as he is a child, does not differ at all from a slave, though he is master of all, but is under guardians and stewards until the time appointed by the father. Even so we, when we were children, were in bondage under the elements of the world. But when the fullness of the time had come, God sent forth his Son, born of a woman, born under the law, to redeem those who were under the law, that we might receive the adoption as sons. And because you are sons, God has sent forth the Spirit of his Son into your hearts, crying out: 'Abba, Father!' Therefore you are no longer a slave but a son, and if a son, then an heir of God through Christ.[20]

---

[20] I will not have much to say about Gal. 4:1-7, not that it is unimportant, but it does not figure heavily in this discussion of the law. Having said that, *the law, its place and its **prescribed duration** undergirds the entire argument*. The apostle's use of the common practice adopted by a patrician in his son's upbringing constitutes a powerful emphasis (by means of this further illustration) of his teaching in Gal. 3:23-25. The father employs a guardian or steward to restrain his son for the duration he himself has stipulated, employs him until his son reaches maturity, and can be set free of the steward's rule, and so be ready to come into his inheritance. Paul, thrilled by what he is saying, outruns his illustration to bring in the idea of adoption (Gal. 4:5-7).

Seven important points before we begin.

First, 'faith' (Gal. 3:23,25). Paul was not speaking about 'faith' as a personal experience – that is, 'believing'. Rather, he was speaking of 'the faith' as the gospel, Christ – that is, 'who and what is to be believed'. In other words, 'faith' here is objective, not subjective.

Secondly, 'to bring us' (Gal. 3:24). These words are not in the original, and should be removed. They have been the unfortunate source of much misunderstanding. Paul did not say the law was given as a child-custodian 'to bring us' to Christ. Rather, the law was in place as a child-custodian 'until' the coming of Christ (Gal. 3:19).

Thirdly, the 'tutor' (Gal. 3:24), Greek *paidagōgos*, 'tutor' (NKJV), 'schoolmaster' (AV), 'in charge' (NIV), 'tutor', literally 'child-conductor' (NASB). Sadly, some of these translations ('schoolmaster' and 'tutor'), even the transliteration 'pedagogue', give the misleading impression that the law was an 'educator', much like *didaskalos* (Rom. 2:20; Heb. 5:2, for example). *This* is not the meaning of *paidagōgos*. The word is a combination of *pais* (child) and *agōgos* (leader), derived from *agō*, 'to drive, to lead by laying hold of, to conduct' with the idea of discipline. As Thayer explained: 'The name was applied to trustworthy slaves who were charged with the duty of supervising the life and morals of boys... The boys were not allowed so much as to step out of the house without them, before reaching the age of manhood... The name carries with it an idea of severity (as of a stern censor and enforcer of morals)'. And, linking this with the previous point, the child-custodian's job was not to *bring* the immature boy anywhere; rather, he had to discipline and protect the boy *until* he reached maturity. During that time, the Jews 'were held prisoners by the law, locked up' by the law (Gal. 3:23, NIV), 'kept under guard by the law', confined by the law.

Fourthly, what 'law' was Paul speaking of? There is no room for doubt. None whatever. Paul was speaking of the entire Mosaic institution. He was not speaking of the moral law, the ceremonial law or the judicial law, allowing the terms for the moment. Nor was he speaking of Jewish misunderstanding of the law, or legalism. Paul said 'the law' and he meant the law, the law of Moses in its entirety. *And he kept to it throughout the passage.*[21]

Fifthly, what of the 'added'? This word must not be misunderstood. The law 'was added' to God's promise to Abraham, given 430 years before the law (Gal. 3:19). Paul did not say that the law was 'incorporated' into the promise, or added to the promise in the sense that the pair made one covenant, a covenant of grace. Quite the opposite, in fact. The law came in as something extra to the promise, a distinct, separate and subordinate economy or system, *not* an alteration of, an adjustment to, or modifier of the promise. The law did not belong to the existing system or promise. It was not part of it. It was something additional, not fundamental. It was an add-on.[22] As the apostle said: 'The law entered' (Rom. 5:20). The Greek word for 'entered' is used only twice in the New Testament (Rom. 5:20; Gal. 2:4). In the latter, it means 'sneaked in'. While

---

[21] Some Reformed commentators are ambiguous on this, or change their mind as they go along, without justification.

[22] It was also temporary (see below), something very different to the promise, which was permanent.

in Romans 5:20 it does not bear the evil sense of Galatians 2:4, nevertheless it possesses the connotation, 'slipped in between', 'came in besides', 'in addition to'. The law slipped in. Paul's emphasis on the law's temporary place in salvation history is obvious here.[23] It ought to be unmistakeable.

The apostle went further. Do not forget the Judaisers' claim that the Abrahamic and Mosaic covenants were one and the same. Paul did not fudge the issue. They could not be more wrong! He was adamant. Going for the jugular, he categorically *contrasted* the two covenants, and let all concerned – the Galatians and the Judaisers – know the consequence of denying the contrast: 'For if the inheritance is of the law, it is no longer of promise' (Gal. 3:18). This he confirmed in Galatians 4:24-26, where he argued that the Abrahamic covenant and the Mosaic covenant were two separate, distinct, covenants, not two parts of the same. What is more, throughout the letter to the Galatians, Paul stoutly preserved this separateness, standing firm against the Judaisers who, as I say, wanted to blend the promise and the law into one.[24]

There is no question but that Paul was thinking of the law's vital, though temporary, role in the unfolding of salvation history. That history is not flat, nor smoothly evolutionary in character. Rather, it is the record of God's interventions. God broke into the history of the world to give Abraham the promise. 430 years later, he intervened again to give Israel the law through Moses. Centuries later, at the right time (Gal. 4:4), he intervened again and sent his Son, the Seed (Gal. 3:19). He intervened again with the gift of the Spirit (Acts 2).[25] To lose sight of Paul's eschatological argument is tragic.[26]

Moreover, as with the previous point, Paul was speaking about the law – the law in its entirety, the law full stop! It was the law, the whole law, that was added 430 years after the promise, and it was the law, the whole law that was temporary in that God intended it to last until the coming of the Seed. There is not the slightest hint that Paul was saying the whole law was given at Sinai, two thirds of which lasted until the coming of the Seed, the remaining one third being eternal.[27]

Sixthly, the 'us'. When Paul said: 'Christ has redeemed *us* from the curse of the law, having become a curse for *us*' (Gal. 3:13), to whom was he referring? Was he speaking of elect Jews? Or was he speaking of the elect, full stop, both Jews and Gentiles? There are strong arguments for both. The problem of the 'us' is not confined to Galatians 3:13-14, of course. It also arises in Galatians 3:23-29 and 4:3-7. It is likely that Paul was speaking primarily of elect Jews – and this is where the emphasis must fall – yet encompassing all the elect, both Jew and Gentile, in Christ's redemption.[28] While

---

[23] See my comments on salvation history in chapter 2.

[24] This, of course, puts the Reformed advocates firmly on the side of those Paul was speaking against!

[25] There is one more intervention to come; Christ's return.

[26] See Isa. 34:4; 65:17; Hag. 2:6-9,21-23; Heb. 12:25-29; 2 Pet 3:3-7. This, of course, takes us back to the continuity/discontinuity debate.

[27] Actually, less than 1% of it.

[28] The arguments in favour of viewing the 'us' as Jews can be summarised thus: while all men, both Jew and Gentile, are sinners, since it was only the Jews who were under the law, its curse could only apply to them, and therefore redemption from the law could apply only to them; since Gentiles are spoken of in Gal. 3:14, it is likely that the Jews were being spoken of in Gal.

historically and actually it was only the Jews who could be said to be 'under the law', Paul probably included the Gentiles on the basis of Romans 2:14-15.[29]

And, *seventhly*, do not miss the unity which the apostle stresses in this passage. The Seed is one (Gal. 3:16), God is one (Gal. 3:20), and believers (whether Jew or Greek) 'are all one in Christ Jesus' (Gal. 3:28). In short, Gentiles do not need to go under the law to belong to the people of God, or to ratify their belonging to that people. They should pay no attention to the Judaisers who want them to submit to the law to make them 'kosher'. In Christ, they, along with believing Jews, 'are all sons God through faith in Christ Jesus'. They, *all* of them, have 'put on Christ', 'are Christ's', and 'are Abraham's seed, and heirs according to the promise' (Gal. 3:26-29), and that without the law.[30]

Having teased out these seven preliminary – but far from trivial – details, we can now get to grips with Paul's argument in Galatians 3:10-25. Trivial details, did I say? If they were to be grasped, it would signal an end to this debate on the believer and the law. Now for the passage. I take it up from Galatians 3:8.

Paul reminded his readers of God's promise to Abraham that through him he would bless the nations, which promise, as the apostle explained, is fulfilled in the calling of the elect (Jew and Gentile) to faith and justification in Christ. This justification, Paul stressed, is by faith in Christ, not by the law. In fact, the law can only curse; it is antithetical to faith. But Christ has redeemed the elect from the law's curse – and in so doing has accomplished the promise God made to Abraham; namely, that the elect, including Gentiles, should 'receive the promise of the Spirit through faith' (Gal. 3:14). This takes us as far as the apostle's earlier rhetorical question: 'Did you receive the Spirit by the works of the law, or by the hearing of faith?' (Gal. 3:2).

3:13; Paul said 'we who are Jews' (Gal. 2:15); note the us/you contrast of Gal. 3:23-25 and 3:26-29; and, finally, the contrast in the Greek between 'us' and 'the Gentiles'.

[29] See chapters 2 and 3 for my reasons. Perhaps Paul was treating the Jews as a special case of redemption (Matt. 15:24; John 4:22), or in their priority over the Gentiles in its order (Luke 24:47; John 1:11; Acts 1:8; 3:26; 10:36; 13:26,46; 28:28; Rom. 1:16; 2:9). As I showed in chapter 3, it may be that Israel and the law served as a paradigm for Gentiles; the Gentiles are answerable to God for the moral standards he has placed upon them and within them, just as Israel was answerable for the law. This is why the Old Testament prophets could condemn the nations for their failure, just as they could condemn Israel for hers – even though the Gentiles and Israel were not under the same law. And this might be the explanation of Paul's warning in Gal. 4:21 and 5:4. For unbelievers, God's 'law' – whatever form it may take – continues to condemn those who are not in Christ and thus have not fulfilled the law. And whatever the arguments over the *us* in Gal. 3, in any event all men need redemption since 'they are all under sin', 'the Scripture has confined all under sin' (Rom. 3:9,22-23; 11:32; Gal. 3:22). All men – Jews and Gentiles – are slaves to sin. See my comments on Rom. 3:19 in chapter 2.

[30] Gal. 3:20 has baffled most, if not all, commentators. I like the following: 'Moses, to whom the Galatians are being tempted to look for membership in the true people of God, is not the one through whom that single family is brought about... The law cannot be God's final word: God, being himself one, desires a single family, but the Mosaic law was given to one race only [the Jews], and therefore cannot put this plan into operation' (N.T.Wright pp169,172). In other words, Gentile believers must not go back to the law. Wright drew attention to the parallel in Rom. 3:30-31. For his full argument, see N.T.Wright pp157-174.

Having cleared the ground thus far, Paul powered on. Even a man's covenant cannot be broken – let alone God's! This principle the apostle worked out in the following verses (Gal. 3:15-18). Nothing can alter, let alone 'annul', God's promise and purpose in the Abrahamic covenant – not even the law! In short, the law cannot contribute to our justification. But neither can it do away with God's earlier promise.

Such statements, of course, raise a question. And Paul asks it! 'If what you have said is true, why ever did God give the law to the Jews through Moses on Sinai?' As the apostle put it: 'What purpose... does the law serve?' (Gal. 3:19). Good question! As always, you can tell whether or not you are getting Paul's drift – does the question that he asks spring to your mind, too? If the law could not justify, and if the law did not abolish the promise, why ever did God give it to the Jews? What purpose did God have in mind when he gave the law to Israel?

Now for the answer! We are left in no doubt since Paul himself answered his own question, and his answer must be definitive, settling the issue once and for all. Here it is. The law? The purpose of the law? 'It was added because of transgressions, till the Seed should come to whom the promise was made' (Gal. 3:19).

There are two points.

First, God's purpose[31] in giving the law was to do with sin; 'it was added because of transgressions' (Gal. 3:19). While this is not easy to interpret, some things are clear. The law was not added because transgressions *existed* – before the law there could be no transgression. Rather, the law brought home the fact that sin (which did exist) was sin against God, it was transgression of his law (1 John 3:4), the law having turned sin into transgression.[32] Men were sinners before the giving of the law, of course, but the law turned sin into transgression – where there is no law, there is no transgression (Rom. 4:15; 5:13). What is more, while the entrance of the law did not create sin, it promoted it, increased it, exhibited it, defined it. This is what the law does. This is why it was 'added'. It exposes sin, and convicts the offender of it (Rom. 3:19-20; 7:7-13). It arouses sin (Rom. 7:5,7-11), brings a curse (Gal. 3:10), slavery (Gal. 4:1-8) and wrath (Rom. 4:15). 'The sting of death is sin, and the strength of sin is the law' (1 Cor. 15:56). 'The law is not made for a righteous person, but for the lawless and insubordinate, for the ungodly and for sinners' (1 Tim. 1:9-10). To break one commandment of the law is to incur the guilt of all (Jas. 2:10-11). As for the Jews, the law was 'added', it was given to them as a prison keeper, prison house, or child-custodian (Gal. 3:23-25). Note Paul's stress on being guarded, confined, restricted, locked up and ruled by the law. So important is this idea, to drive it home the apostle uses the illustrations of slavery (Rom. 6), marriage (Rom. 7), the child-custodian (Gal. 3), the steward (Gal. 4) and Hagar (Gal. 4). 'Moreover, the law entered that the offence might abound' (Rom. 5:20). 'The offence'? What offence? The offence of Adam's sin: 'Through one man sin entered the world, and death through sin, and thus death spread to all men... by one man's offence many died... by the one man's offence death reigned through the one... through one man's offence judgement came to all men, resulting in condemnation... by one man's disobedience many were made sinners' (Rom. 5:12-19). 'Moreover the law entered that the offence' – Adam's offence, and its consequence throughout the human race – 'might abound' (Rom. 5:20). *This* was God's purpose or

---

[31] The 'because' has a forward look; it is a word of purpose.
[32] See chapter 3.

intention in giving the law. It was to make offence 'abound'. In short, the law was to do with sin, transgression, guilt, wrath, curse, death, condemnation, prison and bondage. And it made the offence abound. This is why God 'added' the law. This is why he gave the law to Israel.

So much for the first point.

Secondly, the law was only a temporary economy or system: 'It was added... till the Seed should come' (Gal. 3:19). Paul highlights this temporary nature of the law in two ways. In addition to the word 'added' – which speaks of the law's supplementary role[33] – note the words, 'till the Seed should come'. I draw attention to the *till*. The law was revealed on Sinai to Moses – 'it was added', it 'entered' at that time (Rom. 5:13-14,20; Gal. 3:19) – and it entered the world to last only *until* the Seed should come. This refers first and foremost to the law's historical significance. That is to say, it was a temporary system given to Israel through Moses, 430 years after the promise to Abraham (Gal. 3:17), and lasting *till* or *until* the coming of the Seed. Who is the Seed who was to come? Christ: '"And to your Seed", who is Christ' (Gal. 3:16). So now – do not miss that vital eschatological word, once again – since the Seed, Christ, *has* come, the reign of the law is over, the reign of the law must be over, the law's day is done, its sun has set. This is what the *until* means. Note the *before* and *after* in Galatians 3:23. As Paul stated: '*Before* [the] faith came, we were kept under guard by the law, kept for [shut up to, confined for] the faith which would *afterwards* be revealed' (Gal. 3:23). The time element is very prominent once again – *eis* appears twice in Galatians 3:23-24. In both verses it means 'until'; in neither does it mean 'to'. Paul's argument is that *until* the coming of 'the faith', *until* the coming of the Seed, *until* the coming of Christ, *until* the bringing in of the gospel, it was the time or age of the law.

Not only was it the time of the law: until the coming of Christ, the law *reigned*. The law 'kept under guard' the Jews, imprisoning them, confining them, shutting them up to the coming of the gospel. For, as Paul said, referring to Jewish history from Sinai to the coming of the Messiah, 'the law was our [that is, for the Jews] [child-custodian] to [*eis*, until] Christ' (Gal. 3:24). Until the coming of Christ, the law was disciplining those under its rule, the Jews, shutting them up until the coming of the gospel in Christ. 'The law was put *in charge* until Christ came' (Gal. 3:24, NIV footnote).

'But after [the] faith has come' – that is, now that Christ has come and brought in the gospel – 'we are no longer *under* a [child-custodian]' (Gal. 3:25). 'We', the Jews,[34] said Paul – the Gentiles never were under the law in any case – we are no longer under the law. So how could anybody be under the law since the age of the law is over – now that Christ has come?[35] Now that the faith – the gospel – has come, the law has served

---

[33] See above.

[34] Jews? Jews as Jews? Or converted Jews? Are any Jews under the law today? This takes us far beyond the remit of my book, but since Christ has fulfilled and abolished the law, and its age is therefore over, I am inclined to think the law's old-covenant role has gone. I know that some Jews are still mistakenly waiting for the coming of the Messiah, but if any are still under the law, if the law is still in place, where are the priesthood, sacrifices, *etc.*?

[35] This question has to be answered also by those who mistakenly think Paul was speaking about an individual's experience of the law before conversion. It has especially to be answered by them! See below.

its purpose. 'For the law was given through Moses, but grace and truth came through Jesus Christ' (John 1:17). 'On the one hand there is an annulling of the former commandment because of its weakness and unprofitableness... On the other hand, there is the bringing in of a better hope... For if that first covenant had been faultless, then no place would have been sought for a second... In that [God] says: "A new covenant", he has made the first obsolete' (Heb. 7:18-19; 8:7,13).

All this is reinforced by Paul's use of 'pedagogue'. The pedagogue was a guardian, a child-custodian, whose job it was to restrain a minor from immoral behaviour, and to protect him until he matured. Once the juvenile reached maturity, however, the pedagogue's work was finished. He had no more say over his former trainee. He was out of a job, surplus to requirements. His old power and rule had ended. Paul used this well-known practice to illustrate the law's relationship to the Jews, standing over them, keeping them in line throughout the age of the law.[36] The Mosaic order (the old-covenant administration, economy, dispensation), the law, was the pedagogue which kept Israel in order until the coming of Christ and his new covenant.[37] Once Christ had come, however, believing Jews were no longer under the law (Gal. 3:25). And if Jewish believers are no longer under the law, then, of course, neither are Gentile believers.

Note the repetition of 'under' – the key word – in '*under* guard by the law', '*under* a [child-custodian]', '*under* guardians and stewards' and '*under* the elements of the world', and '*under* the law' (Gal. 3:23,25; 4:2-3,5). The repetition of 'under', and the thrust of the argument, show these phrases are all saying one and the same thing. Which is? The law, bringing in and imposing rules, governed and guarded the way the Jews behaved, confining them *under* itself. The law was over the Jews, they were *under* it, *under* its grip, *under* its power. It revealed sin, and aroused or stimulated it. As we shall see later, Paul says the same thing in Romans 6 and 7. In both Galatians and Romans, the apostle makes it as clear as noonday that there are two stages of salvation history. The former age, 'under law', and the present age, under Christ, 'under grace'. The apostle always heavily contrasts the two. The former age was the age or realm of bondage; the latter, freedom. Now when Paul spoke of 'being under the law', he meant more than being under its curse. He meant being under *it*, under the law as a system, under it as a realm, under it as a rule of behaviour, under the law as a child-custodian, under its reign, under its grip, under its power. It is all a question of maturity, of age, epoch, realm and status. To be under the law is to be under a child-custodian, whereas to be under Christ is to be free. Just as a mature man is no longer under the child-custodian, so the believer is no longer under the law, no longer subject to the imposition of its rule.[38]

---

[36] As I have noted, all this is reinforced by Paul's use of the guardian or steward in Gal. 4:1-7.

[37] See Acts 15. Note the *our fathers nor we* (Acts 15:10) – clearly a reference to the Jews; Peter, a Jew, was speaking about the Jews. I have already noted the reference in Acts 15:21 to synagogues and sabbaths; clearly Jewish – not Gentile – terms. The law distinguished between – divided indeed (Eph. 2:14-15) (see chapters 2 and 15) – Jews and Gentiles, but grace, through trust in Christ, makes them one (Acts 15:7-9; see also John 10:16; 11:52; 17:20-24; Gal. 3:28; Eph. 2:13-22).

[38] This does not mean that the believer has nothing at all to do with the law, but the law is not the rule nor norm for defining his walk with God. I will show how the law plays the role of a believer's paradigm as part of 2 Tim. 3:16-17.

And since this is so, how can believers think of going under the law? After all, the child-custodian only had a job while the child was immature. When the child reached maturity, not only the child-custodian's work, but the child-custodian himself, was finished. Well then, as Paul states so clearly, believers are 'all sons of God through faith in Christ Jesus' (Gal. 3:26). Sons? The apostle uses *huioi* – grown up, mature, sons. And he declares that believers, all believers, the moment they trust Christ, are fully-mature adopted sons of God. Consequently, just as, on reaching maturity, the minor was released from the child-custodian, the believer, being a mature son, cannot possibly be under the law. See Galatians 4:1-7, where the apostle clearly contrasts the infant, *nēpios*, with the son, *huios*. In short, for converted Jews to go back to Moses, or for converted Gentiles – who never had the law – to go under Moses, is unthinkable. Or ought to be.

Here we have it. Galatians 3:10-25 shows us that there have been two great ages, two epochs in human history; first, the age of law from Moses to Christ, and then the age of grace under Christ. And these two ages are sharply contrasted with each other. The law was a temporary or interim measure, a parenthesis, an age which Christ in the gospel brought to an end and did away with. Paul's compelling line of reasoning in this Galatian passage is from start to finish to do with the eschatological, the historical, and he builds his case with invincible clarity and devastating power. The temporary, provisional, age of the law was abrogated with eschatological finality by Christ when he brought in the gospel revelation. Such is Paul's majestic argument. 'All the prophets and the law prophesied until John' (Matt. 11:13). So said the Lord Jesus. Even as he spoke, the age of law was coming to its appointed end. And when Christ died, 'at that moment' (NIV), God tore down the temple curtain (Matt. 27:51; Mark 15:38; Luke 23:45). The age and reign of the law was over. The law had been fulfilled, Christ having brought it to the end that God had always determined for it (Matt. 5:17-18; Rom. 10:4). This is what Paul teaches in Galatians 3:10-25. This section of Scripture, it might well be argued, constitutes the zenith of the apostle's teaching on the law.

But many place a very different construction on the passage. Very different! They say that Galatians 3:19,22-24 speaks of the *personal* experience of conviction of sin during an *individual's* experience of coming to faith in Christ. Paul, they allege, was saying the Spirit uses the law to convict the sinner, closing every avenue but grace, forcing him to Christ for relief from his sins by trusting him for salvation. In other words, the law rules over an individual unregenerate sinner until Christ has come savingly to that individual sinner. Furthermore, the law 'brings us' to Christ (Gal. 3:24). It is not a question of history, at all. It is a personal experience, today. And these teachers, building on this personal idea, say that the preaching of the law is essential in order to prepare the sinner to come to Christ.[39] I spoke of this supposed-preparationism by the law in chapter 4, where I promised to return to it, and explore the biblical text which is (mis)used to support it. I do so now.

---

[39] But even if this is the correct view of the passage – and it most certainly is *not* – Paul's: 'The law was our tutor to bring us to Christ... But after faith has come, we are no longer under a tutor' (Gal. 3:24-25), destroys at a stroke Calvin's third use of the law. On the Reformed view, the law acts as a tutor until the sinner comes to personal faith in Christ, and then that converted sinner is immediately put back under his tutor, the law! How can this be squared with what Paul actually said? And where is the text that states the Reformed view?

This notion of personal preparationism by the law is *not* what Paul was arguing. Not at all! For a start, as I have explained, 'to bring us', is a translators' insertion, and a bad insertion at that. Paul said nothing of the sort. Preparationism's entire edifice is built on this non-existent textual foundation. But preparationism comes to grief on far more than a single text. It is the context!

For a start, consider the immediate context from Galatians 3:10. The apostle was clearly speaking of two ages in the history of the world – before the coming of the Seed, and after. He was not remotely addressing the individual's personal experience. No! He was taking a grand, overall view of the sweep of the history of redemption. Then there is the wider context of Galatians to bear in mind. How preparationism can be made to fit with *that*, I am at a loss to comprehend. The Judaisers got some things wrong, but, after all, they *were* preaching the law – just the job for bringing sinners to Christ! Strange, then, that Paul did not commend them for this part of their ministry, merely fine-tuning the bit they got wrong! And then there is the wider context still – the rest of the New Testament. If the apostle, in Galatians 3:24, had been setting out the way a sinner is brought to Christ, we ought to find several examples of apostolic preaching of the law to Gentiles, especially by Paul. After all, so we are told, this is *the* way for sinners to come to Christ! So where are these examples in Scripture? We find none. Not one! Why did the apostle not take his own medicine? Why did he not make use of this sovereign way of bringing sinners to the Saviour? If, that is, this passage teaches what is claimed for it! Yet he, with the other apostles, saw many Gentile sinners converted to Christ – without first preaching the law to them. Why, Paul told us his method was the very opposite of the idea. He explained how, when wanting to 'win' 'those who are without law', he himself went 'without law' (1 Cor. 9:21). How anybody can argue that the right way to preach the gospel to Gentiles is to begin with the law, when Paul expressly says that he set his face against such practice, baffles me. And certainly his sermons to Gentiles, as documented in Acts 14:15-18; 17:22-32, lend no support whatever to the claim that he preached the law. On the contrary, they amplify and more than justify what he said about his guiding principles (1 Cor. 9:21). As I say, in chapter 4, I fully developed this point.

But let me take time to give one further biblical case to prove that preparationism by the law is wrong. Moreover, it is the obvious case, since it is Paul's choice in Galatians 3:10-25. And what a case! I refer, of course, to Abraham, the pivotal figure in the human race as far as the history of redemption is concerned.[40] Nor must the contextual significance (the Judaisers' attack) be missed: to make his point about conversion, Paul went back, not to Moses, but to Abraham. When we first meet Abraham in Scripture, he is an unbeliever, a pagan, uncircumcised (Rom. 4:1-25), a spiritually-dead sinner without God (Rom. 5:12-14). Yet, in this very state, he is confronted with God's command to quit his homeland (Gen. 12:1-3), which he obeys (Gen. 12:4), receives the promise of God (Gal. 3:16-18), and was later justified by faith (Rom. 4:1-24), and all this without any personal experience of conviction by the law to bring him to Christ. How could he have had a law work? The law was not given for another 430 years (Gal. 3:17)! Even so, he is the prime example in Scripture of

---

[40] Note how Paul uses him again in Rom. 4:9-16 to show that justification is not by circumcision in particular, or by law in general.

believing in Christ for justification (Rom. 4:1-25; Gal. 3:6-29). And this without the law![41]

The tragedy of misunderstanding and misapplying Galatians 3:10-25 is far wider than this question of preparationism, however – though that is serious enough, in all conscience. The Galatian passage is vital for understanding the place and purpose of the law in salvation history. Failure to see *this* point is tragic beyond words. *We must not miss the big picture!* Paul was speaking about the two great epochs – law and grace, law and gospel, before Christ and after Christ.[42] The apostle in this passage most definitely was not concerned with an individual's experience of conviction of sin and subsequent conversion. No! While the individual's experience is, of course, of the utmost importance (to the individual, as it was to Paul – see Galatians 5), the apostle here was speaking of something on a much vaster scale; namely, the historical aspect of the law in the history of salvation. Paul was referring to the law's reign over the Jews in the age before Christ came. The apostle said that the law 'was added because of transgressions, till the Seed should come' (Gal. 3:19). When the Seed came, the law's work was over. That is what Paul said. That is what he meant. To say that the law must be preached before the gospel in order to convict sinners and bring them to Christ is to miss the point and to minimise Galatians 3. As I said when looking at Calvin's uses of the law, Paul was speaking of the historical role of the law, and its temporary nature – 'it was added because of transgressions, till the Seed should come to whom the promise was made' – not of its supposed role in restraining sin in the unregenerate. The idea that the law exists today to do something which was ended nearly 2000 years ago by the coming of the Christ, is remarkable, to say the least. Coming from the other direction, if the law *was* given to bring sinners to Christ, why was it limited to the time that the Seed should come? Surely Calvin, and those who follow him, argue that the law does that work *nowadays*, do they not? Consequently, the notion that Galatians 3:24 justifies the preaching of the law to prepare sinners for Christ is quite wrong. And it is just as wrong to preach the law to believers to sanctify them.

The passage above all is historical in both its meaning and context. It is eschatological. It explains the two great systems of God's dealings with men; namely, through Moses or Christ, by law or by grace (John 1:17). In particular, it sets out the passing of the old age, and Christ's bringing in of 'the time of the new order' (Heb. 9:10, NIV). The historical nature of the Galatian passage must be emphasised. It is absolutely paramount. It cannot be overstated. It certainly can be understated. Worse, it can be ignored. Worst of all, the passage can be warped to make it teach that which Paul never did.

And this of course brings us back to the main issue; namely, Calvin's third use of the law for sanctification. A right understanding of Galatians 3, I say, utterly destroys the idea. How? As I have already noted, even on the Reformer's (mistaken)

---

[41] If, in reply, it is pointed out that Christ did not come into Abraham's conviction of sin, may I ask: But we all believe in progressive revelation, do we not, and therefore we expect clearer light than in Abraham's day, do we not? In any case, my point stands – Abraham was convicted without the law. And he did see Christ! As Christ said: 'Abraham rejoiced to see my day, and he saw it and was glad' (John 8:56). As Paul put it: 'The Scripture... preached the gospel to Abraham beforehand' (Gal. 3:8). Where does it say that it preached the law to him?

[42] BC and AD are not mere convenient calendar divisions invented by men. This, of course, is being whittled away by the use of BCE and CE.

understanding of Galatians 3:24-25, once the sinner has come to Christ, he is no longer under the law. But of course, the idea that Paul was talking about the believer's individual experience is a bad mistake, falling far short of what the apostle really was thinking of. I say it again: *Do not miss the big picture!* The passage teaches there have been two great ages in the history of the world; the age of the law and the age of grace. The age of the law was temporary; it is over now that Christ has come. How then, can the law be the means and the motive for the believer's sanctification? The believer belongs to a totally different age. Grace, not law, is the age in which the believer lives. Grace, not law, must be the means and motive for his sanctification.

What is more, the fact that God gave Abraham and Moses two separate, distinct covenants is utterly basic to Paul's doctrine in Galatians 3:10-25, God having, long before Moses, established his covenant with Abraham – indeed, 430 years before the law (Gal. 3:17). The Judaisers wanted to meld the two covenants into one. Paul would have none if it! The two covenants, he argued, are distinct and contrasting. Being so obvious, it is staggering that anyone should question it. But they do.[43] The spiritual aspect of Abraham's covenant is nothing less than the new covenant. The Mosaic covenant is the law. That these two covenants in question are utterly different is likewise fundamental to understanding the Bible, which takes it for granted, no less. To say otherwise is to make nonsense of Paul's teaching. In the one covenant, God declared to Abraham and to all his spiritual seed what *he* – God – would do; it was God's promise, the covenant of promise (Gen. 15:17-18; Gal. 3:16-17; Heb. 8:6-13; 10:15-17). In the other covenant, God commanded the people through Moses as to what *they* must do: 'You shall... keep my statutes and my judgements, which if a man does, he shall live by them' (Lev. 18:5; Rom. 10:5; and many others), and it was verified by the consent of the people (Exod. 19:8; 24:7). The Abrahamic covenant in the new is unbreakable (Jer. 31:31-34), whereas the Mosaic covenant was conditional; sadly, it was broken (Jer. 31:32). The promise is of faith on the basis of grace; the law was of works, a question of earning and meriting (Rom. 4:1-8; 6:23; 11:6; Gal. 3:11-12,24-25; Eph. 2:8-9). The promise brings blessing; the law brought a curse (Gal. 3:10-14); and so on. Now these are large differences. Differences? *Contrast is the word!* The two are mutually exclusive: 'For if the inheritance is of the law, it is no longer of promise' (Gal. 3:18). 'If those of the law are heirs, faith is made void and the promise made of no effect' (Rom. 4:14). 'You have became estranged from Christ, you who attempt to be justified by law; you have fallen from grace' (Gal. 5:4). 'If by grace, then it is no longer of works; otherwise grace is no longer grace' (Rom. 11:6).[44] How, as many claim, the Mosaic covenant can be thought to be one and the same as the Abrahamic covenant, or that it is 'a fresh administration of the covenant of grace', defies common sense. Worse, it defies Scripture.

As I have already observed, very often we can test our understanding of Paul by looking at the questions he raises after making his staggering assertions. Paul frequently raised objections to his doctrine – we shall meet it again – and here is a case in point. I draw your attention, reader, in particular, to Paul's use of the word 'then': 'What purpose *then* does the law serve?... Is the law *then* against the promises of God?'

---

[43] See chapter 6.

[44] Pointing out the obvious – that in Gal. 5:4 Paul was speaking about justification – cuts no ice. The point I am making at this stage is irrefutable – law and grace are contrasted.

(Gal. 3:19,21). In other words, Paul said, in light of my [Paul's] teaching – which, I admit, sounds so startling – how *then* does the law square with the promise? Now, reader, if the commonly-held Reformed view is right, and the law and the gospel comprise one covenant, if it is essential to preach the law to sinners before preaching the gospel, and if it is essential to take sinners, once converted, back to the law to sanctify them, Paul would never have asked such a (redundant) question as: 'What purpose then does the law serve?' 'Why the law then?' (NASB). Such a question could be raised only by someone who knows the two systems are very different, whose teaching has exposed the difference, and yet who needs to make sure his readers do not denigrate the law. No one who teaches the standard Reformed view needs to ask such a question. It simply does not arise. Nor would his hearers ever think of it. It would never cross their mind. Under his teaching, they are never exposed to thinking the law is different to grace, since he has taught them that the law and the gospel are virtually one and the same covenant. If a Reformed teacher did ask such a question, he would surely be shouted down, dismissed: 'As we all know – and, after all, as *you* taught us – the law serves to prepare the sinner for Christ, and to sanctify the saint. That's the law's purpose. You yourself told us! So why are you asking such a daft question?' Consequently, the fact that Paul raised this very question, using the word 'then', and yet did not give the 'standard' answer, proves he was no advocate of the Reformed first and third uses of the law. Far from it! The truth is, he had to explain how the law fitted in with the promise. The law, he said, was temporary, confining the Jews until Christ came. Thus it is the historical setting of Galatians 3:10-25 which must be grasped. It must not be lost in a welter of words about preaching the law to pagan sinners today. *Do not miss the big picture!*

In the apostle's question, the word 'serve' is not in the original. The original reads: 'Why then the law?' The 'serve' has been added by translators. Very well. But what tense should they have chosen? Is it: 'What purpose *did* the law serve?' Or: 'What purpose *does* the law *now* serve?' The context speaks of the past. This seems, to put it no stronger, to teach that the law has no ongoing function for the believer. But if Paul did ask: 'What purpose *does* the law *now* serve?', why ever did he not reply along the lines of Calvin's threefold use of the law? Why did the Spirit leave it for 1500 years until he made it known to the churches through the Reformer? This is not the same as saying men cannot discuss a problem before it arises – for instance, John Owen did not tackle 'being slain in the Spirit' – for Paul was dealing with the precise issue in hand at this very point. And he was inspired. So why did he not give the classic Reformed answer?

We may put it to the test. Ask any Reformed teacher to tell us the purpose of the law, and he will rattle off Calvin's threefold use. Now ask Paul! Well...?

We may go further. As I have emphasised, the era of the law was temporary.[45] It was only an interlude (but a God-ordained interlude, I hasten to add) in God's great plan for the ages. And God gave Moses the law with the intention that it should last

---

[45] The law of God is eternal; the law of Moses was temporary. I will return to this important distinction between the law of God and the law of Moses in chapter 16 pp222,227. It has nothing to do with Pink's distinction.

only until establishment of the new covenant by Christ (Gal. 3:16-19,24-25).[46] The entire law, not the law's 'mode of administration', was abolished by the coming of Christ.

As for the law of Moses being temporary, note the following: 'In that [God] says: "A new covenant", he has made the first obsolete. Now what is becoming obsolete and growing old is ready to vanish away' (Heb. 8:13; see also 2 Cor. 3:11,13). As for 'vanish away', the same root-word is used in: 'What is your life? It is even a vapour that appears for a little time and then vanishes away' (Jas. 4:14). This opens up an interesting parallel between the temporary nature of the law and the limited, temporary life-span of man: 'The days of our lives are seventy years' (Ps. 90:10). As soon as we are born, we begin to die. 'As for man, his days are like grass; as a flower of the field, so he flourishes. For the wind passes over it, and it is gone, and its place remembers it no more' (Ps. 103:15-16). 'Man is like a breath; his days are like a passing shadow' (Ps. 144:4; see Job 8:9-10; 14:1-2,5-6; Ps. 39:5-6,11-12; 78:39; 89:47; 90:5-6; 1 Pet. 1:24; *etc.*). Our days are 'numbered' (Job 14:5; Ps. 90:12). Similarly, the law of Moses came with a 'sell-by' date stamped on it; it was a temporary, passing shadow which, when its God-appointed task was done, at God's predestined time it would vanish away. And with the coming of Christ and his accomplishment of his Father's purpose, the law's work was over, completed and fulfilled. The age of the law had passed. In addition to this temporary aspect, there is also a parallel – a connection, indeed – between the *frailty* of man and the *weakness* of the law (Rom. 8:3), which 'weakness' we shall explore in the following chapter.

I have spent some time on this section of Galatians because its importance can scarcely be exaggerated. As I have said repeatedly, *do not miss the big picture!* I have laboured the point simply because many Reformed writers claim the two covenants (law and grace) are one and the same, and because they build so much upon it.[47] The fact is, the view we take of Galatians 3:19-20 will largely determine how we think of the believer and the law. Recall Paul's argument thus far. In dealing with the Judaisers, their claim that the covenants are one and the same, and their call for the believers to go under the law, he has drawn on the Galatians' experience. He has appealed to Scripture. He has called upon human reason in using an analogy from everyday life (Gal. 3:15) and applied it to God's dealings with men. He has explicitly set out the temporary nature of the law's reign. He has proved that the Galatians already have all they need spiritually – God's promise, the Christ, and the Spirit – and they have it without the law. How can they think of going to the law in face of the evidence he has produced? What purpose could it serve? The law's sun has set. But, it must be noticed, in light of this, Paul has to answer the question, if this really is the state of things, why then was the law given in the first place? And this is the very question Paul raises and answers! In truth, he has already answered it. The law was not given to believers in the age of the gospel. It was given to Jews before the coming of Christ. And those Jews had to live under the bondage of that law, even though it did not give them any power to meet its demands. But now that Christ has come, that age is over. The law has ceased. It has not ceased in

---

[46] I am not suggesting for a moment that God changed his mind, that his intention in giving the law was thwarted, or anything remotely like it. God always did intend to bring in the law, *but only as a temporary measure*.

[47] See chapter 6.

part or to certain ends. It has ceased. The law, the age of the law, is over. With the coming of Christ, salvation history has entered a new age, the age of the Spirit. Israel's pedagogue, the law, has gone; the Spirit has come. And it is the Holy Spirit, not the law as a pedagogue, who sanctifies the believer. The verb 'led' in Galatians 5:18 comes from the same word as 'pedagogue' – an example of Paul's love of word play.[48] The believer is 'pedagogued' by the Spirit, not the law, now that in the fullness of time Christ has come, and the Spirit has been given. The law's time is finished. Now is the age of the Spirit; now is the time for walking in and by the Spirit.[49]

To sum up Galatians 3:10-25: the law was given through Moses, it was given to Israel, it was given because of sin, it imprisoned and disciplined those under it, it was never intended to be permanent, but to last only until the coming of Christ. How can it be thought that a believer ought to go under the law? To make Gentile believers in the new covenant conform to the law of the old covenant, which was intended to discipline unregenerate Jews in the age before the coming of Christ, is nothing short of incredible.

May I say it just once more: the big picture here in Galatians 3 is of massive importance. *Do not miss it!* And, having seen it, do not forget it!

Galatians 4:12

Brethren, I urge you to become like me, for I became like you (NKJV).
Brethren, I beseech you, be as I am; for I am as you are (AV).
I plead with you, brothers, become like me, for I became like you (NIV).
I beg of you, brethren, become as I am, for I also have become as you are (NASB).

At first glance, this verse seems to have nothing to say on the believer and the law, but the fact is, in all these translations words have been added – words which may actually mislead the reader. Literally, the apostle said: 'Be as I, for I also as you, brothers, I beseech you'. Leaving aside, for the moment, the 'I beseech or urge or plead with you' – over which there is no question – did Paul say that he **had** *become* like the Galatians *were*? Or did he say that he had become like the Galatians *are*? Or did he say that he *is become* like they *were*? Or did he say that he is become like they *are*? And what, in any case, was he speaking about?

I would not be dogmatic. I merely offer the following as a suggestion (but it has the support of noteworthy commentators): 'I urge you to become like me, because I became like you'. In other words, in light of all that the apostle has set out in the letter thus far, he could be saying: 'I urge you to become like me' – that is, one who, being in Christ, lives as I should, dead to the law, since I died to the law (Gal. 2:19-20) – 'because I became like you' – that is, in order to reach you, to win you, I became like you, one who was in bondage (and who is now, by these Judaisers, in danger of being taken under the law). In short, we have the apostle urging the Galatians on the basis of his teaching of 1 Corinthians 9:19-23; Galatians 2:16,19-20; Titus 2:11 – 3:8 and the other passages which we are yet to consider. In effect, Paul was making his readers

---

[48] This will come up time and again. In addition to Gal. 3:24 with 5:18, see Rom. 8:2-4; 9:6; 1 Cor. 9:19-23; 11:3-16; Gal. 6:2,16, and so on.

[49] Once again, this is not to say the law has no place at all in the life of the believer. See chapter 17.

choose between him and Judaisers. 'They want you to go to the law, and live under the law. I don't! I urge you, I plead with you, stay with me!' And, of course, bearing in mind the theme of the letter, he must have had sanctification in his sights. In other words, the apostle was confronting his readers with a choice: 'Is it *going to the law* for sanctification, or is it *going to Christ by the Spirit* for sanctification? What is your position?' In so doing, the apostle was passionately repeating and enforcing all he had taught thus far – bringing the matter to a head, as it were, unashamedly personalising it for the Galatians, forcing them to the biting point, demanding their verdict, but letting them know, in no uncertain terms, what he was desperately longing for.

On the other hand, Paul may have been saying nothing at all about the law. Instead, he may well have been using a kind of proverb to urge the Galatians to love him as much as he loved them.

Although I would not press it, my view is that the former of these two is the more likely, and if so, it adds weight to Paul's argument in Galatians. But whatever the doubts about what Paul said in Galatians 4:12, there is no such question mark over the next section.

And what a section it is! Just before we get into it, may I repeat what I said about Galatians 3:10-25? In what follows, *do not miss the big picture!* This is where the apostle rolls his sleeves up, and, grappling with all his might, wrestles with both with the Judaisers and the Galatians. In so doing, he brings us face to face with one of the greatest of all themes of the new covenant: the believer's freedom in Christ. In arguing out this huge principle, Paul grabs hold of the Judaisers' claim that the promise and the law are one covenant, and shakes it to pieces. Above all, he comes to close quarters with the Galatians and their desire to go 'under the law'. Nobody at the time could be under any illusion as to what he thought about *that*. Nor can we today! Nothing, therefore, *nothing*, could be more relevant to the issue in hand.

Galatians 4:21 – 5:1

Tell me, you who desire to be under the law, do you not hear the law? For it is written that Abraham had two sons: the one by a bondwoman, the other by a freewoman. But he who was of the bondwoman was born according to the flesh, and he of the freewoman through promise, which things are symbolic. For these are the two covenants: the one from Mount Sinai which gives birth to bondage, which is Hagar – for this Hagar is Mount Sinai in Arabia, and corresponds to Jerusalem which now is, and is in bondage with her children – but the Jerusalem above is free, which is the mother of us all. For it is written: 'Rejoice, O barren, you who do not bear! Break forth and shout, you who are not in labour! For the desolate has many more children than she who has a husband'. Now we, brethren, as Isaac was, are children of promise. But, as he who was born according to the flesh then persecuted him who was born according to the Spirit, even so it is now. Nevertheless what does the Scripture say? 'Cast out the bondwoman and her son, for the son of the bondwoman shall not be heir with the son of the freewoman'. So then, brethren, we are not children of the bondwoman but of the free.

I have already looked at this allegory.[50] We are not dealing here with some minor matter. Rather, the apostle is talking about the two covenants which tower over the

---

[50] See chapter 6.

entire range of Scripture; namely, the Abrahamic covenant and the Mosaic covenant. As I have explained, the Abrahamic covenant comprised two parts or strands. The one that concerns us here – as it did Paul in Galatians (Gal. 3:6-29) – is that part of the Abrahamic covenant which came over into the new covenant.

Now for the apostle's teaching. And his teaching is crystal clear in light of the Judaisers' insistence that the two covenants are one. No, retorted the apostle. These two great covenants, the Mosaic (Hagar) and the new in the Abrahamic (Sarah), are chalk and cheese. Not only that. Believers are in the new covenant, and they must not allow themselves to be taken under the old covenant, the Mosaic covenant, the law. Why not? Paul immediately explained, thundering out these words:

For freedom Christ has made us free; stand fast therefore, and do not be entangled again with a yoke of bondage (Gal. 5:1, footnote).
It was for freedom that Christ set us free; therefore keep standing firm and do not be subject again to a yoke of slavery (NASB).

The opening note of Galatians 5 is vital. If grasped, the debate about the believer and the law is over. Freedom! Liberty! LIBERTY! Freedom, that glorious note of the gospel, the sinner's freedom as the result of justification, is Paul's triumphant cry, setting the tone for what follows. Note his abrupt, dogmatic statement: 'For freedom Christ has made us free'. Note the striking way Paul puts it, the emphatic order of his words: 'For freedom Christ has made us free'. Note the seeming tautology, 'for freedom... free', which so powerfully stresses the 'for freedom'. Modern editors, no doubt, would get Paul to tidy up his manuscript. But not the Holy Spirit! Oh, no! Why, it was the Spirit who chose such a terse way of speaking. The form of Paul's Greek, the very sound of his words, and their repetitive nature, reverberates, thumping home his point. By giving his readers (and hearers) a linguistic jolt as they move from Galatians 4:31 to 5:1 – with no chapter or verse divisions, of course – the apostle compels them to pause, draw breath, and ask what is going on. His words would have electrified the Galatian congregation as his letter was read aloud, the listeners sensing that something out of the ordinary – something of high significance – was being put before them. Paul astutely employs this 'outburst' to draw his readers' (and hearers') attention to the climax of his letter. He is forcing the Galatians to sit up, pin their ears back, take notice and think clearly about what they have in Christ, and what, therefore, is being fatally threatened by their desire to submit to the Judaisers' call for obedience to the law. Which is? Freedom! It is freedom which is paramount, and it is freedom which Paul stresses in this punchy, arresting way.

What is this freedom? It is as before – freedom from sin, death and the law; in particular, here, the law. The law, I stress. It is not freedom from the ceremonial law, or freedom from the curse of the law; it is freedom from the law. What is more, it is not merely freedom from the law for justification that the apostle speaks of. Certainly not! In Galatians 5 and 6, Paul is clearly speaking of the justification of the sinner, *and his consequent sanctification*. He is addressing *brethren*, not unbelievers, calling them to 'walk' worthy of God, and his main concern is to tell them that if they try to use the law as the way of sanctification it will inevitably lead to enslavement, bondage to rules, and will never produce the godliness desired. *This* is the theme of the entire letter; and Galatians 5:13-18 is surely its high-water mark. Yes, Paul deals with the danger of going to the law for justification (Gal. 5:2-12) – see below – but it is a grievous mistake to *limit* the believer's liberty, and the threat to it, to justification. Such a restriction indefensibly diminishes the letter to the Galatians. In any case, justification always leads to sanctification and is intimately bound up with it. No! Sanctification is the issue.

Let us remind ourselves of the apostle's rhetorical questions which came earlier in the letter: 'This only I want to learn from you: Did you receive the Spirit by the works of the law, or by the hearing of faith? Are you so foolish? Having begun in the Spirit, are you now being made perfect by the flesh?... He who supplies the Spirit to you... does he do it by the works of the law, or by the hearing of faith?' (Gal. 3:2-5). When the apostle asks: 'Are you now being made perfect?', what is he talking about? Justification? There is no 'being made' about justification! It is instantaneous. No! A man must be deliberately blind if he cannot see that Paul is addressing sanctification here. Moreover, what he is asking is this: 'Are you being sanctified by the law?' That, too, stands out as plain as noonday. Above all, his question is rhetorical, remember. He is not asking out of doubt, seeking instruction. Not at all! He is demanding a response. And the response he demands and expects is... what? Fill in the answer for yourself, reader. Are *you* being sanctified by the law? Are you *seeking* to be sanctified by the law? Do you think it is *possible* to be sanctified by the law? If the answer is: 'Yes', then remember what is at stake – your liberty in Christ. No, I didn't say it. Well, I did – but it was Paul the apostle who told you so, just he told the Galatians.

Having grasped his readers' attention (Gal. 5:1), Paul issues two sharp commands, two commands which follow as a direct consequence of his teaching. The *first*, positive: 'Therefore stand', or 'keep standing firm', virtually a military command putting backbone into unnerved soldiers. The *second*, negative: 'And do not be entangled again', or 'do not be subject again to a yoke of bondage' or 'slavery'. This dramatic verse therefore opens with freedom or liberty, and closes with the risk of the loss of that liberty; namely, slavery or bondage. Liberty, freedom *is* the idea, the crux. Without a doubt, as I said at the start of this chapter, liberty as opposed to bondage is a major leitmotiv throughout the letter (Gal. 2:3-5,11-14; 3:1-18,22-29; 4:1-9,21-31; 5:1,13). This is what the apostle is fighting for. This is why he is sparing no effort in his defence of the Galatians against the Judaisers. It is no academic nicety which concerns the apostle. Paul is wrestling for liberty as opposed to slavery – and that, not in the abstract. Paul is wrestling for the Galatians' liberty. He is wrestling for every believer's liberty; for my liberty and, Christian reader, for *your* liberty. Please keep this personal note in mind as you read on.

Liberty! Christ did not accomplish merely the *forgiveness* of sins for his people; his intention was to *liberate* his people, to *free* them from their sins that they might have *freedom*: 'If the Son makes you free, you shall be free indeed' (John 8:36). Freedom! Liberty! No more slavery! The end of bondage! Christ died to *redeem* his people. To redeem is to purchase, to buy back in order to deliver; especially, to pay a ransom for a slave to set him free from his captivity (Lev. 25:25-26; 27:20; Deut. 7:8; 9:26; and many other verses). Christ shed his blood to redeem his people (Acts 20:28; 1 Cor. 6:20; Gal. 3:13; 4:5; 1 Pet. 1:18-19; Rev. 5:9), to redeem them from the law (Rom. 6:14; 7:4,6; 8:2-4; 10:4; Gal. 3:13,24-25; 5:1,13-18), to redeem them from the enslaving fear of death (Heb. 2:14-15), to redeem them from sin (Tit. 2:14), from its condemnation (Rom. 8:1,33), dominion (Rom. 6:14) and, in eternity, its presence (Rom. 8:23; Heb. 9:12,15). It is a real redemption which Christ wrought. Christ really has freed his people (1 Pet. 2:16) from sin, death and hell. Here, freedom from the law. Believers are free (1 Cor. 7:22; 9:1; 10:29; 2 Cor. 3:17). Truly free! Actually free! Now!

Paul's emphasis on liberty in Galatians 5, as I have pointed out, comes hard on the heels of his allegory or metaphor of Hagar and Sarah (Gal. 4:21-31).[51] Hagar, the slave woman, corresponds to the law given on 'Sinai which gives birth to bondage' (Gal. 4:24). Here we have the sinner's problem – bondage! Problem, did I call it? Ask any slave if he has a 'problem'! Sarah, however, corresponds to the other 'covenant' (Gal. 4:22-24,26), the covenant of freedom, the new covenant. Here we have God's glorious answer for the sinner – freedom! Hagar speaks of the enslaved; Sarah speaks of the free. Do the two make one covenant? Can they be combined? 'What does the Scripture say?' 'Cast out the bondwoman'. And what is Paul's conclusion, his application? Believers 'are not children of the bondwoman but of the free'. Believers are not slaves – they are free. Sinai – the law – spelled bondage; Christ brought freedom. Believers are not children of the law, but children of grace. They must not go back to the law. They dare not go back to bondage. Paul paints the contrast in stark tones. In light of the Judaisers' calling them to go under the law, he presents the Galatians with an ultimatum. It is freedom or slavery.

And he uses the allegory to tell them what they must do: 'Cast out the bondwoman and her son'. He leaves them with no alternative. Paul is not telling them merely not to submit to the law, please note. Rather, they must get rid of every suggestion that they should submit to it. They must not listen to the Judaisers. On no account give them house room! As John, when he faced another set of false teachers, put it to his readers: 'Watch out that you do not lose what you have worked for, but that you may be rewarded fully. Anyone who runs ahead and does not continue in the teaching of Christ does not have God... If anyone comes to you and does not bring this teaching, do not take him into your house or welcome him. Anyone who welcomes him shares in his wicked work' (2 John 8-11, NIV). The Galatians must get their brain in gear, start thinking properly, thinking as new-covenant people, and give up this incredible 'desire to be under the law' (Gal. 4:21). Paul snaps out: 'Do you not hear the law?' Driving home his point, the apostle goes on to tell them some basic truths about the law – after all, the majority of the Galatians were almost certainly Gentiles, and, therefore, largely ignorant of its daily realities. And one thing we can be sure of! The Judaisers certainly wouldn't have told them! See 2 Corinthians 11:12-15. Indeed, the agitators would have acted much as the false teachers Peter wrote against – promising others liberty while they themselves were slaves (2 Pet. 2:19). Speaking of the Judaisers, Paul was adamant: 'For not even those who are circumcised keep the law, but they desire to have you circumcised that they may boast in your flesh' (Gal. 6:13).

So, as I say, Paul lets the Galatians have some home truths to think about, and he pulls no punches. In particular, he stresses that the law enslaves all who are under it, while Christ, at such tremendous cost, has bought freedom for his people – not least,

---

[51] I have already noted how Paul uses the slavery metaphor in Rom. 6, in Gal. 3 (with the pedagogue), in addition to Gal. 4 (with Hagar). See above and chapter 6. Law and slavery are Siamese twins. It is important to note that the slavery of the old covenant, the law, is very different to the slavery of righteousness in the new covenant, which we will met in Romans. The difference is paralleled by the difference between the 'law' in the law of Moses and the law of Christ. I will explore this in chapter 16 p214.

freedom from the law! 'Liberty! Do you really want to put that in jeopardy? Circumcision is only the first step. Oh, I know that's all the Judaisers are calling for at the moment, but if you take that step, let me tell you where you will end up':

It is for freedom that Christ has set us free. Stand firm, then, and do not let yourselves be burdened again by a yoke of slavery. Mark my words! I, Paul, tell you that if you let yourselves be circumcised, Christ will be of no value to you at all. Again I declare to every man who lets himself be circumcised that he is obligated to obey the whole law (Gal. 5:1-3, NIV).

And that means slavery![52]

Furthermore, the apostle presses home the point by referring to the Galatians' own experience. 'Because you are the sons of God, you are free. Don't lose this', he passionately urges them, 'don't be enslaved all over again by going back under the law. You are not slaves. Give up this madness!' This is why he writes to them. This is why he utters his cry, his great cry: 'For freedom Christ has made us free', from which follows his directive: 'Stand fast therefore, and do not be entangled again with a yoke of bondage [slavery, NIV, NASB)]' (Gal. 5:1). Bondage is the very antithesis of the Christian's experience; do not go back to it! Would Christ have set his people free from the prison house (the law) to take them straight back into it? Christ's purpose in coming into the world and going to the cross was to set his people free (Isa. 42:7; 49:9; 61:1-2; Luke 1:74; 4:18).[53] How wrong, then, to fix the manacles of the law onto the saints – as is done when the law is made the rule of sanctification. Believers are free, free from the yoke of bondage – whether God's law, pagan principles or man-made regulations. And this includes what the Reformed call 'the moral law', the ten commandments. None of this will sanctify! And sanctification, do not forget, *is* Paul's concern. Keep in mind the rhetorical questions he posed in Galatians 3:2-5. Is sanctification by the law? Of course not!

The truth is, freedom from the bondage of the law is the very freedom for which Christ made us free. Liberty from the law! Freedom from *the law*, full stop! And this freedom is the release from subservience to the law (Gal. 3:13,22-25; 4:1-9,21-31). Christ has accomplished this through his death and by his resurrection, and by the work of his Spirit (Gal. 2:19-20; 3:2; 4:5-6; Rom. 7:4). Consequently, any dropping back into bondage is utterly out of the question. Or ought to be!

Reader, I hope I am getting through to you. I want you to feel the passion in Paul's words. I want you to get some sense of the depth of his emotion. Desperately anxious lest he should fail, tormented by the thought that the Galatians might be gullible enough to yield to the Judaisers and go under the law, the apostle beseeches them not to do it. 'Don't do it!' He pleads with every fibre of his being. As an advocate in court who, in his closing speech, takes his last chance to appeal for his client's life, his cry is

---

[52] From close observation, I can testify that once a person takes the bait, and gets hooked on the law, there is no limit to it.

[53] Charles Wesley: 'Come, thou long expected Jesus,/ Born to set thy people free;/ From our fears and sins release us,/ Let us find our rest in thee'. We could well add: 'From the law you have redeemed us'.

vehement, earnest and intense. If the Galatians allow themselves to be enslaved all over again, all will be lost. This is Paul's last throw. It is all or nothing![54]

Come to think of it, my illustration of the advocate fails miserably. The advocate is, quite rightly, a professional, disinterested. Not the apostle! He is 'in the pains of childbirth' (Gal. 4:19, NIV). In my mind's-eye, I can see him, tears coursing down his cheeks, his arms outstretched, his fervent words flowing apace.[55] This is how serious it is.

The believer is free from the law. If we do not grasp this fact, we shall never know the believer's rule of holiness. Believers must never allow their freedom to be whittled away. We have to assert it, maintaining it against any and every effort to draw us back into bondage. The Son has made the believer free, and the believer must jealously guard that most precious of commodities – freedom. By nature, we were in bondage; by grace, we now are free. Our duty is to 'stand fast in the liberty by which Christ has made us free'. The law is not the way, either of justification or sanctification. We must not yield an inch. 'Stand fast!'

For the believer's freedom is always exposed to attack – and on two fronts. It was so in apostolic days; it is today. Paul, showing the deepest pastoral concern for the Galatians, now moves on to deal with each of these attacks. Having made his opening basic statement and issued his general command (Gal. 5:1) – it is for freedom that Christ has made you free, and you must never let yourselves be entangled again – he immediately goes on to tackle and demolish these two particular threats to the believer's liberty.

First, in Galatians 5:2-12, he deals with the attack arising out of an attempted misuse of the law in justification. As above, and despite all I have said, I agree with the Reformed at this point, *but I do not **limit** the freedom to justification*. Infinitely more important, nor does Paul. This is precisely where the Reformed career off the rails.

Secondly, in Galatians 5:13ff he deals with the attack arising out of an attempted misuse of the law in sanctification. We are not justified by law; nor are we sanctified by law. It is this second point which is relevant to my book, and on which I will spend more time.

But just a word or two on the first attack.

Paul deals with the attack on justification (Gal. 5:2-12)
By becoming confused about justification, believers can lose the liberty Christ has accomplished for them, and to which he has called them (Gal. 5:1). Indeed, it is far worse than losing liberty: 'You have become estranged from Christ, you who attempt to be justified by law; you have fallen from grace' (Gal. 5:4). This is no storm in a teacup, no much ado about nothing! Of course, there is always a tendency for sinners to go to the law for justification. But it is also a danger for *believers* – to think in terms of

---

[54] See similar cases in Rom. 9:1-3; 10:1; 2 Cor. 11:1 – 12:11; Gal. 1:6-9; Phil. 3:2. Paul gave the Romans the same 'ultimatum' – live for God, in the Spirit, not in bondage to flesh, sin and law (Rom. 6:11-23; 7:4-6; 8:12-14). If you do the latter, 'you will die' (Rom. 8:6,13). Reaping follows sowing (Gal. 6:8). As Christ said: 'You will know them by their fruits' (Matt. 7:16).

[55] This is not at all fanciful. See him with the Ephesians (Acts 20:31); before Agrippa (Acts 26:1,29); at Philippi (Phil. 3:18). In this, he was following his God and Saviour (Matt. 23:37; Luke 19:41; Rom. 10:21).

the law for justification. They need constant reminding that their justification is all of grace. All of it! It is precisely *this* which Paul addresses in Galatians 5:2-12.

The truth is, if believers start to link justification and the law, they will lose their sense of 'no condemnation' (Rom. 8:1), lose their sense of assurance, and they will do so because they will begin to look to works, to the law and to their obedience for justification, instead of looking to Christ, only to Christ, and always to Christ. Satan tries to make them do it, false teachers want them to do it, and the flesh hankers after it. But it is utterly misguided, utterly wrong! For believers to allow themselves to be taken one step along that path is not only foolish; it is completely abhorrent. And there will be no end to it. Circumcision – a speck of yeast, it might be thought – will infect the whole loaf (Gal. 5:9). If the Galatians yield to the Judaisers, if they buy into their teaching, however small a step at first, they will end up 'estranged from Christ... fallen from grace' (Gal. 5:4).[56] Those Judaisers, those agitators...! The apostle could not express his feelings more bluntly, more starkly or more passionately as he cries out to the Galatians:

You were running a good race. Who cut in on you and kept you from obeying the truth? That kind of persuasion does not come from the one who calls you. 'A little yeast works through the whole batch of dough'. I am confident in the Lord that you will take no other view. The one who is throwing you into confusion will pay the penalty, whoever he may be... As for those agitators, I wish they would go the whole way and emasculate themselves! (Gal. 5:7-12, NIV).

Reader, by thinking about what he meant by 'emasculate themselves', and bearing in mind the consequences of it under the law (Lev. 21:20; 22:24; Deut. 23:1), you get some idea of the depth of Paul's emotion here. Stop! Enough of this! Let me call a spade a spade, and spell it out as the Good News Translation does: 'I wish that the people who are upsetting you would go all the way; let them go on and castrate themselves!' *That's* what the apostle said, fulminating against the Judaisers. His righteous anger knows no bounds. The agitators' ruination of the Galatians is staring him in the face. And he hates the very thought of it! Get rid of these law-mongers! Get rid of them!

So far, so good. But this is far from the only threat to the liberty of Galatians 5:1. As I have observed, Paul now goes on to deal with the other danger – the danger that believers will allow themselves to be taken to the law for sanctification.

Let me set the scene. All this talk of freedom – and it is Paul's talk, please remember – might it not easily spill over into licence? If the law is not the believer's rule, what is? *Now this is precisely the point Paul tackles in Galatians 5:13 – 6:10.* The law has

---

[56] I do not want to extend this book into a discussion of the perseverance of the saints. But this doctrine is not, as is so often made out, the same as 'eternal security' and 'once saved always saved'. The biblical doctrine is what it plainly states – the perseverance of the saints. Here, in Gal. 5, it is possible that Paul was addressing those who, though they had professed to be trusting Christ, were, in fact, relying on the law for justification. This is one possibility. On the other hand, the warning passages of Scripture are real. If men – whatever their profession – try to mix the principles of faith and works, grace and law, for justification, they cut themselves off from Christ. The fact is, Paul will not compromise on this principle. Nor should we. Justification is not by the law. I will return to the warning passages.

gone. Freedom in Christ by the Spirit has come. So said the apostle. Yes, but how will this work out in daily practice? How will the Spirit direct the believer? If Paul had not tackled this issue, but left it unresolved, he would have been highly irresponsible. Paul a master-teacher (1 Cor. 3:10)? He would be acting as a cavalier father might, utterly irresponsible in letting his infant wander into a gunpowder factory, having handed the child a lighted taper! There is no need to fear, however. Here we have the apostle's definitive response.

But it is just because the apostle did respond, just because he felt it necessary to explain, that we can be sure that we have truly grasped his meaning: the believer is not under the law for sanctification. If Paul had held the Reformed view, he would never have needed to pen this extended passage on the means and motive of sanctification. Never! This is not the first time I have drawn attention to this point. The fact that Paul needs to 'correct' these 'misunderstandings' is proof positive that he was teaching what I have argued. I cannot over-stress the significance of this. No book which tried to prove the believer is under the law for sanctification, or was written on that basis, would ever need to stress the necessity of good works! But Paul does! Nor is this the last of it! When looking at Romans, we shall see yet again how preaching the gospel properly leaves a man open to the (false) charge of antinomianism. It did the apostle! This simple fact – that the apostle had to correct any misunderstanding about good works – on its own, drives the clinching nail into the coffin of the Reformed view of the law and the believer. Nobody could accuse the Reformed of preaching antinomianism! And, if there was nothing else to say, that fact, by itself, is fatal for Calvin's third use of the law.

Now for the apostle's statement. And what a statement it is!

Galatians 5:13-18

For you, brethren, have been called to liberty; only do not use liberty as an opportunity for the flesh, but through love serve one another. For all the law is fulfilled in one word, even in this: 'You shall love your neighbour as yourself'...[57] I say then: Walk in the Spirit, and you shall not fulfil the lust of the flesh. For the flesh lusts against the Spirit [or spirit],[58] and the Spirit [or spirit] against the flesh; and these are contrary to one another, so that you do not do the things that you wish. But if you are led by the Spirit, you are not under the law.

Do not miss the obvious! Paul is clearly writing to believers – 'brethren', the 'called'. He is writing to them about their liberty in Christ. In particular, he is reasoning with them over the connection between their liberty and the Spirit, and the threat to their liberty by the law. And all is in connection with their sanctification. Finally, do not forget that 'the law' is the law.

As I have already indicated, in this passage Paul is working out his statement in Galatians 5:1. Having, in Galatians 5:2-12, dealt with the first of the two threats to the believer's liberty – going to the law for justification – at Galatians 5:13, Paul takes up the main theme once again, the theme he spelled out in Galatians 5:1, and moves to the

---

[57] See chapters 16 and 17.

[58] There is no way of knowing from the Greek whether it should be spirit or Spirit. The context must decide. I suggest that in Gal. 5:17 it should be spirit, and in Gal. 5:16,18,25 it should be Spirit. See below.

second threat I mentioned – that is, going to the law for sanctification: 'For freedom Christ has made us free; stand fast therefore, and do not be entangled again with a yoke of bondage... For you, brethren, have been called to liberty... Walk in the Spirit, and you shall not fulfil the lust of the flesh... If you are led by the Spirit, you are not under the law'.

Paul's response can be paraphrased thus: what is true for justification is equally true for sanctification. Speaking to believers, he says: 'You are not under the law; you are free'. And in saying this, Paul is making the point once again that to be 'under the law' is the very opposite of being a believer – 'under grace', being free, a child of God, 'led by the Spirit'. To be 'under the law' is to belong to the old age. To be 'under grace', 'not under the law', is to belong to the new age, the new age of grace and redemption, the age of the Spirit. The two states, the two ages, are once again shown to be mutually exclusive. Once again, the law is part of the believer's problem – not the solution.

Now there are two main ways in which these verses are misread. In the first place, some do not see that Paul was speaking about the law, the entire law. Instead, they think Paul was speaking about the curse of the law, especially the ceremonial law, or the law as a covenant – even though he did not say so! Really? It will not do to say Paul was thinking of the tripartite division of the law but 'did not spell it out'![59] Not spell out such a vital step in the argument? The suggestion could only be made by one whose case is desperate! If this is the best which can be offered in defence of Calvin's third use of the law, when confronted by Scripture, not much more need be said! In this way, reader, one of the most glorious of all New Testament statements (Gal. 5:13-18) is watered down, and watered down on the basis of an unbiblical division of the law. This is the first way these verses are misread.

Others, however, think Paul was still tackling the first threat to the believer's liberty; namely an attack upon justification. They claim Paul was still saying the believer is not under law for justification. But, reader, as I have shown over and over again, he was not! Justification leading to sanctification, and the fact that neither of them is by the law – *this* is Paul's theme in Galatians in general, and in Galatians 5:13-18, and on, in particular. 'Walk' (Gal. 5:16,25), 'do' (Gal. 5:17), 'led' (Gal. 5:18) and 'fruit' (Gal. 5:22) are words to do with sanctification, not justification.

In this passage, Paul is making a contrast. Precisely what contrast? Is he speaking, as he was in Galatians 3, of the two ages in the historical sense? Reader, you will recall that some misread Paul in Galatians 3. They think that there he was speaking of the personal experience of believers. But he was not. He was speaking of two historical ages – 'under the law' and 'under grace'; the time before Christ, and the time after Christ; the age of the law, and the age of grace. Here, however, he *is* speaking of the personal experience of believers, and *not* the two ages. Not surprisingly, some who go wrong at Galatians 3, also go wrong here. They think Paul was speaking individually in Galatians 3, and of the two ages in Galatians 5, when in fact he was doing the very opposite. There are indeed two great epochs – law and grace. *But this is not the point of Galatians 5.* It is Galatians 3 which deals with the epochs of law and grace in the history of the ages. Galatians 5:13-18 deals with the epochs of law and grace in the life of the individual believer.

---

[59] I am not making it up! Please see 'Extracts' p439.

Let us look at what Paul says to the individual in Galatians 5. There is always conflict[60] between the flesh and the spirit,[61] he says, and in the unregenerate the flesh will always win (Gal. 5:17). Oscar Wilde said he could resist anything but temptation, and his lifestyle certainly did nothing to contradict his quip! But for you, believer, although you are engaged in a conflict between your flesh and spirit (Gal. 5:16-17), you have the Spirit, and as you walk in the Spirit, the flesh will not defeat you (Gal. 5:16), it cannot defeat you, for 'if [since] you are led by the Spirit, you are not under the law' (Gal. 5:18). The apostle's 'if' does not indicate a doubt. Paul is stating a fact, he is making a case, and he means 'since' (see John 15:20; Rom. 5:10; 6:5; Col. 3:1; *etc.*). 'Since you are regenerate... you are not under the law'.

This is staggering! What is the apostle saying? Just this: in order to overcome the desires of the flesh, a man must be free from the law. In other words, far from the law being the means of sanctification, sanctification is only possible to one who is free from it. It is not merely that the law is *not* the means of sanctification. *Freedom from the law is the only means of sanctification.*[62] This, I repeat, is a staggering statement. And Paul makes it!

Let me remind you of what we learned from Galatians 2:19. In that verse, the apostle moved from justification into sanctification – 'that I might live to God'. What

---

[60] The conflict in Rom. 7:13-24 is not the same as in Gal. 5:16-25. The former is about defeat; the latter, victory. The Spirit is not even mentioned in Rom. 7:13-24, whereas Gal. 5 is emphatic on him and his work.

[61] Should it be 'spirit' or 'Spirit'? Gal. 5:17 has been subjected to much debate. I make the following (very) tentative suggestion: In Gal. 5:16 and 18 read 'Spirit'; the verses are true only of the regenerate. In Gal. 5:17 read 'spirit'; take the verse as a general statement true of all men; the flesh wars against the spirit. 'The spirit indeed is willing, but the flesh is weak' (Matt. 26:41; Mark 14:38); 'I delight in the law of God according to the inward man. But... the law... was weak through the flesh' (Rom. 7:22,23; 8:3); and perhaps some of the several other verses which are usually regarded as speaking of the conflict between the flesh and the Spirit. In the unregenerate, the flesh always wins (Eph. 2:3), its 'weakness' failing to carry out good intentions, and its 'strength' ensuring sin. This means that the 'for' in Gal. 5:17 must be translated as 'the fact is' or 'you see'. In other words, do not read Gal. 5:17 as proof of Gal. 5:16 but rather as an explanation of the need of it. 'Walk in the Spirit, and you shall not fulfil the lust of the flesh' *for the fact is* there is always a conflict with the flesh, and if you do not walk in the Spirit you will be defeated by it. This usage has scriptural warrant. The women came to Jesus' tomb. 'When they looked up, they saw that the stone had been rolled away – for it was very large' (Mark 16:4). This does not mean the stone was rolled away because it was very large; rather, the women had been concerned about the stone (Mark 16:3) and they had reason *for the fact is* it was very large. Again: Simon and Andrew were 'casting a net into the sea; for [the fact is, you see,] they were fishermen' (Matt. 4:18). See also Mark 2:15; 5:42; John 3:16; 4:8; Rom. 7:2; Heb. 3:4; *etc.* In short, I suggest Gal. 5:17 should be put in brackets, as Rom. 7:1; 1 Cor. 16:5; 2 Pet. 2:8. In other words: 'I say then: Walk in the Spirit, and you shall not fulfil the lust of the flesh. (For [the fact is] the flesh lusts against the spirit and the spirit against the flesh; and these are contrary to one another, so that you do not do the things that you wish). But if you are led by the Spirit, you are not under the law'. And, do not forget, the 'but' (*de*) could be 'moreover' or, perhaps, 'indeed'. This, as I say, is my (very) tentative suggestion. So: 'Walk in the Spirit, and you shall not fulfil the lust of the flesh'. Even though you will meet with conflict between the flesh and your spirit (do not forget the apostle's connection between 'flesh' and 'law'), nevertheless, '[moreover, indeed, the truth is,] if you are led by the Spirit, you are not under the law', and you will triumph (2 Cor. 2:14).

[62] As before, the law is part of the problem and not the solution.

is more, he categorically stated that he died to the law 'that' – in order that – 'I might live to God'. As I said at the time, *I cannot overstate the importance of this assertion*. Paul died to the law *in order that* he might live to God. In other words, he was asserting that the law neither justifies nor sanctifies, that the believer is not under the law, either for justification or sanctification. The truth is, he was making the point that to live to God a sinner must die to the law. In short, the law is part of the problem, not the solution! I am not saying a word against the law – the fault lies with the sinner, not the law. But the believer has to be dead to the law in order to live to God. So much for Galatians 2.

And, as I pointed out when looking at Galatians 3:23-25, here in Galatians 5:13-18, Paul, with his love of word play, brilliantly emphasises the point by his use of the verbal form of 'pedagogue' (Gal. 5:18). His readers (and hearers), confronted by his Greek, and not forgetting the earlier illustration, would now make the intended connection: believers are not being led by the law, they are not being 'pedagogued' by the law, but by the Spirit.[63] Because the age of the law is over for them, believers are free from the law (Rom. 6:11-22; 7:3-4; 8:2,21; Gal. 2:16-19; 3:23-25; 5:18). And, because they are free from the law, they can be sanctified.

In short, in Galatians 2, Galatians 3, and now in Galatians 5, the apostle has made the same point. Talk about repeating yourself! Praise God for the repetition, I say! Let me set out the apostle's teaching as succinctly as I can. Believers are not under the law. They must not go under the law. They can only be sanctified because they are not under the law. Because they are not under the law, they have the Spirit. This is how they are to be sanctified. This is how they will be sanctified. This is what Christ died for.

But what about the flesh? Of believers, it is said they 'all once conducted [themselves] in the lusts [gratifying the cravings, NIV] of [their] flesh' (Eph. 2:3). What else could they do? Since 'that which is born of the flesh is flesh' (John 3:6), such behaviour is perfectly natural – the very word! – and only to be expected. But what a glorious change has taken place! Believers have been 'born again... born of the Spirit' (John 3:3,8). Now 'that which is born of the Spirit is spirit' (John 3:6), and 'the Spirit of him who raised Jesus from the dead dwells in [the regenerate]' (Rom. 8:11). 'As many as are led by the Spirit of God, these are sons of God' (Rom. 8:14). Those who 'are led by the Spirit... are not under the law' (Gal. 5:18). 'Sin shall not have dominion over [them], for [they] are not under law but under grace' (Rom. 6:14). 'And those who are Christ's have crucified the flesh with its passions and desires' (Gal. 5:24).[64] These, it must be noted, are statements, not exhortations. They are facts which are true of believers, not duties to be done by them. To be led by the Spirit is to be free of the law, liberated from the reign of sin, and to have crucified the flesh.

Duties (and encouragements) follow, of course. In light of these facts, the facts he has just spelled out, Paul tells believers the breathtaking truth: 'Walk in the Spirit, and you shall not fulfil the lust of the flesh' (Gal. 5:16). 'Walk in the Spirit' is a command. 'And you shall not fulfil the lust of the flesh' is an assertion, a promise. But then comes the consequent exhortation: 'If [since] we live in the Spirit, let us also walk in the

---

[63] Hence 'the law of the Spirit of life in Christ Jesus' (Rom. 8:2), 'the law of Christ' (Gal. 6:2).

[64] See below for more on Gal. 5:24. It marks the transition between Paul's *statements about* believers and his *commands to* them.

Spirit' (Gal. 5:25). Not, please note, let us walk in the *law*, but let us 'walk in the Spirit' – let us 'follow the Spirit's lead, staying in line or step with the Spirit'.[65]

Here we reach the heart of the matter. Sanctification is not by Calvin's third use of the law. Quite the opposite. Calvin could not be more wrong. In order to live a sanctified life, a man has to be delivered from the law, be no longer under the law, but be under grace and walking in the Spirit. In Christ, a man can say: 'I can do all things through Christ who strengthens me', for he has Christ working within him both to will and to do of or for God's good pleasure (Phil. 2:12-13; 4:13).[66] In addressing the Galatians, Paul was writing against Judaisers who were trying to get believers under the law, teachers who were promising them vital power in their spiritual experience if only they would submit to the law, promising that their new life which had begun with the Spirit would be brought to maturity by conforming to the law, that the law was the only sure way of knowing how to live the Christian life, the only way to attain it. The apostle totally and categorically rejected the notion. This, he declared, is nothing other than walking in the flesh and not by the Spirit (Gal. 3:3). Have done with it, root and branch!

It is wrong to try to reduce 'the law' and 'the flesh' to 'Mosaic ceremonies'. The law in Galatians is the whole law. In any case, Mosaic ceremonies never did produce godliness of life! Not even for the Jews! It would be utterly redundant for Paul to tell *the Galatians* not to go under the ceremonies of the law for sanctification! The fact is, Paul did not *compare* 'walking in the Spirit' with being 'under the *ceremonies* of the law'. He *contrasted* 'walking in the Spirit' with being 'under *the law*'. These last two are mutually exclusive, not alternatives (Gal. 5:18). Galatians 5:25 does not say that to walk in the Spirit is to keep the law. The law is not even mentioned. In any case, walking in the Spirit and walking under the law are contrasted, even opposed to each other.

By the way, the Greek for 'under the law' (Gal. 4:4) is precisely the same as in Galatians 5:18. Christ was under the law (Gal. 4:4). The believer is not under the law (Gal. 5:18). And 'the law' is precisely the same. Whatever law Christ was under, the believer is not under. And that law is the law of Moses, all of it.

True, the law of Moses, as part of Scripture, plays a role in the life of the believer,[67] but even so, the New Testament says far, far more about the role played by the Spirit. The fact is, we are living in the age of the Spirit, under 'the law of the Spirit of life [which has] made [us] free from the law of sin and death' (Rom. 8:2). The Spirit not only brings freedom, but his regime is the norm, the pattern, the law, the rule of the new life. He creates, stimulates and rules the believer's new way of living.

And how beautifully balanced all this is. For their sanctification, for their victory in their conflict with the flesh, believers are commanded to walk in the Spirit. They have to do it. It is their duty. It is their responsibility. They have to exert themselves to walk in and by the Spirit, resolutely siding with the Spirit against the flesh. It does not 'just happen'. But neither is it just a human effort. The Spirit shows the way and gives the

---

[65] The 'life in the Spirit' is not the 'ideal life'. It is the believer's actual life.

[66] It will not do to say if we are *sufficiently* possessed of the Spirit, *and yield ourselves to his governance, then*, we no longer need to be under the law, but are free from it. Such glosses cast a long shadow – as I will demonstrate.

[67] As I said above, I will show it takes the role of a believer's paradigm, a part of 2 Tim. 3:16-17.

power. It has nothing to do with 'let go and let God', or any 'passive doctrine of sanctification'. Paul pithily encapsulates it: 'Work out your own salvation with fear and trembling; for it is God who works in you both to will and to do for his good pleasure' (Phil. 2:12-13). Paul's experience and testimony stands as an encouragement to every believer: 'By the grace of God I am what I am, and his grace to me was not without effect'. As for the apostle's work for Christ – and, as he said, he worked harder than all the rest – that could not be credited to him: 'Yet not I, but the grace of God that was with me'. That was what did it; 'the grace of God' was the effective power in his life (1 Cor. 15:10, NIV). The same goes for every believer. Every believer has a responsibility before God; every believer has God's grace to move and enable him to fulfil that responsibility. The law never could – it never can – fulfil this function.

And here, in Galatians, Paul expresses it eloquently when he not only speaks of believers having been 'crucified with Christ', those to whom 'the world has been crucified' (Gal. 2:20; 6:14, both perfect passive), but of their having 'crucified the flesh' (Gal. 5:24, aorist).[68] In the former, Paul emphasises what has happened to them in Christ. In the latter, he stresses their responsibility, participation and action. And, of course, the latter depends on the former. Only the power of Christ could defeat the flesh, but his work enables believers to overcome it.

It is too weak to say 'to walk in the Spirit' is the *best* way to overcome the flesh; it is the *only* way. And it is the *sure* way: 'Walk in the Spirit, and you shall *not* fulfil the lust of the flesh' (Gal. 5:16). The negative is doubled and therefore much strengthened: 'You will assuredly not fulfil the lust of the flesh'. To 'walk in the Spirit', and to be 'led by the Spirit', are virtually synonymous. Believers are under the influence of the Spirit, empowered by the Spirit, guided by the Spirit, and enabled to live their life by the grace of the Spirit.

How did Paul argue his case? By using the word 'walk', the apostle took a Jewish idiom, the language of the Old Testament (as in Ex. 16:4; Lev. 18:4; Jer. 44:23; Ezek. 5:6-7, for instance),[69] and transformed it into 'walk in the Spirit'. And once again, Paul made the choice stark. You can either go over to the Judaisers and live by the law, he said, always checking your life by endless reference to laws and statutes, in an underlying spirit of guilt and fear of punishment – a way doomed to failure – or by constantly referring (the verb is present continuous) to the Spirit. The latter is the right and only way. You began by the Spirit and not by the law, and since you began by the Spirit, you must go on by the Spirit (Gal. 3:2-3,5,14). In contrast to the unregenerate Jew, who was informed only by the external law (Rom. 2:18), you have a renewed and instructed mind (Rom. 12:1-2; Phil. 1:9-10), you have been given the Spirit (2 Cor. 3:3),[70] you have his law (that is, Christ's law, by his Spirit) in your heart (Jer. 31:33-

---

[68] I said I would return to this transition verse. It has its feet in both camps – the facts and the duties. Gal. 5:24, as I say, is in the aorist. It is something which happened in the past (conversion), and continues in the present. In other words, it is both a truth about believers, and a duty for believers to perform.

[69] Do not miss 'walk in the law' or its equivalent. In chapters 16, 17 and 18, we shall see further examples of the way the new covenant takes and uses old-covenant terms.

[70] 2 Cor. 3 does *not* say the Spirit liberates believers from a *false understanding* of the law – namely, that one is justified by keeping it – and this takes them from the *age* of the law into the age of Christ. Nor does the Spirit liberate believers *for* the law, but *from* it.

34; Heb. 8:8-13; 10:15-18), and you delight in it (Rom. 7:22),[71] you have his anointing which 'teaches you concerning all things' (1 John 2:27), and therefore you know God's will. See also Ephesians 3:14-21; Colossians 1:3-12.

This, of course, does not mean that the Spirit *directly* gives the believer all necessary guidance – else why would Paul and the other apostles have spelled out their doctrine and instructions in the Scriptures? As they did. In addition to the passage we are looking at, take one further example:

Brethren, we urge and exhort in the Lord Jesus that you should abound more and more, just as you received from us how you ought to walk and to please God; for you know what commandments we gave you through the Lord Jesus... Therefore he who rejects this does not reject man, but God, who has also given us his Holy Spirit. But concerning brotherly love, you have no need that I should write to you, for you yourselves are taught by God to love one another; and indeed you do so... But we urge you, brethren, that you increase more and more... (1 Thess. 4:1-12).

But the Spirit does more than instruct. Far more! He guides *and* empowers. He gives light *and* life. Above all, he gives life. And it is life in the Spirit, under the Spirit, by the Spirit, not life in and under the law, which is the way of sanctification for the believer. It is life in the Spirit, that life activated by the Spirit, and calibrated by the whole of the written word – the whole of it! – the word rightly nuanced in Christ, that will sanctify the believer – not Calvin's third use of the law.

And another thing! And it is a matter of immense importance. In saying all this, I am not for a moment remotely teaching sinless perfection. Not at all! Sanctification is a process which is never complete in this life. Furthermore, with increased sanctification comes a heightened sensitivity to sin, and a greater perception of one's failure in this regard. Then again, the Christian life is a pilgrimage; indeed, a spiritual warfare (2 Cor. 10:3-4). Conflict there will be (Gal. 5:17; Eph. 6:10-18; 1 Pet. 5:8-9), and skirmishes, even battles, may be – sadly, will be – lost. No! I am not teaching sinless perfection! But neither am I condoning failure! Nevertheless, in the spiritual warfare, ultimate victory is certain: 'Thanks be to God, who gives us the victory through our Lord Jesus Christ' (1 Cor. 15:57). Moreover, as we see here in Galatians, through his liberty from the law, in Christ the believer has glory and joy *now*. This is such an important point, of such relevance to this issue in hand, I must come back to it.[72] Sanctification by Calvin's whip and bridle, sanctification by the law's pricking stimulus to arouse the sluggish ass from his laziness, is patently at variance with the New Testament position of the believer. Calvin's system, a system of fear and guilt and punishment,[73] is utterly at variance with Paul's words to the Galatians – and the tenor of the New Testament in general – the dominant note of the believer's joy and liberty, here and now.[74] In fact,

---

[71] See chapters 17 and 18 for which law is written on the heart in the new covenant.

[72] In chapter 16 p266.

[73] It was Job's way, long before the gospel (Job 31:3,23).

[74] As I have explained, the Reformed are not averse to describing believers as having 'depraved hearts' and being a 'putrid organism'. Some believers seem to think that the pinnacle of spiritual attainment is to be for ever harping on about what miserable sinners we are. This, I feel sure, comes from a misunderstanding and wrong application of Rom. 7. While I fully acknowledge that every believer sins, as I read the New Testament I find a constant emphasis upon glory, triumph, joy, liberty and gladness in Christ. Take Peter. Yes, he certainly wrote about suffering, conflict and such like (1 Pet. 1:6-7,11; 2:12,19-23; 3:9,13-17; 4:1-5; 12-19; 5:1,7-9, just to take

going back to the law, Paul argued, leads to nothing other than a reduced spirituality, a cramped legality. Once again, the law is part of the problem, not the solution.

As we go on, reader, I will put before you many other passages of Scripture which show the true way of sanctification, and never is it by law. It is not based on fear and guilt. The motive and means of holiness are not found in a deterrent which God holds in front of the eyes of his people, or a whip smiting their back, or a goad pricking their side. Paul, *as an unbeliever*, kicked against the goads (Acts 9:5). Why would he advocate such a system for believers? Calvin might. Many contemporary Reformed teachers do. Paul did not! Since, as we have seen so clearly taught in the letter to the Galatians, one of the aims of Christ's coming into the world was to deliver those under the law, to redeem those under the law – to release them from the law – it must be wrong to impose the law upon believers. Wrong? It is tragic, and worse. I am not saying the law is sin, but I am asserting that to impose the law on new-covenant men and women is utterly contrary to the gospel. If anyone objects, let them try telling Paul about it – in light of Galatians 1:6-10; 2:11-21; 3:1-5; 4:8-20; 5:1-12.

The biblical motive and the means of sanctification are very different to this enslaving law-work based on fear. Believer, when you were regenerated, 'you did not receive the spirit of bondage again to fear' (Rom. 8:15), 'a spirit of slavery leading to fear again' (NASB).[75] Quite the opposite! 'Where the Spirit of the Lord is, there is liberty' (2 Cor. 3:17), 'for God has not given us a spirit of fear, but of power and of love and of a sound mind' (2 Tim. 1:7). 'Stand fast therefore in the liberty by which Christ has made us free, and do not be entangled again with a yoke of bondage' (Gal. 5:1).[76] The Spirit is given to a man to take him out of the slavish fear which marked his unregenerate state, never to return to it (Rom. 8:15). Reader, if you are a believer, do not allow yourself to be taken back into guilt-ridden bondage. Stand fast, therefore, in the liberty with which Christ has made you free. And if you are not a believer, look to Christ, and he will set you free.

Now all this raises a vital question. Christ has set his people free, free from the law, yes. But free to do what? There are great dangers – unless this teaching is biblically qualified and understood. True, the believer is free from slavery, but he is also responsible for his life. Liberty is not licence.[77] Christ has not liberated his people to give them a licence for carnal self-indulgence. Consequently, Paul has to make it very clear what kind of life the life in the Spirit is, and what the life in the flesh is. To avoid all misunderstanding, I remind you, reader, of the point I made above. A believer has the inward grace of the Spirit to teach him, but he also has the external word to rule him. It is not either/or, but both. It is light and life.

---

his first letter), but he also had plenty to say on glory, inexpressible joy, liberty and such like. My point is this: in this life, the believer meets trouble through sin, but he also triumphs in Christ. All I ask is, which of the two is the dominant note of the New Testament?

[75] Note the 'again'. Remember how the Reformed think that the sinner, on coming to Christ, is taken from under the law, and then immediately put back there *again*.

[76] In addition to what we have already seen, I will look at such passages in detail as we proceed.

[77] When I was at school, at the end of the winter term we were allowed a certain amount of freedom. But, as the headmaster constantly dinned into us: 'Liberty is not licence!' I'm not sure his repeated harangues made much difference. The poor man, you see, was working with law and not grace!

Paul, of course, answered all these points in the rest of the letter – and, copiously, elsewhere – spelling out the new-covenant position. I will postpone looking at this conclusion to the Galatians in detail, however, until I have examined the other passages of the New Testament which deal with the believer and the law. Then, in chapter 16, I will set out the believer's rule.

For now, let me précis the apostle's concluding words. First, the believer's freedom has a negative aspect – he is not free to give the flesh an opportunity (Gal. 5:13). This must not be minimised: 'Therefore, brethren, we are debtors [we have an obligation, NIV] – [but, NIV] not to the flesh, to live according to the flesh. For if you live according to the flesh you will die' (Rom. 8:12-13). As before, the warning passages of Scripture are real.

Having laid down this searching truth, Paul then thoroughly worked it out as he moved to the end of his letter to the Galatians. Above all, the believer has the Spirit, is led by the Spirit, and will and must produce the fruit of the Spirit. So declared the apostle. This must not be written off – as it is! – as wishy-washy, merely some kind of warm feeling. Far from it! There are solid marks and clear evidences of holiness (Gal. 5:16-26), evidences which can be verified. Paul, please note, used a stronger word for 'walk' in Galatians 5:25 than in Galatians 5:16, employing a word which has the idea of a row (an orderly line) or a rule. It describes a movement in a definite line, such as in a military formation or a dance, a choreography.[78] Nothing vague about this, even though it has been dismissed as such! In short, the believer will and must 'fulfil the law of Christ' (Gal. 6:2). As I say, I will work all this out in chapter 16.

But, reader, the fact that Paul had to answer the charge of lawlessness, rebut its danger, and devote an extended passage to it, proves yet again that he did indeed teach that the believer is free from the law. No such passage, no such warning, would be required in any book which argued the Reformed view of sanctification by the law. Yet Paul gave the same warning to the Corinthians (1 Cor. 8:9); Peter had to do the same thing (1 Pet. 2:16; 2 Pet. 2:19); Jude also (Jude 4,11,13). If the Reformed view had been right, the apostles would never have needed to do any such thing. There is no danger of lawlessness arising from teaching which states that the law is the believer's rule! It only arises when the gospel is taught with the freeness the New Testament warrants and demands. Indeed, the fact that such an accusation can be made, that such an accusation ought to be made, is the acid test for all preachers and teachers, and their doctrine. Let me personalise it: if nobody can accuse us of antinomianism, then we are not preaching the gospel as it ought to be preached – either to sinners for their justification, or to believers for their sanctification!

In closing this chapter, let me repeat the apostle's own way of finishing his letter to the Galatians. It is all here. Bear in mind that although circumcision was at the forefront of the Judaisers' call, Paul had made it abundantly clear to all concerned that it was the whole law which was at stake (Gal. 5:3). Having got that well and truly established, this is how he concluded:

---

[78] The NIV has 'keep in step with'. See also Acts 21:24, 'walk orderly', and Gal. 6:16, 'walk according to this rule'. The idea is going in order, walking in the steps of someone, following an example, directing one's life, being in line with, standing beside, holding to, agreeing with, following. In particular, on Gal. 5:25, 'if or since the Holy Spirit animates us... let us exhibit that control of the Spirit in our life'.

As many as desire to make a good showing in the flesh, these would compel you to be circumcised, only that they may not suffer persecution for the cross of Christ. For not even those who are circumcised keep the law, but they desire to have you circumcised that they may boast in your flesh. But God forbid that I should boast except in the cross of our Lord Jesus Christ, by whom the world has been crucified to me, and I to the world. For in Christ Jesus, neither circumcision nor uncircumcision avails anything, but a new creation. And as many as walk according to this rule, peace and mercy be upon them, and upon the Israel of God. From now on let no one trouble me, for I bear in my body the marks of the Lord Jesus. Brethren, the grace of our Lord Jesus Christ be with your spirit. Amen (Gal. 6:12-18).

Here is the choice. We go the law or to the cross. It cannot be both. So which is it? For Paul, there is no doubt: 'The cross of Christ... the cross of our Lord Jesus Christ... the grace of our Lord Jesus Christ'. Let us ask the apostle: 'How can I be justified? How can I be set free? How can I be sanctified?' His answer is always the same: 'The cross of Christ... the cross of our Lord Jesus Christ... the grace of our Lord Jesus Christ'. And how did he close his letter? Was it: 'The grace of our Lord Jesus Christ be with your spirit, first having gone to Moses to be prepared for Christ, and then taken back to Moses to whip you into sanctification'? No! As he told the Thessalonians, Paul had only one way of closing all his letters: 'The salutation of Paul with my own hand, which is a sign in every letter; so I write. The grace of our Lord Jesus Christ be with you all. Amen' (2 Thess. 3:17-18).

Chapter 10

Romans

If Galatians is the benchmark of Paul's teaching on the law, then Romans 6, 7 and 8[1] is where the apostle sets out his clearest and most extended biblical exposition of the believer's relationship to it.[2] The apostle's extended argument in this passage grew out of his amazing declaration in Romans 5:20, to which I have already referred. Having made such a momentous statement, Paul had to write the next two chapters, and more, to deal with certain objections to what he had said. All chapter (and verse) divisions, it is important to remember, are man-made impositions on Scripture. We are looking at one continuous discourse. In pursuing this argument on the believer and the law, and in order to clarify and drive home his doctrine, Paul first sets out the fundamentals (Rom. 6:1-11), then uses two illustrations – slavery (Rom. 6:12-23)[3] and marriage (Rom. 7:1-6) – following up with plain and categorical statements (Rom. 8). Before looking at this, a reminder of the astonishing declaration which started it all: Romans 5:20.

Romans 5:20

The law entered that the offence might abound. But where sin abounded, grace abounded much more.

Here we have two massive assertions:

> The law entered that the offence might abound.

> Where sin abounded, grace abounded much more.

These two assertions are joined, or contrasted, by the all-important 'but'. Let us examine these two statements in turn.

Take the first. What are the implications of 'the law entered that the offence might abound' (Rom. 5:20)?

First, as we have seen in Galatians, the law entered, entered human history; that is, God intervened in the history of the world to give the law to Israel. And the law is the Mosaic law; that is, God's law. It is not Jewish misunderstanding of the law, the law as a covenant, legalism, the law shorn of its curse, the ceremonial law, or the law as a means of justification. Paul is speaking about the whole law in Romans 5, 6 and (at least) the early part of 7.

Secondly, God gave the law to the Jews so that they would become even more conscious of sin – 'the law entered that the offence might abound'. Before this, of course, sin was in the world (Rom. 5:13), but after the giving of the law, sin was multiplied – in the sense that from now on the Jews had much clearer light and,

---

[1] In addition to looking at these three chapters, I will also glance at Rom. 10.
[2] The extracts for this chapter begin on p448.
[3] As I noted in the previous chapter, Paul uses the slavery metaphor in Rom. 6, in Gal. 3 (with the pedagogue), and Gal. 4 (with Hagar).

consequently, far less excuse (John 9:39-41; 15:22,24; Rom. 4:15). Indeed, following the giving of the law, they had no excuse at all for their sin (Rom. 3:19). More than that, the law turned their sin into transgression (Rom. 4:15; 5:13). The law, let it never be forgotten, was made for and given to sinners (1 Tim. 1:9). That is to say, the Jews were sinners before receiving the law – the law turned them into transgressors.[4] This underlies Paul's argument in Romans 5:12-14. All men from Adam to Moses were sinners, and therefore guilty, under God's wrath, and died, but if they had not broken an express commandment, strictly speaking they had not transgressed. Every transgression is a sin, but not every sin is a transgression. See my note on Galatians 3:19. In light of the accumulated weight of these passages, along with the fact that the law was added through Moses 430 years after the promise to Abraham (Rom. 5:20; Gal. 3:16-17,19), how can any Reformed teacher claim that Adam (before the fall) received the law?

Thirdly, because of the weakness of the flesh, the law incited rebellion against itself, incited transgression – 'the law entered that the offence might abound': 'When we were in the flesh, the sinful passions... were aroused by the law... Sin, taking opportunity by the commandment, produced in me all manner of evil desire. For apart from the law sin was dead... but when the commandment came, sin revived... Sin, taking occasion by the commandment, deceived me, and by it killed me... Sin, that it might appear sin, was producing death in me through what is good [that is, the law], so that sin through the commandment might become exceedingly sinful' (Rom. 7:5-13).

And *fourthly*, following the above, the sum total of sin in the world was much greater after the entrance of the law than before. Note what Paul said: 'The law entered *that, in order that, so that,* the offence might abound'; God gave the law with this purpose.

In other words, once again, the law is a part of the sinner's problem, and not the solution.

So much for the apostle's first assertion in Romans 5:20.

The second is truly astounding: 'The law entered that the offence might abound. But where sin abounded, grace abounded much more'. God, through Moses, gave the law to make sin's offence abound, but grace came through Jesus Christ (John 1:17), so that where sin abounded God might make his grace abound *much more*. Note how, as we have seen before, Paul piles on the hyperbole – 'abound much more'.

Above all, of course, it is the implications of the 'but' in Romans 5:20 which are so far-reaching. How much hangs on such a short word!

Romans 5:20 raises questions. It even raises eyebrows in some quarters. Clearly this is the climax of Paul's doctrine of justification. As he has proved, justification is not by the law. Far from it. It is by grace (Rom. 3:20 – 5:21). But once a person is justified... what then? Where is the law now? The law cannot justify. Can it sanctify? That is the question. I have already spoken of the unbreakable connection between justification and sanctification. In what he goes on to say following Romans 5:20, the apostle works out the doctrine of practical godliness and fruit-bearing for those who are justified; that

---

[4] Christ, of course, was unique. Though he was a Jew 'born under the law' (Gal. 4:4), the law did not make him a transgressor. There was no sin in him at all (2 Cor. 5:21; Heb. 4:15; 7:26-27).

is, sanctification. He has to – after speaking so unguardedly about salvation being by grace, and not by the law. 'Where sin abounded, grace abounded much more' (Rom. 5:20).

'Where sin abounded, grace abounded much more'! 'That's all very well', says an objector to the apostle's doctrine, 'but surely such teaching spells the end of the law, and inevitably leads to antinomianism, does it not? Have you thought this out, Paul? Haven't you been irresponsible, to say the least? Think, man! What safeguards will your teaching raise against sin? What bulwark against antinomianism? How will it produce holiness? Can a believer do what he wants, how he wants, when he wants, live careless of questions of sin and godliness, even saying sin is godliness? Surely you will need to spell out very clearly – and do it now! – that the believer is under the law for sanctification. If you do not, antinomianism must be the result': 'What shall we say then? Shall we continue in sin that grace may abound?' (Rom. 6:1).

Paul has one dismissive, short reply to all such talk: 'Certainly not!' (Rom. 6:2). Perish the thought! It is utterly unthinkable. But notice, reader, what Paul does not say. It is his silence which is so important here, so telling. *He does not say that the believer is under the law, after all!* Certainly not! In fact, as we shall see, it is the believer's very freedom from the law of Moses which leads to his deliverance from the dominion of sin, and produces a godly life!

Even so, *these* are the sort of questions which Paul's doctrine *must* provoke; that is, if this is what Paul was saying. Do we find such questions? We certainly do! A glance through Romans 6 and 7 will prove it. We know, therefore, we are drawing the right conclusions from Romans 5:20, because it is precisely these sort of objections and questions which led to Paul's response in Romans 6 and 7.

One thing we must be clear about, *and must not forget*: as we enter Romans 6 and 7 we find Paul speaking about the fruit and effect of justification. *He is not telling his readers – believers – how to be justified.* The apostle, having fully explained the way of justification (Rom. 3:20 – 5:21), immediately goes on to the *consequences* of it (Rom. 6:1). Dealing with freedom from the *power* of sin, not merely its penalty, he speaks of the end of sin's rule, the end of its dominion (Rom. 6:14), not merely of its forgiveness or pardon. No longer talking about the *sinner* and the law, he now deals with the *saint* and the law. I am not saying the apostle has altogether finished with justification – of course not – but having no need to explain again *how* a sinner is justified, he now moves on to tackle *the effects and consequences of justification* for someone who *is already* justified. How does a believer avoid sin? More, how does he cultivate holiness? This is what Paul is concerned with in these chapters. So whatever Romans 6 and 7 say about sin or law, and the relationship believers have with either or both, these chapters say it to those who have been justified, and say it for their sanctification. In other words, he is dealing with the precise issue that my book is all about. Here we have the definitive answer to the relationship of the believer, the law and sanctification.

This is to state the obvious. After all, as Paul explained, he was writing to people who have 'been set free from sin' and become 'slaves of righteousness', and writing to tell them to submit themselves 'as slaves of righteousness for holiness' (sanctification, NASB, including margin) (Rom. 6:18-19). To this end, he could speak of the *former* way of life of his readers – their pre-conversion, pre-justification days – 'when you were slaves of sin', and so on (Rom. 6:20), immediately following this up with the momentous contrast: 'But now having been set free from sin, and having become slaves of God, you have your fruit to holiness' (resulting in sanctification, NASB) (Rom. 6:22). '*But now*'! As I keep saying, this 'but now' is vital. It (or, in the context, 'now') comes again and again in Romans – indeed, throughout the New Testament (Rom. 3:21; 5:9,11; 6:22; 7:6; 8:1; 11:30; 11:31 (second 'now' in NIV, NASB); 16:26; see also John 15:22,24; Acts 17:30; 1 Cor. 15:20; Gal. 4:9; Eph. 2:12-13; 5:8; Col. 1:26; Heb. 8:6; 9:26; 12:26; 1 Pet. 2:10). Although I address the individual aspect of these chapters – the 'but now' for the individual believer – it is the *eschatological* 'but now' which is at the root of the apostle's argument. Paul speaks of the age from Adam to Moses – before the law; then the age of Moses – the reign of the law; and then the age of Christ by his Spirit – after the law, the reign of grace. Once again, it is this towering view of salvation history, and, in particular, the contrast between the age of the law, and the age after the law, which is vital. Paul is here clearly contrasting the realms of law and grace, the realms of the old age and the new, both in history *and* in the believer's personal experience. Above all, here, the latter – but securely based on the former. Without the historical, eschatological 'but now', there would be no personal 'but now'.

'But now'. How frequently does it come up! 'Something far-reaching has happened to you', the apostle declared. 'You have been converted, you have been justified. And something follows this justification, as sure as night follows day. You are new creatures, living in a new realm, producing new works'. *Sanctification*, progressive growth in grace, is the theme.

Why do I stress this so strongly, even though it is obvious? Because so many will persist in trying to avoid the conclusions of Romans 6, 7 and 8 by talking about justification. In so doing, they grievously miss the point. I apologise, reader, for labouring it, but the consequences of getting this wrong are tragic. In these chapters, and there is no question of it, Paul develops the doctrine of sanctification.

Before we get to grips with the detail of the actual teaching, let me say just a little more on that large and important negative I raised a moment ago. Think about what we do *not* read in Romans 6. Paul does not make the obvious rejoinder if one wants to promulgate Calvin's use of the law. Paul's answer – Romans 6 and 7 – to the objections prompted by Romans 5:20, *ought* to have been, according to the Reformed system, along these lines:

Please understand that when I say 'law' in Romans 6, when I say the saint is no longer under the law, I don't mean *law*; what I mean is the *ceremonial* law. The believer *is* still under the *moral* law as a perfect rule of righteousness. You objectors misunderstand me when I say the believer is not under law. He is, after all, still under the law – not for justification, of course, but for sanctification. If you grasp this, it will put a stop to all talk about lawlessness, all talk of antinomianism. In short, believer, you must realise that you *are* under the law – not as a covenant, of course – but as a perfect rule of life. You *are* under the law for sanctification. Nevertheless, you may rest assured, that though you inevitably fail, the law cannot condemn you, even though you are under the law for sanctification. In any case, God will accept a good try.

Paul says nothing of the sort. Nothing of the sort! The truth is, as we shall see, he says the very opposite. Let me repeat that. *He says the very opposite.* He says the believer is no longer under the law (Rom. 6:14), since he has died to it (Rom. 7:4). And it is the sinner's death to the law which enables him to be sanctified. In fact, the apostle declares that, until a man has died to the law, he never can be sanctified.

In other words, Calvin's third use of the law could not be more wrong. Rather than the believer having to go under the law for sanctification, he has to be dead to it in order to be sanctified.

Romans 6:1-23

What shall we say then? Shall we continue in sin that grace may abound? Certainly not! How shall we who died to sin live any longer in it? Or do you not know that as many of us as were baptised into Christ Jesus were baptised into his death? Therefore we were buried with him through baptism into death, that just as Christ was raised from the dead by the glory of the Father, even so we also should walk in newness of life. For if we have been united together in the likeness of his death, certainly we also shall be in the likeness of his resurrection, knowing this, that our old man was crucified with him, that the body of sin might be done away with, that we should no longer be slaves of sin. For he who has died has been freed from sin... Therefore do not let sin reign in your mortal body, that you should obey it in its lusts. And do not present your members as instruments of unrighteousness to sin, but present yourselves to God as being alive from the dead, and your members as instruments of righteousness to God. For sin shall not have dominion over you, for you are not under law but under grace. What then? Shall we sin because we are not under law but under grace? Certainly not! Do you not know that to whom you present yourselves slaves to obey, you are that one's slaves whom you obey...? But God be thanked that though you were slaves of sin, yet you obeyed from the heart that form of doctrine to which you were delivered. And having been set free from sin, you became slaves of righteousness... Just as you presented your members as slaves of uncleanness, and of lawlessness leading to more lawlessness, so now[5] present your members as slaves of righteousness for holiness. For when you were slaves of sin, you were free in regard to righteousness... But now[6] having been set free from sin, and having become slaves of God, you have your fruit to holiness, and the end, everlasting life. For the wages of sin is death, but the gift of God is eternal life in Christ Jesus our Lord.

A sinner is justified by faith in Christ (Rom. 1:16 – 5:21). This faith unites him to Christ. Christ died, the believer died with him. Christ was raised, the believer is raised with him (Rom. 6:1-11). Christ ascended and sits in glory; the saint is seated with him (Eph. 1:20; 2:6). The believer is free of the slavery of sin (Rom. 6:6-7,11). He must not be stupid, go back to his former way of life and allow sin to dominate him again (Rom. 6:11-13; Eph. 4:17-24; 1 Pet. 1:14-15; 4:1-4). Imagine a liberated slave fixing the manacles back on his wrist! Imagine a believer submitting to his old bondage to sin! Indeed, he will not, he cannot, 'for sin shall not have dominion over you, for you are not under law but under grace' (Rom. 6:14).

'Just a minute! Think of the consequences of what you are saying! What kind of life will *that* doctrine produce?'

Well, for a start, *that* doctrine is not *my* doctrine – it is Paul's! And he has already answered the objection. The believer cannot go back to the old slavery, and sin. He dare not, it is unthinkable: 'What then? Shall we sin because we are not under law but under grace? Certainly not!' (Rom. 6:15). So thunders the apostle. Before his

---

[5] Note the 'now'.
[6] Note the 'but now'.

conversion, the believer was a slave of sin, but now he is not; he is a slave of righteousness (Rom. 6:17-18). In his former slavery to sin he produced sin and death (Rom. 6:19-21). Now, being the slave of God, the slave of righteousness, he produces holiness (Rom. 6:22-23).

It should be obvious by now that I am not preaching sinless perfection. I do not say that a believer cannot sin. Of course not! But there is all the difference between 'sinning', and 'living in' or 'being a slave' to sin; between 'being in the flesh', and 'the flesh being in you'; between 'a sense of desertion', and 'living without God'; between 'a sense of darkness', and 'living in the kingdom of darkness'. I am not – *not* – teaching sinless perfection. But I am restating Paul's doctrine: the unbeliever is a slave to sin; the believer is not. John said: 'Whoever abides in [Christ] does not sin. Whoever sins has neither seen him nor known him. Little children, let no one deceive you. He who practices righteousness is righteous, just as he is righteous. He who sins is of the devil... Whoever has been born of God does not sin, for his seed remains in him; and he cannot sin, because he has been born of God' (1 John 3:6-9). NASB has 'sins... sins... practices sin... practices sin... sin'; NIV has 'keeps on sinning... continues to sin… does what is sinful... continue to sin... go on sinning'.[7] Above all, I say again, although I talk as though *I* am saying this or that, all I have done is quote the apostle and try to enforce what *he* is saying! And at the heart of Paul's doctrine is this glorious statement: 'For sin shall not have dominion over you, for you are not under law but under grace' (Rom. 6:14).

Let us look at it in more detail.

A slave is obliged to obey the master who owns him. Obliged? Precious little choice has he! As long as he has breath in his body, he belongs, body and soul, to his master, and is at his constant beck and call, day and night. Once the slave dies, however, he is no longer under the ownership, the rule or control of his former master; he is free. Paul uses this fact – and extends it – to say that the believer, having died to his former master, is now under a new slave-master; he is 'under new management'. 'If anyone is in Christ, he is a new creation; old things have passed away; behold, all things have become new' (2 Cor. 5:17).

Of course, as with all illustrations – even Paul's – the similitude breaks down. If a slave dies, he is buried; he can't be anyone else's slave! But this is the merest quibble. Paul is not illustrating the economics or politics of the slave market, or talking about the work of an undertaker. He is speaking about conversion. The minor details of the illustration are trivial and irrelevant. What is the main idea? Just this: a sinner trusting Christ, is united to Christ, dies to sin, dies to the law, is 'raised from the dead' to 'walk in newness of life' (Rom. 6:4-11), and so becomes the slave of Christ. His old master was sin. His new master is Christ. Now the real power behind the old slavery was the law: 'The strength of sin is the law' (1 Cor. 15:56). The word 'strength' means 'power'. It was the law which gave sin its power, and it was through the law that sin worked its power. Hence, when Paul says to the believer: 'Sin shall not have dominion over you, for you are not under law but under grace' (Rom. 6:14), his point is that coming to faith in Christ brings redemption from slavery. It brings release, freedom from the reign of both sin and the law, which are in a sense one and the same. Not, I hasten to add, that the law is sin – but the very fact that Paul needed to say as much

---

[7] See chapter 16 p232.

(Rom. 7:7), shows, yet again, that we are on the right track. It is the *reign* of law, to be 'under the law', and the *reign* of sin, to be 'under sin', which are one and the same *in their effect*. Which is? Death! (Rom. 6:23; 7:5,9-11,13). To be delivered from sin is to be delivered from the law. Thus, all believers can say that in Christ we have 'been set free from sin', we 'also have become dead to the law... we have been delivered from the law, having died to what we were held by' (Rom. 6:18,22; 7:4,6). In other words, Romans 6:14 *is* true, however amazing it may sound: 'Sin shall not have dominion over you, for you are not under law but under grace'.

To be under the law is to be under the dominion of sin. To be under grace is to be liberated from the rule of law and the dominion of sin, for, as I explained in the previous chapter, when looking at Galatians 3:2-3, 'by the flesh' and 'in the flesh' are virtually one and the same with 'under the law' and 'by the works of the law'. Freedom from the law is essential if the sinner is to be free from sin. The power of sin is the law (1 Cor. 15:56). To be 'under the law' is to be in the old age, the age of the old covenant. To be 'under grace' is to be in the new. These two positions are mutually exclusive. Paul is speaking objectively when he speaks of 'under the law' and 'under grace'. He is not speaking of a man's feelings or understanding.

This is easily proved. As so often with Paul – in fact, as I indicated earlier, Romans 6 and 7 illustrate the very point – in order to drive home his argument, he asks a question, a question which naturally would be raised by an objector who has understood the teaching, *but can hardly credit it*. The objector asks his question to make sure he has heard aright: 'Can I believe my ears, Paul? Did you really say *that*? Did you *mean* it? Surely... if you mean what it sounds like, then...'.

Reader, think about the objector's immediate outburst in this case. Paul has just said: 'Sin shall not have dominion over you, for you are not under law but under grace'. The objector replies: 'What then? Shall we sin because we are not under law but under grace?' (Rom. 6:14-15).

I must stress this. The question in Romans 6:15, though bluntly dismissed by Paul, needs to be asked, and inevitably will be asked of all who teach scripturally on the law, since the biblical teaching on the matter sounds so startling. The usual Reformed teaching, of course, would never, could never, can never, provoke such a question. And this is as fatal a mark against it as anybody could wish. Biblical teaching on the law and sanctification *must* provoke such a response, such a question – just as biblical teaching on the law and justification must provoke the response of Romans 3:5,7-9; 6:1. I noted this in the previous chapter. The asking of such questions is a litmus test for preachers of the gospel. Sadly, those who advocate the biblical position on Romans 6 and 7 are dismissed as antinomians, but the fact is, unless a man can be accused of antinomianism he is not preaching the gospel properly. Paul met it; many others have. Even so, the unjust accusation hurts! *Not* to get it, however, ought to hurt far more!

Furthermore, the very fact that such a question can be asked – that such a question ought to be asked – proves that Paul really was equating the reign of sin and the reign of law. Of course, Paul's answer is a resounding: 'Certainly not!' (Rom. 6:15), but as I have pointed out, he did not put the objector's mind at rest by saying: 'You have misunderstood me. Of course the believer may not sin. After all, he is under the law still – for sanctification. The believer's life may be defined as law-keeping, and this law, the moral law, is the ten commandments. This perpetual, unchanging and

164

inflexible law is the believer's perfect pattern and rule'.[8] No! The apostle said nothing of the sort. Rather, he went on to amplify his teaching on the two forms of slavery – slavery to sin, and slavery to righteousness – and to make even more absolute his meaning.[9] To paraphrase: 'You were the slave of sin, but now[10] you are the slave of righteousness' (Rom. 6:16-23). 'That is to say', he declares, 'what I stated in Romans 6:14 stands triumphantly uncorrected. The truth is: "Sin shall not have dominion over you, for you are not under law but under grace"'.

Paul relentlessly hammers home the point. There are two slave-masters in the experience of the human race, and only two. Every person is a slave to the one or the other – either to Satan, law and sin, on the one hand, or to Christ, grace and holiness, on the other. There is no middle path. And how a person lives will show which master he serves. If he is under law, he will produce sin (Rom. 7:8-11). If he is under grace, he will produce holiness, fruit to God. Note the 'therefore' and the 'for... for' of Romans 6:12-14. Paul, having proved that justification is by faith, addresses believers, commanding them: '*Therefore* do not let sin reign in your mortal body' – speaking of their sanctification – and giving them the reason: '*For* sin shall not have dominion over you, *for* you are not under law but under grace'. Do not miss the 'but'.

Remember, this is the first time since Romans 5:20 that Paul has mentioned 'the law'. On that occasion he spoke of the law with regard to its increasing sin. Consequently, when he now speaks of the law, following the change brought about by Christ (in Rom. 6) – that is, when he said that the believer is 'not under the law' (Rom. 6:14) – he surely speaks of freedom from the law in *that same sense*; that is, the believer is free from the law's power to increase sin. In other words, the believer is free from the law, free from its dominion, so that he can live a godly life. In short, it is freedom from the law which is the essential ingredient of sanctification. The truth is, the believer has to be freed from the law in order to be rid of the dominion of sin. The law certainly does not help in freeing him from it.

It is vital to see that Romans 6:14 is a statement, not a command or an exhortation. Nor is it something which might be true of some specially holy or advanced believers. It is a statement of fact about *all* believers, about each and every believer, even the newest believer. Sin will not have dominion over any believer. Why not? Because no believer – without exception – is under law. Every believer – without exception – is under grace. Note Paul's dogmatism; no believer is under law. This is the fixed and final, permanent truth for every believer. There is no exception. Paul is categorical. To be under Christ is to be free of the law.

In short, sanctification, which inevitably follows on from justification, is only possible because the believer is liberated from the law. The law gives strength and

---

[8] See chapters 5 and 9. Paul in Rom. 6 is not speaking merely of the sin-defining role of the law, that the believer is under the law really, but not as it defines sin! Not at all! But in any case, if the believer is not under the law in the sense of defining sin for him, and yet the law is his *perfect* rule, what does define sin for the believer in the Reformed system? If the law defines holiness, it must of necessity define sin.

[9] Let me repeat an earlier note. The slavery of the old covenant, the law, is very different to the slavery of righteousness in the new covenant. The difference is paralleled by the difference between the 'law' in the law of Moses and the law of Christ. I will explore this in chapter 16 p214.

[10] Note the 'but now' – from Rom. 6:22.

power to sin; it exposes it, but affords no power to overcome it. The law cannot get sin off the throne, let alone keep it off. Rather, it adds to the believer's problem, since it arouses sin. Either the law or grace rules; not both. *This* is what Paul is saying. He is not looking back to the believer's justification. He is looking forward to the life of the believer, following hard upon his justification, a life lived out in fruitfulness to God. And he is speaking of the power needed – and supplied by God – to live a godly life now that a person is converted and justified. What is that power? How is it communicated? How is a believer sanctified? By the law? Certainly not! The only power is in the gospel, by the Spirit. This is the only way grace is supplied to overcome sin and produce holiness. By Christ, in Christ, the believer can do all things. The law cannot give the believer a motive for holiness, it does not encourage holiness. All it can do is work fear and guilt and wrath and misery and defeat. But Christ breaks Satan's kingdom, grip and reign, and gives his Spirit not 'by the works of the law', but 'by the hearing of faith' (Gal. 3:2). The law can never break the dominion of sin. Never! Grace, by the Holy Spirit, is the only way sin's rule and power is destroyed in a believer. Christ alone can do it. Christ has done it! As soon as he is in Christ, and only because he is in Christ, the sinner begins to live a sanctified life. But he can do it only as he reckons on the benefits arising out of his union with Christ – not least, that he is liberated from the law – and works out those benefits in his daily experience, striving after holiness, looking constantly to Christ alone. In short, sanctification is not by the law, but by grace; not by the law, but by the gospel; not under Moses, but under Christ.

And this is what God has promised and procured in Christ for all his elect on coming to faith: 'Sin shall not have dominion over you, for you are not under law but under grace' (Rom. 6:14).

Romans 7:1-6

Do you not know, brethren (for I speak to those who know the law), that the law has dominion over a man as long as he lives? For the woman who has a husband is bound by the law to her husband as long as he lives. But if the husband dies, she is released from the law of her husband... she is free from that law, so that she is no adulteress, though she has married another man. Therefore, my brethren, you also have become dead to the law through the body of Christ, that you may be married to another – to him who was raised from the dead, that we should bear fruit to God. For when we were in the flesh, the sinful passions which were aroused by the law were at work in our members to bear fruit to death. But now[11] we have been delivered from the law, having died to what we were held by,[12] so that we should serve in the newness of the Spirit and not in the oldness of the letter.

Marriage is Paul's second illustration setting out the believer's relationship to the law. Under the marriage law upon which Paul bases his argument, a woman is bound to her husband, she is bound to obey him. If the husband dies, however, she is no longer married to him, she is no longer under his rule. Moreover, she is free to marry another man. Thus speaks this law of marriage.

Paul starts by saying he is speaking 'to those who know the law' (Rom. 7:1). Who were they? This seemingly simple question raises some important issues about the

---

[11] Note the 'but now'.

[12] Note the recurring description of the law as that which brings bondage (as in Acts 15:10; Gal. 2:4-5; 3:22-23; 4:22-26,30-31; 5:1, for instance).

readers of the letter. Paul was writing to believers, both Jews and (probably mostly) Gentiles, and referring to the Mosaic law.[13] There is no problem with this. In addition to converted Jews and proselytes, Paul was speaking to converted Gentiles. These Gentiles, in their pre-conversion days, by nature had the work of the law in their heart, a rudimentary knowledge of the law (Rom. 2:14-15). In addition, following their conversion, they had begun to learn about the Old Testament, including the law. Thus these Roman believers could be said to 'know the law', even the Mosaic law, including the ten commandments.

Notice, Paul said they *knew* the law; not that they were under it. As I have explained in chapters 2 and 3, even though the Gentiles did not have the law, there are a (very) few passages in the New Testament which seem to address believing Gentiles as though they had been under the law in their pre-conversion days. This passage might be one such. Might. But, it is important to note, the apostle does not say his readers were *under* the law. They *knew* it, was all he said. Some of his readers might well not have been married – they certainly weren't *under* any marriage law. Even so, they *knew* what that law said. In addition, the experience of the Jews, who of course were under the Mosaic law, is used by Paul (Rom. 7:4) as a paradigm, or representative of the position of all sinners, whether Jew or Gentile.

Now to get to grips with the illustration. Its main thrust is clear: the death of a spouse ends a marriage, and the survivor is free to marry again. The spiritual point Paul is making is that the believer, before his regeneration and conversion, was married to the law (whether or not as a Jew or a Gentile is irrelevant). In his believing, he died with Christ, and this ended his marriage to the law. As a consequence, he is free to marry again, and to be fruitful in that new marriage. In truth, the believer *has* married again. He has married Christ (Rom. 7:1-6), and this, not only that he *might* be fruitful, but that he *should* be, and *will* be. Do not miss the parallel with Paul's illustration in Romans 6; namely, the believer has died with Christ, and this has ended the believer's slavery to the reign of sin and law. Here, he has died to the law.

The illustration, like that of slavery, breaks down. A literal reading of the analogy means the wrong spouse has died. In the illustration, the law – the first husband – died, leaving the living spouse free to marry again, whereas the point of the illustration is that even though it is the believer who has died, it is the believer, nevertheless, who has married again, and is now married to Christ. In other words, according to the analogy, the dead spouse has remarried![14]

But this, as before, is the merest quibble. The point is that death ends the legal obligations of marriage. Indeed, it ends the marriage state. Likewise, the relationship between the sinner and the law ends when the sinner comes to faith in Christ, since by faith the believer is united to Christ in his death, and has died in and with him. The believer, therefore, is no longer married to the law. He is married to Christ. Whereas the unbeliever under the law must submit to the law – as a wife to her husband – the

---

[13] The apostle could have been referring to, say, the Roman law of marriage. But it is almost certain (in my view it is certain) that he was speaking of the Mosaic law, particularly the seventh and tenth commandments of the decalogue. The context, before and after, is convincing. In Rom. 7:7, Paul quoted the tenth commandment as an illustration of the law he was speaking of. In Rom. 7:10, he referred to Lev. 18:5, which, in Rom. 10:5, he rightly attributed to Moses and his law, and which, in Gal. 3:12, he argued is a part of the Mosaic law.

[14] As with the slavery illustration; the slave died and thereby became the slave of another!

law has no rule, governance or jurisdiction over the believer. He is dead to it.[15] He is at liberty, free from the law, married to Christ, and under his rule, under his law. 'We have been delivered from the law', said Paul (Rom. 7:6). 'Delivered'? The apostle uses a strong word – 'discharged', 'set at liberty', 'set free'. Believers are totally discharged or set free from the law. It has no authority over them any longer, it rules them no more. Just as a man, when he dies, is discharged from all obligations to the law,[16] so it is with the believer. He has complete freedom from all obligations to the Mosaic law as a rule of life.

As I have already recognised, there is an issue about the unconverted Gentile and the law. Very well. But whatever view one takes of that, the undeniable fact is the believer (Jew or Gentile) is most definitely not under the law. And in this debate that is what counts! We are talking about the believer and the law. And of that there is no doubt. The believer is free of the law, and married to Christ and, therefore, under his sole governance.

As before, to be 'under the law' means far more than the law defining sin. This is claimed! But Paul was saying far more than that! Marriage speaks of far more than defining something. We are talking about a regime, a jurisdiction, a state. To be married to the law is to be under the rule of the law, under the rule, the headship or jurisdiction of Moses. In marrying Christ, is the believer to think of Christ as merely defining holiness for him? To be married to Christ is to be under his rule and headship.

The illustration must not be glossed away. Its full import must be allowed to stand. Indeed, it must dominate further discussion. When a man dies and his wife remarries, is she under the authority of her new husband or her old? Certainly not the old! The fact is, her former husband is no longer her husband at all. His death ended that marriage. It would be unthinkable, even ridiculous, if a woman, being remarried after her first husband's death, deferred to the authority of her former (dead) husband. The fact is, that authority does not even exist![17] 'No one can serve two masters' (Matt. 6:24); that is, no servant (Luke 16:13) can. We are in the realm of headship, rule and governance. No wife can obey two husbands, one dead and the other alive. The fact is, she can have only one husband! The picture is plain. The unregenerate sinner is married to the law, but when the Spirit regenerates and converts him, he dies to the law, and is united to Christ by faith. From now on, he is no longer under the law, but under Christ; no longer under *its* rule, but *his*. Instead of being in his first, unfruitful marriage – to the law – he is now in a marriage – to Christ – in which he produces fruit to God through his union with the Redeemer (Rom. 6:22; 7:4).

And this is the climax of the passage. 'Fruit to God' can be produced only by those who have died to the law. Those who have not died to the law can produce nothing but 'fruit to death'. As long as we are married to the law, we cannot be married to Christ, and thus there is no possibility of being sanctified. Our bondage to the law has to cease. Then, and only then, can we start to live a new life in relationship to Christ. The old

---

[15] Many confuse the illustration and say the law has died. It has not. The believer has.

[16] Once again, it is the merest quibble to point out that an executor has to discharge the debts of the deceased. Paul is not dealing with the law of probate, but with the ongoing life of the believer.

[17] Again, it is the merest quibble to talk of the respect the woman has for her former husband, now dead. As with all biblical illustrations, we must grasp the main point.

relationship must end, and this can only happen by death. It is only as we are married to Christ, free from the law, that we can be sanctified.

Let me reinforce a vital point. In these verses, we are *not* talking about justification. We are talking about the fruits and effects of justification; namely, sanctification. And as we have seen in other passages, far from teaching that a believer is under the law for sanctification, Paul says the very opposite. Unless a man is dead to the law, and married to Christ, he will never produce fruit to God; he will never be sanctified. In his first marriage – to the law – he produced sin and death. In his second marriage – to Christ – he produces righteousness. Paul especially underlines the fact that it is the believer's very freedom from the law which enables him to be sanctified. Staying under the law would make it impossible. The truth is, the opposite would occur. Sin would be aroused or excited by the law, and sin being stimulated, death would be the inevitable result. The law, therefore, cannot be the perfect rule for sanctification. As I have argued from Galatians 2:19; 5:13-18, far from the law being the means of sanctification, sanctification is only possible to one who is free from it. It is not merely that the law is *not* the means of sanctification. *Freedom from the law is the only means of sanctification.* Christ has set his people free from the law in order that they might be sanctified.

Phew! Let us pause for breath, and take stock! Read over once again the first six verses of Romans 7 – in more than one version – read them aloud – and just let the apostle's words sink in. If the above is *not* what he is saying – then what *is* he saying? And whatever answer you come up with, go on to verse 7 and ask yourself whether or not your explanation would promote the apostle's question.

Although this sounds startling, frightening, shocking to those who hold Calvin's third use of the law, I am convinced that what I have put before you, reader, is the plain teaching of the apostle. And the law we are talking about is, I remind you, the Mosaic law, including the ten commandments. As so often, some try to say that Paul is here speaking about justification, about the penalty, demands and curse of the law, or about the law as a works covenant, claiming that, although the believer has died to the law as a curse, and so on, the law still stands as his rule of life. Paul is saying nothing of the sort! *He says the very opposite!* The believer has died to the law. It is simply not possible to divide or tinker this 'having died' into having died to the *curse* of the law but being alive to its *rule*.

In any case, Romans 7:1-6 is not concerned with justification. Romans 7:4 is saying the same as Romans 6:14, using a different illustration. Neither passage is limited to justification. Paul is not saying that believers are dead to the law as a way of justification. Paul is speaking about the two realms, the two ages – law and grace – in both historical and personal terms. The full force of the eschatological 'but now' (Rom. 7:6) must be grasped. The believer is living in a totally different and new age. He was a slave; he is free. His first marriage has ended; he is re-married. The two states – the former and the present – are totally incompatible. They cannot be cobbled together. The believer is not partly slave (and partly free), partly married to the law (and partly married to Christ). 'But now', thunders Paul (Rom. 7:6), with his sights set on the huge contrast between the new and old age for the believer, 'we have been delivered from the law, having died to what we were held by'.

Nor is Paul talking about a *misunderstanding* or *misuse* of the law, and contrasting *that* with the Spirit. He is contrasting the old covenant and the new, the old age and the new. The believer is in the new covenant, free from bondage to the law, and thus he will serve God by the Spirit, being in a totally new condition of life (2 Cor. 3:6), and he will bear fruit to God's praise (Rom. 6:22-23). Note the continuing – dominating – role for 'but now' in Paul's argument. Discontinuity and contrast are the words! See Romans 3:21; 5:9,11; 6:22; 7:6; 8:1; 11:30; 11:31 (second 'now' in NIV, NASB); 16:26.

That this is the teaching of Romans 7 is easily proved. As before, in order to drive home his point, Paul asks a question, a question which naturally would be raised by an objector – or doubter – who has understood what Paul is teaching, *but can hardly credit it*. The objector asks his question to make sure he has heard Paul aright. Reader, consider the objector's immediate outburst in this case: 'Is the law sin?' (Rom. 7:7). 'Is the law sin?' What a question! But the fact that such a question can be asked – that such a question ought to be asked – and that very question Paul actually *did* ask – proves that Paul *is* once again equating the reign of sin and the reign of law. Of course the answer to the question is a resounding, No! 'Certainly not! On the contrary... the law is holy, and the commandment holy and just and good'; it is 'spiritual', declares the apostle (Rom. 7:7,12,13-14,16). Notice what Paul does not say: 'Oh, you have misunderstood me. Of course the law is not sin! How can it be? The believer is still under it as a perfect rule of life!' He says nothing of the sort. In fact, *he says the very opposite*. The believer has died to the law; he had to die to the law in order to be sanctified. Even so, the objector's question needs to be asked, and will be asked of those who teach scripturally on the law. As before, Reformed teaching would never – could never – provoke such a question. If Paul had taught that the believer is married to the law, under the law – whether the moral law or whatever – nobody would have dreamt of asking: 'Is the law sin?' *But he did ask it!* The law is certainly not sin. No, it is not. But neither is the believer under the law.

The position is clear: the saint is no longer under the law (Rom. 6:14; Gal. 3:24-25; 5:18); he is delivered, freed or released from it (Rom. 7:6; 8:2). In fact, he has died to it (Rom. 7:4; Gal. 2:19). Think of that! *Died* to the law. The believer died to the law when he died with Christ (Rom. 6:1-8; Gal. 2:19-20). As for Christ himself, after he had died, he was no longer under the law *in any respect*. 'It is finished' (John 19:30), he cried, speaking of many things, I realise, but not excluding his relationship to the law. He had fully satisfied it, and all its claims were met. He had fulfilled it (Matt. 5:17-18). Christ *fulfilled* the law, I say again. He did not arbitrarily destroy it, demolish it, invalidate it, violate it, explain it away, dismantle it, or repeal it. He fulfilled it, and therefore completed it.[18] Christ is now not under it. He was once! But, having been born under the law (Gal. 4:4), lived under it, and then died, cursed, under it (Gal. 3:13), having risen again, he is freed from it. Similarly, the believer died with Christ to the law, was freed from it so that he might produce holiness and righteousness (Rom. 7:4), *in order that* he might produce holiness and righteousness. No wonder the apostle declares: 'Christ is the end of the law for righteousness to everyone who believes' (Rom. 10:4).[19]

---

[18] See below, especially pp236,498.

[19] One 'explanation' of Rom. 7:2-6 is to say a believer has two natures, his old nature has died, leaving his new nature married to the law! This is bizarre. The believer is not a spiritual schizophrenic! He does not have two natures. He is human! Christ alone has two natures. As for the believer, *he* has died – he, not his 'old nature' – and he – he, not his 'new nature' – is

Any serious work on the law will – must – take full account of Romans 6:14 – 7:6. I freely admit this doctrine is amazing. But it is the apostle's doctrine, and it is true of every believer. The believer, in Christ, has died to the law so that he can be sanctified. This is what Paul teaches. Calvin, however, in his third use of the law, effectively says that in order to be sanctified, the believer must be re-married to the law – though on easier terms! Calvin was wrong!

I now move on to Romans 8. Before I do, a passing glance at the rest of Romans 7.

A passing glance at Romans 7:14-25

Why do I largely pass over Romans 7:14-25? To discuss it thoroughly would considerably extend my book, and the inevitable (and, I am afraid, inconclusive) debate about the 'I' would only confuse the issue. Many are concerned about 'the man of Romans 7', but the main topic of the chapter is, in my opinion, the inadequacy of the law (Rom. 8:3). In Romans 7, Paul argues that the law does not deliver from the rule of sin. The sinner cannot sanctify himself by the law. The truth is, the law makes his problem worse, so that he must be delivered from the law in order to be sanctified. The apostle makes this clear by setting out the experience of an unconverted Jew[20] faced with the law and trying, by law, to be right with God and to be holy. This unconverted Jew finds that the law cannot save him. It cannot justify him, nor can it sanctify him. Although the man says things which no regenerate believer could ever say, he also shows that he has some desire to be right with God, and to please him. He is, without fear of contradiction, a complicated man! Whether or not 'the man' of the passage is a real man, one man or a composite drawn by the apostle for the purposes of illustration, is, to my mind, an open question. But *this* is not the point of the passage! The point is *this*: the man, whoever or whatever he is, finds no relief by the law – not for his sin nor for his desire after holiness.

This, in brief, is how I read the passage. It fits entirely into both the immediate and wider context of the letter, whereas the normal Reformed view – that the passage speaks of the believer in his highest spiritual state – clearly makes the apostle guilty of denying the truths about the believer he so explicitly lays out, both before and after. As for the first part of Romans 7:25, this is not integral to Paul's argument – in fact it destroys it. Rather, it represents Paul's irrepressible outburst as he was recording this Jew's experience. He could not help himself spelling out – shouting out – that although

---

married to Christ. Another 'explanation' is to claim that, in Rom. 7:6, Paul was saying believers have been delivered, not from the law of God, the law of Moses, but from another law altogether; namely, the law of sin, which is defined as the law of God taken over by sin. But Paul was speaking about the law, not the law 'taken over' by anything! Another 'explanation' is to say Paul was speaking about the law 'as a script, a mere piece of writing' – the letter (Rom. 2:29) – that is, this writing divorced from the Spirit, and this is what is old, obsolete, and valueless. But when Paul said: 'We have been delivered from the law, having died to what we were held by, so that we should serve in the newness of the Spirit and not in the oldness of the letter' (Rom. 7:6), he meant believers are delivered from *the law*, not a piece of writing read without the Spirit. Paul distinguished between the Spirit and the law, not between the Spirit and the letter, or between two opposing approaches to the law. The believer's spiritual life is maintained and ruled by the Holy Spirit *in contrast to* the rule of the law. See chapter 15 for a closer examination of 'the letter'.

[20] Possibly, probably?, himself when he was in that condition. For ease of argument, I will take the man, at least as far as verse 13, to be Saul of Tarsus. Some think the man of Rom. 7 is Israel.

this Jew finds no relief from the law, there is relief – in Christ! If, reader, you put the first part of Romans 7:25 in brackets (as is justifiable), it all reads as it should and makes perfect sense. Compare my comments on Romans 2:4-11.

In any case, overall, Romans 7:7-25 is a digression in Paul's main argument. It should, as a whole, be put into brackets. It is in Romans 8:1 where Paul picks up the main thread of his argument he began in Romans 5:12, developed through Romans 6 and the early verses of Romans 7, and temporarily put to one side at the start of Romans 7:6. Let me set out what I mean, taking up the passage from that verse:

But now we have been delivered from the law, having died to what we were held by, so that we should serve in the newness of the Spirit and not in the oldness of the letter... There is therefore now no condemnation to those who are in Christ Jesus, who do not walk according to the flesh, but according to the Spirit. For the law of the Spirit of life in Christ Jesus has made me free [freed you] from the law of sin and death...

Note Paul's reiterated 'now', his emphasis on justification leading to sanctification, on the Spirit, and the believer's freedom from the law in the matter of 'serving' or 'walking'. In light of that, let us now move on to Romans 8.

Romans 8:1-4

There is therefore now no condemnation to those who are in Christ Jesus, who do not walk according to the flesh, but according to the Spirit. For the law of the Spirit of life in Christ Jesus has made me free [has freed you] from the law of sin and death. For what the law could not do in that it was weak through the flesh, God did by sending his own Son in the likeness of sinful flesh, on account of [for] sin: he condemned sin in the flesh, that the righteous requirement of the law might be fulfilled in us who do not walk according to the flesh but according to the Spirit.

Note the emphatic 'therefore now'. Paul, seizing the reader's (listener's) attention, picks up his argument[21] from chapters 6 and 7:1-6, which stemmed from Romans 5:12-21, and stresses once again the 'now', the new age in the history of salvation, the new era inaugurated by Christ in his death and resurrection.[22]

Note also, once again, the intimate connection between justification – 'no condemnation' – and sanctification – those 'who do not walk according to the flesh, but according to the Spirit', and 'the righteous requirement of the law... fulfilled in us who do not walk according to the flesh but according to the Spirit'.[23] The word 'walk' shows we are firmly located in the realm of practical godliness, and not (merely) justification. Believers are not only freed from the condemnation of the law, but they have received the Spirit (Rom. 8:9) to live a life to the glory of God. We are dealing,

---

[21] And it is an argument! Take, for instance, the word *gar*, 'therefore', a word used by a man engaged in reasoning out an argument. In Rom. 8, it appears in verses 2,3,5,6 and 7 (twice). And that in addition to *dioti*, 'because' (verse 7) and *de*, or *ei de*, 'so', 'but' or 'and' in verses 8,9 (twice), 10 (twice) and 11, besides other arguing words (*ara, dia, alla*, and so on) ('then', 'on account of', 'but', and so on). We are not dealing with isolated 'proof-texts'!

[22] Not only is Paul's opening in Rom. 8 emphatic, it is ungrammatical – for the same reason as his opening of Gal. 5 – which see. There is widespread disagreement about the precise import of the 'therefore'. My view is as above. It does *not* refer to Rom. 7:25.

[23] It makes no difference if, as is most likely, 'who do not walk according to the flesh, but according to the Spirit' is not in Rom. 8:1; it is in Rom. 8:4. See NASB, NIV, NKJV footnote.

therefore, with the believer's life in the Spirit, the life of one who is no longer condemned. In a word, sanctification.

The word 'law' appears four times in this passage; 'the law of the Spirit of life in Christ Jesus', 'the law of sin and death', 'the law', and 'the righteous requirement of the law'. There is no question about the third and fourth; both refer to the Mosaic law.

But what of the first law, 'the law of the Spirit of life in Christ Jesus'? This law, 'the law of the Spirit of life in Christ Jesus' is said to be a liberating law – it 'has made me free' (Rom. 8:2). Therefore it cannot be the Mosaic law. That law was a law of bondage. This law 'has made me free from the law of sin and death' (Rom. 8:2)! It cannot be the very same law!

And that leads to consideration of the second law, 'the law of sin and death' (Rom. 8:2), 'the law of sin' (Rom. 7:25). What law is that? Is it the dominion of sin, sin likened to, or personified as, a slave-master, the enslaving power which leads to death? Or is it 'the law of God' as it stimulates sin and condemns the sinner? I think the latter. After all, as the apostle said in the context, when the law of God struck home in his own heart, this is how it appeared to him, this is how it was – it aroused sin in him, deceived him, made him captive, and killed him (Rom. 7:5,7-11,13,23); it made him wretched (Rom. 7:24). The law of God is 'the law of sin and death', which fails utterly to bring peace (Rom. 8:1-8; see also Rom. 3:19; 4:15; 5:20-21; 7:7-25; 1 Cor. 15:56; 2 Cor. 3:7,9).[24]

Putting this together, 'the law of the Spirit of life in Christ Jesus' – that which liberates from the law of Moses – is clearly the antithesis of the law of God. The believer is now 'in Christ Jesus', whereas he was before 'under the law', under its rule and power. But no longer. His condition is the very opposite of being under the law; he is under grace. He is under the principle of grace, the reign of grace, 'the law of the Spirit of life in Christ Jesus'. Paul is once again contrasting these two realms or reigns – the reign of law and sin with the reign of grace. The apostle never tired of the theme! The believer is in the new covenant; a new principle or power reigns in him. The gospel, 'the law of liberty' (Jas. 1:25; 2:12),[25] has, by the Holy Spirit, freed him from the old regime of law, sin and death. By using the phrase, 'the law of the Spirit', Paul is engaging in word play – as we have seen, a favoured technique of his.[26] Here, he plays with the word *law*, contrasting the *law* of Moses – 'the *law* of sin and death' – with 'the *law* of the Spirit of life'. Paul does this to highlight yet again that the Spirit, on the basis of Christ's work, liberates the believer from the old age or realm of the law – both in its condemnation, and in its grip, its enslaving power.

The believer dare not go back under the law (Rom. 3:19 – 8:17; Gal. 3:10; 4:21-31). Its rule has gone for him (2 Cor. 3:6-11; Gal. 3:25; 4:28 – 5:1; Eph. 2:15; Col. 2:14), lock, stock and barrel. The law is not made for a righteous man (1 Tim. 1:9). Just as he dare not go under it for justification, so he must not go under it for sanctification. The

---

[24] Rom. 7:5,7-11 does not refer to the regenerate. Paul was speaking of his pre-regenerate days. The law did not *produce* sin in him, since it is good and spiritual (Rom. 7:7-16), but sin used the law to *arouse* sinful desire in him. It was sin – not the law – which was the cause of the trouble, producing death through the law. Note, as I have shown (see chapter 4), Reformed teachers wrongly argue that the law *restrains* the unregenerate from sin. Paul said he found it aroused sin in him!

[25] I will return to this.

[26] For more on Paul and his play on words, especially over 'law', see chapter 16 p216.

law is obsolete (Heb. 8:13). Its time is over. The age of the law has passed. And, as for the age, so for the individual. Though the law is good in itself, of course, being the law of God, nevertheless it cannot handle the flesh, it cannot cope with the flesh, it cannot conquer the flesh. To put it bluntly, the flesh is too strong for it. The truth is, the flesh has so weakened the law, flesh is master, and thus law cannot conquer sin. And this is true not only for justification, but also for sanctification; especially, in this context, sanctification.[27]

The point is made every day. Governments are for ever passing new laws to try to change moral behaviour – but man immediately seeks a way round the law, finding the law stimulates him to break it, and so on. Take a child. Forbid him to look in a certain cupboard. What will he inevitably do? Take the speed limit. That which was intended to be the maximum becomes the minimum. Take tax laws. Some accountants sit up all night after the Budget preparing new strategies for their clients to avoid tax in line with the laws just announced. Examples are legion. As I write, the Prime Minister has just delivered a speech in which he has admitted the obvious; namely, that the Government (by passing laws) cannot stop men and women being obese. C.S.Lewis observed the obvious but largely ignored: 'You cannot make men good by law'.[28]

And what is this 'righteous requirement of the law' (Rom. 8:4) which is fulfilled in those who walk according to the Spirit? It is not 'the law' itself, but 'the righteous requirement of the law', which Paul speaks of. The law, it seems, is not so important as that which it intends, its purpose, its end, its 'righteous requirement', which is 'love' (Gal. 5:13-16; 1 Tim. 1:5). Note also the singular, 'requirement', not 'requirements'; 'the righteous requirement of the law' is its *one* great end or purpose. And it is, said Paul, this 'righteous requirement of the law' which is fulfilled in believers. The end of the law – 'the commandment which was to bring life' (Rom. 7:10) – the purpose of the law, its majestic goal, all that the law wants, all this is produced in those who live by the Spirit.

'What the law could not do in that it was weak through the flesh, God did by sending his own Son... that the righteous requirement of the law might be fulfilled in us' (Rom. 8:3-4); that is, believers. Echoes here of Galatians 4:4-5.[29] By Christ's work, 'the righteous requirement of the law' is 'fulfilled in us'. 'Fulfilled', 'fulfilled in us'! Clearly, this is something which God in Christ has done *for* and *in* believers, not something to be done *by* believers trying to keep the law. Paul here *describes* believers; he does not tell them to fulfil the law. God, by his Son, Christ Jesus, accomplished the fulfilment of the righteous requirement of the law, and it is this perfect obedience of Christ, his righteousness, which is imputed and imparted to believers. Thus Christ fulfilled the law, and believers have fulfilled it in him. Christ's work imputed to them by the Spirit accomplishes their justification. Christ's work being imparted to them by the Spirit accomplishes their sanctification. And it is this sanctification which is the evidence and fruit of the fulfilment of the righteous requirement of the law in believers

---

[27] It has been suggested that Paul was here saying the opposite; namely, that through the Spirit, the law holds a new power which produces the believer's sanctification. The verses cannot bear such an interpretation – except by drastically altering the translation of the text of Rom. 8:3; which is precisely what has been done. See 'Extracts' p464.

[28] Lewis: *Mere* p367.

[29] See chapter 6 p93.

in and by Christ. Do not miss the trinitarian emphasis. Paul has taken us up onto high ground here.

This is what Paul speaks of here. Christ is the only one who has power to deal with sin. What the law cannot do, he has done. This is the contrast the apostle is making. He spells out what Christ did (and does), and what the law was (and is) too weak to do. The Spirit takes the place of the outward law in the life of the believer, and thus enables the believer to 'fulfil' it. Christ did not abolish the law in the sense of ignoring or getting rid of its purpose. Quite the reverse! Christ, by the Spirit, accomplishes that very purpose in his people. Note how Paul does not say the law is now 'obeyed' or 'kept' or 'done' by believers – the usual way of talking about keeping the law – but he says that what the law requires is now 'fulfilled' in believers. Note the passive. Note the word itself: 'fulfilled'! – a word of immense significance in New Testament terms. Christ set the tone right at the start: 'Do not think that I came to destroy the law or the prophets. I did not come to destroy but to fulfil. For assuredly, I say to you, till heaven and earth pass away, one jot or one tittle will by no means pass from the law till all is fulfilled' (Matt. 5:17-18). As Paul said in Galatians 5:14, the Spirit is the 'fulfilment' of the law, its goal, end or aim – which is, to bring about righteousness. The law, though holy, righteous and good (Rom. 7:12), being weak, could not bring about the righteousness that God required. It is the Spirit who has been given to believers in order to effect, to 'fulfil', the law in them, and so establish that righteousness which the law demanded but was unable to produce. Paul was not talking about 'law-works', law-observance, but conformity to Christ (Rom. 8:29), renewal of mind so that the believer can live to God's pleasure (Rom. 12:1-2). This is why Paul, when spelling out the details of the believer's obedience (Rom. 12:1 – 15:13), declares that 'the righteous requirement' of the law is love of neighbour – which 'fulfils' the law (Rom. 13:8). Even though the occasion was ripe for the apostle to make the point if he wished, Paul does not speak of keeping dietary laws, for example – expressly ruling them out – but of 'righteousness and peace, and joy in the Holy Spirit' (Rom. 14:17). Yes, 'fulfilled' is a massive New Testament word.

The believer is no longer guilty for his sins, no longer under condemnation. Yes, but far more is also true of him. The believer is now able to live a life pleasing to God; that is, a righteous life. Long before reaching Romans 8, Paul has taught that the law could never justify, that it could never take away guilt and condemnation, but now he is stressing something more. He is, once again, taking us ever higher – developing and enforcing what he has been setting out from Romans 6. 'The law of the Spirit of life in Christ Jesus' has enabled the believer, the man who is 'in Christ', to live 'not after the flesh', but 'after the Spirit'. He is no longer living 'under the law' but 'under grace'. The purpose of the Father's plan, the design of Christ's redemption, and the culmination of the Spirit's work – which goal is one and the same – is not merely to have a forgiven people, a justified people. No! It is to have a fruitful people, a holy people, a people who glorify the triune God (Rom. 7:4,6; 8:4,8-14; Eph. 5:25-27; 1 Pet. 1:15-16, and many more); in other words, a sanctified people. But just as the law cannot produce this justification, neither can it produce this sanctification.

How sad it is that many Reformed commentators stop short of this in connection with the law. They are rightly adamant that the law cannot justify, but are unable to admit that it cannot sanctify. They stress that justification and sanctification can never be separated, yet too often they themselves separate them at this very point. But if only they would do as Scripture does, and keep the union between justification and sanctification, it would signal the end of the debate concerning the believer and the law. The law is removed, eliminated, taken away. The believer is no longer enslaved to it, or married to it, but he is enslaved and married to Christ. Thus the law is fulfilled in the believer. What the law could not do, Christ has done. What the law cannot do, Christ does. And what goes for justification goes equally for sanctification. This is the teaching of Romans 6 – 8. How distressing it is to see this lost in a welter of petty-fogging, unscriptural get-out clauses such as 'ceremonial law', or 'law as a covenant and not a rule', and all the rest of it. Get-out clauses? Who wants to 'get out' of Paul's magnificent, breath-taking argument of Romans 6 – 8? It could be argued that it is the peak of all biblical revelation! Let us rejoice in it!

Romans 10:4

Christ is the end of the law for righteousness to everyone who believes.

This verse makes only a modest contribution to the debate about the believer and the law, since, as I have shown,[30] its context is to do with the contrast between law and grace in the matter of justification. Yet there is just a little more to be said. The law is the Mosaic law. The point here is this: 'Christ is the *end* of the law for righteousness to everyone who believes'. What, precisely, does this mean? How is Christ the *end* of the law for righteousness?

There are several possible meanings of 'end' – the two leading contenders being 'termination, finish' and 'fulfilment, completion, goal'. Which is it? Is it: 'Now that Christ has come, the law's role has *terminated*, the law has been brought to an end as far as righteousness is concerned'? Or is it: 'Now that Christ has come, the *goal* of the law has been fulfilled, completed'? A strong case can be made for both on grounds of biblical usage, but the weight of evidence, based on the context, clearly points to the first, 'termination'. Christ, I quickly add, has brought the law for righteousness to an end, terminated it, because he has 'fulfilled' it. This rightly combines both meanings; Christ abolished the law by fulfilling it. But 'fulfilment' on its own is not enough here. Although it is a vital aspect of Romans 10:4, 'fulfilment' is not Paul's point. Yes, Christ did say he had come to fulfil the law and the prophets, that all must be fulfilled (Matt. 5:17-18), but he stated, just before his death, that 'this which is written must still be accomplished... For the things concerning me have an end' (Luke 22:37). While 'fulfilled', therefore, makes good sense here, it does not go far enough. Christ terminated the law, bringing it to its terminus. There is a time element here. With the coming of Christ, the authority of the law of Moses is over, terminated. The idea of 'goal', of course, is also present – as in a race, the tape marks not only the finish, but also the goal. The whole point of the race is to get to the tape. In short, Christ brings the age of the law to an 'end', and he also is its 'goal', that which the law was looking forward to. Christ ended, fulfilled and completed the law-era of salvation history, and inaugurated the new age of grace. It is the continuity/discontinuity question,[31] and the corresponding 'but now', which we have met again and again. The law had been pointing to Christ. 'Moses indeed was faithful in all his house as a servant, for a

---

[30] See chapter 6 for Rom. 10:5-6.
[31] See chapter 6.

testimony of those things which would be spoken afterwards [that is, Christ and the gospel]' (Heb. 3:5). Now Christ has come and ended the law's reign.

I am not saying that Christ has ended all connection with the law for the believer, that Christ has removed it from Scripture. Not at all! The Mosaic law is still part of God's word, and as such is profitable for the believer as part of 'all Scripture' (2 Tim. 3:16-17). But Christ is the law's fulfilment and end, and he can only be truly appreciated in the light of the law. I will take up this question of the way the believer should – must – read and profit from the law, and have more to say on it. Even so, the believer lives his life in Christ, not through and under the law of Moses. His day-to-day life is to be ruled primarily by the teaching of Christ and his apostles, not by the law. The glorious truth is this: the believer lives in the Spirit, and the Spirit lives in the believer. The child of God lives in the realm of the Spirit, not the law. Christ has ended the law for his people.

As I explained, my purpose in looking at Romans 10:4 has been modest. The verse deals with justification, and says nothing directly about sanctification. But Christ *is* the end of the law for righteousness for the believer, and the verse does say *that*. As the apostle had already said: 'Therefore, my brethren, you also have become dead to the law through the body of Christ' (Rom. 7:4; see Gal. 2:19-20). And this means the believer's standing before God and his approach to God are based not upon law but upon Christ. This will have large implications when I come to explain the biblical rule of life for the believer.

Let me close this look at Romans with a reminder of these words from Paul, words which are true of all believers:

Sin shall not have dominion over you, for you are not under law but under grace... Therefore, my brethren, you also have become dead to the law through the body of Christ, that you may be married to another – to him who was raised from the dead, that we should bear fruit to God. For when we were in the flesh, the sinful passions which were aroused by the law were at work in our members to bear fruit to death. But now we have been delivered from the law, having died to what we were held by, so that we should serve in the newness of the Spirit and not in the oldness of the letter... For what the law could not do in that it was weak through the flesh, God did by sending his own Son in the likeness of sinful flesh, on account of [for] sin: he condemned sin in the flesh, that the righteous requirement of the law might be fulfilled in us who do not walk according to the flesh but according to the Spirit... For Christ is the end of the law for righteousness to everyone who believes (Rom. 6:14; 7:4-6; 8:3-4; 10:4).

Too good to be true? Believer, this *is* the truth about yourself. This is *your* 'but now'. Believe it, treasure it, and do not allow yourself to be robbed of it. Above all, live in the light of it, bask in the warmth of it, and feast off the good of it.

Chapter 11

2 Corinthians 3

Do we begin again to commend ourselves? Or do we need, as some others, letters of commendation to you or letters of commendation from you? You are our letter written in our hearts, known and read by all men; clearly you are a letter of Christ, ministered by us, written not with ink but by the Spirit of the living God, not on tablets of stone but on tablets of flesh; that is, of the heart. And we have such trust through Christ towards God. Not that we are sufficient of ourselves to think of anything as being from ourselves, but our sufficiency is from God, who also made us sufficient as ministers of the new covenant, not of the letter but of the Spirit; for the letter kills, but the Spirit gives life. But if the ministry of death, written and engraved on stones, was glorious, so that the children of Israel could not look steadily at the face of Moses because of the glory of his countenance, which glory was passing away, how will the ministry of the Spirit not be more glorious? For if the ministry of condemnation had glory, the ministry of righteousness exceeds much more in glory. For even what was made glorious had no glory in this respect, because of the glory that excels. For if what is passing away was glorious, what remains is much more glorious. Therefore, since we have such hope, we use great boldness of speech – unlike Moses, who put a veil over his face so that the children of Israel could not look steadily at the end of what was passing away. But their minds were blinded. For until this day the same veil remains unlifted in the reading of the Old Testament, because the veil is taken away in Christ. But even to this day, when Moses is read, a veil lies on their heart. Nevertheless when one turns to the Lord, the veil is taken away. Now the Lord is the Spirit; and where the Spirit of the Lord is, there is liberty. But we all, with unveiled face, beholding as in a mirror the glory of the Lord, are being transformed into the same image from glory to glory, just as by the Spirit of the Lord.[1]

In seeking the resolution of the tension over the believer and the law, nobody could pretend that 2 Corinthians 3 carries the same weight as Galatians or Romans. No! But whatever decision we arrive at concerning the believer and the law, we must not fail to get to grips with the apostle's teaching in this chapter, and make sure that our stance takes it fully into account. And more! Our view must thrive in face of 2 Corinthians 3. Indeed, it must arise directly from it.

As so often in New Testament times, Judaisers were, once again, on the attack; this time at Corinth. As always, Paul stood up to them:

For such are false apostles, deceitful workers, transforming themselves into apostles of Christ. And no wonder! For Satan himself transforms himself into an angel of light. Therefore it is no great thing if his ministers also transform themselves into ministers of righteousness, whose end will be according to their works. I say again, let no one think me a fool. If otherwise, at least receive me as a fool, that I also may boast a little. What I speak, I speak not according to the Lord, but as it were, foolishly, in this confidence of boasting. Seeing that many boast according to the flesh, I also will boast. For you put up with fools gladly, since you yourselves are wise! For you put up with it if one brings you into bondage, if one devours you, if one takes from you, if one exalts himself, if one strikes you on the face. To our shame, I say that we were too weak for that! But in whatever anyone is

---
[1] The extracts for this chapter begin on p469.

bold – I speak foolishly – I am bold also. Are they Hebrews? So am I. Are they Israelites? So am I. Are they the seed of Abraham? So am I (2 Cor. 11:13-22).[2]

Note the apostle's emphasis upon boasting and boldness. Broadening this, note the word 'glory', 'glorious' or 'glorify', appearing, on my count, twenty-three times in the letter, mostly in the third chapter. 'Glory' is the theme of the entire letter; 'glory' is certainly the theme of 2 Corinthians 3. In particular, the apostle glories and boasts in connection with his ministry. This is the issue he focuses on when confronting the false teachers at Corinth, with their boasting and self-exaltation. See, in particular, 2 Corinthians 10 – 12.[3]

And that leads us directly to the central aspect of Paul's argument, the fundamental core of his case against the Judaisers. His ministry is more powerful and more glorious than theirs. That is his claim. They boast. Very well! He, too, can boast. What is more, he will boast! Further, he can outdo them in their boasting. And he does! How? Is it because he is a better preacher, and all the rest of it, than they? No! In some senses, he might be regarded as a poorer preacher (1 Cor. 1:17; 2:1,3-4,13; 2 Cor. 10:10; 11:6) – though, in these letters to Corinth[4] (see for instance, 1 Cor. 4:10; 2 Cor. 11:19,21), it must not be forgotten, irony is never far below the surface with the apostle. No! What makes the difference between him and the law-mongers is 'commendation', that pet theme of the Judaisers. They are forever on about it! They demand letters of commendation. That is why Paul speaks of commendation so frequently in this letter (2 Cor. 3:1; 4:2; 5:12; 6:4; 10:12,18), and stands up to his detractors on the issue: 'Letters of commendation? Well, I've got them!' Really? 'Oh yes!' He addresses the Corinthians plainly: 'You are my letters! You believers! Every one of you at Corinth! Bits of paper? I don't need bits of paper! My gospel success, my spiritual power, my sufferings, and God's evident approval of my ministry, as revealed in the lives of others, you Corinthians in particular – there's my "commendation"' (2 Cor. 3:1-3; 4:2; 5:11 – 6:4; 10:13-18; 12:11-12; see also 1 Cor. 3:6; 9:1-2). 'Now then, the Judaisers – what's theirs? Let's hear it!' (2 Cor. 10:12-18). As he had told them in his first letter: 'I do not write these things to shame you, but as my beloved children I warn you. For though you might have ten thousand instructors in Christ, yet you do not have many fathers; for in Christ Jesus I have begotten you through the gospel... Now some are puffed up, as though I were not coming to you. But I will come to you shortly, if the Lord wills, and I will know, not the word of those who are puffed up, but the power. For the kingdom of God is not in word but in power. What do you want? Shall I come to you with a rod, or in love and a spirit of gentleness?' (1 Cor. 4:14-21).[5]

But even this fails to get to the root of the apostle's argument. The fundamental difference between his ministry and that of the Judaisers lies in something much more radical than its evident power, as compared to theirs.

---

[2] There are hints of it in his first letter also (1 Cor. 4:14-21; 5:6-8). See immediately below. Do not forget the Judaisers' mistaken claim that the Abrahamic and Mosaic covenants are one, and that if Gentiles want to become children of Abraham they must be circumcised – and that this, in turn, means coming under the law.

[3] On my count, the words 'boast' or 'boasting' come 28 times in the letter, 18 of which occur in these three chapters.

[4] And elsewhere.

[5] He is not contradicting 1 Cor. 4:1-5. Remember, he calls himself 'a fool' for boasting, explaining that he was forced into it (2 Cor. 11:16-23; 12:6,11).

The truth is, the Judaisers' ministry is in a totally different realm, a different age, a different system to the apostle's. They are really living in the age and ambience of the law, and their ministry shows it. Theirs is an old-covenant ministry. Paul, however, lives in the realm of the Spirit, and his ministry is that of the new covenant. *This* is what makes all the difference. His boasting, power and commendation come from his being in the realm of the Spirit, and not in the realm of the law. Paul's power does not come from himself (2 Cor. 2:16; 3:5; 4:7-12,16-18; 6:3-10). Not at all! He can boast, yes, but only because God in Christ has made him competent, 'sufficient', as a minister (1 Cor. 15:10; 2 Cor. 3:5-6). And this sufficiency derives directly and inevitably from his being in the new covenant, his labouring in the realm of the Spirit, and his use of spiritual weapons appropriate to that covenant (2 Cor. 6:7; 10:3-5):

Do we begin again to commend ourselves? Or do we need, as some others, letters of commendation to you or letters of commendation from you? You are our letter written in our hearts, known and read by all men; clearly you are a letter of Christ, ministered by us, written not with ink but by the Spirit of the living God, not on tablets of stone but on tablets of flesh; that is, of the heart. And we have such trust through Christ towards God. Not that we are sufficient of ourselves to think of anything as being from ourselves, but our sufficiency is from God, who also made us sufficient as ministers of the new covenant, not of the letter but of the Spirit; for the letter kills, but the Spirit gives life... We do not war according to the flesh. For the weapons of our warfare are not carnal but mighty in God for pulling down strongholds, casting down arguments and every high thing that exalts itself against the knowledge of God, bringing every thought into captivity to the obedience of Christ (2 Cor. 3:1-6; 10:3-5).

And *this* is the heart of the matter – the new covenant. *This* is what makes the difference between the Judaisers and the apostle. They labour in the letter, the law; he labours in the Spirit, in the gospel. And it is not only, as it were, the message that is different. The power, the boasting, the glory of the apostolic ministry, its very ethos, lies in that it is a ministry of the new covenant, not the old. With the change of covenant, the entire ministry has changed.

Let me stress this. Remember the chicken and the egg? Which comes first – the change of covenant, or the evident power? There is no doubt about it. It is as plain as a pikestaff. Paul does *not* argue that since he possesses power and glory, there must have been a change of covenant. No! What he says is, since the old covenant had a glory, the new covenant must have even greater glory – which it has – and, as a consequence, he has that power and glory, and the Judaisers do not. It is all a result of the change of covenant. He is in the new covenant; they are in the old. And it shows.

The Judaisers, locked in the old covenant, preaching the law, are using thrash and slap[6] to enforce their doctrine, hitting the Corinthians into line. So much so, the apostle can rebuke the Corinthians: 'You put up with it if one brings you into bondage... if one strikes you on the face'. Paul will have none of it: 'To our shame, I say that we were too weak for that!' (2 Cor. 11:20-21). Taking this line, Paul, of course, is being ironical. It is not a question of weakness. He is not weak! Not at all! He is in a different covenant to the Judaisers! He has no intention whatsoever of hitting the Corinthians. Severity might be required, as a last resort. If so, he will not shirk it: 'Being ready', he says, 'to punish all disobedience when your obedience is fulfilled' (2 Cor. 10:6). But

---

[6] How about 'whip'?

that is not his forte: 'Therefore I write these things being absent, lest being present I should use sharpness, according to the authority which the Lord has given me for edification and not for destruction' (2 Cor. 13:10).[7] Read again the above-extract from his first letter.

So, in 2 Corinthians 3, having made his point about the two covenants, in order to make sure that the Corinthians really do take it on board – since it is so easily and so often forgotten or whittled away (never more so than today!) – the apostle then launches into a comparison of the two. A comparison? He *contrasts* them, irrefutably spelling out the contrast in a series of devastating terms, deliberately polarising the two covenants as starkly as he can.

Before we glance at these contrasts, however, we must bear in mind that although Paul uses neither of the phrases, 'the old covenant', or 'the law', what else could he be talking about? And he certainly does use 'Old Testament' – which might easily be translated 'old testament'. In fact, he uses *palaias diathēkēs*, literally 'old covenant' (verse 14). And when he refers to 'tablets of stone... the letter... the letter... the ministry of death, written and engraved on stones... the ministry of condemnation' (verses 3,6,7,9) and speaks of Moses (verses 13,15), there is no doubt whatsoever that he is speaking of the old covenant, the entire Mosaic economy, the law, including the ten commandments, which he contrasts with 'the new covenant' (verse 6), the work and realm of 'the Spirit' (verses 6,8,17-18).

I say it again, there can be no doubt. Paul *is* contrasting the old and new covenants. He is not contrasting certain aspects of the two covenants, certain man-made and artificial segments of the covenants (none of which exist in Scripture). No! He is, root and branch, contrasting the old and new covenants.

And what a devastating series of contrasts he draws between the two! But, yet again, even that is not quite right. Although I will now list the contrasts, they do not actually form a list; they make one continuous line of reasoning. Do not miss the apostle's use of 'but... for... but... but if... so that... for if... for even... for if... therefore...' (verses 6-12) – all of which, I grant, are small Greek words in themselves, yet all of them are mighty words of reasoned argument. And when they follow hard, one after another, what an argument it is! What reasoning! So let us get away from a proof-text and bullet-point mentality, let us get away from a 'list-driven' Christianity, and let us get a firm grip on the apostle's argument. Indeed, let his argument grip us!

Nevertheless, in contradiction of what I have just said, in order to make things as clear as I can, I will now list the various contrasts the apostle draws.

Each of these, on its own, would constitute a powerful-enough statement of contrast between the old and new covenants. Gathered together, in one small section of Scripture, they form an invincible catalogue, demonstrating beyond all fear of contradiction that the old and new covenants, far from being one covenant, are chalk and cheese. Not only that. As these statements make plain, the old covenant was, in comparison with the new, outward, weak, fading, useless and is now, with the completion of the redeeming work of Christ, and his resurrection, obsolete.

And that is not all:

---

[7] For more on this, see chapter 16 p264.

The old covenant was to do with the flesh; the new covenant is the covenant of the Holy Spirit (verses 3,6,8).

The old covenant was an outward covenant, written on stones; the new covenant is an inward covenant, written on the heart (verses 2-3,7).

The old covenant killed; it spelled death; the new covenant is life (verses 3,6-7).

The old covenant was deliberately temporary, designed by God to be so; the new covenant is permanent; it remains (verses 11,13).

The old covenant had glory, but its glory was lesser and fading; the new covenant has a glory which exceeds, excels, being so much greater than the glory of the old covenant (verses 7-11).[8]

The old covenant condemned; the new covenant is saving (verse 9).[9]

The old covenant spelled bondage; the new covenant brings liberty (verses 12,17).

What a phenomenal series of statements! Breathtaking! But even so, we still have not reached the apostle's ultimate point! No! We have not yet got to the fundamental conclusion and application of his words in this chapter. So let us do it now.

Let me remind you, reader, of what I argued in my *The Priesthood of All Believers*, when looking at this passage. I have two things in mind: 'Ministry' goes far wider than 'pulpit work'. What is more, we must not confine the 'ministry' in question to that of the apostle:

[In] 2 Corinthians chapters 2 to 4, without question Paul *is* speaking of his own ministry, and that of his fellow-apostles and fellow-workers, yes... But notice how the apostle uses 'we' in these three chapters. Sometimes by 'we' he does mean, perhaps, just himself, maybe with other apostles and fellow-workers in mind (2 Cor. 2:17; 3:1; 4:7-15), although it is not absolutely certain in all these cases. But notice how he quickly moves into 'you' (2 Cor. 3:1-3). So what should we make of the 'we' and 'ours' in the next verse, leading on to the words I quoted above? And it is, I think, unlikely that the 'we' in 2 Corinthians 3:12-18; 4:16-18; leave alone 5:1 and on, should be limited to Paul himself, or to Paul and his fellow-apostles. In any case, it is undeniable that *all* Christ's people are kings, priests and prophets by reason of their union with Christ. The prophets foretold it, and Christ established it. Not in a literal sense, of course, but in a spiritual sense. Believers, therefore, are ministers. I think we may justly argue that they are 'competent'; all of them are 'competent as ministers'. Each believer has God's Spirit and can, to a measure, teach others. The point can be broadened. God equips all his people to fulfil that particular ministry which he has for each of them. To deny it is to fly in the face of the provisions of the new covenant (Isa. 54:13; 61:6; Jer. 31:31-34; 33:14-22; Zeph. 3:9-10; John 6:45; 2 Cor. 1:21-22; 1 Thess. 4:9; 5:11; Heb. 8:8-12; 10:15-18; 1 Pet. 4:10-11; 1 John 2:20-21,27; 5:20).

Why do I reiterate that here? I do so for this reason. Although the apostle is dealing primarily with his ministry as opposed to the ministry of the Judaisers, the principles he sets out apply to all believers. All believers are, from the moment of their conversion,

---

[8] Note the apostle's 'deliberate tautology' – without redundancy, of course.
[9] 'Righteousness', *dikaiosunē*, 'justification'. But this does not mean that the apostle is speaking only about the law for justification. 'Righteousness' here includes the whole of salvation, not excluding sanctification. The context proves it.

in the new covenant; indeed, they are ministers of the new covenant – all of them, without exception, both men and women. So what Paul says about himself, he actually says about all believers. And that which lies behind his power and glory, and brings about that power and glory, lies behind every believer, and produces that same power and glory in them. Yes, I know it sounds staggering, but it is the truth! 'Ministry' is far more than 'preaching', and new-covenant ministry is something every believer engages in. When a sinner is converted, when he 'turns to the Lord' (verse 16), all is changed (2 Cor. 5:17). From that moment, he (or she) has the Spirit of God, and now lives under the new covenant, in the realm of the Spirit – with all that entails in terms of life and liberty and glory:

In Christ... When one turns to the Lord, the veil is taken away. Now the Lord is the Spirit; and where the Spirit of the Lord is, there is liberty. But we all, with unveiled face, beholding as in a mirror the glory of the Lord, are being transformed into the same image from glory to glory, just as by the Spirit of the Lord (2 Cor. 3:14-18).

And the upshot of all this? How can any new-covenant person think of going back to the old covenant? How can any new-covenant teacher think of instructing believers to submit to the old covenant? In light of 2 Corinthians 3 it ought to be utterly out of the question. But, sadly, as is all too evident, Reformed teachers persist in trying to mix the old and new covenants. They think they are doing the saints a service when they pick up – to use Calvin's words – the whip of the law to smite lazy asses. The truth is, in so doing, they risk (to put it no higher) coming under the apostle's reproof so pointedly set out in this chapter.

If I may use an illustration. Reader, what would you think of a man who insisted on lighting a candle for illumination when he was sitting in the glare of the full mid-day sun at the height of summer? What would you think of him putting on his thermals at such a time? You would think him mad or, at the very least, ill!

Well, this is the age of the Spirit. Do not go back to the flesh! Keep to the gospel. Do not allow yourself to be taken back to the law. The law is the flickering candle; the gospel is the meridian sun.

Can this be right? Is this really what the apostle is saying? We have a way of finding out. Bearing in mind what we have seen so far in this chapter, along with material I have not dealt with – that is, Moses' veil, the blindness of the natural man's heart, the removal of the veil in Christ – all of which leads up to the triumphant conclusion of the chapter with its exuberant declaration of life, liberty and joy of believers, let us glance at the way the apostle goes on in chapter 4:

Therefore, since we have this ministry, as we have received mercy, we do not lose heart. But we have renounced the hidden things of shame, not walking in craftiness nor handling the word of God deceitfully, but by manifestation of the truth commending ourselves to every man's conscience in the sight of God. But even if our gospel is veiled, it is veiled to those who are perishing, whose minds the god of this age has blinded, who do not believe, lest the light of the gospel of the glory of Christ, who is the image of God, should shine on them. For we do not preach ourselves, but Christ Jesus the Lord, and ourselves your bondservants for Jesus' sake. For it is the God who commanded light to shine out of darkness, who has shone in our hearts to give the light of the knowledge of the glory of God in the face of Jesus Christ. But we have this treasure in earthen vessels, that the excellence of the power may be of God and not of us. We are hard pressed on every side, yet not crushed; we are perplexed, but not in despair; persecuted, but not forsaken; struck down, but not destroyed – always carrying about in the body the dying of the Lord Jesus, that the life of Jesus also may be manifested in our body. For we who live are always delivered to death for Jesus' sake, that the life of Jesus also may be manifested in our mortal flesh. So then death is working in us, but life in you. And since we have the same spirit of faith, according to what is written: 'I believed and therefore I spoke', we also believe and therefore speak, knowing that he who raised up the Lord Jesus will also raise us up with Jesus, and will present us with you. For all things are for your sakes, that grace, having spread through the many, may cause thanksgiving to abound to the glory of God (2 Cor. 4:1-15).

I leave you, reader, to judge whether or not what I have said here really has caught the spirit of 2 Corinthians 3. If it has, then it should signal the end of the debate about the believer and the law. The believer is in the new covenant; every believer (whether man or woman) is a minister of the new covenant. The new covenant is the air we breathe, the kingdom in which we live, the governance under which we thrive. The notion that *we* – the children of the new covenant – should mix law and gospel, old covenant and new, let alone elevate law over gospel, ought to be utterly out of the question.

Chapter 12

Philippians 3:2-12

Beware of dogs, beware of evil workers, beware of the mutilation! For we are the circumcision, who worship God in the Spirit, rejoice in Christ Jesus, and have no confidence in the flesh, though I also might have confidence in the flesh. If anyone else thinks he may have confidence in the flesh, I more so: circumcised the eighth day, of the stock of Israel, of the tribe of Benjamin, a Hebrew of the Hebrews; concerning the law, a Pharisee; concerning zeal, persecuting the church; concerning the righteousness which is in the law, blameless. But what things were gain to me, these I have counted loss for Christ. Yet indeed I also count all things loss for the excellence of the knowledge of Christ Jesus my Lord, for whom I have suffered the loss of all things, and count them as rubbish, that I may gain Christ and be found in him, not having my own righteousness, which is from the law, but that which is through faith in Christ, the righteousness which is from God by faith; that I may know him and the power of his resurrection, and the fellowship of his sufferings, being conformed to his death, if, by any means, I may attain to the resurrection from the dead. Not that I have already attained, or am already perfected; but I press on, that I may lay hold of that for which Christ Jesus has also laid hold of me.[1]

Once again, we meet yet another church under attack from Judaisers; this time at Philippi. As always, the agitators wanted to take the believers under the law, especially, in those early days, with respect to circumcision. But, as I have shown, it was 'the law' which was the issue. As before, the Judaisers mistakenly argued for the oneness of the Abrahamic and Mosaic covenants, and that if Gentiles want to become children of Abraham they must be circumcised – that is, they must go under the law of Moses. And again, as always, Paul stood up to the Judaisers. He would have none of it, and he was prepared to 'fight it out' every inch of the way. Opening his account in the most abrupt manner, even to the extent of starting with his conclusion, he twice commanded his readers to 'beware' of the false apostles, to beware of their teaching and their practice. Moreover, he chose a highly insulting way of defining those he had in his sights, calling them 'dogs' and 'evil workers'. Notice, further, the apostle's use of Jewish terminology, and his calling upon one of his favourite devices – word play.[2] None of this was an accident. Right from the start (Phil. 3:2-3), the apostle was deliberately setting the tone for what he wanted to say.

He was categorical. Despite the plausible claims of the Judaisers, all believers, without any resort to the law, are the true people of God, the true Israel: '*We* are the circumcision, who worship God in the Spirit, rejoice in Christ Jesus, and have no confidence in the flesh' (Phil. 3:3).[3] In other words, he was telling the Philippians, in no uncertain terms, that they ought to have every confidence that, entirely in Christ, only in and through Christ, and without any reference to the law, all was well between them and God, and that they should on no account entertain any notion of going under

---

[1] The extracts for this chapter begin on p471.

[2] This is evident in the 'concision' and 'circumcision' of the AV. But it is also evident in the apostle's Greek *kata-tomē* and *peri-tomē*.

[3] We shall meet this again when we consider 'the Israel of God' (Gal. 6:16).

the law. No law-works, no Jewish rites, were necessary. Their rejoicing, their boasting in Christ and his work alone, proved beyond question that through the Redeemer they were already right with God. They were justified. Hence, they must not encourage the Judaisers, they must not listen to their teaching, they must shut their ears, minds and hearts to the claims of the law-mongers, those evil dogs.

But Paul did not leave it there. He went on to do far more than merely declare these facts. As I say, he fought it out, blow by blow, with those who were trying to impose the law on believers. Let me trace it out.

At every point, he stood his ground; at every stage, he proved that his Jewish credentials matched those of the false teachers. More, they out-did them. His claims for law-works were impeccable. What about theirs? Circumcision? Could the Judaisers stay with Paul on that? He himself had been circumcised the eighth day, which, of course, put him in the topmost bracket (Gen. 17:12; Lev. 12:3; Luke 1:59; 2:21). Let them match that, if they could. That's the first thing. And so he goes on. He had been born a Jew – *born* a Jew; he was no proselyte. He had his genealogical qualifications. What were theirs? And what about the law? Could they match his devotion to the law as a Pharisee? What about zeal for God? Had he not shown remarkable enthusiasm for the public glory God – even to the dedication of his life to the fanatical persecution of the church – Christ in his people (Acts 9:5)? As for the observance of the law, he had, in his own eyes, and in the eyes of others, been blameless. True, his righteousness would have been, at best, external, and not without at least a tinge of self-righteousness, but nevertheless he certainly passed muster as a law-conforming Jew. No one could contradict him. The Judaisers couldn't match him – let alone beat him – on that score, that's for sure! Compare Galatians 1:13-14.

But when Christ confronted Saul of Tarsus on his approach to Damascus, all his religion based on the law collapsed in ruins, all his law-righteousness, all his self-righteousness, crumbled to dust and ashes. He was in the dust – and so was his religion! Seeing Christ, he realised, there and then, that all his law-religion amounted to nothing – to less than nothing. As a matter of fact, he saw it all as a 'loss', a negative weight. A negative weight? In what way? There, in the dust before Christ, he saw that all his zeal, all his law-keeping, all his Jewish credentials, all his observances – about which he had boasted so much, and of which he had thought so highly – he saw that all that, far from bringing him to God, far from enabling him truly to worship and serve God, actually kept him from knowing the true and only way of righteousness. The law was not part of the solution to his problem, after all. Far from it! Indeed, the law, and his striving to keep it, was an integral part of the problem itself! Confronted by Christ, he saw that justification came not by his observance of the law, but, entirely and only by trust in the obedience and sacrifice of the Lord Christ himself. And thus, relinquishing all his former hopes based on the law, he trusted Christ alone.

And now, thirty years after that experience outside Damascus, writing this letter, he is still of the same opinion. Indeed, he is even more convinced than he had been then. He has gone even further. He now realises that it isn't just his Jewish credentials and the law which gets in the way of his knowing God and worshipping him aright – anything and everything other than Christ, or in addition to Christ, would keep him from salvation. As a result, he now reckons *everything* apart from Christ to be a loss: 'Yet indeed I also count all things loss for the excellence of the knowledge of Christ

Jesus my Lord' (Phil. 3:8). All things! Nothing could compare with Christ; nothing would compare with Christ in his estimation.

But it was not only that he *counted* such things as loss. For Christ, he could say: 'I have [actually] *suffered* the loss of all things, and count them as rubbish, that I may gain Christ and be found in him, not having my own righteousness, which is from the law, but that which is through faith in Christ, the righteousness which is from God by faith' (Phil. 3:4-9). Nothing that the Judaisers could offer him, or demand from him, could in any way come close to Christ and salvation by him. The law? Let them have the law! Nothing could compare to Christ! Everything other than Christ – everything, including his Jewishness and his law-observance, he knew to be rubbish.[4] To yield an inch to the Judaisers would take him back into the morass from which Christ had extricated him.

So far, so good. We can all agree. Justification is not by the law. It is by faith in Christ, apart from law-works. Righteousness comes to the believer from God through faith, without the law. Very good. So what's the fuss? Just this. Notice how the apostle goes on:

Yet indeed I also count all things loss for the excellence of the knowledge of Christ Jesus my Lord, for whom I have suffered the loss of all things, and count them as rubbish, that I may gain Christ and be found in him, not having my own righteousness, which is from the law, but that which is through faith in Christ, the righteousness which is from God by faith; that I may know him and the power of his resurrection, and the fellowship of his sufferings, being conformed to his death, if, by any means, I may attain to the resurrection from the dead. Not that I have already attained, or am already perfected; but I press on, that I may lay hold of that for which Christ Jesus has also laid hold of me.

I refer, in particular, to these words: 'That I may *know* [Christ] and the *power* of his resurrection, and the *fellowship* of his sufferings, *being conformed to* his death, if, by any means, I may *attain to* the resurrection from the dead. Not that I have already attained, or am already perfected; but I *press on*, that I may *lay hold of* that for which Christ Jesus has also laid hold of me'.

What is *their* significance? Up to and including verse 9, the apostle has been talking about justification. There is no question of it. Justification is by Christ through faith, and not by the law. Very well. *But at verse 10, Paul moves from justification into sanctification.* There is no question of it. He now begins to talk about the experience of knowing Christ *after* justification. He speaks of enjoying Christ's power in his life, sharing in Christ's sufferings, being more and more conformed to Christ, pressing on, laying hold of the hope for which Christ had taken hold of him and saved him. By using such language, it is clear that the apostle is now thinking, not about justification, but about his way of life after justification; namely, sanctification.

This is such a vital point, I must underscore it. We must not miss the apostle's emphasis here. He is speaking about his life, his experience, his daily walk, *after his justification.* Paul wants to enjoy Christ, to grow up into Christ, to experience Christ,

---

[4] 'Rubbish' is almost certainly a better translation than 'dung' (AV). The 'rubbish' was the bones, the worthless detritus of food, thrown to the 'dogs' – yet another example of the apostle's fascination with the play of words – having already called the Judaisers 'dogs'. Right then! Do the dogs want the scraps? They are welcome! If they want the law, let them have their submission to the law!

and do so more and more, day by day. He is justified, yes, but he is not satisfied in knowing that he is justified as a forensic fact. He wants to 'lay hold of' all that Christ intended when he 'laid hold of' him (Phil. 3:12). He yearns to attain to it all, he wants to be 'perfected' (Phil. 3:11-12). He longs to go on to feel, to experience, to enjoy Christ, and to do so throughout the rest of his life and in every aspect of his life – and to do so more and more. His course and his sight are ever 'upward' (Phil. 3:14). He wants to 'apprehend' (Phil. 3:13). When the apostle speaks of knowing Christ (Phil. 3:10), he uses *ginōskō*, to know by personal experience.

In all this, the apostle is clearly thinking of sanctification! *This* is what he desires! Listen to the way in which he expresses himself in the verses which follow, as he urges the Philippians to join him in pursuing the same course:

If, by any means, I may attain to the resurrection from the dead. Not that I have already attained, or am already perfected; but I press on, that I may lay hold of that for which Christ Jesus has also laid hold of me... Brethren... forgetting those things which are behind and reaching forward to those things which are ahead, I press towards the goal for the prize of the upward call of God in Christ Jesus. Therefore let us, as many as are mature, have this mind... let us walk by the same rule, let us be of the same mind. Brethren, join in following my example, and note those who so walk, as you have us for a pattern (Phil. 3:11-17).

Spurgeon, who certainly grasped what Paul was speaking about, closed his sermon on the passage:

I desire that you should feel the resurrection power. We have many technical Christians, who know the phrases of godliness, but know not the power of godliness. We have ritualistic Christians, who stickle for the outward, but know not the power. We have many moral religionists, but they also know not the power. We are pestered with conventional, regulation Christians. Oh, yes, no doubt we are Christians; but we are not enthusiasts, fanatics, not even as this bigot. Such men have a name to live, and are dead. They have a form of godliness, but deny the power of it. I pray you, my hearers, be not content with a truth till you feel the force of it. Do not praise the spiritual food set before you, but eat of it till you know its power to nourish. Do not even talk of Jesus till you know his power to save. God grant that you may know the powers of the world to come, for Jesus' sake! Amen.[5]

Even so, granting all we have seen thus far, still we have not finished with the apostle's words in this passage. Do not forget the context. Paul is addressing the Philippians in light of the Judaisers' attack upon them. *That* is what prompted the apostle to speak in this way at this time. And so, he now swings back, weeping, to those 'dogs', those 'evil workers', 'the enemies of the cross of Christ'. Having spelled out the things *he* is longing for and looking for – as a result of the grace of God in Christ – he lists the things *they*, the Judaisers, cherish, the things *their* doctrine produces. Furthermore, mincing no words, he states the end to which they are going (Phil. 3:18-19). Once again, he pulls no punches. As for the Judaisers, they are 'the enemies of the cross of Christ... whose god is their belly, and whose glory is in their shame – who set their mind on earthly things'. He himself, however, is looking for eternal glory. *They* can only expect 'destruction'. Full bellies now, and eternal damnation to follow! Strong stuff! I fail to see how the apostle could have made his meaning any more stark.

---

[5] Spurgeon: *Metropolitan* Vol.35 p216.

What has all this to do with the believer and the law? A great deal. Remember, the Philippians were believers before the Judaisers got at them. Paul himself had preached the gospel to the Philippians, and done so without any mention of the law. And he had seen them converted and baptised (Acts 16). But these false teachers had now come to Philippi and were preaching the law to these believers, and calling upon them to submit to it. In light of this attack upon the Philippians – the attempt to get believers under the law – how heavily the apostle lays into the Judaisers! He punches with all the weight he can muster. He misses no 'trick'. He pulls out every stop. This is no 'secondary' matter, no grey area. The believer and the law just do not mix. The Philippians must not think of going under the law. Under no circumstances must they yield to the Judaisers, however plausible their claims, however authoritative their demands. Think of what their doctrine produces. Think of the end to which it is taking them.

Very well. Believers must not ever think of going under the law. For justification? Of course not! Submit to the law for justification? Never! And Paul says it loud and clear (Phil. 3:2-9).

But as we have seen, Paul did not leave it there. He knew very well what the Judaisers were up to. He knew what fish they were preparing to fry. And he wouldn't have it at any price. The law will not justify you, he assures the Philippians. Nor will it sanctify you.

Ah! Here we reach the crunch. After all, the Philippians were believers already and therefore justified. Sanctification was the main concern. And, according to Paul, the law will no more sanctify than it will justify. This was the issue at Philippi. It is the very thing Paul deals with from verse 10 and on. And *this* is the very issue on which I am writing.

Now, if ever there was a time and a place where the apostle should have set out Calvin's third use of the law, this is it; that is, if he believed it. If Calvin was right, at the end of verse 9, the apostle would have said – should have said – words to the effect that, although the law has no part to play in the sinner's justification, it does, of course play a vital part in the saint's sanctification. The fact that the apostle – though speaking so plainly and so earnestly about sanctification, and doing so when expressly refuting men who wanted to take believers under the law – says nothing of any place for the law in that sanctification, is of massive importance in this debate. It must not be missed, glossed over or ignored.

Let me spell it out. The Judaisers were attacking the Philippians, pressing them to submit themselves to the law, and Paul laid into them, punching as hard as he could – including 'dogs' and 'rubbish' – stopping up every loophole, destroying every argument. But, according to the Reformed view, he failed miserably as a teacher. For he left the Philippians with quite the 'wrong' impression. He left them believing that everything in the Christian life – principally, justification, sanctification and glorification – are in and through Christ, and not by law; so much so, under no circumstances whatever must they go under the law, and submit themselves to it. This is the unmistakeable impression he left the Philippians with.

But in doing so, according to advocates of Calvin's third use of the law, Paul made a dreadful mistake. He was terribly remiss. Apparently, we have to believe, the apostle failed to make himself clear. He should have stated the Reformed view on this vital issue. And this is precisely the point at which he should have stated it, and stated it *unambiguously*. He could have done it, once and for all. It is perfectly easy to do it. Let me show you. The apostle should have said something along these lines: 'Do not go under the law for justification. Trust Christ and Christ alone. But, of course, having trusted Christ for your justification, you must submit to the law for sanctification. That is what I do, myself. You, too, must submit to the law for sanctification. The law will be the motive and the means of your sanctification. It is your perfect rule'.

But he did not say it. He said nothing of the sort. In fact, he left the distinct impression that believers should not submit to the law under any circumstance. He told them that Christ is all. And so he made a dreadful 'mistake', a 'mistake' which has cost millions of believers dear. Don't forget that the apostle was meeting this problem everywhere. Why did he not do the one thing necessary, and spell out Calvin's threefold use of the law, once and for all? What a world of trouble he would have saved.

Enough of this! An inspired man, a man who was concerned about getting a singular instead of a plural (Gal. 3:16), would never make such a puerile blunder as this; he would never miss such an open goal or fail to grasp such a golden opportunity. In fact, if he really did make such a mistake, I fail to see how he can be thought of as a master-teacher (1 Cor. 3:10). And do not forget, as I have just said, he was inspired by the Holy Spirit. Why didn't the Spirit spell it all out through his servant? After all, Christ promised that the Spirit would lead his apostles into all truth (John 16:13).

I simply cannot accept this kind of talk. It verges on the blasphemous. There is only one possible deduction. Calvin's view that the believer must submit to the law in order to be sanctified is utterly wrong. And in putting it like that, I am failing to use the strength of language employed by the apostle. I should use his word. I will use it, and call it 'rubbish'.

As he had said earlier in the letter: 'Only let your conduct be worthy of the gospel of Christ' (Phil. 1:27) – not, you notice, 'worthy of the law of Moses'. Paul did not press the law upon his readers in order to produce godliness – neither as its rule nor motive. Rather, he had rounded on those who were trying to do it. Not only that. He stressed the gospel for sanctification. Moses? Go to Christ! Go to Christ, look to Christ, for all things! I say it again, believers must never think of going under the law for sanctification.

Chapter 13

1 Timothy 1:5-11

We know that the law is good if one uses it lawfully, knowing this: that the law is not made for a righteous person, but for the lawless and insubordinate, for the ungodly and for sinners, for the unholy and profane, for murderers of fathers and murderers of mothers, for manslayers, for fornicators, for sodomites, for kidnappers, for liars, for perjurers, and if there is any other thing that is contrary to sound doctrine, according to the glorious gospel of the blessed God.[1]

Paul is speaking of the law of Moses, as the context – both before and after – makes clear. Although verse 9 refers to 'law' (no article in the Greek, NIV – but see footnote) and not 'the law', this poses no problem. The fact is, as I explained in chapter 1, the lack of the article strengthens the concept of 'the law' as the law of Moses. In any case, in verse 8 it is 'the law'. Furthermore, in verse 7, Paul speaks of Judaisers, teachers of the Mosaic law, and in verses 9 and 10, clearly he is referring to the ten commandments. So whatever the passage teaches, it teaches concerning the Mosaic law, including the ten commandments.

But, in the first instance, take Paul's words as applicable to 'law' in general: 'Law is not made for a righteous person'. This is self-evident. A law is enacted to deal with an offence. Litter is commonly thrown in the streets; the authorities respond by passing a law against litter-louts. Certain dogs bite; a law is passed against dangerous dogs. And so on, *ad infinitum*. Law has to do with sin, not righteousness. Sin leads to the introduction of law. This is true in general, but it is also true in particular – as here – of the law of Moses. Some men murder, so God forbids it, and brings in a law against it. By this law, he exposes the sin, turns it into transgression (Rom. 4:15), and sets up punishments for it. 'By the law is the knowledge of sin' (Rom. 3:20). 'Moreover the law entered that the offence might abound' (Rom. 5:20). The law 'was added because of transgressions' (Gal. 3:19).[2] And the law always curses all offenders for each and every offence: 'Cursed is everyone who does not continue in all things which are written in the book of the law, to do them' (Gal. 3:10; Deut. 27:26).

Though it deals with sin and sinners, the law itself is 'good' (*kalos*): 'We know that the law is good' (1 Tim. 1:8), 'good, excellent in its nature and characteristics, and therefore well-adapted to its ends... good in its substance and nature'.[3] The same word is used in Romans 7:16 in reference to at least the ten commandments, which, in passing, is a further confirmation of the first point I made; it *is* the law of Moses we are thinking about. This law is 'well-adapted to its ends'. It is these 'ends' or purposes, or God's design in giving the law, which must be thought about.[4] And that design Paul

---

[1] For more on this, and an examination of 1 Tim. 1:5, see chapter 16 p250. The extracts for this chapter begin on p474.

[2] See my remarks on 'transgressions' in chapters 9 and 10.

[3] Thayer.

[4] See chapter 9 for my comments on Gal. 3 dealing with the purpose of the law.

immediately spells out; that is, 'the law is not made for a righteous person, but for the lawless and insubordinate' (1 Tim. 1:9).

Now this 'good' law can be misused, even abused: 'We know that the law is good' – but only 'if one uses it lawfully' (1 Tim. 1:8). 'Lawfully'? Yes, indeed. It must be used as it was intended by the lawgiver; that is, for the purpose he designed, and for the goal he intended. It must not be used for a purpose for which it was not intended, nor applied to a person outside its remit. Let me illustrate. To try to prevent murder, a law is passed against the use of knives. It would be manifestly absurd to apply this law to chefs, butchers, fish-filleters and surgeons engaged in their normal duties. It would bring the law into disrepute – make 'an ass' of it.

To whom does the law *not* apply? We know 'that the law is not made for a righteous person' (1 Tim. 1:9). To whom *does* it apply, therefore? For whom *is* it made? It is made for the lawless, the unrighteous, the ungodly, the profane, and so on (1 Tim. 1:9-10). Who is this lawless person? He is *anomos*, one 'departing from the law, a violator of the law, lawless, wicked, godless'.[5] The same word is used for 'the lawless one' (2 Thess. 2:8), 'he in whom all iniquity has as it were fixed its abode'.[6]

Let us look at this a little more closely. Who is this righteous person, the one to whom the law does *not* apply? This person must be either a believer or an unbeliever. And the 'righteousness' must be 'true' righteousness (in the sense, say, of Romans 8:4) or 'false' righteousness – that is, external righteousness or self-righteousness.

Let me consider the possibilities.

Is the 'righteous person' an unbeliever who is truly righteous? No! Self-evidently, such a person does not exist.

Is the 'righteous person' an unbeliever who is righteous in an external way? Zacharias and Elizabeth (Luke 1:5-6) and Paul (Phil. 3:6) are cited as examples by those who argue in this way. If so, then we have to believe the law was not made for such people – it had nothing to do with Jews such as these. Obviously, once again, quite wrong. If not, we end up with the absurdity that the law was not made for Jews such as Zacharias and Elizabeth, and Paul before his conversion, when we know it *was* made for such (Rom. 7:7-12). They were Jews, weren't they?

Is the 'righteous person' an unbeliever who is self-righteous? Take Paul. We know he did not keep the law (Rom. 7:7-12). In fact, it was he himself who argued that 'there is none righteous, no, not one' (Rom. 3:10). In Philippians 3:6, he was saying no more than he did in Acts 26:5: in his own opinion – and that of others – before conversion, he was a righteous man, when all the time, as he later found out, he was self-righteous! So, if the 'righteous person' of 1 Timothy 1:9 refers to a self-righteous man, then Paul was really saying the law is not made for such. If so, I would like to know for whom it *is* made! Jesus regarded self-righteousness as a sin, and a common sin at that (Luke 16:15; 18:9), and whatever else the law is to do with, it is to do with sin (Rom. 3:20; Gal. 3:19, for instance). So the law is made for sinners – including the self-righteous.

Coming closer to the matter about which the apostle was writing to Timothy: are we really to believe that Paul was concerned that Judaisers were trying to get self-

---

[5] Vincent Vol.2 p1016; Thayer; Arndt and Gingrich.
[6] Thayer.

righteous people, non-believers, to submit to the law? And that, because of his concern, he wrote to Timothy and told him point-blank that the law was not made for self-righteous or externally-righteous unbelievers? Is this what we have to understand? Nonsense!

Surely the false teachers were trying to get *believers* to submit to the law. *That* was the threat. Paul was concerned with the danger to believers, wasn't he? At this point, he was not in the least worried about what the Judaisers might be trying to do to unbelievers, and whether or not those unbelievers were externally conforming to law or self-righteous hypocrites. It was *believers* he was concerned with. He was anxious because Judaisers were trying to get *believers* under the law. *That* is what Timothy had to sort out and put a stop to. The law was not made for *believers*, said the apostle.

Let me move on to the positive. In general, the righteous person means one who is good, 'a good person', but the context takes it further. It here means 'a justified person'. The 'righteous person' of verse 9, in the context, is a believer, a child of God. After all, Paul was dealing with false teachers at Ephesus – those who were deceiving and misleading *believers*, trying to bring *them* under the law. The false teachers were not trying to bring merely respectable, decent, 'good' people under the law. They were teaching *in the church*. They were trying to get *believers* under the law. Paul was dealing with the issue of the believer and the law. 'The law is not made for a righteous person'. Here, therefore, the righteous person is a godly person, a believer, one who is justified. The law is not designed for the believer, since the believer is 'not under law' (Rom. 6:14), as 'the glorious gospel of the blessed God' (1 Tim. 1:11) repeatedly affirms (Rom. 6:14-15; 7:4-6; 8:2; Gal. 5:18; Eph. 2:13-15; Col. 2:13-17).

All this is highly significant for the question in hand. It was wrong of these Judaisers to try to impose the law upon believers, to try to bring them under the law. Thus it is, to try to make the law the rule and spur for the believer, in order to stir him to sanctification, must be a gross misuse of the law. God did not design his law or introduce it for that purpose. The law has to do with the sinner and his sin, not the saint and his holiness. This is a basic tenet of the gospel. Note the 'according to' (verse 11). The fact that the law is not made for a righteous man is according to the gospel. This is what Paul taught (1 Tim. 1:10-11). And since, in my book, we are dealing with the believer, one who is a 'righteous' man, a justified (the same word in Greek) man (Rom. 5:19; 8:33), we may say that the apostle's declaration means, therefore, that it is simply not fitting to bring such a man under the rule of the law. In fact, it is quite out of place. It is wrong! The believer has died to the law through Christ (Rom. 7:4-6; Gal. 2:19-20) who is 'the end of the law for righteousness to everyone who believes' (Rom. 10:4). If Timothy allowed the Judaisers to get their way, and the law was brought into the church at Ephesus to be taught as the perfect rule for believers, he would be guilty of tolerating a serious misappropriation of the law. The law was not designed for that purpose. It was not designed for believers, full stop, but for the lawless and disobedient.

This, of course, smites a heavy blow at the heart of the Reformed view of the law, as expressed in Calvin's third use. It will not do to say that Paul was speaking about the Mosaic law marred or distorted by human tradition; that he was talking about the condemning power of the law; that he was telling Timothy to watch out for those who misuse the law to introduce 'spells' concerning ancestors; that he was talking about the *self*-righteous man. All of which have been suggested. Paul was speaking of the justified man, not merely the morally upright, and saying the law is not made for *him*.

The fact is, if any of these alternatives are right, and Paul was saying that these particular uses or abuses of the law are not made for a righteous man, then it can only mean that the law itself – the law – *is* made for a righteous man after all! And Paul was making a dreadful mistake. In fact, from the Reformed point of view, far from attacking these teachers at Ephesus, Paul should have commended them. He should have told Timothy to encourage them! They were doing precisely the right thing; they were getting believers to submit to the law. And if these teachers (and Timothy) were not quite clear about it, and one or other of those suggested alternatives *had* messed things up a bit, and that *that* was the problem he was dealing with, Paul should have instructed them and fine-tuned their thinking on the law – like Aquila and Priscilla did for Apollos on another matter (Acts 18:26). In short, he should have praised these teachers, at least for aiming in the right direction and trying to impose the law on believers, since the law in its third use *is* made for a righteous man! This, apparently, is the very person for whom it is made! Why, according to Calvin, it is its principal use!

Paul, however, declared the exact opposite. These teachers were *false* teachers. They had to be stopped. The law must not be imposed on believers. 'The law is not made for a righteous person'. The law must be used for the purpose God gave it, and no other. It must be used 'lawfully'. It must not be misused by trying to make it do something for which it was never intended. The one thing which Paul says here about the believer and the law is that the law is not made for him!

Of course I am not saying that because the law is not made for a righteous man, it has no relevance in his life. But I am certainly saying it is not his pattern, standard or perfect rule. These Judaisers wanted believers under the law, and Paul wouldn't have it at any price.[7]

As 1 John 3:7 declares: 'He who practices righteousness is righteous, just as he [Christ] is righteous'. The justified person will show it by godly works (Jas. 2:14-26). The law is not made for such a person. It is made for the opposite, for the sinner, the ungodly, the non-justified person, the person who is yet in his sin, the person whose ungodly works demonstrate that he is still an unbeliever (Rom. 6:19-23; Gal. 5:16-24; 1 Pet. 4:1-3, for instance). That is to say, God gave the law to the Jews when they were in that condition and for that purpose.

Paul is not here setting out the proper way for the believer to use the law. Not at all! That is not his purpose. He is dealing with false teachers. That's who he has in his sights. As he taught the Romans and the Galatians, believers are in Christ, have the Spirit, and so the law is fulfilled in them. They belong to a new age; thus, they are not under law (Rom. 6:14 – 7:6; Gal. 4:28 – 5:1). The atmosphere of this passage in Timothy – with its talk of the law, lawless, insubordinate and ungodly men, and fornication, sodomy, murder, lying, kidnappers and the like – is surely at variance with

---

[7] I say little about the reconstructionist's view that the law is the law for the Christian man and for a Christian society. What is a 'Christian society'? It does not exist. And if it did, it would not need the law. Why not? Because we know 'the law is not made for a righteous person, but for the lawless and insubordinate, for the ungodly and for sinners' (1 Tim. 1:9-10). Would a 'Christian society' need a law against blasphemy or murder for instance? If the answer is yes, then what distinguishes a 'Christian society' from a 'non-Christian society'? This passage on its own destroys the reconstructionist's claim; it says the opposite.

the sanctification of believers. I do not pretend that saints are immune to sin. David is too glaring an example for me to suggest such a thing. And, sadly, there is no shortage of contemporary examples. Who is without sin? I certainly do not claim it for myself! But are we really to understand that believers are to be taught, nourished, trained and disciplined in an atmosphere of *law* against sodomy, murder, adultery and the like? Is this really the height of Christianity? Is this the spirit of the New Testament? How does this fit with 1 Corinthians 6:9-11? Paul was clear: fornicators, sodomites, homosexuals and the like 'will not inherit the kingdom of God'. 'And such were some of you', he exclaimed. 'But you were washed, but you were sanctified, but you were justified in the name of the Lord Jesus and by the Spirit of our God' (1 Cor. 6:9-11). If ever there was a place for the apostle to set out Calvin's third use of the law, 1 Corinthians 6 is it. But what mention did Paul make of the law to sanctify these ex-homosexuals, ex-drunkards, and so on?

None! Paul did not take the Corinthians to Moses to keep them clean, and growing in godliness. He took them to Christ and the Spirit: 'The body is not for sexual immorality but for the *Lord*, and the *Lord* for the body. And God both raised up the *Lord* and will also raise us up by his power. Do you not know that your bodies are members of *Christ*?' he thundered. 'Shall I then take the members of *Christ* and make them members of a harlot? Certainly not!... Or do you not know that your body is the temple of the *Holy Spirit* who is in you, whom you have from God, and you are not your own? For you were bought at a price; therefore glorify God in your body and in your spirit, which are God's' (1 Cor. 6:13-20). 'Those who live should live no longer for themselves, but for him who died for them and rose again' (2 Cor. 5:15). *This* is the 'law' for believers – the law of Christ; not the law of Moses. The law of Christ is the means and motive of sanctification. Believers are not sanctified by the law of Moses; it is by Christ, by considering him, his blood, his present work as intercessor and advocate, his coming again, their union with him, and so on. I will return to this and develop it in chapter 16.[8]

In a word, believers ought not to be brought under the law of Moses. It is not designed for them. Paul said so in 1 Timothy 1:8-11. They live in a totally different realm. And, therefore, we should not be surprised to discover that, having opened his first letter to Timothy with 'Jesus Christ... the Lord Jesus Christ... Jesus Christ our Lord...', as with the Corinthians, the apostle went on to speak of Christ: 'I thank Christ Jesus our Lord... the grace of our Lord was exceedingly abundant, with faith and love which are in Christ Jesus... Christ Jesus... Jesus Christ... Christ Jesus... Christ... Christ Jesus... God was manifested in the flesh, justified in the Spirit... the Spirit... Jesus Christ... Christ... the Lord Jesus Christ... our Lord Jesus Christ...', continuing the theme in his second letter: 'Jesus Christ... Christ Jesus... Christ Jesus our Lord... Christ Jesus... our Saviour Jesus Christ... Christ Jesus... the Holy Spirit... Christ Jesus... Jesus Christ... Jesus Christ... Christ Jesus... Christ... Christ Jesus... Christ Jesus... the Lord Jesus Christ... the Lord Jesus Christ be with your spirit. Grace be with you'. And, of course, 'the Lord... the Lord... the Lord...'.[9]

Moses? The law? For the believer? No! Christ, the Spirit and grace!

---

[8] As I will show, the concept of 'law' in the law of Christ is very different to its concept in the law of Moses.

[9] And I may have lost count!

Chapter 14

Hebrews

If any book in the New Testament disproves the Reformed idea that the Sinai covenant and the new covenant are one and the same, it must be Hebrews, which makes it clear beyond a doubt that these two covenants are very different – indeed, that they are mutually exclusive – and that the Mosaic covenant has been abolished in Christ.[1] I will be brief on this – having dealt with it in other places throughout the book and elsewhere[2] – but since it has large implications for the issue of the believer and the law, and since Hebrews deals with it so fully, it would be wrong not to take at least a glance at what it says on the two covenants.

But before I get to individual passages, may I suggest, reader, that you read (aloud) Hebrews 7:11 – 10:18? May I further suggest that you read it again, in a version or two different to the one you normally use? To my mind, the argument is overwhelming. We have a new covenant, a new priesthood, a new order, a new system, a new sacrifice, a new commandment... new everything. Except, according to Reformed teaching, the law! And yet the law is the covenant, and the covenant is the law! Whatever else is new under the new covenant, it must be the law! Hebrews 7:11 – 10:18, I say, is irrefutable evidence that it is so.

Now for individual passages.

Take Hebrews 2:1-4, which reads:

Therefore we must give the more earnest heed to the things we have heard, lest we drift away. For if the word spoken through angels proved steadfast, and every transgression and disobedience received a just reward, how shall we escape if we neglect so great a salvation, which at the first began to be spoken by the Lord, and was confirmed to us by those who heard him, God also bearing witness both with signs and wonders, with various miracles, and gifts of the Holy Spirit, according to his own will?

Note the contrast drawn between what 'we have heard' and 'the word spoken through angels'. The writer, clearly, was referring to the gospel and the law. As a consequence, let me start again. Note the contrast drawn between the two covenants, and note, further, just how stark this contrast is. And we are talking of the contrast between the gospel and the law, between the new and the old covenants. One covenant is 'the things [which] we have heard... so great a salvation', which is the gospel. The other is 'the word spoken through angels', which is the law (Acts 7:53; Gal. 3:19). The old covenant was concerned with 'transgression and disobedience' in that every sin 'received a just reward' or retribution or penalty. The new covenant is also concerned with sin, but instead of bringing punishment, it brings salvation. The contrast could not be more sharply made. The new covenant is far superior to the old, and that is why 'we must give the *more* earnest heed to the things *we* have heard', since these things are so

---

[1] The extracts for this chapter begin on p476.
[2] See chapter 6, and my *Battle*; *Infant*; *Priesthood*.

much better than what was heard under the Mosaic covenant. If this point is ignored, many errors ensue. Confusion over the believer and the law is one such.

Take Hebrews 7:11-22 and 8:6-13:

Of necessity there is also a change of the law... On the one hand there is an annulling of the former commandment because of its weakness and unprofitableness, for the law made nothing perfect; on the other hand, there is the bringing in of a better hope, through which we draw near to God... Jesus has become a surety of a better covenant... But now[3] he has obtained a more excellent ministry, inasmuch as he is also mediator of a better covenant, which was established on better promises. For if that first covenant had been faultless, then no place would have been sought for a second. Because finding fault with them, he says: 'Behold, the days are coming, says the LORD, when I will make a new covenant with the house of Israel and with the house of Judah – not according to the covenant that I made with their fathers in the day when I took them by the hand to lead them out of the land of Egypt... This is the covenant that I will make... I will put my laws in their mind and write them on their hearts...'. In that [God] says: 'A new covenant', he has made the first obsolete. Now what is becoming obsolete and growing old is ready to vanish away.

If these words are not plain enough, I fear nothing will suffice. Once again, a clear contrast is drawn between the two covenants. On the one hand, we have 'the first covenant', 'the law', 'the former commandment'. And on the other 'a second', 'a better covenant which was established on better promises', 'a new covenant'. Christ, in bringing in the new covenant, has abrogated the old. Why have a new covenant, if the old covenant, the obsolete covenant, is still up and running? What place is there for a covenant that has vanished away? In particular, how can there be three *new*-covenant uses (*à la* Calvin) for something which is obsolete, grown *old*, and has vanished?

Take Hebrews 9. The same contrast between the covenants is drawn yet again. The old covenant, the law, was done away with at 'the time of reformation' (Heb. 9:10), 'the time of the new order' (NIV); that is, by the work of Christ. And, as far as benefits go, the new covenant is on a totally different plane to the old. The first covenant was all outward, it accomplished no salvation, and it has been done away with. But when we come to the new, how very different the story. God has always required blood sacrifice since 'without [the] shedding of blood there is no remission' (Heb. 9:22). Consequently, in the old covenant, blood was continually offered 'according to the law' (Heb. 9:22); namely, 'the blood of goats and calves... the blood of bulls and goats and the ashes of a heifer' (Heb. 9:12-13). How pointedly this is contrasted with the blood sacrifice of the new covenant, 'the blood of Christ', 'his own blood' (Heb. 9:12-14). Note the double contrast. *First*, the many sacrifices under the law are contrasted with the one sacrifice of Christ (see also Heb. 10:1-4,10-14). *Secondly*, the blood of animals is contrasted with the precious blood of Christ (see also 1 Pet. 1:18-19). What conclusion ought to be drawn from such contrasts? 'How much more shall the blood of Christ... cleanse your conscience from dead works to serve the living God? And for this reason he is the mediator of the new covenant'. It was necessary that Christ should redeem from 'the transgressions under the first covenant' because the first covenant was useless to save. It was more than 'necessary', however; it is the very thing which

---

[3] Note the 'but now'.

Christ *did* in bringing in the new (Heb. 9:11-15). How is it possible for covenant theologians to say these covenants are one and the same?

Take Hebrews 10:1-20,28-29.

For the law, having a shadow of the good things to come, and not the very image of the things... He takes away the first that he may establish the second... The Holy Spirit also witnesses to us; for after he had said before: 'This is the covenant that I will make with them after those days, says the LORD... then he adds: 'Their sins and their lawless deeds I will remember no more'... Anyone who has rejected Moses' law dies without mercy... Of how much worse punishment, do you suppose, will he be thought worthy who has trampled the Son of God underfoot, counted the blood of the covenant by which he was sanctified a common thing, and insulted the Spirit of grace?

Omitting the 'and' in Hebrews 10:1, which is not in the original, the verse reads: 'For the law, having a shadow of the good things to come, not the very image of the things, can never...'. Once again, we have a contrast, and more than a contrast. They – the shadow and the image – were *opposed* to each other. See Colossians 2:17. And the contrast, the opposition, is between the law and the gospel. There is a large, basic, fundamental difference between the two covenants, between the law and the gospel, which difference governs many issues – in particular, the believer and the law. It is the continuity/discontinuity issue once again.

The rest of Hebrews 10 goes on to draw the same contrast between the two covenants, and comes to the same conclusion as earlier passages, but from the opposite point of view; namely, punishment, not mercy. The two covenants both carried punishments, but since the new covenant is superior to the old, it is only to be expected that the punishments under the new covenant are far more serious than those under the old.[4] And they certainly are: 'Anyone who has rejected Moses' law dies without mercy... Of how much worse punishment, do you suppose, will he be thought worthy who has trampled the Son of God underfoot, counted the blood of the covenant by which he was sanctified a common thing, and insulted the Spirit of grace?' (Heb. 10:28-29). Yes, 'of how much worse punishment'? How can the covenants be the same? Their punishments are as different as their benefits.

Hebrews 12:18-29 stresses exactly the same distinction between the two covenants. The old covenant was physical; the new is spiritual. Mount Sinai is sharply contrasted with Mount Zion (Heb. 12:18,22). The old covenant was issued with burning and blackness, darkness and tempest (Heb. 12:18); the new is full of joy and happiness. The old brought terror, fear and trembling – even for Moses (Heb. 12:19-21); the new brought peace and salvation. The old said: 'Stay away, keep off' (Heb. 12:20); the new cries: 'Come and welcome'. It is utterly impossible for these two covenants to be the same.

Isaac Watts:

> *Curs'd be the man, for ever curs'd,*
> *That does one wilful sin commit;*
> *Death and damnation for the first,*
> *Without relief, and infinite.*

---

[4] As before, the warning passages are real.

Thus Sinai roars, and round the earth
Thunder, and fire, and vengeance flings;
But Jesus, thy dear gasping breath
And Calvary, say gentler things:

'Pardon and grace, and boundless love,
Streaming along a Saviour's blood;
And life, and joy, and crowns above,
Obtained by a dear bleeding God'.

Hark! How he prays (the charming sound
Dwells on his dying lips): 'Forgive!'
And every groan and gaping wound
Cries: 'Father, let the rebels live!'

Go, ye that rest upon the law,
And toil and seek salvation there,
Look to the flame that Moses saw,
And shrink, and tremble, and despair.

But I'll retire beneath the cross;
Saviour, at thy dear feet I'll lie!
And the keen sword that justice draws,
Flaming and red, shall pass me by.[5]

The Mosaic covenant was abolished in Christ. And since the Mosaic covenant, the law, has been abolished in Christ, how can it be the perfect rule for the believer? Does the believer live on Mount Zion for justification, and, at the same time, live on Mount Sinai for sanctification? We are expressly told that as believers we have not come to Sinai (Heb. 12:18)![6]

If I may interject a personal note, when I preach the passage, I start by asking the congregation what mountain they are living on. In the discourse, I set out the two mountains in question, and ask them which of the two they are living on. Their answer makes all the difference in the world – and in eternity! Make no mistake! They are living on one of the two – not both! As we all are!

How anybody can read Hebrews and come away with the impression that the law and the gospel are the same covenant, or that believers are under the law as a perfect rule, utterly baffles me.

---

[5] *Gospel Hymns* number 394.
[6] I would not press it, but Heb. 12:18 has all the appearance of destroying preparationism by the law, too.

Chapter 15

The Law Written

There are several places in the New Testament where the law in its *written* aspect is spoken of, where it is described as 'the law of commandments contained in ordinances', 'the letter', and so on.[1] This written law, Scripture explains, is at enmity with those it holds in its grip. It is a 'ministry of condemnation', a 'ministry of death' for those who are under it. Above all, these New Testament passages declare that, for his people, Christ has dealt with this 'letter', this 'law of commandments contained in ordinances', this 'written and engraved' law which was against them. He has removed it. They are no longer under it. In short, these passages concerning the written law teach the very same as we have seen in Romans 6:14; 7:4,6; 8:4, Galatians 3:25-26; 5:18, and elsewhere.

Here are the passages in question:

But now we have been delivered from the law, having died to what we were held by, so that we should serve in the newness of the Spirit and not in the oldness of the letter (Rom. 7:6).

God... made us sufficient as ministers of the new covenant, not of the letter but of the Spirit; for the letter kills, but the Spirit gives life. But if the ministry of death, written and engraved on stones, was glorious, so that the children of Israel could not look steadily at the face of Moses because of the glory of his countenance, which glory was passing away, how will the ministry of the Spirit not be more glorious? For if the ministry of condemnation had glory, the ministry of righteousness exceeds much more in glory. For even what was made glorious had no glory in this respect, because of the glory that excels. For if what is passing away was glorious, what remains is much more glorious (2 Cor. 3:5-11).

[Christ]... having abolished in his flesh the enmity; that is, the law of commandments contained in ordinances... putting to death the enmity (Eph. 2:14-16).

[Christ] having wiped out the handwriting of requirements that was against us, which was contrary to us. And he has taken it out of the way, having nailed it to the cross (Col. 2:14).

These four passages speak about the same thing, making the same point to the same sort of people. They speak to believers, teaching them the truth about their past and present relationship to the law. These passages tell us that the law was the *letter*, the law *written* and *engraved* on stones, the law of commandments contained in *ordinances*, the *handwriting*. And addressing believers, these passages all say this written law was a ministry of *condemnation*, at *enmity* with or *against* them. And they all say the written law, which was against them, was by Christ's work and gift of the Spirit *passing away*, *abolished*, or *wiped out*, so that believers are *delivered from* it.

Let me deal with the words I have just emphasised.

The Greek for *delivered from*, *passing away* and *abolished* means 'to cause to cease, to put an end to, to do away with, annul, abolish, to make invalid'. Thus Romans 7:6, 2 Corinthians 3:11 and Ephesians 2:15 all speak of the same thing; namely, of the end of the law, of its being abolished, of its being done away with, of its being put away, its being made to cease. In other words, believers are released from the law by

---

[1] The extracts for this chapter begin on p478.

200

the work of Christ. He has done away with it. The word is used elsewhere in the New Testament, to speak of making the law *void*, of *destroying* the body, of *putting away* childish things and of *abolishing* death (Rom. 3:31; 1 Cor. 6:13; 13:11; 2 Tim. 1:10).[2] This makes the meaning of our passages very clear. The law, for believers, has been abolished, put away, destroyed, made invalid, brought to an end, made void.

A different word is used in Colossians 2:14, translated *wiped out*. It means 'to wipe off, wipe away, obliterate, erase, blot out, remove, destroy'. Hence it speaks with a similar voice to the other passages; Christ has obliterated the law for believers, wiped it away, erased it. Note the three steps. He 'blotted it out'. Is that enough? No! 'He took it out of the way'. Is *that* enough? No. He 'nailed it to his cross'. It is finished, over and done with, for ever.

Ah! But what is the 'it'? What, precisely, has been abolished, done away with, removed by Christ? What have believers been delivered from? *This* is the issue. It is the law (Rom. 7:6; Eph. 2:15), the killing letter, the ministry of death and condemnation written on stones (2 Cor. 3:6-7,9), 'the handwriting of requirements' (Col. 2:14). It is the law which is blotted out, not the law in 'so far as it was against us and cursed us'. The law! Sadly, however, there is a great deal of confusion over this. Let me look at it in more detail.

Take the Ephesian passage. Paul spoke of 'the law', 'the law of commandments', 'the law of commandments contained in ordinances'. What did he mean? He was speaking of the law of Moses written on stones and written in Scripture, the Mosaic law in its entirety. The same goes for the Corinthian and the Colossian passages.[3] There is no difference between 'the letter' which 'kills... the ministry of death, written and engraved on stones... the ministry of condemnation' (2 Cor. 3:5-11), 'the enmity; that is the law of commandments contained in ordinances... the enmity' (Eph. 2:14-16), and 'the handwriting of requirements that was against us, which was contrary to us' (Col. 2:14).

In 2 Corinthians 3, Paul was certainly referring at least to the ten commandments given at Sinai. *They* were written on stones (Ex. 34:28; Deut. 4:13; 5:22; 10:4). Moreover, the Greek word for *letter* or *writing* in Romans 7:6 and 2 Corinthians 3:6, is the same as in Romans 2:27; namely, the written code, the written law of Moses, 'his writings' (John 5:47). And this, it goes without saying, is the law, including the ten commandments. Furthermore, in Romans 7:7, Paul quoted the tenth commandment. In addition, the Greek word for *commandments* in Ephesians 2:15 is used in Ephesians 6:2, speaking of the fifth commandment. So 'the law of commandments' (Eph. 2:15) must include the ten *commandments*. Furthermore, it is the word which is used repeatedly in Romans 7:8-13, where Paul undeniably was speaking of the decalogue, the commandments of the law, that law which God gave to Moses. In the Ephesian passage, Paul declares that the law of Moses itself is the dividing wall of hostility between Jews and Gentiles, and that Christ made peace between Jews and Gentiles by

---

[2] While I recognise that Rom. 3:31 states that the gospel establishes the law and does not make it 'void', I am drawing attention to the use of the word 'abolish', which is used of the law in the other texts. As for Rom. 3:31, see chapter 6 where I observed that Christ accomplished the justification of his people under the law – by keeping it perfectly and undergoing its punishment for sin – thus establishing it. As I have also noted, and will show, the believer's sanctification is an aspect of Rom. 3:31.

[3] But see below.

destroying this hostility, the dividing wall, by abolishing the law of commandments in ordinances itself – that which gave rise to the hostility. This is further confirmed by the Greek word for *law* which is used in Ephesians 2:15 and many other places, including Romans 7; Galatians 3 and 4; and 1 Timothy 1:8-9. It refers to 'the Mosaic law – the volume or its contents', including the ten commandments. It is the whole of the Mosaic law, the ten commandments in particular, which 'passes [fades] away' (2 Cor. 3:11,13; Heb. 8:13).[4] What is more, the Greek word for *ordinances*, which is used in Ephesians 2:15 and Colossians 2:14, means 'the rules and requirements of the law of Moses', and is linked as above with *commandments*. There is no doubt, therefore, that these four passages – in Romans 7, 2 Corinthians 3, Ephesians 2 and Colossians 2 – speaking of the written law, all refer to the Mosaic law including the ten commandments.

Exodus 34:27-28 is a crucial passage, showing that 'the ten commandments' and 'the words of the covenant' are one and the same. The Reformed tripartite division of the law founders on this passage. The Mosaic law given at Sinai is one indivisible law, and this statement (Ex. 34:27-28) paints the background for Paul's declaration about its abolition. It is the law of Moses as a whole, and in all its parts, which has passed away, and this includes the ten commandments. 'The whole law' is embraced in Paul's declaration.[5]

It is abundantly plain, therefore, that the four passages in question speak about one and the same thing; namely, the Mosaic law, that same law as is spoken of in Romans 6:14; 7:1-12; 8:2-4 and Galatians 3:10-25; 4:21-25; 5:14,18. If you have any doubt, reader, please read these passages, and compare them with the passages in question in this chapter. They all speak of the same law – the Mosaic law, including the ten commandments – and they consistently speak of it in terms of its rule, bondage, curse, enmity, requirements, and so on, and they consistently speak of its removal for believers by the work of Christ. So the believer – the person who has the Spirit of the Lord – is no longer in bondage, because in Christ 'there is liberty' (2 Cor. 3:17).[6]

As we saw in chapter 11, in 2 Corinthians 3:3-18, Paul was contrasting the glory of the gospel with that of the Mosaic economy, contrasting the ministries of the old and new covenants, contrasting their relative glories. The old covenant was to do with the flesh; the new covenant is the covenant of the Holy Spirit (verses 3,6,8). The old covenant was an outward covenant, written on stones; the new covenant is an inward covenant, written on the heart (verses 2-3,7). The old covenant killed; it spelled death; the new covenant spells life (verses 3,6-7). The old covenant was deliberately temporary, designed by God to be so; the new covenant is permanent; it remains (verses 11,13). The old covenant had glory, but its glory was lesser and fading; the new covenant has a glory which exceeds, excels, being so much greater than the glory of the

---

[4] In chapter 9, I drew the comparison with man's likeness to a temporary and vanishing 'vapour' in Jas. 4:14 and associated passages.

[5] See chapter 7.

[6] Now a question might suggest itself. Since, as I have explained in chapter 2, the law was given to the Jews and not to the Gentiles, how were these Gentiles ever under this 'handwriting' in the first place? How were they under the law? The answer is Romans 2:14-15. Gentiles have 'the work of the law written in their hearts'. See chapter 3 for an examination of Rom. 2:14-15. This same difficulty arises elsewhere of course; Rom. 7:1-6, for instance. One thing is certain, however. If any Reformed writer wants to limit 'the law' in these passages to the ceremonial law, he needs to explain how the Gentiles were ever under the ceremonial law. See below.

old covenant (verses 7-11). The old covenant condemned; the new covenant is justifying (verse 9).[7] The old covenant spelled bondage; the new covenant, liberty (verses 12,17). Note the new/old contrast; the new is established, the old is abolished; the new has power, the old was useless and ineffective.

The enmity of the law in Ephesians 2:14-16 came about because of its divisive nature. God built this separation into the law, making it a fundamental aspect of the law. As we saw in chapter 2, God gave the law to Israel, and only to Israel, as a special mark to separate the Jews from the rest of mankind. The law separated Jew and Gentile, and both were separated from God (Rom. 3:19-20; 4:15; 5:20; 7:7-11). And this law can be none other than the law of Moses, the whole of it. The same goes for Colossians 2:14. Christ abolished the law, by fulfilling it. By his death, he has freed believers from the law. They are no longer under the law but under grace (Rom. 6:14). The word 'ordinances' must not be misunderstood. Paul was not talking about what Reformed people call the ceremonial law – he was talking about the whole law expressed in particular rules, regulations, commands and ordinances. It certainly included the fourth commandment – the sabbath. After all, the sabbath was a principal dividing marker between Jew and the rest of mankind (Ex. 31:12-18; Neh. 9:13-14; 13:14-22; Ezek. 20:5-26).

As for Romans 7:6, 'the oldness of the letter' is the law. It is called 'the letter' simply because it was an external written code, written on the two tablets of stone, and then in Scripture. Both the old and new covenants were (are) written; the old, externally on stone and in the pages of Scripture; the new, in Scripture and, above all, in the heart. The old was a killing covenant; the new brings life. 2 Corinthians 3:6 is a parallel passage. Christ has set believers free from the law.

In short, these four passages on the written law, Romans 7:6, 2 Corinthians 3:5-11, Ephesians 2:14-16 and Colossians 2:14, teach the same doctrine as we have seen in many other places of Scripture; namely, Christ has set his people free from the law of Moses. It cannot be, therefore, the believer's perfect rule of godliness.

Sadly, it is not unknown for Reformed writers to gloss these passages. Let me give some examples.

Some say the law in question is the ceremonial law

This is a frequent claim, but inconsistently made. Some argue for instance that Ephesians 2:14 refers to 'the ceremonial law', but Romans 7 is the entire Mosaic law. And yet these two passages, as I have shown, speak of precisely the same law. Some argue that it was only the ceremonial law which divided Jew and Gentile. Yet they also admit that the ten commandments, like the ceremonies, were given to Israel. Some make much of the word 'ordinances' in Ephesians 2:14-16, deducing Paul was not talking about the ten commandments. But this is a mistake. Even in the ten commandments, there are ordinances, 'rules and regulations'. Were these not an

---

[7] As I have explained, although the apostle spoke of 'justification' in 2 Cor. 3:9, he was encompassing much more; indeed, the whole of salvation. No sinner was saved by keeping the law. To clutch at a straw here, and try to use this verse to limit the passage – and all the other passages – to the law for justification is simply not worthy of serious teachers. If Calvin's third use of the law depends on such puerile exegesis, its case must be desperate.

integral part of 'the Mosaic code' and its 'stipulations'? Does Colossians 2:14 not refer to the Mosaic law, including the ten commandments? Who wrote the handwriting in Colossians 2:14? and where did he write it? In other words, what or whose is 'the handwriting of requirements' which has been 'wiped out'? I have answered all these questions. There can be no doubt that the writing and law of commandments which was against us includes the ten commandments, not merely the so-called 'ceremonial law'. Ephesians 2:14-15 is 'the law with its commandments and regulations'; not the *ceremonial* law.[8] If anybody should try to argue that the 'that is' of Ephesians 2:15 proves Paul was referring to the ceremonial law, they should bear in mind that the translators have added the 'that is'; Paul didn't write it!

As for the ordinances in the ten commandments, take the fourth. Sabbath law was full of ordinances – ordinances about work, the family, servants, animals and immigrants. And the number of sabbath ordinances contained in the rest of Moses' writings is, I might say, legion. So even if Paul had been speaking about the ordinances which flesh out the commandments, and not the commandments themselves, he would have destroyed the Reformed case: Christ, apparently, has delivered us from the sabbath *because he has delivered us from all its ordinances*. And if he has delivered us from the fourth commandment, he has delivered us from the entire system (Jas. 2:10-11). Since Reformed sabbatarians claim Christ has removed all ceremonial laws for his people, how can they argue for the retention of a commandment so obviously ceremonial?

And, reader, do not forget, when Paul was writing to the Ephesians and Colossians, he was writing to Gentiles. Were they ever under the ceremonial law (allowing the term) with all its Jewish fasts, feasts, foods, offerings and circumcision? Were the Ephesians labouring under such things before conversion? Was that their problem? No Reformed writer – as far as I am aware – has ever suggested that Gentiles were under what the Reformed call the ceremonial law. Where and when did God ever command and require – I use the word 'require' advisedly in light of 'handwriting of *requirements*' (Col. 2:14) – where did he command and require Gentiles to observe the fasts, feasts, offerings and circumcision? Did Christ die to release Gentiles from *Jewish* feasts and rituals? Paul was not saying that Christ abolished the law of ceremonies, destroying its binding power. I am glad Christ has done far more than that for his people.

The Ephesian passage teaches us that the Jews were distinguished from the Gentiles, separated from them, that there was 'a middle wall of division between' them. This barrier, this wall of division, this demarcation line between the two, primarily comprised 'the law of commandments contained in ordinances'. True, circumcision had become in the Jewish mind the great divider, the most visible, the most obvious, divider (Eph. 2:11),[9] the one the Jews boasted of more than any, but the fact is the Gentiles 'at that time... were without Christ, being aliens from the commonwealth of Israel and strangers from the covenants of promise, having no hope and without God in the world' (Eph. 2:12). Especially were they separated from the Jews – and from God – by the fact that God gave his law, 'his word... his statutes and

---

[8] See chapter 17 for an examination of the seeming contradiction between this view of Eph. 2:14-16 and Eph. 6:1-3 where Paul quoted the law in his teaching on the care of children.
[9] Not only was circumcision an obvious separating mark, so were the sabbath and dietary laws.

his judgements', 'the law of commandments contained in ordinances', to the Jews and not to them (Ps. 147:19-20). They were not under the pedagogue of the law as were the Jews (Gal. 3:23-25). As I have shown, God gave his law to Israel and to no others.[10] What law was this, which distinguished the Jews from the Gentiles? The law of Moses. All attempts to restrict this to a part of the law are very wide of the mark.

Some say the law in question is the judicial law

Disagreeing with those who think it was the ceremonial law which divided Jew and Gentile, some think it was 'the judicial law' which did it; it was the 'civil regulations' which comprised 'the wall of partition'. Oh? How is it then that we are told (Ex. 31:12-18; Neh. 9:13-14; 13:14-22; Ezek. 20:5-26) that the sabbath[11] was given to the Jews as a sign to mark them out from all other nations, that it was a central part of his covenant with Israel, his special people (Deut. 4:1-8,44-45; 5:1-3; 29:1,10-15,25,29)? I mention this because the sabbath is not, of course, according to Reformed writers, part of the judicial law, but the moral! What is more, if Christ shed his blood to remove the handwriting of the *judicial or social* law, he must have died to grant his people liberty to eat pork, wear garments of mixed yarns, and so on.[12] The idea is preposterous. And, as before, who will claim that the Gentiles were ever under the *Jewish* civil law?

Some show a reluctance to take the passages seriously, especially in their works on the sabbath

I have noted a seeming unwillingness on the part of some, or an inadequate examination of the passages, in their works on the law or the sabbath, to face up to John 1:17, 2 Corinthians 3:6-11, Ephesians 2:15 and Colossians 2:14, passages of high significance in this debate. Why is it that, in their works on the sabbath, so many Reformed writers seem reluctant to tackle these passages? And, even when they do, they frequently introduce (contradictory) glosses to circumvent them. Why?

Various other escape routes

Romans 7:6, Ephesians 2:15 and Colossians 2:14 clearly teach that the law is abolished; the believer is free of it. Christ did not abolish the entire law except the ten commandments. He abolished the law. Paul did not say that the believer is free of the law only in the sense of obtaining justification by it, that he is no longer under its curse. Christ has wiped out the law for the believer. Above all, Paul was not speaking only of justification when writing to the Ephesian and Colossian believers. The context of Colossians 2 is not justification but sanctification. The letter starts with justification, but Paul's aim was his readers' sanctification. By reading the letter through in one sitting, this becomes very clear. See especially Colossians 1:9-14; 2:6-10,16 – 4:18. In particular, in his letter, the apostle was not only telling the Colossians that there is no justification by law work – he was telling them there is no sanctification by the law,

---

[10] See chapter 2 for more on the law as the wall of partition.
[11] See chapter 7.
[12] Or does this come under the *ceremonial* law?

either. He was speaking of justification leading to sanctification. See Ephesians 4:1 –
6:24; Col. 1:10,22-29; 2:6,16-23; 3:1 – 4:18. Reader, you may verify this from
Ephesians 2, for instance. Note how justification (Eph. 2:8-9) leads to sanctification
(Eph. 2:10) which leads directly to Ephesians 2:11 and on, beginning with the word
'therefore' (Eph. 2:11-22).

The ten commandments were written by the finger of God on two tablets of stone
(Ex. 31:18; 32:14-15; 34:1,28; Deut. 5:22) – and it was *precisely* this system, the
temporary ministry of death, written on stones, which was abolished when Christ
fulfilled the law (2 Cor. 3:7,11). It is not only the glory of the law which was done
away with – it was the law itself.[13] 2 Corinthians 3:11,13 proves it. Yes, the glory of
the old covenant was fading – but only because the old covenant itself was fading! It
was temporary (Gal. 3:19,23-25); it was being annulled (Heb. 7:18); it was 'becoming
obsolete and growing old' and was 'ready to vanish away' (Heb. 8:13). But, please
note, it was *the entire system of law* which Christ abolished, not merely its glory. It was
not merely the glory of the law which was becoming obsolete, growing old and ready
to vanish away – it was the law *itself*. Indeed, only the covenant could be said to be
'abolished', not its glory. In any case, the evasion is the merest quibble. If the law has
lost its glory, it has lost everything! For those who think it is just the glory of the law
which is gone, what now of the suggestion that we are to think that Christ leads his
people back to Moses? If this is so, it means that the law, far from losing its fading
glory, has greater glory under Christ than ever it had under Moses! But Christ took
away the first – law – to establish the second – grace (Heb. 10:9). Moses has given way
to Christ. Christ has superseded him. Christ is better: 'For this one has been counted
worthy *of more glory* than Moses... Moses indeed was faithful in all his house as a
servant, for a testimony of those things which would be spoken afterwards [that is,
Christ and the gospel], but Christ...' (Heb. 3:1-6). Once again, reader, see John 1:17.

Christ and his covenant have more glory than Moses and his covenant. Therefore, if
the Reformed are right, and sinners, on conversion, are taken under Moses for their
sanctification, then they are taken under a covenant that has less glory than the new
covenant Christ established for them. This, it seems to me, can only mean that the
Reformed end up with a system that gives Moses more glory than Christ. Nonsense!

Nor will it do to try to argue that the law *as a piece of writing*, independent of the
Spirit, was done away with, and *that* was the old, obsolete thing which was abolished,
not the law itself. Such a view, of course, prepares the way for asserting Calvin's third
use of the law, in which the Spirit takes up that same law and uses it as the perfect rule
in the believer's life. In plain English, it is not done away with after all! Rather, it is
made stronger! No! 'The letter' means 'the law in its written aspect'. 'The letter' is
contrasted with 'the Spirit' (Rom. 2:29; 7:6; 2 Cor. 3:6), as is 'the law' (Rom. 7:6; Gal.
5:18). 'The letter' therefore is 'the law', not the law without the Spirit.

The four passages we have looked at in this chapter, which all concern the written law,
Romans 7:6, 2 Corinthians 3:5-11, Ephesians 2:14-16 and Colossians 2:14, all teach
the same doctrine as we have seen in many other places of Scripture; namely, Christ
has set his people free from the law of Moses. It therefore cannot be the believer's
perfect rule of godliness.

---

[13] See the previous chapter.

True, the old covenant had a glory. But the new covenant is better, superior, and its glory, therefore, is all the greater. The old covenant of death and condemnation, which was temporary, has gone. The new covenant, of Christ, of the Spirit, brings justification, and is permanent. What is more, it brings sanctification leading to glorification. Beyond all doubt, the new covenant is more glorious than the old. Notice how Paul, in 2 Corinthians 3, takes his argument on to sanctification, the transformation of believers. It is as Christ is preached, believed and looked to – in other words, as the new covenant is declared and received – that believers, having and realising their freedom in Christ, are transformed more and more into his image:

Behold what manner of love the Father has bestowed on us, that we should be called the children of God... Beloved, now we are children of God; and it has not yet been revealed what we shall be, but we know that when he [Christ] is revealed, we shall be like him, for we shall see him as he is. And everyone who has this hope in him purifies himself, just as he is pure (1 John 3:1-3).

If that is not 'the law of Christ', what is it? If such passages do not tell us the motive, the spur, the way, and the aim of sanctification – with no mention whatever of 'the law' – what do they tell us?

Part Four

The Believer's Rule

The Law Is Not the Believer's Rule. So What Is?

Chapter 16

The Believer's Rule

Although the believer is not under the law, he is not law-less; he is under the law of Christ – the meaning of 'law' in the law of Christ – the eschatological setting of 'law' – the law of Christ – Galatians 6:2 and its context – the law of Christ cannot be confined to the ten commandments – two biblical examples – the law of Christ cannot be the old law; it must be new; it must be his own law – a seeming contradiction – Christ is the giver of his law – its binding nature – love its goal – love its motive – its penetrating nature – Christ gives power to keep his law – it is not independent of Scripture – it is all about what a believer is – the law of Christ is Christ himself – further New Testament examples – the law of Christ brings glory to the believer now – the choice – examples from the writings of men

Before I start, I have to offer an apology. Although I have tried hard to keep this chapter in bounds, and to make it as systematic as I can, I have, nevertheless, failed to do as well as I had hoped. I considered breaking it into parts, but that would accomplish nothing. In short, I have to admit defeat, leaving the end-result, I am afraid, somewhat unwieldy.

In a sense, however, I am relieved. As I understand the law of Christ, as I discover it set out in the pages of the New Testament, I find it to be of such a nature or character that defies simplistic systematisation. The decalogue, of course, can be set out in ten straightforward commands; even the law of Moses can be set out as one rule after another. But you cannot possibly do that with the law of Christ. Notwithstanding, this is not a weakness of the law of Christ; it is, in fact, one of its greatest glories. The law of Christ is not a 'law' in the Mosaic sense at all.

Nevertheless, I am sorry that I have not been able to do better. I am sure others could set out Christ's law in a more user-friendly way than I have been able to manage. But there it is. May I suggest, reader, that you make full use of the epigraph at the head of this chapter. I hope it will help!

Now for the chapter itself. Let me preface it with some words which I wrote right at the start:

I realise that in writing this book I leave myself a hostage to fortune. 'Physician, heal yourself!' But I do not send this book out into the world because I have attained to the standard I spell out. I make no pretence of that! I do not boast about it, but it is the sad fact. I am a sinner. I fall short. The best closing prayer I ever heard was: 'Lord, make us as good as others think we are'. Even so, remember, reader, every sermon you have ever heard, every prayer you have said 'Amen' to, every hymn you have ever sung, and every book you have ever read, was produced by a sinner – a sinner, like yourself!

Those words were never more applicable than they are now.[1] I am not saying that what I set out is easy to attain to. Nor do I claim perfection for myself (or anyone else who

---

[1] The extracts for this chapter begin on p481.

takes the same line as I do on the law). But let us be clear about it. Lack of perfection is a sad fact of life for every Reformed and evangelical writer on sanctification, for every advocate of Calvin's third use of the law – not excepting Calvin himself, the Puritans, or the most earnest devotee of the Westminster Assembly documents. New-covenant writers do not have a monopoly on sin and failure! I am not excusing our sin, but we are all sinners – *all* of us (2 Chron. 6:36). If sermons can be preached (and heard), and books can be written (and read), only by those who have reached the standard set out in such sermons and books, I guess our pulpits, churches and book shelves will be more or less empty. Or else our sermons and books won't be saying very much worth thinking about! This, I hope it is understood, is not my version of a blank cheque for laxity; it is meant to strike a note of realism.

The question which has to be settled is: What is the New Testament way of sanctification?

As we have seen, the law cannot be the believer's perfect rule. And we know why. How can the letter which kills (2 Cor. 3:6), the ministry of death (2 Cor. 3:7), the ministry of condemnation (2 Cor. 3:9) which brings wrath (Rom. 4:15), the old, obsolete, letter (Rom. 7:6; Heb. 8:13) which brings a curse (Gal. 3:10), which arouses sin (Rom. 7:5,9), kills (Rom. 7:9-11) and makes the offence abound (Rom. 5:20), which is not of faith (Gal. 3:12), which could not give life (Gal. 3:21), which believers are not under (Rom. 6:14) – indeed, to which they have become dead, and are delivered from, so that they can be married to Christ (Rom. 7:1-6) – how can *this* be the perfect rule of life for the believer?

Ah, but if the believer is not under the Mosaic law, does this mean that he is under no law at all? Is he law-less, and therefore may be lawless? Far from it!

Although the believer is not under the law of Moses, he is not law-less; he is under the law of Christ

The believer really is free – in particular, set free from sin (Rom. 6:22), and free from the law (Gal. 5:1). But liberty is not licence. There is a rule for believers to live by. They are 'under law towards Christ', that 'perfect law of liberty'. They are ruled by 'the law of Christ', following 'this rule', 'walk[ing] by the same rule', having taken Christ's 'easy yoke', being taught by the Spirit 'to observe all things' which Christ commanded (Matt. 11:28-30; 28:20; 1 Cor. 9:21; Gal. 6:2,16; Phil. 3:16; Jas. 1:25; 2:12).[2]

The believer is free in Christ, he is free from the law, yes, *but this does not mean he is free to sin*. Holiness of life is an essential mark of the true believer (Heb. 12:14), not an optional extra. It is impossible to be justified *and stop there*. Justification is not the terminus! A justified man must go on to be a sanctified man.[3] Justification and sanctification are always linked in Scripture.[4] Justification, which is by grace through

---

[2] I will give my reasons for taking Gal. 6:16; Phil. 3:16; Jas. 1:25; 2:12 to be the law of Christ.

[3] As I have explained, sanctification is not the goal. Glorification is! But my concern in this chapter, as it has been throughout the book, is progressive sanctification.

[4] In chapter 9 p124, I spoke of this, including the disagreement between the Anabaptists and the Reformers over it.

faith without works, leads to sanctification; that is, good works (Eph. 2:8-10). 'You know that everyone who practices righteousness is born of [God]' (1 John 2:29). The outward evidence of justification (which cannot be seen) is sanctification (which can and must be seen). Justification is a declaration by God *about* the believer. Sanctification is a work of God *in* the believer. And God never declares a sinner righteous in his sight without also working in him to make him righteous in the sight of men. To the believer, God imputes righteousness, but he never does this without also imparting it. 'Faith by itself, if it does not have works, is dead'. To the man who claims to be justified by faith even though he has no works – no sanctification – to prove it, James retorts: 'Show me your faith without your works' – an impossibility – 'and I will show you my faith by my works... O foolish man... faith without works is dead' (Jas. 2:14-26).

Of course, while there are strong connections between justification and sanctification, there are big differences. In particular, while justification is instantaneous and perfect, sanctification is progressive and never complete in this life. It is this progressive sanctification which concerns us here – the believer's obedience to Peter's closing injunction: 'Grow in the grace and knowledge of our Lord and Saviour Jesus Christ'. This, surely, is the way to bring about the apostle's desire: 'To [Christ] be the glory both now and for ever' (2 Pet. 3:18). Nor is it without significance that Peter had opened his letter by praying: 'Grace and peace be multiplied to you in the knowledge of God and of Jesus our Lord' (2 Pet. 1:2). This growing experience of the grace and knowledge of Christ, and the fruits and effects of it, are what I mean by 'sanctification'.[5]

Sanctification, therefore, is not a mere desirable for the child of God; it is obligatory (Gal. 5:13-18; 1 Thess. 4:1-7). It is a matter of obedience to a command: 'Pursue... holiness [the sanctification, NASB], without which no one will see the Lord' (Heb. 12:14).[6] 'As he who called you is holy, you also be holy in all your conduct' (1 Pet. 1:15). Believers are to perfect 'holiness in the fear of God' (2 Cor. 7:1).[7] 'Let everyone who names the name of Christ depart from iniquity' (2 Tim. 2:19). Those who are not sanctified 'will not inherit the kingdom of God' (1 Cor. 6:9-11, NIV).[8] And so on.

Hence, for the believer there is no question as to whether sanctification is required. Of course it is! Nor is there any question as to whether the believer is under a rule of life. Of course he is! But since the law of Moses is not that rule, what is? We know that in Christ 'there is an annulling of the former commandment because of its weakness and unprofitableness, for the law made nothing perfect [or complete]' (Heb. 7:18-19). This perfection is not limited to justification; it includes sanctification. The law made *nothing* perfect. (Compare Rom. 8:3-4; Phil. 3:12; Heb. 12:23). Nothing! And this

---

[5] 'Grace and peace' (or the equivalent) at the opening of so many New Testament letters is no make-weight (Rom. 1:7; 1 Cor. 1:3; 2 Cor. 1:2; Gal. 1:3; Eph. 1:2; Phil. 1:2; Col. 1:2; 1 Thess. 1:1; 2 Thess. 1:2; 1 Tim. 1:2; 2 Tim. 1:2; Tit. 1:4; Philem. 3; 1 Pet. 1:2; 2 Pet. 1:2; 2 John 3; (Jude 2); Rev. 1:4).

[6] The legalist wants salvation *by* his holiness, *by* the merit of it, *because* of it, but he cannot. An antinomian wants it *without* holiness, but God will not allow it. The true believer knows he cannot be saved *by* his holiness, nor *without* it.

[7] There is a huge difference between godly and carnal fear.

[8] I do not say this merely because of the 'sanctified' in verse 11. I say it because it is the tenor of the passage. Believers are justified and sanctified, *but they must show it in their lives. Or else!*

includes both justification and sanctification. So what *will* make believers perfect or complete? Since God 'has made the first [covenant] obsolete' (Heb. 8:13), what has replaced it?[9] What – precisely – is the rule by which the sanctification of a believer is to be measured? Even more important, what is the spur or motive for this sanctification? Above all, what is the means of sanctification? While it is right to be concerned about *what* we ought to be doing, and *why*, the most difficult question is *how* we are to do it! In this chapter, I am setting out what I see as the biblical answer to these questions. And that answer is 'the law of Christ'. This is 'the believer's rule'.

But herein lies the makings of a misunderstanding. Let me explain the meaning of 'rule' in this connection. It does not mean a list of regulations. Far from it. The believer's rule is far bigger than this. Why, it is not like it at all! Similarly, the word 'law' in 'the law of Christ' does not mean 'law' in the Mosaic sense. So what does it mean?

The meaning of 'law' in the law of Christ

This is a crucial point. I am claiming that the believer is not under the law of Moses, but under the law of Christ. Now, in saying this, am I splitting hairs? that is, despite all I have said, fundamentally the Reformed and I really agree, after all? Do we both think a believer is sanctified by law, that he is under law, and that we mean the same sort of thing when we say 'law'? In other words, does the only difference between us come down to the Reformed use of the ten commandments, 'the law of Moses', for their rule, while I argue for another set of commandments – 'the law of Christ'? In short, when all the semantics are boiled down, in effect we agree; the believer is under law! Is this what it amounts to? If so, have I been 'obsessed with disputes and arguments over words... useless wranglings' (1 Tim. 6:4-5), 'a question of words and names' (Acts 18:15), striving 'about words to no profit, to the ruin of the hearers' (2 Tim. 2:14)?

The answer to all those questions is a resounding No! I have not!

Let us start with the law of Moses. The believer is not under the law of Moses. The various scriptures – the many scriptures – we have looked at teach that the believer is *not* under law. Of course, my explanation of these passages, and my deductions from them, may be wrong. That this is possible, I admit at once. But if so, what *do* they teach?

I have gone still further. From these scriptures, I have argued that believers are not under law – not under law *per se*. In fact, it is only because believers have died to the law that they can possibly be sanctified (Rom. 7:4,6; Gal. 2:19). If so, how can they be under 'the *law* of Christ'?

It all hinges on the word 'law'. 'The law of Moses' and 'the law of Christ' are (in the common parlance) very different beasts; that is, they are very different 'entities', 'systems', 'regimes'. And they are poles apart, not only in content, but in their whole basis, approach, ethos, outlook, attitude and mindset. It is all to do with 'Moses' and 'Christ' (John 1:17). The two laws belong to two distinct, contrasting ages, and are very different 'laws'. The law of Moses is a list of specific rules – the decalogue is *ten* commandments, after all. The law of Christ, however, is far wider, far bigger. And I

---

[9] The answer is in the verse.

am not thinking of a hundred commandments instead of ten! (Or, rather, a thousand commandments instead of the more-than six hundred in the Mosaic law!) The law of Christ is not a list at all. This is the point I am striving for. The law of Christ is a principle, an all-embracing principle. Anything more different to a list of rules, especially a list of 'do nots', would be hard to imagine. Christ's law is inflexible, but there is certain flexibility within it. Within limits, differences of judgement are allowed under Christ (see Rom. 14:1 – 15:7; Phil. 3:15-16, for instance). This is a remarkable aspect of the law of Christ. In general, law allows no room for conscience. In particular, the Mosaic law allows none. Summarising the essential difference between the two 'laws', the law of Moses and the law of Christ, we are talking about the difference between precept and principle.

The word 'law' takes different meanings in Scripture, according to the context. I established this right at the beginning. In the New Testament, 'law' often carries all the overtones of Jewish law, the *torah*, but not always. Sometimes it means 'principle' or something similar. Take 'the law of faith' (Rom. 3:27). I have already noted that Paul was not speaking about the 'law' of faith, in the sense of substituting faith in Christ for obedience to Mosaic commandments – in effect, one set of rules replaced by another. Rather, the idea is 'principle', the principle of faith. 'The law of the Spirit of life in Christ Jesus' (Rom. 8:2), is another example. Many teachers have rightly called on other words in trying to get to grips with this concept – 'principle', 'ordinance', 'norm', 'system', 'doctrine', 'teaching', 'order', 'method', 'demand', 'arrangement', 'force' or 'reign'.[10] Paul spoke of 'a pattern' (Phil. 3:17). Boasting is excluded, said Paul. 'By what law?' On what basis? By what principle? Not by substituting faith in Christ for works under Moses. No! Boasting is excluded by the fact that the concept of works, obedience to law, has gone, and has been replaced by a totally new principle or system or arrangement (Rom. 3:27-28). Indeed, it is a new age, 'the time of the new order' (Heb. 9:10, NIV). Law has been replaced by gospel.[11]

So why did Paul use 'law' in Romans 3:27, and speak of 'the *law* of faith'? Why did he not use something like 'principle'? Above all, why did he not coin a word? This is a most interesting question. It seems a contradiction in terms. 'The law of faith', I ask you! Obviously, the apostle had good reason for his choice.[12]

Could it be because of the high regard the Jews had for the law? Or because the apostle wanted to avoid the charge of novelty? Was it a Hebraism? Could it amount to nothing more than 'the doctrine or prescript of faith'? Could Paul have been using 'law' the way Greek-speaking Jews of the first century used it – in a general sense – just as we do today, when speaking of 'the [so-called] law of averages', 'the laws of music', 'the law of unintended consequences', 'the law of diminishing returns', and the like. As I say, it is a fascinating question: Why did Paul use the word 'law' in 'the law of Christ'?

---

[10] See chapter 17.

[11] See chapters 6 and 10.

[12] See chapter 18 for the close parallel with Paul's deliberate use of the term 'Israel' in 'the Israel of God' (Gal. 6:16). I will show that this describes the people of the new covenant. The law of Moses was for Israel after the flesh. The law of Christ is for spiritual Israel, the Israel of God. Paul showed that both 'law' and 'Israel' have been taken over and *transformed* in the new covenant. And do not forget Paul's love of word play!

Almost certainly Paul was drawing upon the Septuagint, the translation of the Old Testament into Greek for Jews with no Hebrew, completed just over a hundred years before Christ, the version most often quoted in the New Testament. After all, this was the way the Greek-speaking Jews – who could not understand Hebrew – read or heard the Greek word for 'law'. Did this matter? A great deal! They read it and *understood* it as a Greek word (*nomos*), not reading into it all the ideas and associations of the Hebrew word (*torah*) which it translated. Most of the scattered Jews of the time would have never read the law of Moses – they didn't have a copy of the Hebrew Scriptures, and, at best, would have only heard it read. In any case, as I have explained, most of them couldn't understand Hebrew. All this is highly relevant to Paul's use of the word – and even more relevant to the way his non-Hebrew readers would have understood him.

And, of course, the same goes for us today. When Paul uses *nomos* in connection with the law of Moses, we should think in Jewish terms, but when used in connection with the law of Christ, we should think in this Greek way. In addition, the *torah* was more than rules and regulations.[13] And in the new covenant, Christ is the *torah* in that his teaching is his *nomos*, and he himself *in toto* reveals God and what he requires of his people. I will return to this weighty point.

Then again, we must remember, Paul loved word play. He used it with 'law' in Romans 3:27: 'Where is boasting then? It is excluded. By what *law*? [The *law*] of works? No, but by the *law* of faith'. He used it in Romans 8:2-4: 'For the *law* of the Spirit of life in Christ Jesus has made me free from the *law* of sin and death. For what the *law* could not do in that it was weak through the flesh, God did by sending his own Son in the likeness of sinful flesh, on account of sin: he condemned sin in the flesh, that the righteous requirement of the *law* might be fulfilled in us who do not walk according to the flesh but according to the Spirit'. He used it in 1 Corinthians 9:19-23, when he explained the way in which he approached sinners with the gospel, how he accommodated himself to his hearers, so that 'I might win the more'. In particular, he said: 'To those who are without *law*, [I became] as without *law* (not being without *law* towards God, but under *law* towards Christ), that I might win those who are without *law*'.[14] It is very likely, therefore, that when he spoke of being 'under law towards Christ', 'under Christ's law', Paul deliberately chose to use 'law', precisely because of the association his word play entails. In particular, the apostle engaged in word play in 'the law of Christ' (Gal. 6:2). For 'law', we could also speak of the standard, the norm, the principle of Christ. (See earlier on 'the law of faith').

The law of Christ! What a staggering choice of phrase! As I have said, 'the law of Christ' is a seeming contradiction in terms. And look where the apostle coined it – at the end of Galatians! Galatians, of all places! After all he has said in the letter, it seems as though Paul must have blundered, forgotten himself and written an absurdity. It has been rightly called 'a breathtaking paradox'; 'the law of Christ', indeed! But of course the apostle hadn't blundered! He knew what he was doing! By using such provocative

---

[13] Let me repeat an earlier note. The meaning of *torah* is 'teaching', 'doctrine', or 'instruction'; the commonly accepted 'law' gives a wrong impression. We should, perhaps, think in terms of 'custom, theory, guidance or system' (see Wikipedia).

[14] Rom. 9:6; Gal. 6:2,16; Phil. 3:3; 2 Thess. 3:11 (NIV); Philem. 10-11 are further examples of word play. God himself does it; see Mic. 1:8-16. Christ did it – see below. See chapter 10 for comments on Rom. 8:1-4.

language, latching on to the word 'law' and attaching it to 'Christ', Paul was deliberately drawing attention to what he was saying. He was a teacher! He wanted the Galatians to understand and remember! And what was he saying? Bearing in mind Paul's entire argument throughout the first five chapters of the letter, 'the law of Christ' must be, at the very least, different to the law of Moses. I go further. It must be in stark contrast to the law of Moses.

Word play. Christ himself engaged in it: 'Take my yoke upon you... For my yoke is easy and my burden is light', he said (Matt. 11:29-30).[15] The concept of a 'yoke' was current in such phrases as 'yoke of the *torah*' and 'yoke of the commandments'. Clearly, however, Christ was speaking of a new yoke, an altogether different kind of yoke – 'my yoke' – not the old yoke of Moses, nor the Mosaic law as expounded by Christ. Christ, I repeat, was speaking of his *own* law, not the Mosaic law reinterpreted. There is a clear contrast between Christ's yoke and the yoke of the law. The Jews would have recognised at once Christ's word play, and would have readily grasped the substitution he was claiming, the substitution of himself and his law in the place of Moses and his law. The contrast is clear. The *Didache*, probably dating from about 80-140, called Christ's commandments 'the Lord's yoke'. What a contrast there is between the two yokes. Christ's is easy (Matt. 11:30),[16] the opposite of Moses' (Acts 15:10,28; Gal. 5:1). An easy *yoke*? What is this? Yet another contradiction in terms.

And this raises the very point – the vital point – I am trying to make. Christ has his law, his yoke for his people, but this is not a new list of laws replacing the old list (although, of course, there are specific commands for believers to obey in the gospel; witness the abundance of such in the letters of the New Testament). In speaking of the law of Christ, Paul was not referring to a new set of ten commandments, using 'law' in the old sense. We are talking about the *new* covenant. The old law has been replaced by the new. And the phrase makes its appearance, remember, at the end of Galatians. The apostle, having resolutely stood up to the Judaisers, having endured personal stress in publicly rebuking Peter, and having taught the Galatians so thoroughly – all of which he had done in order to rescue believers from the bondage of the Mosaic law – would not, as he closed his letter, bind believers with an even tighter and heavier yoke. It would have be unthinkable! He was not setting out a new legalism with the commands of Moses replaced by the commands of Christ. For sanctification, what is wanted is not mere conformity to a set of rules, especially negative, but consecration, dedication and likeness to Christ.

In short, while the law of Christ is a real law, it is a *new* law, a law very unlike the law of Moses. Consequently, when we speak of Christ's *yoke*, 'the believers' *rule*', 'the *law* of Christ', we should not think in Jewish terms, of the *torah*. Rather, we should think in terms of the broader, fuller, first-century meaning of the Greek word *nomos*. This is the way to understand 'the law of Christ', since this was the way the non-Hebrew-speaking believers of the first century (the overwhelming majority) would have understood Paul's words, written in Greek. We must put the same overtones on 'the *law* of Christ' as they did, and not impose Jewish nuances on the phrase.

---

[15] See Christ's play on 'rock' in Matt. 16:18.

[16] Is there another word play here (in the Greek) between *chrētos* (easy) and *christos* (anointed, Christ)?

Paul saw Christ as the new Moses in a new covenant, teaching his own law, a new *torah*, with the idea of *torah* qualified as above. So it would be better to think of the law of Christ, not as a set of rules, commandments and prohibitions, but rather as a life-principle within the believer empowered by the Spirit of Christ. It is Christ's teaching, life, death, and resurrection, and the coming of his Spirit upon and in his people, and the deposit of all truth from Christ into which he led the apostles (John 14:26; 16:12-15), which is the believer's new *torah*, the law of Christ. The law of Christ is not a list. It is power! 'The kingdom of God is not a matter of talk but of power' (1 Cor. 4:20, NIV).

This last point was weighty enough, but now – not an intentional pun, I assure you reader – I want to raise the level of the discussion even further; that is to say, I want to return to the 'but now'.

The eschatological setting of 'law'

The most important point in this entire debate is the historical or eschatological setting of the Mosaic law in connection with salvation; that is, the 'but now' we have come across time and again in our look at various sections of Scripture – notably Galatians 3 and Romans 5 – 8. In this 'but now', we have met the two epochs of salvation history, law and grace, especially noting the temporary nature of the epoch of law in that history. Intertwined with all this we have the law of God, the law of Moses and the law of Christ. In 1 Corinthians 9:19-23, Paul made a distinction between the law of Moses and the law of Christ, at the very least implying that, in the new covenant, the law of Christ has replaced the law of Moses as the law of God. This very important, though subtle, point, must not be missed or ignored. Linking it with the eschatological setting of law and grace, we may say that in the one age – the age of law – the law of Moses was the law of God, but in the present age – the age of the Spirit – the law of Christ is now the law of God. And it is only this fact which puts consideration of the law of Christ onto its proper footing. What we are talking about in 'the law of Christ' is far more than a question of mere word play by Paul, however intriguing. I go further. It is this eschatological fact which gives the key to the understanding of the many scriptures which speak of rejoicing in the law. For believers, this rejoicing is in the law of Christ.[17] I have noted how easy and tempting it is to conflate various texts without recognising the different use to which 'law' may be put in the context of each passage. Dire results follow.

The point I have just made is of such immense importance, I must restate it. The law of God! 'The law of God', as a phrase, runs throughout Scripture. When the context is the old covenant, 'the law of God' must be read as the law of Moses, the law God gave to Israel through Moses at Sinai. When the context is the new covenant, 'the law of God' must be read as the law of Christ. It is all the law of God, yes, but the change of covenant is fundamental. I do not know of any weightier point than this throughout my book. Let me make it as clear as I can:

---

[17] See chapters 9 and 10. None of this, as I have explained, means there is no part for the law of Moses to play for the believer (2 Tim. 3:16-17).

When, in Scripture, we meet 'the law of God', we must ask ourselves which covenant we are talking about. If it is the old covenant, then 'the law of God' is the 'the law of Moses'. If it is the new covenant, then 'the law of God' is 'the law of Christ'.

The law of Christ: A summary

Having cleared the ground, we are now able to answer the question I posed. What is this rule, this principle, this system, arrangement, pattern, this norm, or basis upon which believers live a life of godliness, and grow to spiritual maturity? It is the law of Christ. What is this law of Christ?

There are three main views: The law of Christ is the law of Moses as interpreted and fulfilled by Christ. Or it is a nebulous concept void of content. Or it is the new code, norm, new 'law' of the new covenant. I will tackle all three.

Clarity is essential. You have every right, reader, to dismiss my book if I fail to make my meaning clear. The believer's rule must be simple to comprehend.[18] In New Testament times, it was, apparently, well understood by believers, most of whom did not have a university or seminary training in theology or logic, so it must be simple for believers to grasp nowadays. Just as an understanding of the answer to the question: 'What must I do to be saved?', ought not to require a theological degree, neither should it require a PhD to the answer to the questions: 'What must I do to be sanctified? How can I do it? Why should I do it?' Clarity and simplicity, I reiterate, are paramount. If believers have to master a manual of systematic theology in order to get to grips with the law of Christ, most of them will have to give up before they start! Above all, of course, if they are attempting to hit the wrong target, trying attain the wrong standard by the wrong method, using the wrong motive and the wrong means, they will be in serious trouble – to put it mildly!

It doesn't take a genius to work out that in saying these things I have been talking about the Reformed way of sanctification. As I have demonstrated, and a glance at the extracts will confirm, to get to grips with the ramifications of Calvin's third use of the law, one needs to be nimble in spiritual metaphysics, and be master of a certain sort of logic. If nothing else, this must be a fatal mark against the Reformed way of attempting sanctification, since such demands exceed the abilities of most believers. They certainly defeat me!

Coming to the biblical way of sanctification, the law of Christ is not 'a haze of imprecise ethics' which leaves the believer 'adrift, without a definite objective' – though this is said. True, the New Testament does not *directly* set out the law of Christ, certainly not in the same way as the Old Testament set out the law of Moses. For the reasons I have already given, this is impossible! The law of Christ is not that kind of entity. Rather, Scripture sets out *principles* which the believer has to apply in differing circumstances. This, of course, is not a weakness in the law of Christ. Quite the opposite, in fact. It is one of its towering strengths. And it is one of the vital aspects of the newness of the new law compared to the old.

Compare, on the one hand, a list of instructions imposed on a child with, on the other, a set of principles a mature adult lives by. The weakness of a code comprising

---

[18] *Comprehend*, I said. I did *not* say simple to *live out*! Nor, as I have admitted, have I found it easy to systematise.

detailed specific commands, as distinct from general principles, can be seen in the dilemma of being forced to choose between two of the rules when they conflict over a particular issue. For instance, if a driver, stopped at red traffic lights, hears the wail of the siren and sees the flashing blue light of an ambulance closing up behind him, does he remain where he is and so block the road for the ambulance? Or does he, without police instruction, ease over the line? If he does the latter, he breaks the law! But whatever he does, he will break a law of some sort. Working on principle tells him to ease over the line if no one is at risk. The law of the land tells him to stay where he is and delay the ambulance. External law cannot produce appropriate action! Grace, not an external law, is wanted! Such examples could be multiplied times without number. Law (in its legal sense) does not produce holiness! Remember the big picture!

The law of Christ: Galatians 6:2 and its context

I have already drawn attention to the significance of the place where the phrase, 'the law of Christ', first saw the light of day; that is, Galatians 6:2. Paul coined[19] the phrase as he drew to the climax of his major statement on the law, doing so by a telling play on words. Not only that; the immediate context of the phrase is Christ himself. This bears repeating. Christ is the context of his law. Believers have the Spirit of Christ (Gal. 4:6); Christ is formed in them (Gal. 4:19); his 'appropriation' of Leviticus 19:18 covers everything in their lives (Gal. 5:14).[20] This contextual link with Christ is strengthened further if, as is likely, Paul, in Galatians 5:22-23, was giving a short description, a thumb-nail sketch, of Christ's character. It is in this context that we meet 'the law of Christ' (Gal. 6:2). 'Against such there is no law' (Gal. 5:23).[21] So what am I saying? Christ is the believer's – the **CHRIST**ian's – pattern; the believer is to live like Christ, and show Christ to others (Gal. 4:14; 6:17). Those who live like Christ have no need of the Mosaic law to rule them. In any case, it couldn't do the job; the Mosaic law could never produce Christ-likeness. Only Christ, with his law, can do that!

But he can and he does! Remember John 1:17! Of course, while the transformation to Christ-likeness will be complete only in eternity, nevertheless, it begins here and now – at the moment of regeneration. Remember Paul's glorious conclusion to his discourse on the new covenant: 'Now the Lord is the Spirit, and where the Spirit of the Lord is, there is freedom. And we, who with unveiled faces all reflect the Lord's glory, *are being transformed into his likeness* with ever-increasing glory, which comes from the Lord, who is the Spirit'. And it wasn't long before he was explaining 'that *the life of Jesus* may also be revealed in our body... that *his life* may be revealed in our mortal body' (2 Cor. 3:17-18; 4:10-11, NIV; see also Rom. 8:29; 1 Cor. 15:49; Phil. 3:21; Col. 3:4; 1 John 3:2).

Getting back to Galatians, as the context shows, Paul is here preparing the way for his last, climactic, argument (in Galatians) about the law of Christ, beginning at Galatians 6:1. Do not forget the ground we have covered. These verses do not come as

---

[19] I repeat an earlier note. It is especially important here – emphasising the newness of what we are thinking about: 'Coining' does not mean, as so often it is assumed to mean, 'copying'. It means, 'inventing'. As before, this and Paul's word play will be reinforced in chapter 18 when I look at 'the Israel of God', a phrase in the same context, please note (Gal. 6:16).
[20] See the next chapter.
[21] See also 1 Tim. 1:8-11. See below and chapter 13.

bullet points, set down in glorious isolation. Remember what is going on at this stage in the letter. The apostle is doing all he can to stop the Galatians yielding to the Judaisers and their call for them to go under the law; he is piling on the pressure. He has already told his readers that they, as believers, are not under the law of Moses. They can't be. They mustn't be. He has already commanded them not to go back to bondage. He has pleaded with them not to do it. Now he tells them that they are under the law of Christ. And this law of Christ, as we shall see, is not the old law of Moses, not even re-vamped. Such a thing would be unthinkable! In the context of the letter to the Galatians, believers must be under Christ, under Christ's own new law for his people. Believers, by the Spirit must walk as Christ did, follow his example and obey his commands. How would Christ (as a man)[22] live in my present circumstances? *This* is the context for the law of Christ.[23]

To bring out the contrast between Paul's way and the Reformed way of sanctification, let me remind you, reader, of Calvin's third use of the law, as a whip for lazy asses. If this is granted – the law playing the part of a whip for sluggish asses – believers, no less! – it would establish *fear* based on guilt as the motive. I know Calvin said that servile fear, slavish service, is useless,[24] but, as so often with Calvin, he wanted his penny and the bun. I have acknowledged there is a big difference between godly fear (which is an essential) and carnal fear (which is wrong). I suggest Calvin's whip produces a slavish fear. I cannot see how a whip can do anything else.[25]

Now, as I have shown, this fear is totally out of place. Fear is not the fulfilment or purpose or aim of the law under which saints are found. Rather, the believer must love – not fear. And if he does love, that love will ensure that he wants to meet all the commands – even those not written in the ten commandments. It will ensure he seeks to please God, to keep the revealed will of God, and to live a holy life even in areas not specified by the law; that is, in matters which were unknown in the days of Sinai.

Moses did not specify a rule to cover all circumstances for all time. To ask him to provide a rule for believers under all conditions is to ask the impossible. No written rule – written on stone or paper – could possibly meet such a demand. The law for the believer must be the gospel, written on the heart. And when I say 'gospel', I am talking

---

[22] I will not repeat this every time. I am not, of course, suggesting that believers are to be like Christ as God.

[23] See below for more contextual confirmation of the link between the law of Christ and Christ himself, including what I call the 'balancing contrast' in Heb. 10:28-29.

[24] See 'Extracts' p360.

[25] The extracts will verify it. Calvin: 'The law was given, that it might make you guilty – being made guilty, might fear'. 'The law is the everlasting rule of a good and holy life... The law... not only contains a rule of life as to outward duties, but... it also rules their hearts before God and angels... The law acts like a whip to the flesh, urging it on as men do to a lazy sluggish ass... a constant stimulus, pricking him forward'. 'The law, so far as it is a rule of life, a bridle to keep us in the fear of the Lord, a spur to correct the sluggishness of our flesh... is as much in force as ever, and remains untouched'. 'It annexes to works a reward and a punishment; that is, it promises life to those who keep it, and curses all transgressors. Meanwhile it requires from man the highest perfection and most exact obedience. It makes no abatement, gives no pardon, but calls to a severe reckoning the smallest offences'. Oh, I know Calvin had his self-contradicting get-outs – and I have quoted them – but it will not wash! A whip on the back of a lazy ass can produce nothing but fear as the motive for obedience. I will not repeat this note every time, but it should be borne in mind whenever appropriate in what follows – which is quite often!

about that which is alive and life-giving, a vital principle. New demands, new questions, new temptations are being raised all the time for the believer. To imagine that a precise code of practice delivered in ten commandments to Moses on Sinai, 3500 years ago, could possibly cover all these new eventualities, is a remarkable, not to say, ridiculous, suggestion. Praise God, the law of Christ attempts nothing of the sort. It does not set norms in concrete which hardened 2000 years ago, but gives the believer principles to apply to every new circumstance: 'What would Christ say and do in this situation? How would Christ react? What does Scripture teach me about all this?' And, of course, the believer has the Spirit to enable him to love and obey God in his word. As I say, the law of Christ is a living force, a living principle and power.

Let me illustrate. As I write, the government is trying desperately to think of ways to police the internet. They want to legislate to prevent harm by its abuse. It is – surprise, surprise – proving difficult! The present legislation is manifestly inadequate; in the current jargon, 'not fit for purpose'. 'The fact is', we hear repeatedly, 'when the present law was drafted (only a few years ago), nobody envisaged this internet explosion, and the sheer volume of electronic traffic we should have to cope with'. Quite! Thus it is with law – always! Fix it in concrete today, cover every eventuality today – and tomorrow it will be exposed as not up to the job. What is the answer? Governments do not have it. But there is an answer. Grace! The grace of Christ, the power of his Holy Spirit, in the gospel. That's the answer! If the heart and mind of every internet user was ruled perfectly by grace, there would be no need of a law to prevent internet abuse (nor need of keys, courts, prisons, and so on). Law never produces godliness. Only grace can do that! And grace does it! That is why we must be gospel preachers – in life, in pulpit and with pen.

The law of Christ cannot be confined to the ten commandments

As I explained in chapter 5, it is claimed that the ten commandments define the believer's behaviour, and nothing else can. Not to teach the ten commandments as the believer's rule, is to leave the Christian all at sea, living without a sure guide, and with no clear aim, or so it is said. Moses, it seems, is a safer and clearer guide than Christ. It is only the ten commandments, so we are told, which can protect us from the dangerous consequences of error and immorality.

How wrong can one be? What a woeful misrepresentation of the New Testament! The truth is, the boot is on the other foot! But I do not 'snipe at the ten commandments' when I say they must not be used for a job for which they were never intended! Nor do I have the disease of 'Sinaiphobia' which makes me say the Mosaic law code is invalid. I do not destroy morality. I am not one of the 'cranks who foment against Sinai', an antinomian who wants to obliterate the ten commandments, and never refers to the law but to attack it. On the other hand, I certainly do not think *all* the Mosaic law is valid for believers today. Nor do I think we should recite the Creed to remind us of what to believe, and the commandments to tell us what to do. As for the imitation of Christ, and imitation of the apostles as they imitated Christ, this is only one part of Christ's law, but it is a part, and must not be dismissed as vague, hazy, undefined or imprecise. Such comments are highly offensive. (Actually they are worse than offensive. They run counter to Scripture. See John 13:15; Rom. 15:3,5,7; 1 Cor. 11:1 with 1 Cor. 4:16; Eph. 5:1-2; Phil. 3:17; 4:9; 1 Thess. 1:6; 1 Pet. 2:21; 1 John 2:6). I will return to this. Paul certainly points to Christ as one to be copied. But this does not imply any separation between the teaching of Christ and his person; both are one, inseparably so. By the way, all the criticisms I have just raised in this paragraph have actually been levelled, in print, mostly by Reformed teachers, against people like me. As the extracts will show, I am not making them up.

The New Testament will not sustain the claim that the ten commandments constitute the believer's perfect rule. After all, in 2 Timothy 3:15-17, Paul spoke of 'the holy Scriptures... all Scripture' – *all* Scripture, please note, not only the law, and certainly not merely the ten commandments – 'all Scripture... is profitable for doctrine, for reproof, for correction, for instruction in righteousness, that the man of God may be complete, thoroughly equipped for every good work'. And if Paul was not referring to sanctification in saying this, to what was he referring? Furthermore, Christ's prayer for his people – 'sanctify them by your truth. Your word is truth' (John 17:17) – is surely relevant here. It is very interesting to see what Reformed writers – who elsewhere are so eager to tell us that the law is the rule and means of sanctification – say about this prayer and statement of Christ. They agree that Christ declared the word of truth to be the rule of true sanctification – the word, mark you, the entire word, not merely the ten commandments; the word of truth, especially the doctrine of Christ (John 14:6),[26] the gospel. I fully endorse this, of course, but how these writers could still claim that *the law* (and only the ten commandments, at that!) is the believer's perfect rule of sanctification, I simply cannot fathom. As John, the apostle, said, believers keep Christ's commands – obey his law; that is, they keep his word (1 John 2:3-6), his entire word, not merely the ten commandments. As I will demonstrate, while Reformed writers claim the law of Moses is the believer's rule, when they come to call for sanctification they inevitably turn to the gospel!

The reason is not hard to find. The ten commandments cannot possibly be the perfect rule for believers. Does the decalogue set out all that Christ requires of his people? Does it contain *all* that is needed for sanctification in *all* the life of the believer? It is, after all, said to be the *perfect* rule. Those who say it is, that it contains all that is required, are virtually denying progressive revelation.[27] Moreover, as I have noted, we need a living law which will enable us to deal with the new circumstances which are arising all the time – by now, well-past the time of revelation. And we have it. It is called the law of Christ.

However, those who want us to submit to the ten commandments as our perfect rule of life claim that the ten commandments are God's final word, and, though these commandments do not explicitly contain all that is required, they do so *implicitly*.

---

[26] I find 2 John 9 interesting – 'the doctrine, the teaching of Christ' (see AV, NKJV, NIV, NASB). Could this be speaking of the 'the law of Christ'?

[27] On progressive revelation, see chapter 6. Without trying to enter another minefield, but just to illustrate the point, those who sing only Psalms never sing of the full glories of Christ in the gospel, except as prophesied in old-covenant terms. They miss the fullness of the New Testament. Similarly, the ten commandments cannot possibly contain *all* the teaching of the New Testament. While on this note of comparison, is there no parallel between, on the one hand, claiming to sing Psalms, but in some way or another circumventing the imprecatory portions, the portions which speak of perfection, portions which speak of dancing and orchestral instruments, and, on the other, claiming to be under the law but not its penalties? For more on interpreting the Psalms in the new covenant, see chapter 18.

The Believer's Rule

What of this? Take the fifth commandment. This is said to apply to everyone in all the variety of their many relationships, governing *every* situation in which the believer finds himself, *every* relationship.[28] This needs serious thought and proof; the consequences have to be faced! Under certain circumstances, for instance, the law exacted the death penalty for breaking this commandment (Ex. 21:15,17; Lev. 20:9; 21:9; Deut. 21:18-21). How can this be avoided if the law is the perfect rule of life for believers? Furthermore, if the Reformed view is right, the death penalty will have to be carried out when the fifth commandment is broken in any of the relationships which the Reformed think it encompasses; in other words, in *all* human relationships. On this basis, there's going to be a great many executions, I fear. Of course, I know the Reformed convince themselves that they can have the law without its penalties. But they can't!

By the way, when the Reformed try their technique on the ten commandments, they are in fact trying to make the old-covenant law act as though it were the law of the new covenant. In so doing, they are destroying their own principle and going against their own rubric. I am sure the New Testament warrants us to read the old covenant through the lens of the new, through Christ. The Reformed, however, argue that the law of Moses stands inviolate – but immediately proceed to violate it, change and apply it in ways it was never intended, watering down its penalties, if not removing them altogether, all the time castigating those who openly argue the biblical principle. The familiar pot and kettle, I think.

To continue: that the New Testament *occasionally* refers to the commandments and applies them to believers, I fully admit – yes, as it does other parts of the Old Testament[29] – but it is too great a leap to argue from this that the ten commandments themselves stipulated these very applications. Surely, when the apostles applied the commands to believers they were introducing something new, were they not?

The fact is, as much as we might desire a neat little summary of what God requires of us as believers, we shall desire in vain. Certainly the ten commandments do not provide it. But the New Testament (especially) does spell out what Christ requires. Christ's example and commands, the apostolic examples and commands, the inward working of God's Spirit, and his new-covenant use of the Mosaic law and the prophets as recorded in the Scriptures – these form the law of Christ. Christ promised: 'The Holy Spirit, whom the Father will send in my name... will teach you all things, and bring to your remembrance all things that I said to you... The Spirit of truth... will guide you into all truth... He will glorify me, for he will take of what is mine and declare it to you. All things that the Father has are mine. Therefore I said that he [the Spirit] will take of mine and declare it to you' (John 14:26; 16:13-15). And in saying this, Christ was not promising light only; he was promising both light *and* life.

Let me prove that we are talking about the law of Christ. How did Paul urge holiness on his readers? By the law of Moses? Certainly not! Consider two passages.

---

[28] Ezek. 34:2; Matt. 15:4; Rom. 12:10; 13:8; Eph. 5:21; 1 Pet. 2:17 are used as proof-texts for the claim that the fifth commandment applies 'to everyone in their several places and relations'. I leave you, reader, to judge whether these verses establish the point, and especially whether the commandment itself taught it.

[29] See chapter 17.

The law of Christ: Two biblical examples

First:

For the grace of God that brings salvation has appeared to all men, teaching us that, denying ungodliness and worldly lusts, we should live soberly, righteously, and godly in the present age, looking for the blessed hope and glorious appearing of our great God and Saviour Jesus Christ, who gave himself for us, that he might redeem us from every lawless deed and purify for himself his own special people, zealous for good works (Titus 2:11-14).

Note the apostle's argument: It is '*the grace of God that brings salvation*' – not the law, but grace – which teaches believers to 'live soberly, righteously, and godly in the present age'. Paul told Titus to 'speak *these* things' (Tit. 2:15). This is the way to produce godliness, he said. Preach Christ! Remind believers that Christ accomplished their justification, and that this is inevitably connected to their sanctification. Stress this. Stress that it is all in Christ and through Christ! This is what the apostle demands of Titus. Christ himself is the sanctification of believers – its motive, means and measure: 'Our great God and Saviour Jesus Christ... gave himself for us, that he might... purify for himself his own special people, zealous for good works'. Christ is not only 'righteousness... and redemption' for those who are in him. He is also their 'sanctification' (1 Cor. 1:30).[30] The commencement, continuance and completion of sanctification is always ascribed to God's grace in Christ. Spurgeon:

The way of salvation by grace... is the best promoter of holiness in all the world... Salvation by grace promotes good works far better than the teaching of salvation by works ever did, for those who hope to be saved by their works have generally very scanty works to be saved by, and those who put works aside altogether as a ground of hope, and look to grace alone, are the very people who are most zealous to perform good works... Law! There is no power for holiness in it! Law drives our spirits to rebellion, but love has magic in it. Has God forgiven me? Did Christ die for me? Am I God's child? Has he forgiven me, not because of anything I did, but just because he would do it, out of love to my poor guilty soul? O God, I love you. What would you have me to do? There speaks a man who will perform good works, I warrant you, sir: and while he will tread under foot with the deepest detestation any idea that he can merit anything of God, he is the man who will lay himself out, as long as he lives, for the honour of that dear Lord and Master by whose precious blood he has been redeemed. The law does not furnish me with a constraining principle, but the gospel does. The law treats me like a mere hireling, and a hireling can never serve with the zeal which is born of love... Oh yes, the doctrine of salvation by grace, by teaching men to love, transforms them, and makes new creatures of them... People... whereas they resolved to be good, and to give up vice, and to practice virtue... never did it till they believed in Jesus; and when they believed in him, love to him made service easy, and sin hateful, and they became new creatures in Christ Jesus, by the Spirit's power. There is the pith of it all. If you want to get rid of the guilt of sin, you must believe in Jesus; but equally, if you would be rid of your lusts, you must believe in him; for from his side there flows not merely blood but water – blood to take away your criminality, and water to take away tendencies to sin – so that henceforth you shall not serve sin, or live any longer therein.[31]

---

[30] I am not going back on my remarks about the word 'sanctification' in this verse. My case does not depend on the accident of words. The context is progressive sanctification.

[31] Spurgeon: *Metropolitan* Vol.19 pp682-683.

May I express the hope that all who have a high regard for Spurgeon really will weigh his words here, and weigh them very seriously? I am sure he has caught the spirit of the new covenant. I endorse his sentiment – without reservation. What about you, reader?

Verse and chapter divisions in Scripture are artificial impositions on the text, which, more often than not, seriously damage if not ruin the flow of the argument.[32] Here is a case in point. Paul's line of reasoning, which he put before Titus, carries over into the next chapter: 'This is a faithful saying, and these things I want you to affirm constantly, that those who have believed in God should be careful to maintain good works. These things are good and profitable to men' (Tit. 3:8). 'These things I want you to affirm constantly', 'I want you to stress these things' (NIV), 'I desire you to strongly insist on these things'. Stress, strongly insist on, or affirm constantly *what* things? The necessity for good works? Yes, but not only that. In order to produce these good works in his hearers, Paul told Titus to stress, to affirm constantly, 'the kindness and love of God our Saviour', to lay emphasis on our salvation, and to insist that it is 'not by works of righteousness which we have done, but according to his mercy he saved us' through the regenerating grace 'of the Holy Spirit, whom he poured out on us abundantly through Jesus Christ our Saviour, that having been justified by his grace we should become heirs according to the hope of eternal life' (Tit. 3:4-7). *These* are the things which must be stressed in order to produce good works. So said Paul.

Thus, God's grace, not the law, regulates our lives. Notice, reader, the absence of the law here and in the context – except this:

There are many insubordinate, both idle talkers and deceivers, especially those of the circumcision, whose mouths must be stopped, who subvert whole households, teaching things which they ought not... Rebuke them [the Cretans] sharply, that they may be sound in the faith, not giving heed to Jewish fables and commandments of men who turn from the truth... Avoid foolish disputes, genealogies, contentions, and strivings about the law; for they are unprofitable and useless (Tit. 1:10-14; 3:9).

I draw attention especially to these words in the immediate context of this call for sanctification: 'Avoid... strivings about the law; for they are unprofitable and useless' (Tit. 3:9). Where, now, is Calvin's third use of the law? Naturally, I expect advocates of Calvin's third use of the law to respond by saying that they are not 'striving'. I quite agree. Except... whenever the law is on the agenda, it is never long before striving raises its head. Witness the Jews in Christ's day! And let me make a suggestion: try setting the cat of Calvin's view of the fourth commandment among Reformed pigeons! Feathers will be ruffled, if not fly, I predict, and 'striving' will soon follow.

I said I would mention two passages at this time; here is the second: 'Only let your conduct be worthy of the gospel of Christ' (Phil. 1:27) – not, you notice, 'worthy of the law of Moses'. Paul did not press the law upon his readers in order to produce godliness – neither as its rule nor motive. Rather, he stressed the gospel. This becomes all the more significant when we bear in mind what Paul had to face, and what he said about it, in Philippians 3 – which we have looked at.[33]

Christ's law makes gospel promises the motive for holiness (2 Cor. 7:1). It is the nature of God (1 Pet. 1:15-16) and the believer's relation to him (Eph. 5:1; 1 Pet. 1:14,17), the

---

[32] This is why a paragraph Bible is so much more valuable than a verse Bible.
[33] See chapter 12.

mercies of God (Rom. 12:1; Eph. 4:32), the name, person and attributes of Christ and the believer's relation to him (1 Cor. 1:10; 2 Cor. 10:1; Eph. 5:2; Phil. 2:5; Col. 3:1), the believer's calling (Eph. 4:1; 1 Pet. 2:11), the redemption Christ accomplished (1 Pet. 1:17-21), the hope of Christ's return (Col. 3:4-5; 1 Thess. 5:8-11; 2 Pet. 3:10-12; 1 John 3:1-3), and so on, which Christ in his law makes the motive for obedience. The bulwark against wicked men, lawless (NIV), unprincipled (NASB) men, is for believers to 'grow in the grace and knowledge of our Lord and Saviour Jesus Christ' (2 Pet. 3:17-18). So runs the law of Christ. The promotion of godliness, and the defence against lawlessness, is not by the law of Moses. Where is the New Testament text which commands believers to grow in the law? Sanctification is by the grace of the Lord Jesus Christ. What else could it be, should be, in the new covenant?

And that takes us on to the next point.

The law of Christ cannot be the old law; it must be new; it must be his own law

As we have seen, for the believer – the one who has been brought into Christ by faith through grace, and who knows that what the law could not do for him, God has done in Christ (Rom. 7:24-25; 8:1-4) – the law not only belongs to the old age, historically speaking, but it belongs to the time of his own personal bondage and death. The Spirit has liberated him from his bondage, so that he does the will of God from his heart (Eph. 6:5-6), producing 'the fruit of the Spirit' (Gal. 5:22). Under such circumstances, under the 'but now', how can the *old* law be the rule for such a *new* man in such a *new* age? The believer is not under the old system – the law – nor under the old system with a new label. No! He is under a new system, the gospel. He lives in 'the time of the new order' (Heb. 9:10, NIV). Christ has replaced Moses; grace has replaced law. 'The law of the Spirit of life in Christ Jesus' has set him 'free from the law of sin and death' (Rom. 8:2). The rule of law has gone; the rule and reign of grace has come (Gal. 3:24). He is no longer married to the law, but to Christ (Rom. 7:1-6). Christ, as master and husband, is the lawgiver for his people in the new covenant. Their Redeemer is their ruler.

Christ *is* the lawgiver for believers, the promised 'Ruler' (Matt. 2:6), of whom it was prophesied: 'The government will be upon his shoulder... Of the increase of his government... there will be no end, upon the throne of David and over his kingdom, to order it and establish it with judgement and justice' (Isa. 9:6-7). His people, his subjects, believers, are under his government, under his law, 'the law of Christ' (Gal. 6:2). To Christ, it is said: 'Your throne, O God, is for ever and ever; a sceptre of righteousness is the sceptre of your kingdom. You have loved righteousness and hated lawlessness' (Heb. 1:8-9, quoting Ps. 45:6-7).[34]

As a husband in his own right, Christ rules his bride, his people, by his own law, not by the law of their old husband, Moses.[35] Christ gives his people *his own* law. He does

---

[34] See below for more on Christ as lawgiver. See chapter 18 for my reasons for the way I interpret the prophets.

[35] To make the point, I have taken the liberty of changing the figure slightly, and personified the law as Moses. But there is ample scriptural warrant for it (see, for instance, Luke 5:14; 16:29,31; 24:27; John 5:45; 2 Cor. 3:15).

not send them to Moses. He does not give them a mere reinterpretation of the Mosaic law. Just as we have two different covenants, two different slave-masters, two different marriages, so we have two different laws.[36] Christ has replaced Moses as lawgiver; grace has replaced law (John 1:17).

And, of course, it goes deeper than that, much deeper. The realm of grace is altogether different to the reign of law. Both Moses and Christ command their subjects, but only Christ with his grace gives power to obey; only Christ gives life. Whereas the law of Moses was written on stone, the law of Christ is written on the heart. Whereas the law of Moses was a list of requirements which men had to do – or else! – grace brings the Spirit's power to enable the believer to love and obey his Lord's commands. Believers are not law-less or lawless. They gladly wear Christ's yoke. Obedience is their badge of discipleship (Matt. 11:28-30; John 13:34-35; Gal. 6:2). The same grace that saves them also sanctifies them. What is more, as I have shown, the whole concept of 'law' has changed under the gospel. Christ gave his disciples 'a *new* commandment' (John 13:34). Not only did he not send them back to the old law, he did not send them back to the old *system* of law.

Again, if 'the law of Christ' really is the ten commandments, why did Paul coin the phrase 'the law of Christ'? Why did he not make use of a perfectly biblical (though rare) phrase such as 'the ten commandments'? If that's what he meant, why didn't he say so? Or why did he never say – or imply – that the new law is really the same as the old law, with a change of label? '*All* things have become new', he said (2 Cor. 5:17). 'All things'! It is not only the label which is new!

But what of John, who said: 'I write no new commandment to you, but an old commandment which you have had from the beginning... Let that abide in you which you heard from the beginning... For this is the message that you heard from the beginning, that we should love one another... And this is his commandment... Not as though I wrote a new commandment to you, but that which we have had from the beginning: that we love one another' (1 John 2:7-8,24; 3:11,23; 2 John 5-6). How can the commandment be both 'old' and 'new'? And what was the 'beginning'? Was it creation, or Christ's discourse at the last supper, or the start of their Christian life? Certainly not the creation. The commandment is new because it is the gospel, Christ's law, new in the new covenant, new and only for believers. There is a new emphasis. There is a new quality – it is not 'love your neighbour *as yourself*' (Lev. 19:18; Matt. 19:19; 22:39; Rom. 13:9; Gal. 5:14; Jas. 2:8), only, but 'love your enemies' (Matt. 5:43-44), and, above all, love *as God in Christ loved*. There is a new extent – the 'neighbour' – is far more extensive in the new covenant than in the old. And it is always new. It is a new teaching, a new law, for a new people in a new age.

New! What does the Bible mean by the word? In the Old Testament, while 'new' can be something renewed or repaired, it can be something fresh, new. As applied to the prophecies of the new covenant,[37] there can be no doubt as to which it is. It is 'a freshly made', 'new' covenant. It certainly is not an old covenant 'renewed' or 'repaired'. And this is borne out by the two main New Testament words for 'new'. One is 'new, unused, unknown, unheard of, recently made, in contrast to the obsolete,

---

[36] And, I would add, 'for two different Israels'. See chapter 18.
[37] See chapter 18.

superior to the old,[38] something of a new kind, novel, unprecedented, previously non-existent'. The other is 'new, fresh, recently born'. The former refers to 'new' primarily as to quality, whereas the latter more to 'new in time'. As for the *new* covenant, it is a covenant new in quality,[39] not the old covenant repaired.[40]

Now, while I accept that there are few explicit references to the new covenant in the New Testament, its *principles* permeate it.[41] The concept of the new covenant is far more widespread than it would seem judging by the number of direct uses of the term. In the *New* Testament, it is no surprise, then, to find Christ saying: 'No one puts a piece from a *new* garment on an old one; otherwise the *new* makes a tear, and also the piece that was taken out of the *new* does not match the old. And no one puts *new* wine into old wineskins; or else the *new* wine will burst the wineskins and be spilled, and the wineskins will be ruined. But *new* wine must be put into *new* wineskins' (Luke 5:36-38).

And what of other scriptural passages which, while they do not use the phrase 'new covenant', nevertheless speak of it? It is important to take full account of these many indirect references and allusions[42] to 'newness', since so much hinges on a right understanding of the two covenants, especially the contrast between the *old* and the *new* covenants.

Take for instance:

But you have not so learned Christ, if indeed you have heard him and have been taught by him, as the truth is in Jesus: that you put off, concerning your *former* conduct, the *old* man which grows corrupt according to the deceitful lusts, and be re*new*ed in the spirit of your mind, and that you put on the *new* man which was created according to God, in true righteousness and holiness (Eph. 4:20-24).

Note the contrasting words which speak so forcibly of the change from the old to the new *and, especially, the direct practical consequences and effects which follow from this change*. Here we have it. In their unregenerate days, believers were *old* men in Adam, 'but now' in the *new* covenant they are *new* men who have a *new* mind, a *new* attitude, a *new* heart, a *new* life and who of course participate in *new* worship. The significance of this *new*ness is made clear. Christ's law is written on the heart of those in the *new* covenant. For example, the *old* ways of lying, stealing, bad speech, immorality and idolatry are out of the question for believers; *old* worship has gone, and true spiritual worship has come (Eph. 4:25,28-29; 5:3,5,18-21). All this flows from the *new* life arising in the *new* man in the *new* covenant, the law written on the heart producing this *new* spiritual life.

---

[38] If something is *kainos*, it is superior to that which is not.

[39] In the New Testament, *kainos* is far more frequent than *neos*, which in connection with 'covenant' is used only in Heb. 12:24.

[40] The radical thought of newness is disliked by many.

[41] How many *explicit* apostolic references are there to Christ's *own* teaching? See Acts 20:35; 1 Cor. 9:14; 11:23-25; 1 Tim. 5:18. See extract from Fee: *1 Corinthians* pp291-292.

[42] Asides or indirect allusions are often more powerful than direct statements. By way of illustration, take the scores of indirect references to Christ's deity. For example, those passages which link God and Christ in such a way that, if Christ is not God, the writer is playing with fire (John 5:16-47; 1 Cor. 12:4-6; see 3-11; Gal. 1:1,3; 1 Thess. 3:11; 2 Pet. 1:2 and many, many more). What mere man would need to say: 'My Father is greater than I' (John 14:28)? And so on. Compare Isa. 41:4; Rev. 1:8,11; 21:6; 22:13.

Take Colossians 3:1-11. Those who 'were raised with Christ', who 'have put off the *old* man with his deeds, and have put on the *new* man who is re*new*ed in knowledge according to the image of him who created him' – that is, men and women of the *new* covenant – are *new* creatures. The *old* life has ended. The law written on the heart produces the opposite of immorality, idolatry and lying. It generates the positive aspects of godliness, love and true spiritual worship (Col. 3:5,9,12-17), and so on.

Paul argued with the Galatians, demanding an answer: How can *you* – you *new*-covenant people, the people of Galatians 3:26-29 – go back to ritual, superstition and idolatry? The suggestion is out of the question (Gal. 4:9-10). You dare not go back to the *old* ways, whether it be Judaism or paganism, or any combination of the two.[43] Paul reasoned likewise with the Romans. You men and women of Romans 12:1ff, live a *new* life. You have a living fellowship with other saints. You have the power to live this *new* life, the grace to offer *new* service and to enjoy *new* fellowship (Rom. 12:2-8; 13:9-10; 14:1ff) because the spiritual desire rises in your heart by the Spirit since you are members of the *new* covenant. Reader, do not forget the obvious; Romans 12 comes after, and as a consequence of, Romans 6 – 8. The New Testament is not a series of disjointed texts. Keep the big picture in mind!

Again, as evidence that the concept of the new covenant really does pervade the New Testament, think of all the *new* things found in Christ: *new* cloth (Matt. 9:16; Mark 2:21; Luke 5:36); *new* wine (Matt. 9:17; Mark 2:22; Luke 5:38; compare Acts 2:13 and Eph. 5:18); *new* doctrine (Acts 17:19); a *new* lump (1 Cor. 5:7); a *new* covenant (Matt. 26:28; Mark 14:24; Luke 22:20; 1 Cor. 11:25, 2 Cor. 3:6; Heb. 8:8,13; 9:15; 12:24) or *new* testament (Heb. 9:15, AV); the believer is a *new* creation (2 Cor. 5:17; Gal. 6:15), a *new*born babe (1 Pet. 2:2), a *new* man (Eph. 2:15; 4:24; Col. 3:10); he comes to God in a *new* and living way (Heb. 10:20), keeping a *new* commandment (John 13:34; 1 John 2:8) in *new*ness of life (Rom. 6:4) and *new*ness of heart and spirit or Spirit (Ezek. 11:19; 36:26; Rom. 7:6), having a *new* name (Isa. 62:2; Rev. 2:17; 3:12), singing a *new* song (Rev. 5:9; 14:3); Christ has now made all things *new* (2 Cor. 5:17; Rev. 21:5), and will do so especially in eternity, where the saints will dwell in the *new* heavens and the *new* earth in the *new* Jerusalem (2 Pet. 3:13; Rev. 3:12; 21:1-2,5).

Think of all the *old* things put away by Christ: the *old* covenant has been abolished (Heb. 8:13), *old* things are gone (2 Cor. 5:17); for the believer, the *old* man has gone (Rom. 6:6) with his *old* sins (2 Pet. 1:9); the believer no longer lives in the *old* way (Eph. 4:22-23; Col. 3:9), serving God with the *old* leaven (1 Cor. 5:7-8). The *old* cloth and *old* wine have had their day (Matt. 9:16-17; Mark 2:21-22; Luke 5:36-38).[44]

Again, think of all which is conjured up by the lovely word *former*; the believer can talk about the passing away of *former* things including his *former* conduct or way of life (Eph. 4:22), his *former* lusts (1 Pet. 1:14); indeed, he looks forward to the time when all the *former* things (Rev. 21:4) will be done away with. Unbelievers have no *former* – and therefore no *new* – experience. Such belongs entirely and only to those

---

[43] See chapter 9, where I examined this passage in Galatians in detail.

[44] Luke 5:39 seems to contradict the point – old wine tastes better than new wine. But there are two comparisons running alongside each other. The one I am speaking of is not to do with taste! It is to do with power. If new wine is put in old wineskins, the lively production of gas will burst the old, dried-up leather. New, lively, effervescent wine needs new wineskins to cope with the release of explosive energy. The power, the energy of the new covenant cannot be contained within the obsolete old covenant, with its old law.

who are in the *new* covenant, to those who have been taken out of the *former* covenant. Similarly with *no longer* (Isa. 62:4).

And this concept of the change of covenant is not only found in the 'accident' of words, but the very doctrine of the gospel is based upon it. More, it *is* the gospel. Let me explain. Every human being is a sinner, since every human being is born a sinner (Job 14:4; Ps. 51:5; Rom. 3:23), born a creature 'of the flesh' (John 3:6), 'a natural man' with 'a natural mind' who cannot understand, appreciate, receive or inherit spiritual things, 'the things of the Spirit of God' (1 Cor. 2:14; 15:50). Consequently, every human being, if he is to 'see the kingdom of God', let alone 'enter' it (John 3:3,5), must be 'born again... born of the Spirit' (John 3:3,5,7), 'born... of God' (John 1:13), 'born again, not of corruptible seed but incorruptible, through the word of God' (1 Pet. 1:23). And once a sinner has been born again – regenerated – he has been 'delivered... from the power of darkness and conveyed... [translated, AV] into the kingdom of [Christ]' (Col. 1:13). Every child of God was born, naturally, of the flesh, and was flesh, but has become a spiritual man by the work of God the Holy Spirit within him. This is nothing less than being brought into the new covenant. My point is that even though the words 'new covenant' might not be mentioned in a particular passage, the New Testament is constantly appealing to believers to live out what they are in that new covenant; namely, not to live as fleshly or carnal, but to live as spiritual, as children of God (Rom. 6:11-23; 7:1-25; 8:1ff; 1 Cor. 3:1-3; Gal. 5:13-26; 1 Pet. 1:14; 2:1-3). Other phrases are used to convey the same. Take Ephesians 4:17-32; 5:1 – 6:9, for example.

And this ties in with what I have said about the believer's rule. The believer must and will keep the law of Christ. Why? How? By this inward working of the Spirit, this living power of the Spirit in the new covenant, as we have seen in Galatians 5:13-25, for example. The saints are spiritual people because they have the work and grace of the Spirit in them under the new covenant. My point is that the saints must and will obey the law of Christ because of this new covenant, because they are regenerate. They cannot do anything else. As Peter put it:

Simon Peter, a bondservant and apostle of Jesus Christ, to those who have obtained like precious faith with us by the righteousness of our God and Saviour Jesus Christ: Grace and peace be multiplied to you in the knowledge of God and of Jesus our Lord, as his divine power has given to us all things that pertain to life and godliness, through the knowledge of him who called us by glory and virtue, by which have been given to us exceedingly great and precious promises, that through these you may be partakers of the divine nature, having escaped the corruption that is in the world through lust. But also for this very reason, giving all diligence, add to your faith virtue, to virtue knowledge, to knowledge self-control, to self-control perseverance, to perseverance godliness, to godliness brotherly kindness, and to brotherly kindness love. For if these things are yours and abound, you will be neither barren nor unfruitful in the knowledge of our Lord Jesus Christ. For he who lacks these things is short-sighted, even to blindness, and has forgotten that he was cleansed from his old sins. Therefore, brethren, be even more diligent to make your call and election sure, for if you do these things you will never stumble; for so an entrance will be supplied to you abundantly into the everlasting kingdom of our Lord and Saviour Jesus Christ (2 Pet. 1:1-11).

It is all here. Believers, having been regenerated, having partaken of the divine nature, are equipped with God's power, enabling them to live a godly life, all being calibrated by Scripture; in particular, apostolic instruction. But notice also that, on the basis of this grace – 'for this very reason' – believers have to work out their salvation in progressive sanctification, leading to everlasting glory. This is the law of Christ.

Reader, I have put these passages before you to point out how much the doctrine of the new covenant permeates the New Testament. In truth, it dominates it. 'Newness' is *the* concept, not surprisingly, since we are, after all, talking about the *New* Testament, the age of the '*new* testament', the '*new* covenant'. And it is the very 'newness' of the new covenant, and the weight which Scripture gives to this newness, which makes it utterly incongruous to regard the law of the old covenant as the perfect rule of life for believers.[45] How can it be? After all, believers are children of the *new* covenant! All things have become new (2 Cor. 5:17). *All* things! And this negates the idea that the law of Christ is not a new law but is the old law of Moses. But a new law is precisely what it is! A new commandment Christ gave us (John 13:34).

Of course, I recognise that both laws come from God, and that both aim for the same – love for God and neighbour (Matt. 22:37-40), but even so the law of Christ *is* a new law: 'A new commandment I give to you' (John 13:34). This commandment is not another statement of the law of Moses, revised, more fully expounded or differently administered (that favoured word of Reformed writers). It is a new law. It is an entirely new entity.

Above all, there is an eschatological contrast between the past and present in terms of the old and new covenants. It is, as always, the 'but now' that we have met time and again. The Gentiles are now included in the people of God, included – and this is the point – *included apart from the law*, that separating marker of the old covenant. The people of the new covenant are 'signed' by the Spirit, and the Spirit alone. The law, though spiritual (Rom. 7:14), and having a certain glory (2 Cor. 3:7), did not carry with it the Spirit's power. How could it? It was written on stone, it was a dead letter, which could give neither life or liberty but, consisting of a code of requirements, led to death (Rom. 2:29; 7:6; 2 Cor. 3:5-7). In the new covenant, however, the Spirit writes his gospel on the heart (2 Cor. 3:3), he circumcises the heart (Rom. 2:29), and does so with an eternal glory, giving life through Christ to those in the new covenant, changing them into glory (2 Cor. 3:4-18), all of it being the ministry of the Spirit himself (2 Cor. 3:8,17-18). The new covenant has replaced the old, and this is demonstrated by the gift of the Spirit, according to the terms of the promise of Jeremiah 31:31-34 joined with Ezekiel 36:22 – 37:14. The old covenant failed, simply becoming a code or set of rules dividing Jew and Gentile; the new, by the Spirit, brings in all that God promised. This is the eschatological point. Now, in this gospel age, whether a man is a Jew or a Gentile, if he has the Spirit, he is spiritually alive in the new covenant, and this without the law of Moses – which, as we know, is now 'obsolete' (Heb. 8:13).

A seeming contradiction

In saying that the law of Christ is not the law of Moses – not even a 'law' in the Mosaic sense – I am not implying that God's demands under the gospel are easier than the demands of the law. Far from it. Why, the new covenant is more searching than the

---

[45] This is not to go down the Marcion road. Marcion rejected the Old Testament, saying the God revealed there was not the God of the New Testament. I am not remotely approaching this notion! I abhor it!

old. As we saw in Hebrews, to sin against Christ's law is far worse than sinning against Moses: 'Anyone who has rejected Moses' law dies without mercy on the testimony of two or three witnesses. Of how much worse punishment, do you suppose, will he be thought worthy who has trampled the Son of God underfoot, counted the blood of the covenant by which he was sanctified a common thing, and insulted the Spirit of grace?' (Heb. 10:28-29).[46] Clearly, it is more culpable to sin under the new covenant than the old.

Furthermore, church life plays a vital role in the law of Christ; in particular, under this heading, the discipline of church life. Take the case of incest at Corinth, over which the believers were – yes – boasting! Paul rebuked them. They should have 'been filled with grief' (NIV) over it, and removed the offender. The apostle went on, setting out the way in which the law of Christ must be applied in such cases:

In the name of our Lord Jesus Christ, when you are gathered together, along with my spirit, with the power of our Lord Jesus Christ, deliver such a one to Satan for the destruction of the flesh, that his spirit may be saved in the day of the Lord Jesus. Your glorying is not good. Do you not know that a little leaven leavens the whole lump? Therefore purge out the old leaven, that you may be a new lump, since you truly are unleavened. For indeed Christ, our Passover, was sacrificed for us. Therefore let us keep the feast, not with old leaven, nor with the leaven of malice and wickedness, but with the unleavened bread of sincerity and truth. I wrote to you in my letter not to keep company with sexually immoral people. Yet I certainly did not mean with the sexually immoral people of this world, or with the covetous, or extortioners, or idolaters, since then you would need to go out of the world. But now I have written to you not to keep company with anyone named a brother, who is sexually immoral, or covetous, or an idolater, or a reviler, or a drunkard, or an extortioner – not even to eat with such a person. For what have I to do with judging those also who are outside? Do you not judge those who are inside? But those who are outside God judges. Therefore 'put away from yourselves the evil person' (1 Cor. 5:1-13; see also Matt. 18:15-19; Acts 5:1-11; 8:18-23; 2 Thess. 3:6-15).

Do not miss the references to the law – the Passover and the extract drawn from several repeated Deuteronomy passages. As we have seen, the law of Christ knows how to make full – but properly nuanced – use of the law of Moses. Do not miss the reference to leaven – echoes of Galatians 5:9. And while the severity aspect of the law of Christ stands out a mile, do not forget that its application at Corinth had a reforming effect, and all was put right (2 Cor. 2:5-11). This, too, is another heart-warming aspect of Christ's law. But the point at issue stands. The law of Christ is anything but hazy sentimentalism, vague ethics, however often such dismissive terms are used by its ill-informed critics. Iron sits within the velvet.

The fact is, however, here we have what seems to be yet another contradiction. How can the new covenant be *more searching* than the old, and to sin against Christ's law be *far worse* than sinning against Moses' law, and yet at the same time the 'law' of Christ, his 'yoke', his 'burden', be 'easy' and 'light'?[47]

How do Reformed teachers deal with this? As I showed in chapter 7, they say the law of Christ is the law of Moses shorn of its condemnation. I called this 'pulling the law's teeth'. The new law, according to this, is something *less* than the old, *less* severe. It is the old law *minus* the difficult part. Reader, how can this be reconciled with the

---

[46] See chapter 14. See below where I speak of the 'balancing contrast' in these verses.

[47] See earlier where I spoke of one aspect of this seeming contradiction.

fact that the new covenant is more penetrating than the old? Instead of explaining the problem, this approach explodes it!

What is the biblical answer? How can the new covenant be more penetrating than the old, and yet be easy and light? Clearly, although the Bible states the seeming contradiction, there can be none. As to the severity aspect of Christ's law, contrary to the Reformed approach, no teeth are to be pulled. The warnings of the new covenant *are* to be taken seriously and given their full weight. There must be no getting round them by semantics. The warning passages are real.

The fundamental sin of the new covenant is to depart from Christ. I have just quoted Hebrews 10:29. What sin does the verse warn against? Nothing less than the deliberate, wilful (Heb. 10:26) forsaking of Christ, the bitter rejection of him and his Spirit.[48] Whoever breaks Hebrews 10:29 'has trampled the Son of God underfoot, counted the blood of the covenant by which he was sanctified a common thing, and insulted the Spirit of grace'. 'Worse punishment' than under Moses awaits such a man! And this warning note is sounded again and again throughout the letter to the Hebrews (Heb. 2:1-3; 3:12-14; 4:1,11; 6:4-8; 10:26-39; 12:14-17,25-29). Take also Romans 8:6,13: 'To be carnally minded [to have the mind of the flesh] is death... If you live according to the flesh you will die'. And Galatians 6:8: 'He who sows to his flesh will of the flesh reap corruption, but he who sows to the Spirit will of the Spirit reap everlasting life'. I have repeatedly noted the reality of the warning passages. They are not hypothetical. They are not put in Scripture as 'bogey men'. They are unfeigned. They mean what they say, and they say what they mean.

Perseverance under Christ, holding to him and his law, is a sure mark of grace, the ultimate proof of spirituality. To depart from Christ is the worst of all sins. We are Christ's 'house... *if* we hold fast the confidence and the rejoicing of the hope firm to the end' (Heb. 3:6). 'For we have become partakers of Christ *if* we hold the beginning of our confidence steadfast to the end... And we desire that each one of you show the same diligence to the full assurance of hope until the end... See that you do not refuse him who speaks' (Heb. 3:14; 6:11; 12:25). 'The gospel... by which... you are saved, *if* you hold fast' to the apostolic word, the gospel (1 Cor. 15:1-2). 'He who endures to the end shall be saved' (Matt. 24:13).

Is the punishment under the new covenant severe? It is indeed. To break the law of Christ – to reject Christ, to turn back from him, to forsake him – leads to: 'I never knew you; depart from me, you who practice lawlessness' (Matt. 7:23; see verses 13-29). How harrowing, then, is Christ's question: 'Do you also want to go away?' There is only one satisfactory reply: 'Lord, to whom shall we go? You have the words of eternal life. Also we have come to believe and know that you are the Christ, the Son of the living God' (John 6:67-69). The ultimate testimony which counts is this: 'I have fought the good fight, I have finished the race, I have kept the faith' (2 Tim. 4:7). Believer, Christ will 'present you holy, and blameless, and above reproach in his sight – *if* indeed you continue in the faith, grounded and steadfast, and are not moved away from the hope of the gospel' (Col. 1:22-23).

But just a moment! Surely all believers sin? Sadly, they do! Well, when a believer sins, does he bring condemnation upon himself? Does he lose his salvation? Certainly not! Let me explain. As I have said, the law of Christ is far more than a list of rules. In

---

[48] Do Matt. 12:31-32; Mark 3:29; Luke 12:10 speak of this?

truth, it is not that at all. It is an entirely new system. As I will show, to submit to the law of Christ is to yield to him, to receive him as Lord and Saviour, to honour and obey him, to learn of him, to cleave to him, to abide in him, to continue in him, to have him formed within, to have his Spirit, to walk according to his Spirit. Now although a believer may stumble into sin, this is a far cry from deserting the Redeemer.[49] While I would not excuse the least sin, there is a world of difference between *failing* Christ and *forsaking* him. The believer sins; sadly, it is so. But God has made abundant provision for such (1 John 1:5-10; 2:1-2, for instance). Nevertheless, the warnings are real. If professing believers do turn their back upon Christ, and abandon him, they will come under the severest of all judgements: 'For if, after they have escaped the pollutions of the world through the knowledge of the Lord and Saviour Jesus Christ, they are again entangled in them and overcome, the latter end is worse for them than the beginning. For it would have been better for them not to have known the way of righteousness, than having known it, to turn from the holy commandment delivered to them' (2 Pet. 2:20-21). This, it goes without saying, is far worse than under Moses.

This, then, is the biblical answer to the seeming contradiction. I realise that this, in itself, raises other problems, problems connected with God's sovereignty, his purpose and decree. On the one hand, I know that God will bring all his elect to everlasting glory. I rejoice in it. But I also know that each one of the elect has to come individually to faith in Christ and has to continue in Christ. I do not try to reconcile these two. I believe them both because I find them both revealed in Scripture. However much I explored these matters, I would still end up with a seeming contradiction, something beyond my wit to understand or explain. But this happens so often with me, I do as I always do: after trying to reconcile the paradox as far as I can within biblical parameters, I accept the remaining tension, and press on by faith. And it not just me! All believers find the same. Of course they do! Unless, that is, they are prepared to trim Scripture to fit their system!

So, although I will deal with the gentle, kindly aspect of Christ's law as I go on,[50] its severity aspect is real. We must take the warnings seriously. In the final analysis, to break the law of Christ is to depart from Christ, to desert him, to live according to the flesh. And the consequences are indescribably bad. But the law of Christ is far from negative. Although I have spent a little time on this negative aspect of it in order to tackle a seeming contradiction, there is far more to be said on the positive side. 'But you, beloved, building yourselves up on your most holy faith, praying in the Holy Spirit, keep yourselves in the love of God, looking for the mercy of our Lord Jesus Christ unto eternal life... Now to him who is able to keep you from stumbling, and to present you faultless before the presence of his glory with exceeding joy, to God our

---

[49] In chapter 10, I drew attention to the difference between 'being in the flesh' and 'the flesh being in you'. I also quoted: 'Whoever abides in [Christ] does not sin. Whoever sins has neither seen him nor known him. Little children, let no one deceive you. He who practices righteousness is righteous, just as he is righteous. He who sins is of the devil... Whoever has been born of God does not sin, for his seed remains in him; and he cannot sin, because he has been born of God' (1 John 3:6-9). NASB has 'sins... sins... practices sin... practices sin... sin'; NIV 'keeps on sinning... continues to sin... does what is sinful... continue to sin... go on sinning'. He does not 'sin wilfully' (Heb. 10:26), 'sin deliberately' (NIV). He does not live in the *realm* of sin.

[50] That is, I will say more about the 'easy' (the opposite of burdensome) and 'light' (easy to be kept) aspect of Christ's law.

Saviour, who alone is wise, be glory and majesty, dominion and power, both now and for ever. Amen' (Jude 20-21,24-25).

It is time to develop this positive aspect of the law of Christ. What is it? Who gave it? And to whom is it given?

Christ is the giver of his law

It must be so. It is, after all, 'the law of Christ'! Christ has given his law to his believing, redeemed, people; hence, 'the law of Christ'. Take the Sermon on the Mount (Matt. 5 – 7). In addressing his disciples (Matt. 5:1-2), while Christ made use of the Mosaic law, he clearly promulgated a new law, his own law. Let me prove it.

Christ the giver of his law: The Sermon on the Mount

Addressing his disciples, Christ took the Mosaic law for his springboard or starting point, saying again and again: 'You have heard that it was said... but I say to you' (Matt. 5:21-22,27-28,31-32,33-34,38-39,43-44). Four things should be noted: *First*, the link between Moses and Christ. Christ was preaching a new law, but this did not involve any disloyalty to the old law. The Mosaic law is, as I keep restating, part of 'all Scripture', and therefore 'profitable' (2 Tim. 3:16-17). The law of Christ knows how to make proper use of the law of Moses. But it has to be 'proper'. *Secondly*, note the contrast between Moses and Christ: 'It was said... but *I* say'. *Thirdly*, Christ always cut deeper than Moses. Instead of making obedience an external matter, Christ made (his) law-keeping a matter of the heart, which is far more penetrating and searching. *Fourthly*, note Christ's jaw-dropping conclusion to the discourse: 'Therefore whoever hears these sayings of mine' (Matt. 7:24,26). The point was grasped by the crowd, even though they gasped at what the Lord had said: 'And so it was, when Jesus had ended these sayings, that the people were astonished at his teaching, for he taught them as one having authority, and not as the scribes' (Matt. 7:28-29).

There is no doubt about it – the crowd saw it – Christ did not regurgitate other men's thoughts; he did not even replicate Moses. *He gave his own law*. And he gave it *in his own name and on his own authority*. Furthermore, he spoke unmistakeably as the new lawgiver: 'I say to you', giving the people 'these sayings of mine'. And how frequently it is recorded throughout the Gospels that he did such a thing! I refer to 'Jesus said', 'I say', 'my words', *etc*. These are not always merely explanatory; in context, they show Christ's authority. A glance at a concordance under 'verily I say' or 'verily, verily' (AV), 'assuredly' or 'most assuredly' (NKJV), 'I tell you the truth' (NIV), 'truly I say' or 'truly, truly' (NASB), will confirm the point. Christ could not have made the position any clearer. He called for obedience to his words (Matt. 7:24-29; Luke 6:46-49). Above all, see Matthew 28:20.

Let us take this further. As for the Mosaic law, Christ dogmatically states that he, and he alone, has the right to give its true, spiritual, interpretation, as he uses it in his own law. In other words, Matthew 5 – 7 is not a repetition of the Mosaic law spelled out or recast for believers. Far from it! It is Christ's own law. And, it goes without saying, it is a true law. In this Sermon, Christ does not offer advice; he issues his law and does so with majestic authority, raising the question of obedience right at the dawn of the new age. Moses was the lawgiver for the old Israel. Christ is the lawgiver for his new Israel. But there is a difference. Whereas the law of Moses was not, strictly speaking, his law, but God's, Christ did give his *own* law. In this, Christ explicitly demonstrates that he is greater than Moses (Heb. 3:1-6); his law, likewise. I am not going back on what I said earlier. Christ's law is not the same sort of law as the Mosaic yoke. Let me stress this: 'law' under Christ is not at all the same as 'law' under Moses. Christ's law is love, the fruit of the Spirit (Gal. 5:22), worked out by those walking in the Spirit. Christ delineated all this in his Sermon on the Mount.

This is contested. Some think Christ was not issuing a new law at all. Rather, it is said, he was calling for a recovery of that which had been lost under the Pharisees, he was correcting their misunderstanding of Moses, their distortion of his law.[51] While there is some truth in this, it does not exhaust what Christ was doing – not by a long chalk. 'You have heard... it has been said', declared Christ, over and over again (Matt. 5:21,27,31,33,38,43), and each time he was quoting *Moses*, not the scribes or Pharisees. True, the Pharisees did reduce the meaning of the law, ruining it by their tradition, and Christ told them so (Matt. 15:1-9; Mark 7:5-13). But this explanation on its own simply does not measure up to what was going on in the Sermon on the Mount, where Christ did not quote the rabbis, but Moses. Yes, Christ did expound and elucidate certain points of the law. Even so, he took Moses far beyond the import of his original words, occasionally rescinding or adding to him, not merely clarifying or rubber-stamping him. Christ is greater than Moses, and he certainly shows it here. He did not do as the scribes who appealed to Moses (or others) as their authority. Rather, he showed himself to be Lord. He taught on his own authority, towering above all who came before him, including and especially, Moses. In short, Christ not only took some principles from the Mosaic law and made them more intense; he upheld others, in particular the love commandment,[52] and made others redundant. The fact is, Christ was not renewing the Mosaic covenant at all, but, right at the start, he was instituting his own law for the new covenant. He was setting out a new law, under a new covenant, in a new age, for new men.[53]

Christ the giver of his law: A look at Matthew 5:17-18
But what did Christ mean by saying he had not come 'to destroy the law or the prophets. I did not come to destroy but to fulfil. For assuredly, I say to you, till heaven and earth pass away, one jot or one tittle will by no means pass from the law till all is fulfilled' (Matt. 5:17-18)? I have already glanced at this,[54] but I now examine the way some use Christ's words to try to blunt his emphasis on the newness of his law in the Sermon on the Mount. It is claimed that Christ here was not setting out anything new, but 'explaining', 'establishing' or 'upholding' the law, declaring its real or intended meaning in light of Pharisaical efforts to get round its full significance.

While, as I have agreed, there is some truth in this, it fails to grasp what Christ was saying. It is worse. The word 'fulfil' (*plēroō*) cannot here mean 'establish'. By no stretch of the imagination can Christ's words of contrast: 'You have heard... but I say to you' (Matt. 5:21-48), be construed as Christ *establishing* the Mosaic law. Christ's 'do not swear at all', does not *establish* Moses' 'not [to] swear falsely' (Matt. 5:33-34); 'not to resist an evil person', does not *establish* 'an eye for an eye' (Matt. 5:38-39); nor

---

[51] The rendering, 'said *by* them' (Matt. 5:27, AV), is incorrect (see NKJV, NASB, NIV, *etc.*).
[52] Lev. 19:18. See the next chapter.
[53] Note the eschatological point once again.
[54] In chapters 6 and 10 pp96,170; see also 'Extracts' p498.

does 'love your enemies' *establish* 'love your neighbour' (Matt. 5:43-44). In these instances, at least, Christ was not establishing the Mosaic law, but was specifying something quite different and far more penetrating.

Nor will it do to say that Christ was establishing the law by explaining it, giving its intended meaning – which is precisely what the Jews of Christ's day expected of the Messiah they were looking for. Take the commands I have just quoted; 'not [to] swear *at all*' cannot be squeezed out of 'not [to] swear *falsely*'; 'not to resist an evil person', cannot be the full meaning of 'eye for an eye'; nor can 'love your *enemies*' be the intended meaning of 'love your *neighbour*'. As before, in these instances, Christ was not setting out the intended meaning of the Mosaic law, but was specifying something quite different, something new and far more penetrating. Christ was not *expounding* the Mosaic law. He was setting out his own law.

This, too, has been contested – along these lines: Take Matthew 5:27-28. Christ forbade heart adultery. Now if Christ's teaching had been new then what he taught could not have been known under Moses. Yet the Old Testament did prohibit heart adultery. Christ therefore could not have been teaching anything new. Thus, so it is claimed, Christ was making explicit what was already implicit in the seventh commandment, not setting out a new law in contrast to Moses. Rather, he was correcting the mistaken, current understanding taught by the Pharisees.

In reply, I readily agree, of course, that the Old Testament speaks of the heart (Ps. 66:18; Prov. 7:25, for instance), and the tenth commandment in particular – the one Paul found most searching (Rom. 7:7-11) – is concerned with covetousness (Ex. 20:17), a matter of the heart. Yes. But to leap from this to say that all that Christ intended was to show that the ten commandments have a meaning that was patently there, if only the Jews had had the wit to see it, reads far more into (or out of) the old covenant than is biblically warranted. What is more, paradoxically, it is also too limiting, far too-cramped a view of what Christ was actually doing here. Christ, in giving his law, used the old law, yes, but in this Sermon on the Mount Christ *was* saying something new, something beyond the commandments as they stood. This, to put it no stronger, raises a question mark over the Puritan way of applying the ten commandments in fine detail far beyond their stated remit.[55]

What is more, if Christ was saying nothing more than the law of Moses had already said, then of course he could not have been saying anything new. But, quite clearly – as the crowd realised – he was! And, of course, he used the contrasting-word 'but', 'but I say...'. So he must have been saying more than was in the ten commandments. He was!

Take the rabbis, the experts on the law. Christ was going far beyond them – they did not stress 'inwardness', the heart (Matt. 15:1-20; Mark 7:1-23). For instance, they did not emphasise the heart in their interpretations of Jeremiah 31. On that vital passage, see chapter 18.

In short, to claim that Christ was reinterpreting the Mosaic law, explaining the law, or merely making clear what was already in the law, and not giving his own new law, at once proves too much and, at the same time, fails to give sufficient weight to the contextual evidence of the startling newness of Christ's authority and teaching. What do I mean? If all Christ was doing was restating the ten commandments, and removing the clutter of Jewish misunderstandings, it seems rather like the proverbial nut and

---

[55] See 'Extracts' p363.

sledgehammer. The nut would seem to be miniscule, and the hammer colossal – since, don't forget, all this led up to the cross![56]

Certainly, Christ did not ignore or attack the law, saying something totally alien to Moses. But Christ in his law shows the way to use and apply the Mosaic law *under the new covenant*;[57] that is, as seen in Christ's fulfilment of it. And 'newness' is the word; Christ was saying something new compared to Moses. Those who disagree have to come to terms with Matthew 5:18-19: if Christ was establishing Moses' law, then believers must observe all the commandments of the law – including the sacrifices. This, of course, is unthinkable. I have already shown that the common ploy of damage-limitation by narrowing the demand to 'the moral law' will not work – the technique being wholly without biblical warrant. If Christ was establishing Moses' law, then it was the whole law he was establishing, even the 'least' commandment.[58] This, in itself, destroys the case.

To sum up: 'establish' will not work here. Christ was not 'establishing' the Mosaic law.

But what if 'fulfil' is taken to mean 'extend' or 'deepen'? Was Christ taking the law 'further' by speaking of the heart, and not simply the external, when he spoke of murder/hate and adultery/desire?

Indeed he was. Take the sin of impurity. Christ condemns no sin as much as this; and this, not only in the act, but in the thought (Matt. 5:28). See John 8:1-11, the woman taken in adultery. The way in which Jesus dealt with this woman – and the Jews – exquisitely illustrates the point. The Jews, imbued with the law of Moses, embroiled in it, thought in terms of the external act; 'in the very act', they stressed (John 8:4). That's it! The act! Don't worry about the heart! Christ, responding in his own time and way, in his law drove them, piercingly, to the heart – above all, their own hearts! Why did the men drift off? I don't think it takes much working out! They had dragged the woman there – what about the man? Indeed, how many of them, I wonder, had actually committed adultery themselves? I go further. How many, in Christ's terms (Matt. 5:28) had committed adultery with this wretched woman, even as they, hauling her before Jesus, had been ogling her? Christ's law, plainly, went much deeper and further than Moses' law. His words cut them to the heart (compare Acts 2:37). Yes, he certainly 'deepened' Moses. The men found it so that day. And look at the way Jesus dealt with the woman herself. Compare *that* with the way they dealt with her! 'Mercy

---

[56] Time and again, the Jews wanted to kill Jesus, both for the things he said and for his miracles – which often challenged their view of the law, and provoked them not least over the sabbath. See, for instance, Matt. 12:14; John 5:16-18; 7:1,19,25-30,44; 8:37-40,59; 10:31; 11:53. Do not forget the wider context. Take Luke 6:11. I would include in this – like Luke – not only the healing of the man with the withered arm on the sabbath, which Christ did so provocatively (Luke 6:6-10), but his parable of the garments and the wineskins (Luke 5:36-39). Opening a sermon on this passage, I asked the congregation: 'Why ever would you crucify a man who told pretty stories?' The answer is of course that Jesus did not tell pretty stories. Here, he was telling the Jews the old covenant was over. Worn out garments, dried wineskins and a withered arm! The Jews understood him, and they didn't like it.

[57] For more on this, see chapter 18.

[58] By the way, which of the ten commandments do the Reformed think is the least? According to Matt. 23:23; Luke 11:42, the 'least' commandments made their appearance outside the so-called moral law.

triumphs over judgement!' (Jas. 2:13). Could we wish for a better illustration of John 1:17?

Or of this:

The word of God is living and powerful, and sharper than any two-edged sword, piercing even to the division of soul and spirit, and of joints and marrow, and is a discerner of the thoughts and intents of the heart. And there is no creature hidden from his sight, but all things are naked and open to the eyes of him to whom we must give account.

The men certainly found it so that early morning. And what about this?

Seeing then that we have a great high priest who has passed through the heavens, Jesus the Son of God, let us hold fast our confession. For we do not have a high priest who cannot sympathise with our weaknesses, but was in all points tempted as we are, yet without sin. Let us therefore come boldly to the throne of grace, that we may obtain mercy and find grace to help in time of need (Heb. 4:12-16).

Was not the woman a forerunner of the truth of it?

Getting back to the 'fulfil' in the Sermon on the Mount, and broadening the context: Matthew's very frequent use of *plēroō* – 16 times – makes it probable – I would say, certain – that he was thinking in terms of the eschatological. Let me explain. Christ was not abandoning the law, but was bringing out what the law had pointed to. He 'fulfilled' it – the very word he used! Christ was showing continuity with the old covenant, yes, *but also discontinuity*, in the sense of shadow giving way to reality as the new age came in. Moses anticipated Christ, foreshadowed him, but Christ was unique, and so was his teaching. It was new: 'No man ever spoke like this man!' (John 7:46). He alone has the words of eternal life (John 6:68).

Incidentally, it was the confession of John 7:46 which needled the Jewish authorities into taking matters into their own hands, inciting them to try to trap Jesus with 'the case' of the woman taken in adultery, as recorded in John 8:1-11. But they soon found they had bitten off more than they could chew. All they succeeded in doing was to expose the great gulf between their use of the law when approaching the sinner, and the way Christ dealt with the woman – and, incidentally, with them. As I say, the law of Moses and the law of Christ are very different things, as this episode plainly shows.

Getting back to Matthew 5:17-18, there is one further point. Christ said he had not come 'to destroy the law or *the prophets*. I did not come to destroy but to fulfil'. Notice: as with the law, so with the prophets. Just as the prophets (speaking of Christ's first coming) have been fulfilled by Christ, and, therefore, their day is over, so with the law. Consequently, in the same way as we read and use the prophets where Christ has now fulfilled them, so must we read and use the entire law, since he has fulfilled it all. As I will argue in chapter 18, this has an important bearing on our understanding of the Old Testament prophecies of 'the law' in the new covenant.

Let me pull all this together. From the Sermon on the Mount, we have learned that the believer's rule is not the old law established, continued, deepened, extended, enlarged or more fully explained. While there are elements of truth in all that, it falls a long way short of the facts. The Sermon on the Mount is Christ's own law. And in saying that, I mean more than that Christ promulgated his law in this address. He did. But remember the eschatological. In giving his law, Christ was acting in fulfilment – note the word –

of God's eternal decree. The Godhead had determined that Christ would bring in the new covenant at the appointed time. That time had now come. It was the time of 'fulfilment'' (see Luke 9:31; 21:22; 22:37, all NIV). Writing to the Corinthians, Paul could tell them they were living in the time of 'the fulfilment of the ages' (1 Cor. 10:11, NIV). Thus Christ, right at the start of his ministry, sets out his new law for his new-covenant people. It is the eschatological moment, the 'but now'. Not to grasp this, but to fall back into the Reformed way of restricting the Sermon on the Mount to some sort of re-hash of Moses, is to make an abysmal mistake. Christ, having come into the world in order to fulfil the Mosaic law, in his own law not only interprets and applies Moses' law to the believer in the new age, and does so in his own unique way, but in so doing he promulgates his own law. Christ is the lawgiver of his new-covenant people, and it is his own – new – law which he gives them. *This* is the point of Matthew 5 – 7. Anything less, diminishes the Lord of glory. If all Christ was doing was enforcing Moses' law, then Hebrews 3:3 will have to be rewritten. Moses, after all, is worthy of greater honour than the Lord Jesus! And John 1:17 will have to be recast. The law came by Moses, that's the major point; Jesus Christ enforced Moses' law, yes, but that's all. Really? As for me, I will stick with what Scripture actually says. Christ has greater glory than Moses. While, in Matthew 5 – 7, he used Moses' law, Christ undoubtedly declared his own law. Moses certainly was the instrument God used to give his (God's) law to Israel, yes, but Christ himself, and in his own right, and at the appointed time, issued his own law to his new Israel. The law came by Moses. But Jesus Christ brought grace and truth.

And it was not only in the Sermon on the Mount where Christ set out his terms for discipleship in the new covenant. He did it again and again (Matt. 10:5 – 11:1; 20:25-28; Luke 14:26-35; John 8:31-32). Above all, it was at the final supper with his disciples (Luke 22:14-38; John 13 – 16) where Christ spelled out his law. God through Moses had given his law to the nation of Israel in the old covenant at Sinai; Christ gave his law (Gal. 6:2) to the new Israel, the Israel of God (Gal. 6:16) in the new covenant at the last supper.[59]

As I have said repeatedly, do not miss the eschatological in all this. We are at the watershed of the ages. None of this happened 'by chance'. All was determined by the Godhead. Moreover, God had clearly promised it down the ages. Indeed, supremely, and most appositely, it was by Moses – yes Moses – that he had prophesied this momentous act of Christ.

Let me explain.

Christ the giver of his law in fulfilment of prophecy
The fact that Christ so often rightfully displayed himself as the lawgiver of his people should cause us no surprise. After all, in Deuteronomy 18:15-19 Moses had predicted:

The LORD your God will raise up for you a prophet *like me* from your midst, from your brethren. Him you shall hear, according to all you desired of the LORD your God in Horeb in the day of the assembly, saying: 'Let me not hear again the voice of the LORD my God, nor let me see this great fire any more, lest I die'. And the LORD said to me: 'What they have spoken is good. I will raise up for them a prophet *like you* from among their brethren, and will put my words in his mouth, and he shall speak to them all that I command him.

---

[59] See chapter 18 where I justify my claim that the church is the Israel of the new covenant.

And it shall be that whoever will not hear my words, which he speaks in my name, I will require it of him'.

'A prophet like me', said Moses. So, as Moses gave his law to Israel,[60] so now, 'but now', at the appointed time, the promised Messiah appears among men. 'Like Moses' – greater by far than Moses (John 1:17; Heb. 3:1-6) – Christ, the lawgiver, has come! The prophecy is fulfilled. Christ, the new Moses, is here! Christ the lawgiver for his new Israel! Clothed with the Spirit, lifting up his voice, Christ reveals himself as this mighty lawgiver, fulfilling, not only God's prophecy through Moses, but also through Isaiah: 'Behold! My servant... I have put my Spirit upon him; he will bring forth justice to the Gentiles... He will bring forth justice for truth... And the coastlands shall wait for *his law*' (Is. 42:1-4; Matt. 12:17-21). 'The LORD is our judge, the LORD is our lawgiver, the LORD is our King' (Isa. 33:22). Again, on the mountain where Christ was transfigured, when Peter wanted to put Moses and Elijah (the law and the prophets) on the same level as Christ, the Father in no uncertain terms immediately spelled out his Son's uniqueness and authority as the lawgiver over his people: 'This is my beloved Son, in whom I am well pleased. Hear *him*!' (Matt. 17:4-5; Luke 9:35). Christ is the believer's only teacher. He himself declared: 'You call me teacher and Lord, and you say well, for so I am' (John 13:13). As the Sun of Righteousness (Mal. 4:2) full-shining, he makes the lesser lights of the Old Testament (the law and the prophets) fade away (Heb. 8:13). Again, Christ linked himself very much to Moses in this matter of law-giving. When addressing the Jews, he expostulated: 'If you do not believe his writings, how will you believe *my words*?' (John 5:47), a staggering juxtaposition unless he is – as he is – all he claimed to be. Peter in Solomon's porch confirmed it, preaching 'Jesus Christ' of whom 'Moses truly said to the fathers: "The LORD your God will raise up for you a prophet like me... *Him you shall hear in all things, whatever he says to you*. And it shall be that every soul who will not *hear that prophet* shall be utterly destroyed from among the people"' (Acts 3:20-23. Compare Deut. 34:8 with Deut. 34:10-12). Mary's words are most apt: 'Whatever *he says* to you, do it' (John 2:5).

Again, as the writer to the Hebrews put it:

God, who at various times and in various ways spoke in time past to the fathers by the prophets, has in these last days *spoken* to us *by his Son*... Therefore we must give the more earnest heed to the things we have heard, lest we drift away. For if the word spoken through angels[61] proved steadfast, and every transgression and disobedience received a just reward [retribution], how shall we escape if we neglect so great a salvation, which at the first began to be *spoken* by the *Lord*, and was confirmed to us by those who heard him... Consider... Christ Jesus, who was faithful to him who appointed him, as Moses also was faithful in all his house. For this one has been counted worthy of more glory than Moses, inasmuch as he who built the house has more honour than the house... Moses indeed was faithful in all his house as a servant, for a testimony of those things which would be spoken afterwards, but Christ as a Son over his own house, whose house we are if we hold fast the confidence and the rejoicing of the hope firm to the end... Anyone who has rejected Moses' law dies without mercy on the testimony of two or three witnesses. Of how much worse punishment, do you suppose, will he be thought worthy who has trampled the Son of God underfoot? (Heb. 1:1-2; 2:1-3; 3:1-6; 10:28-29).

---

[60] Or rather, as an agent he received God's law for Israel.

[61] That is, the giving of the law at Sinai. Angels spoke the old law; Christ spoke the new.

Note the link with Moses; 'Christ Jesus... as Moses'. Note the contrast with Moses: 'Moses indeed was... but Christ'. To reject Moses' law was bad enough, but to reject the Son of God is far worse. Note that Moses' chief work was to prophesy of Christ and his covenant: 'Moses... was faithful... for a testimony of those things which would be spoken afterwards'. Incidentally, notice how these words confirm what I said on the Sermon on the Mount. Moses testified of Christ. Christ is the goal, the end, the fulfilment; Moses was the signpost. Those who want to argue against what I deduced from the Sermon on the Mount, and persist in maintaining that Jesus enforced, explained and established Moses in order to bring the believer under the law of Moses as his perfect rule, will have to do the same as before; namely, they will have to recast Hebrews 3:5-6 also. Apparently, the writer to the Hebrews got it the wrong way round. He should have said that Christ was faithful in explaining all that Moses spoke! And, he could have added, he should have added, he surely would have added, that Moses' law, therefore, indisputably is the perfect rule for the believer – now that Christ has fully clarified what Moses was saying!

Let us get back to reality: the passage itself. Note the emphasis upon speaking; both Moses and Christ *spoke*. Note the emphasis upon hearing. Those under Moses had to hear him, and those under Christ have to hear *him*. But there is a contrast; Moses was a **servant** *in* his house, whereas Christ is a (the) **Son** *over* his house. Christ rules his house, arranges it, orders it. If Moses gave his law to Israel, how much more does Christ give *his* law to *his* people. Moses was a (mere) go-between. Moreover, as I have said, Moses did not give *his* law to Israel. He gave *God's* law to them. He was the agent. Angels spoke the law to Moses who then passed it on to Israel. How very different with Christ. He spoke his law directly to his people. Christ spoke of 'my commandments' (John 14:15,21; 15:10; see also John 15:12,14,17; compare John 8:43,47,51). Jesus drove it home even harder: 'If anyone keeps my word he shall never see (or taste) death'. The Jews got the point, but didn't like it (John 8:51-53). Nevertheless, Christ enforced it further still (John 8:54-55). Moses, nor any other prophet, nor any apostle, did (would dare to do) such a thing. Yes, of course, the apostles instructed believers. But they instructed, as apostles, in Christ's name, under Christ's authority. Take one example: 1 Corinthians 11:17,23. On rare occasions (1 Cor. 7:25, for instance), Paul gave his 'judgement' or advice, having no direct command from Christ. But this was rare, and was clearly flagged. See 2 Corinthians 8:10. But Christ spoke as one with God the Father, one who had the right and authority to lay down laws for his people. Matthew 28:18-20 is the standing ordinance of Christ for his people throughout this age. Christ did not issue advice or make a request. Who else can say: 'This is my commandment' (John 15:12), and: 'Keep my commandments' (John 14:15,21,23,24; 15:10,12,14,17)? Finally, we are told that this law of Christ, this 'salvation', which 'at the first began to be spoken by the Lord', 'was confirmed to us by those who heard him'.

God, when he declares: 'This is my beloved Son... Hear him!', commands men to hear the one to whom he has 'committed all judgement... and has given him authority to execute' it, and is demanding that all men honour Christ as they honour himself, declaring him to be the Son of God with power, to be both Lord and Christ, the one to whom he has given power over all flesh, all power in heaven and earth, a name above every name in this world, or in that which is to come, whom he has commanded all the angels of God to worship, and whom he has appointed to judge the world in righteousness. More than all this, when Christ speaks, it is the commandment of him who is 'God manifested in the flesh', the word who, in the beginning, was with God – was God – by whom all things were made – without whom nothing was made, who is 'our great God', as well as 'our... Saviour' who is 'over all, God blessed for ever'. It is the commandment of him who, by an act of will, formed the universe, and, by an act of will, can and will dissolve that same universe. It is the commandment of one infinite in wisdom and power, in righteousness and goodwill; and, just because it is *his* commandment, it must be, no less than the old law, like himself, 'holy and just and good'. It is a commandment, then, that cannot be neglected or disobeyed, without incurring the deepest guilt and greatest danger. To disobey this commandment is to disobey not only a divine messenger, but a divine person, God himself, Immanuel, 'God with us' (Matt. 1:23; 17:5; 28:19-20; John 1:1-3; 5:19-27; Acts 2:36; 17:31; Rom. 1:4; 7:12; 9:5 (AV, NASB); Eph. 1:21-23; Phil. 2:9-11; 1 Tim. 3:16; Tit. 2:13; Heb. 2:3). This is Christ's *own* commandment to his *own* people, a commandment which did not and could not exist until he came and issued it. Beyond all question, it is 'a new commandment'. Reader, think of the arrogance of Jesus if he had been a mere man. Take these words from John:

He whom God has sent speaks the words[62] of God, for God does not give the Spirit by measure. The Father loves the Son, and has given all things into his hand... Jesus... said: 'My doctrine is not mine, but his who sent me. If anyone wills to do his will, he shall know concerning the doctrine, whether it is from God or whether I speak on my own authority... I do nothing of myself, but as my Father taught me, I speak these things... I speak what I have seen with my Father... If anyone hears my words and does not believe... He who rejects me, and does not receive my words, has that which judges him – the word that I have spoken will judge him in the last day. For I have not spoken on my own authority; but the Father who sent me gave me a command, what I should say and what I should speak. And I know that his command is everlasting life. Therefore, whatever I speak, just as the Father has told me, so I speak... The words that I speak to you I do not speak on my own authority; but the Father who dwells in me does the works... He who does not love me does not keep my words; and the word which you hear is not mine but the Father's who sent me' (John 3:34-35; 7:16-17; 8:28,38; 12:47-50; 14:10-11,24).

In light of this momentous testimony, what else can we say but that Christ is the only lawgiver for his people? Moses is not the lawgiver for believers. There is no question of it. Christ fulfilled and ended the law of Moses, giving his people, as their prophet, as the Son of God himself, his own law (Heb. 1:1-2). Believers, liberated from the law of Moses, are now under the law of Christ. The Son has made us free. 'If you hold to my teaching, you are really my disciples. Then you will know the truth, and the truth will set you free... If the Son sets you free, you will be free indeed' (John 8:31-32,36, NIV). Believers are free. Nevertheless, in seeming contradiction, they are also slaves. But, wonder of wonders, both their freedom and their new slavery are entirely bound up with Christ: 'He who is called in the Lord... is the Lord's freedman... Christ's slave. You were bought at a price; do not become slaves of men' (1 Cor. 7:22-23). Believers are Christ's slaves because Christ, having set them free (John 8:36; Gal. 5:1), rules over them in his own law.

---

[62] Note the plural.

The last supper, and Christ's discourse

Let us look a little more closely at Christ giving his law to his people. During that final Passover celebration, Christ broke with centuries of Jewish tradition to do something absolutely new, something truly staggering. Taking the bread and the cup, he established his supper to serve as a perpetual reminder of himself in the new covenant, and this by way of command to his disciples: 'This is my body which is given for you; do this in remembrance of me... This cup is the new covenant in my blood, which is shed for you' (Luke 22:19-20). And 'supper being ended' (John 13:2), Jesus, having washed his disciples' feet, gave them more of his law:

You call me teacher and Lord, and you say well, for so I am... I... your Lord and teacher... have given you an example, that you should do as I have done to you... If you know these things, blessed are you if you do them (John 13:13-17). A new commandment I give to you, that you love one another; as I have loved you, that you also love one another (John 13:34). Believe... in me... believe me (John 14:1,11). If you love me, keep my commandments (John 14:15). He who has my commandments and keeps them, it is he who loves me (John 14:21). He who does not love me does not keep my words; and the word which you hear is not mine but the Father's who sent me (John 14:24). Abide in me (John 15:4). This is my commandment, that you love one another as I have loved you (John 15:12). You are my friends if you do whatever I command you (John 15:14). These things I command you, that you love one another (John 15:17). Remember the word that I said to you (John 15:20). Ask... (John 16:24). Be of good cheer (John 16:33). The kings of the Gentiles exercise lordship over them... But not so among you; on the contrary, he who is greatest among you, let him be as the younger, and he who governs as he who serves (Luke 22:25-26).

Loving obedience to me, said Christ, spelling out his law for his disciples, is the badge of all true believers, the evidence of their spirituality: 'By this all will know that you are my disciples, if you have love for one another' (John 13:35). 'Abide in me... By this my Father is glorified, that you bear much fruit; so you will be my disciples' (John 15:4,8) – and in no other way! 'If you keep my commandments, you will abide in my love' – and in no other way! – 'just as I have kept my Father's commandments and abide in his love' (John 15:10). Earlier, I made the claim that to keep the law of Christ is to cleave to him; to break his law is to desert him. Here is the proof. 'Abide in me'! He who could say: 'I bestow upon you a kingdom' (Luke 22:29), had every right to give his people the rule and pattern of that kingdom. And so he did. As I noted earlier, Christ established obedience to his law right at the start of the new age.

King Jesus gives his law to his people

Think how many commands Christ gave his disciples after his resurrection (Matt. 28; Mark 16; Luke 24; John 20 – 21; Acts 1:1-8). As it is recorded: 'He through the Holy Spirit [gave] commandments to the apostles' (Acts 1:2). The kingship of Christ, his office as his people's lawgiver, is nowhere more clearly spelled out than in Matthew 28:18-20:

All authority has been given to me in heaven and on earth. Go therefore and make disciples of all the nations, baptising them in the name of the Father and of the Son and of the Holy Spirit, teaching them to observe all things that I have commanded you; and lo, I am with you always, even to the end of the age.

Christ is King. Yes, Christ *is* King – now. Judging by outward circumstances, it does not appear so. Not all his enemies are yet destroyed. Even so, he reigns at this very moment (1 Cor. 15:25-26). He is King. Through all the fog of prejudice, political intrigue, abject impotence, unmitigated venom and despicable cringing that surrounded the Lord Jesus at his 'trials', one thing, at least, shines out like a beacon: Christ is King (John 18:33-39; 19:2-3,12,14-15,19-22)! Pilate failed miserably that day, but in one respect he deserves credit: 'Pilate wrote a title and put it on the cross. And the writing was: JESUS OF NAZARETH, THE KING OF THE JEWS... written in Hebrew, Greek, and Latin'. The Jewish bigwigs did not like it; they did not like it at all: 'Therefore the chief priests of the Jews said to Pilate: "Do not write: 'The King of the Jews', but: 'He said: "I am the King of the Jews""'. Pilate answered: "What I have written, I have written"' (John 19:19-22). And there it stands impregnable in Scripture: JESUS... THE KING!

And King he is! The prophets time and again foretold his kingship over an increasing and endless kingdom (Ps. 89:3-4,29,35-37; Isa. 9:6-7; 16:5; Dan. 2:44; 7:14,18,27; Zech. 9:9-10, and so on).[63] Just before Christ's birth, the angel Gabriel announced to Mary that her 'son... Jesus... will be great and will be called the Son of the Most High. The Lord God will give him the throne of his father David, and he will reign over the house of Jacob for ever; his kingdom will never end' (Luke 1:31-33, NIV). Christ's entry into Jerusalem on the donkey we know 'took place to fulfil what was spoken through the prophet [Zech. 9:9]: "Say to the daughter of Zion, see, your King comes to you..."' (Matt. 21:1-11, NIV). 'The whole crowd of disciples began joyfully to praise God in loud voices... "Blessed is the King who comes in the name of the Lord!"' (Luke 19:37-40, NIV). In commissioning his people for their work – spreading the gospel, baptising converts, teaching them, and so on – Christ could claim: 'All authority (power, AV) has been given to me in heaven and on earth. Go therefore... and lo, I am with you always, even to the end of the age' (Matt. 28:18-20). Power! Authority! Lordship! Christ is King, now, in this age! Christ is King, as Christ himself claimed (Luke 23:2-3), and the early church preached (Acts 17:7). 'Now... we see Jesus... crowned with glory and honour' (Heb. 2:8-9).

Christ is now *seated* in heaven, the sacred writer drawing attention to what this tells us about the Redeemer's *finished* sacrificial work (Heb. 1:3; 8:1; 10:12; 12:2). But there is another aspect to it. Rulers, kings, sit on their thrones. Commoners stand in their presence. To be seated, to remain seated, speaks of power and authority, governance (1 Kings 22:19; Is. 6:1; Jer. 17:25; 22:4,30). Well, Christ is now seated at God's right hand as King, with authority, in power (Ps. 110:1; Matt. 26:64; Mark 16:19; Acts 2:33-36; Rom. 8:34; Eph. 1:20; Col. 3:1; Heb. 1:8-9; 2:8-9; 1 Pet. 3:22; Rev. 3:21). All the angels of God worshipped him, the King, at his birth (Heb. 1:6), and heaven's gates triumphantly opened to welcome him, the returning King of glory, following his resurrection (Ps. 24:7-10).

And, being a King, Christ has a kingdom. And that kingdom has a law governing its members. And we know that Christ is the one who issues the law of his kingdom and exercises the rule over it. He is *the* lawgiver of his people. Christ's own law, 'the law of *Christ*' (Gal. 6:2), not the law of *Moses*, is the law of his kingdom. Christ said of his sheep, they 'hear *his voice*', 'they know *his voice*', 'they will hear *my voice*... My sheep hear *my voice*... and they follow *me*' (John 10:3-4,16,27). Christ does not send them to Moses to hear *his* voice!

---

[63] See chapter 18 for reading the prophets in this way.

Isaac Watts:

The law by Moses came,
But peace, and truth, and love
Were brought by Christ (a nobler name),
Descending from above.

Amidst the house of God
Their different works were done;
Moses a faithful servant stood,
But Christ a faithful Son.

Then to his new commands
Be strict obedience paid;
O'er all his Father's house he stands
The Sovereign and the head.[64]

Nor did the giving of Christ's law stop at the last supper or with his discourses after his resurrection. As he had explained at the last supper: 'I still have many things to say to you, but you cannot bear them now' (John 16:12). Consequently, the apostles – having received the law of Christ from the lawgiver, and having received the promised Holy Spirit who brought to their remembrance *all* things which Christ had said to them, and who guided them into *all* truth (John 14:26; 16:13) – spelled out Christ's law for all Christ's disciples for all time. The apostolic writings are replete with the notion: 'Be mindful of the words which were spoken before by the holy prophets, and of the commandment of us, the apostles of the Lord and Saviour' (2 Pet. 3:2). The gospel, 'the way of righteousness', is called 'the holy commandment' (2 Pet. 2:21). The apostles taught 'the law of Christ' (Gal. 6:2), 'this rule' which is to be observed by the Israel of God (Gal. 6:16),[65] commanding believers to 'walk by the same rule' (Phil. 3:16),[66] and to 'consent to wholesome words, even the words of our Lord Jesus Christ, and to the doctrine which accords with godliness' (1 Tim. 6:3; Tit. 1:1).[67] The apostles commanded Christ's people to be sanctified, instructing them in the matter (1 Cor. 14:37; 1 Thess. 4:1-12; 2 Thess. 3:4-15). They gave instructions about family life (Eph. 5:22-33; 6:1-4; Col. 3:18-21), the work place (Eph. 6:5-9; Col. 3:22-25; 4:1), church life (1 Cor. 11:17-34; 1 Tim. 3:14-15), the way believers should conduct themselves in the State (Rom. 13:1-7; 1 Pet. 2:13-17), and so on. They also commanded other teachers to do the same on the authority of the apostles and their instructions (1 Tim. 4:11; 5:7; 6:2,17; 2 Tim. 2:2,14; 4:1-5; Tit. 2:1-15; 3:1-2,8,14). And all was in the

---

[64] Gadsby: *Hymns* number 50.
[65] Is 'this rule' of Gal. 6:16 the law of Christ? I think so. It is the believer's norm, the principle of Gal. 6:15. It is not the law of Moses. Gal. 5:25 does not support the claim that it is; that law is not even mentioned.
[66] Is 'the same rule' of Phil. 3:16 the law of Christ? I think so. Although 'rule' probably was not in the original, even so it is clearly implied. We could use 'principle', or (NASB) 'standard', or 'precept', 'doctrine of Christ', 'the rule of faith as opposed to works'.
[67] Are these 'wholesome words' the law of Christ? I think so. Leaving aside the first 'even' (supplied by the NKJV), consider the 'and' in 'the words of our Lord Jesus Christ, *and* to the doctrine'. This 'and' is *kai* which – see discussion in chapter 18 – may be translated 'even'. If so, 'the words of our Lord Jesus Christ, *even* the doctrine which accords with godliness' form the law of Christ. In other words, Christ's teaching is that which leads to and promotes godliness. And Christ's teaching includes the apostles' teaching, of course.

name of Christ himself: 'Now I plead with you, brethren, by the name of our Lord Jesus Christ...' (1 Cor. 1:10).

Nor did Christ give his law by word only. By his actions, he set the 'example' (Matt. 11:29; 16:24; John 13:14-15; Rom. 14:3,15; 15:1-3,7; 1 Cor. 11:1; 1 Pet. 2:21-24; 1 John 2:6). And in this he was followed by the apostles and their 'pattern' (1 Cor. 11:1; Phil. 3:17; 1 Thess. 1:6; 2 Thess. 3:7-9). As Paul put it: 'Finally, brethren, whatever things are true, whatever things are noble, whatever things are just, whatever things are pure, whatever things are lovely, whatever things are of good report, if there is any virtue and if there is anything praiseworthy – meditate on these things. The things which you learned and received and heard and saw in me, these do, and the God of peace will be with you' (Phil. 4:8-9).

All this, gathered together in Scripture, is the abiding rule of Christ's people until the end of the age. It is his inflexible law. The law of Christ cannot be confined to the ten commandments given to Israel, any more than the Atlantic can be contained in a thimble. Can the whole of Scripture be confined to sixteen verses? The law of Christ summarises and encapsulates the Mosaic law (Lev. 19:18; Matt. 7:12; 22:36-40; Rom. 13:8-10; Gal. 5:14; 6:2), not the other way round. Christ's law is precisely that – Christ's own law for his people. What else should we expect with the bringing in of the new covenant? Do not forget the eschatological 'but now'! Forget it? Glory in it!

The law of Christ: Its binding nature

Furthermore, the law of Christ does not merely describe the life of the believer; it *prescribes* it. It does not set out the ideal. It sets out the *essential* – and the *inevitable* – since regeneration leads inevitably to holiness of life (Eph. 2:8-10; 4:20-24). All of which is delivered in Scripture to the believer as a *command*, not a suggestion. Which is to say that believers are under the law of Christ as the rule of life, a true law, a real law, binding upon his people and normative for them. Believers are under authority, Christ's authority. I cannot over-stress this. Let's have done with the ridiculous objection that what I am advocating is 'wishy-washy'. *Christ's law is a real law, a proper rule.* This is brought out very clearly by the context in which the phrase, 'the law of Christ', is introduced; namely Galatians 6:1-2. Paul, addressing the 'brethren', spoke of 'a man... overtaken [caught] in any trespass'. Trespass? Yes. Paul was speaking of a believer going where he ought not. Paul had just been speaking of walking, keeping in step with the Spirit. When he said 'trespass' he used a word which means taking a false step, wandering from the right path; hence a lapse, a sin, a trespass, taking a forbidden path. And this shows, if there had been any doubt, that I am not teaching sinless perfection in this life. Sadly, believers sin! The point is this: when we read of a trespass, a transgression, we are in the realm of law (Rom. 4:15). As I have shown, this law (in Gal. 6) is not the law of Moses, but the law of Christ (Gal. 6:2).[68] To break the law of Christ, therefore, is to commit a real sin, a real trespass. As we have seen, the law of Moses turned sin into trespass. This means, therefore, that Christ's law is itself a real law.

---

[68] Link Gal. 6:1 with Matt. 18:15. The sin in question might be in Paul's list (Gal. 5:19-21), the opposite of Gal. 5:22-23, which as I explained earlier, is a thumb-nail life of Christ.

Putting it another way, the believer is not free of commandment. Certainly not! 'This is [God's] *commandment*: that we should believe on the name of his Son Jesus Christ and love one another, as he gave us *commandment*' (1 John 3:23). And lest there be any mistake, this *is* a command, which *has* to be obeyed: 'Now he who keeps his *commandments* abides in him, and he in him' (1 John 3:24).[69] I emphasise this. It is not, with respect to Calvin, 'kind advice'. Nothing is being offered to us here – certainly not 'advice'; we are being commanded – in love, yes – but being commanded by our King and lawgiver. 'And now I plead with you... not as though I wrote a new *commandment* to you, but that which we have had from the beginning: that we love one another. This is love, that we walk according to his *commandments*. This is the [his, NIV] *commandment*, that, as you have heard from the beginning, you should walk in it' (2 John 5-6). 'Let the peace of God *rule* in your hearts... Let the word of Christ dwell in you richly' (Col. 3:15-16). In other words, let the peace which Christ provides rule you, let the word which he gives – which concerns himself – dwell in you. This is nothing less than telling believers they must obey the law of Christ, the word which Christ issues to his people. 'Let' does not imply an option! Believers are under authority; Christ's authority.

'Obedience' is a key word in the vocabulary of believers, and it has an enormous bearing on both justification and sanctification. Note how Paul opened and closed his letter to the Romans: Christ gave 'grace and apostleship for [to bring about, NASB] *obedience* to the faith [of faith, NASB] among all nations for his name' (Rom. 1:5). The 'gospel and the preaching of Jesus Christ... made known to all nations, according to the commandment of the everlasting God, for *obedience* to the faith' (Rom. 16:25-26). Obedience is not only a key 'word'; without it, we have nothing and are nothing. Believers are those who are '*obedient* to the faith' (Acts 6:7); that is, they have '*obeyed* from the heart that form of doctrine to which [they] were delivered' (Rom. 6:17). God's elect are sanctified 'for *obedience*' to Christ (1 Pet. 1:1-2) who is 'the author of eternal salvation to all who *obey* him' (Heb. 5:9), having 'purified [their] souls in *obeying* the truth' (1 Pet. 1:22). Unbelievers, on the other hand, are disobedient (Heb. 3:18; 4:6). They 'do not know God, and... do not *obey* the gospel of our Lord Jesus Christ' (2 Thess. 1:8; 1 Pet. 2:7-8; 4:17-18; see also Acts 5:29,32; 26:19; Rom. 2:8; 6:16; 10:16,21; 15:18; 16:19; 2 Cor. 2:9; 7:15; 10:5-6; Gal. 3:1; Eph. 2:2; 5:6; Phil. 2:12; Col. 3:6; 2 Thess. 3:14; Tit. 1:16; 3:3; Heb. 4:11; 11:8; 1 Pet. 1:14,22).

The law of Christ: Love is its goal

This has come up time and again in these pages, and more is to follow. I apologise for the spreading nature of the material, but it cannot be helped. The law of Christ defies clever bullet-points. And this, moreover, gets pretty close to what it is all about! That love is the goal of the law of Christ is a truth that is written large across the whole of

---

[69] As before, to obey the law of Christ is to abide in him; to depart from Christ is the ultimate breaking of his law. 'They went out from us, but they were not of us; for if they had been of us, they would have continued with us; but they went out that they might be made manifest, that none of them were of us' (1 John 2:19). Christ, giving his law at the last supper, clearly made a huge and abiding impression on John. As Christ promised, the Spirit brought it all back to his mind (John 14:26; 16:12-15).

the New Testament, and trying to tie it up in neat little packages is a forlorn task – but let me make the effort.

Take 1 Timothy 1:5. *First*, what is the right translation? Is it: 'Now the purpose of *the* commandment is love from a pure heart' (AV and NKJV)? Or is it: 'Now the goal [or purpose] of *this* command is love' (NIV)? The NASB got it right: 'The goal of *our instruction* (commandment) is love'. In short, the goal or end of apostolic instruction or 'charge' is love from a pure heart. *Secondly*, was Paul speaking of the law of Christ or of Moses? Not the law of Moses. In the New Testament, the particular word used here is never used of the Old Testament law. But Paul did use it when writing: 'You received from us how you ought to walk and to please God; for you know what commandments we gave you through the Lord Jesus' (1 Thess. 4:1-2); that is, you know what charges or injunctions or instructions *we* gave you. Clearly, the apostle was speaking not about the ten commandments, but the rule of Christ, apostolic instruction, the goal of which is love (Gal. 5:6).

In short, *the gospel* is the believer's rule, and the mark or sign or fulfilment or goal of this rule is love. 'Above all... things put on love, which is the bond of perfection' (Col. 3:14). Love fulfils the law, and love binds all other graces into one. The love in question is 'the love of God' which 'has been poured out in our hearts by the Holy Spirit who was given to us' (Rom. 5:5). Support for this view of 1 Timothy 1:5 comes from 1 Timothy 6:14, where Paul charged Timothy to 'keep this commandment without spot, blameless until our Lord Jesus Christ's appearing'. Several meanings have been suggested for the 'commandment' spoken of in this verse, but Paul was speaking of those obligations Christ places upon believers in the gospel (Matt. 28:20; John 15:10,14). In other words, it is Christ's law which Timothy must keep. And the goal of this law is love.

As for 'the law of Christ', note the correspondence between Romans 13:8-10; 15:1-2 and Galatians 5:14; 6:2 in the matter of 'fulfilling' of the Mosaic law.[70] Paul issues a general demand for the love of one's neighbour, as did Jesus, and this leads to various exhortations for the practical outworking of the theme. Paul's climaxes – the example of Christ (Rom. 15:1-3,5,7), and the keeping of the law of Christ (Gal. 6:2) – are one and the same; Christ's example and Christ's law are one. And what does this mean in practice? 'Walk in love, as Christ also has loved us and given himself for us' (Eph. 5:2), 'live a life of love' (NIV). Love is the goal of the law of Christ.

Of course, love for one's neighbour was an integral part of the Mosaic law – the second of the two great commandments (Lev. 19:18; Matt. 22:37-40). But in Christ's law there is something absolutely new about this command to love: 'This is my commandment', said the Saviour, 'that you love one another *as I have loved you*' (John 15:12). Now there's a standard! Who has the audacity – the mad arrogance – to dismiss *this* as 'woolly'? I will come back to this in a few moments.

But let me first say a few words on the inbuilt motive of the law of Christ. Love is not only the goal of the law of Christ; it is its motive. In contrast, the motive for Calvin's way of sanctification must be fear. The lazy ass fears the whip, and stirs

---

[70] The law in these places, of course, *is* the Mosaic law. This raises an interesting question. Does Paul here destroy what he has so carefully established? Certainly not. He is *not* exhorting believers to keep the Mosaic law because they are under it as their rule of sanctification. Rather, he is saying that by keeping the law of Christ the law of Moses is fulfilled – note the passive. See the next chapter where I explore this more fully, especially in light of Gal. 5:3.

himself simply to avoid another dose of the same. But love is the motive for the believer to obey Christ in his law.

The law of Christ: Love is its motive

Love is not only the goal of the law of Christ; it is its motive. Christ's law does not read: 'Brethren, because God spoke on Sinai in terrifying terms, we ought to love one another'. No! Fear is not its motive. How does it read? 'In this is love, not that we loved God, but that he loved us and sent his Son to be the propitiation for our sins. Beloved, if God so loved us, we also ought to love one another' (1 John 4:10-11). 'If [since] God so loved us, we also ought to love'. Or again: 'And be kind to one another, tender-hearted, forgiving one another, even as [just as, NIV] God in Christ [also, NASB] forgave you. Therefore be imitators of God as dear children. And walk in love, as Christ also has loved us and given himself for us' (Eph. 4:32 – 5:2). 'Even as [just as, NIV] God... as Christ also has loved us...'. It is 'the love of Christ [which] compels [that is, urges, impels] us' (2 Cor. 5:14); not the law of Moses.[71] Guilty fear is *not* the motive, I say again. Paul could tell believers: 'You did not receive the spirit of bondage again to fear, but you received the Spirit of adoption' (Rom. 8:15). 'God has not given us a spirit of fear, but of power and of love and of a sound mind' (2 Tim. 1:7). 'There is no fear in love; but perfect love casts out fear, because fear involves torment. But he who fears has not been made perfect in love. We love him because he first loved us' (1 John 4:18-19). Or, as it should be: 'We love because he first loved us' (NKJV footnote, NASB, NIV). In light of this, how can Calvin's whip be the driving force behind our sanctification? Love is.[72] The love of God for us in Christ is the moving cause of our love. Christ died 'that those who live should no longer live for themselves, but for him who died for them and rose again. Therefore, from now on, we...' (2 Cor. 5:15-16). The Spirit gives the believer the mind of Christ (1 Cor. 2:16), and so helps him keep his law.[73] Love is the driving force for godliness.

Coming at it from the other direction, when a believer sins, he does not go back into his former state, he does not go back under the spirit of bondage, guilt and fear, 'under the law'. Why not? Because it is not law (in the Mosaic sense) that he has sinned against, but love. The thought of this, of course, wounds him far more.

This is the sum of it: 'By this we know that we love the children of God, when we love God and keep his commandments. For this is the love of God, that we keep his

---

[71] Paul was not saying that believers try to keep the law of *Moses* because of their sense of *Christ's* love to them.

[72] A passing thought: some, who take a similar line to me on the law and sanctification, write hymns of joy about Christ's law. Do the Reformed sing about Calvin's third use of the law? Do they thank God for the whip? If they need a start, let me make a suggestion: 'Lord, I thank you for your whip,/ For lazy ass am I./ I thank you that the law now smites/ And drives me to obey'.

[73] But this is not to be divorced from Christ's own teaching, in particular, and the entire Scripture, in general. On the law of Christ not being independent of Scripture, see below. As above, there is vast difference between carnal, slavish fear – fear of the whip – and godly fear – reverence for God. 2 Cor. 7:1; Eph. 5:21; Phil. 2:12; Heb. 12:28; 1 Pet. 1:17; 2:17; *etc.* surely come into the latter class. I am not saying there is no warning or rebuke in the law of Christ; discipline, 'reproof' and 'correction' come into it (see 1 Cor. 5; 1 Tim. 5:20; 2 Tim. 3:16, for instance).

commandments. And his commandments are not burdensome' (1 John 5:2-3). Why should believers 'live no longer for themselves'? Because the law of Moses commands them not to? and smites them for not doing so? Not at all! Rather, they love God and love others because of the love of Christ who died for them (2 Cor. 5:14-15). Love is the motive in Christ's law.

To sum up thus far: Christ is the lawgiver. His law is binding. It is a real law. Love is its goal. Love is its motive.

The law of Christ: Its penetrating nature

As we have seen, many ill-informed and dismissive comments have been made by those who pour scorn upon those of us who advocate the law of Christ, and not the law of Moses, as the believer's rule. Speaking for myself, I do not merely resent this. It is a travesty. Worse, it is a direct offence against the Lord Christ himself! Christ's law is *not* foggy sentiment. He is *not* content with a woolly obedience, a vague profession of some sort of 'love'. Christ demands total, unstinted, constant and continual obedience, out of the highest possible motives – because he loved me, because of all he is, and because he has taught me to love him. And, at the highest pitch of all, the believer, as Christ declares, has to 'keep my [Christ's] commandments... just as I [Christ] have kept my Father's commandments' (John 15:10). Note the 'just as'. This is what Christ requires. This is what pleases him. He demands the same quality of obedience from his people as that which he himself gave to his Father. Let *that* sink in! Moreover, such obedience not only pleases Christ, this is what makes his people truly happy: 'If you know these things, blessed [happy, AV] are you if you do them' (John 13:17).[74] More, obedience is essential; it is no option. And if anyone dares to dismiss this obedience to the gospel as sentimental vagueness, I urge him to think seriously about what he is doing. On a coming day, he will have to explain his words to Christ, the one who commands his people to show their love to him by obedience to his commandments, his law, and to do so with the same quality of obedience as he himself, while he lived on earth, showed to his Father.

As I have hinted, this section and the previous two are intimately linked. To make myself clear, and to do what I can to put a stop to those who scoff at this loving obedience as the fulfilling of the law of Christ, at the risk of annoying some readers, let me draw attention, yet again, to the way God himself raises this obedience to the highest possible level. I can do it in no better way than by emphasising the appropriate phrases in the following extracts:

If you keep my commandments, you will abide in my love, ***just as*** I have kept my Father's commandments and abide in his love. These things I have spoken to you, that my joy may remain in you, and that your joy may be full. This is my commandment, that you love one another *as* I have loved you (John 15:10-12).

Receive one another, ***just as*** Christ *also* received us, to the glory of God (Rom. 15:7).

Be kind to one another, tender-hearted, forgiving one another, ***even as*** [***just as***, NIV] God in Christ [*also*, NASB] forgave you. Therefore be imitators of God as dear children. And walk in love, *as* Christ ***also has*** loved us and given himself for us (Eph. 4:32 – 5:2).

---

[74] This is more than a warm feeling, of course. Such people are truly blessed in God's eyes.

Husbands, love your wives, *just as* Christ *also* loved the church and gave himself for her... *just as* the Lord does the church (Eph. 5:25,29).

In light of biblical commands of this nature and weight, all foolish, dismissive talk – cheap talk! – about the so-called inadequacy or vagueness of the law of Christ should cease forthwith. Such scorning of the law of Christ verges on the blasphemous.

The law of Christ: Christ gives power to keep it

One would think, judging by Reformed writings, the burning question for the believer is to know right from wrong. The believer, apparently, is constantly puzzled as to *what* he should be doing.[75] But is this right? True it is that all believers have problems in this area, but it is not their *main* problem. Far from it. Most believers are only too well aware of *what* they should be doing. It is the actual doing of it, *how* they are to do it, which is their real difficulty. However Romans 7:13-25 may be interpreted, its words strike a chord with every saint! As has been well said, it's not the scriptures I don't understand which bother me; it's the ones I do!

One of the glories of the new covenant is that Christ does not merely *tell* believers they are *obliged* to show their love for God by their obedience to him. Nor does he stop at giving them only the *motive* for obedience. *Christ also gives his people power to keep his law.* It is not that they have a law written on stones, nor (merely) that they have the written word in Scripture; *that* is not their power to obey.[76] Believers obey God in Christ, they love him and his people, because they are regenerate (1 John 4:7), because they are in the new covenant, because Christ died for them, because the Spirit in-dwells them. *This* constitutes the *means* of their obedience. 'He who does not love me does not keep my words' (John 14:24). 'As you therefore have received Christ Jesus the Lord, so walk in him, rooted and built up in him and established in the faith, as you have been taught' (Col. 2:6-7). 'But concerning brotherly love you have no need that I should write to you, for you yourselves are taught by God to love one another... But we urge you, brethren, that you increase more and more' (1 Thess. 4:9-10). 'The anointing which you have received from him abides in you, and you do not need that anyone teach you; but as the same anointing teaches you concerning all things, and is true, and is not a lie, and just as it has taught you, you will abide in him' (1 John 2:27).[77] A moment or two ago, I referred to 1 John 4:19: 'We love because he first loved us' (NKJV footnote, NASB, NIV). I said God's love in Christ is the motive for our love. Now I go further. It is also the source, the spring of it. God's love to us both moves us to love, and enables us to love. And such love leads to godliness.

---

[75] And he has to turn to the law of Moses – specifically, the ten commandments – to tell him! It is, after all, supposed to be his perfect rule!

[76] As below, I am not dismissing the written word in saying this. It has a vital part to play, but the believer's obedience is more than a legal obedience or conformity to an external law. Above all, the written word does not supply the power to live a godly life. We need both word *and* Spirit. Too many stress the word at the expense of the Spirit. Some, I admit, do the opposite. We need both. Without the Spirit, the word is powerless. In the new covenant, God gives us both.

[77] As above, not that this means there is no need for external instruction. See below. See the next chapter for an extract on 1 John 2:27.

This is no spineless sentiment. As Paul said: 'If [since] we live in the Spirit, let us also walk in [by, NASB] the Spirit' (Gal. 5:25).[78] Notice how Paul set out the governing principle – 'since we live in the Spirit' – closely following it up with an exhortation. Since 'we live in the Spirit', since this is our position, on this basis, because of this, 'let us also walk in or by the Spirit' (Gal. 5:25). This, I say, is not spineless. Nor must it be dismissed as anarchy. Liberty is not licence, an excuse for carnal self-indulgence. Believers will live by the Spirit; believers must live by the Spirit. True, the apostle cast his words in the form of an exhortation, but even so there is a firmness about them. There is an unbreakable link between living in the Spirit and walking in the Spirit, and the believer has to demonstrate it. And what is promised to those who carry out this injunction? 'Walk in the Spirit, and you shall not fulfil the lust [that is, desires] of the flesh' (Gal. 5:16). The double negative in the Greek makes this statement very strong indeed. It is only the Spirit who is powerful enough to enable believers to overcome the flesh, but he can – and he *will*. Paul said so!

Berridge proved it. So much so, he was moved to pen a hymn on the subject in his own typically quaint, but expressive, style:

> *Run, run, and work, the law commands,*
> *Yet finds me neither feet nor hands;*
> *But sweeter news the gospel brings;*
> *It bids me fly, and lends me wings.*
>
> *Such needful wings, O Lord, impart,*
> *To brace my feet and brace my heart;*
> *Good wings of faith and wings of love*
> *Will make a cripple sprightly move.*
>
> *With these a lumpish soul may fly,*
> *And soar aloft, and reach the sky;*
> *Nor faint nor falter in the race,*
> *But cheerly work, and sing of grace.*[79]

Concerning this power or ability to keep the law of Christ, two things should be noted: it is only the Spirit of God who can bring about the required obedience, but Christ promises and gives his Spirit to his people to enable them to obey. Consequently, it is only believers who can obey Christ's law.[80] Christ commands no one but believers to keep his law. Only those who are regenerate can appreciate the motive for sanctification, have the desire for it, and have the grace to produce it.

And this is precisely where the new-covenant emphasis upon the heart is so necessary. The new covenant meets the believer's *every* need. The believer not only

---

[78] As above, Paul was *not* saying to walk in the Spirit is to live in accordance with the law of Moses. Gal. 5:25 and the passage which follows does not teach it. Rather, it shows the *contrast* between life under the Spirit and life under the law of Moses, not their *sameness*.

[79] Berridge: *Sion's* number 150; Gadsby: *Hymns* number 49. Berridge had: 'Run, John, and work'.

[80] In passing, it is the utmost folly – and worse – to try to get the unregenerate to obey Christ's law. It is impossible to try to produce the life of a Christian without first being made a Christian. We must preach the Lord Christ as Saviour, and see sinners converted, before we try to sanctify them. Incidentally, nowhere does this apply more forcefully than in children's work! Addressing children as believers is, in my experience, commonplace – and disastrous!

knows what he should do, he is given grace to help him do what he knows he ought to do. The Spirit does far more than record the rule of Christ in Scripture. He does far more than explain the rule, far more than tell the believer what he has to do. He gives grace and power to live according to that rule, and grace to *want* to live it out. He works in the heart and will, as well as in the mind.

But lest I should be misunderstood, it is necessary at this point to answer another question. How, precisely, does the believer know what is required of him? Where and how does he discover what godliness is?

The law of Christ: It is not independent of Scripture

Although I have cast this in a negative form, the truth is, the entire Scripture *is* the law of Christ. The inward work of the Spirit and the external law of Christ are also linked the other way about. And in this we discover the perfection of God's design. What do I mean? Just this: the believer is free; he is not under the law of Moses; he has the Spirit. Now there are obvious risks in stressing the point.[81] Liberty might degenerate into licence. But it is at this very danger-point where the perfection of God's design stands out in all its glory. Let me explain.

God has put in place written, outward controls, guides and directives; the Scriptures. The Scriptures, I stress, not merely the ten commandments: 'Sanctify them by your truth. Your word is truth' (John 17:17). 'All Scripture is... profitable for doctrine, for reproof, for correction, for instruction [training] in righteousness' (2 Tim. 3:16). But as I have said, it is not the Spirit *or* the word; it is both at one and the same time. The undoubted emphasis, however, falls clearly on the person and power of the Spirit (Gal. 5:16,25); only the Spirit can turn the written word into practical obedience. God in the new covenant does not bypass the external, written revelation of Scripture, and make it redundant – not at all! – but he gives a love of that law, that promise, that revelation, that Scripture; he gives a heart desire to obey it and walk in its ways. There is no question of driving any wedge between the inward Spirit and the outward word. The two are inextricably linked. God has given his word, but he also gives individual heart-grace to his people to stir them to want to live according to that written word, and to enable them to do so and thus produce fruit to his glory. In short, the Spirit directly writes Christ's law upon the believer's heart, in addition to having inspired men to write it large in the Scriptures. It is inward and outward, both. Moreover, all this is accompanied with the Spirit's inward witness (Rom. 8:1-4,16; Heb. 8:7-12; 10:15-18).[82]

---

[81] As I warned in earlier notes. But this risk occurs with all aspects of the gospel. Take just one example: salvation through faith can be made to sound like easy-believism; Eph. 2:8-10 and Jas. 2:14-26 are the correctives. See Rom. 3:5-8; 6:1,15; Jude 4. True gospel-preaching is always marked by such a possibility. Without it, it is not *true* gospel-preaching! I raised this in chapters 9 and 10.

[82] As I have already mentioned in connection with Luther as opposed to the Anabaptists, an emphasis upon 'light' rather than 'life' is a marked feature of many who adopt a Reformed stance (or something akin to it) on the church; that is, tick the credal statement – even though you don't understand, let alone accept, it all – and you're in! Those who live in this particular glasshouse ought to be careful about castigating Anglicans who sign the 39 Articles but don't believe them or, at least, ignore them. This practice is just as wrong when the credal statement in

In short, the external aspect of the law of Christ – the written word of God – calibrates its inward aspect – the indwelling Spirit – and the inward Spirit stimulates and enables the believer to live under the external aspect of Christ's law; in other words, to be godly. What wisdom God displays in all this! Those who have the Spirit, from the heart can say before God – at the very least, it is their heart's desire: 'I have not departed from your judgements, for you yourself have taught me. How sweet are your words to my taste, sweeter than honey to my mouth! Through your precepts I get understanding; therefore I hate every false way... Direct my steps by your word' (Ps. 119:102-104,133). See the entire Psalm![83]

Just now, I said only those who are regenerate have the motive, desire and grace to produce sanctification. And this leads to a bigger point. Sanctification is not only what a believer *does* but, supremely, what a believer *is*.

The law of Christ: It is all about what a believer is

A believer's *doing* inevitably comes out of a believer's *being* – what he is – and it shows what he is (compare Prov. 20:11). Godly action comes from a godly person. A holy life is produced by a holy man. Sanctification is not so much what we *do*, as what we *are*. It is because of what we are that we do certain things and not others – not the other way round. In other words, we do not do certain things in order to make ourselves believers, but we do certain things because we are believers. Christ told us so: 'Out of the abundance of the heart the mouth speaks. A good man out of the good treasure of his heart brings forth good things, and an evil man out of the evil treasure brings forth evil things'. 'A good tree cannot bear bad fruit, nor can a bad tree bear good fruit... Therefore by their fruits you will know them'. Figs do not come from thorns, nor grapes from a bramble. To apply the figure, as sin arises in the heart of the ungodly, and shows itself in ungodliness, so holiness arises in the heart of the believer, and shows itself in godliness (Matt. 7:16-20; 12:33-35; 15:17-20; Mark 7:18-23; Luke 6:43-45; Eph. 4:17-21). It is the heart! The heart must be changed before sanctification can ever be on the agenda.

But how does this change of heart come about? By the mighty work of the triune God himself in the provisions of the new covenant, and in no other way: 'I will make a new covenant... I will put my law in their minds, and write it on their hearts' (Jer. 31:31-33). 'I will sprinkle clean water on you, and you shall be clean... I will give you a new heart and put a new spirit within you; I will take the heart of stone out of your flesh and give you a heart of flesh. I will put my Spirit within you and cause you to walk in my statutes, and you will keep my judgements and do them' (Ezek. 36:25-27). 'I will... I will... I will'. So runs God's repeated, glorious assurance. And, in fulfilment of these prophecies, 'the Spirit of the living God' writes Christ's law on the heart (2 Cor. 3:3). Believers are 'bondservants of Christ' who have been given grace to do 'the will of God from the heart' (Eph. 6:5-6). And, as God promised, so he has done: 'I will

---

question is the Westminster or the 1689 Particular Baptist Confession, or the equivalent. Tozer spoke of 'the difference between the religion of creed and the religion of the Spirit... Among religious persons of unquestioned orthodoxy there is sometimes found a dull dependence upon the letter of the text without the faintest understanding of its spirit' (Tozer: *Root* pp37-38) – or, in many cases, understanding or believing what they have signed! We need both light and life!

[83] I am not, of course, teaching sinless perfection!

put my law in their minds, and write it on their hearts' (Jer. 31:33; Heb. 8:10; 10:16). The heart has always been paramount with God.[84] He has always demanded obedience from the heart, not a mere external obedience and conformity to rules (Deut. 10:16; 11:13; 13:3; 26:16; 30:2; Josh. 22:5; 1 Sam. 12:20,24; 16:7; Ps. 15:1-5; 16:7; 24:4-6; 40:6-8; 51:10; Jer. 4:4; 9:26; Ezek. 18:30-31; 44:7,9; Joel 2:12; Matt. 22:37; Mark 12:30-34; Luke 8:15; 10:27; Acts 7:51; 2 Cor. 5:12; Eph. 6:5-6; Col. 3:22; Heb. 10:5-9; 13:9; 1 Pet. 3:4, for instance). Hence Isaiah's complaint, taken up by Christ: 'These people... honour me with their lips, but their heart is far from me' (Isa. 29:13; Matt. 15:7-9; Mark 7:6). It is the heart which counts above all (Rom. 6:17; 10:6-10). This is where sin arises in man (Prov. 22:15; Matt. 15:18-20; Mark 7:18-23; Acts 7:51,54; Rom. 2:5; Eph. 4:17-19; 2 Pet. 2:14). The heart is 'deceitful above all things, and desperately wicked' – it is only God, who searches it and knows it secrets (Ps. 44:21; Jer. 17:9-10); it is in the heart God requires truth – in the innermost parts – he calls for his law in the heart (Deut. 6:6; Ps. 37:31; 40:8; 51:6; 119:11; Isa. 51:7; Jer. 31:33; Rom. 12:2; Eph. 4:23; 1 Pet. 1:14). He knows what men are thinking in their heart (Ps. 10:3-4,13-14; 14:1; 53:1; Ezek. 14:3-7; Rom. 3:10-18; Heb. 4:12-13; 2 Pet. 2:14). Christ rebukes the hard, unbelieving heart (Mark 16:14). God requires 'a new heart and a new spirit' (Ezek. 18:31), has promised it (Deut. 30:6; Jer. 24:7; 31:31-34; 32:38-41; Ezek. 11:19-20; 36:25-27), and now gives it in the new covenant (Luke 24:32; John 6:44-45; 7:38-39; 14:16-17; Rom. 5:5; 6:17; 1 Cor. 2:8-16; 2 Cor. 3:3; 4:6; 1 Thess. 4:9; Heb. 8:10-11; 10:15-16,22; 1 John 2:27).

The believer's daily godliness, as I say, comes out of what he is in his heart. The rule of the new covenant, the gospel, 'the law of the Spirit of life in Christ Jesus' (Rom. 8:2), is internal, liberating and sanctifying, delivering; it sets the believer free from 'the law of sin and death'. This law of the Spirit is not the law of Moses, but is a living principle, a law which gives life through the Spirit (Gal. 3:2-5). Of course, this does not set aside the two great commandments of the law (Deut. 6:5; Lev. 19:18; Matt. 22:37-40), since 'love is the fulfilment of the law' (Rom. 13:10). Rather, it takes the two great commandments, and enables the believer to keep them in newness of Spirit – better, spirit, or the Spirit (Rom. 8:4; Gal. 5:16-18) – not in the oldness of the letter (Rom. 7:6), as Christ's freeman (John 8:32; 2 Cor. 3:17), and not Moses' prisoner or bondslave (Gal. 3:24-25; 4:3-7). This obedience is a willing obedience (Ps. 110:3; Rom. 1:5; 6:17), and not a legal duty. No wonder Paul could speak of his 'delight in the law of God according to the inward man' (Rom. 7:22) – since the Spirit enabled him so to do, having renewed him in love to God and his children.[85] The law the apostle delighted in, of course, was far more than the ten commandments; it was the full revelation of God culminating in the gospel, even Christ himself (see immediately below).

---

[84] See earlier and chapter 18.
[85] Even so, Rom. 7:22 seems at odds with its context – but, as I mentioned in chapter 10, I do not pretend to fully understand Rom. 7:13-25, apart from that which stands out a mile; namely, the law cannot justify or sanctify. In general, it is the absence of the Spirit in Rom. 7:7ff which dominates the section. See below. Even so, the law of God in the new covenant is far more than the law of Moses. In this chapter (see also chapter 18), I have already given reasons for my vital assertion that in the old covenant the law of God was the law of Moses, but in the new covenant it is the law of Christ.

Thus the glories of the old covenant pale in comparison with those of the new (2 Cor. 3:7-13). The new covenant makes the former covenant vanish (2 Cor. 4:18; Heb. 8:13), like the sun renders the candle obsolete. Even though they knew what God required (1 Sam. 16:7; 1 Chron. 29:17; Ps. 147:10-11), the Jews largely thought only of the external, and were content with it; Christ is not (Mark 7:1-16; Luke 11:39-40). The Jews, in general, were satisfied with outward conformity; Christ demands the heart (Jer. 11:20; Eph. 6:5-6; 1 Pet. 3:3-4). The believer's measure of things is not outward, but of the heart (2 Cor. 5:12); or should be. It is tragic when otherwise, 'for the things which are seen are temporary, but the things which are not seen are eternal' (2 Cor. 4:18).

To sum up thus far: Christ is his people's lawgiver. His law is binding. It is a real law. Love is its goal. Love is its motive. It is a penetrating law. Christ gives power to keep it. It is not independent of Scripture. It is all about what a believer is.

But there is one further point to make. And it is the ultimate point, the supreme point.

The law of Christ is Christ himself

Who can plumb the depth of Paul's words: 'We preach Christ crucified... the wisdom of God... But of him you are in Christ Jesus, who became for [to, NASB] us wisdom from God' (1 Cor. 1:23-24,30)? Christ, the wisdom of God? Christ became wisdom for us? What does this mean? Wisdom! What a word for Paul (a converted Jew, an ex Jewish-teacher) to conjure with! Surely he had in mind the excellencies of wisdom found in Job 28; the first nine chapters of Proverbs, and such passages as Psalm 104:24; 136:5; not forgetting, of course, 'wisdom is the principal thing; therefore get wisdom' (Prov. 4:7). The point is: the apostle *unreservedly applied this scriptural language to Christ.* Thus he could declare that Christ 'is the image of the invisible God, the firstborn over all creation. For by him all things were created that are in heaven and that are on earth, visible and invisible, whether thrones or dominions or principalities or powers. All things were created through him and for him. And he is before all things, and in him all things consist... in whom are hidden all the treasures of wisdom and knowledge' (Col. 1:15-17; 2:3). What telling statements! What staggering claims! How sweeping! How weighty! How significant!

Let me stress this. The Jews of Paul's day continued to think in terms of the *torah*, the law – principally the Proverbs – when speaking about wisdom, and the Gentiles were not backward in boasting of their intellectualism, their culture of 'wisdom' and 'philosophy'. It was to all such (1 Cor. 1:22-24) that Paul preached only 'Jesus Christ and him crucified', that he declared he was 'determined' to preach Christ, preaching him as 'Christ crucified... the wisdom of God' (1 Cor. 2:2,7).[86] His meaning could not be clearer. Let Jews and Greeks boast of their wisdom. Believers will boast of Christ and his cross (Gal. 6:14). Believers know that in the new covenant, Christ is their wisdom. Christ is wisdom, full stop! Christ himself is the word of God (John 1:1; Heb. 1:2). CHRIST IS WISDOM!

---

[86] Note how many times Paul used 'wisdom' (or 'foolishness') in the context of 1 Cor. 1:18 – 2:16, and on to 3:18-20.

The translation of 1 Corinthians 1:30 is debated. Its mistranslation has led to an ingrained misinterpretation and consequent misunderstanding. The AV gives the impression that Christ is four things for believers – wisdom, righteousness, sanctification and redemption. The NKJV makes a demarcation between wisdom and the other three: 'Christ Jesus... became for us wisdom from God – and righteousness and sanctification and redemption'. The NIV goes further with 'wisdom from God – that is, our righteousness, holiness and redemption'. Which is right? The last. Paul is saying that Christ is wisdom – this is the principal thing – wisdom which comprises righteousness, sanctification and redemption. The apostle is not listing four separate entities. Furthermore, Paul is speaking objectively. Christ is made by God to be wisdom. True, he is made wisdom 'for us'; in Christ, therefore, believers have wisdom. But this is because he himself is wisdom. Being wisdom, *Christ* is his people's wisdom; that is, they are justified, sanctified and redeemed in and by Christ. They 'are complete in him' (Col. 2:10).

Let us get to grips with this. We are approaching something of high significance. More! It is vital! Paul (as a converted Jew, as an ex Jewish-teacher) knew full well that, in the Old Testament, wisdom was closely associated with the law: 'Be careful to observe [the statutes and judgements, the commandments, the law]; for this is your wisdom and your understanding' (Deut. 4:6). 'The fear of the LORD is the beginning of wisdom; a good understanding have all those who do his commandments' (Ps. 111:10). This intimate connection between the law and wisdom had been ingrained in Paul, right from his days as Saul of Tarsus. How striking, then, that Paul, writing to Greeks and Jews, called the gospel 'wisdom' (1 Cor. 2:6-7). Writing to Timothy, 'the holy Scriptures', he said, bring wisdom, for they 'are able to make you wise for salvation' (2 Tim. 3:15). Moreover, the apostle emphasised wisdom in his prayers for believers – that they would be given 'the spirit of wisdom and revelation in the knowledge of [God]' (Eph. 1:17), being 'filled with the knowledge of his will in all wisdom and spiritual understanding' (Col. 1:9). And he commanded believers to 'let the word of Christ dwell in [them] richly in all wisdom' (Col. 3:16). Above all (1 Cor. 1:23-24,30) – above all, I stress – he proclaimed that Christ himself is wisdom. See also Romans 10:6-8, where Paul quoted Deuteronomy 30:11-14, which referred to the law, and yet applied it unreservedly to Christ. Christ is the total, complete fulfilment of the law.

So let me spell it out: Christ is the new *torah*! Let me say that again. *In the new covenant, Christ, being wisdom, is the believer's **torah***. Oh, that it might sink in! Christ is the *torah* of the new covenant. In light of this, can it really be argued that the law at Sinai was God's final word? that the ten commandments comprise the believer's *perfect* rule? Does Matthew 5 – 7; John 13 – 16, especially John 13:34; Hebrews 1:1-4, not shout otherwise? *Christ* is God's final word! Christ is all!

What am I saying? I am trying to do the impossible and get down on paper that which the New Testament reveals to be the topmost stone of the arch of Christ's law. In the new covenant, Christ is the believer's wisdom; that is, Christ is his people's law. Christ *himself* is the law of Christ. He not only gave, brought, taught the word of God; *he is the word of God itself*. See John 1:1-18. He declared himself to be the truth: 'I am... the truth' (John 14:6), a statement of tremendous import. He did not claim to have truth, or bring truth; he did not claim to be *a* truth! No! 'I AM **THE** TRUTH'. 'His name is called "The Word of God"' (Rev. 19:13). Let me quote some of the opening words of John's gospel:

In the beginning was the Word, and the Word was with God, and the Word was God. He was in the beginning with God... In him was life, and the life was the light of men... That was the true light which gives light to every man coming into the world... And the Word became flesh and dwelt among us, and we beheld his glory, the glory as of the only begotten of the Father, full of grace and truth... And of his fullness we have all received, and grace for grace. For the law was given through Moses, but grace and truth came through Jesus Christ. No one has seen God at any time. The only begotten Son, who is in the bosom of the Father, he has declared him (John 1:1-18).

And Christ himself, *he himself as his law*, is revealed in the gospel. So important is this, let me make it as clear as I can:

Christ himself is the law of Christ

'Anyone who has rejected Moses' law dies without mercy on the testimony of two or three witnesses. Of how much worse punishment, do you suppose, will he be thought worthy who has trampled the Son of God underfoot, counted the blood of the covenant by which he was sanctified a common thing, and insulted the Spirit of grace?' (Heb. 10:28-29). Note the 'balancing contrast' in Hebrews 10:28-29. The law of Moses is balanced by, contrasted with... what? It can only be the law of Christ. Which is? 'The Son of God... the blood of the covenant... the Spirit of grace'. Once again, the law of Christ is not a list of rules. The law of Christ is Christ himself.

Putting all this together, it is clear that, in the new covenant, Paul saw Christ as the wisdom of God, the new law, the law of Christ, the believer's *torah*, the believer's *nomos*, the believer's perfect rule. Thus the law of Christ is nothing less than his person, his words and works. Believers are to live as Christ lived, do as Christ would do, think as Christ would think, speak as Christ would speak. They must obey Christ's words and follow Christ's example. They must 'walk just as he walked' (1 John 2:6). Christ is their wisdom, Christ is their law, Christ is their life. Christ himself, Christ's words, Christ formed and living in his people (Gal. 2:20; 4:19; Eph. 3:17; Col. 1:27; 3:4) by his Spirit, is the motive, the means and standard of their sanctification. The believer lives, thinks, feels, speaks, acts and suffers as Christ. 'As he is, so are we in this world' (1 John 4:17). Believers are in Christ, and Christ is in them, as almost-countless scriptures declare.

Consider: 'Looking unto Jesus' (Heb. 12:2). How do we become Christians? By looking unto Jesus: '*Look* to me, and be saved' (Isa. 45:22). 'As Moses lifted up the serpent in the wilderness, even so must the Son of Man be lifted up, that whoever *believes* in him should not perish but have eternal life' (John 3:14-15). And what did God instruct Moses to do? 'Make a fiery serpent, and set it on a pole; and it shall be that everyone who is bitten, when he *looks* at it shall live. So Moses made a bronze serpent, and put it on a pole; and so it was, if a serpent had bitten anyone, when he *looked* at the bronze serpent, he lived' (Num. 21:8-9). Christ told us: 'My Father's will is that everyone who *looks* to the Son and believes in him shall have eternal life, and I will raise him up at the last day' (John 6:40, NIV). What will bring about our final consummation as Christians? Looking to, looking at, Jesus! 'We know that when he [Christ] is revealed, we shall be like him, for we shall *see* him as he is' (1 John 3:2). 'For now we *see* in a mirror, dimly, but then face to face' (1 Cor. 13:12). Just so!

Christ prayed for it: 'Father, I desire that they also whom you gave me may be with me where I am, that they may *behold* my glory' (John 17:24). Ah! But what about the in-between? We began by looking to Jesus. We shall end by looking to Jesus. What is it that keeps us walking in godliness? Looking to Jesus! 'We... *beholding* as in a mirror the glory of the Lord, are being transformed into the same image... by the Spirit of the Lord' (2 Cor. 3:18). 'Let us lay aside every weight, and the sin which so easily ensnares us, and let us run with endurance the race that is set before us, *looking* unto Jesus, the author and finisher of our faith' (Heb. 12:1-2). In short: '*Seek* those things which are above, where Christ is... *Set your mind* on things above' (Col. 3:1-2). Looking to Jesus! Looking to Jesus is how we begin the race; looking to Jesus is how we continue and finish the race; and looking to Jesus is our glory at the end of the race. Looking to Jesus; not Moses, not the law, not baptism, not anything or anybody else. The Lord Jesus Christ! Only the Lord Jesus Christ! Looking to him! Looking only to him!

The New Testament, I admit, does not explicitly state that Christ is the new law for his people (no more than it states, say, the trinity), but it is written large for all to read. Christ is God's final word to man. And this takes us back to Hebrews 1:1-4. Christ is all.

Reader, this is what I understand by the law of Christ. Christ is his people's lawgiver. His law is binding. It is a real law. It is a penetrating law. Love is its goal. Love is its motive. Christ gives power to keep it. It is not independent of Scripture. It is all about what a believer is. Above all, it is Christ himself formed in his people by his Spirit. Christ is all.

The law of Christ in use: Further New Testament examples

The rule for God's people – the new Israel, a new creation – is faith which works by love (Gal. 5:6; 6:15-16). The New Testament does cite the commandments of the Mosaic law, of course, yet it never leaves them as bare commandments, but always links them to Christ and the new age of the gospel he brought in. It always interprets and applies them by who and what Christ is and has done. Let me work this out a little with some practical examples from Scripture.

How does Christ teach a godly man and woman to behave in marriage? What is their motive for a biblical marriage? Is it the law of Moses? Is it the seventh commandment? No! It is Christ – his love and his death (Eph. 5:22-33). The new-covenant wife will submit to her husband as her head, not merely because of some command, but because she, from her heart, wants to submit to him just as the church submits to Christ as the head of the church (Eph. 5:22-24) – 'as is fitting in the Lord' (Col. 3:18). The new-covenant husband will be faithful to his wife, not merely because the law of Moses commands him to be faithful, not because he will be punished if he is not, but because he delights to be faithful, and God helps him to be faithful, and gives him the desire to be faithful. He will love his wife 'just as Christ also loved the church'; he will nourish and cherish his wife, 'just as the Lord does the church' (Eph. 5:25,28-29). How much higher, therefore, how much more spiritual, is the law of Christ than the law of Moses. The Spirit enables the new-covenant wife and husband to live together in loving obedience to Christ, under his law, walking 'in accordance to this rule' (Gal. 6:2,16) which Christ has written upon their hearts (Jer. 31:33; Heb. 8:10; 10:16).

How does Christ teach believing children to obey their parents? 'Children, obey your parents *in the Lord*'. And godly parents must 'bring up' their children 'in the training and admonition *of the Lord*'. Certainly Paul referred to the fifth commandment in giving this instruction, but he did so *in support* of the gospel rule, not as its origin (Eph. 6:1-4).[87]

Why should a believer not lie? What stops him lying? Is it merely the ninth commandment? Or is it: 'Put off... the old man... be renewed in the spirit of your mind... put on the new man which was created according to God, in true righteousness and holiness. Therefore, putting away lying, "Let each one of you speak truth with his neighbour", for we are members of one another' (Eph. 4:22-25)? In other words, is it the law of Moses, or the law of Christ? 'Do not lie to one another, since you have put off the old man with his deeds, and have put on the new man who is renewed in knowledge according to the image of him who created him, where... Christ is all and in all' (Col. 3:9-11).

How does the law of Christ teach believing servants (employees) the way to behave? First comes the apostolic command: 'Bondservants, be obedient to... your masters... with fear and trembling, in sincerity of heart... not with eye service... but... with good will'. But what is the motive? What is the spur? What is the power to help believing servants carry out this command? It is Christ: 'Bondservants, be obedient to... your masters... *as to Christ... as bondservants of Christ*, doing the *will of God* from the heart... *as to the Lord*... knowing... [you] will receive... *from the Lord*...' (Eph. 6:5-8). What is the motive for a believer to show love to a weaker brother? It is Christ: 'We then who are strong ought to bear with the scruples of the weak, and not to please ourselves. Let each of us please his neighbour for his good, leading to edification. *For even Christ* did not please himself... Now may the God of patience and comfort grant you to be like-minded towards one another, *according to Christ Jesus*... Therefore receive one another, *just as Christ* also received us, to the glory of God' (Rom. 15:1-7). And so on, and so on.

Never did the apostles wield the whip of Moses' law when trying to produce godliness. Never! Nor did they try to bind the consciences of believers by the law. Never! I am, needless to say, using Reformed terminology to describe what they say is the New Testament way of sanctification. The law stressed the negative – 'you shall not'. The apostles, however, majored on the positive.[88] They did not over-emphasise

---

[87] I will return to this in the next chapter.

[88] At least some Reformed teachers try to justify their third use of the law for the believer as showing love for God, but this leads, inevitably, to a list of negatives – never to put anything before God, not to murder, not to commit adultery, not to steal, not to lie, not to covet. Is this the biblical approach to holiness for a believer? Of course there are negatives, but how about 'loving, being faithful, being generous, telling the truth, sharing', *etc.*? In short, why not describe holiness as the New Testament overwhelmingly does in its commands to believers? Which is? Positively, 'to be like Christ'. Should a believer aim not to be a law-breaker – or to be like Christ?

punishment. On the contrary, they spoke of gain and reward.[89] The notion of a whip is utterly out of step with the spirit of the New Testament, replete as it is with words like 'urge', 'appeal', 'implore', 'request', 'desire', and so on.[90]

Of course, there is a negative side to sanctification. Believers must not only cultivate the good, they must shun the bad. But just as the Mosaic law is not the motive for seeking the good, neither is it the way to avoid the evil. Believers are not warned against sin on the basis of the Mosaic law. Take, for instance, Paul's description of pagans. He speaks of 'the futility of their mind... their understanding darkened... ignorance... blindness [hardening, NIV] of their heart... past feeling [having lost all sensitivity, NIV]... lewdness [sensuality, NIV]... uncleanness with greediness' (Eph. 4:17-19). How does the apostle warn believers against this? On the basis of the law of Moses? Certainly not! Rather: 'But you have not so learned Christ, if indeed you have heard him and have been taught by him, as the truth is in Jesus' (Eph. 4:20-21).

And, of course, in this 'learning Christ' it is impossible to miss echoes of Matthew 11:28-30; 28:20. The New Testament does not say: 'For to me, to live is *Moses*', but it does say: 'For to me, to live is *Christ*' (Phil. 1:21). The believer is not under the law of Moses; he is under the gospel; that is, he is under the law of Christ. The result is, the motive for holiness and practical obedience – and the means for attaining it – is Christ, his relationship to Christ, and what Christ has done for him, to him and in him. This is the way to avoid sin and produce holiness. The New Testament does not remotely warrant a culture of whip, fear and guilt to produce godliness in the believer. Quite the reverse. The uniform teaching of the New Testament demonstrates beyond all doubt that godliness comes through the believer's sense of the love of God in his soul. The more the love of God is shed abroad in the believer's heart (Rom. 5:5), the greater the sense the believer has of the wonder of his Father's love towards him and the untold benefits of his Saviour's sacrifice at Cavalry on his behalf, the more he is moved to gospel obedience. What will make him give up the world (1 John 2:15-17)? True enough, John commands us not to love the world, but scan his entire letter. What aspect of the law of Moses does he lay on believers? And what does he tell us of Christ? The truth is, the more the believer sees of Christ, the more he values him, the less the world proves attractive to him.

In the words of Helen H.Lemmel:

> *Turn your eyes upon Jesus,*
> *Look full in his wonderful face,*
> *And the things of earth will grow strangely dim,*
> *In the light of his glory and grace.*

And as Ora Rowan put it:

> *What has stripped the seeming beauty*
> *From the idols of the earth?*
> *Not a sense of right or duty.*
> *But the sight of peerless worth.*

---

[89] Which is the better way, of course. Take an everyday illustration. If the authorities wish to encourage prompt payment of taxes, will they be better employed in fining late-payers, or offering a reduction for early-payers?

[90] Note the lack of 'he who whips with the law, let him whip with vigour' in Rom. 12:6-8.

> *Not the crushing of those idols,*
> *With its bitter void and smart;*
> *But the beaming of [Christ's] beauty,*
> *The unveiling of his heart.*
>
> *Who extinguishes their taper*
> *Till they hail the rising sun?*
> *Who discards the garb of winter*
> *Till the summer has begun?*[91]

Let me take three New Testament books to make my point; I refer first to 2 Corinthians. The church at Corinth was in a shocking state. It needed urgent, desperate reformation of behaviour, both in private and in public. In short, the Corinthians needed to get a grip on sanctification, both as individuals and as a church. The question is: How did the apostle set about it? Did he scourge the Corinthians? He did not! He was concerned to 'spare' them. He did not stand over them, whip in hand: 'Not that we have dominion over your faith', he said (2 Cor. 1:23-24). Reader, as you peruse the following, pick up the tone, read the apostle's heart, and ask yourself if you think Paul was a whip-master over Corinthian whipping-boys, or was he trying to move them by Christ and love:

O Corinthians! We have spoken openly to you, our heart is wide open. You are not restricted by us, but you are restricted by your own affections. Now in return for the same (I speak as to children), you also be open... Open your hearts to us. We have wronged no one... I do not say this to condemn; for I have said before that you are in our hearts, to die together and to live together... We have been comforted in your comfort... I speak not by commandment, but I am testing the sincerity of your love... And in this I give advice... I do not mean that others should be eased and you burdened... Now I, Paul, myself am pleading with you by the meekness and gentleness of Christ... I beg you that when I am present I may not [have to] be bold with that confidence by which I intend to be bold against some, who think of us as if we walked according to the flesh... Oh, that you would bear with me... I am jealous for you with godly jealously... I fear, lest somehow... your minds may be corrupted... Did I commit sin in humbling myself that you might be exalted...? Why? Because I do not love you? God knows!... I will not be burdensome to you... I will very gladly spend and be spent for your souls; though the more abundantly I love you, the less I am loved. But be that as it may, I did not burden you (2 Cor. 6:11-13; 7:2-3,13; 8:8-13; 10:1-2; 11:1-11; 12:14-16).

Paul was no whip-master to the Corinthians. Nevertheless, they had such! Paul could say to the Corinthians: 'You put up with it if one brings you into bondage... if one strikes you on the face' (2 Cor. 11:20). Such teachers (almost certainly Judaisers; see chapter 11) tried to hit them into line. What did Paul think of it? 'To our shame, I say that we were too weak for that!' (2 Cor. 11:20-21). In saying this, Paul, of course, was being ironical. It was not a question of weakness. He had no intention whatsoever of hitting the Corinthians. Even when things had reached a tragic state of carnality at Corinth, still Paul asked: 'What do you want? Shall I come to you with a rod, or in love and a spirit of gentleness?' (1 Cor. 4:21). The gospel answer is obvious, surely. I know,

---

[91] *Psalms and Hymns* number 308. The old, dead leaves of the beech hedge do not have to be picked off laboriously by hand each spring; the new leaves, fed by the rising of the living sap, will force them to lose their grip. Remember the fable of the contest between the wind and the sun to see which could make the man remove his overcoat.

as a last resort, discipline is necessary (1 Cor. 5; 2 Cor. 13:2-3), but how can the way of sanctification be by whip and stick? How far removed it is from the law of Christ. 'Therefore I write these things being absent, lest being present I should use sharpness, according to the authority which the Lord has given me for edification and not for destruction' (2 Cor. 13:10).

I said I would look at three books; now for the second: Paul's letter to Philemon, a small book, often passed over – but, as for the matter in hand, a gem. Paul wanted a certain course of action from Philemon. He wanted a godly, sanctified response. How did he go about it? What use did he make of the law to move Philemon? None whatsoever. Did he whip him? He did not! Why, Paul did not even command him! He refused to do so. As he said:

Though I might be very bold in Christ to command you what is fitting, yet for love's sake I rather appeal to you... I appeal... Without your consent I wanted to do nothing, that your good deed might not be by compulsion, as it were, but voluntary... Yes, brother, let me have joy from you in the Lord; refresh my heart in the Lord. Having confidence in your obedience, I write to you knowing that you will do even more than I say... The grace of our Lord Jesus Christ be with your spirit. Amen (*passim*).

Finally, the apostle, writing to the Thessalonians:

We were gentle among you, just as a nursing mother cherishes her own children. So, affectionately longing for you, we were well pleased to impart to you not only the gospel of God, but also our own lives, because you had become dear to us. For you remember, brethren, our labour and toil; for labouring night and day, that we might not be a burden to any of you, we preached to you the gospel of God... You know how we exhorted, and comforted, and charged [implored] everyone of you, as a father does his own children, that you would walk worthy of God who calls you into his own kingdom and glory... Now may the God of peace himself sanctify you completely; and may your whole spirit, soul and body be preserved blameless at the coming of our Lord Jesus Christ (1 Thess. 2:7-12; 5:23).

I realise, of course, that a father sometimes has to use the rod on his wilful child (Prov. 13:24; 19:18; 22:15; 23:13-14; 29:15-17). But any true father, surely, only reaches for the rod as the last resort. What is more, the loving father regrets its use. He only employs the rod because he has to. In a sense, he feels defeated when using it. Surely, reader, love is the real motive, the true spur, the proper attitude in all of this? No good father wants to produce a child who is afraid of him, a son who obeys in order to avoid another lashing with the whip, does he? That were to produce a cringing, cowering slave. The aim, surely, is to produce a mature and loving son, one who gladly obeys from the heart; more, one who is able to decide wisely for himself. And if this is true in the case of family relationships, how much more so in the gospel.

These three letters, reader, show us the New Testament way of bringing about godly obedience.[92]

---

[92] I can only suggest, reader, that as you read the New Testament you look out for such things. Take 'these things I write to you, so that you may not sin' (1 John 2:1). What things? The law of Moses? Let the context decide. The entire letter of 1 John is the context – yes, of course – but what of the immediate context. Glance at 1 John 1:5 – 2:2. What does the apostle major on? Is it not the forgiveness of sins, propitiation by the blood of Christ? And what of the seemingly ridiculous way John goes about his work? He writes so that we will not sin, yet he immediately

As we saw, especially when looking at Galatians 5, the New Testament speaks of the believer in terms of his *present* liberty, his *present* joy, his *present* glory. And this glory is intimately connected with Christ, the believer's redemption in Christ from the law, and the indwelling of the Spirit. In short, the law of Christ not only sanctifies the believer; it brings him liberty and joy in that sanctification, as part and parcel of his sanctification. The sanctification and the joy are Siamese twins. I said I would return to this matter. I do so now.

The law of Christ brings glory to the believer now

This glory, this joy, this liberty, as I say, is no mere tack-on to sanctification; it is no side-effect. Rather, the believer's liberated joy in Christ is an integral component of his holy walk before God in Christ, and an essential mark of it. It is one of the crowning glories of the new covenant. Let me prove it.

In the spiritual warfare, we know that ultimate victory is certain: 'Thanks be to God, who gives us the victory through our Lord Jesus Christ' (1 Cor. 15:57). 'Thanks be to God who always leads us in triumph in Christ' (2 Cor. 2:14). 'We are more than conquerors through him who loved us' (Rom. 8:37), 'we overwhelmingly conquer' (NASB). *But this note of triumph must not be confined to heaven.* It is a present felt-experience for the believer. Listen to the Lord Jesus, addressing his disciples on the subject of 'joy', just before his crucifixion:

These things I have spoken to you, that my joy may remain in you, and that your joy may be full... Most assuredly, I say to you that you will weep and lament, but the world will rejoice; and you will be sorrowful, but your sorrow will be turned into joy. A woman, when she is in labour, has sorrow because her hour has come; but as soon as she has given birth to the child, she no longer remembers the anguish, for joy that a human being has been born into the world. Therefore you now have sorrow; but I will see you again and your heart will rejoice, and your joy no one will take from you. And in that day you will ask me nothing. Most assuredly, I say to you, whatever you ask the Father in my name he will give you. Until now you have asked nothing in my name. Ask, and you will receive, that your joy may be full (John 15:11; 16:20-24).

In saying this, of course, the Lord was speaking of the joy the disciples would experience after his resurrection, following hard upon their grief at his arrest, trial, crucifixion and burial. In that (as it seemed to them at the time) cataract of unmitigated disaster, their hopes had been dashed, buried with Christ (Luke 24:17-21), and they had proved by bitter experience the truth of the Psalmist's words: 'Hope deferred makes the heart sick' (Ps. 13:12). Even so, as the Psalmist had also declared: 'Weeping may endure for a night, but joy comes in the morning' (Ps. 30:5). Furthermore, as above, Christ had promised that their joy would return. And so it did: 'He showed them his hands and his side. Then the disciples were glad when they saw the Lord' (John 20:20). As the two on the way to Emmaus described it: 'Did not our heart burn within us while he talked with us on the road, and while he opened the Scriptures to us?' (Luke 24:32).

---

talks in this vein: 'And if anyone sins, we have an advocate with the Father, Jesus Christ the righteous'. Is it not clear? What is the motive for the believer's holiness? Christ, his death, and God's forgiveness of sins.

Moreover, joy was not an experience just for the disciples, and at that time. Abundant life in Christ (John 10:10) for *all* believers begins at regeneration, and glory and joy for *all* believers have come *now*: Though '*now* you do not see [Christ], yet believing, you rejoice [now, at this very moment] with joy inexpressible and full of glory'. And why? Because you are 'receiving the end of your faith – the salvation of your souls' (1 Pet. 1:8-9). So that 'we all... beholding... the glory of the Lord, are being transformed into the same image from glory to glory... by the Spirit of the Lord' (2 Cor. 3:18). Listen to Christ addressing his Father in his prayer for *all* (John 17:20) his people: 'Now I come to you, and these things I speak in the world, that they may have my joy fulfilled in themselves... The glory which you gave me I have given them' (John 17:13,22). 'I have given', please note, not 'I will give'. The faith that takes a sinner to glory brings glory to the sinner – now. And this because believers are spiritual, not fleshly; because they are under grace, not law; because they have the Spirit (Rom. 6:14; 8:1ff; Gal. 5:18); and all because they are perfectly justified in Christ (Rom. 5:19; 8:1; 2 Cor. 5:21; Eph. 5:25-27; Heb. 10:14).[93] 'The righteous sings and rejoices' (Prov. 29:6).

'This is all very well. But can't we have a bit of realism? Let's face life as it is'.

Of course! I agree that realism is wanted, that realism is essential. But it must be *biblical* realism![94] And biblical realism is what I am setting out. Yes, believers are intimately acquainted with sin, affliction, personal trial, failure, disappointment and suffering. What is more, until Christ returns, there will be no 'golden time'; rather, false teaching, declension, defection and apostasy will increase.[95] The apostles experienced it in their time.[96] Even so, believers do triumph and overcome in these afflictions. Romans 8 is surely the greatest of all biblical statements on the theme. In this chapter, the apostle pulls no punches, he runs away from no difficulty with his talk of 'tribulation, distress, persecution, famine, nakedness, peril, sword, death', but neither does he fail to sound the note of jubilation. Fail to sound it? He revels in it:

You did not receive the spirit of bondage again to fear, but you received the Spirit of adoption by whom we cry out: 'Abba, Father'. The Spirit himself bears witness with our spirit that we are children of God, and if children, then heirs – heirs of God and joint heirs with Christ, if indeed we suffer with him, that we may also be glorified together. For I consider that the sufferings of this present time are not worthy to be compared with the glory which shall be revealed in us.

'Hang on! We know all that. Why are you telling us this in a book on the law?' For this reason: nothing could be more apposite. Do not miss the opening note of Romans 8. The apostle gets to the root of the matter right from the start:

There is therefore now no condemnation to those who are in Christ Jesus, who do not walk according to the flesh, but according to the Spirit. For the law of the Spirit of life in Christ

---

[93] See the same argument in 1 John 2:3-11,27,29; 3:1-15,18-19,22-24; 4:1-16,21; 5:1-5,18-21. In fact, the entire first letter of John is taken up with the theme.

[94] And not only for the believer and his comfort. This is the way to witness to the world. Believers have trials, but they triumph in Christ. They triumph now, and will gloriously triumph in eternity. The world needs to see this. Now!

[95] Matt. 24:3-28; Mark 13:4-23; Luke 21:7-17; 1 Tim. 4:1-3; 2 Tim. 3:1-9; 4:1-4; *etc.*

[96] Acts 15:1; 20:29; Rom. 16:17-18; 1 Cor. 15:12; 2 Cor. 11:3-4,12-15; Gal. 2:4-5,11-21; 2 Thess. 2:2-3,7; 1 Tim. 1:19-20; 5:15; 6:3-5,10; 2 Tim. 2:17-18; 4:9-18; Tit. 1:9-16; 3:9-11; 2 Pet. 2:1-22; 1 John 2:18-23; 4:1-6; 2 John 7-11; 3 John 9; Jude 4-19; *etc.*

Jesus has made me free from the law of sin and death. For what the law could not do in that it was weak through the flesh, God did by sending his own Son in the likeness of sinful flesh, on account of sin: he condemned sin in the flesh, that the righteous requirement of the law might be fulfilled in us who do not walk according to the flesh but according to the Spirit... You are not in the flesh but in the Spirit, if indeed the Spirit of God dwells in you.[97]

Building on that magnificent opening, the apostle is soon proclaiming, and proclaiming with tremendous confidence, the believer's glory – both present and ultimate. Paul makes it clear: the believer's assurance flows directly from the fact that he is in Christ, and that, being in Christ, he has been redeemed from the law, and is now under the law of Christ, 'the law of the Spirit of life in Christ'. And that 'law of the Spirit of life in Christ' has set him 'free from the law of sin and death'. Free! He is set at liberty! And nowhere does this 'law of the Spirit of life in Christ', the believer's liberty in Christ, better prove its worth than at the lowest point in the darkest night; namely the believer's physical dissolution and death. *That* is what the apostle teaches in Romans 8. *This* is biblical realism!

Death! Is that enough realism for you? The believer, like all who were born sons of Adam, has to meet that dread, last enemy – death (1 Cor. 15:26). And, make no mistake, death is an enemy (Heb. 2:15). What does the New Testament have to say to a believer confronted by the grim reaper? Anything? Of course it does! In light of the return of Christ, and the glorious resurrection to come, the child of God can, at that very moment when standing before the open grave of a long-loved fellow-believer who has just died, lift his heart and voice as he calls out in exultation: '"O death, where is your sting? O hades, where is your victory?"'. 'Thanks be to God, who gives us the victory through our Lord Jesus Christ' (1 Cor. 15:55-57).

Just a minute! Don't rush on! Did you notice my deliberate omission? Let me quote the passage properly:

'O death, where is your sting? O hades, where is your victory?' ***The sting of death is sin, and the strength [or power] of sin is the law.*** But thanks be to God, who gives us the victory through our Lord Jesus Christ (1 Cor. 15:55-57).

Reader, do you see what I am driving at? In the midst of all his rejoicing over death and hades, catch hold of the apostle's seeming irrelevance about the law: 'The sting of death is sin, and the strength [or power] of sin is the law'. What an odd thing for him to say, and in such a place! What an odd thing to do – to make a doctrinal statement about the law, and make it while standing in the graveyard! Why did the apostle stray into this jarring aside here, at such a time as this? *Because it is neither jarring nor an aside.* He did not stray, and what he said is certainly not irrelevant! Doctrine is never irrelevant! Anything but! The apostle – or this believer quoting him at such a moment – knows that victory over death is accomplished through the Saviour's own death and resurrection. More, he knows that Christ's victory over death is accomplished through his victory over sin. Above all, and this is the point, the apostle teaches us that victory over death is accomplished *because Christ has been victorious over the law*. And just as Christ's victory over the law is complete, so is his victory over death.

The bereaved believer, therefore, being in Christ, being united to Christ, has the assurance that death – though at this moment seemingly all-conquering – is in fact

---

[97] We could have started with Rom. 5:1-11, if not before, not forgetting Rom. 6 and 7.

utterly defeated. And he is sure of this because he knows that Christ has redeemed his people from the law. United to Christ, when he rose, they rose (Rom. 6:1-14; Eph. 2:6; Col. 2:12-13; 3:1), and he (and they) rose triumphant over sin, law and death. In particular, Christ has redeemed the brother or sister who, at this moment, is being laid in the grave – redeemed him or her from the law. So that, while this bereaved believer, as he stands at the graveside, certainly feels the sting of death, at this moment he also glories in the victory that Christ has accomplished. *This* is the biblical realism I have been talking about. *This* is the note of triumph which Paul puts at the heart of the believer's confidence. And it all hinges on Christ's ending of the law for all believers.

You see, reader, in writing this book, I have not been engaged in a theological knockabout with the Reformed just for the fun of it. The fact that Christ has redeemed his people from the law is of unspeakable comfort to the believer at the nadir of his life: at the graveside of a long-loved fellow-believer – wife or husband or whatever; and, not least, when contemplating his own death. Redemption, remember, means liberty! Liberty from sin, from death and the law. And liberty means liberty at such a time – especially at such a time! What is more, if this sense of freedom from sin, freedom from death – and all through freedom from law – through the finished work of Christ, brings blessed consolation to the believer in the darkest hour, and in the bleakest of circumstances, how gloriously it must sustain and enliven the child of God 'through *all* the changing scenes of life'!

Of course, I readily acknowledge that death is the curse of the law, the result of the condemnation brought about by the law, but to try to restrict the apostle's glorious statement to one aspect of the law is wrong, and sadly diminishes one of the highest accomplishments of the gospel. As I have proved, it can't be done biblically. What is more, observe the connection Paul makes between law and sin, every bit as much as between law and death. And when he says that the law gives sin its strength or power (1 Cor. 15:56), the apostle is clearly thinking of far more than sin's power to curse in death; he is undoubtedly including sanctification as well as justification. The same goes for Romans 8:1-4, the triumphant opening of that greatest of all chapters on the subject. To take this liberty from sin and to restrict it to liberty from sin's curse – and therefore liberty from the law's curse – is tragic. Liberty from sin means not only liberty from the curse or *penalty* of sin and death; it means liberty from the *power* of sin and death (and, in eternity, the *presence* of sin and death). And it all comes through Christ setting his people free from the law. So much so, if liberty from the law can afford such benefit at the point of the believer's death, how much it must afford throughout the believer's life. *This* is the point I am trying to make.

'Talk about clutching at straws! A bit thin, isn't it?' Far from it! In addition to Romans 8, consider 2 Corinthians 1:3-11 (NIV). Think about the apostle's heavily repeated (nine-fold) emphasis on 'comfort... comfort... comfort' in 'troubles, patient endurance, sufferings, hardships, pressure, despair, deadly peril', and the like. The question is: Where did Paul go for comfort in all these 'changing scenes of life' and death? He went to Christ! He went to Christ's death and resurrection: 'Just as the sufferings of Christ flow over into our lives, so also through Christ our comfort overflows... that we might not rely on ourselves but on God, who raises the dead'. And it isn't long before the apostle is moving the argument on and securing it firmly in the glories of the new covenant, in the redemption which Christ wrought for his people – not least, in obtaining their freedom from the law. Read 2 Corinthians 2:4 – 3:12

(NIV), and see! Yes, the apostle knows 'great distress and anguish of heart and with many tears'; but, he says, 'but thanks be to God, who always leads us in triumphal procession in Christ and through us spreads everywhere the fragrance of the knowledge of him'. Where does Paul find such confidence? 'Are we beginning to commend ourselves again?' Not at all!

Such confidence as this is ours through Christ before God. Not that we are competent in ourselves to claim anything for ourselves, but our competence comes from God. He has made us competent as ministers[98] of a new covenant – not of the letter but of the Spirit; for the letter kills, but the Spirit gives life. Now if the ministry that brought death, which was engraved in letters on stone, came with glory, so that the Israelites could not look steadily at the face of Moses because of its glory, fading though it was, will not the ministry of the Spirit be even more glorious? If the ministry that condemns men is glorious, how much more glorious is the ministry that brings righteousness! For what was glorious has no glory now in comparison with the surpassing glory. And if what was fading away came with glory, how much greater is the glory of that which lasts! Therefore, since we have such a hope, we are very bold.

So much so, in concluding this section of his letter, the apostle can declare: 'Now the Lord is the Spirit, and where the Spirit of the Lord is, there is freedom. And we, who with unveiled faces all reflect the Lord's glory, are being transformed into his likeness with ever-increasing glory, which comes from the Lord, who is the Spirit' (2 Cor. 3:17-18, NIV). This 'ever-increasing glory', this ever-increasing glory, *now* – brought about by freedom from the law – is no phantom. This is no straw that I am clutching!

Nor has the apostle finished! In continuing with his letter to the Corinthians, Paul has even more to say on the subject. Read 2 Corinthians 4:1 – 5:6. Do not miss: 'For God... made his light shine in our hearts to give us the light of the knowledge of the glory of God in the face of Christ. But we have this treasure in jars of clay to show that this all-surpassing power is from God and not from us' (2 Cor. 4:6-7, NIV). As the apostle declares:

With that same spirit of faith we also believe and therefore speak, because we know that the one who raised the Lord Jesus from the dead will also raise us with Jesus and present us with you in his presence. All this is for your benefit, so that the grace that is reaching more and more people may cause thanksgiving to overflow to the glory of God. Therefore we do not lose heart. Though outwardly we are wasting away, yet inwardly we are being renewed day by day. For our light and momentary troubles are achieving for us an eternal glory that far outweighs them all. So we fix our eyes not on what is seen, but on what is unseen. For what is seen is temporary, but what is unseen is eternal (2 Cor. 4:13-18, NIV).

Then again, within a few verses the apostle is listing his many trials – including 'through glory and dishonour, bad report and good report; genuine, yet regarded as impostors; known, yet regarded as unknown; dying, and yet we live on; beaten, and yet not killed' – nevertheless showing he has overcome – 'sorrowful, yet always rejoicing' (2 Cor. 6:8-10, NIV). As he later explains: 'I am greatly encouraged; in all our troubles my joy knows no bounds. For when we came into Macedonia, this body of ours had no

---

[98] See my *Priesthood* and *Pastor* for proof that 'ministers' must not be limited to 'professional men standing in a pulpit'. As the context proves, while he was speaking of his own apostolic 'ministry', Paul was including all believers, men and women, and young and old. All new-covenant members are 'ministers'.

rest, but we were harassed at every turn – conflicts on the outside, fears within. But God, who comforts the downcast, comforted us by the coming of Titus, and not only by his coming but also by the comfort you had given him. He told us about your longing for me, your deep sorrow, your ardent concern for me, so that my joy was greater than ever' (2 Cor. 7:4-7, NIV).

Do not forget, reader, the doctrine which underpins all this rejoicing in the midst of suffering: the new covenant. Do not forget the glorious statements in 1 Corinthians 15:56 and 2 Corinthians 3:1-18. Believers have exuberant confidence in all their troubles, and they have such confidence entirely and only because they are in Christ, and because Christ has accomplished so much for them, and in them. 'The sting of death is sin, and the power of sin is the law. But thanks be to God! He gives us the victory through our Lord Jesus Christ' (1 Cor. 15:56-57, NIV). And if for death, then for all our troubles: 'The sting of all *our* troubles, including death, is sin, and the power of sin is the law. But thanks be to God! He gives *us* the victory in all *our* troubles, including death, through *our* Lord Jesus Christ'. And all because we have been delivered from the law, the condemning covenant of death, and have been made partakers of the new covenant, 'the ministry of the Spirit... the ministry that brings righteousness', the 'ministry' that has 'surpassing glory... glory... which lasts!' As a consequence, 'therefore... we are very bold' (2 Cor. 3:7-12, NIV).

In this vein, the apostle presses on (2 Cor. 11:16 – 13:14). Repeatedly confessing his 'weakness', he does so in order to bring his argument to a glorious climax. He had prayed for the removal of his thorn. No! said Christ: 'My grace is sufficient for you, for my power is made perfect in weakness'. Feeling the force of Christ's argument, grasping what his Lord and Saviour was saying, Paul responds in exultation: 'Therefore I will boast all the more gladly about my weaknesses, so that Christ's power may rest on me. That is why, for Christ's sake, I delight in weaknesses, in insults, in hardships, in persecutions, in difficulties. For when I am weak, then I am strong... For to be sure, he was crucified in weakness, yet he lives by God's power. Likewise, we are weak in him, yet by God's power we will live with him' (2 Cor. 12:9-10; 13:4, NIV).

And what is the kernel of Christ's argument? Grace! 'My grace'! Grace, not law! Do not miss it, reader! Grace, Christ's grace bringing Christ's power, is the core of the new covenant – both for justification and sanctification; above all, for unspeakable joy for the believer in and through it all. The law? Where does the law come into all this? Silence![99] Grace is the heart of it: 'It is good that the heart be established [strengthened, NIV] by grace' (Heb. 13:9). Thus, as the apostle concluded his Corinthian letter (in words which, because they have become so familiar to us, grievously, they seem to have lost nearly all meaning): 'May the grace of the Lord Jesus Christ, and the love of God, and the fellowship of the Holy Spirit be with you all' (2 Cor. 13:14, NIV).

In short, reader, we have come full circle from Romans 8:1-4: 'The law of the Spirit of life in Christ Jesus *has* made me free from the law of sin and death. For what the law could not do in that it was weak through the flesh, God *did* by sending his own Son'.

Now the apostle's experience, while more dramatic than most, is the experience of all who are in Christ. The conflict and the comfort, the sufferings and the joy, are, all of

---

[99] In this letter, in addition to the silence on the law, note the twelve references to 'grace', the recurring themes of the death and resurrection of Christ (2 Cor. 1:5,9; 4:10-14; 5:14-15; 8:9, not to mention allusions to it), and the Spirit (2 Cor. 1:21-22; 3:1-18; 5:5; 6:6; 13:14).

them, an integral part of their sanctification (Heb. 12:1-29). 'The most severe trial' and 'overflowing joy' (2 Cor. 8:2, NIV) are theirs, and at one and the same time. And the underlying reason for the joy is that every believer can say with full assurance:

Since *I* died with Christ, *I* believe that *I* shall also live with him, knowing that Christ, having been raised from the dead, dies no more. Death no longer has dominion over him... Sin shall not have dominion over *me*, for *I* am not under law but under grace... *I*... have become dead to the law through the body of Christ, that *I* may be married to another – to him who was raised from the dead, that *I* should bear fruit to God... *I* have been delivered from the law... that *I* should serve in the newness of the Spirit and not in the oldness of the letter... The law of the Spirit of life in Christ Jesus has made *me* free from the law of sin and death. For what the law could not do in that it was weak through the flesh, God did by sending his own Son for *me*... *I* through the law died to the law that *I* might live to God. *I* have been crucified with Christ; it is no longer *I* who live, but Christ lives in *me*; and the life which *I* now live in the flesh *I* live by faith in the Son of God, who loved *me* and gave himself for *me* (Rom. 6:8-9,14; 7:4,6; 8:1-4; Gal. 2:19-20).

Reader, I do not want to play the hypocrite. Please bear in mind my opening remarks to this chapter. I do not say these things because I have attained to them. I say them because I believe them to be scriptural, and I say them now, not only to instruct you, but to stir my own heart. The truth is, of such doctrine as I have set before you, too often, with William Cowper, I have to confess:

Sweet truth, and easy to repeat!
But when my faith is sharply tried
I find myself a learner yet,
Unskilful, weak, and apt to slide.[100]

And, with Anne Steele:

Forgive my doubts, O gracious Lord,
And ease the sorrows of my breast;
Speak to my heart the healing word,
That thou art mine – and I am blest.[101]

But, and this is the point, God in Christ *does* forgive and renew. And, above all, my weakness – and weakness of every other believer (including Paul, Cowper and Steele) – does not in the least affect the truth of the glories of the new covenant. Indeed, the new covenant is needed by – and by God's grace in Christ the new covenant is established for – 'such as sinners be'.[102]

Why am I going into all this? Because, reader, it captures the essence of what I want to assert under this heading. And 'assert' is the very word. I want to *assert* it. I want to 'lay it on the line'. I have been looking at two ways which men claim to be the way of sanctification. The way of sanctification, of course, is nothing less than the Christian life itself.

Well, then, on the one hand, we have sanctification by the law of Christ – through trial and suffering, yes, but also with a glorious sense of liberty and overcoming joy through Christ's redemption – not least, in his deliverance of his people from the law;

---

[100] *Gospel Hymns* number 591; Gadsby: *Hymns* number 323.
[101] Anne Steele number XLII; *Gospel Hymns* number 575; Gadsby: *Hymns* number 957.
[102] Charles Cole (*Gospel Hymns* number 396; Gadsby: *Hymns* number 984).

that is, deliverance from the rule, power and reign of law, not merely its curse. The word is 'exuberance'! New Testament believers, in all their trials and sorrows, were exuberant. I cannot resist another reference. Read Hebrews 10:32-34. And do not forget the apostolic talk of all-surpassing power, boundless and overflowing joy! *This* was the experience of the New Testament believers. It must be ours. It can be ours. It is ours, in Christ.

The various scriptures I have quoted in this section have set out the law of Christ in action. In *action*, I stress. This is no ivory-tower theory! What is more, these scriptures are wholly representative of the uniform teaching of the New Testament, with its realistic recognition of the believer's sins, fears, trials and disappointments, but, also, its constant emphasis on his present joy, liberty, confidence and triumph in all his circumstances. This is the first way of sanctification. It is the new-covenant way.

On the other hand, we have sanctification by the law of Moses as a whip smiting lazy asses, beating 'putrid' sinners into holiness. This must inevitably produce servile fear as the motive for godliness – ask any ass, cowering from his approaching master, whip in hand! As for this second way, the Reformed way of sanctification – which I think is fairly delineated as the fear-and-guilt-and-punishment system – what can we say? How can it possibly produce the believer's exuberance so patently written across the pages of the New Testament? I do not detect any joy in being whipped! I put it to you, reader, the consequence of the Reformed way of sanctification is utterly foreign to the New Testament.

I cannot put it better than Calvin himself. Arguing from Romans 8:15, Hebrews 12:18-22 and Galatians 4:25-26, he drew the obvious lesson: 'The sum of the matter comes to this: the old covenant[103] filled the conscience with fear and trembling – the new inspires it with gladness... Liberty and joy... neither was derived from the law; but... by the law they [that were under it] were oppressed like slaves, and vexed with a disquieted conscience'.[104] So why ever did Calvin make believers go under the law? Of course, he had his get-out clauses, but, as I have shown, they do not stand scrutiny. The point is, under the law – and that is precisely where Calvin wanted believers to be for sanctification, under the law – there is no liberty or joy, but only 'a disquieted conscience'. My point exactly! The opposite of the New Testament!

Here, then, are the two ways. Like the two covenants, they are chalk and cheese. And they present us with a choice. No! They *confront* us with a choice.

The choice

Here we come to the crunch. In these pages I have not been engaged in an academic debate about the niceties of two equally acceptable ways of sanctification. One is wrong; the other, right. It comes down to a stark choice. To see believers sanctified, we preach Moses or Christ. Some will say I am polarising the debate. Not so. It has been polarised for a very long time. The choice *is* clear. We have to make it! We preach law

---

[103] Calvin had Old Testament (and New Testament), but as I have shown he was really talking about the old and new covenants, 'covenant' being, as Calvin's editor elsewhere argued, the right translation: '"Covenant" is a more faithful translation than "Testament"; and a careful investigation of the meaning of *diathēkē* would contribute greatly to elucidate many passages of Scripture' (the editor in Calvin: *Commentaries* Vol.21 Part 1 p137).

[104] Calvin: *Institutes* Vol.1 pp394-395.

or grace. Only one is right. Too many today are arguing as Calvin, wanting to lash the saints with the whip of the law, or at least binding them with rules – often man-made – all of which produces outward conformity. But that is all!

To try to make the law serve as the believer's perfect rule is to make a grievous mistake. With the coming of Christ, the age of the law is over. God's people are under no whip. It is utterly incongruous for a minister of the gospel to be preaching the law of Moses as the sanctification rule for the children of the new covenant.

As I say, we have to make a choice. Sadly, if we reject Calvin's third use of the law, we know what awaits us. Opprobrium, on a serious scale! But to maintain that the law of Christ – the gospel in the hands of the Holy Spirit – is the way of the believer's sanctification – this is to take the path marked out so clearly for us in the pages of the New Testament.

It has been argued that the teaching I have been putting forward is 'doctrinal antinomianism'. I deny it. It has also been claimed that the position is unworkable. I deny it. Why am I so definite? Because it is the *biblical* position. Therefore it must be workable. It is workable. To say otherwise is to say something very serious about God and his revelation, and to say it to his face. Do I need to spell it out?

I go further. What we have seen is the *only* means of sanctification. In fact, I take my stand with these so-called 'doctrinal antinomians' – allowing the term, for argument's sake – contrary to the Reformed who claim the law is the way to produce sanctification. It is the duty and privilege of preachers to extol God's free grace in Christ, both for justification and sanctification. Preaching the law will do neither.

And it is not only doctrinal antinomians! As we have seen, Paul plainly taught that it is only by dying to the law that we can be married to Christ and so be sanctified (Rom. 7:4,6; Gal. 2:19). I guess this makes Paul a doctrinal antinomian!

The law of Christ in use: Examples from the writings of men

Now it is interesting to find that, although in theory, Reformed writers say Calvin's third use of the law is the way of sanctification, when it comes to the practice of calling for it, they adopt a very different course. For all their categorical claims about sanctification by the law, it is not unknown (to put it mildly) for Reformed teachers, when they get down to practical details, instinctively to leave Moses and turn to the gospel. Of course they do! Examples are legion. The fact is, every believer who tries to argue for the Reformed use of the law as the way of sanctification, has to contradict his claim. The Reformed believer does not walk according to the law, and the Reformed preacher does not produce sanctification by preaching the law. I have no hesitation in asserting it. It is only in Reformed text books on the law that such a course is set out. But when they expound the New Testament (rather than their systems, Confessions and the like), and appeal to believers, Reformed preachers are bound to preach Christ! Though they might claim the law is the complete and unchangeable rule and system for the behaviour of believers, when they call us to holiness, what do they speak of? What will *encourage* us, *stir* us, *spur* us to do it? What is the *motive*? What is the *means*? If the law is a *complete* system and rule of duty, should it not supply its own motive and means? Yet time and again, Reformed teachers rightly – scripturally – argue that believers must remember that they are the elect of God, think of the price Christ paid for their redemption, dwell on Christ's suffering – these are the motives to subdue our sins and stir up our obedience. It is the consideration of Christ – his person, work, offices, his love for his people, and so on – these are the motives for godliness. The love of Christ, the blood of Christ, the grace of God, liberty from the law, the new birth, the indwelling of the Spirit, fatherly discipline, these are the motives Scripture uses. Love must be the root, and the gospel is the only source of it. It is the love of Christ for his people, and their love for God which makes the principal motive for obedience. It is grace, grace all the way, grace from first to last, which leads the believer to deny himself and walk in the ways of God. I am not making these things up! All can be found in Reformed writings, and in abundance!

As you can plainly see, reader, while the Reformed claim is that the law is the 'complete system' for producing godliness, 'the perfect rule', when it comes to the crunch, the theory is quietly jettisoned and Christ and grace are preached. In short, sanctification comes by the gospel. Grace is the believer's rule, not the law. It is grace which is the perfect and complete rule and system. All this can be found in works which call for godliness – irrespective of whether the writers take the Reformed position on sanctification or not.

I must make space to quote at least one Reformed writer to demonstrate the point. Take Abraham Booth as an illustration of what I am saying. Booth was categorical: 'The moral law, in particular... is the rule of our obedience. It is a complete system of duty; and considered as moral, is immutability the rule of our conduct'. Here we have the standard Reformed position. As you know, reader, I deny it, and have argued against it. Is it true that for the believer, the decalogue is *the* rule? A *complete* system? I am sure it is not. But my question now is this: Did Booth himself believe it? It is most enlightening to read his comments when he came to the section where 'we may now consider the principal motives that are used in the book of God to stir up the minds of believers to seek a larger enjoyment of sanctification, and to abound in every good work'. It is one thing to know what we ought to do, but what will *encourage* us, *stir* us, *spur* us to do it? What is the *motive*? What is the means? If the law 'is a *complete* system of duty', should it not supply its own motive and means? Well, what did Booth list as the 'principal motives' for sanctification, as found in Scripture?

These:

Believers are exhorted to obedience from the consideration of their distinguishing characters as the elect of God and a peculiar people. The purchase which Christ has made of his chosen, and the unequalled price he paid for their deliverance, afford a charming, a constraining motive to be holy in all manner of conversation... The sufferings of Christ on the cross... Considerations [such as] these [are] most happily calculated to mortify our lusts and quicken our graces; to make us loathe sin and love the law[105] as being holy, just and good... Consider him in... circumstances of unparalleled woe, and see whether it will not fire your heart with holy zeal, and arm your hands with an heavenly resolution to crucify every lust, and to mortify every vile affection... Behold the Redeemer's love to his Father's law... Reflect upon this, believer, and see whether it will not prove a noble incentive to labour, and strive after a more perfect conformity to its holy precepts... Then you will see that as the Lord, out of love to your soul and honour to the law, refused not to die the most infamous death for your salvation, you are laid under the strongest obligations to love his name, and reverence the law, to confide in his atonement, and imitate his example. When

---

[105] But see chapter 18 where I show 'the law' in the new covenant is far richer than the ten commandments.

the Christian considers that his whole person is the object of redeeming love, and the purchase of Immanuel's blood... By such considerations as these... the love of a dying Saviour, and the infinite efficacy of his atoning blood... love to him would be more fervent... how patient would [he] be... thankful... ardent... holy... useful... peaceful... joyful... happy indeed. The purchase made by the holy one of God is therefore a noble, constraining motive to holiness of life...

The Christian should often meditate on the nature and excellence of his high, holy, heavenly calling. Being called by grace... How gracious, how glorious the design of God... The mercies of God... the free pardon of all [his] sins... constitute the noblest attractive of the heart... 'For you are not under the law, but under grace'. Here grace is described as having dominion. Here grace reigns. This consideration the apostle applies as a powerful motive to holy obedience. The filial relation in which believers stand to God, and their hope of life eternal, constitute another motive to answer the same end. The inspired writers frequently take notice of that sublime relation... to promote a suitable conduct. And, surely, the children of God should act from nobler principles, and have more elevated views, than the slaves of sensuality and the servants of sin. A consideration of their heavenly birth... inheritance... the indwelling of the Holy Spirit... the promises... [even] those chastisements, with which the Lord, as a father, corrects his children... because he loves them...

That these are all the motives to obedience, with which the Scriptures furnish believers, and which they are bound to keep in view, [Booth admitted], I am far from supposing; but they, I conceive, are some of the principal [motives]... It also appears that... no obedience is acceptable to God except it proceeds from a principle of love... It is the gospel of reigning grace, under the agency of the Divine Spirit, which produces true holiness in the heart, and furnishes the Christian with such excellent motives to abound in obedience... The gospel only can furnish us with principles and motives to obedience, as will cause us to take delight in it... Be it your concern, believer, to keep in view the many inducements to holiness with which the book of God abounds and urges on you... As nothing is a more powerful persuasive to holiness than a consideration of the love of Christ and the glory of God that are manifested in the atonement made on the cross, let that be the subject of your frequent meditation... Love to God is the only principle of true obedience... Grace, that very grace which provided, reveals and applies the blessings of salvation, is the master who teaches, is the motive which induces, and the sovereign which sweetly constrains, a believer to deny himself, and to walk in the ways of holiness.[106]

Is it not clear? While Booth claimed the law is the 'complete system' for producing godliness, when it came to the crunch, he dropped his theory and turned – quite rightly – to Christ. And how he preached him! Not only that. Booth provided plenty of Scripture references to support his claims. If only he had regarded 'the law', as it applies to the believer, in its new-covenant sense (see chapter 18), he would have admirably set out what I am trying to say. As it was, Booth very effectively destroyed his own case and showed that the law of Christ, not the law of Moses, is the complete system for the believer's sanctification. The law of Christ supplies the rule, the motive and the means of godliness.

I am sure that Booth is not alone. Indeed, I know he is not![107] For all their dogmatic and sweeping claims for the law, when it comes to it I wonder how many Reformed believers really do try to use the law of Moses for sanctification.[108] I wonder how many

---

[106] Booth pp201,208-217.

[107] For more examples, see 'Extracts' p511.

[108] For all the glowing Prefaces and Introductions to *The Practice of Piety* by Lewis Bayly, I wonder how many who manage to read Bayly – or who write the fulsome commendations – actually carry out his dictats in daily practice.

Reformed teachers actually teach the law for sanctification. I know that if they preach the text of Scripture, and not their Confession or theological system, then, like Booth, they will do something very different. Like Booth, they will be bound to turn to the law of Christ. If they are preaching the law of Moses as the perfect rule of sanctification, then they must be preaching their system and not Scripture. I appeal to them: don't only parrot your oft-repeated tag – *sola Scriptura* – mean it and do it! Establish your case from Scripture; then, and only then, turn to the Confessions, catechisms, creeds and your Puritan 'divines'. Moreover, when you do, if you find that they fail to speak according to what the Bible says, reject them. That is what *sola Scriptura* means!

And when we do turn to Scripture, what do we find? I cannot put it better than Booth himself did: 'Grace, that very grace which provided, reveals and applies the blessings of salvation, is the master who teaches, is the motive which induces, and the sovereign which sweetly constrains, a believer to deny himself, and to walk in the ways of holiness'. Reader, you will have to go a long way to better Booth's words. I can't improve on them. They express what I have been trying to say throughout my book, and what I want to feel, know and experience day by day.

Nor can I improve on Anne Steele:

> *Be all my heart and all my days*
> *Devoted to my Saviour's praise;*
> *And let my glad obedience prove*
> *How much I owe, how much I love.*

And:

> *Jesus, my Lord, in thy dear name unite*
> *All things my heart calls great, or good, or sweet;*
> *Divinest springs of wonder and delight,*
> *In thee, thou fairest of ten thousand, meet.*
>
> *Do I not love thee? ah, my conscious heart*
> *Nor boldly dares affirm, nor can deny;*
> *Oh, bid these clouds of gloomy fear depart,*
> *With one bright ray from thy propitious eye!*
>
> *Do I not love thee? can I then allow*
> *Within my breast pretenders to thy throne?*
> *Oh, take my homage, at thy feet I bow!,*
> *No other Lord my heart desires to own.*
>
> *Take, take my passions in thy sovereign hand,*
> *Refine and mould them with almighty skill;*
> *Then shall I love the voice of thy command,*
> *And all my powers rejoice to do thy will.*
>
> *Thy love inspires the active sons of light,*
> *With swift-wing'd zeal they wait upon thy word;*
> *Oh, let that love, in these abodes of night,*
> *Bid my heart glow to serve my dearest Lord.*
>
> *Come, love divine, my languid wishes raise!*
> *With heavenly zeal this faint, cold heart inflame,*
> *To join with angels in my Saviour's praise,*
> *Like them obey his will, adore his name.*

But can the mind, with heavy clay oppressed,
To emulate seraphic ardour rise?
While sin pollutes her joys, forbids her rest,
How can she join the worship of the skies?

Yet he commands to love and to obey,
Whose hand sustains those happy spirits there;
In him, my soul, who is thy guide, thy stay,
In him confide, to him commit thy care.

Jesus, my Lord, oh give me strength divine!
Then shall my powers in glad obedience move;
Receive the heart that wishes to be thine,
And teach, oh teach me to obey and love![109]

And so I come to the end of trying to set out what I understand to be the law of Christ, the believer's perfect rule of life. Yet again, I can only apologise for the unwieldy nature of the material I have put before you. Read the New Testament is my counsel. Read it and mark how often it declares and works out the truth that Paul so succinctly declared to the Philippians: 'For to me, to live is Christ' (Phil. 1:21). This, I submit, and not the way spelled out by John Calvin, is the new-covenant way of sanctification.

I realise, of course, that sincere and searching objections can be raised to what I have delineated, objections which demand an answer. What about those New Testament passages which speak of the ten commandments – or their summary in the two great commandments – love to God and love to neighbour? Again, Paul quoted the law – or otherwise alluded to it – in appealing to believers. How does this square with the view that the believer is not under the law? And there are yet more objections. As far as I can see, they amount to seven in total. They must be faced and answered. Some I have touched on in passing, but I will deal more fully with all of them in the following couple of chapters.

---

[109] Anne Steele numbers CI and CXIV.

Chapter 17

The Believer's Rule:
Seven Objections: The First Six

'The law of Christ' appears but once in Scripture – if believers are not under the law of Moses, what will stop them being utterly lawless? – why does the New Testament apply the Mosaic law to them? – why did James say that believers who keep 'the perfect law of liberty' will be blessed? and why did he say that believers will be judged by that law? – why did Paul say that 'keeping the commandments of God is what matters' (1 Cor. 7:19)? – why are believers told they know God only if they keep his commands?

Reader, we are reaching the conclusion of my book. I have tried to show that believers, for their sanctification, are not under the law of Moses, but under the law of Christ. In short, I reject Calvin's third use of the law. But, as I said at the close of the previous chapter, objections are raised to this doctrine. To them I now turn.[1]

If believers are not under the law of Moses, where does this leave the ten commandments? What is the relationship between the law of Moses and the law of Christ? Does the law of Moses have nothing to say to the child of God? What about the two great commandments of the law (Lev. 19:18; Deut. 6:5; Matt. 22:37-40)? Is the believer lawless? Can he do whatever he wants? And if the believer is not under the law of Moses as a rule of holiness, why did Paul quote the ten commandments when writing to believers? As he did (Rom. 13:8-10; Gal. 5:14-15; Eph. 6:1-4). Further, what of 'the perfect law of liberty' (Jas. 1:25; 2:8-13)? And what of Paul's statement that 'keeping the commandments of God is what matters' (1 Cor. 7:19)? And what of 1 John 2:3-5, and similar passages, which tell us 'we know that we know him, if we keep his commandments'? And what of passages which teach us that the law is written on the heart by the Spirit in regeneration (Heb. 8:7-13; 10:15-16)? Does all this not mean that the law of Moses must after all be the rule of holiness for believers?

These are real and valid objections, and I wish to examine them fairly. I will address seven altogether; the first six in this chapter, and the seventh objection – because it will take more space – in the next chapter.

Objection 1: The phrase, 'the law of Christ', appears only once in Scripture. Can it, therefore, be as important as I have made it out to be?

The phrase, 'the law of Christ', appears but once in Scripture.[2] So it does. In Galatians 6:2. But very close parallels appear in other places: 'The law of the Spirit of life in Christ Jesus' (Rom. 8:2); 'under law towards Christ' (1 Cor. 9:21) or 'Christ's law' (NIV); and, of course, elsewhere – please see below. But let us take it as read; 'the law of Christ' as a phrase appears but rarely – once in the entire word of God.

---

[1] The extracts for this chapter begin on p528.
[2] How many times did Paul use the phrase 'the law of Moses'? Once only (1 Cor. 9:9).

So what? As I have shown, 'the ten commandments' appears as a phrase but three times in the Bible, and 'new covenant' but four. What conclusion should we draw from *that*? We are told 'we have the mind of Christ', but once (1 Cor. 2:16). The same goes for 'the Spirit of Christ' (Rom. 8:9), 'the sufferings of Christ' (2 Cor. 1:5), 'a letter of Christ' (2 Cor. 3:3), 'the gospel of the glory of Christ' (2 Cor. 4:4), 'the power of Christ' (2 Cor. 12:9), 'the word of Christ' (Col. 3:16),[3] 'partakers of Christ' (Heb. 3:14), and so on. I am not for a moment suggesting that these phrases are not important, that their equivalent does not appear elsewhere, or – above all – that the ideas they encapsulate are not written large in Scripture. I am simply showing that this first objection to 'the law of Christ' is puerile. I am also claiming that although 'the law of Christ', as a phrase, is rare, its principles dominate the New Testament.

For those who are still hesitant, many things which, though not *explicitly* stated in Scripture, are, nevertheless, true. They can be – and are – properly deduced from Scripture. After all, words and phrases such as 'the trinity', 'unconditional election', 'particular redemption', 'the righteousness of Christ' or 'Christ's righteousness', 'the free offer', 'duty faith', 'believer's baptism', 'progressive sanctification', 'church membership' and 'closed communion' don't appear at all in Scripture. What are we to deduce from *that*? Surely, we should ask that whether or not the phrase appears in Scripture, does the idea?

One final word on this before I move on. Many of those who read my book will quite happily use such phrases as 'personal Saviour', 'open-air work', 'quiet time', 'pastoral ministry', 'theological college', 'Bible college' or 'seminary', 'Sunday school', 'mission' or 'missionary', 'evangelism', 'covenant of works', 'covenant of grace', and 'Confession of faith', perhaps without realising that they appear nowhere at all in Scripture. Do they all appear in Scripture as concepts?

To sum up: what now of the objection about the infrequency of 'the law of Christ'? What is more, this phrase *does* appear in Scripture. So, if what I have said about it is wrong, what *does* it mean?

Objection 2: If believers are not under the law of Moses, what will stop them being utterly lawless?

To ask such a question is, at best, to betray a gross misunderstanding of what I have argued for. The truth is, I have expressly written against it – over and over again. Even so, the question is still asked. In fact, the question is not always asked. Those who say the gospel – and not the law of Moses – is the believer's rule, are *alleged* to subvert the gospel because they have no interest in the law, and are dismissed out of hand. If they have not already arrived, it is claimed, such people are on the high road to antinomianism, with all its attendant evils. How can believers take such a route, runs the argument, when patently the New Testament demands godliness? Such teaching as I have set out, so it is said, will lead to an end of all sanctification, to lawless Christians living sinful lives, to a subversion of the gospel, to Christians living as they like, making them worse than criminals, abandoned to their own personal whims, governed by a hazy, vague and imprecise subjectivism. And so on. All this is said.

---

[3] But see Rom. 10:17 (NIV, NASB); 'the word of God' (NKJV).

Reader, this cannot go unchallenged. Placing even the best construction on such accusations, we are left with a nasty taste. There is, at the very least, an implication that people like me do not recognise stealing and adultery and such like as sin. Really! Do advocates of the law of Christ, not the law of Moses, as the believer's perfect rule, teach that believers are free to blaspheme and murder and lie? that they can live as they like? that they are answerable only to themselves? that they need not love God and man? Just because believers are not under the law of Moses, it does not mean they are lawless. To be a believer and to be law-less is a contradiction in terms. Under Christ, believers are under a far more probing law than the law of Moses. Believers must not only avoid murder; they must not even hate; indeed, positively, they must love! Love, the very principle of Christ's law.

I am saying that Christ's law in the gospel, as found in his example and commands, and in the declarations, commands and instructions of his apostles, is the perfect rule for believers. Christ's law is a true law, and to break his law is to sin. It is most objectionable – it is offensive – to have this dismissed as living by 'individual opinion', 'nothing but vague subjectivism', or 'a haze of imprecise ethics'. If I may presume to caution any who use language of this kind: be careful against whom you are speaking. Have I not quoted Christ and his apostles time and again saying the sort of things you reject in such pejorative terms?

What will stop believers being lawless? The law of Christ! The law of Christ will stop believers being lawless – by the power of the indwelling Spirit under the terms of the new covenant. Believers are neither lawless nor law-less. I go further: nothing but the law of Christ, as employed by the Spirit, will produce heart-godliness. The Reformed system claims that being under the law is the only way to produce godliness. God, through Paul, says the direct opposite (Rom. 6:14; 7:4-11). All this I have set out in the previous pages.

Some professing believers, I concede, might claim that sin is tolerable or even a sign of grace, but I have never met any. Nevertheless, I can say what I think of such in a few words. However they dress up their doctrine, they are utterly mistaken and deceived. They are a disgrace to the gospel. They are condemned by Jude 4. They are no friends of what I have said about the law of Christ. Believers, being under the law of Christ, are duty-bound to 'adorn the doctrine of God [their] Saviour in all things' (Tit. 2:10) – and the New Testament leaves us in no doubt as to what *that* entails!

Objection 3: If believers are not under the law of Moses, why does the New Testament apply the law to them?

If, as I have claimed, believers are not under the law, why does the New Testament appeal to the ten commandments? The Reformed have no problem with this, of course. It is just what would be expected.

But wait a minute! Is it? The New Testament does use the ten commandments when addressing believers, yes. But how does it do it? And how often does it do it? Surely, if the Reformed view is right, the New Testament should always – always! – be drawing the attention of believers to the ten commandments; 'as the ten commandments say' should be a constant refrain. After all, the Reformed say that the ten commandments are the believer's perfect rule. If so, shouldn't the New Testament be always pointing believers to the ten commandments – to that which is their 'perfect' rule? But we do not find it so.

Let us clear away some loose thinking. And there is need! We meet plenty of sloppy – not to say, shoddy – exegesis when the Reformed turn to these passages, and try to make their case. For instance: Paul did not *impose* the fifth commandment on the believers at Ephesus (Eph. 6:1-3). Christ and the apostles did not *always* refer believers to the law when they wanted to speak of godliness. Nor does the New Testament show that *frequently* meditating upon the law is the *best* way to live a sanctified life, or to be stirred to it. Nor does it repeat and enforce *all* the ten commandments. These things are claimed. Do we get the impression that believers in the New Testament were turning to the law and *frequently* meditating upon it as the *best* way to discover God's will for their lives, and stirring them to godliness? I think not! What evidence do we have that Gentile believers in that time had, or had even seen, a copy of the ten commandments?[4] To think Gentile believers had (let alone pored over) a copy of the law (in Greek or Hebrew) is wildly fanciful.

The truth is, reader, where does Paul *ever* tell believers they are under Moses' law? Where does he *ever* tell believers they must regard the law of Moses as their norm, their rule? Which commandment of the ten does Paul *ever* tell believers they must obey? The silence is deafening. These significant facts cannot be ignored. Yes, Paul *used* the law when *exhorting* believers – though even this is rare – but he never commanded believers to obey the Mosaic law.[5]

Having cleared the ground in general, let me now go on to consider those particular places where Paul does appeal to the ten commandments when writing to believers.

Consider Romans 13:8-10
Owe no man anything except to love one another, for he who loves another has fulfilled the law. For the commandments: 'You shall not commit adultery, you shall not murder, you shall not steal, you shall not bear false witness, you shall not covet' – and if there is any other commandment – are all summed up in this saying; namely: 'You shall love your neighbour as yourself'. Love does no harm to a neighbour; therefore love is the fulfilment of the law.

The love Paul spoke of is love for men – particularly, if not expressly, believers – not love for God. As to the 'law' in question, there can be no doubt. Both the wider context – Paul's overwhelming use of the word throughout Romans – and especially the immediate context – in which some of the ten commandments are quoted (Rom. 13:9) – make it clear that Paul, writing to believers, was here speaking about the Mosaic law,[6] the ten commandments in particular. The upshot is, Paul undoubtedly quoted some of the ten commandments when writing to the believers at Rome. This is agreed.

But notice what Paul did not do. He did not make the law the be-all and end-all of his teaching. He did not make the law its climax. *Notice further what Paul did not say.* He did not tell the believers – nor remind them of what, according to Reformed teaching, they are supposed to have been fully aware of – that they are, of course,

---

[4] See my extract in the previous chapter regarding most Diaspora Jews and their lack of the Hebrew Scriptures.

[5] See below where I show how the apostle was prepared to draw on all sorts of sources to make a point.

[6] He quoted Lev. 19:18. See below for more on this point.

under the law of Moses. Strange silence! Not exactly a proof that Calvin's third use of the law is wrong, I grant you, but from the Reformed point of view, certainly odd! Rather, the apostle said that love fulfils the law (Rom. 13:8,10; Gal. 5:14). 'Fulfil'! How many times we have met this word before! Love, said Paul, *fulfils* the law. And we know that, in this regard, old-covenant regulations do not count: 'For in Christ Jesus, neither circumcision nor uncircumcision avails anything, but faith working through love' (Gal. 5:6). I realise that Paul was speaking of justification in this last verse, but the point is justifying faith will show itself by love – not by trying to keep the law of Moses! It is by faith a believer is justified, and it is as his faith works by love that he shows his sanctification.

While love does not dispense with the law – rather it fulfils it – Paul certainly did not say the law of Moses is the regulative norm for believers; he did not impose it upon them. He did not say it is their rule. He did not say believers must strive to keep it. *Nor did he imply it.* He simply cited examples from the ten commandments, making the point that love is the real end, the 'fulfilment', of the law. And in order to drive the point home, Paul says it twice in this brief paragraph (Rom. 13:8,10). *This*, I say, is the point. Furthermore, if the apostle's citing of the ten commandments really does prove that the law is the believer's perfect rule, does the same apply to nature and pagan poets? After all, see Acts 17:28-29; 1 Corinthians 11:14; Titus 1:12-13. No! Paul briefly quotes the ten commandments to say that love fulfils them.

'Fulfil' is a strong word. What does it mean? It does not here mean 'sum up'. Rather, we are, once again, in the realm of the eschatological. It also reminds us of something Paul said earlier in Romans: God has done a work through his Son in order 'that the righteous requirement of the law might be fulfilled in us who do not walk according to the flesh but according to the Spirit' (Rom. 8:3-4). I refer you, reader, to chapter 10 and my remarks on those verses. Linking that passage and this, both in the same book, remember, with no chapter/verse divisions, Paul, it is evident, is speaking of believers, those who are redeemed by Christ, who are indwelt by the Spirit, who belong to the new age of the Spirit, who are no longer under 'law', 'but now' are in Christ – the one who is the 'end of the law' (Rom. 10:4). And what does Paul say of these believers? Believers, who love one another, have satisfied, fulfilled the demands of the law as far as their conduct towards their fellow-men is concerned.

But, I hasten to add, as the context also makes clear, this does not mean that love has replaced the commandments; love *fulfils* the law, it does not replace it. Believers still need the written word, including the law of Moses – but they need all the word, including all the law, not merely the ten commandments. The entire word teaches them, reproves them, corrects them, instructs and trains them (2 Tim. 3:16-17). And this word, I repeat, includes the Mosaic law in all its entirety – properly nuanced in line with the New Testament, of course. But it also includes apostolic commands. And love is the fulfilling of it. Love is the purpose of the commandment – whether we understand it to refer to the precise command Paul gave Timothy (1 Tim. 1:5), or to the whole of Scripture, including the law. The law is 'all summed up' in love (Rom. 13:9). The believer, one of God's people, a member of the new covenant, is no longer under the law of Moses, the law for Israel, the old-covenant people of God. On the contrary, he is under a new law, 'the law of Christ' (1 Cor. 9:19-21; Gal. 6:2). And at the heart of Christ's new law lies that commandment of Moses – namely, the commandment to love our neighbour as ourselves (Lev. 19:18; Gal. 6:2 with 5:13-14).

There is not a hint of a suggestion that Romans 13:8-10 is a list of rules for believers. Indeed, such a thing would have destroyed what the apostle is, in fact, saying. Consider the context. Paul has been dealing with practical godliness right from Romans 12:1. We can go back even further. From Romans 6:1, he has been dealing with sanctification.[7] On reaching Romans 13:9, Paul cites several of the ten commandments to illustrate the point that love is the great fulfiller of the law. Love is the great motive and spur for godliness. Love is both its test and standard: 'He who loves another has fulfilled the law... Love is the fulfilment of the law' (Rom. 13:8,10). And how does the apostle go on? By sundry commands and exhortations. Ah, but why? Why 'do this' and 'do that'? Because the law says so, because we are under regulation, because otherwise we might get lashed with Calvin's whip? Not at all! Why should we be godly? Because Christ is coming, because our salvation is getting daily nearer (Rom. 13:12). Avoid carnality, Paul demands. But how? By this:

Put on the Lord Jesus Christ, and make no provision for the flesh... the Lord... the Lord... the Lord... the Lord... the Lord... the Lord... Whether we live or die, we are the Lord's... Christ... Lord... We shall all stand before the judgement seat of Christ... the Lord Jesus... Christ... joy in the Holy Spirit... Christ... Christ... Christ Jesus... glorify the God and Father of our Lord Jesus Christ... just as Christ... Jesus Christ... by the power of the Holy Spirit... Jesus Christ... sanctified by the Holy Spirit... Christ Jesus... Christ... the Spirit of God... Christ... Christ... Christ... I beg you, brethren, through the Lord Jesus Christ, and through the love of the Spirit... in the Lord... in Christ Jesus... in Christ... in Christ... in the Lord... in Christ... in Christ... in the Lord... in the Lord... in the Lord... in the Lord... Christ... Lord Jesus Christ... The grace of our Lord Jesus Christ be with you. Amen... the Lord... The grace of our Lord Jesus Christ be with you all. Amen (Rom. 13:11 onwards).

Otherwise you 'do not serve our Lord Jesus Christ' (Rom. 16:18). In conclusion:

Now to him who is able to establish you according to my gospel and the preaching of Jesus Christ, according to the revelation of the mystery kept secret since the world began but now[8] made manifest, and by the prophetic Scriptures made known to all nations, according to the commandment of the everlasting God, for obedience to the faith – to God, alone wise, be glory through Jesus Christ for ever. Amen (Rom. 16:25-27).

If this does not set Romans 13:8-10 in its proper context, nothing will. The suggestion that Paul is imposing the law of Moses upon believers is incredible. The sense of anticlimax – to return to Moses after nearly thirteen chapters of teaching on the glory of Christ in the gospel – would be intolerable. Paul does not go back to Moses. Of course not! In contrast, he rises to the Lord Jesus Christ. 'Christ' is what he leaves ringing in their ears. Christ!

Let me summarise the passage. As I have already said, the argument runs from Romans 12:1. Paul, having reached Romans 13, lays the foundation and measure of sanctification, 'love' (Rom. 13:10), and then moves on to the eternal hope believers have in Christ (Rom. 13:11-12), and the consequent holiness of life this must produce, both in a negative sense – things to 'cast off' (Rom. 13:12) – and in a positive sense – 'let us put on... put on the Lord Jesus Christ, and make no provision for the flesh' (Rom. 13:12-14). Paul then takes up the issue of 'things indifferent' (Rom. 14:1-23; 15:1-7). Notice the absence of a list of rules and regulations – the law approach. And

---

[7] See chapter 10.
[8] Note the 'now'.

not only an absence of regulations! Observe how the apostle gives believers an *overall principle* by which to order their lives. And what is this principle? It can be summed up as the law of Christ. Note the references to Christ. In addition to references to 'the Lord', it is Christ and his work which are specifically and repeatedly used as the believer's motive and touchstone (Rom. 14:6-10,14-15,18; 15:1-3,5-7). And Moses is not mentioned once! Above all, notice Paul's final word on the subject: 'Therefore receive one another, *just as Christ also received us*, to the glory of God' (Rom. 15:7). As in the previous chapter, I draw attention yet again to this paramount comparison, this staggering comparison: 'Just as...'! Is this what Reformed critics mean by 'wishy-washy'?

Thus the believer has to take a far more spiritual stance than merely looking up a code of practice and seeking to obey it. How mistaken it is, therefore, to say that Paul, at the start of Romans 12, takes up the law and wields it to teach believers their duties. By his use of 'the will of God', the apostle does not mean 'the law of God'. Certainly, 'the will of God' cannot be confined to the ten commandments, a mere sixteen verses (thirty-two, with the repeat) of Scripture. It is the entire revealed will of God – 'all Scripture' (2 Tim. 3:16-17). As Christ prayed for his people: 'Sanctify them by your truth. Your word is truth' (John 17:17). 'Your word' – your entire word! The apostle does not tell the believer to keep the law. He does not say the law is the rule, the norm, the standard of the Christian life. That could not be right.

Paul, in Romans 13:8-10, shows that he is not against the law. He does not attack Moses. He is not an antinomian. The work of Christ in the gospel fulfils the law in the believer. But this does not mean that Paul here re-issues the law. How could he? He has already taught that believers, living by the Spirit, are enabled by him to love one another – and that this is what the law wanted to produce but could not. Paul is not making the law the rule for believers in Romans 13:8-10, and thus going back on what he set out a few pages before (Rom. 6:14; 7:1-6). Believers have died to the law!

Consider Galatians 5:13-14
Here is another place where Paul, when writing to believers, quotes the Mosaic law, or a kind of summary of it – but not, in fact, one of the ten commandments. When looking at Galatians, I said I would return to the passage. I do so now:

You, brethren, have been called to liberty; only do not use liberty as an opportunity for the flesh, but through love serve one another. For all the law is fulfilled in one word, even in this: 'You shall love your neighbour as yourself'.

Paul does not here destroy what he has so carefully established in the rest of his letter to the Galatians. Of that we may be sure. After all that he has said, he is not at this late stage putting forward 'the moral law', the ten commandments, as the believer's rule. And if he is, he chooses a singularly inept way of doing it, since he quotes from Leviticus.[9] The law here is, without question, the Mosaic law. Consequently, if Reformed teachers want to use this passage to say the moral law is binding on believers as their perfect rule, it proves too much for them. They must extend their view of the law far beyond the ten commandments. 'The law', in Galatians 5:14, is the law of Moses.[10] It is, literally in the Greek, 'the whole law'.

---

[9] See above for Paul's use of Lev. 19:18 in Rom. 13:8-10. See also below.

[10] Not the law of Christ. See chapter 9.

But why did Paul quote from Leviticus? Why this emphasis upon 'love your neighbour'? We have met this reference to Leviticus 19:18 before, and will meet it again. This is noteworthy. Whereas before Christ's use of it, and Paul wrote his letters to the churches, there are no explicit references to the verse in Jewish writings, in clear contrast, in the New Testament this verse is the most frequently quoted passage from the Pentateuch (Rom. 13:9; Gal. 5:14; Jas. 2:8). This can only mean that the emphasis on Leviticus 19:18 is particularly and specially a gospel emphasis, and must have come from Christ himself, who first used it in this way (Matt. 5:43; 19:19; 22:39; Mark 12:31; Luke 10:27).

Notice Paul's emphasis upon 'fulfilled' once again. Paul is certainly not establishing the Mosaic law as the believer's rule, the commandments of which are to be obeyed in every particular. Love is the fulfilment of the law, and this love is possible only to those who have the Spirit. To try to establish Calvin's third use of the law from this passage, is to miss the point of what Paul is saying, and to miss it badly. He is not exhorting believers to keep the law. He is stating a fact. By their life of love, he declares, all the law is fulfilled. And he puts it in the passive, 'the law is fulfilled'. I am not word-spinning. Paul is not commanding them to 'fulfil the law'; he is telling them 'the law is fulfilled' – two very different things. Paul speaks of believers and the fulfilment of the law in three places (Rom. 8:4; 13:8-10; Gal. 5:14), and in none of them does he command believers to fulfil the law. Rather, as believers walk according to, by or in the Spirit, the law is fulfilled, he says. We have already met this important passive. Paul says the righteous requirement of the law is *fulfilled* in believers (Rom. 8:4), but never says believers have to *do* or *keep* the law.

So what is the issue? It is no accident that 'fulfilled' (Gal. 5:14) and 'fullness' (Gal. 4:4) come from the same root word (which is, significantly, the same word as in Matt. 5:17), *plēroō*. The truth is, Paul is expounding the theme he has stressed so much in this letter; namely, the eschatological. The age of the law is over. The 'fullness' of the time has come (Gal. 4:4). Christ has come. The faith, the gospel, has come. And this has huge consequences for the individual. 'All the law is fulfilled' in believers by their obedience to Christ and his law in this new age. They are a new creation. And this is what Christ said he came to accomplish (Matt. 5:17).[11] And this is the issue in Galatians 5:13-14.

Paul, it must not be forgotten, is directing his remarks to those 'who desire to be under the law' (Gal. 4:21).[12] To Paul, such a desire is unthinkable, the stock-in-trade of false teachers, the Judaisers. He stresses the believer's freedom from the law (Gal. 4:21-31; 5:1,13), and this context of Galatians 5:13-14, both narrow and wide, must not be forgotten or ignored. It is the eschatological point all over again, worked out in individual experience. Paul is speaking of the believer's freedom (Gal. 5:1), the freedom he has by the work of the Holy Spirit. The believer has been rescued from this present evil age (Gal. 1:4).

As for 'all the law', Paul meant 'the whole law', the entire law of Moses; that is, not so much individual commands, but the law in its entirety and purpose. Compare Romans 8:4. The literal Greek, 'the all law', is 'odd' in that Paul put the 'all' in a peculiar place, and this is significant. Moreover, Paul put the definite article – 'the' – in

---

[11] See pp96,170,236,498.
[12] The Reformed get caught in this net.

a strange position too. None of this would have been lost on the original readers; 'the all law' is 'the entire law', 'the heart of the law', the fulfilment of the law's purpose.[13]

As I have pointed out, 'loving one's neighbour' is not a soft option, not a lowering of the standard of the law. To dismiss the thesis of my book by such a device is too tempting for some; they wave it away as something vague and hazy – 'imprecise ethics'.[14] Not at all! The very imprecision in defining 'love' and 'neighbour', and how this can vary according to time and circumstance (Gal. 6:10),[15] makes Christ's law *all the more demanding* than Moses' law. While Christ does not call for conformity to rules, a ticking-of-the-boxes approach to sanctification – which, in truth, is no sanctification at all – neither does he call for a warm, vague feeling towards other believers. He wants, he demands, a real, practical and concentrated love, the sharing of goods and money, even – wait for it – even to the laying down of one's life for the brethren, all because Christ laid down his life for us (Rom. 15:1-3; 1 John 3:11-18)! And we are to have the mind of Christ in this (Phil. 2:5)! Think of that! I hesitate, I shrink back, even as I write the words and cite the passages! How do they strike you, reader, as your read them? 'Soft option', indeed!

Galatians 6:2 is apposite here. The law of Christ is that law of love which Christ taught in John 13:34-35; 15:12, and so on. In bearing one another's burdens, believers are obeying the law of their Lord. When they fail to do this, they break his law. Believers keep the law of Christ, the essence of which is love, and they do so out of gratitude to him for his love to them. To break his law, therefore, is to show gross ingratitude to him for his love. Clearly, the law of Moses and the law of Christ are in contrast. Paul was saying the bearing of one another's burdens, under Christ's law, is infinitely better than keeping the external Moses' law.

Of course, an emphasis upon the believer's freedom, unless accompanied by the equally biblical emphasis on the all-embracing law of Christ, can be turned into an excuse for all sorts of carnal behaviour. This, it goes without saying, is utterly wrong. In declaring that 'all the law is fulfilled in one word' (Gal. 5:14), in declaring that 'all are summed up in this saying, namely: "You shall love..."' (Rom. 13:9), Paul was not jettisoning the Mosaic law, saying it no longer had any place or value. Nor was he replacing the Mosaic law by a warm feeling. Certainly he was not abandoning all restraint. But nor was he imposing the law of Moses upon believers.

To sum up: the comments made above on Romans 13:8-10 apply with equal validity here. In Galatians 5:14, Paul was not imposing the Mosaic law on believers.

---

[13] What of the seeming contradiction between Gal. 3:10-12; 5:3 and Gal. 5:14? See 'Extracts' pp536-537 for my views. In brief, in Gal. 5:3, Paul was speaking of the attempt to earn justification by 'doing the law', which can be only by 'doing the whole law', 'the observance of all that the law requires' (Gal. 3:12; 5:3). This is impossible for fallen man. *Hence the negative overtones*. In Gal. 5:14, however, Paul was speaking of the new-covenant provisions Christ brought in, by which he gives people grace to 'fulfil the whole law', giving them his Spirit to enable them to live a sanctified life which expresses love (see Rom. 8:3-4). 'The love of God' – the sense of God's love to his people – 'the love of God has been poured out in our hearts by the Holy Spirit who was given to us' (Rom. 5:5). Thus the Spirit enables believers to love in return (Luke 7:36-50; 1 John 4:7-11,19) and so 'fulfil the whole law'. *Hence the positive overtones*.

[14] See above and the previous chapter.

[15] Because the 'neighbour' in Lev. 19 referred to a fellow-Israelite, it is probable that the focus here is love to fellow-believers. Leaving aside Gal. 6:10, is there any reference in Galatians as to how believers should relate to unbelievers?

Rather, he was continuing his theme of the epoch of the Spirit having superseded the epoch of the law, and the relevance of this triumphant 'but now' to the believer. It is tragic, it is a travesty, to reduce such a momentous argument by trying to claim Paul was making the ten commandments the believer's rule.

Consider Ephesians 6:1-3

Children, obey your parents in the Lord, for this is right. 'Honour your father and mother', which is the first commandment with promise: 'that it may be well with you and you may live long on the earth'.

Paul, clearly addressing godly children, here commanded them to obey their parents in the Lord; he said this is right. And he backed up his command by referring to, alluding to the law. *But he did not quote the law as the rule under which believers live.* Rather, he used the law as a paradigm, a model of good behaviour for believers, not as a rule which he imposed upon them. He simply reminded his readers that the Jews had this fifth commandment with its associated promise of possession of the land of Canaan – which promise he stressed. He was challenging his readers: If the Jews had this commandment, and this promise, how much more should believers live a sanctified family-life! What greater benefits are promised to them than to Israel of old! If the Mosaic law spoke of Canaan, how much more does Christ promise to his people today! This is what he was saying.

But if it is still maintained that the commandment must come over unchanged as part of the believer's perfect rule, *then so must the promise*. We cannot pick-and-mix! In other words, we shall have to admit that we have made a serious mistake in dismissing the 'prosperity gospel'. In the new covenant, obedience, after all, does bring huge material benefit, here and now. Mind you, depending on how strictly we interpret the promise, we might all have to move to the Middle East and settle in 'the land'. Hmm! A bit far-fetched? Surely, the apostle was using the commandment as an illustration or paradigm to encourage sanctified family-life among believers. This is what he was doing. He was certainly not imposing the commandment on them, nor was he promising them material prosperity for obedience!

And this is made all the more evident if we bear in mind that the issue of family life – here, the attitude of godly children to their parents – is but one example of the apostolic call for sanctification among many. This stands out all the more if the entire passage concerning practical godliness, the three chapters, Ephesians 4 – 6, is read in one sitting. Paul's total argument, its overall force, must be kept in mind. Which is? The believer must obey – he will obey – the gospel, and do so in practice, not by thinking he is under the rule of the law of Moses, but by thinking of his calling as a believer, imitating God his Father, living as a child of light, and being filled with the Spirit, and so on; above all, by thinking of Christ – I estimate that 'Christ' or 'Jesus' appears some nineteen times in these three chapters. And what is at the heart of these chapters? 'Christ... loved the church and gave himself for her, that he might sanctify and cleanse her with the washing of water by the word, that he might present her to himself a glorious church, not having spot or wrinkle or any such thing, but that she should be holy and without blemish' (Eph. 5:25-27). The cross! The cross leading to the believer's holiness! This is what Paul says to the believer. As the believer walks by the Spirit, living out the life of Christ, keeping his eye and heart on Christ and his cross, so he fulfils the law, fulfils it as it were indirectly. True, in addressing this particular topic, Paul quotes the fifth command to illustrate and enforce his call for godly children to be sanctified at home, but the apostle does not impose the command on believers; he simply uses the law as a paradigm for this godly behaviour.

What am I talking about? What is this 'paradigm' business? I have noted it on several occasions. Now is the time to establish and develop what I mean by it.

The law as a paradigm

While Paul does not make the law the rule under which believers live, he does not go to the other extreme and ignore the law or say it is of no use whatsoever. From the rich treasury of the entire Old Testament, Paul draws various lessons, types, illustrations, analogies and examples. In particular, he cites the Mosaic law, quotes it, illustrates and supports his doctrine with it, and gives examples from it. Of course he does – the New Testament quite rightly treats the Old Testament as the Scriptures, pointing to Christ, foreshadowing him (Col. 2:17; Heb. 8:5; 10:1). In Hebrews 8:5, two words are used, 'copy' and 'shadow'. A copy is not the real or original, but it shows what the real thing is like; inadequately, yes, but nevertheless usefully. A shadow bespeaks the existence of the real, solid thing. True, a shadow is colourless, blurred and flat, but this does not detract from the glory of the original. In fact, it adds to it. Shadows are vital to an artist in conveying a sense of reality and solidity. In 'pure' water-colours, the lights are formed by painting in the darks, and deepening the darks enhances the lights. The Old Testament may be shadow, but how greatly it highlights the New! Paul, therefore, used the entire old covenant, including the law, to enforce his doctrine: 'Christ, our Passover, was sacrificed for us' (1 Cor. 5:7), for instance. But this is not to say he preached Moses, or that he imposed Moses on believers. He preached Christ, making use of Moses to preach Christ.

This is what I mean by using the law as a paradigm – which is what Paul did, and what we should do. But the law must be used lawfully, properly nuanced[16] under the new covenant. The law, a component of 'all Scripture', has its role to play in the life of the believer, and part of that role is as a paradigm. But this is not the same as saying that every part of the Old Testament, down to its minutest detail, has authority over the believer, nor that the law is his perfect rule. The New Testament *uses* the Old, but its system of sanctification is not based upon it. The basis of new-covenant ethics is Christ, not the ten commandments. The law of Christ *uses* all the law of Moses to illustrate its claims. It *borrows* from it – but that only *occasionally*. Above all, it is not *based* upon it.

Having set this out with regard to Ephesians 6:1-3, let me further illustrate what I am saying by reference to 1 Corinthians. In that book, Paul several times alludes to the Mosaic law. I emphasise this. He alludes to the law, the whole law, all the law – not just the so-called 'moral law'. Paul draws on the entire law, including the Passover (1 Cor. 5:6-8), the removal of offenders from Israel (1 Cor. 5:9-13), the non-muzzling of the ox while treading the grain (1 Cor. 9:8-12), people and priests eating the sacrifices (1 Cor. 9:13-14; 10:18), Israel's sins in the wilderness (1 Cor. 10:1-11), the use of foreign languages (1 Cor. 14:21), and woman's submission (1 Cor. 14:34). But not

---

[16] In chapters 7 and 9, I spoke of this. What I am setting out is very different to those who say the law is binding in every detail, but at the same time 'modify' it by cutting out its punishment, or in splitting it into three, and so on. I am simply doing what the New Testament does with the law. It never plays Reformed 'ducks and drakes' with it.

once does Paul tell believers they are under the law. Never once does he tell them that they must keep Moses' precepts. Not once does he speak of the law as a list of rules which govern the life of the believer. Instead, he uses the law to give the believer a paradigm, an example, an illustration of the Christian life. 'These things happened to them as examples and were written down as warnings for us, on whom the fulfilment of the ages has come' (1 Cor. 10:11, NIV). That is to say, the apostle uses the Old Testament in general, and the law in particular, as a pattern, a model, an illustration of his teaching, to help his readers understand his instructions for godliness, and to encourage them in obedience – including the need for purity, for proper financial support of gospel teachers, warning against sin, against the misuse of foreign languages in meetings, showing the right way for a woman to show her submission, and so on. Certainly this is the main way in which Paul uses the law in, say, 1 Corinthians. He appeals to the law as a paradigm for godliness. The same goes for 2 Corinthians. Paul uses the law as a paradigm in the matter of holiness (2 Cor. 6:14 – 7:1), the giving of money (2 Cor. 8:15), and the need for two or three witnesses to confirm a case (2 Cor. 13:1). But, as before, never does he turn the law into the believer's rule. In short, he takes his own medicine and uses the law lawfully (1 Tim. 1:8). He is *not* dividing the law into three bits, disposing of two, and setting up 'the moral law' as a rule; rather, he uses the entire law to illustrate new-covenant principles for believers. While the law of Moses very usefully serves as an illustration of the believer's behaviour, or an allusion to it, it cannot be the believer's perfect rule.

So, for instance, on not muzzling the ox, Paul takes the law but makes it say something different to what it originally said, applying it to the present circumstances of the believer, showing how the new covenant uses the old as a paradigm for the proper financial support for those who labour in the gospel (1 Cor. 9:1-18). Paul backs his argument by reference to the law: 'Do I say these things as a mere man?' he asks. 'Or does not the law say the same also?'[17] Reader, where did 'the law say the same also'? Where did it say that a gospel preacher needs and must receive financial support to do his work? It said it in the new-covenant reading of Deuteronomy 25:4. Listen to Paul: 'For it is written in the law of Moses: "You shall not muzzle an ox while it treads out the grain"'. Pause, reader! A literalist, an old-covenant reader, has to argue that Deuteronomy says nothing about financial support for a preacher of the gospel. And he is quite right – on *old-covenant* principles; the verse is concerned with allowing an ox to eat some corn as it works the treadmill, and that is all. But listen to Paul, reading the law through new-covenant eyes:

Is it oxen God is concerned about? Or does he say it altogether for our sakes? For our sakes, no doubt, this is written, that he who ploughs should plough in hope, and he who threshes in hope should be partaker of his hope. If we have sown spiritual things for you, is it a great thing if we reap your material things?... Do you not know that those who minister the holy things eat of the things of the temple, and those who serve at the altar partake of the offerings of the altar? Even so the Lord has commanded that those who preach the gospel should live from the gospel (1 Cor. 9:9-14).

The Jews, no doubt, should have realised that the principle applied to more than oxen. All who labour ought to partake of the benefit of their labour. Surely oxen should not

---

[17] In writing to Timothy, he used the same paradigm, saying 'the Scripture says' (1 Tim. 5:17-18).

be treated better than men! Even in the old covenant, the humane treatment of oxen served as a paradigm for labour-relations. But it is only in the full light of the gospel that the spiritual point is made clear. This is the way the old covenant serves as a paradigm for the new. This is the way believers should use the Mosaic law, not as a binding rule down to its last Jewish detail.[18]

There are many such examples. In that same section, Paul cited temple-practice (1 Cor. 9:13-14; 10:18). Before that, he had raised the Passover. I know, like the sabbath, the Passover slightly anticipated Sinai (Ex. 12 and 16), but, again, like the sabbath, the Passover was in fact an integral part of the Sinai covenant. In any case, both came very heavily into the law, and both played an enormous part in the life of Israel under the law. Now then, what did Paul command the Corinthians? 'Purge out the old leaven, that you may be a new lump, since you truly are unleavened. For indeed Christ, our Passover, was sacrificed for us. Therefore let us keep the feast, not with old leaven, nor with the leaven of malice and wickedness, but with the unleavened bread of sincerity and truth' (1 Cor. 5:7-8). Let us think about that for a moment. Believers must get rid of yeast, and keep the feast of Passover. Hang on a minute! Do believers keep the feast as Moses stipulated? Do they keep the feast at all? They do not! If they did, it would be anathema to the Lord, would it not – since it would be an offence against the person and finished work of Christ? It would be tantamount to saying he had not died, and had not, by the shedding of his blood, redeemed his people. The truth is, of course, Paul was not talking about keeping any literal feast! Nobody in their right mind would think it![19] He was telling believers to get rid of all worldly contamination, and live godly lives for Christ, live sincerely and scripturally for the glory of their Redeemer. The apostle simply used the Passover as a paradigm to drive home his point. What he was not doing was to make the law the believer's rule.

Similarly, old-covenant worship had an altar. So does the new: 'We have an altar from which those who serve the tabernacle have no right to eat' (Heb. 13:10; compare 1 Cor. 10:14-22). This verse – and its context – encapsulates precisely the right way for Christians to apply old-covenant terms. The altar of the new covenant is spiritual. Only the regenerate can partake of its sacrifices. The kingdom of God is spiritual; it does not consist of foods (Heb. 13:9); 'the kingdom of God is not eating and drinking, but righteousness and peace and joy in the Holy Spirit' (Rom. 14:17). When we are told 'to go forth to [Christ], outside the camp' (Heb. 13:13), who thinks we are to make a move to a physical place? Likewise, who (apart from the revivalist with his 'altar-call') thinks that in order to obey Christ's command to 'come to me' (Matt. 11:28), a person

---

[18] I am not supporting the Puritan way of making the law teach every new-covenant matter in advance. There is all the difference between *that*, and looking back, through the gospel to the law and seeing an illustration.

[19] But the unthinkable does happen. I know of a professing believer, once Judaisers had got a toehold, religiously get rid of yeast products, eat unleavened bread for the requisite number of days, and then, on the 'right' day, eat roast lamb while standing up, deliberately-timed at sunset. I know of another who seriously contemplated smearing blood on the front door – with hyssop, I wonder? How long will it be before such people, staff in hand, sandals on feet, cloak tucked in, eat the whole lamb, innards and all, burning the remains the next morning, and doing it all in a rush? And what about the Feast of Tabernacles, the New Moon, and all? Bizarre! And sad. And worse. For Christ has fulfilled all the Jewish shadows, and abolished them! Heb. 7 – 10 is categorical; in particular, Heb. 9:10; 10:9,18.

has to leave his seat and make a physical movement? Again, the city we seek in the new covenant is not the physical Jerusalem (Heb. 13:14). It is the heavenly, spiritual Jerusalem (Gal. 4:25-26); believers 'have come to Mount Zion and to the city of the living God, the heavenly Jerusalem' (Heb. 12:22). The saints of the Old Testament[20] were conscious of the very same thing (Heb. 11:10,13-16).[21]

Yes, I know the Reformed have their answer ready. 'Believers are under the moral law. All that stuff is ceremonial'. Oh? I have already shown how that technique only works as long as you are willing to do what Scripture never does, and break the law into convenient bits. The Bible will never warrant it; it always treats the law as indivisible. In any case, it misses my point. I am simply showing that Paul would use anything and everything from the law to enforce his doctrine on believers – the ten commandments, feasts, whatever. But never once did he impose any of those things upon believers as their perfect rule. He simply used anything and everything from the law as a paradigm. *That* is my point. So, whether or not any particular example comes from the ten commandments or any other part of the law (allowing, for argument's sake, such a division to exist), the Reformed gloss is utterly irrelevant.

Furthermore, Paul would use any source to enforce his teaching, not only the law. Moses, of course, was in a different league to the following, but the apostle was prepared to cite nature (Acts 14:15,17; 17:24-29; Rom. 1:20; 1 Cor. 11:14), history (Acts 14:16; 17:30; 1 Cor. 10:1-13), superstitious pagan and idolatrous practices (Acts 17:22-23; Rom. 1:21-23; 1 Cor. 10:18-22), and the writings of pagan poets, prophets and philosophers (Acts 17:28; Tit. 1:12-13), common sense and every-day practice (1 Cor. 9:7,10-12), the facts of life (1 Cor. 11:11-12; 12:12-31), and so on. But he made none of these the basis for his teaching, nor was he saying these constituted a norm for believers. Rather, he was making use of all these resources to draw analogies, and thus illustrate his doctrine.

In short, when addressing believers, the New Testament sometimes quotes and draws lessons from the whole law, yes, but this is a far cry from saying that the ten commandments are binding on believers as their rule of life. As we have seen time and again, Paul never adopts the Reformed threefold division to limit 'the law' to 'the moral law', and so make the ten commandments the believer's perfect rule. On the contrary, the apostle makes the commands of the entire law to serve as a paradigm or example, illustration, specimen, instance or model of the behaviour which is required of believers. And that is all! I say again: new-covenant men use all the law – we do not select a mere 1% or less of it! No! The Reformed may call us antinomians. Let them! They need to use the mirror! For, unlike them, we use all the law – *but we only use it the way the New Testament does when it applies it to believers!* And never does it make the law the believer's rule.

Let me confirm that this *is* the right way to read those places in the New Testament where the law is so used. Take 1 Peter 1:15-16: 'As he who called you is holy, you also be holy in all your conduct'. Why? 'Because it is written'. Where is it written? In the law (Lev. 11:44-45; 19:2; 20:7). What is written in the law? 'Be holy, for I am holy'. If the Reformed view is right, then it follows that since believers must be holy because

---

[20] Who were, of course, in the new covenant.
[21] See the next chapter for more on the way to interpret the Old Testament. Heb. 4:1-10 uses the sabbath as a paradigm for believers.

God in the law told the Jews they had to be holy, then it follows that *that very law therefore is binding on believers as their rule*. Will the advocates of Calvin's third use of the law call upon this passage in 1 Peter for support? I doubt it. Although Peter quoted from the law, he did not quote from that part of the law which Reformed writers like to say is binding upon the saints. The fact is, turning to Leviticus, the apostle quoted from a passage (Lev. 11:1-47, especially verses 44-45) which commanded the Jews as to what kind of animals, fish, reptiles and insects they could or could not eat. He also quoted from another passage (Lev. 19:1-37, especially verse 2) which commanded the Jews to keep the fifth commandment; to keep the sabbaths (note the plural, reader; it was *all* the sabbaths they had to keep); to keep the second commandment; and to keep listed regulations for eating the sacrifices, reaping at harvest time, and so on. And he quoted from yet another passage (Lev. 20:1-27, especially verse 7) which commanded the Jews to stone idolaters, to execute all who cursed a parent or committed adultery, and so on. Is *this* law binding upon believers? Is it authoritative over them in every minute detail?

Of course not! It is the principle which counts. *As* the Jews had to be holy because God is holy, *so* believers must be holy. But this is not to say that the law, which God imposed upon the Jews, now forms the rule for believers! Rather, it serves as an illustration, exemplar or paradigm: *as* God never changes, and is always holy, and always requires holiness in his people, *so* believers must be holy. As I have shown more than once, this is the vital principle and demand. *As* God has forgiven his people, *so* they must forgive (Eph. 4:32). 'As... so' is the key here. Compare also Matthew 18:23-35.

For another instance of the use of the law in this way, see Romans 12:19-21, where believers are instructed: 'Beloved, do not avenge yourselves, but rather give place to wrath'. Why? 'For it is written'. What is written? 'Vengeance is mine, I will repay'. So says the Lord (Rom. 12:19; see also 1 Thess. 4:6; Heb. 10:30). But, reader, *where* did the Lord say this? In the law. Ah! but, I ask every Reformed reader, in which of your three categories of the law did God put it? You will not find it in what you like to call 'the moral law'! The original you will find in Deuteronomy 32:35, among the last words of Moses to the Jews before his death. Does *this* constitute the believer's rule?

The fact is, the New Testament is its own interpreter in all these matters: 'Whatever things were written before were written for our learning' (Rom. 15:4), and 'these things became our examples... All these things happened to [the Jews] as examples, and they were written for our admonition, upon whom the ends of the ages have come' (1 Cor. 10:6,11). 'Whatever things'! In short: 'All Scripture is given by inspiration of God [better, God-breathed, God breathed them out], and is profitable for doctrine, for reproof, for correction, for instruction [training] in righteousness' (2 Tim. 3:16). 'All Scripture'! But this is a far cry from asserting – as the Reformed want to assert – that what they call 'the moral law' is binding on believers as their rule of life. I say again, it is 'whatever things, all these things, all Scripture', not just the ten commandments. The Old Testament does not give us all we need. If it does, why the New Testament?

In saying this, I do not say believers may be less holy than the Jews. Far from it: 'Unless your righteousness exceeds the righteousness of the scribes and Pharisees, you will by no means enter the kingdom of heaven'. And Jesus spelled out what he meant: 'You have heard that it was said to those of old... But I say to you...' (Matt. 5:20-22). If you have any suspicion that I am teaching believers to be lawless, reader, I ask you to re-read the previous chapter.

Nor am I saying a word against the law. Paul never argues that 'the Mosaic law is a bad thing'. Quite the opposite! But the fact is the time of the law of Moses is over. It has had its day. No doubt the child-custodian was good for the child (Gal. 3:24; 4:1-2), but hardly appropriate for a grown man! The law is not the norm of the Christian life. The law must be viewed through the new covenant.[22] While the law still has relevance for the believer, it is not Moses but Christ who is his people's lawgiver (Deut. 18:15-19; John 5:46-47; Heb. 3:5-6). The believer reads Moses, and gains from him, but it is Christ, the one of whom Moses prophesied, the one who fulfilled the law of Moses, whom believers are under. Christ is Lord, even of Moses. This is how and why Paul speaks as he does in 1 Corinthians 9:20-21. And he speaks for all believers everywhere and at all times. It is Christ, not Moses, who is his people's lawgiver.

In short, while the New Testament makes occasional use of the law of Moses in order to illustrate the law of Christ, this does not mean that believers are under the law of Moses as their rule of life.

Objection 4: If believers are not under the law of Moses, why did James say that believers who keep 'the perfect law of liberty' will be blessed? and why did he say that believers will be judged by that law?

In other words, what of James 1:25 and 2:8-13? Do these passages not teach that the believer is under the law of Moses as the rule of life? This is what James wrote:

He who looks into the perfect law of liberty and continues in it, and is not a forgetful hearer but a doer of the work, this one will be blessed in what he does... If you really fulfil the royal law according to the scripture: 'You shall love your neighbour as yourself', you do well; but if you show partiality, you commit sin, and are convicted by the law as transgressors. For whoever shall keep the whole law, and yet stumble in one point, he is guilty of all. For he who said: 'Do not commit adultery', also said: 'Do not murder'. Now if you do not commit adultery, but you do murder, you have become a transgressor of the law. So speak and so do as those who will be judged by the law of liberty. For judgement is without mercy to the one who has shown no mercy. Mercy triumphs over judgement.

Here we have yet another quotation of Leviticus 19:18, and the call for its fulfilment in the life of the believer. This serves as an important link with what has gone before, and, moreover, since they are relevant here, and set the tone for the present discussion, I refer you, reader, to the remarks I made earlier.[23]

What is 'the law of liberty'? Unless we get this right, we shall be all at sea. Just because we meet the word 'law', we must not assume that James was referring to the Mosaic law, nor the ten commandments in particular. Here, once again, we often run smack into sloppy exegesis. 'The law of liberty' cannot possibly be the law of Moses – it could never be called *that* – which was anything but a law of *liberty*. Words and phrases such as curse, bondage, child-custodian, locked up, and slavery are biblically associated with Moses' law. And, as before, the quotation from Leviticus 19:18 (Jas.

---

[22] For the Anabaptist position on this, and their citation of various laws no longer applicable to believers, see chapter 6 with extracts.

[23] See above p286.

2:8) is sufficient to scotch this idea that the law here is the ten commandments. But, as I have indicated, it does more than this. It raises the discussion to a higher plane. As I have argued, with the apostolic use of Leviticus 19:18, following on from Christ's use of it, we are firmly in the realm of Christ, not Moses, as lawgiver. Although the law of Moses plays its part in the believer's life, it is not the believer's perfect and entire rule, and certainly not his rule of *liberty*. Freedom is never associated with the law of Moses, but with Christ: 'For freedom [he, Christ] has made us free' (Gal. 5:1, footnote). We have to 'stand fast... in the liberty by which Christ has made us free' (Gal. 5:1). 'Law' and 'freedom' are joined only by Christ. 'If the Son makes you free, you shall be free indeed' (John 8:36). (See also John 8:31-32; Rom. 6:18,22; 8:21; 1 Cor. 7:22; 2 Cor. 3:17; Gal. 4:31; 5:13; 1 Pet. 2:16).[24]

In any case, as the context makes clear, James 1:18-25 is speaking of 'the word', the Scriptures: 'He brought us forth by the word of truth... Receive with meekness the implanted word, which is able to save your souls. But be doers of the word, and not hearers only, deceiving yourselves. For if anyone is a hearer of the word and not a doer, he is like a man observing his natural face in a mirror; for he observes himself, goes away, and immediately forgets what kind of man he was. But he who looks into the perfect law of liberty and continues in it, and is not a forgetful hearer but a doer of the work, this one will be blessed in what he does'. There is no break of thought between verses 24 and 25. 'The perfect law of liberty' is not the law of Moses. It is something far bigger. It is the word 'which is able to save', the Scriptures. We are back in the realm of 2 Timothy 3:16-17 once again. The 'law of liberty' is the 'word of truth', the word by which God regenerates sinners, 'the faith of our Lord Jesus Christ', the saving word (Jas. 1:18,21), the gospel. James 1:25 must not be treated out of context, in isolation.

What is more, in James 2:8-13, we have a contrast between the law of liberty and the law of Moses. James, having referred to what he called 'the royal law according to the Scripture' (Jas. 2:8), which is Leviticus 19:18 in the hands of Christ,[25] immediately moved to another law – which he called 'the law' (Jas. 2:9,11), 'the whole law' (Jas. 2:10), making reference to some of the ten commandments, noting how God, in the law of Moses, had demanded absolute and perfect obedience to every commandment, condemning the least transgression. Turning to his readers, James said: 'So speak and so do as those who will be judged by the law of liberty' (Jas. 2:12). He did not say, 'as those who will be judged by "the law", or by "the law of Moses", or by "*this* law"'. This is important. It must not be missed. If he had used any of these phrases, James would in the context have been referring to the law of Moses, but by calling it 'the law of liberty', he was distinguishing it from the law of Moses. He was making a contrast with the law of Moses. He was speaking of another law, the 'royal law', the fulfilment of Leviticus 19:18 (Rom. 13:9; Gal. 5:14), which can be none other than 'the law of Christ' (Gal. 6:2), 'this rule' by which the Israel of God must walk (Gal. 6:16; Phil. 3:16), 'the law towards Christ' or 'Christ's law' (1 Cor. 9:21), 'the law of faith' (Rom. 3:27),[26] 'the law of the Spirit of life in Christ Jesus' (Rom. 8:2), the gospel. *This* is the law by which believers must live and by which they will be judged; not merely the ten

---

[24] See chapters 9 and 10, for instance.
[25] Could the 'royal' have any reference to the law of Christ *the King*?
[26] 'Law' in Rom. 3:27 could aptly be translated 'rule'. In other words, 'the rule of faith'.

commandments. *This* is the easy yoke and light burden which Christ enables his people to delight in, that law which encompasses the entire word of God, and therefore includes and encapsulates the ten commandments and all the Mosaic law as part of Scripture, but that law *as interpreted and applied by Christ and the apostles in the new covenant.*[27]

As a consequence, these verses in James, far from proving that the law of Moses is a perfect rule for believers, do the very opposite. They prove that the complete word, especially the gospel, the law of Christ, by the power of the Holy Spirit, is 'the perfect law of liberty'. The gospel is the law of liberty because it shows the way to true liberty, true freedom, the freedom from sin, the Mosaic law, God's wrath, and death, through Christ (John 8:31-32,36). It not only *shows* it; it *brings* it! Christ's law is perfect freedom. It is the perfect law of liberty, governing 'the Lord's freedman' (1 Cor. 7:22) through love and gratitude (Rom. 12:1; Tit. 2:11-12). The motives of the gospel are mercy and grace, not fear. The obedience of the gospel is an obedience performed out of gratitude or thankfulness, not fear. Believers have the Spirit, the Spirit of liberty, the one who makes them free, and enables them to serve God gladly and freely. Because it contains within it spirit and life, coming with and by the Holy Spirit, the law of Christ is, therefore, rightly called 'the perfect law of liberty'. *That* law is perfect, and it does bring liberty for the believer. And it is *that* law which makes believers more and more like Christ, holy and blameless before God. And this is the law by which believers must live, and by which they will be judged.

This objection, therefore, falls to the ground.

Objection 5: If believers are not under the law of Moses, why did Paul say that 'keeping the commandments of God is what matters' (1 Cor. 7:19)?

Yes, it is true, Paul did say that, for a believer, 'keeping the commandments of God is what matters' (1 Cor. 7:19). But *what* commands? It is simplistic – and wrong – to say that this means 'keeping the law of Moses'; and even more, to say it is the ten commandments. The context makes this abundantly plain. 'Circumcision is nothing' (1 Cor. 7:19), said Paul, and this, of course, is fatal to the view that believers are under the law, since circumcision is part of the law (John 7:19,22; Rom. 2:25; Gal. 5:3). How could Paul require believers to keep Moses' law as a perfect rule, yet call part of it 'nothing'?

What is more, if the ten commandments comprise the believer's perfect rule, why did Paul issue a command in the immediate context of this verse? Why did Paul, speaking of a believer, saying that he should keep the station of life he had when he was called by grace (1 Cor. 7:17-24), declare: 'This is the rule I lay down in all the churches' (1 Cor. 7:17, NIV)? '*I* lay down'? I thought the ten commandments are supposed to be the believer's *perfect* rule. When is 'perfect' not perfect? Evidently, that 'perfect' rule lacked something here. Perhaps Paul was simply restating one of the ten commandments? If so, which? What is more, if he was restating or explaining one of the ten commandments, could he really have claimed he was laying something down? Surely, he *was* saying something entirely new, wasn't he? He was laying down a new rule, wasn't he? The answers are obvious. Well, then, if the apostle was laying down a

---

[27] See the next chapter for more on this vital qualification.

rule which is not covered by the ten commandments – and, make no mistake, that is precisely what he was doing – how can verse 19 mean that *all* that counts is that believers should keep the ten commandments? How can the ten commandments be *the perfect* rule?

So what is this 'keeping the commandments of God'? What did Paul mean? Paul was laying down a principle for believers; in this case, concerning marriage, and the station in life in which they found themselves (1 Cor. 7:1-24). He told them it does not matter what they were before they were converted – Jew or Gentile, slave or free – trying to change their situation or background is irrelevant: 'Keeping the commandments of God is what matters'. In short: 'Obey Scripture! Do what God tells you. Get on with living the spiritual life in obedience to his word'. This is what Paul was saying. God's word? Yes, indeed. All of it! And, of course, he was including in this the very things he was teaching at that very time. In other words, Paul was telling believers they must keep the law of Christ. He was speaking of 'obedience to the faith' (Acts 6:7; Rom. 1:5; 6:17; 16:25-26), the 'law [or rule] of faith' (Rom. 3:27). He was telling the Corinthians that sanctification is the proof of justification. It is the teaching of James 2:14-26; namely, 'faith without works is dead'. A believer shows his faith by his works. It is impossible to show faith without works. 'Keeping the commandments of God is what matters' (1 Cor. 7:19), not rites and ceremonies, not trying to rewrite one's history – especially over the matter of circumcision. 'For in Christ Jesus, neither circumcision nor uncircumcision avails anything, but faith working through love' (Gal. 5:6). Paul, within a few verses within the same letter, reiterated the point: 'For in Christ Jesus, neither circumcision nor uncircumcision avails anything, but a new creation. And as many as walk according to this rule, peace and mercy be upon them, and upon the Israel of God' (Gal. 6:15-16).

Above all, linking 1 Corinthians 7:19 with Galatians 6:15-16, just quoted, we see a definite and clear connection between the believer's new creation and keeping the commandments of God. Paul was writing to the called, the redeemed (1 Cor. 7:17-24). As before, reader, notice the eschatological aspect of all this. Paul, having dismissed a principal rite of the old age – circumcision – stressed the keeping of the commandments on the basis of the new creation, the new covenant. It would seem incongruous to say the least, therefore, if he were, in the same breath, to tell believers to keep the commands of the old order. Paul was talking about the law of Christ, not the law of Moses.[28]

This objection, therefore, falls to the ground.

Objection 6: If believers are not under the law of Moses, why are they told that they know God only if they keep his commandments?

This objection is the same as the previous. It is based on 1 John 2:3-5; 5:2-3, and similar passages, which tell us 'we know that we know him, if we keep his commandments'. I quoted several such passages in chapter 16 when speaking of the law of Christ. For instance: 'If you love me, keep my commandments' (John 14:15). 'He who has my commandments and keeps them, it is he who loves me' (John 14:21).

---

[28] As I note before, the believer's sanctification is one aspect of Rom. 3:31.

'You are my friends if you do whatever I command you' (John 15:14). And so on. As for 1 John, consider 1 John 2:2-8; 3:22-24; 4:21; 5:2-3.

The explanation is patent: these passages all speak of the law of Christ. All of them! We are talking about Christ's commands, 'his commandments', 'as he gave us commandment' (1 John 3:23). None of them speak of the law of Moses.[29] None of them! They tell us, yet again, that the evidence of saving faith is the obedience of faith, obedience to the commandments of Christ, submission to Christ's rule.

Consider the following: 'The dragon was enraged with the woman, and he went to make war with the rest of her offspring, who keep the commandments of God and have the testimony of Jesus Christ' (Rev. 12:17). 'Here is the patience of the saints; here are those who keep the commandments of God and the faith of Jesus' (Rev. 14:12). These commandments are not to be limited to the ten commandments. Why not? Because we know that John 'bore witness to the word of God, and to the testimony of Jesus Christ' (Rev. 1:2), not simply to the ten commandments. That is why he was in exile on Patmos: 'I, John, both your brother and companion in the tribulation and kingdom and patience of Jesus Christ, was on the island that is called Patmos for the word of God and for the testimony of Jesus Christ' (Rev. 1:9). This is why the martyrs had been slain: 'I saw under the altar the souls of those who had been slain for the word of God and for the testimony which they held... I saw the souls of those who had been beheaded for their witness to Jesus and for the word of God' (Rev. 6:9; 20:4). 'Here is the patience of the saints', then. It is the keeping of all God's commandments – the old-covenant commandments as nuanced through Christ, and the new-covenant commands directly – the entire word of God, especially in connection with the Lord Jesus Christ; in a nutshell, 'the law of Christ'. The rule for believers, as before, is not the law of Moses, but the law of Christ.

As I indicated at the start of the chapter, I want to answer seven objections which are raised against the claim that the law of Moses is not the rule for believers. The seventh objection – to do with the Old Testament prophecy of the new covenant – demands a chapter of its own to do it justice. I now turn to it.

---

[29] See chapter 16 p228 for my comments on 1 John 2:7 concerning 'the old commandment is the word which you heard from the beginning'.

Chapter 18

The Believer's Rule:
The Seventh Objection

The objection: if believers are not under the law of Moses, why is the law written on their hearts in the new covenant? – 1 Peter 1:8-12 – a vital point – an objection (Eph. 3:1-6) – Jeremiah 31:31-34 – 'the Israel of God' (Gal. 6:16) – conclusion

Calvin's third use of the law is wrong. The law of Moses is not the believer's rule. In this chapter, I look at the seventh and most important objection to this claim. Far from demolishing the case, however, it confirms it. Indeed, it is its strongest support.[1]

Objection 7: If believers are not under the law of Moses, why is the law written on their hearts in the new covenant?

And the law *is* written on a believer's heart in the new covenant, written by the Spirit in regeneration. The terms and promises of the new covenant, prophesied in Jeremiah 31:31-34, and set out in Hebrews 8:6-13 and 10:16-17, are these:

Behold, the days are coming, says the LORD, when I will make a new covenant with the house of Israel and with the house of Judah – not according to the covenant that I made with their fathers in the day that I took them by the hand to lead them out of the land of Egypt, my covenant which they broke, though I was a husband to them, says the LORD. But this is the covenant that I will make with the house of Israel after those days, says the LORD: I will put my law in their minds, and write it on their hearts; and I will be their God, and they shall be my people. No more shall every man teach his neighbour, and every man his brother, saying: 'Know the LORD', for they all shall know me, from the least of them to the greatest of them, says the LORD. For I will forgive their iniquity, and their sin I will remember no more.

How should we interpret and apply such prophecies? What are the general principles? Specifically, of what time was Jeremiah speaking? To whom does this prophecy apply? And to what law does it refer?

As to the time in question, in the first instance, of course, Jeremiah was speaking to the people of his own day; his words had relevance for them in their particular circumstances. But *that* does not exhaust the import of the passage – not by a long chalk. Jeremiah was clearly speaking of what he called 'the days [which] are coming', 'after those days'. What 'days' are these?

Next, he addressed 'the house of Israel and... the house of Judah', saying God would make 'a new covenant' with *them* in those 'days'. Of whom was he speaking? There are two main views. Some think he was speaking of the spiritual blessing of national Israel at the end of the gospel age; namely, a general conversion of the Jews, and a covenant which God will make with the Jewish nation in those days. Others,

---

[1] The extracts for this chapter begin on p543.

however, think the prophecy refers to the church, the new or spiritual Israel, and speaks of the new covenant with every child of God throughout this gospel age. Some believe both.

Then there is the 'law' of which Jeremiah prophesied. In Jeremiah's day, of course, 'the law' was the entire law of Moses, just as 'Israel and Judah' in Jeremiah's day meant 'the nation of Israel'. But Jeremiah was a prophet, and his words were a prophecy. What does 'the law' mean in the days of which he was speaking, the days of this new covenant? *That* is the question. As above, there are two main views, dividing in precisely the same way as over the first question. Many think Jeremiah's prophetic use of 'law' refers to the law of Moses, the ten commandments in particular; others think it is the law of Christ. But there is a great deal of inconsistency. As I will show, many want to regard the 'Israel and Judah' as spiritual Israel, but keep the law as the law of Moses.

Whatever answers to these questions we arrive at, three things must be borne in mind.

First, we must not assume our answers, but work them out scripturally. We must not assume, for instance, that 'law' must mean the law of Moses. The 'law' does not automatically mean that. I have already dealt with this. 'The law of faith' (Rom. 3:27), 'the law of the Spirit of life in Christ Jesus' (Rom. 8:2), 'the law of liberty' (Jas. 2:12) and 'the law of Christ' (Gal. 6:2) – these are not the law of Moses! In any case, is it not possible – to put it no stronger – that a prophecy of a *new* covenant might be concerned with something other than the law of the *old* covenant, the law of Moses? We must not assume that 'the law' for this new-covenant people is the same as for the old-covenant people of God. Nor must we assume the people are the same. Might not a new covenant speak of a new law for a new people? And it is a *new* covenant: 'I will make a *new* covenant... *not according to* the covenant that I made with their fathers in the day that I took them by the hand to lead them out of the land of Egypt'.

Secondly, we must be consistent. If Jeremiah's use of 'Israel and Judah' is a prophecy of a new Israel, then a similar conclusion and 'change' of meaning must apply to 'law'. It will not do to say that one part of the passage – 'Israel and Judah' – becomes 'new' in the prophecy, but the other – 'the law' – does not. A new Israel requires a new law.

Thirdly, if it is the law of Moses that is written on the heart in the new covenant, then it is the law of Moses – all of it! It is quite wrong to whittle this down to the ten commandments, blithely assuming it is so. If it is the law of Moses, the complete law, that is written on the heart of every believer, the consequences will have to be lived with![2]

Clearly, all this raises a very important point of biblical interpretation. Did Jeremiah prophesy the law of Moses would be written on the hearts of the Jews? Or did he prophesy the law of Moses would be written on believers' hearts? Or did he prophesy the law of Christ would be written on the hearts of Jews at the end of the age? Or did he prophesy the law of Christ would be written on believers' hearts now? In other words, how should we read Old Testament prophecies such as this? That is, should we read them as predicting old or new-covenant blessings to old or new-covenant people?

---

[2] Consequences? Every believer will have heart love for, and devote heart obedience to, the sacrifices, observance of the festivals, dietary laws, and so on.

Naturally, the prophecies were delivered, in the first instance, to Jews in old-covenant language and terms, but are they to be understood in that way in the days of the new covenant?

What tools has God given us so that we might do the job – and come to a definitive, biblical answer to such questions? It is high time we looked at the key passage.

A look at 1 Peter 1:8-12

Peter, addressing believers, could say to them:

> Believing, you rejoice with joy inexpressible and full of glory, receiving the end of your faith – the salvation of your souls. Of this salvation the prophets have inquired and searched carefully, who prophesied of the grace that would come to you, searching what, or what manner of time, the Spirit of Christ who was in them was indicating when he testified beforehand the sufferings of Christ and the glories that would follow. To them it was revealed that, not to themselves, but to us they were ministering the things which now have been reported to you through those who have preached the gospel to you by the Holy Spirit sent from heaven (1 Pet. 1:8-12).

Peter speaks of 'the prophets'. We need have no doubt that he includes Jeremiah. After all, what we read here can be properly extended to '*all* the prophets', as Peter himself observed (Acts 3:24; 10:43), and as Christ himself warranted (Luke 24:27).

Note the 'now' in Peter's words: 'The prophets... prophesied of the grace that would come to you... They were ministering the things which *now* have been reported to you' – reported by the apostles to believers, he meant, of course. There is no question about what Peter has in mind when he uses 'now'. He is referring to nothing less than the eschatological change brought about by the coming of Christ and his establishment of the new covenant, as predicted by the prophets and 'reported' by the apostles. Peter is certainly not writing about some supposed millennial age *after* this present gospel age. Not at all. He is talking about 'now', the 'but now' we have met so often throughout these pages. (Compare John 15:22,24; Acts 17:30; Rom. 3:21; 5:9,11; 6:22; 7:6; 8:1; 11:30; 11:31 (second 'now' in NIV, NASB); 16:26; 1 Cor. 15:20; Gal. 4:9; Eph. 2:12-13; 5:8; Col. 1:26; Heb. 8:6; 9:26; 12:26; 1 Pet. 2:10). There is no doubt about Peter's theme, I say. It is the sufferings of Christ, the salvation which those sufferings accomplished, and the glories that have *now* followed the finished work of Christ.

We know that the prophets – all of them – prophesied of these things (Matt. 1:22-23; 5:17; 13:17; 26:56; Mark 1:2-3; Luke 1:70; 10:24; 18:31; 24:25,27,44; John 1:45; 6:45; Acts 3:18-25; 10:43; 13:40; 24:14; 26:22; 28:23; Rom. 1:2; 3:21; 16:26; 2 Pet. 3:2). Interestingly, Peter informs us about the reaction of various parties to those prophecies. Angels, who had no personal interest in these matters, who could have no personal interest in them, nevertheless were curious. The prophets themselves, who would not live to see the fulfilment of their prophecies, even so were deeply interested, inquisitive and probed into it all. So, if angels were curious, and the prophets explored these things, how much more should we, as believers – those who inherit these benefits – how much more should we be taken up with them?

What is more, *we* have the enormous advantage of living in the time of the 'but now'. 'But now' Christ has come, and because he has 'now' poured out his Spirit to teach us all truth, and to glorify the Son of God by declaring the truth to us through the apostles (John 14:26; 16:13-15; Heb. 2:3; 2 Pet. 1:16-21; 1 John 1:1-4), we 'now' have had all these things made clear to us by the Spirit through the apostles. So says Peter. We are living in the time of the 'now'. If we could ask the prophets to explain their prophecies, they would not be able to help us much. Now... if only we could ask the apostles! They would be able to give us the definitive interpretation and explanation. If only!

Well... we *can* ask them. We can ask them how *they* read the prophets. They have told us, over and over again. All we have to do is open the New Testament and let them speak! This is the key. That is to say, to understand, interpret and apply the prophets, we must submit our minds to the apostles' teaching drawn from those prophets, and their (the apostles') exposition of the Old Testament prophecies. How did the Spirit teach the apostles to understand, explain and interpret the prophets? *That* must be definitive for us.

We have no lack of material to guide us. Take the prophecy of Amos 9:11-15. Its terms are old covenant, Jewish; that is, they concern David's tabernacle, Edom, the rebuilding of the cities of Israel in Canaan to form a settlement which will never come to an end, and so on. But the new-covenant fulfilment of Amos 9:11-15 is spiritual. It has nothing to do with tabernacle, temple or vineyards. It is gospel success among the Gentiles. This may surprise some, but James told us so (Acts 15:13-18). As we have seen, the issue which brought this to a head in the early church was conflict over the way Gentiles could be saved, enter the church and go on to sanctification, and, in particular, the part to be played in all this by the law. James cited Amos, indeed 'the prophets' (Acts 15:15), to show that God had predicted the very thing which was now taking place – namely, the calling of the Gentiles by grace, without the law. Thus James showed the way to read 'the prophets'.

Isaiah 2 speaks of 'the word that Isaiah the son of Amoz saw concerning Judah and Jerusalem' (Isa. 2:1). A literalist views this as for the Jews. 'In the latter days', Zion 'shall be established on the top of the mountains, and shall be exalted above the hills' (Isa. 2:2). This must mean, to the literalist, that the physical hill of Zion will be higher than Everest! Some try to mitigate this by saying, without warrant, that it will be the highest mountain *in Israel*, which, in any case, is still considerable – Mount Hermon being over 9000 feet (3000m)! What is more, literally 'all nations shall flow to it', climbing this mountain (about 2 or 6 miles high! – depending on Hermon or Everest) to learn the ways of God (Isa. 2:2-3), 'for out of Zion shall go forth the law, and the word of the LORD from Jerusalem' (Isa. 2:3). And, to the literalist, this will apply to the Jews, 'the house of Jacob', who will say: 'Let us walk in the light of the LORD' (Isa. 2:5). So much for the literal interpretation of this Old Testament prophecy. How does the New Testament understand it?

In the first place, what is the reference to 'the latter days'? Isaiah declared these words in the Old Testament, of course, and he was referring to the age of the New Testament. 'The last days' started with the first coming of Christ (Heb. 1:1-2). Peter knew he was in 'the last days' when he preached at Pentecost (Acts 2:16-17). John could say 'it is the last hour' (1 John 2:18). 'The last days' or the 'latter times' or 'the last time' or 'these last times' all refer to the gospel age (1 Tim. 4:1; 2 Tim. 3:1; 1 Pet. 1:20; 2 Pet. 3:3; Jude 18). Christ has come 'at the end of the ages... to put away sin by the sacrifice of himself' (Heb. 9:26); 'the ends [fulfilment, NIV] of the ages have come' upon us (1 Cor. 10:11). There is no biblical warrant whatsoever for saying 'the last days' refer to the millennium, allowing such an age to exist.

Next, take these two mountains, Sinai and Zion. Sinai is mentioned by name only four times in the New Testament; twice by Stephen when speaking of the physical location where God spoke to Moses (Acts 7:30,38), and twice by Paul when speaking of the old covenant (Gal. 4:24-25). Zion is mentioned seven times in the New Testament; twice in the phrase, 'daughter of Zion', in reference to the actual Jerusalem (Matt. 21:5; John 12:15), four times with reference to the gospel or the church (Rom. 9:33; 11:26; Heb. 12:22; 1 Pet. 2:6), and once where the prophetical view of the reader will colour his interpretation (Rev. 14:1). In Heb. 12:22, 'Zion' must be figurative; the 'heavenly Jerusalem' cannot be the literal city in the Middle East. Note the contrast between Israel and the church. Israel came historically to a physical mountain; believers do not – they come to Christ. Furthermore, nobody can believe that all those addressed in the letter to the Hebrews were actually living at Zion. And yet the writer speaks of them as having come to Mount Zion – not for a fleeting visit as tourists, but permanently living there. The verse cannot refer to believers going to heaven when they die, since that is future, and the verse speaks of a past experience ('you have come') which has led to their present salvation, and its consequences. The writer to the Hebrews goes on to explain this spiritual experience they are enjoying now. The context is the new covenant (Heb. 12:24).

So when the prophets promised that in the latter days God would elevate Zion and send his law out of Zion (Isa. 2:3; Mic. 4:2), they were not speaking literally of the Mosaic law being preached in a physically raised Jerusalem; they were predicting the worldwide advance of the gospel. The fact is, they were going further. They were making an implicit contrast between the old covenant from Sinai, and the new covenant from Zion. Sinai and Zion are two very different places; the law of Sinai and the law of Zion are two very different laws. But laws they both are! Let us not run away with the idea that just because they are not under the law of Sinai, believers are lawless. They are under the law of Zion, the law of Christ (1 Cor. 9:20-21; Gal. 6:2). And what a contrast there is between Sinai and Zion (Gal. 4:24-26). The same goes for the two laws. Moses ascended Mount Sinai to receive the law and so give it to Israel; Christ reigns on Mount Zion: 'I have set my King on my holy hill of Zion' (Ps. 2:6), from where he issues his law: 'For law will proceed from me' (Isa. 51:4), and will run throughout the world: 'The coastlands shall wait for his law' (Isa. 42:4). 'The LORD is well-pleased for his righteousness' sake; he will exalt the law and make it honourable' (Isa. 42:21). Who can think that this 'law' is just the ten commandments? Or even the entire books of Moses? Surely it must be the gospel. It is, beyond question, the entire word of God, particularly in its revelation of Christ. *This* is the way to read the prophets. At this point, reader, it is worth glancing back into chapter 14, and re-reading Isaac Watts' hymn on the contrast between the law and the gospel.

The same goes for 'Jerusalem'. In Galatians 4:25-27, Paul distinguished two Jerusalems; namely, the literal, the earthly 'Jerusalem which now is, and is in bondage with her children', and the spiritual Jerusalem, the church, 'the Jerusalem above [which is] free, which is the mother of us all'. Then he quoted Isaiah 54:1, applying it to the spiritual – not the literal – Jerusalem. *This* is how to read the prophets.

Take the prophecy of Zion in Isaiah 28:16, 'Behold, I lay in Zion a stone for a foundation, a tried stone, a precious cornerstone, a sure foundation; whoever believes will not act hastily'. The New Testament use of this (Rom. 9:33; 10:11; 1 Pet. 2:6) clearly indicates that the prophet was predicting gospel times, especially Christ himself. The literal, old Zion was destroyed in AD70 (completed in AD135). The Zion in question is the heavenly Jerusalem, the church.

Such things are repeated times without number. Prophecies in the days of the old covenant were given in Jewish terms – how else could they be given? – and often given figuratively. They must be interpreted with this in mind. To read them literally when they are written figuratively, would be to make a foolish, not to say grievous, mistake. Likewise, to read them as literal for the Jews, when the New Testament applies them spiritually to the church, is another bad mistake.

For instance, a literal interpretation of Joel 2:28-32 demands remarkable astronomical signs; Acts 2:14-21 gives the right way to interpret the passage. Does anyone expect a literal fulfilment of Joel 3:1-2,12-16? If so, how deep will men be standing on one another's shoulders in the Valley of Jehoshaphat? Will the mountains of Judah literally run with wine and milk, and a fountain overflow from a newly-built temple (Joel 3:18)?

Take the prophet Hosea. A literalist must expect the establishment of a reunited and massively enlarged Israel, living in material abundance under king David (Hos. 1:10-11; 2:16-23; 3:5). The New Testament shows the proper interpretation of these passages, however; namely, the calling of Jews and Gentiles under Christ in the gospel (Rom. 9 – 11, especially Rom. 9:25-26). And the same goes for the other prophecies which the apostle quoted in writing those chapters. Paul applied Hosea 1:10 and 2:23 to the calling of the Gentiles (Rom. 9:24-26), yet Hosea 1:8-11 itself speaks only of the children of Israel. The context of Hosea 1 is the defection and judgement of Israel, and God's surprising mercy to them despite their departure from him. The same applies to Hosea 2:23. The word 'Gentiles' does not appear in Hosea, except in Hosea 8:8, and this has no connection whatsoever with their salvation. A literalist, an interpreter wedded to the old-covenant, Jewish explanation, would never see – could never see – the calling of the Gentiles in Hosea. *But Paul did.*

Take Ezekiel: surely no one expects the setting up again of David as king, his reign to last for ever – which means he as Israel's king will never die (Ezek. 34:23-31; 37:24-25) – and the rebuilding of the temple with all its apparatus of priesthood and sacrifice, including altar, offerings, feasts and holy-days (Ezek. 37:26-28; 40:1 – 46:24). And, reader, please note, with regard to these sacrifices and offerings, if literally restored, they must be for atonement for sin (Ezek. 43:13-27; 45:17-25), not merely for commemoration, as some try to say. Are we to expect Israel to have a prince again, a prince who will have sons, who will have an allotment of land, the inheritance of which is to be maintained according to property laws which distinguish between royal sons and servants (Ezek. 44:3; 45:7-8; 46:2,16-18)? Is the land yet to be reallocated according to the tribes (Ezek. 45:1-8; 47:13 – 48:29)? Who will the aliens be (Ezek. 47:21-23)? Will the tribal settlement be in rectangles (Ezek. 45:1-8; 48:1-29)? Will the observance of the new moon and the sabbath be re-established, literally (Ezek. 44:24; 45:17; 46:1-4,6,12)? Of course not! Ezekiel's prophecy is fulfilled in the new covenant. See how it is applied to the believer in 2 Corinthians 6:14 – 7:1. The same goes for Isaiah 52:7-12; 61:4-7 and 66:20-21, and so on.

Again, take Zechariah: surely no one expects a restoration of Jewish fasts and feasts (Zech. 8:19; 14:16), the setting up of the tribes again (Zech. 12:12-14),[3] and annual visits by all the peoples of the earth to Jerusalem for worship at the Feast of Tabernacles (Zech. 14:16-19), including sacrifices on the temple altar (Zech. 14:20-21), do they? If so, what do they make of: 'The Most High does not dwell in temples made with hands' (Acts 7:48)? What do they make of Hebrews 7 – 10; in particular, Heb. 9:10; 10:9,18?

God swore to his 'servant David': 'Your seed I will establish for ever, and build up your throne to all generations... His seed also I will make to endure for ever, and his throne as the days of heaven... His seed shall endure for ever, and his throne as the sun before me; it shall be established for ever like the moon' (Ps. 89:3-4,29,36-37). How are we to understand this? Was God saying the kingdom of Israel would last for ever, with one of David's descendants reigning as king? This cannot be. The kingdom, ruined, its royal line broken by the captivity (which was spoken of in the immediate context, Ps. 89:38-51), was not restored after the Jews' return. Even if it had been, still it would have fallen far short of the categorical terms of the prophecy. Nor, allowing the possibility for sake of argument, will a temporary restoration of the kingdom in the millennium – albeit lasting for a thousand years – and which will end in ruin, meet the case.

God was speaking of the *endless* reign of *Christ* – he is the seed of David (Gal. 3:16) – the endless reign of Christ over his seed, his elect (Isa. 53:10). The angel, speaking to Mary, before the birth of her son, said of Jesus: 'He will be great, and will be called the Son of the Highest; and the Lord God will give him the throne of his father David. And he will reign over the house of Jacob for ever, and of his kingdom there will be no end' (Luke 1:32-33). This is none other than that which was prophesied by Isaiah: 'Unto us a child is born, unto us a Son is given; and the government will be upon his shoulder... Of the increase of his government... there will be no end, upon the throne of David and over his kingdom, to order it and establish it with judgement and justice' (Isa. 9:6-7).

The point is that the new-covenant fulfilment and application of old-covenant language, terms, ordinances, promises, prophecies and commandments, strips out the external, Jewish element as we pass from the Old to the New Testament, since it has been abolished in the change of covenant. The writer to the Hebrews, writing nearly two thousand years ago, described these things as then being 'obsolete and growing old... ready to vanish away' (Heb. 8:13). This is how the New Testament reads the Old. It is the way *we* must do it. The application is to be spiritual and inward, not literal and external. No longer is there any concern over land, an earthly kingdom, a physical temple, physical circumcision, and so on. Such things pale into insignificance – indeed, into oblivion – in the light of the true interpretation, which is Christ and the gospel. The New Testament is its own interpreter.

Let me say just a little more on this. We must allow the New Testament to set the agenda. It is quite wrong, for instance, to read the New Testament in light of the Old. I have dealt with this at length already. We understand and appreciate the Old through

---

[3] Those who think Rev. 7:4-8 refers to the literal tribes of Israel have to explain why none from the tribe of Dan will be included, why both Joseph and Manasseh are included, but not Ephraim, and whether or not they take the 12,000 to be literal, and, therefore, exact.

the lens of the New. And there is a further point. We all have our systems of theology, and our schemes of prophecy. Very well. But, where necessary, those systems and schemes must fall before Scripture. As we have seen repeatedly, we must resist the temptation to trim Scripture to make it fit our system or scheme. Sadly, for many, the system comes first. It is a temptation to us all. But if we force Scripture to fit our scheme, not only are we committing a wrong, we are bringing grievous trouble and misery, not only to ourselves, but to those who adopt our scheme and follow the track we have marked out. We must not do it! 'Let God be true...'.

A vital point

Now for another point. And a big one, at that. In all this, the apostles did not, as is sometimes claimed, draw a *parallel* between Jews and Gentiles. I stress this. The New Testament way of using these prophecies is not by drawing a parallel; it talks about their *fulfilment*. 'Fulfilment'! This is *the* word, as we have seen time and again. Nor does the New Testament ever say it is making just a local application of these prophecies, a mere interpretation of them, leaving the fulfilment to a later age. No! It always talks in terms of 'just as it is written', 'this is what was spoken', 'this is' (Acts 2:16,25,34; 3:22; 4:11,25; 8:32; 13:33-35,40,47; 15:15; 28:25-26, for instance); that is, events in apostolic days were the fulfilment of the prophecies. By no stretch of the imagination can a temporary (albeit 1000 years long) Jewish kingdom, which will end in ruin, be greater than the everlasting kingdom of believers under the gospel. For that to happen, we should have to regard a temporary (albeit 1000 years long) Jewish kingdom, which will end in ruin, as being the *fulfilment* of the prophecies, while the gospel (which has already lasted for nearly 2000 years) is a mere local *application* of them. Fantastic nonsense!

Take Hosea, whose prophecy I referred to earlier. The prophet spoke of the northern tribes of Israel. He did not include the Gentiles in his prophecy; Paul applied this to the church. Paul was speaking of Gentiles and not Jews. Paul was *not* merely drawing an analogy.[4]

So, I say again, the New Testament writers did not, as is claimed, draw a *parallel* between Jews and Gentiles, or draw an *analogy*. Rather, rightly *interpreting* the verses, they showed us the way to read the prophets and their prophecies. Let me restate this. The New Testament way of using these prophecies is not by drawing a parallel. It talks about their fulfilment. Fulfilment, I say again. Let 'fulfilment' ring in our ears. It is vital (Matt. 5:17-18 – all of Matthew!; Acts 3:18; Rom. 8:4; Gal. 5:14; 6:2, for instance). Nor does the New Testament ever say it is making a local application of these prophecies, a mere *interpretation* of them, leaving the *fulfilment* to a later age. No! It always talks in terms of 'just as it is written'; that is, events in apostolic days were the *fulfilment* of the prophecies. Which is? When the Old Testament predicts a renewed Israel and the expansion of the kingdom, it is, in fact, predicting Christ, the gospel and the church. And in so doing, the apostles gave us the definitive way to

---

[4] But what about his use (Rom. 10:20-21) of Isa. 65:1-2? If Isaiah was speaking of Israel, once again we have an Old Testament promise of blessing for Israel (Isa. 65:1) fulfilled in the church. Yet if, in fact, in Isa. 65:1, the prophet was speaking about the Gentiles, but, in Isa. 65:2, was speaking about Israel – as I think – then no explanation of Paul's use of the passage is required. In 1 Pet. 2:10, Peter applied Hos. 1:10; 2:23 in the same way as Paul in Rom. 9:25-26, which seems to suggest that Hos. 1:10; 2:23 were a kind of 'proof-texts' in New Testament times.

understand the Old Testament in this matter. We know the apostles set out God's final revelation, his last word, in Christ. As a consequence, the key with which the apostles unlocked and applied the Old Testament must be our key also. And, bear in mind, never once do we come across any evidence of apostolic practice to the contrary.

What I am saying is sometimes dismissed with the pejorative, 'Replacement Theology'! Replacing what with what? Replacing Israel by the church. Well, if it is a 'replacement', who did the replacing? *I* didn't! The writers of the New Testament did it – men who were led into all truth! I am simply repeating and enforcing their words. For my part, that is enough to silence all dismissive talk of 'Replacement Theology'. The apostles who could write, for instance – and this is just a sample – the words of Romans 2:28-29; 9:6-8; Galatians 3:7,9,28-29; 5:6; 6:15; Ephesians 2:11-18; Philippians 3:3; Colossians 3:11 and 1 Peter 2:9-10, have, I am convinced, made their position perfectly clear. Abuse may make a smoke screen, but Scripture shines through the fog!

Notice, once again, that all this applies to '*all* the prophets' (Luke 24:27; Acts 3:24; 10:43). In every prophet, therefore, we may find Christ and the gospel. More, in every prophet we *must* find Christ and the gospel. So much so, even before the full revelation of the new covenant, before the 'but now', Christ could speak severely to his disciples:

O foolish ones, and slow of heart to believe in all that the prophets have spoken. Ought not the Christ to have suffered these things and to enter into his glory?... These are the words which I spoke to you while I was still with you, that all things must be fulfilled which were written in the law of Moses and the prophets and the Psalms concerning me (Luke 24:25-26,44).

No wonder Christ, 'beginning at Moses and all the prophets... expounded to them in all the Scriptures the things concerning himself' (Luke 24:27). No wonder, also, that Paul, informing the Jews in Antioch in Pisidia of the atrocious sin of the Jews in Jerusalem in crucifying Christ, could put it like this: 'Those who dwell in Jerusalem, and their rulers, because they did not know' – that is, because they were ignorant, because they did not recognise (1 Cor. 2:8), because they would not recognise – 'those who dwell in Jerusalem, and their rulers, because they did not know him [Christ], nor even the voices of the prophets which are read every sabbath, have fulfilled them in condemning him' (Acts 13:27-28). Note that. The Jews should have known; they had 'the voices of the prophets which are read every sabbath'. The prophets told them what to expect – if they had had eyes to see it. And what goes for the Jews in Christ's day, goes for us today – and more so. We have the Scriptures fully revealed and completed. The 'but now' has come. More light? More responsibility!

The evidence, I submit, is overwhelming. *This* is the way to read the old covenant today; namely, to look for its spiritual fulfilment in Christ. And, at the very least, therefore, it encourages us to search for Christ in all the Scriptures: 'You search the Scriptures', or 'Search the Scriptures'; 'these are they which testify of me' (John 5:39).[5]

---

[5] I am reminded of the man who commented on a sermon he heard: 'Not enough of Christ in it for me'. 'But Christ was not mentioned in the text', came the reply. 'Wherever you are in England, you will find a road that will take you to London', the man responded. 'Every text has a way to Christ. It is the preacher's job to find it'. Spurgeon commended Robert Hawker for the

An objection

But what of Ephesians 3:1-6? Since Paul called the church 'a mystery', 'which in other ages was not made known to the sons of men', how, it is asked, could it have been revealed in the Old Testament? As a matter of fact, some go so far as to allege that the Old Testament contains no information about the church at all. Is this right? Certainly not! Scripture uses 'mystery' as a precise technical term, speaking of something which cannot be known by man unless God reveals it to him, something beyond discovery by human effort or ability (see Eph. 1:9; 6:19; Col. 1:27; 2:2; 4:3; 2 Thess. 2:7; 1 Tim. 3:9,16). It is *not* something hard to grasp, or vague, abstract or indefinite. To claim that 'the mystery' is the church, and that the church therefore was not revealed in the Old Testament, is wrong on more than one count. First, the mystery, said Paul, was not the church, but *something about the church*; namely, 'that the Gentiles should be fellow-heirs, of the same body, and partakers of [God's] promise in Christ through the gospel' (Eph. 3:6), and that God had planned this from all eternity. The mystery was not simply that Gentiles would be saved, but that in the new covenant, God in Christ would form believing Jews and Gentiles into one body, the church, breaking down the separating wall between them. *That* was the mystery. In the second place, Paul did not say that the fact that Jews and Gentiles would form one body was *totally unknown* in the Old Testament. Far from it! He said this mystery 'in other ages was not made known to the sons of men, *as it has now been revealed* by the Spirit to his holy apostles and prophets' (Eph. 3:5). As? The word means 'in the same manner as, just as, exactly like', 'in such a way as'. In other words, it had been made known before, but not to the same extent, not with the same clarity as it is under the apostles.

And this is entirely consistent with 1 Peter 1:8-12, to which I will return in a few moments. As Peter assures us, the prophets knew they were handling things they did not entirely comprehend, and it was only when the Holy Spirit made these things fully known to the apostles and the New Testament prophets – 'but now' – that men really began to understand many of the Old Testament prophecies. But it is wrong to say that the Old Testament made no mention at all of the church. The fact is, the Old Testament prophets were continually pointing men to Christ, the gospel and the church, even though the prophets themselves did not fully grasp what they were speaking about, and knew they had not grasped it.

In short, Ephesians 3:1-6 does not in the slightest militate against the claim that we must read the prophets through new-covenant eyes, and see Christ, the gospel and the church in them. Not at all. It enforces it. In light of it, we should expect to find the glories of the gospel and the church spoken of in the Old Testament, but not so clearly as in the New. None of this, of course, supports the Reformed system of ordering the affairs of the church by the Old Testament. I have fully explained my position elsewhere.[6]

I go back to the key passage, 1 Peter 1:8-12. Speaking of 'the salvation of your souls', received through faith in Christ, Peter said:

---

way he always saw Christ in the Psalms – even though, as Spurgeon said, he sometimes saw him where he was not!

[6] See my *Infant*; *Pastor*; and chapter 6 in this present volume, in particular. By claiming that Israel was the Old Testament church, covenant theologians inevitably open a Pandora's box, less the 'Elpis'.

Of this salvation the prophets have inquired and searched carefully, who prophesied of the grace that would come to you, searching what, or what manner of time, the Spirit of Christ who was in them was indicating when he testified beforehand the sufferings of Christ and the glories that would follow. To them it was revealed that, not to themselves, but to us they were ministering the things which now have been reported to you through those who have preached the gospel to you by the Holy Spirit sent from heaven (1 Pet. 1:10-12).

If we could have asked prophets: 'Of what are you prophesying when you speak of the elevation of Zion, the going forth of the law from Zion, and the worldwide effect of it?', and so on, there is no doubt as to their reply: 'There are things we do not know. We do not know the precise timing and circumstances of the events we predict (1 Pet. 1:11), but we know the suffering Messiah is coming, and following hard upon his death and as a consequence of it, unspeakable glories will come, salvation is coming, grace is coming' (1 Pet. 1:10-12). Isaiah, for instance, would have said that the coming Messiah must suffer for his people, suffer for their sins, even unto death. Nevertheless – and because of this – untold glories must follow. 'God has revealed to me', Isaiah would have said, 'that the Messiah "shall see his seed... he shall see the labour of his soul... by his knowledge my righteous servant shall justify many, for he shall bear their iniquities. Therefore I will divide him a portion with the great, and he shall divide the spoil with the strong" (Isa. 53)'. The prophets would have been unanimous: 'We will not live to see it', they would have said; 'it is for others' (1 Pet. 1:12). We are very curious about what we are speaking of, what it means, the timing of it all and how, precisely, it will come about (1 Pet. 1:10-12). Despite our partial understanding, and despite its coming only after we are dead, come it will'.[7]

There is no hint of a suggestion in the New Testament that they would have said: 'We are predicting a physical restoration of Israel, and the re-instating – indeed, the exaltation of – the old-covenant law and worship'. The truth is, it is the very opposite; 1 Peter 1:10-12 tells us they were predicting the grace which would come to the church, not the law to the Jews.[8]

Consider such passages as Luke 24:27,44-47; John 1:45; Acts 3:18,25; 7:52; 8:30-35; 26:22-23; 28:23; Romans 1:2; 3:21; 16:26; 1 Peter 1:10-12. Unless we see Christ in the Old Testament – both law and prophets – we shall never read it and them aright. 'For the testimony of Jesus is the spirit of prophecy' (Rev. 19:10). Everything in the Old Testament points forward to Christ, and everything in the New Testament is centred in him. This is the way to read the Bible. There is both a continuity and a discontinuity. To deny one or the other, or to confuse the two, is to make a grievous mistake. As Peter told the Jews: 'Those things which God foretold by the mouth of all his prophets, that the Christ would suffer, he has... fulfilled'. Moses spoke of Christ, 'yes, and all the prophets, from Samuel and those who follow, as many as have spoken, have also foretold these days' (Acts 3:18-24). How categorical – '*all* the prophets...

---

[7] This raises some interesting questions. How deeply did the disciples, for instance, probe the matter? They were surprisingly ignorant of Christ's impending suffering – even though he repeatedly warned them of it (Mark 9:31-32; 10:33-34; Luke 9:22,44-45; 12:50; 18:31-34; 22:15-23; 24:7,25-26). The same goes for the resurrection. It was only after the resurrection and Pentecost that things fell into place (John 2:19-22; 12:16; 14:26; John 20:9; Luke 24:1-8,44-49). See note immediately following.

[8] Following on from the previous note, the prophets had got closer to the meaning than the disciples – let alone the Jews – in Christ's time (Luke 24:21; Acts 1:6-8).

have... foretold *these* days'. Yet so many claim to see a restoration of a national Israel near the end of this age – or after it – in almost 'all' if not 'all the prophets'![9]

Note the words, 'not to themselves, but *to us* they were ministering' (1 Pet. 1:12); *to us*, that is, to believers, in this gospel age. *This* was revealed to the prophets. They knew *that* much. I concede that they could not have gone so far as to say something like: 'The law has been added... till the Seed shall come... The law has been put in charge as our child-custodian until the coming of Christ' (compare Gal. 3:19,24) – that had to wait for the 'but now' of Christ, followed by the outpouring of the Spirit on the apostles. Principally, of course, it had to wait until God revealed it to his people through Paul, writing to the Galatians. Even so, the prophets did know that they were ministering to us. And, the fact remains, *we have* entered into the promised glories, and done so *now*.

Further, while many people will allow that the prophets spoke of Christ in terms of his suffering, note Peter's assertion that the Spirit, through the prophets, 'testified beforehand the sufferings of Christ *and the glories that would follow*' (1 Pet. 1:11). I acknowledge that these glories will culminate in the second coming of Christ and the ushering in of the eternal state (1 Pet. 1:4-5,13), but they are by no means confined to that day. Peter could say that 'God... raised [Christ] from the dead and gave him glory' (1 Pet. 1:21). The glories of which Peter spoke – and of which the prophets testified – are nothing less than the glories of the new covenant. As I have pointed out, to say that the saints *will* 'rejoice with joy inexpressible and full of glory', and leave it there, is sadly to miss the point. The truth is, 'though now you do not see him [Christ, that is], yet believing, you rejoice with joy inexpressible and full of glory' (1 Pet. 1:8). In other words, while it is true that the saints *will* rejoice in the age of the new heavens and the new earth, the wonder of the gospel – the wonder of the new covenant – the wonder of the grace Christ has brought in, even now, by his sufferings – is that the saints rejoice *now*, at this very time, despite their grief through 'various trials' (1 Pet. 1:6). This is a vital part of 'the glories that would follow'. It is not at all surprising, therefore, to hear Christ explaining that the prophets – who realised they were handling something very wonderful – 'desired to see what you see, and did not see it, and to hear what you hear, and did not hear it' (Matt. 13:17; Luke 10:24). 'These all died in faith, not having received the promises, but having seen them afar off were assured of them, embraced them' (Heb. 11:13). This 'not having received the promises', however, does not apply to us! In the new covenant, it is to those of us who are believers – 'upon whom the ends of the ages have come' (1 Cor. 10:11) – that these things belong. They are ours. We *have* received the fulfilment of these promises.

Take Peter's sermon after the miraculous healing of the cripple (Acts 3:11-26). The apostle was explicit. This miracle, he said, is part of that which 'God foretold by the mouth of all his prophets... Yes, and all the prophets... as many as have spoken, have... foretold these days' (Acts 3:18,24). And what events were unfolded in 'these days', of which Peter was speaking? The sufferings and resurrection of Christ (Acts 3:13-18). But not only that! Why, the very context tells us what the apostle was referring to. He was making proper capital out of the miracle they had all just witnessed. The prophets foretold that, too! Oh yes, said Peter, the prophets foretold these days of suffering. But, in addition, notice how he opens his sermon: 'Men of Israel, why do you marvel at

---

[9] I do not think the present state of Israel, founded in May 1948, remotely fulfils the prophecies.

this?... The God of Abraham, Isaac and Jacob, the God of our fathers, glorified his servant Jesus, whom you delivered up and denied...' (Acts 3:12-13). The fact is, Peter was talking about the prophets who 'testified beforehand the sufferings of Christ *and the glories that would follow*'. Here was one of the glories!

Making a proper application of this, the apostle immediately commanded the people to repent, promising them salvation – under the striking expression, 'that your sins may be blotted out, so that times of refreshing may come from the presence of the Lord' (Acts 3:19). He was, of course, addressing Jews, and making Jewish allusions. Listen to Isaiah, quoting God himself: 'I, even I, am he who blots out your transgressions for my own sake; and I will not remember your sins... I have blotted out, like a thick cloud, your transgressions, and like a cloud, your sins' (Isa. 43:25; 44:22; see also Ps. 51:1,9; Isa. 1:18; Jer. 50:20). And: 'I will pour water on him who is thirsty, and floods on the dry ground; I will pour my Spirit on your descendants, and my blessing on your offspring. They will spring up among the grass like willows by the watercourses' (Isa. 44:3-4; see also Isa. 41:17-20; Ezek. 34:26-27; Joel 3:18). Compare John 4:13-15; 6:35; 7:37. And Peter's hearers – Jews – certainly would have grasped what he what talking about. Furthermore, they would have realised that the apostle was declaring Christ to be God Almighty in human flesh.

Ah! But what about Acts 3:20-21? 'That he may send Jesus Christ... whom heaven must receive until the times of restoration of all things, which God has spoken by the mouth of all his holy prophets since the world began'. Doesn't this mean that everything Peter was saying refers not to his own time – that is, our time – but to the millennium which will be ushered in at the return of Christ?

I do not think so. Let me quote Acts 3:19-21 fully:

Repent therefore and be converted, that your sins may be blotted out, so that times of refreshing may come from the presence of the Lord, and that he may send Jesus Christ, who was preached to you before, whom heaven must receive until the times of restoration of all things, which God has spoken by the mouth of all his holy prophets since the world began.

Working on the basis that Peter *was* talking about the millennium, would somebody give me the explanation of – and connection between – his command to repent and the 'that... so that... that'? Nobody disputes, surely, that Peter was commanding his hearers to repent there and then. Surely he was also promising them that, upon their repentance, God would blot out their sins – there and then. On this basis, the first 'that' falls naturally and easily into place. Very well. Where, then, in this unbroken sentence, does the apostle leap from present experience to the millennium? At what point does he make this leap? Does it come between 'blotted out' and 'so that'? In other words, Peter commands his hearers to repent, 'so that times of refreshing may come from the presence of the Lord, and... the times of restoration' will come – come in the sense of the millennium? If so, would somebody explain to me how the repentance of sinners two thousand years ago would produce the millennium, yet to come? There is no baulking the 'that' and the 'so that'. The first part of the statement and promise leads to the second, and is instrumental in producing it. The repentance is the instrument, the means by which the blotting out, and all the rest, are produced. There is no evading this, I repeat. I must say that I am utterly at a loss to make the connection between repentance under Peter's preaching in Acts 3, and a millennium yet to come.

For my part, I believe the apostle was telling the Jews that if they repented, there and then they would receive the joys and sweets of sins forgiven. He enforced this, as I have shown, by reference to the prophets – a reference with which they would have been familiar. By the promise that God would 'send Jesus Christ', therefore, I am convinced that Peter was not speaking of the second coming of Christ, but of the first coming of Christ, and now, supremely, the preaching of the gospel, the preaching of the person and work of Christ – which he himself had just engaged in, and to which he referred in Acts 3:26: 'To you first, God, having raised up his servant Jesus, sent him to bless you, in turning away every one of you from your iniquities'. See also Isaiah 57:19; Acts 10:36; 13:32,38; Ephesians 2:17. It is at this point – when he has exhausted the implications of the 'that' and 'so that', that the apostle moves to make a declaration about Christ's return and – as the prophets foretold – the eternal glories which will then be ushered in. I have already recognised that 'the glories which follow', though they speak of this present time, will only be totally accomplished in the eternal glory.

This is what the apostle is talking of. To shunt *all* these blessings to the (supposed) millennium, is I think not only a mistake. It runs contrary to the context. And it robs believers of the glories which are now theirs – *now* theirs, I say.

'Those things which God foretold by the mouth of all his prophets, that the Christ would suffer, he has... fulfilled'. Moses spoke of Christ, 'yes, and all the prophets, from Samuel and those who follow, as many as have spoken, have also foretold these days' (Acts 3:18,22-24). 'To [Christ] all the prophets witness' (Acts 10:43). Let us, therefore, do as Philip when he was asked by the eunuch concerning Isaiah 53: 'Of whom does the prophet say this?' 'Philip... beginning at this scripture, preached Jesus to him' – and preached him for the conversion and baptism of the eunuch. In short, he preached in new-covenant terms (Acts 8:26-38).

In this regard, I find Acts 24:14 intriguing; Paul believed 'everything that agrees with the law and that is written in the prophets' (NIV), 'in accordance with the law' (NASB).[10] So do we, as he did – as fulfilled by Christ in the gospel; that is, in the new covenant. The key word is *kata*, a word very rich in meaning. Here it means 'according to'; perhaps, 'agreeably to', 'in accordance with', 'in concord with' (see also Matt. 7:12; Luke 1:70; 16:29,31; 24:27,44; John 1:45; 5:39-47; Acts 3:22-24; 10:43; 26:6,22-23; 28:23; Rom. 3:21; 1 Pet. 1:10-12). What Paul did *not* say was that he was a keeper of the *torah*, and that 'the Way' is nothing other than keeping the Mosaic law.

Having covered all that ground – but it is vital background material – we are now able to go back to where we left off, and consider the major Old Testament prophecy of the new covenant – the one which is cited by those who raise this seventh objection. In light of all that we have seen, we are now able to deal with it properly.

A look at Jeremiah 31:31-34
Let me start by retracing my steps. The law *is* written on a believer's heart in the new covenant, written by the Spirit in regeneration. The terms and promises of the new

---

[10] Notice what Paul did *not* say. He did not say: 'I do all that the law requires'. Nor did he say: 'I am bound by the law'. Nor did he say: 'The law is the perfect rule by which I live'. Above all, he did not set out Calvin's three uses of the law, especially the third! Why ever not – if he believed it? In the context, it would have utterly floored his critics. And, of course, it would have saved believers a great deal of trouble down the centuries.

covenant, prophesied in Jeremiah 31:31-34, and set out in Hebrews 8:6-13 and 10:16-17, are these:

Behold, the days are coming, says the LORD, when I will make a new covenant with the house of Israel and with the house of Judah – not according to the covenant that I made with their fathers in the day that I took them by the hand to lead them out of the land of Egypt, my covenant which they broke, though I was a husband to them, says the LORD. But this is the covenant that I will make with the house of Israel after those days, says the LORD: I will put my law in their minds, and write it on their hearts; and I will be their God, and they shall be my people. No more shall every man teach his neighbour, and every man his brother, saying: 'Know the LORD', for they all shall know me, from the least of them to the greatest of them, says the LORD. For I will forgive their iniquity, and their sin I will remember no more.

After all we have seen, we know how we should interpret this prophecy. We need be in no doubt. Jeremiah was predicting the coming of Christ and the setting up of the new covenant. God was announcing that in that new covenant, he would write his law – the law of Christ – upon the hearts of believers.

Moving from the general, to the specific, the New Testament directly quotes this prophecy, and interprets and applies it. I refer, of course, to Hebrews 7:18-19,22; 8:6-13; 9:24-28; 10:1-18. How does the writer of the letter to the Hebrews interpret this prophecy? Literally or spiritually? The literal interpretation of Jeremiah's prophecy and its context would entail the setting up of David's kingship once again (Jer. 30:9), the rebuilding of Jerusalem (Jer. 30:18; 31:38-40), its establishment for ever (Jer. 31:40), and the reinstatement and immense enlargement of the priesthood with its sacrificial ministry (Jer. 31:14; 33:17-18,21-22). Did the writer to the Hebrews speak of such things? Certainly not! That there was a physical restoration of the Jews to their land after their captivity in Babylon, I do not deny, but we are left in no doubt as to the New Testament fulfilment of Jeremiah's prophetic words; which is, the gospel, the new covenant (Heb. 8:6-13).

In a lengthy extract drawn from the prophet, and a detailed exposition of that extract, the writer to the Hebrews is explicit as to how we should read, interpret and apply Jeremiah. May I suggest, reader, that you read Hebrews 7:18-19,22; 8:6-13; 9:24-28; 10:1-18, and do so out loud? If you do, I think things will soon become exceedingly clear. Having already spoken of a change of law under the gospel, and that change a 'necessity' (Heb. 7:12), the writer to the Hebrews contrasts the new 'law' with the Mosaic law, which he called 'old', 'obsolete', and 'ready to vanish away', 'disappear' (NIV) (Heb. 8:10,13). Note how he speaks of 'now... now... now, once at the end of the ages' (Heb. 8:6; 9:24,26). Note the 'us' and 'we' (Heb. 7:19; 9:24; 10:10,15). Note the utter lack of a whiff of a suggestion that there will be another fulfilment – a greater fulfilment – of the prophecy, which will come in some future Jewish kingdom. In fact, the whole context is that the prophecy was being fulfilled there and then – even as the writer was penning his letter. It was the present experience of the early believers. And it is ours, now, as believers. The passage speaks for itself. On its own, it is conclusive.

In short, Jeremiah's prophecy of Israel and Judah (Jer. 31:31-34) is to be understood spiritually, of believers. The law of which he prophesied, and which is fulfilled in the new covenant, is not the law of Moses, but the law of Christ, the gospel. The hill of Zion, Jerusalem, spiritually, is the church (Gal. 4:24-26; Heb. 12:22-23; Rev. 14:1-5) –

which is called the *new* Jerusalem (Rev. 21:2); the temple is the church (Eph. 2:19-22; see also 1 Cor. 3:9,16; 2 Cor. 6:16; and I would include 2 Thess. 2:4).

What now, then, of the objection to the case I have made out for the believer's rule – the objection based on the fact that, in the new covenant, the law is written on believers' hearts? It is no objection at all. Right at the start of this chapter, I remarked that, properly understood, Jeremiah's prophecy is, in fact, the strongest biblical proof for the rebuttal of Calvin's third use of the law. For 'the law' in Jeremiah's prophecy, is nothing other than the law of Christ. It is not the law of Moses; no, not even limited to the Reformed view of the law – 'the moral law'. Neither Jeremiah, nor any other prophet, nor, come to that, any New Testament writer, ever used the phrase. As I have observed, they wouldn't know what it meant. The truth is, God, through Jeremiah, promised that with the coming of his Son, he would set up the new covenant and, by his Spirit, write Christ's law in the hearts of all his people.

This point is further strengthened when we consider that most intriguing of phrases, 'the Israel of God', coined by Paul in Galatians 6:16.

'The Israel of God' (Gal. 6:16)
As many as walk according to this rule, peace and mercy be upon them, and upon the Israel of God.

In chapter 16, I gave my reasons for regarding 'this rule' as the law of Christ, but I now ask: Who or what is 'the Israel of God'? The verse is unique, and presents several difficulties, punctuation – which has to be supplied – being one of them. Without getting involved in a convoluted discussion, let me say that, along with the majority, I take the punctuation as above, placing the comma after 'rule' and before 'peace'.[11] But what of 'the Israel of God'? This is the only time Paul used the phrase. Indeed, as I have said, it is unique in the whole of Scripture. What did the apostle mean by it? Above all, what of the 'and' in '*and* upon the Israel of God'? And why did Paul pen a piece of such remarkable, if not awkward, Greek? And why did he do it here – at the end of Galatians?

Let me tackle the 'and' first. When Paul said '*and* the Israel of God', was he using 'and' as 'and also'? In other words, was Paul speaking of two distinct groups – on the one hand, those who were living according to Christ's rule, *and also*, on the other, the Israel of God? If so, the Israel of God could not have been walking according to Christ's rule. Therefore, they were unbelievers; in fact, they were unbelieving Jews. But what an odd way of expressing it! 'The Israel of God', apparently, counter-balances 'as many as walk according to this rule'. This is not convincing. Quite the

---

[11] The two possibilities are: 'As many as by this rule shall walk, peace upon them and mercy, and upon the Israel of God'; in other words, 'peace' and 'mercy' both belong to 'as many as shall walk by this rule'. That is one possibility – the one I accept. Or: 'As many as by this rule shall walk, peace upon them, and mercy [and] upon the Israel of God'; in other words, 'peace' belongs to 'as many as shall walk by this rule', but 'mercy' belongs to 'the Israel of God'. That is the other – the one I reject. There is a second point; 'peace' and mercy' are in reverse order to every other occasion of their conjunction in Scripture (1 Tim. 1:2; 2 Tim. 1:2; Tit. 1:4; 2 John 3; Jude 2). The order in Gal. 6:16 is 'illogical', although it occurs in the Nineteenth Benediction in the liturgy of the synagogue, which Paul might have been using. But this does not explain the structure of Gal. 6:16.

reverse! It is hard – for me, impossible – to accept that Paul called unbelieving Jews 'the Israel of God'. Why did he not use 'the circumcised' or 'the circumcision', his usual terminology (Rom. 3:30; 4:9; 15:8; Gal. 2:7-9,12; Eph. 2:11; Tit. 1:10, for instance), and which would have aptly fitted the context? What is more, if he was speaking of unbelieving Jews, it means that Paul desired peace and mercy upon them, every bit as much as he did upon those who belong to Christ. This is unthinkable. Why would Paul wish peace and mercy for those who did not see eye to eye with him on Galatians 6:14-15, who were not believers? For their salvation, he would pray, yes (Rom. 9:1-3; 10:1), but a desire for 'peace and mercy' does not translate into a desire 'that they might be saved'. In any case, concern for the salvation of unbelieving Jews is foreign to the context, both immediate and throughout the letter. And if he was including the Judaisers in 'the Israel of God' – as he ought, if he was speaking of unbelieving Jews – I cannot see how Galatians 6:16 can be made to fit with Galatians 5:12.

Not only is it very unlikely (it is unthinkable!) that Galatians 6:16 teaches that Paul prayed for 'peace and mercy' for both believers and unbelievers, it is hard to see how the verse teaches that Paul prayed for two sorts of believers – Gentile and Jewish.[12] The idea that the people of God can be divided into Gentile believers and Jewish believers is utterly foreign to Galatians,[13] and is surely eliminated by John 10:16; 11:52; 17:20-23; Ephesians 2:11-22.[14] Paul never does such a thing. So this kind of division cannot be the meaning of 'and the Israel of God'.

The fact is, Paul was not praying for two groups at all. The 'and', *kai*, can be translated 'namely', 'even' or 'that is', and this is how it should be read here: 'Peace and mercy to all who follow this rule, even to the Israel of God' (NIV).[15] Indeed, the word is sometimes best left untranslated. The upshot is, Paul prayed that 'peace and mercy be upon them, [that is, namely, even] upon the Israel of God'. In other words, he desired peace and mercy upon all who walk according to Christ's law; that is, all believers. 'The Israel of God', therefore, is an all-encompassing term for all believers, for all – for 'as many as', whether Jews or Gentiles – for all who live according to Christ's law.

But why did Paul choose the term 'the Israel of God'? Why did he not say 'the elect', or 'the saints', or 'the church', or some such? Why did he use 'Israel'? This is the most interesting question of all. We find its answer by re-considering our parallel discussion, in chapter 16, of Paul's choice (and in the same context – and, as always, the context must be king) of the word 'law' in 'the law of Christ' (Gal. 6:2). When thinking about *that*, I asked why Paul did not use another, neutral word for 'law', saying he must have had good reason for his use of the old Jewish word. It could only

---

[12] Nor was Paul thinking of ministers, on the one hand, and private believers, on the other. I have not made up these 'explanations'. As always, they are seriously suggested by various writers.

[13] Moses, through his law, divided men, whereas Christ unites. This is a vital part of Galatians.

[14] See also Ezek. 34:23-31; 37:24-28.

[15] There is scriptural warrant for it, not least in Galatians. For instance: 'But even (*kai*) if we, or an angel from heaven, preach any other gospel to you than what we have preached to you, let him be accursed' (Gal. 1:8). 'And the rest of the Jews also played the hypocrite with [Peter], so that even (*kai*) Barnabas was carried away with their hypocrisy' (Gal. 2:13). 'Knowing that a man is not justified by the works of the law but by faith in Jesus Christ, even (*kai*) we have believed in Christ Jesus' (Gal. 2:16). 'Even (*kai*) so we' (Gal. 4:3).

have been deliberate. I called 'the law of Christ' a staggering phrase, a breathtaking paradox, and noted how intriguing was Paul's choice of such a loaded term as 'law'. I also commented on his word play over 'law'. Above all, I noted the important part played by the eschatological aspect of law and grace.

All this applies equally to Paul's use of 'Israel' here and elsewhere. His word play, for instance, is clearly at work in his astounding statement that 'they are not all Israel who are of Israel' (Rom. 9:6). At once the spotlight shines upon 'Israel'. Paul, there can be no question of it, meant his readers to sit up and take notice. We know that 'Israel', as a word, had enormous resonance for the Hebrew people. It was peculiarly their own name, their self-designation as the covenant people of God; outsiders called them Jews. This is significant. Whenever we come across 'Israel', we have something noteworthy, something precious. 'The Israel of God' (Gal. 6:16), therefore, must be exceedingly significant; not only 'Israel', but '*the* Israel', even 'the Israel of *God*'!

Then again, it is clear that in leading up to his use of 'the Israel of God' (Gal. 6:16), Paul has had 'Israel according to the flesh' in mind. Note his emphasis on law, circumcision, flesh and boasting (Gal. 6:12-13). This is what I meant by the context. Then comes his thunderous: 'But God forbid that I should boast except in the cross of our Lord Jesus Christ, by whom the world has been crucified to me, and I to the world' (Gal. 6:14), which prepares the way for his shattering statement: 'For in Christ Jesus, neither circumcision nor uncircumcision avails anything, but a new creation' (Gal. 6:15) – an unmistakeable echo of Galatians 5:6. I say shattering, and so it is in light of the context. Paul could not have picked a more emotive topic to make his point for those tempted to go to the law – circumcision, of all things. How often he has spoken of it in this letter in one way or another (Gal. 2:3,7-9,12; 5:6,11-12; 6:12-13,15). The truth is, 'the circumcision' or 'the circumcised' was a euphemism for 'Israel' (Acts 10:45; 11:2; Rom. 3:30; 4:9,12; 15:8; Gal. 2:7-9,12; Eph. 2:11; Col. 4:11; Tit. 1:10). But circumcision, or lack of it, is of no concern, says Paul. All that matters is to be 'in Christ', to be a new creation, to boast in nothing but his cross. 'And as many as walk according to *this* rule, peace and mercy be upon them'. *They* are 'the Israel of God' (Gal. 6:16). Furthermore, in his use of 'peace and mercy', unmistakeable Jewish overtones are evident once again. As I say, Paul's readers would not have missed all this emphasis upon Israel; 'the Israel of God' would have assumed enormous significance for them. The phrase was no idle choice, one grabbed out of the air, but was deliberate, calculated to produce maximum effect.

And not the least aspect of the phrase's fascination lies in the fact that 'the Israel of God' is virtually impossible to express in Hebrew. It is entirely a New Testament phrase and concept. All this indicates that Paul had a special purpose in coining[16] 'the Israel of God', every bit as much as when he coined 'the law of Christ'. As with 'law', so with 'Israel'; the significance of both lies in the eschatological period we are talking about.[17] Which Testament are we in? Which covenant are we talking about? 'The law

---

[16] As before, I deliberately use the word 'coin'.

[17] By eschatological, I do not mean some supposed restoration of national Israel in the millennium, which is utterly foreign to Galatians (and everywhere else, as far as I can see). As I have explained at large, Paul has been speaking about the eschatological 'but now'. 'Once at the end of the ages, [Christ] has appeared to put away sin by the sacrifice of himself' (Heb. 9:26). 'The ends of the ages have come' upon us (1 Cor. 10:11). 'Now', 'but now' (Rom. 3:21; 5:9,11; 6:22; 7:6; 8:1; 11:30; 11:31 (second 'now' in NIV, NASB); 16:26; see also John 15:22,24; Acts

of Moses' was for 'Israel after the flesh' (1 Cor. 10:18) in the old covenant. 'The law of Christ' is for 'the Israel of God' in the new. Both 'law' and 'Israel' have been taken over and transformed in the change of covenants. Paul, in the same context, using the two weighty Jewish words, pregnant with meaning, 'law' and 'Israel', coined two new-covenant phrases, 'the law of Christ' and 'the Israel of God'. It is a classic demonstration of how the New Testament writers (Paul in particular) use the language, rites and titles of the old-covenant people, Israel, and apply them to the new-covenant people, the church. 'Passover', 'circumcision', 'sabbath', 'altar', 'sacrifice', 'priest', 'temple', *etc.* have all come over and been transformed.[18] Likewise with 'law' and 'Israel'. The law of Christ is the new law for the new people. As the Israel of the Old Testament had its law, the law of Moses – so the Israel of the New Testament has its law, the law of Christ.

Linking this with Jeremiah's prophecy of the new covenant, we can, once again, face up to the two questions. Who are the 'Israel' and 'Judah'? What is the law? These two questions are inextricably linked through the historic change of epoch in redemption history. The law of Moses gave way to the law of Christ (Gal. 6:2), and Israel after the flesh gave way to the Israel of God (Gal. 6:16). Let me use the despised word, 'replacement'; I am not ashamed of it: 'the law of Christ' has replaced 'the law of Moses', and 'the Israel of God' has replaced 'Israel after the flesh'. There is a contrast between the 'Israel of God' and the 'Israel after the flesh' (1 Cor. 10:18) The 'Israel of God' is the spiritual Israel, the whole body of believers whether Jew or Gentile, those who are governed by this rule. On them, peace and mercy abide, since they are the true Israel of God. All this, of course, was fully determined in God's decree, accomplished by Christ, and is being applied by the sovereign Spirit.

This is confirmed by other scriptures. 'We are the circumcision, who worship God in the Spirit, rejoice in Christ Jesus, and have no confidence in the flesh' (Phil. 3:3). 'He is not a Jew who is one outwardly, nor is circumcision that which is outward in the flesh; but he is a Jew who is one inwardly; and circumcision is that of the heart, in the Spirit, not in the letter; whose praise is not from men but from God' (Rom. 2:28-29; see also Rom. 4:12; 9:6-8; Gal. 3:7,9,28-29; 5:6; 6:15). In Christ, all believers, Jew and Gentile, are 'circumcised with the circumcision made without hands, by [better, in] putting off the body of the sins of the flesh, by the circumcision of Christ' (Col. 2:11). Such are now 'a holy nation, his own special people... now the people of God' (1 Pet. 2:9-10; see also Tit. 2:14; Heb. 2:17). Note the 'now' – '*now* the people of God'. Before conversion, Gentile unbelievers 'were without Christ, being aliens from the commonwealth of Israel and strangers from the covenants of promise, having no hope and without God in the world'.[19] But after conversion, Gentile believers (and Jewish, of course) 'have been brought near by the blood of Christ' (Eph. 2:11-13). Christ has reversed all the negatives. Gentile (and Jewish) believers are in Christ, they are one body in Christ, citizens of the true Israel, they partake of the covenants of promise, have hope and God in the world. I underline, in particular, the fact that the saints are Israelites indeed (see John 1:47; Rom. 9:6). They form 'one new man', 'one body', one

---

17:30; 1 Cor. 15:20; Gal. 4:9; Eph. 2:12-13; 5:8; Col. 1:26; Heb. 8:6; 9:26; 12:26; 1 Pet. 2:10). I cannot stress too much the 'but now'.

[18] For more in this vein, see below.

[19] Jewish unbelievers, of course, although Israelites, were without Christ, and so on, but Paul is addressing Gentiles at this point.

'household', 'one 'building', one 'temple', one 'dwelling place' of and for God (Eph. 2:14-22). All believers – Jew and Gentile – are Abraham's children (Rom. 4). In truth, they are the 'children of promise' (Gal. 4:28), God's adopted children, no less (Rom. 8:14-17; Gal. 4:5-7). They are, in short, the Israel of God.

'As many as walk according to this rule, peace and mercy be upon them, and [even] upon the Israel of God', therefore, is the climax – and a fitting climax, at that – to Paul's letter to the Galatians. It is not a mere add-on. Moreover, Paul is not at this late stage introducing a new subject – such as some future blessing for the Jews. Far from it. He is summing up his letter, drawing the threads together. 'The Israel of God'! All through his letter, Paul has been working towards, not the 'Israel after the flesh', but the 'Israel of God'; 'peace and mercy be upon *them*'. And, coupled with this, of course, he has been defending his readers – stirring his readers – against the attacks of the Judaisers, showing believers that holiness is not by the law of Moses (Gal. 3:2-5), but by the law of Christ.

Galatians 6:16 is not sufficient, on its own, to come to a clear decision about the believer and the law, especially in connection with Jeremiah 31:31-34. No! For that, I can only refer you, reader, to the abundant biblical evidence I have already cited. Galatians 6:16 is only one part of this, I accept. Nevertheless, it is a part! And it is all very well to say what we *cannot* deduce from the verse, but what *was* Paul saying? After all, he used the phrase, 'the Israel of God'! He must have meant something by it! If he was not thinking of what I have said, then what was he thinking of? I contend that both parts of Jeremiah's prophecy – 'the law' and 'Israel and Judah' – are transformed by the epochal change of covenant. The parallel use of eschatological terms in Galatians and Hebrews concerning the replacement of the law by the Spirit, to my mind clearly establishes that 'the Israel of God' (Gal. 6:16) is not 'Israel after the flesh'. I do not agree with the suggestion that 'the Israel of God' are the elect Jews, not the church. Nor do I think that Justin Martyr (*c.* AD160) was the first to call the church 'the Israel of God'. I am convinced Paul used 'Israel' in this way in Galatians 6:16. And it is all of a piece with the rest of the New Testament teaching about the eschatological 'but now'.

Christ has come. It is the age of the Spirit; the age of the Mosaic law is over. No more is it Israel according to the flesh, but Israel according to the Spirit. No longer is it the bondage of Mount Sinai in Arabia, but the liberty of the spiritual Zion. The law of God is now the law of Christ.

And this, I submit, confirms the view of Jeremiah 31:31-34 which I have set out. The prophet was not speaking of the law of Moses being written on the hearts of Jews. Nor was he saying that the law of Moses would be the believer's rule under the gospel. The new covenant, of which Jeremiah prophesied, is an inward covenant, inward through the indwelling Christ, he himself being the new law, by his Spirit, 'written on the hearts' of believers. The law within the believer is nothing less than Christ living and formed within. As the apostle could declare to the Colossians: 'I became a minister according to the stewardship from God which was given to me for you, to fulfil the word of God, the mystery which has been hidden from ages and from generations, but now has been revealed to his saints. To them God willed to make known what are the riches of the glory of this mystery among the Gentiles: which is Christ in you, the hope of glory' (Col. 1:25-27).

Nor was Jeremiah the only prophet to speak of the new covenant. Take God's promise through Isaiah: 'All your children shall be taught by the LORD' (Isa. 54:13; John 6:45). Again, through Ezekiel: 'I will give them one heart, and I will put a new spirit within them, and take the stony heart out of their flesh, and give them a heart of flesh, that they may walk in my statutes and keep my judgments and do them; and they shall be my people, and I will be their God... I will sprinkle clean water on you, and you shall be clean; I will cleanse you from all your filthiness and from all your idols. I will give you a new heart and put a new spirit within you; I will take the heart of stone out of your flesh and give you a heart of flesh. I will put my Spirit within you and cause you to walk in my statutes, and you will keep my judgments and do them' (Ezek. 11:19-20; 36:25-27; see also Ezek. 16:59-63). Nor, for obvious reasons, is the doctrine of the new covenant confined to the Old Testament![20]

The *doctrine* of the new covenant (despite its relative rarity as a *phrase*) is written large throughout the entire Bible. It pervades everything; it is a major concept in Scripture. Take Isaiah 42, where God was addressing the Messiah, Christ (Matt. 3:17; 12:17-21; 17:5): 'Behold! My servant whom I uphold, my elect one in whom my soul delights' (Isa. 42:1). God commanded the people to 'sing to the LORD a *new* song', having addressed Christ thus: 'Behold, the *former* things have come to pass, and *new* things I declare; before they spring forth I tell you of them' (Isa. 42:9-10). This was a foretelling of the *new* covenant which would be established by Christ. 'Do not remember the *former* things, nor consider things of old. Behold, I will do a *new* thing' (Isa. 43:18-19; Jer. 31:22). God described this *new* thing: 'I will even make a road in the wilderness, and rivers in the desert... waters in the wilderness and rivers in the desert, to give drink to my people, my chosen' (Isa. 43:19-20), and 'a woman shall encompass a man' (Jer. 31:22), something unheard of! God assured his people that they would 'hear *new* things', things they had not known (Isa. 48:6), 'be called by a *new* name' (Isa. 62:2), and eventually live in a '*new* heavens and a *new* earth' (Isa. 65:17; 66:22). The *new* song to be sung by the elect is a repeated theme of the Psalms (Ps. 33:3; 40:3; 96:1; 98:1; 144:9; 149:1). No wonder, since God promised to 'give... a *new* heart [to] and put a *new* spirit within' his people (Ezek. 36:26; 11:19-20), fulfilling his command that they should 'get [themselves] a *new* heart and a *new* spirit' (Ezek. 18:31).[21]

When the Psalmist spoke of the godly man, and recorded that 'his delight is in the law of the LORD, and in his law he meditates day and night' (Ps. 1:2), naturally, he was thinking of the law of Moses. Of course he was, since he was living in the days of the old covenant. But as a prophet, was he saying that the believer in the age of the Spirit would delight in, and day and night meditate upon, the law of Moses? Or, as so many (mis)define the law, the ten commandments? Reader, if you are a believer, does this describe you? When you ask God: 'Open my eyes, that I may see wondrous things from your law' (Ps. 119:18), and tell him: 'Oh, how I love your law! It is my meditation all the day' (Ps. 119:97), are you thinking only – or primarily – of the Mosaic law? Or do you read, delight in and meditate upon the entire Scripture, and especially the gospel of our (your) Lord and Saviour, Jesus Christ? 'Consider *him*' (Heb. 12:3)! Surely the staunchest advocate of Calvin's third use of the law would not

---

[20] For the New Testament, see chapter 16.
[21] See chapter 16 p228 for the importance of 'new' and 'heart'.

spend *all* his time in the law, would he? Nor would he spend *more* time in the Old Testament than the New, would he? And when reading and interpreting the Old, would he not do so in terms of the New? Reader, when you cite, sing or otherwise use, say, Psalm 3:4; 5:7; 18:6; 20:2-3; 24:3; 27:4-6; 48:9,12; 50:5; 51:18-19; 54:6; 65:4; 122; 128:5; 134; 141:2, what is going through your mind? If you were to be washed up on a desert island, and could have only one leaf of Scripture, would you select Exodus 20 or Romans 8? To ask such questions is to answer them.[22]

In all this, please do not forget the vital distinction I drew when setting out the believer's rule in chapter 16. This is what I said:

When, in Scripture, we meet 'the law of God', we must ask ourselves which covenant we are talking about. If it is the old covenant, then 'the law of God' is the 'the law of Moses'. If it is the new covenant, then 'the law of God' is 'the law of Christ'.

Here is where it comes into its own.

Conclusion

What has all this to do with the objection raised against the claim that I have made – namely, that the ten commandments cannot sanctify? that the ten commandments do not form the believer's perfect rule? Everything! God demands heart obedience, heart experience, heart worship, but man cannot provide it. The good news is that God, by his grace, through Jeremiah (and others) promised that he would set up a new covenant and do this very thing, writing his new law, the law of Christ, upon his people's hearts. More than that, at the appointed time, God sent his Son into the world to establish this new covenant, to die for his people to redeem them, and to earn the gift of the Holy Spirit for them, and so write his law upon their hearts.

Thus the new-covenant man inevitably delights in obedience, and gives God heart worship and service, not a grudging conformity to irksome rules imposed from without. To any who object to my use of 'irksome', I can only suggest they re-read passages such as Acts 15:5,10,24; Galatians 2:4-5; 3:21-25; 4:21 – 5:1,13, noting words such as 'trouble', 'slavery', 'bondage', 'locked up', and 'prison' which are coupled with the law, and words such as 'freedom' and 'liberty' which are associated with the new covenant. The truth is, the believer serves God in Christ in glorious freedom. Why? How? Because God's Spirit enables the believer to *delight* in the law (the entire word of God, especially the gospel) from his heart, where the Spirit writes it (Ps. 1:2; 19:7-8; 37:31; Jer. 31:33; Rom. 7:22; Heb. 8:10; 10:16).

Take just one example. God commands his people to 'love one another fervently with a pure heart'. How can they do it? What grace and power does God give them to enable them to obey? Let the new covenant speak: 'Since you have purified your souls in obeying the truth through the Spirit in sincere love of the brethren, love one another fervently with a pure heart, having been born again, not of corruptible seed but incorruptible, through the word of God, which lives and abides for ever' (1 Pet. 1:22-23). That's how believers can do it – 'having been born again'. They can do it, they will do it, because they are regenerate, because they have the Spirit of God, because

---

[22] Believer, have you not found that you can open the New Testament anywhere and turn it into prayer without adjustment? Do you find you can do the same with, say, Deut. 28:58-68; 1 Kings 8:14-53; Ps. 18:20-24; 109:1-20? What about Isa. 58:13-14 with Ex. 35:2-3; Jer. 17:21-27?

they are 'partakers of the divine nature' (2 Pet. 1:4), and because they are newly 'created to be like God in true righteousness and holiness' (Eph. 4:24, NIV).

So, while believers are under a far more searching regime in the new covenant, far more incisive than the Jews under the old covenant, while the law of Christ is far more penetrating, far more demanding, than the law of Moses, Christ provides so much more than Moses. God demands all. God promises all. Christ accomplished all. Christ gives grace to enable his people to love and obey his law from the heart, and thus glorify God.[23]

'The law was given through Moses' – BUT – 'grace and truth came through Jesus Christ' (John 1:17).

As to this seventh objection militating against my claim that the law of Moses is not the believer's rule, the opposite is the case. It actually constitutes its greatest proof.

---

[23] In saying this, I do not imply that there were no regenerate people in the Old Testament. While, as I have pointed out (see chapter 6), the position of Old Testament believers is 'somewhat anomalous', Abraham (before the law was given), Moses (who was given the law), and David (after the law had been given), are typical of those who lived and died trusting in the coming Messiah, and are rightly counted among the men and women of faith (John 8:56; Heb. 11). The Psalmist spoke for all new-covenant people of both ages when he said: 'Oh, how I love your law!' (Ps. 119:97). 'Love' is a heart word. Throughout Psalm 119, note the connection between 'law', 'precepts', 'judgements', and so on, and such words as 'heart' or 'whole heart', 'rejoice', 'delight', 'longing', 'love', and the like. The man who prefers the law above 'thousands of shekels of gold and silver' shows us where his heart is (Matt. 6:21). See also Ps. 1:2; 40:8. The fact that there were new-covenant people living in the Old Testament, of course, is why I can quote their words! There is no difference between David and Paul: 'I delight in the law of God according to the inward man' (Rom. 7:22). As I have made clear, it is all 'the law of God', but in the old covenant it is 'the law of Moses', while in the new it is 'the law of Christ'. In saying this, of course, I am not going back on my comments on Rom. 7:14-25; I am deliberately not defining the man in question.

Conclusion

Reader, before I take my leave of you, may I address you personally?[1] You are either an unbeliever or a believer. My book has been written with the believer in mind, and most of my remarks have been made on that basis. It is, after all, a book on the believer and the law. But what if you are an unbeliever? You do not need the law. You need Christ. You need to be right with God – to be justified. The law will never justify you. Never! It can only condemn you. 'But', do I hear you say, 'I have no thought of being right with God by keeping his law. None whatsoever!' No? Perhaps not. But when I began this book, I used the word 'incipient'. I come back to it now. Many are *incipiently* seeking justification by the law. What do I mean? While some do overtly argue for justification by law-keeping, many more, who might not mention the law of God, nevertheless still hope to be right with God through their works – 'incipiently' seeking justification by law. Indeed, I know that every unbeliever is bent on a course of getting right with God, and this by works or self-effort. We meet examples of it in Scripture, and daily experience confirms it. I notice that the Jews who addressed Christ, and the Philippian jailer who addressed Paul and Silas, all had the same thing in mind: they wanted to know what they could do to be saved, to be right with God (John 6:28; Acts 16:30). 'Do'! It is ingrained in us, this love of trying to earn our way to God. Ask any man in the street, and it will not be long before he is telling you: 'I do my best!' 'Do'! In other words, works! Yes, even professed atheists, for all their confident talk, still base their hopes upon their doings and their deservings. But works will never save. Never. God is absolute in holiness, and demands perfection from us. Reader, you will never make it! So give up trying to get right with God through your works. It can't be done! Give it up, I say! Even your best works are no better than 'filthy rags' in his sight (Isa. 64:6). Moreover, even if you could live perfectly from now on, you could never atone for your sins of the past. Repent of your sins, therefore (Acts 3:19; 17:30), trust Christ, submit to Christ, obey Christ, and you will be saved (Acts 6:7; 16:31; Rom. 1:5; 16:26; Eph. 2:8-9). Christ's blood will wash away your sins (1 John 1:9), and Christ will become your righteousness (1 Cor. 1:30). Otherwise you will perish (Luke 13:3,5; John 3:16,18; Acts 13:41; 2 Thess. 2:10-12). The law of God will not save you. And if *God's* law can't save you, what hope is there for your own puny works and standards? I say it again. You do not need law. You need Christ.

And now I make a final appeal to you who are believers in our Lord Jesus Christ, you who trust him for your everlasting salvation. You know you are beyond condemnation in Christ (Rom. 8:1). *But you also know that you must be holy in your personal experience*. The grace of God which has brought you salvation has taught you it is so; godliness is essential (Tit. 2:11-14). The New Testament commands you to 'pursue... holiness, without which no one will see the Lord' (Heb. 12:14). Why? 'Unless your righteousness exceeds the righteousness of the scribes and Pharisees, you will by no means enter the kingdom of heaven' (Matt. 5:20). In Christ you are righteous, and now you must live out that righteousness day by day.

---

[1] The extracts for this chapter begin on p556.

Ah! But how to attain this godliness? *That* is the question. You have been justified by grace through faith, but how will you be sanctified? *That*, I say, is the question. In these pages I have set before you two ways. One by law, the other by grace. One by fear, the other by love. One wrong, the other right. I have tried to demolish the former, and establish the latter.

This is the choice before you. But, in truth, there is no 'choice' about it. God has revealed his mind to us in Scripture. It is our task, by his Spirit to understand that revelation and to put it into practice in our lives. So, the fundamental question is not, for example, what Calvin said or did not say on the matter, or what the Confessions state or do not state about it. The issue is, what does the Bible – the New Testament, above all – teach us about the part played by the law of Moses in the sanctification of the believer?

Right at the start, I admitted the biblical tension over the believer and the law. I am convinced that the right resolution of that tension is to get to grips with the eschatological 'but now', written so plainly across the pages of the New Testament; in other words, to realise that the believer is living in the age of the new covenant. 'But now', or its equivalent, one of the greatest of all biblical expressions, has come up time and again throughout these pages. It was bound to, since it comes up time and again across the New Testament. 'But now' must be given its due weight. The significance of the discontinuity nestled within that 'but now' cannot be overstated. The coming of Christ into the world, his redeeming work on the cross, his glorious resurrection and the consequent out-pouring of the Holy Spirit, brought the age of the law to an end, and ushered in the new covenant, the new age, the age of the Spirit, the age of the gospel.

It all starts with justification. The Scriptures could not be more clear: 'By the deeds of the law, no flesh will be justified in his sight, for by the law is the knowledge of sin. *But now* the righteousness of God apart from the law is revealed, being witnessed by the law and the prophets, even the righteousness of God, through faith in Jesus Christ, to all and on all who believe' (Rom. 3:20-22). The age of the law has gone, 'but now' the age of the Spirit has come, and the righteous demands of the law are fulfilled in the people of the new covenant. 'But now', therefore, there is no place for the law in the justification of the sinner.

But the 'but now' does not end with justification; nor must it be limited to justification. The New Testament – Paul, in particular – proves that it is utterly wrong to impose the law upon believers for sanctification. Indeed, it is only because the believer has died to the law, that he can be sanctified (Rom. 7:1-6). The New Testament, unlike Calvin, never whips believers with the law to prevent sin and produce godliness. It preaches Christ. The gospel, not the law, is both the rule and motive for the believer's sanctification. In short, sanctification is not by the law of Moses!

To say this, however, raises hackles. If we tell men such things, so it is said, we shall encourage all manner of sin. It will lead to antinomianism. It will open the flood-gates of iniquity. It will never produce godliness. Such critics are wrong. They could not be more wrong! They fly in the face of Scripture.

Listen to John. Far from producing antinomianism, publishing the grace of God in Christ is the way to sanctify a believer (1 John 1:5 – 2:2). Yes, that is what the apostle said. The more the freeness of the grace of God in Christ is exalted, the more the glories of Christ are set forth, and the more these are applied to the believer, the more the believer is moved to holiness. That is what John taught us:

This is the message which we have heard from him and declare to you... The blood of Jesus Christ his Son cleanses us from all sin. If we say that we have no sin, we deceive ourselves, and the truth is not in us. If we confess our sins, he is faithful and just to forgive us our sins and to cleanse us from all unrighteousness. If we say that we have not sinned, we make him a liar, and his word is not in us. My little children, these things I write to you, so that you may not sin. And if anyone sins, we have an advocate with the Father, Jesus Christ the righteous. And he himself is the propitiation for our sins, and not for ours only but also for the whole world.

To be sanctified, this is what we need. We need to have our minds and hearts set upon Christ. We need preaching that will set Christ before us in all his glorious grace. We need to hear, to meditate upon, to enjoy, to feel the rich freeness of our complete and utter perfection before God in and through Christ. And this is what will produce sanctification, this is what will move us to godliness to the glory of God. So says Scripture.

This doctrine – that sanctification comes by the grace of God and not the law of Moses – is feared and resented by many. And they are not averse to writing against both it and those who advocate it – doing so in the sternest of terms. Yes, it does sound absurd to tell believers that if they sin they have an advocate, and that upon their confession and repentance they will be forgiven – *and to tell them this beforehand*. Yet John states that *this* is the very way to produce godliness: 'These things I write to you, so that you may not sin'. And what are 'these things'? That 'the blood of Jesus Christ... cleanses us from all sin'; and 'if we confess our sins, he is faithful and just to forgive us our sins'; and 'if anyone sins, we have an advocate with the Father, Jesus Christ the righteous. And he himself is the propitiation for our sins'. *These* are the 'these things I write to you', says John, 'so that you may not sin'. Free grace is the spur of sanctification. No, say the critics; that's the way to produce sin. They could not be more wrong!

And 1 John 1:5 – 2:2 is not the only place where the New Testament says that to proclaim and to grasp the freeness of the grace of God in Christ is the way to sanctify a believer. It always speaks of free grace in Christ as the preventative of sin, and the producer of holiness. It asserts it over and over again. It is always holding Christ before us. And not, primarily, as an example. Overwhelmingly, Christ is held before us as the great and glorious Redeemer, the one who, in obedience to his Father, out of the love God has for sinners, because of the grace of God towards sinners, yielded his life as the blood sacrifice on the cross. Faith in this Christ and his sacrifice is not only justifying; it is sanctifying, too. Read, for example, the letter to the Romans, starting at Romans 3:21. Read the letter to the Ephesians, and John's first letter. Read Titus 2:11 – 3:8. And so on. I say it again, it is not by the preaching of law, wrath and fear, that the believer is sanctified. True, the wrath of God must be preached to believers, but even this is to rouse them to think of the love of God to them, and of all they have been freed from, and so to stir them to greater gratitude and, therefore, greater sanctification. Christ, his cross – this is the motive for sanctification. And this is what I have argued for.

Listen to Elisabeth Charles. It is all here:

Never further than thy cross,
Never higher than thy feet;
Here earth's precious things seem dross,
Here earth's bitter things grow sweet.

Gazing thus our sin we see,
Learn thy love while gazing thus,
Sin, which laid the cross on thee,
Love, which bore the cross for us.

Here we learn to serve and give,
And, rejoicing, self deny;
Here we gather love to live,
Here we gather faith to die.

Pressing onward as we can,
Still to this our hearts must tend;
Where our earliest hopes began,
There our last aspirings end.

Till amid the hosts of light,
We in thee redeemed, complete,
Through thy cross made pure and white,
Cast our crowns before thy feet.[2]

Hear Paul: 'The message of the cross is foolishness to those who are perishing, but to us who are being saved it is the power of God... We preach Christ crucified... to those who are called... Christ the power of God and the wisdom of God... I determined not to know anything among you except Jesus Christ and him crucified' (1 Cor:1:18,23-24; 2:2). Here it is: Christ and his cross. This is what Paul preached. 'Ah!' you say, 'of course – for justification. Quite!' No! Well, yes, to be sure, for justification. But look! In saying this, the apostle is writing to believers, to those who are called. He is writing to believers who are surrounded by unbelieving Jews and Greeks. He is writing to the church at Corinth – spiritually infantile, riddled with party spirit, jealousy, carnality, the cult of men, incest, internecine law-suits, marriage problems, disorder, false teaching about the resurrection, and all the rest. How is he going to set it right? Where will he begin? By setting out his stall. And what does he offer the believers? What does he preach to the believers? What does he teach the believers? What will he not be diverted from? Christ and him crucified! Yes, for justification, but here, supremely for sanctification. Paul did not say he preached the law to produce sanctification. He said he preached Christ. He said he preached nothing but Christ. He said that he was 'determined not to know anything... except Jesus Christ and him crucified' (1 Cor. 2:2; see also 1 Cor. 1:23; Gal. 3:1).

Paul wrote those words, I say again, to believers! He preached Christ to sinners for their justification, yes, but he also preached Christ to saints for their sanctification. He opened his letter by reminding the Corinthians that they are 'those who are *sanctified* in Christ Jesus' (1 Cor. 1:2). Then, right at the heart of the passage I am quoting, lies this: 'You are in Christ Jesus, who became for us wisdom from God – and

---

[2] *Christian Hymns (Old)* number 222.

righteousness and *sanctification* and redemption' (1 Cor. 1:30). Sanctification![3] The Corinthians stood in desperate need of reformation, both personal and corporate. In short, they needed to be more sanctified. What better place for the apostle to hammer the law! What better time! But what did he say to believers who needed radical improvement in practical godliness? 'I preach Christ. I will preach nothing but Christ and him crucified!'

Believer, do you need, do you want, power and wisdom to grow in grace and live for God's glory? Of course you do! Well, here it is! Look to Christ! Look to his cross! Here is 'power and wisdom'. It all comes from the cross. So said the apostle.

Fanny Crosby understood it: 'Jesus, keep me near the cross'. Sinners need to be brought to the cross to be saved. Of course! But, having come to the cross, having trusted Christ for salvation, what next? To be sanctified, do they move on from the cross, move beyond the cross, and go the law as their perfect rule? Fanny Crosby let us know what she thought: 'Jesus, keep me near the cross'. She wanted to walk day by day under its shadow. Just so! It is saints who need to be kept close to the cross, and to walk with Christ in the shadow of his cross:

> *Near the cross! O Lamb of God,*
> *Bring its scenes before me;*
> *Help me walk from day to day,*
> *With its shadows o'er me.*

> *Near the cross I'll watch and wait*
> *Hoping, trusting ever,*
> *Till I reach the golden strand,*
> *Just beyond the river.*[4]

Did Fanny have it right, or not? I have given you my opinion, reader. What do you think? She was writing as a believer, remember, and writing for believers. Her words have been sung time and again by countless believers. I have sung her hymn as a believer. And so have you. Did I mean it? Did you? Will you sing it now? Does it bring tears to your eyes? Are you not determined to live for your crucified Saviour and Lord? Then stay close to the cross!

At the risk of annoying some readers, I cannot resist quoting yet another hymn. This time by Antoinette Bourignon, translated by John Wesley. I do not wonder that Wesley brought these words into English. I, for one, am glad he did:

> *Come, Saviour, Jesus, from above!*
> *Assist me with thy heavenly grace;*
> *Empty my heart of earthly love,*
> *And for thyself prepare the place.*

> *O let thy sacred presence fill*
> *And set my longing spirit free!*
> *Which pants to have no other will,*
> *But day and night to feast on thee.*

---

[3] I repeat an earlier note. I am not going back on my remarks about the word 'sanctification' in such texts. My case does not depend on the accident of words. The context of the entire letter is progressive sanctification.
[4] *Christian Hymns (Old)* number 688.

While in this region here below,
No other good will I pursue;
I'll bid this world of noise and show,
With all its glittering snares, adieu!

That path with humble speed I'll seek,
In which my Saviour's footsteps shine;
Nor will I hear, nor will I speak,
Of any other love but thine.

Henceforth may no profane delight
Divide this consecrated soul;
Possess it thou, who hast the right,
As Lord and Master of the whole.

Wealth, honour, pleasure, and what else
This short-enduring world can give,
Tempt as ye will, my soul repels,
To Christ alone resolved to live.

Thee I can love, and thee alone,
With pure delight and inward bliss:
To know thou tak'st me for thine own,
O what a happiness is this!

Nothing on earth do I desire,
But thy pure love within my breast;
This, only this, will I require,
And freely give up all the rest.[5]

Back to the apostle. His declaration to the Corinthians was no flash in the pan. Hear Paul again, this time to the Colossians. His desire, he explained, was to 'present every man perfect in Christ Jesus. To this end I also labour', he said, 'striving according to his working which works in me mightily' (Col. 1:28-29); that is, his aim was the complete sanctification of every believer.

And this, I accept, is the desire of all who put forward the Reformed view of the law. I do not doubt it for a moment. It is mine also. The question is, how shall we reach this end? What did the apostle say and do? 'Christ... we preach, warning every man and teaching every man in all wisdom, that we may present every man perfect in Christ Jesus' (Col. 1:27-28). This, I say, was the means he used to produce the sanctification he desired. And this is the means we must use too. The NIV translation of Hebrews 3:1 sums it up: 'Therefore, holy brothers, who share in the heavenly calling, fix your thoughts on Jesus, the apostle and high priest whom we confess'. It is the only way. 'Fix your thoughts on Jesus'.

Talking of Colossians 1:27-29, reader, may I suggest that you read through the entire letter to the Colossians in one sitting? It will take only a few minutes. As you do, note how Paul tried to reach his goal – the sanctification of the saints. How many times did he mention Moses? Not once. How many times did he mention Christ? Two score and more. What arguments did he use to produce sanctification? What motives? What standard did he set? Christ! It was all from Christ, all of Christ, all to Christ, and all for

---

[5] *Christian Hymns (Old)* number 687.

Christ. What place did he see for the law of Moses? None. Rather, he put Christ before his readers. The only time he referred to the law of Moses was to say it is 'wiped out' (Col. 2:14). Christ is the motive, Christ is the means, Christ is the standard: 'As you therefore have received Christ Jesus the Lord, so walk in him... You are complete in him' (Col. 2:6,10). Neither God's law nor human regulations have any 'value against the indulgence of the flesh' (Col. 2:14-23). On the contrary: 'If [since] then you were raised with Christ, seek those things which are above, where Christ is... for you died, and your life is hidden with Christ in God' (Col. 3:1-3). 'Even as Christ forgave you, so you also must do... Whatever you do in word or deed, do all in the name of the Lord Jesus... for you serve the Lord Christ' (Col. 3:13,17,24). The faith can be summed up as 'the mystery of Christ' (Col. 4:3). In short, believers are under 'the law of Christ'.

There are two principal parts to our present experience – justification and sanctification. Both are in Christ, both are by Christ, and both are from Christ. Yes, sanctification is by the word and Spirit, the word of God and the Holy Spirit. But what do we find written all across the pages of Scripture? What is the ultimate message of the Bible, what does the Bible proclaim above everything else? Did I say 'what'? It is not 'what'! It is 'who'! It is Christ! Christ is 'in all the Scriptures' (Luke 24:27,44-46). And what did Christ promise that the Spirit would do? 'He will teach you all things, and bring to your remembrance all things that I said to you... He will guide you into all truth', yes! But what, supremely, will the Spirit do through that truth? Christ told us: 'He will glorify me, for he will take of mine, and declare it to you. All things that the Father has are mine. Therefore I said that he will take of mine and declare it to you' (John 14:26; 16:13-15). Is it not clear enough?

In the 'Introduction', I quoted the request of the Greeks to Philip: 'Sir, we wish to see Jesus' (John 12:21). I also said I wanted my book to point to Christ's person and work, and I made my purpose clear with the uncompromising title: *Christ is All*. Reader, I hope you have discovered Christ written large in these pages, and seen him as the unambiguous climax of all I say. I hope you have found that Christ is indeed all in all – and not only in these pages, but, above all, in your heart.

Take justification. Believers are in Christ (Col. 1:2), they are regenerated by Christ (Col. 2:11), they have faith in Christ (Col. 1:4), they are redeemed in Christ, through his blood (Col. 1:14), they are reconciled to God in Christ (Col. 1:21-23), they are indwelt by Christ (Col. 1:27), they know Christ (Col. 2:2), they have received Christ as Lord (Col. 2:6), they are rooted and built up in Christ (Col. 2:7), they are united to Christ (Col. 2:12), they died with Christ (Col. 2:20), they were raised with Christ (Col. 3:1), they are alive with Christ (Col. 2:13), they are hidden with Christ in God (Col. 3:3), Christ is their life (Col. 3:4), and they have everything in Christ (Col. 2:10).

Take sanctification. Believers are to serve Christ (Col. 1:7; 3:24; 4:7,12,17), to walk in Christ (Col. 2:6), to live worthy of Christ (Col. 1:10), to please Christ (Col. 1:10), to be built up in Christ (Col. 2:7), to base everything on Christ (Col. 2:8), to forgive as Christ (Col. 3:13), to let the word of Christ dwell in them richly (Col. 3:16), to give thanks to God through Christ (Col. 3:17), to make their homes fitting for Christ (Col. 3:18-21), as their employment practices (Col. 3:22). Indeed, whatever they do must be as to Christ (Col. 3:17,23), aiming for perfection in Christ (Col. 1:28), looking to Christ for their reward (Col. 3:24).

Believer, you need to be holy before God and men – to be sanctified. Therefore trust Christ, submit to Christ, obey Christ (John 13 – 15; 1 Cor. 9:21; Gal. 6:2,16; 1 John 2:3-8; 3:22-24; 4:21; 5:2). Christ is your sanctification (1 Cor. 1:30).

In short, everything is found in Christ and only in Christ (Col. 2:17). Believers 'are complete in him' (Col. 2:10). Having Christ, they have the sum and substance of it all: 'Christ is all and in all' (Col. 3:11).

CHRIST *IS* ALL

Extracts with Comments

Here are the extracts I omitted from the main text. While I have been unable to check these extracts as thoroughly as usual, and for this I apologise, nevertheless, they possess integrity and stand scrutiny. The disadvantages of supplying such 'unchecked' extracts are, I hope, heavily outweighed by allowing you, reader, access to important statements from many others. Of course, if you wish to use this material for yourself, you should verify it from the originals. I have, where necessary, modernised both spelling and grammar without altering the sense. Finally, much of what follows, I vehemently disagree with. The rest, I strongly endorse. Which is which, I hope, should be obvious. On a technical point, while in the body of the book I waited until I dealt more fully with the believer's rule before setting out my reasons for saying that the law which is written on the believer's heart is the law of Christ, in the extracts I largely assume it from the start.

I have gathered the extracts into some sort of order, but, even so, this section of my book inevitably retains the sense of a collection of disjointed observations. To try to set everything out in order would have taken me back to what I wanted to avoid in the first place; namely, including the quotations in the main body of the text!

INTRODUCTION

A salutary reminder from Lloyd-Jones before we start: 'Sanctification is always subsidiary. It is a real error to regard sanctification as an end in and of itself. But it is often regarded as such. That is... because so many approach the whole of the Christian life in a purely subjective manner – they start and end with themselves and their problems'. So what is the real end in personal experience? Glorification! 'How often do you think of your coming glorification? How often have you heard sermons on glorification? The whole emphasis [today] is on sanctification'. 'But sanctification is only a part of the process that leads to glorification'. 'We are so miserably subjective, because we fail to think of salvation in terms of what God has ultimately planned and purposed for us. His end is our glorification. Sanctification is designed to prepare us for [the] glory that awaits us' (Lloyd-Jones: *Sons* pp151-152; *Final* pp1-2,261).

Karlberg: 'Discussions on the topic of Paul and the Mosaic law continue to occupy some of the best minds in contemporary theology. The complexity of the issues involved and the importance of the subject for a biblical theology of the Old and New Testaments and for Christian dogmatics account for the current preoccupation with this topic' (Karlberg p36).

Harris: 'The law has ever furnished a subject of disputation in the church from the time of its earliest records' (Harris p36). Zaspel: The law is 'such a rewarding area of study [because of] the wide range of biblical and theological issues which it touches. The study takes the student from the many passages bristling with exegetical challenges to hermeneutical issues such as redemptive history and typology and on through theological categories such as ecclesiology, soteriology, even eschatology. But most rewarding of all, as we should expect, the study finds its culmination in the person and work of Christ. It is to this end that our study should always lead us' (Zaspel p145).

A reconstructionist would say: 'The Christian is obligated to keep the whole law of God as a pattern of sanctification and... this law is to be enforced by the civil magistrate where and how the stipulations of God so designate' (see Good p270).

As for various definitions of an antinomian, consider the following. An antinomian has been defined as one who denies 'the validity of the law in the life of the spirit: it implies a distrust of all forms or rites of worship and stated rules of morality'. Or, an antinomian is 'one who holds that the moral law is not binding on Christians... For antinomians not only the law of Moses but all human laws [are] inapplicable to the elect'. And how about this for a loose, not to say, wild definition: 'The antinomian position is that the sabbath was unknown before the giving of the law' (Adamson and Folland p81; Hill: *Liberty* pp214,217; Lee p7).

As for labels hindering rational discussion, Armstrong: 'I tried to engage in serious discussions with theologians from several sides of this historic hermeneutical divide. The response was often distressing. Labels were easy to come by in such discussions: dispensationalist, antinomian, sabbath breaker, libertine, *etc.* And from the other side I came to see more clearly-used names such as legalist, covenantalist, federalist, *etc.* The names of the living and the dead were often invoked to prove points. The atmosphere was anything but conducive to the earnest pursuit of truth with love for grace and God's covenants' (Armstrong p12).

For a typical Reformed statement, the Westminster Confession: 'God gave to Adam a law... by which he bound him, and all his posterity, to personal, entire, exact and perpetual obedience... This law, after [Adam's] fall, continued to be a perfect rule of righteousness; and, as such, was delivered by God upon Mount Sinai in ten commandments' (Westminster Confession chapter 19, sections 1 and 2).

Loose Reformed statements: 'With the fall, Adam lost his "Sunday"'. 'God who made men, has given them a law by which to live [namely, the ten commandments]... It can be summed up like this: 1. We may worship no one else but the true God... 4. We must keep Sunday as a special day, set apart for God, and complete our work on the other six days... Sin is breaking of this law'. 'The law was placed in the ark [in the tabernacle]... The law, therefore, remains for the church as the rule of life' (Lee p7; Benton p3; Malcolm Watts p21). Hulse moved straight from the Lord's day to the English Sunday to the sabbath, equating all three (Hulse: *Sunday*; *The Puritans* pp135-138). In light of this, I find it astonishing that he could say: 'Meticulous exegesis within the context of the transition of the old covenant to the new is the only way we will be certain of what is meant by the word *law*' (back-cover Bayes). Quite. But it rather depends on 'meticulous'. Judging by this sample, we shall have to re-define the word. One might say he wasn't even 'scrupulous'. The truth is, it is 'quite amusing to read in an evangelical writer that one might keep the fourth commandment by gathering round a cosy fire on the [Sunday] to read John Bunyan – when one knows that what the fourth commandment really stipulated for gathering round a fire on [Saturday] was the death penalty (Ex. 31:15; 35:2)'. 'This straight tie-up between the Old Testament sabbath and the New Testament seems to be something of a theological confidence trick. [As an example:] "On the first day of the week the Lord rose from the dead... This day is the Lord's day, and as such is the sabbath which God had instituted at creation". Hey, presto!...the trick is done... [a] sleight of hand' (Michael Eaton: *Encouragement* p9; Wesson p65). Brian Edwards: 'The Bible... doesn't use the two phrases "moral law" and "ceremonial law"'. That ought to make us pause and think! Edwards had his response ready: 'However, Jesus clearly implied a distinction between the two. In Mark 10:19, he reminded a young man of the moral law and told him to keep the ten commandments; but in John 4:21-24, he told the Samaritan woman that the ceremonial, or religious, law was coming to an end, and that soon there would be no special value in the temple at Jerusalem as a place of worship... In Gal. 3:23, [Paul] says that the ceremonial law was like a guard to make sure we didn't break free from God and make up our own rules' (Brian Edwards p7). Really? I am afraid that I fail to see that Edwards has done anything more than argue in a circle. He assumes the thing, inserts it as a gloss, and claims to have proved it! Why bother to try? Just state the assumption with confidence, and get on with it! What is more, are we to assume that Edwards thinks the Jewish ceremonial law guarded us Gentiles? Hmm!

Loose definition of a neonomian: 'To deny the necessity of the preceding work of the law in gospel preaching smacks of Dr Daniel Williams' neonomianism' (Ella: *John Gill and the Cause* p91).

'Preparation is the hidden issue in the [New England] antinomian crisis of 1637'. 'The increasing preoccupation with the conscience in the light of the law continued "till the strain proved too great, and antinomianism set in"'. 'The legalistic tendencies in early Puritanism, against which the antinomians had reacted, had been reasserted and firmly established in what came to be called neonomianism' (Miller pp53-67; Kendall p169, quoting Nuttall; K.M.Campbell p77).

McClain: 'Much of the controversy which has attended the Christian doctrine of salvation by grace has arisen about the place of the "law" in relation to the Christian believer who is saved by grace. This was true in the days of the apostles, and it has likewise been true down through the centuries of church history. This was the subject of discussion in... Acts 15... It was also the occasion of the writing of Paul's sharpest letter, the letter to the Galatian churches. This is an endless battle, but every generation in the church of God must meet the issue for itself. Various motives – some good and some evil – have raised the issue. Recently [McClain was writing in 1954] it has been raised by teachers and writers with the best of intentions. These men have been grieved and disturbed by the failure of Christian people to live the kind of life the word of God expects [demands] of those saved by grace.

As a remedy for this distressing condition in the churches, they have proposed that we turn back to the law. We have failed, they argue, because we have not laid upon the members of the churches the obligations of the "moral law". The path of success in both the Christian life and the work of the church, they say, will be found in getting the Christian people to see that they are still under the moral law of God. It is quite astonishing to find how widely this opinion is held and advocated' (McClain pp5-6). So it is. Hence my book.

In addition to the above, see Bayes p103; Bruce: *Paul* p260; Calvin: *Treatise* pp272-273; Daniel: 'Antinomianism' pp176-190; Curtis Evans pp305-325; Fairbairn: *Typology* Vol.2 pp161-163; Gadsby: *Works* pp5-6,39-41,63-65,70-71,98-100 (on the numbering of the pages in Gadsby, note that after the Preface, there is *A Memoir* with page numbers 7-144. Then follows a Preface followed by the *Works* with page numbers 5-315. I have cited this volume as Gadsby with page numbers, but not indicated the section); Gay: *Offer*; *Infant*; *Particular*; Miller pp219-225; Tow 1986, pp23-27; Witherington p341.

CHAPTER 1: WHAT IS THE LAW?

Michael Eaton: 'The term ["law"]... is used [by many] in a quite confusing manner. In [much] evangelical theology, "the law" does not refer, as it ought, to the totality of the Mosaic legislation given by God through Moses to Israel. It refers instead to a code of morality and spirituality heavily influenced by Thomas Aquinas in the 13th century... and further developed by the Reformers of the 16th century and the Puritans of the 17th' (Michael Eaton: *Encouragement* pp9,103,128; *Living* pp131-132,151).

Wells: 'When many speak of "the law" [they] have in mind only the decalogue or ten commandments. That meaning has an honoured history in the church, but as far as I can see the Scripture does not use the phrase in that way. If it does, it is a rare and uncharacteristic use' (Wells p44).

Barcellos: 'The word "law" in the New Testament may refer to the law of Moses exclusively or to the whole of the Old Testament' (Barcellos pp21,62).

John Murray: In Rom. 3:19; 7:1, 'the law assumed to be known is surely the written law of the Old Testament, particularly the Mosaic law. Paul uses "law" in this sense (Rom. 3:19; 5:13; 1 Cor. 9:8,9; 14:21,24; Gal. 3:10,19)' (Murray: *Romans* Vol.1 pp105,240).

Lloyd-Jones: 'There has been some argument as to what the term law [in Rom. 3:19] means – whether it just means the law of Moses, or whether it means the whole of the Old Testament Scriptures. There is a good deal to be said for both points of view. Personally, because of the context, I tend to agree with those who say it means the whole of the Old Testament' (Lloyd-Jones: *Righteous* pp220-221).

Fairbairn: 'There can be no doubt that the word "law" is used both in the Old and New Testament Scriptures with some latitude' (Fairbairn: *Typology* p77).

'In the vast majority of places where the word "law" appears in Paul, the reference is to the Jewish law – the law of God given to Israel through Moses, recorded in the first five books of the Bible and transmitted from generation to generation'. 'More than 90% of the occurrences of *nomos* in Paul refer to the Mosaic law' (Bruce: *Paul* pp259-260; Moo: *Romans* p145).

'Law' without the article 'may reflect rabbinical usage of the Hebrew word (*torah*) without the article, almost as if it were a proper noun'. 'Law' in Rom. 7:7-12 means 'the Mosaic law'. The best approach is 'letting the immediate context... determine the meaning [law] has in any particular Pauline statement'. 'The omission of the article is no problem for this interpretation'. 'Law' without the article means the Mosaic law. In Gal. 4:21, 'the fact the one reference has the article and the other has not has no significance for the meaning here or (elsewhere)' (Bruce: *Paul* p260; Daniel Fuller p97; Moo: *Romans* pp145-146,388; Dunn p245).

Bayes: 'It seems extremely unlikely that the apostle would use the key word with varied meaning... The law [in Romans is the law of Moses] the *torah* in its entirety' (Bayes pp88,90).

In addition to the above, Edgar H.Andrews pp80-84; Barcellos p14; Bigg: *Pursuit* p87; Bolton pp54-55; David Brown p37; Bruce: *Romans* p52; Chantry: *Righteous* pp70,80; Michael Eaton: *Encouragement* pp48-49,67-70; Daniel Fuller p80; Gill: *Body* Vol.2 pp33-34; Lloyd-Jones: *Atonement* p117; Moo: *Romans* pp247-250; Murray: *Romans* Vol.1 pp122-123; Owen: *Dominion* pp542-543; Philpot: *Meditations* p388; Reisinger: *Tablets* p35; Zens: *Studies* pp39-40.

CHAPTER 2: TO WHOM DID GOD GIVE THE LAW?

'The Jews alone have the special gift of the law'. 'The law of God... the Lord did not deliver it by the hand of Moses to be promulgated in all countries, and to be everywhere enforced; but having taken the Jewish nation under his special care, patronage and guardianship, he was pleased to be specially its legislator, and as became a wise legislator, he had special regard to [the Jewish nation] in enacting laws' (Reisinger: *Tablets* p46; Calvin: *Institutes* Vol.2 p665; Wendel p197).

Moo: 'While Paul can sometimes imply that Gentiles have some kind of relationship to the Mosaic law (*e.g.*, Rom.2:14-15; 6:14-15; 7:1-6), he also generally accepts the usual conceptualisation of first-century Judaism: Jews are, by definition, the people who "have the law" while Gentiles do not (see Rom. 2:12-13; 3:19-20; 1 Cor. 9:20-21)' (Moo: 'Galatians' p16).

A loose Reformed statement: 'The ten commandments... came to *us* on Mt Sinai' (Thackway p438, emphasis mine). They did not. 'God himself spoke them to all *Israel*'.

'The law was given to Israel... for three main reasons. First, it was intended to function as a code regulating the national life of the [nation of Israel]... Second, the law was intended, as Paul tells in Gal. 3:19-24, to prepare the Jews for the coming of Christ. This it did, says Paul, by acting as a gaoler and tutor. As gaoler, it kept men [that is, Jews] "shut up" in custody, under bondage, forced to shoulder a burden of observances which, as Peter said, "neither our fathers nor we were able to bear" (Acts 15:10; Gal. 3:23). As tutor, it made them ready for Christ by convincing them that they were sinners needing a Saviour (Gal. 3:24)... And then third, the law was meant to act as a "wall of partition" (Eph. 2:14) between Jew and Gentile, keeping the Jews from the pagan ways of surrounding nations and isolating them for the moral and spiritual training that God planned to give them'. Why did God give the law to Israel? 'The answer... lies in the unique status of the nation of Israel. With them God was entering into special, covenantal relationship' (Packer: *Understanding* pp10-11; Zaspel p147).

Luther: 'Ex. 20:1... makes it clear that even the ten commandments do not pertain [were not given] to us. For God never led us out of Egypt, but only the Jews' (quoted by Zaspel p165).

Philpot: 'It is true that the law says: "You shall love the Lord your God"... But to whom does God say it? To his own people Israel, for it is thus prefaced: "Hear, O Israel"... (Deut. 6:4). If you read the connection, you will see that God does not there call upon *all men* to love him... but he bids Israel to love the Lord *his* God (his in covenant); and then goes on to enumerate the blessings which God had given, and which he would further give by bringing him into the promised land... To take such a command as: "Love the Lord"... disassociated from all the promises connected with it, and distinct from its peculiar bearing upon the children of Israel as God's covenant people, is to confuse the whole doctrine of law and gospel. We, as Gentiles, are not under the law in the same sense as the children of Israel were. It was never made a covenant with us in the same way as it was with them, for it was revealed to them in connection with the ceremonial law,[1] under which the Gentiles never were... We are not under the law in the same way as the children of Israel were; and therefore what was commanded them in connection with peculiar promises does not apply to us as Gentiles, who have no interest as Gentiles in those peculiar [special] promises. The want of seeing this grand primary truth has caused nearly all the confusion which on this point generally pervades the creeds and confessions of churches, and catechisms, and the

---

[1] See chapter 7 where I deal with this unbiblical way of dividing the law.

writings of good men in the days of the Puritans' (Philpot: 'Three' pp58-59, emphasis his; *Dead* pp10-11).

Loose Reformed statements: 'God gave to Adam a law... by which he bound him, and all his posterity, to personal, entire, exact and perpetual obedience'. 'This law, after [Adam's] fall, continued to be a perfect rule of righteousness; and, as such, was delivered by God upon Mt Sinai in ten commandments'. 'Adam heard as much in the garden, as Israel did at Sinai, but only in fewer words and without thunder' (Westminster Confession chapter 19, sections 1 and 2; Lightfoot, quoted by Kevan: *Grace* p60; Michael Eaton: *Encouragement* p228).

Such loose statements answered: Moo: 'Not only is there nothing in Paul to suggest that Adam was given the (Mosaic) law... but it also runs counter to what is a point of crucial theological significance [that is, salvation history] for Paul [and everybody else]: that the law is not the primary locus for the fulfilment of God's purposes... but that it has a subordinate role, coming long *after* the establishment of God's salvific [saving] promise to Abraham and his heirs' (Moo: *Romans* p429, emphasis his).

Verduin: The 'lawless' men of Acts 2:23 were not 'lawless in the sense of "wicked", but "lawless" in the Jewish sense – "without the law". In other words, they were law-less... The Jews prided themselves on being law-havers, the only people to whom God had given his law; this put all the rest in the "lawless" category... [Christ was crucified by the Jews who used] the Gentiles, the without-the-law people... [as] their tool' (Verduin: *Anatomy* p71).

In Gal. 2:15, 'Jews by nature [are contrasted with] sinners of the Gentiles [or] Gentile sinners'. 'Sinners [and] Gentiles [are] here.. synonymous... those who, by definition were lawless (outside the law)'. 'The idea is that Gentiles by nature are outside the circle of the old covenant, do not have the law... and therefore are by definition (but also by nature and choice), beyond the pale – sinners'. 'Gentiles... do not have the law' (Dunn pp132-133; Witherington p173). The law, not just the so-called ceremonial law.

Edgar H.Andrews: 'As far as I can tell, the New Testament does not propagate the idea that we must necessarily preach the law to the unconverted, to bring them under conviction, before presenting the gospel. On the contrary, whenever Paul refers to the content of his evangel, he tells us that he preaches "Christ" (see, for example, Rom. 1:1-4,9,16-17; 1 Cor. 1:23; 2:2; 2 Cor. 2:12; 5:18-21; Gal. 1:16; Eph. 3:8; Phil. 1:18; Col. 1:27-28)' (Edgar H.Andrews p182).

As Heb. 7:11 makes clear, 'there cannot pass a law of covenant between God and man without a priesthood. This is here taken for granted. Indeed, further, [the inspired writer] takes it for granted that the law and priesthood are answerable one to another; such as the law is, such is the priesthood' (Gouge p501). Quite. As Israel alone was given the priesthood, Israel alone was given the law. Gouge, however, could not help dropping in the usual Reformed caveat: 'The law was given to "the nation of the children of Israel, for to them *in special* was the law given"' (Gouge p501, emphasis mine). No! It was given to them *alone*! Rom. 9:4, which Gouge cited, says nothing about the Jews *in special*; it says God gave certain things to the Jews and to the Jews *uniquely*. Did God give 'the adoption, the glory, the covenants... the service of God, and the promises' to the Jews *in special*? It was to them *only*. Gouge also thought 'the law is here in special meant the ceremonial law' (Gouge p501). I disagree. See the following note.

This law cannot be confined to the so-called ceremonial law or the law of priesthood. 'I look not on it as suited unto the design of the [inspired writer] in this place... The levitical priesthood... was appointed by God, or confirmed by law, yet it was a far greater advancement that therewith *the whole law* was given, and thereon did depend, as [the writer] declares in the next verses... *The whole law is intended...* That *whole law* was given by the voice of God out of the tabernacle whereof Aaron was the minister... So that the people in the largest sense may be said to receive *the law* under that priesthood'. Having said this, Owen undid it all: The writer 'in this place has especial respect unto the law as it was the cause and rule of religious worship', he said. He felt the writer was speaking of 'the law of commandments contained in ordinances', excluding 'the moral law' (Owen: *Hebrews* Vol.3 Part 2 pp423-425, emphasis mine). How Owen could think that at least the first three commands had nothing to say about 'religious worship' baffles me. For a more detailed examination of the mistaken Reformed divisions of the law, see chapter 7.

Anticipating what follows in the next chapter, Lloyd-Jones: 'Whereas... [the Gentiles] have never heard the law that was given by Moses, and are in no sense, therefore, "under the law", they nevertheless have a moral consciousness. And it is because they have this that they are responsible – they can be judged in terms of that moral consciousness which they possess. In that sense they are a law unto themselves. In other words, they do not come under the law of Moses but they come under this – we must not call it the law, but this kind of other law which is in terms of their moral consciousness, and which leads to a sense of responsibility' (Lloyd-Jones: *Righteous* p117).

Rom. 3:19

Bayes: 'The natural reading of [Rom. 3:19] identifies the previous catena as the law, thus equating it with the entire Hebrew Bible, and makes the point that the Jewish law addresses specifically those whose sphere of being it demarcates [that is, the Jews], whom it identifies as one subsection of "all the world", and it is read as such by most commentators' (Bayes p89).

John Murray: 'The law speaks to those who are in the law... The question arises: How extensive is this sphere of the law's application? Does its relevance apply only to those who had the Old Testament, namely, the Jews to whom the oracles had been committed (Rom. 3:2)?... There can be no question but here [Rom. 3:19] is the note of all-inclusive universality, especially in the words "the whole world". Paul includes the Gentiles who did not have the law in the sense of the Old Testament or of specially revealed law (Rom. 2:14)... This establishes the all-important consideration that although the Gentiles did not have the Old Testament law, and in that sense were without law, yet they were not outside the sphere of the judgement which the Old Testament pronounced. This is saying that the descriptions given in those passages quoted [in Rom. 3:9-18] were characteristic of the Gentiles as well as of the Jews and the corresponding judgement rested upon them to the end that they all might be without excuse and be condemned in the sight of God' (Murray: *Romans* Vol.1 pp106-107).

Let me return to an extract I have already used. Lloyd-Jones: 'There has been some argument as to what the term law [in Rom. 3:19] means – whether it just means the law of Moses, or whether it means the whole of the Old Testament Scriptures. There is a good deal to be said for both points of view. Personally, because of the context, I tend to agree with those who say that it means the whole of the Old Testament... But in the end, of course, it does not really matter very much whether you take it to mean the whole Old Testament or simply the law of Moses. What the apostle is asserting is that the law speaks particularly to those who are under the law. The Old Testament, of course, is primarily addressed to the Jews, and therefore it speaks to the Jews... What he is saying, therefore, is that the very oracles of God, of which the Jews boasted, prove in and of themselves that the Jews are under condemnation, and are as much under the wrath of God as are the Gentiles. The Jew believed that though the Gentile was under the wrath of God, he himself was not... Why has [Paul] been at such great pains to prove that the Jews are under the wrath of God in exactly the same way as the Gentiles? Paul tells us here that he had two objects in view... The first object is "that every mouth may be stopped"... The second object... is that "all the world may become guilty before God"... He is anxious to prove the universality of the condemnation: Jews, as well as Gentiles, every mouth, the whole world... There are no exceptions, none at all' (Lloyd-Jones: *Righteous* pp220-221,224).

Calvin's editor: 'We must bear in mind that... [in Rom. 3:19] the words "that every mouth"... and "that all the world"... were added, not so much as to include the Gentiles, *as to include the Jews*, who thought themselves exempted. No doubt the Gentiles are included, but the special object of the apostle evidently seems to prevent the Jews from supposing that they were not included. In no other way can the connection between the two parts of the verse be understood' (editor's note in Calvin: *Commentaries* Vol.19 Part 2 p130, emphasis mine).

Moo: 'Paul's chief purpose throughout Rom. 1:18 – 3:20 is not to demonstrate that Gentiles are guilty... but that Jews bear the same burden' (Moo: *Romans* p206).

Haldane: The law speaks 'to the Jews... and... it does so in order that the mouths of *all*, without distinction, may be stopped. If God should try the Jews according the law, they could not stand... The law brought against the Jews... accusations and reproaches... "All the world" [Rom. 3:19] – that is to say both Jews and Gentiles. The first clause of [the] verse, though specially applicable to the Jews, proves that since they, who enjoyed such peculiar privileges, were chargeable with those things of which the law accused them, the rest of mankind... must also be under the same condemnation... This expression, then, must include the whole of the human race... Who can be excepted? Not the Gentiles, since they have all been destitute of the knowledge of the true God. Not the Jews, for them the law itself accuses' (Haldane pp122-123, emphasis his).

Kruse: 'In Rom. 3:10-18 the apostle uses a catena of scriptural quotations from the Psalms and Isaiah to underline the fact that (unbelieving) Jews as well as (unbelieving) Gentiles are under the power of sin. These quotations apply to the Jews well, Paul argues, because what the "law" (here referring to the passages just quoted...) says, it says to those under the law, *i.e.*, Jews (Rom. 3:19a). The law says this about those under it, so that every mouth may be stopped and the whole world held accountable to God (Rom. 3:19b). Paul's train of thought appears to be that if the Jews, who so often took the high moral ground over against the Gentiles, are declared to be under the power of sin by their own "law", then clearly all peoples stand guilty before God, Jews as well as Gentiles' (Kruse pp184-185).

Loose Reformed statements: 'All humankind is guilty of transgression of God's law. The law at Sinai... reinstitutes the original law of creation... The law works wrath, and those under the law, whether the law of Moses or the law of creation, are under the curse of God for transgression (compare Hos. 6:7 and Isa. 24:5)'. 'The moral law (the ten commandments)'. 'God the Creator has imposed his law on all created beings – angels and men alike[2] – as the objective expression of his will'. 'It is clear that God imposed his moral law on man from the very beginning'. 'That law was written on the hearts of all men (Rom. 2:14-15)'. (I will deal with this slipshod statement in the next chapter). 'It was reinstituted

---

[2] I find the idea that angels must not commit adultery or lie, and must keep the sabbath, interesting to say the least! Malcolm Watts thought the ten commandments would apply in the eternal state, 'where all are made to keep it finally and eternally' (Malcolm Watts p22). Again, I find it astonishing that Watts could think that glorified saints will have anything to do with a law against adultery – when we know there is no marriage in heaven (Matt. 22:30). Will there be any place in *eternity* for a law on the sabbath? Will the glorified saints keep a weekly sabbath from sunset to sunset – when there will be no more sun to set (Rev. 22:5), and when time and divisions of time 'will be no more'? Does Watts' remarks not suggest that when some Reformed teachers read the word 'law', they cannot seem to restrain the amount of praise they heap upon it? Compare the way reason seems to fly out of the window when Reformed teachers, Calvin in the van, come across the word 'baptism'.

in the time of Moses'. 'The moral law is that law which directs and binds people in moral duties'. 'It has been given for the ordering of moral duties in this world'. 'The summary of this moral law is in the decalogue or ten commandments'. After the fall, 'the moral law continued to bind men'. 'From Adam onwards... men were subject to the moral law. Indeed, unbelievers were under that law as a covenant'. 'The [moral] law was declared from Mt Sinai'. 'The moral law had fallen into obscurity and so at Sinai... we may be certain that this law from Mt Sinai was intended not for the Jews only, but for the world'. 'The law has universal reference'. '*All* the ten commandments were in the world before Mt Sinai... God made Adam and Eve with an instinct for the ten commandments. Their conduct conformed to them [that is, they kept all the ten commandments perfectly] in that originally perfect world'. This included the fourth, 'one of the most important... the sabbath commandment... the fourth commandment... a creation ordinance... permanent' (Karlberg p37; Alderson pp4-5; Malcolm Watts pp20-21; Thackway pp437-438, emphasis mine). Phew!

Some common sense from Spurgeon: 'Even with the light of nature, and the light of conscience, and the light of tradition, there are some things we should never have believed to be sins had we not been taught so by the law. Now, what man, by the light of conscience, would keep holy the sabbath day – suppose he never read the Bible and never heard of it?... Not by any possibility could he find out that the seventh part of his time should be set apart to... God... But I should like to know where they could discover that there was a certain seventh day to be set apart to God... I cannot conceive it possible that either conscience or reason could have taught them such a command' (Spurgeon: *New* Vol.1 p286).

In short, as McClain said: 'As a written law, it was given in the form of a covenant to Israel alone... Ex. 19:3-5; 24:7; 34:27; Deut. 31:26... Dr Sampey writes: "It was to Israel that the decalogue was primarily addressed, and not to all mankind"' (McClain pp31-32).

In addition to the above, Edgar H.Andrews pp78-80; Brown: *Hebrews* pp337-338; Chantry: *Righteous* pp114-115; Cullmann; Michael Eaton: *Encouragement* pp48-49,78-79; Fairbairn: *Typology* Vol.2 pp99-100; Gay: *Particular*; *Infant*; Charles Hodge: *Romans* p80; Hubner p33; Lloyd-Jones: *Final* pp29-31; Moo: *Romans* pp25-27,145,314-316,422-423,435; Murray: *Romans* Vol.1 pp69-70.

Hong set out the connection between transgression (*parabasis*) and sin (*hamartia*): '*parabasis* is a legal term, referring to a concrete act of breaking a promulgated law or an explicit command. The term *parabasis* is not something which is antecedent to, but something which is subsequent to, the coming of the law. According to Rom. 4:15; 5:14, there was *hamartia* but no *parabasis* between Adam and Moses because the law had not yet been given' (Hong p356). 'The point here [Rom. 5:12-14,20; Gal. 3:19] being that *parabasis* [transgression] is what happens when miscellaneous sin (*hamartia*) is confronted by a specific command' (N.T.Wright p172, citing Barrett).

'Gentiles are to be distinguished from Jews in that they "do not have the law" (Rom. 2:14). Therefore, Gentiles are said to be "without the law" (Rom. 2:12). When Paul thinks of those who have the law (Jews) and those who do not have the law (Gentiles), he distinguishes between sin and transgression. Gentiles, even though they do not possess the law, still sin. "All who have sinned without the law will perish without the law" (Rom. 2:12). Transgression can be distinguished from sin, for "where there is no law there is no transgression" (Rom. 4:15)... Gentiles did not transgress the law, for they did not have the written law. But even though they did not transgress a written law, they still sinned, in that they violated the will of God. Paul argues that those who lived between the time of Adam and the time of Moses sinned, even if they did not transgress a specifically revealed commandment as Adam did, or as the Israelites did under the Mosaic covenant (Rom. 5:14)... Even though Gentiles did [do] not technically live under the Mosaic law, they are still considered to be in the realm of the law, for they have the law [the work of the law – precision is needed here, DG] written on their hearts, and know what God expects of them. Such a view seems to be reflected in Galatians, where the desire of the Gentiles to submit to the law is described as a return to paganism. Such an indictment makes sense if Paul sees the Gentiles in a sense to be under the law' (Schreiner pp77,80).

In Rom. 2:14-15, 'the "law" in question is the law of Moses, the body of commandments given by God through Moses to the people of Israel at Mt Sinai'. The Gentiles are 'without law... both law in the abstract and the Mosaic law. The principle laid down is general, though... with special reference to the law of Moses'. 'Paul uses the word *nomos* (law) consistently[1] throughout Romans... [It] refers to the law of God, the law of Moses... the law of God... the *torah* as a complete system... the *torah* in its entirety' (Moo: *Romans* pp149-151; Vincent Vol.2 p676; Bayes pp88-90).

True, it is Gentiles not *the* Gentiles, but this makes no difference: 'There is no good reason to suppose that this does not apply collectively to the Gentiles'. 'The Jews possessed the one authentic revelation of knowledge and truth (Rom. 2:20). By contrast, the Gentiles exist without the gift of that special revelation of God... not having the law... Paul is simply stating the fact that the Jews were entrusted with God's revelation while the Gentiles were not' (Murray: *Romans* Vol.1 pp72-73; Bayes p89).

Loose Reformed statements: 'What the Gentiles possess is the ten commandments, though not necessarily in the identical form as they appear in the decalogue... What the Jews get *via* special revelation the Gentiles get by general revelation'. 'God... has imposed his law on all created beings'. 'It is clear that God imposed his moral law [that is, the ten commandments] on man from the very beginning'. 'That law was written on the hearts of all men (Rom. 2:14-15)' (Barcellos pp81-82; Alderson p4).

---

[1] Not quite. As I have explained, occasionally Paul meant 'principle', 'force' or 'norm'. But the general point made by Bayes (writing in defence of the Reformed position) was right, and should not be jettisoned by the Reformed when writing on the law!

Should the comma in Rom. 2:14 come just before 'by nature', or just after? 'Some scholars argue that... the latter [option] is to be preferred... [but] the majority of modern translations adopt the former'. 'Taking "by nature" with the verb "do" makes better sense... as do all major English translations' (Kruse pp178-181; Moo: *Romans* p149).

The three possibilities: '(1) Gentiles who fulfil the law and are saved apart from explicit faith in Christ; (2) Gentiles who do some part of the law but who are not saved; (3) Gentile Christians who fulfil the law by virtue of their relationship to Christ'. Moo thought 'the second alternative is the best' (Moo: *Romans* pp148-149). I agree. Please note, Moo's order and mine are different.

Bayes: 'The most common interpretation [is] that these are Gentiles in general, and Paul is observing that the practices even of Gentiles do sometimes coincide with the requirements of God's law' (Bayes p103). The fact is, however, Bayes was preparing the ground to state: 'The most satisfactory reading of these verses is... that Paul, without specifying the fact, has in mind Gentile *Christians*. He is inviting the Jewish members of the Roman church to look around their own congregation for the evidence that what he says is true... Paul clearly sees a place for the law in the life of the Gentile believer'. And even in this, he had a bigger fish to fry; namely, to defend Calvin's third use of the law. 'Paul is deliberately leaving the term unspecific as yet, as he builds up his case gradually'. This, to put it mildly, is not at all convincing. Even so, Bayes felt able to reassure his readers: 'However, he himself has Gentile Christians in mind' (Bayes pp104,107).

Bayes made a loose statement equating 'the law' with 'the work of the law' written on their hearts in Rom. 2:14-15: 'It is my contention that the two phrases are synonymous; Paul is making no distinction between them' (Bayes p105). This is wrong.

The 'work of the law' is *not* the same as 'the works of the law': '"The works of the law" are the carrying out of *all* those things which the law requires'. 'By "the work of the law"... is to be understood what the law requires... the work which God requires or demands... that is, such work as the law prescribes and requires'. '"The work of the law" [is equivalent to] conduct corresponding to the law' (Kruse p68, emphasis mine, supported by Karlberg p36; Calvin's editor in Calvin: *Commentaries* Vol.19 Part 2 p97; Vincent Vol.2 p676; see Schreiner pp41-45).

Statements, which I do not accept, from those who argue that Paul was speaking of regenerate Gentiles: 'There is much to be said for it'. 'Since the time of Augustine the orthodox interpretation had applied this verse [Rom. 2:14], either to the Gentile converts, or to the favoured few among the heathen who had extraordinary divine assistance'. 'The doers, according to the context, are believing pagans who demonstrate the works of the law written in their hearts'. 'Rom. 2:14 may well refer to the fulfilment of the covenant promise of Jer. 31:33 among Gentile believers'. '[I] believe the better translation puts the "naturally" with "not having the law" with the understanding that the law... is the Mosaic law: "Gentiles which have not the law *naturally*". Gentiles are naturally bereft of the Mosaic law, yet they will judge [condemn?] those who have the law because of a greater law of Christ put in the hearts [of] those among the Gentiles called and regenerated of God'. 'Rome's conclusion is due to the faulty assumption that the "Gentiles" in Rom. 2:14-15 are unbelievers, as opposed to Jer. 31:33, which teaches that God writes his law on the hearts of believers as a sign of the new covenant in Christ. It is better to see in Rom. 2:14-15 Gentiles who have been circumcised in the heart (Rom. 2:26-27), who are obeying the law of the Holy Spirit written by God on the hearts (Heb. 8). It is not that Gentiles *do* the law naturally. It is rather that Gentiles do not *have* the law naturally... yet do his law because of the work of God in regeneration by the Spirit'. '"The work of the law written in their hearts" (Rom. 2:15) [is the] "dispensation of God's grace"'. 'There is a *clear* allusion here to Jer. 31:33-34' (Michael Eaton: *Encouragement* p118; Sanday and Headlam p60; Colin Brown pp177,923; Zins pp33-34, emphasis his; Bayes pp104-105, emphasis mine).

Such statements go wildly beyond the facts. 'In general, the Puritans (old and new) did not accept the new-covenant view of the passage [Rom. 2:14-15]'. That is, they rightly did not think that Paul was talking about Gentile believers. Of course not! He was speaking about 'Gentiles [who, as Gentiles, were] not without a law engrafted in their conscience, whereby they had common dictates about good and evil'. 'But you must not... compare this with that gracious promise in Jeremiah, of God writing his law in the hearts of his people'. Rather, it was 'small defaced relics [of the law written on Adam's heart but] by his fall defaced and [almost] obliterated'. 'The unregenerate man has some natural knowledge of what the law requires'. 'The transcript of God's own holiness that he has written first of all in the heart of every man and then published in codified form in the law of Moses. This is the argument of Paul in Romans 2:14-15' (Kevan: *Grace* pp59-60,72-73,227; Gouge p576; Kevan: *Experience* p40).

The law here cannot be the ten commandments: 'We have never discovered a single instance of anyone knowing, by nature, the sabbath law'. 'These Gentiles do not have the law of Moses [written on their hearts; rather] there is within them a law... this law is the impact of God's general revelation on their consciences... Paul does not say that these Gentiles reveal "the law" written on their hearts, as is said of God's redeemed people [in the new covenant], but that they show "the work of the law" written on the hearts... What law is this? The law expressed in God's general revelation, which teaches even Gentiles that there is a difference between right and wrong, that wrong is punished and right is rewarded'. Gentiles 'did certain things... commanded by the law, which proved they had, by their original constitution, a discernment of the difference between right and wrong' (Reisinger: *Tablets* p47; Hoekema pp197-198; Haldane: *Romans* p90).

Moo: 'The Gentiles [in question] are unbelievers... Gentiles are, indeed, "without the law" when one is thinking from the typical Jewish perspective of the law as the law of Moses... Gentiles certainly have some knowledge of God's moral demands – "law" in the generic sense. And when God condemns them, he does not do so without their having any understanding of his demands upon them... Paul is speaking not of all Gentiles nor of only a very small number of Gentiles, but, generically, of Gentiles as Gentiles... Paul's point is that Gentiles outside of Christ regularly obey their parents, refrain from murder and robbery, and so on... [are] a law to themselves [as having an innate measure of the] knowledge of divine moral standards... These Gentiles, while not possessing the law of Moses, nevertheless have access to knowledge of God's will for them... Paul continues to speak of those Gentiles who manifest in their behaviour an innate awareness of God's moral demands... "The work of the law"... is probably no more than a "collective" variant of "the things of the law"... the "work", the conduct, that the law demands... [possibly the covenant] God gave to Noah for all human beings [instilling] certain basic moral requirements' (Moo: *Romans* pp149-151,169-171).

John Murray: 'It is true that the sense of obligation is engraven upon the moral constitution of man. It is the apostle Paul who says that the Gentiles, who have not the law [yet] do by nature the things of the law, [who] in [doing] that... show the work of the law written in their hearts, their conscience also bearing witness and their thoughts accusing or else excusing them. Man has a conscience and that means that in some *vague* sense at least he recognises that there is a distinction between right and wrong... "In our present fallen condition it is impossible to excogitate a standard of duty which shall be warped by none of our prejudices, distorted by none of our passions, and corrupted by none of our habits... It is only of the law of the Lord, as contained in the Scriptures that we can justly say: It is perfect"' (Murray: *Collected* Vol.1 pp196-197, in part quoting John Henry Thornwell, emphasis mine).

Lewis: 'First... human beings, all over the earth, have this curious idea that they ought to behave in a certain way, and cannot really get rid of it. Secondly... they do not in fact behave in that way. They know the law of nature' – better, they have 'the work of the law written in their hearts' – but 'they break it. These two facts are the foundation of all clear thinking about ourselves and the universe we live in... We know that men find themselves under a... law which they did not make, and cannot quite forget even when they try, and which they know they ought to obey... God... left us a conscience, the sense of right and wrong: and all through history there have been people trying (some of them very hard) to obey it [even though] none of them ever quite succeeded' (Lewis: *Mere* pp326,335,352).

'If anything in the life of the Gentiles corresponds to the Jewish law, it is the voice of conscience, which shows that "what the law requires is written on their hearts" (Rom. 2:15)"'. 'The law of conscience... is the unwritten law, and belongs to those who, like the ancient heathen, had no immediate revelation from God. [Since I have been] favoured with a revelation of God's will in his word, I do not need this [unwritten] law, for it is superseded by the revelation which God has given of himself in the Scriptures of truth; but in the same way as I have already spoken of the two commandments of the law being absorbed into the gospel and regulated by it, so the law of natural conscience is absorbed into the spiritual conscience, as quickened, enlightened and directed by the word of truth' (Bruce: *Paul* p260; Philpot *Gospel Standard* 1861 pp97,157-158; *Dead* pp27,36-37).

Let me return to an extract from Lloyd-Jones: 'Whereas... [the Gentiles] have never heard the law that was given by Moses, and are in no sense, therefore, "under the law", they nevertheless have a moral consciousness. And it is because they have this that they are responsible – they can be judged in terms of that moral consciousness which they possess. In that sense they are a law unto themselves. In other words, they do not come under the law of Moses but they come under this – we must not call it the law, but this kind of other law which is in terms of their moral consciousness, and which leads to a sense of responsibility... The apostle does not say that they show the "law" written in their hearts; he says that they show the "work" of the law written in their hearts. Now why did he vary the expression? Well, it is important that he should have done so because he is not teaching here... that the Gentiles are people who have the law of God written on their hearts. That is not what he is saying... If you observe or read about any pagan race, you will find that they refrain from certain things. The Gentiles, however ignorant they may be, have got ideas about murder and robbery and thieving and such like things, and you will find that this kind of moral sense is very highly developed among certain pagan tribes. Now that is what he means by the "works of the law".[2] The law says you must not do this, you should not do that. And these people show quite plainly in their conduct that they know something about this, because they punish murder and they punish robbery and theft, and they teach their children that they should not steal, and so on... "Their thoughts the meanwhile accusing or else excusing one another". The word "thoughts" is not a very good translation here. What it really means is "reasonings". "Their reasonings also between one another accusing or else excusing one another". Paul is saying, in effect: "You know, do you not, that these Gentiles who have never heard the law of Moses often have arguments among themselves as to whether a certain thing is right or whether it is wrong. Not only that, they have disputes and debates between one another as to whether what a certain man has done is right or not. They condemn one another and then they try to excuse themselves. They would not do all this unless they had got a standard"... And this, again, is universally true. Go to the most primitive tribes in the world and you will find they are always doing this sort of thing... And the very fact that people do that is the final proof of the fact that they have this moral sense, this moral consciousness, this ability to differentiate between right and wrong and between good and evil'. Lloyd-Jones then tackled the wrong view of the

---

[2] I do not know why Lloyd-Jones used the plural. Was it a printing mistake?

passage: 'There are those... who say that the apostle is here teaching that there is a kind of natural law which is written in the hearts of all men; that the same law which God gave to the children of Israel through Moses was originally written in the hearts of all men and remains in the hearts of all pagans who have never heard of the Mosaic law at all. [This is a] false argument, [a] false deduction... [All the Gentiles have is] some *vague* notion of his power and deity' (Lloyd-Jones: *Righteous* pp117-121,125, emphasis mine).

Kruse: 'It is... best to stay with [this] option'; namely, 'Gentiles, who do not possess the law, do instinctively what the law requires' (Kruse pp178-179).

Bayes: This does not mean 'that there are non-Jewish doers of the law who will be... justified... [but there is] occasional and incidental right behaviour by Gentiles' (Bayes pp104,106).

Calvin: 'There is indeed imprinted on the hearts of men a certain conviction respecting the existence of God; for none are so barbarous as not to have some sense of religion: and thus all are rendered inexcusable, as they carry in their hearts *a* law [not, you notice, *the* law – see below] which is sufficient to make them a thousand times guilty. But at the same time the ungodly... bury this knowledge... they suppress it as much as they can; indeed, they even strive to extinguish... this knowledge'. 'Since then all nations, of themselves and without a monitor,[3] are disposed to make laws for themselves, it is beyond all question evident that they have some notions of justice and rectitude... which are implanted by nature in the hearts of men. They have then *a* law, though they are without law: for though they have not a written law, they are yet by no means wholly destitute of the knowledge of what is right and just'. Paul 'sets nature in opposition to a written law, meaning that the Gentiles had the natural light of righteousness, which supplied the place of that law by which the Jews were instructed, so that they were *a* law to themselves'. 'The Gentiles are those spoken of: God gave them no outward law, but the law of nature which is inward' (Calvin: *Commentaries* Vol.15 Part 1 p51; Vol.19 Part 2 pp96-99, including editor's note, emphasis mine).

Bunyan: Possibly it speaks of 'the very Gentiles, and barbarous people, that fall far short of the light that we have in these parts of the world... [who do not have the law] written as we have; that is, in our Bibles' (Bunyan: *Doctrine* p195).

Zaspel: '"The law was given through Moses" (John 1:17), to be sure, but of course that is not to say that before Moses there was no law from God. Indeed, we so take this for granted that when we read in the Old Testament of pre-Mosaic sinners judged for their wickedness we never [rarely?] stop to ask what law code it was which they had violated and to which they were held accountable. We very naturally and very rightly understand that *they knew better*. And, in fact, if we [could] stop to ask the question of... Paul, his answer would be the same: *they knew better*. It is this very point he expounds at some length in Rom. 1 – 2... The Gentiles are not condemned for their violation of the terms of Sinai; for to them the Sinaitic legislation was never given (Rom. 2:14). Rather, they are declared culpable for suppressing the truth that was *in them* (Rom. 1:18-19). These things they knew to be wrong, independent of the formal legislation of Sinai... [As for] the Gentile who "keeps the requirements of the law"... this could hardly imply that the Gentiles "who have not the law" of Moses are in fact fulfilling every requirement of it. Clearly, [Paul] means only that they observed principles of righteousness which were in keeping with those contained also in the law of Moses. It is in this sense alone that Gentiles can be said to "fulfil the law" (Rom. 2:27). Again, it is evident that there is a law – a standard of moral righteousness – that is independent of Mosaic legislation. Divine law is published universally within every man; it is a standard of righteousness that exists independent of any formal codification. To restate

---

[3] A significant word in light of Gal. 3:23-24.

the point, those who violated the eternal moral precepts of divine law before [the giving of the law to Israel through] Moses knew better... [Consider] those Gentiles of Moses' day who were "far off" (Eph. 2:13) from the law which he mediated to Israel... We are not surprised that the prophets who went to such people did not, in order to establish their guilt, hold before them the tablets of stone [Amos 1 – 2, for instance]. Their sin constituted rebellion against God, yes, the [work of the] law of God written on their hearts. As men made in God's image, they knew better. And when their "iniquity became full", they were judged accordingly... The picture we see of divine law in the Old Testament, both in pre-Mosaic times and in "extra-Mosaic" contexts, is one of inner witnesses, conscience. God's image in man impresses within him an intuitive sense of right and wrong. Formal code or no, it was a sufficiently clear rule of life which all men, in varying degrees, have both obeyed and suppressed. And it is to this that men were and are justly held accountable' (Zaspel pp145-149, emphasis his).

Although I have already quoted the following extract from Moo, I re-quote it here to let him develop it further: 'While Paul can sometimes imply that Gentiles have some kind of relationship to the Mosaic law (*e.g.*, Rom.2:14-15; 6:14-15; 7:1-6), he also generally accepts the usual conceptualisation of first-century Judaism: Jews are, by definition, the people who "have the law" while Gentiles do not (see Rom. 2:12-13; 3:19-20); 1 Cor. 9:20-21)' (Moo: 'Galatians' p16). Moo: 'The Jews become, as it were, representative of human beings generally. If the Jews, with the best law that one could have, could not find salvation through it, then *any* [and every] system of works is revealed as unable to conquer the power of sin. The "bottom line" in Paul's argument, then, is his conviction that sin creates for every person a situation of utterly helpless bondage. "Works of the law" are inadequate not because they are "works of *the law*" but, ultimately, because they are "works". This clearly removes the matter from the purely salvation-historical realm to the broader realm of anthropology. No person can gain a standing with God through works because no one is able to perform works to the degree needed to secure such a standing. The human inability to meet the demands of God is what lies at the heart of Rom. 3... [Taking Rom. 7:4 as an illustration] we suggest that Paul views the Jewish experience with the Mosaic law as paradigmatic for the experience of all people with "law". Israel stands in redemptive history as a kind of "test case", and its relationship with *the* law is *ipso facto* applicable to the relationship of all people with that "law" which God has revealed to them (Rom. 2:14-15). In Rom. 7:4, then, while being "put to death to the law" is strictly applicable only to Jewish Christians, Paul can affirm the same thing of the whole Roman community because the experience of Israel with the Mosaic law is, in a transferred sense, also their experience' (Moo: *Romans* pp217,417,428,433, emphasis his).

In addition to the above, Bunyan: *Doctrine* p186; W.D.Davies pp115-116; Michael Eaton: *Encouragement* p48; Gouge p576; Lloyd-Jones: *Righteous* p116,129-134; Moo: *Romans* pp145,152; Murray: *Romans* Vol.1 p71; Newton pp101-107,118-121; Thayer.

CHAPTER 4: CALVIN'S FIRST AND SECOND USES OF THE LAW

'In his earliest publications', Calvin showed a 'precocious knowledge of... the Fathers... notably... Augustine'. For the *Institutes*, 'he read with close attention a great many works of the Fathers... However, the influence of... Augustine upon the Reformer is more important and may even be said to be unique of its kind. He makes... Augustine his constant reading... quotes him at every opportunity... He borrows from... Augustine with both hands... [Yet] Calvin made the closest study of the Bible – the whole of it – and... he had a more remarkable knowledge than any other Reformer of the Old Testament, [and took] the Scriptures alone [for] normative value for faith, which cannot be claimed for the Fathers... Calvin does not hesitate to part company with them when ever they seem to him to deviate from the straight path of Scripture'. But as Calvin himself said: 'Augustine is so wholly with me, that if I wished to write a confession of my faith, I could do so with all fullness and satisfaction to myself out of his writings'. Calvin borrowed 'with both hands... Luther, Augustine... Bucer... [and] has laid himself the most widely open to the reproach of legalism so often laid against him... We can hardly deny that there is a certain legalism about [his threefold use of the law], tending to efface the antinomy between the law and the gospel, upon which Luther had been so insistent'. Wendel went on to try to relieve Calvin of this in respect to the believer. I disagree. It has been claimed that it was 'the legalism of Rome and... the antinomianism of the sects' which led the Reformers to what has been called – I beg to differ – 'a consistent, well developed doctrine enshrined in their well-known emphasis on the threefold use of the law' (Wendel pp11,19,123-125,200,204-205; Calvin: *Calvin's Calvinism* p38; Donald Macleod: 'Luther' p5).

Preparationism

Pettit on preparationism: 'No point in New England theology was more significant for religious introspection than how much a man could do under the law to predispose himself for saving grace, or how much through preparation he could dispose God to save him...'. Following the triumph of the preparationism of Hooker and Shepard in the New England antinomian controversy of 1637, the New Englanders could not agree with the Westminster Confession Chapter 9 when it stated that 'man... is not able... to prepare *himself* to salvation. In the Cambridge Platform of 1648 they drew attention to their problems over Chapter 10 of the Confession and its claim that in effectual calling 'man... is *altogether* passive therein' (Pettit pp18,164, emphasis mine).

Calvin taught preparationism by the law. In his own words: 'First, by exhibiting the righteousness of God – in other words, the righteousness which alone is acceptable to God – it admonishes every one of his own unrighteousness... convicts, and finally condemns him. This is necessary, in order that man... may be brought... to know and confess his weakness and impurity... So soon... as he begins to compare [his own powers] with the requirements of the law, he has something to tame his presumption. How high soever his opinion of his own powers may be, he immediately feels that they pant under the heavy load, then totter and stumble, and finally fall and give way. He, then, who is schooled by the law, lays aside the arrogance which formerly blinded him... After he is forced to weigh his conduct in the balance of the law, renouncing all dependence on [his] fancied righteousness, he sees that he is at an infinite distance from holiness... In the law we behold, first, our impotence; then, in consequence of it, our iniquity; and, finally, the curse as the consequence of both... To this effect is the apostle's declaration, that "by the law is the knowledge of sin" (Rom. 3:20). By these words, he only points out the first office of the law as experienced by sinners not yet regenerated'.

But, according to Calvin, the law has contrasting effects on the reprobate and the elect. The former might well 'give up all hope and rush headlong on despair... owing to their obstinacy'. The law's effect on the elect, however, is altogether different. God uses it to bring them to Christ. His purpose is: 'That divesting themselves of an absurd opinion of their own virtue, they may perceive how they are wholly dependent on the hand of God; that feeling how naked and destitute they are, they may take refuge in his mercy, rely upon it, and cover themselves up entirely with it; renouncing all righteousness and merit, and clinging to mercy alone, as offered in Christ to all who long for it and look for it in true faith... Augustine... writes... "the law orders, that we, after attempting to do what is ordered, and so feeling our weakness under the law, may learn to implore the help of grace... The utility of the law is, that it convinces man of his weakness, and compels him to apply for the medicine of grace, which is in Christ... God enjoins what we cannot do, in order that we may know what we have to ask of him... The law was given, that it might make you guilty – being made guilty, might fear; fearing, might ask indulgence... The law was given, in order to convert a great into a little man – to show that you have no power of your own for righteousness; and might thus, poor, needy, and destitute, flee to grace"' (Calvin: *Institutes* Vol.1 pp304-307).

Calvin, in trying to justify his lack of scriptural support for his view, was patronising and sweeping: 'Of this... we have so many proofs, that there is not the least need of an example... For all who have remained for some time in ignorance of God will confess, as the result of their own experience, that the law had the effect of keeping them in some degree in the fear and reverence of God, till, being regenerated by his Spirit, they began to love him from the heart' (Calvin: *Institutes* Vol.1 pp308-309).

Helm rightly maintained, against Kendall (see Kendall p26), that Calvin *did* teach preparationism (Helm: *Calvin* pp61-70). But the English Puritans, according to Kendall, followed Theodore Beza, not Calvin: 'There is nothing in Calvin's doctrine that suggests, even in the process of regeneration, that man must be prepared at all – including by the work of the law prior to faith' (Kendall p26). Clearly this is a mistake. Kendall spent a woefully inadequate time (Kendall pp27-28) on Calvin's view of the law as expressed in his *Institutes*, got his threefold division wrong, and omitted vital passages. And even though Miller thought that if the New England Puritans had followed Calvin they would *not* have adopted preparationism (Miller p56), Pettit noted Miller's misreading of the point (Pettit p40). Nevertheless, as Pettit observed: 'In orthodox Reformed theology of the 16th century no allowance had been made for the biblical demand to prepare the heart for righteousness... Preparation was heretical. It was, in fact, forbidden by Reformed dogmatics' (Pettit vii, p2). It depends, of course, on the definition of 'orthodox' and 'preparation'. It mostly hinges on '*self*-preparation'.

Ulrich Zwingli and Peter Martyr, for instance, did not believe in preparation at all (Pettit pp16,31-47). But Calvin *did*: 'For the emergence of preparation from Reformed theology, Calvin's position adds a significant dimension... While he held that man is totally depraved, and can do nothing of his own to prepare for grace, he did not deny preparation as such' (Pettit pp39-40). It could have been put a little stronger. Calvin: 'The law was the grammar [school] of theology, which, after carrying its scholars a short way, handed them over to faith to be completed... The law is a preparation for Christ'. I know Calvin was here speaking of the Jews: 'Paul compares the Jews to children, and us to advanced youth... Under the reign of Christ, there is no longer any childhood which needs to be placed under a schoolmaster, and that, consequently, the law has resigned its office' (Calvin: *Commentaries* Vol.21 Part 1 pp108-109), but Calvin, in his *Institutes*, applied the passage (Gal. 3:24-25) to sinners in general. In addition, even in his *Commentary* Calvin broadened the scope: 'What remains but that faith shall take its [the law's, or the training of childhood's?] place? And so it does, when *we*, who are destitute of a righteousness of *our* own, are clothed by it[?] with the righteousness of Christ. Thus is the saying accomplished, "he has filled the hungry with good things" (Luke 1:53)... It would be unjust, and in the highest degree unreasonable, that the law should hold *believers* in perpetual slavery... *We* are freemen... By faith *we* have obtained... *our* freedom' (Calvin: *Commentaries* Vol.21 Part 1 pp109-110, emphasis mine).

In other words, according to Calvin believers were under the law, and so made to feel their need of Christ, before conversion. Leaving aside the fact that here Calvin was at best ambiguous, a great deal depends on the definition of preparation. Pettit was speaking of the Reformed emphasis 'on the utter depravity of man and his inability in any way to influence God or to predispose *himself* for saving grace' (Pettit p2, emphasis mine). Calvin certainly did not teach *self*-preparation.

In a confusing section, Calvin: 'Some... are unfit to receive the grace of Christ, until they are completely humbled. This the law does by making them sensible of their misery, and so disposing them to long for what they previously imagined they did not want. Others have need of a bridle to restrain them from giving full scope to their passions, and thereby utterly losing all desire after righteousness... Those, therefore, whom [God] has destined to the inheritance of his kingdom, if he does not immediately regenerate, he, through the works of the law, preserves in fear, against the time of his visitation, not, indeed, [with] that pure and chaste fear which his children ought to have, but a fear useful to the extent of instructing them in true piety according to their capacity... Under the guidance of the law... the sinner, terrified at the prospect of eternal death... turns to the mercy of God as the only haven of safety. Feeling his utter inability to pay what he owes to the law, and thus despairing of himself, he bethinks him of applying and looking to some other quarter for help... Hatred of sin, which is the beginning of repentance, first gives us access to the knowledge of Christ, who manifests himself to none but miserable and afflicted sinners, groaning, labouring, burdened, hungry, and thirsty, pining away with grief and wretchedness' (Calvin: *Institutes* Vol.1 pp308,318,526. See also *Commentaries* Vol.2 Part 1 pp313-316; Vol.3 Part 1 pp196-199).

Helm took Kendall to task for misreading Calvin in this extract (Helm: *Calvin* p67) – but Calvin was confusing and ambiguous, if not contradictory! Not only did the Reformer mix up his first two uses, he actually returned to the issue in hand when he was on his third use (Calvin: *Institutes* Vol.1 p318), and, possibly, beyond (Calvin: *Institutes* Vol.1 p526).

Calvin, of course, thought 'repentance is not made a condition in such a sense as to be a foundation for *meriting* pardon' (Calvin: *Institutes* Vol.1 p526, emphasis mine). He was speaking of the *way* God brings sinners to Christ through the law, not their *warrant* for coming. Nor did Calvin think sinners can prepare themselves. He had no time for the notion that 'divine grace [is] preceded by any will of ours... Away, then, with all the absurd trifling which many have indulged in with regard to preparation' (Calvin: *Institutes* Vol.1 pp246-247). God invites and commands sinners in the gospel, yes, but in their own power they cannot obey (see Calvin: *Institutes* Vol.1 pp245-247,255-261,276-277,281-284,291; Helm: *Calvin* pp60-61; Kendall pp20-21).

Calvin was not alone in sowing the seed of preparationism. For the part played by Johann Heinrich Bullinger and Calvin, see Pettit pp22-47. 'The acknowledging of sin is a certain preparative unto faith', Bullinger argued; fear of God, sorrow for sin, and love for Christ – 'these preliminary motions', as Pettit called them – 'prepare an entrance and make a way for us to Christ himself' (Pettit p37).

'For the emergence of preparationism in Puritan thought [Calvin's position] points toward untold consequences'. 'Calvin's system had left various gaps still unstopped, which later divines sought to fill'. 'It is clear that the Reformers firmly emphasised the necessity of the law as a discipline preparatory to faith. Only the law can create a sense of need. Only the law...'. The law's 'function is to create a sense of need'. 'It makes [the sinner] a child of wrath, appreciative of the propitiation'. 'It is of no use trying to sew with the silken thread of the gospel unless we pierce a way for it with the sharp needle of the law' (Pettit pp39,42; French p246; Donald Macleod 'Luther' pp8-9; Spurgeon: *Lectures* p181). See also Bunyan: *Doctrine* p198; Lloyd-Jones: *Atonement* p25; Zens: *Studies* pp37-39,43-44; Michael Eaton:

Encouragement pp9,222; Kendall pp37-41,45,59-61,100-101,106,114-116,119-121,160-163,193,199; *etc.*

These large consequences are not always admitted: 'Among the Puritans there are *occasional* inconsistencies in this matter' (Thomas p12, emphasis mine). Is that all?

A brief account of the history of these consequences: 'Richard Greenham... was among the first in the post-Marian period [to preach in such a way that] the notion of the heart prepared thus emerged within a scriptural framework... In Puritan thought, preparatory activity must be examined in terms of the law and the gospel' (Pettit pp13,15). Pettit was arguing that 'in orthodox Reformed theology' the law work 'is reduced in time to the moment of conversion itself... so that man is virtually wrenched by the law into gospel grace', whereas the lengthening of the process into a series of stages was post-Calvin (Pettit pp16,217-218). 'The first thing', said Greenham, 'is preparation, [to be] humbled with the [law]'. Richard Rogers took Greenham's work further, and enunciated a system of preparation by 'stages, [the] first work [of which is to be] pricked in the heart by the preaching of the law... Richard Rogers and Richard Greenham... point to a crucial concern for later developments in Puritan thought... The very fact that spiritual preachers began to think of regeneration as a process, rather than as a moment in time, meant that conversion itself no longer implied immediate assurance of final election... With [Arthur] Hildersham... the steps leading up to effectual conversion were given full elaboration for the first time, beginning with the work of the law'. The process went on – and on. Under William Perkins, Richard Sibbes, John Preston and William Ames, Puritan preparationism flourished (Pettit pp50-85).

'In a host of sermons and tracts that went far beyond Calvin, [the English Puritans] broke down the operation of faith into a succession of recognisable stages. William Perkins... identified ten stages in an individual's acquisition of faith. The first four were preparatory. [One of Perkins' stages] was so critical, it received a great deal of attention from Puritan writers, and was [itself] broken down into several stages' (Morgan: *Visible* p68). See Pettit pp17-18. And not only English Puritans; some Anabaptists held to a law work before faith. See the extract in chapter 6, for instance, from Philips pp235-237. For New England see Pettit.

This was 'substantially beyond what Calvin did'. Perkins' four 'works of preparation [were followed by] four stages of grace'. For Perkins, 'the receiving of Christ involves five steps... precise... [stages] which could be drawn out. John Winthrop, for instance [first] felt the power of the word about the age of eighteen (1606)... [under] Ezekiel Culverwell... But... reading in Perkins and other Puritan writers [he knew he had not yet reached a state of grace]. At about the age of thirty (1618) [however] the work of preparation was finally ended', and Winthrop was assured (Beeke pp88-90; Morgan: *Visible* pp71-72). Twelve years! 'By preparation they meant a period of prolonged introspective meditation and self-analysis in the light of God's revealed word' (Pettit p17).

Crofton 'direct[ed] the unconverted to comply with the summons to repent... Sit with care, constancy, and conscience under the word of truth and gospel of grace... Study the nature of God... Sit close to the work of self-scrutiny... Sit loose to the world... See the shortness of life... Seriously expect approaching judgement... Seriously apprehend the possibility... of pardon... Soak the heart in the blood of Jesus... Linger not in what you will be rid of... Sue for [repentance] at the hands of God... The Puritan evangelist's message was: Start reaching now!' (Packer: *Among* pp230-231).

Flavel: 'The very order of the Spirit's work in bringing men to Christ, shows us to whom the invitation and offers of grace in Christ are to be made'. This is utterly wrong! See my *Offer*; *Particular*. Flavel again: 'No man will or can come to Christ by faith, till convictions of sin have awakened and distressed him, John 16:8-9. This being the due order of the

Spirit's operation, *the same order must be observed in gospel offers and invitations'* (Flavel p177, emphasis mine). Once again, this is utterly wrong. It is pure hyper-Calvinism! Contradicting himself, Flavel added: 'How happily that universal particle *all* is inserted in Christ's invitation, for the encouragement of sinners'.

Clarkson: 'How does the Lord work faith?' Clarkson, setting out 'in what manner, by what steps and degrees, the Lord ordinarily proceeds when he brings a sinner to believe [admitted at once that] there are some extraordinary cases where the Lord proceeds not in the ordinary method... and... [even] in ordinary cases there is a great variety in respect of circumstances...'. Even so: 'A discovery of sin which the Lord makes by the law and by the Spirit... The Lord convinces him that all those dreadful things which are denounced against sin belong to him... The soul is wounded with apprehensions of sin and wrath, the weight of them lie heavy on his soul, they enter as iron into his soul... [The] inquiry how he shall avoid this misery, what shall he do to be freed from that burden of sin and wrath... A renouncing of all unsafe ways... [The] revelation of Christ... Hope. Though he despair as to himself, yet the Lord keeps him from despairing as to Christ... Self-abhorrence... Hopes that he may find mercy with God, and probability that he may have pardon through Christ, fill him with indignation against sin, and himself for sin; makes him condemn himself and justify God, though he should proceed against him with the greatest severity... Valuing Christ... When he... sees the excellency, all-sufficiency of Christ [revealed] in the gospel, his thoughts of Christ are raised... Discourses of Christ are not tedious now; he thinks he can never hear enough of them... Strong desires after Christ... A persuasion that the Lord would have them believe that Christ is willing they should rest on him for pardon and life... He resolves to comply with the Lord's invitation... The Lord [reveals] his faith to him, possesses him with an apprehension that he does truly believe... From this assurance proceeds sometimes peace, sometimes comfort, sometimes joy, triumph and glorying in God...'. Until the sinner is 'brought... to be willing to accept Christ as he is offered, till then he has no ground to expect pardon and life from Christ. Till then he has no encouragement to rely on Christ for it. *Till then we cannot press it on him as his duty...*[1] But for the sensible sinner... it is his next duty to cast himself upon Christ for life and salvation...'.

Having taken his hearers into such a fearful mire – Bunyan's Slough of Despond – nevertheless Clarkson still felt able to assure them: 'Legal terrors are no parts of faith or conversion; they are neither essential nor integral parts... These are no conditions of any promise. The Lord has not promised faith... to these legal preparations... These are not necessary antecedents of faith, though they be usually antecedents of faith, yet not necessarily; though they ordinarily go before faith, yet not always... He who finds in himself undoubted effects and evidences of faith need not question the truth of his faith for want of legal humiliation, so that he who finds in himself the clear evidences of a preparedness for Christ, need not be discouraged from coming to him for want of these legal terrors, because they do not always go before faith, at least in the same degree with it' (Clarkson pp78-91,96-97,127-136, emphasis mine). Do not miss the Reformed double-talk in all this. As for my reference to Bunyan – Bunyan was not teaching that the Slough of Despond was – as so many think – the experience of a believer. Pilgrim entered the Slough *before* he had his sins forgiven. I am grateful to one of my readers who told me of the girl who, when asked: 'Have you come through the Slough of Despond?', replied: 'I did not come that way'. As for Bunyan's years of torment through his lack of assurance as a believer, see Morden pp51-65. And where and how did Bunyan find relief? Looking to Christ: 'I must go to Jesus... Then with joy, I told my wife: "Oh now I know, I know!"' (Bunyan: *Grace Abounding to the Chief of Sinners* sections 261-264 in Google Books).

---

[1] This is pure hyper-Calvinism, utterly contrary to Scripture!

Alleine: 'I have a prescription that will cure you all infallibly. Follow these directions... Hear, then, O sinner, as ever you would be converted and saved, take the following counsel'. Alleine now spelled out sixteen steps. These included a sense of the impossibility of salvation in an unconverted state, 'a thorough sight and lively sense and feeling of your sins... strive to affect your heart with a deep sense of your present misery... settle it in your heart that you must look out of yourself' – when he was telling his readers to do the very opposite! – 'and away from your own doings... renounce all your sins... make a solemn choice of God for your portion... accept the Lord Jesus in all his offices... resign all your powers and faculties, and your whole interest to be his... choose the laws of Christ as the rule of your words, thoughts and actions... You must chose them all... for all times... This must be done deliberately and understandingly... all this [must] be completed in a solemn covenant... take heed of delaying... attend conscientiously upon the word, as the appointed means for your conversion...' – note, the reader is not yet converted! – 'strike in with the Spirit when he begins to work upon your heart... set upon the constant and diligent use of serious and fervent prayer... forsake all evil company, and forbear the occasions of sin... set apart a day to humble your soul in secret by fasting and prayer, to work a sense of your sins and miseries upon your heart... read over a through exposition of the commandments, and write down the duties omitted, and sins committed by you'. Thus, concluded, Alleine: 'I have told you what you must do to be saved' (Alleine pp100-124). Compare all this, for instance, with the words of Paul to the jailer (Acts 16:31). If it is protested that the jailer was awakened, and, I suppose, had gone all through Alleine's stages in a few seconds, how about Paul addressing the sinners in the Areopagus (Acts 17:30)?

Bolton: 'God gave the law.. to reveal sin and to awaken the conscience, and to drive men out of themselves, and bring them over to Christ... God gave the law to [reveal] sin... that when we were convinced of sin, we might look out for and prize a Saviour... The law serves the cause of the gospel because, convicting men of their works of condemnation, it prepares them to seek the grace which is found in the gospel... Thus the law remains, an instrument in the hand of the Spirit, to [reveal] sin to us, and humble us for it, that so we might come over to Christ... When the law has come to [sinners]... with an accusing, convincing, humbling, killing power, oh then, Christ is precious, the promise is precious, the blood of Christ is precious' (Bolton pp81,86; see Kendall p193).

Boston: 'Whosoever... would enter into the covenant of grace,[2] must, in the first place, have a faith of the law... for which cause, it is necessary that the law, as well as the gospel, be preached to sinners... [The] faith of the law consists in a belief of... three things... That he is a sinner... a lost and undone sinner, under the curse of the law... [and] his utter inability to recover himself. [This] faith of the law [which brings] a legal repentance... is our schoolmaster to bring us unto Christ; and the faith of the law makes way for the faith of the gospel... Not that either this legal faith or legal repentance is the condition of our welcome to Christ and the covenant of grace: our access to Christ and the covenant is proclaimed free, without any conditions or qualifications required in us to warrant us sinners... to believe on Jesus Christ... But they are necessary to move and excite us, to make use of our privilege of free access to Christ and the covenant; insomuch that none will come to Christ, nor embrace the covenant, without them in greater or lesser measure'. Boston, still not clear of danger, moved on to the notion of the 'sensible sinner', illustrating his point by the physician; it is only those who know they are sick who send for the physician, but the fact that they are sensible of their sickness 'is not the condition for his curing them, but for their employing him' (Boston: *Beauties* pp588-591).

In consequence: 'The constant message of Puritan preachers [meant]... in order to be sure one must be unsure'. 'The surest earthly sign of a saint was his uncertainty; and the surest

---

[2] See chapter 6.

sign of a damned soul was security'. 'Indeed, argued Perkins, the absence of doubt meant that one was damned... worrying about one's salvation was itself a sign that one was saved'. 'By emphasising the importance of continuing doubt, as did Perkins... [he] opened the gates to a new legalism'. 'Apart from his teaching on the self-confirming value of perpetual doubt... the process of conversion as expounded by William Perkins was upheld by English evangelicals for three centuries as the normative Christian experience' (Morgan: *Visible* p70; Michael Watts pp173-174,178-179).

Not all agree with this assessment. Perkins and his 'desperate quest for assurance of election... must not be exaggerated' (Wakefield p74). The facts contradict Wakefield, however. Preachers tried to mitigate the effects and ended up in the oddest of places. Sibbes urged sinners to 'civility and religion, and wait the good time till God shine on them in mercy' (Sibbes: *Lydia's* pp522-523). 'To sermon attenders who had not yet "closed with Christ in a promise", [New England] ministers also preached the duty of civil and spiritual obedience, but as a form of conviction and "humiliation" rather than thankfulness. "Legal" obedience, though not sanctified, was better than no obedience at all' (Stout pp24,41).

Vain attempts have been made to distinguish between the ordinary from the extraordinary methods God uses: 'Both Calvin and the Puritans taught that, *typically*, conversion to Christ comes about through a preparatory period of conviction of sin brought about by the preaching of the law. But neither Calvin nor the Puritans laid down *rigid rules* to which all Christian experience must conform'. The 'preparatory work of the law [is that] which the Lord does *ordinarily* make use [but] the Lord does not always observe the same plan with men'. 'The way of calling men unto the saving knowledge of God... the efficient cause of this work is the Holy Ghost; the preaching of the word, especially the law, being the instrument which he makes use of. [But] God is pleased to exercise prerogative and sovereignty in this whole matter, and deals with the souls of men in unspeakable variety. Some he leads [in one way, others in another]' (Helm: *Calvin* p81, emphasis mine; Guthrie pp23-24, emphasis mine; Owen: *Spirit* pp349,351,360-361).

Others were not so flexible. Hooker: 'The soul of a poor sinner *must* be prepared for the Lord Jesus, before it can receive him'. Preston: 'No man can come to Christ, *except* the law be a schoolmaster to bring him to Christ. [For] a perfect work of the gospel the knowledge of the law *must* precede'. Sibbes: 'Before we can come from nature to grace, we *must* come under the law'. Whitefield: 'First we hear Moses' voice, we hear the voice of the law; there is no going to Mount Zion *but* by way of Mt Sinai; that is the right straight road... They *must* hear the voice of the law... you *must* hear the voice of the law before ever you will be savingly called unto God'. Sears: 'A man *must* learn Sinai before he comes to Zion' (quoted by Miller p64, emphasis mine; quoted by Kendall p121 and Lloyd-Jones: *Sons* p207, emphasis mine; Sibbes: *Excellency* p339, emphasis mine; Whitefield (Tegg) pp784-785; (Banner) p114 (quoted with approval by Lloyd-Jones: *Sons* p220, emphasis mine); Sears p133, emphasis mine).

Of course, 'everyone must have wrought in him the preparatory work of which Jesus spoke before he can or will come to Christ. Everyone who has not had that work wrought in him does not want to come to Christ' (Sears p132). *This* is not the issue! Nor is it *all* the Reformed demand!

Jonathan Edwards at one stage doubted his 'interest in God's love and favour... because', he said, 'I cannot speak so fully to my experience of that preparatory work, of which the divines speak... [and] I do not remember that I experienced regeneration, *exactly in those steps*, in which divines say it is generally wrought'. Later, he felt some relief concerning his 'trust and affiance in Christ, and with delight committing of my soul to him, of which our divines used to speak, and about which I have been somewhat in doubt'. Yet, later still: 'Whether I am now converted or not...'. Even so, he vowed to use 'for helps some of our old divines' (Jonathan Edwards' *Diary* xxiv,xxxv,xxxvi, emphasis mine). My advice? When in a hole, stop digging! In a more biblical vein, look to Christ!

As Baxter: 'For those doubts of my own salvation, which exercised me many years, the chiefest causes of them were these... because I could not distinctly trace the workings of the Spirit upon my heart *in that method* which Mr Bolton, Mr Hooker, Mr Rogers, and other divines describe... I was once [inclined] to meditate on my own heart... I was continually poring either on my sins or wants, or examining my sincerity... but now, though I am greatly convinced of the need of heart-acquaintance... yet I see more need of a higher work, and that I should look often upon Christ, and God, and heaven, [rather] than upon my own heart' (Baxter pp10,113, emphasis mine). Spot on!

Goodwin: 'We were held under John Baptist's water, of being humbled for sin... Happy is that soul that in conversion or calling was pitched first on Christ... Happy it is with some whose lot it is that their conversion work begins with Christ. Next after their humiliation for sin, they are pitched upon Christ' (Goodwin p346, misquoted by Packer: 'Puritan' p20).

Preparationists ought to listen to Wheelwright: 'To preach the gospel, is to preach Christ... and nothing but Christ' (Miller p60). And start doing it!

Joseph Hart: 'Nothing but thy blood, O Jesus,/ Can relieve us from our smart;/ Nothing else from guilt release us,/ Nothing else can melt the heart./ Law and terrors do but harden/ All the while they work alone,/ But a sense of blood-bought pardon/ Soon dissolves a heart of stone' (*Gospel Hymns* number 159 verse 2; Hart: *Hymns* number 54, p71). Now, if any preparationist should latch on to Hart's 'work alone' to argue that preparationism by the law is essential as long as it works *with* the gospel, he should remember that the law is supposed to prepare the sinner to be fit *for* the gospel. And Hart immediately spoke of the sinner in question having 'a sense of blood-bought pardon'. The law never gives any sinner 'a sense of blood-bought pardon'! Consequently, I cannot see how Hart's hymn can be used for preparationism. Quite the opposite!

Spurgeon had a good deal to say on the subject. We should 'tell a sinner that foul and filthy as he is, without any preparation or qualification, he is to take Jesus Christ to be his all in all. [He does not need] months of law work... I solemnly warn you, though you have been professors of faith in the Lord Jesus Christ for twenty years, if your reason for believing in Christ lies in this, that you have felt the terrors of the law... it is a false reason, and you are really relying on your experience and not upon Christ [and you are lost]'. He dismissed preparationism, making feelings and such like the warrant for faith, as 'absurd... legal... boasting... changeable... utterly incomprehensible... unacceptable to the awakened sinner... false and dangerous' (Spurgeon: *Metropolitan* Vol.9 pp533-538).

He had issued the same warning three years before, saying such men 'give descriptions of what a sinner *must* be before he may come to Christ, which actually represent what a saint *is*, after he has come to Christ' (Spurgeon: *New* Vol.6 pp397-398, emphasis his). While Packer criticised Spurgeon for his insufficient care, he also recognised he had a point. As Packer said: 'By concentrating on this preliminary work of grace, and harping on the need for it to be done thoroughly... [Puritan] writers effectively discouraged souls from going straight to Christ in their despair' (Packer: 'Puritan' pp19-21).

Interestingly, contradictorily, in light of the above, Spurgeon told his students to preach the law when addressing sinners with the gospel (Spurgeon: *Lectures* p181)! And he was not averse to it in his preaching. See Spurgeon: *New* Vol.1 pp289-292; Vol.3 pp170-176; *Metropolitan* Vol.20 pp553-560; Vol.28 pp284-285; Vol.32 pp25-34; Vol.33 p325; Vol.34 pp132-144.

Yet he could also say: 'Sinners say they are to get ready for Christ, and fools they are for saying it' (Spurgeon: *Metropolitan* Vol.19 p732). 'Fling away any preparations, fitnesses... and take my Lord Jesus as empty-handed sinners take him. Meet him just as he is, and just as you are' (Spurgeon: *Metropolitan* Vol.21 p372).

Boston: 'Now in calling you to embrace the covenant, you are called indirectly, and by consequence, to this faith in the law; namely, to believe that you are sinners in life, heart and [disposition]; lost and undone, under the curse; and utterly unable to recover yourselves. Yet it is not saving faith, nor does it instate [install, fit, put into, launch] one in the covenant of grace; that is peculiar to another kind of believing' (Boston: *Beauties* p591).

Hulse got it badly wrong – in fact, in cavalier fashion, he wrote-off a countless number of believers at a stroke: 'The moral law is God's schoolmaster to bring us to his Son... The person who has no experience of God's law has no experience at all!... The law is essential... because it alone can humble proud sinners... The moral law [the ten commandments] impressed upon the conscience is God's way of conviction... If our experience of Sinai is light... then our grasp of and gratitude for the gospel will be equally shallow... The law has a vital role to play both before and after conversion. As the Old Testament precedes the New, so does the law precede the gospel... To safeguard those who have truly repented but who have experienced a minimum of conviction of sin is important... The nature and the role of the law cannot be over-estimated in these days when there is so much feeble preaching. Let us bring back the schoolmaster that we might expect many more applicants who welcome obedience to the gospel. The law is able to drive men to Christ and cause them to look for, and, if possible, storm the very gates of heaven to be sure that they are reconciled to God' (Hulse: *Believer's* pp67-77).

Really? Hulse was clearly going way beyond Scripture in making such assertions, and gratuitously hurting true believers who cannot trace out what he considers to be an 'experience of God's law'.

And what about this from Kendall, summarising Preston? 'The upshot is that we must concentrate on our attitude towards the law rather than our receiving the righteousness of Christ' (Kendall pp119-121). Are such men *gospel* preachers? As Spurgeon thundered: 'We ought to know how much of these qualifications are needed... I demand of all legal-gospellers distinct information as to the manner and exact degree of preparation required' (Spurgeon: *Metropolitan* Vol.9 p534).

The Particular Baptist Confession of 1644 rightly and expressly denied preparationism: 'The tenders of the gospel to the conversion of sinners is absolutely free, no way requiring, as absolutely necessary, any qualifications, preparations, terrors of the law, or preceding ministry of the law' (Lumpkin p163).

Not all the spiritual descendants of the 1644 Particular Baptists have kept to this biblical position, however. Gill: 'Nor does [God] anywhere invite, encourage, or by his messengers, entreat all men to be reconciled to him... I do not find that any such [that is, "insensible of their state and condition"] are exhorted to believe in Christ for salvation; but as sensible of it'. Gadsby described 'the characters addressed' by Christ, and invited by him: they 'are heavy laden with a sense of their own guilt before a righteous God, and labouring under it as an intolerable burden; ardently panting for deliverance, but feel themselves yoked down by the killing letter, accompanied with a sense of God's just wrath, as revealed in his holy laws, so can get no rest to their souls. Such poor souls the blessed Saviour sweetly invites to come unto him; that is, believe in and rest upon him for salvation... Poor sinners are addressed as subjects of convictions, and certain impressions'. The Gospel Standard Articles: 'We believe that the invitations of the gospel, being spirit and life (that is, under the influence of the Holy Spirit), are intended only for those who have been made by the blessed Spirit to feel their lost state as sinners and their need of Christ as their Saviour, and to repent of and forsake their sins... We believe it would be unsafe, from the brief records we have of the way in which the apostles, under the immediate direction of the Lord, addressed their hearers in certain special cases and circumstances, to derive absolute and universal rules for ministerial addresses in the present day under widely-different circumstances... Therefore, that for ministers in the present day to address unconverted persons, or indiscriminately all in a mixed congregation, calling upon them savingly to repent, believe, and receive Christ, or perform any other acts dependent upon the new creative power of the Holy Ghost, is, on the one hand, to imply creature power, and, on the other, to deny the doctrine of special redemption' (Gill: *Cause* pp152,164; Gadsby: *Works* pp304-307; Articles 24,32 and 33).

John Brown had it right: 'The free and unrestricted nature of the invitation [to Christ]... deserves notice. Not only is the descriptive character of those invited, 'those who thirst', common to all human beings, but the invitation is so fashioned, that no human being can find the shadow of a reason for thinking himself excluded... It is not: "If any man be deeply sensible of his guilt, depravity and wretchedness, let him come to me and drink". Such are invited; but if that were all, as some have taught, thus, however unintentionally, clogging with conditions the unhampered free offer of a free salvation, men might think that till they had brought themselves, or were in some way or other brought, into a state of deep contrition, and earnest seeking after pardon, and holiness and salvation, it would be presumption in them to come to Christ, or even look towards the Saviour for salvation. But the invitation is: "Whosoever wishes to be happy, let him come to me, sinful and miserable as he is, and in me he shall find salvation. If you are not a brute, if you are not a devil – however like the one in sensuality, or the other in malignity – you are invited. If you are on earth, not in hell, you are invited"' (Brown: *Discourses* Vol.2 pp9-10).

Archibald G.Brown, Spurgeon's successor, wrote an account of the conversion of an uneducated costermonger, one Bill Sykes. Sykes would refer to what he called, 'that little bit'. 'That little bit about Christ taking my place, and how he had my punishment for me'. Brown commented: 'Would the Christian worker behold conviction of sin? Then let him try "that little bit". Sin never appears so sinful as when viewed in the light that breaks from Calvary. The "green hill far away" surpasses Sinai's splintered peaks in convincing power. It is when a man measures his sinfulness by the cross that he gains a true conception of its magnitude. You may tell a man until you are hoarse that he is a drunkard, a liar and a reprobate. He will hear, and, perhaps, believe you; but no sorrow is begotten in the hardened soul. Tell him "that little bit", and, in beholding Christ, he sees himself, and sees himself through his tears. Denunciation may shiver a heart, but substitution melts it. Ice smashed is still ice. Ice thawed is no longer ice. What worker for God is there who has not, over and over again, seen the magic power of "that little bit" to make the iceberg soul to weep itself away'.

Brown quoted from John Newton's hymn: 'I saw one hanging on a tree,/ In agony and blood,/ Who fixed his languid eyes on me,/ As near his cross I stood./ Sure, never to my latest breath,/ Can I forget that look;/ It seemed to charge me with his death,/ Though not a word he spoke./ My conscience felt and owned my guilt,/ And plunged me in despair,/ I saw my sins his blood had spilt,/ And helped to nail him there'. Brown went on: 'It is "that little bit" that melts away pride, prejudice, hardness, coldness, and makes a man sob forth – "God be merciful to me the sinner"' (Archibald G. Brown pp7-8).

Let Robert Traill, writing in 1692, bring this section to a close: 'Is it desired that we should forbear to make a free offer of God's grace to the worst of sinners? This cannot be granted by us... 1 Tim. 1:15. This was the apostolic practice, according to their Lord's command (Mark 16:15-16; Luke 24:47)... Shall we tell men that unless they are holy they must not believe on Jesus Christ? that they must not venture on Christ for salvation till they are qualified and fit to be received and welcomed by him?[3] This would be to forbear preaching the gospel at all, or to forbid men to believe on Christ. For never was any sinner qualified for Christ. He is well qualified for us (1 Cor. 1:30), but the sinner out of Christ has no qualification for Christ but sin and misery. Whence should we have any better but in and from Christ?... Suppose an impossibility, that a man was qualified for Christ, I boldly assert that such a man would not, nor ever could believe on Christ – for faith is a lost, helpless condemned sinner's casting himself on Christ alone for salvation, and the qualified man is no such person. Shall we warn people that they should not believe on Christ too soon? It is impossible that they should do it too soon. Can a man obey the great gospel-command too soon? (1 John 3:23), or do the great work of God too soon? (John 6:28-29)' (Traill pp153-154).

For more extracts on preparationism, see p420.

So much for Calvin's first use of the law. Now for the second.

Calvin, in his own words: 'The second office of the law is, by means of its fearful denunciations and the consequent dread of punishment, to curb those who, unless forced, have no regard for rectitude and justice... It is true, they are not on this account either better or more righteous in the sight of God. For although restrained by terror or shame... their heart is by no means trained to fear and obedience. [Indeed], the more they restrain themselves, the more they are inflamed, the more they rage and boil, prepared for any act or outbreak whatsoever, were it not for the terror of the law... The feeling of all who are not yet regenerate... is, that in regard to the observance of the law, they are not led by voluntary submission, but dragged by the fear of force... [Indeed], this tuition is not without its use, even to the children of God... When, by fear of divine vengeance, they are deterred from open out-breakings, though, from not being subdued in mind, they profit little at present, still they are in some measure trained to bear the yoke of righteousness' (Calvin: *Institutes* Vol.1 pp307-308). An astonishing statement, this, for the gospel age!

Bolton: The 'principal and chief [end] for which the law was promulgated [was] to restrain transgression... God has given a law to set banks and bounds... to men's sins and sinful affections... binds and restrains [sin]'. Bolton offered no verse which speaks of the law restraining sin. The passages he did cite (Rom. 2:8-9; 5:13-14; Gal. 3:19; 2 Tim. 3:16), say no such thing. But while he had no *scripture* to support him, he *was*, however, able to list 'Jerome and Chrysostom [as among those who] understand [the words in Gal. 3:19] to refer to the restraining of transgressions' (Bolton pp78,80,84).

This is wrong. As Hendriksen said: 'The context [in Galatians]... refutes the interpretation, favoured by some, that Paul here views the law as a means of checking or restraining transgressions' (Hendriksen: *Galatians* p140). As Bolton himself said, showing the Reformed propensity for double-speak on the law: 'The law was given to uncover and reveal transgression, and this, I conceive, is *the true meaning* of the apostle's words in Gal. 3:19... that is, *chiefly*, that the law might... reveal and discover sin... The apostle seems to say the same thing in Rom. 5:20' (Bolton p80, emphasis mine).

Gill shot himself in the foot: The law is of use 'to restrain sin... the law... deters men from sin... though by such restraints, it does but rise and swell, and rage more within, like a flood of water stopped in its course' (Gill: *Body* Vol.2 p39). A man must have a remarkable talent if he can believe such opposites of his own making.

Calvin also shot himself in the foot: The idea that the law restrains sin 'agrees with the saying of philosophers... yet, owing to the corruption of our nature, its instruction tends

---

[3] This is the reality. Preparationism starts by talking about the sinner being fit enough to believe, but it can so easily morph into the sinner being fit enough for Christ to receive him.

only to increase transgressions, until the Spirit of regeneration come[s], who writes it [begging the question as to which law is written on the heart in the new covenant; see chapter 18] on the heart; and that Spirit is not given by the law, but is received by faith. The law excited in us evil emotions, which exerted their influence through all their faculties; for there is no part which is not subject to these depraved passions. What the law does, in the absence of the inward teacher, the Spirit, is increasingly to inflame our hearts, so that they boil up with lusts'. Calvin's editor: Sinful passions are 'occasioned by the law... made to abound by the law' (Calvin: *Commentaries* Vol.21 Part 1 pp100-101; Vol.19 Part 2 pp249-250; the editor cited Rom. 5:20; 7:8).

John Murray quite rightly recognised that the law aroused sin. Commenting on Rom. 7:8, he declared: 'Then the commandment... entered into [Paul's] consciousness – it came home with power and authority. Sin was then aroused to activity. It was no longer dead. And it took occasion to stir up all manner of covetous lust. *It did this through the instrumentality of the commandment*; the sinful principle *was aroused* to all manner of desire contrary to the commandment *through the commandment itself*' (Murray: *Romans* Vol.1 p251, emphasis mine).

Whitefield: 'You never throw off your cloak in a storm, but you hug it the closer; so the law makes a man hug close his corruptions (Rom. 7:7-9)... But when the gospel of the Son of God shines into their souls, then they throw off the corruptions which they have hugged so closely; they hear his voice saying, Son, daughter, be of good cheer, your sins, which are many, are all forgiven you' (Whitefield (Tegg) p785; (Banner) p114).

Even so, Poole followed Calvin's first two uses: The law was given 'either to restrain sin' – quoting 1 Tim. 1:9, which says nothing of the sort – 'or to make men see that they stood in need of Christ' – quoting Rom. 7:13, which says nothing of the sort (Poole p650).

John Brown, commenting on Gal. 3:19, dealt with both. Quoting Albert Barnes (to refute him): 'The law was given... to disclose the true nature of sin; to deter men from committing it... to be preparatory to... the work of redemption through the Redeemer', Brown called this the 'ordinary interpretation'; that is, the Reformed view – Calvin's first two uses of the law. Acknowledging Barnes had set it out 'very well', Brown immediately pointed out the obvious; namely '*till* the Seed should come...' 'is quite inconsistent with this exegesis'; that is, it is quite inconsistent with the idea that the law was given to restrain sin and to bring sinners to Christ. Why? Simply this: if the law *was* given to deter men from sin, to bring them to Christ, and so on: 'Why was it limited to the time that the Seed should come?' (Brown: *Galatians* pp149-150). Surely Calvin and those who follow him argue that the law restrains sin and brings men to Christ *nowadays*, do they not? Indeed, Barnes himself had made this very point when he added the words: 'This use of the law still exists'.

Please remember that so many who so strongly advocate Calvin's first two uses of the law, also say the opposite. Calvin himself did. Read the extracts once again. I wonder which aspect of each contradiction the Reformed really do believe, after all.

In addition to the above, Brooks Adams pp217,219,230-231,235-248; James Truslow Adams p170; Bremer p113; Brook Vol.3 pp70,157; Calvin: *Institutes* Vol.1 pp21-25; Dix; Duffield p60; Erikson pp71-107; Gay: *Battle*; *Infant*; *Offer*; *Particular*; *Septimus*; Horn pp19-37; Howe pp215,224-231,233-234; Hulse: '1689' p5; Kendall pp110-113,125-138,163,167-182; Levy and Young v; Lloyd-Jones: *Puritans* p350; Mather Vol.1 pp252-253,266-268,347,386,389-390; Vol.2 pp508-509,511,513,516; Miller pp3,53-67,214,222; Morgan: *Dilemma* pp134-154; *Visible* pp96-97; Murray: *Lloyd-Jones* pp721-726; Pettit pp86-157,161-162,176-177,183-189,205,210-211,221,238; Ruether and Keller pp167-169,174; Stout pp25,35,37-42,202-207,322-324; Wendel pp134-144,198-206; Witherington pp268-269.

CHAPTER 5: CALVIN'S THIRD USE OF THE LAW

Calvin: 'The third use of the law (being also the principal use, and more closely connected with its proper end) has respect to believers in whose hearts the Spirit of God already flourishes and reigns. For although the law [begging the question as to which law is written on the heart in the new covenant; see chapter 18] is written and engraved on their hearts by the finger of God, that is, although they are so influenced and actuated by the Spirit, that they desire to obey God, there are two ways in which they still profit from the law. For it is the *best* instrument for enabling them daily to learn with greater truth and certainty what that will of the Lord is which they aspire to follow, and to confirm them in this knowledge... Then, because we need not doctrine merely, but exhortation also, the servant of God will derive this further advantage from the law: by frequently meditating upon it, he will be excited to obedience, and confirmed in it, and so drawn away from the slippery paths of sin... The law acts like a whip to the flesh, urging it on as men do to a lazy sluggish ass. Even in the case of a spiritual man, inasmuch as he is still burdened with the weight of the flesh, the law is a constant stimulus, pricking him forward when he would indulge in sloth... It cannot be denied that it [the law] contains a perfect pattern of righteousness... one perpetual and inflexible rule... The doctrine of the law... remains... that... it may fit and prepare us for every good work... The general end contemplated by the whole law [is] that man may form his life on the model of the divine purity... The law... connects man, by holiness of life, with his God... [It is] one perpetual and inflexible rule... The law... is given for the regulation of the life of men, so that it may be justly called the rule of living well and righteously... By the word "law"... we understand what peculiarly belonged to Moses; for the law contains the rule of life... and in it we find everywhere many remarkable sentences by which we are instructed as to faith, and as to the fear of God. None of these were abolished by Christ... The law is the everlasting rule of a good and holy life... The law... not only contains a rule of life as to outward duties, but... it also rules their hearts before God and angels... The law acts like a whip to the flesh, urging it on as men do to a lazy sluggish ass... a constant stimulus, pricking him forward' (Calvin: *Institutes* Vol.1 pp309-311,356; *Commentaries* Vol.3 Part 1 p196; Vol.22 Part 1 p167; Vol.21 Part 1 p119; Vol.15 Part 2 p220, emphasis mine).

'It is here that [Calvin] has laid himself the most widely open to the reproach of legalism so often laid against him... We can hardly deny that there is a certain legalism about this' (Wendel pp200-205).

Calvin contradicted himself: 'What is drawn forth by constraint, or servile fear, cannot please God... It is possible that a man may be affected with reverence towards the law of God; but... God requires from us no slavish service' (Calvin: *Commentaries* Vol.2 Part 1 p381; Vol.6 Part 1 p477).

Others had said the same as Calvin's main position – before Calvin. Bucer, for instance: 'The law... to those who are endowed with the Spirit... is in no sense abolished, but is so much the more potent in each one as he is richly endowed with the Spirit of Christ' (Wendel p205).

Many have followed Calvin: 'The moral law does for ever bind all, as well justified persons as others, to the obedience thereof... The law... is of great use to [believers]... as a rule of life, informing them of the will of God and their duty, it directs them and binds them accordingly'. 'The decalogue, or ten commandments... is called the moral law because it is the rule of life and manners... The Scripture is a banquet, and the moral law is the chief dish in it... It is an exact model and platform of religion; it is the standard of truth... Though the moral law is not a Christ to justify us, it is a rule to instruct us... The law of God is a hedge to keep us within the bounds of sobriety and piety... We say not that [the believer] is under the curse of the law, but the commands... The moral law... remains as a perpetual rule to believers... Every Christian is bound to conform to it... Though a Christian is not under the condemning power of the law, yet he is under its commanding power... They who will not have the law to rule over them, shall never have the gospel to save them'. 'The law was given to be a spur to quicken us to duties. The flesh is sluggish, and the law is... a spur or goad... to quicken us in the ways of obedience' (Westminster Confession chapter 19, sections 5 and 6; Watson pp10,34; Bolton p83).

Some astonishing statements from Calvin's followers on the law: 'Although true believers are not under the law as a covenant of works, to be thereby justified or condemned, yet it is of great use to them as well as others, in that as a rule of life, informing them of the will of God and their duty, it directs and binds them to walk accordingly... It... is of use to the regenerate to restrain their corruptions... the law encourages to [their doing good] and deters from [their doing evil]' (The Baptist Confession of 1689, chapter 19.6). The law 'is of use to saints and true believers in Christ... to point out the will of God unto them; what is to be done by them, and what to be avoided; to inform them of, and urge them to their duty... to be a rule of life and conversation to them; not a rule to obtain life by, but to live according to... It continues as a rule of walk and conversation to them' (Gill: *Body* Vol.2 pp39,41). 'A believer... is under perpetual and indissoluble obligation to conform to [the law] as a rule of conduct... If the [moral] law be not a rule of conduct to believers, and a perfect rule too, they are under no rule; or, which is the same thing, [they] are lawless' (Andrew Fuller: *Antinomianism* p339; *Moral* p891). 'A third... and essential use appears to the believer... The believer's sanctification can only be attained in practice by giving him a holy rule of conduct. Such a rule is the law. It is to be assiduously observed as the guide to that holiness which is the fruit of adoption' (Dabney p354). 'The law is a rule of life for believers... [While] the Reformed do full justice to [Calvin's] second use of the law... they devote even more attention to the law in connection with the doctrine of sanctification' (Berkhof p615). The law shows 'the believer the will of God and his duty to his fellows' (*We Believe* pp26-27). 'The law of the Lord is not only for the soul that needs conversion, but also for the nurture and warning of the converted' (Tow p29). 'Avoid as you would a deadly snake any man who denies the law of God is the Christian's rule of life. The law, not the gospel, is the rule of our sanctification' (Pink quoted by Murray: *Pink* p104; quoted by Daniel: *Hyper* p638).

Some more: 'The pedagogic work of the law is not... confined to the unbeliever nor is it confined to our pre-conversion experience. It is vitally important, also, in the life of a Christian'. Donald Macleod quoted Calvin: The law 'exacts much more of [believers] than they are able to offer... This is vital... Day by day the law exposes his ungodliness... The function of the law [is] to sustain [the sense of need], bringing it home to us continually that all our righteousness is as filthy rags... It also exasperates and stirs up our depravity... The effect of the law upon our depraved hearts is akin to the effect of the sun on any putrid organism. The law suggests sins, even in the very act of forbidding them. It provokes resentment of God's authority. It creates a slavish fear of penalty which itself is incompatible with love, the very essence of obedience' (Donald Macleod: 'Luther' p9, quoting Calvin's Genevan Catechism). Are these *gospel* ministers speaking?

Yet more: Believers 'have returned to the moral law for direction in sanctification... Nothing but the moral law can define for us what sanctified behaviour is... As New Testament writers discuss the moral law they frequently and naturally turn to the ten commandments... How is love to God and neighbour to express itself?... To answer this the apostles always return to the ten commandments... How readily the New Testament binds the ten commandments upon Christian consciences' (Chantry: *Righteous* pp72,84-86,96-97,114). May I ask what scripture passages would justify that last from Chantry?

Some of Calvin's followers have admitted that voices have been raised against Calvin's view. First, a somewhat muted round of support for Calvin from Bayes: 'The law does have an[!] ongoing role as a binding authority in the life of the Christian believer'. It is 'the instrument [of sanctification, with its] directing [or] binding power' in the life of the believer. 'In Calvin's understanding of sanctification... the Spirit is the agent and the law the instrument. Employed by the Spirit, the law is, in the life of the believer, a power for exciting obedience'. 'Calvin's emphasis [was] on the law as an instrument of the Spirit, invested with power for the sanctification of the Christian'.

But Bayes also referred to opponents of Calvin's view: During the so-called 'antinomian controversy in Puritan New England... in 1637, and the years immediately following... John Wheelwright... [argued that] the believer's sanctification [is] not in the law, but in Christ... The leaders of the New England establishment... held, contrary to the [so-called] antinomians, that... the law... has... the power to direct the believing life'. Bayes found 'the omission of reference' in the Particular Baptist Confession of 1644 'to the directing power of the law in the life of the believer... noteworthy... noteworthy that [John] Brine', the 18th-century Particular Baptist, failed to 'mention the law as itself instrumental in the believer's sanctification', whereas 'advocates of [Calvin's] third use understand the law as [a] rule in an instrumental sense' (Bayes pp6,15-19,27-29,51,102,111-112,115-117, 119,124).

More from Calvin's followers: 'The law... has a position of centrality... in man's sanctification (in that man grows in grace as he grows in law-keeping, for the law is the way of sanctification)... Man's sanctification is by means of the law of God... Law [is] the way of holiness... Paul never attacked the law as the way of sanctification... [Acts 15] clearly established or sustained the law as the way of sanctification... [including] even the dietary aspects of the law... The believer is under "the law of the Spirit of life in Christ"' (Rom. 8:2)' (Rushdoony pp3-4,7,732,734). 'When people say... that they are not under the law as a rule of life, that is a terrible thing to say' (Malcolm Watts p22). Speaking for myself, I find many of the Reformed statements quoted in this chapter to be 'terrifying', if not 'terrible'.

Some have tried to argue a difference between the two givings of the law. Spurgeon did (Spurgeon: *Metropolitan* Vol.33 pp325-326). Bunyan: The first issuing of the law 'does more principally intend its force as a covenant of works [whereas the second was] as a rule, or directory, to those who are already found in... Christ; for the saint himself, though he is without law to God, as it is considered the first or old covenant, yet even he is not without law to him as considered under grace, "not without law to God, but under the law to Christ" (1 Cor. 9:21)'. This (second) giving of the law is 'a rule, or directory, to those who are already found in... Christ'. Bunyan argued this from the record that when God first gave the law, 'he caused his terror and severity to appear before Moses... (Ex. 19:16; Heb. 12:18-21). But when he gave it the second time, he caused all his goodness to pass before Moses... (Ex. 34:6-8)'. Who, in Scripture, ever argued thus? By that I mean, that although I recognise the scriptural references, I do not recollect any scriptural writer making such deductions from the two givings of the law.

Bunyan has been misunderstood in the following: 'When this law with its thundering threatenings attempts to lay hold of your conscience, shut it out with a promise of grace... the Lord Jesus is here... and here is no room for the law. Indeed, if [the law] will be content with being my informer, and... leave off to judge me, I will be content; it shall be in my sight, I will also delight therein; but... I being now made upright without it, and that too with the righteousness which this law speaks well of and approves, I may not, will not, cannot, dare not, make it my Saviour and judge, nor suffer it to set up its government in my conscience... The sum then of what has been said is this, the Christian now has nothing more to do with the law, as it thunders and burns on Sinai, or as it binds the conscience to wrath and displeasure of God for sin; for from its thus appearing, it is freed by faith in Christ. Yet it is to have regard thereto, and is to count it holy, just and good'. Although it sounds as though Bunyan had got it right, unfortunately he was only speaking of justification, not sanctification, saying the law cannot now condemn the believer. As he said in another place: The 'law is a rule for everyone that believes to walk by, but not for justification' (Bunyan: *Christian* pp535-536; *Vindication* p99).

Let us get back to Scripture, and hence come to the right view: 'In fact, the only place in Paul's letters where he appears unambiguously to quote Mosaic law as applicable to Christian believers is Eph. 6:2'. That the believer is under the law which must curse him for the least failure is 'a sentiment... so grossly repugnant to the gospel of Christ I do not for a moment hesitate to renounce. Sanctification in principle or in practice is not by the law. The law is not the means by which the Holy Spirit operates in making the redeemed a holy people, and cannot, therefore, be the means by which we attain a holy character. Sanctification by the law is as contrary to sound doctrine as justification by the law...'. The Anabaptist Waterland Confession of 1580, the second Mennonite (Anabaptist) Confession: 'The intolerable burden of the Mosaic law with all its shadows and types was brought to an end in Christ and removed from the midst of his people... A man... regenerated and justified by God through Christ, lives through love (which is poured out into his heart through the Holy Spirit) with joy and gladness, in all good works, according to the law and precepts and customs enjoined on him by God through Christ' (Moo: 'The Law' p216; George Wright pp231,234; Lumpkin pp41-43,49,57).

Slipshod Reformed statements: 'The law was given to Israel... because they had been redeemed... The law was added at Sinai as the necessary standard of life for a redeemed people... The very grace that redeemed Israel carried with it the necessity of revealing the law to Israel'. [God] 'had already redeemed them... [The Hebrews] were to keep the commandments *in gratitude* for what the Lord had already done for them; [namely, that] he had already redeemed them' (Pink: *Law* pp5-6; Chantry: *Covenants* p13, emphasis mine). Assertion is one thing, but could we be given the scriptural proof?

Such slipshod statements corrected: 'The Christian... has undergone a new exodus... [and] stood at the foot of a new Sinai... under a new *torah*... incorporated into a new Israel... and... enter[ed] a new covenant' (Davies pp146,223,225).

Again, those who think, as the Reformed do, that the fifth commandment governs 'everyone in their several [various] places and relations', must bear in mind that under certain circumstances the law exacted the death penalty for breaking the fifth commandment (Ex. 21:15,17; Lev. 20:9; 21:9; Deut. 21:18-21). 'It is difficult... to see on what grounds this penalty could be avoided'. If not, 'one comes very close... to setting case laws against the fifth commandment itself'. Is the decalogue 'the law of Christ'? 'There are important reasons for answering... negatively... It is beyond dispute that the display of the excellencies of God found in Jesus Christ is primarily his moral excellencies. Can we really believe that all this is *fully* anticipated in the decalogue?... Only on the assumption that the ten commandments explicitly or implicitly contain all of this same revelation can we think of putting them on the same level as the Lord Jesus himself'. But many have thought they could. 'The Puritans, for example, repeatedly show that they believed that the decalogue contained implicitly all the demands of God as reflected in his moral character. But the evidence for that [so-called] fact was always wanting, as indeed it would have to be, if there is such thing as progressive revelation... The ten commandments... could not have functioned as a compact summary of all moral law. And they never did among the Jews' (Wells pp45-47, emphasis mine. See Westminster Shorter).

Harking back to Calvin himself: The law is 'of use to the regenerate... the threatenings of it serve to show what their sins deserve, and what afflictions in this life they may expect from them, although freed from the curse thereof threatened in the law' (Westminster Confession chapter 19, section 6). Where, in the New Testament, do we find this? If the apostles felt the law was this useful to the regenerate, one would expect to find it repeatedly throughout their writings.

Andrew Fuller put his finger on one of the problems for the Reformed: Can 'the whole of Christian obedience be formally required in the ten commandments?... Certainly it is not... Neither the ordinance of baptism, nor that of the supper, is expressly required by them; and there may be [there are – an infinite, ever-developing number!] other duties which they do not, in so many words, inculcate'. Even so, Fuller tried to argue that these were 'virtually required' by the ten commandments (Andrew Fuller: *Moral* p890). Do not miss the vagueness! And some Reformed dismiss as 'hazy' the view that I and many others set out!

Gadsby exposed the vagueness in his reply to Fuller: 'Which is as much as to say, that the infinitely wise Jehovah Jesus has given to his spouse a perfect rule for her behaviour, though this rule does not expressly contain those things he wishes her to observe. So that what Gaius[1] says upon the subject plainly amounts to this, that the law is a perfect imperfect rule'. Gadsby was not in any way decrying the ten commandments, of course: 'Who objects to the perfection of the ten commandments? I know no one who does except Gaius, and men like him. I believe the law to be holy, and the commandment holy, just, and good, a perfect transcript of the perfections of God; and it stands as a perfect rule of life *to all that are under it* [emphasis mine], and that too in its primitive purity, *without any alteration whatever* [emphasis mine]. Surely Gaius has forgotten himself. It is *he* [Gadsby's emphasis] that objects to its perfection, for he tells us, "that as a covenant, it is dead to the believer"'. I pause. Gaius [Fuller] was badly adrift here in more than one way. The Bible never says the law has died; it is the believer who has died to the law. To let Gadsby go on: 'Now, if the law was originally a perfect rule, how comes it to pass that it must undergo so painful an operation as death to constitute it a rule? If this is not treating the law with contempt, it will be difficult to know what is... To say that the condemning power of the law is taken away, so that, though the believer cannot keep it, it does not condemn him, positively robs the law of its authority and perfection... For what is a law without power to inflict punishment on transgressors? If this is not making void the law, what is? for I read of no penalty annexed to the law of works, but that of a curse' (Gadsby: *Works* pp7-8,12). Would some Reformed writer care to refute Gadsby?

Reformed teachers squirm at this point. See for instance Westminster Confession chapter 19, section 6: The law is 'of use to the regenerate... the threatenings of it serve to show what their sins deserve, and what afflictions in this life they may expect from them, although freed from the curse thereof threatened in the law'. Although there is truth in this – see chapter 18 – it seems to me that Reformed writers want to have their cake and eat it! If the law *is* the believer's perfect rule, it must stand absolute in its entirety, curses and all; if, however, it is a paradigm – see chapter 17 p289 – then its curses may and can be used to illustrate the glories of the gospel.

Gadsby again, this time exposing the futility of trying to distinguish between the law as a covenant and the law as a rule: In the Sermon on the Mount, it 'is beyond a doubt... the Lord points out the authority of the law. [First] to convince his disciples of their impossibility of keeping it; but in all that he says upon the subject, he never once mentions any difference between the law as a covenant of works and a rule of conduct, but speaks of it in its fullest sense... therefore evident it is, that such men, who preach the law as a rule of conduct to believers, are the men who break the commandments, and teach men so, by saying it is dead as a covenant, and that its condemning power is taken away; which is as much as to say, the law is your perfect rule of conduct, but if you fall short of obedience, it has no power to hurt you. If this be not sporting with the law, I am at a loss to know what is... Who is it that deprecates the law – the man that, by a precious faith in Jesus Christ,

---

[1] Fuller, himself – see Andrew Fuller: *Dialogues* pp294-308.

gives it its full demand, and so establishes it; or the man that first kills it, and then takes it for a perfect rule of conduct, and gives it but a partial obedience at best? The latter must be the man that deprecates the law' (Gadsby: *Works* p16).

Gaius (Andrew Fuller) had asked: 'Are believers at liberty to profane the sabbath?' By raising the sabbath, Fuller, no doubt, had thought he had floored his opponents. In fact, he had bitten off more than he could chew! Gadsby was rightly scornful in reply. He pointed out that in the fourth command, God demands the keeping of the *seventh* day. He asked: 'Now, are we at liberty to work on the *seventh* day, and set apart the *first* day for worship, and yet the law remain a perfect rule of conduct? Does the law allow us to reverse its commands, so that when it says *the seventh* is the sabbath, and *in it* you shall *not* work, are we to understand by such terms, that the seventh is *not* the sabbath, and in it we *are* to work? If the law, as a perfect rule of conduct, allows us liberty to reverse its commands, it follows that when it says [we are not to kill, steal and bear false witness]... that we *are* at liberty to kill, steal and bear false witness... Does it not appear that those men who enforce the law of works as a perfect rule of conduct to believers, while they can reverse the fourth command, open a wide door for all ungodliness? I wonder how Gaius could ask the above question, and not blush at the same time, seeing he is the man that thinks we *are* at liberty to profane the sabbath!' (Gadsby: *Works* pp12-13, emphasis his).

The sabbath, of course, is one of the hard nuts the Reformed have to crack. Calvin's view on the sabbath, for instance, makes awkward reading for them. As for my view on the sabbath, I hope to publish on it. In short, believers are to keep the Lord's day – but this is not the sabbath. The sabbath itself fell with the old covenant, fulfilled by Christ, who is himself the believer's sabbath.

Gadsby replied to the Reformed critic who stupidly accused those who did not subscribe to the Reformed view of the law of 'losing their reverence for the Lord's day'. Gadsby admitted there would be some of whom this was true, but this was not generally the case. Indeed, he retorted – and, reader, I must say I feel a huge sympathy with him – 'there are thousands who profess to believe that the law of works is the believer's rule of life who profane the Lord's day' – even though they lambast people like me for our views on the law! He roundly told his critic: 'You should recollect that the law says: "The seventh day is the sabbath", not the *first* [Gadsby's emphasis]. You must not go to the law of works, sir, to prove that the first day of the week is set apart for the worship of God; you are obliged to come to the rule of those whom you oppose for proof of that'. That is to say, those who argue that the law of Moses is the believer's rule have to go to the gospel for this particular law. 'The law does not allow those who are under it to reverse its commands. Profaning the Lord's day is likely to arise from the sentiment which affirms the law to be the believer's rule, and at the same time maintains that it is right to do any lawful work on the seventh day, and sets apart the first in its room, contrary to the express command of God in that law. You know, sir, that in London there are what they call Seventh Day Baptists, and they are *consistent* Baptists [emphasis mine], if the law of works be their rule of life' (Gadsby: *Works* pp41-42).

Consider the logic of making the law the perfect rule of sanctification for the believer while at the same time saying it cannot justify the unbeliever. Boston delineated the two laws: 'The law of works is the law [which is to] be done, that one may be saved' and 'the law of Christ [which] is the law of the Saviour, binding his saved people to all the duties of obedience... The law of works, and the law of Christ, are in substance but one law, even the ten commandments'. Two very different laws, one for justification by obedience to the commands, the other for sanctification, yet these two laws 'are in substance but one law' comprised of precisely the same commandments? How can this be? The ten commandments are both an insupportable burden and an easy yoke! Boston thought he reconciled these impossibilities thus, in terms of 'a difference [which] is constituted between the ten commandments as coming from an absolute God out of Christ to sinners, and the same ten commandments as coming from God in Christ to them. [It is] utterly groundless [to say] that the original indispensable obligation of the law of the ten commandments is in any measure weakened by the believer's taking it as the law of Christ, and not as the law of works... The law of the ten commandments [remaining the same throughout, issued by the same God, was first] the natural law... written on Adam's heart on his creation, while as yet it was neither the law of works nor the law of Christ... Then it became the law of works... The natural law of the ten commandments (which can never expire... but is obligatory in all possible states of the creature...) is, from the moment the law of works expires as to believers, issued forth to them [again]... in the channel of the covenant of grace... Thus it [now] becomes the law of Christ to them; of which law also the same ten commandments are likewise the' substance. What about the law of Christ? After all, the two laws, according to Boston, consist of precisely the same commandments but ' in the threatening of this law [the law of Christ, that is] there is no revenging wrath; and in the promises of it no proper conditionality of works; but here is the order of the covenant of grace'. In other words, all men are always under the law, the same law which demands the same obedience and warns of the same punishments as ever it did since it has not changed in one iota, nor indeed can change; but, apparently, when dealing with any particular man, the law has to ask itself which sort of man it is dealing with. If the man is under the law as the law of works it punishes him when he transgresses; if he is under it as the law of Christ, it pardons him. 'Thus the ten commandments stand, both in the law of works and in the law of Christ at the same time... but as they are the [substance]... of the law of works, they are actually a part of the law of works; howbeit, as they are the [substance]... of the law of Christ, they are actually a part, not of the law of works, but the law of Christ. And as they stand in the law of Christ... they ought to be a rule of life to a believer... they ought [not, however] to be a rule of life to a believer, as they stand in the law of works' (Fisher pp24-27).

George Wright put some sense back into the argument: 'If... after proclaiming Christ as the end or consummation of the law, and the consequent deliverance of believers from the law, I should study to promote their morals by insisting: "The law must still govern you, and be your rule of life", I should gainsay my own doctrine, pull down what I had built, and expose myself to the just reproach of every wise man in the household of faith as an unfaithful steward, handling the word of God [foolishly] by leading souls from Sinai to Zion for salvation, and from Zion to Sinai for good morals' (George Wright: p232).

Neophytus – Fisher's young Christian – exposed the Reformed dilemma: 'Sir, I do not know well how to conceive this freedom from the law, as it is in the covenant of works'. Nomista – Fisher's legalist: 'Sir, I must confess, I do not know what you mean by this distinction'. Fisher's answer: 'The truth is... the law of the ten commandments, as it is the [substance] of the law of works, ought not to be a rule of life to a believer', but 'the law of the ten commandments, as it is the [substance] of the law of Christ, ought to be a rule of life to a believer', but not as it is the substance of the law of works, of course. 'So far as any man comes short of the true knowledge of this threefold law... so far he comes short both of the true knowledge of God and of himself' (Fisher pp24-27,155-171). Reader, did you get it? The ten commandments are the rule of life to the believer as they are part of the law of Christ, but not as they are part of the law of works! So the believer is not obliged to be faithful to his wife if that means he obeys the law of works, but he is to be faithful to his wife if he obeys the law of Christ! Hmm!

'If the moral law could justify, what need was there of Christ's dying?... We say not that [the law] saves, but sanctifies' (Watson pp10,34). I ask: If the moral law can sanctify, what need is there of the Holy Spirit and the New Testament? I am indebted to Zens: *Studies* p64, for the essence of this question.

Calvin: 'The law... will act only in the capacity of a kind adviser, and will no longer lay a restraint upon your consciences... In regard to believers, the law has the force of exhortation, not to bind their consciences with a curse, but by urging them, from time to time, to shake off sluggishness and chastise imperfection... What Paul says, as to the abrogation of the law, evidently applies not to the law itself, but merely to its power of constraining the conscience'. 'A kind adviser', please note. If so, the law cannot be a rule, can it? The same goes for 'exhortation' and 'urge'. Law does not advise, exhort or urge. It rules! And it punishes those who offend.

On the other hand, Calvin did what he so often did – and wanted it both ways: 'The law not only teaches, but also imperiously demands. If obedience is not yielded... if it is omitted in any degree, it thunders forth its curse... By the term law, Paul frequently understands that rule of holy living in which God exacts what is his due, giving no hope of life unless we obey in every respect; and, on the other hand, denouncing a curse for the slightest failure'. Again: 'We ought to imitate the prophets, who conveyed the doctrine of the law in such a manner as to draw from it advices, reproofs, threatenings and consolations, which they applied to the present [that is, contemporary] conditions of the people... We ought to make known the judgements of God; such as, that what he formerly punished he will also punish with equal severity in our own day' (Calvin: *Commentaries* Vol.21 Part 1 p164; *Institutes* Vol.1 pp310-311,366; *Commentaries* Vol.7 Part 1 xxx).

Spurgeon put some common sense into the frame: 'The old law shines in terrible glory with its ten commandments. There are some who love the law so much, that they cannot pass over a sabbath [that is, the Lord's day – Spurgeon equated the two] without its being read in their hearing, accompanied by the mournful petition: "Lord, have mercy upon us, and incline our hearts to keep this law". Nay, some are so foolish as to enter into a covenant for their children, that "they shall keep all God's holy commandments, and walk in the same all the days of their life". Thus they early wear the yoke which neither they nor their fathers can bear, and daily groaning under its awful weight, they labour after a righteousness which cannot be found... O, when will all professors, and especially all professed ministers of Christ, learn the difference between the law and the gospel? Most of them make a mingle-mangle, and serve out deadly potions to the people, often containing but one ounce of gospel to a pound of law, whereas, but even a grain of law is enough to spoil the whole thing. It must be gospel, and gospel only... How it makes a man live close to Christ!... It leads me to seek after purity and holiness'. I pause. What was the 'it'? Was it the law? It was not! It was 'preaching Christ to sinners as sinners'. And what verse did he use to drive home his point? Was it a verse speaking of the law? It was not! Rather, it was: 'As you have received Christ Jesus the Lord, so walk in him' (Spurgeon: *Metropolitan* Vol.9 pp529,540).

McClain: '1. There are at least three possible ways in which a theological system can be constructed for the purpose of putting the Christian under the law: (a). A system which would place the Christian under the total law, including all its elements and penalties. This is pure Judaism. (b). A system which would place the Christian under the [so-called] moral law and its penalties. This is moral legalism. (c). A system which would place the Christian under the [so-called] moral law stripped of its proper penalties. This might be called a "weak and beggarly" legalism (*cf*. Gal. 4:9)'. This, of course, is the Reformed view.

McClain went on: '2. It is this third system that deserves the severest criticism. (a). It employs an unscriptural terminology, taking only one element of the law and divesting even that of its sanctions, and then calls it "the law of God". In the Bible, "the law" is a unity which includes all its elements with its penalties. (b). Claiming to honour the law of God, [this] system actually dishonours the law, especially because it reduces the holy law of a holy God to the level of mere good advice... (c). This ultimately moves in the direction of theological disaster, bringing and compounding confusion into our views of sin, salvation, of the work of Christ and even of the doctrine of God. (d). Worst of all, this abstraction of the moral element from the ceremonial element in the Old Testament law, and its imposition upon the Christian as a rule of life, has a grave spiritual and moral danger...

3. The word of God condemns unsparingly all attempts to put the Christian believer "under the law". The Holy Spirit through... Paul gave to the church the book of Galatians for the very purpose of dealing with this heresy. Read this letter over and over, noting carefully the precise error with which the writer deals. It is not a total rejection of the gospel of God's grace, and a turning back to a total legalism. It is rather the error of saying that the Christian life, having begun by simple faith in Christ, must thereafter continue under the law or some part of it. This is clear from the apostle's indignant charge: "This only would I learn of you: Did you receive the Spirit by the works of the law, or by the hearing of faith? Are you so foolish? Having begun in the Spirit, are you now made perfect in the flesh?" (Gal. 3:2-3). Little wonder that he begins the chapter with a cry of astonishment: "O foolish Galatians, who has bewitched you, that you should not obey the truth...?" (Gal. 3:1)' (McClain pp50-52). For my arguments – and for a continuation of this extract from McClain, see chapter 9.

Bennett spoke of the need for the 'stretching' of 'Westminster theology... in the direction of the new-covenant theology' in the area of 'our whole relationship now to the Mosaic law and covenant'. In other words, Bennett was rightly about to expose some of the large and serious deficiencies in the Westminster documents concerning the believer and the law. 'Common ideas in Westminster theology are that we are no longer under the law for our justification, but we are still under it as a rule of life for our sanctification'. 'Without denying an element of truth in this, on the whole [this is too weak – DG] it is not what the New Testament teaches'. Referring to Rom. 7:1-6, Bennett declared: 'Whoever exactly the man of Rom. 7:14ff. is, one thing is clear: Paul's main purpose in writing the passage was to show that the law cannot sanctify – the corollary of Rom. 7:16... The old saying that the law sends us to Christ to be justified, and then Christ sends us back to the law to be sanctified is not right, but a dangerous half-truth... In this matter, the Heidelberg Catechism scores a major victory over the Westminster Catechisms: it depicts most theology as grace, and ethics as gratitude, and reflects Calvin's view that Sunday is not a Mosaic sabbath... whereas the Larger Catechism from Westminster sometimes gives the impression that law is a major power in sanctification, and both it and the Westminster Shorter in effect define even the gospel as an aspect of law: see questions 5 and 3 respectively... This has the unfortunate consequence of introducing the gospel, not as a wonderful piece of news to rejoice in, believe and celebrate, but as something we are to believe, *i.e.*, as part of our duty – which, of course, it is, but that's not the main point of it. The Bible is not fundamentally a book about law, but an announcement of some wonderfully good news about historical events... In the latter half of the 20th century, it would have been good if the revival of interest in historic Reformed literature in Britain had not concentrated quite so much on the 17th-century writers, powerful in searching the heart as many of them are, and/or that some kind of... health warning had been printed on the dust jackets, instead of the impression being given that this was the best stuff ever written since the Bible... Not only must we understand and apply the Mosaic law from a clear stand within the new covenant, as well as see ourselves as under grace, not law, in the whole of the Christian life... we must... see that our duties as believers and churches centre on the law of Christ (1 Cor. 9:21; Gal. 6:2), with the Mosaic law incorporated into it in a subsidiary way, provided it is interpreted rightly' (Bennett: 'Use' pp12-14). On the whole, excellent, though I would strengthen Bennett's words at one or two places. I will, of course, be returning to the themes flagged up in this extract.

In addition to the above, Barcellos pp61-68; Calvin: *Commentaries* Vol.8 Part 1 p421; Curtis Evans pp305-325; Gay: *Battle*; *Infant*; Harris pp44-45; Kruse p216; Lloyd-Jones: *Law* pp259-260; Murray: *Romans* Vol.1 p274; Reisinger: *Tablets* pp77-78; *Law* p24.

CHAPTER 6: THE BUTTRESS OF THE REFORMED CASE
COVENANT THEOLOGY

Covenant theology

We cannot find any warrant in Scripture for such an expression as 'the covenant of grace made between the three persons of the adorable trinity' (*Sears* pp113-114).

For a detailed, sympathetic history of covenant theology, see Robert Letham. In brief, it runs as follows: Although Augustine raised some of the issues, they remained dormant until the Reformation. 'Interest in the covenant developed in a big way in Reformed theology', beginning with Zwingli. I pause. It is significant that the development of covenant theology originated with Zwingli. He, of course, was, at first, at one with the emerging Anabaptists, and their view of the discontinuity of the Testaments, but he drew back, and, as Letham explained, by June 1525 was teaching 'covenant unity', which he applied to baptism. From this early start, the snowball of covenant theology began to roll, growing all the time, until it got its *imprimatur* in its 'classic statement' at the Westminster Assembly – though this was far from unanimous. Although Letham admitted covenant theology has 'a problem of definition' – indeed, it has an extraordinary talent for the exposure of differences among its proponents – nevertheless he himself was in no doubt: 'We can begin to think in terms of covenant theology, for in some sense "covenant" has become a lens through which to examine a wide area of theology'.

I pause once more to note that admitted inherent difficulties in covenant theology have not stopped its advocates making covenant theology the filter through which they read theology (and Scripture). This, it seems to me, exposes the fundamental issue with covenant theology. Instead of being the cart, it has become the horse. Instead of Scripture ruling theology, covenant theology now rules Scripture.

The major stumbling block (but not the only stumbling block) for covenant theologians is, of course, the place of the law, and, intimately connected with it, the so-called covenant of works. Letham: 'There have been some differences [among covenant theologians] over the place of the Mosaic covenant, differences that are widely recognised as intra-mural and more apparent than real'. I can only remark that this smacks of whistling in the dark! The covenant of works, Letham explained, though it was hinted at by Augustine, and again in 1562 by Ursinus, owes its inception to Dudley Fenner in 1585. Following Fenner, 'a spate of theologians' produced works on the newly-defined covenant, but 'it was by no means universally taught at this time', and was not adopted by any Confession until Westminster, sixty years later. And 'even in the 1640s, unanimity was lacking in the existence of this covenant'. Indeed, some were opposed to the notion. Ever since – to this very day (even down to my effort) – 'the covenant of works has come under severe criticism', and many, including covenant theologians themselves, have raised insurmountable problems with it. James B.Torrance, for instance, argued that it has produced a legal approach to the gospel, 'with disastrous consequences for both theology and piety'.

One more stumbling block before we move on. What about 'the covenant of redemption'? Although Olevianus had hinted at the idea of this covenant in 1585, it had to wait until Cocceius (1648) and Owen[1] produced their works. This, too, has met with stiff opposition from other covenant theologians. Letham summarised their objections: it leads to error over the trinity; indeed, the covenant of redemption itself is explicitly 'not trinitarian at all'. It sets the will of the Father and the Son in opposition. It excludes the Holy Spirit. In short, as Letham stated: 'The formulation is mistaken' (Letham pp1-39).

---

[1] See, for instance, apuritansmind.com/covenant.../john-owen-and-the-covenant-of-redemption

Adding my tuppence worth, I say that covenant theology itself, and not just the covenant of redemption, is a mistaken imposition on Scripture, and the cause of enormous, even eternal, damage to many souls. Neither its history, nor its contemporary disagreements among its staunchest advocates, do anything to reassure me. Those who object should read the originals, and not be content with the glossy eulogies of today's covenant-campaigners.

Berkhof claimed that Kaspar Olevianus 'was the real founder of a well-developed federal theology'. 'The covenant made between God and Adam in creation, what Reformed dogmaticians from the late 16th century up to the present have identified as the covenant of works... [is] that [so-called] doctrine of Scripture which has exercised so pivotal a role in Reformed semantics'. 'The doctrine of the covenants' – that is, covenant theology – 'is at the core of [Reformed] theology, and the health of any theological system depends on its understanding of this truth. It would be nearly impossible to overstate the central importance of the biblical teaching' – that is, according to Chantry, Reformed teaching – 'on covenants'. 'This covenant theology is at the heart of Calvinism. Where it is misunderstood or opposed, usually Calvinism declines very quickly' – which is a significant though strange claim since 'Calvin, it is generally agreed, was not a covenant theologian, in that covenant concepts were never the organising principle of his theology' (Berkhof pp211-212; Karlberg p41; Chantry: *Covenants* pp1,6; Pettit pp39-40).

VanGemeren: 'Reformed theology is an expression of a continuity system'. 'For nearly 500 years the covenant concept has given unity to Reformed theology. The history of Calvinism reveals a consciousness of unity between the Old Testament and the New Testament... This inherent fondness for unity has fostered federal or covenant theology, but not without complication. The covenant idea has been attacked from without and within, has undergone philosophical developments beyond biblical recognition, and has been the basis for the progression and the setback of Reformed doctrine, and is still being used as a way of distinguishing Reformed from non-Reformed systems of theology... The inception of "covenant" as a unifying concept is not Calvin's major contribution to theology... It is clear from the *Institutes* that he develops the unity of the covenant most consistently in his confrontation with the Anabaptists. The Anabaptists emphasised the differences between the Old and New... Like Calvin, Bullinger... was opposed to the Anabaptist emphasis on discontinuity... However, the covenant is not yet [that is, at that time] an over-arching motif... The development from Calvin to federal... theology has not gone without criticism. Some criticism is well-deserved, because federal theologians operated with a mistaken concept of covenant and abstracted the covenant motif increasingly... from the Bible... James B.Torrance has explained how federal theology confused "covenant" with "contract"... [resulting] in an inversion of law over grace, which explains the legalism associated with covenant theology' (VanGemeren pp37-86).

The fall out of covenant theology has been heavy. For instance, the antinomian controversy in New England in the 1630s arose out of 'a distinction between such as were under a covenant of works, and such as were under a covenant of grace'. 'Covenant theology... was an essential ingredient for the emergence of preparation'. 'A phenomenon of Calvinism everywhere in the [17th] century was a tendency to analyse the process of regeneration into a series of moments, but that strain which invented the federal theology was impelled... to set off an initial period wherein he who is about to believe begins to learn what to expect'. But Stout said Miller over-emphasised 'the legalistic and intellectualistic dimension of covenant theology' (Mather Vol.2 pp508-516; Pettit p11; Miller pp55,59; Stout pp38,325).

'Some of the Reformers reintroduced the logical system of biblical interpretation based either on Aristotelian logic, or later, on Ramusian logic'. Consequently, 'deductions according to reason were [regarded] as authoritative as the [sacred] text'. 'The antinomian controversy was conducted largely in logical, rationalistic terms rather than by means of exegesis... [with] the prevalence of scholastic or moralistic preaching, and the use of philosophical distinctions and terminology on the part of many Puritan preachers'. One of the followers of Anne Hutchinson in New England defiantly dismissed the Puritan preachers as 'black-coats that have been at the Ninniversity... your learned scholars'. Howe sadly had to admit there had been an 'aptness to lay greater stress... upon some unscriptural words in delivering Scripture doctrine... [The advocates of covenant theology] handed back and forth the ball of hypothesis, until their fine-spun theses came in many ways to resemble the intricate casuistry of the medieval schoolmen and none but minds drilled in ratiocination could follow them'. 'Religious though their hearers were, and accustomed to lucubration and theory, we cannot suppose that the full complexities of the thought of Puritan ministers were delivered to ordinary churchgoers, nor put into books intended for their everyday reading'. All the more pity, then, that Reformed theologians have not more closely heeded Bullinger's observation: 'It seems to me a notable point of folly to go about to tie matters of divinity to precepts of logic' (K.M.Campbell pp77-79; French pp246-247; quoted by Pettit p36).

Covenant theologians have their internecine differences, and some are prepared to own it in print: 'There are different representations respecting the parties in the covenant of grace. Some considered... others [considered]... and still others... distinguish two covenants [of grace], namely, the covenant of redemption... and... the covenant of grace. [There is a] great deal of confusion that is incidental [to one of these] representations, [whereas another] is easier to understand'. God is the first party in the covenant of grace, but, according to Reformed teachers themselves, 'it is not easy to determine precisely who the second party is... Reformed theologians are not unanimous in answering this question. Some say [one thing]... others assert [another]... The great majority of them, however, maintain that [God] entered into covenant relationship with the elect or the elect sinner in Christ... Even unregenerate and unconverted persons may be in the covenant'. Boston rejected 'the old and widely accepted way of distinguishing the covenant of redemption... from the covenant of grace'. Jonathan Edwards said 'he did not agree with how [Boston] set forth the covenant of grace. Indeed, he says he does not understand his scheme... The real significance of covenant theology, as it passed from Bullinger to the Puritans, was not that it solved anything'. 'Although it stemmed from a branch of Reformed thinking which wanted to avoid scholastic definitions and mechanical metaphors, its real significance was its conscious ambivalence' (Berkhof pp265,273,288-289; John Macleod p147; Pettit p219).

'What induced these theologians to speak of the covenant as made with the elect in spite of all the practical difficulties involved?' Among Reformed teachers, 'there have been several deviating opinions respecting the Sinaitic covenant'. In light of all this internal dissension, the answer to the following question raised by Berkhof would seem to be self-evident: 'Why did this doctrine [of the covenant] meet with little favour outside of Reformed circles?' (Berkhof pp273,298-300; see Boston: *Memoirs* xxviii).

Covenant theologians often try to argue that all the covenants boil down into one: 'The covenant made with all the fathers in so far from differing from ours in reality and substance, that it is altogether one and the same: still the administration differs'. 'All the historic covenants (with Abraham, Moses, David or Christ)... in all ages, dispensations or covenants... the... covenant of grace... is the abiding kernel of every historic covenant... the unity of all covenants'. 'There is but one covenant of grace (of promise) with varying administrations'. 'Every biblical covenant since the fall is revealed by God as a form of *the* covenant of grace. None since Eden has been a covenant of works'. 'None of the biblical covenants since Eden operates on the "law of works" (Rom. 3:27)'. 'All biblical covenants... are but varying administrations of the covenant of grace'. The covenant of grace 'is essentially the same in all dispensations, though its form of administration changes'. In particular, 'the covenant of Sinai was *essentially* the same as that established with Abraham'. 'Little need be said respecting the New Testament dispensation of the covenant'. 'The covenant of grace, as it is revealed in the New Testament, is essentially the same as that which governed the relation of Old Testament believers to God'. 'The covenants mentioned in the Old Testament are like sub-headings falling under a major heading'. 'They are steps leading up to the full revelation of God's covenant of grace which finally finds its fullest expression in what we call the new covenant' (Calvin: *Institutes* Vol.1 p370; Chantry: *Righteous* pp46,103; *Covenants* p13, emphasis mine; Berkhof pp279, 297,299, emphasis his; Hulse: *Restoration* p52).

Those who dare to question it are given rough treatment. Calvin: 'Some madmen of the sect of the Anabaptists' dared to disagree and were guilty of a 'pestilential error'. Chantry deplored the fact that some dare to assert that the 'old covenants are now rescinded' (Calvin: *Institutes* Vol.1 pp369-370; Chantry: *Covenants* p8).

The right view: 'We... agree in asserting the unity of God's purpose through the ages, but the selection of the word "covenant" to describe this unity [has] lent itself to important misunderstandings'. 'In the New Testament the word "covenant" is almost always used to assert discontinuity. The evidence for this is overwhelming'. 'This... strongly suggests that no such covenant is referred to in the New Testament'. 'The covenant under which Christians now live is called *new*'. 'Whatever else this covenant may be, it will be unlike the Mosaic covenant. The Mosaic covenant was one thing; this covenant is another'. 'The Lord declares its substantive dissimilarity to the covenant that preceded it'. 'The strong contrast between the Lord Jesus Christ, as the central figure in the new covenant, and his predecessors, argues strongly for a newness that recognises a large measure of discontinuity'. In Heb. 1:1-2, 'the writer... gives us three contrasts... By ignoring the common use of *covenant* in the New Testament' to indicate discontinuity – see above, 'theologians have tended to subsume all the covenants under the single "covenant of grace", and in the process have largely ironed out the important differences between them'. 'The new covenant is *plainly* superior to the old'. 'While scholars [believers] may not agree on what exactly the 'not like' [of Jer. 31:32] entails, it [is necessary for] everyone to discover [think out] in what way or ways the two covenants are different'. Even covenant theologians have to admit 'the fundamental and most obvious difference between the old and the new, namely, that the new is NEW', listing thirteen differences between the Abrahamic covenant and the new covenant (Wells pp22-24; Hoch pp61-62, emphasis mine; Hulse: 'Covenant' pp24-25).

The law, the old covenant, was temporary. God always intended it to be so. 'The law was a necessary part of God's plan, but not his final word... The *torah* is [was] given for a specific period of time, and is [was] then set aside – not because it was a bad thing now happily abolished, but because it was a good thing whose purpose has now been accomplished... The Christian no longer lives under the *torah*, but this is not because the *torah* is a bad thing now happily done away. Part of membership in the new-covenant family, which is not demarcated by *torah*, is... the true understanding of *torah*, precisely as a God-given deliberate temporary dispensation... *torah*... is [was]... a deliberately temporary dispensation... Christians have left the realm of... *torah*, coming out from the place where it could exert a hold over them' (N.T.Wright pp168,181-182,191-192,195). I will substantiate these points as we come to specific New Testament passages (especially Rom. 7; 2 Cor. 3; Gal. 3; Hebrews).

Sadly, many contemporary Particular Baptists – Baptists, of all people – seem eager to become covenant theologians: 'Currently one may observe the Puritan-Reformed orientation of the [Particular Baptist] family moving in the orbit of the Second London Confession [1689] and gravitating toward an ecclesiastical system which will, unless arrested, move into a modified covenant-theology and Presbyterial form of church polity' (Good p255).

The 2012 Carey Conference, for instance, organised by *Reformation Today*, made its position clear on covenant theology. Mostyn Roberts: 'I came away from this conference encouraged as a Calvinist; as a Baptist; and as a 1689 Baptist – it did seem as if the Carey Conference were trying to pin its colours to the mast of [that is, over] the new-covenant theology issue. After the Q & A session, the chairman said that he could hear the nails in the coffin of new-covenant theology; I am not so sure, as error [*sic*] is tenacious but, for whatever reason, its voice was not heard above a squeak at this conference [surprise, surprise!]. Erroll Hulse insisted that we are not going to accept any tinkering with the 1689 (meaning presumably no asserting an ambivalent position on the law, as the 1644 Confession is supposed to do)'. And Oliver certainly gave a glowing review of Greg Nicholl's *Covenant Theology* (*Reformation Today* pp33-40). By the way, there is nothing 'ambivalent' about the law in the 1644. On the law, it is not Calvinistic, full stop!

These would-be covenant-theologian Baptists are quite determined, and, even though they have to confess that there are some insoluble conundrums at the heart of the system, they are not averse to dismissive name-calling, and the raising of bogey-men: 'Some panic-stricken Baptists have been so foolish as to abandon covenant theology by adopting a false kind of dispensationalism – setting up the old covenant against the new'. The covenant of works is 'something of a mystery', but if we reject the concept, 'we do not have the biblical way of thinking – we are simply sinners thinking' (Hulse: 'Covenant' p20; Thomas pp14-15). Thus, in a stroke, Thomas writes off countless worthy men and women!

Yet even covenant theologians have to admit: 'The widespread denial of the covenant of works... makes it imperative to examine its scriptural foundation with care'. 'It must be admitted that the term... is not found in the first three chapters of Genesis'. The practice is 'justified' by reference to 'trinity' (Berkhof p213; Chantry: *Righteous* p45; *Covenants* p2).

The answer to that, of course, is that '"trinity"... stands for a teaching of the Bible which cannot be expressed with any single Bible word' (Wells p25). 'Covenant', however, is a biblical word, and should be used only in the way the Bible uses it.

Covenant theologians claim that 'the parallel which Paul draws between Adam and Christ... can only be explained on the assumption that Adam, like Christ, was the head of a covenant... The righteousness of Christ is imputed to us [the elect], without any personal work on our part to merit it. And... this... [is] a perfect parallel to the manner in which the guilt of Adam is imputed to us. This naturally leads to the conclusion that Adam stood in covenant relationship to his descendants' (Berkhof pp213-214).

But this, in turn is answered by another covenant theologian: 'This administration has often been denoted "The Covenant of Works" [but] the term is not felicitous... [and] it is not designated a covenant in Scripture. Hos. 6:7 may be interpreted otherwise [than the usual Reformed view] and does not provide the basis for such a construction of the Adamic economy... It should never be confused with what Scripture calls the old covenant or the first covenant (Jer. 31:31-34; 2 Cor. 3:14; Heb. 8:7,13). The first or old covenant is Sinaitic. And not only must this confusion in denotation be avoided, but also [so must] any attempt to interpret the Mosaic covenant in terms of the Adamic institution. The latter could apply only to the state of innocence, and to Adam alone as representative head. The view that in the Mosaic covenant there was a repetition of the so-called covenant of works, current among covenant theologians, is a grave misconception and involves an erroneous construction of the Mosaic covenant, as well as a failure to assess the uniqueness of the Adamic administration... The obedience Christ rendered fulfilled the obedience in which Adam failed... but it would not be correct to say, however, that Christ's obedience was the same in content or demand. Christ was called on to obey in radically different conditions, and required to fulfil radically different demands. Christ was a sin-bearer and the climactic demand was [for him] to die. This was not true of Adam. Christ came to redeem; not so

Adam. So Christ rendered the whole-souled totality [of?] obedience in which Adam failed, but under totally different conditions and with incomparably greater demands'. Unfortunately, Murray thought 'the Mosaic covenant was distinctly redemptive in character and was continuous with and extensive of [as?] the Abrahamic covenants' (Murray: *Collected* Vol.2 pp49-50,58).

Moo, though right, was too cautious: 'The inability of the law to save or justify is a point that all sides in this debate agree on. The point at issue is whether Paul [in Gal. 3:15 – 4:7] intends to confine his critique of the law to this point, or whether he is making a more sweeping claim about the law in the new-covenant era. Traditional covenant-theology has carefully distinguished between the law as a "concept of works" and the law in its regulatory significance, arguing that believers are freed from the former but still obliged to the latter. "New-covenant theology", on the other hand, asserts that believers are free from all aspects of the Mosaic law. I think that Galatians lends support to this more inclusive understanding. First... *nomos* in Galatians refers to the law of Moses, and Paul gives no hint that he restricts his focus to a particular function of the law, or to a particular part of the law' (Moo: 'Galatians' p14).

Continuity/discontinuity

'It is difficult to think of any problem that is more important or fundamental than the relationship between the Testaments. There are two Testaments; no one questions that. How do they form one Bible?' 'The two Testaments may be unified just as certainly through discontinuity as through continuity. Both continuity and discontinuity are a part of the unity of the Biblical revelation'. 'Few issues are of greater significance to biblical theology and, ultimately, to systematic theology as the relation between the Testaments'. 'The immensity of the issue... so vast an issue'. 'The law, and indeed all of the Hebrew Scriptures are to be read... primarily Christologically. Though previously Paul had read all of life through the lens of the law, now [after conversion] he reads it all from the viewpoint of his faith in the eschatological Christ'. 'Issues of continuity and discontinuity between the Testaments are some of the most difficult to grasp in all of theology'. Jonathan Edwards: 'There is perhaps no part of divinity attended with so much intricacy, and wherein orthodox divines do so much differ, as stating the precise agreement and difference between the two dispensations of Moses and Christ'. The issue arose 'at every major disputation between Reformed and Anabaptist thought... [The] Anabaptists provoked the discussion to a greater extent than is usually admitted'. 'Calvin... emphasises the continuity... Beza... stresses the difference...[Beza thought] the ignorance of this distinction between the law and the gospel is one of the principal causes and roots of all the abuses' which have corrupted Christianity (Paul D.Feinberg pp110,128; Moo: 'The Law' pp203-204; Witherington pp220,267,342; Barcellos p7; quoted by Armstrong p20; Belcher and Martin p21; Kendall pp37-38).

Moo: 'Privileging the New Testament over the Old Testament.. is grounded in core convictions about the progressive nature of revelation... The larger issues of continuity and discontinuity between the Testaments... are of such a nature that, almost by definition, the Old Testament has little decisive to say on the matter. Again – and I want to say this very clearly – I am not claiming that the Old Testament can be ignored, or its meaning overridden at will. But I am claiming that the very nature of the questions we are dealing with... – such as the relationship of the new covenant to the old, or the nature of continuity and discontinuity in the law of God – means that decisive evidence will not come from the Old Testament but from the New Testament... Of course, all Christians read the Bible through the lens supplied by Christ and his fulfilment of Scripture.[2] But this lens is more

---

[2] It is interesting to compare the following. Moo, above. Moo again: 'The Old Testament law... must [now] always be viewed though the *lenses* of Jesus' ministry and teaching' (Moo: 'Galatians' p25). Again: 'Though previously Paul had read all of life through the *lens* of the law,

important in "new-covenant theology" than in some other Reformed traditions... A second defining characteristic of new-covenant theology is its insistence that the scriptural revelation is structured in some fundamental way by a temporal contrast between the old covenant and the new. The choice of the language "new-covenant theology" is therefore, to some extent, polemically driven, setting itself in contrast to... "covenant theology"... "New-covenant theology" highlights the shift from the "old" covenant to the "new", and takes very seriously the biblical "salvation history"... The movement gives more credence to this biblical scheme in its final "putting together" of biblical revelation... We will... have to emphasise the "new" in the new covenant, dismissing the attempts to soften the language speaking of a "renewed" covenant' (Moo: 'Galatians' pp3-5,8).

'The difficulty regarding the *newness* of the new covenant is inseparable from the larger debate regarding the relationship between the Testaments... Systems of *continuity* tend to opt for a renewed old covenant. Systems of *discontinuity* opt for either a new replacing old as the covenantal rule' – which is my (DG's) position – or one or other of the dispensational views – which I (DG) reject. 'In other words, entire theological systems are called into question if the new covenant is [regarded as] a partially emended old covenant', on the one hand, or, 'a replacement for the old covenant' on the other. I (DG) reject the dispensational view which leads to 'a divided covenant for... two distinct peoples of God: Israel and the church' (Hoch pp57-58,73 emphasis his).

The position of Old Testament believers was 'somewhat anomalous'. They were in the new covenant and therefore delighted in God's law (Ps. 119), but at the same time they were under its burden. Calvin recognised this but tried to limit it to the 'observance of ceremonies'; that is, the ceremonial law. But their bondage was to the law, the entire law. 'Believers under the law were not destitute of the filial character; but the law, under which they were, infused even into *their* feelings and services something servile' (Moo: *Romans* pp422-423; Calvin: *Institutes* Vol.1 pp394-395; Brown: *Galatians* p234, emphasis mine). Calvin, as we have seen ('Extracts' p360), although he also said the opposite, wanted believers under such servility.

On Gal. 4:24: '"Covenant" is a more faithful translation than "Testament"; and a careful investigation of the meaning of *diathēkē* would contribute greatly to elucidate many passages of Scripture'. 'Originally, Christians used the term "new testament" to refer to the new covenant... It was not until the 3rd century that the term "New Testament" became common as a designation for the Christian Scriptures' (the editor in Calvin: *Commentaries* Vol.21 Part 1 p137; Bercot p472).

The Anabaptists: 'We believe in and consider ourselves under the authority of the Old Testament, in so far as it is a testimony of Christ; in so far as Jesus did not abolish it; and in so far as it serves the purpose of Christian living. We believe in and consider ourselves under the authority of the law in so far as it does not contradict the new law, which is the gospel of Jesus Christ'. 'The Anabaptist characteristic distinction between the Old and New Testaments is most clearly enunciated in the work of Pilgram Marpeck... There is no question about Marpeck's allegiance to the Bible as the word of God. Yet for Marpeck there was an absolute distinction between the Old Testament and the New'. Marpeck

---

now [after conversion] he reads it all from the viewpoint of his faith in the eschatological Christ' (Moo: 'The Law' pp203-204). Thielman: The law is to be 'interpreted through the eschatological *lens* of the gospel' (Thielman p35). Zaspel: Moses 'is not now to be ignored; but the law he gave remains relevant only insofar as it is read through Christian *lenses*' (Zaspel pp158-159). Letham: 'We can begin to think in terms of covenant theology, for in some sense "covenant" has become a *lens* through which to examine a wide area of theology' (Letham pp2-3). Which is right? We all wear spectacles when we read Scripture in general, and the law in particular. Do we read it through Christ or covenant theology? Or what?

argued this by drawing on 'the transitory nature of the Old Testament when compared to the eternal nature of the New. In the Old there is symbol; in the New the essence of that which is symbolised. The Old Testament speaks of Adam, sin, death and law; the New Testament centres in the message of redemption through the risen Christ... Thus... the New Testament alone became the rule of faith and practice for the Anabaptists. Marpeck saw all sorts of dire consequences for Christendom in the failure to interpret the Old Testament properly, [blaming the men of Münster and Calvin] in this regard'. Marpeck drew heavily upon Galatians and Hebrews for his view. 'For all Anabaptists the Bible was the only rule of faith and practice for discipleship and the church. The biblical revelation was held to be progressive. The Old Testament was preparatory and partial, whereas the New Testament was final and complete. All of the Scriptures, they insisted, must be interpreted Christologically, that is, through the mind of Christ'. 'It is possible that Marpeck was influenced greatly by Martin Luther's early emphasis on the utter difference between law and gospel in developing his covenant theology'. 'Marpeck compiled an entire book of over 800 pages... on the theme of the contrast of the two Testaments on a multitude of topics: forgiveness, rest, faith, sword, offerings, *etc*. The period of the old covenant is called "yesterday", while the era of the new is called "today"' (Estep pp141-144,148; Wenger p177).

'For the Reformers, the total Bible was to be taken as a flat book, with every text having the same kind of authority, regardless of its place in the Bible, when it served their purposes... The religious government of the Old Testament could be an example for the State Church in the 16th century without reference to what happened to that government under divine providence in the Old Testament, or what Jesus did about being a king... The Anabaptists were the only mission group of the Reformation to make clear the fundamental distinction between the Old Testament and the New... Over against the "mainstream magisterial" Reformation for which in all history there has been but one age since the covenant with Abraham... the Anabaptists spoke... of the old covenant and the new... The significance of the relationship between [the] Testaments is enormous in practical consequences' (Yoder pp19-20).

'Anabaptism was not fully conformant to Reformation Protestantism, in that it refused to place the Old Testament on a parity with the New, choosing rather to make the new covenant of Christ supreme, and relegating therefore the Old Testament to the position of a preparatory instrument in God's programme. This important basic attitude toward the two Testaments has significant theological consequences, with its bearing on the concept of the church... as well as on ethical questions'. 'Baptism is not the counterpart of circumcision therefore'. The Anabaptists were dogmatic: 'We are not children of the Old Testament but of the New... [They] complained loudly that the weapons which the Reformers used in the battle [with them] were taken from the Old Testament arsenal. They looked upon the policy of sliding from the Old Testament to the New as a master evil, one from which all sorts of evils come' Verduin: *Stepchildren* pp209-210, in part quoting Bender).

'It would seem... that the Reformers, in their haste to find the [Anabaptists] guilty of heresy at this point, were themselves led into error, the error of not appreciating the teaching, found so unmistakeably present in... Hebrews, for example [as well as Romans and Galatians], that the Old Testament is superseded by the New. One can go very far indeed... in saying that there is a discontinuity between the Old Testament and the New before one lands in error as great as that of the man who refuses to accept the discontinuity that the New Testament plainly teaches'. 'The Anabaptists were sometimes accused of rejecting the Old Testament as Scripture. Because they categorically rejected the circumcision-baptism analogy so important for the retention of infant baptism and because they refused to allow the old-covenant ethic to attenuate that of the new, it was *assumed* that the Old Testament was not a part of their Bible. Evidence that any Anabaptist leaders rejected the Old Testament Scriptures has yet to be adduced... It hardly needs to be pointed out that [the] aberrant groups [Münster, for example] have no claim to be considered as Anabaptist groups, even though the assertion is at times made that their attitude toward the Old Testament is Anabaptist' (Verduin: *Stepchildren* pp210-211; Klassen: 'Studies' p80, emphasis mine).

Calvin tended 'to efface the antinomy between the law and the gospel upon which Luther had been so insistent... Calvin exposed himself to the reproach of having blurred the clear distinction that... [some other] Reformers had established between the law and the gospel, or... [exposing himself to the reproach of] having placed the Old and New Testaments on exactly the same level. By also insisting as he did upon the part played by the law, and attributing an active function to it in the Christian life, he gave further cause for the complaints that were addressed to him on this subject... The comparison that Calvin draws between the two Testaments leads him, in effect, to differentiate them by their chronological position in the plan of salvation, rather than by their content... Bucer had similarly affirmed that so far as the substance is concerned there is no difference between the two Testaments... Calvin [agreed]: "The apostle not only makes the people of Israel like and equal to us by the grace of the covenant but also in the meaning of the [so-called] sacraments"... Did not Bucer also say that, as to their substance, the [so-called] sacraments of the old and new covenants were identical?... Calvin... [argued that] the substance or the ground of the two Testaments is identical' (Wendell pp205,208-214).

Grievous consequences followed, as night follows day. For instance, the Presbyterians at the Westminster Assembly argued for their view of church government on what they called 'Jewish subordinations [which, they said,] do concern us as well as them... we may... urge an argument... from subordinations in the Jewish Church to prove a subordination still... there should be subordinations now in the Christian Church, that was then in the Jewish'. 'In other words, Israel's levitical order is seen to constitute a model for the church'. Again: On the premise 'that one and the same covenant, which was made to Abraham in the Old Testament, is for substance the same with that in the New; and this under the New Testament the very same with that of Abraham's under the Old...'. I pause. Shepard wrote of what he called the double covenant – the parent's and God's, the external and the internal covenant, the elect and the church seed. He saw nothing wrong in all the members of a believer's household, being 'visibly godly or the children of such' being church members, whether the children were 'good or bad'. I pause again. Federal holiness covered it all, according to Shepard; the children may be unbelievers, of course, but even so be 'faithful federally'. What if these children grow up profane? They are still church members 'until they are cast out', but for this they must 'positively reject the gospel, [otherwise] they are to be accounted of God's church'. Shepard admitted such churches would be 'mixed with many chaffy hypocrites, and often profane persons', but he thought all is well since 'ordinarily God gathers out his elect' from such 'corrupt churches' (Diprose pp137-138; Shepard in Murray: *Reformation* pp379-405). Would some Reformed teacher like to establish this from the New Testament? After all, it is published by the Banner of Truth, one of the leading contemporary Reformed publishing houses, and read and presumably believed and practiced by present-day Reformed men and women.

A world of trouble would have been avoided if the Reformers had heeded the Anabaptists at this point. Take Dietrich Philips: 'True ministers... rightly divide the word of God between the Old and New Testaments, between the letter and the Spirit'. Philips was scathing about the use of Mosaic laws to 'exercise dominion over the consciences of men'. Taking up Deut. 13:5, 'that God through Moses commanded that the false prophets be put to death', he pointed out the obvious: 'If, according to the Old Testament command, false prophets were to be put to death [today – as of course they were in Philips' days, by Romanists and Reformers, who both were masters at applying the old covenant to the church!], then... likewise the higher powers would be obliged to put to death not only the false prophets but also all image worshippers, and those who serve idols, and who counsel other people to commit sacrilege (Ex. 22:18), and all adulterers, and all who blaspheme the name of the Lord, and who swear falsely by that name, all who curse father and mother, and profane the sabbath (Ex. 20:7; Deut. 27:16); for they are all alike condemned to death by the law as well as the false prophets are... God through Moses had commanded to kill the false prophets; that is a command of the Old and not the New Testament... In all false and anti-Christian congregations these [following] things are not found: namely, no real new birth; no real distinction between law and gospel, that brings forth fruit, and by which people truly repent and are converted from unrighteousness unto the living God (Matt. 3:8; Luke 3:8); no true knowledge of the eternal and only God, who is life eternal, the fullness of wisdom and of righteousness, that is manifested by the keeping of the commandments of God (John 17:3...); no true confession of the pure, holy and spotless humility; no scriptural baptism or Lord's supper; no Christian washing of the feet of saints (John 13:5-17) in the quietness of true humility; no key to the kingdom of heaven; no evangelical ban or separation [that is, church discipline]; no shunning of the temples of idolatry nor false worship; no unfeigned brotherly love; no God-fearing life nor keeping of the commands of Christ; no persecution for righteousness' sake. All these ordinances and evidences of true Christianity are found in no anti-Christian congregations in correct form, but everywhere the reverse and opposite'. Yet the fact is, 'all things have become new through Jesus Christ (Rom. 7:6); the oldness of the letter and of the flesh has passed away, and the upright new being of the Spirit has been ushered in by Jesus Christ (2 Cor. 5:17)' (Philips pp235-237,240-243,253-256).

And Menno Simons: 'To swear truly was allowed to the Jews under the law; but the gospel forbids this to Christians'. Sebastian Franck complained of 'wolves, the doctors of unwisdom, apes of the apostles, and antichrists [who] mix the New Testament with the Old... and from it prove [the legitimacy of]... [the] power of magistracy... [the] priesthood; and praise everything and ascribe this all forcibly to Christ... And just as the popes have derived all this from it, so also many of those who would have themselves called evangelicals hold that they have nobly escaped the snare of the pope and the devil, and have nevertheless achieved... nothing more than that they have exchanged and confounded the priesthood of the pope with the Mosaic kingdom... If [that is, since] the priesthood cannot be re-established out of the old law, neither can [Christian] government... be established according to the law of Moses'. In all this, Franck listed the sabbath along with circumcision, kingship, temple and sacrifices, as old-covenant externals (quoted by Stuart Murray pp101-102; Franck pp151-152).

Discontinuity: the 'but now'
Lloyd-Jones aptly entitled his opening chapter on Rom. 3:21-22: 'The Great Turning Point – "But Now"'. As he said, it is these two words, 'but now', which are vital. 'What then is their meaning and import?' He answered his question: 'They do two main things. First and foremost they provide us with a contrast... to all the old law position, to our being under the law in any shape or form. But in addition to that, of course, the "but now" brings in the time factor... What [Paul] is saying is, "NOW" this thing that has happened [Christ has come, and so on] has changed everything'. Having rightly stressed the continuity between the law and the gospel – "the law and the prophets witnessed to" the gospel – Lloyd-Jones then spoke of: 'What the position was under the law... but it is no longer like that. Something new has happened – "now". The great turning point in all history had just taken place: that was the coming of the Son of God into the world. So that we are living in a new age – the "now". It is no longer the old, it is the new age. It has arrived... This is a most important word to watch, therefore, as you read the New Testament; there is a contrast between what once was and what is now' (Lloyd-Jones: *Atonement* pp23,28-29,34-38,40).

John Murray on the same verses: 'Paul is emphasising not only the contrast between justification through the works of [the] law and justification without the law... but he is also emphasising the *manifestation* of the latter which came with the revelation of Jesus Christ.

Now, in contrast with the past... This does not mean for Paul that justification without the law was now for the first time revealed and that in the earlier period all that men knew was justification by works of law. It is far otherwise. To obviate any such discrepancy between the past and the present Paul expressly reminds us that this righteousness of God now manifested was witnessed by the law and the prophets. He is jealous to maintain in this matter as in other respects the continuity between the two Testaments. But consistently with this continuity there can still be distinct emphasis upon the momentous change in the New Testament in respect of *manifestation*. The temporal force of the "now" can [must!] therefore be recognised without impairing either the contrast of relations or the continuity between the two periods contrasted' (Murray: *Romans* Vol.1 pp108-109, emphasis his).

Many Reformed teachers do not accept this discontinuity, or at least its emphasis; take Charles Hodge: 'The words "but now"... may be regarded as merely marking the transition from one paragraph to another, or as a designation of time, "now", *i.e.*, under the gospel dispensation' (Charles Hodge: *Romans* p88).

Lloyd-Jones rightly dismissed this: 'We must emphasises the word "now", and we do so for this reason. It is not brought in here as a kind of grammatical connection. It is not that the apostle is just saying: well, we have been seeing how no attempt to justify oneself by means of the law can possibly succeed, "but now" by way of contrast there is this other way. It included that. But I believe that the word "now" is used by the apostle in order that he might emphasise also the historical aspect of this matter' (Lloyd-Jones: *Atonement* p40). Speaking for myself, I am sure the 'but now' speaks both of contrast and the historical – the eschatological.

Charles Hodge overstated his case: 'The evangelical doctrine of justification by faith is the doctrine of the Old, *no less than* the New Testament' (Charles Hodge: *Romans* p102, emphasis mine).

As Kruse expressed it: 'The "now" here seems to be [is!] more than an inferential particle. While it does signal that what is to follow will draw out the implications of what has already been said, it also indicates that God has acted in the present time, the great eschatological now, to manifest his righteousness apart from the law' (Kruse p189).

As Moo put it: 'The phrase ["but now"] could have purely logical force... but it is much more likely [it does!] to preserve its normal temporal meaning... "But now" marks the shift in Paul's focus from the old era of sin's domination to the new era of salvation. This contrast between two eras in salvation history is one of Paul's most basic theological conceptions... Rom. 1:18 – 3:20 has sketched the spiritual state of those who belong to the old era: justly condemned, helpless in the power of sin, powerless to escape God's wrath. "But now" God has intervened to inaugurate a new era, and all who respond in faith – not only after the cross, but, as Rom. 4 will show, before it also – will be transferred into it from the old era. No wonder Lloyd-Jones can exclaim: There are no more wonderful words in the whole of Scripture than just these two words "But now"' (Moo: *Romans* p221).

'In... Luke and Acts... the law should be interpreted in light of salvation history. Now that the new covenant has arrived in Jesus Christ, the law no longer occupies centre stage. The law must be interpreted in light of Jesus Christ and his coming. It was the will of God to keep the law during the old era of salvation history, but the law... is no longer normative now that Christ has come' (Schreiner p179).

Law and gospel
As far as justification goes: 'Central to the Reformers' teaching about salvation was their distinction between "law" and "gospel"'. Yes, for justification, but not sanctification. And Calvin's third use of the law has become so ingrained, 'so intimately have the two directories of law and grace been accustomed to be blended, that many a believer is found

thinking, and speaking, and acting unconsciously as a Jew. Men have gone on unconsciously confounding things that differ'. 'The history of covenant theology shows a tendency to overplay the *continuity*, and not do justice to the revealed *discontinuity* of the two covenants'. This continuity shows itself in that 'God is the author of both'. 'There is an obvious overlapping of commandments regarding the love of God and one's neighbour, the honouring of one's father and mother, doing no murder, committing no adultery, not stealing, lying or coveting. There are other common commandments... to pay the labourer, aid the poor, not intermarry with pagans, avoid gluttony and drunkenness, not indulging in impure thoughts, not taking revenge' (Moo: *Romans* p644; Harris p45; Zens: *Studies* p41; Hoch p62). Yes, there is continuity. I certainly do not deny it. But...

Thielman: 'The law of Moses... stands both in continuity and in discontinuity with the "word of faith". The law is continuous with the gospel because it led the way to Christ, but it is discontinuous with the gospel because it spells the end of the Mosaic covenant'. Matthew, Luke, John, Paul and the writer to the Hebrews 'are all unified in the conviction that [the Mosaic law] has been overwhelmed by the life, death and resurrection of Jesus. Much of the Mosaic law, both at the level of structure and specific commands, has been creatively appropriated in this new, eschatological situation. Still, too much of the law has been omitted or radically reinterpreted for the emphasis to fall on the continuity between law and gospel. Continuity is present, but the gospel is something new' (Thielman pp31,182). Thielman's words are the more significant since he is a Presbyterian. I will not repeat this every time I quote him, but the comment stands.

Gal. 4:21-29

Witherington: 'It is probably a mistake to read Gal. 4 in the light of 2 Cor. 3 where there is a clear contrast between an old and a new covenant...[3] [but] one must add that Paul closely connects the Abrahamic and new covenants; indeed it is plausible [it is certain!] that here Paul is thinking of the fulfilment of the Abrahamic covenant in the new one'. Dunn: 'The passage as a whole is clearly constructed in a sequence of contrasts... antithetical correspondences (antinomies)'. Dunn, however, went only so far as to say: 'It is tempting to understand the two covenants as the old and new covenant' – amazingly rejecting this obvious truth, claiming 'only one covenant is at issue here – the covenant with Abraham', even though he listed 1 Cor. 11:25; 2 Cor. 3:6; Heb. 8:6-13, and went on to tackle Gal. 4:24, which he read as, 'one of these covenants is from Mount Sinai and gives birth to slavery'.

Witherington rightly corrected this: 'Dunn has failed to grasp the radical character of Paul's argument... It is the argument of the agitators, not Paul, that the Mosaic covenant is an extension of the Abrahamic covenant'. This puts covenant theologians on the side of the agitators against Paul (Witherington pp330-332; Dunn pp244,249-250).

But covenant theologians will not have it: 'At bottom there were not two covenants, but two dispensations of one and the same covenant of grace'. 'These two women... represent... two covenants, [that is,] two distinct affirmations of God's one and only covenant of grace'. So how could Paul say the Mosaic covenant, if it really was the covenant of grace, enslaved? It was only 'as the Jews and Judaisers actually viewed it... law (as interpreted by the Judaisers)'. To confuse the Mosaic covenant with the covenant of works – to deny it is the covenant of grace is 'the most common error'. 'The majority of our holy and most learned divines concur [in saying] that though the law is called a covenant, yet it was not the covenant of works... but it was the same covenant in respect of its nature and design under which we stand under the gospel, even the covenant of grace, though more legally dispensed to the Jews. It differed not in substance from the covenant of grace'. 'The covenant of grace under the law is called by such divines... the old covenant... and under

---

[3] That is to say, 2 Corinthians was written after Galatians.

the gospel... the new covenant. [These] holy and most learned divines', saw the oldness of the old covenant simply as a way of describing its 'legal administrations', its obscurity, and so on. But even so 'the new and old covenants, the covenants of law and gospel, are both of them really covenants of grace, only differing in their administrations'. 'Covenant theologians generally [regard] phrases like "first covenant" and "old covenant" as referring, not to the Mosaic covenant, but to the whole age between Adam's fall and Christ's [first] coming'. 'We insist that [in the Mosaic covenant] there was nothing else than a fresh administration of the covenant of grace, so that in actual substance it is the same as the covenant entered into with Abraham' (Ridderbos p176; Hendriksen: *Galatians* pp182,187; Thomas p15; Bolton pp99-100; Heppe quoted by Zens: *Studies* pp22-23).

This is quite wrong. The Mosaic (Hagar) covenant in question 'was formed on a servile principle, "do and live"'. And Calvin himself admitted as much: 'The legal covenant makes slaves'. Even so, despite stating this obvious truth, Calvin dropped back into: 'The gendering to bondage... denotes those who make a wicked abuse of the law, by finding in it nothing but what tends to slavery'. But, as Calvin himself said: 'The two covenants... are the mothers of whom children unlike one another are born; for the legal covenant makes slaves, and the evangelical covenant makes freemen' (Brown: *Galatians* p234. Calvin: *Commentaries* Vol.21 Part 1 pp137-138). It was not 'abuse' of the old covenant that produced bondage; it was the old covenant itself!

Covenant theologians are guilty of double-speak: 'The same covenant of grace... [was] made with Abraham, [was] renewed at Sinai... [yet] donning the appearance of the covenant of works' (Heppe quoted by Zens: *Studies* p23). See my other works, and throughout these pages, for plenty of other examples of Reformed double-speak.

I see the double-speak in Calvin's extended section on 'The Difference Between the Two Testaments' (Calvin: *Institutes* Vol.1 pp387-399). Calvin set out five major differences between the two. As for the fourth, Calvin stated: 'In Scripture, the term "bondage" is applied to the Old Testament, because it begets fear, and the term "freedom" to the New, because productive of confidence and security... The Old Testament filled the conscience with fear and trembling, the New inspires it with gladness. By the former the conscience is held in bondage, by the latter it is manumitted [freed from slavery] and made free'. He spelled out the reasons. So far, excellent. Yet in that same section, while admitting the five major contrasts, he nevertheless claimed 'that they all belong to the mode of administration rather than the substance', which they certainly do not! For 'testament', of course, we should read 'covenant'. I remind you of an earlier extract: '"Covenant" is a more faithful translation than "Testament"; and a careful investigation of the meaning of *diathēkē* would contribute greatly to elucidate many passages of Scripture' (the editor in Calvin: *Commentaries* Vol.21 Part 1 p137).

Karlberg: 'The law at Sinai... reinstitutes the original law of creation in a manner appropriate to the Mosaic dispensation of the economy of redemption... The legal demand of the Mosaic law, which obligation appeared as a reinstatement of the original demand placed upon the first Adam at creation, [was] the reintroduction of the covenant of works [but] modified'. In light of this, how could Karlberg then add: 'The covenant of law under Moses was, after all, a renewal of the single covenant of grace spanning the entire age from the fall to the consummation'? So much so, the law of Moses and the gospel were simply different 'dispensations of the covenant of grace'. 'The Mosaic covenant was, assuredly, an administration of the covenant of grace'. And this, even though he had previously admitted: 'The law works wrath and those under... the law of Moses... are under the curse of God for transgression... The curse of the Mosaic law had been laid upon the entire house of Israel, comprising both the elect and the non-elect... The function of the Mosaic law was chiefly negative' (Karlberg pp37,39,40). I cannot fathom such schizophrenia.

Andrew Fuller: 'Strictly speaking, men are not now under the covenant of works, but under the curse for having broken it. God is not in covenant with them, nor they with him. The law, as a covenant, was recorded, and a new and enlarged edition of it given to Israel at Mt Sinai; not however, for the purpose of "giving life" to those who had broken it; but rather as a preparative for a better covenant' (Andrew Fuller: *Worthy* p171).

What about this for arguing black is white? Witsius thought Adam was under the covenant of works which 'in substance [corresponded] with what is expressed in the ten commandments'. After Adam fell, God instituted a 'new covenant of grace' with him. Witsius based this on the fact that when God says 'new, he makes the first old' (Heb. 8:13). 'It is indeed true, that the [writer], in that place, does not speak precisely of the covenant of works, but of the old economy of the covenant of grace... Yet we properly build on his [that is, the writer to the Hebrews as interpreted by Witsius] reasoning' (Zens: *Studies* pp24-25,92-93, quoting Witsius). I do not apologise for the word – Hermann Witsius was a great man, I have no doubt, but this is rubbish!

What about the Puritans, the masters of covenant theology? They were confused as to what the New Testament means when it refers to the first and second covenants, the old and new covenants. In fact, taken as a body, they were all at sea on the law: 'In expressing this covenant there is a difference among the learned. Some make the law a covenant of works, and upon that ground [they say] that it is abrogated. Others call it a subservient covenant to the covenant of grace, and make it only occasionally, as it were, introduced, to put more lustre and splendour upon grace. Others call it a mixed covenant of works and grace; but that is hardly to be understood as possible, much less as true. I therefore think that opinion true... [which says] that the law by Moses was a covenant of grace... It is not possible to make an accurate classification of the Puritans on the basis of their views about the Mosaic covenant, because many of them held several of the different [even contradictory] views in varying combinations. On the whole, however, they can be divided into two groups on this subject; those who regarded the Mosaic covenant as a covenant of works, and those who regarded it as a covenant of grace. [The majority fell into] line with the earlier Protestant theologians who minimised the difference between the Old Testament and the New, and regarded the law of Moses and the gospel of Christ "as different forms of the one covenant of grace"... The outcome of the Puritan debate was that, on the whole, it was agreed that the Mosaic covenant was a form of the covenant of grace; and this view was embodied in the [Westminster] Confession of faith... These differences of interpretation are discouraging' for advocates of Calvin's view of the law based on covenant theology (Kevan: *Grace* pp113-117,120-121). All advocates of covenant theology – not excluding Particular Baptists (and Kevan himself was one such) – should weigh these words.

Bunyan had a peculiar view of the twofold giving of the law at Sinai: 'The first does more principally intend its force as a covenant of works', whereas the second, he claimed, was as a rule to those who are in Christ: 'The covenant of works, or the law... is the law delivered upon Mt Sinai to Moses, in two tables of stone, in ten particular branches, or heads; for this see Gal. 4'. 'This law... delivered to Moses... in substance, though possibly not so openly, was given to the first man Adam' (Bunyan: *Christian* p535; *Doctrine* pp179-259). If any reader agrees with Bunyan, would he or she kindly email me, and give me the biblical proof of it?

How about this for opaqueness? 'According to Petto the interpretative key is found in the New Testament passages referring to the old and new covenants. If one reads the pertinent passages, Heb. 8, Gal. 3-4, or 2 Cor. 3, for instance, the contrast between the grace exhibited in the new covenant[4] comes not from the covenant of works made with Adam, but with the covenant made with Israel at Sinai. This covenant is the one which is placed in opposition to the new covenant. Some of the authors, however, who argue strongly for the Mosaic covenant being one of grace, are the same ones who also argue for the identification of the old covenant with the covenant of works with Adam; or else they see no contradiction when the old-covenant passages from Hebrews are used in connection with the covenant of works. However, the old covenant, treated as a covenant of works, appears inconsistent with the view of the Mosaic covenant as an administration of the covenant of grace... John Owen rejected the Mosaic covenant as being a covenant of grace... Of course, neither did he accept it as a covenant of works' (Strickland p29). So what *do* covenant theologians think?

Antinomista put the question which has to be answered by the Reformed: 'Were the ten commandments, as they were delivered to [the Israelites] on Mount Sinai, the covenant of works or not?' Boston: 'As to this point, there are different sentiments among orthodox divines... It is evident to me that the covenant of grace was delivered to the Israelites on Mt Sinai... But that the covenant of works was also... delivered to the Israelites on Mt Sinai, I cannot refuse'. Fisher: 'The covenant of grace and... the covenant of works... the ten commandments were the [substance] of both covenants'. Boston: 'I conceive the two covenants to have been both delivered on Mt Sinai to the Israelites... [both] the covenant of grace... [and] the covenant of works... There is no confounding of the two covenants of grace and works... According to this account of the Sinai transaction, the ten commands, there delivered, must come under a twofold notion or consideration; namely, as the law of Christ, and as the law of works... The transaction at Sinai... was a mixed dispensation; there was the promise or covenant of grace, and also the law; the one a covenant to be believed, the other a covenant to be done'. Nomista put his finger on the flaw: 'The Lord never delivers the covenant of works to any that are under the covenant of grace'. Fisher: 'Indeed it is true', but...! Boston: Since God gave the commandments twice on Sinai, this means it 'is not strange' that the ten commandments fulfil these two contradictory roles. Even so, Boston realised he was clutching at straws: 'Whether or not... some such thing is intimated, by the double accentuation of the decalogue, let the learned determine' (Fisher pp53-59,76-77).

Reader, learned or not, can you 'determine' what Boston was on about? If you are a Reformed believer, which covenant are you under? As you know, according to your teachers and your Confessions, you are under the law – but are you under it as the covenant of works or the covenant of grace? Are you under the law as given to Moses the first time, or the second? Do you know? Does it matter? Where does the New Testament talk like this?

Berkhof: 'The Sinaitic covenant included a service that contained a positive reminder of the strict demands of the covenant of works. The law was placed very much in the foreground, giving prominence once more to the earlier legal element... But the covenant of Sinai was not a renewal of the covenant of works [but grace and the] divine message of salvation... The Jews lost sight of the latter aspect, and fixed their attention exclusively on the former... They regarded the covenant ever increasingly, but mistakenly, as a covenant of works'. Chantry: 'The covenant of works breathes a curse... Such an emphasis upon cursing in the covenant of works, not blessing... It is a world under the curse of the covenant of works.. the curse of the covenant of works... the curse of the covenant of works... the very curse which hangs over [sinners'] heads in the covenant of works... The covenant of works

---

[4] Something must be missing here. Petto was trying to resolve 'the contrast between the grace exhibited in the new covenant' and what? I presume it was 'the works required in the old covenant'.

breathes a curse... cursing in the covenant of works... under the scheme of works cursing, not blessing... came... If [men] do not flee to Christ for grace, they must receive the curse. Gal. 3:10a: "As many as are of the works of the law are under the curse"... The Most High expects perfect and perpetual obedience to each and every statute in his moral law. Deut. 27:26 is quoted in Gal. 3:10: "Cursed is everyone that continues not in all things which are written in the book of the law, to do them"... The operative principle in the covenant of works is "do for ourselves"... Gal. 3:10-12: "All who rely on observing the law are under a [the] curse...". Under the covenant of works, the curse... Gal. 3:13: "Christ has redeemed us from the curse of the law..."'. How odd then to read Chantry's dismissal of 'dispensationalists' and 'the new breed of Calvinistic Baptists' who dare to call the Mosaic covenant the covenant of works. 'It is possible... to slip into reading the moral law with the glasses of the covenant of works', but it really is not so. Oh no! It is, after all, the covenant of grace. What is more: 'Every biblical covenant after the fall is revealed by God as a form of the covenant of grace. None since Eden has been a covenant of works... None of the biblical covenants since Eden operates on the "law of works"... All have as their mainspring the "law of faith"' (Berkhof p298; Chantry: *Covenants* pp4-6,9-13). So – the law – which is it? The covenant of works or the covenant of grace?

Boston again. As we have seen, he is prone, at the very least, to be confusing on this subject. Will he do any better this time? 'The unbelieving Israelites were under the covenant of grace made with their father Abraham externally... but under the covenant of works made with their father Adam internally... Further, as to believers among them, they were internally... as well as externally, under the covenant of grace; and only externally under the covenant of works, and that, not as a covenant coordinate with, but subordinate and subservient to, the covenant of grace'. Boston was trying to answer the objection 'that... the same persons, at one and the same time, were both under the covenant of works, and under the covenant of grace... is absurd'. So it is, of course. Oh no, it is not, said Boston. Take the Jews. Then followed the above paragraph. Having, he felt, sorted it all out, Boston declared: 'In this there is no more inconsistency than in the former' (Fisher p54). No! No less inconsistency, either! Reader: Did Boston get it any clearer for you this time?

J.G.Vos had no time for the concept of two basic or primary covenants, 'the covenant of works' and 'the covenant of grace'. Staggeringly, however, he felt he could assert: 'The advocates of covenant theology reject "this common belief in two basic covenants". [They] hold that the really basic covenant is the one covenant of grace... The two halves of the Bible should be regarded not as separate covenants made by God with mankind, but as records of the way in which the one covenant was administered in two different ways for necessary reasons' (quoted by Zens: *Studies* p27).

Let's back to biblical reality. Edgar H.Andrews: In Gal. 4:21-29 'Paul's message is clear. The two covenants are distinct, opposed and mutually exclusive... There are two covenants, one being the Sinai covenant represented by Hagar, and the other the covenant of promise represented by Sarah... There are two covenants... distinct... opposed... mutually exclusive... The Sinai covenant was, by its very nature, a covenant of works... How are men brought into bondage by the law? By the endless and futile search for obedience to that law: endless, because it is a task from which man can never rest; futile, because everything man does is tainted by sin and therefore cannot satisfy God. It is because Moses' covenant requires men to work for God's blessing that it brings them into bondage... The false idea that salvation can be obtained by such works is rightly called "legalism". However, there is another kind of bondage to the law that can be experienced even by true believers, who understand they can be justified only by faith. This occurs when Christians seek holiness or "sanctification" by the deeds of the law, and has been called "nomism"... There is persuasive evidence in the letter that Paul is [mainly – DG] worried about nomism. If Paul's concern is limited to legalism (which denies men salvation through Christ), why does he write such a letter to people whom he treats throughout as already being saved?

(See Gal. 3:1-3,26-29; 4:6-9; 5:7-10,13)... The overwhelming evidence is that Paul regarded them as true believers who were being confused and led astray by false doctrine. There was a danger of apostasy [yes, Gal. 3:4; 5:2-4], but there was a greater danger of true believers being entangled with a yoke of bondage. The danger is present today when the law is urged upon believers as the primary pattern for Christian living... The two covenants give rise to... two peoples. The "children" of the old Jerusalem are those who remain in bondage to the old covenant, made at Sinai. This bondage can take the form of legalism; namely, the idea that man can be justified by the works of that law. But (among believers) it can also take the form of nomism, in which the law of Moses is seen as necessary in some manner for a believer's sanctification or holiness. By contrast, the "children" of the heavenly Jerusalem... are free. They have been delivered from the power and penalty of sin, and thus from the clutches of the law. They are no longer in bondage to the requirements and sanctions of the law. But they are not without law, being subject to the rule and law of Christ, which is written in the hearts. They are enabled to keep this new law by the indwelling Spirit. Thus Paul established that the two covenants... are opposed and mutually exclusive. We can belong only to one "Jerusalem", not both. Any attempt to merge law and gospel into a single system is doomed to failure' (Edgar H.Andrews pp234-256).

Andrews has made some vital points which must not be forgotten. His words serve as an admirable end to this section.

Lev. 18:5 and Deut. 30:12-14
On Rom. 10:3-8, Gal. 3:12, (Lev. 18:5), Moo: 'The law... refers in this verse, as usually in Paul, to the Mosaic law'. This is the view of 'the great majority of scholars... [Paul's] purpose in quoting Lev. 18:5 is succinctly to summarise... the essence of the law: blessing is contingent on obedience...'. Moo rejected the notion that Paul was merely using biblical language to express his own thoughts: 'This solution will not work... [Rom. 10:6] looks like the introduction to a quotation... The best explanation for Paul's use of the Deut. 30[:12-14] text is to think that he finds in this passage an expression of the grace of God in establishing a relationship with his people. As God brought his word near to Israel... so God now brings his word "near" to both Jews and Gentiles that they might know him through his Son Jesus Christ and respond in faith and obedience. Because Christ, rather than the law, is now the focus of God's revelatory word (see Rom. 10:4), Paul can "replace" the commandment of Deut. 30:11-14 with "Christ"... As Paul therefore uses Lev. 18:5 to summarise the essence of "the law", so he quotes Deut. 30:12-14 to encapsulate "the gospel"'. John Murray: 'Paul appropriates [Lev. 18:5] as... suited to express the principle of law-righteousness... We should not perplex the difficulties of the passage by supposing that the apostle takes a passage concerned with law-righteousness and applies it to the opposite, namely, faith-righteousness'. Bruce thought Deuteronomy might be an 'anticipation' of the new covenant, but he confessed: 'It is not so easy for us as it was for Paul to draw a distinction between' the two passages in the law. Kruse noted how Paul 'adds his own comments... by which he makes the [Deuteronomy passage] speak of the gospel he proclaims. This seems, on first reading to be a very [sic] arbitrary use of the Old Testament... What is clear... is that Paul in Rom. 10:5-8 uses different parts of the law... to contrast faith-righteousness with law-righteousness. It is also clear that Paul uses Deut. 30:12-14 to emphasise that, just as the law was not something hidden and distant from the Israelites, so also the gospel of faith-righteousness is not something hidden or distant – it is freely available to both Jews and Gentiles'. As Kruse had earlier commented on Rom. 3:21: 'It is important to note that, by saying that this righteousness has been manifested 'apart from the law', the apostle makes it clear that it is therefore available to "all who believe", both the Gentiles (who do not have the law) and Jews (who have the law but do not keep it' (Moo: *Romans* pp636,648,651-654; Murray: *Romans* Vol.2 pp51-52; Bruce: *Romans* p204; Kruse pp189,229-232). See Schreiner pp59-64.

Could the law justify?

The biblical answer is, yes. But the obedience would have to be perfect. This, however, is heavily contested today.

One 'modern view' is that there never was any justification by the law; the Jews never thought it: 'The works of the law' were not done by the Jews as 'good works done to amass merit... for in principle Judaism was not a religion in which the law was observed for this reason, but simply because it was required under the terms of the Mosaic covenant'. '[Daniel] Fuller argues that Mosaic law – no less than the gospel proclaimed by Jesus – required only the obedience of faith, and repudiated the idea that works merit divine blessing' under the law (Kruse pp67-69; Karlberg pp36-37; Daniel Fuller xi; pp66-88; back-cover). Schreiner: 'Virtually all scholars agree that there is no warrant for this idea' – namely, that salvation could be earned by the law (Schreiner p29). Of course, I agree that no sinner could possibly keep the law; nevertheless, perfect obedience to the law would earn justification (Rom. 7:10). Schreiner did not give the verse its due weight. Even so, in what he did (weakly) say about it, he contradicted himself: 'The law at one level may have been given to bring life (Rom. 7:10), but it actually failed miserably to do so and increased transgressions instead' (Schreiner p81). Apart from 'may have been given' – it *was* given (Rom. 7:10)! – first-rate. See also his answer to his own question: 'Is Perfect Obedience to the Law Mandatory for Salvation?': 'The short answer to this question is "yes"... Perfect obedience to the law was necessary for salvation' (Schreiner pp53,57). So, as Schreiner said: 'Paul insists that the whole law must be kept to obtain justification... Paul argues that the law is not a solution but part of the problem... (Rom. 5:20)' (Schreiner pp45,81).

An alternative 'modern view'; namely, it was all a question of 'misunderstanding'. The Jews thought they could obtain justification by law-works, but this arose out of their misunderstanding of the law; the law itself never promised justification for good works: 'In the New Testament... across its pages we find Judaism's soteriology to be fundamentally at odds with the teachings of Christ... The fatal error of the Judaisers lay in their *misunderstanding* and *misuse* of the Mosaic law; the Jews thought that salvation could be obtained on the basis of works-righteousness. Obedience to the law was thus *mistakenly* viewed as the meritorious grounds of salvation; that is, life everlasting'. 'As regards the doctrine of salvation, the New Testament lays out the clear-cut, irreconcilable differences between the teaching of Judaism and the Old Testament... [Lev. 18:5] and its New Testament citations [referred only to] life and prosperity in the land of Canaan... temporal life in the promised land... temporal blessing(s)'. The curse of the law was 'exile in a foreign land... the Babylonian exile'. Israel served as a type which finished in AD70 when 'the ancient, theocratic kingdom of Israel was finally abolished' (Karlberg pp36-40, emphasis mine).

Bayes started on the right note: 'It is not the mere having of the law which will lead to justification, but doing it' (Bayes p103). Surprising, then, that he argued so strongly against the possibility of justification by law: 'The weakness of the law in terms of justification is simply that justification is something with which the law has never had anything to do' (Bayes p144. See also Bayes pp115,117,123). This is seriously wrong, as I have shown in the body of the book. Significantly, Bayes made, as far as I have discovered, but one passing reference to Rom. 7:10 (Bayes p92). Incidentally, Daniel Fuller did not even mention the verse, and Kevan, in *Grace*, mentioned it only in passing, and did not mention Rom. 10:5. Is this not strange?

So what about Rom. 10:3-6? Bayes: 'The subject of the passage [Rom. 10:3-6] is justification, [but it was] Israel's *misunderstanding* of the law as a route to righteousness... The weakness of the law in terms of justification is simply that justification is something with which the law has never had anything to do... It will be clear that I [Bayes] am not endorsing the traditional Protestant interpretation of Galatians... The old interpretation of

Galatians said that the reason why justification is not by the law is that no one is able to fulfil it, and that the purpose of the law is to demonstrate that fact. I am arguing that the reason why justification is not by the law is that God never intended that it should be... The law never had a justifying role... To harmonise [Gal. 3:12 and Rom. 10:5] is not easy'. But it is! As Bayes himself admitted: 'The law was a matter of doing'. The New Perspective: 'Some Jews in Paul's day *misunderstood* the teaching of the Old Testament and thought in terms of personal merit... Jews did not generally consider the law as a hurdle to be jumped or a burden to be carried in order to gain acceptance with God, but as a gift showing the path in which they should walk as those already accepted by him. They therefore were to obey the law as the way of life'. But did Thompson go further? I find him confusing. On the one hand, it appears he virtually blamed Paul – it could be described as *his* misunderstanding: 'When Paul speaks about people seeking a righteousness of their own, according to the law (Rom. 10:3; Phil. 3:9), that is *his interpretation* [emphasis his] of what people were advocating. In other words, although *his opponents would not see it that way* [emphasis mine], their view *in effect* [emphasis his] meant self-reliance and reliance on what was temporary (the law)'. I – DG – think Thompson was arguing that these Judaisers were not actually saying what Paul mistakenly thought they were saying. Rather 'it is more likely... that they too [like Paul] believed that membership in God's people is based on the grace of God, and that they were demonstrating their faith by insisting on the keeping of the law' (Bayes pp115-123,144,153,155,164,173; Michael Thompson pp9,13,18, all emphasis mine, except where stated).

The traditional view – mine (DG – I think it is the *biblical* view): 'The law... in theory set forth a means of justification... [In Rom. 2:7,10,13; 7:10:] Paul agreed with the Jewish belief that justification could, in theory, be secured through works'. But 'while... one could be justified by doing the law in theory, in practice it is impossible'. 'This issue is related in traditional Reformed theology to the debate over the existence and nature of the "covenant of works" and the place of the law within that covenant... The law embodies, in its very nature, the principle that perfect obedience to it would confer eternal life (see Rom. 2:13; 7:10). It may be this principle that Paul intends to enunciate here *via* the words of Lev. 18:5. However... Paul's... purpose in quoting Lev. 18:5 is succinctly to summarise what for him is the essence of the law: blessing is contingent on obedience. It is the one who *does* the works required by the law who must find life through them. The emphasis lies on the word "doing" and not on the promise of "life"'. 'Paul clearly accords to the law a theoretically life-giving potential (Rom. 7:10)'. Paul 'denies that it is a practical possibility to keep the law so as to secure that life. For no one after the fall has the capacity to fulfil the law perfectly; and only such perfect fulfilment would lead to the securing of eternal life' – which was precisely what Christ did (Gal. 4:4-5) (Moo: *Romans* pp155-156, 211-217,439,637,648-649; 'The Law' p212, emphasis his).

On Gal. 4:4-5, Bayes thought Christ coming under the law 'is most likely a statement of his Jewish identity'. This is woefully inadequate. Being 'born under the law', as Witherington said, 'makes [it] quite clear that Jesus was born a Jew, but it does not [in itself] tell us in any *full* way what Jesus' relationship to the law was'. Nevertheless, when combined with the following verse, 'the purpose of Christ's coming and being under the law' is spelled out: 'He came to set [elect] Jews free who were confined under the law'. 'Christ bore the law's curse when he died (Gal. 3:13)'. Bayes: 'Christ alone is the man who has attained life by doing the things of the law'. Calvin: 'Salvation can only be procured by [the law] if its precepts be exactly fulfilled. Life is indeed promised in it, but only if whatever it commands be complied with' (Bayes p136; Witherington p288, emphasis mine; Bayes p123; Calvin: *Commentaries* Vol.3 Part 1 p200).

What about the Puritans, those masters of covenant theology? Did they think justification was possible by the law? According to Kevan: 'All the Puritans were agreed... the Mosaic law... was not given by God as a means of justification'. Of course: 'There is no hope of [*fallen* man] winning God's favour by law-keeping'. And, as Bruce said: 'Anyone who – in theory, at least – gained life through keeping the law gained it as the reward which his achievement had earned. It was a matter of work and merit. But anyone who failed to keep the law – and that meant everyone [except Christ] – could therefore make no claim to such a reward. The law, which pronounced blessing and life on those who obeyed it, pronounced cursing and death on those who disobeyed it. If those who disobeyed it were nevertheless admitted to blessing and life, it could not be on the score of [their] merit, but on the ground of God's grace' (Kevan: *Grace* pp118-119; quoted by Karlberg p42, quoting Bruce: 'Christ' pp54-55).

Poole: 'Life, in the law, is promised to those who do the things it requires'. Speaking of 'the life promised to the observation of the law, not a temporal life only is to be understood, but eternal life also'. Sadly he qualified 'the law [here as] the law contained in ordinances' (Poole pp649-650). It is not; it is the law, full stop!

Bolton wrongly maintained: 'The law is not incompatible with grace'. As he himself recognised: 'The law stood upon such opposite terms; therefore it must be a covenant of works'. The law stood 'upon opposite terms' to the gospel, this being 'manifest, for in one case there is a command to do, and in the other to believe...[Lev. 18:4-5, Ezek. 20:11 and Gal. 3:12:] "He that doeth them shall live in them"'. If it had been '"live *by* them"', he would have conceded. Instead he thought the *in* 'explained' the passages in his favour. But see NKJV, NASB, NEB, NIV. On Rom. 10:5-11, Bolton: 'The law *seems* upon opposite terms to grace'. If he could think of a reply, he reasoned, 'if' the objection 'can be cleared, then all is done'; that is, all would be right with this point of Reformed theology. If the objection cannot be cleared, then the edifice collapses, of course. '"Do this and live"', said Bolton, 'was not spoken of the law abstractly and separately considered, but of the law and the promise jointly; not of the law exclusively, but of the law inclusively, as including the promise, and as having the promise involved with it. [But] life is not by doing, but by believing. [In] "do this and live"', God was testing men to see if they would go that way, and once they found they could not '"do this and live"', they might better see, admire, adore and glorify the mercy of God who has given a promise, and sent a Christ, to save those who were not able to do anything towards their own salvation'. He wondered if '"do this and live" has reference merely to a temporal and prosperous life in the land of Canaan'. Or, perhaps, God was speaking 'to Christ, who has fulfilled all righteousness for us, and purchased by his own obedience'. Bolton: 'I will lay down six or seven particular matters for consideration' to prove that law and grace are not opposite. Having listed these six points, he then tried to wash his hands of the responsibility: 'Some of these six points I reject entirely, and I cannot heartily go with any of them, but I state them to show the variety of interpretations... I will give briefly my own thoughts of the matter... I conceive the opposition between the law and the gospel to be chiefly of man's own making. Men should have been driven to Christ by the law, but instead they expected life in obedience to it. This was the great error and mistake'. In the end, he felt he had 'answered the... great query' regarding the law (Bolton pp10,84,102-109). His publishers agreed. I do not. I think he was all at sea!

Charles Hodge: 'The law... is viewed in a twofold aspect... First, it was that original covenant of works, demanding perfect obedience, whose conditions must be satisfied in order to [bring about] the reconciliation of men with God. Christ, by being made under the law, Gal. 4:4, and fulfilling all righteousness, has redeemed those who were under the law. He delivered them from the obligation of fulfilling its demands as the condition of their justification before God. In this sense they are not under the law. Compare Rom. 6:14; 7:4,6; Gal. 5:18; Col. 2:14... Christ by his death has freed us from the law. We are no longer under the law but under grace. Rom. 6:14. We are no longer required to seek salvation on the ground of obedience to the law, which says: "Do this, and live", and "Cursed is every one that continues not in all things written in the book of the law, to do them". Christ has freed us from the law as a covenant of works, by himself being made subject to it, Gal. 4:5; by bearing its penalty, Gal. 3:13; by his body, Rom. 7:4; by the body of his flesh, Col. 1:22; by his cross, Col. 2:14... The "abolishing" [Eph. 2:14-15], therefore... does not consist in setting the law aside, or suspending it... [but] is causing it to cease; or rendering it no longer binding by satisfying its demands, so that we are judicially free from it; free not by the act of a sovereign but by the sentence of a judge; not by mere pardon, but by justification... The antithetical ideas always presented in Paul's writings... are the law and grace, the law and the gospel, the system which says: "Do and live", and the system which says: "Believe and live"' (Charles Hodge: *Ephesians* pp130-135). Hodge, it seems to me, wanted it both ways.

Better, as Moo: 'It was God acting through his Son who accomplished "what the law could not do" [Rom. 8:2]... The Spirit can liberate the believer from sins and death only because in Christ and in his cross God has already "condemned" sin: "For what the law could not do, in that it was weakened by the flesh, God did: by sending his own Son in the [likeness] of sinful flesh and concerning sin he condemned sin in the flesh" [Rom. 8:3]... It is God himself who has done what the law could not do, and he has done it through the sending of "his own Son". In most references to the "sending" of the Son the focus is on the incarnation. But... Paul's application of the language is broader, with a particular focus on the redemptive death of the Son (*cf.* also Gal. 4:4)' (Moo: *Romans* pp474-479).

Reisinger got it in one: 'If the ten commandments are not a legal/works covenant that can afford life and righteousness [as a reward for obedience], then we believers have no righteousness. Our righteousness is an earned righteousness. It was earned by Christ keeping some law covenant that had the authority to award obedience with life and righteousness. What other law covenant, besides the covenant at Sinai, could Christ have possibly been "born under" to earn this righteousness for us? Did [Christ] endure the curse of a covenant of grace or a legal covenant of works when he died on the cross? Let the readers find the answers to these questions in their own theological system if they can' (Reisinger: *Tablets* p73).

As did Gadsby: 'The apostle says, as many as are of the works of the law are under the curse, and this is the ceremonial law, think you? Surely not; for that preached Jesus [in shadows]. The curse, or the sentence of death, is in the law of works. A man must do violence to his own understanding before he can think this is the ceremonial law' (Gadsby: *Works* p69).

And, surprisingly, so did Calvin: 'Christ... became subject to the law. Why? He did so in our room that he might obtain freedom for us'. 'Christ chose to become liable to keep the law, that exemption might be obtained for us'. Despite his earlier remarks, according to Kevan, the Puritans also spoke of justification by Christ's 'obedience in fulfilling the law, [by which] the Son of God performed for us all things contained in it, that we might have right to life everlasting, and that according to the tenor of the law... Christ doing the whole law, whereby he purchased righteousness for us'. Christ's saving work was 'by suffering the punishment due to sin, which is the curse of God; and the perfect keeping of the law, without which there can be no deliverance from sin and condemnation'. God was so 'set upon his law, that when Christ did undertake for mankind, if Christ had not satisfied every part of the law that was required, if there had been one jot of the law unfulfilled, all mankind must have perished'. The necessity of 'Christ's... active conformity to the law of God'. 'Citations in the same strain can be multiplied almost indefinitely'. 'At that very time when Jesus Christ did hang on the cross on Mt Calvary, was buried, rose again from the dead, and ascended up above the clouds, at that very time was all the law fulfilled for righteousness. He is the end of the law; mark, he is the end of the law for righteousness. But if there were anything yet to be done for justification, which was not then done, there could not be an end put to the law for righteousness for everyone that believes. But in that there is an end put to the law for righteousness by Jesus for all the elect of God, Christ having once fulfilled it for them, it is manifest that there was not anything then left undone by Christ'. 'The end of the law is its fulfilment, the performance of what it requires in order to attain life: and Christ in this respect is its end, having rendered to it perfect obedience' (Calvin: *Commentaries* Vol.21 Part 1 p118; Kevan: *Grace* pp142-144; Bunyan: *Vindication* p99; see *Doctrine* pp188-206; the editor in Calvin: *Commentaries* Vol.19 Part 2 p384).

Matt. 5:17-18

A word of warning: watch out for sleight of hand. For example: 'Christ professes "that he came not to destroy the moral law" (Matt. 5:17), and that the least of them should not be abrogated in his kingdom of the New Testament' (Bayly p171). By the way, which, according to Reformed, is the least of the ten commandments? According to Matt. 23:23; Luke 11:42, the 'least' commandments made their appearance outside the so-called moral law.

John Brown, as almost always with him, got it right: 'Many interpreters... consider [Matt. 5:17-18] as a declaration that it was not our Lord's intention to abrogate the moral law. There are, however, insuperable objections to this mode of exposition. We have no right to restrict the term "law" to the moral part of the Mosaic institution: and there can be no doubt with a careful reader of the New Testament, that our Lord *did* come to abrogate the law of Moses. It belonged to the temporary, as well as a typical, economy'. From Gal. 3:19,25, Eph. 2:14-15 and Col. 2:14, the law 'having served its purpose, it was to cease'. Christ did not come to destroy (*kataluō*) the law and the prophets; that is 'to invalidate, to represent as of no authority, or of diminished authority, those former revelations of the divine will... I apprehend the word "fulfil" is used in the sense of "complete", "fill up", "perfect"... Our Lord came to complete divine revelation, both inasmuch as he came to do and suffer those things which were to form the subject of that part of the divine revelation which yet remained to be given, and inasmuch as, by his Spirit, through the instrumentality of his apostles, he actually made that revelation'. In effect, Christ was saying: 'I do not come to demolish' the former revelation; 'my purpose is to carry forward and complete [it]'. Hence '"the law", the Mosaic institution, ceased to be of obligation; it had served its purpose; it entirely, as a system, passed away. "The middle wall of partition" was completely taken down'. Barcellos: 'What Christ does to the law and the prophets, the whole Old Testament, is to bring them to redemptive-historical maturity... The law of God, even the whole of the Old Testament... [finds] its realisation in him' (Brown: *Discourses* Vol.1 pp168-172, emphasis mine; Barcellos p65).

See 'blossom' extract from Edgar H.Andrews on pp416,498.

Whither covenant theology?

John Murray: 'It would not be... in the interests of theological conservation or theological progress to think that the covenant theology is in all respects definitive and that there is no further need for correction, modification, and explanation... It appears to me that the covenant theology, notwithstanding the finesse of analysis with which it was worked out and the grandeur of its articulated systematisation, needs recasting' (quoted in part by Zens: *Studies* p46 and in part by Daniel Fuller p79). He could go further! Recasting? Rejecting, more like.

In addition to the above, Geoff Adams pp80-94; Arndt and Gingrich; Bender: 'Pacifism' pp168-169; Berkhof pp262-301; Bigg: *Pursuit* pp90-100; Brown: *Galatians* pp140-141; Clifford: *Atonement* p13; Horton Davies Vol.1 p283; Vol.2 pp6,311-313; Michael Eaton: *Encouragement* p110; Engelsma pp4-5; Curtis Evans pp305-325; Friesen p173; French pp246-251; Gadsby: *Works* p14; Gay: *Battle*; *Infant*; *Particular*; *Priesthood*; George pp346,352; Hendriksen: *Galatians* p134; Hulse: *Restoration* p51; Kendall pp39,57-58; Kevan: *Grace* p161; Klassen: 'Studies' pp80-88; Kruse pp83-84,107-108,213-215; Latourette Vol.1 pp18-19; Lloyd-Jones: *Final* pp417-419; Stuart Murray pp97-124;

Reisinger: *Tablets* pp3-13; Snyder pp87-100; Strickland p32; Thayer; *The New* pp267,729,1005; *The Mennonite* pp49-54; Thomas p20; Verduin: *Anatomy* pp110-111; Wenger pp176-179; Williams: *Radical* xxviii, pp274-275,304,410,674-675,828-834; Witherington p247; Zaspel pp150,155-159; Zens: 'Covenant' Part 1 p3.

McClain: 'Several answers, all evasive in character, have been given to the question: Is the Christian believer under the law? For the most part they are based upon wrong or inadequate definitions of law. (a). Some argue that the believer is under the moral law, but not under the ceremonial law. (b). Others say that we are under the moral law, but not under its penalties. (c). Still others assert that we are under the moral law as a rule of life, but not as a way of salvation. Another way of saying the same thing is that we are under the law for sanctification, but not for justification. (d). Another view is that we are under the Sermon on the Mount, but not under the law of Sinai. (e). A rather curious view advanced recently (by A.W.Pink) is that the Christian believer is under "the law of God" but not under "the law of Moses". According to this scheme, "the law of Moses" is the entire system of law recorded in the Pentateuch, whereas "the law of God" is limited to the ten commandments! That such distinction between "the law of God" and "the law of Moses" cannot stand is clear from the Scriptures... Luke 2:21-24,39; Mark 7:8-13... We will not be misled by any of the above erroneous views if we hold fast to a complete definition of the divine law; namely, that the law of God in the Bible is one law, including moral, ceremonial and civil elements, and inseparable from its penalties... To be "under the law" in the biblical sense is to be under the law of God – the entire Mosaic legal system in its indivisible totality – subject to its commands and liable to its penalties. Now the word of God declares plainly that the Christian believer is not "under the law". At least four times, simply and without qualification, the New Testament asserts this great truth (Rom. 6:14-15; Gal. 5:18; 1 Cor. 9:20 footnote, NIV, NASB)... The Christian believer is not under the law in any sense as a means of salvation or any part of it... Rom. 3:20... In Rom. 6:14, the Scripture declares not only that the law as law has absolutely nothing to contribute in the accomplishment of the believer's sanctification, but on the contrary the freedom from the law's bondage is actually one indispensible factor in that important work of God in the soul... [Rom. 7:1-6]... Rom. 8:3-4... The Christian is "delivered from the law". This is the central argument of Rom. 7... Rom. 10:4... The conclusion must be that the law itself as law, for the Christian, has been "abolished"... 2 Cor. 3... Col. 2:14' (McClain pp41-49).

In short, the policy seems to be: Carry a salt cellar filled with escape-glosses. On hitting a difficult text, give the salt cellar a liberal shake, and hey presto, the job is done. One of the glosses will do the trick.

Reformed escape route: Divide the law into three bits
Colin Hart: 'Theologians down the ages, and especially the Reformers, have made the very helpful[1] distinction that the Bible contains three types of law: the moral, the civil and the ceremonial. The ceremonial laws have been fulfilled in Christ... The civil laws of Israel are not necessarily binding on people and nations today. But the moral law has not been done away with. It is still in force and binding on everyone whether a believer or an unbeliever' (Hart in Mackay pp6-7). Strong on assertion, Hart offered no scriptural support. He did, however, cite Augustine, Aquinas, the Thirty-Nine Articles, the Westminster Confession, the Lutheran Formula of Concord. When Mackay, himself, came to make the point, his arguments were thin (Mackay pp28-29) – Ex. 20:18-19; Deut. 5:4; 18:16; 'ten is a symbol of completeness'; Ex. 31:18; 32:15-16; their emplacement in the ark; the ten commandments being 'the general terms and policy... [followed by] the detailed stipulations'. Others must judge for themselves whether or not Mackay's suggestions bear the weight of the vital structure Mackay went on to build upon them. For myself, I have no doubt about the answer.

---

[1] It may be 'helpful' to the Reformed cause, but is it scriptural?

I agree with this: 'There is no evidence that [Paul] makes some sort of hermeneutical distinction between the ritual [ceremonial] law and the moral law in Scripture'. 'The popular hermeneutical attempt to divide Moses' law into so many parts and then interpret New Testament statements of the passing [end, abolishing, wiping out, annulment] of the law accordingly is simplistic, nor can it be maintained exegetically. [Ex. 34:27-28 is] of critical significance here'. 'No dividing of Moses will fit here. The legislation of Sinai is an inseparable unit'. '"The whole law" stands or falls together as an indivisible unit'. The Reformed division of the law is 'an unwarranted assumption [which] proceeds to a foregone [an assumed, a predetermined] conclusion... that the decalogue is the expression of God's eternal moral law. These are matters which demand exegetical support but which find none. [The study of the law] renders the complex and apparently artificial tripartite division of Moses irrelevant. Such difficult hermeneutical grids are simply unnecessary. [The Reformed position is based on] hermeneutical presuppositions' (Witherington pp177,220; Zaspel pp154-155,161-162).

Edgar H.Andrews, quoting James Denney: 'Paul nowhere draws any distinction in the law between ceremonial and moral precepts. The law for him is one, and it is the law of God' (Edgar H.Andrews p89). Bigg: 'The Bible habitually describes the old covenant as God's law, the law of the Lord, the law of Moses or simply "the law", without any distinguishing between moral and ceremonial aspects' (Bigg: 'Fulfilling' p20).

Some Reformed writers try to draw back a little. Take Chamblin: The Reformed threefold division of the law 'can be misleading'; both Testaments 'normally use the term "law" to speak of the *whole* Mosaic law'. Even so, he clung to Reformed 'distinctions', but engaged in damage limitation by talking of 'three dimensions... rather than... three kinds of law' (Chamblin p183, emphasis his). It will not wash!

Another attempted 'defence': 'The classic Confessions provide evidence of the threefold division of the law, but do not put it in precise terms' (Letham p32). I think it is quite easy to translate. If there had been clear scriptural proof, these 'classic Confessions' would not have failed to latch on to it!

Where did the threefold division of the law come from? Michael Eaton: 'In the 13th century a theologian named Thomas Aquinas was powerfully influential and wrote *Summa Theologica* (A Summary of Theology), which includes many pages on "The Old Law", the law of God given on Sinai. Thomas Aquinas formulated a doctrine of law using as a framework the thought of the Greek philosopher Aristotle, plus Paul and Augustine. He divided the law into three. The *moral* laws are the basic principles of right and wrong. For Aquinas they are the same as "natural law", the basic law on everyone's conscience which can be deduced by unaided reason without the need of God's word'. I pause. Oh? What about the sabbath? – bearing in mind the sabbath is not the same as the Reformed 'one day in seven'. Eaton: 'The *ceremonial* laws are the Old Testament legislation about sacrifices and holy days, and so on. Aquinas thinks this part of the law is abolished, and is "not only dead, but also deadly". Then there are the *judicial* laws which are regulations concerning justice which were special to the nation of Israel. He taught that judicial laws were abolished and are "dead since they have no binding force but [they are] not deadly", and that if a ruler imposed them he was not guilty of sin'. 'It was Thomas Aquinas, especially, who popularised in theological circles the habit of using the phrase "the law" to designate a moral code extrapolated from the ten commandments' (Michael Eaton: *Living* pp131-132; *Encouragement* pp9,103). But, according to Richard N.Longenecker, the threefold division started with Tertullian (about 200) (Schreiner p89).

'Aquinas... gathered up the threads from Christian and classical antiquity, from the wisdom of the Arabs and the philosophy of the medieval Jews into an integrated theological system'. Of Aquinas and his mentor, Albert Magnus: 'The ridiculous oddity of many of their expressions, the hideous barbarity of their style... They neither defined their terms accurately... nor did they divide their subject with perspicuity and precision'. As for Aquinas, 'his definitions are often vague or obscure, and his plans or divisions, though full of art, are frequently destitute of clearness and proportion'. 'His teaching became the basis of Roman Catholic doctrine'. 'Aquinas was named as the authoritative exponent of orthodox theology, and his *Summa Theologica* was placed on the altar below only the Bible and the Decretals'. From that time 'in the Roman communion his influence has never ceased'. 'To this day... Aquinas is the principal intellectual influence in the Catholic Church; and there are experts prepared to say that, even yet, the fullness of his personal contribution to thought has scarcely begun to be known'. Hughes, a Roman Catholic, went on to speak of what he called the 'vast syntheses... in orderly, systematic fashion... [in which] truths... were explained' (Bainton: *Reformation* p11; Mosheim Vol.1 p623; Michael Eaton: *Living* p132; Durant p929; Walker pp244-245,525; Hughes p27). Hmm!

But, as Michael Eaton observed: 'At the time of the Reformation in the 16th century the gospel preachers [re]discovered the gospel of the Bible... They saw clearly what Paul meant when he said we are not "justified by the works of the law". So they rejected the teaching of Aquinas and others that justification comes by a mixture of faith and love and other aspects of godliness, including law-keeping. They said that salvation comes by Jesus' righteousness being given to us, and that it is grasped by faith only. However, they accepted [that is, they retained] Thomas Aquinas' division of the law into three' (Michael Eaton: *Living* pp132).

They did this, even though, as Cunningham said: 'The works of Aquinas afford some useful materials; not so much... for establishing the truth from the word of God, but for answering objections, founded upon general considerations of a philosophical or metaphysical kind'. Talk about faint praise! And as Dickens observed: 'It might well be contended that even the Reformers erred through their inability to throw off the vainglorious scholastic spirit, to avoid rebuilding, all too high above the documents, the exciting but insecure towers of ratiocination' (Cunningham Vol.1 p424; Dickens p340). The fact is, as Wendel observed: 'As for scholastic authors... Calvin knew them much better than he is commonly said to have done... The instruction he received... left direct traces in the vocabulary of Calvin, who readily employs the terminology in use in the schools. This influence also appears in his persistent taste for dialectical definitions. Does this mean that, with regard to the scholastic definitions themselves, Calvin's attitude was other than purely negative? It has been proved that he studied the works of... Anselm... Peter Lombard... and... Thomas Aquinas, whom he quotes word for word'. Helm (writing in *The New*): 'The influence of Aquinas on Protestantism must not be minimised. Though what were regarded as his (and others') speculative excesses and unbiblical errors were repudiated at the Reformation, the Augustinian character of much of his theology was gratefully recognised... The influence of Thomas will always be felt where philosophical theology is pursued vigorously'. Blanchard: 'It can still be claimed that Aquinas' influence is "greater than ever"' (Wendel pp126-127; *The New* p61; Blanchard p42). For Aquinas' influence on John Owen, see Cleveland *passim*.

The upshot is, as Bayes put it: 'The Reformed constituency has... *traditionally assumed* the validity of the threefold division of the law into its moral, ceremonial and judicial parts' (Bayes p3, emphasis mine). Another case of damning with faint praise, I should say. How flimsy a basis upon which to build so vast an edifice!

Moo, with a magnificent understatement, recognising that in writing against the usual Reformed division of the law he was 'running smack up against a cherished and widely taught tradition', declared: 'The basic difficulty' with the position is that the New Testament never takes it (Moo: 'The Law' pp217-218). As he said elsewhere: 'The Reformed tradition has often divided the Mosaic law into three categories – moral, ceremonial and civil – but it does not hold up under scrutiny'. He raised several objections.

He spoke of the difficulty (I would say, impossibility), 'even within the ten commandments, to distinguish between what is "moral"... and what is not... More important, Jews in Paul's day [did the Jews ever? I cannot find it] did not divide the law up into categories; on the contrary, there was a strong insistence that the law was a unit and could not be obeyed in parts. This being the case, we would require strong evidence from within the New Testament to think that the word *nomos* in certain texts can apply to only one part of the law'. This, of course, is utterly lacking. Moo continued: 'Jesus reference to "more important matters in the law"[2] is followed immediately by an insistence that all the commandments must be obeyed'. Moo then referred to Gal. 5:3 and Jas. 2:10 (Moo: 'Galatians' pp14-15).

Robert Reymond tried to justify the threefold division biblically. In 1 Cor. 7:19, he alleged: 'Paul distinguishes here between the ethical and the ceremonial, that is, between the permanent and the temporary aspects of the law, insisting on the essentiality of keeping God's moral law while at the same time insisting on the non-essentiality and insignificance of keeping the ceremonial law'. But this is arguing backwards and reading law-division into the text. Let me quote the verse: 'Circumcision is nothing and uncircumcision is nothing, but keeping the commandments of God is what matters'. No reader – simply starting with the verse and having no preconceived idea, picked up from Aquinas or one of his devotees – would arrive at Reymond's division of the law and his consequent response to it. As he himself pointed out, his view is 'contrary to what most studies have concluded' (Reymond: *Paul* p477). In fact, it is utterly unscriptural!

Though Maurice Roberts was another to try, his slipshod paper contained self-contradiction, caricature, question-begging and circular argument. He characterised new-covenant theology as the view of those who regard the ten commandments as abrogated – yet on the same page, he allowed that such people think 'the sixth, seventh and eighth' commands 'are in place today', 'but others are altered to suit our new-covenant status'. Later, we are told that 'new-covenant teaching... regards the ten commandments as binding only insofar as they are explicitly re-affirmed in the New Testament'. So... which is it? What, according to Roberts, *does* new-covenant theology say about the ten commandments? Roberts went on: 'In the order of Scripture, moral law comes first (Ex. 20)', that 'God is said to have written the moral law on the heart of man' (Rom. 2:15), and that 'the moral law is of great use to us as believers. It is our rule of life' – this last, a statement of enormous import, one which requires proof, of course, not just assertion. The sabbath, as always, is the nut which has to be cracked. Roberts simply asserted that 'the weekly sabbath' is still in place, moving straight into the Lord's day. That this is easier to assert than to prove, everybody knows. Roberts more or less assumed Eph. 2:15 and Rom. 4:9 to be 'the ceremonial law'. He rebuked those who 'introduce analogies... without clear biblical warrant'. Hmm! In the Sermon on the Mount, Roberts asserted, 'it is evident that our Lord intended to state that the moral law, as such [why 'as such'?] will remain in force till the end of the world... The context makes it clear that we are being informed about the moral law only'. I pause. What about Matt. 5:38 for a start? Is that the moral law? Roberts: Jesus was 'clearing up certain falsehoods which had been taught by Jewish tradition'. Much of Roberts' article was taken up with showing that the Bible distinguishes between various laws as regards their weight, which nobody in this debate doubts. But how this establishes the threefold division beats me, I am afraid. When he quoted Mic. 6:6-8, Roberts' case would have been stronger if he could have quoted the prophet replying to the question as to what does God require, thus: 'Keep the decalogue!', but he couldn't. And I'm struck by the in-built weakness of his statement: 'Paul virtually recites the ten commandments at one

---

[2] Which some might regard as a hint of a division in the law. As above, according to Matt. 23:23; Luke 11:42, the 'least' commandments made their appearance outside the so-called moral law.

point (Rom. 13:9)' (Roberts pp1-10. I have changed many of the upper case 'Moral Law', 'Ceremonial Law', *etc.*) Apart from the missing 'sabbath', do not miss the 'virtually recites'. If the Reformed are right, I for one would expect the apostles to be hammering *all* the ten commandments on almost every page, at least when they turn to sanctification – which they do exceedingly often, but *rarely* using the commandments! Odd, surely, from a Reformed perspective! I will return to many of these issues, but I fail to see that Roberts has established the threefold division.

More weighty should have been Iain D.Campbell's contribution – at least, to judge by the title of his paper: 'The Threefold Division of the Mosaic Law'. Under such a heading, he should have given those of us who disagree with the threefold division something serious to think about. Maybe I have failed to grasp what he said, but it did not dent my convictions. Indeed, if the Trades Descriptions Act applies to the giving of papers at Christian Conferences, then this particular paper may have some difficulty in meeting its requirements. Take his closing claim: 'The burden of this paper has been that the obsolescence of the Sinai covenant does not mean the abolition of the decalogue'. If so, then out of his own mouth, Campbell admitted that he did not keep to the remit he had been given. He should have stuck to the title of his paper! By the way, whoever said the ten commandments are abolished? The old covenant is abolished, yes, but the ten commandments are still part of God's word, and, as I will make clear, play their part in Christ's law. Indeed, the old covenant, as a whole, still plays its part in Christ's law. The fact is, Campbell moved the goal-posts in order to say many good things about the law – which, in this debate, nobody ever doubted! – but what about the matter in hand; namely the threefold division? *That* was the issue.

On that topic, Campbell devoted a meagre 20% of his paper to what he called 'Exegetical considerations'; that is, biblical arguments. The rest was taken up with Confessions, history, new-covenant theology and Reformed theology, which nobody questions, *and on this issue strictly has nothing to say*. The scriptural argument – which is what is wanted – according to Campbell, can be set out in three points: 'First, there is the manner in which the decalogue was given, distinguishing the ten commandments from all other precepts... Second, there is the subsequent Old Testament reflection on the law of God, which expresses continuing delight in "the law" while anticipating the impermanence of some features of the Mosaic legislation... Third, there is the use of the concept of "law" in the Gospels and Pauline letters, where both dominical [Christ's] and apostolic teachings distinguish the ten commandments from all other material'. On that last, however, Campbell quoted Hendriksen to admit that 'Jesus cites only from the second table of the law'. This admission, it would seem to me, blows a hole in Campbell's third heading – if quotation of the ten commandments establishes the threefold division, how does that fit with the absence of the first table in Jesus' teaching? Overall, I cannot see that Campbell has got anywhere near establishing the threefold division from Scripture. And since he derided the use of the phrase 'new-covenant theology' – because, as he said: 'I fail to find the phrase... anywhere in the Bible' – may we hope that we shall soon hear no more talk of 'the threefold division of the law'? – which, as everybody knows, is another phrase conspicuous by its absence in Scripture. As is the sleight of hand, 'older covenant' instead of the biblical 'old covenant' – the former appearing in Campbell's paper.

Notwithstanding this paucity of scriptural justification, Campbell made some hefty claims for the threefold division of the law: 'The nature of the work of Christ, both in its intrinsic value and its salvific ends, cannot be adequately understood except in the light of the threefold division of the law... Without the threefold division of the law, it is impossible to have an adequate definition of sin, in the light of which the gospel may be preached to man as fallen... Our understanding of the atonement in its nature, design and effects is impoverished without the threefold division of the law... The nature of sin – the nature of the cross – the nature of salvation – the nature of the Christian life – all of these require to read the Bible carefully[!]. When we do, we will see not only that the threefold division of the law... has merit,[3] but that without it, none of these issues can be adequately understood or expressed'. Phew! That puts people like me in our place alright! We have not only got the law wrong, but apparently, we have failed to understand sin and the atonement, and can't preach to sinners into the bargain. Really? What *have* we got right? Anything? In addition, Campbell (in part, quoting Boston!) made some quite staggering claims; such as: the law was in Eden – Adam and Eve 'broke all the ten commands at once... Adam heard as much in the garden [of Eden] as Israel did at Sinai, only in fewer words and without thunders'. Furthermore, we come across some weak claims: 'May the threefold division of the law be justified? On what basis might we justify it? There are, it seems to me, several important standards of biblical testimony *which point in this direction*... [which are] *further reinforced* by four important theological considerations'. Christ's incarnation, and the linking of Sinai and the mount of transfiguration, 'itself, *it seems to me* [Campbell], to *underscore* the traditional classification'. Really? How about 'establish'? When oh when are we going to get a Reformed teacher establishing the threefold division from Scripture? After all this, I am not surprised to read Campbell's admission: 'Even within Reformed theology... there is a growing dissatisfaction with the threefold division' (Campbell pp1-37, emphasis mine). I am glad to hear it. I hope more Reformed teachers will reconsider this fundamental flaw in their argument. Once this has been abandoned, Calvin's third use of the law will have to go, too.

Michael Eaton: 'It became the habit among Christians to talk about "the law" but mean only certain bits of the law of Moses (actually less than 1% of it!) and to say it was a "rule of life" for the Christian'. 'We now need to ask the question: "How much of the traditional teaching of the churches [on the law] has grasped hold of Paul's teaching?" And the answer is: "Not much! Most of it is Aquinas more than Paul!"' Harris: 'The law is spoken of in Scripture as one thing' (Michael Eaton: *Living* pp131-132; *Encouragement* p128; Harris p37).

Aquinas, holding the threefold division, argued that the decalogue differs from the rest of the law by reason of the fact that God gave 'the precepts of the decalogue, while he gave the other precepts to the people through Moses' (Aquinas Vol.2 pp246-248). Bolton set out the typical Reformed view: 'The word "law" signifies the moral, judicial and ceremonial law... The main difficulty... concerns the moral law... The ceremonial law was [merely] an appendix to the first table of the moral law... This law... is abrogated... The judicial law... was [merely] an appendix to the second table [of the moral law]... That part of the judicial law which was typical of Christ's government has ceased, but that part which is of common and general equity remains in force... All the controversy arises from... the moral law... which is summed up in the decalogue'. Thackway joined in: 'The law God gave to Israel falls into separate categories. It has inbuilt distinctions... The ceremonial law ended at Calvary... The judicial law ended in AD70... Certain aspects are to continue, such as the death penalty for murder (Gen. 9:6; Rom. 13:4), and other laws that have influenced the statute books of civilised nations... The moral law (the ten commandments) remains, because it is clearly in a category by itself. [God accompanied] their promulgation with unparalleled expressions of his majesty and holiness: smoke, fire, earthquake, cloud, darkness and trumpet blast. This is so different from the way he gave the ceremonial and judicial laws to Moses afterwards' (Bolton p56; Thackway pp437-438).

Really? How does this fit in with Ex. 31:18? At Sinai, God gave the ten commandments to Moses on the stone tablets *after* 'he had made an end of speaking with him'. What was God saying in all that speaking? When did he begin to speak to Moses? Was is at Ex. 24:12-18

---

[3] It is not a question of whether or not the threefold division 'has merit'. The question is, does it have scriptural warrant?

or Ex. 19:1? Whenever it was, it included a mass of sundry laws and regulations about all sorts of matters, including the tabernacle. 'These are the commandments' – that is, the entire revelation at Sinai, including the whole of Leviticus – 'which the LORD commanded Moses for the children of Israel on Mount Sinai' (Lev. 27:34 – the closing verse of the book). We know the law of Moses comprised all the laws and commandments that the LORD had commanded Israel (1 Kings 2:3; Neh. 8:1, for instance), and yet this is also called the law of God (Neh. 8:8,18, for instance). Consider Neh. 9,10,13. Note the repeated 'law', 'laws', 'law of God', 'law of Moses', or their equivalents, with citations from all parts of 'the law', including the sabbath from the ten commandments. In short, the ten commandments and all the other laws comprised one law, the law of God, the law of Moses. When the Israelites finally went into captivity, God set out the reason for their captivity. They had failed to keep his commands and statutes, 'according to all the law [the entire law, NIV] which I commanded your fathers, and which I sent to you by my prophets' (2 Kings 17:13). These commands came from the decalogue and, for instance, Moses' instructions in Moab (2 Kings 17:7-17), all encompassed in 'the statutes, the ordinances, the law, and the commandment which he [the LORD] wrote for you' (2 Kings 17:35). See also Deut. 29:1; 31:9,24-26; 33:4; 2 Kings 21:8; *etc.* Take the phrase, 'the book of the law' or 'the book of the covenant' (Ex. 24:7; Josh. 8:31-34; 23:6; 24:26; 2 Kings 14:6; 22:8-11; 23:2; 2 Chron. 17:9; 34:15,30; Neh. 8:1-3,18; 9:3; Gal.3:10). Take 'the whole law' (2 Chron. 33:8; Gal. 5:3; Jas. 2:10). These are interchangeable, referring to the same thing, and we know that it comprised God's entire revelation at Sinai (two givings) and the renewal in Moab (Ex. 24:4; Josh. 8:35). Above all, in this context, it contained the ten commandments (Josh. 23:6-7,11,16; 24:14-26; 2 Kings 22:17; and, above all, Jas. 2:10-11). Furthermore, we know the ten commandments comprised the covenant (Ex. 34:28; Deut. 4:13). Indeed, without any proof-text, the notion that the book of the law did not contain the ten commandments is ludicrous, yet this must be the case if the Reformed are right to distinguish the ten commandments in the way they do. *But the Bible nowhere makes the Reformed distinction.* The logical outcome of the Reformed view would appear to be that the ten commandments formed the law of God, while the rest formed the law of Moses! As for God speaking to Israel through Moses, we know that Moses was in a class of his own as a prophet (Num. 12:6-8; Deut. 34:10-12; see also Hos. 12:13). Consequently, when God spoke to the people through him it was as close as could be to God speaking directly to the people. It is quite wrong to try to drive a wedge between the two. The Jews didn't: 'We are Moses' disciples. We know that God spoke to Moses' (John 9:28-29). Christ knew they relied on Moses, which, as Paul said, meant the law (John 5:45; Rom. 2:17). And, of course, we have: 'The law was given through Moses... Did not Moses give you the law?... The law... was added... was appointed through angels by the hand of a mediator' – who was, of course, none other than Moses! (John 1:17; 7:19; Gal. 3:19). Moses and the law – the whole law – are virtually synonymous in this context.

John Brown got some common sense back into the argument: Heb. 12:18-28 'opens with a very striking comparative view of the two economies, the Mosaic and the Christian... The Sinaitic dispensation – rigid in its requirements, terrible in its sanctions, severe and unbending in its whole character... That economy was established at Sinai... To be under that economy is here figuratively represented as being of the congregation of Israel at Sinai at the giving of the law; and the severe character of that economy is indicated by a most graphic description of the terrific natural and supernatural phenomena by which its establishment was accompanied. Instead of saying in simple words: "You are not under the law, that severe and wrathful economy"... "You are not of the congregation of Israel who came to Mt Sinai, and from its cloud-capped summit received, amid clouds, and darkness, and thunder, and lightnings, a fiery law"... The circumstances of the giving of the law were in accordance with its genius as a divine economy. The people of Israel in a "waste, howling wilderness", standing in speechless terror at the foot of a rugged mountain enveloped with black clouds, now agitated by tempest, now partially illuminated by flashes of lightning, while from the midst of a devouring fire, towering above the summit of the mountain, and flaming up to heaven, an unearthly trumpet uttered its spirit-quelling notes, and the voice of Jehovah proclaimed the statutes of that all-perfect law, which forbids sin in all its forms and degrees, and requires the unreserved submission of the mind and heart, and the undeviating obedience of the whole life – were a striking emblem of the situation of all under that dispensation which was then established – a dispensation of which the leading features were strongly marked in these circumstances... The [inspired author's] statement, then, is equivalent to – "The law – the Mosaic economy – is a system, the leading characters of which, marked in the circumstances of its establishment, are externality, obscurity and severity"' (Brown: *Hebrews* pp643,644,650).

A word of warning! Challenging the unbiblical Reformed threefold division of the law, is a risky business. Take Chantry. Starting with the weakest of warrants for the practice, nevertheless he was soon letting fly: 'Historically the church of Christ has distinguished between three types of law – moral, ceremonial and judicial (or civil). But legalists and antinomians take great care to show that the Bible never uses the terms "moral law", "ceremonial law", or "judicial law"'. Reformed 'pastors and creeds [however] have followed biblical guidelines [which and where?] in speaking of the permanent moral law and of the temporary ceremonial and judicial (or civil) laws'. 'Although the ceremonial and judicial (or civil) laws were rescinded in Christ, the moral law remained in force'. 'While distinctions between moral, ceremonial and judicial laws are of the utmost importance, a caution is necessary'. Scriptural proof would seem to be essential. Where is it? 'All three kinds of law are woven very tightly into a unified covenant administration in Moses. Seldom can a text be labelled entirely moral, ceremonial or civil'. 'In many instances all three are intertwined so that it is seldom possible to make such neat identifications... The ten commandments are the glaring exception'. 'It is not devotion to tradition, but love of Scripture which drives us back to the position of the creeds. Moral law remains. Ceremonial and judicial laws of Moses have passed away. We must wrestle [which Chantry himself did not do] with these distinctions in understanding God's word'. Any questioning of the Reformed position is 'quibbling [of] lazy minds'. Note Chantry's abrupt and inconsistent change of 'law' from 'moral law' to 'the covenant administration of Moses' (Chantry: *Righteous* pp68-98,101-123; *Covenants* pp5-6).

This cannot go unanswered! I wonder how many heresies have had historical, pastoral and credal support? I wonder, also, how few there are who have ever dared to question mainstream theology, who, for their pains, have not been nicknamed, labelled and blackballed? I cannot resist repeating a note from the body of the book: When will the Reformed put the Bible before their creeds and Confessions? If any take offence at my question, let them answer this: How many Reformed men preach the Confession or the Catechism – Heidelberg, Westminster, 1689 or...? Every man that has done it makes one too many!

Let's get back to scriptural sense. 'In the vast majority of places where the word "law" appears in Paul, the reference is to the Jewish law – the law of God given to Israel through Moses, recorded in the first five books of the Bible and transmitted from generation to generation'. 'The Jews did not divide up their law into moral, judicial and ceremonial precepts. For them it was a whole, covering God's revealed will for all areas of their common life. The Christians have had to divide it'. Oh? Why? For what scriptural – as opposed to credal – reason? 'The term "moral" is nowhere to be found in the Scriptures, and to me it appears that calling the law of works the "moral" law is a constant perplexity... "The moral law" is an ambiguous term among divines'. Listen to Calvin; yes, Calvin: We must be 'quit of the trifling of the false prophets, who in later times instilled Jewish ideas into the people'. 'The false prophets' were talking about the fourth command, trying to divide the command into its ceremonial part and its moral part, saying the ceremonial part is abrogated while leaving the moral untouched; they were 'alleging that nothing was abrogated but what was ceremonial in the commandment... while the moral part remains – *viz.* the observance of one day in seven. But this is nothing else than to insult the Jews' (Bruce: *Paul* pp259-260; Wells p47; Gadsby: *Works* pp33,70,101-102; Fisher p28; Calvin: *Institutes* Vol.1 pp343-344). Calvin, it seems to me, here effectively destroyed his own doctrine.

McClain: 'The law is one law – an indivisible unity. While it is unquestionably true that at least three elements – moral, ceremonial and civil – appear within this law, it is wrong to divide it into three laws... This is clear from the New Testament references. James [speaks of]... "the whole law... guilty of all" (Jas. 2:10). On the "all" of this text, Oesterley writes that the Greek *panton* is equivalent to "all the precepts of the *torah*". The same viewpoint is expressed by... Paul in Gal. 5:3... and Christ declares... (Matt. 5:19), thus upholding the essential unity of the law. That the "least commandments" referred to by our Lord are set forth in the Pentateuch, and not merely those of the [so-called] "moral law", or the few contained in the Sermon on the Mount, is perfectly clear from the context (Matt. 5:17-18), where the identification is unmistakeable. He is speaking about the law of Moses... Meyer, writing on Matt. 5:17, says: "In *nomos*... to think merely of the moral law is erroneous: and the distinction between the ritualistic, civil and moral law is modern". [Actually, several hundred years, now!]. Peake declares: "This distinction between the moral and ceremonial law has no meaning in Paul"... Godet: "In general, the distinction between the ritual and moral elements of the law is foreign to the Jewish conscience, which takes the law as a divine unity". Thus he argues that Paul must have held this view. In his able article on New Testament law, J.Denney points out an interesting fact in the New Testament use of the term. With one exception, he maintains, a quotation from the Septuagint version of Jer. 31:33 in Heb. 8:10; 10:16, the word "law" in the New Testament is always found in the singular... [Classical writers would say 'the laws' of Athens or whatever]. This almost invariable singular form [in the New Testament] points to the unity of divine law as opposed to merely human laws... In this Sermon on the Mount, our Lord... is reaffirming in the strongest kind of language the unity and inviolability of the Mosaic law... All three elements of the Mosaic law are present. That the moral element is present needs no special argument, for the greater part of the sermon is devoted to this element. It is not so generally recognised that the ceremonial element of the Mosaic law is also present. Matt. 5:23-24... Alford declares that "the whole language is Jewish, and can only be understood by Jewish rites". It is also very clear that the Sermon on the Mount contains references to the civil element of the Mosaic law. In Matt. 5:21... the judgement referred to is "that of the local courts of Deut. 16:18", and the phrase "in danger" means "legally liable to". In the next verse, our Lord [speaks of being]... " in danger of the council". The "council" here is without question the great court of the Sanhedrin... We are thus in the realm of Jewish civil jurisprudence as outlined in the Mosaic law... Not only are the three elements of the Mosaic law present in the Sermon on the Mount, but the penalties of that law also appear' (McClain pp8-10,12-14).

Finally, why all this fuss over such an elementary question? If anyone was asked to give the scriptural warrant for Christ having abolished the old covenant, he could rattle off, say, 2 Cor. 3:7-11; Heb. 7:11-12,18-22; 8:13; 9:15; 10:9; 12:18-24. I think that would establish the case. Of course, other things could then be considered, but, at least, we would have weighty, direct scriptural evidence placed on the table. Why is it then, that on such a basic issue as the threefold division of the law, no Reformed teacher, it seems, can set out the corresponding *scriptural* evidence? To do it, would put an end to the debate once and for all.

Reformed escape route: The trouble is all down to misunderstanding

Calvin: 'Paul seems to abrogate the law, as if nowadays it did not concern believers'. Seems? Calvin went on: The apostle 'could not help contrasting the law with the gospel, as if they were in opposition to each other... Not that they were really so... [His] controversy was with those who *interpreted* [the law] *amiss*... the absurd mixture which the false apostles introduced'. Berkhof claimed Rom. 4:13-15 and Gal. 3:17 speak 'only [of] the law as it functioned in [the Sinaitic] covenant, and this function only as it was *misunderstood* by the Jews'. Michael Thompson: 'Some Jews in Paul's day *misunderstood* the teaching of the Old Testament [and Rom. 10:3 and Phil. 3:9 reflect Paul's] interpretation of what people were advocating'. This sort of argument was answered by Moo: 'If "misunderstanding" the law was the root problem, God would certainly not have had to resort to so drastic a step as the death of his Son to set us free from its "rule"' (Calvin: *Commentaries* Vol.3 Part 1 p199; Berkhof p297; Michael Thompson pp9,18; Moo: *Romans* p415).

Fairbairn on 2 Cor. 3:7: The verse refers to 'the decalogue in its naked terms and isolated position... as contemplated by a spirit utterly opposed to the gospel – the spirit of Rabbinism'. Wrong! It was nothing to do with Rabbinism. Fairbairn answered it himself on 2 Cor. 3:11: 'The two tables... formed the material of a covenant, which was intended to last only till the great things of redemption should come; when a new covenant... should be introduced... The former... being from its very nature transitory' (Fairbairn: *Law* pp372,375, emphasis mine).

Bayes: 'The Judaisers... could have been Gentiles [in the churches of Galatia] who had come to the conclusion that the Jewish law is binding upon believers'. This flies in the face of 'the traditional understanding' which, as Bayes himself weakly admitted 'seems incontrovertible'. Dunn: 'That the trouble-makers or agitators... were Jews is... fairly obvious... It is equally clear that the troublemakers were also Christians, or at least saw themselves as such' (Bayes p135; Dunn pp9-10).

The point is, if it was all a question of Jewish misunderstanding, or Rabbinism, why ever did Christ have to die? A clear explanation to the Jews would have sufficed. Are believers not under *a Jewish misunderstanding* of the law (Rom. 6:14)? Have believers died to a *Jewish misunderstanding* of the law (Rom. 7:4; Gal. 2:19)? What the law could not do, Christ has done (Rom. 8:3-4) – was it because of *Jewish misunderstanding*? And so on.

Reformed escape route: Distinguish between a covenant and a rule
Edgar H.Andrews: 'That the law was a covenant is the key to its proper understanding. It means that the law stands or falls as a single entity. With a covenant, you cannot pick out the bits you like and ignore the rest. As Paul himself argues in Gal. 3:15, even a covenant between men, once it is confirmed, cannot be amended by addition or (he implies) subtraction' (Edgar H.Andrews p83). Note how the people promised to do 'all the words' (Ex. 24:3). All!

The Reformed, however, show few inhibitions. Take Malcolm Watts who, starting with a whacking gloss, soon had it all sewn up: 'Christ has delivered us from the law in its covenant form. We are not under the law as a covenant of works... [But] we are under it as a rule of life'. It would be nice to be offered substantial scriptural proof for such far-reaching assertions. When may we expect it? Fisher: 'It is generally laid down by our divines, that we are by Christ delivered from the law as it is a covenant'. Boston quickly 'corrected' Fisher: 'But not as it is a rule of life'. Tow: The law is 'abolished in the sense that (1) as a covenant of works, it has failed to bring salvation, and (2) as an exhibition of Christ only by shadowy ceremonies, it is set aside when the reality appears'. Barcellos: 'The whole law of Moses... has been abolished... Christ's death annulled the law of Moses... The New Testament clearly abrogates the whole old covenant, including the decalogue [but only] as it functioned under the old covenant.. The coming and death of Christ and the inauguration of the new covenant now condition its application... As far as our sanctification goes... the Old Testament is still authoritatively *binding* on the church... The whole Old Testament is authoritative between the two advents of Christ, down to its minute detail... The whole Old Testament, the law and the prophets, is... ethically *binding* until the eternal state comes'. John Macleod: 'The profound distinction that lies between the law as a covenant of life and death, under which our Lord came, and the moral law as an exponent or rule of obedience which furnishes an index to the will of God for the obedience of his creatures [referring to] the valid distinction between the law as a covenant and the law as a rule of life'. This, Macleod called 'the good old divinity of our Reformers and their school'. Macleod castigated those who treat 'as a mere figment of the theological schools that the distinction should be drawn between the law as a covenant of life or of death and the law as a rule of obedience' (Malcolm Watts p22; Fisher p60; Tow pp28-29; Barcellos pp61-68; John Macleod pp136-137,155, emphasis mine).

Some comments are called for. If 'the Old Testament is still authoritatively binding on the church... the whole Old Testament...', may we expect believers to stone for adultery? Will they give up pork? Will they exact the death penalty for sabbath breaking? As for the confident distinction between the law as a covenant and as a rule, may we given the scriptural proof?

As Gadsby answered (Andrew Fuller's) claim that though 'as a covenant, believers are dead to the law [nevertheless it is still] the moral law as the rule of conduct to believers: Why does not [Fuller] bring forward the scripture that makes any distinction between the law as a covenant and as a rule of conduct?... If the believer is under it, he must be under it in the sense in which it was given, for Jesus declared that not one jot or tittle of it shall fail till all shall be fulfilled; so, if the believer is under it, he must be under its curse, for "as many as are of the works of the law are under the curse". The Scriptures give us no account of any [middle way] between being under the law and being dead to the law, for "what things soever the law says, it says to them who are under the law" (Rom. 3:19). And... "you also are become dead to the law, by the body of Christ" (Rom. 7:4); and... "sin shall not have dominion over you", and the reason [Paul] assigns for it is, "because you are not under the law, but under grace" (Rom. 6:14). But how believers can be said to be freed from the law (Rom. 8:2), delivered from the law (Rom. 7:6), not under the law (Rom. 6:14), dead to the law (Rom. 7:4; Gal. 2:19), and yet be under it as a perfect rule of conduct, is a mystery to me, nor does Gaius' letter [that is, Fuller's letter] unfold the mystery... They say that it is as a covenant of works that they are thus free from [the law], and not as a rule of life; but ask them to produce a passage of Scripture to prove this, and that points out the difference between the law as a *rule* and a *covenant*; and they are totally at a loss to find such a scripture, for the Bible will not furnish them with one' (Gadsby: *Works* pp5,7,70).

Philpot, in his turn, set out some weighty arguments against the Reformed view. As he said, the law 'must be taken as a whole'. As for the Reformed view – that 'we may be dead to [the law] as a covenant, and yet alive to it as a rule' – observing that if he took the lease of a farm, he was obliged to keep the rules of the lease, since these rules governed his way of farming: 'The lease and the rules... form but one instrument, are written on the same paper, sealed with the same seal, and signed with the same signature. In a similar way... I cannot discard the law as my covenant, and yet make it a rule of my life; for the covenant and its rules must necessarily form one and the same instrument' (Philpot: 'Three' pp88-91; *Dead* pp17-18).

W.D.Davies, in short compass, set out a few biblical facts of life: 'Throughout the Old Testament passages could be quoted where the covenant stands for the *torah* or for laws commanded by Yahweh'. He cited Num. 15:31; Deut. 29:1-9 [the whole chapter]; Josh. 23:16; Judges 2:19-20; 2 Kings 17:15; Hos. 6:7; 8:1 (W.D.Davies p260). In other words, the Old Testament allows no such distinction as the Reformed seem so confident of. And if the Old Testament does not, where does the New?

In any case, as Zaspel declared: 'The decalogue *is* the statement of the covenant. Much hermeneutical and theological confusion has resulted from a failure to appreciate this identification. The ten words to Israel *are* the covenant; apart from this foundational summary statement (the decalogue), there is no covenant at all. [Ex. 34:27-28 is] of critical significance here' (Zaspel p149, emphasis his).

Kevan, however, tried to argue black is white: 'There can be commandment without covenant, and there can be covenant without commandment; and there can also be a close relation between them'. Without proof, he asserted: 'The important thing to understand, however, is that they are not only distinguishable, but separable... Happily, the Puritans themselves drew attention to the necessity of observing this distinction between commandment and covenant', and criticised other Puritans who failed 'carefully to separate the ideas of command and covenant'. Bolton: 'We are freed from the law... We are freed from the ceremonial law... We are freed from the moral law'. I pause. Yes, that is what he said! He immediately explained: 'Freed from it, first, as a covenant, say our divines... Take it, as do many, in the sense that we are freed from the law as a covenant. The law may be considered as a rule and as a covenant. When we read that the law is still in force [where do we for a believer?], it is to be understood of the law as a rule, not as a covenant. Again, when we read that the law is abrogated, and that we are freed from the law, it is to be understood of the law as a covenant, not as a rule'. 'The believer is freed from the law as a covenant, and hence from its judgements, sentences, condemnations, curses and accusations... The law... as a covenant... could not be given, for then God would have acted contrary to himself... Therefore he gave it as a rule... a rule of walking with God... The believer is freed from the rigour of the obedience required in the law' (Kevan: *Grace* pp148-151; Bolton pp28,38,40). So there you have it, reader. The believer is under the law as a rule (without the nasty penalties), but not as a covenant (with its penalties). On what basis can you rest assured of this? Scripture? Oh no! 'Our divines'! I have a request: Would some supporter of Bolton please email me with a definition of 'Reformed', paying particular attention to the question of authority? I thought 'Reformed' was at least as 'strict' as 'evangelical', and that an integral part of being an evangelical was to regard *Scripture* – not 'our divines' – as our authority. It is all very well bandying the Latin tag *sola Scriptura*, but when is *sola* '*sola*'? (I am well-aware of the Westminster Confession's get-out clause).

Let me develop this a little. Donald Macleod dismissed Philip Doddridge on the trinity because, said Macleod, 'Doddridge's approach reflects a simplistic biblicism'. While I have no intention here in exploring the rights and wrongs of Doddridge on the trinity, nor am I interested in whether or not the Reformed believe every word of their Confession (though I strongly suspect they do not!), I am interested in Macleod's approach to Doddridge. What did he find 'simplistic' in Doddridge? Doddridge stressed and acted on *sola Scriptura*! This, according to Macleod, rules him out as serious teacher. Macleod: 'There is nothing whatever in the Reformation slogan, *sola Scriptura,* to preclude the use of creeds and Confessions in the church'. Of course not! But too often in Reformed circles, while *sola Scriptura* remains a noble-sounding slogan, the real weight lies with those afore-said creeds and Confessions – as I have demonstrated. Macleod went further, putting his finger on what he considered to be the real issue with Doddridge's appeal to Scripture only: 'The real difficulty with Doddridge's appeal to the sufficiency of Scripture is that the writers of the New Testament never faced the precise issues raised by Arianism and therefore made no pronouncement upon it' (Macleod: 'God' pp121-138). In other words, unless we have the creeds, Councils and Confession of the Fathers, seeing we've only got the Bible, we've had it! Now this really does give the game away. Macleod has made a statement of immense consequence, and done so in print. It is truly appalling. Yes, I mean it! Let Alan Clifford expose it: 'Does Macleod realise what he is pleading for? Isn't he suspiciously close to the Roman Catholic view that the Bible requires the magisterial pronouncements of dogmatic tradition to safeguard its true meaning?' (Clifford: *Doddridge* pp245-251). Reader, whether it is Rome, the Reformed, Baptists or Uncle Tom Cobley, while, in our darkness, we make proper use of the candles other men have left behind, unless Scripture is paramount, in reality as well as in slogan, we are nothing but papists of one shade or another. 'Give us a pope to tell us what to believe!' There are far more popes about than that aged gentleman who lives in the Vatican, and there are more papal bulls in circulation than evangelicals and the Reformed usually admit. And those bulls aren't all issued at Rome! It is altogether too possible to turn the Westminster, the 1689, or whatever, into a papal pronouncement, set in stone, untouchable *and all-authoritative*.

Getting back to the point at issue, George Wright was right to 'renounce [the] distinction [between covenant and commandment] as frivolous and absurd' (George Wright p229).

Pull the law's teeth

Let Chantry set the Reformed scene: 'It must be observed that the moral law in the hand of Moses had a flavour that it does not have in the hand of Christ'. 'Rigid and unrelenting administration of the law for the children's good is found in Israel of old. Harsh chastisements for violations warn the immature against disobedience and prevent excessive transgressions. These judicial appendages have fallen away from the fourth commandment with the coming of Christ. Mature heirs of God's house, filled with the Spirit, need no severe rod or childish regulations' (Chantry: *Righteous* pp135-136).

It is the old story. Strong on assertion, but signally weak, pitifully weak, on biblical proof. Nevertheless, he was only taking after Calvin: 'The law... requires from man the highest perfection and most exact obedience. It... calls to a severe reckoning the smallest offences'. 'The law, so far as it is a rule of life, a bridle to keep us in the fear of the Lord, a spur to correct the sluggishness of our flesh... is as much in force as ever, and remains untouched'. 'It annexes to works a reward and a punishment; that is, it promises life to those who keep it, and curses all transgressors. Meanwhile it requires from man the highest perfection and most exact obedience. It makes no abatement, gives no pardon, but calls to a severe reckoning the smallest offences'.

Fear not, said Calvin: 'All such qualities of the law, Paul tells us, are abolished'. 'When Paul contrasts the law with the gospel, he speaks only of the commandments and threatenings'. 'Nor are we [believers] to be deterred or shun its [the law's] instructions, because the holiness which it prescribes is stricter than we are able to render'. 'It does not now perform toward us the part of a hard taskmaster, who will not be satisfied without full payment'. And this must be a relief to the Reformed, since 'the law requires a perfect righteousness, it cannot be received by any mortal fruitfully [because] however any one may study to obey God, yet he will still be far from perfection'. Indeed, among 'the children of God, even after they are regenerated... [none] will be found who can perform the law... because the keeping of it is impossible, on account of its extreme rigour'. However, despair not, reader; that is, if you believe Calvin: in the gospel the 'rigorous requirement [of the law] is relaxed [so that] the will to obey is pleasing to God instead of perfect obedience'. True, said Calvin, believers fail to keep the law, 'but in the gospel God receives, with fatherly indulgence, what is not absolutely perfect. [The] severe requirement [of the law] is relaxed, so that the vices under which believers still labour are no obstacle to their partial and imperfect obedience being pleasant to God'.

Not a single text is offered, reader, in the vain hope of trying to prove this unbiblical notion! And, I cannot resist pointing out, Calvin's followers have the gall to accuse others of antinomianism! A classic case of beams and motes. Calvin again: 'We must be freed from the fetters of that law, if we would not perish miserably under them'. 'But what fetters? Those of rigid and austere exaction, which remits not one iota of the demands, and leaves no transgression unpunished'. As he had said a moment or two before: 'The law not only teaches, but it also imperiously demands. If obedience is not yielded, indeed, if it is omitted in any degree, it thunders forth its curse'. 'To redeem us from this curse, Christ was made a curse for us'. Did you spot it reader? 'To redeem us from *this* curse, Christ was made a curse'. *This* curse? According to Calvin, Christ died to redeem his people from the '*rigid* and *austere* exaction' of the law. If we have that 'righteousness in that forgiveness of sins by which we are freed from the rigour of the law', then we are not under the '*rigid* and *austere* exaction' of the law. 'In the way of the Lord, believers are apt to stumble', of course, but 'let them not be discouraged because they are unable to satisfy the demands of the law'. 'The performance of their duties is not rejected on account of their present defects, but is accepted in the sight of God, as if it had been in every respect perfect and complete' (Calvin: *Commentaries* Vol.21 Part 1 pp109-110; Vol.6 Part 1 p477; *Institutes* Vol.1 pp310; *Commentaries* Vol.2 Part 1 pp413-414; *Institutes* Vol.1 p311; *Commentaries* Vol.21 Part 1 pp163-164).

What an appalling catalogue of scripturally-unjustified assurances! Wendel exposed the root of the trouble in it all: 'Here we find ourselves deep in the problem of Christian liberty'. As Wendel observed, Calvin got round the 'problem' by 'the line of conception that [he] developed'. According to Calvin, 'the law was not in itself abrogated by... Christ, but only the slavery and malediction attaching to it... Christians therefore remain subject to the law, but not in the same way as the Jews used to be... And in this modification of the function of the law... as Calvin conceives, Christian liberty consists. Clearly, to grasp his thought, we must envisage... the three aspects or "parts" he believes he can distinguish in this notion' (Wendel p203). Many do claim that they can 'envisage' Calvin's 'three aspects', and, therefore, are able to swallow his 'notion'. I, for one, cannot. As I keep asking: May we be shown all this from Scripture?

The Puritan, Jeremiah Burroughs, speaking of the moral law, spelled out some of the features of its 'rigour': 'It requires hard things of those who that were under it... not only hard, but impossible things, impossible to perform by those that are under it... The law exacts all of us under the condition of perfection. The law accepts nothing but that which is complete and absolutely perfect in every way, both [*sic*] in regard to the principle from whence, the manner how, the rule by which, and the end to which it requires absolute perfection... The law accepts no surety. It must be done in our own persons. It is like a severe creditor who will be paid the utmost farthing, and only by us... The law requires constancy... The law exacts the obedience it requires in a violent way upon all that are under it... Upon any breach of the least thing it breaks the soul by its severity... It... gives no strength at all to do what it requires... It strikes at our life in all that it does... Upon any breach it binds the soul to eternal death by the strongest bonds that possibly can be... Once it is offended, amends can never be made by anything we are able to do... The law accepts no repentance... it shows no means of deliverance... Instead of mortifying any of our sins, it rather stirs them up and makes them more'.

Wow! Spot on, Mr Burroughs. What now for the Reformed doctrine of bringing believers under the law? Have no fear – that is, if you are willing to take the Reformed escape route. Burroughs was. He confidently assured believers – who, according to the Reformed system, are under the moral law as the perfect rule of their sanctification – that they escape this 'rigour': as 'for the rigour of the law... you are free from [it]. Though there is much required, *upon some endeavours there may be remission*... It is a vain plea of many people [unbelievers] to say that they do what they can, they desire well and endeavour well'; for unbelievers, this is useless. Ah! But what of believers? 'This is something [that is, this plea works for] those who are children [of God] and have freedom by Christ... God is not strict to mark what is done amiss by his children... If there is even a will, a desire in you, God accepts the will for the deed' (Burroughs pp121-128,136-137, emphasis mine).

Those who can believe the assurance can sleep easy. So let Watson repeat it: 'The decalogue, or ten commandments... is called the moral law because it is the rule of life and manners... We say not that [the believer] is under the curse of the law, but the commands... To obey the law in a legal sense – to do all the law requires – no man can... but in a true gospel-sense, we may *so* obey the moral law as to find acceptance. This gospel obedience consists in *a real endeavour* to observe the whole moral law. "I have done your commandments" (Ps. 119:166); not, I have done all I should, but I have done *all I am able* to do; and where my obedience comes short, I look up to the perfect righteousness and obedience of Christ, and hope for pardon through his blood. This is to obey the moral law evangelically; which, though it is not to satisfaction, yet it is to acceptation... Every Christian is bound to conform to it; and to write, *as exactly as he can*, after this copy... Though we cannot, by our own strength, fulfil, all these commandments, yet doing... *what we are able*, the Lord has provided encouragement for us... Though we cannot *exactly* fulfil the moral law, yet God for Christ's sake will *mitigate the rigour* of the law, *and accept of something less than he requires*; God in the law requires exact obedience, yet he will *accept of sincere* obedience... He will see the faith, and *pass by the failing*. The gospel *remits the severity* of the moral law. Where our personal obedience comes short, God will be pleased to accept us in our Surety' (Watson, pp10,12,34,36, emphasis mine).

But, reader, do you think he established his assurances from Scripture? *That*, after all, is the question!

Sibbes: 'The same duties are required in both covenants... In the covenant of works, this must be taken in the rigour; but under the covenant of grace, as a sincere endeavour proportional to the grace received... it must have an evangelical mitigation' (Sibbes: *Bruised* p59, emphasis mine). Oh? What scripture gives us this assertion and assurance?

Calvin on pulling the law's teeth: 'The whole lives of Christians ought to be a kind of aspiration after piety, seeing they are called unto holiness (Eph. 1:4; 1 Thess. 4:[1-8])'. I agree. See also Heb. 12:14. But, he went on: 'The office of the law is to excite them to the study of purity and holiness by reminding them of their duty'. I pause. Calvin, you notice, offered no passage to justify this remarkable claim.

And now we run into trouble. 'By the cross of Christ, [believers] are free from the condemnation of the law... so that in Christ alone they can rest in full security... [The apostle] asserts the right of believers to liberty of conscience... Consciences obey the law, not as if compelled by legal necessity; but being free from the yoke of the law itself, voluntarily obey the will of God. Being constantly in terror so long as they are under the dominion of the law, they are never disposed promptly to obey God, unless they have previously obtained this liberty... They indeed make many efforts, but the flesh partly enfeebles their strength, and partly binds them to itself. What can they do while they feel that there is nothing of which they are less capable than to fulfil the law? They wish, aspire, endeavour, but do nothing with requisite perfection. If they look to the law, they see that every work which they attempt or design is accursed... Nor can anyone deceive himself by inferring that their work is not altogether bad, merely because it is imperfect, and, therefore, that any good which is in it is still accepted of God. For the law demanding perfect love condemns all imperfection...'. I break off. Here we reach the crunch. What solution did Calvin propose to escape the impasse? Let him tell us: 'For the law demanding perfect love condemns all imperfection, *unless its rigour is mitigated*', emphasis mine.

Right! Let's have the scriptural proof that the rigour of the law is mitigated. Calvin: 'See how our works lie under the curse of the law if they are tested by the standard of the law. But how can unhappy souls set themselves with alacrity to a work from which they cannot hope to gain anything in return but cursing? On the other hand, if freed from this severe exaction – or rather, from the whole rigour of the law – they bear themselves invited by God with paternal lenity, they will cheerfully and alertly obey the call, and follow his guidance'. Very well, but Calvin has not yet established the case. What he said by way of assurance would indeed be remarkably liberating – if he could prove that the believer is under the law, but not its rigour. How did he set about *this* vital task? He went to Mal. 3:17,

God's promise to those who feared him that he would spare them as a man spares his son. Calvin sucked as much as he could out of this lemon. In my view he got more juice than was there: 'The word "spare" evidently means indulgence, or connivance at faults, while at the same time service is remembered'. Connivance? He then turned to Heb. 11:2, and how God 'estimates them merely by faith'. Then he went to Rom. 6:14 – 'Sin shall not have dominion over you, for you are not under the law, but under grace'. The apostle, said Calvin, 'comforts' believers 'by adding that they are freed from the law. Although you feel that sin is not yet extinguished, and that righteousness does not plainly live in you, you have no cause for fear and dejection, as if God were always offended because of the remains of sin, since by grace you are freed from the law, and your works are not tried by its standard' (Calvin: *Institutes* Vol.2 pp131-134).

I can only assume that Calvin thought that if he said a thing often enough, and used enough double-speak, men would believe him. If I read him aright, he was saying believers are not under the law for justification, but they are under it for sanctification. Nevertheless, they are not under the rigour of the law, so all is well. He certainly quoted one or two scriptures, but whether or not an unbiased reader would consider them relevant to the issue in hand, whether or not they prove Calvin's case, I can only say I have my doubts. After all, the only relevant text, Rom. 6:14, proves beyond all question that on the matter of sanctification, the believer is not under the law. I know of no text in the entire Bible which tells me that believers are under the law, but not its rigour. As for Rom. 6:14, I will look at that more fully in chapter 10.

Yet Reformed teachers want it both ways. In contradiction of the above, they insist that the law *is* the rule for the believer, and that its authority is stronger for the believer than the sinner. Take John Macleod: 'The obligation of the law of God as an index to his preceptive will [that is, that which God has revealed as his requirement] is not made void by the faith that rests on the surety obedience of the Saviour [that is, Christ's obedience as the substitute for sinners, earning their salvation]. No, the obligation in response to the gracious salvation of the gospel is one that *is more intense* than man was under as a creature... The obligation of the law as an index to God's will, or as a rule of life, is one that lies upon man as man. It is one from which there is for him *no escape*. It lay upon man while still unfallen. It lies upon him in his state of sin and misery. It will lie upon man when he is lost for ever, and is forever unable to answer the end of his being. *It lies upon man redeemed* and saved and brought home to heaven... By becoming a new creature the believer does not cease to be a creature; and the obligations of creaturehood hold good... This same law when broken did not lower its terms' (John Macleod pp134-136, emphasis mine).

So which is it, after all? May I ask any Reformed reader: Which Reformed teacher do you believe? Do you think you are under the law with its teeth drawn? Or with its teeth intact? What does your preferred teacher say? What does Scripture say? If you put that last question to me, my answer is: Rom. 6:14; 7:4-6; Gal. 3:25; 5:1, and such like.

Gadsby challenged Reformed logic: 'Some will tell you that they are free from it as it was given to Moses, but *now* it is in the hands of Christ, and in his hands it is a *rule of life* to the believer; but if you ask them whether the law in the hands of Christ can do anything less than curse for transgression, some of them will say it cannot; and so what advantage can be had for its being in the hands of Christ, I cannot tell! For it can but curse in the hands of Moses, and if it can do no less in the hands of Christ, where is the difference?' (Gadsby: *Works* p70, emphasis his).

George Wright: 'The law of Sinai is the law of Sinai, and not the law of Zion by an *imaginary* separation of the commands from the curse. The sanctions of the law belong *essentially* to the law; and to separate one from the other is to make void the law'. William Kelly: 'If we were really under the law for [our] walk, we ought to be cursed, *or you destroy its authority*'. Witherington: The curse falls on *all* [emphasis his] those who are under the law and do not remain in *all* [emphasis his] of it so as to do *all* of it... If [believers] submit to the Mosaic law they will... indeed be subject to such a curse, if, that is, they fail to keep *all* the law' (George Wright p235; quoted by Kent p88; Witherington p233, emphases mine unless otherwise stated).

The Reformed will not have it. Boston: 'The ten commandments... [are] obligatory in all possible states of the creature, in earth, in heaven, or hell'. Incredible! Thomas Taylor, the Puritan: 'The first difference is that the gospel is called "grace", whereas the law does not acknowledge the word. Indeed, the two are opposed, to be under law and to be under grace... What a killing letter the law is, which commands inward and perfect righteousness, for nature and actions, and that in our own persons! It promises life upon no other condition than that of works, and these must be perfect. The law wraps us under the curse of sin, and enfolds us in the justice of God, without showing any mercy at all. Now to be under grace is to be freed from all this bondage'. Taylor ruined this by the usual Reformed gloss: 'To be under the law is not to be [that is, it does not refer to believers being] under it *as a rule of life*, for so all believers on earth... indeed the saints and angels in heaven are under it'. Incredible! (Fisher p26; Taylor p174, emphasis mine).

Let Govett put it right: 'Before his death, Moses writes out the book of the law, and gives it to the Levites to put in [the side of (AV) beside (NKJV, NIV)] the ark (Deut. 31:22-26). And in that book, a curse is levelled against every one who should omit to obey any part of the law (Deut. 27:26; Gal. 3:10; Jas. 2:10-11). Here then is the iron girdle which runs with stern grasp round the whole circuit of the law. The law in all its parts, moral, judicial, ceremonial, makes up one great whole. Obedience to one part with neglect or refusal of another, lays the transgressor under the curse' (Govett p8). I will refer to Govett more than once. He is worth listening to. Bear in mind the opinion of Spurgeon: 'Mr Govett wrote a hundred years before his time, and the day will come when his works will be treasured as sifted gold' (schoettlepublishing.com/biographies/rgovett.htm). Perhaps not all of them!

Let a Reformed commentator have the last – excellent – word: 'Could man perfectly fulfil the law, he might expect life from it, and salvation to his obedience to it; but the law curses him that continues not in all that is written in it' (Poole p649). And that goes for whatever hat the law is wearing – no matter what the Reformed may claim. And if the believer is under the law, he is condemned for the least offence of it!

At the risk of annoying sympathetic readers (if there are any!), let me finish with a sentence summarising my view of these Reformed extracts attempting to justify their escape routes*: long on assertion; short on Scripture*. Until these two are reversed, I, at least, remain to be convinced.

In addition to the above, Edgar H.Andrews pp86,90; Bayes back cover; Bigg: *Pursuit* pp88-89; Benton p3; Bromiley p29; Brooks Vol.6 p464; Calvin: *Institutes* Vol.2 p663; *Commentaries* Vol.3 Part 1 p200; Cunningham Vol.1 p423; Michael Eaton: *Encouragement* pp46-50,74-76,78,101-104; Friesen pp131-136; Gay: *Infant*; *Priesthood*; Gill: *Body* Vol.2 p34; Hessey p6; A.A.Hodge pp403,637; Hulse: *Sunday*; *Puritans* pp135-138; Latourette Vol.1 pp509-514; Vol.2 pp1088,1102,1361-1362,1429; Lee p7; John Macleod pp137-138; Moo: 'The Law' pp210-211; Mosheim Vol.1 p579; Vol.2 pp198-200; Owen: *Indices* p608; Reymond: *Contending* pp307-318; Schaff Vol.5 pp659-677; Simon pp76-82,91-92,109-110; Malcolm Watts p21; Wesson p65; Westminster Confession chapter 19, sections 1-6; Witherington p341.

Bengel: 'The conjunction ["but"] is elegantly omitted' but 'a "but" was to be looked for here... To grace and truth, the law gives way' (Bengel p254).

W.J.Dumbrell: 'Revelation of a preliminary character (*torah*) came through Moses, but... the full gift of revelation, grace as fully revealed, came through Jesus Christ... There seems... a convincing level of opposition which is being drawn between two spheres of revelation in John 1:17' (Dumbrell pp34-35)

Let us hear from some Reformed teachers. Tow missed the mark badly when he dismissed the 'but' in John 1:17 as 'an English will o'the wisp raised up by the translators from an empty Greek text [in order to introduce] a resplendent Christ and not to dismiss a waning Moses' (Tow p27). But as to the temporary status of the law – which Tow in effect ridiculed – what about 2 Cor. 3:11 and Heb. 7:18; 8:13, as cases in point? Rushdooney: 'There is no contradiction between law and grace. [Believers are] the people of the law'! (Rushdooney pp6,8-9). Two staggering assertions in light of the New Testament.

On John 1:18, Pink was good: 'A remarkable contrast is pointed. In the past, God, in the fullness of his glory, was unmanifested... but now, God is fully revealed... This contrast... How profoundly thankful should we be that the dispensation of law has passed, and that we live in the full light of the dispensation of grace' (Pink: *John* Vol.1 pp47-48). He wrote at large on the contrast (Pink pp43-48).

On John 1:17, Ryle was weak: 'This verse *seems* intended to show the *inferiority* of the law to the gospel... It does so by putting in strong contrast the leading characteristics of the Old and New dispensations – the religion which began with Moses, and the religion which began with Christ' (Ryle: *John* Vol.1 p41, emphasis mine). I have emphasised Ryle's weakness.

Calvin left no loophole. Not many would go as far as he: 'But we must attend to the antithesis, when [John] contrasts the law with grace and truth; for his meaning is, that the law wanted [that is, lacked] both of them (the law had neither the one nor the other)' (Calvin: *Commentaries* Vol.17 Part 2 p52). What now of Calvin's third use of the law? Are believers under that which contains no 'grace and truth'? Is *that* their *perfect* rule?

Philips: The law was 'the word of command, given by God through Moses on Mount Sinai with such a terrifying voice... [which] condemns the inward uncleanness of nature... condemns the wicked desire and inclination which are contrary to the law of God; for whoever reads the law with unveiled countenance must be terrified at God's wrath (Rom. 3:20; 7:7; 2 Cor. 3:13-16; Ex. 34:33,35; 20:19ff; Heb. 12:19)'. 'The law is given by God, not that it might bring with it perfect righteousness, salvation and eternal life (for by the deeds of the law shall no flesh be justified, Rom. 3:20; Gal. 2:16)'. 'The law teaches the knowledge of sin'. '*But* the gospel is the word of grace. It is the joyful message of Jesus Christ'. 'He... says in the gospel (Matt. 11:28-30): "Come unto me, all you that are heavy laden, and I will give you rest... Take my yoke upon you, for my burden is light and my yoke is easy"'. 'This is the true gospel, the pure doctrine of our God, full of grace and mercy, full of comfort, salvation and eternal life, given to us by God from grace without our merits and works of the law, for the sake of the only eternal and precious Saviour Jesus Christ, who made himself subject to the law for our sake, and became the fulfilment of the law unto eternal salvation for all believers' (Philips pp226,235-236, emphasis mine).

Some Reformed writers get the point. Poole: 'There is an eminent difference between [Moses] and Jesus Christ. The law is nowhere called grace, neither does it show anything but duty and wrath; it shows no remission, if the duty is not done, nor affords strength for the doing of it'. Sibbes wrote of the need 'to know distinctly the difference between the covenant of works and the covenant of grace, between Moses and Christ; Moses without all mercy breaks all bruised reeds, and quenches all smoking flax. For the law requires... personal... perpetual... perfect obedience... and from a perfect heart; and that under a most terrible curse, and gives no strength, a severe taskmaster, like Pharaoh's requiring the whole tally, and yet giving no straw. Christ [however] comes with blessing after blessing even upon those whom Moses had cursed, and with healing balm for those wounds which Moses had made'. 'Another aggravation of sins against the gospel is, that they sin against the better covenant. The first covenant was: "Do this and live" – against which all sinned, and were under the curse. But now we are under a more gracious covenant, a covenant of mercy: "Believe in the Lord Jesus Christ and we [*sic*] shall be saved". Therefore sin now must needs be more heinous'. Tasker: 'The contrasts in this verse are not only between law and grace, and between Moses and Jesus, but between *was given* and *came*' (Poole p280; Sibbes: *Bruised* pp58-59; *Misery* p389; see also *Excellency* pp201-305; Tasker p49, emphasis his).

Taylor got off on the right foot: 'The first difference is that the gospel is called "grace", whereas the law does not acknowledge the word. Indeed, the two are opposed, to be under law and to be under grace... What a killing letter the law is, which commands inward and perfect righteousness, for nature and actions, and that in our own persons! It promises life upon no other condition than that of works, and these must be perfect. The law wraps us under the curse of sin, and enfolds us in the justice of God, without showing any mercy at all. Now to be under grace is to be freed from all this bondage... And here is another difference between the law and [the] gospel; comparing the two, the apostle calls the law a killing letter, and its ministry a ministry of condemnation and death; but the gospel he calls a quickening spirit, and the ministry of the Spirit, and the ministry of righteousness'. Having correctly handled an objection to his doctrine, based on a misunderstanding of Ps. 19:7 – 'there the law, in a more general sense of the word, comprehends the whole doctrine of the covenant of life and salvation' – Taylor continued: 'The law is no instrumental cause of faith, repentance, or any grace'. He expanded on this as far as justification goes. He cited Gal. 3:2 to prove that sinners do not receive the Spirit by the law. But he also included 'our sanctification... in the chain of our salvation', excluding the law as 'the instrumental cause of it; [which] shows that we are saved by grace alone... A third difference between the law and the gospel' arises because the law 'was restricted to the Jews only. In that covenant there was always a difference made, and a wall of partition set up between Jew and Gentile... After the [giving of] the law there was a distinction between Jew and Gentile; God made a covenant with the former, took them into his teaching, and passed by the other. To the Jews alone pertained... the covenant, the giving of the law, the service of God'. The gospel, however, is 'common to all people'. In the greater light granted to men through the New Testament as compared to the Old, and this 'not shining (as before) to the Jews alone, but to the Gentiles also', Taylor saw 'a fourth difference' between the law and grace. 'Paul affirms that the ministration of the Spirit is far more glorious than that of the law, which he calls the ministration of death (2 Cor. 3:7)' (Taylor pp12,174-179).

Taylor, however, ruined this by the usual Reformed gloss: 'To be under the law is not to be [that is, it does not refer to believers being] under it as a rule of life, for so all believers on earth' are, he said, adding – amazingly – 'indeed the saints and angels in heaven are under it'! (Taylor p174). What? If law and grace, law and gospel, are 'opposed', how can the law be a rule of life for the saints? Have words lost all meaning? Taylor watered down the biblical meaning of 'the law' by claiming 'to be under law' means only 'to be under its yoke, which we nor our fathers were able to bear'. In other words, when his system required it, he replaced the biblical phrase, 'the law', by the Reformed gloss, 'the condemnation or curse of the law'. In short, whereas John 1:17 contrasts law and grace, with no qualification, Taylor merely contrasted the condemning power of the law and grace. In effect, his system would not allow him to accept that law and grace really are contrasted and opposed, although he had said they are. For the Reformed believer – since the law according to Taylor is a rule of life – the law and the gospel are hand in hand. John, in effect, did not write John 1:17; or else he did not mean it!

Bolton stated the Reformed position: 'The law is not incompatible with grace'. But, he had to admit, this proposition is 'more knotty' to deal with than the issue as to whether or not the 'Christians are freed from the moral law as a rule of obedience' – and this itself he had previously called one of 'the greatest knots in the practical part of divinity'! (Bolton pp51,77). He could say that again about these propositions being 'knotty'. They run directly counter to plain scriptures, not least John 1:17!

Without being patronising, I do hope that any advocates of Calvin's third use of the law reading this (if there are any who have got this far!), will seriously weigh the Puritans' admissions in this chapter, and elsewhere. At key points in their system, they have to introduce serious glosses, unwarranted glosses, into Scripture, and, even after they have done that, they still end up with what they call 'the greatest knots' and things 'more knotty'! Remember, reader, we are talking about the way of sanctification for each and every believer – an essential for *every* believer, including the weakest and newest believer, not just those who are expert in unravelling theological and philosophical knots!

In addition to the above, see Gay: *Battle*; *Infant*; Hendriksen: *John* p91; Henry Vol.5; Hutcheson pp19-20; Lloyd-Jones: *Righteous* pp92-93; Rushdooney p303; Ryle: *John* Vol.1 pp35-37.

CHAPTER 9: THE BIBLICAL CASE
GALATIANS

Witherington: 'There is no letter where the law is a more crucial or central subject than Galatians'. Karlberg called it 'the benchmark for Paul's theology on the law' (Witherington pp341-356; Karlberg p36).

'Beginning with Galatians has a certain logic. It is... the first letter Paul wrote, it focuses on a key issue... salvation history, and it has the highest occurrences of *nomos* ("law") of any New Testament book... Paul's focus in Galatians is on salvation history. The inability of any law to justify sinners is a minor note, faintly heard in such texts as Gal. 3:10. But the major note Paul sounds in this letter is a temporal argument: for the Galatians to voluntarily put themselves under the law would be to sever their relationship to Christ (Gal. 5:2-4) because the law of Moses was intended by God to rule the people of God only until the Messiah came. Now that the Messiah is here, the law is no longer is no longer directly applicable to his followers. This claim gets to the heart of... "new-covenant theology"' (Moo: 'Galatians' pp8-12).

Silva, on the theology of the Judaisers: 'It seems rather obvious that the Judaisers insisted on the compatibility between the Abrahamic and Sinaitic covenants... We have no reason whatever to think that the Judaisers argued for the annulment or even the alteration of the Abrahamic covenant. On the contrary, every indication we have – considering the thrust of the argument in Gal. 3:7,29 as well as Rom. 4:9-17 – is that Judaisers wanted Gentiles to participate in the Abrahamic inheritance. This blessing, they argued, could be received only by submitting to circumcision and thus becoming Jews (cf. Acts 15:1,5)' (Silva pp190-191). There is more to it. Yes, the Judaisers majored on circumcision (and possibly dietary laws) but it was the entire law which was the issue – as Paul told all concerned – the Galatians, the Judaisers and us today (Gal. 5:3).

Bayes: 'It is generally agreed that *nomos* generally refers in Galatians to the Mosaic law'. Moo: 'The Mosaic law... is clearly what the New Testament writers mean 95% of the time when they use the word "law"' (Bayes pp135-136; Moo: 'The Law' p218).

Dunn: 'Freedom is the leitmotiv of the letter... "Freedom" [is] the word which [here] encapsulated the gospel for Paul... "our freedom in Christ"'. Witherington: 'The heart of [Paul's] message [was] the freedom which we have in Jesus Christ' (Dunn pp260-261; Witherington p137).

Witherington: Paul was defending 'the positive benefits one has in Christ, including being set free from... the Mosaic law'. The false teachers 'will attempt to impose the Mosaic law upon [their] Gentile converts or else say that Gentiles cannot have fellowship (in particular, table fellowship) with Jewish Christians. In short they want a church that is either united in the strict observance of the Mosaic law... or else two churches. To neither of these options will Paul accede'. Bayes rightly took it as read that the attack was over 'the issue of the law'. Dunn: 'The concerns of this group's members [that is, the infiltrators] would be... to ensure that the new movement within Judaism remained true to the principles and practices clearly laid down in the *torah*' (Witherington pp136-137; Bayes p132; Dunn p99).

Some Reformed teachers will not have this. They try to limit the 'freedom' to 'freedom from the curse of the law, from the law as a way of salvation, and from the ceremonial observances which that law demands... a tremendous effort to attain salvation by law-works'. 'The bondage of the ceremonial law' (Hendriksen: *Galatians* p80; Poole p644). Not at all! As we shall see, Paul in Galatians is concerned with the way a sinner is justified *and then sanctified*; particularly the latter. And this, he argues, is not by the law. In fact, freedom from the law is not only the believer's privilege in Christ; it is the only way he can be sanctified. *This* is what Paul teaches! Calvin, with his third use of the law, could not have got it more wrong!

Let me close this opening section with some sterling remarks from Govett. Not only do they give an excellent overview of Galatians, he makes many statements containing, in my opinion, unanswerable arguments on the believer and the law, in light of which every defender of Calvin's third use of the law needs to respond to. I paraphrase his words: 'We challenge our brethren to' answer him. As he said: 'Silence here is the confession of defeat'. Tackling the Reformed claim that the law is abolished as far as justification goes but not for sanctification, Govett made the point that 'if this distinction is not maintained in the New Testament, it is fatal to our brethren's plea. Let us trace its consequences if applied to the [letter to the] Galatians':

'1. If it is a valid distinction, it would provide an escape through all the difficulties which the apostle meets with in that letter. (1). Paul goes up to Jerusalem, and takes with him the Gentile Titus (Gal. 2:1). The Pharisaic party press for his circumcision. Paul refuses it persistently. To have yielded, would have been to give up the truth of the gospel. But now, why could Paul not have made answer to their demands in such terms as these: "I utterly refuse the circumcision of Titus as necessary to his justification, but if you seek it only as an accordance with the law as a rule of life [for sanctification], I do not object". How was it that this proposal came neither from them, nor from Paul, nor from any of the inspired apostles, prophets or teachers? (2). Apply it to the next case – Paul's collision with Peter at Antioch. If the distinction suggested is valid, how was it that Paul put so unfair a construction on Peter's conduct? How was it that we do not have Peter's reply in terms of this distinction? "Why are you so unjust, Paul, as to suppose that I am observing the laws of Jewish diet [actually it was Jewish laws against association with Gentiles] as a matter touching justification? I am not; I am keeping them solely as a rule of life; and you yourself admit that the Mosaic law is in part the believer's rule of life". (3). By the same line of argument, the Galatians could defend themselves against the apostle's attacks (Gal. 3). It would apply also to his assertion of the temporariness of the law (Gal. 3:15-25). "We admit that the institutes of Moses have passed away as a means of justification, but not as a rule of life". (4). The same distinction would serve the Pharisaic teachers of Galatia. Submission to that extent would, no doubt, have screened Paul from persecution (Gal. 5:11; 6:12-14). Could he have said: "I own the decalogue as binding on all Christians", the severity of Jewish persecution would have been blunted. Could the Judaising teachers have said: "We teach circumcision at present as a wise yielding to the Jewish rule of life, not at all involving a belief in justification by works", the force of Paul's argument would have been lost'.

'2. Consider again, had the supposed distinction been scriptural, it must have been prominent and conspicuous in apostolic controversy then, as it is in the controversy now. (1). The apostle taxes the Mosaic law with being in its nature temporary and abolished now (Gal. 3:15-25), a yoke of bondage (Gal. 4:21 – 5:3), a rule only to the slave and to the child (Gal. 3:23; 4:1), hostile to faith and to Christ (Gal. 3:1-14; 5:1-4), a rule for the fleshly, not for the spiritual (Gal. 4:21-31; 5:16-18; 1 Tim. 1:9). He affirms that it only condemns and curses (Gal. 3:9-14) the sons of fallen Adam. (2). With regard to our position as believers, he declares that we are not under it, are dead to it, are delivered from it, redeemed from its slavery. But if our opponents' views are true, that is but half the truth; and these representations are only one-sided and mischievous, through the omission of the necessary counterbalancing statements. There must needs have been, in the same letter, the assertions – that in a certain sense we are under the law, alive to it, serving it; that in part it is abiding, the school of liberty, the rule of the spiritual, the guide of those who are in Jesus, and able to sanctify them. These statements must have appeared on our opponents' theory, both as arising out of the Holy Ghost's perfection of view and guidance, and as springing out of the apostle's honesty and love for the truth – even if his antagonists had not seen them. Amidst

Paul's charges against the Mosaic law, we must have heard these tones of candid confession. These sentiments must have risen to the surface in the arguments of his opponents. They must have been mirrored in the apostle's replies to the objections. If Paul admitted that a part of the law was binding on the Christian, the arguments, both of himself and of the Judaising teacher, must have turned on the question: "How much of the law is to be observed? How do you sever between the part observed and part rejected?" Both would have felt: "This is the fairest point of attack; this is the hardest to defend". Is there any such passage to be found in this letter? We challenge our brethren to point it out. Silence here is the confession of defeat... Look now at both the Galatians and the 15th of Acts and we shall see that the Pharisaic believers pressed the claims of the law of Moses as a whole, and Paul resisted it as a whole, of one quality and obligation throughout. "It was necessary to circumcise them and to command them to keep the law of Moses" (Acts 15:5). "You must be circumcised and keep the law". "We gave no such command" (Acts 15:24)'.

'3. Again, the argument of some texts applies equally against the law, whether we suppose the believer to keep it as a means of justification, or with a view to sanctification only... [Take the curse for one failure in] Gal. 3:10. Here the curse strikes equally all who are of the law's party and put themselves under its rule, whether in order to sanctification or to justification. For its curse lights on all who break it in but one point. You who are under it as the rule of life, are you not guilty of [say] coveting, or of evil desires? If so, you are cursed! If under the law, you are under the curse, so long as you are a sinner, not only in act, but in feeling. A law is not merely a rule, or a piece of advice;[1] 'it is a command connected with a penalty which is to be carried out, not for the good of the party smitten, but in the spirit of justice, destroying the offender... Herein it differs from the commands of grace given by our Lord Jesus to the sons of God, which are commands with penalties, but to be executed in the spirit of mercy as chastisements designed for the good of those enduring them. You cannot say: "I accept the decalogue as a rule without a penalty, to be carried out by mercy" [that is, you have no right or warrant to impose any such terms upon God and his law!] So taken, it ceases to be law. You make void the law by [your view of] grace. But no! The Christian is "not under law, but under grace", a new principle, which both justifies and sanctifies (Rom. 3:24; Tit. 2:11-12)' (Govett pp33-38).

Well, there it is – both Govett's statements and his (and my) challenge. This is such a serious matter, I really must ask for a Reformed or evangelical response. No! A biblical response!

Gal. 2:1-13
Both inexplicably and inconsistently – in light of his later outstanding comments, to which I will make copious reference – John Brown here (Gal. 2:1–11) thought the problem is the 'ceremonial law' (Brown: *Galatians* p75). This was a very serious mistake. Michael Eaton got it right: 'Although Paul was very concerned with the issue of circumcision and table-fellowship, he explicitly makes the point in Gal. 5:3 that one cannot pick and choose between parts of the Mosaic covenant. One must take it that the Christians' relationship to the "whole law" has been in mind all along. There may be some uncertainty about the main concern of the Judaisers, but what concerns Paul is the "whole law"' (Michael Eaton: *Encouragement* p97).

Hubner: 'Since the Gentile Christian, Titus, was not compelled to be circumcised, Gentile Christians must not be compelled to obey the law nor to observe it. Titus represents [is typical of?] all Gentile Christians, and circumcision stands for the whole law... From Paul's standpoint circumcision means *a fortiori* an obligation to obey the whole law... This is what he is... making clear [in] Gal. 5:3... the consequences of circumcision... the *torah* and

---

[1] *Touché* Calvin and his talk of the law being 'a kind adviser' (Calvin: *Commentaries* Vol.21 Part 1 p164).

enslavement to it. Thus circumcision is rejected in order to reject the *torah*... If freedom from circumcision is conceded, this can be understood only as freedom in principle from the *torah*... It is specifically circumcision which implies the obligation to obey the whole *torah*. But if the obligation to obey that prescription falls, then so does the stipulation that one is obliged to keep the law. If there is a dispensation from circumcision, then the *torah* itself comes to lack any foundation... For anyone who breaks out from edifice of the *torah* the very cornerstone of circumcision brings about the collapse of the entire structure... Only total obedience to the law is obedience to the law at all'. As to the escape route of dividing the law into bits moral and ceremonial: 'This is precisely what Paul does *not* say – quite apart from the fact that we are importing a distinction into the Mosaic law here which cannot be found as such in ancient or at least in Jewish thought, where, in fact, there is no clear-cut distinction made at all between the cultic and the moral aspect' (Hubner pp21-25).

Witherington: 'Paul deals with the Mosaic law as a whole... he never once speaks of "laws"... but only of "the law" (119 times)... "the whole law" (Gal. 5:3,14)'. 'In other words, Paul connects the ritual [that is, ceremonial] law, including the distinctive boundary rituals, to the rest of the law, and says that one entails the other'. 'We must thus conclude that by "works of the law" Paul means actions performed in obedience to the Mosaic law, or more specifically acts performed in response to *any and all* commandments of the law'. Ridderbos: The whole law, '*ho pas nomos*: the law considered as a unit as distinguished from the individual commandments' (Witherington p177, emphasis mine; Ridderbos p201).

Bayes: 'It is the clear teaching of this letter that the law, in some sense at least, has no ongoing place in the life of the believer... The law as a total religious system... the epoch of the law is utterly finished... Consequently, Paul can make the general statement about all Christians: "You are not under the law" (Gal. 5:18)' (Bayes p165). What an admirable statement! It is to be hoped that no escape route lies buried in the words 'in some sense'. If not, in less than fifty words, Bayes would have seemed to have answered his own book in defence of the Reformed system, and destroyed his own case.

Dunn: 'Paul himself clearly experienced his new faith in Christ as a "liberation"; this is one of the most consistent notes in his major letters, often with a similar depth of feeling expressed (Rom. 6:17-22; 7:3[-4]; 8:2,21; 1 Cor. 7:22; 9:1; 10:29; 2 Cor. 3:17), and is a central emphasis in this letter in particular (Gal. 4:7,26,30-31; 5:1,13)... He saw the false brothers as enforcing [slavery] on his converts, forcing them to exchange their freedom (from the law as traditionally understood) for slavery – that is, for a dependence on the law rather than directly on God's Spirit; see also Gal. 5:22-23,25... Paul... [saw it as] an illegitimate perversion of the freedom of the gospel... He took his stand for the sake of the Gentile converts in general, including the Galatians' (Dunn pp100-101).

Gal. 2:16-21

Harking back to my previous extract from John Brown – where he showed staggering inconsistency – here he was admirable: '"The law" [in Gal. 2:16-21 is] the Mosaic law... any law... the law'. As was Hendriksen: 'The Old Testament law... God's law... the law... the law of Moses'. As Poole: It is 'the law of Moses, whether ceremonial or moral... the moral law; nor [is] it the ceremonial law only [but] the law of God... the law of Moses'. And Barnes: 'The law of Moses... any law – ceremonial or moral'. And Witherington: 'There is little dispute... that when Paul speaks of "the law" here he means the Mosaic law' (Brown: *Galatians* p93; Hendriksen: *Galatians* pp101-103; Poole pp646-647; Barnes Vol.6 pp321,324; Witherington p175). We seem to be agreed. So let's stick with it throughout the letter, not just in this paragraph. The law is the law of Moses.

Bayes rightly argued the 'bondage' was to 'impose upon themselves the slavery of a works-based religion... by the works of the law'. This raises large and important issues (Bayes p134). See the penultimate extract of this section for Witherington's list.

Kruse spoke of the modern views of justification, the 'increasing reluctance to accept the traditional Reformation view of "the works of the law"... as good works in order to amass merit before God, upon which they could rely for salvation'. But I am totally convinced that Paul *was* writing here against the notion that sinner can be justified by observance of the law. I am with Moo: 'Traditionally, [Rom. 3:20] has been understood as a denial that a person can earn salvation by doing anything; no "works", however "good" – even those done in obedience to God's holy law – can bring a person into relationship with God... [The] Jews in Paul's day... believed that, indeed, they could get into relationship with God by obedience to the law. Many modern interpreters... question this [traditional] explanation... I think, however, that, properly nuanced, the traditional view remains the best explanation of the Pauline polemic' (Kruse p78; Moo: *Romans* p212). I put it stronger. This *is* what Paul is saying.

John Brown: 'By the law having had its full course... I am completely delivered from the law. The law has no more to do with me, and I have no more to do with it in the matter of justification. And this freedom from the law is at once necessary and effectual to my living a truly holy life – a life devoted to God... To justify, to sanctify, is... an impossibility to the law'. Witherington: Believers are 'no longer under the law's jurisdiction, no longer obligated to keep the law, no longer under the law's power, free from the law's curse and its demands'. 'They now [live] in a new sphere of influence, namely Christ, or to put it another way, they [are] now part of the eschatological new creation. They [are] now under a new mandate, namely the law of Christ'. Gal. 2:19 'suggests [too weak! – death to the law is *essential*] that one must die to the law, in order to live to God'. Michael Eaton: 'Restoring the law is transgression'. 'Not to abandon the law is itself to transgress the law. This is not always understood'. Quite! 'Returning to Mosaism leads to transgression'. 'Release from the *torah* enables sanctification'. Ridderbos: 'The apostle contrasts the living unto God with the dying unto the law. By the first term of the contrast is meant the God-directed, God-consecrated life. The possibility of living thus was, however, given him only *after* he had died to the law'. 'And this death Paul has now died *so that* he might live unto God'. Edgar H.Andrews: 'Notice the word "that" [in Gal. 2:19], meaning "in order that" or "so that". The Scripture is telling us here that we must die to the law before we can live spiritually. Our relationship to the law must be dissolved before we can serve God. [Andrews quoting Longenecker:] In Pauline usage, "to die to" something is to cease to have any further relation to it' (Brown: *Galatians* pp96,165; Witherington pp188-189; Michael Eaton: *Encouragement pp*97-99; Ridderbos pp103-104, first two emphases mine, the third his; Edgar H.Andrews pp116,122).

Edgar H.Andrews: 'How can Paul say the law has been "destroyed" when Jesus says the opposite? When Jesus refers to "the law and the prophets" in Matthew, he is actually talking about the Old Testament Scriptures, not the law of Moses. However, Moses' law forms part of those Scriptures, so the question remains a fair one. The word "destroy" must be understood in its context in each case. Christ said he came "not to destroy, but to fulfil". But in fulfilling the law, he rendered it redundant. For example, the Mosaic priesthood was swept away, being replaced by Christ's high priesthood (see Heb. 7 – 9). So, in one sense, fulfilment can be seen as destruction, since it renders obsolete that which is fulfilled. The purpose of the flower is fulfilled when its petals fall, leaving the seed-pod to ripen. The blossom is destroyed in the very act of fulfilment. So it is with the law. [Longenecker, quoted by Andrews:] The phrase... "those things that I annulled/annihilated/destroyed" [Gal. 2:18]... refers to the law as both the basis for justification and a necessary form of life. The aorist tense of the verb... has in mind a past, once-for-all act – that time of conversion when one ceased to rely on the Mosaic law for either justification or the supervision of life, but turned to Christ for both acceptance before God and the pattern for living' (Edgar H.Andrews pp109-110). In other words, the law is not the way of sanctification.

John Brown: 'This freedom from the law is at once necessary and effectual to... living a truly holy life'; that is, sanctification. Paul went on: 'I am a dead man with regard to the law, but I am a living man in regard to Christ. The law has killed me, and by doing so, it has set me free from itself. I have no more to do with the law. The life I have now, is not the life of a man under the law, but the life of a man delivered from the law'. Kruse: 'Paul argued that the law was not the regulatory norm for Christian living, for Christians had died to the law (ending their relationship with it) so that they might live to God... Thus whatever might be the function of the law in the life of the believer... it was never to be rebuilt to function as a standard by which believers (whether Jews or Gentiles) *must* live'. Ridderbos: 'The law can no longer use him. He is what a dead servant would be to his master... [Making] void the grace of God... was the essence of [Paul's] controversy with Peter. And that is the consequence of what the Galatians are doing also, if they... permit themselves to be brought under the law. That, too, is the thing that will be sharply and forcefully said in the sequel, beginning immediately at Gal. 3:1' (Brown: *Galatians* p97; Kruse pp71,113, emphasis his; Ridderbos pp104-107).

Dunn called Paul's conversion 'that encounter... with the risen Christ. [It] so completely turned upside down his understanding of the law... that the law ceased from that time to exercise the same hold over him... He became dead to what had previously been his primary motivating force. The thought is stark, but it is not made easier by taking "through the law" as a reference to 'the law of faith' (Rom. 3:27); nor is the issue here to be translated simply into ritual versus moral law... [His conversion] meant, for Paul, an irreversible change: to return under the law was for him as inconceivable as for one who enjoys life beyond death to return to life before death, life under death... His encounter with Christ resulted in the possibility [better, the inevitability] of living to God liberated from the constraints of the old life... All this was possible, as Paul is about to make clear, because his dying and new life were a sharing in Christ's death and risen life (*cf.* Rom. 6:8-11; 7:4). By implication, Christ's death was also a dying through the law and to the law in order that the constraints of the law might be lifted (*cf.* Gal. 3:13-14)'. On Gal. 2:19-20: 'The thought is stark... the language is startling' (Dunn pp143-145).

Witherington listed some of the consequences of a works-based religion. He included: 'Does the law still have a function in the new economy of God? Should one add obedience to the law to faith in Christ as the agitators were urging in Galatia? What should the role of the Mosaic law be in the life of a Christian believer?' He made this telling observation: 'It cannot be stressed enough that throughout all of Paul's acts of persuasion that follow, Paul is arguing with *Christians* about the proper and improper ways of getting on with their Christian lives. In other words, even though Paul will at points give his converts a reminder about how they got into the [church] of God, this argument is not basically about getting in, nor even about how one stays in, but rather about how one goes on in Christ and with the aid of the Holy Spirit... The Mosaic law and obedience to it is not, in Paul's view, how one got into Christ, how one stays in Christ, or how one goes on in Christ. It is no longer what defines and delineates who the people of God are and how they ought to live and behave' (Witherington pp171-172, emphasis his). This is of the utmost importance. That sanctification is not by the law, is not merely a truth; it is a major theme in Galatians.

Let Moo close this section, and lead us on to the next: 'Justification by faith... while perhaps not the main theme of Galatians or even of this section of the letter, is a critical aspect about the truth of the gospel that Paul needs to establish. What perhaps is not as often appreciated, but which is made tolerably clear by the justification language in Gal. 5:4-5, is that the justification involved here is not simply entrance into the Christian life. The issue in Galatia, as the following paragraph, Gal. 3:1-5, reveals so clearly, is not how one begins the Christian life, but how one continues it. Paul challenges the Galatians to "continue" in the same way as they have begun. He does not deny that the Galatians have been justified when they first came to Christ... but the rhetorical exigencies of the Galatian crisis require Paul to focus on the continuation and culmination of the Christian life. The focus of the letter, then, is on what we might call "ultimate justification", vindication on the day of judgement. And this vindication, Paul insists, will come by means of faith and not law, or "the works of the law" (Gal. 2:16 [three times]; 3:2,5,10... [And] there can really be no doubt that *nomos* in Galatians refers (with one possible exception [Gal. 6:2?]) to the law of Moses' (Moo: 'Galatians' pp9-11). There are no chapter/verse divisions in the original, of course.

Gal. 3:1-5

Witherington: Paul opened Gal. 3:1-5 'with a bang in the form of an exclamation followed by a series of questions'. Hendriksen, however, seriously – badly, appallingly – glossed the passage: 'By what avenue were you first made conscious of having the Holy Spirit in your hearts? Was it by the avenue of rigorous bondage to ceremonial ordinances?' Not at all! The Galatians did not receive the Spirit by the law – the law, full stop! John Brown got it right: 'When God gave you the Spirit... was it in consequence of your yielding obedience to the Mosaic law?' Calvin was rightly corrected by his translator: 'Did you receive [the Holy] Spirit... by conformity to the law of Moses?' (Witherington p200; Hendriksen: *Galatians* p113; Brown: *Galatians* p113; note by Chandler added by the translator to rectify Calvin's sad 'silence' on the matter in Calvin: *Commentaries* Vol.21 Part 1 p81).

Liversidge: 'The Galatian letter is often presented as the case for *salvation* by faith. Though it can be used in that way, it is more correctly seen as the case for *perfection* by faith. We are not only to begin in faith but also to go on into mature Christian experience by faith (Gal. 3:3)' (Liversidge p10, emphasis mine).

Pink got it wrong: 'The central issue raised in Galatians is not what is the standard of conduct for the believer's life, but what is the ground of the sinner's salvation'. As I say, quite wrong! Galatians *is* about sanctification – but it is about far more than sanctification's *standard*. Paul sets out the 'how' of it – by setting out the way not to get it; namely, by the law. Ridderbos, too, failed to get Paul's meaning: 'What is indicated in the letter to the Galatians is the inadequacy of the law for salvation' – unless, of course, he included sanctification as well as justification in 'salvation' (Pink: *Law* p21; Ridderbos p22). As did Hubner. He started right: 'In Galatians, Paul reproaches the Galatian congregations with being on the point of placing themselves under the dominion and bondage of the law; or, more precisely, of renewing such bondage'. Sadly, he then careered off the rails: 'He considers that the Galatians are in danger of seeking to be justified by the works of the law' (Hubner p15). Not at all. Gal. 3:1-5 proves Hubner wrong. Apart from certain sections (principally Gal. 2:15-17,21; 5:2-12), the apostle's primary concern in Galatians is sanctification. The truth is, Paul 'considers that the Galatians are in danger, *above all*, of seeking to be *sanctified* by the works of the law'. And that is why Galatians is so relevant to the issue in hand.

Witherington got it right: 'I must reiterate... what I have said before. Paul's primary concern in this letter is with how the Galatians will go on in Christ... Justification is not the main subject of this letter; it is brought into the discussion about how the Galatians should behave as Christians, and whether they should "add" obedience to the Mosaic law to their faith in Christ. Paul's response is that precisely because they did not come to be in Christ by obeying the law... they should *not* [emphasis his] now add obedience to the Mosaic law to their faith in Christ. Rather they should continue as they started in Christ, walking in the Spirit and according to the law or norm or example of Christ... A crucial point... Paul's subject in this letter is not how one gets into the Christian fold, nor how one stays in the Christian fold, but how one goes on with one's Christian life... The Galatians are thinking of adding obedience to the law to faith in Christ. In Paul's view this is changing horses in the middle of the stream... [He] will have nothing to do with the notion that Christians ought to add obedience to the Mosaic law to faith in Christ... Notice... the present continual tense ["being made perfect" (Gal. 3:3)]. This is the issue Paul must primarily discourse on in what follows – how they will go on in the present and into the future as Christians, *not* how they began... [On Gal. 3:12:] The issue is how God's people shall live, how they shall go on in their Christian life' (Witherington pp175,214,235,346, emphasis mine, unless otherwise stated).

What are 'the works of the flesh'? Witherington: 'Paul... associates works of the flesh with being under the law in some way'. Dunn: 'The parallelism between Gal. 3:2-3 clearly links "Spirit" and "faith" on the one side and "flesh" and "works of the law" on the other'. Fee: 'Ever and always in Paul this [that is, the flesh] describes those outside of Christ... Such people neither submit nor can they submit to God's *torah*... The reason they cannot submit to God's *torah* is that they live apart from the Spirit' (Witherington p395; Dunn pp155-156; Fee: *Empowering* p542).

Witherington: The emphasis in the Greek upon '"works of the law" [Gal. 3:2]... is the bone of contention and the cause for writing this letter' (Witherington p210).

Kruse: 'Paul seeks to show the Galatians that both justification *and progress in the Christian life* are independent of the works of the law... [On Gal. 3:3, Paul's argument] relates to the Galatians' experience of the Spirit. This [third] question, however, relates not to the initial reception of the Spirit but rather the Spirit's role in the ongoing life of believers... Just as they began their new life as believers with the Spirit (and independently of the works of the law), so they must seek its completion in the same way... As the Christian life is begun, so it is to be completed. There is no more place for the "works of the law" in the ongoing Christian life than there was at its beginning... It is faith, not the works of the law, which is important in the ongoing Christian life' (Kruse pp73-76, emphasis mine).

On Gal. 3:1-5, Bayes was right to say: 'The channel for [the Galatians']... experiences associated with their... justification... was not the law'. But he went far too far when he said: 'Paul's *main emphasis* in this passage is that... the law simply is not God's method for endowing his people with his Spirit at the time of their justification'. Bayes argued this because he thought Paul's 'central teaching [in Galatians was] that the law was never given as a way of justification'. But as he had already said on Gal. 3:21: This 'statement... comes to the heart of Paul's argument about the weakness of the law in this letter: his fundamental point is that the law does not have the power to justify, *nor to achieve the true life which is the inseparable concomitant of justification*' (Bayes pp137,150-151,163, emphasis mine). Precisely! A pity Bayes did not hold on to that last – it would have saved him writing his book – or else enabled him to write a very different book!

Let Poole close this section and lead us on to the next: 'The ordinances of the law were... commanded by God; yet they, being temporary institutions, never intended by God to continue longer than the coming of Christ, and the law being but a schoolmaster to lead to Christ, Christ being now come, and having died, and risen again from the dead, they became useless... It spoke great weakness, therefore, in the Galatians, to begin with what was... perfect (the embracing of the gospel, and Christ there exhibited for the justification of sinners), and to end in what was... imperfect... [that is, going to the law for sanctification!] and so [the apostle] calls them foolish, for beginning in the Spirit... and then apostatising... to a carnal life... Their folly is argued from their thinking to be made perfect by the beggarly elements and worldly rudiments of the law, whereas they had first begun... with the... perfect doctrine of the gospel' (Poole p648). I hope there was no hidden escape route in Poole's use of 'ordinances'. As long as we read his words as referring to 'the law', all is well. After all, that is what the apostle declared. And in so doing, he annihilated Calvin's third use of the law!

Gal. 3:10 – 4:7

John Brown on Gal. 3:10-25: The law here 'is obviously the Mosaic institution viewed as a whole. It is neither what has been termed the moral law, nor the ceremonial law, nor the judicial law, which theologians have been accustomed to treat of as three distinct codes; but it is the whole arrangement or covenant under which the people of Israel were placed at Sinai'. Calvin: 'Paul does not speak of the moral law only, but of everything connected with the office held by Moses'. Witherington: 'Paul is deliberately trying to speak in more general terms about the law, not just about particular laws. Paul does not wish to focus just on a curse appended to a particular set of Mosaic laws, but one which pertains in general to those "under the law"'. Kruse: 'Here the law must be understood as God's law, not as a legalistic misunderstanding of it... "Law" here is best understood to denote the requirements of God's law, not legalism'. Moo rightly dismissed 'the hypothesis that Paul is speaking here of the "misunderstood" law of Jewish legalists, [as] little short of incredible [in light of his] explanation [here] for the purpose of the law in salvation history' (Brown: *Galatians* p148 Calvin: *Commentaries* Vol.21 Part 1 p99; Witherington p232; Kruse p84; Moo: 'The Law' p212). A first-rate set of extracts. Let us go on with this in mind: whatever we find Paul saying, he is saying it about the law, the law of God, the law of Moses, the entire law, including the ten commandments, no 'ifs, buts or maybes', no glosses. In other words, can we let Paul tell us what we are to believe – not the other way about?

Longenecker: 'What ties all four... statements [in Gal. 3:19] together is the emphasis on the inferior status of the Mosaic law [with respect] to the promise given in the Abrahamic covenant – an inferiority expressed in terms of the law's temporary status, its purpose and function, and the manner in which it was given. In these four statements... Paul states the theme for all that follows in Gal. 3:19 – 4:7'. Quoting Ernest DeWitt Burton, Longenecker then spoke of 'the law as supplementary and hence subordinate to the [Abrahamic] covenant... The law in the apostle's thought forms no part of the [Abrahamic] covenant, [it] is a thing distinct from it, in no way modifying its provisions... The whole clause, "until the Seed to whom the promise referred should come", sets the limit during which the law continues. Thus the covenant of promise is presented... as of permanent validity, both beginning before, and continuing through, the period of the law and afterwards; the law, on the other hand, is temporary, added to the permanent covenant for a period limited in both directions'. First class!

Longenecker moved to the law's role in 'supervising life': The apostle 'uses the analogy of the pedagogue in [Gal. 3:24-25] and the illustration of a son in a patrician household in [Gal. 4:1-7], for these figures were particularly suggestive... in nuancing what he means by "we were held prisoners by the law"... Paul says quite clearly that [the law] functioned in this manner "until faith (that is, *ten pistin*, 'the faith' that came with Christ) should be revealed" (Gal. 3:23; *cf.* Gal. 3:19). This suggests [it means!] that some [major, massive] difference in the divine economy took place with the coming of Christ, with that difference being that righteousness is now apart from the law (*cf.* Rom. 3:21) – yet without in any way nullifying the promise... [The phrase] *eis Christon* must be taken here in the temporal sense of "until Christ". With the coming of Christ, the supervisory function of the law ended, just as the services of a pedagogue end when his charge comes to maturity. Any endeavour on the part of a son who has reached maturity and come into possession of his inheritance to revert back to the supervision of an administrative guardian would be a reversion to childishness – it would in fact be a return to what Paul calls "the elemental teachings/principles of the world". For when God moves forward in his redemptive economy, any reversion or standing still becomes a "worldly" act, no matter how good or how appropriate such a stance once was'. Excellent, once again. This scriptural teaching must not be forgotten.

Longenecker then came to the crunch: 'The relevance of all this for the question of Christians and the Mosaic law'. 'What then should we say as to the relevance of Paul's pedagogue analogy of Gal. 3:24-25, his illustration of a son in a patrician household in Gal. 4:1-7, and his overall argument of Gal. 3:19 – 4:7 for the question of Christians and the Mosaic law?' he asked. 'In Gal. 3:19 – 4:7, Paul has given us an important answer [*the* answer!] to a perennial problem of Christian theology and lifestyle – an answer that needs to be highlighted, particularly in evangelical circles today'. How right this is! It was right in 1982, when Longenecker wrote, and it is still right today! That is why I have produced this book! As Longenecker concluded: 'God's purpose in redemption has always been to bring his people to a full realisation of their personal relationship with him as sons, and to a full possession of their promised inheritance. So with the coming of Christ, Paul insists that "we are no longer under the supervision of the law" (Gal. 3:25) and "no longer a slave, but a son... and also an heir" (Gal. 4:7). It is for this reason that Judaism speaks of itself as being *torah*-centred and Christianity declares that it is Christ-centred, for in Christ the Christian finds not only God's law as [a] standard pre-eminently expressed, but also as a system of conduct, set aside in favour of guidance by reference to his teachings and example and through the direct action of his Spirit. Thus Paul proclaims that "Christ is the end of the law in its connection with righteousness to everyone who believes" (Rom. 10:4, understanding the much disputed *telos* as properly "termination" and not just "goal"). It is such concept that Paul has nuanced by his use of the pedagogue analogy of Gal. 3:24-25, and by his illustration of a son in a patrician household of Gal. 4:1-7, and it is such concept that Christians need to recapture today'. I pause. How right this is! 'Otherwise we are in danger of being "half-Judaisers" – that is, of denying the Judaisers soteriological legalism [that is, salvation by the law], but retaining their insistence on the necessity for a nomistic lifestyle [that is, sanctification by the law]'. I pause again. This is precisely the Reformed position! As Longenecker went on: 'Gal. 3:19 – 4:7, however, was given as a corrective to such thinking. It sets before us one important feature of the answer to the question concerning Christians and the Mosaic law' (Longenecker pp57-61). A first class statement!

What of the Reformed view that the promise and the law form one covenant? What does Paul's teaching in Gal. 3:19 – 4:7 have to say about that? Quite a bit! John Brown: 'The law was added or appended. It was a separate subordinate institution, not an alteration of *or addition to* the original arrangement'. Witherington rightly dismissed the idea that the role of the law and the promise are 'integrated'. In Gal. 4:24: 'Paul sees the Abrahamic covenant and the Mosaic covenant as two separate covenants, not two parts of one covenant... Paul is trying to maintain their separation, while the agitators presumably were seeing them as blended together... Salvation history is not developmental or evolutionary but apocalyptic or interventionist'. Lloyd-Jones, commenting on 'the law entered' (Rom. 5:20): 'There was a state of affairs already existing; but now into that situation something else comes. It is not so much that it creates a new situation; it comes in alongside of the other situation. If we understand this principle we are at once more than halfway to an understanding of the function of the law. The very word "added alongside", that Paul uses here, tells us that the law, in and of itself, is not something that is of fundamental importance to us. It is something additional, it is something that has come in for the time being, for a particular function. It is not fundamental... it is something that enters, an addition, something that "comes in alongside of"'. Kruse: '"Added" [speaks of] a supplementary role for the law' (Brown: *Galatians* p149; Witherington pp255,266; Lloyd-Jones: *Assurance* pp284-285; Kruse p91, emphasis mine).

McClain: 'Gal. 3:19. The verb "added" indicates that the law was not primary in God's dealings with sinners. The covenant and promises of God were first. The law was added. And the divine reason is found in man's "transgressions". This general statement will be amplified in more specific statements. But the heart of the matter is that the giving of the law is related to man's sin. There is a time element in the matter – the law was given because of transgressions until "the Seed should come to whom the promise was made".

Thus the giving of the law was neither first nor is it final with God in saving sinners or dealing with the problem of sin. It was "added" and temporary' (McClain pp24-25).

What about the 'us' of Gal. 3:13? John Brown was unequivocal: Paul was referring to elect Jews: 'Gentile believers were, previously to their conversion, under sin and condemnation, as well as the Jewish believers; but not being subject to the Mosaic law, they could not be considered as exposed to its curse, and, of course, they could not be... redeemed from a curse to which they were never subject'. Machen: 'On the whole, it is probable' that Paul meant elect Jews. Bayes: 'The word "us" here [Gal. 3:13] probably refers in the first instance to the Jews as those who were under the law... The reference to the Gentiles in [Gal. 3:14] suggests that Paul is thinking here [Gal. 3:13] only of the Jews... In the primary sense, the curse of the law can be applicable only to the Jews, since it was only to them that the law was given'. Michael Eaton: 'The "we" is generally taken to refer to include Jewish and Gentile Christians. Yet there are indications that this is an exclusive "we" and refers only to the people of Israel [Gal. 2:15]'. Dunn: 'The "we" here will, unusually, mean "we Jews"': Paul was thinking so much in Jewish terms... that he naturally spoke as from a Jewish standpoint... Hence the "all/you" emphasis of Gal. 3:26-29 in contrast to the "we" of Gal. 3:23-25'. Witherington: 'When "we" occurs in the earlier part of the letter it consistently refers to "we" Jews or more often "we" Jewish Christians' (Brown: *Galatians* pp129-130; Machen p179; Bayes p154; Michael Eaton: *Encouragement* pp104-108; Dunn pp197-198; Witherington pp199,235-238,267,269,288). He thought the first place in the letter where 'we' means 'all believers' is Gal. 5:25 (Witherington p413).

Moo, however, was not quite so sure: 'The first-person plural verbs and pronouns used throughout Gal. 3:23 – 4:5 could point in this direction, but Paul's use of this first-person is notoriously difficult to pin down'. Even so, drawing on Rom. 2:12,14-15; 1 Cor. 9:20-21, Moo admitted Paul 'principally confines the law to Jews. While dogmatism is out of order... it may be the case that [Paul is speaking of] we Jews... [The question] has significance for the question of the status of Gentiles in the Old Testament. Were they, in any sense, "under the law"?... Perhaps it is best to view Israel's experience with the law as paradigmatic of all nations. While, then, the Gentiles would not be "under the law" in the same sense as Israel, they would be responsible for those moral standards that God had laid upon them'. I (DG) think of Rom. 2:14-15 in this connection. Moo: 'The Old Testament prophets can condemn the "nations" because of this standard. And in addition, the nations would be under the condemnation brought by their failure to live up to those standards for which God made them responsible... Paul's warning in Gal. 4:21 and 5:4 to the effect that Gentile Christians who place themselves "under the law" are "alienated" from Christ suggests the continuing relevance of this function of the law. Thus, the fulfilment of the law brought by Christ is applicable only to those who become joined to him by faith; for those outside of Christ, both Jew and Gentile, God's "law" continues to condemn' (Moo: 'The Law' p213; see also 'Galatians' p16).

Hubner: 'All mankind [are] under sin – the Jews under the law... The enslaving power under which Jews and Gentiles stood [is] in essence the same' (Hubner p33). If so, Moo thought 'the transition to the Gentiles [in the letter] would then be made in Gal. 4:5' (Moo: 'The Law' p213).

John Brown: '"God sent forth his Son, born of a woman, born under the law" (Gal. 4:4). So far was the imposition of the law on the Gentiles from being the object of [Christ's] coming, one of its designs was to deliver the Jews from under it'.

On 'God's purpose' 'because of transgressions' (Gal. 3:19), Kevan: 'The writings of the apostle direct our attention to the forward look, or purposive meaning, of the word "because"... The startling affirmation which Paul makes here is that the law was added to "promote" transgressions: it was to "create" or "to increase transgressions"... The law did not, of course, "create" transgressions in the absolute sense: its function was to cause sin to be exhibited as breach of law, and thus as something incurring penalty'. Thielman: 'Although there is no transgression where there is no law (Rom. 4:15), sin and its penalty of death still exist because of Adam's disobedience. The law makes it possible to "reckon" (*ellogeō*) sin precisely as transgression against one or more of God's commandments; but it only made worse the rebellion against God that was in the world from the time of Adam's transgression... The law, Paul says, played an important but subsidiary role in salvation history: it transformed Adam's transgression of a single commandment into Israel's rebellion against a whole range of God's commandments'. Ridderbos: 'From Rom. 4:15; 5:20 it becomes apparent... that Paul means... the law was given, so to speak, to call forth the transgressions, and make them manifest... that by means of the law sin should come out into the open and multiply itself. The law makes guilt and evil greater (Rom. 5:20)... Up to [Christ's] coming, the law had to bring sin out more and more, and, by reason of human wickedness, call it into existence'. Kruse: 'The law's function was to restrain Israel morally until the coming of Christ... The corollary, as Paul does not hesitate to point out, is that once the promise is fulfilled, and faith has come, then believing Israel is no longer under the law (Gal. 3:25). And if Jewish believers are no longer under the law, then neither are Gentile believers' (Kevan: *Experience* pp30,34; Thielman p25; Ridderbos pp137-138; Kruse pp93-94).

We now come to a very important subsection. The temporary nature of the law is clearly established by the apostle in Gal. 3:15 – 4:7. So much so, Calvin's second and third uses of the law must be wrong. The law was added as a temporary measure, and its role ceased with Christ, having been fulfilled by him. It is useless – it is wrong – to try to limit this 'temporary' to certain aspects of the law. Remember what we have seen. With the exception of Gal. 6:2, 'the law' means the law, the entire law of God, the law of Moses, including the ten commandments.

Moo: 'The clear temporal limits that Paul places on the law in this section [Gal. 3:15 – 4:7] would not naturally be taken to apply to only one part of the law. It is the law of Moses in its totality that "was added" (Gal. 3:19), "430 years" after the promise (Gal. 3:17), and that was to last only "until the Seed to whom the promise referred had come" (Gal. 3:19)... These clear temporal indications suggest strongly that Gal. 3:24 should not be translated... "Therefore the law has become our tutor *to lead us* to Christ", but... "So the law was put in charge of us *until* Christ came"... and therefore lends no support to the so-called [that is, Calvin's] "second" [use]... of the law (to show people their need of God, and so lead them to Christ)' (Moo: 'Galatians' pp15-16, first emphasis his; second, mine).

Now for another vital issue – the law as a slave-master. 'Under', *hupo*, repeated, Moo called 'the key word' (Gal. 3:23,25; 4:2-5). The repetition of '"under" [and] the flow of the context... [shows] these descriptions are interrelated and mutually interpreting... The law imposed rules, guarded behaviour, and served to reveal, confine under, and stimulate sin... The similarity to Rom. 6:14-15 is obvious. In both contexts, an earlier stage of salvation history, *hupo nomon* ["under law"], is contrasted with the present era (denoted by *hupo charin* ["under grace"] in Romans) with particular stress on the freedom enjoyed in the latter state. And, as in Romans, not to be *hupo nomon* seems clearly to include not being bound to the law as a code of conduct. For when one reaches maturity, one no longer needs the 'pedagogue' to direct, guide and correct one... [The law] no longer stands as the authoritative norm for living out one's relationship to God' (Moo: 'The Law' pp213-214).

Moo also argued that the apostle's use of 'under the law' confirms the pedagogue's temporary role as a custodian: 'Confirmation of this point may be found in another key phrase that Paul uses in this context [Gal. 3:15 – 4:7] and elsewhere in Galatians: "under the law". Paul uses the phrase "under [the] law" (*hupo nomon*) five times in Galatians and six times elsewhere (Gal. 3:23; 4:4,5,21; 5:18; see also Rom. 6:14-15; 1 Cor. 9:20 [four occurrences]). The omission of the article in each instance does not indicate that Paul is thinking of divine "law" in general or of law as a principle...; the "law" in question is so well known that there is no need to make the word *nomos* definite. As the context in each case makes clear, the law to which Paul refers is the Mosaic law, the *torah*. Reformed interpreters have often interpreted the phrase as a reference to the condemnation pronounced by the law'. Moo, in reply, was not strong enough. While he admitted there is some support for this,[2] 'other evidence points in a different direction... [Take] the *paidagōgos* in Gal. 3:24... This word, as we have seen, denotes, not the cursing effect of the law, but its custodianship of the people of Israel during the time of their "minority". A second reason for preferring this broader interpretation of the phrase is Paul's assertion in Gal. 4:4 that Jesus was himself "born under [the] law". Since Jesus was not born subject to the curse (although he later voluntarily and vicariously took it upon himself; *cf.* Gal 3:13), the phrase here cannot mean "under the curse of the law". Jesus, Paul is stressing, was a Jew and lived as one who was subject to the requirements of the Mosaic law that had been given to oversee the Jewish people. Like most other phrases about bondage in the context, then, "under the law" refers to a status of close supervision and custodial care, a situation that eventually gives way to a time of maturity and freedom'. Moo developed his argument by reference to Rom. 6:14-15; 7:4; 1 Cor. 9:20-21 (Moo: 'Galatians' pp17-20).

Hong, taking a different view to that of Moo, argued that being 'under the law' means under 'slavery', and this includes its 'curse'. He argued from Gal. 3:23; 4:4-5,21; 5:18 with Gal. 3:22,25; 4:2-3, alleging this 'primarily refers to the existence of the Jews before the coming of faith (Gal. 3:23-25)'. He went on: 'However, with the coming of Christ, the bondage of the law was brought to an end (Gal. 3:25)'. From this he claimed, if being "under sin" refers to the slavery of the evil power of sin [Gal. 3:22-23][3]... then we are not permitted to see any positive element in being under the law'. Hong developed his case extensively throughout his paper. 'Paul employs the pedagogue metaphor in order to describe vividly the enslavement of the law'. The same goes for the guardian (Gal. 4:1-7). 'The coming of faith... corresponds to the coming of Christ'. As for Christ being 'born under the law' (Gal. 4:4), Hong did not shy away from the inevitable conclusion of his argument: 'What Paul means here is that at his birth Christ took upon himself the curse which the Jews had incurred because of their non-fulfilment of the law... This points to the deep condescension of his incarnation (*cf.* Phil. 2:7). This humiliating incarnation is the first significant step of Christ's redemptive work'. I pause. If so, this has a bearing on the debated subject of Christ's active and passive obedience. Hong concluded: 'For Paul, the law functions as an enslaving power, seen from the perspective of the history of salvation' (Hong pp354-372).

Whichever view on this is right, there is no doubt that the law brought slavery. With the work of Christ, however, that slavery has been abolished, Christ having fulfilled the law and liberated his people from it – from the law, not merely its curse. Believers are no longer under the law, no longer slaves of the law. They are free! For them, the law has came to an end.

Reformed teachers fly in the face of this, placing an altogether different interpretation on the apostle's words. Watson: 'The law of God is a hedge to keep us [believers] within the bounds of sobriety and piety'. Poole tried to suck the meaning out of Christ's words (Matt. 11:13): 'The *ceremonial* law from [this] time began to die' (Watson p10; Poole p49, emphasis mine).

Not at all. Michael Eaton: 'The contrast that flows through this section refers to epochs of world history before and after the coming of Jesus. The law [was] an interim measure until

---

[2] See Hong immediately below.

[3] As above, Moo disputed this interpretation (Moo: 'Galatians' p17).

the coming of Jesus... For Paul the law [was] only an interim measure and the total Mosaic covenant is abrogated'. John Brown: 'The law was added to the promise as a temporary appendage, and did not abrogate it; but the gospel takes the place of the law, and thus abolishes it'. Dunn called the law 'an interim measure... until [the problem of transgression] could be dealt with definitively and finally in the cross of Christ... The contrasting epochs can be summed up simply by their most characteristic features – law (for Israel) and faith... The interim epoch of the law... the restrictive character of that epoch... is underlined by every phrase: "confined"; limited in scope and provisional in comparison with faith; faith "revealed" with immediacy (*cf.* Gal. 1:12,16) and with eschatological finality, in contrast to the law given through intermediaries. This limited, provisional role of the law is reinforced by the imagery of the next two verses [Gal. 3:24-25], as carried over also into Gal. 4:1-10'. Bayes: 'Paul sees "the law" as a definite epoch in the life of the Jewish people... The epochal status of the law implies that it is [better, was] a bracketed period within human (and specifically Jewish) history, that the epoch denominated "the law" is [better, was] not of unending duration... The law as viewed by Paul in this letter [was] "a parenthetic epoch"... [In Gal. 3:23-24] the word "faith" is used with objective force, the time note serving to emphasises the fact that Paul is talking here about the law and faith as successive epochs... It is important to stress that these verses... are concerned with the Jews... Paul's point is that the Jews were subjected by God... to the oversight of the epoch of the law, only until, and with a view to, the coming of Christ... The disciplinary nature of the law was its power to keep the Jewish hope on course towards the Messiah. The epoch of the law was thus a parenthesis... This powerful role of the law in Jewish life for a particular epoch, reached its goal, and therefore came to its conclusion "when the fullness of the time had come" (Gal. 4:4), when the Jewish hope was realised in the sending by God of his Son. In the next verse... Paul defines the twofold purpose of his coming in true humanity as a member of the Jewish race. The first purpose of his coming was to redeem those who were under the law' (Michael Eaton: *Encouragement* pp107-108; Brown: *Hebrews* p662; Dunn pp190,198; Bayes pp136,142,147-150). Bayes, in saying this, it seems to me, has gone a long way to destroying his own case. The law was temporary. The faith, the gospel, has come. So – how can the law be the believer's perfect rule?

Now for a misunderstanding with very serious consequences, based on a bad translation. I refer to 'schoolmaster'. McClain, said Gal. 3:24 (AV) 'has been the source of considerable misunderstanding. The apostle certainly did *not* write: "The law was our schoolmaster to bring us unto Christ". The words "to bring us" do *not* occur in the original text. The whole idea of the law serving as a schoolmaster conducting the sinner to Christ, as Lightfoot has declared, ought to be "abandoned". The *paidagogos* (schoolmaster) of ancient times was a slave who exercised restraint over the child until he was made a son. So the law was the *paidagogos* until Christ came and sonship was acquired by faith in him. The law does not bring men to Christ, therefore' (McClain pp28-29, emphasis mine).

So we have two things to bear in mind: the temporary age of the law, and the law's slavery. Paul is not talking personally here, but in an epochal sense, and talking in terms of bondage. Despite this, many persist in saying Gal. 3:19,22-24 speaks of the personal experience of conviction of sin, and an individual's experience of coming to faith in Christ. Paul, they allege, was saying the Spirit uses the law to convict the sinner and lead him to faith in Christ for salvation. In other words, the law rules over an individual unregenerate sinner until Christ has come savingly to that individual sinner. See chapter 4 for Calvin on Gal. 3:24. Hendriksen agreed: 'The law... serves [the promise], by revealing our sinfulness and leading us to Christ... When by God's grace the sinner has learned to see himself in the light of the law... he yearns for Christ... Some hold that "faith" must here be interpreted in the objective sense (religion, doctrine) as in Gal. 1:23'. Quite right, too! But he did not agree: it means the individual, personal 'subjective activity of believing in [Christ]... The law performed a useful function... to bring sinners to Christ, having aroused within them a sense of guilt and yearning for salvation through him'. But Hendriksen wanted his penny and the bun, however, when he had also rightly spoke of 'the old dispensation... the Christ of history... Now *before* this faith in the Christ of history arrived, hence during the old dispensation, "we", says Paul, "were kept in custody" under the law' (Hendriksen: *Galatians* pp132,141,145-146, 152, emphasis his). So which is it?

Even Calvin was prepared to admit: 'The law does not efficaciously lead men to God'. And Bayes used the proper name when he rightly spoke of 'the *assumption*... often made that Paul is thinking of the function of the law... to bring the sinner to self-awareness as a transgressor... It is doubtful... whether this is Paul's meaning here'. But there is no 'doubt' about it! Of course it isn't Paul's meaning! Witherington: 'Nothing is said about the pedagogue leading a person to a teacher, and so it is in all likelihood [weak; it is certainly] unwarranted to speak of the law leading a person to Christ'. Bruce: 'There is no evidence that Paul ever used the law in this way in his apostolic preaching' (Calvin: *Commentaries* Vol.2 Part 1 p414; Bayes p142, emphasis mine; Witherington p265; Bruce: *Paul* p265).

Broadening the picture of preparationism, Lloyd-Jones was wrong to say that until he reached Rom. 3:21, Paul had been preaching the law to bring sinners to Christ. He was doing nothing of the sort. He was teaching *believers* that the law cannot save the Jews but only condemn them. The Gentiles, too, for their part, were condemned. And, in Rom. 3:21, the apostle cut right across the law when he thundered out the 'but now' of the gospel. Yet Lloyd-Jones was adamant that Paul was taking Calvin's line of preparation by the law: The apostle was 'doing precisely that... In true evangelism you must always start with a law work' (Lloyd-Jones: *Atonement* p25). As I say, he was not!

The best Chantry could come up with was: Without the moral law of God 'the gospel will offer no one knows what to sinners... No doubt [Paul] wielded [weak; if Paul did what Chantry alleged, why not produce the evidence?] the ten commandments in preaching as he did in his letters [and where did he do that?]... In the task of bringing men into the kingdom, the moral law and the gospel are the two major instruments in the arsenal of the Spirit... The moral law... is ever present at the heart of conviction, new birth, repentance and faith... A belief in the mercy of God through Christ will have no effect if preached without the moral law... [Without the moral law, Christ's] cross is a quaint story which provokes curiosity and sad emotions, but it makes little sense to modern man... If only the multitudes were instructed in the moral law! [Then] the loveliness of Christ and imputed righteousness found in the gospel would make sense to them' (Chantry: *Righteous* pp74,90-93). What an incredible – grievous – statement from such a fine man in a work published by such a reputable publishing house!

Crisp rightly argued: 'Men are mistaken if they think that the law makes them to see their own vileness; for a gracious sight of our vileness is only the work of Christ... It is Christ alone who opens the eyes of men to behold their own vileness and filthiness' (Crisp: *Christ* Vol.1 p25).

John Brown: 'It has been common to connect the words "shut up" with the concluding clause "to the faith"... and to consider the words as conveying the idea that the design and effect of the command and threatenings of God's law, on the mind of an awakened sinner, is to close every avenue of relief but one, and shut him up to accept of the free and full salvation of Christ by believing the gospel. But though this is a truth, [is it?] and an important one, it is not the truth taught here'. Chantry rightly described Brown as 'excellent... as the bright noonday sun shining on the text of' Gal. 3. Consequently, Chantry agreed with Brown: Many Reformed 'Christians [have found in Gal. 3:24-25] a favourite New Testament illustration – the schoolmaster to bring us to Christ. This illustration is widely understood to mean the moral law brings conviction of sin to a man's heart and thus was a schoolmaster to send him to Christ for grace'. Now, as I have shown, this is precisely what Chantry himself believed: 'It is a truth taught by the Bible...[4] yet it is not the truth taught in Gal. 3:24-25. To hold on to that interpretation will fog the passage. Paul's meaning is that the Mosaic order (covenant administration, economy, dispensation) was a schoolmaster to bring men [Jews] to the new covenant in Christ'. But, even going as far as this, Chantry still failed to grasp the apostle's meaning in the pedagogue. 'Schoolmaster' is quite wrong. Brown, when dealing with 'the law was our tutor [pedagogue] to bring us to Christ' (Gal. 3:24), made the point again: 'These words have often been [mis]applied to express the idea that it is by the commands and threatenings of God's law brought home to the conscience of the sinner by the effectual working of the Holy Ghost, that he is induced to believe the revelation of mercy, and gladly receive Christ Jesus as the only and all-sufficient Saviour. But this, though a very important truth,[5] is obviously not what the apostle means... "to bring us" [is not in the original but] is a supplement, and is one of those supplements which might well [ought to] have been omitted... "Before the faith of Christ came" (Gal. 3:23)... is just equivalent to "before the Christian revelation was given"'. Poole: 'Before... the doctrine of the gospel, or Christ himself, was revealed' (Brown: *Galatians* pp171-173; Chantry: *Righteous* pp101-102; Poole p651).

Moo: 'What does Paul here [in Gal. 3:15 – 4:7] assert the role of the law to have been in the history of Israel? The answer hinges on how we understand the word *paidagōgos*... Some interpreters think the word suggest that the law was given to "teach" Israel; to be their "schoolmaster to bring us [them?] unto Christ"... But this is almost certainly wrong. The *paidagōgos* in the ancient world was a slave who was responsible to watch over a young child. He was not a teacher, but a guardian or "nanny"'. Even this does not go far enough; 'nanny' is too benign. 'The imagery Paul uses here therefore suggests the idea of the law as a guardian over the people of Israel in their "minority". And this same sense is strongly reinforced by the imagery of "under-age" children, under the supervision of "guardians and trustees" in Gal. 4:1-7. The important point to make here is that this imagery does not suggest that Paul is thinking of the temporary role of the law in restricted terms, such as the giving of life or securing of the inheritance. The *paidagōgos* has nothing to do with a child's securing the inheritance. But, as the child's supervisor and custodian, he does issue instructions to the child. Paul therefore implies, in his salvation-historical argument of Gal. 3:15 – 4:7, that the law once had an instructional role in the life of the people of God [that is, Israel – DG] that it no longer has' (Moo: 'Galatians' pp16-17). I would be more definite than Moo (with his 'almost certainly', 'suggests' 'does not suggest', 'implies') in drawing the conclusion. I would also strengthen the final point. The law has lost its supervisory role for Israel, and it never had it for Gentiles. And the atmosphere, as I have said, is far less benign. The law enslaved, kept in bondage.

Packer started well, but went off the rails at the end: 'The law was intended, as Paul tells in Gal. 3:19-24, to prepare the Jews for the coming of Christ. This it did, says Paul, by acting as a gaoler and tutor. As gaoler, it kept men [Jews] "shut up" in custody, under bondage, forced to shoulder a burden of observances which, as Peter said, "neither our fathers nor we were able to bear" (Acts 15:10; Gal. 3:23)'. At this point, sadly, Packer careered off the apostolic track: 'As tutor, it made them ready for Christ by convincing them that they were sinners needing a Saviour (Gal. 3:24)' (Packer: *Understanding* p10). That is not the meaning of Gal. 3:24.

Dunn: 'By "we" Paul still thinks as a Jew... who recalls his own coming to faith in Christ, *after* his earlier experience... "under the law"... We Jews... What has come to an end, clearly, is the law's role precisely as "custodian" of Israel' (Dunn pp199-200, emphasis mine).

---

[4] Is it? Where is it found?
[5] Is it? Where is it found?

Calvin: 'Was it necessary that [the law] should last only until the coming of Christ?... For if so, it follows that it is now abolished. The whole of that administration... was temporary'. Superb! Sadly, however, Calvin ruined all: 'And yet I do not admit that, by the coming of Christ, the whole law was abolished. The apostle did not intend this, but merely that the mode of administration... must receive its accomplishment in Christ'. Calvin, it seems, simply could not allow Paul to stand uncorrected. Even though he admitted Paul 'affirms that, under the reign of Christ... the law has resigned its office...', Calvin could not resist a qualification. Paul said *the law* lasted until Christ, but Calvin tried to make him say that *the Mosaic administration of the law* lasted until Christ. Calvin *had* to make Paul fit his system: 'The law *so far as it is a rule of life, a bridle to keep in the fear of the Lord, a spur to correct the sluggishness of our flesh...* is as much in force as ever, and remains untouched' (Calvin: *Commentaries* Vol.21 Part 1 pp101,109-110, emphasis mine).

Not at all! Staggeringly, Calvin: 'The imprisonment by the law is here proved to have been highly generous in its character'. What! Bondage, slavery – generous? But Dunn had the same opinion: 'This role attributed to the law is essentially positive... What Paul had in mind was almost certainly a *protective* custody... He saw the law's role... as providing some protection for Israel during the time when sin ruled supreme in "the present evil age" (Gal. 1:4) before the coming of Christ'. No! 'the present evil age' is the age from the fall of Adam until the second coming of Christ, '*this* present age' (NKJV), not the age between Sinai and Calvary (or Pentecost). As Dunn said on Gal. 4:4-5: 'The law's functioning in effect as one of the elemental forces to enslave. [Christ came to redeem,] purchasing a slave in order to redeem him... the slavery in question being that to "the elemental forces of the universe"... including the law'. And yet again, on Gal. 4:25: 'Paul defines the relationship to which Sinai gave birth [that is, "under the law"] as one of slavery (the children of slaves being themselves slaves). [And again, on Gal. 4:31:] Those who were still "under the elemental forces", including "under the law", were still in a condition of slavery' (Calvin: *Commentaries* Vol.21 Part 1 p107; Dunn pp197,198-199,216,250,259 emphasis his). The law was Israel's custodian; it kept the people in bondage!

Reformed people still want to argue that the Mosaic covenant can be thought to be one and the same as the Abrahamic covenant 'a fresh administration of the covenant of grace' (See Zens: *Studies* pp41-44).

'What purpose... does the law serve?' Paul's answer to his own question must be the definitive statement on the matter, settling the issue once and for all. Witherington: 'It is scarcely an exaggeration to say that how one views Gal. 3:19-20 will go a long way to determining how one understands Paul's view of the Mosaic law... Paul... has appealed to the Galatians' experience, to Scripture, and to human reason and reflection using an analogy between human and divine covenants. Paul has contended that the Galatians already have... promise, Christ, the Spirit – in short [all] the status and the spiritual benefits they need. Submitting to the law would neither be necessary nor beneficial in such a situation. Paul then must answer the question which would surely follow... Why then was the law given at all if this is the case?' Yes, indeed: 'Why then?' Witherington had earlier answered the question: 'The law was not given to govern those who were already mature in the faith, much less to those who already had the Spirit to guide and empower proper Christian living. The law was given to those [that is, the Jews] whose life needed to be structured by following certain clear precepts... [who] needed to live by careful observance of the commandments, not [to believers, who need to live] by making faith judgements [in] one situation or another... The law's function, according to Paul, was to keep God's people [that is, the Jews] in line and in bounds; it could not, however, empower them to observe it. They were to live by the law, but they could not be enlivened or empowered by it'. With the coming of Christ, this time had now passed. And as Witherington said: 'There is nothing in the way Paul puts this matter that suggests that he [was] talking about the cessation of only some of the purposes of the law. Paul's argument has to do with the eras of salvation history, and in his view the coming of the Seed changed the eschatological state of affairs and brought to a close the age when the law had a necessary and indeed crucial function in the life of God's people [that is, the Jews]... Paul says nothing in Gal. 3-4 about any ongoing functions of the law past the time when Christ arrived on the scene... It is the Holy Spirit, instead of the pedagogue, [who] forms the virtues in the life of the Christian (Gal. 5)... It is no accident that the verb 'led' [in Gal. 5:18] is the verbal form of... part of the word pedagogue... It is past time to put the law to rest, for the fullness of time has arrived, the Messiah has come, the Spirit has been bestowed... The time for submission to the law is past, but the time for walking in the Spirit... is now' (Witherington pp235,246-247,252,254,261-262,266-267,275).

Thielman: 'Why then, did God give the Mosaic law? Paul claims in Galatians that it was a temporary institution, operative until the coming of Christ and designed to enclose all things under sin (Gal. 3:19 – 4:7). In the age of fulfilment, its divinely appointed function is complete, and it passes from the scene. Gentiles join the people of God, therefore, not through accepting the yoke of the law, but in the same way that God reckoned Abraham to be righteous – through faith alone (Gal. 3:6-9)' (Thielman pp19-20).

Schreiner: 'There is abundant evidence in Paul that the old covenant had an interim character and that it is no longer operative since the coming of Christ. It is imperative that Christians today understand that we do not live any longer under the old covenant, but the new covenant that has been inaugurated in Jesus Christ... Paul's use of the phrase "under law" should be understood in redemptive-historical terms. Those who are under the law are also under the dominion and authority of sin. The history of Israel under the Mosaic covenant confirms the truth that those who lived under the law were subject to sin's mastery. Paul proclaims that believers are no longer under the law. A new era of salvation history has been inaugurated, and hence we have further evidence to confirm... [that] the law has been abolished now that Christ has come. Believers are no longer under the law' (Schreiner pp71,75-76). I agree with Schreiner: 'It is imperative that Christians today understand that we do not live any longer under the old covenant'. Imperative, yes, but I am afraid that too many believers are in practical bondage. Paul did not write his letter to the Galatians for fun. It was a very real danger for them. It is for us!

Edgar H.Andrews: 'Having served its purpose of leading the believing remnant of Jews to Christ, the law became redundant [Gal. 3:25]. Paul therefore seems to teach that the law has no ongoing function, at least in the lives of believers. Is this indeed what Paul is saying? Does the law of Moses have no current role?... [In Gal. 3:23-25] Paul is silent... regarding any current role for Moses' law. There are several possible reasons for this emphasis on the past. The first and most straightforward is that Paul does not regard the law as having any current function whatever. We have already seen, when considering Gal. 2:17-18... that the believer is dead to the law. Certainly, the law and its works can play no role in the believer's justification or standing with God. Furthermore, as we shall see... sanctification (however it is understood) is the work of the Spirit, not of the law... Romans is at one with Galatians in rejecting any role for the Mosaic covenant in the life of the believer... (so also is Hebrews). Paul's rejection of the law is not reserved exclusively for the Galatians; [it goes without saying that] he is wholly consistent on this subject... Finally, the New Testament teaching on practical holiness is perfectly clear, and relies in no way on the works of the law, as we shall see when we consider Gal. 4, 5 and 6...'. Paul's question in Gal. 4:9 does not mean, 'of course', that they were 'reverting to their former idols, but rather seeking to embrace the law of Moses. Yet, declares Paul, to do this would be to return to the selfsame bondage from which Christ had once delivered them. It was difficult for the Galatians to grasp the fact that submission to the law was tantamount to a return to idolatry. There seems such a world of difference between the two. Yet both idolatry and legalism, asserts Paul, belong to the same philosophical genre; they both represent "the elements of the world" (Gal. 4:3) from which Christ has set his people free... There are many today who, like the Galatians, fail to discern between true Christian faith and the efforts of the flesh. Paul had earlier reprimanded his readers asking: "Having begun in the Spirit, are you now being made perfect by the flesh?" (Gal. 3:3). Law imposed from without appeals only to the flesh and is inimical to spiritual life, "for the letter kills, but the Spirit gives life" (2 Cor. 3:6). Only God's law, written in the heart of the believer by the indwelling Spirit can bring forth true holiness of life' (Edgar H.Andrews pp179-180,217-218). See chapter 16 for what 'law' that is.

Govett, on Gal. 3:24-25: 'The law was originally a teacher. It was the instructor of the Jews. It was the picture-alphabet given to the world's earlier years, to instil into the mind the simplest elements of truth, and to prepare the way for the real education of the gospel. Christ is our teacher now: Moses is set aside, as no longer suited for the sons of God. "One is your Master, even Christ" (Matt. 23:8). We have not to co-ordinate teachers, partly Moses and partly Christ (John 13:13-14)' (Govett p18). Of course, Christ uses Moses – as all the Scriptures – but Govett's point stands.

For more extracts on preparationism, see p348.

Gal. 4:12
According to Lightfoot, in Gal. 4:12, Paul was saying: "'I appeal to you. I laid aside the privileges, the prejudges of my race; I became a Gentile, even as you were Gentiles. And now I ask you to make me some return. I ask you to throw off this Judaic bondage, and to be free, as I am free"'. Witherington: 'If the Galatians will imitate Paul in his rejection of the yoke of the law which was part of his past, and in his pursuit of walking in the Spirit and according to the pattern of Christ and the freedom [which] that provides... 1 Cor. 9:21... Paul... wants them to grow up to full maturity in Christ... living on the basis of the Christ pattern, even as Paul is doing' (Lightfoot: *Galatians* p173; Witherington pp307-308). See also Ridderbos pp164-165, Hendriksen: *Galatians* pp169-170; Edgar H.Andrews pp222-223,232. This must not be limited to justification. If Paul was talking about not going back to the law, he meant it with regard to sanctification as well as justification. Indeed, he particularly meant sanctification here, writing to believers in the letter to the Galatians.

But John Brown preferred: 'It is equivalent to the expostulation: "Why should you dislike me who so cordially loves you?"' (Brown: *Galatians* pp210-212).

Gal. 4:21-31
As we come to this passage, which holds within it so much that is of tremendous significance to the matter in hand, let us bear in mind that many of the Reformed regard the two covenants – the Mosaic and the Abrahamic – as one covenant of grace. How this can be maintained in face of Gal. 4:21-31 defies my understanding – and not only mine, judging by what now follows. Some parts of these extracts have already made their appearance, but I include them here to give the full sense and flow of what these writers are saying.

Edgar H.Andrews: In Gal. 4:21-29, 'Paul's message is clear. The two covenants are distinct, opposed and mutually exclusive... There are two covenants, one being the Sinai covenant represented by Hagar, and the other the covenant of promise represented by Sarah... There are two covenants... distinct... opposed... mutually exclusive... The Sinaitical covenant was, by its very nature, a covenant of works... How are men brought into bondage by the law? By the endless and futile search for obedience to that law: endless, because it is a task from which man can never rest; futile, because everything man does is tainted by sin and therefore cannot satisfy God. It is because Moses' covenant requires men to work for God's blessing that it brings them into bondage... The false idea that salvation can be obtained by such works is rightly called "legalism". However, there is another kind of bondage to the law that can be experienced even by true believers, who understand they can be justified only by faith. This occurs when Christians seek holiness or "sanctification" by the deeds of the law, and has been called 'nomism'... There is persuasive evidence in the letter that Paul is [mainly – DG] worried about [this] nomism. If Paul's concern is limited to legalism (which denies men salvation through Christ), why does he write such a letter to people whom he treats throughout as already being saved? (See Gal. 3:1-3,26-29; 4:6-9; 5:7-10,13)... The overwhelming evidence is that Paul regarded them as true believers who were being confused and led astray by false doctrine. There was a danger of apostasy [yes, Gal. 3:4; 5:2-4], but there was a greater danger of true believers being entangled with a yoke of bondage. This danger is present today when the law is urged upon believers as the primary pattern for Christian living... The two covenants give rise to... two peoples. The "children" of the old Jerusalem are those who remain in bondage to the old covenant, made at Sinai. This bondage can take the form of legalism; namely, the idea that man can be justified by the works of that law. But (among believers) it can also take the form of nomism, in which the law of Moses is seen as necessary in some manner for a believer's sanctification or holiness. By contrast, the "children" of the heavenly Jerusalem... are free. They have been delivered from the power and penalty of sin, and thus from the clutches of the law. They are no longer in bondage to the requirements and sanctions of the law. But they are not without law, being subject to the rule and law of Christ, which is written in the hearts. They are enabled to keep this new law by the indwelling Spirit. Thus Paul established that the two covenants... are opposed and mutually exclusive. We can belong only to one "Jerusalem", not both. Any attempt to merge law and gospel into a single system is doomed to failure' (Edgar H.Andrews pp234-256).

Spurgeon: 'There cannot be a greater difference in the world between two things than there is between law and grace... He is not far from understanding the gospel theme in all its ramifications, its outlets, and its branches, who can properly tell the difference between law and grace... Between law and grace there is a difference plain enough to every Christian, and especially to the enlightened and instructed one; but still, when most enlightened and instructed, there is always a tendency in us to confound the two things. They are as opposite as light and darkness, and can no more agree than fire and water; yet man will be perpetually striving to make a compound of them – often ignorantly, and sometimes wilfully. They seek to blend the two, when God has positively put them asunder... The two women – Hagar and Sarah... are the types of the two covenants... The Hagar covenant – the covenant propounded on Sinai, amidst tempests, fire and smoke... That is the covenant of law, the Hagar covenant' (Spurgeon: *New* Vol.2 pp121-122).

Moo, yet again, I am afraid, rather weaker than he ought to have been: 'The specific identity of these covenants [in Gal. 4:21-31]... is debated... But the context makes it more likely that Hagar stands specifically for the Mosaic covenant, since Paul compares Hagar's status as a "slave woman" with the law, which the Galatians are in danger of becoming "enslaved" to (Gal. 5:1). And it is likely that Sarah represents the Abrahamic covenant, to which Paul has explicitly referred in Gal. 3:17. But Paul has, of course, defined the Abrahamic covenant in strictly Christological terms. Christ is the "Seed" who inherits the Abrahamic promise. So, even in Gal. 4, the covenant contrasts is not so much between two parallel covenants, but between an "old" covenant that was in force for a period of time, and a covenant that, while initiated in Abraham's time, has only come into full force with the coming of Christ' (Moo: 'Galatians' pp6-7). As I say, too weak. Gal. 4:21-31 is clear and definite on these issues.

Gadsby cast his thoughts on Gal. 4:21 – 5:1 into a hymn: 'What! must the Christian draw/ His comforts from the law,/ That can do nothing but condemn?/ If this be Zion's rule,/ Then unto Hagar's school,/ Must Sarah send her free-born son./ But the bond-woman's son/ With such shall not be one;/ Isaac alone is lawful heir;/ So Abra'm must obey,/ And Ishmael send away,/ Nor Hagar must continue there' (Gadsby: *Hymns* number 522).

By the way, I notice that those who oppose the Reformed view of the law are prepared to write and sing hymns about their view. Is there a hymn celebrating and rejoicing in

Calvin's third use of the law – whip, lazy asses, and all – let alone his first two uses? They who sing only paraphrases of the Psalms do sing about the law, yes, but I seriously question whether they have Calvin's third use in mind when they do.

Gal. 5:1-12
Gal. 5 is not Paul's first reference to liberty; see Gal. 2:3-5,11-14; 3:1-18,24-29; 4:1-5,21-31 (Kruse p112). But this is the great theme of this chapter, especially in its opening.

Dunn spoke of 'the abruptness of the exclamation [at the opening of Gal. 5]... the redundancy of expression ("for freedom... set free") underlining its character as *freedom* – freedom given the place of emphasis ("for *freedom*"), freedom as characterising the gospel from beginning to end, freedom as the goal of the divine act of liberation... Since the eye of the reader would not run smoothly over the grammatical bridge between Gal. 4:31 and Gal. 5:1, the reader would be forced to pause, and thus to signal to his Galatian audiences a statement of importance to follow. The predominance of long vowels in the Greek and repetition of the theme of freedom (noun and verb) would also serve to give the exclamation the resonance and forcefulness of a slogan or epigrammatical summary which brought to focus the burden of the whole letter' (Dunn p261, emphasis his). Bear in mind that originally there was probably only one reader – the rest were hearers.

Edgar H.Andrews: 'What a rallying cry is this [Gal. 5:1]! "Stand fast!" is a term borrowed from the battlefield... 1 Cor. 16:13. We have a battle on our hands today... Our freedoms in Christ are constantly under attack. They are attacked by legalism and nomism [among other things]... "Do not be entangled again with a yoke of bondage", warns the apostle (Gal. 5:1). By "yoke of bondage", he clearly means enslavement to the law... By contrast, the "yoke" of Christ is easy, and his burden light (Matt. 11:30). To be yoked to Christ is to be at rest (Heb. 4:10)... Paul said, do not be entangled "again"... The freedom of conscience that believers have in Christ is easily lost when legalism, nomism and the doctrines of men are introduced into the church. How, then, may we avoid the "yoke of bondage"?... We must never lose sight of the person and work of Christ. He must be the central theme of all our preaching and teaching, and the example for all our practice... By what rule should we live? We are to walk in the Spirit of Christ, bringing forth his fruit (Gal. 5:22-25)... As long as our religion centres upon Christ, both in its doctrine and practice, we shall remain free. Lose that perspective, however, and bondage will ensue. We become slaves if our Christianity becomes focussed on mere doctrine, on religious duties, on ethics, on rules and regulations' (Edgar H.Andrews pp262-264). How true this is!

Hubner: 'Why does Paul place so much emphasis on the function of the law as the location of enslavement? He does it because for him everything depends on emphasising the freedom which the Galatians have already acquired. You are free because you are the sons of God, you are free because you believe. This is the concern which he passionately propounds: do not lose your freedom, do not gamble it away, do not let yourselves be enslaved again... The existence of the believer is not a state of subordination. *The nerve [centre] of the argument lies here...* so everything leads up to the great cry: "Christ has freed you for freedom", from which follows the summons, "so stand fast... and do not submit again to a yoke of slavery" (Gal. 5:1)... Paul therefore reminds the Galatians that prior to their conversion to Christ, they had experienced the dominion of the weak elements of the world. They had themselves experienced the fact that so long as one submits to them they can really dominate and subject men... He appeals to the Galatians' self-understanding. His reproach... implies the question: Is your existence again to be determined by fear? Now it is perfectly clear that the Galatians certainly did not want this... But... they are living... on the basis of the works of the law – on what one establishes in terms of quantitatively determinable deeds... Thus the Galatians are... betraying their freedom... It has not dawned on them what freedom really is... If they [stand fast in the] freedom – even, and indeed particularly... freedom from the Mosaic law – then everything else will be given' (Hubner pp34-35, emphasis mine). I am afraid it is not only the Galatians of whom it can be said: 'It has not dawned on them what freedom really is'. Too many believers today are in bondage. The Reformed, of course, are credally so – being whipped by the law, as Calvin taught them. But bondage is not restricted to Calvinists.

Dunn: 'The whole reason for [Paul's] writing to the Galatians is summed up in his passionate cry of Gal. 5:1. And the depth of feeling which so strongly motivated the writing, and which moves disturbingly [mostly just] beneath the surface throughout, bursts through once again in the forcefulness of the appeal. Paul must have felt that this was it! Like a lawyer pleading for a client in danger of being found guilty of a capital offence, he must have seen this as the critical moment. If he could not convince his Galatian audiences now, he might never have another chance; his work with them and their freedom in Christ might be lost irretrievably. Caught up in the movement of his argument and the depth of concern for the Galatians, his diction at this point must have assumed new tones of intensity and vehemence. The consequence is a passage almost unique within Paul's letters in its passionate forcefulness, in its polarisation of choice, and in its dismissal of those opposing him'. The delightfully capitalised-heading Ridderbos chose for his comments on the passage was: 'FOR THE LAST TIME: EVERYTHING OR NOTHING!' (Dunn p260, citing Rom. 9:1-3; 2 Cor. 11:12-20; Gal. 1:6-9; Phil. 3:2 as 'coming close'; Ridderbos p185).

What is this freedom? The usual Reformed glosses – freedom from the ceremonial law, or freedom from the law for justification – will not do. Such escape routes are woefully inadequate, let alone unbiblical. The immediate context, for a start, just will not allow it. Michael Eaton: 'Although Paul was very concerned with the issue of circumcision and table-fellowship he explicitly makes the point in Gal. 5:3 that one cannot pick and choose between parts of the Mosaic covenant. One must take it that the Christians' relationship to the "whole law" has been in mind all along. There may be some uncertainty about the main concern of the Judaisers but what concerns Paul is the "whole law"' (Michael Eaton: *Encouragement* p97).

Bayes tried to restrict those 'who desire to be under [the] law' (Gal. 4:21) to those who wanted to be under the law 'for the purpose of justification... The freedom which Christ has achieved for his people is to be prized; all attempts to deprive believers of their liberty resulting from the enslaving tendency, which has arisen among the Gentiles, of seeking justification by the works of the law, must be resisted... Seeking justification by the works of the law' was Bayes' pitiful view of the problem: 'The problem at Galatia was that these Gentile Christians had fallen into the belief that it was necessary to keep the law for justification... It was necessary that the Galatians should understand... the implications of their heretical doctrine of justification by works of the law... It is important to keep in mind [Paul's] fundamental purpose in this letter, which is to correct a Gentile misunderstanding of the way of justification revealed in the Old Testament. The Galatians had come to the... conclusion that the Hebrew Scriptures taught that justification had to be achieved through the works of the law... The embracing by the Galatians of the law for justification represents... a retreat from Christ. The misuse of the law by the Galatians is leading them into a self-inflicted slavery... To use the law as a path to righteousness, Paul insists, must inevitably lead to bondage to rules and regulations... It is necessary, therefore, Paul insists, that the Galatians reject the law as a way of justification... The allegory thus serves to highlight... the consequences of the erroneous doctrine of justification through the law. The law is weak when justification is the theme' (Bayes pp158-163). This is an appalling misreading of Galatians. As we have seen, Paul is concerned with justification, yes, but he does not leave it there. Indeed, defending justification by faith is not the 'fundamental purpose in this letter'. We know what that is. Right at its heart, both literally and essentially, lies Gal. 3:1-5. Justification is not by the law. *Neither is sanctification.*

Hendriksen, however, was of a similar mind to Bayes: 'The context indicates that [Paul] is thinking particularly of freedom from the law... deliverance from the curse which the law pronounces upon the sinner'. But as Hendriksen himself pointed out: 'Freedom is more than deliverance' (Hendriksen: *Galatians* p192). And Bayes himself admitted that the Galatians were already 'justified through their faith in Christ' (Bayes p160). Above all, of course, the apostle led on directly to sanctification (Gal. 5:13 and on). It is quite wrong – and utterly foolish – to stop short! If Reformed exegetes can so glaringly – or is it deliberately? – miss Paul's purpose... words fail!

Ridderbos was much better: Believers 'in communion with the death of Christ... die to sin [and the law], so that its lordship is broken and the freedom of the life unto God is born... They are liberated from the curse as well as from the power of sin, and so their life can be a life unto God... [They] are not born for bondage, but for freedom, and are educated in it. Not the law, nor the thing they themselves must do, but grace, that which they have received in Christ, determines their life... Very emphatically the freedom of the believers is placed in the foreground here as the purpose of Christ's redemptive work... Christ did not set us free for slavery but for freedom! By this freedom is meant dismissal from subservience to the law (*cf.* Gal. 3:13,22-25; 4:1,2,21-31)... This took place – such [is] the thrust of *Christ set us free* – through the death and resurrection of Christ which, through the power of the Spirit, also works life and freedom in believers (*cf.* Gal. 2:19,20; 3:2; 4:6; Rom. 7:4). And therefore the falling back into subservience is inexplicable and inexcusable'. A little earlier he had said: 'The Galatians [must] not... let themselves succumb to the clutches of the Judaisers. Rather, they must avoid this contact with a slave-principle, and defend themselves against it. Else the inheritance may escape them'. And Hendriksen also saw it: 'Is it not ridiculous to imagine that Christ would have opened for us the gate of our prison... merely to transfer us to another prison? Surely, he set us free in order that we might indeed be and remain free [from] the yoke of slavery, including its many regulations, augmented subsequently by man-made traditions' (Ridderbos pp105-106,178-179,182,186; Hendriksen: *Galatians* pp192-193).

But Bolton, the Puritan master on the law, certainly showed his schizophrenic attitude to the law: 'Christ has freed us from the law: that is another part of our freedom by Christ. "You are delivered from the law, that being dead wherein we were held; that we should serve in newness of spirit, and not in the oldness of the letter" (Rom. 7:6). "I through the law am dead to the law, that I might live unto God" (Gal. 2:19). "If you are led by the Spirit, you are not under the law" (Gal 5:18). "You are not under the law, but under grace" (Rom. 6:14). This then is another part of our freedom by Christ: we are freed from the law. What this is we shall now consider. We are freed from the ceremonial law, which was a yoke which neither we nor our fathers were able to bear (Acts 15:10) [offering no proof that Acts 15:10 refers to what he called the ceremonial law]. Yet this is but a small part of our freedom...'. Believers are free from 'the law as a covenant. We are freed from the moral law... We are freed from the law as that from which life might be expected on the condition that due obedience was rendered... The believer is freed from the law as a covenant, and hence from its judgements, sentences, condemnations, curses and accusations... [However] I must tell you that the law in its directive power remains with the believer. This must needs be plain from the words: "The law, which was four hundred and thirty years after (the promise), cannot disannul [cancel, annul] (the promise), that it should make the promise of none effect" (Gal. 3:17)'.

I pause. How that historical fact makes Calvin's third use of the law plain, baffles me. Bolton, however, ploughed on, undeterred: The law 'after our justification by the promise [is] a rule of walking with God, so that in all things we might please him'. Bolton then turned to the believer's 'freedom from the rigour of the law... The believer is freed from the rigour of the obedience required in the law. He is not freed from the requirement of exact obedience, but from that rigour of obedience which the law required as a condition of salvation'. Even so, 'the law requires the full measure of obedience; it abates nothing in the command... [Yet] believers... are freed from the rigour of the law'.

Why did Bolton bother to quote the Scriptures if he was going to drive a coach and horse through them? He thought the doctrine of the believer's freedom to be among 'the greatest knots in the practical part of divinity'. He quoted Rom. 6:14; Gal. 3:19; 4:4-5; Rom. 8:2; Gal. 5:18; Rom. 10:4; 1 Tim. 1:8-10, saying: 'There seems therefore to be a great deal of strength in the Scripture to prove the abrogation of the law, that we are dead to the law, freed from the law, no more under the law... I only quote [the Scriptures] to let it be seen with what strength the Scriptures seem to hold out... for the abrogation of the law'.

Despite this, he was convinced that 'the law remains as a rule of walking for the people of God... The law... still remains a rule of life to the people of God... Though we disown the law in respect of justification, yet we establish it as a rule of Christian living... and declare the continuation of it now under the gospel as an exact rule to direct Christians in their walk and obedience,.. The law still remains as a rule of obedience under the gospel...The law in the substance of it remains a rule of walking or obedience to them in Christ... We cry down the law in respect of justification, but we set it up as a rule of sanctification. The law sends us to the gospel that we may be justified; and the gospel sends us to the law again to inquire what is our duty as those who are justified... So while you are in the wilderness of the world, you must walk under the conduct of Moses; you must live in obedience to the law'.

Nevertheless, Bolton warned his readers: 'It is a hard [it is utterly impossible!] lesson to live above the law, and yet to walk according to the law. But this is the lesson a Christian has to learn, to walk in the law in respect of duty, but to live above it in respect of comfort, neither expecting favour from the law in respect of his obedience, nor fear harsh treatment from the law in respect of his failings... Let us learn to walk in the law as a rule of sanctification... The law is a yoke of bondage... [yet, even so] walk in the duties of the law, but with a gospel spirit. The law is to be acknowledged as a rule of sanctification' (Bolton pp28-76,219-220). I want to play fair with Bolton. To let him speak for himself, reader, you should read the original in its entirety. Nevertheless, I think I have made good my assertion regarding his schizophrenic attitude to the law. I can quite see how Bolton got all this from the Reformed Confessions, but where he found it in the New Testament I am at a loss to discover.

As for schizophrenia, try putting together these statements from Kevan: 'It cannot be too often said that law-keeping can never be the means of sanctification, but it will most certainly be its result'. 'Grace is more commanding than law', 'it is a mark of spiritual infancy... to be under law'. 'The law, from the beginning, has been a means of grace'. In our sanctification we are left 'within the law as a rule of life' (Kevan: *Experience* pp30,38,48-49,59,66,68,77; Zens: *Studies* p36). Really? Are Christians really supposed to be this schizophrenic?

John Brown, contrary to such men, thought the liberty is 'much more general and extensive than' liberty from the Mosaic law, but includes liberty from 'the doctrines and commandments of men... The apostle plainly refers to the subjection to the law. [Christians must] assert their freedom, and guard against the admission of any principle, or the submission to any imposition, that may entangle their consciences and strip their obedience, even to Christ's law... What an admirable system is pure Christianity!... How deeply we should study it! How jealously should we guard it against corruption!... How grateful... should all be who have reason to hope that they are in possession of this liberty! He whom the Son makes free is free indeed! Every man is naturally a slave; and he only is truly free whom grace has made a freeman... Let those who have this freedom... receive the truth in the love of it, and that truth will make them free; and as it is this truth believed which gives this spiritual freedom, so it is the continued belief of this truth which alone can enable them, in opposition to all the attempts of their spiritual enemies to entangle them again in bondage, to "stand fast in the liberty wherewith Christ has made us free"' (Brown: *Galatians* pp252,254-256).

Reader, do not misjudge my purpose in making the comments I do. I am not interested in scoring points. That's too easy! There are plenty of open-goals! No! The fact is, I am convinced that not a few believers woefully fail to grasp the glorious freedom we have in Christ. I include myself! It is a tragedy. A proper understanding of Gal. 4:31 – 5:1 would go a long way to putting things right.

Gal. 5:13-26

As I have explained, in light of his teaching on the law, Paul has to distinguish between liberty and licence. The believer is free. But how will this produce holiness? In this paragraph, Gal. 5:13-26, Paul makes it very clear.

Dunn: 'How [can] freedom be prevented from lapsing into licence...? If the law... [does] not provide the blueprint for daily conduct, what [does]? This is the burden of what follows (Gal. 5:13 – 6:10)... freedom... and Spirit... replacing law... It is now incumbent on [Paul] to explain how the Spirit [functions] to provide a viable pattern of living. A theology of freedom, particularly freedom from the law, which [does] not explain how that theology [translates] into daily living would have been a theology of irresponsibility' (Dunn p285. See Witherington p376). There is no need to fear. Paul sets it all out.

Dunn: '"Stand therefore", [Paul] cried, almost like a military commander rallying wavering troops'. Kruse: 'In this passage [Gal. 5:13-14, which is based on Gal. 5:1] believers' freedom from the law is assumed'. Witherington: 'What is going on here, is a contrast between freedom and slavery, two conditions the Galatians [and all believers] must choose between'. Paul's use of 'the allegory [of Sarah and Hagar] is... to aid the Galatians' decision-making process by emphasising the enslaving results of submitting to the law'. And by the command, 'cast out the bondwoman and her son', Paul was telling his readers 'not only are they not to submit to the law, but they are to remove the source of temptation to follow it'. Matera: 'Flesh and Spirit represent two different ways of living. The Galatians must choose one or the other; they cannot choose both' (Dunn p262; Kruse p103; Witherington pp326,328,395).

Now for a slipshod approach by Masters: 'What does the apostle mean when he said... "But if you are led by the Spirit, you are not under the law" [Gal. 5:18]?' Masters gave three answers to his question: 'We are not under the law in three senses, but we always remain under its authority'. What Scripture did he offer for this far-reaching claim, this categorical adjustment of the apostle's words? None! I can only presume he wants us to believe it because he says it.

He moved immediately into the first of them: 'First, let us dismiss the heresy of the Judaisers. We are not under the ceremonial law of the Jews, which was the teaching system that came to an end with the coming of Christ our Saviour'. I pause. Was *this* the heresy of the Judaisers? Where are we told that they wanted believers to be under the ceremonial law? Indeed, can we be given one scripture which uses the phrase 'the ceremonial law'? I am well aware that the Judaisers were majoring on circumcision (and, possibly, food laws) – but which ceremonial law-commandment is that? No, I have not forgotten John 7:22. In any case, Masters missed the point by a mile. In this very chapter, Paul has made it clear that you cannot pick and choose with the law: 'If you become circumcised, Christ will profit you nothing'. What? How can the apostle say such a thing? Because 'every man who becomes circumcised... is a debtor to keep the whole law' (Gal. 5:2-4). Consider: 'For on the one hand there is an annulling of the former commandment because of its weakness and unprofitableness, for the law made nothing perfect; on the other hand, there is the bringing in of a better hope, through which we draw near to God... But now he has obtained a more excellent ministry, inasmuch as he is also mediator of a better covenant, which was established on better promises. For if that first covenant had been faultless, then no place would have been sought for a second' (Heb. 7:18-19; 8:6-7). Are we to understand that when the writer to the Hebrews wrote those words, he was talking about the ceremonial or teaching aspect of the law?

Masters: 'Secondly, we are not under the moral law in the sense that we are not under its condemnation'. I pause yet again. Notice how Masters here calls on, and unites, two Reformed escape routes. Split the law into parts – here the moral – and then pull its teeth – not under its condemnation. Very convenient! But can we have the scriptural proof, please? Masters supplied none. Oh, he did go on to definite assertion: 'It is still the law of God, representing the character of God, his standards, desires and tastes, but it is no longer the instrument of our eternal condemnation. If we have come to Christ, then [it means that] Christ has died for us and taken the punishment that by the law should be meted out to us. We are free from that punishment which comes from disobedience to the law, and no longer under the its threatening cloud of judgement. Our salvation no longer depends on our success in keeping the law, but on Christ's atoning death, and on having his righteousness imputed to us, earning heaven for us'.

I pause again. What a confusing of things which ought to be kept distinct! Masters' comments were all about justification. But he was supposed to be commenting on Gal. 5:18 which is manifestly a verse about sanctification. Furthermore, note the sleight of hand – moving from the moral law to the law. Again, can we be given the scripture which says that Christ has pulled the law's teeth? I, for one, fail to see how the law can still be the law, God to be the same God of the same law as he was before Christ's death, and yet the law – still the same law, of the same God – has now lost its teeth. I simply do not get it. I thought the law was inexorable, unchangeable, for ever settled. Calvin certainly thought it was, as I showed in chapter 6. How about Ps. 119:89; Matt. 5:18; Luke 16:17, for a start?

Masters did go on to speak about sanctification: 'However, although we are free from the condemnation of the law, we desire to keep it, with the help of the Holy Spirit, because we love God and long to please him. We are not under the condemnation of the law, but we are under the delight of the law (Rom. 7:22)'. Three things bother me about this. First, I thought the apostle said: 'But if you are led by the Spirit, you are not under the law' (Gal. 5:18), and this was the verse Masters was expounding. I cannot see how his words match those of the apostle. Secondly, what a leap! Could we be offered proof that 'the law' of Rom. 7:22 is 'the law' of Gal. 5:18? And that man who rejoices that he is not under the law, and yet at the same time delights in that same law, must have a strange spiritual and emotional make-up. If he can say both things – that is, if 'the law' is the same in both verses, which it is not! – he is a remarkable man. Masters might be that man; Paul was not. Thirdly, Rom. 7:1-6, is explicit that sanctification is only possible to the man who had died to the law. So how can he be sanctified by being under it?

Masters: 'The third sense is which we are not under the law is this: we are not under it as the source of our strength for righteousness. This is just as well, because the law does not supply help and strength' (Masters pp22-23).

As for me, I will stick with Paul actually said: 'But if you are led by the Spirit, you are not under the law' (Gal. 5:18).

On Gal. 5:13-15, Edgar H.Andrews: 'Liberty in Christ. We are free from bondage, from the law and from its curse. We are free! But there is another danger; namely, that of lawlessness (or antinomianism). Liberty is not the same as libertarianism. Freedom from the law does not mean freedom to indulge the [flesh], or to sin with impunity... Heb. 12:14. But (and here lies an important distinction) this practical righteousness is to be attained through the Spirit, not through the law. These verses begin one of the most important passages in Scripture on the Holy Spirit and the believer... Freedom from the law can be misused. Without the external compulsion and restraint of rules and regulations, the... flesh can, in principle, run riot... Jude also highlights the problem of libertarianism... (Jude 4). How does Paul deal with this danger? He does not re-impose the law, or some substitute for it, but simply instructs the Galatians to make a better choice. It lies within their ability, and their desire, to reject the sinful tendencies of the [flesh]; to refuse temptation and choose to do good rather than evil (though... not to the point of sinless perfection). There is parallel teaching in... Rom. 6:15-19... Sin no longer has dominion over [believers] (Rom. 6:14), and they are now free to obey righteousness. This is the essence of their God-given liberty, and only those who *do* 'follow holiness' are truly exercising the liberty that Christ has given them. To use this liberty as an excuse to indulge the [flesh] is, therefore, a contradiction in terms. Any who do so have not understood the meaning of Christian liberty, for liberty and lawlessness are bitter enemies, not companions. The believer's power to reject sin derives from the indwelling Spirit of God... Those who embrace the law are in danger of neglecting the Spirit... by contrast, those who cultivate the fruit of the Spirit seek to imitate Christ... Gal. 2:20; Heb. 12:2. Their actions and attitudes are dictated by the Spirit within, rather than by external rules. Of course, these actions and attitudes must be validated by Scripture... Nevertheless, it remains true that the believer is led by the Spirit of Christ in his actions and attitudes [Gal. 5:18]... Gal. 5:14... The mutual service Paul wants to see is prescribed in the law; indeed, says the apostle, it encompasses the law. Yet, ironically, such love can never be a reality if it is based on duty to an external rule. Here lies the weakness of the law: it can prescribe love but cannot produce it. This quality of love must be born of, and energised by, the indwelling Spirit of Christ... One further matter; namely the "fulfilment" of the law in the life of the believer. Paul's proposition is not that believers do the law, but that "the righteous requirement of the law is fulfilled in us" (Rom. 8:4). The distinction is important... The apostle's teaching on Christian liberty was frequently misunderstood. Because he proclaimed that "Christ is the end of the law for righteousness" (Rom. 10:4), he was accused of preaching lawlessness and encouraging sin (Rom. 3:8; 6:15). This remains a common source of controversy today... How do we acquire practical righteousness? How does the believer, justified as he is through the work of Christ, live out his life in a manner pleasing to God? Some teach that, for the believer to honour God, his practical life must be regulated by [what they call] the moral elements of the law of Moses; in other words, the ten commandments must be his "rule of life". Galatians offers no support for this idea. Paul's attitude to the law... is very clear. Its purpose is never to justify, nor to help a man please God in lesser ways... Gal. 5:14... Rom. 8:3-4... The righteousness requirement of the law is actually satisfied, or "fulfilled" in the lives of those who "walk according to the Spirit" or are "led by the Spirit" (Rom. 8:14)... In a pragmatic sense, the righteous requirement of the law is fulfilled in the believer. The believer, led by the Spirit, does bear fruit in harmony with the law in terms of practical righteous living' (Edgar H.Andrews pp279-287, emphasis his).

Moo: '"Under law" designates the status antithetical to the status of the believer. To be "under grace", free children of God, "led by the Spirit", means to be living in the new age of redemption, and no longer in the old age that was characterised by, and dominated by, the law... Life in the Spirit is put forward by Paul as the ground of Christian ethics, *in contrast to* life "under law"' (Moo: 'The Law' p215, emphasis his). But 'if Christians are no longer "under the law", what will guide and empower their conduct? Paul answers in terms of the Spirit and (surprisingly, perhaps) the law. Christians enjoy the indwelling presence of the Spirit. By "walking" by the Spirit (Gal. 5:16) and "keeping in step with the Spirit" (Gal. 5:25), believers will develop those character traits that should mark God's people... In Gal. 5:14, [the apostle] proclaims that "the entire law is fulfilled in keeping this one command: 'Love your neighbour as yourself'". How does the love command of Lev. 19:18 "fulfil" the law? It may mean simply that [love] is so central to the law that one is not really obeying the law if love is not present. Paul highlights love, not to displace the law in any sense, but to point to its true meaning and essence. But the language of "fulfil" suggests [it does more than suggest!] that Paul means something [far] more radical than this. Vital to understanding Paul's perspective on the law is to recognise a principal distinction in his writings between "doing" and "fulfilling" the law. Nowhere does Paul say that Christians are to "do" the law, and nowhere does he suggest that any but Christians can "fulfil" the law.[6] "Doing" the law refers to that daily obedience to all the commandments that was required of the Israelites. "Fulfilling" the law, on the other hand, denotes that complete satisfaction of the law's demands that comes only through our identification with Christ (Rom. 8:4) and our submission to that commandment which Christ put at the heart of his new-covenant teaching: love. It is the love of others, first made possible by Christ (hence the "new" commandment, John 13:34), that completely satisfies the demand of the law. The other reference to "law" in this concluding section of Galatians comes in Gal. 6:2' (Moo: 'Galatians' pp20-21). I will leave Moo's remarks on Gal. 6:2 to the relevant section in chapter 16 – but they should, of course, be read in conjunction with the above.

Reformed writers grievously misread this by opting for one or other of their escape routes. According to Poole, believers are not under the law in the sense of being 'under the curse of it, or coaction [that is, compulsion, restraint, force, coercive jurisdiction – *Shorter*] of it, and an obligation to the performance of the ceremonial law'. Calvin: 'When the condemnation of the law is removed, freedom from ceremonies follows as a necessary consequence; for ceremonies mark the condition of a slave' (Poole p658; Calvin: *Commentaries* Vol.21 Part 1 p164).

Others take a different tack. Bayes: 'It is the clear teaching of this letter that the law, in some sense at least, has no ongoing place at all in the life of the believer'. Quite right! This, of course, virtually destroys the thrust of his book! Nevertheless, it was not long before he got back on to the Reformed track: 'However, there is another sense in which, it seems, the law does have an ongoing role in the believing life... The context for Paul's teaching on liberty is specifically the matter of justification'. It is not! It is justification leading to sanctification, and the fact that neither of them is by the law – *this* is the theme of Galatians in general, and the context of Gal. 5:13-18 in particular. 'It seems necessary to accept that Paul distinguishes, at least in his mind, though he does not spell it out, between the different aspects of the law which have come to be described in theological tradition as the moral and ceremonial law'. I break in. Not only a totally unjustified statement, but, even if it had been right, still damning by faint praise! 'It seems necessary to accept that Paul distinguishes, at least in his mind, though he does not spell it out...'. Really! If, to defend the Reformed position, we have to resort to guessing what might or might not have been in the apostle's mind – or, rather, putting our own thoughts into his mind – why bother with the apostle in the first place? Aren't we supposed to be getting our thinking from Paul, not the other way about? Is this the best defence of Calvin's position?

Bayes went on: 'Paul puts great stress on the work of the Spirit'. It is 'necessary... to examine the relationship between the Spirit and the law'. When Paul said: '"If you are led by the Spirit, you are not under the law"', Bayes thought he was speaking of 'the totality of the law as an epoch, now superseded by the epoch of the Spirit' (Bayes pp165-168). Quite right. There are indeed two great epochs – law and grace. *But this is not the point of Gal. 5.* Bayes' words have come two chapters too late. It is Gal. 3 which deals with the epochs of law and grace in the *history* of the *ages*; Gal. 5:13-18 deals with the epochs of law and grace in the *life* of the *individual*.

I agree, of course, with Dunn: 'The law still has a positive role... so long as it does not conflict with the "from faith, by the Spirit" life-orientation... particularly Gal. 5:18 – "if you

---

[6] We may go further. In every believer, by Christ's work, by 'the law of the Spirit of life in Christ Jesus', 'the righteous requirement of the law [is] fulfilled' (Rom. 8:2-4).

are led by the Spirit, you are no longer under the law"'. Fee: 'Paul herewith places the flesh and the law on the same side of things over against the Spirit... Everything before Christ, which was fundamentally eliminated by his death and resurrection and the gift of the eschatological Spirit, belongs to the same "old age" sphere of existence. In that sense the Spirit stands over against both the flesh and the law, in that he replaces the latter and stands in opposition to the former. Although Paul does not say so here, the argument of Romans 6 – 8 demonstrates that *torah* was helpless in the face of the flesh, while the Spirit is not, and for that reason [the Spirit] replaces *torah*'. Fee quoted Bruce: 'For Paul... the law and the flesh belong to the same pre-Christian order' (Dunn p200; Fee: *Empowering* p438). See Hoch pp62-63.

It is vital to recognise that the conflict in Rom. 7:13-24 is not the same as in Gal. 5:16-25. The former is about defeat; the latter, victory. The Spirit is not even mentioned in Rom. 7:13-24, whereas Gal. 5 is emphatic on him and his work. Witherington: 'It is a mistake to try and read back into the discussion in Gal. 5 what we find in Rom. 7' (Witherington p377; see Witherington pp394-395; see Lloyd-Jones: *Law* pp230-232).

On: 'If you are led by the Spirit, you are not under the law' (Gal. 5:18), Kruse: 'The implication of this surprising statement is that being free from the law is intimately connected with overcoming the desires of the flesh'. Paul brilliantly emphasised the point by using the verbal form of 'pedagogue' in Gal. 5:18. Witherington: This 'is no accident'. Taylor: 'To such the Holy Spirit becomes a schoolmaster [better, child-custodian]' (Kruse p105; Witherington p396; Taylor p10). Quite! The Spirit, not the law!

Nothing here, of course, about 'let go and let God'. Witherington: The believer does not life a godly life 'by accident or chance... effort and resolve is required on the part of the Christian. "If [since] we live in the Spirit, let us also walk in the Spirit" (Gal. 5:25)'. Not, let us walk in the law, but let us 'follow the Spirit's lead, staying in line or step with the Spirit'. Ridderbos: 'He is the new life-principle of freedom (*cf.* 2 Cor. 3:17)... The Spirit must also become the norm, the rule, of this manifestation of life. He creates a new life-style... This new manner of life must be made manifest, must be distinguishable... For the believers this walking by the Spirit remains a constantly renewed mandate and a continuous exertion'. Dunn: This 'call... is so important: there must be that inward resolution and determined discipline to side with the Spirit *against oneself* in what is an ongoing and inescapable inner warfare, so long as the flesh continues to be a factor (that is, for the duration of this earthly life)' (Witherington pp394,413; Ridderbos p210; Dunn pp299-300, emphasis his).

On Gal. 5:25, Dunn: 'Paul does not see the Spirit as an anarchic power disruptive of all order; [rather, he] continues to warn against treating the freedom given by the Spirit as a licence for self-indulgence' (Dunn pp317-318; see Dunn p297).

John Brown got close – but, surprisingly for him, not close enough – when he said that 'to walk in the Spirit' is 'the *best* means of obtaining dominion over the flesh'. It is the *only* way. But it is the *sure* way: 'Walk in the Spirit, and you shall *not* fulfil the lust of the flesh' (Gal. 5:16). The negative is doubled and therefore much strengthened: 'You will assuredly not fulfil the lust of the flesh'. You will 'certainly not'. But Brown was right when he said: 'To "walk in the law of the Lord" is to regulate our conduct according to its precepts. To "walk in the Spirit", is to act like spiritual persons... through the faith of the gospel, by the agency of the Holy Spirit... to live habitually under the influence of the faith of Christ, and those dispositions which it naturally inspires'.

Unfortunately, Brown was a little weak in the section which followed: 'This will put a more effectual check on the desires of the flesh than the most rigid observance of Mosaic ceremonies. Nothing mortifies pride, malignity, and impure desire, these lusts of the flesh, like walking in the Spirit'. Weak because, in addition to his continued use of the notion that walking in the Spirit is the *best*, 'more effectual way of godliness' – when, as I have pointed out, it is the *only* way – Brown inexplicably compared 'walking in the Spirit' with 'observance of the Mosaic ceremonies', when Paul plainly said 'the law'. Brown should have stuck with his (almost constant) correct reading of 'the law' in Galatians – namely the Mosaic law, the law, the whole law.

But Brown got back on to the right road when he said: '"To be led by the Spirit" is another figurative expression, signifying to be influenced by the new mode of thinking and feeling to which the Spirit by the faith of the gospel forms men. To "walk in the Spirit" and to be "led by the Spirit", are nearly synonymous. The active influential nature of the Spirit is perhaps somewhat more clearly brought out in the last of these modes of expression. They who are thus influenced are not under the law. It has been ordinary [usual] to consider this verse as stating that all who are the subjects of the leading influences of the Holy Ghost are delivered from the law, in its covenant form, from its condemning, and irritating, and commanding power. This proposition, if rightly explained, contains much important truth, but it does not, I apprehend, at all express the apostle's meaning... "The law" is here, as generally throughout this letter, the Mosaic law... And what the apostle says is: If you are influenced as you ought to be by these views and affections which grow out of the faith of the gospel, you will not be among those who seek to subject themselves to the Mosaic law, you will distinctly see that you stand in no need of it, and its genius does not correspond to the character of the new and better order of things which the Messiah has introduced, and refusing to submit to what are now nothing better than "commandments of *men*", you will "walk at liberty, keeping *God's* commandments". They who are led by the Spirit spontaneously, by "a law written on their hearts", follow that course which God approves, and have no need of the pedagogy of the law from which [Israel] has been delivered. The great practical lesson taught us by this passage is that the true way of mortifying sin, and making progress in holiness, is to yield our minds and hearts more and more up to the transforming influence of divine truth' (Brown: *Galatians* pp291-293,298-299, first emphasis mine; others, his) See Dunn p297; Witherington p393.

On the whole, a high-quality statement by Brown, in which he effectively destroyed the Reformed position. I would, however, had introduced 'looking to Christ' in his last sentence. To be 'led by the Spirit' is, indeed, to yield to the truth, but, as Jesus himself taught us, the Spirit leads us through the truth to Christ himself (John 14:26; 16:12-15). And, of course, 'the truth' is the entire Scripture (John 17:17; 2 Tim. 3:16-17), not just the law of Moses. And, don't forget, the law of Christ is that law which is written on the believer's heart.

Fairbairn: 'When the believer receives Christ as the Lord his righteousness, he is not only justified by grace, but he comes into a state of grace, or gets grace into his heart as a living, reigning, governing principle of life. What, however, is this grace but the Spirit of life in Christ Jesus? And this Spirit is emphatically the Holy Spirit; holiness is the very element of his working; every desire he breathes, every feeling he awakens, every action he disposes and enables us to perform, is according to godliness. And if only we... are... possessed of this Spirit...'. I pause. Fairbairn inexplicably qualified this otherwise splendid statement with these words: 'And if only we are *sufficiently* possessed of this Spirit, *and yield ourselves to his direction and control*, we no longer need the restraint and discipline of the law; we are free from it', emphasis mine. What a gloss! It casts a long shadow – see below.

To let him continue: 'We no longer need the restraint and discipline of the law; we are free from it, because we are superior to it. Quickened and led by the Spirit, we of ourselves love and do the things which the law requires... [For] one who has become a partaker of grace, the law, considered as an outward discipline placing him under the yoke of manifold commands and prohibitions, has for him ceased to exist'. Fairbairn spoke of the law written in the believer's heart, 'the law of the Spirit of life in his inner man; emphatically,

441

therefore, "the law of liberty": his delight is to do it; and it were better for him not to live, than to live otherwise than the tenor of the law requires... Like Paul, he can say with king-like freedom: "I can do all things through Christ strengthening me"... for I have him working in me both to will and to do of his good pleasure'.

Good! Except... Fairbairn was thinking of the Mosaic law, and consequently did not work out the full implication of what he had said. Seemingly unable to trust the power of the Spirit and the plan of grace by which God has determined to sanctify his elect, Fairbairn sought safety in the law. This is the long shadow of which I spoke: 'The law is... needed to present continually before the eye of the mind a clear representation of the righteousness which, through the grace of the Spirit, believers should be ever striving to attain. While that grace is still imperfect, they are necessarily in danger of entertaining low and defective views of duty... But the law stands before them, with its revelation of righteousness, as a faithful and resplendent mirror, in which they may behold, without any danger of delusion or mistake, the perfect image of that excellence which they should be ever yielding to God... Thus the freedom of the Spirit is a freedom only within the bounds and limits of the law; and the law itself must stand, lest the flesh, taking advantage of the weakness of the Spirit's grace, should in its wantonness break forth into courses which are displeasing to the mind of God' (Fairbairn: *Typology* Vol.2 pp165-167,173-175).

In other words, Paul might say it, but it is not truly practical. Paul: 'Walk in the Spirit, and you shall not fulfil the lust of the flesh... If you are led by the Spirit, you are not under the law... If we live in the Spirit, let us also walk in [or by] the Spirit' (Gal. 5:16,18,26). No, declared Fairbairn: 'The law is... needed... continually... The law stands... Thus the freedom of the Spirit is a freedom only within the bounds and limits of the law; and the law itself must stand...'. No! Paul said what he said, and he meant what he said! True, no believer is perfectly sanctified in this life – that is why he has the Spirit, the entire word of God (John 14:26; 16:12-15; 17:17; 2 Tim. 3:16-17), and, with the law of Christ written in his heart, goes on, looking unto Jesus, growing in the grace of Christ. But in all this he really does have the Spirit, and he really is free from the Mosaic law. As John Brown on Gal. 4:5: 'So far was the imposition of the law on the Gentiles from being the object of [Christ's] coming, one of its designs was to deliver the Jews from under it'. Therefore, going back to the law, Paul argued, as Michael Eaton put it: 'Results only in diminished spirituality'. John Murray: 'The reception of the Holy Spirit does not have the effect of a relapse into that slavish fear which characterised the pre-Christian state' (Brown: *Galatians* pp195-196; Michael Eaton: *Encouragement* pp115-116; Murray: *Romans* Vol.1 p297).

How Calvin and his colleagues could live with Gal. 5:13-26, I do not know. Calvin: 'There are two things to consider in the law. That is to say, the teaching, which is the rule for right living... The doctrine of the law exists to show us how our life ought to conform to the will of God. The second point is its rigour, since it declares to us that whoever fails in a single point will be cursed, and it promises salvation only to those who perfectly observe its commandments. As long as this rigour is in force, we are entirely bereft of the hope of life and under the condemnation that the law announces. For there has never been a single mortal man who has acquitted himself with respect to what it requires. Hence if the law with its appendages has authority over us, then everyone is without hope. For to satisfy its requirements is impossible. Nor can its condemnation be avoided. For this reason, the only remedy that remains is to be set free from such a bondage. This deliverance is given to us in the gospel when it is said to us that we are no longer under the law'. Did Calvin really mean by this that the believer is free from the law? He did not! 'The doctrine [the law] remains in effect in order to guide in the right direction; only the curse is removed... Liberty only has to do with the law's curse or rigour'. Bucer: 'The law... to those who are endowed with the Spirit... is in no sense abolished, but is so much the more potent in each one as he is richly endowed with the Spirit of Christ' (Calvin: *Treatises* pp271-273; quoted by Wendel p205).

In other words, Paul might say it, but Calvin, Bucer *et al* will gloss it. Paul: 'Walk in the Spirit, and you shall not fulfil the lust of the flesh... If you are led by the Spirit, you are not under the law... If we live in the Spirit, let us also walk in [or by] the Spirit' (Gal. 5:16,18,26). No glosses!

Dunn, except at one point, put the proper view of the passage: 'The mistake [Paul] was seeking to counter was the persuasive teaching... that the new life begun with the Spirit was brought to its completion by conforming to the requirements laid down by the law for Jews and proselytes, that the only sure means of gaining direction on how to live was by reference to the law...'. Precisely so! And this 'persuasive teaching' is the Reformed position in a nut-shell. Now what did Paul think about it? As Dunn noted: 'This Paul saw as just another form of pandering to the flesh, by over-valuation of [the law],[7] and amounted to an abandoning of the Spirit (Gal. 3:3)'. Paul argued his case by selecting a 'metaphor [which] is typically Jewish... "Conduct oneself"... Paul, therefore, is deliberately using the language of Old Testament moral obligation... Paul would be well aware of the typical Old Testament use of the metaphor: the conduct looked for was "to walk in (God's) law(s)/statutes" (as in Ex. 16:4; Lev. 18:4; Jer. 44:23; Ezek. 5:6-7)... By speaking instead of a "walk by the Spirit", Paul is deliberately posing an alternative understanding of how the people of God should conduct themselves – not by constant reference to laws and statutes, but by constant reference (the verb is present continuous) to the Spirit; and not to the Spirit as norm, but to the Spirit as resource... The emphasis on the Spirit is [of course] consistent with Paul's emphasis in Gal. 3:3 – that the Galatians should continue as they began. This means he is putting considerable weight on what they had experienced – as an experience of acceptance by God (Gal. 3:14), sonship to God (Gal. 4:6), of liberty (Gal. 5:1,13), and now of guidance for daily living. He must therefore have been envisaging a life-style and decision-making which constantly referred back to that inward fact or consciousness of the Spirit's presence, and which sought to bring it to expression in daily life (so Gal. 5:25). The contrast with "walking in God's laws" likewise implies an inward rather than an outward reference point in matters of ethical decision. This is... what Paul had in mind when he spoke confidently of a discerning of God's will by virtue of a renewed mind (Rom. 12:1-2), in contrast with the traditional Jewish confidence of discerning matters by instruction from the law (Rom. 2:18); so too particularly Rom. 14:22 and Phil. 1:9-10. In other words, this counsel reflects Paul's assumption [no! – assurance] (as in 2 Cor. 3:3) that those who had been given the Spirit thus also [know] the eschatological experience looked for in Jer. 31:33-34 – an immediate knowledge of God, an enabling to know what God's will [is] in particular instances' (Dunn pp294-296). On the whole, an admirable commentary on Paul's words.

Note Dunn's use of 'alternative' and 'contrast' in the above, the very reverse of Bayes who thought Paul in Gal. 5:25 'stressed to walk by the Spirit is to live in accordance with the law' (Bayes p173). The verse says nothing of the sort – the law is not even mentioned – but since it is the only place Bayes raised the verse, I cannot follow his argument further. In his introduction to the section starting with Gal. 5:25, Dunn said: 'That the exhortations are concrete but general and not prescriptive in close detail marks the *difference* between an ethic of the Spirit and an ethic of law' (Dunn p317, emphasis mine). Once again, first class.

Nobody is arguing – surely it goes without saying – that the Spirit leads the believer without reference to Scripture? As I have said, time and again, the Spirit leads through the Scripture to Christ (John 14:26; 16:12-15; 17:17; 2 Tim. 3:16-17). The believer lives in the Spirit, under the entire word of God, looking to Christ, with Christ's law written on his heart. The fact is, he does not live under the law of Moses! Witherington: 'Life in the Spirit,

---

[7] Dunn limited 'the law' to 'physical rite and ethnic identity'. Paul said 'the law' and, as I have proved, he meant the law.

not life lived under the Mosaic law, should mark the Christian life... It is saying too much to argue that the Spirit provides *all* the necessary guidance in the fight against the flesh (otherwise this letter is pointless, as is the later discussion of the law of Christ)'. Dunn: 'However qualified, we should not lose the point of Paul's exhortation here: that the key to moral effort and acceptable conduct lies in the prompting of the Spirit from within, not in the constraints of the law from without; that moral living springs from inward engagement and motivation enabled from God rather than from outward compulsion'. Mussner, quoted by Dunn: 'The Christian ethic is no longer a law-ethic but a Spirit-ethic!' (Witherington pp393,396-397,415, emphasis his; Dunn pp296-297).

Dunn commenting on: 'If you are led by the Spirit, you are not under the law' (Gal. 5:18), wrote: 'The reference to the law once again is no accident. Paul's [statement] here is aimed precisely at those who were being persuaded that the Jewish law provided the necessary directions and rules for their daily conduct'. *Touché* the Reformed! 'His concern, therefore, has been to show that a life-style determined by the Spirit gives them all that they need and more. No external constraint or rule-book is capable of countering "the desire of the flesh" adequately. What is needed is the Spirit [and] the law written within (Jer. 31:33-34), to provide an inner drive of greater and more enduring strength...But Paul's concern here goes further. The point here is to reinforce the message that such a Spirit-led life is quite other in character from one "under the law"... To put oneself thus "under the law" was to look once again for an answer to "the desire of the flesh" in a written code, an outward constraint; whereas in the age of fulfilment introduced by Christ, it was the circumcision of the heart, an effective inner force which was now available. To put oneself "under the law", in other words, was to look in the wrong direction for salvation [sanctification?]' (Dunn pp300-301).

Dunn's choice of 'salvation' is surprising here, unless he meant 'full salvation including sanctification'. After all, he has been speaking about believers and their moral and ethical choices, and their overcoming the flesh, *etc.* In other words, like Paul he has been dealing with sanctification, 'how the people of God should conduct themselves'. But 'sanctification' is a biblical word Dunn did not seem to use.

Edgar H.Andrews: In Gal. 5:16-21, 'Paul's message is that the law and the flesh are co-conspirators against grace and the Spirit... "Walk in the Spirit"... The outward conduct of the believer is to be dictated and controlled by an inward, spiritual principle. It is not to be dictated by external laws... The Holy Spirit indwells believers and guides them in their thinking, their attitudes and their behaviour. He pours out God's love in their hearts, so that they are motivated by love rather than selfishness and covetousness. He leads them to a growing understanding of truth through the Holy Scriptures, so that the Bible, in its entirety, becomes their "rule of life" as they seek the glory of God in all that they do... "But if you are led by the Spirit, you are not under the law" (Gal. 5:18). Here the apostle defines the relationship of the believer to the law *in the context, not of justification, but of personal holiness.* What connection is there, then, between righteous living and freedom from law? The verse has important implications... Paul's concern was not only with apostate legalists, but also with the threat which the law, when misapplied, poses to genuine believers... What, then, is the apostle telling us? Very simply that, for the believer, the indwelling Spirit has supplanted the external law as the controlling principle that guides his conduct. Had Paul intended to teach that the law, or any part of it, should be the Christian's "rule of life", here was his opportunity to do so. [But] what does he say? He tells us that those led by the Spirit are not beholden to the law with respect to righteous living. Indeed, he [goes – not "seems to go"] further; being led by the Spirit and being ruled by the law are mutually exclusive... Of course... those who are Spirit-led will fulfil the righteous requirements of the law... but this will not be because they subject themselves to the law, but because they are guided by the indwelling Spirit in conformity to the *whole* of God's word and the example of Christ... Led and empowered by the indwelling Spirit of God, and taught in the objective principles

444

of the Holy Scripture, the believer seeks to conform his life to the will of God' (Edgar H.Andrews pp287-293,296-297, emphasis his). In addition, the believer has the law of Christ written in his heart.

Let me say it again: liberty is not licence. Dunn: 'Freedom is a heady mixture. The removal of old constraints can easily lead to a wider breakdown of discipline. The forces marshalled to break through the earlier servitude may lose direction and cohesion, once that purpose has been attained. Liberty once gained might easily become the occasion for the licence of self-indulgence... Paul... was all too conscious of the dangers of the theme... Freedom [is] a call not merely *from* the older enslavement, but also a call *to* a new responsibility. The freedom of God has both aspects, otherwise it is not God's freedom. The liberty which does not ask: "Liberty for what?" is a dangerous commodity... Consequently it was necessary for Paul now to spell out what life in accordance with the Spirit really [means] and how it [contrasts] with life on the level of the flesh' (Dunn pp284-287,295).

Ridderbos noted Paul's use of *stoichein* for 'walk' in Gal. 5:25. This is a 'more rigid' word than his choice in Gal. 5:16, and 'the idea of a row or rule is contained in it. It is used for movement in a definite line, as in military formations or in dancing'. Thayer: 'If the Holy Spirit animates us... let us exhibit that control of the Spirit in our life' (Ridderbos p210; Thayer p589).

Believers are free, but they are responsible; they have duties, but they have liberty in Christ. On Gal. 5:22-26, Edgar H.Andrews: 'Fruitfulness in Christian living is the direct result of the Spirit within... The good works done by believers flow naturally from the activity of the Spirit within. It is by this "fruit" that the Holy Spirit's presence is demonstrated and his power declared. One who is led by the Spirit cannot avoid bearing fruit... Spiritual fruit is not only the evidence of spiritual life. Even more important is the fact that it glorifies God... John 15:8... Matt. 5:16... The indwelling Spirit does not compel us to carry out particular actions, as if we were robots under alien control. He rather induces in our hearts and minds those Christ-like attitudes, which then issue in specific acts that glorify God. It is the believer himself who is responsible for translating these attitudes into good deeds... Exhortations... which abound in Scripture would not be necessary if Christians automatically produced good works without conscious thought or effort... The Spirit within gives us the attitudes, desires and intentions to do so, but it is our responsibility to put these intentions into effect... Paul's point is that such Spirit-led behaviour transcends the requirements of any law, even that of Sinai. Thus... Rom. 8:4. Paul's conclusion also means that the fruit of the Spirit cannot be interpreted as a new law imposed upon believers, replacing that of Moses. The whole point of this passage is that spiritual fruitfulness supersedes external law as the spring and basis of moral action... The fruits of the Spirit are attitudes that control and dictate actions, rather than the actions themselves. Thus the believer's manner of life flows from a genuine inner principle, not from adherence to an external law. It is the believer himself who is responsible for translating these attitudes into good deeds... Fruitfulness in Christian living is the direct result of the indwelling Holy Spirit... It is the responsibility of the believer to mortify the sinful tendencies of the flesh and thus live in a manner that honours Christ. Spirit-led behaviour transcends the requirements of any law. Spiritual fruitfulness supersedes external law as the spring and basis of moral action' (Edgar H.Andrews pp298-306).

Christopher Idle: 'Freedom and life are ours/ For Christ has set us free!/ Never again submit to powers/ That lead to slavery:/ Christ is the Lord who breaks/ Our chains, our bondage ends,/ Christ is the rescuer who makes/ The helpless slaves his friends./ Called by the Lord to use/ Our freedom and be strong,/ Not letting liberty excuse/ A life of blatant wrong:/ Freed from the law's stern hand/ God's gift of grace to prove,/ Know that the law's entire demand/ Is gladly met by love./ Spirit of God, come, fill,/ Emancipate us all!/ Speak to us, word of truth, until/ Before his throne we fall:/ Glory and liberty/ Our Father has decreed,/ And if the Son shall make us free/ We shall be free indeed!' (*Baptist* number 528).

On the note of 'triumph', Tozer: 'The unique thing about the early Christians was their radiant relation to a person. " The Lord", they called him tenderly, and when they used the term they gave it its own New Testament meaning. It meant Jesus Christ who, a short while before, had been among them, but was now gone into the heavens as the high priest and advocate. It was this engrossment with a victorious person that gave verve and vibrancy to their lives, and conviction to their testimony. They bore witness joyously to the one who had lived as a true man among men... They accepted his claim to be invested with authority over everything in heaven, earth and hell... Jesus was Lord... sovereign head... Hence they never presented him as Saviour merely... Today we hold the same views, but our emphasis is not the same. The meek and lowly Jesus has displaced the high and holy Jesus in the minds of millions. The vibrant note of triumph is missing in our witness... So we sing pop choruses to cheer our drooping spirits and hold panel discussions in the plaintive hope that someone will come up with the answer to our scarce-spoken complaint. Well, we already have the answer, if we had but the faith and wisdom to turn to it. The answer is Christ victorious high over all. He lives for ever above the reach of his foes. He has but to speak and it is done; he need but command, and heaven and earth obey him. Within the broad framework of his far-looking plans, he tolerates for a time the wild outlawry of a fallen world, but he holds the earth in his hand, and he can call the nations to judgement whenever he wills. Yes, Christian pilgrim, we are better off than the sad church can see. We stand in Christ's triumph. Because he lives, we live also. "Thanks be to God who gives us the victory through out Lord Jesus Christ"' (Tozer: *Root* pp69-71).

Conclusion to Galatians
Let McClain bring this chapter to a close. Picking up where it all began – with Paul's rhetorical and rasping questions in Gal. 3, – McClain: 'The word of God condemns unsparingly all attempts to put the Christian believer "under the law". The Holy Spirit through... Paul gave to the church the book of Galatians for the very purpose of dealing with this heresy. Read this letter over and over, noting carefully the precise error with which the writer deals. It is not a total rejection of the gospel of God's grace, and a turning back to a total legalism. It is rather the error of saying that the Christian life, having begun by simple faith in Christ, must thereafter continue under the law or some part of it. This is clear from the apostle's indignant charge: "This only would I learn of you: Did you receive the Spirit by the works of the law, or by the hearing of faith? Are you so foolish? Having begun in the Spirit, are you now made perfect in the flesh?" (Gal. 3:2-3). Little wonder that he begins the chapter with a cry of astonishment: "O foolish Galatians, who has bewitched you, that you should not obey the truth...?" (Gal. 3:1)'.

McClain continued: 'And having pursued his devastating argument against this type of legalism through Gal. 3 into Gal. 4, showing that the redemption of God in Christ has set us free from all the bondage of the law, he again asks with irony: "But now, after that you have known God, or rather are known of God, how do you turn again to weak and beggarly elements, whereunto you desire again to be in bondage?" (Gal. 4:9). And then he adds: " I am afraid of you, lest I have bestowed upon you labour in vain" (Gal. 4:11). "You did run well; who did hinder you that you should not obey the truth?" (Gal. 5:7). As for the preacher [or writer or friend] who had introduced this heresy among the flock, Paul writes by inspiration of the Holy Ghost: "He that troubles you shall bear his judgement, whosoever he [or she] may be" (Gal. 5:10)'.

McClain hit the nail on the head: 'That this matter was no mere case of theological hair-splitting (as some today are accustomed to charge) is made clear in the very beginning of the book of Galatians. In seeking to add some modicum of law to the gospel of God's grace, these legalistic teachers are preaching "another gospel" (Gal. 1:6). Paul hastens, however, to add that what they are preaching is really "not another" gospel at all, for the very meaning of the term "gospel" excludes all works of law. And so, strange as it may seem to some, for anyone to add any law (no matter how worthy) to the simple good news of God's grace in Christ, is actually to destroy the gospel as gospel! It is no longer gospel at all! If even the smallest item of the law should be added to the gospel and made binding upon believers...' (McClain pp51-53).

Very serious words, but not too serious. I hope any advocate of the law as the believer's rule who is still reading my book – if there is one such reader – will reflect upon them.

In addition to the above, Edgar H.Andrews; Arndt and Gingrich; Barnes: *New* Vol.6 pp344-345,352; Bayes pp131,173; Bigg: *Pursuit* pp100-106; Brown: *Galatians*; Bruce: *Apostolic* pp31-42; Calvin: *Institutes* Vol.1 p308; Vol.2 p281; *Commentaries* Vol.3 Part 1 pp196-199; Vol.21 Part 1 p163; Chantry: *Sabbath* pp84-86,97; Crisp: *Christ* Vol.4 pp218-219; Dunn; Michael Eaton: *Encouragement* pp114-119,123; Fee: *Empowering* xxiii; Friedmann pp82,84-85; Gay: *Particular*; Hendriksen: *Galatians*; Horn pp19-37; Kautz pp113-114; Kingdon pp83-84; Klassen: 'Studies' p82; *Neither* pp28-36; 'Radical' pp138-146; Kruse; Lloyd-Jones: *New* pp155-158; *Law* pp230-232; *2 Peter* p88; Moo: *Romans* pp211-217; Stuart Murray pp186-205; Oliver p132; Philips pp235-237; Reisinger: *Tablets* pp82-83; Ridderbos; Sattler pp250-252; Shaw p199; Spurgeon: *1866* p259; Verduin: *Anatomy* pp184-188; Williams: *Spiritual* pp80,235-237,366-367; Witherington.

CHAPTER 10: THE BIBLICAL CASE
ROMANS

Rom. 5:20

'The law entered that the offence might abound' (Rom. 5:20). Entered? Cullman: 'Slipping in between'. Kruse: 'Paul sees the law as part of the human predicament, not the solution to it' (Cullmann p265; Kruse p203).

Lloyd-Jones on Rom. 5:20: 'The law – let us be quite clear about this – in verse 20 means the law that was given through Moses on Mount Sinai, not the moral law only but the ceremonial law also, in fact the whole of the law' (Lloyd-Jones: *Assurance* p284).

Rom. 6

Let Moo set the scene. He spoke of two dangers we will meet if we get the connection between justification and sanctification wrong. First, if we mistakenly put them into separate compartments: 'We can forget that true holiness of life comes only as the outworking and realisation of the life of Christ in us. This leads to moralism or legalism in which the believer "goes it on his own", thinking that holiness will be attained through sheer effort, or ever more elaborate programmes, or ever-increasing numbers of rules'. The second danger: 'But if... justification and sanctification [are mistakenly] collapsed together into one, we can neglect the fact that the out-working of the life of Christ in us is made *our* responsibility. This neglect leads to an unconcern with holiness of life, or a "God-does-it-all" attitude in which the believer thinks to become holy through a kind of spiritual osmosis'. What is the biblical position? 'Paul makes it clear, by [Rom. 6:1-14], that we can live a holy life only as we appropriate the benefits of our union with Christ... That holiness of life can be stifled if we fail continually to appropriate and put to work the new life God has given us'. Moo quoted Burroughs, who saw Christ 'as a fountain [from which] sanctification flows into the souls of the saints: their sanctification comes not so much from their struggling, and endeavours, and vows, and resolutions, as it comes flowing to them from their union with him' (Moo: *Romans* p391, emphasis his).

Moo again: 'In Rom. 6... the main issue is not freedom from the *penalty* of sin, but freedom from the *power* of sin. If sin is not to rule over the believer (Rom. 6:14), more than forgiveness would seem to be [it is!] necessary. After all, justification in itself could simply free the believer to sin with impunity – which is precisely the objection raised in Rom. 6:1. In the context, then, there is every reason to think that "not being under the law" involves more than being free from condemnation... The last reference to *nomos* before Rom. 6:14 comes in Rom. 5:20, where the law is pictured as an instigator of sin: "The law was added so that the trespass might increase". If the law functioned historically to increase sinning, one would expect "not [being] under the law" to describe the condition of freedom from that instigation of sin' (Moo: 'The Law' p211, emphasis his). Moo, as so often, gets it right, but is too apologetic about it.

Moo again: 'In Rom. 6:14-15, Paul contrasts being "under the law" with being "under grace". These assertions are closely related to Rom. 7:4, in which he claims that Christians have "died the law". Traditional Reformed (and especially Puritan) exegesis has viewed the contrast here as between justification and condemnation. Christians [they allege] are free from the law's condemnation, for their status "under grace" has delivered them from the law as a "covenant of works", in which every infraction had to receive its penalty... But it is questionable whether this is all that Paul means'. Yet, again this is too weak – the Reformed claim is obviously wrong. Paul meant far more than what they claim, as the context makes abundantly clear. Moo: 'The issue in Rom. 6 is not freedom from the *penalty* of sin, but from the *power* of sin... In the context, then, "not being under the law" must involve more than freedom from the law's condemnation'. Arguing from Rom. 5 – 8, 'where Paul employs the metaphors of slavery, freedom, and transfer from one regime or power to another, to denote the new status of the believer', Moo went on: 'Christians die to sin and are joined to Christ (Rom. 6:1-11); are set free from sin and enslaved to God and righteousness (Rom. 6:15-23); die to the law (Rom. 7:4); being set free from it (Rom. 7:6), so as to be joined to Christ (Rom. 7:4); are released from the sphere of the flesh (Rom. 7:5; 8:9), and placed within the sphere of the Spirit (Rom. 7:6; 8:9). That Paul would designate another such transfer from one regime to another by speaking of Christians as no longer under law but grace, makes good sense'. It does more than that! It is precisely what he does say! 'His [the apostle's] point, then, is that the Christian lives in a new regime, no longer dominated by the law with its sin-producing and condemning power, but by Christ and the Spirit' (Moo: 'Galatians' pp18-19, emphasis mine). In short, the apostle is talking about sanctification – and sanctification comes because the Christian is no longer under the law. Calvin's third use of the law could not be more diametrically opposed to the truth of Scripture.

Let me show how many Reformed writers get this disastrously wrong. Alderson: 'When a verse like Rom. 6:14 asserts that Christians are "not under law but under grace", the writer means that Christians are not required to keep the law in order to obtain justification' (Alderson p8). Woefully adrift! The context destroys it in one blow.

John Murray was wrong to say on Rom. 6:19,22: 'Notwithstanding the opinion of some of the most able commentators... *hagiasmos*... does not most suitably refer to a process but to the state of holiness or consecration... The rendering "holiness" of the AV is more suitable than the ambiguous word "sanctification"'. Not at all! But Murray was right to say: 'The dedication of the believer, and the end to which this dedication is directed have in view the holiness of heart and life without which no man shall see the Lord (*cf.* Heb. 12:14; 1 Cor. 1:30; 1 Thess. 4:3-4,7)' (Murray: *Romans* Vol.1 p234).

Lloyd-Jones got it right. See his *New*. Note his repeated use of 'holiness and sanctification, sanctification and holiness, sanctification, sanctify... sanctification [which] is a progressive process' (Lloyd-Jones: *New* pp258,260,262,265,269,293,297-299, often several times on each page). Spot on!

Fairbairn, having explained that 'believers in Christ are not under the law as to the ground of their condemnation or justification before God', went on: 'But this is not the only aspect in which the apostle affirms believers now to be free from the law, nor the respect at all which he has in view in the sixth and seventh chapters of his letter to the Romans; for the subject he is there handling is not justification, but sanctification. The question he is discussing is not how... we may be accepted as righteous before God; but how, being already pardoned and accepted in the Beloved, we ought to live. In this respect... he affirms that we are dead to the law, and are not under it, but under grace – the grace, that is, of God's indwelling Spirit, whose quickening energy and pulse of life takes the place of the law's outward prescriptions and magisterial authority... According to... the apostle... believers are not under the law as to their walk and conduct; or as he says elsewhere, "the law is not for the righteous": believers "have the Spirit of the Lord; and where the Spirit of the Lord is, there is liberty"'. Fairbairn rightly dismissed as 'very strange [and] untenable' – the notion that Paul was still speaking about justification – 'considering how plain and explicit the apostle's meaning is' (Fairbairn: *Typology* Vol.2 pp163-165). Excellent!

But Fairbairn rightly raised a pertinent question. Pertinent? The *essential* question, the apostle's own question (Rom. 6:15). Moreover, he went on to give the biblical answer: 'But is not this a dangerous doctrine? For where now is the safeguard against sin? May not each do as he wishes, oblivious of any distinction between holiness and sin, or even denying its existence, as regards the children of God, on the ground that where no law is, there is no transgression? To such questions the apostle's reply is: "God forbid" – so far from it, that the freedom he asserts from the law has for its sole aim a deliverance from sin's dominion, and a fruitfulness in all well-doing to God' (Fairbairn: *Typology* Vol.2 p165). The believer, of course, is not antinomian, he is under law – the law of Christ (see chapter 16). I said Fairbairn's question is essential. Of course it is. It is the question that must be asked of Paul and his astounding doctrine. *But it is never asked of any advocate of Calvin's third use of the law.* So how can Paul's doctrine and Calvin's doctrine be the same – since they do not provoke the same response? Indeed, they provoke diametrically opposite responses.

The answer is of course; they are anything but the same! Let me remind you of Calvin's disastrous view of the believer and the law: 'The law acts like a whip to the flesh, urging it on as men do to a lazy sluggish ass. Even in the case of a spiritual man, inasmuch as he is still burdened with the weight of the flesh, the law is a constant stimulus, pricking him forward when he would indulge in sloth... It cannot be denied that it [the law] contains a perfect pattern of righteousness... one perpetual and inflexible rule... The doctrine of the law... remains... that... it may fit and prepare us for every good work' (Calvin: *Institutes* Vol.1 pp309-311). This sets out – as clear as noonday – the answer to the question I asked just above. It would be a mark of an imbecile to wonder if such a doctrine could produce antinomianism. Why is it possible – inevitable – to ask Fairbairn's (Paul's) question of Paul, but impossible to ask it of Calvin? What does that tell us?

Bayes, defending Calvin's third use of the law: 'In both cases [before and after conversion], the law of God is the standard against which human life is assessed... Holiness as the believer's way of life, contrasts with lawlessness, because it involves actually living in obedience to the law of God. This brings us to the major issue: the implication of [Rom. 6:19, "present your members as slaves of righteousness for holiness"] is that the law does have ongoing status in the believing life... in that the sanctified life of the Christian may legitimately be defined as a life of law-keeping. The authentic Christian life takes its description from the moral law of God, and finds expression in a ready and deliberate obedience to that law'. Bayes, acknowledging Rom. 6:14 and the following verses as one of the 'negative indicators' – meaning one 'of those texts which might seem to pose a problem for the view that Paul asserts the ongoing relevance of the law for the believer' – said: 'It is the law in its sin-defining function that the believer is not under... In the sphere of the Spirit, the law stands before the believer as the definition of holiness, and becomes in the Spirit's power, a force in the believing life for the reproduction of its own demands' (Bayes pp111-112,115-117).

Not at all! Let Lloyd-Jones set us on the right road: 'To be "under sin", and to be "under the law" are the same thing, and we need to be delivered from sin as we need to be delivered from the law' (Lloyd-Jones: *Law* p311).

'The strength of sin is the law' (1 Cor. 15:56). Thayer: 'Sin exercised its power... through the law' (Thayer).

Bruce on Rom. 6:22: '"The return you get is sanctification". And this, in fact, is the subject of the present section of the letter (chapters 6 – 7). Those who have been justified are now being sanctified; if a man is not being sanctified, there is no reason to believe that he has been justified'. Bayes: 'Here Paul is contrasting the life of the believer with the pre-conversion state. In each case, he compares life with slavery... The former life of... Christians entailed slavery to "uncleanness to lawlessness, leading to lawlessness", while the Christian life is slavery "to righteousness leading to holiness"' (Bayes p111; Bruce: *Romans* pp142-143).

Moo on Rom. 6:14: 'These words are to be understood of a promise that is valid for every believer at the present time: "Sin shall certainly not be your lord – now or ever!"' 'The promise is confirmed by the assurance that "you are not under law but under grace"' (Rom. 6:14 linked to Rom. 3:19-21,27-28; 4:13-15; 5:13-14,20 and, especially Rom. 5:20 and 7:1-6). 'As in all these references, *nomos* here must be the Mosaic law, the *torah*. And, while most of the (Gentile) Christians in Rome have never lived "under the law", the situation of the Jews under the Mosaic law, as we shall see in Rom. 7:4, is used by Paul as representative of the situation and need of all people... It is clear that Paul is speaking in these passages of the law *as God gave it*'.

'Under law' cannot be explained away as Jewish misunderstanding, nor by taking any other Reformed escape routes. In particular, Moo said, as for 'confining the phrase only to the notion of condemnation [this] fails to grasp the salvation-historical contrast that Paul sets up here'. 'This explains why Paul can make release from the law a reason for the Christian's freedom from the power of sin: as he has repeatedly stated, the Mosaic law has had a definite sin-producing and sin-intensifying function; it brought "knowledge of sin" (Rom. 3:20), 'wrath' (Rom. 4:15), 'transgression' (Rom. 5:13-14), and an increase in the severity of sin (Rom. 5:20). The law, as Paul puts it in 1 Cor. 15:56, is "the power of sin". This means, however, that there can be no final liberation from the power of sin without a corresponding liberation from the power and lordship of the law. To be "under law" is to be subject to the constraining and sin-strengthening regime of the old age; to be "under grace" is to be subject to the new age in which freedom from the power of sin is available'. Of course: 'We cannot conclude from this verse that the believer has no obligation to any of the individual commandments... Still less... that Christians are no longer subject to "law" or "commandments" at all – for *nomos* here means *Mosaic* law, not "law" as such'.

As Moo noted, Paul was not here speaking against legalism. When Paul wants to speak of legalism, 'he uses phrases like seeking justification "on the basis of" (*ek*) the law (*cf.* Rom. 10:5; Phil. 3:9) or through "works of the law" (Gal. 2:16; *etc.*) to designate it. In other words, it is not the word *nomos* itself that denotes "legalism" in Paul, but various phrases in which the law... is falsely understood as the basis for salvation. In the context of Rom. 6 – 7, the "legalistic" meaning is particularly inappropriate. For the condition of being "under the law" and the release from that situation though incorporation into Christ's death (Rom. 7:4) clearly imply that being under the law is an objective condition that is quite independent of anyone's attitude toward or understanding of the law' (Moo: *Romans* pp387-390; 'The Law' pp210-211, emphasis his).

Lloyd-Jones: 'I am very ready to agree with the vast majority of commentators who say that it not only means the Mosaic law, but also law in general, law as a principle... There are only two positions; we are either "under law", or else we are "under grace"... The term "law"... obviously means, not the ceremonial law, but the demands of the [so-called] moral law' (Lloyd-Jones: *New* pp182,196; see whole section beginning on his p179).

John Murray: '"Law" in this case must be understood in the general sense of law as law... It is not to be understood in the sense of the Mosaic law *as an economy*... Law must be understood... in... general terms of law as commandment'. Rom. 6:14 is concerned with the bondage of sin. 'Law can do nothing to relieve the bondage of sin. [Rather] it accentuates and confirms that bondage. It is this... feature of the impotency of the law that is particularly in view... The word "grace" sums up everything that *by way of contrast* with law is embraced in the provisions of redemption. Believers have come under all the resources of redeeming and renewing grace which find their epitome in the death and resurrection of Christ. The virtue which ever continues to emanate from the death and resurrection of Christ is operative in them through union with him. All of this the expression "under grace" implies. And, in terms of this passage and of the subject with which it is concerned, there is *an absolute antithesis* between the potency and provisions of law and the potency and provisions of grace. Grace is the sovereign will and power of God coming to expression for the deliverance of men from the servitude of sin' (Murray: *Romans* Vol.1 pp228-229, emphasis mine).

Pink started right: 'Rom. 5 and 6... treat of justification and its consequences', but ruined it when he alleged that Paul's statement: '"You are not under law, but under grace", [signifies] you are under a system of gratuitous justification'. Far from it! By this stage, Paul has clearly moved to sanctification. Pink, however, pushed on, quoting Moses Stuart: 'The contrast is not between the law of Moses and the gospel of Christ, as two economies or dispensations; rather, it is a contest between law and grace as the principles of two methods of justification... "Not under law" [signifies] not keeping the law in order to be saved'. Once again, this is quite wrong. Look at the context! Paul is well into sanctification by this stage. Why – as Pink (and Stuart) surprisingly, but rightly, went on to say: 'Christians are not under the law, as an actual, effectual, adequate means of justification *or sanctification* [emphasis mine], and if they are so, their case is utterly hopeless; for ruin must inevitably ensue'. Quite right, I say. Most odd, then, for Pink to argue: 'In what follows, to the end of the chapter, the apostle shows that though the believer is "*not* under law" as the ground of his justification, nevertheless he *is* under the law as a rule of his Christian life [emphasis his]' (Pink: *Law* pp16-17). How could he get it so wrong – especially seeing he had so clearly understood the apostle's point? Could it be that the system had to be preserved at all costs?

Bruce got Rom. 6:14 right: 'The implication of these words is as astounding for traditional theological ethics as [it was] in the first century. To be under law – not only the law of Moses but the law of God – means to be under the dominion of sin. To be under grace – the grace of God brought near in Christ – is to be liberated simultaneously from the rule of law and the dominion of sin'. Kruse called Rom. 6:14 a 'surprising statement... because it implies that the law is something from which people must be freed in order to escape sin's dominion, rather than something which helps them to escape from it. In Rom. 7:1 – 8:13 Paul picks up this theme again to show that people must indeed be freed from the law to escape sin's dominion' (Bruce: *Paul* p267; Kruse pp205-206). Just so. On the believer and the law, Calvin was precisely180 degrees out.

Edgar H.Andrews: 'Rom. 6:15-19... Sin no longer has dominion over [believers] (Rom. 6:14), and they are now free to obey righteousness. This is the essence of their God-given liberty, and only those who *do* "follow holiness" are truly exercising the liberty that Christ has given them. To use this liberty as an excuse to indulge the [flesh] is, therefore, a contradiction in terms. Any who do so have not understood the meaning of Christian liberty, for liberty and lawlessness are bitter enemies, not companions. The believer's power to reject sin derives from the indwelling Spirit of God' (Edgar H.Andrews p280, emphasis his). And the law of Christ is written on his heart.

Owen on Rom. 6:14: 'The law gives no strength against sin to them that are under it, but grace does. Sin will neither be cast nor kept out of its throne but by a spiritual power and strength in the soul to oppose, conquer and dethrone it. Where it is not conquered it will reign; and conquered it will not be without a mighty prevailing power: this the law will not, cannot, give... God... rules only by the law or by grace, and none can be under both at the same time. In this sense the law was never ordained of God to convey grace or spiritual strength to the souls of men; had it been so, the promise and the gospel had been needless: "If there had been a law given which could have given life, truly righteousness should have been by the law" (Gal. 3:21). If it could have given life or strength, it would have produced righteousness, we should have been justified by it. It exposes sin and condemns it, but gives no strength to oppose it. It is not God's ordinance for the dethroning of sin, nor for the destruction of its dominion'. The law given to Israel on Sinai, Owen observed, administered no spiritual strength or grace; it could only 'judge, curse and condemn... It is not God's ordinance for the dethroning of sin, nor for the destruction of its dominion... There is, therefore, no help to be expected against the dominion of sin from the law. It was never ordained of God to that end; nor does it contain, nor is it communicative of, the grace necessary to that end (Rom. 8:3). Wherefore, those who are "under the law" are under the dominion of sin. "The law is holy", but it cannot make them holy who have made themselves unholy... It... can do them no good, as to their deliverance from the power of sin. God has not appointed it to that end. Sin will never be dethroned by it; it will not give place to the law'.

On the other hand: 'It is otherwise with them that are "under grace". Sin shall not have dominion over them; strength shall be administered to them to dethrone it. "Grace"... as we are here [Rom. 6:14] said to be under it, and as it is opposed to law, it is used or taken for the gospel... To be "under grace" is to have an interest in the gospel covenant and state, with a right to all the privileges and benefits of it, to be brought under the administration of grace by Jesus Christ – to be a true believer... One principal difference between the law and the gospel' is the power or otherwise to defeat the dominion of sin. 'The law guides, directs, commands all things that are against the interest and rule of sin. It judges and condemns... it frightens and terrifies the consciences of those who are under its dominion'.

But if the law is asked what power it can supply against sin, 'here the law is utterly silent'. Indeed, it only adds to the trouble since 'the strength of sin is the law'. The only power is the gospel: 'But the gospel, or the grace of it, is the means and instrument of God for the communication of internal spiritual strength to believers. By it they do receive supplies of the Spirit or aids of grace for the subduing of sin and the destruction of its dominion. By it they may say they can do all things through him that enables them... The law gives no liberty of any kind; it genders to bondage, and so cannot free us from any dominion – not that of sin, for this must be by liberty. But this we have... by the gospel'.

Having spoken of 'our deliverance from the law and its curse' under the gospel, of our translation 'by grace into a state of glorious liberty; for by it the Son makes us free' – freedom by the Spirit, quoting 2 Cor. 3:17 in support, Owen went on to make a most important statement: 'The law does not supply us with effectual motives and encouragements to endeavour the ruin of the dominion of sin in a way of duty; which must be done, or in the end it will prevail'. All the law can do, is to work 'fear and dread... The very promise of it ["do this, and live"] becomes a matter of terror, as including the contrary sentence of death upon our failure in its commands'. Nothing but grief, sadness, discouragement is found by the law, 'no life, activity, cheerfulness or courage... Hence those who engage themselves into opposition to sin, or a relinquishment of its service, merely[1] on the motives of the law, do quickly faint and give over'. Grace, on the other hand, said Owen, is attended with power. Whereas 'Christ is not in the law; he is not proposed in it, not communicated by it' – the gospel reveals Christ; Christ is the great deliverer – 'he alone ruins the kingdom of Satan, whose power is acted in the rule of sin... The like may be spoken of the communication of the Holy Spirit... but we receive this Spirit not "by the works of the law", but "by the hearing of faith" (Gal. 3:2)... The law and its duties... can never destroy the dominion of sin... The internal efficient cause of this liberty... whereby the power and rule of sin is destroyed in us, is the Holy Spirit himself' (Owen: *Treatise* pp542-552,554).

If Owen has not effectively destroyed the Reformed third use of the law to sanctify the believer, then words have lost all meaning.

Rom. 7
Moo on Rom. 7: 'The main topic... is the Mosaic law'. Rom. 7:1-6 'contains the main point that Paul wants to make in this chapter' (Moo: *Romans* pp409-410).

---

[1] I do not know what Owen meant, precisely, by this. The law does play a part in sanctification, in that it serves as a paradigm for godly behaviour, and is part of Scripture, all of which God uses to sanctify his people (John 17:17; 2 Tim. 3:16-17). According to the *Shorter*, one of the meanings of 'merely' since 1601 – a significant date as far as Owen is concerned – is 'actually'.

What of: 'Those who know the law' (Rom. 7:1)? Kruse: 'This expression, taken on its own, could simply refer to people who know about any system of marriage law, but in the context Paul would seem to have in mind the Mosaic law, from which, he argues, believers have been set free. Therefore the expression has significance for discussions about the readership and the purpose of Romans. It is not as helpful to us in this connection as it might first appear, however, because it is susceptible of several interpretations. Within the overall context of Romans, "those who know the law" could refer to (i) Christian Jews (who made up part of the Roman church); (ii) Gentile Christians who had formerly been proselytes; (iii) Gentile Christians who had formerly been loosely attached to the synagogue as God-fearers; (iv) Gentile Christians who had gained an understanding of the law and the Old Testament since they joined the church'. John Murray: 'We are not to regard this ["those who know the law"] as in any way restrictive – [Paul] is not distinguishing between those who know and those who do not. All are credited with this knowledge'. Lloyd-Jones said Paul was writing not only to Jews 'but to all who are Christians... to Jews and Gentiles who had been converted'. Vincent: Paul was addressing 'all Christians, not only Jews but Gentiles who are assumed to be acquainted with the Old Testament'. Moo: 'It is almost certain... that Paul here refers to the Mosaic law, but no implications about the ethnic background of his audience can be derived from the fact' (Kruse p207; Murray: *Romans* Vol.1 p240; Lloyd-Jones: *Law* p15; Vincent Vol.2 p699; Moo: *Romans* p412).

Kruse: 'This analogy [Rom. 7:1-6] and its application constitute one of the clearest expressions of Paul's [doctrine] that Christians (Jews as well as Gentiles) are completely freed from all obligations to the Mosaic law as a regulatory norm. Like a person who has died they have been discharged from all obligations to the law... Underlying this notion of freedom from the law is the assumption that the period of the law has been brought to an end with the coming of Christ'. Moo: 'Paul argues that a person's bondage to the law *must* be severed in order that he or she may be put into a new relationship with Christ... Death severs relationship to the law... but... not only... does Paul... illustrate the general principle that "a death frees one from the law"... he also sets up the theological application... in which severance from the law enables one to enter a new relationship'. John Murray: 'Rom. 7:1-6 is to be connected with what the apostle had stated in Rom. 6:14... In [the] earlier context the statement gives the reason or ground of the assurance that sin will not have dominion over the believer. There is, however, at that point no expansion or validation of the proposition that the believer is not under law... Now at Rom. 7:1, he returns to the question of release from the law and shows how this discharge has come to be'. Bruce: 'Death breaks the marriage bond – and death breaks a man's relation to the law. When Paul applies the analogy, we are conscious of a reversal of the situation; the believer in Christ is compared to the wife, and the law is compared to the husband, but whereas in the illustration it was the husband who died, in the application it is not the law that has died, but the believer; the believer has died with Christ – and yet it is still the believer who, no longer bound to the law, is free to be united with Christ. If, however, we put the matter in simpler terms, we can express Paul's meaning easily enough: as death breaks the bond between a husband and wife, so death – the believer's death-with-Christ – breaks the bond which formerly yoked him to the law, and now he is free to enter into union with Christ. His former association with the law did not help him produce the fruits of righteousness, but these fruits are produced in abundance now that he is united with Christ. Sin and death were the result of his association with the law; righteousness and life are the product of his new association; for (as Paul puts it elsewhere), "the letter kills, but the Spirit gives life" (2 Cor. 3:6)... Such an attitude to the law must have seemed preposterous to many of [Paul's] readers then [adding, somewhat dryly], it has seemed preposterous to many of his readers since' (Kruse pp207-208; Moo: *Romans* pp409,413-414, emphasis mine; Murray: *Romans* Vol.1 p239; Bruce: *Romans* pp144-145). Here we have it. The believer, in Christ, has died to the law so that he can be sanctified. Calvin's third use of the law, however, effectively says that in order to be sanctified, the believer must be re-married to the law – though on easier terms!

Edgar H.Andrews: 'Paul's metaphor [of death] is uncompromising. The believer has not died partially to the law, for death is total. He has not died temporally to the law, for death is final. His relationship to the law has not undergone some subtle change; it has been terminated. The believer's subjection to the law, his obligation to perform its requirements, has been swept away, "through the body of Christ". What does this mean? It means two things. First, the believer is freed from the law through the perfect obedience that Christ yielded to the law during his earthly life. Secondly, he is delivered from the punishment for his law-breaking through the death of Christ on his behalf. Thus the law can no longer make any demands upon the believer, either in respect of obedience, or in respect of punishment for transgression. Those demands have been fully and finally met by the man Christ Jesus. Is the believer, then, without law? Not at all. We are not "without law towards God, but under law towards Christ" (1 Cor. 9:21). The context in which Paul makes this statement makes [it]... clear... that the "law towards Christ", to which Paul did submit, was something other than the law of Moses'. Andrews quoting Denney: 'When the apostle tells us that through the law he has died to the law (Gal. 2:19), or that we have died to the law through the body of Christ (Rom. 7:4), or that we are not under law but under grace (Rom. 6:14)... he means that nothing in the Christian life is explained by anything statutory, and that everything in it is explained by the inspiring power of that death which Christ made all our responsibilities to the law his own' (Edgar H.Andrews pp89,114).

Compare that with this from Brian Edwards: 'In 1 Cor. 9:21, Paul states clearly: "I am not free from God's law but am under Christ's law"... Paul is saying that as a Christian he is to live under the authority of the law of God, but motivated and controlled by Christ's law of love' (Brian Edwards p8). While there is considerable merit in this statement, far more care is needed. The word 'law' appears eight times in two verses. Paul is clearly playing with words to make a point. Commentators, therefore, must show more respect than Edwards showed here for the apostle's nuances. Edwards has made some massive claims. It would have been nice to have a clear definition of his terms, and a biblical substantiation of those claims. I admit that I have drawn this extract from a deliberately simplified presentation of the issues – and I am not patronising when I commend the effort – but there should have been a big health warning to the effect that far more detailed exegesis is required. Although Edwards owned the law is 'a very big issue' over which believers disagree (Brian Edwards p3), nevertheless, as I say, 'Andy' and 'Jane' should have been made to realise that Edwards was attempting the impossible.

John Murray: 'What is this law?... The law... is surely the written law of the Old Testament, particularly the Mosaic law. Paul uses "law" in this sense (Rom. 3:19; 5:13; 1 Cor. 9:8-9; 14:21; Gal. 3:10,19) and there is no need to look for any other denotation [such as the "ceremonial" law] here... The law binds a man as long as he lives, and the implication [better, Paul's teaching] is that when he dies that dominion is dissolved... The writing [in Rom. 7:6] may refer to the two tables of stone on which the ten commandments were written or to the fact of the law as contained in Scripture' (Murray: *Romans* Vol.1 pp240,246).

Bolton was at best hesitant on Rom. 7:1-3, which verses, he could only grudgingly admit, 'seem' – seem? They do! – 'to speak of the abrogation of the law... That the apostle here speaks of the moral law is evident from the seventh verse [of Rom. 7]; and that believers are freed from it, see the sixth verse and others [Rom. 6:14; 8:2; 10:4, Gal. 3:19; 4:4-5; 5:18; 1 Tim. 1:8-10]. There seems, therefore, to be a great deal of strength in the Scripture to prove the abrogation of the law, that we are dead to the law, freed from the law, no more under the law' (Bolton pp52-53). A grudging admission this – but grudging or not, it destroys Calvin's third use of the law – which Bolton wanted so much to defend.

Pink: 'We have been discharged from the law... more accurately' translates Rom. 7:4. Bayes: Rom. 7:4 'is substantially the same point as that made in Rom. 6:14... Older commentators often... understood this to mean that believers are dead to the law as a way of salvation and justification'. He rightly dismissed this, but sadly simply repeated his earlier far-from-adequate statement: 'Paul's main point has been that in the sphere of the flesh the law has a sin-defining function' (Pink: *Law* pp18-19; Bayes p117, who was returning to his 'proof-text', Rom. 6:19). Really! Can Reformed writers not allow Scripture to speak for itself? When a man is bereaved, has his marriage ended in the sense of 'defining' him or something? Is that all?

Let us turn from such half-hearted – and worse – comments, such running away from facts, to Philpot – who got it right: 'The first husband is the law, and the second husband is Christ... Which is to be the rule of the wife's conduct when [she is] re-married; the regulations of the first or of the second husband?... When he [the first husband] is dead, have not all his rules and regulations [over her] died with him? And is his wife not entirely liberated from his control? If he is dead to her, she is equally dead to him. All his authority over her has ceased. And what should we think... of a wife who, instead of seeking to please her present husband, was always referring to the rules and regulations of her former partner...?' Philpot graphically contrasted the two husbands – the law and Christ. The first was 'extremely harsh, [having] ruled [the woman] as with a rod of iron, always keeping her in bondage and terror... a cruel tyrant... Her second husband [is] a most affectionate and loving spouse... Is not the rule of love, as the rule of the second marriage, in every respect superior to the rule of command, which was the rule of the first?... The apostle has so clearly and beautifully opened up the subject... in Rom. 7:1-4... [that] I wish that you might read this portion... in the light of the Spirit, and then you would see how thoroughly dead the believer is to the law, both as a covenant and a rule, by virtue of his union to [Christ]'. Gadsby: 'I am inclined to think that if any woman who has married a second husband were to be told that she must be under her first husband's laws, both she and her husband would treat such an assertion with contempt' (Philpot: 'Three' pp92-93; *Dead* pp22-23; Gadsby: *Works* p19).

Striking the right note on Rom. 7:4-6, Fee: 'In keeping with the argument of Gal. 5:13-24, both the law and the flesh belong to the past, on the pre-Christ, pre-Spirit side of eschatological realities. The death of Christ and the gift of the Spirit have ended *torah* observance. [To say] that "the law" to which believers have died is merely "the law's condemnation"... is to miss the eschatological and covenantal character of much of this language as well as to read into the text something neither Paul says nor implies' (Fee: *Empowering* p504). Just so! Did he have anybody in mind, do you think?

Moo quoted Calvin's view – 'delivered from the law insofar as it has power to condemn' – which has become 'virtually the "orthodox" view in Reformed theology'. Moo drew attention to Rom. 5 – 8 where 'Paul focuses not so much on the condemnation that comes when the law is disobeyed... as [overwhelmingly!] on the failure of the law to deal with the problem of sin. [Linking] the inability of the law' (Rom. 8:3), the stimulation the law gives 'sin in the person who is "bound" to it' (Rom. 7:4-6), the law's production of sin (Rom. 7:5,8), and its making the sin-problem worse (Rom. 7:9-11,13), Moo went on: 'This suggests [too weak] that, as in Rom. 6:14, Paul in Rom. 7:4 is viewing the law as a "power" of the "old age" to which the person apart from Christ is bound. The underlying conception is again salvation-historical, as is suggested by the "letter"/"Spirit" contrast in Rom. 7:6. Just as, then, the believer "dies to sin" in order to "live for God" (Rom. 6), so he or she is "put to death to the law" in order to be joined to Christ. Both images depict the transfer of the believer from the old realm to the new. As long as sin "reigns", God and righteousness cannot; and neither, as long as law "reigns", can Christ and the Spirit... In being released from the law... the believer is, naturally, freed from the condemning power of the law. But we introduce categories that are foreign to Paul – at least at this point – by distinguishing

456

between the law in its condemning power and the law as a "rule of life"'. Moo issued a necessary warning: From this verse we cannot conclude 'that the law can play no role at all in the life of the believer' (Moo: *Romans* pp414-416). Quite. I, myself, have never said it. Rather, I keep saying the opposite! What is more, let us stop worrying about what the apostle *did not* say, and concentrate on what he *did* say. The believer has died to the law! *Died* to it! The law no longer rules him. What does *this* say about Calvin's third use of the law?

Lloyd-Jones on Rom. 7:6: '"We have been delivered from the law". This is a very strong word... Some translate it as "discharged", "set at liberty", "set free". We are no longer under the law; we have had a complete discharge from it'. Speaking of every believer, Lloyd-Jones continued, the law 'has no authority over him any longer; he has finished with' it. The question is, of course, 'in what sense has the Christian been delivered from the law?' First of all, 'the law which held us could not justify us, as we were told back in [Rom. 3:20]. We are freed from that'. So far, so good; all are agreed. Then, and of the utmost significance, he took up the issue over which the Reformed clash with Scripture: 'But the point about which the apostle is most concerned here is that we are delivered from the inability of the law to sanctify us. While we were under the law we could never be sanctified. The law can no more sanctify us than it can justify us. While we were held there we could not be joined to the one who can sanctify us as well as justify us. We had no freedom; but now we have been delivered. Now there is the possibility of sanctification. If I can get out of the clutches, as it were, of that first husband, and be joined to another, there is hope for me. There was no hope while I was under the law; but now I am set free. I am delivered from my inability to experience sanctification. This what the apostle is particularly concerned to emphasise'.

I break off. Lloyd Jones then had a most intriguing passage: 'But [Paul was] concerned also to emphasise something further... namely, the work of the law in aggravating and inflaming our sins'. 'The law of God always leads to death... the law of God leads to sin; it aggravates it, it inflames [it]... it always produces death'. But, as he said earlier: 'We have been set free from this tendency of the law to aggravate our problem... we have now been delivered from the law' (Lloyd-Jones: *Law* pp85-87,287-294). In this paragraph, note Lloyd-Jones' use of 'our' – 'the work of the law in aggravating and inflaming our sins'. Was he being a little lax here – or was he being precise? Rom. 7:5,7-11 does not refer to the regenerate. Paul, there, was speaking of his pre-regenerate days. The law did not produce sin in him; no, it is good and spiritual (Rom. 7:13-16). But sin used the law to arouse sinful desire in him. It was sin – not the law – which was the cause of the trouble. See Kruse p212. But did Lloyd-Jones deliberately use 'our' – speaking of believers? If so, then in one stroke he has obliterated Calvin's third use of the law. The law produces holiness in the believer (Calvin). The law arouses sin in the believer (Lloyd-Jones)! In any case, let us not forget what Lloyd-Jones said in the previous paragraph: 'We are delivered from the inability of the law to sanctify us. While we were under the law we could never be sanctified'. If that does not sound the death knell for the Reformer's third use of the law, what does?

Sadly, those who advocate the biblical position on Rom. 5 – 8 are often dismissed as antinomians. When preaching Rom. 8:15, Lloyd-Jones met the accusation head-on: 'You are surely inciting people to sin by speaking in this way'. He had his reply ready: 'I am quite happy about such a charge, for it is the charge that was brought against Paul...True preaching of the gospel in its fullness always exposes itself to the charge of antinomianism'. Gadsby: 'If any poor sinner, who has felt the authority of the law in his conscience and has been condemned by it, and who knows by experience that the letter kills, that the law works wrath, who has been led by the Spirit to the fountain open for sin and uncleanness, and has had the blood of sprinkling applied to his guilty conscience, and thereby has been brought to rejoice in Christ Jesus, know that his sins are forgiven, and his iniquities blotted out; who has entered into Christ as his rest, and has been enabled by the

Spirit to drink of the water of life, and has felt the precious bond of love, which has united Christ as his head and him together, cast out fear, and helped him to say with the inspired apostle: "I, through the law, am dead to the law, that I might live unto God: I am crucified with Christ, nevertheless I live; yet not I, but Christ lives in me" (Gal. 2:19-20); and again: "But now we are delivered from the law, that being dead wherein we were held, that we should serve in newness of spirit, and not in the oldness of the letter" (Rom. 7:6); I say, should any of this class venture to prove that the believer is dead to Moses, his first husband, and married to Christ; that he is ruled by the precious laws [*sic*] of Christ, his second husband, and thereby vindicate the honour of his dear head, who has redeemed him, and saved him, and made him free; the best character that [legal critics]... can give such a man, is a "pulpit libertine"' (Lloyd-Jones: *Sons* p228; Gadsby: *Works* pp6-7).

And now for an incredible contribution by a Reformed writer. Bayes thought that Paul was] 'beginning a new section' in Rom. 7:5. He further proposed 'a rather [very!] different translation of Rom. 7:6' to argue that Paul was not saying believers 'have been delivered from the law', the law of God, the law of Moses, but that they have been delivered from another law altogether; namely, 'from the law of sin, which is the law taken possession of by sin'. Bayes also made very significant changes to the text of Rom. 8:3, concluding that those who 'speak in terms of the Christian life as maintained and controlled by the Holy Spirit in contrast with life under the commandments of Moses [are mistaken]. Paul's distinction... is emphatically not between the Spirit and the law, but between the Spirit and the letter, which are seen as two antithetical approaches to the law. It is not as if the law has no further relevance for the Christian believer [of course not!]: it is the law as letter, as a mere piece of writing viewed in independence from the Spirit which is old and obsolete, and which, according to Rom. 2:29, never was of any value. [It is only] in the sphere of the flesh [where this matters]. However, in the sphere of the Spirit... the law is taken up by the Spirit to be the definition [of?] and empowering for authentic Christian experience'. This falls so far short of that which Paul actually wrote, it is staggering. Indeed, it is diametrically opposed to what Paul said! 'We have been delivered from the law', declared Paul. Of this law, Bayes himself had said: 'Paul uses the word *nomos* (law) consistently throughout Romans... [It] refers to the law of God, the law of Moses... the law of God' (Bayes pp88,118-119). If Bayes' defence of the Reformed position depends on such exegesis as he set out here, not much need be said.

Bunyan took an inadequate view: 'Once [these husbands][2] are become dead to you,[3] as they then most certainly will when you close with the Lord Jesus Christ, then I say, your former husbands have no more to meddle with you, you are freed from their law... The sum then of what has been said is this, the Christian now has nothing more to do with the law, as it thunders and burns on Sinai, or as it binds the conscience to wrath and displeasure of God for sin; for from its thus appearing, it is freed by faith in Christ. Yet it is to have regard thereto, and is to count it holy, just and good' (Bunyan: *Christian* p536). Why not let Paul tell us what he told us – and leave it at that?

Boston: 'If you have a saving interest in Christ's death, you are dead with him to the law also... (Gal. 2:19-20)... Our Lord Jesus took on our nature to satisfy the law therein; the whole course of his life was a course of obedience to it, for life and salvation to us; and he suffered, to satisfy it in what of that kind it had to demand, for that effect. In a word, he was born to the law, he lived to the law, and he died to the law; namely, for to clear accounts with it, to satisfy it fully and get life and salvation for us with its good leave. He was "made under the law, to redeem them that were under the law" (Gal. 4:4-5). And when once it fell

---

[2] For some reason Bunyan introduced the plural to say the believer has died to his former husbands, namely, 'sin and... righteousness which is of the law'.

[3] Why not stick with the biblical expression? The believer has died to the law!

upon him, it never left exacting of him, till it had got the utmost farthing,[4] and he was quite free with it, as dead to it (Rom. 7:4). In token whereof, he got up the bond, blotted it out, yes, rent it in pieces, nailing it to his cross (Col. 2:14). Now, Christ became dead to it, dying to it in his death on the cross: so that the holiness and righteousness of the man Christ did thereafter no more run in the channel in which it had run before, namely, from the womb to his grave – that is to say, it was no more, and shall be no more for ever, obedience performed to the law for life and salvation[5] – these having been completely gained and secured, by the obedience he gave it from the womb to the grave'.

Christ died to the law, and believers died to the law, says the Scriptures; believers died with Christ to the law 'as a covenant of works', said Boston, but not as the rule of sanctification. In other words, in effect the believer has *not* died to it! Even so, Boston went on to argue, perfectly soundly: 'Your obedience will run in another channel than it did before your union with Christ, even in the channel of the gospel. You serve in newness of spirit, in faith and love'. Excellent. How strange then to read this from Boston: 'The frowns of a merciful Father will be a terror to you, to fright you from sin'. Boston offered no verse in support. Then he contradicted himself: 'Love and gratitude will prompt you to obedience... You will not continue to serve in the oldness of the letter, as before; at what [which?] time the law was the spring of all the obedience you performed... you being alive to the law, and dead to Christ (Rom. 7:6)... If by faith you wholly rely on Christ's righteousness, the holiness of his nature, the righteousness of his life, and his satisfaction for sin, how is it possible but [that] you must be dead to the law? for the law is not of faith (Gal. 3:12)' (Boston: *Beauties* pp524-526). So which is it? Is the believer under the law or the gospel for sanctification? Is he moved to sanctification out of terror, or out of love and gratitude?

Amazingly, from Rom. 7 of all places, Rushdooney tried to claim that the regenerate 'are now alive to the law' (Rushdooney p736), a noteworthy example of contemporary theological-alchemy!

Let us get back to what Scripture actually says. Moo: 'The antithesis is not between the *misunderstanding* or *misuse* of the law and the Spirit, nor even, at least basically, between the outer demand and the inner disposition to obey, but between the old covenant and the new, the old age and the new... The believer, released from bondage to the law, can [better, will] serve in the new condition created by God's Spirit, a condition that brings life (2 Cor. 3:6) and fruit pleasing to God (Rom. 6:22-23)' (Moo: *Romans* pp421-422, emphasis mine).

And, finally, a splendid contribution from Lloyd-Jones: 'Let me put it plainly and clearly. The apostle teaches here that it was essential we should be married to [Christ]; because until we are married to him we shall never bear this fruit. We were married to the law, but the law was impotent; it could not bring forth children (fruit) out of us. But we are now married to one who has the strength and the virility and the potency to produce children even out of us. It is his strength that matters... Here is the real purpose of the marriage; we need one whose seed is so powerful, who can so impregnate us with his own holy nature that he will produce holiness even in us. That is why we are married to him, in order that "we should bring forth fruit unto God". His strength is so great, his might is so potent, that even out of us he can bear this progeny of holiness... This therefore is the apostle's argument. He says in effect: You had to be delivered from your marriage to the law before you could produce this fruit. You had to die to that law, that old marriage had to be

---

[4] At the time, the smallest British coin. In the US, the equivalent would be the mill, 0.001 of a dollar.

[5] Note the gloss. If one is dead to the law, one is dead to it – not dead to it merely in certain respects and for certain purposes. Because of his theological system, Boston was limiting his otherwise excellent statement to justification – when, clearly, the scripture he quoted (Rom. 7:4) comes from a passage dealing with sanctification.

dissolved, in order that you might be married to this mighty one who can produce the fruit in you. And he says it has happened. The central object of salvation is holiness. I would not hesitate to assert that it is sinful to say that you can stop at justification even temporarily, or say that a man can be justified and not sanctified. It is impossible... You cannot stop at justification... The whole object, the whole movement of salvation is to make us holy. So from the moment we are joined to him the process begins. From the moment of the marriage and the union... his power begins to work... and... we are already bringing forth something of this fruit, which is "holiness unto God"' (Lloyd-Jones: *Law* pp66-67).

What a superb elaboration of the apostle's words! Lloyd-Jones was hitting the bull's eye time and again in Romans. And there's more to come. Read on! I must say I do hope Lloyd-Jones' 'appreciators' are keeping up!

Rom. 8

Moo on Rom. 8:1-4: 'The combination "therefore, now" is an emphatic one, marking what follows as a significant conclusion... These verses pick up various themes from chapters 6 – 7 to restate the reassuring message of Rom. 5:12-21... The "now" alludes to the new era of salvation history inaugurated by Christ's death and resurrection'. Kruse: 'Those who are in Christ are freed from the condemnation of the law, and have become recipients of the Spirit (Rom. 8:9)... Justification and new life in the Spirit might be able to be separated in discussion; they cannot be separated in experience'. Fee: 'At issue throughout is not the problem of forgiveness, *i.e.*, of dealing with "sins", but with the tyrannical nature of indwelling sin' (Moo: *Romans* p472; Kruse p216; Fee: *Empowering* p529). In other words, sanctification.

Fee on 'the ungrammatical nature' of the opening verses of Rom. 8: It 'is most likely due to two factors. [It was] Paul's concern over *torah* – as ineffective and therefore now obsolete – which caused him to start with this matter; and his tendency, when referring to the work of Christ, to make it the central focus... [But] *torah*'s time is past, because... of what Christ has done to... sin and the flesh, and... its purpose is now fulfilled by the Spirit... The concern is once more with *torah* – as obsolete... The law, a good thing in itself, was ill-equipped to take on the flesh (*cf.* Rom. 7:14); in fact, the law was left in a weakened state by the flesh, meaning that in the matter of sin our "flesh" was stronger than *torah*; indeed the flesh proved *torah* helpless, thus "weakened". What the law was incapable of doing, of course, in its "weakened condition" was to deal with the problem of indwelling sin, which issues in death. This failure of *torah*... leads to the central focus of the sentence: Christ as God's way of effectively dealing with both sins and the flesh... In rendering *torah* obsolete and ineffectively dealing with sin, Christ has opened the way for the Spirit to "fulfil" the very purpose for which *torah* existed but which it was unable to provide: righteousness. Thus... primarily through the work of Christ, but in the last instance through the ongoing work of the Spirit – God has brought the time of the law to an end, the very point of Rom. 7:1-6. Even though one may recognise *torah* for what it is, God's good and holy thing, its ineffectiveness with regard to sin has finally rendered it basically finished; it is now "the *oldness* of the letter", replaced through the effective work of Christ by "the *newness* of the Spirit"... All of the "sin" and "flesh" language in this passage is directly attributable to Paul's singular concern, the intended contrast between *what Christ did* and *what the law was incapable of doing* – namely, dealing effectively with sin and the flesh... The Spirit himself fulfils *torah* by replacing it, and he does so by enabling God's people to "fulfil" the "whole of *torah*"... In bringing the time of *torah* to an end, God did not thereby eliminate its purpose, but through the Spirit has brought that very purpose to fruition. After all, Paul does not say that *torah* is now "obeyed" or "kept" or "done" – the ordinary language for *torah* observance – but that what *torah* requires is now "fulfilled" *in us*... As in Gal. 5:14, the Spirit is regarded as the "fulfilment" of the goal or aim of *torah*, namely, to bring about righteousness. Thus *torah* is here described in language reminiscent of Rom. 7:12. *Torah* was not evil; on the contrary, it was good, holy and righteous. But it proved ineffective to bring about the righteousness that it called for. Hence the reason for the coming of the Spirit, to effect, that is to "fulfil", the righteousness that *torah* called for but could not produce. But what is being fulfilled is not "*torah* observance"... The "righteous requirement" of *torah* turns out to have little or nothing to do with "observance". It has everything to do with being conformed unto the likeness of Christ (Rom. 8:29), and having one's mind renewed (by the Spirit) so as to know and live in ways that are good and pleasing to God (Rom. 12:1-2). Thus, when Paul comes to the particulars in Rom. 12:1 – 15:13, "the righteous requirement" of *torah* takes the form of love of neighbour – which "fulfils *torah*" (Rom. 13:8) – or "righteousness, peace, and joy in the Holy Spirit" – which have nothing to do with food laws as such (Rom. 14:17)' (Fee: *Empowering* pp528-537, emphasis his).

McClain: 'In Rom. 8:1-4... we are told that there can be no condemnation to them which are in Christ Jesus. The reason for this exemption is found in our freedom from the law, which in fallen man could only stimulate sin and finally bring death. What the law could not do, God in Christ did for us at Calvary, when he made an offering for sin. The moral result of this way of saving men is that the righteousness of the law is "fulfilled in us". The verb is passive, not active in form. "It is not our doing, though done in us"' (McClain p77, quoting Denny).

Although I included some of this in the extracts on Galatians (to make full sense to what Andrews was saying at that time), Edgar H.Andrews, on 'the "fulfilment" of the law in the life of the believer', declared: 'Paul's proposition is not that believers do the law, but that "the righteous requirements of the law is fulfilled in us" (Rom. 8:4). The distinction is important... The apostle's teaching on Christian liberty was frequently misunderstood. Because he proclaimed that "Christ is the end of the law for righteousness" (Rom. 10:4), he was accused of preaching lawlessness and encouraging sin (Rom. 3:8; 6:15). This remains a common source of controversy today... How do we acquire practical righteousness? How does the believer, justified as he is through the work of Christ, live out his life in a manner pleasing to God? Some teach that, for the believer to honour God, his practical life must be regulated by [what they call] the moral elements of the law of Moses; in other words, the ten commandments must be his "rule of life"... Paul's attitude to the law... is very clear. Its purpose is never to justify, nor to help a man please God in lesser ways'. Nor can it sanctify: 'Gal. 5:14... Rom. 8:3-4... The righteousness requirement of the law is actually satisfied, or "fulfilled", in the lives of those who "walk according to the Spirit" or are "led by the Spirit" (Rom. 8:14)... In a pragmatic sense, the righteous requirement of the law is fulfilled in the believer. The believer, led by the Spirit, does bear fruit in harmony with the law in terms of practical righteous living' (Edgar H.Andrews pp283-287).

Now for some important technical details. The word 'law' appears four times in Rom. 8:1-4. Paul spoke of 'the law of the Spirit of life', 'the law of sin and death', 'the law', and 'the righteous requirement of the law'. The first law, 'the law of the Spirit of life' is a liberating law – it 'has made me free' (Rom. 8:2). This is not the law of Moses! It is the gospel. As Moo stated: 'Throughout his letters, and not least in Romans, Paul pictures the Mosaic law as ranged on the opposite side [to] the Spirit, righteousness and life'. This phrase, the *law* of the Spirit, 'suggests' [to weak!] 'an intentional play on the word [*law*], as Paul... contrasts the *law* of Moses [the second *law* of the verse, the *law* of sin and death] with... the "*law* of the Spirit who confers life"... The Spirit... is God's Spirit, coming to the believer with power and authority, who brings liberation from the powers of the old age, and from the condemnation that is the lot of all who are imprisoned by those powers'. The third use of 'law' (Rom. 8:3), *nomos*, 'is now clearly the Mosaic law', and the fourth use, 'the righteous requirement of the law' (Rom. 8:4), speaks of 'the righteousness demanded by the law... God's law... Old Testament laws'. Kruse: '"The law of the Spirit of life" [is] the liberating power of the Spirit' (Moo: *Romans* pp474-482, emphasis mine; Kruse p217).

461

One of the main sticking points is the second law, 'the law of sin and death' (Rom. 8:2). Clearly, in the above, Moo regarded the second law as the law of Moses. This is my view also. Others are not so sure. Kruse thought 'the law of sin and death' is 'the dominion of sin'. Bruce: 'Perhaps it is the dominion or dictate of sin, which in [Rom. 6] is personified as the slave-master'. In Rom. 7:25, '"the law of sin" and the law of God are set in sharp contrast. [But] "the law of sin" could be an aspect of the law of God'. But how can the law of God be called 'the law of sin and death'? Can it be called such? 'Yes, in so far as it stimulates sin and passes sentence on the sinner'. Now for some more from Moo. Slightly drawing back from his remarks in the previous extract, Moo thought taking 'the law of sin and death' as the Mosaic law 'fits both the context and Paul's theology', [he] slightly [preferred] "the binding authority of sin that leads to death"' (Kruse p217; Bruce: *Romans* p272; Moo: *Romans* p476). I remain convinced that the second law is the Mosaic law.

Lloyd-Jones got close, but dropped in to the Aquinas-Reformed mode. Commenting on 'the law of sin and death' (Rom. 8:2), he said: 'It means the moral law of God,[6] and especially the law that God had given through Moses in the ten commandments'. No! It is the law of Moses, full stop. This includes the ten commandments, yes, but as we have seen, apart from very obvious and very few exceptions, 'the law' in Romans means at least the Mosaic law in its entirety; certainly not the ten commandments only. As Lloyd-Jones himself went on: 'It is "the law" about which he has been writing from the beginning of this letter... The law condemns [Rom. 3:19]... the law is always the great cause of condemnation [Rom. 4:15; 5:20-21; 7:13; 1 Cor. 15:56; 2 Cor. 3:7,9]... The law of God leads to sin [Rom. 7:7-12]... The law... always produces death [Rom. 7:13-25]... What is it that has set me free from the law? The answer is: "The law of the Spirit of life in Christ Jesus"... [which is] obviously the opposite of the law of God... We as Christians are no longer in the position in which we were before we became Christians; since we are "in Christ Jesus" our whole position has been changed... We were "under law", we were under the rules and the reign and the power of the law. But now we are in an entirely different position... the opposite of being "under the law"... What has set me free from the law of sin and death? It is the grace of God in Christ Jesus... the gospel... the opposite to the "law" is "grace", and "the reign of grace" is contrasted with "the reign of sin"... The principle, or the ministration, or the covenant, of the Spirit of life in Christ Jesus freed me from the law of sin and death. In other words, the apostle is saying that we are under a new covenant now, under a new testament; there is a new principle or power reigning over us and in us. The gospel has set us free, we are under "the law of liberty"... by the Holy Spirit... The gospel has freed us, and the gospel frees us through the Spirit... Before it was the "power of the law" that was the chief power in us, and led us to sin and to captivity, to defeat and death. Now, we have been set free and delivered from all that; we are in a new realm... We are not "under law", we are "under grace"... We have nothing to do with the law from the standpoint of salvation now; we have finished with it; we are dead to it' (Lloyd-Jones: *Law* pp285-293).

Let me comment on this from Lloyd-Jones. With the caveat I raised, absolutely superb. Indeed, even with the caveat – perhaps, *especially* with it (he was confining his remarks to the ten commandments, remember) – he was shattering Calvin's third use of the law. I do hope all 'devotees' of Lloyd-Jones (not excluding his publishers) remember what he said here. His books are bought by the thousand. Are they read by the thousand? As for those who do read him, do his words affect their view of the law, the believer and sanctification?

Thielman, commenting on Romans, said: 'The "law of sin and death" must be the Mosaic law, since Paul's references to the Mosaic law in the preceding paragraphs have... linked it

---

[6] Very interesting! Allowing it to stand, it deals the death knell to the Reformed gloss which says the believer is free from the ceremonial law but under the moral law as a rule of life. That law, said Lloyd-Jones, is the law that leads to death!

consistently with sin and death. From this law, Paul says, believers have been "set free", an echo of his claim in Rom. 7:3 that the believer "is free from the law". Their freedom from the Mosaic law has been secured by "the law of the Spirit of life in Christ Jesus", an echo of Paul's claim in Rom. 7:4-6 that the believer's death to the law "through the body of Christ" means that "we serve in the newness of the Spirit, not in the oldness of the letter". This new law, then, is both the believer's unity with Christ's death, and the work of the Spirit in the believer's life. It is reminiscent of the "law of faith" in Rom. 3:27, which God also instituted through the death of Christ (Rom. 3:25), and with which he replaced the Mosaic law... Through this "law of the Spirit of life in Christ Jesus" (Rom. 8:2), believers can now fulfil God's law, a law that is, however, different from [to] the Mosaic law' (Thielman pp27-28). Remembering Thielman's background, what a magnificent testimony to the truth!

On: 'What the law could not do in that it was weak through the flesh, God did by sending his own Son... that the righteous requirement of the law might be fulfilled in us' (Rom. 8:3-4) – 'fulfilled'! – Barcellos, in part: This means 'those living in conformity to the requirements of the law by the work of Christ wrought by the Spirit in them'. Kruse: 'The fulfilment of the law in believers is... not achieved because they are continuously careful to observe its many stipulations'. He was almost right to go on: 'Rather, it is fulfilled in them as they walk according to the Spirit, and as by the Spirit they put to death the deeds of the flesh (Rom. 8:13)'. Better, Moo: 'God not only provides in Christ the full completion of the law's demands for the believer, but he also sends the Spirit into the hearts of believers to empower a new obedience to his demands' (Barcellos p44; Kruse p219; Moo: *Romans* pp481-485).

It is never said of believers that they 'do', *poiein*, the law; they – and only they – 'fulfil', *plērouv*, it (see Edgar H.Andrews p286).

Now for another massive pronouncement by Lloyd-Jones: 'The righteousness of the law is fulfilled in us in two ways. The righteousness of Christ is "imputed" to us; but, thank God, the righteousness of Christ is also "imparted" to us... The second is the process of sanctification... Paul's argument everywhere... is not merely that we are no longer guilty... [but] the apostle rejoices that we are now able to bring forth fruit unto God – that is, positive righteousness... The apostle is saying here that the law could not deliver me from the guilt and condemnation it pronounced upon me; *but still more important*, that it could not give me positive righteousness... But, thank God, "the law of the Spirit of life in Christ Jesus" has given it me. I am "in Christ" and because of that I walk "not after the flesh", but "after the Spirit". I am no longer walking under the law; I am no longer "under the law"; I am "under grace"... First and foremost this means our justification, and that we are "clothed with the righteousness of Jesus Christ". *But again I insist*... that we must not stop at that point, as some of the great commentators do... Christ has fully satisfied the demands of the law... and because all this has happened in and through Christ there is no more that the law can do to us who are "in Christ". Christ has exhausted all the possibilities of the law with respect to us, he is "the end of the law". So the law can say nothing to me, and, as far as the believer is concerned, is powerless... the law is eliminated... the law is taken away... The law having been removed, Christ having fulfilled it in every way, I am free to be married to [Christ]; I am married to him. His power is now in me delivering me... Thus is the righteousness of the law fulfilled in me. We do not stop at justification, we go further. The moment the Christian is "in Christ" sanctification has begun... The learned commentators with whom I am disagreeing are at great pains elsewhere to say that you must never separate justification and sanctification, yet they themselves separate them here... The law could never save us... We are in a state [by nature] in which we have to be set free from "the law of sin and death"... That having been done, we can be united to [Christ] and the power of his life. And the Spirit that was in him is in us, and thus the righteousness of the law is fulfilled in us' (Lloyd-Jones: *Law* pp304-306,337,339-342, emphasis mine).

In the above, note the words I have stressed: 'But still more important... but again I insist', *and what follows*! And let me get rid of his euphemisms. Let me not mince words. Lloyd-Jones was exploding the Reformed view of sanctification by the law. 'The great commentators... the learned commentators', of course, are the leading Reformed men. I say it again. I hope that all who 'follow' Lloyd-Jones will either answer him – refute and disown him here – or else submit their thinking to Scripture, abandon 'the great and learned commentators' on this issue, come out into the open, and start arguing for the biblical view of the law, the believer and sanctification.

So, in light of all this, how do the Reformed cope with Rom. 8:1-4? Bayes, for instance, stuck valiantly to his last: 'Here, then, we have a declaration of the ongoing relevance of the law to the believer. The believing life, it appears, is not a life in which the law has no place; rather through the Spirit, the law acquires a new power towards the believer's sanctification' (Bayes p102).

How did Bayes manage to arrive at a conclusion which so obviously turns Scripture on its head? First, he altered the translation of the text of Rom. 8:3. Let me try to simplify the very complicated argument which this involves. I do so by drawing attention to his changes. This is how he translated the verse: 'For this *being* the law's inability *while it used to be* weak *in the sphere of* the flesh...'. These are very important changes from the accepted reading, and they significantly alter the meaning of the text. How? They introduce a time element where none exists. The law *used to be* weak, according to Bayes, but, he implied, it is no longer weak. Quite the opposite, he thought! Under the gospel Christ has given it strength to play a vital role, a powerful role, in the life of the believer; I might say, an all-powerful role. These are large issues. Are the textual changes – on which they are based – justified? The argument is, as I say, complicated. Significantly, however, Bayes had to confess that at almost all of the 'seven grammatical points' of his proposed translation, he was taking a line different to 'most' commentators. At various points he admitted he was at variance with the 'common understanding of the construction'; 'parting company from [*sic*] most modern commentators', though keeping company with 'the Greek Fathers'; 'most modern commentators prefer' something different; 'it does not seem inappropriate to argue that this particular use might be a unique exception'; 'the fact that the patristic authors could [take my (Bayes') line] must count against the absolute conclusiveness of otherwise normal biblical usage'; 'I am proposing... [whereas] most commentators prefer...'; 'I am reading it as... [but] the significance [of this]... is largely overlooked by commentators... It seems to me... the only commentator whom I have read who appears to do any justice at all to the imperfect tense [that is, who agrees with me, Bayes,] is Karl Barth... although I would not wish to endorse [Barth's] statement as precisely as Barth means it'; 'this is often translated [in such a way]... [but] I have arrived at my proposed translation...' (Bayes pp84-87). In this sophisticated way, the plain teaching of the apostle is turned on its head. I, for my part, will stick with the almost-universally held text. Besides, both the immediate context of Rom. 5 – 8, and the analogy of faith, support the usual translation against that proposed by Bayes. And the context is always king!

Let me end this section with this simple, but telling, summary of its teaching by H.Cockrell: 'In chapters 6, 7 and 8 of his letter to the Romans, Paul makes three statements concerning the believer's relationship to the law: "not under the law" (Rom. 6:14); "dead to the law" (Rom. 7:4); "free from the law" (Rom. 8:2)... A new position... a new partner... a new power' (Cockrell: 'Relationship' p116). Simple! No sophistication! Scriptural!

Rom. 10
Moo: In Rom. 10:4-6, '*nomos* almost certainly refers the Mosaic law'. Better, omit the 'almost'; there is no doubt about it. 'The context here shows that *nomos* must mean what it consistently does in Paul; the Mosaic law, the *torah*'. Moo listed three possible meanings of

the word 'end', *telos*: 'termination' in a temporal sense; 'goal' or 'purpose'; and 'result' (Moo: 'Galatians' p26; 'The Law' p207; *Romans* p638). Further: 'Christ is the end of the law, so that there might be righteousness available to everyone who believes... The... most important issue is the meaning to be given to the word *telos*... It is necessary to use several English words, or a phrase, to capture the meaning of this word in this kind of context. Looking at other occurrences of this word in Paul... and in light of his broader theology, we would argue that Christ being the *telos* of the law means that he is the point of culmination for the Mosaic law (note the TNIV rendering: "Christ is the culmination of the law"). He is its "goal", in the sense that the law has always anticipated and looked forward to Christ. But he is also its "end" in that his fulfilment of the law brings to an end that period of time when it was a key element in the plan of God. Both ideas are clearly present in the context'. 'Rom. 10:4, therefore, presents elements of both continuity and discontinuity. Christ is that to which the law has been pointing; now that he has come, a whole new situation with respect to the place of the law in the life of the people of God exists... This interpretation of Rom. 10:4 results in a meaning quite similar to our conclusions on Matt. 5:17' (Moo: 'Galatians' pp26-27).

Calvin: In Rom. 10:5, Paul was 'comparing the law and the gospel'. 'Do you see how [Paul] makes this the distinction between law and gospel: that the former attributes righteousness to works, the latter bestows free righteousness apart from works? This is an important passage, and one that can extricate us from many difficulties if we understand that the righteousness which is given us through the gospel has been freed from all conditions of the law. Here is the reason why [Paul] so often opposes the promise to the law, as things mutually contradictory'. 'Therefore, in the promises of the gospel there must be something distinct and different [to the promises in the law], unless we would admit that the comparison [which Paul makes] is inept. But what sort of difference will this be, other than that the gospel promises are free and dependent solely upon God's mercy, while the promises of the law depend upon the condition of works?' 'Paul unequivocally teaches that the law, in commanding, profits nothing (compare Rom. 8:3). For there is no [sinner]... who can fulfil it'. Calvin got it wrong when he alleged that 'the gospel has not succeeded the whole law in such a sense as to introduce a different method of salvation'. Justification under the law was by works; under the gospel, it is by faith. And Calvin ruined all when he said: 'When the whole law is spoken of, the gospel only differs from it in respect of clearness of manifestation'. The gospel is better than the law only because it is clearer? Really? True, though, the gospel 'confirms the law, and proves that everything which it promised is fulfilled' (Calvin: 'Appendix' pp104-106; *Institutes* Vol.1 pp366-367).

Charles Hodge: 'Christ has abolished the law... by fulfilling it. He has abolished the law as a rule of justification... The whole Mosaic economy having met its completion in him, has by him been brought to an end... When Christ came, the old legal system was abolished, and a new era commenced... His coming and work put an end to its authority, we are no longer under the law, but under grace... It is because Christ is the fulfiller of the law, that he is the end of it... Christ... by fulfilling abolishes the law... Christ is the end of the law... In him all [its] demands are satisfied'. Calvin's editor: 'The end of the law is its fulfilment, the performance of what it requires in order to attain life: and Christ in this respect is its end, having rendered to it perfect obedience. This... meaning is most consistent with the words which follow, and with the apostle's argument' (Charles Hodge: *Romans* pp336,343; Calvin: *Commentaries* Vol.19 Part 2 pp383-384).

Haldane, however: 'From the moment a man believes in [Christ] the end of the law is attained in that man; that is, it is fulfilled in him, and he is in possession of that righteousness which the law requires... Christ... by his obedience has fulfilled the law in every form that men have been under it, that his obedience or righteousness might be imputed as their righteousness to all who believe'. While this undoubtedly is a truth, it is not the truth which Paul was teaching here. He did not say that 'the possession of righteousness' is the end of the law; he said Christ is. For Haldane's view to be right, as John Murray observed, Paul should have said 'the end (or purpose) of the law is Christ'. This, however, would have made the construction 'awkward if not impossible' (Haldane: *Romans* pp502-503; Murray: *Romans* Vol.2 p49).

Daniel Fuller preferred 'goal [or] completion [rather than] termination'. As did Bayes; if it is 'termination [then] this verse becomes a negative indicator for the ongoing status of the law' (Daniel Fuller xi and pp84-85; Bayes pp119-123); that is, if Rom. 10:4 is read as 'termination', it will militate against Calvin's third use of the law, which he, Bayes, was defending. A most interesting comment – in light of the following extract!

John Murray: 'There are... objections to this ["fulfilled"]... Though the word "end" can express aim or purpose, preponderantly, and particularly in Paul, it means termination, denoting a terminal point... In this letter, and in the context, the antithesis is between the righteousness of the law as that of works, and God's righteousness as the righteousness of faith... The view most consistent with this context is, therefore, that the apostle is speaking in verse 4 of the law as a way of righteousness before God and affirming the relation that Christ sustains to this conception. The only relation that Christ sustains to it is that he terminates it... "to every one who believes"'. Kruse agreed: The law 'now that Christ has come... has no role now in establishing righteousness' (Murray: *Romans* Vol.2 pp49-50; Kruse p229).

Moo: 'These considerations require that *telos* [adopts] a temporal nuance: with the coming of Christ the authority of the law of Moses is, in some basic sense, at an end'. The idea of 'goal' is also present – like a race, the tape marks not only the finish, but also the goal. The whole point of the race is to get to the tape. In short: 'Christ is the "end" of the law (he brings its era to a close) and its "goal" (he is what the law anticipated and pointed towards)... As Christ consummates one era of salvation history, so he inaugurates a new one... We see in this key verse [Rom. 10:4]... elements of both continuity and discontinuity. Christ is that to which the law has been pointing; now that he has come, a whole new situation with respect to the place of the law in the life of the people of God exists'. Christ has not ended all law for the believer; 'nor is [Paul] saying that the Mosaic law is no longer part of God's revelation or of no more use to the believer. The Mosaic law, like all of Scripture, is "profitable" for the believer (2 Tim. 3:16) and must continue to be read, pondered, and responded to by the faithful believer'. But, at the same time, 'our relationship with God is now found in Christ, not through the law; and our day-to-day behaviour is to be guided primarily by the teaching of Christ and his apostles rather than by the law. On the other hand, Jesus and Paul also caution us against severing Christ from the law. For he is its fulfilment and consummation, and he cannot be understood or appreciated unless he is seen in light of the preparatory period of which the law was the centre' (Moo: *Romans* pp638-643; 'The Law' pp207-208).

See 'blossom' extract from Edgar H.Andrews on pp416,498.

On Rom. 10:4, Bruce: 'It is plain that Paul believed and taught that the law had been in a major sense abrogated by Christ. "Christ is the end of the law", he wrote, "that every one who has faith may be justified". The age of the law, which was never designed to be other than a parenthesis in God's dealing with mankind (Gal. 3:19; Rom. 5:20a), had been superseded by the new age, which might variously be called the "age of Christ", with reference to Christ's reigning at the right hand of God (1 Cor. 15:25, quoting Ps. 110:1), or "the age of the Spirit", with reference to the Spirit's presence with the people of Christ on earth as a pledge of their eternal inheritance in the resurrection life (Rom. 8:10ff)... Now, as he [Paul] learned, "Christ is the end of the law, that everyone who has faith may be justified" (Rom. 10:2-4). The affirmation that "Christ is the end of the law" has been variously understood. The word "end" (*telos*) can mean "goal" or "terminus", and here it probably means both. Christ, for Paul, was the goal of the law in the sense that the law was a temporary provision introduced by God until the coming of Abraham's offspring in whom the promise made to Abraham was consummated; the law, in other words, "was our custodian until Christ came, that we might be justified by faith" (Gal. 3:19,24). But Christ was also, for that reason, the terminus of the law: if, as Paul says, the law was a temporary provision, the coming of Christ meant that the period of its validity was now at an end. Some of Paul's interpreters have tried to modify the starkness of this statement; others have tried to sharpen it, or at least to extend its scope... But what he is concerned with in his statement that "Christ is the end of the law" is the place of the law in man's approach to God; the *prima facie* meaning of the statement is: now that Christ has come, there is no more place for law in man's approach to God. To the thinking of many, this is a hard saying, which lies open to the charge of antinomianism – a charge which Paul met and rebutted in his own day [as in Rom. 3:8; 6:1ff]... In the Reformed tradition derived from Geneva, it has been frequently said that, while the man in Christ is not under law as a means of salvation, he remains under it as a rule of life [Calvin: *Institutes*, 2.7.12-15]... It should not be imagined that [this] has Pauline authority. According to Paul, the believer is *not* under law as a rule of life – unless one thinks of the law of love, and that is a completely different kind of law, fulfilled not by obedience to a code but by the outworking of an inward power. When Paul says: "Sin will have no dominion over you, since you are not under law but under grace" (Rom. 6:14), it is the ongoing course of the Christian life that he has in view, not simply the initial justification by faith – as is plain from the point of the antinomian retort which Paul immediately quotes: "What then? Are we to sin because we are not under law but under grace?" (Rom. 6:15). Again, it is sometimes said that Christ is the end of the ceremonial law (including not only the sacrificial cultus but circumcision and the observance of the sacred calendar) but not the moral law [Calvin: *Institutes* 2.7.17]... Once more... [this claim] has no place in Pauline exegesis. It has to be read into Paul, for it is not a distinction that Paul himself makes' (Bruce: *Paul* pp262-266. See also Bruce: *Romans* pp56,203). An excellent summary, this, including the law's eschatological place in salvation history.

Summary of 'the law' in Romans

Thielman: 'Paul believed that the Mosaic law, although in itself good, was closely allied with sin. It both revealed sin (Rom. 3:20; 7:7) and was used by sin to increase rebellion against God (Rom. 5:20; 6:14; 7:5,8,11). Christ's death and God's Spirit, however, have released the believer from this deadly alliance between the law and sin (Rom. 7:4-6; 8:2), and have brought the era of the Mosaic law to its divinely appointed close (Rom. 9:30 – 10:13)... All this means that the believer no longer looks directly to the Mosaic law for ethical guidance, but instead relies on God's renewal of the mind, and on the teachings of Jesus for direction (Rom. 12:1-2; 13:8-10; 14:1 – 15:13; Jer. 31:33-34). Since the teachings of Jesus include elements of the Mosaic law, some continuity between the two exists (Rom. 13:8-10; *cf.* 15:4). Nevertheless, believers have been released from the law (Rom. 7:4-6), its entanglement with sin (Rom. 6:14-15; 7:5,7-25; 8:2), its now obsolete ethnic boundaries (Rom. 2:28-29; 3:28-30; 4:16-17; 10:5-13), and its penultimate provisions for atonement (Rom. 3:25-26; 12:1). It is therefore impossible to say that the Mosaic law, as it was commonly understood in Paul's time, supplies the substance of his moral vision' (Thielman pp33-34).

In addition to the above, Arndt and Gingrich; Barcellos pp45,65; Bayes pp81-83; Brown: *Discourses* Vol.1 pp167-170; W.D.Davies p26; Friesen pp98-110; Friedmann pp82,84-85; Kautz pp113-114; Kevan: *Experience* pp33-34; Kingdon pp83-84; Klassen: *Neither* pp28-36; 'Radical' pp138-146; Kruse pp163-169,202,207-208,212,218,226-228; Laicus; Lloyd-Jones: *New*; *Law*; *Final* p331; Moo: *Romans*; Murray: *Romans*; Stuart Murray pp186-205; Philips pp235-237; Plumer: *Romans* p504; Reymond: *Paul* pp475-476; Rushdoony pp2-3; Sattler pp250-252; Shaw p199; Thayer; Tow pp29-31; Verduin: *Anatomy* pp184-188;

Williams: *Radical* p832; *Spiritual* pp80,113,127; Witherington p327; George Wright pp236-238; Zaspel pp155-159; Zens: *Studies* p63.

CHAPTER 11: THE BIBLICAL CASE
2 CORINTHIANS 3

N.T.Wright: 'Though most of the discussion of Paul and the *torah* focuses inevitably, and rightly, on Romans and Galatians, one can be easily lulled by this into thinking that the task is more or less complete when those two letters are dealt with. But 2 Corinthians, a noble and remarkable writing worthy of close consideration in itself, and not merely as a footnote to other letters, raises in its third chapter, though from a different angle, several of the central issues' in connection with the believer and the law (N.T.Wright p175).

On the chicken and the egg – see chapter 11 for my use of the conundrum in establishing which came first, the glory or the change of covenant – N.T.Wright observed: 'It is not difficult to assess Paul's purpose in 2 Cor. 3:7-11. He wishes to argue that his ministry possesses *doxa*, glory... to counter any suggestion that an itinerant preacher with a poor speaking style and a prison record is not fit to be an apostle of the Lord of glory. He argues, not by means of demonstration ("what I mean by glory is *x*: you can see that I possess *x* because...") but, in the first instance, with an *a fortiori*: the ministry of the old covenant had *doxa*, so that of the new must have even more. He makes this point in the different ways:
(a) verses 7-8: the ministry of the old covenant was that of the "letter", written on stone, and was an administering [administration, dispensation – even though the latter word was rejected by Wright] of death (Paul is obviously picking up the themes of verses 3,6); that of the new is of the life-giving Spirit. We may compare Rom. 8:10; 1 Cor. 15:45. (b) verse 9, explaining this (*gar*): the ministry of the old covenant was one of condemnation... that of the new in one of justification. This point is then amplified in verse 10: it is as though, by comparison, the old has come to have no glory at all. (c) verse 11, offering further explanation (*ei gar*): the old covenant was destined to be abolished; the new is destined to remain. Thus, if Paul's readers acknowledge that he is a minister of the new covenant, they must see that his ministry possesses *doxa*, however surprising that may be' (N.T.Wright pp177-178).

As I noted at the start of chapter 11, I have referred to 2 Cor. 3 in several places throughout my book. As a result, the relevant extracts appear at various places also. But I now repeat one which seems particularly pertinent to what I say in chapter 11. On 2 Cor. 3:7-18, Kruse: 'Paul had occasion to compare and contrast the glory of the apostolic ministry with that of Moses... Here Paul compares and contrasts the ministries of the old and new covenants... [He] was contrasting the lesser splendour of the ministry of the law to the greater splendour of the ministry of the gospel'. Sibbes, in his 'considerable volume' on 2 Cor. 3:17-18, spoke of three 'distinct properties and prerogatives of the gospel in which it excels the law, [following which,] by inferences drawn from these properties... the apostle more largely illustrates the transcendent glory of the gospel, and how far it exceeds the glory of the law' (Kruse pp151-153,155; Sibbes: *Excellency* pp202-205). Sibbes worked this out over the next 100 pages or so.

Kring on 2 Cor. 3:7-11: 'The main point of these verses is... very clear. The old covenant had a definite glory. [But] the new covenant is superior and therefore the glory of the new covenant is greater that that of the old... Paul... proceeds to present a series of three arguments from the lesser to the greater (verses 7-8,9-10,11). If the old-covenant ministry had glory, then the new covenant *must* exceed it in glory... First... the old covenant was a ministry of death... Second... the old covenant was a ministry... of condemnation... Third... the temporary duration of the old covenant'. The old covenant, Paul contrasts with 'the ministry of the Spirit... the new covenant, which brings justification... The new covenant remains. It is permanent... The conclusion' that the new covenant is more glorious than the old 'is inevitable'. Among Kring's 'points for reflection', he rightly saw an application 'in the realm of sanctification'. How are believers 'transformed?... Our preaching must be Christocentric. We must determine to know nothing but Jesus Christ and him crucified.

From the law of Moses and the prophets and the Psalms, from the Gospels, the Acts, and the letters, to the book of Revelation, we must preach him who is the very image of the invisible God, so that unveiled new-covenant believers will be transformed more and more into the same likeness!' (Kring pp105-106,111,113-114, emphasis his. See the entire article Kring pp99-115).

CHAPTER 12: THE BIBLICAL CASE
PHILIPPIANS 3:2-12

Calvin: 'There is an elegant play upon words. [The Judaisers] boasted that they were the circumcision; [the apostle] turns aside this boasting by calling them the concision; that is, those who rend and divide the church, inasmuch as they tore asunder the unity of the church' (Calvin: *Commentaries* Vol.21 Part 2 p87).

Phil. 3:10 and on
Thayer on 'know', *ginōschein*: The word 'denotes a discriminating apprehension... a knowledge grounded on personal experience'.

In the following extracts, I draw attention to the way in which Reformed commentators, without exception, state that Paul is speaking of justification *and* sanctification. Notice how all these commentators, without exception, ascribe sanctification to Christ. Notice, finally, that all these commentators, though elsewhere they might argue for sanctification by the law, when they come to explain the apostle's words, rightly make no mention whatsoever of the law for sanctification.

Calvin: Paul 'points out the efficacy and nature of faith – that it is the knowledge of Christ, and that, too, not bare or indistinct, but in such a manner that the power of his resurrection is felt... But as it is not enough to know Christ as crucified and raised up from the dead, unless you experience, also, the fruit of this, he speaks expressly of efficacy or power. Christ therefore is rightly known when we feel how powerful his death and resurrection are, and how efficacious they are in us... Having spoken of that freely-conferred righteousness, which was procured for us through the resurrection of Christ, and is obtained by us through faith, he proceeds to treat of the exercises of the pious, and that in order that it might not seem as though he introduced an inactive faith, which produces no effects in the life. He also intimates, indirectly, that these are the exercises in which the Lord would have his people employ themselves; while the false apostles pressed forward upon them the useless elements of ceremonies'.

I pause. Calvin was, of course, perfectly right to state that the Judaisers wanted the Philippians to be circumcised – a rite, or ceremony. But we must not get misled by Calvin's words. As Paul says, you cannot pick and mix, you cannot stop at circumcision: 'I testify... to every man who becomes circumcised that he is a debtor to keep the whole law' (Gal. 5:3). The false apostles were majoring on circumcision, true, but the point is Paul does not say that believers must go under the law apart from circumcision – which he could not say, in any case – since no man has the right to play fast and loose with God's law. No. His point is, believers should not go under the law, full stop. As Calvin himself observed: 'I confess, indeed that Paul there [Gal. 3:13; 5:1-4] treats of ceremonies, because he was [as here in Philippians] contending with false apostles who were plotting to bring back into the... church those ancient shadows of the law which were abolished by the advent of Christ. But, in discussing this question, it was necessary to introduce higher matters, on which the whole controversy turns' (Calvin: *Institutes* Vol.2 p132).

Quite! The higher matter in question is, of course, the law. Sadly, as I showed in the extracts on Reformed escape routes, Calvin dropped back into his usual misguided vein on the law, but, even so, he hit the nail right on the head here. Circumcision may have been the little local difficulty; the real issue is the law.

To let Calvin go on: 'Christ crucified is set before us that we may follow him through tribulations and distresses; and hence the resurrection of the dead is expressly made mention of that we may know that we must die before we live. This is a continual subject of meditation to believers as long as they sojourn in this world' (Calvin: *Commentaries* Vol.21

Part 2 pp98-99). As I have observed, Calvin was clearly speaking of sanctification – with no mention of the law! Hmm!

Hendriksen: 'When God justifies his child, he also sends forth his sanctifying Spirit into the heart. Hence, from the divine side, the link between righteousness imputed and righteousness imparted is the Holy Spirit; from the human side – ever dependent on the divine – the link is the gratitude of faith. Now "that I may know him" refers to a knowledge not only of the mind but also of the heart... The apostle... wants to gain as full an understanding of Christ's person and love as possible. He is not satisfied with anything short of perfection. When he expresses his yearning to know Christ, he has in mind not only or even mainly the learning of certain facts about Christ, but also and especially the sharing of certain experiences with him, as clearly indicated by the rest of [Phil. 3:10-11]. He wishes to be entirely "wrapped up" in Christ, so that Jesus will be "all the world" to him... He longs for an ever-increasing supply of the power that proceeds from the risen and exalted Saviour... It was that same resurrected Christ who sent his Spirit into Paul's heart for the purpose of sanctification. Christ's life in heaven is ever the cause of Paul's new life (John 14:19). Paul desires a growing supply of this cleansing power, this dynamite that destroys sin and makes room for personal holiness and for effective witness-bearing' (Hendriksen: *Philippians* pp167-168). As above, Hendriksen was clearly speaking of sanctification – with no mention of the law! Hmm!

Robert Johnstone: 'As regards deliverance from guilt, when "Jesus was delivered for our offences, and was raised again for our justification", we so died in him, in the sight of God, that the law has no longer any claim upon us for punishment; and so we rose in him, as to pass out into the sphere of full blessed acceptance with God, and adoption into his family. As regards sanctification, we live though the fellowship of Christ's life; and yet at the same time, being in a wicked world, we have "a fellowship of his sufferings, being fashioned after the likeness of his death"... Vital religion impels to ardent longing and persistent effort after progress in holiness... The power of the gospel when received by faith... [gains] commanding influence over the nature [disposition]... Progress is the law [the principle] of the new life... The goal before the apostle's mind, in speaking of the persistent spiritual efforts of his life, [is] perfect conformity in everything to the will of God, to the image of Christ... Let us "abide in Christ", remembering that he "is made of God to us" no less our "sanctification" than our justifying "righteousness"... We shall hear our Saviour's voice behind us, saying: "This is the way, walk in it"; and we shall have grace given to walk therein' (Johnstone: *Philippians* pp271,284-286,305). As above, Johnstone was clearly speaking of sanctification – with no mention of the law! Hmm!

Daille: 'The apostle... goes on to recount the excellent fruits of this righteousness of God which he possessed in Christ, saying, "that I may know him, and the power of his resurrection"... It appears that the apostle, having spoken sufficiently of our righteousness in Christ, these words more properly relate to the efficacy of his resurrection for our sanctification... In this our day, is not our doctrine misunderstood and calumniated...? Do they [Papists (and other Judaisers)] not say: "Since you are justified by faith alone, what inducement have you to perform good works? But, O adversaries, it is to perform good works that I am justified"'.

I pause. Daille was right. We are justified in order to be sanctified (and eventually glorified) (Rom. 8:30; Eph. 1:4; 2:8-10; 4:1,24; Col. 3:10; Tit. 2:14). A true sense of our justification – not the law – is the motive and spur for our sanctification. To let Daille go on: 'This divine righteousness of Christ has been communicated to me in order that I may be transformed into his image; that I may know the power of his resurrection, and that I may be like him, a new creature; that I may love God, not to lay him under obligation to me... but to acquit myself in a small degree of the immense debt I owe him. I love him because he has loved me... Behold, then, the two principal fruits of our justification by Christ Jesus, deeply to feel and experience. First, the power of his resurrection. And secondly, the fellowship of his sufferings, being made conformable unto his death. This is the path by which God conducts us to the third and highest point of all happiness; it being very [*sic*] certain that if we suffer and die with Christ, we shall live and reign with him... Such, my brethren, is the gain which the apostle found in Christ. First, he obtained a perfect and assured salvation, a righteousness of God by faith of Jesus Christ. Secondly, a blessed and happy experience of the power of the resurrection of his Lord. And, thirdly, the glorious fellowship of his sufferings, in order to attain at last to the resurrection and eternal life... Let us then, dear brethren, seek to receive this divine power in our hearts. Let us attentively contemplate this beautiful and glorious life, which he has placed before our eyes by rising from grave... and in which is everything that can be desired to render us perfectly happy. And having seen so beautiful an object, how could we have any affection for the trifles of earth? O unhappy earth, where time and death consume all things, none but Christ my Saviour has escaped your vanities... Let us not fear, then, to travel that road wherein his footsteps can be traced. Let us be partakers, not with patience merely, but with joy, of his sufferings and of his death. Let us believe that these sufferings, and this death, will add to our glory and happiness, since they render us conformable to the Son of God, and conduct us to the enjoyment of his immortality' (Daille pp200-205). As above, Daille was clearly speaking of sanctification – with no mention of the law! Hmm!

Henry: 'The apostle was as ambitious of being sanctified as he was of being justified. He was as desirous to know the power of Christ's resurrection killing sin in him, and raising him up to newness of life, as he was to receive the benefit of Christ's death and resurrection in justification... That he might be conformable unto him, and this also is meant of his sanctification... Observe... whence our grace comes – from our being apprehended of Christ Jesus. It is not our laying hold of Christ first, but his laying hold of us, which is our happiness and salvation... not our keeping hold of Christ, but his keeping hold of us... It is of great use in the Christian course to keep our eye upon heaven. This is proper to give us measures in all our service, and to quicken us every step we take... Eternal life... is in Christ Jesus; through his hand it must come to us, and is procured for us by him. There is no getting to heaven as our home but by Christ as our way'. As above, Henry was clearly speaking of sanctification – with no mention of the law! Hmm!

Poole: 'As consequent... [Paul] here insists upon sanctification... Being found in [Christ], after justification and sanctification, he doubts not to be glorified... for which end, or for this purpose, to be perfectly sanctified and glorified at the resurrection... he eyed Christ... "Let us walk by the same rule"... the unerring word of God, exemplified in the condescending love of Christ, whom he had proposed to their imitation, in whom he was found, and the fellowship of whose sufferings he desired to know more perfectly, being heavenly-minded, in opposition to those who became enemies to his cross... The rule of faith, love and a Christian life, or heavenly conversation, which he elsewhere calls a walking in the Spirit, and according to the Spirit in opposition to walking in and after the flesh (Rom. 8:1,5; Gal. 5:16)...' (Poole pp698-699). Note those last two passages! As above, Poole was clearly speaking of sanctification – with no mention of the law! Hmm!

Reader, what now of Calvin's third use of the law for sanctification?

On 'law' in 1 Tim. 1:5, Kent: 'The Greek word in question 'is never used in the New Testament to refer to the Old Testament law'. Hendriksen rightly saw the verse as a reference to the 'charge to the church': 'The charge is in reality the sum and substance of *all* Christian admonition... Love is the fulfilment of the law (both tables, Mark 12:30,31) as well as the essence of the gospel. Hence what is stated in the present passage is in exact harmony with... Gal. 5:6... It is best to understand the commandment as the obligations which are upon believers as a result of the gospel. These obligations are viewed as a single entity because they are the practical obligation arising from the gospel... Timothy's conduct is to be in such harmony with the standard in the gospel that he will be spotless and blameless' (Kent pp83,202-203; Hendriksen: *I & II Timothy* p61).

On 1 Tim. 1:8-9, Vincent: 'The nature of the proper use of the law – [its] use according to its design – is indicated by the next clause'; that is, 'the law is not made for a righteous person, but for the lawless and insubordinate'. Who is this lawless person? He is one 'departing from the law, a violator of the law, lawless, wicked... godless' (Vincent Vol.2 p1016; Thayer; Arndt and Gingrich). Kent: That 'law is not [made] for a righteous man must mean the member of the church. For a Christian to be called "righteous" is to say he is justified (exactly the same word in Greek)... (Rom. 5:19; 8:33). Hence the impropriety of applying the law to Christians is obvious. The believer has died to the law's demands in the person of his substitute, Christ ("the end of the law [for righteousness] to everyone who believes", Rom. 10:4). To bring the law into the church at Ephesus as a guide[1] for Christians, was to miss the purpose of the law. It was not designed to form motives of integrity. Christians have something far better: [the grace of] the Holy Spirit who continually guides from within... The fact that the Mosaic law was intended not for the righteous ones but for sinners is in accord with (*kata*, verse 11) the gospel message' (Kent pp86-88). And, of course, the law of Christ is written in the believer's heart.

Moo was not strong enough: It 'probably means that the law is not binding on Christians' (Moo: 'The Law' p216). It certainly is not!

Kruse: 'The mistake which the false teachers were making evidently was that they were continuing to lay upon their hearers certain demands of the Mosaic law... The law, though good, was not intended to be used in that way... for those in Christ... but only for "the lawless and disobedient"' (Kruse p266). The point is: the Judaisers were totally out of order because believers *per se* are not under the law (Rom. 6:14-15; 7:4-6; Gal. 2:19; 3:25).

Hendriksen was woefully inadequate, glossing the text with both hands. While he agreed 'the law' here is 'the Mosaic law', he ruined this by trying to say that Paul was really speaking about 'the law... buried under a load of "traditions" which nullify its very purpose... or when it is used as a "take-off" point for spell-binders about ancestors'. And as for the 'righteous man', Hendriksen did not agree Paul was referring to the justified man, the believer. Paul, according to Hendriksen, meant the *self*-righteous, those who 'considered themselves to be good by nature... "righteous" in their own eyes [who] consider themselves to be' righteous. Furthermore, Hendriksen did not consider that justification is in view at all: 'It certainly seems very probable that we are here in the moral, not in the forensic realm... "Righteous" is best understood as the opposite of "'lawless, insubordinate, impious, unholy, profane...'" all of which terms have to do with sins in the moral-spiritual realm'. Vincent agreed: '"Righteous"' does not here mean 'in the Pauline

---

[1] I do not altogether agree with this way of expressing it. The law *is* a part of the believer's guide since it is an integral part of Scripture and therefore comes under the remit of 2 Tim. 3:16-17. What Paul did *not* do was to bring the law into the church at Ephesus as 'the (perfect) rule'.

sense of justified by faith'. Rather, it means 'morally upright... "righteous"' is the opposite of 'the lawless and insubordinate... the ungodly and... sinners'. However, when commenting on the verses which close the passage, 1 Tim. 1:10-11; namely, 'sound doctrine, according to the glorious gospel of the blessed God', Vincent rightly declared: 'It is not denied that Christ is the source of true righteousness... According to Paul, the man who is not under the law is the man who lives by faith in Christ. Paul emphasises this. It is faith in Christ which sets one free from the law. Here, the man for whom the law is not made (verse 9) is the man who is ethically conformed to the norm of sound teaching... The sound teaching is according to the gospel... The connection is with the whole foregoing statement about the law and its application (verse 9ff.) [Paul] substantiates what he has just said about the law, by a reference to the gospel' (Hendriksen: *I & II Timothy* pp64-65; Vincent Vol.2 p1017). In other words, Vincent would seem to have shown where and how he was wrong in his earlier comment.

Not surprisingly, Poole glossed 'the law': 'By "the law" is to be understood the [so-called] moral law [that is, the ten commandments], (though possibly not excluding the law of Moses, consisting in many ordinances)'. Then he got it right: 'By the "righteous man" [is to be understood] one in whom a principle of divine grace is planted, and, from the knowledge and love of God, chooses the things that are pleasing to him, and is ardent and active to do his will... It is evident that it [that is, the law] is directed to the wicked'. But then he ruined all by adding this glaring gloss to the apostle's words: 'The law was not made for a righteous man, *as to its condemning office*'. As Poole himself had said earlier, the law 'is good to men when it is used for the end to which God gave it'. Pink agreed with Poole's last comment, adding these words: 'The apostle contrasts the design of the law as it respected believers and unbelievers' (Poole p774, emphasis mine; Pink: *Law* p24).

Barcellos was ambivalent on the 'righteous man'. On the one hand, he could agree that the righteous are those who are 'seeking to conform to the law', and go even further and say '"the righteous person" is anyone in external conformity to the law, whether Christian or non-Christian... These "righteous" ones are those who conform to the law... A "righteous person... is already conforming to it'. Yet he could also agree that 'the "righteous" are... those living in conformity to the requirements of the law by the work of Christ wrought by the Spirit in them', citing Rom. 8:4. So, which is it? A respectable man or a true believer? Reymond also wanted it both ways: 'The law is not "made" for the "righteous"... that is, the obedient man who is already moulding his life in accordance with it. Of course, in saying this, Paul is not denying the law's relevance for Christians' (Barcellos pp43-44; Reymond p477). As for that last from Reymond, neither am I. But nor am I saying, as Reymond did, the law is 'the norm or standard of the Christian life' (Reymond: *Paul* p476). I find Reymond's assertion utterly incomprehensible in light of the New Testament. Is this a *gospel* minister speaking? I can hear Moses saying the equivalent for the Jews, but...!

Rushdooney paid but scant attention to the verse. In over 800 pages of his massive *Institutes* on the law, he mentioned the verses only twice; once when quoting Luther, and the other to speak about homosexuality. Not once did he actually get to grips with the words. And what he said was this – indeed he baldly asserted: 'The law is... the law for Christian man and Christian society' (Rushdooney pp9,21,256). Astonishing! The apostle said precisely the opposite. Why do these men bother with Paul? Why not write a book just giving us their own preconceptions? And what is a Christian society?

Fee got it right: 'It is clear that Paul's intent here is not to argue for a correct, Christian, use of the law. Rather, he is pointing out the folly of the false teachers, including the fact that they use the law at all... Paul reflects a point made earlier in Galatians, that those who have the Spirit and bear its fruit have entered a sphere of existence in which the law no longer performs it legal functions (Gal. 5:22-23)' (Fee: *1 & 2 Timothy* p45). As I said a few moments ago, believers *per se* are not under the law (Rom. 6:14-15; 7:4-6; Gal. 2:19; 3:25).

CHAPTER 14: THE BIBLICAL CASE
HEBREWS

John Brown aptly noted the 'beautiful contrast between the... "letter that kills", the ministration of condemnation and death – and the salvation, the revelation of mercy, the ministration of justification and life'. Plumer: 'It is right [for] us to follow the Scriptures and distinguish between the Mosaic and the Christian dispensations. Many and great errors proceed from a neglect to do this' (Brown: *Hebrews* p75; Plumer: *Hebrews* p85).

On Heb. 8:13, based upon the quotation from Jeremiah, Brown observed that the inspired writer 'draws an inference from the language in which the prophet speaks of the new covenant, as to the abrogation of the Sinaitic covenant. The terming of this order of things *new*, implies the former order was become *old – antiquated*; for why have a new covenant, if the original one can serve the purpose? The *new* covenant has been introduced. The former is now *old*; and, as *old*, is about to vanish away' (Brown: *Hebrews* p374, emphasis his).

On Heb. 10:1, as Plumer observed: 'In this verse, shadow and image are *directly opposed* to each other'. Owen: 'There is a great difference between the shadow of good things to come, and the good things themselves actually exhibited and granted unto the church. This is the fundamental difference between the two testaments, the law and the gospel, from whence all others do arise, and (into which) they are resolved' (Plumer: *Hebrews* p386, emphasis mine; Owen: *Hebrews* Vol.4 Part 1 p429).

Thielman: 'Nothing could be clearer from the argument of Hebrews than that the author believed the Mosaic law to be obsolete. Its obsolescence is revealed supremely in its inability to accomplish what Christ's death had effected... The entire law is obsolete, moreover, not simply the portion of the law that regulates the priesthood and the sacrifices. It is true that the author uses the term "law" (*nomos*) principally to refer to these sections of the Pentateuch, but he also provides unequivocal hints that his argument takes the entire Sinaitic covenant into its sweep. In Heb. 9:15-22, he makes the term "first covenant" synonymous with "every commandment spoken by Moses according to the law" (Heb. 9:19). Similarly, in Heb. 10:28, the law – whose penalties for disobedience have been superseded by greater penalties in the new covenant – is the entire "law of Moses" (*cf.* Heb. 2:2-3). This is confirmed by the author's understanding of sabbath celebration in terms of participation in the eschatological rest of God (Heb. 4:3-11).[1] The entire Mosaic covenant, therefore, and not merely a part of it, has been superseded by the new covenant: the change in priesthood has required not merely a change in some laws pertaining to the priesthood, but a different law entirely (Heb. 7:12)... For the author of Hebrews, therefore, the Mosaic law occupies a firmly fixed place within Christian theology; but it is firmly fixed in both the positive and negative sense of that expression. It stands as the immoveable framework upon which Christian understanding of the person and work of Christ hangs. But it can never become the edifice itself. Without it, the death of Christ is only the crucifixion of a man named Jesus outside the walls of Jerusalem, who, like any other crucified man of his time, did not want to die. With it, Jesus' death represents the consummation of the redemptive purposes of God – the final goal for which the patriarch, matriarch, lawgiver, prophet and sage eagerly hoped. If the Mosaic law is allowed to rise out of its firmly fixed place and move into a position of prominence, the result is disaster. Those who allow this to happen, says the author, are trampling the Son of God underfoot, considering the blood of the covenant unclean, and insulting the Spirit of grace (Heb. 10:29). On the basis of the Mosaic law itself, they can only expect the most severe judgement (Heb. 10:28-31)'

---

[1] I hope Thielman was including in this the believer's present rest in Christ – not reserving it all for eternity.

(Thielman pp131-132). With the hope expressed in my note, another masterly statement by Thielman.

In addition to the above, Geoff Adams pp87-94; Gay: *Battle*; *Infant*; Hoch pp70-71,73.

katargeō: 'To cause to cease, to put an end to, to do away with, annul, abolish, to make invalid'. *exaleiphō*: 'To wipe off, wipe away, obliterate, erase, blot out, remove, destroy'. *entolē* is used of 'the commandments of the Mosaic law, that which God prescribed in the law of Moses, particular precepts as distinguished from the body or sum of the law'. *nomos* refers to 'the Mosaic law – the volume or its contents'. *dogma* means 'the rules and requirements of the law of Moses' (Thayer; Arndt and Gingrich).

Bolton: 'By the "handwriting of ordinances", I conceive is not meant the ceremonial law alone, but the moral law also... We can here observe the successive steps which the apostle sets out. "He has blotted out". But lest this should not be enough, lest any should say, It is not so blotted out, but [that] it may [still] be read, the apostle adds, "he took it out of the way". But lest even this should not be enough, lest some should say: "Yes, but it will be found again and set against us afresh", he adds, "nailing it to his cross". He has torn it to pieces, never to be put together again for ever' (Bolton pp31-32). First-rate! But Bolton put a fly in the ointment – adding his own gloss; namely, 'so far as it was against us and bound us over to the curse'. Bolton simply failed to get the point the apostle was making! Or, did he get it, but simply had to trim (that is, expand!) the apostle to make him fit his system?

Let's get back to Paul! Lloyd-Jones on Rom. 7: 'What law is this?... [Some] say that this is a reference only to the law as given through Moses... Some even go further and say that it refers to the ceremonial part of [the Mosaic] law alone, and to nothing else... It would be quite unprofitable to spend time in refuting these false expositions. [What Paul said] is true of the Mosaic law, certainly, but not only of the Mosaic law... [Paul] is referring, of course [please note], to the written moral law that was given through Moses to the children of Israel. They referred to it as the "writing" because God wrote it on the tables of stone which he gave to Moses' (Lloyd-Jones: *Law* pp15,92). I must say, I like Lloyd-Jones' 'of course', although I wish he had not introduced the unnecessary 'moral law'. Nevertheless, bearing in mind what the Reformed mean by it, I am rather glad he did, and I find I now like Lloyd-Jones' 'of course' very much indeed! Do the Reformed?

Kruse: In the Ephesian passage, 'Paul says that it is the law of Moses itself which gives rise to the dividing wall of hostility between Jews and Gentiles... Christ made peace between Jews and Gentiles by destroying the dividing wall (that is, the hostility), and by abolishing the law of commandments [expressed – Kruse's addition] in ordinances which gave rise to the hostility' (Kruse pp263-264).

Zaspel: 'It is the Mosaic legislation in its entirety and the decalogue specifically that Paul said "fades away" (*katargesas*, 2 Cor. 3:11; *cf. exaleipsas*, Col. 2:14)... [Ex. 34:27-28 is a passage] of critical significance... where God identifies "the ten commandments" as "the words of the covenant". No dividing of Moses will fit here'. Nor anywhere else! 'The legislation of Sinai is an inseparable unit, and this statement (Ex. 34:27-28) must inform the apostolic declaration of its abolition. It is the Mosaic code as a whole and in all its parts that has passed away, and the apostolic declarations to that end must therefore be seen to embrace even the decalogue... "The whole law" stands or falls together as an indivisible unit. It would be wrong to forget this stated, essential unity of the old covenant/decalogue when reading New Testament statements of the covenant's/law's abolition... The statements are as broad and inclusive as they appear' (Zaspel pp154-155). 'It would be wrong to forget this...', I agree, but that is precisely what the Reformed do when they force Scripture to support their system. In fact, they more than 'forget' the apostolic statements; they gloss them to make them say the opposite!

On 2 Cor. 3:7-18, Kruse: 'Paul had occasion to compare and contrast the glory of the apostolic ministry with that of Moses... Here Paul compares and contrasts the ministries of the old and new covenants... [He] was contrasting the lesser splendour of the ministry of the law to the greater splendour of the ministry of the gospel'. Sibbes, in his 'considerable volume' on 2 Cor. 3:17-18, spoke of three 'distinct properties and prerogatives of the gospel in which it excels the law, [following which,] by inferences drawn from these properties... the apostle more largely illustrates the transcendent glory of the gospel, and how far it exceeds the glory of the law' (Kruse pp151-153,155; Sibbes: *Excellency* pp202-205). Sibbes worked this out over the next 100 pages or so.

On Eph. 2:14-15, Vincent: 'The enmity was the result and working of the law regarded as a separative system; as it separated Jew from Gentile, and both from God. See Rom. 3:20; 4:15; 5:20; 7:7-11... Law is general, and its contents are defined by *commandments, special injunctions*, which injunctions in turn were formulated in definite *decrees*'. Fairbairn: 'The law of commandments in ordinances is but another name for the Sinaitic legislation, or the old covenant'. On Col. 2:14: 'What here is meant by the handwriting in ordinances... there can be no doubt, was the law, not in part but in whole – the law in the full compass of its requirements' (Vincent Vol.2 p852; Fairbairn: *Law* pp458,466-467). Yet in his *Typology* Vol.2 pp175-177, Fairbairn contradicted himself, calling this last 'the ceremonial law', 'those ceremonies', 'the purifications of the law', 'the Old Testament ceremonies', 'the ceremonies of Moses'. No! 'The law' is the law.

On Eph. 2:14-15, Charles Hodge: 'Christ abolished the Mosaic law by fulfilling all its types and shadows... the abolition of the Mosaic law removes the wall between the Jews and Gentiles. This is what is here taught... This was done by abolishing the law... He abolished the law... Having by... his death abolished the law... Christ by his death has freed us from the law. We are no longer under the law but under grace, Rom. 6:14... The law which Christ has thus abolished is called "the law of commandments in ordinances". This may mean the law of commandments with ordinances... or it may refer to the form in which the precepts are presented in the law... as commands... giving the contents of the law... The idea is probably the law in all its compass, and in all its forms, so far as it was a covenant prescribing the conditions of salvation, is abolished. The law of which the apostle here speaks is not exclusively the Mosaic law... it is the law of God in its widest sense... not merely the law of Moses... [But] (in the passage before us), special reference is had to the law in that particular [that is, the Mosaic] form... The doctrine of the passage... is that the middle wall of partition between the Jews and Gentiles... has been removed by Christ having, through his death, abolished the law in all its forms' (Charles Hodge: *Ephesians* pp130-131,134-136). Do the Reformed agree with Hodge here? If so, how can the 'abolished' law, which 'Christ by his death has freed us from', be the believer's perfect rule for sanctification?

On Rom. 7:6, John Murray: '"The oldness of the letter" refers to the law, and the law is called the letter because it was written. The writing may refer to the two tables of stone on which the ten commandments were written or to the fact of the law as contained in Scripture. It is law simply as written that is characterised as oldness, and the oldness consists in the law. This is apparent not only from the context where the apostle has been dealing with the powerlessness of the law to deliver from sin, and the confirmation it adds to our servitude, but also from the parallel passage in 2 Cor. 3:6. The contrast there between the letter and the Spirit is the contrast between the law and the gospel, and when Paul says "the letter kills, but the Spirit makes alive", the letter is shown by the context to refer to that which was engraven on stones, the law delivered by Moses'. Charles Hodge, like Murray, rightly called 2 Cor. 3:6 one of the 'parallel passages... The letter [refers to] the law [which] is so designated because the decalogue, its most important part, was originally written on stone, and because the whole law, as revealed to the Jews, was originally written in the Scriptures, or writings... Believers then are free from the law, by the death of Christ' (Murray: *Romans* Vol.1 p246; Charles Hodge: *Romans* p219). See my comment at the end of the previous paragraph.

Barcellos: 'The middle wall of separation was the law of the old covenant... the old or Mosaic covenant' (Barcellos p67). True, the law is used in the new covenant as a paradigm (see chapter 17), but, as Paul said, the law divided Jew and Gentile before the coming of Christ. Barcellos spoiled his comment by qualifying 'law' by adding 'as old-covenant law' (Barcellos pp67-68), a redundant phrase since that is precisely what the Mosaic law was! Let me illustrate. Take these two statements: *First*, the levitical sacrifices were old-covenant sacrifices. *Second*, the spiritual sacrifices of believers are new-covenant sacrifices. The first, as it stands, is a tautology. Linked with the second (fully explained – see my *Priesthood*), however, it is a powerful statement, emphasising the fundamental contrast of the two covenants, the oldness of the old covenant and the newness of the new covenant, and the radical difference in the nature of the sacrifices. So it is with Barcellos' phrase: 'old-covenant law'. The law of Moses is the old-covenant law. The law of Christ is the new-covenant law. And these two 'laws' are utterly different – not only in content, but in nature. I do not for a moment think that Barcellos meant *that*. Thus his phrase was redundant.

Fee, linking Rom. 6:14 and 7:6 with Rom. 2:29 and 2 Cor. 3:6: 'The contrast between Spirit and "letter" has nothing to do with the several popularisations of this language [euphemism for "Reformed glosses"]; *e.g.*, between "the spirit and letter" of the law, or between "internal and external", or between "literal and spiritual"... [The language of the biblical text] is eschatological and covenantal language. "Letter" has to do with the old covenant that came to an end through Christ and the Spirit... The new has thus replaced the old, which was ratified by Moses and Israel on Sinai and characterised by "written regulations requiring obedience"' (Fee: *Empowering* pp507-508).

For Kring on 2 Cor. 3:7-11, see the extracts for chapter 11.

In addition to the above, Arndt and Gingrich; Barcellos pp37-38,40; Bayes pp118-119; Baynes pp42-43; Calvin: *Commentaries* Vol.21 Part 1 pp233-234,237-238; Vol.21 Part 2 pp188-189; *Sermons* pp196-197; Chantry: *Righteous* pp117,135; *Sabbath* pp33-35,57; Jonathan Edwards: *Sermons* pp93-103; Fee: *Empowering* pp301,683; Haldane: *Sanctification* pp670-702; Hendriksen: *Ephesians* pp134-135; *Colossians* pp120-121; Kruse p260; Lee p8; Lloyd-Jones: *Way* pp208-210; Pink: *Law* p20; Pipa; Rushdoony p738; Thayer; *The Baptist Confession of 1689*, Chapters 19 and 22; Tow p32; Witherington p343.

CHAPTER 16: THE BELIEVER'S RULE

Introduction
Calvin: 'Christ... justifies no man without also sanctifying him. These blessings are conjoined by a perpetual and inseparable tie... They are both inseparably comprehended in Christ... You cannot possess him without being made a partaker of his sanctification... The Lord... bestows both... never the one without the other' (Calvin: *Institutes* Vol.2 p99). But Calvin was wrong to say 'the Lord... bestows both *at once*'. Sanctification is a life-long process. The main point stands, however. Although I have argued against making the law of Moses the believer's rule, I have, nevertheless, argued equally strongly that the believer must be progressively sanctified. No holiness of life? No conversion! Whatever else might be said about me or my book, I am not an antinomian!

Berridge: 'A legalist would see the Lord *by* his holiness, by the merit of it, but he cannot; and an antinomian would see the Lord *without* holiness, but he must not. Thus a Christian man can neither see the Lord *without* holiness, nor *by* it. Which though a truth, may seem a mystery to many' (Berridge: *Unmasked* p312, emphasis his).

See Moo: 'The Law' p208 for his listing of the 'three main positions' on the law of Christ – the law of Moses as interpreted and fulfilled by Christ; a nebulous concept void of content; the new code, norm, 'law' of the new covenant. The third is what I argue for.

'Law' in 'the law of Christ', and its equivalent: Why did Paul use 'law'?
Calvin on Gal. 6:2: 'The word "law", when applied here to Christ, serves the place of an argument. There is an implied contrast between the law of Christ and the law of Moses. If you are very desirous to keep a law, Christ enjoins on you a law which you are bound to prefer to all others, and that is, to cherish kindness towards each other. He who has not this has nothing' (Calvin; *Commentaries* Vol.21 Part 1 p173). Excellent. See Witherington pp424-426. Charles Hodge: '"Law" is not used in its ordinary sense. The general idea, however, of *a rule of action* is retained' (Charles Hodge: *Romans* p100, emphasis his).

Why did Paul use the word 'law' in Gal. 6:2 (and elsewhere)? Calvin's editor suggested that Paul used it 'because the word, law, was in high veneration among the Jews'. Poole: 'Some think' Paul used 'law' 'in condescension to the Jew's custom of speaking, who are so much delighted with the name of law, and so that he might not be suspected of novelty: but as most [think], it is a Hebraism, denoting no more than the doctrine or prescript of faith'. Moo rightly referred to Paul's 'rhetorical play on words', later noting 'the broader meaning' of 'law' among the Greek-speaking Jews of the first century, in such phrases as '"the (laws) unwritten rules of war", "the (laws) customs of war", "the law of historical writing", and "the (laws) norms of music"'. This phrase, *the law of the Spirit* (Rom. 8:2) 'suggests [too weak!] an intentional play on the word [*law*], as Paul... contrasts the *law* of Moses [the second *law* of the verse, *the law of sin and death*] with... the "*law* of the Spirit who confers life"'. C.K.Barrett drew attention to the important part played by the Septuagint in the way Greek-speaking Jews – who could not understand Hebrew – would grasp the meaning of 'law'. They, of course, read *nomos* in their version of the Old Testament. Did this matter? A great deal! They 'understood it as a Greek word and did not import into it all the connotations of the Hebrew word (*torah*) that it translated'. Witherington: 'Most ancients, including most Diaspora Jews, would not have read the law since they did not have copies or easy access to copies of the Hebrew Scriptures [which most of them could not read, in any case], but rather [would] have only heard it read' (Calvin: *Commentaries* Vol.19 Part 2 p148; Poole p489; Moo: *Romans* pp146,249-250,475-476, emphasis mine; Barrett pp75-76; Witherington p328). When speaking of the *law* of Christ, we could speak of the standard, the norm, the principle of Christ. See earlier references to 'the law of faith', and Witherington pp175,412,424.

Hays elegantly described 'the law of Christ' as 'a breathtaking paradox'. Ian H.Thompson agreed: 'In the context of Galatians [he found it] intriguing that Paul chose such a loaded term as "law"... when he could have written 'the teaching of Christ' or even "the gospel"' (Ian H.Thompson p129). It is more than 'intriguing'. By his play on words, Paul was making a vital point. On 1 Cor. 9:19-23, as Fee remarked, Paul 'can scarcely resist a play on words... "under law toward Christ", "under Christ's law", Paul uses the word "law", of course, because of the word play involving "law" compounds' (Fee: *1 Corinthians* pp429-430; see also pp148,566). Similarly, take Christ's use of 'yoke' (Matt. 11:29-30). The concept of a 'yoke' was current in such phrases as 'yoke of the *torah*' and 'yoke of the commandments'. Christ was speaking of a new yoke, an altogether different kind of yoke – 'my yoke' – not the old yoke of Moses; nor, in Chamblin's words, 'the [Mosaic] law as [Christ] expounds it' (Chamblin p189). Christ's law is the new law for the new-covenant people. For more on word play, see chapter 10 for comments on Rom. 8:1-4. Rom. 3:27; 9:6 and Philem. 10-11 are further examples; Hendriksen: *Matthew* p504; Chamblin p189. Is there another word play in Matt. 11:28-30 between *chrētos* (easy) and *christos* (anointed, Christ)?

While I agree with W.D.Davies: 'Paul must have regarded Jesus in the light of a new Moses, and... recognised in the words of Christ a *nomos tou Christou*... [by which] he meant that the actual words of Jesus were for him a new *torah*', I would qualify the understanding of *torah*. Indeed, I agree with Dodd – whom Davies quoted – that the law of Christ should not be thought of as 'the *torah* of Jesus... but (as)... an immanent principle of life... determined by the Spirit of Christ'. Davies again: '*Torah*... is not merely to be understood in the restricted sense of legislation... Paul would think of Jesus as the *torah* of God not only in the sense that his words were a *nomos* but that he himself *in toto* was a full revelation of God and of his will for man... We are... right[1] in finding a *contrast* between the yoke of Christ's teaching or law and that of the *torah*. Taking the yoke of the *torah* was a familiar Rabbinic expression. In Matthew, clearly there is a substitution of Christ for the *torah*, and Christ... is pictured after the image of the *torah*'. The *Didache*, probably dating from about 80-140, called 'the commandments of Jesus' the Lord's yoke, '*zugos tou kuriou torah*'. 'To the totality of the teaching, life, death and resurrection of Jesus, Paul... ascribe[d] the significance of a new *torah*. But... the advent of Christ meant... the advent of the Spirit... In short, Paul found in Christ both *torah* and Spirit... There is found... not only a "Christifying" of the Spirit but also a "Christifying" of the *torah*; Spirit and *torah*... are coincident... in Christ' (W.D.Davies pp144,149-150,223, emphasis mine).

Fee: 'This does not mean that in Christ a new set of laws has taken the place of the old, although in terms of specifics it would certainly refer to those kinds of ethical demands given, for example, in Rom. 12 and Gal. 5 – 6, so many of which do reflect the teaching of Jesus'. In speaking of the law of Christ, Paul was not referring 'to a code of precepts to which a Christian man is obliged to conform' (Fee: *1 Corinthians* pp429-430). It is altogether a new system. Brown, on John 13:33-35: 'The words... rather show *how*, than say *why*, a Christian should love a Christian' (Brown: *Discourses* Vol.2 p500, emphasis his).

Kruse: Paul, 'having fought to deliver Gentile believers from the yoke of the Mosaic law, [was not guilty of] immediately placing upon them the heavier yoke of Christ's law (understood as a collection of the many injunctions such as those found in... Matt. 5 – 7)... For Paul, to live [under Christ's law] would not have been a new legalism based on the commands of the historical Jesus and the exalted Christ' (Kruse pp106,129-130).

On Gal. 6:2, Edgar H.Andrews: '"The law of Christ" stands in contrast to the law of Moses. It is an inner principle rather than an external precept, and is fulfilled as we bear spiritual

---

[1] Davies had 'we are probably right'. I have no doubt about it!

fruit... The believer is not without law. He is no longer under the law of Moses, but is controlled and motivated by a higher principle; namely, "the law of the Spirit of life in Christ Jesus" (Rom. 8:2)' (Edgar H.Andrews pp309-312). Andrews was clear that the law of Christ is *not* 'another set of rules, different perhaps from Sinai's, but of the same essentially, external nature'. Of course, Christ's law is of a totally different nature to the Mosaic law – just as the new-covenant people differ from the old-covenant people.

Thielman: 'For Paul... the law of Christ [is] Jesus' own teaching and example. Although it had absorbed elements of the Mosaic law, this was a different law and formed the new norm for the people of God during the period of the dawning eschaton [that is, the gospel age]'. 'Paul may have formulated the phrase "the law of Christ" to demonstrate that this new law replaced "the law of Moses". "The law of Moses" was a standard way of referring to the Jewish law... in Scripture... (Josh. 23:6; 2 Kings 23:25; Dan. 9:11)'. 'Two different laws are in view here: the law of Moses, which builds a wall of division between Jew and Gentile, and the law of Christ, which breaks it down' (Thielman pp19,43).

Jackson spoke of 'the weakness of a supposedly all-embracing ethical code', such as the law of Moses. 'The Christian faith is a personal relationship between man and God, and it does not present us with such a code of detailed rules; rather, God has given us certain guiding principles and expects us to our daily actions upon them, the Holy Spirit guiding us in judgement in answer to humble prayer and study' (Jackson p20). This is the law of Christ.

Denney: 'In the Christian religion, as... Paul understood it, nothing statutory could have any place. To give a legal authority to any formal precept, ethical or ritual, is to shut the door of hope, and open again the door of despair. It is to contemn [treat with contempt] the Spirit, who is Christ's gift, and the cross, by which he won [the gift], and to renounce the liberty with which he has made us free... Paul was not an antinomian (for the just demand of the law is fulfilled in all Christians), but he was certainly an anomian. He recognises no law in the church but the law of the spirit of life in Christ Jesus, and while that is both law and impulse, it is essentially personal, and can never be reduced to a statutory form... All legalism is eliminated when the law is described as having its fulfilment in love (Rom. 13:10; Gal. 5:14), and "the law of Christ" is explained as "bearing each other's burdens" (Gal. 6:2). Legalism, in short, and Christianity (life in the Spirit) are to... Paul mutually exclusive ideas... The idea that the existence of Christianity depended on them ["a legal creed and a legal organisation"] could only have seemed to him a fatal contradiction of all that Christianity meant'. Superb! Calvin's third use of the law, it goes without saying, flies in the face of this scriptural argument.

The eschatological setting of 'law' – the law of Christ is not the law of Moses
Despite the extracts above, many think it is! The law of Moses, John Macleod argued (John Macleod pp134-138,155), is the believer's rule of obedience 'which [is] the law of Christ'. Thus Macleod confused – conflated – the law of Moses – 'a yoke of bondage' (Acts 15:10) – with the law of Christ – 'the yoke of Christ' (Matt. 11:29-30). See chapter 16.

Luther: 'Some would bind us at this day to certain of Moses' laws that like them best, as the false apostles would have done at that time [in Galatia]. But this is in no wise to be suffered [allowed]. For if we give Moses leave to rule over us in anything, we are bound to obey him in all things. Wherefore we will not be burdened with any law of Moses. We grant that he is to be read among us, and to be heard as a prophet and a witness-bearer of Christ; and, moreover, that out of him we may take good examples of good laws and holy life. But we will not suffer [allow] him in any wise to have dominion over our conscience. In this case let him be dead and buried, and let no man know where his grave is (Deut. 34:6)' (Luther: *Galatians* p453).

To make the Mosaic law the believer's rule, as Harris argued, 'tends to lead the children of God into bondage... A believer is redeemed from the law, he is dead to the law... it cannot attach to him in any way whatever. It is no longer the rule by which he walks, because being suitable for the relationship of master and servant, it is not suitable for the relationship of father and son. The end proposed to those under the law was obedience unto life: "This do and you shall live"... But the believer *has* life: "He that has the Son has life". It is that from which he sets out, not that which he is pursuing' (Harris pp38-39, emphasis mine). In other words, since the law of Moses had to be obeyed to bring life, and since the believer already has life, the believer is no longer under the law of Moses. He does not need life. He has it! Harris made the same mistake as others, however, when he said the law is dead to the believer.

The law of Moses cannot be the law of Christ. On: 'The law made nothing perfect [or complete]' (Heb. 7:18-19), Owen: 'It made "nothing", that is, none of the things which we treat about, "perfect"'. John Brown: 'Some consider the "perfection" here spoken of as referring to expiation... others, to sanctification... [the] spiritual transformation of character; others, to true, permanent, everlasting happiness. I am disposed to think that the word is intended to comprehend all these ideas... [The law] did not give real, far less perfect, sanctification. [Brown quoted Eberard:] Some consider the "perfection" here spoken of as referring to expiation... others, to sanctification... [the] spiritual transformation of character; others, to true, permanent, everlasting happiness. I am disposed to think that the word is intended to comprehend all these ideas... [The law] did not give real, far less perfect, sanctification' (Owen: *Hebrews* Vol.3 Part 2 p471; Brown: *Hebrews* pp337,344).

On the eschatological setting of 'law', Moo: 'The Christian is no longer bound to the Mosaic law; Christ has brought its fulfilment. But the Christian *is* bound to "God's law" (1 Cor. 9:20-21; *cf.* "God's commands" in 1 Cor. 7:19 and 1 John *passim*). "God's law" is not [now], however, the Mosaic law, but "Christ's law" (1 Cor. 9:20-21; Gal. 6:2), because it is to Christ, the fulfiller, the *telos* of the law (Rom. 10:4), that the Christian is bound... Failure to observe this distinction [between the law of Moses and the law of God] has resulted in considerable confusion and misunderstanding' (Moo: 'The Law' pp217-218, emphasis his; see Witherington pp424-425). He could say that again!

On 1 Cor. 9:20-21, Moo: 'Paul's point... is that he as a Christian is not subject to the rule and authority of the Mosaic law, but he willingly gives up that freedom, and conforms to that law when evangelising Jews... Paul wants to guard against any idea that he has no more obligations to the law of God. Indeed, while not being "under the law", he recognises a continuing obligation to "God's law", in the form of "Christ's law" (the Greek is *ennomos Christou*). The conceptualisation of this text provides as neat a summary of my view [Moo's, and mine – DG] of the law as the New Testament affords. It suggests that "God's law" comes to his people in two forms: to Israel in the form of "law", *torah*, and to Christians in the form of "Christ's law". Here we find the "new-covenant theology" emphasis on two contrasting covenants worked out in terms of two different "laws". But the key question remains: How different are they?' 'To answer this question', Moo said, 'we return to Galatians'; in particular, to Gal. 5:13 – 6:2. 'To recapitulate: ...The teaching of the New Testament on the matter of the law of God is neatly summarised in the distinctions that Paul draws in 1 Cor. 9:20-21: the law of Moses, the *torah* ("law" simply), was given to the people of Israel to govern them until the coming of the Messiah; since his coming, the people of God are governed by the "law of Christ". Biblical law, in other words, is firmly attached to the temporal two-covenant structure that is the hallmark of "new-covenant theology"' (Moo: 'Galatians' pp20,27). Moo went on the look at what he called 'certain important nuances [which] need to be added if this view is to fit all the biblical data'. I have discussed the topics in question throughout my book.

John Brown: 'The doctrine of the gospel undoubtedly is that Christians are not subject to the Mosaic law; that nothing is obligatory on a Christian's conscience merely because it is contained in the law of Moses; and that the system of divine administration under which they are placed in consequence of their connection with Christ, is not a system of strict law under which the rule is: "Do and live"' (Brown: *1 Peter* Vol.1 p397; see also pp355-356,397-402,417-418). Excellent, though I do not agree with Brown when he tried to distinguish between the law as a rule and a covenant.

Harris: 'The believer is not... without law to God, but that rule [the law] that subsisted between the Lord and the servant [does] not apply to this new relationship... Many a Christian... [however] does not stand fast in that liberty wherewith Christ has made him free: "For you are all children of God by faith of Jesus Christ". And, not rejoicing in the liberty of sonship, they [do not] see... their calling to be to walk as "obedient children, not fashioning themselves according to their former lusts in their ignorance, but as he who has called them is holy, so are they to be holy in all manner of conversation". They still look to the law as their rule, and "receive the spirit of bondage again to fear", questioning... the extent of the obedience required, instead of returning the answer of a willing heart unto a loving Father. The law deals in formal enactments, but the Spirit, who is liberty, [deals] more in the application of some great and acknowledged principles. What law could accurately define the measure and quality of the obedience of a child to a parent?'

The believer's 'liberty makes him not lawless to God... It is indeed blessed liberty into which we are called as children of God, but it is a high and holy responsibility. "Be therefore followers (imitators) of God *as* [emphasis mine] *dear children* [emphasis his], and walk in love". The perfectness of the Father's love is the only standard proposed to the children: "Be... perfect, even as your Father which in heaven is perfect". Just in proportion as the relationship is raised in dignity from that of a servant to that of a son, so is the standard of obedience raised also. The law might tend to tutor the flesh, but the Spirit alone [can] serve God. "If you are led of the Spirit you are not under the law", and this applies to the law as a rule of life; for... this passage is not concerning justification, but Christian conduct: "This I say then: Walk in the Spirit, and you shall not fulfil the lusts of the flesh"... Jesus... [was] made under the law, meeting every one of God's requirements, even fulfilling all righteousness... He had the right and title to have entered into life, because he had kept the commandments... Freedom from the yoke of bondage is not that we may be without law to God, but that we may be obedient children... The consideration of the remainder of the apostle's statement, as to a Christian being "under law to Christ", will most plainly prove that he is in no sense whatever under *the* [emphasis his] law. "The law is not made for a righteous man, but for the lawless and disobedient, for the ungodly and sinners, for unholy and profane"' (Harris pp39-41). Note how Harris combines several themes I have already set out in more detail. Echoes here also of the Anabaptists who 'continually distinguished between the covenant of servitude and that of sonship' (Williams: *Radical* p832). See Jackson pp19-20.

Thielman summarised 'the law' in Romans and Galatians: 'In both Romans and Galatians, Paul argues that the era of the Mosaic law has passed away. Paul says this explicitly in passages where he speaks of the believer having been "released" (*katargeō*) from the Mosaic law (Rom. 7:2,6; *cf.* Gal. 2:19), and of the law's temporary function of identifying, punishing and increasing sin. This function, Paul says, has now ceased with the coming of Christ and the Spirit (Gal. 3:19-25; 4:1-5; 5:18; Rom. 3:20; 5:20; 6:14-15; 7:1-25; 8:2). Paul also implies the cessation of the Mosaic era when he claims that central elements of the Mosaic law such as circumcision (Gal. 5:2,6; 6:15), dietary regulations (Gal. 2:11-14; Rom. 15:14), the observance of special days (Gal. 4:10; Rom. 14:5-6), and the temple cult (Rom. 3:25-26; 8:3; 12:1) are no longer necessary'.

'In Galatians, Paul says explicitly, and in Romans he implies, that the new era has brought with it a new law, "the law of Christ" (Gal. 6:2). In Galatians, Paul links this law to the teaching of Jesus by saying that it is fulfilled when believers "bear one another's burdens", a statement that echoes Jesus' own summaries of the law's second table in terms of "the golden rule" and Lev. 19:18 (Matt. 7:12; 19:19; 22:39; Mark 12:31; Luke 10:27; *cf.* Luke 6:31). Paul's independent use of Lev. 19:18 to summarise the law's requirements (Gal. 5:14; Rom. 13:8-10), and his claim that an unloving insistence on the Mosaic law's dietary regulations is a transgression (Gal. 2:18), increase the likelihood that he considered Jesus' teaching on love for neighbour to be part of this new "law of Christ". The new law, then, incorporates parts of the Mosaic law within it, but apparently only insofar as the teaching of Jesus reaffirms their validity'.

'The demise of the Mosaic law and the introduction of the law of Christ does not mean, however, that the Mosaic law ceased to function as authoritative Scripture for Paul. Specific passages within the Mosaic law, such as the Abrahamic narrative (Gal. 3:6-18,29; 4:21 – 5:1)[2] and the decalogue (Rom. 13:9), continue to offer guidance to the Christian community – indeed, like all the Scriptures, they were written precisely for the Christian community (Rom. 15:4) – but they are interpreted through the eschatological lens of the gospel' (Thielman pp34-35).

Thielman again: Matthew, Luke, John, Paul and the writer to the Hebrews 'all... agree that the Mosaic law is no longer the authoritative norm by which God's people should live... [that] the authority of the Mosaic law to regulate the lives of God's people has passed away. In this sense, Jesus' proclamation, ministry, death and resurrection represent a break with the past... In place of the Mosaic covenant, all five authors put something new... a new covenant... (Heb. 8:8-13; 9:15; 10:11-18)... Jesus' ethical teaching has replaced the Mosaic law (Matt. 5:1 – 7:29; John 13:34; 14:15,21,23-24; 15:10-17). Paul and Luke embrace both notions (1 Cor. 9:21; 11:25; Gal. 6:2; Rom. 3:21-30; Luke 22:20; 6:12-49)... Four of the five authors appear to claim that Jesus established a new "law" for his disciples... John... portrays Jesus as a new Moses... It is often said that Paul believed the Mosaic law had been replaced in the new era by the leading of the Spirit. Unlike the Mosaic law, it is thought, Pauline ethics lack specificity'. This allegation is false: 'Evidence exists for just such a concrete body of ethical demands. Paul speaks explicitly of "the law of Christ" (Gal. 6:2; *cf.* 1 Cor. 9:21)... Thus, a concrete body of ethical teaching replaces the instructions of the Mosaic law in Matthew, Luke-Acts, John and the Pauline letters. If by the term "law", we mean detailed legislation in which, to paraphrase Hebrews, every transgression and infraction receives a commensurate penalty, then we cannot properly call this teaching a new law. But if we use the term more broadly to refer to specific ethical guidelines backed up by a general promise of blessing for obedience and woe for disobedience, the phrase "new law" seems [too weak!] to be an appropriate way of describing this material. Despite the replacement of the Mosaic covenant with a new covenant and a new "law", all five authors agree that the Mosaic law continues in some sense to be valid. It is valid both because it provides the theological structure for the gospel, and because it constitutes a rich repository of specific ethical material for the newly-constituted people of God... The five... authors... are all unified [united] in the conviction that [the Mosaic law] has been overwhelmed by the life, death and resurrection of Jesus. Much of the Mosaic law, both at the level of structure and specific commands, has been creatively appropriated in this new, eschatological situation. Still, too much of the [Mosaic] law has been omitted or radically reinterpreted for the emphasis to fall on the continuity between law and gospel. Continuity is present, but the gospel is something new' (Thielman pp176-182). As I have already

---

[2] Abraham pre-dated the Mosaic covenant, of course. But see Thielman pp15-18 for an explanation of his meaning.

observed, Thielman's words are all the more significant since they come from a Presbyterian.

And Aquinas, while he certainly plays a large part in establishing the immensely damaging, unscriptural threefold-division of the law, he did have some good things to say on 'the new law'. On Heb. 7:12, the change of priesthood: 'The priesthood is twofold... the levitical priesthood, and the priesthood of Christ. Therefore the divine law is twofold; namely, the old law and the new law... The law that brings all in a perfect way of salvation could not be given until the coming of Christ... The new law is the law of the New Testament. But the law of the New Testament is instilled in our hearts (Jer. 31:31-33; Heb. 8:8-10)... The new law is chiefly the grace itself of the Holy Ghost, which is given to those who believe in Christ... The new law is in the first place a law that is inscribed on our hearts, but that secondarily it is a written law... The priesthood of the New Testament is distinct from that of the Old... Therefore the law is also distinct... The new law is compare to that of the old as the perfect to the imperfect... The new law fulfils the old by supplying that which was lacking in the old law... The end of the old law was the justification of men. The law, however, could not accomplish this... In this respect, the new law fulfils the old by justifying men though the power of Christ's death. This is what the apostle says (Rom. 8:3-4)... Wherefore the new law is called the law of truth, while the old law is called the law of shadow or of figure' (Aquinas Vol.2 pp211-212,321,326-328). So, even Aquinas must have agreed, the law of Christ is most definitely not the law of Moses.

The law of Christ: Gal. 6:2 and its context

Those 'who manifest these traits' (Gal. 5:22-23), said Witherington, 'have no need of law, in this case, the Mosaic law... Christ is the Christian's standard, and to the extent they manifest Christ-like qualities... they appear as Christ among others (*cf*. Gal. 4:14; 6:17)... This is [yet] one more argument against submitting to the Mosaic law... This remark is especially appropriate here because it prepares, as [does] Gal. 5:24-26, for Paul's final argument [in Galatians] about the law or standard of Christ which begins at Gal. 6:1' (Witherington pp411-412,416). According to Witherington, Paul was almost certainly making use of the Galatians' knowledge of Aristotle, very much as he used the Cretan poets (Tit. 1:12-13). Be that as it may, in the main text I give more contextual confirmation of the link between the law of Christ and Christ himself. In short, as Witherington put it: 'By what rule or standard will the Christian community live and be shaped? Paul's answer is that the community is to be cruciform and Christological in shape. It is to follow his example and the pattern of Christ and walk in and by the Spirit. It is, in short, to follow the law of Christ which is not identical with the law of Moses... The law of Christ is not the Mosaic law intensified or in a new guise' (Witherington pp342,345).

John Brown on Gal. 6:2: 'There seems to be [there is!] a tacit contrast between the law of Moses and the law of Christ. [The] fulfilling of the law of Christ [is] infinitely better [than] a keeping of the law of Moses'. Lightfoot: 'The law, *not of Moses*, but of Christ'. Michael Eaton: 'In light of the *total thrust* of Galatians the force of the phrase *must be* in antithesis to Mosaic law' (Brown: *Galatians* p326; Lightfoot: *Galatians* p216, emphasis mine; Michael Eaton: *Encouragement* pp113-114 emphasis mine).

Let me return to Moo, and the extract from his 'Galatians', when he was looking at Gal. 5:13 – 6:2. Moo was answering the question: 'What will guide and empower' believers – seeing they are not under the law? The answer, as he said, contains two components – the Spirit and, 'surprisingly, perhaps', the law. Ah! But which law? 'The other reference to "law" in this concluding section of Galatians comes in Gal. 6:2... The interpretation of the phrase "law of Christ" is central to my [Moo's and mine – DG] argument. Unfortunately, Paul provides little contextual information.[3] We have, however, already noticed that Paul

---

[3] Is it because the early believers knew full-well what the apostle was talking about?

uses similar language in 1 Cor. 9:21, where, the context suggests [it makes it plain!] "the law of Christ" is distinguished from the Mosaic law. Coupled with the claim that Christians are no longer "under the (Mosaic) law", this makes it unlikely[!] that the "law of Christ" is the Mosaic law interpreted and fulfilled by Christ. Rather, the phrase is more likely [to be] Paul's answer to those who might conclude that his law-free gospel provides no standards of guidance for believers. On the contrary, Paul says, though no longer directly responsible to Moses' law, Christians are bound to Christ's law. In what does this "law" consist? Since... Gal. 5:14..., the demand for love [must be] a central component of the "law of Christ". But it is unlikely that Paul confines the law to this demand alone, for, as we have seen, Paul also stresses in this context the fruit-bearing ministry of the Spirit. Coupled with the centrality of the Spirit in Paul's teaching about what it means to live as a Christian, this strongly suggests that the directing influence of the Spirit is an important part of this law of Christ... Jer. 31:31-34... Ezek. 36:26-27. It is more difficult to determine whether the law of Christ includes specific teachings and principles... I think it highly probable [it is certain!] that Paul thought of the law of Christ as including within it teachings of Jesus and the apostolic witness, based on his life and teaching'. Moo, in part, quoting Longenecker: 'The law of Christ "stands in Paul's thought for those prescriptive principles stemming from the heart of the gospel (usually embodied in the example and teachings of Jesus), which are meant to be applied to specific situations by the direction and enablement of the Holy Spirit, being always motivated and conditioned by love". Does the "law of Christ" include Mosaic commandants? Of course. We may expect that everything within the Mosaic law that reflected God's "eternal moral will" for his people is caught up into and repeated in the "law of Christ"' (Moo: 'Galatians' pp21-22). On the whole, a fine statement, but, as so often, Moo could have been stronger at certain points. The biblical evidence is overwhelming – 'the law of Christ' cannot be confined to the ten commandments.

Not, however, for the Reformed advocates of Calvin's third use of the law! Kevan: 'The law [of Moses]... is the Christian's rule of life... The law of Moses is none other than the law of Christ'. Again; 'To leave the Old Testament and come into the New, is to find this function of the law [of Moses] as the Christian's rule of life made abundantly clear' (Kevan: *Moral* p7; *Evangelical* p13). Chantry argued that believers 'have returned to the moral law' – the ten commandments, he meant – 'for direction in sanctification... Nothing but the moral law can define for us what sanctified behaviour is' (Chantry: *Righteous* p72). 'Once deny that the decalogue is a synopsis of the moral law, and men are sent into a haze of imprecise ethics. They are adrift, without a definite objective standard by which to judge righteousness... Those who snipe at [see my reply below] the ten commandments never give their hearers an objective canon of moral law to follow... Without a brief compendium of the moral law, every reading of the Bible is a redesigning of the blueprint of righteousness' (Chantry: *Righteous* pp80-82).

What an arrogant and misguided set of assertions! As something of an (amusing) aside, let me quote Kevan advising believers that if they 'recite the Creed to keep in memory what they must believe', they should similarly 'recite the Commandments to keep in memory what they must do' (Kevan: *Experience* p71). Is how a *gospel* minister should speak?

To return to Chantry. For those who do not take Moses as their guide to the Christian life but prefer Christ, Chantry had a word of caution: 'A study of Jesus' life can be complex... The ten commandments are comprehensive enough to embrace all his pure works and compact enough to serve as a rule in our finite judgement. [It is] only those who have been unable to shake off the mental categories given them by the decalogue [who] have avoided dire heresies'. Under Moses, in other words, believers are safer and have clearer light than under Christ! 'How varied are the systems which claim to imitate Jesus!' snapped Chantry. Reader, are we to believe that those who follow Moses see eye to eye? Do the Reformed? But Chantry posed a fundamental question here. If we do not make the ten commandments our rule, where shall we go? 'Is there an objective expression of the righteousness of

Christ' outside the law?, Chantry asked (Chantry: *Righteous* pp82-83), obviously expecting the answer, No. But there is reader, there is. Read on! Imitation of Christ, and imitation of the apostles as they imitated Christ, is only one part of Christ's law, but it is a part. And it must not be dismissed as vague or imprecise. See Rom. 15:3,5,7; 1 Cor. 11:1 with 1 Cor. 4:16; Eph. 5:1-2; Phil. 3:17; 4:9; 1 Thess. 1:6; 1 Pet. 2:2; 1 John 2:6. I will return to this. Those who dismiss such a battery of texts will have to answer to the one who inspired them.

For now, consider W.D.Davies: 'Again and again [Paul] holds up the historical Jesus for imitation'. But this does not mean 'that there was any departmentalism in the mind of Paul whereby the teaching of Jesus was artificially separated from the person of Jesus... Any such dichotomy was alien to the apostle... he not merely referred to the words of Jesus, but also to his character. Thus he holds up certain qualities of the historic Jesus which [are] to be imitated... Paul's greatest doctrinal statements subserve his ethical exhortations; when Paul had to impress certain ethical duties upon his converts he appealed to what Jesus essentially was and did... In the mind of the apostle... the teaching and character of Jesus were inextricably bound together... The life of Jesus and his words are for Paul an inseparable unity' (W.D.Davies pp88,147-148). Spot on! It is offensive to see this arrogantly and ignorantly written off as 'a haze of imprecise ethics... without a definite objective standard'.

Incidentally, I do not 'snipe at the ten commandments' when I say they must not be used for a job for which they were never intended! I do not have the disease of 'Sinaiphobia' which makes me want to 'eliminate any [every?] Mosaic code as invalid for New Testament times'; I do not 'viciously pull down the moral law of God'; I am not one of the 'cranks who foment against Sinai', one of 'neo-antinomians who demand the rash [or any other sort of] obliteration of the ten commandments [and who] forbid us to compare Jesus' words and conduct with the decalogue', one of those 'who want to snatch the ten commandments from Christian hands', one of the 'assailants of the decalogue', or one of the 'ten commandment abolitionists' (Chantry: *Righteous* pp73-74,82-84,86-87). How did Chantry get away with such a splenetic caricature and dismissal of sincere believers who do not buy into Calvin's third use of the law? What were his publishers thinking of? Strong arguments are always welcome, even when used in determined opposition, but outbursts such as this? Methinks the Reformed teacher protests too much! As the preacher's notes had it: 'Argument weak here. Shout!' By the way, was Chantry saying *all* the Mosaic law is valid for believers today? Hmm!

Let nobody allege that those who take the position I am trying to enunciate have no time for the ten commandments, and have nothing to say on them. I had given abundant evidence to the contrary. Michael Eaton concluded his thorough examination of Exodus 19 – 24 in the *Theology for Beginners* series with these words: 'For the Christian, the law [of Moses] is part of the system that has been abolished. But he does not throw it away as uninteresting or unimportant. He is not under it; but he fulfils it. He is not under the law; he is under Christ. When he reads the law, he sees it as a signpost pointing to Jesus. He sees it as a shadow, sketching for him a higher level of living. Does he abolish the law? Certainly it is abolished for the Christian. But it is not abolished because it is thrown away as worthless. It is abolished because it gets fulfilled in another way. Does the Christian despise the law? Not at all. He fulfils it by the Holy Spirit. He fulfils its call for righteousness. Then he enters into the tabernacle, and even presses on to the holy of holies. Once again, worship will be the way in which he gives recognition to his King' (Michael Eaton: *Applying* p178).

Wells was right: 'We must... acknowledge that the New Testament offers us little exposition that *directly* explains what this law [the law of Christ] is'. But I also agree with him when he immediately added: 'Nevertheless, we have the materials for determining the question' (Wells p40, emphasis mine, and a vital emphasis, at that). This, of course, is one of main differences between the law of Moses and the law of Christ. The former is specific in minute and precise detail; the latter deals in principles.

Bruce: 'The law belongs to the old age, the age of [the believer's] spiritual powerlessness' and worse – his bondage and death; 'the Spirit is the earnest [deposit, advanced payment, foretaste] of the new age, in which [the] man, liberated from the bondage which is inevitable under [his] old age, can "do the will of God from the heart" (Eph. 6:6) or... "produce the fruit of the Spirit" (Gal. 6:22)'. Lloyd-Jones: 'The opposite of "law" is "grace", and the law of the Spirit of life in Christ Jesus means "the rule of grace", the "reign of grace". It is the way of faith in Christ Jesus... We are no longer under that old law called "the letter"; we are under the law of the Spirit now... "the law of the Spirit of life in Christ Jesus"... the "perfect law of liberty". What a paradox! "Law of liberty"! [James] means "a way", "a reign"; it is "the reign of grace" and that is a reign or law "of liberty"'. On Rom. 7:1-6, Burroughs called this a part of the 'joyful sound of liberty you [believers] have by the gospel: your lawgiver is none other than he who is your husband. You have to deal with none other, now, in the matters of your soul, but with him who is your husband and your advocate, by whom all is ruled... You now have to deal with Christ your lawgiver' (Bruce: *Paul* p274; Lloyd-Jones: *Law* pp290-291; Burroughs p135).

Taylor translated Tit. 3:8: 'I desire you to strongly insist on these things [Tit. 3:4-7]'. Calvin: Paul 'means that [the grace of God] ought to hold the place of instruction to us to regulate our life well'. Hendriksen: 'Let Titus then stress those matters [as listed in Tit. 3:4-7]... the purpose being that those who have their faith fixed on God... may be careful to apply themselves to noble deeds. They should concentrate their thought on such deeds of gratitude, applying themselves with diligence to their performance, and making this their chief business' (Taylor p286; Calvin: *Commentaries* Vol.21 Part 2 p317; Hendriksen: *I & II Timothy* pp393-394). Notice the absence of the Mosaic law here and in the context – except this, in the following verse: 'But avoid... strivings about the law; for they are unprofitable and useless' (Tit. 3:9). See Gadsby: *Works* p19.

But advocates of the Reformed view of the law disagree; they think the law of Christ is the law of Moses. Malcolm Watts: 'I take it to mean... that Christ has delivered the law [the ten commandments, Watts meant] to his people having already fulfilled its righteousness, and secured heaven for us. Now he gives us the law as the guide for our holiness and our righteousness'. Reymond on Rom. 13:10 and Gal. 5:6,13: 'The norm or standard of the Christian life is the law [of Moses], and the motive power to keep it is the new life in Christ, that is, life in the Spirit, which exhibits itself as a life of obedience which is the expression of love. Love finds its direction and parameters in the law of God' (Malcolm Watts p22; Reymond: *Paul* pp476-477; see Kruse p106). Incidentally, the view I am putting forward does not in any way approximate to saying that 'love is... content-less or only a warm and undefined feeling' – I will supply plenty of evidence to the contrary – nor does it set love 'in opposition to the law' (Reymond: *Paul* p477). But neither can the law of Christ be confined to the ten commandments, nor to a legalistic system in general. And Scripture does say that 'love is the fulfilment of the law' (Rom. 13:10).

Christ gives his people *his own* law; he does not send them to Moses! Witherington: 'By "the law of Christ", Paul does not mean Christ's interpretation of the still binding Mosaic law... The apostle who is capable of speaking of two covenants in Galatians, and of a new covenant in 2 Cor. 3, is also perfectly capable of speaking of two different laws' (Witherington pp424-426). And, I would add, 'for two different Israels'. See chapter 18.

Packer: 'What Paul calls "the law of Christ" (Gal. 6:2) is specifically and concretely a law for the redeemed... Christ's exposition of God's eternal law is given in terms of the particular situation of the believer, and of nobody else. It is a statement of God's law as it applies to the citizens of God's kingdom. The only man to whose condition it speaks directly is the born-again Christian. From this we can see what was new about the law of Christ, as compared with the law of the old covenant. Christ's law was new in the same sense in which Christ's gospel of the kingdom was new... First, we find a new depth of exposition... The second fresh feature in Christ's restatement of the law is a new stress in application' (Packer: *Understanding* pp9-10). Good as far as it goes, but there is more to the newness of Christ's law than this.

Dunn on 'the law of Christ', made several points, coming finally to what he called 'the most striking of all... the parallel between Rom. 13:8-10; 15:1-2 and Gal. 5:14; 6:2; not least the common theme of "fulfilling" the law (Rom. 13:8,10; Gal. 5:14...)'. I pause. The law in question, of course, is the Mosaic law. This raises an interesting question: Does Paul here destroy what he has so carefully established? Certainly not. He is not exhorting believers to keep the Mosaic law because they are under it as their rule of sanctification; rather, he is saying that by keeping the law of Christ, the law of Moses is fulfilled – note the passive. See chapter 17, where I explore this more fully, especially in the light of Gal. 5:3. To let Dunn continue: 'In both cases the call for love of neighbour, in echo of Jesus' teaching, is followed by a series of practical exhortations illustrating this love. In Romans, the climax comes with clear allusion back to Rom. 13:8-10, and with explicit evocation of the example of Christ (Rom. 15:2-3). In Galatians, the climax comes by referring to the law of Christ at the equivalent point and with the equivalent function: fulfilling the law of Christ (Gal. 6:2) [therefore] means following the good example of Christ in seeking the good of the neighbour (Rom. 15:2-3)... We must speak [therefore of the law of Christ as] at least of Christ's self-giving treated as a paradigm for Christian relationships' (Dunn pp322-323).

Schreiner: 'The law of Christ should be defined as the law of love. We see in 1 Cor. 9 that Paul's flexibility and sacrifice on behalf of his hearers represents the same kind of sacrificial love that Christ displayed in going to the cross. The life of Christ... exemplifies the law of love. It would be a mistake to conclude that there are no moral norms in the law of Christ, for Rom. 13:8-10 makes it clear, as do many other texts in Paul, that the life of love cannot be separated from moral norms' (Schreiner pp103-104).

The 'new command' in John's letters

As for John Brown: 'Though the commandment... cannot now be called a new one, as if just issued... for from the beginning of the gospel [John 13:34] it was announced as the distinctive command of our one lawgiver – yet it may well be called new... for no one gave it until he did it... and... it was a law to which you were strangers, till you assumed his light and easy burden'. And as to Christ's command, Brown was clear: 'Paul calls it "the law of Christ"' (Brown: *Discourses* Vol.2 p501). Stott thought the apostle was speaking of the command 'they had known... from the outset of their Christian life... It was as old as the gospel itself'. Stott referred to 1 John 2:24, 'that... which you heard from the beginning', calling it 'the gospel, the apostolic teaching, the original message which had been preached' (Stott pp97,117,143,209). Calvin: 'These were the first elements of the gospel, that *they* had been... taught from the beginning... [John] calls it "old", not because it had been taught the fathers many ages before, but because it had been taught *them* on *their* very entrance into [*their* spiritual] life... It had proceeded from Christ himself, from whom *they* had received the gospel' (Calvin: *Commentaries* Vol.22 Part 2 pp177,198, emphasis mine). Calvin's editor drew attention to the fact that John told his readers *they* had had the commandment, 'which *you* have had', 'from the beginning' (Calvin: *Commentaries* Vol.22 Part 2 p177, emphasis his).

The whole Bible is to be used for sanctification – not just the ten commandments

On John 17:17, Hutcheson: 'The instrumental cause of... sanctification... the word of truth is the means and instrument of sanctification... The truth of God is the rule of true sanctification... The truth of God... has... a special influence in the matter of daily sanctification... The word of command... the word of promise... and the word and doctrine of the cross of Christ... [is] the rule and touchstone of sanctification... a means and instrument of it... The truth of God... is only to be found in the word of God' (Hutcheson pp364-365). Do not miss: 'The word and doctrine of the cross of Christ... [is] the rule and touchstone of sanctification... a means and instrument of it'. Hutcheson did not mention 'law' once, and all but one of his supporting verses (and that Ps. 12:6) came from the New Testament. I am not complaining, just observing that the Reformed argue tooth and nail for the law, but when their system is out of sight they argue biblically.

But surely Calvin will stick to his guns, won't he? Calvin: Christ spoke of 'the means of sanctification... "The word" here denotes the doctrine of the gospel... Whoever departs from the gospel as the means [of sanctification] must become more and more filthy and polluted'. How does that fit with his third use of the law? Consistency surely requires: 'Whoever departs from the law of Moses as the means [of sanctification]'! I am not complaining – just observing that Calvin must have forgotten his third use of the law at this point. Hendriksen: 'The truth [by which the believer must be] governed [so that] this sanctification can take place, [is] God's redemptive revelation in Christ, as the ultimate standard of life and doctrine. This truth is embodied in Christ, in him alone. He is the truth [John 14:6]. [The] word [which the believer must] live according to [is] the truth of God revealed in [the] message which [the apostles] had received from [Christ]'. Where does this leave the third use of the law? Manton knew that God sanctifies by the Scriptures; but, as he said, 'the truths delivered in the word may be referred to two heads – law and gospel... In this place Christ chiefly intends the gospel' (Calvin: *Commentaries* Vol.18 Part 1 pp179-180; Hendriksen: *John* p361; Manton: *Sermons* pp296,304). Well, there you have it; Reformed writers arguing that the gospel is the way the believer is sanctified!

Unsurprisingly, Edgar H.Andrews got it right: 'The believer's rule of life is the whole Bible, not just part of it... Certainly, Moses' law and the law "written in the heart" have some things in common, but they remain two distinct laws. They overlap, but they are not the same. Both teach me, for example, that I must not defraud my neighbour, but only the law of Christ teaches me to go the second mile, and love my enemy. The Sermon on the Mount is sometimes (wrongly, I believe) said to be Christ's exposition of the ten commandments. The fact is that the Sermon on the Mount introduces entirely new concepts of morality. To despise a fellow-human being is akin to murder. To lust in the heart is akin to adultery. When a building is demolished, the builders may use some of the old material to rebuild on the same site. Some valuable items may be carefully preserved for inclusion in the new edifice. But the old building is nonetheless destroyed, and the construction that replaces it nonetheless new! So it is with the law of Moses and the law of Christ... New Testament teaching... goes beyond the law in defining God's moral standards upon men, as in the Sermon on the Mount, or the "practical" sections of Paul's letters. Again, the nature and character of God is revealed most clearly in Christ, as Heb. 1:1-3 states unequivocally. The law, therefore, takes its natural place as part of Scripture...'.

'As regards sanctification, the law can be accorded no special place today in the life of the believer; that is, no place *over and above* the rest of Scripture. To suggest that the ten commandments are in some *special* way the Christian's rule of life does an injustice to the whole body of New Testament teaching on Christian conduct... It is often said that the Sermon on the Mount is nothing more than an exposition of the ten commandments, but this is not the case. The Sermon on the Mount refers to "these commandments" (Matt. 5:19), but the context is the entire Old Testament, not just the decalogue. Again, only three of the ten commandments are referred to in the sermon, either directly or indirectly, whereas it embodies an abundance of moral and spiritual instruction which is nowhere implied in the decalogue. This specifically New Testament teaching includes such things as reconciliation, the permanence of marriage, a forgiving spirit, love for our enemies, self-effacing charity, prayer, fasting, our attitude to material wealth, confidence in God's providence, the tests of genuine faith and a life built upon the rock (that is, obedience to Christ's teaching). It cannot be adequate to suggest that Christian morality and holiness of life stem in some special way from the decalogue...'.

'There is a real danger that believers may revert to law-keeping in the mistaken belief that this makes them more "spiritual" and thus more acceptable to God. Paul's purpose [in Gal. 4:1-3] is to point out that the very opposite is true. That is, submission to the law begets bondage, and belongs to the "world" from which Christ has delivered his people, rather than the kingdom of God... [Believers] are free from the law, no longer subject to its requirements or its penalties. Are they, then, a lawless people, having no law? Not at all. They are under a new law, even the rule and law of Christ (1 Cor. 9:21; Gal. 6:2)... The law of Christ is an altogether more demanding law than that of Moses. Yet believers can keep it, because it is written in the hearts and because they are enabled by the indwelling Holy Spirit (Jer. 31:31-33). Their obedience is not perfect, for they are still sinners. But they do not rest on the perfection of their law-keeping for either salvation or holiness. Christ is their redemption and their sanctification, and his blood keeps on cleansing them from all sin (1 Cor. 1:30; 1 John 1:7-9)' (Edgar H.Andrews pp112-113,182-183,203,252, emphasis his).

The law of Christ is not a neat set of rules replacing the ten commandments
Wells: 'As soon as we see that the demand for a *compact* rule of life is neither found in the Scriptures nor implied by them, we are prepared to receive from Christ a *comprehensive* law based on the new-covenant documents. No slogan, not even Scripture, can contain it, but it is clearly there, as it must be if Jesus Christ is Lord'. Wells suggested 'its parameters; [namely,] the commands of the Lord Jesus himself... the demands laid upon believers in the books of the New Testament, the new-covenant documents... the further illumination of the Holy Spirit... [and]... the examination of the Old Testament law with the idea in mind of finding those things that are in keeping with the explicit demands of Christ in the New Testament. In these, it seems to me, we have the law of Christ' (Wells pp47-48, emphasis mine; Crisp: *Christ* Vol.4 p117). As I have explained, I would add 'the example of Christ' (1 Pet. 2:21; 1 John 2:6) to the list. See Lloyd-Jones: *New* pp158-162.

Bennett: In 1 Cor. 5, 'Paul is concerned, as he always was in his letters, not to give the impression that the law – Mosaic, Mosaic contextualised into the new covenant, or even straightforward Christian law – is the centre of our faith, or that it has the ability to motivate us in obedience; instead, Christ and his atonement is [*sic*] the centre, and our motivation is that our Passover lamb has died to save us, as well as that we have now been made new by his saving work (1 Cor. 5:7) [see also 2 Cor. 5:17]. As those loved and rescued by Christ, we can and must live out the sanctifying change that he has wrought in us; because this is a fact in our communion with God, and not just a law written on stone, or set in Scripture, we want to obey him, and we can' (Bennett: 'Use' pp6-7).

Jesus his people's lawgiver: The Sermon on the Mount: General comments
In addition to what follows, see also Edgar Andrews immediately above and on Gal. 2:16-21 p416.

Thielman: 'In four places in his Gospel, Matthew shows that he believes Jesus' own teaching is a replacement of the Mosaic law. Jesus' own words, including his affirmation of the Mosaic law's ultimate goal and many of its specific requirements, constitute not a new interpretation of the Mosaic law but a supersession of it'. In particular, in the Sermon on the Mount, 'Jesus replaces Moses, and his teaching replaces the Mosaic commandments. Just as Moses spoke from a mountain, so Jesus speaks from a mountain here. Just as Moses gave commandments with the intention that his hearers should keep them, so Jesus intends that his commandments should be kept. Just as Moses spoke with authority, so Jesus speaks with an unsurpassed authority. Jesus and his teaching, in short, have superseded Moses and the law' (Thielman pp 69,71).

Govett: 'Let us now turn to another field in which the loftiness of the new rule of life is more fully exhibited. I refer to the Sermon on the Mount, in which the Saviour's doctrine is compared with that of Moses in many and most important points. The main difference between the two systems consists in this – that Moses' law embodies the spirit of JUSTICE; the teaching of our Lord, the spirit of MERCY. It is from this fundamental distinction that the superiority of the new rule of life flows... Jesus came in no hostile spirit against the law or the prophets. Both were sent by his Father; both must receive their entire fulfilment ere they passed away, as it was designed that they should. But... there is no "unseemly opposition" here...'.

'The Saviour begins to compare his new standard with the old. He takes the second table of the decalogue, and shows how much more he requires than Moses demanded of old. The Saviour announces his commands with the most studied contrast to the law: a contrast which has been blunted to English readers by our translation. We read [in the AV of Matt. 5:21]: "You have heard that it was said *by* those of old time", instead of "*to*", which beyond just question is the correct rendering; and which is given in the margin [of the AV, and is the translation in the NKJV, NIV; the NASB has "the ancients were told"]. [Christ] begins with the sixth command. The law forbade murder, and announced to the murderer the judgement of the appointed court. Jesus assures his disciples that even anger between brethren would come before his future court; and that a malicious word would expose the utterer to the danger of hell-fire. Here is a heightening indeed of the offence and of the penalty. That which was no misdeed against the law of Moses is now to be visited with a sentence greater than that belonging to the highest crime under the law (Matt. 5:21-22)'.

'When he speaks of the seventh command, there is a similar raising of the standard. That which was no misdeed at all as reckoned by Moses is by Jesus announced to be adultery, and exposed to the visitation of Gehenna. With like words does Jesus exalt the rule of life concerning theft, false witness and coveting a neighbour's goods (Matt. 5:27-30)'.

'But he does not halt at the decalogue. That was not the Jew's entire rule of life'. Let me pause. What a very important point this is. It must not be missed. The ten commands comprised only a part of the rule for Jews. So, how can the Reformed argue for believers to be under a more restricted rule than the Jews were? 'The Saviour therefore shows how his new commands rise above and set aside the law. He forbids divorce in cases permitted by Moses. Moses allowed oaths and vows... the Saviour forbids them... Moses' general doctrine was that goodness and kindness were to be exhibited towards men, specially towards the holy nation of Israel; but it admitted of two exceptions – criminals and enemies... Criminals... pity was forbid (Deut. 13:8; 19:21). The enemies of Israel might be smitten to death with the sword. The priests with the trumpets of God were to encourage and bless their warfare. Now [under the law of Christ] this is forbidden. The law of grace is to encircle even the cases excepted by Moses. The disciple is not to prosecute the offender; nor is he permitted on any occasion to take the sword against a foe. His Father in heaven is sparing criminals and enemies; he is to resemble him (Matt. 5:38-48)'.

'Jesus next drops a word of warning. He confesses the extreme difficulty to fallen man of a rule of life so high and heavenly as this. 'Tis a narrow gate and a strict way indeed! But he tells us not to imagine that he was asking of disciples born of God only conduct such as might be exhibited by the lowest of mankind. Was such a life difficult indeed? Yes, but an especial reward was also promised thereto. Were they born again of God? Let them show it by grace like that of the Father in heaven'.

'In regard of religious service, the Saviour next exalts the standard greatly beyond the law. Moses... required only that the offerer should be a circumcised Jew, not ceremonially unclean, and that the offering... should be without blemish. But now our Lord brings into view the motives of the worshipper... (Matt. 6:1-18)'.

'The law promised, and gave as its blessing, treasures on earth. Filled barns and overflowing storehouses were the sign of Jehovah's favour. Now the disciples were to give up these for treasures in heaven, and for a recompense at the resurrection of the just (Matt. 6:19-34). Under the law, to be a magistrate and ruler was an honour, rightly desired by an Israelite... The Saviour now forbids this to his disciples... (Matt. 7:1-2). The law admitted to its sacred rites every circumcised descendant of Abraham. No matter how sensual, bloodthirsty, deceitful and unbelieving a Jew might be, he had a right to partake of the Passover. Judas the betrayer had as good a right to the Paschal lamb as our Lord. Wicked as a high priest might be, if he were not ceremonially unclean, he had a right to enter the holiest. But that defect is removed in the Saviour's new scheme. His disciples were to exclude from the sacred rites appointed by our Lord all the unclean and unrenewed in spirit (Matt. 7:6)'.

'Thus I have rapidly gone over the Sermon on the Mount, and have exhibited our Lord as indeed the author of a new doctrine, affecting all the Christian's life, and standing in constant contrast with the commands of the Mosaic law. Jesus is no mere expounder of Moses'. What a vital point this is! 'Most would make Jesus only a land-surveyor, pointing out afresh the old boundaries of the fields, scraping from the surface the stones, the moss and lichens which in the course of ages had covered them; or rooting from their neighbourhood the brambles that concealed them. But now evidence in plenty has been adduced to prove that this view is mistaken. Moses brought LAW: Jesus brought GRACE (John 1:17). The prophet who was to come, according to God's own promise, was not merely one who was to recall attention to the words spoken by Moses. He was to bear a new doctrine ["his law" (Isa. 42:4)]: and woe to him that refused it! The two schools of doctrine taught by Moses and by Christ, respectively, have been briefly presented. You, my reader, must decide by which you will be led. Some, as the Saviour foresaw, would prefer the old and easier rule of life. For them, he draws the consequence of such a choice... (Matt. 5:20)' (Govett pp48-53).

Let me emphasise this last point. As Govett rightly shows, the law of Christ is more penetrating than the law of Moses, and its punishment ultimately more severe. In the body of the book I have explained what is meant by this. The warning passages are real! Please remember Jesus' words about judgement were largely delivered to his disciples and for them! Most evangelicals today are quite content to forget the context and apply them to unbelievers. So, taking up Govett's expression, those who opt for the Mosaic law as the way of sanctification have actually opted for the 'easier rule of life' – the wrong one, but easier!

Bruce, referring to 1 Cor. 9:21 and Gal. 6:2: 'The law of Christ... is not less difficult than the law of Moses... The Sermon on the Mount... sets a much higher standard for human behaviour than do the ten commandments' (Bruce: *Spreading* p120. See Gadsby: *Works* p20). Christ gave his law; this is why it is called the law of Christ.

Now for the other side of the coin. I have already quoted Kruse arguing from Gal. 6:2; I return to it: Paul, 'having fought to deliver Gentile believers from the yoke of the Mosaic law', was not guilty of 'immediately placing upon them the heavier yoke of Christ's law (understood as a collection of the many injunctions such as those found in... Matt. 5-7). The law of Christ is love... [which is] the fruit of the Spirit (Gal. 5:22)... It is only in the lives of those freed from the law, and walking by the Spirit, that the law of Christ is fulfilled' (Kruse p106). 'For Paul, to live [under Christ's law] would not have been a new legalism based on the commands of the historical Jesus and the exalted Christ, but probably a life lived in the service of Christ out of gratitude for his amazing love, in which the commands of Christ were gladly obeyed' (Kruse pp129-130). This is the point. See below.

So, paradoxically, Christ's law is both more penetrating and yet easy (Matt. 11:30). As with the severity aspect of Christ's law, in the body of the book I say more about the 'easy' (the opposite of burdensome) (Thayer), 'kindly' (Arndt and Gingrich; Hendriksen: *Matthew* p505) and 'light' (easy to be kept) (Thayer) aspect of Christ's law.

W.D.Davies: 'Jesus... preached a new *torah* from the Mount and yet... remained loyal to the old *torah*... Paul... believe[ed] that loyalty to the new law of Christ did not involve disloyalty to the *torah* of his fathers... Jesus is deliberately set before us as a new lawgiver who is greater than Moses; the "Sermon" on the Mount [in part] is the counterpart of the "Sermon" on Sinai'. Lloyd-Jones: Christ 'does not hesitate to assert... that he, and he alone, is able to give the spiritual interpretation of the law that was given through Moses... He does not hesitate to speak of himself and to regard himself as the lawgiver: "I say to you"' (W.D.Davies pp73,149; Lloyd-Jones: *Studies* Vol.2 p331).

Christ is his people's lawgiver. Zaspel: 'His authority is supreme, and his law is obligatory'. Luther: 'Moses is a teacher and doctor of the Jews. We have our own master, Christ, and he has set before what we are to know, observe, do, and leave undone'. Wells: 'It is [the] priority of Jesus that the New Testament is concerned to maintain against all competitors... This priority of the Lord Jesus... is so evident in the Sermon on the Mount' (Zaspel p156; Luther, quoted by Armstrong p17. Luther went on to show how Moses is still useful to believers; Wells p42. I would not limit this to the Sermon on the Mount. Note 'Jesus said', 'I say', 'my words', *etc.*, outside the Sermon on the Mount. See Zaspel p166.

This approach to the Sermon on the Mount, however, has been contested. Chamblin claimed that Christ was issuing 'a call to *rediscover* the Old Testament and to obey certain *existing* demands of the Mosaic law... Jesus is not expounding a new law... It marks the *rediscovery* of a quality of obedience which the [Pharisees] have lost' (Chamblin p191, first two emphases his; the last, mine). Chamblin added that the Sermon also 'marks an intensifying or escalating of obedience owing to the dawn of the kingdom'. In saying this, Chamblin was getting closer to what Christ was doing, but still not reaching the newness of his law.

Hendriksen was another to resist the proper understanding of the Sermon on the Mount, arguing that Christ was contrasting his words with those of 'the *expounders* of the law, the rabbis... the ancient interpreters [of Moses]' (Hendriksen: *Matthew* pp295-318, emphasis mine. See also p504). Barcellos, similarly, said Christ was contrasting 'the law of Moses and *the false understanding* evidenced in the hypocrisy of the scribes and Pharisees... They distorted the law of Moses by settling for externalism' (Barcellos pp75-76, emphasis mine; see also Pink: *Sermon* p79; Pink: *Sermon* p80 made much of 'said *by* them' (Matt. 5:27, AV), but this rendering is incorrect (see NKJV, NASB, NIV, *etc.*). It is claimed that Christ here was saying that he was not setting out anything new but rather was 'explaining', 'establishing' or 'upholding' the law, declaring its real or intended meaning in light of Pharisaical efforts to get round its full significance. 'Advocates of a strong measure of continuity between Jesus' teaching and the law' argue this way (Moo: 'The Law' p204). This was precisely what the Jews of Christ's day expected: 'When the rabbis taught... that the Messiah... would bring a new law, they thought of that law as new not in the sense that it would be contrary to the law of Moses but that it would explain it more fully' (W.D.Davies p72). True, the Pharisees did reduce the meaning of the law, they did ruin it by their tradition, and Christ told them so (Matt. 15:1-9; Mark 7:5-13). But as Lloyd-Jones said, this explanation on its own 'is totally inadequate... The Sermon on the Mount does expound and explain the law at certain points – but it goes beyond it' (Lloyd-Jones: *Studies* Vol.1 pp14,221-223,232-233, for instance).

Zaspel, likewise: 'In short, [Christ] is exercising his prerogatives as the "greater than Moses", the new interpreter of the will of God... Jesus, rather, exercised the prerogative of lordship... [The] new-covenant perspective provides a Christocentric focus which takes seriously Christ's claims of lordship. It is, in fact, a theology of lordship... Christ fulfils and stands above all that came before him. Unlike the scribes whose highest appeal was to Moses, Jesus teaches on his own authority, an authority that is unique' (Zaspel pp156-157,162-163).

Witherington: 'Christ [not only] endorsed a certain amount of the principles within the Mosaic law as part of his own teaching, in particular the love commandment [Lev. 19:18; see chapter 17], but he also declared void other parts, and intensified yet other parts of the Mosaic law. In other words, he was not engaging in an act of mere covenant renewal, but offering a new covenant between God and his people, which required a new law' (Witherington p424).

John Brown: 'It has been supposed by some very judicious interpreters that the word "fulfil" here means fully to expound, to bring out the true meaning, in opposition to the false glosses of the Jewish teachers... and they have thought that there is here a reference to what they consider as the expositions of the law which follow... I scarcely think this formed so great a part of [Christ's] teaching... and I more than doubt if the statements which immediately follow [in the Sermon on the Mount] are, strictly speaking, expositions of the law' (Brown: *Discourses* Vol.1 pp169-170). Putting aside all the negatives, Christ is establishing his own law, a new law, for his people.

This is questioned. Barcellos, for instance: 'Christ is stating *explicitly* what was already contained *implicitly* in the seventh commandment. He is not instituting a contrastive and new law in Matt. 5:28. Instead, he is correcting the faulty exegesis of the day' (Barcellos pp72-76, emphasis his).

Not at all! As John Brown said: 'It has been supposed by some, that our Lord's object is to expound the law of the ten commandments, and to show, by a few examples, its exceeding breadth and spiritual reference. They suppose that our Lord asserts that the sixth commandment forbids not only murder, but malignant feeling; and the seventh not only adultery, but impure desire. That the divine law does take cognisance of the thoughts and intents of the heart, there can be no doubt, [or] that malignant feeling and impure desires are sins in the estimation of him who looks on the heart; but whether the sixth and seventh commandments, strictly speaking, do forbid anything but what, in plain terms, they prohibit, is a totally different question, and one which, I apprehend, our Lord's statements do not furnish us with the means of answering. There is nothing, either in the way of direct statement or otherwise, to lay a foundation for the conclusion that our Lord [in this passage] had it for his object to show that the law of the ten commandments had a hidden, recondite, spiritual meaning, besides the literal signification of the words in which it is couched' (Brown: *Discourses* Vol.1 pp175-176). In other words, there is no warrant for the Reformed trying to make the Mosaic law say more than it did. This, of course, to say the least, raises a large question mark over the Puritan way of applying the ten commandments in fine detail far, far beyond their stated remit. I noted this in chapter 5. The law of Christ had to wait for Christ himself to establish it.

The 'mark of "inwardness" [which is] in the new covenant... does not seem to have been very influential in Rabbinic Judaism. We do, indeed, read of the law being in the heart, but the idea is not prominent [in Rabbinic teaching]... In [Rabbinic] interpretations of Jer. 31 no emphasis is laid on this' (W.D.Davies p225). The truth is, Christ was going far beyond the rabbis, setting up his own, new law. On Jer. 31, see chapter 18. Stronger, and better, Brown: 'No sin is more strongly prohibited in the law of Christ than impurity' (Brown: *Discourses* Vol.1 p192). And this, not only in the act, but in the thought. This is no better exemplified than in John 8:1-11. The Jews, imbued with the law of Moses, could only think in terms of the external act; Christ, in his law, drove them to the heart – above all, their own heart!

Pink caricatured the position I have outlined. I, nor any of the writers I have quoted, allege that 'Christ... proceeded to pit himself against [the law and the prophets,] affirming that Moses taught one thing and he quite another' (Pink: *Sermon* p79). Even so, there is the heavy contrast I have already spoken of. And I, along with others, do say that Christ in his law shows the way to use and apply the Mosaic law *under the new covenant*; that is, as seen in Christ's fulfilment of it. I further claim he was saying something new compared to Moses, and the rabbis.

Jesus his people's lawgiver: The Sermon on the Mount: Matt. 5:17-18

I know I have already quoted this, but it bears repetition here. Edgar H.Andrews: 'How can Paul say the law has been "destroyed" when Jesus says the opposite? When Jesus refers to "the law and the prophets" in Matthew, he is actually talking about the Old Testament Scriptures, not the law of Moses. However, Moses' law forms part of those Scriptures, so the question remains a fair one. The word "destroy" must be understood in its context in each case. Christ said he came "not to destroy, but to fulfil". But in fulfilling the law, he rendered it redundant. For example, the Mosaic priesthood was swept away, being replaced by Christ's high priesthood (see Heb. 7 – 9). So, in one sense, fulfilment can be seen as destruction, since it renders obsolete that which is fulfilled. The purpose of the flower is fulfilled when its petals fall, leaving the seed-pod to ripen. The blossom is destroyed in the very act of fulfilment. So it is with the law' (Edgar H.Andrews p109).

Moo: *plēroō*, to make full, fill up, complete, accomplish, fulfil (Thayer), speaks 'of salvation history which pictures the entire Old Testament as anticipating and looking forward to Jesus... It is likely that the "fulfilment" of Matt. 5:17 means that Jesus' new, eschatological demands do not constitute an abandonment of the law but [rather] express that which the law was all along intended to anticipate. The continuity of the law with Jesus' teaching is thereby clearly stressed, but it is a continuity on the plane of a salvation-historical scheme of "anticipation-realisation"' (Moo: 'The Law' pp205-206). 'The linchpin in interpretations of this text is the word "fulfil" (*plēroō*). Some interpreters argue that Jesus' claim in Matt. 5:17 relates to him personally: in his ministry, and, especially his death and resurrection, he will bring to pass all that is written about him in the Old Testament. But the context, which focuses exclusively of Jesus' teaching, is decisively against this view. Jesus is talking about how, in his teaching, he would fulfil "the law and the prophets". This last phrase also suggests a focus on teaching. The phrase can refer to the Old Testament as a whole, but Matthew uses it quite distinctively to describe what we might call the "commanding" aspect of the Old Testament (Matt. 7:12; 22:40). Those who contend for a strong measure of continuity between Jesus' teaching and the law argue that Jesus' fulfilment of the law consists of [in] of his "establishing" or "upholding" the law, giving it its real intended meaning in response to Jewish attempts to evade its full significance. But while "fulfil" could have this sense, and the contrast with "abolish" would also fit this understanding, the idea that Jesus here simply "expounds" the law suffers from two grave difficulties. First, the context does not support it. In the "antitheses" of Matt. 5:21-48, Jesus does not simply re-establish the true meaning of the law. No exegesis of the *lex talionis* (eye for eye) would lead to the conclusion that one is not to resist one who is evil (Matt. 5:38-39); loving neighbour in Lev. 19:18 means to love the fellow-Israelite, not, as Jesus demands, to love the enemy (Matt. 5:43-47). Nor does the Old Testament demand to keep one's oath lead naturally to the conclusion that one is to refrain from oaths... (Matt. 5:33-37). To be sure, some of the requirements of Jesus seem to be directed against a perversion of the teaching of the law current among some Jews of his day; hatred of the enemy (Matt. 5:43) is certainly not Old Testament teaching. But the fact remains that Jesus' own demands go considerably beyond any fair exegesis of at least most of the actual texts he quotes; nor do most of his demands find support anywhere in the Old Testament. Jesus' pairing of his teaching with quotations from the Old Testament in the antitheses do not fall into a single pattern. Moreover, the startlingly "*I say to you*" suggests that Jesus teaching here arises from his own unique position within salvation history'.

I pause. I would strengthen 'suggests' – see the extracts immediately below. Moo continued with another alternative: 'If Jesus is not expositing the law, then, perhaps he is "deepening" or "radicalising" it. This popular way of conceiving the relationship between Jesus' teaching and the Old Testament here fits the first two antitheses (murder-anger; adultery-lust) quite well. But, again, it does not explain all the antitheses well at all. Moreover, it does not do justice to the Matthew use of the world "fulfil" – and this is also the second objection to the "exposition" view. The word "fulfil" (*plēroō*) is central to Matthew's theological vocabulary; in addition to Matt. 5:17, he uses it fifteen times, in comparison with Mark's two and Luke's nine uses. Ten occurrences come in the introductions to the distinctive Matthean "formula quotations" (Matt. 1:22; 2:15,17,23; 4:14; 8:17; 12:17; 13:35; 21:4; 27:9), two more in general statements regarding Jesus' fulfilling of the Scriptures (Matt. 26:54,56), one in the reason given for Jesus' baptism, and two others have no theological significance (Matt. 13:48; 23:32). "Fulfil" is therefore *the* word that Matthew uses to depict Jesus' relationship to the Old Testament in general. It clearly extends beyond the usual idea of "prophecy-fulfilment". Matthew claims that the history of Israel reaches its "fulfilment" in Christ (*cf.* Matt. 2:15); and, in a text particularly relevant for Matt. 5:17, Matthew has Jesus declaring that "all the prophets and the law prophesied until John" (Matt. 11:13). The whole Old Testament, according to Matthew, has a "prophetic" quality: its law and its history, as well as its prophecies. Matthew presents a theology of salvation history which pictures the entire Old Testament as anticipating and looking forward to Jesus'.

'In light of this distinctive Matthean usage of "fulfil", I [Moo] think it likely that Jesus "fulfils" the law and the prophets by teaching the eschatological "law of the kingdom" which Old Testament law was all along anticipating and planning towards. Jesus, apparently, in response to objections to the nature of his early preaching, asserts the continuity of the law with his teaching, But it is a continuity on the plane of a salvation-historical scheme of "anticipation-realisation". How are we then to understand the strong emphasis on continuity found in Matt. 5:18-19? These verse are indeed difficult: but difficult for *any* view that seeks to integrate all the New Testament teaching on the law. For, taken at face value, these verses appear to insist that every single commandment of the law remains binding on God's people as long as the earth shall last – and this, of course, stands irreconcilable conflict with the claim of many New Testament pages (see Hebrews specially) that most of the commandments in the Mosaic law are no longer binding on the church. Critical scholars simply attribute these verses to a conservative Jewish faction in the early church. Evangelicals offer various explanations. Some argue that Jesus is thinking here only of the "moral" law – but we have already argued that this was not a well-established category in first-century Judaism'. I pause. I go further. To impose such a filter on the text is clearly an imposition without biblical warrant. If one takes that line, one might as well go the whole hog and just cut it out of Scripture altogether! 'The best option, then, is simply to argue that these verse be read in context: the law that remains in force and that must be taught in the kingdom is the law *as Jesus has fulfilled it*'.

'I conclude from these brief remarks on this key text that Jesus is making two key points: 1. his teaching stands in continuity with the Old Testament law; and 2. it is his teaching, not the law as such, that provides the "rules" for life in the kingdom. The Old Testament law is not to be abandoned. Indeed, it must continue to be taught (Matt. 5:19) – but interpreted and applied in light of its fulfilment by Christ. In other words, it stands no longer as the ultimate standard of conduct for God's people, but must always be viewed though the lenses of Jesus' ministry and teaching. This conclusion is in keeping with Jesus' general approach to the Old Testament law in the Gospels. He rarely cites the Old Testament as substantiation of his demands (and most of these appear in polemical contexts). He presents himself as authority greater than the law itself, as the "I say to you" formula implies, and as he claims quite plainly in Mark 2:28... And he charges his followers to teach their disciples what *Jesus* had taught (Matt. 28:16-20)' (Moo: 'Galatians' pp23-26, emphasis his). And that takes us neatly on to the next section.

Jesus his people's lawgiver: 'My commandments'

Ryle: 'Let us notice how our Lord speaks of "my commandments". We never read of Moses or any other servant of God using such an expression. It is the language of one who was one with God the Father, and had the power to lay down laws and make statutes for his church'. Berridge: 'Who has a right to say: "Keep my commandments", but God? If Jesus is only a creature, he has no right to require that obedience at my hands which is due only to God. Neither [*sic*] Moses, prophets, nor apostles say: "Keep my commandments"' (Ryle: *John* Vol.3 p81; Berridge: *Outlines* p107).

On John 15:12, John Brown asked: 'Who is this who speaks? Whose commandment is this?' He answered: 'It is the commandment of "a teacher sent from God..."'; and who, therefore, might "speak with authority – not as the scribes", saying not: "This is my request – this is my advice" – but "this is my commandment".[4] It is the commandment of the prophet whom God had promised to raise up like Moses... It is the command of him whom the Father has "sent and sealed", and respecting whom he has proclaimed the most excellent glory: "This is my beloved Son, in whom I am well pleased; hear him". It is the commandment of him to whom the Father has "committed all judgement", and whom he has required all to honour, as they honour himself, whom he has constituted both Lord and Christ, to whom he has given power over all flesh, all power in heaven and earth, a name above every name in this world, or in that which is to come, whom he has commanded all the angels of God to worship, and whom he has appointed to judge the world in righteousness. More than all this, it is the commandment of him who is "God manifest in the flesh", "the word who, in the beginning, was with God – was God – by whom all things were made – without whom nothing was made", who is "the great God", as well as "our Saviour" who is "God over all, blessed for ever". It is the commandment of him who by an act of will formed, and by an act of will can dissolve, the system of the universe. It is the commandment of one infinite in wisdom and power, in righteousness and benignity; and, just because it is *his* commandment, it must be, like himself, "holy and just and good". It is a commandment, then, that cannot be neglected or disobeyed, without deep guilt and great danger. To disobey this commandment is to disobey, not only a divine messenger, but a divine person...'.

'But there is something more than this in the case before us. This is a commandment which he claims as *his own*, in a peculiar sense... It is *his own* [emphasis mine] commandment to *his own* [emphasis mine] people – a commandment which could have no existence till he came... "a new commandment"... There is something in these words: "This is my commandment", that would bear the mark of arrogance, did they come from any mere man. There is nothing like them in the writings of the prophets and apostles. They never command in their own name. It is not *their* commandments, but *God's* commandments, which they announce. It belongs only to him whose name alone is Jehovah, to ground the obligation of a requisition on his own authority, and to say: '"This is my commandment", and *therefore* you should obey it". "This is my commandment", "a commandment, not

---

[4] Hendriksen weakly and confusingly spoke of 'the authoritative *advice* Jesus gives' in Matt. 11:28-30 (Hendriksen: *Matthew* pp505-506). Not at all! Jesus commanded! Remember Calvin's 'kind adviser' when talking about the law (see pp367,414). For all their dismissive talk, and accusations of antinomianism, Christ's law is more penetrating than the Reformed set out with their system.

mere counsel; and not only one of my commandments, but, in a sense quite peculiar, *my commandment*'' (Brown: *Discourses* Vol.3 pp317-319, apart from the notes above, emphasis his). What a powerful 'discourse' on 'my commandments'! Christ is his people's lawgiver; not Moses.

On Matt. 28:19-20, Carson: 'The focus is on *Jesus'* commands, not Old Testament law' (Carson p598, emphasis his).

John Smyth's Short Confession of Faith in 1610: 'Acknowledge him' – the Son of the living God – 'to be the only... lawgiver... whom we must trust, believe and follow. In him is fulfilled, and by him is taken away, an intolerable burden of the law of Moses, even all the shadows and figures... And as the true promised prophet he has manifested and revealed unto us whatsoever God asks or requires of the people of the New Testament; for as God, by Moses and the other prophets, has spoken and declared his will to the people of the Old Testament, so has he in these last days, by his Prophet [that is, Christ] spoken unto us... and has showed by doctrine and life, the law of Christians, a rule of their life, the path and way of everlasting life'. The Dordrecht Confession of 1632, 'the most influential of all Mennonite (Anabaptist) Confessions, [spoke] of the law of Christ, which is the holy gospel, or the New Testament... Christ... caused it to be declared, that all men without distinction, if they are obedient, through faith, follow, fulfil and live according to the precepts of the same, are his children and rightful heirs' (Lumpkin pp66,70,105).

Harris: 'Let it ever be borne in mind, that because we are called to liberty, even the liberty of sons, because we are already made the household of God, and have our mansions prepared in it, that the Lord Jesus as head over that house, claims our allegiance to him. It is because we belong to heaven that he exercises this authority over us, in order that we may walk worthy of our high and holy calling. It is because we are sons, and if sons then heirs, heirs of God and joint heirs with Christ, that the Son who has made us free, shows us how to use that freedom in service to the Father' (Harris p46).

Taylor: 'The ministry of grace is another law, the law of faith, to which we are bound; and this law can not only command, as the former [that is, the law of Moses], but [it] can also give grace and power to obey and perform the commandment... And those who give up their names to Christ, must not expect to be lawless, for they come to take a yoke upon them, and learn of him; yes, they are bound to fulfil the law of Christ (Gal. 6:2), a new commandment (John 13:34). So Christians must still be under commandment. Neither would Christ by any other touchstone try [test, prove] the love of a professor unto himself, than by keeping and obeying his word... It is no matter to you that grace has appeared, nor any benefit unto you that it brings salvation, unless you are also instructed by it in the lessons following' (Taylor pp174-175,182-183).

Taylor included these words: 'And this is the doctrine of grace... The doctrine of the gospel is a schoolmaster [better, child-custodian], and full of instruction,[5] in which it differs not from the law... Though they teach the same things, yet they differ in the manner of teaching'. To put it mildly, I do not agree with this way of expressing it. It stems from the mistaken view that the law and the gospel are one and the same, just different administrations. How anybody could think that the law and the gospel teach the same thing, but only in different ways, baffles me. If it were so, why ever do we have the gospel – is it the same as, but just clearer than, the law? Is that what Christ came, lived, died and rose again for – to give us another way of saying the same thing? A bit more light, perhaps? Really! At this point, Taylor pp182-183; see also p12 was wrongly arguing that believers

---

[5] Taylor was misled by 'schoolmaster'. As I have explained, the law was not a schoolmaster; it was a child-conductor. The emphasis is not upon education, but on discipline, even with severity.

are under the law of Moses for sanctification. Now we know. To be able to maintain Calvin's third use of the law, this is the kind of theological gymnastics such law-advocates have to be nimble at.

Balthasar Hubmaier, in 1527: 'God sent Christ, the [Good] Samaritan, the Eternal Physician, to administer the wine of the law which enables the fallen soul to know what is righteous in God's sight, and the oil of the gospel to enable it to do right... Christ... is the Alpha and Omega (Rev. 1:8), the beginning and the end of the fulfilment of the divine commandments (Col. 1:19)... Our perfection is in him' (paraphrased by Williams: *Spiritual* pp113,127). See George Wright pp236-238.

W.D.Davies spoke of 'those places in the Pauline letters where Paul is clearly dependent upon the words of Jesus... Those words permeate *all* his ethical exhortations. Moreover, at the most personal point of all his letters we cannot help tracing the impact of the teaching of Jesus... It is surely from the words of his Lord that he had made the shattering discovery of the supreme importance of the motive behind any act... [or] thought... He had learnt of Christ'. Davies, noting that Christ by 'friend and foe [was given the title] Rabbi... throughout the Gospels [where] the importance of Jesus as teacher shines clear, [also remarked on] the extreme deference with which [Paul] refers to the words of the Lord, and his almost unconscious references to them show that his mind was permeated with his sayings; his converts are they who have learnt Christ' (W.D.Davies pp138-144, emphasis mine).

Fee, on the rarity of explicit apostolic reference to the words of Christ: 'This [1 Cor. 7:10] is one of the rare instances in Paul's extant letters when he appeals directly to the teaching of Jesus (*cf.* 1 Cor. 9:14; 11:23; 1 Tim. 5:18), which fact means neither that Paul lacks authority nor that Jesus does not ordinarily count as authority for him. The clue is to be found in 1 Cor. 7:12, where, in contrast to this parenthetical insertion, he says: "I, not the Lord". Christ is always Paul's ultimate authority. When he has no direct command, he still speaks as one who is trustworthy (verse 25) because he has the Spirit of God (verse 40). Two reasons suggest themselves as to why he does not appeal more often directly to Jesus: (1) From his point of view his ethical instructions *all* come from the Lord. If he does not appeal more often to the sayings of Jesus themselves, that is because such teachings are the *presupposition* of his own. The "ways" of Jesus are lived out and taught in the "ways" of the apostle (see on 1 Cor. 4:16; *cf.* 1 Cor. 11:1). Hence he feels no need for such an appeal. Those ways have already been taught before he writes his letters, so that he simply appeals to prior instructions (*cf.* 1 Thess. 4:1-2,11-12). (2) But for many other issues that arose in Gentile churches, Paul speaks on his own authority (which of course derives from the Lord), precisely because Jesus did not address such questions [and he had expressly made provision for this, John 14:26; 16:12-15]. However, in this present matter, on which Paul probably had *not* previously given instruction, there is a Jesus word, so he appeals to it. In verses 12-16, on the other hand, where the issue lies outside the province of Jesus' own life-setting, it is Paul who speaks, not the Lord' (Fee: *1 Corinthians* pp291-292, emphasis his). Fee's sane comments are in stark contrast to, and a stout rebuttal of, some bizarre (not to say, blasphemous) comments made on this by some modern-day Judaisers (see, for instance, revelations.org.za/Passion.htm).

'What are Christ's commandments?' asked John Brown. He replied: 'The whole revelation of the divine will, respecting what I am to believe, and feel, and do, and suffer, contained in the Holy Scriptures, is the law of Christ. Both volumes of the Holy Scriptures are the work of the Spirit of Christ... The commandments of Christ include whatever is good, and whatever God has required of us... These are the commandments of our Lord Jesus. Now to keep these commandments, is just to make them the rule and reason of our faith and conduct... The commandments and the sayings – the words – of our Lord... are not to be confined to what was, strictly speaking, preceptive in our Lord's teaching; they include all the communications he has made, directly or indirectly, in his personal teaching, or by the holy prophets and apostles. All his words may be termed his commandments, as they were all a revelation committed to him by the Father, and commanded to be given by him to the world: "The Father has given me a commandment what I should say, and what I should speak" [John 12:49]; and therefore, all of them have a high authoritative character; the doctrines, as we are accustomed to call them, being intended to regulate human opinion, just as really and as extensively as the precepts were intended to regulate all human disposition and conduct. The whole revelation is "the law of the Lord"... It is obviously impossible, in a discourse of this kind,[6] that I should [be able] to lay before you all the commandments of our Lord, by keeping which we are to continue in his love – for the commandments of Christ include the whole preceptive part of the inspired volume, with the exception of those ritual and political statutes which refer to the introductory dispensations which have passed away' (Brown: *Discourses* Vol.3 pp85-86,161,286). Brown listed a few of 'the most comprehensive and important of our Lord's commandments to his disciples', Matt. 6:19-20,33; 10:8; 16:24; Luke 12:15; John 13:34. See also Marbury p366.

Moo: 'My quarrel with traditional Reformed theology is not over whether the Old Testament contains eternal moral law, but how we are to discover what it is. We have no "red-letter" Old Testament[7] that identifies those laws; and... it is difficult even within so short and obviously important a text as the decalogue to distinguish the eternal from the temporary. We know what is eternally valid from the Old Testament law by its being included in the teaching of Jesus and the apostles. This is the "law of Christ" to which we, as God's new-covenant people, are now bound... While my Reformed colleague might argue that we are bound to whatever in the Mosaic law has not been clearly overturned by New Testament teaching, I argue that we are bound only to that which is clearly repeated within New Testament teaching' (Moo: 'Galatians' p31).

Karlberg appears to have misunderstood the believer's rule. 'We maintain', he declared, 'that if the commands of Christ are binding, then they are normative for Christian conduct' (Karlberg pp40-41). I could not agree more. Perhaps the misunderstanding arose over the phrase 'the law of God', which Karlberg was discussing. As I noted earlier, the law of God was the law of Moses in one epoch of salvation history, but is now the law of Christ in the age of the new covenant. Thus the proper comparison is between the law of Moses and the law of Christ. The fact is, while the law of *Moses* is not binding on the saints, the law of *Christ* is. And, as I have explained, the *law* of Moses is a very different entity to the *law* of Christ. The law of Moses (read through new-covenant glasses) can describe Christian behaviour, but it does not prescribe it. See Kruse p104.

On Gal. 6:1-2, Witherington: 'We must be dealing here with some sort of law that Paul [saw] his converts as already under, and in the future, in some danger of violating'. This must be 'the law of Christ' (Gal. 6:2) (Witherington pp421-422). He linked Gal. 6:1 with Matt. 18:15. Dunn suggested the sin in question might be found in Paul's list (Gal. 5:19-21), the opposite of Gal. 5:22-23, which as I explained earlier, Dunn thought was 'a kind of character-sketch of Christ' (Dunn pp310,319). To break the law of Christ, therefore, is to commit a real sin, and this means that Christ's law is a real law. And this shows, if there had been any doubt, that I am not teaching sinless perfection in this life. Sadly, believers sin! See Dunn p319.

Consider Gal. 6:16; Phil. 3:16; 1 Tim. 6:3
Is 'this rule' of Gal. 6:16 the law of Christ? I think so. Dunn thought it is 'clearly the norm by which [Paul and every believer] lives' (Dunn p343). John Brown thought it 'is obviously the principle laid down in the preceding verse' (Brown: *Galatians* p381). Bayes agreed but

---

[6] Or in a mere book like mine, or – without being facetious – on two tablets of stone.

[7] The American system of marking the words of Christ in red.

went further: 'It amounts to a life lived in accordance with the moral law of God which had originated from Christ', which I would call the law of Christ. Bayes however, fell back to the Reformed position: 'It is probably correct... to understand Paul to mean... the law... as the pattern for the believing life', by which he meant the law of Moses. As I showed in chapter 9, oddly Bayes turned to Gal. 5:25, saying, 'Paul stressed that to walk by the Spirit is to live in accordance with the law' (Bayes p173). I repeat my earlier comment: to my mind the verse says nothing of the sort – the law is not even mentioned – but since it is the only place Bayes raised the verse, I cannot follow his argument further. Indeed, as I explained in a note in chapter 9, Gal. 5:25 and the passage which follows shows the *contrast* between life under the Spirit and life under the law, not their *sameness*. See Dunn pp295-296,317.

Is 'the same rule' of Phil. 3:16 the law of Christ? I think so. Although the phrase in question probably was not in the original, 'nevertheless, that is the idea' (Hendriksen: *Philippians* p177). Hendriksen cited Gal. 6:16; he used 'principle'. NASB uses 'standard'.

On Phil. 3:16, Johnstone used 'precept', 'principle' and 'doctrine of Christ': 'As regards deliverance from guilt, when "Jesus was delivered for our offences, and was raised again for our justification", we so died in him, in the sight of God, that the law has no longer any claim upon us for punishment; and so we rose in him, as to pass out into the sphere of full blessed acceptance with God, and adoption into his family. As regards sanctification, we live though the fellowship of Christ's life; and yet at the same time, being in a wicked world, we have "a fellowship of his sufferings, being fashioned after the likeness of his death"... Vital religion impels to ardent longing and persistent effort after progress in holiness... The power of the gospel when received by faith... [gains] commanding influence over the nature [disposition]... Progress is the law [the principle] of the new life... The goal before the apostle's mind, in speaking of the persistent spiritual efforts of his life, [is] perfect conformity in everything to the will of God, to the image of Christ... Let us "abide in Christ", remembering that he "is made of God to us", no less our "sanctification" than our justifying "righteousness"... We shall hear our Saviour's voice behind us, saying: "This is the way, walk in it"; and we shall have grace given to walk therein' (Johnstone: *Philippians* pp271,284-286,301-305).

On Phil. 3:16, Lightfoot called the 'rule' 'a correct gloss' added by the translators. He spoke of 'the rule of faith as opposed to works', linking it with Gal. 6:16 (Lightfoot: *Philippians* p154). Poole: 'That very canon in exact conformity whereunto God's Israel might be sure of the best peace (Gal. 6:16; Phil. 4:7). The unerring word of God, exemplified in the condescending love of Christ, whom he had proposed to their imitation... The rule of faith, love, and a Christian life, or heavenly conversation, which he elsewhere calls a walking in the Spirit, and according to the Spirit, in opposition to walking in and after the flesh (Rom. 8:1,5; Gal. 5:16)' (Poole p699).

Are these 'wholesome words' (1 Tim. 6:3) the law of Christ? I think so. Leaving aside the first 'even' (supplied by the NKJV), consider the 'and' in 'the words of our Lord Jesus Christ, *and* to the doctrine...'. This 'and' is *kai* which – see discussion of *kai* in chapter 18 – may be translated 'even'. If so, we have 'the words of our Lord Jesus Christ, *even* to the doctrine which accords with godliness', which I take to be nothing less than the law of Christ. Hendriksen described this as the 'truths which issued from Christ's mouth and were exemplified in his life and death'. Of 'the truth which is according to godliness' (Tit. 1:1), Hendriksen said it 'is in the interest of, promotes, godliness, the life of Christian virtue, the spirit of true consecration' (Hendriksen: *I & II Timothy* pp195,340). On Tit. 1:1, Taylor spoke of the law of Christ (Gal. 6:2) (Taylor p12).

The law is not the motive for obedience; love for Christ is

And motive is all-important! Tozer: 'In the sight of God, we are judged not so much by what we do, as by our reasons for doing it. Not *what* but *why* will be the important question when we Christians appear at the judgement seat to give account of the deeds done in the body' (Tozer: *Root* p89, emphasis his).

John Brown: 'Every lover of Christ keeps Christ's commands implicitly, impartially, cheerfully and perseveringly, and no man who is not a lover of Christ keeps his commandments in any, far less in all, of these ways... If I love Christ, I will keep his commandments *implicitly*; that is, I will do what he bids me, because he bids me... If I love Christ, I shall keep his commandments *impartially*... If I do anything, just because Christ commands me to do it, I shall "do whatsoever he commands me"... If I love Christ, I shall keep his commandments *cheerfully*; I shall reckon it a privilege to obey his law, "to be under the law to Christ". The thought, that they are the commandments of him whom I love' – more, of him who loves me – 'because of his excellencies and his kindness, makes me love his law, for it must be excellent because it is his, and it must be fitted to promote my happiness for the same reason. And I have pleasure in pleasing him, and I am pained when I am aware of having offended him; and, therefore, I have satisfaction in doing what I am sure will please him, for he has commanded it. There are many who do many things which Christ has commanded, not because they love either him or his law, but because they are afraid if they do them not, they must go to hell; and because they hope if they do them, they shall get to heaven. Their spirit is the spirit of bondage. But it is otherwise with the lover of Christ...'.

'If I love Christ, I shall keep his commandments *perseveringly*... If I love Christ... if I love him really, I can never cease to love him; and if I never cease to love him, I shall never cease to obey him... If I am not persevering in keeping his commandments, it is a proof, not only that I do not love him, but that I never have loved him... This is the only way in which a disciple can continue in his Master's... love. If he be unduly self-indulgent or self-reliant, if he does not follow his Lord fully, if he becomes weary in well-doing, if his love to the brethren and to all men waxes cold, if he allows the world to occupy a place in his attention and affection to which it is not entitled, in a word, if he neglects or violates any of his Lord's commandments, he, just in that measure, does not – cannot – continue in his Master's love... Every disciple of Christ will find that in keeping his commandments is the great reward of enjoying, and knowing that we enjoy, his complacent approbation; and that this cannot continue to be enjoyed, if any of these commandments are knowingly neglected or violated... [John 15:10]...'.

'If we would continue in his love, we must keep his commandments, *as* he kept the Father's commandments. His obedience was the obedience of *love*, and so must *ours* be... He delighted to do the will of his Father. It was his meat to finish *his* work; and so must be our obedience to him. We must run in the way of his commandments with enlarged hearts. We are to keep them, not so much because we *must* keep them, as because we choose to keep them; or, if a necessity is felt to be laid on us, it should be the sweet necessity resulting from perfect approbation of the law, and supreme love to the lawgiver. His obedience to the Father was universal – it extended to every requisition of the law. There was no omission – no violation; and in our obedience to our Saviour, there must be no reserves – there must be no allowed omissions or violations – we must count his commandments to be in all things, what they are – right – and we must abhor every wicked way. His obedience to the Father was persevering. He was faithful to death; and so must *we* be. It is he who endures to the end, that so continues in the Saviour's love as to be saved... It is *thus*... – thus only – by keeping the commandments of our Lord, as he kept the commandments of his Father, that we shall continue in his love, as he continued in his Father's love'.

Brown not only set out the range of Christ's law, and the manner of keeping it, but he set out the motives for obedience. I forbear to quote at length, but Brown specified the motives for continuing in the love of Christ, by keeping his commandments; for 'thus "will you resemble your Lord and Master" – thus will you minister to his enjoyment – thus will you obtain solid permanent happiness to yourselves...' (Brown: *Discourses* Vol.3 pp87-89,287-296, emphasis his).

Brown had earlier said: 'Now... that we have been abundantly furnished with the means of arriving at a right resolution of the question, it comes back on each of us: "Do you love me?" I am afraid there are those... who, if they bring in a verdict according to the evidence, will be obliged to say: "Lord, you who know all things, you know I do not love you. I do not keep your commandments implicitly, impartially, cheerfully, perseveringly; I do not submit to your dispensations [providences] humbly and patiently, I do not love your word, I do not love your day,[8] I do not love your people, I do not love your cause, I do not love you". You dare not say this, but you feel it to be true. Now, if it be so, do not attempt to conceal the fearful truth from yourself. It cannot be concealed from "him with whom you have to do". Rather look the broad fact in the face, that you may distinctly perceive its true character. You do not keep HIS commandments, whose will all nature, inanimate and irrational, obeys – whose commandments the angels do, "hearkening to the voice of his word". This is he whom "you will not have Lord over you"; he whom "God has made both Lord and Christ"; he who is "Lord of all". This is he of whom Jehovah speaks by Moses: "I will raise up a prophet... And it shall come to pass, that whosoever shall not hearken unto my words, which he shall speak in my name, I will require it of him" [Deut. 18:15-19]. Reflect for a moment. Why do you not keep his commandments? Is not his law "holy, just and good"? Is it not right to "hear him who speaks from heaven"? Think what the end must be of disregarding his authority, and disobeying his laws: "As for these, my enemies, who would not have me to reign over them, bring them forth, and slay them before me". It is they only "who do his commandments, that have a right to the tree of life, and that shall enter in through the gates into the city". "Oh, foolish people, and unwise!" But you not only do not keep his commandments – that is bad enough – but you do not love him...'.

'You cannot reach heaven, nor escape hell, if you do not keep Christ's commandments; and you cannot keep his commandments if you do not love him, for he values not obedience but where it is the fruit, the expression, of love... By keeping his words... [believers] manifest and prove their love to [Christ]... To keep the words or commandments of our Lord, is a phrase [and duty] of very comprehensive meaning. It includes the keeping them pure and entire as Christ has given them; the keeping them in the mind as habitual subjects of thought – the keeping them in memory; and it includes, too... the keeping them as commandments – the turning them to the practical purpose which they are intended and fitted to serve. They must be kept as he gives us them. We must not detract from them; we must not add to them; we must in no way modify them; we must keep them as we have got them; we must not mingle them with human ordinances, or traditions or speculations [Deut. 4:2]... Everyone who really loves him, thus keeps his commandments and words; and... the man who does not thus keep his commandments and words, does not love him... He who loves our Lord with that love which grows out of the faith of his words, must be characterised by habitually keeping his commandments in all their various aspects in which we have considered that wide-reaching expression... The appropriate use of the statements now made is, serious self-examination. Is the character delineated mine? Have I Christ's words? Have I understood and believed the gospel? Do I love Christ? And am I showing my love for Christ by keeping his words?' (Brown: *Discourses* Vol.3 pp90-91,163-166). Brown then delivered an impassioned plea for sinners to turn to Christ (Brown: *Discourses* Vol.3 pp166-169).

---

[8] This should be understood as the Lord's day, not the sabbath.

Brown again: 'Christians, these illustrations [and doctrines] have not served their proper purpose with you, if they have not induced the determination and the prayer, "I *will* keep the commandments of my God". "O that my ways were directed to keep his statutes. Then shall I not be ashamed, when I have respect unto all your commandments. I *will* keep your statutes: O forsake me not utterly". "I *will* keep his law continually, for ever and ever; and I will walk at liberty, and delight myself in his commandments, which I love" [see Ps. 119:5-8,44,45,47]. If they have had this effect, your own experience will soon furnish you with a better commentary than any human exposition on these words: "If you keep his commandments, you shall continue in his love, even as he kept his Father's commandments, and continued in his love. His joy shall remain in you, and your joy shall be full". Then will you have the evidence in yourselves, of that of which the world is not easily persuaded, that "the Christian life is the path of genuine happiness, and that the greater the progress is in the graces and excellencies of the spiritual character, the greater is the experience of that consolation and joy which the world cannot give, and cannot take away"' (Brown: *Discourses* Vol.3 pp295-296, emphasis his). See M'Cheyne pp1-12 for *the love of Christ* constraining believers to live godly lives.

Reader, I hope you did not miss it. In the above, notice how Brown, speaking about Christ, 'my commandments', 'Christ's law', moved seamlessly into scriptural extracts which apply to God, his word, his law. For example: 'hearkening to the voice of his word', 'him with whom you have to do', 'holy, just and good', 'hear him who speaks from heaven'. All these are words which belong to God and his word, his law, yet they are applied, by Brown, without the slightest tremor, to Christ and his law. Now, that this proves that Brown knew Christ is God, is patent. Yes. *But it also demonstrates that Brown knew that 'the law of Christ' is the 'the law of God'.* And so it is. As I have explained, in the old covenant 'the law of God' was 'the law of Moses'; in the new covenant, 'the law of God' is 'the law of Christ'. This, as I have stated, is a point of massive significance.

Compare the above with this. On 2 Cor. 5:14, Malcolm Watts added an extraordinary gloss, without warrant: 'Believers try to keep the law [of Moses] because they are deeply affected by God's amazing love toward them' (Malcolm Watts p22). *That* is not the teaching of the New Testament! Believers try to keep *the law of Christ* because they are deeply affected by God's amazing love toward them. In fact, believers *want* to keep Christ's law because they are deeply affected by God's amazing love toward them.

As Dodd put it: 'That Christ loved us and died to save us is the most moving fact in Paul's universe. And he so died "that those who live should no longer live for themselves". His love puts a moral constraint upon us. Accordingly, the stamp of Christ will be upon the whole of the Christian's daily activity. The "law of Christ" is binding upon him in all things. That law is apprehended inwardly by the activity of the indwelling Spirit of Christ, for it is the Spirit [who] gives us "the mind of Christ"' (quoted by W.D.Davies pp144-145). Dodd went on: 'But it would be a mistake to divorce this thought from a direct reference to the historic teaching of Jesus Christ'. On the law of Christ not being independent of Scripture, see below.

When a believer sins, as Lloyd-Jones noted, 'whatever may be the condition and the feelings of the backslider, even at his worst, he is still not back in or under the spirit of bondage and of fear'. Why not? Because 'he is conscious that he has not sinned against law, but against love'. The thought of this, of course, wounds him far more than sinning against law ever could do. Yet the truth stands: 'But the believer, however grievously he may sin, does not go back "under the law"; he realises that his sin is a sin against love' (Lloyd-Jones: *Sons* p227). See Gadsby: *Works* p14.

By the way, to try to get the *unregenerate* to obey Christ's law does far more harm than good. Lloyd-Jones: 'It is sinful and insulting to God to believe that morality or righteousness is possible apart from [God in Christ]... Men thought that you could still have Christian conduct and behaviour without the vital experience... There is no true evangelism without putting these things in the right order. The primary purpose of evangelism is to bring men and women to God, to the right relationship to God, to have a right attitude to God. Nothing must come before that. No benefit must even be considered before that. We must not offer Christ in any capacity before we have started with that' (Lloyd-Jones: *Gospel* pp359-364).

As Dunn observed, there are 'controlling factors', external norms, to qualify the inward work of the Spirit – see chapter 9, where I quoted Dunn pp295-296. Paul 'calls upon an external norm (the law of Christ),[9] as well as the inward principle of the indwelling Spirit. It is precisely such norms which are necessary to prevent a too-exclusively focussed Spirit-ethic from degenerating into the attitudes illustrated in Gal. 5:13a, 26'. Just so! But 'at the same time, we should recall that at the head of both the main paragraphs in this section [in Galatians] Paul puts the first emphasis on the leading of the Spirit (Gal. 5:16,25): it is only the Spirit [who] can make the norm a dynamic motivating power, only the Spirit [who] can enable that sustained love of neighbour so fully illustrated by Jesus' (Dunn p324).

The law of Christ is what a believer is, not so much what he does
And now for a very important matter. Contemporary calls for sanctification are too often made in terms of conformity, a consequence of (knowingly or unknowingly) making the law the believer's rule of life. What am I talking about? Preaching which concentrates on action – recipe preaching – and a response which is satisfied with externals, often negatives at that. Let me illustrate. I knew a woman who told an elder that she was backsliding. Leaving aside the rights and wrongs of that, what do you think the elder said in reply? 'You can't be. You're still coming to the meetings'! Examples of sanctification being defined in terms of concentration on dress, Bible version, cultural issues, and so on, are legion. I am not saying these things are unimportant. But biblical sanctification, and biblical preaching for it, begins with the heart. It leads to action, yes, but it begins with the heart. This is in complete accord with Jesus' teaching (Matt. 15:1-20; Mark 7:1-23). The law of Christ, properly understood and preached, is what we need.

Lloyd-Jones: 'The biblical emphasis is on *being* rather than doing. It is a positive state. True Christians are not so much people who do certain things, as people who *are* something, and because of what they *are*, then they do those things' (Lloyd-Jones: *Life* p424, middle emphasis his; the other two, mine).

Lewis: 'We might think that God wanted simply obedience to a set of rules: whereas he really wants people of a particular sort' (Lewis: *Mere* p371).

Tozer: 'Historically, the west has tended to throw its chief emphasis upon doing, and the east upon being. What we *are* has always seemed more important to the oriental; the occidental has been willing to settle for what we *do*. One has glorified the verb *to be*; the other, the verb *to do*... Out of deep inner confusion, arises the antagonism between being and doing, and the verb upon which we throw our emphasis puts us in one of the two [classes]: we are *be*-ers or we are *do*-ers, one or the other. In our modern civilised society, the stress falls almost wholly upon doing... Being has ceased to have much appeal for people, and doing engages almost everyone's attention. Modern Christians lack symmetry' (Tozer: *Root* pp72-73, emphasis his).

The penetrating nature of the law of Christ
In addition to extracts which appear elsewhere, consider the following, which I take to be from the pen of Reisinger as editor of *Sound of Grace* in an 'Open Letter to Dr Sproul': 'Dr

---

[9] I regard the law of Christ as the norm; its written aspect is its external aspect.

Sproul, please explain why your magazine labels new-covenant theology as antinomian when we not only affirm just as strongly as you that the Christian is not only under clear objective ethical commandments in the new covenant, but we also insist those new-covenant laws are even higher than those written on stone. How is it possible for our belief in a *higher* law to be turned into *anti* law? Your September [2002] issue of *Tabletalk* condemns us as heretics simply because we believe that our Lord Jesus Christ is a true lawgiver in his own right and, as such, gives higher and more spiritual laws that anything Moses ever gave. Why do we deserve the odious label of "antinomian" simply because we believe that Christ replaces as the new lawgiver in exactly the same way he replaces Aaron as high priest?' (Reisinger: 'Open' p3, emphasis his).

The law of Christ is Christ himself

In the new covenant, Christ himself is the believer's wisdom; that is, Christ himself is his people's law. Christ himself is the law of Christ. On 1 Cor. 1:30, W.D.Davies: 'The evidence suggests that... "wisdom... is constituted... of righteousness, sanctification and redemption" is the best' translation. Morris: 'The Greek seems... to mean that these three are subordinate to wisdom, and explanatory of it'. Fee: It is not 'that Christ has been made these four things for believers. Rather, God has made him to become wisdom... true wisdom... to be understood in terms of the three illustrative metaphors' (W.D.Davies pp154-155; Morris p50; Fee: *1 Corinthians* p86).

In the new covenant, Christ is wisdom, and he is his people's wisdom (see W.D.Davies pp147-176). Deut. 30:11-14 referred to the law, and yet Paul applied it unreservedly to Christ in Rom. 10:5-13. Since this has been pressed too hard in an attempt to make it fit Paul's wisdom Christology, Moo cautioned: 'The association of Christ with wisdom is perhaps not as widespread nor as important to Paul's Christology as some have made it' (Moo: *Romans* p653). W.D.Davies: 'The appeal to this passage in proof of Paul's wisdom Christology does not carry conviction' (W.D.Davies p154). Even so, Davies was right to note: 'What is highly significant... is that the passage quoted from Deut. 30:12-14 refers to the *torah*... whereas Paul applies it to Christ' (W.D.Davies p154). *This* is my point. Christ is his people's law. Spiritual life begins with union with Christ; union with Christ is the believer's life.

W.D.Davies: 'To be a Christian is to re-live, as it were, in one's own experience the life of Jesus, to die and to rise with him, and also at the same time to stand under the moral imperative of his words... Not only did the words of Jesus form a *torah* for Paul, but so also did the person of Jesus. In a real sense, conformity to Christ, his teaching and his life, has taken the place for Paul of conformity to the Jewish *torah*. Jesus himself – in word and deed or fact – is a new *torah*'. As Davies admitted, 'it is true that at no point in the Pauline letters is the recognition of Jesus as a new *torah* made explicit in so many words'. Nevertheless, this fact is clearly taught and implied – especially in 2 Cor. 3 and 4, where Paul proved that 'Jesus, not the *torah*, was the true revelation of the divine glory and the divine light. This probably means... that Jesus [is] a new *torah*... Jesus has replaced the *torah* at the centre of Paul's life'. But '*torah*... is not merely to be understood in the restricted sense of legislation... Paul would think of Jesus as the *torah* of God not only in the sense that his words were a *nomos* but that he himself *in toto* was a full revelation of God and of his will for man'. And this takes us back to Heb. 1:1-3. John Brown: 'When a man becomes a true Christian, "Christ is formed in him"; that is, Christ's mode of thinking and feeling becomes his. The mind that was in Christ is in him. He has the spirit [Spirit] of Christ; so that he thinks as Christ thought, feels as Christ felt, speaks as Christ spoke, acts as Christ acted, suffers as Christ suffered. He is just an animated image of Jesus Christ. This, and nothing short of this, is to be a Christian' (W.D.Davies pp148-149; Brown: *Galatians* p226). I say it again. Union with Christ is the key. This is how spiritual life begins, how it continues, and how it will be consummated – united for ever with Christ in glory.

Zens: 'The rule of the new Israel is a new creation... faith which works by love... the keeping of God's commandments (Gal. 6:15-16; 5:6; 1 Cor. 7:19). The citations of Old Testament commands come to us, [it is true, but] not as bare commandments, but only as contemplated in their relationship to Christ and the new age he has inaugurated' (Zens: *Studies* p57).

Now glance at the alternative. The law stressed the negative – 'you shall not'; the apostles, however, majored on the positive. See Reymond: *Paul* p474. Travelling the negative road, trying to justify the Reformed third use of the law, Reymond asked: 'How does one show concretely his love to God and to his neighbour, as Christ commands?' Reymond's answer consisted mainly of negatives – 'never putting anything before [God]... not murdering... not committing adultery... not stealing... not bearing false witness... not coveting'. Oh dear! It shows the negative nature of the Reformed approach to holiness. Of course there are negatives, but how about '*loving, being faithful, being generous, telling the truth, sharing*', *etc.*? In short, why not describe holiness 'as Christ commands' in the New Testament? Which is? Positively, 'to be like Christ'. Should a believer aim not to be a law-breaker, or to be like Christ?

Crisp: 'Run through the several branches of sanctification, and you find that every particular is begun, continued, and perfected through the favour and bounty of God in Christ' (Crisp: *Christ* Vol.4 p117).

Reformed teachers (at best) ignore the sanctifying power of the gospel when they wrongly give it to the law. Witsius, for instance, claimed that 'the promises of grace [ought to] be referred to the gospel, all injunctions of duty... [belong] to the law' (quoted by Zens: *Studies* p35). Really? What version of the New Testament do such teachers possess?

I have already quoted from Archibald G.Brown, Spurgeon's successor, and his account of Bill Sykes, who would refer to what he called, 'that little bit'. 'That little bit about Christ taking my place, and how he had my punishment for me'. Brown: 'It would be no evil thing, but a matter for thankfulness, if there were a widespread impatience... in all congregations – a refusal to sit quiet unless "that little bit" was given to the people. Everything lies in it. All truths spring out of it or circle round it. It is the acorn that contains within itself every limb and twig of the forest king. It is the centre of the solar system of grace. All the doctrines march in their courses round the cross. Whatever else the Christian worker may leave behind him, let him be sure that he carries "that little bit". It works what nothing else can or ever will. Would he gain the attention of his audience? Let him tell "that little bit". There is a never failing freshness about the theme... There is a heavenly fascination about the theme. The best cure for empty sanctuaries is plenty of "that little bit"'. And, I would, 'that little bit', and plenty of it, is the way to holiness. As Brown concluded: 'We vowed that, God helping us, "that little bit" should be set as the central gem in every sermon preached henceforth. Fellow-preachers, teachers, labourers, may God make us all great on "that little bit"' (Archibald G.Brown pp7,10). In other words, let us follow the apostle (1 Cor. 1:23; 2:2), and preach Christ and him crucified – both for justification *and for sanctification*.

The law of Christ brings glory to the believer now
Fee on 1 Cor. 15:56-57: 'Anyone who has heard this paragraph read at a Christian funeral senses the dissonance these words seem to bring into the argument'. It is not, of course! 'So much so... some have [wrongly] argued this verse is a gloss'. 'Although it is something of an aside, it is not difficult to see its relevance... [Sin] is the deadly sting that has led to death. Thus, Christ's victory over the latter is evidence that he has overcome the former as well. The second line ["the power of sin is the law"] is the puzzler... Nowhere [in this letter] do the issues that have arisen... reflect concern over the law' – 'although see 2 Cor. 3:4-18, which implies that the Corinthians were not untrained in this kind of understanding of the

law'. 'Its point is simple, and is spelled out in detail in Rom. 7: The relationship of law to sin is that the former is what gives the latter its power... Rom. 5:13... condemnation... 2 Cor. 3:6... The law, which is good, functions as the agent of sin because it either leads to pride of achievement, on the one hand, or reveals the depth of one's depravity and rebellion against God, on the other. In either case, it becomes death-dealing instead of life-giving... In exulting in Christ's victory over death, Paul [sees and declares] that that victory is the *final* triumph over the sin that brought death into the world, and over the law that has emboldened sin. But since both sin and the law have already been overcome in the cross, this compendium prefaces a final doxology [1 Cor. 15:57-58] that thanks God for present "victory" as well' (Fee: *1 Corinthians* pp805-807, emphasis his). That is to say, Christ has gained not only the *ultimate* triumph for the child of God, but that ultimate victory s realised here and now in the believer's any and every difficult and grievous circumstance. And at the core of that victory is freedom from the law.

Calvin on 1 Cor. 15:57: 'Death has no sting with which to wound except sin, and the law imparts to this sting a deadly power. But Christ has conquered sin, and by conquering it has procured victory for us, and has redeemed us from the curse of the law (Gal. 3:13). Hence it follows, that we are no longer lying under the power of death. Hence, although we have not as yet a full discovery of those benefits, yet we may already with confidence glory in them, because it is necessary that what has been accomplished in the head [Christ] should be accomplished, also, in the members. We may, therefore, triumph over death as subdued, because Christ's victory is ours. When, therefore, he says, that victory has been given to us, you are to understand by this in the first place, that it is inasmuch as Christ has in his own person abolished sin, has satisfied the law, has endured the curse, has appeased the anger of God, and has procured life; and further, because he has already begun to make us partakers of all those benefits. For though we still carry about with us the remains of sin, it, nevertheless, does not reign in us: though it still stings us, it does not do so fatally, because its edge is blunted, so that it does not penetrate into the vitals of the soul. Though the law still threatens, yet there is presented to us on the other hand, the liberty that was procured for us by Christ, which is an antidote to its terrors' (Calvin: *Commentaries* Vol.20 Part 2 p65). Calvin, even here, though good, could not shake off his connection with the law. Christ has liberated his people from the law – not merely its curse and condemnation. It is this total liberty that brings joy to the believer.

Gill: 'The strength of sin is the law; not that the law of God is sinful, or encourages sin: it forbids it under the severest penalty... But thanks be to God who gives us the victory... over sin the sting of death, over the law the strength of sin, and over death and the grave; and which will be the ground and foundation of the above triumphant song in the resurrection morn, as it is now at this present time of praise and thankfulness to God: and it is all through our Lord Jesus; he has gained the victory over sin... Christ has obtained a victory over the law; he has stopped its mouth, and answered all its demands; he has been made under and subject to it; he has obeyed its precepts, and borne its penalty, and has delivered his [people] from the curse and condemnation of it, so that they have nothing to fear from it; it is dead to them, and they to it. He has also abolished death... He has conquered the grave... Now this victory, in all its branches, is given by God to believers; they are made to share in all the victories of Christ their head, and are more than conquerors through him' (Gill: *Commentary* Vol.6 p273).

Examples of teachers appealing for sanctification
For all their claims about sanctification by the law, as far as I can tell, Reformed teachers, when they get down to practical details, instinctively leave Moses and turn to the gospel. Of course they do! That is what the New Testament does! Examples are legion. We have come across plenty already. In fact, I doubt whether any – apart from modern Judaisers, of which there is no lack – actually overtly preach the law in all its proper ramifications when calling believers to holiness. But, as always, it is the incipient variety which is so insidious. Many

evangelicals may not know they are Calvinistic on the law, but there are many incipient advocates of Calvin's third use of the law – far more than would care or like to think they are. In this section, however, I concentrate on men – whatever their theoretical position – who are actually preaching for sanctification, and doing so in a biblical way. As you will see, the law is conspicuous largely by its absence. George Wright went further: 'Every believer that holds the [Reformed] sentiment practically contradicts what he asserts and contends for in words. In no instance does he walk according to the law, either in act or principle' (George Wright p233).

Take Spurgeon: 'I am persuaded that nothing but the blood of Jesus will kill sin. If you go to the commandments of God, or to the fear and dread of hell, you will find such motives as they suggest, to be as powerless in you for real action, as they have proved themselves to be on the general world; but if you remember gratefully that the first death of sin in you was by the blood of Jesus, you will firmly believe that all the way through you have overcome by the same weapon... You must get to Christ, nearer to Christ, and you will overcome sin' (Spurgeon: *Metropolitan* Vol.15 pp417-418.).

How did Berridge deal with the subject? He started with the futility of cobbling together the two covenants. He had his own striking way of expressing it: 'This [new] covenant is too glorious for nature to behold; she shrinks from the dazzling sight, fears woeful consequences from it, and, trembling for morality, beseeches the vicar to marry Moses unto Jesus, and couple the two covenants. From this adulterous alliance springs the spurious covenant of faith and works, with a spruce new set of duties, half a yard long, called legally evangelical, or evangelically legal, unknown to Christ and his apostles, but discovered lately by some ingenious gentlemen. However, Jesus does not thank old nature for her fears. He has promised in his covenant to provide a new heart, and good feet, as well as justification and pardon; and what he promises he will perform. Jesus does not want [need] the staff of Moses; nor will the master of the house suffer [tolerate] an alliance with his servant... Now the blessings of this covenant were all purchased by Jesus, and are lodged in his hand to dispose of; free pardons to bless a guilty sinner, free grace to sanctify his nature, with full power to lead him safe to Canaan... For a century past the noble building of God's grace has been shored up with legal buttresses; Moses is called in hastily to underprop his master, Jesus'.

He asked what the effect of this was. Did it produce godliness? It did not! There is only one way. As Berridge had rightly claimed: 'Everyone who is born of God is made to hunger for implanted holiness, as well as thirst for imputed righteousness. They want a *meetness* for glory, as well as *title* to it, and they know they could not bear to live with God, unless renewed in his image. Heaven would not suit them without holiness, nor could they see the face of God without it... Where imputed righteousness is... received by the Spirit's application, it produces love to Jesus, tender love with gratitude. And this divine love not only makes us willing to obey him, but makes us like him; for God is love. Christian holiness springing from the application of imputed righteousness is a glorious work indeed; far exceeding moral decency, its thin shadow and its dusky image. It is true devotedness of heart to God, a seeking of his glory, walking in his fear[10] and love, rejoicing in him as a reconciled Father, and delighted with his service as the only freedom. Full provision is made for this holiness in the new covenant; and Jesus the noble King of Israel bestows it upon his subjects' (Berridge: *Unmasked* pp291-292,295-296,337-338, emphasis his).

---

[10] In these extracts, the word 'fear' will come up several times. There is a wrong 'fear' – as produced by Calvin's whip, for instance. There is a right 'fear of God', associated, as here, with 'love'. The two 'fears' are chalk and cheese. I will not repeat this note every time, but it should be borne on mind.

Berridge composed a hymn on the theme: 'A sinner's claim to heavenly bliss,/ Rests on the Lord's own righteousness;/ Our legal debts he came to clear,/ And make a *title* full and fair./ Yet holiness the heart must grace,/ A *meetness* for his dwelling place;/ No filthy souls in heav'n appear,/ They cannot breathe in holy air./ The faith that feels the Saviour's blood,/ And finds in Christ a title good,/ Rebellious lusts will conquer too,/[11] And build the soul divinely new./ And where no work of grace is wrought,/ Nor holiness with hunger sought,/ Such barren souls for all their boast,/ Are sinners dead, and sinners lost./ May Jesus' grace to me convey/ Much pow'r to watch, and will to pray,/ Much seeking of the things above/ Much store of faith, and fruits of love./ More broken hearted let me be,/ And more devoted unto thee;/ More sweet communion with thee find,/ And more of all thy heavenly mind' (Berridge: *Sion's* number 161, emphasis his).

And another. Having written: 'By Christ's obedience fully paid,/ A soul in law is righteous made;/ For what can justice say?/ When every debt is well discharg'd,/ The debtor sure must be enlarg'd,/ And sing and march away', Berridge went on: 'Yet also Jesus, by his grace,/ Gives meetness for his dwelling place,/ And sanctifies the heart;/ His peace creates the tempers[12] kind;/ And love, to all good works inclin'd,/ Fills up the Christian part./ Then let my Lord impute to me/ His own obedience full and free,/ As title to his bliss;/ And let his Spirit too implant/ All Christian graces that we want,/ As pledge of happiness' (Berridge: *Sion's* number 219).

As he said elsewhere: 'For Christ comes not with pardon alone... but he brings also a spirit of life and power'. Berridge, of course, understood the need for the written word alongside the inner witness: 'The apostles also give many rules to direct the walk of faith, and often couple faith with love or obedience' (Berridge: *Observations* p161; *Unmasked* p307).

Oddly, in light of the above, Berridge still thought 'Jesus Christ explained the moral law... for a rule of life to believers... It becomes a rule of life in the Mediator's hand'. And Berridge pp306,336-337 was using 'the moral law' in the usual Reformed sense. See also Berridge: *Outlines* pp134-135; Berridge: *Observations* p182.

Manton: 'Faith, working to sanctification, apprehends the love of God, the blood of Christ, the promises, [the] precepts of the word; and by all these it is ever purging and working out corruption. By apprehending the love of God [Gal. 5:6]... Shall I love that which God hates? "Oh! do not this abominable thing that I hate", [says God] (Jer. 44:4). Faith represents God pleading thus: Is this your kindness to your friend? Do I thus requite God for all his kindness to me in Christ?... Heb. 9:14... "The blood of Christ"... is an excellent purger... Faith apprehends the blood of Christ to purge the conscience, it waits for the sanctifying virtue of his blood, and the grace purchased thereby. So faith makes use of the promises... 2 Cor. 7:1'. See his development of 'our many advantages in Christ. We have not only encouragement offered, but help... Christ will give what he requires' (Manton: *Sermons* pp299-300,302). See also Rainsford pp317-322.

John Brown: 'Let Christians seek clearer views, more settled convictions, respecting the death of Christ as the great atoning sacrifice, and their own interest in it as not only the price of their pardon, *but the means of their sanctification*; and let them open their minds and hearts to all those powerful motives, from such a variety of sources, which urge them to live devoted to him who died devoted for them; to glorify him whom they have so long dishonoured; to deny ungodliness and worldly lusts, and to live soberly, righteously and godly in the world; constantly seeking to be more and more disconformed to this world, by being more thoroughly transformed by the renewing of their minds, and proving the good, and perfect, and acceptable will of God' (Brown: *1 Peter* Vol.2 p318, emphasis his). Brown

---

[11] 1 John 5:4 was cited.
[12] Temper, as in disposition, attitude, frame of mind.

was commenting on 1 Pet. 4:1, which he translated as: 'Arm yourselves with this same thought', the 'thought' being: 'He that has suffered in the flesh has been made to rest from sin'. Brown argued that Peter was saying the same as Paul in Rom. 6. 'Reckon yourselves to be dead indeed to sin, but alive to God in Christ Jesus our Lord' (Rom. 6:11). In other words, sanctification comes as believers think of their union with Christ and the benefits which flow from it. This 'thought' is 'the instrumental means of sanctification'. '"This thought" being in our mind, habitually in our mind, is essential to our sanctification. We cannot be sanctified if it is not in our mind; and, if it really is habitually in our mind, sanctification is a matter of course' (Brown: *1 Peter* Vol.2 pp270-321. See also Vol.1 pp220-221,318-319).

Now for Gadsby, who clearly felt the criticism levelled against him and others for preaching the law of Christ as the believer's rule: 'The glorious gospel is a revelation of Jehovah's will to Zion, and this glorious goodwill towards the objects of his everlasting love is a bright transcript of his glorious nature, as the God of grace and truth. Herein are revealed his wisdom, power, love, grace, righteousness, peace, life, holiness, justice, faithfulness, light, mercy and truth. And is this glorious revelation destitute of a rule for the government of those favoured characters to whom it is made known? Is not the nature and will of God the standard of all real obedience? Surely it is; and in this glorious gospel it shines in all its beauty and excellencies. Must it, then, be so, that a man must be styled a pulpit libertine, and the doctrines he preaches be called foul dogmas, [when in fact] whose chief concern it is to glorify the Triune Jehovah, in vindicating his adorable perfection, in setting forth his beauties in the gospel of his grace, in directing poor sinners to this glorious subject for life and salvation, and in exhorting them to be followers of God as dear children? If this must be our lot, the Lord enable us to bear it patiently. Some tell us that the gospel is good news, and therefore cannot be a rule of obedience; but they should recollect that we read of obedience to the gospel; so of course it must be a rule of obedience. These gentlemen speak as if the child of God considered nothing good news but a free pardon of all his sins. But the characters they call pulpit libertines have not so learned Christ. They are enabled by divine grace to rejoice in a full and free pardon of all their sins, and at the same time consider his yoke easy and his burden light. They count the whole of God's will to his holy hill of Zion good news, both in its declarations of mercy, its promises, and doctrines of grace, and in its invitations, precepts and exhortations. They cannot believe that it would be a proof of a loving obedient child to call everything his father said bad news and heavy tidings, except when he told him he pardoned all his folly. The whole will of God, as King in Zion, is to them sweeter than honey and the honeycomb... Through the riches of God's grace, we know what it is to love him, and feel a pleasure in keeping his commandments, for they contain no yoke of bondage nor killing letter'. Gadsby explained. He regarded 'so speak and so do as those who will be judged by the law of liberty' (Jas. 2:12), and, 'only let your conduct be worthy of the gospel of Christ' (Phil. 1:27), as references to this gospel rule. As to the latter, 'Paul thought the gospel a sufficient rule; else why does he say: "*Only...?*". James calls it a perfect law (Jas. 1:25)'.

Quoting Gal. 6:15-16, Gadsby continued: 'Now, if the gospel is a perfect law, and a perfect rule of [life], and if the believer is to walk according to this rule, and to be judged by this rule, [indeed], if he is to fight and overcome by the same rule, and if as many as walk according to it are to expect peace, then surely the gospel is a competent rule... We read of the obedience of faith, and we are expressly told that the law is not of faith, and the word declares that if there had been a law given which could have given life, [truly] righteousness should have been given by the law... Now if the Father's commandment is life everlasting, and the law of works does not contain this everlasting life, and if the obedience of faith is to obey from the heart the doctrines of this everlasting gospel (Rom. 6:16-17), how comes it to pass that the killing letter [the law of Moses] contains the whole of Christian obedience?... "Nevertheless, to the degree that we have already attained, let us

walk by the same rule" (Phil. 3:16)'. Gadsby asked: What is 'that rule that Paul speaks of?'
Since Paul had just said that he was 'forgetting those things which are behind' (Phil. 3:13),
and this included the law of works (Phil. 3:4-9), then 'if this rule be the law of works, I am
wonderfully mistaken... Yet this is the rule Paul walked by; so he was not without a rule,
though he had left his old rule behind. And thus it is with every believer under heaven, for
he is dead to his old rule... And the way in which he now walks is not the old way of works,
but he walks by faith in Jesus Christ, the way, the truth and the life' (Gadsby: *Works* pp8-
11,20 emphasis his). See chapter 17 for more on 'the perfect law of liberty' as found in Jas.
1:25; 2:12. See Brinsmead in Zens: *Studies* p50.

Philpot made three telling points: '1. Why the law is not the believer's rule of life. 2. What
is his rule. 3. A disproof of the objection cast upon us that our views lead to doctrinal or
practical antinomianism'. Philpot explained his terms: By 'the law', he meant 'chiefly,
though not exclusively, the law of Moses'. By 'a rule of life', he meant 'an outward or
inward guide, by following which a believer directs his walk and conversation before God,
the church and the world'. And he emphasised that he was dealing strictly, 'wholly and
solely', with a believer. Following this explanation, Philpot struck some heavy blows. He
noted first of all that the law 'must be taken as a whole'. Philpot showed that believers are
not under the law 'either as a covenant or as a rule [but]... they [are] free from its curse as a
condemning covenant, and from its commands as a galling yoke, which neither they nor
their fathers could bear (Acts 15:10)'.

Above all, on this point he quoted Gal. 6:15-16 to show that it is not the law but 'the
Spirit's work on the heart [which] is held out... as the rule of a believer's walk. [In short,]
my first reason... for rejecting the law as believer's rule of life is that... I cannot separate a
covenant from the rules of the covenant; if I take the latter, I also take the former. Nor is
this a trifling matter, for by [taking the law as my rule] I virtually put myself under the
curse of the law... I forsake the gospel of the grace of God, which is sufficient to guide me
as well as to save me... [The law] is strictly a covenant of works; it knows nothing of
mercy, reveals nothing of grace, and does not communicate the blessed Spirit (Gal. 3:2)'.

As a consequence, he asked: 'Why, then, if I am a believer in Christ, and have received his
grace and truth into my heart, am I to adopt for the rule of my life that which does not
testify of Jesus either in word or in my conscience? If I am to walk as a believer, it must be
by a life of faith in the Son of God (Gal. 2:20). Is the law my rule here? If it is, where are
those rules to be found? "The law is not of faith" (Gal. 3:12). How, then, can it lay down
rules for a life of faith? A rule to influence and guide a believer's whole life must be very
express and comprehensive. It must embrace beginning, middle and end of a Christian life;
be adapted to all the circumstances, and direct the whole course of his walk before God, the
church and the world. But where is this to be found in the law of Moses? I find, then, [the
law as the believer's rule is in] every way defective. If I am to walk with God, it gives me
neither help nor instruction; for it is silent about Christ and salvation; and all it says is: "The
man who does them shall live by them" (Gal. 3:12). If I wish to walk as becomes a believer
with the church, what help will the law give me there? To walk as such must be by the law
of love as revealed in Christ, and made known by the power of God. If I am to walk in the
ordinances of God's house, are those to be found revealed in the law? Must I then take that
as my rule how to walk in the house of God, which does not even recognise the existence of
a... church, and holds forth no ordinance but that of circumcision? Paul writes to Timothy a
number of directions [as to] how he should behave himself in the house of God, which is
the church of the living God (1 Tim. 3:15). These were rules for Timothy to walk by. But
are they law or gospel? Moses or Christ? works or faith? By what rule am I to walk as a
minister?... The ten commandments[?]... But where in these ten commandments is the
ministry of the gospel even hinted at? How, then, can [they] direct my walk as a minister of
Jesus Christ?... Surely it is casting a great reflection on the precepts and example of our
blessed Lord, and the injunctions of his apostles in the New Testament, to go back to the

law, when we have before our eyes a gospel so pure, holy and precious. Or if I am to walk as becomes my profession before the world, is it by shaping my life by the ten commandments, or by the precepts of the gospel?... I reject the law as my rule [because of] its imperfection. I have a better and more perfect rule, and therefore do not need it'.

Philpot referred to 2 Cor. 3, the contrast between the letter and the Spirit, pointing out that the choice was between being 'ruled by the killing letter, which can only minister condemnation and death', and being ruled by 'that which ministers the Spirit, righteousness and life... Which [is] the better rule?' he demanded. Is it the law of Moses? 'I am not against this law... though I do not consider it to be a believer's rule of life; for it has most important uses, and therefore I cannot be against it as long as it is confined to those uses'. He cited 1 Tim. 1:8. While the law cannot be 'a rule of life for a believer, who is... a righteous man, [nevertheless] it has its uses, and important ones'. But, he argued, for all true believers, 'the gospel, not the law, becomes their guiding, ruling principle'. He explained: 'Believers in Christ [are] not under the law of nature and conscience, like the Gentile, nor under the law of Moses, like the Jew, but under the grace of the gospel and the teaching and guiding of the blessed Spirit... The gospel, as a law of liberty and love, fulfilled and absorbed the law of Moses, and thus became the believer's rule of life... [Believers] are set free that they may serve – serve in newness of spirit and not in the oldness of the letter... This is true liberty – liberty not to sin, but from sin [Matt. 1:21]. Being made free from the guilt of sin by the blood of sprinkling, from the filth of sin by the washing of regeneration, from the love of sin by the love of God shed in their heart, from the power of sin by the efficacy of grace, and from the practice of sin by the fear of God as an inward fountain of life, they become servants to God, have their fruit unto holiness, and the end, everlasting life (Rom. 6:17-22). This is the religion I contend for' (Philpot: 'Three' pp88-92,97,154,161-162; *Dead* pp16-22,28,32,41-43). I would not put it in quite this way. The law is still useful to the believer – as a paradigm. See chapter 17.

Philpot had more to say on the believer's rule. He asked of the believer: 'Is he without rule? without law? a lawless wretch who because he abandons[13] the law of Moses for his rule, has no guide to direct his steps?' Philpot gave this notion short shrift: 'I answer, God forbid!' Having quoted 1 Cor. 9:21 – 'under law towards Christ' – and noting the absence of the article *the* in the original – he went on: 'The believer then has a guiding rule which we briefly call the gospel'. Philpot saw 'two main branches' of this: 1. The gospel as written by the divine finger on the heart.[14] 2. The gospel written by the blessed Spirit in the word of truth. Philpot rightly observed: 'These do not form two distinct rules, but one is the counterpart of the other; and they are mutually helpful, and corroborative of each other'. He asked: 'What is the main use of a rule but to lead? But who can lead like a living guide? How can a dead law lead a living soul? The very proof that we are children of God is that we are led by the Spirit [Rom. 8:9,11,13-14]; and this inward leading becomes our guiding rule. Can you want a better?... The living guide is that holy and blessed Spirit who "guides into all truth" (John 16:13); and if he guides into all truth, are not his guidings a rule, and a sure rule too, by which he leads and directs both heart and feet? Here is the main blessedness of the work of grace upon the heart, that the leading and guiding of the blessed Spirit form a living rule every step of the way; for he not only quickens the soul into spiritual life, but maintains the life which he gave, and performs (or finishes, margin) it until the day of Jesus Christ (Phil. 1:6)'.

As Philpot pointed out: 'There is not a single part or particle of our walk and conduct before God or man which is not revealed and inculcated in the precepts of the gospel'. Of

---

[13] Strange word to use! The believer has died to the law. Did Philpot mean 'rejects' or 'does not accept'?

[14] Echoes here of Denck in Williams: *Spiritual* p98.

course, he admitted, not every last detail involved in our obedience is spoken of in Scripture, but God has revealed 'most blessed principles, enforced by every gracious and holy motive, and [this revelation forms], when rightly seen and believed, a most perfect code of inward and outward conformity to the revealed will of God, and of all holy walk and conduct in our families, in the church and in the world... A believer has a rule to walk by which is sufficient, and more than sufficient, to guide him every step of the way; for if he has the internal quickenings, teachings and leadings of the Spirit to make his conscience tender in the fear of God, and has the law of love written upon his heart by the finger of God; and if besides this he has the precepts of the gospel as a full and complete code of Christian obedience, what more can he want to make him perfect in every good word and work? Can the law do any of these things for him? Can it give life, in the first instance, when it is a killing letter? Or can it maintain life, if it is not in its power, in the first instance, to bestow it? And, even as a moral code, is it not most imperfect and defective, when put side by side with the full, perfect and complete precepts of the gospel?' (Philpot: 'Three' pp93-95; *Dead* pp23-26). Philpot dealt with the nonsensical view that the two parts – the internal and the external rule – might clash (see Philpot: 'Three' p95; *Dead* p25).

Gadsby again: 'The gospel's the law of the Lamb;/ My soul of its glories shall sing;/ With pleasure my tongue shall proclaim/ The law of my Saviour and King;/ A sweet law of liberty this;/ A yoke that is easy and mild;/ Of love it the precious law is,/ Unknown unto all but a child./ The law of the Spirit of life,/ That takes the old yoke from our neck,/ Proves Zion to be the Lamb's wife,/ And Zion with beauty does deck;/ Provides her a clothing divine,/ And makes her all-glorious within;/ Nor angels are clothèd more fine,/ Nor can it be sullied with sin' (Gadsby: *Hymns* number 523).

George Wright spelled out 'the way of true holiness... the grounds of my practical sanctification', stressing the word 'practical'. How will a believer be sanctified? 'Not under the law... which is the strength of sin, nor in the yoke of a commandment by which sin will take occasion to work in me all manner of [evil desire]... Making the law my rule will not advance me one step towards the holiest of all'. So much for the negative. What of the positive? Just this: 'My sanctification in the person of Christ by federal union, by which I stand in his glorious holiness; my sanctification by the blood of Christ, by which my sin is purged away; my sanctification by the indwelling of the Spirit of Christ as the immediate cause of all holy principles, affections and motives; [these] are the grounds of my *practical* sanctification by the truth, as the Spirit himself guides me into the truth, writes it on my heart, and makes the word work effectually within me' (George Wright p239, emphasis his).

As so often with those who disagree with the Reformed view on the law, George Wright was strongly criticised because, it was said, he 'holds sentiments repugnant to practical godliness'. Wright responded by saying he 'uniformly and earnestly insist[ed] upon the obligation of believers to obey the preceptive will of the Redeemer... in spirit, word and actions' (quoted by Dix p129). Although Dix said Wright 'was ambiguous' on the law (Dix p129), I think not. Dix did not seem to see that Wright was properly distinguishing between the law of Moses and the law of Christ. In the *Memorials*, Bland said 'George Wright herein *very clearly* expounds his convictions concerning the law and the gospel' (George Wright p228, emphasis mine). On the other criticism levelled against Wright, that he said 'that believers have nothing to do with the law in any sense whatsoever' (quoted by Dix p129), I am unable to comment. True, in the source I have – Wright's letter on 'The Law and the Gospel' in his *Memorials* – he said nothing about the law having a place in the life of the believer – as a paradigm, for instance – but whether or not Wright did teach what was alleged against him, I am unable to say. If he did, he was wrong. The fact, however, that Wright was a respected and profitable minister over many years – long influential in 'ensuring doctrinal orthodoxy' in the New Association of Suffolk Strict Baptists formed in

1830 (he was secretary until 1865) (Dix p128) – must throw some doubt on the accusation. For Bland's assessment of Wright, see Dix p119.

John Eaton, who played a large part in the controversies of the 1640s, has long been smeared as an antinomian; (see Bayes pp9-11, for instance). Speaking for myself, however, I find Eaton's words have gospel savour and sweetness. If the Reformed school prefer Calvin's whip and bridle, they are welcome to them; give me that which Eaton called 'the mighty power of the gospel, to true sanctification'. Listen to him expand upon the subject, reader, and judge for yourself: 'The laying out of the excellency of free justification works also this powerful effect; namely, that it is the only means to eradicate, and utterly root out that inbred original corruption... The true joyful knowledge of [the benefit of justification] is the only powerful means to... sanctify us, and to make us truly to love, fear and trust in God, working in us the true evangelical repentance; in sincerity hating sin, because it is sin, and in truly loving all holiness and righteousness: and thus it is God's holy fire that inflames his people with right thankful zeal of God's glory, in careful and diligent walking in all God's commandments' (quoted by Bayes p10, from John Eaton p456 and on). Bayes doubted 'this doctrinal antinomian position' 'can in fact be consistently sustained' (Bayes p11). Bayes dismissed what he called 'doctrinal antinomianism'. It 'sees the preacher's responsibility as the extolling of free grace, and argues that the preaching of the law hinders sanctification' (Bayes p51). Although this fairly sums up my position, reader – that it can be rightly called antinomianism, I deny. What is more, the answer to Bayes' doubt that Eaton's position is workable is this: Is it scriptural? *That* is the only question. If it is not, then it is of no consequence; not only is it not workable, it is utterly wrong. On the other hand, if it *is* scriptural, then it *must* be workable. In case my meaning is not clear, what would you think of somebody asking if Acts 16:31 is workable? Well, as for justification, so for sanctification. First establish the biblical position. Whatever *that* is, self-evidently it must be workable!

Brainerd proved the workability of Christ's system in the 1740s. In his Journal he set out the doctrine he preached to the Indians, and its effect. Having taught them about the fall and their need of Christ, Brainerd preached 'Christ crucified... making him the centre and mark to which all my discourses among them were directed. It was the principal scope and drift of all my discourses to this people... to open his all-sufficiency and willingness to save the chief of sinners, the freeness and riches of divine grace', and so on. He said how he had been helped 'to dwell upon the Lord Jesus Christ, and the way of salvation by him, in the general current of my discourses... God was pleased to help me "not to know anything among them, save Jesus Christ and him crucified"... This was the preaching God made use of for the awakening of sinners'. But this was not the only effect of such preaching. 'It is worthy of remark... that numbers of these people are brought to a strict compliance with the rules of morality and sobriety, and to a conscientious performance of the external duties of Christianity, by the internal power and influence of divine truths – the peculiar doctrines of grace – upon their minds; without their having these moral duties frequently repeated and inculcated upon them, and their contrary vices particularly exposed and spoken against'.

In this, Brained was definite. It was the same doctrine, he testified – the preaching of Christ – which both awakened the Indians *and reformed them*; that is, led to their sanctification: 'This was the continued strain of my preaching... and these were the doctrines' – their complete ruin in themselves and 'the glorious and complete remedy provided in Christ for helpless, perishing sinners, [Christ whom he] offered freely... These were the doctrines, this was the method of preaching, which was blessed of God for the awakening, and, I trust, the saving conversion, of numbers of souls, and which were made the means of producing a remarkable reformation among the hearers in general... No vice' was left untouched, Brainerd asserted, mentioning drunkenness and marital unfaithfulness in particular, but including 'all other vicious practices'. By preaching Christ to the Indians, he saw them converted and leaving off their sins, 'some of [which] I never so much as mentioned'. It was the preaching of Christ which did the work. 'And when I did at any time mention their wicked practices, and the sins they were guilty of... it was not with design, nor indeed with any hope, of working an effectual reformation in their external manners by this means [but] to excite them with the utmost diligence to seek after that great change, which if once obtained... would of course produce a reformation of external manners in every respect... The happy effects of these peculiar doctrines of grace, which I have so much insisted upon with this people, plainly show, even to demonstration, that instead of opening the door to licentiousness, as many vainly imagine, and slanderously insinuate, they have a direct contrary tendency... And happy experience, as well as the word of God, and the example of Christ and his apostles, has taught me, that the very method of preaching which is best suited to awaken in mankind... to excite them earnestly to seek after a change of heart, and to fly for refuge to free and sovereign grace in Christ... is like to be most successful toward the reformation of their external conduct. I have found that close addresses, and solemn applications of divine truth to the conscience, tend directly to strike at the root of all vice; while smooth and plausible harangues upon moral virtues and external duties, at best are likely to do no more than lop off the branches of corruption, while the root of all vice remains untouched'. Brainerd did not fool himself. He did not pretend all his hearers were converted; nor did he claim there is never a need for preaching what he called 'morality... and external duty'. But, he testified most strongly, it was his experience, confirming Scripture, that it was the preaching of Christ which produced the results he aimed for – both saving and sanctifying (Brainerd in Jonathan Edwards Vol.2 pp416-418). Note also how Brainerd strongly denied that this kind of preaching is antinomian – no matter how many 'vainly imagine' it is – or falsely accuse us of it!

John Eaton warned against adopting Calvin's third use of the law, complaining that too many were doing it in his time: 'With the coming of the Messiah, the time of the law expired, and with it the legal whippings of the people of God by fear... We ministers of this glory of the gospel, too many among us, do not only limp in our practice, and lisp in our speech, but even halt downright... that is, in not preaching and opening the glory of free justification... We slide back to the legal preaching of the Old Testament, from which, we, not understanding the intention of God in such high commending, and sharp exacting of works and legal righteousness, do fetch our principal vein of preaching... All our main labour is to command things that are right, and to forbid wicked doings, to promise rewards to followers of righteousness, and, though threaten punishment to the transgressors... we confound the Old Testament with the New' (Bayes pp10-11, in part quoting John Eaton p113 and on). I repeat Eaton's complaint about preachers today. That is why I have written this book!

Gadsby, addressing a person who still regarded the law of Moses as the believer's rule – in other words, one who accepted Calvin's third use of the law – said: 'I will propose to you a few questions:

'1st. If the law is the believer's rule of life, [I] shall thank you to tell me what is intended by the letter written by the apostles and elders, and sent to the believing Gentiles, as recorded in Acts 15, and shall expect you to explain the chapter.
2ndly. [I] hope you will tell me what the apostle means in the first six verses of Rom. 7; where he says that the believer is dead to the law, and free from the law; and let me know how that law can be his rule, when he is dead to it, and as free from it, as a woman is from her husband when she has him buried. Should you be disposed to say that the believer is dead to it as a COVENANT but not as a RULE of life, you will no doubt, point to those scriptures which make a distinction between the law as a covenant and as a rule of life; for unless you do this, you will not move me.
3rdly. You will have the goodness to inform me what is intended by the first four verses of Rom. 8; and let me know how it comes to pass that the law of the Spirit of life in Christ has made me free from the law of death, and yet that law of death (called in another place the

killing letter) is my rule of life; and how it is that it is my rule of life after it has killed me, and I am made free from it?

4thly. You will read 2 Cor. 3, and let me know how it is that administration of death, written and engraven on stones, is the living man's rule of life, and how this can be consistent with what the apostle observes in verse 11, where he says "it is done away", and in verse 13, where he says, "it is abolished". Now, my dear sir, you are to tell me how that law which is done away with and abolished still remains the believer's perfect rule of life.

5thly. You will also show me how it is that the law was our schoolmaster to bring us to Christ, that when faith is come we are no longer under a schoolmaster, and yet that this schoolmaster is our only rule of life after faith is come (Gal. 3:24-25).[15]

6thly. You will inform me how it is that if we be led by the Spirit we are not under the law, and yet that law is a perfect rule of life to that man who is led by the Spirit (Gal. 5:18). There are many things in the letter to the Galatians which you will find worthy of your attention in this business. I hope you will read the whole.

7thly. I shall expect you to tell me how it is that the handwriting which was against us, and contrary to us, is taken out of the way, and nailed to the cross (as Col. 2:14), and yet remains a perfect rule of life. Should you be disposed to say that the ceremonial law is here intended, you will tell me how that law, which was the gospel in its day, came to be against the believer, and what there was in it contrary to him.[16]

8thly. You will sure to inform me how it is that the law which was not made for a righteous man is the righteous man's rule (1 Tim. 1:9).

9thly. As Christ was made under the law, to redeem them that were under the law (as in Gal. 4:4-5), you will say how it comes to pass that they still remain under it in any sense that Christ was made under it, seeing he was made under it to redeem them from under it.

10thly. But as whatsoever the law says, it says to them who are under the law (as Rom. 3:19), and as the believer is not under the law (as Rom. 6:14; Gal. 5:18), you will inform me what the law says to them who are not under it.

11thly. If the law contains the whole of the revealed will of God, as to the matter of obedience... you will let me know upon what ground you prove that unbelievers have no right to be baptised, and partake of the Lord's supper...

12thly. You will inform me how it is that while men contend for the law being a perfect rule of life to believers, and call those ill names who do not, [many of them who contend for the law being a perfect rule] can and do, openly, knowingly, and designedly, break the fourth commandment every week. You will inform me whether doing *every* sort of work on the seventh day is walking according to that rule which says: "You shall not do *any* work, no, not so much as to kindle a fire" (Ex. 35:3).

13thly, and lastly. You will inform me how it is that Christ is the end of the law for righteousness to every one that believes, (Rom. 10:4), and yet that the believer, who is got to the end of the law at once, namely, by faith in Christ, must come back again, and begin at the beginning, by taking it for a perfect rule of life' (Gadsby: *Works* pp72-75, emphasis his).

Gadsby said he received no reply. Indeed, he found it necessary to correct false reports which his critic had circulated. Gadsby still received no satisfaction on the points he had raised. I do not intend to be patronising when I respectfully ask Gadsby's questions of any reader who feels I have gone astray in setting out the believer's rule. May I ask that you act as Priscilla and Aquila, and explain to me 'the way of God more accurately' (Acts 18:26), and do so from Scripture? I shall be grateful.

---

[15] As I have made clear, I disagree with Gadsby's view of Gal. 3:24-25. See chapters 4 and 9. Nevertheless, Gal. 3:25 invincibly makes Gadsby's point.

[16] I would also like to know the *scriptural* warrant for such a division of the law.

John Murray: 'The basis and spring of sanctification are union with Christ...' (Murray: *Romans* Part 2 p109).

McClain: 'The standard of life for Christians... is the will of God in the context of his grace given in our Lord Jesus Christ as revealed perfectly in the entire written word of God. This is so important that it should be memorised. The essential elements are: (a). The will of God. (b). In the context of his grace. (c). Given in our Lord Jesus Christ. (d). Revealed in the entire word of God written... The written word fixes our attention on Christ himself... The written word fixes our attention on the love of Christ... The written word of God also directs our eyes to the work of Christ...The written word of God also opens our eyes to the words and commandments of Christ...' (McClain pp54-63). McClain supported these claims with a score of scriptures.

Berridge, in a letter he wrote in 1773, not only set out the only way of sanctification – the gospel way – but he had stern – nevertheless, proper – warnings for those who try any other way (for my purpose, Calvin's third use of the law): 'The clearer sight we get of Christ, and the sweeter views we have of our adoption, [then] the more our hearts are filled with love, joy, peace and all the fruits of the Spirit, which is sanctification. When Jesus gives a clearer view of his dying love, he always accompanies that view with the graces of the Spirit. The heart is filled at the same time with pardon and holiness, with justification and sanctification; so that if we desire to be holy, we must seek to be happy in the Saviour's love, must seek a clear evidence of our adoption, and labour to keep it clear... No sweet, humble, heavenly feelings, no sanctifying graces are found but from the cross. Jesus says: "He that eats my flesh and drinks my blood, has (or possesses) eternal life" [John 6:54] – where he shows how eternal life (which must comprise the whole, of spiritual life) is obtained; *viz.*, by eating his flesh and drinking his blood; *i.e.*, by feeding on his atonement. Thus all divine life, and all the precious fruits of it, pardon, peace and holiness, spring from the cross... Get holiness by clear views of the cross, and find eternal life by feeding on the Saviour's flesh and blood. Was not a lamb sacrificed every morning and evening in the Jewish temple? And was not this intended to show us that we must feed on Christ's atonement every day, and derive all our life, the life of peace and holiness, from his death? Upright people are often coming to me with complaints, and telling me that since they received pardon, and have been seeking sanctification (as a separate work), their hearts are become exceeding dry and barren. I ask them how they find their heart when Jesus shows his dying love. They tell me: Full of peace and love, and every heavenly feeling. Then I answer: Jesus hereby shows you that holiness, as well as pardon, is to be had from the blood of the cross. Labour therefore to get your conscience sprinkled every day with the atoning blood, and sanctification will ensue [as a matter] of course... All fancied sanctification, which does not arise wholly from the blood of the cross, is nothing better than Pharisaism; and if persisted in will end in Pharisaism... Men profess and preach they are first justified by the blood of Christ, and then [sanctified] by their own obedience... If we would be holy, we must get to the cross, and dwell there; else [with] all our labour and diligence, and fasting and praying, and good works, we shall yet be void of real sanctification, destitute of those humble, sweet and gracious feelings which accompany a clear view of the cross. But mere doctrinal knowledge will not give us this view; it only proceeds from a lively faith wrought in us by the Prince of life. A legal spirit helps forward our mistake in the matter of sanctification... Both pardon and holiness spring from the blood of the cross, the root of merit is dug up thereby, and Christ is all in all... All heavenly graces are called fruits of the Spirit. Hence we [wrongly] conclude that pardon must spring peculiarly from the blood of the cross, and holiness must be a separate work of the Spirit. But though all gracious feelings are the Spirit's fruits, yet that fruit is bestowed at the foot of the cross; eternal life is found by eating the Saviour's flesh and drinking his blood' (Whittingham pp378-382).

I remind you of my epigraph, Col. 3:11, and Spurgeon preaching it: 'The apostle was arguing for holiness. He was earnestly contending against sin, and for the maintenance of Christian graces, but he did not, as some, who would like to be thought preachers of the gospel, resort to reasons inconsistent with the gospel of free grace. He did not bring forward a single legal argument... He knew that he was writing to believers, who were not under the law but under grace, and he therefore fetched his arguments from grace, and suitable to the character and condition of "the elect of God, holy and beloved". He fed the flame of their love with suitable fuel, and fanned their zeal with appropriate appliances...

He... goes on to declare that the believer's life is in Christ, "for you are dead, and your life is hid with Christ in God". He infers holiness from this also... he then brings forward... that in the... church, Christ is the only distinguishing mark... Now, as the only distinction which marks the Christian from other men, and the only essential distinction in the new world of grace, is Christ, we are led to see beneath this fact a great underlying doctrine. In the realm of grace, things are what they seem. Christ is apparently all, because he is actually all. The fact of men possessing Christ is all in all in the church, because in very deed Christ is all in all. All that is real in the Christian, all that is holy, heavenly, pure, abiding and saving, is of the Lord Jesus. This great granite fact lies at the basis of the whole Christian system; Christ is really and truly all in all in his church, and in each individual member of it...

This little text is yet one of the greatest in the whole Bible... It is like one of those rare gems which are little to look upon, and yet he who carries them bears the price of empires in his hand. It would not be in the compass of arithmetic to set down the value of this sapphire text. I might as soon hope to carry the world in my hand as to grasp all that is contained in these few words. I cannot navigate so huge a sea, my skiff is too small, I can only coast along its shore. Who can compress "all things" into a sermon [or a book!]? I will warrant you that my discourse this morning will be more remarkable for its omissions than for what it contains, and I hope that every Christian here will be remarking on what I do not say; for then I shall have done much good in exciting meditations and reflections. If I were to try to tell you of all the meaning of this boundless text, I should require all time and eternity, and even then all tongues, human and angelic, could not avail me to compass the whole. We will swim in this sea, though we cannot fathom it, and feast at this table, though we cannot reckon up its costliness...

How this... rebukes the coldness of saints. If Christ be all in all, then how is it we love him so little? If he be so precious, how is it we prize him so little?... Christ is all, my brethren, yet look how little we offer to him... God stir us to holy fervency, that if Christ be all for us, we may be all for Christ...

Christ is all in all; therefore, "put on, as the elect of God, holy and beloved, tender mercies, kindness, humility, meekness, longsuffering". The exhibition of the Christ-life in the saints is the legitimate inference from the fact that Christ is all to them. If Christ is all, and yet I being a Christian am not like Christ, my Christianity is a transparent sham, I am nothing but a base pretender, and my outward religiousness is a pompous pageantry for my soul to be carried to hell in – nothing more. It is a gilded coffin for a lifeless spirit... Without Christ you are nothing, though you be baptised, though you be members of churches, though you be highly esteemed as deacons, elders, pastors. Oh, then, have Christ everywhere in all things, and yet constrain men to say: "To that man, Christ is all in all; I have marked him; he has been with Jesus, and has learned of him, for he acts as Jesus did"' (Spurgeon: *Metropolitan* Vol.17 pp457-468).

Under the law of Christ, the believer has liberty and glory now
But not under the law! I return to a previous extract from Calvin. Arguing from Rom. 8:15; Heb. 12:18-22; Gal. 4:25-26, he drew the obvious lesson: 'The sum of the matter comes to this: the old covenant[17] filled the conscience with fear and trembling – the new inspires it

---

[17] Calvin had Old Testament (and New Testament), but as I have shown he was really talking about the old and new covenants, 'covenant' being, as Calvin's editor elsewhere argued, the

with gladness... Liberty and joy... neither was derived from the law; but... by the law they [that were under it] were oppressed like slaves, and vexed with a disquieted conscience'.[18] So why ever did Calvin make believers go under the law? Of course, he had his get-out clauses, but, as I have shown, they do not stand scrutiny. The point is, under the law – and that is precisely where Calvin wanted believers to be for sanctification, under the law – there is no liberty or joy, but only 'a disquieted conscience'. My point exactly!

In addition to the above, Arndt and Gingrich; Barcellos p21; Barnes: *New* Vol.4 p92; Bayes p173; Bennett: 'Primer' p34; Bigg: *Pursuit* pp106-109,112-176; Bruce: *Romans* p52; Calvin: *Commentaries* Vol.16 Part 2 pp314-315; Chamblin p182; W.D.Davies p37; Decker pp293-294; Fairbairn: *Typology* Vol.2 pp165-166; Fee: *1 Corinthians* p85: *Empowering* pp812-814; Friedmann pp82,84-85; Andrew Fuller: *Moral* p890; Gadsby: *Works* p7; Hendriksen: *Matthew* p506; Hoch 59,69-73,98; Kautz pp113-114; Kingdon pp83-84; Klassen: *Neither* pp28-36; 'Radical' pp138-146; Lumpkin pp41-43,49,57; Moo: *Romans* pp145,247-248; Murray: *Romans* Vol.1 pp122-123; Philips pp235-237; Plumer: *Romans* p138; Reymond: *Paul* pp489-491; Ryle: *Luke* Vol.1 pp317-318,320; *John* Vol.3 p225; Sattler pp250-252; Spurgeon: *Metropolitan* Vol.9 pp529-540; Vol.12 p259; Vol.15. pp417-418; Thayer; Michael Thompson p7; Verduin: *Anatomy* pp184-188; Wells pp45-46; Westminster Shorter; Williams: *Spiritual* p80; Witherington pp343,407.

Appendix: Michael Servetus

It was as I was putting the last of the concluding touches to the final checking of the mss that I was shown a copy of the thirty letters written by Michael Servetus to Calvin, taken from his *The Restoration of Christianity* of 1553. At a glance I could see that Servetus had challenged Calvin (and I mean challenged!) over many things, including his view of the law, and I felt I had to make room for it. Hence this Appendix. Of course, I know I am putting the lid on Reformed reaction to my book, ensuring, if there had been any doubt before, that I shall be blackballed. In the (I fear) vain hope of trying to stem the deluge of criticism I am pretty sure to get, let me say that just because I quote a man it does not mean I always endorse his way of putting it. May I also remind you, reader, that right at the beginning I said that just because I agree with a man on certain statements he made about the law, it does not follow that I agree with him everything he ever said – not even about the law!

Enough! Let Servetus speak for himself. If the only way we can preserve our credal credentials is by silencing men we disagree with – which seemed to be the policy in those far-off days (has it quite gone away?) – then our case must be desperate. The press is open for those who wish to refute Servetus' views – or mine, for that matter.

Servetus, as is well known, held heretical views. (Just in case it needs saying, I, too, think some of his views were heretical). As is also well known, for these views he was executed by fire. (Which, let me say, was a wicked thing to do – even for heresy). And as is further well known – though it is too often played down – Calvin was heavily implicated in his death. Indeed, the fact that Calvin was so heavily implicated in Servetus' death ought to serve as a warning to all who go to the law of Moses to maintain and enforce the gospel. Of course, Rome slaughtered far more that the magisterial Reformers, but of what relevance is that? Two wrongs never made a right! What is more, the entire emphasis upon law comes from the medieval Church – Rome! Calvin never did manage to get rid of his medievalism in this regard. In fact, with the death of Servetus, Calvin was only following his medievalism to its logical conclusion.

---

right translation: '"Covenant" is a more faithful translation than "Testament"; and a careful investigation of the meaning of *diathēkē* would contribute greatly to elucidate many passages of Scripture' (the editor in Calvin: *Commentaries* Vol.21 Part 1 p137).
[18] Calvin: *Institutes* Vol.1 pp394-395.

While Servetus was no Anabaptist, he certainly showed some of their hallmarks; he staunchly opposed infant baptism, for instance. And Calvin had no qualms about lumping him with the Anabaptists – one advantage being, I suppose, he could catch as many birds as possible at one go when letting fly with his invective. For instance, Calvin said of Servetus: 'That monstrous miscreant, Servetus, and some madmen of the sect of the Anabaptists... Servetus, one of their masters... Servetus, not the least among the Anabaptists, nay, the great honour of this crew... Servetus has supported his friends the Anabaptists' (Calvin: *Institutes* Vol.1 p369; Vol.2 pp549-550,554). According to Bainton, 'Servetus... was at once a disciple of the Neo-platonic academy at Florence and of the Anabaptists' (Bainton: *Servetus* p4).

Unfortunately, in gathering all my extracts from Servetus in this Appendix, even though his comments have relevance at various places throughout my book, I might give the impression that at times Servetus glossed. If so, as I have shown, time and again, that wouldn't make him unique! But, in order to clear him of the accusation, please consult what I say on each of the relevant passages; namely, Rom. 6 – 7, 2 Cor. 3, Gal. 3 and 4, and so on. You will then see my supporting arguments for the claims Servetus makes – even though he himself does not always include the intermediate steps in his letters to Calvin. Finally, although it will tend to over-simplification, by means of headings I will introduce some systematisation into the letters.

Consider first the 23rd letter, entitled 'Slavery of the Law, Freedom of the Spirit' (Servetus pp111-125). Servetus tells Calvin:

Christ fulfilled the law. 'God wanted the law to be placed in accordance with temporal progressions until Christ came; and Christ wanted the same... In the first place, Christ, in his own person, did not dissolve the law. But he fulfilled it in every way... Nothing of that which is spiritual in the law has been dissolved. Christ dissolved nothing in the law which corresponds to the true intention of the legislator.[19] For Christ is the purpose of the law'.

Christ has freed us from the law, including the ten commandments – as illustrated by the sabbath. 'Christ is the perfect liberator. Christ has rescued us from every bond and indenture to the law into complete freedom. Therefore, the force of the law itself has been utterly destroyed. (Understand the force of the law as the authority to bind, a yoke of slavery, a bond of obligation by which we [that is, those who are under it] are necessarily constrained under determined penalties). Although we do a great many of the things that are contained within the law of Moses, nevertheless we do not do them according to the force of the law, but because the Spirit teaches us to do what must be done. In this sense, we say that the law of the decalogue has been abrogated. That this law does not constrain us can be seen from the commandment of the sabbath.[20] The force of other injunctions has also expired and ceased; they do not have the power to bind or authority to constrain us. Nor do the customary rules of punishment employed there have any application for us'.

The law was given only to Israel. 'From the first commandment, it is established that God gave the law of the letter only to whom the people he led out of Egypt' – that is Israel, and not all men in general.

The believer is free from the law. 'The law of sin and death, as Paul attests, was the law of the decalogue from which, he says, we have been freed (Rom. 7 and 8): "We have been freed from the law of the decalogue which was the law of death to which we were subjected". A "ministry of death" and "ministry of condemnation" he calls the law of the

---

[19] That is, 'God's designed end or purpose in giving the law – Christ'.
[20] Servetus, of course, was shooting a sitting duck by tackling Calvin on the sabbath, as I have shown (see p103).

decalogue written in stone, and teaches us that it has been abolished or that it has reached its end (2 Cor. 3)... Therefore, it has reached its end, and the law of the decalogue has been abolished. The law of the decalogue was terrible; it killed; it increased sin; it gave rise to anger; it was an excuse for sin and was an opportunity for transgression because of the frailty of our flesh; for this reason it has been destroyed... When the law has been abrogated, it means that the decalogue has been abolished'.[21]

The claim that believers are under the law but not its curse is a pipe-dream. '"Christ redeems us from the execration and curse of the law" (Gal. 3). This curse and execration were the effect of the law of the decalogue, as Paul teaches throughout. If everyone under the law of the decalogue has been cursed for not fulfilling all its commands, and you, too, are under the law of the decalogue, then you are all cursed. But in point of fact, Christians are neither under a curse or under that law. We have not approached this frightful mountain on which the law of the decalogue was given (Heb. 12). In other words, we do not accept the law of the decalogue. Paul spoke about the law of the decalogue, saying that "it was not established for us who are just" (1 Tim. 1)'.

Believers are not under the law, including the ten commandments – it was only temporary, and was fulfilled by Christ. 'Regarding it, [Paul] says, the law was given for the time because of transgression until Christ came (Gal. 3). But now that discipline has been abrogated (Gal. 3 and 4), there cannot be a more clear lesson [than that] of Paul on this matter: "It is the law of commandments as posited in ordinances that Christ has abrogated" (Eph. 2)... The antiquity of the letter was the decalogue itself; now, because it has been abolished, there is a newness of spirit (Rom. 7 and 2 Cor. 3)'.

To be free from the law does not lead to sin and lawlessness. 'Thus, from this abrogation of the law, Paul's objection immediately follows (Rom. 6): "Therefore, is it proper to sin because we are not under the law?" Is it permitted to do anything contrary to the decalogue because the decalogue no longer binds us? Are we now permitted to fornicate, thieve, lie and murder? "By no means". On the contrary, just the opposite, if we have been regenerated. The Spirit teaches thus, those who are in Christ. The Spirit of Christ teaches us always to block the works of the flesh which are works of sin after we have crossed over from the flesh to the Spirit... In sum, Paul says we are not under the law, but under grace. Those who are under grace are not under the law'.

The motive for obedience is a vital consideration. Believers are under the law of Christ, and their obedience is a willing obedience, not a compelled obedience as slaves. 'You will object that it is all the same whatever you do whether by the force of the law or according to the teaching of the Spirit. On the contrary, it makes the greatest difference. For the Spirit gently instructs us like children; it does not force us like slaves. The law of the rock is rigid. The Spirit gently teaches and gives strength in order that, aided in life and taught better things, we may sin far less. But if we should sin, we have an easy remedy. These gifts of the liberator are outstanding. This liberation from the yoke and the bond of curse through Christ benefits us lest our consciences be as terrified as the consciences of [the Jews] were always frightened. If we sin, we are not immediately cursed to death like them. The remedy was not at hand for them as it is for us, but they were compelled to seek expiation with the blood of beasts, being always in terror... For us there is a genuine [real] and immediate expiation if we but seek forgiveness from Christ, if we but confess our sins, as John says'.

The law of Moses is not natural law. 'There are those who maintain that the decalogue is still in force, saying that its moral judgements are perpetual laws of nature. But we make this objection to them: "What is perpetual from nature is not so from Moses because it was

---

[21] See the main text of my book for taking 'the law' to be 'the ten commandments' in these passages.

before Moses". If you utter these statements about nature, you will not [be able to] give them the force of a law that curses because such cursing was not known except through the law, nor such wrath, except through the law'.

The believer is not under the law. 'The law has been abolished, and we are no longer under the law nor under its wrath... Paul... speaks... "... But now through Christ I have been freed from the law". Therefore, Paul is not under the law as you imagine it. On the contrary, his view is that the law has been abolished as he announces in the beginning of this chapter [Rom. 7], because he constantly understands it as the law, the law of the decalogue, and gives examples based on it [throughout Rom. 7]'.

The law of Christ is not the law of Moses, not even the ten commandments. '"I shall not give you a decalogue on stone tablets", said God [in Jer. 31:31-35], "but the faith in Christ on the tablets of your heart"... Jeremiah in chapter 31, already cited, and the [writer] in Hebrews 8 teach that this [old] covenant has been abolished. Ezekiel in chapter 16 teaches that the same covenant as written on tablets, which they had promised to observe, has been abolished'.

The law made nothing perfect. 'Therefore, the law of the decalogue has been abolished. God does not now receive us among his own under that covenant, but only through faith in Jesus Christ, his beloved Son. Paul calls the decalogue a testament of slavery given in the covenant given to Moses at Sinai[22] and now abolished (Gal. 4). The law of the decalogue led to no perfection; therefore, it has been abrogated because of its weakness and uselessness (Heb. 7). I beg you, when did we who were born from the Gentiles, and were living without the law, enter into the law of Moses? Or does faith which frees others, make us captive to it?'

In his 24th letter, under 'On the Scripture in the Church' (Servetus pp128-129), Servetus tells Calvin:

Christ gives his Spirit to his people in the new covenant. 'It is sometimes granted to us firm heaven to have a sincere, inner love with the full passion of the heart, and this, at that time, to fulfil the law. For "he who loves another has fulfilled the law", as Paul says. This is everywhere granted to those who have been regenerated and delightedly taste the things of heaven'.

Christ in his law brings joy. He does not prepare sinners by the law of Moses, nor does he sanctify saints by the law of Moses. 'Moreover, in order that you may understand better that in this spiritual doctrine of Christ there is no legal bond nor a precept to slavery, but that grace has been freely given as a heavenly gift, consider thoroughly the evangelical [gospel] joy at Christ's arrival in its entirety, and the announcement of exuberance that is far different from the law.[23] Because we were completely captive to the sin of Adam and the slavery of the law, Christ who is most pious [righteous, holy] came and announced joy and freedom to these who believe. He teaches us to believe, and he gives to us his gifts, without obligation.[24] He does not compel us with the law, but he offers benefit to those

---

[22] Servetus had 'given in the Sinai'. Surely something along the lines I have suggested is missing.

[23] I wish Servetus had been a little clearer here. I take it that he is saying, as I argued in the body of my book, that with Christ's triumph (John 19:30), resurrection and gift of the Spirit, believers enter into glorious liberty, and that this is announced, as we see throughout the New Testament, with 'exuberance'.

[24] That is, we are not expected to pay for them. We are, of course, obliged to serve our new master, but it is a willing, free service that he expects and deserves from us. We do not serve as slaves – the point that Servetus had already made.

wishing [willing] to believe. Later those, too, who had believed were taught heavenly things without the compulsion of the law... Thus is the entire gospel of the kingdom, the most joyous news with gifts for the present. Does giving such heavenly gifts free of obligation mean imposing the slavery's yoke?'

In the 25th letter, under 'The Mosaic Law and the Christian Law' (Servetus pp129-138), Servetus tells Calvin:

The law could justify. '"If you want to enter life, keep the commandments" (Matt. 19). The possibility of the consequence follows from the possibility of what precedes... Paul says that righteousness is twofold being the righteousness of the law and righteousness of faith (Rom. 10). Will you say that one part of this division is nothing? In every division, the parts must be taken as something. In that passage, Paul defines the righteousness of the law, and therefore he expresses his opinion that it is something'.

In closing this 25th letter, Servetus addresses Calvin with a plea, treating him rather as a teacher might a recalcitrant pupil who had failed to get his homework right: 'Therefore, Calvin, stop twisting the law against us or arguing so violently for its observation as if you had to perform it with the Jew. May God, who always took pity on the Jews, take also pity on you. Amen'.

Finally, under 'Judgements and Forgiveness' (Servetus p139), the 26th letter, in an obvious allusion to Gal. 3 and 4, Servetus tells Calvin of:

The temporary nature of the law as a child-custodian. 'The entire legislation of Moses was abolished, and as Paul testifies, we are not permitted to re-establish again [*sic*] what has been destroyed. The law given to the boy or the slave ceases when the slave changes from being a slave into a freeman or the boy passes from boyhood into manhood, and he becomes exempt from the power of his pedagogue and previous master'. The translators referred to Rom. 7:2-6; 1 Cor. 13:11.

As I claimed – and as you can see, reader – Servetus challenged Calvin over his view of the law. Alas, we do not have Calvin's replies – except in passing in his *Institutes* and *Commentaries*. Leaving aside the strength or weakness of his arguments in those places, Calvin certainly showed no reticence in heaping abuse on his correspondent. As I have observed, it is a risky business engaging with the Reformed over the law – as I shall no doubt prove by personal experience!

CHAPTER 17: THE BELIEVER'S RULE: SEVEN OBJECTIONS
THE FIRST SIX

Objection 2: If believers are not under the law of Moses, what will stop them being utterly lawless?

Philpot: 'Do we then set aside the two great commandments of the law?' Calvin: 'We must here observe, the exemption from the law which Christ has procured for us does not imply that we no longer owe any obedience to the doctrine of the law, and may do whatever we please' (Philpot: 'Three' p95; *Dead* p26; Calvin: *Commentaries* Vol.21 Part 1 p119).

But Andrew Fuller was one to get the wrong end of the stick. He listed what he thought were the consequences of saying the believer is not under the law as a perfect rule: 'It strikes at the root of all personal religion, and opens the flood-gates to iniquity... Those who imbibe this doctrine talk of being sanctified in Christ, in such a manner as to supersede all personal and progressive sanctification in the believer'. The dire consequences, he asserted, include utter lawlessness and claims of sinless perfection. Indeed, 'by disowning the law... men utterly subvert the gospel... If the law is not a rule of conduct to believers, and a perfect rule too, they are under no rule; or, which is the same thing, are lawless... I am aware that those who deny the law to be the rule of a believer's conduct, some of them, at least, will not pretend [claim] to be lawless. Sometimes they will profess to make the gospel their rule; but the gospel, strictly speaking, is not a rule of conduct, but a message of grace, providing for our conformity to the rule previously given'. Arguing from Rom. 4:15, Fuller claimed: 'If [since, that is] there is no sin but what is transgression of the [moral] law, there can be no rule binding on men which is not comprehended in that law... [1 Cor. 9:21 means that] believers... are under greater obligations to [obey the law] than any men in the world. To be exempt from this is to be without law, and, of course, without sin... I have been told that believers are not to be ruled by the law... but by love; and that it is by the influence of the Spirit that they are moved to obedience, rather than by the precepts of the law'. He had several replies, one being: 'The question is not: What moves or causes obedience? But: What is the rule of it?' If we claim love is the principle of the believer's life, we 'reduce our obligation to the standard of our inclinations?' In other words, if we do not regard the ten commandments as the *perfect* rule of life, can we live as we like? Certainly not! And where in my book have I said anything which bears any resemblance to this: 'We are not obliged to love either God or man, and it is no sin to be destitute of love to both'? Is this the inevitable consequence of saying the law of Moses is not the believer's rule? Fuller thought it was (Andrew Fuller: *Dialogues* p300; *Moral* p891; *Antinomianism* p339).

A damning catalogue indeed – if it were true! I will not deal with each of Fuller's points here – I have done that in the body of the book. Much as I admire Fuller, he has lashed out here, badly missing the mark. It is not that I do not like what he said – I don't! – but it is so patently unscriptural. It just was not worthy of so fine a writer. I am not belly-aching. As I say, I have answered all Fuller's points.

Now... stand by for an appalling tirade from Chantry: 'Even criminals have a code of ethics... There is honour among thieves'. Regarding those who do not take Calvin's route concerning the law, Chantry posed some rhetorical questions: 'Are we abandoned to nothing more than individual opinion in our search for a definition of a moral code of holiness? Is there nothing but vague subjectivism to guide us into paths of righteousness?' Having made these insinuations by interrogation, Chantry asked: 'What is the yardstick by which we may measure what is good and right and acceptable to a holy God? The standard of righteousness must be defined'. I agree, wholeheartedly. But Chantry, of course, claimed the ten commandments are that perfect definition: 'Once deny that the decalogue is a synopsis of the moral law and men are sent into a haze of imprecise ethics' (Chantry: *Righteous* pp77-78,80). But see Michael Eaton: *Encouragement* pp119-123. I do not want to fault a man for a word, but I thought the Reformed look upon the ten commandments as *the* synopsis of the moral law, not a synopsis of it. Indeed, I thought they looked upon it as the moral law itself. As before, I welcome strong, scriptural comment, even in opposition, but how did Chantry's verbal abuse get published? Not only is it nasty, it verges on the libellous. Likening believers to 'criminals' and 'thieves' – actually putting them lower than criminals and thieves – because they dare to question Calvin's third use of the law! I ask you!

Gadsby, having met Fuller and Chantry's like, had his answer ready: 'Now our [Gadsby was being ironical] preachers in general say that if we are not under the law, then we are at liberty to sin. I wonder whether... they would have the courage to get their pen and scratch out [Rom. 6:14]. Scratch it out, and say it ought not to be in the Bible, if you insist upon it that not to be under the law is the high road to sin. God says it is just the reverse. While we were under the law, and it comes with its commanding and condemning authority, it stirs up sin'. In saying this, Gadsby was, of course, referring to Rom. 7:7-11. 'But when we are brought to be "dead to the law by the body of Christ"... grace makes the heart tender, brings us to have holy freedom with God, and delivers us from the reigning power of sin, for sin shall not reign. True enough, now and then it will kick up a riot; but rioting is not reigning' (Gadsby: *Sermons* p72).

I agree with Wells: 'We must be absolutely clear that the category "law" is indispensable to the church' (Wells p40). The church is not law-less! But which law is the believer under? I can only repeat what I have said many times. The believer is not under Moses; he is under Christ. Not to be under the law of Moses is not to be lawless or law-less, however, since the believer is under the law of Christ. And Christ's law is a real law.

McClain: 'If you preach the grace of God for salvation, you will be warned that some may use the doctrine of grace as licence to go on sinning... We admit the warning is often based on fact. Even in the early church, there were some who actually turned "the grace of our God into lasciviousness [lewdness, NKJV, a licence for immorality, NIV] (Jude4). But in the case of such men, the basic trouble was not merely that they had broken the [so-called] moral law (for in this sense all have sinned), but that they were denying 'the only Lord God and our Lord Jesus Christ" (Jude 4, NKJV). They were "ungodly men", Jude writes, not saved men at all, "before of old ordained to this condemnation". Distressing as such cases are, it will do no good at all to change our message from grace back to law. Such a retreat can only deepen the disaster. Certainly these high-handed sinners should be warned of their final doom, and urged to flee to Christ from the wrath to come. But we as preachers must never forget that the law can neither regenerate men nor make them good. Only the grace of God can do that...'.

'Furthermore, if you preach this gospel of God's grace, you are likely to be charged with antinomianism. But this charge is nothing new in the history of the church... Paul himself was accused of the same thing (Rom. 3:8). Therefore we need not be too much surprised to meet the same charge today. As a matter of fact, unless you are charged thus sooner or later, you are probably not preaching the good news of God's grace as it ought to be preached. For it has been truly pointed out that only the true doctrine of grace can be caricatured as a form of antinomianism. You may be sure you will never be charged with antinomianism as long as you are willing to compromise the message of grace with the smallest modicum of law. But the charge is false when levelled against the preacher of salvation by grace. For in the gospel of salvation by grace alone in Christ we are honouring the law and establishing the law. By his death, our Lord Jesus Christ satisfied in full all the law's holy and just demands. The real antinomians are the legalists, for they either take only one element of the law, or they strip it of its penalties, or they soften and relax its demands; to this extent they are against (Greek *anti*) the law' (McClain pp73-74).

Touché Calvin, Fuller, Chantry *et al.*

Objection 3: If believers are not under the law of Moses, why does the New Testament apply the law to them?

This is an important section. My point is that while the New Testament does apply the law to believers, it does so infrequently, and then only as a paradigm, never as a binding rule. But it is prepared to apply 'the law', not just the ten commandments. One of the great faults with the Reformed system is that in order to avoid having to apply much of the law that they would find awkward, not to say distasteful, they have to resort to their escape routes. This is wrong. Besides, it is entirely unnecessary. Take the law of Moses as a paradigm. Take any portion of the law, view it through Christ, and so apply it to the believer. *This is exactly what the New Testament does.* And, I say again, this is a far cry from dividing the law without warrant into bits, discarding most, and then making a certain selected portion ('the moral law') the binding, perfect rule for the believer. The New Testament never does that.

Let me clear away some of the fog of loose thinking and writing. Alderson, for instance, stated that in Eph. 6:1-3, 'Paul makes no apology for *imposing* the fifth commandment on his Ephesian readers' (Alderson pp5-6, emphasis mine). Of course he didn't apologise for something he didn't do! Calvin: 'When Christ or the apostles are treating of the perfect life, they *always* refer believers to the law... It is the *best* instrument for enabling them daily to learn with greater truth and certainty what that will of the Lord is which they aspire to follow, and to confirm them in this knowledge... by *frequently* meditating upon it, [they] will be excited to obedience' (Calvin: *Commentaries* Vol.3 Part 1 p69, emphasis mine; *Institutes* Vol.2 p309, emphasis mine). Always, best, frequently? Would someone who agrees with Calvin please email me and show me this from the New Testament? Pink: 'The New Testament repeats and enforces all the ten commandments' (Pink: *Law* p22). Does it? How about the fourth? Despite his unjustifiable statement, with its sweeping implication, yet Pink could also say, on the same page: 'To be led by the Spirit is incompatible with being under the law'. I know Pink was glossing the Scripture by applying this to justification – in which gloss he was wrong; it applies, as I have shown, to sanctification also. The fact is, in that last, Pink made a bigger statement than he realised.

I must comment on that paragraph. *All the statements in the main extracts in that paragraph are false.* Kruse: 'Paul rarely, if ever, cites the law of Moses simply as a command to be obeyed by believers' (Kruse p122). I would go further. Where does Paul *ever* tell believers they are under Moses' law? Where does he *ever* tell believers they must regard the law of Moses as their norm, their rule? Which command of the ten does Paul *ever* tell believers they must obey? The silence is deafening. This significant fact must be given due weight. Yes, Paul *used* the law when *exhorting* believers, but even such a use is rare. See Michael Eaton: *Encouragement* pp121-123.

Of course, as Fairbairn said: 'The relation of believers under the New Testament to the law has been a fruitful subject of controversy among divines. This has arisen chiefly from the apparently contradictory statements made respecting it in New Testament Scripture'. Bayes: 'On the one hand there is a set of texts [in Romans] which appear *prima facie* to accord the law no status whatsoever in the believing life. On the other hand, there are further texts which... seem to teach that the law has a vital place'. Bruce: 'To gain a clear understanding of Paul's attitude to the law is notoriously difficult'. Calvin: 'Paul, after having dealt with Christian liberty... in his letter to the Romans, and having said that we are free and absolved from the subjection of the law, nevertheless still leads us back to this doctrine, teaching us that it is fitting for us to observe it. How then do we square these views: that the law no longer holds us in bondage, yet its doctrine still remains in effect for governing our life?' (Fairbairn: *Typology* Vol.2 pp161-163; Bayes p103; Bruce: *Paul* p260; Calvin: *Treatises* pp272-273).

Very well! I hope my book has clearly set out my view on this seeming paradox. I strongly disagree with Bruce's 'explanation': 'The difficulty arises in some measure from' what he called 'the ambivalence in [Paul's] thinking and language on the subject'. I do not for a moment accept the suggestion that Paul was 'ambivalent'. But the fact of tension is nothing strange. There is, for instance, a seeming tension between, on the one hand, the need of being taught by those whom Christ has gifted, and who teach on the basis of the written word, and, on the other, the inner anointing of the Spirit (1 John 2:27). This tension has erupted from time to time; with the Quakers and their inner light, for example. There are contemporary examples of it also. The fact is, however, it is not either/or; it is both. Similarly there is a tension, or seeming paradox, over God's decree to save the elect and his expressed desire to save all men, over the place of prayer in light of God's decree, *etc.* We live by faith with these seeming paradoxes.

The Reformed have a solution to the dilemma over the law – a solution of sorts; pull the law's teeth! Calvin, followed by very many, thought – wrongly, as I have proved (see chapter 7, for instance) – that the solution was to say 'this liberty only has to do with the law's curse or rigour'. Citing Gal. 5:1,13 and 1 Pet. 2:16, he concluded: The law 'does not cease to be a good and salutary doctrine, although it no longer exercises such severity on us as it does the ungodly... The Scripture shows us that the ancient ceremonies have been abolished and that we are no longer required [it is more than that; we are forbidden to observe them] to observe them (Col. 2:16) and in general that our consciences are not restrained by external things' (Calvin: *Treatises* p273).

Bolton also saw the dilemma and tried to solve it. He agreed 'there seems.. to be a great deal of strength in the Scripture to prove the abrogation of the law, that we are dead to the law, freed from the law, no more under the law'. But 'on the other hand, there are some scriptures which seem to uphold the law, and which say that the law is still in force... Upon these varieties of texts... men have grounded their varieties of opinions for the abrogation, or the obligation of, the law'. What was Bolton's solution? 'There is no question but the Scripture speaks truth in both; they are the words of truth; and though they seem here to be as the accusers of Christ [at his trial before Pilate], never a one speaking like the other, yet if we are able to find out the meaning, we shall find them... both speaking the same things'. Bolton's solution was, as so often with Reformed teachers, to take refuge in what he saw as the tripartite division of the law, and, as I have noted (see chapter 7), to concentrate on what he and almost all others call the moral law: 'All the controversy arises from the third part, the moral law... It is one of the great disputes in these days [the 1640s; it still is], whether this moral law is abrogated... whether believers are freed from the moral law... Are believers freed from obedience to the moral law; that is, [freed] from the moral law as a rule of obedience?'

Having listed various approaches to the question, he declared: 'Acknowledge the moral law as a rule of obedience and Christian walking, and there will be no falling out [between us; in other words, if you concede, and agree with me, then I will not argue!], whether you take it as promulgated by Moses, or as handed to you and renewed by Christ'. Bolton was referring to John 13:34, the words of Christ: 'A new commandment I give to you'.

Bolton moved to 'two propositions', the first of which concerns us at this point. It reads: 'That the law, for the substance of it... remains as a rule of walking to the people of God... If these two propositions are made good... the doctrines of the abrogation of the law and of freedom from the law will both fall to the ground'. In dealing with his first 'proposition', having once again emphasised that he was talking about the ten commandments, Bolton then proceeded to give several testimonies from 'the Reformed Confessions'. Admitting, however, that the words of men have no authority in themselves – he then turned to the word of God (Matt. 5 – 7; Mark 10:19; Rom. 3:31; 7:12,22,25; 10:4; 13:8-10; 1 Cor. 9:21; Eph. 6:1; 1 Thess. 4:3-4,7; Jas. 2:8; 1 John 2:4; 3:4), and argued: 'Therefore, since Christ, who is the best expounder of the law, so largely strengthens and confirms the law... since faith does not supplant, but strengthens the law; since the apostle so often presses and urges the duties commanded in the law; since Paul acknowledges that he served the law of God in his mind, and that he was under the law to Christ; I may rightly conclude that the law... still remains a rule of life to the people of God'.

This, of course, is the point at issue – and, reader, it is the very point which has to be proved! Bolton, I contend, was wrong in his conclusion. However, having himself explored several objections to it, Bolton came to the place where felt he could state: 'The law sends us to the gospel for our justification [after which] the gospel sends us to the law to frame our way of life. Our obedience to the law is nothing else but the expression of our thankfulness to God who has freely justified us, that "being redeemed, we might serve him without fear" (Luke 1:74). Though our service is not the motive or impelling cause of God's redeeming of us, yet it is the purpose of our redemption... "Therefore, brethren, we are debtors" (Rom. 8:12). If Christ has freed us from the penalties, how we ought to subject ourselves to the precepts! If he has delivered us from the curses, how we ought to study the commands! If he paid our debt of sin, certainly we owe him a debt of service! This was the great end of our redemption; he redeemed us from bondage and brought us into freedom, from slavery to service... He has freed us from the *manner* of our obedience, but not from the *matter* of our obedience. We now obey, but it is from other principles, by other strength, unto other ends, than we did before'.

Bolton went on: Before we were justified, our law-works, we thought, 'were for justification and life; now' that we have been justified through faith, however: 'They are for other ends – to glorify God, to dignify the gospel, to declare our sincerity, to express our thankfulness. Before, we obeyed, but out of compulsion of conscience; now we obey out of the promptings of [grace, the Spirit of God],[1] which, so far as it works, works to God... Let not Moses take the place of Christ; but at the same time, make a right use of Moses... Let the servant follow the Master; let Moses follow Christ; the law, grace; obedience, faith; and then all act their proper and designed parts... Let the righteousness of the law be fulfilled in us; let us not walk after the flesh, but after the Spirit (Rom. 8:4)... The substance of the law is a rule of obedience to the people of God, and that to which they are to conform their lives and their walk now under the gospel'. Let me repeat this point: Bolton, addressing 'all believers', gave them this counsel: 'Make a right use of Moses'. I wholeheartedly agree with this last – at least, as it reads.

But I do not agree with what the Puritan meant! Bolton showed what *he* meant when he quoted the following comment: 'Live as though there were no gospel; die as though there were no law. Pass the time of this life in... this world under the conduct of Moses'. This reminds me of the advice to preach as an Arminian and pray like a Calvinist! He repeated his dreadful sentiment, saying: 'While you are in the wilderness of this world, you must walk under the conduct of Moses; you must live in obedience to the law... The substance of the law is a[2] rule of obedience to the people of God, and that to which they are to conform their lives and their walk now under the gospel' (Bolton pp53-62,72-76 emphasis his). See Zens: *Studies* p44. Fairbairn agreed with Bolton; he said that the law is the 'special instrument... for keeping alive in men's souls a sense of duty' (Zens: *Studies* p36, quoting Fairbairn: *Law* p289).

---

[1] Bolton had 'nature'; he meant the divine nature, the inward working of the Spirit of God (2 Pet. 1:4, and many other places).
[2] I would have thought Bolton would have used 'the'. What, in Bolton's terms, are the other rules? Can there be more than one *perfect* rule? Bolton is not alone in saying such a thing, of course; the comment applies wherever it is used by Reformed writers.

I will not deal with Bolton's individual points here, having done so throughout my book. But here you have it. Believers must walk under Moses. One would think that John 1:17; Rom. 6:14; Rom. 7:4,6; Gal. 3:25; 5:1, and such like, had never been written.

Compare Crisp: 'Either we are the ministers and messengers of Christ, or the ministers of Moses'; 'it is to be lamented... we are too much ministers of Moses, pressing and thundering the wrath of God... publishing unto men the working out of their own salvation by their own works, according to the law' (Crisp: *Christ* Vol.1 p164; Vol.2 p5).

In Rom. 13:8-10, as to the 'law' in question, there can be no doubt. Take the context. Consider, first, the wider context – that is, Paul's overwhelming use of the word throughout Romans. Then consider especially the immediate context, in which some of the ten commandments are quoted (Rom. 13:9). Both contexts make it clear that Paul, writing to believers, was here speaking about the Mosaic law. He quoted Lev. 19:18. (I have spoken of this in connection with the ten commandments). And the apostle said that love fulfils the law (Rom. 13:8; Gal. 5:14). In short, we are talking about the Mosaic law. Kruse: 'This text has important implications for our understanding of the relationship of Paul's gospel to the Mosaic law. It indicates again that his gospel is not antinomian, for it results in the fulfilment of the law. This does not however mean a reinstatement of the law. Rather the effect of Paul's gospel is that believers, walking by the Spirit, are enabled to love one another, so that what the law sought, but was unable to produce, is fulfilled in them. Understood in this way, Paul's teaching does not involve inner contradiction or conflict. The apostle, having argued that believers have died to the law in Rom. 7:1-6 is not reinstating it again [*sic*] as a regulatory norm for them in Rom. 13:8-10'. Is the 'love' in question love for all men in general, or love between believers? John Murray thought love for all men (Murray: *Romans* Vol.2 pp159-160); Kruse thought love between believers (Kruse pp237-238), as did Haldane: 'Christians ought not only to love one another continually, but to abound in love more and more' (Haldane: *Romans* p588). Calvin ridiculously thought it is the obedience of believers to princes, to magistrates (Calvin: *Commentaries* Vol.19 Part 2 pp484-486). See also Moo: *Romans* p814.

In Rom. 13:8-10; Gal. 5:14, 'fulfil' does not mean 'sum up'. Rather, we are in the realm of the eschatological once again. See Witherington pp382-383. Witherington: 'The consummation of faith' – not merely justification – 'is not found in doing works of the Mosaic law, but by doing loving works of piety and charity'. He rightly spoke of 'this high note' (Witherington p370). See Murray: *Romans* Vol.2 p161; Kruse p238.

How mistaken was Reymond, therefore, to say: 'When Paul, beginning in Rom. 12, takes up the moral outworking of justification, he does so by picking up his earlier emphasis on God's law. Only now he does so by speaking of the law under the synonym of "the will of God"... Here Paul calls on the Christian to use his renewed mind to discern and obey God's law... The norm or standard of the Christian life is the law' (Reymond: *Paul* p476). This cannot be right. 'The will of God' cannot be confined to the ten commandments, a mere sixteen verses (thirty-two, with the repeat) of Scripture; it is the entire revealed will of God – the 'all Scripture' of 2 Tim. 3:16-17. See John 17:17.

To bring out the contrast between Paul's way and the Reformed way of sanctification, let me remind you, reader, of Calvin's third use of the law: 'The law acts like a whip to the flesh, urging it on as men do to a lazy sluggish ass. Even in the case of a spiritual man, inasmuch as he is still burdened with the weight of the flesh, the law is a constant stimulus, pricking him forward when he would indulge in sloth... It cannot be denied that it [the law] contains a perfect pattern of righteousness... one perpetual and inflexible rule... The doctrine of the law... remains... that... it may fit and prepare us for every good work' (Calvin: *Institutes* Vol.1 pp309-311). See Michael Eaton: *Encouragement* pp81-82. I know Calvin said that servile fear, slavish service, is useless (see 'Extracts' p360), but he wanted the penny and the bun! I have acknowledged there is a big difference between godly fear (which is an essential) and carnal fear (which is wrong). I suggest Calvin's whip produces *nothing but* a slavish fear.

Rom. 8:3-4; 13:8-10, Moo: 'Christians who love others have satisfied the demands of the law *in toto*... and they need therefore not worry about any other commandment'. But, I hasten to add, as the context also makes clear, this does not mean that love has replaced the commandments; love *fulfils* the law, it does not replace it. Dunn: 'The contrast should not be reduced to the simple one of law *versus* love (or law *versus* Spirit, or law *versus* faith)'. Moo: 'The Christian, who belongs to the new-covenant people of God, is no longer "under the (Mosaic) law", the law for the old-covenant people of God; he is under a "new law", "the law of Christ" (see Gal. 6:2 and 1 Cor. 9:19-21). And central to this new law is a command that Christ himself took from the Mosaic law and made central to his new demand: the command to love our neighbours as ourselves (*cf.* Gal. 6:2 with 5:13-14)' (Moo: *Romans* pp814-817; Dunn p271).

Moo: 'Paul [says] Christians "fulfil" the law (*cf.* especially Rom. 8:4), but nowhere does he require that Christians "do" it. The distinction is not just a semantic one. "Fulfilling" the law in Paul is attached not to the obedience of precepts, but to the attitude of love and the work of the Spirit. For even in Rom. 8:4 the meaning is not that the Spirit enables us to do the law, but that because we are indwelt by the Spirit, the law *has been fulfilled in us*. Thus, the continuity of God's demand (the law must be fulfilled.) is met by a discontinuity in method (not in "doing" but in love and by the Spirit)' (Moo: 'The Law' pp209-210, emphasis his).

On Gal. 5:13-14, Dunn: 'Paul is continuing to address the same people as before, those "who desire to be under the law" (4:21)... [The law in question is] unmistakeably... the Mosaic law'. Witherington: 'It must be kept steadily in mind that the context of this discussion is Paul's emphatic assertion of eschatological freedom (Gal. 5:1) brought about in the Christian's life by the Holy Spirit. This is part of what it means to have been rescued from this present evil age (Gal. 1:4)' (Dunn pp289-290; Witherington pp381-383).

As for 'all the law' (Gal. 5:14), Dunn suggested 'the whole law, the law seen as a whole rather than as an aggregation of individual commandments'. Witherington drew attention to the literal Greek, 'the all law', pointing out that the 'odd' position of the 'all' 'must have some significance. [And] the exceptional position of the definite article' adds to this. Paul is speaking of 'the whole substance of the law... the basic substance or heart of the law, or at least that which fulfils the law's basic intent and design'. Similarly, Moo: 'It may be that the unusual placement of the article in the phrase' – 'the all law' (Gal. 5:14) – is intended to highlight this unitary demand of God' (Dunn p288; Witherington p380; Moo: 'The Law' p209). See Lightfoot: *Galatians* p208.

John Brown oddly (for him), and wrongly, argued that 'the law' in Gal. 5:14 'does not signify the Mosaic law, but the law by which Christians are bound to regulate themselves; for, as the apostle elsewhere says, though completely free from the obligation of the Mosaic law, they are "not without law to God, but under the law to Christ". It is what the apostle calls "the commandment", when he says: "The end of the commandment is love out of a pure heart, and of a good conscience, and of faith unfeigned"... and [it is] what... James terms "the perfect law of liberty", and "the royal law", in opposition to the law of bondage' (Brown: *Galatians* p287), referring to 1 Tim. 1:5; Jas. 1:25; 2:8. Zens did not see the point I am making (Zens: *Studies* p45). He thought Brown's words – as above on Gal. 5:14 and as below on Gal. 6:2 – 'most instructive'. With my caveat about right words on the wrong verse, I wholeheartedly agree with Zens (and Brown), of course.

On New Testament quotation of Lev. 19:18, Dunn: 'Explicit references to Lev. 19:18 are lacking in Jewish literature before Paul... In contrast, Lev. 19:18 is the Pentateuchal passage most often cited in the New Testament... The stimulus to focus thus on Lev. 19:18 must therefore be peculiarly Christian and is best explained as deriving from Jesus himself'. Kruse: 'Paul is defining love in terms of the law, not reinstating the Mosaic law as a regulatory norm, every part of which believers must obey'. As Calvin said: 'Love is the capstone of the law'. And, as he pointed out, it is only 'the Spirit of God [who] forms us to such love' (Dunn p291. Witherington p383 agreed but noted a Qumran reference. Kruse pp103-104; Calvin: 'Appendix' p105).

'Loving one's neighbour' is not a soft option, it is not a lowering of the standard of the law. To dismiss the thesis of my book by such a device is too tempting for some; as we have seen, they wave it away as something vague and hazy – 'imprecise ethics'. Not so! Bigg: 'Full weight should be given to Jesus' key statement that the two greatest commandments in the law are those urging wholehearted, unqualified love for God and neighbour (Deut. 6:5; Lev. 19:18; Matt. 22:34-39). Such a verdict becomes even more important when we accept that everything else in the Mosaic law, as well as the Old Testament prophets, is derived from these all-embracing moral principles (Matt. 22:40). This means, among other things, that *the two greatest commandments are more fundamental than the ten commandments*. They also merit the description "timeless". Indeed, the continuing validity of: "Love your neighbour as yourself" is well illustrated by its repeated use in the New Testament. No wonder love has such a high profile in the apostolic writings (*e.g.*, John 13:34; Rom. 13:8-20; 1 Cor. 13; Eph. 5:2; Col. 3:14; 1 Thess. 1:3; 3:12; 4:9-10; Jas. 2:8; 1 Pet. 4:8; 1 John 3:11-23; 4:7-21)... For each of the ten commandments, what carries over from the old covenant to the new is the inner kernel or moral instruction pertinent to God's people in every age. These constitute the *timeless* aspects of the ten commandments... Deut. 6:5; Lev. 19:18... The entire old covenant depended on these two moral requirements (Matt. 22:34-40). As abiding spiritual principles they were [are] valid *for all time*. The highest expression of love for God and neighbour *at that time* was in the ten commandments...We are not subject to any part of the law of Moses *as it stands in Exodus-Deuteronomy* because we are not Israelites living und the old covenant. Paul's argument in Gal. 3:15-25 shows that the law was an interim measure [coming] between Abraham and Christ, the promised Seed, and was "added... *until* the Seed... had come" (Gal. 3:16-19)... Many of the laws we are to obey reveal continuity from the old covenant to new. Thus stealing, lying, slander and revenge were sinful in Moses' day, and are still sinful now (Lev. 19:11,16,18; Rom. 12:19; Eph. 4:28; Col. 3:8-9). The underlying reason for these and other continuities is that they express the permanently valid commandments: "Love you neighbour as yourself". This commandment encapsulates the "righteous requirement of the law", which is is to be [it is!] *fulfilled* in those who walk according to the Spirit (Rom. 8:4; 13:9). Paul summed it all up by affirming that *the law is fulfilled through manifestations of Christian love* (Rom. 13:8-10)... Let us take seriously the crucial importance, underlined by Jesus himself, of the two greatest commandments, which involve love for God and neighbour (Matt. 22:34-40). Our approach will be truly biblical when we treat these, rather than the ten commandments, as the foundation for all Christian ethical conduct. Let us handle the ten commandments in the way the New Testament handles them – in terms of continuity and discontinuity... Let us repel any suggestion that we are being "antinomian" (against law) if we oppose the idea that the ten commandments constitute God's moral law and the rule of life for Christians today. By adopting Paul's position, and joyfully accepting that we are subject to the law of Christ (1 Cor. 9:21; [Gal. 6:2]), we will actually be more "law-abiding" than anyone who tries to keep the ten commandments' (Bigg: 'Fulfilling' pp21-23, emphasis his).

Dunn also quashed the notion that the biblical call for 'love' is 'imprecise': 'On the contrary, just because it is less prescribed beforehand what love of the neighbour demands, and depends on who the neighbour is and his/her situation in each particular instance, *it is all the more demanding*. Moreover, the demand is open-ended: we do not know beforehand who our neighbour might be at any one time (see also... Gal. 6:10)... It is a call for a practical love, a concentrated love, not a vague feeling for humankind stretched so thin as to be non-existent'. I agree, further, with Dunn when he once again observed how an emphasis upon 'the freedom of the Spirit can easily degenerate' into all sorts of carnal behaviour, unless it is accompanied by the equally biblical emphasis on the all-embracing law of Christ. Carnal behaviour 'is the lot of those who throw over the law without a principle as penetrating as love of neighbour to guide them, and without a genuine commitment to serve one another. Without that, the call to freedom can open a floodgate which sweeps away every foundation' (Dunn pp289,292-293, emphasis mine; Witherington pp384-385). Because the 'neighbour' in Lev. 19 referred to a fellow-Israelite, Witherington thought the focus here is love to fellow-believers. 'Almost nothing in this letter is about how Christians should relate to outsiders', but he noted Gal. 6:10. See his extract from Chrysostom, who contrasted the one who 'transgresses the law' with 'the other [who] transcends it'.

Brown on Gal. 6:2: '"The law of Christ" seems here plainly to be the law of mutual love, so often and so explicitly enjoined, and so powerfully and affectionately enforced – John 13:34-35; 15:12... When Christians bear one another's burdens, they obey the law of Christ; and when they do not, they violate that law... It is a very powerful motive with the Christian mind to reflect: "If I do this, I do what is well pleasing to my Saviour – what he has required of me as a proof of my love and obedience – and if I do not do this, I displease him, I trample on his authority, I dishonour his name". There seems [weak!] to be a tacit contrast between the law of Moses and the law of Christ. It is as if the apostle had said: "This bearing one another's burdens is a far better thing than those external observances which your new teachers are so anxious to impose on you. To be sure, it is not like them, a keeping of the law of Moses, but infinitely better, it is a fulfilling of the law of Christ – the law of love"' (Brown: *Galatians* pp325-326).

But what of the seeming contradiction between Gal. 3:10-12; 5:3 and Gal. 5:14? On the one hand Paul (and the law) demanded total obedience to the law, 'doing the law', 'keeping the whole law', 'continuing in all things which are written in the book of the law' – which Paul spoke of with negative overtones. On the other hand, he spoke of the 'fulfilling of the law', 'fulfilling the whole law', with positive overtones. How can these be reconciled? Dunn: 'On this contrast, many an attempt to exegete and expound Paul's thought has run aground... His position at this point has rarely been appreciated'. Dunn rightly noted the escape route – of trying to say a different law is in view – is useless; 'the whole law' is 'the Mosaic law' throughout. He went on: The apostle's 'position at this point has rarely been appreciated' – 'least of all by those who can only understand Paul's theology as an out and out rejection of the law as a still important yardstick for Christian conduct' (Dunn pp289-291). See Kruse p104. As for that last from Dunn, let me say it yet again, contrary to what may be said about me, I do nothing of the sort! The law is a part of Scripture and thus is useful to the believer (2 Tim. 3:16-17) – as long as it is used 'lawfully' (1 Tim. 1:8); that is, biblically. With Dunn and Witherington, I reject Hubner's claim that Gal. 5:3 and Gal. 5:14 do not both speak of the entire Mosaic law (Dunn p290; Witherington p380; Hubner p37).

So what is the solution to the seeming contradiction? Kruse suggested '"doing the law" denotes the observance of all that the law prescribes [Gal. 3:10-12; 5:3], whereas "fulfilling the law" [Gal. 5:14] means living a life in which the great moral concerns of the law are exemplified, even though many of the actual regulations of the law... are not observed' (Kruse p104). To my mind, the cases are different. For a start, the law-phrases in Gal. 5:3 and 5:14 are not the same – even though Moo spoke of 'an unlikely distinction between' the two (Moo: 'The Law' p210). In the first, 'there is reference to all the detailed prescriptions of the law'; in the second, as I have already noted, there is reference to the 'heart of the law' (Witherington p380). Moreover, in Gal. 5:3, Paul was speaking of the attempt to earn justification by 'doing the law', which can be only by 'doing the whole law', 'the observance of all that the law requires' (Gal. 3:12; 5:3). This is impossible for fallen man. *Hence the negative overtones.* In Gal. 5:14, however, Paul was speaking of the new-covenant provisions Christ brought in, by which he gives people grace to 'fulfil the whole law', giving them his Spirit to enable them to live a sanctified life which expresses love (see Rom. 8:3-4). 'The love of God' – the sense of God's love to his people – 'the love of God has been poured out in our hearts by the Holy Spirit who was given to us' (Rom. 5:5). Thus the Spirit enables believers to love in return (Luke 7:36-50; 1 John 4:7-11,19) and so 'fulfil the whole law'. *Hence the positive overtones.*

In Eph. 6:1-3, Paul alluded to the law. See Charles Hodge: *Ephesians* pp356-357. *But the apostle did not quote the law as the rule under which believers live.* Kruse: 'Paul appeals to the law more as a paradigm of good behaviour for those in the Lord, than as a regulatory norm under which believers still serve'. Michael Eaton: 'The total flow of argument' [in Eph. 4 – 6] must be noted'. Linking Eph. 6:1-4 with Rom. 8:1-4, he added: 'To be sure, Paul *mentions* the law: in the long run the ten commandments are fulfilled by those who obey the Spirit. The question is, how does this come about? Not, apparently, by putting oneself directly under the law, but by being full of the Spirit. If one walks by the Spirit deliberately one fulfils the law accidentally... The law is fulfilled indirectly by walking in the Spirit... The fact that Paul can refer to some of the commands of the decalogue does not negate the fact that he makes minimal use of the [law] in his exhortations to Christian godliness'. The absence of the rule of the law of Moses, in Paul's setting out of the law of Christ for believers, could not be more clear (Kruse p265; Michael Eaton: *Encouragement* pp122-123,240-241, emphasis mine). Of course, as Reymond said, Paul could quote the fifth command 'with the assumption that the Christian community would recognise and accept the abiding significance of the law'. I also agree with him, Paul did 'not quote the law to make it binding'. But I disagree when he said Paul quoted it 'because it is binding'. Not so. It is a paradigm. Reymond realised this; listing some of Paul's 'allusions' to the Old Testament, he said: 'Paul... underscores by citing other Old Testament passages to state his ethical teaching' (Reymond: *Paul* p478). Just so! But citing and alluding to the law is one thing; treating it as the binding rule is another.

Hoch: 'The New Testament writers certainly used the Old Testament as their Bible. But did they require Gentile believers to abide by the Mosaic covenant as their rule of faith and practice?' No, of course not! 'Paul preached Christ, not Moses'. But the point is this: 'One can still preach from the Old Testament using it typologically, illustratively, analogically and rhetorically as the New Testament writers themselves do, without bringing in the Mosaic covenant as the continuing rule of life for Christians'. Luther, having observed that Christ, not Moses, is the believer's master, went on: 'However, it is true Moses sets down, in addition to the laws, fine examples of faith and unbelief, punishment of the godless, elevation of the righteous and believing – and also the dear and comforting promises concerning Christ which we should accept... This... is to be noted well for it is really crucial. Many great and outstanding people have missed it, while even today many great preachers still stumble over it. They do not know how to preach Moses or how to regard his books' (Hoch p70; see Armstrong p17).

Barcellos claimed the law is authoritative and binding upon the believer for sanctification, but qualified this by saying the work of Christ 'modified' or 'conditioned' its application under the new covenant. As to this last, I agree. In fact, it is precisely what I am saying here – unless, of course, he meant by 'modify', 'pull the law's teeth!' I agree with Barcellos when he said: 'The whole Old Testament is inspired of God and still profitable for men... under the new covenant'. I do not limit this – as Barcellos did here – to 'men in the Christian ministry', unless, which I doubt, he was giving 'ministry' its full New Testament meaning – see my *Priesthood*; *Pastor*. The law, in particular, as part of 'all Scripture', has its part to play in the life of the believer, and that part is as a paradigm. So I do not say the law is 'null and void', 'cancelled in all respects', that 'Christ's people are to have nothing to do with the law of the Old Testament'. Nor do I think Christ came 'to obliterate the law'.

On the contrary, I agree that 'the law of God, even the whole Old Testament, has its *place* under Christ, finding its realisation in him and its modified application in his kingdom... The Christian ethic involves the whole Bible. The abrogation of the old covenant does not cancel the utility of the Old Testament'. Of course not. I, for one, have never written anything remotely like it. In short, 'the law is the same [but] its application is modified to fit the conditions brought on [in] by the death of Christ and the inauguration of the new covenant'. As I say, I am at one with Barcellos in this – unless he was saying that the Mosaic law (however he defines it) is the law of Christ. I emphasise his use of 'utility' and 'place'; the law is useful and has its place in the life of the 'believer'. As I have explained, I would prefer 'nuanced' to 'modified'.

But as for these 'modified conditions' – the way the law is used in the new covenant – we must let the New Testament teach us. I vehemently disagree with Barcellos when he says 'the whole Old Testament is authoritative [in this age] down to its minute detail... still binding... [in] all its parts'. We must be shown New Testament evidence for such sweeping statements. They carry enormous consequences. How about Matt. 5:38-39? Are the sacrifices and feasts still 'binding'? And how about the punishments (see Ex. 21:15,17; Lev. 20:9; Deut. 21:18-21, just for a start). The key word, I repeat, is 'place'. It *is* binding, *in its place*. But what is the law's place in the new covenant? Certainly it is not the believer's rule; rather it serves as a paradigm to illustrate and enforce the law of Christ. Barcellos realised he was in a minefield. Having asserted that the law is 'authoritatively binding on the church', he nevertheless had to admit the difficulties of his position. What did he do with these difficulties? 'Casting aside all the difficult questions that arise concerning the specific application of this thesis', he said, and ploughed on. But this is not the way to deal with Scripture. Nor is it fair or helpful to the believer who wants to know, precisely, how the law applies to him in his specific circumstances. The one thing a believer cannot do – and teachers in particular dare not do – is to cast aside all difficulties when trying to come to grips with Scripture. It is precisely the difficulties which need to be addressed! Imagine a physician taking the same route as Barcellos – casting aside all difficulties connected with the understanding of a disease and its proposed cure! But notice how admirably Barcellos caught the biblical principle by his use of 'borrows': 'The New Testament clearly abrogates the whole old covenant, including the decalogue, as it functioned within the old covenant, and yet borrows from its documents... for new-covenant ethics'. Excellently put. But Barcellos went far too far when he called the decalogue 'the *basis* for new-covenant ethics' (Barcellos pp61-69,87-88, emphasis mine). The basis of new-covenant ethics is Christ, not the ten commandments. The law of Christ *uses* all the law of Moses to illustrate its claims, it *borrows* from it, but it is not *based* upon it.

Kruse: Paul did not speak of the law 'as a set of demands to be observed as a regulatory norm; rather it provided believers with a paradigm for Christian behaviour... Paul's predominant appeal to the law in 1 Corinthians is as a paradigm for Christian behaviour. By appealing to the law in this way, Paul was not reinstating its demands as a regulatory norm, but rather finding in the law... instructive examples of the way in which God dealt with his people, and of the ways in which they were to relate to one another'. Fee: 'Paul well understood the paradigmatic, analogical character of the law... By their very nature, the laws, which are limited in number, do not intend to touch all circumstances; hence they regularly function as paradigms for application in all sorts of human circumstances... It should be noted... that Paul does not speak to what the law originally meant... He is concerned *with what it means*, that is, *with its application to their* [the believers in 1 Corinthians] *present situation*' (Kruse pp119,145. See also pp156,160,265; Fee: *1 Corinthians* pp214-220,406-409,451-452, emphasis mine). Witherington p220 also made the point, but timidly. See Barcellos p68.

On 1 Tim. 1:8, Harris: The law 'may be used lawfully as the expression of God's mind with respect to a variety of actions. It may be used lawfully too as exhibiting any great principle of divine conduct; as such the apostle uses it, when insisting on children obeying their parents in the Lord, where he shows that there was in the law an express promise to obedient children. So again he uses it lawfully when he presents it as the general expression of the Divine mind, that labour is entitled to support [1 Cor. 9:8-9]... If we [do not use it in this way] we deprive ourselves of the benefit of God's own expressed mind on a great variety of subjects, and therefore of that wisdom which comes from above. But fully allowing all this, I would assert that the believer who proposed to himself the law for his rule would constantly be walking disorderly as a disciple of Christ. It was given by Moses for a specific purpose... "It made nothing perfect"... We are under law to Christ, not to Moses' (Harris pp41-42).

John Murray nearly got it right: 'The Old Testament was designed to furnish us in these last days with the instruction necessary for the fulfilment of our vocation to the end, and that it is as *written* it promotes this purpose' (Murray: *Romans* Vol.2 p199, emphasis his). Murray was not precise enough here. Instead of '*the* instruction', he should have said: 'The Old Testament furnishes *some* of the instruction [or,] furnishes illustrations and examples'.

Zaspel quoted Luther: 'That Moses does not bind the Gentiles can be proved from Ex. 20:1, where God himself speaks... This text makes it clear that even the ten commandments do not pertain to us'. I pause. 'Do not pertain' – that is, were not given. The law – not just the ten commandments – do 'pertain' to the believer, I hasten to add, in the sense that Moses, though he is not the believer's lawgiver, is one of his teachers. As I have said, the law acts as a paradigm, an illustration, an example for the believer, but it is not his perfect rule. To let Luther continue: 'For God never led us out of Egypt, but only the Jews. The sectarian spirits [Judaisers] want to saddle us with Moses and all the commandments. We will just skip that. We will regard Moses as a teacher, but not regard him as our lawgiver' (Zaspel p165).

Witherington: Paul 'believes that law has had its day and has ceased to be the standard that Christians must live by... It follows that the Christian cannot unreflectingly apply this or that verse of the Mosaic covenant to the lives of Christians without asking if this or that imperative or principle has in fact been reaffirmed in the new covenant'. We have to ask: 'Where does this leave Moses?' Zaspel raised the question and answered it: 'Clearly, he has taken a back seat'. But this does not mean Moses has no relevance whatsoever for the believer. He is in the back seat, yes, but he is still in the car, and has much to contribute. The fact is, Moses 'is not now to be ignored; but the law he gave remains relevant only insofar as it is read through Christian lenses. Moses can no longer be read by himself. His fulfiller [Christ] has come, and it would be wrong to ignore him [Christ] for Moses' sake. Moses himself would not allow this; we must hear this prophet who is like – but greater than – Moses (Deut. 18:15-19). We read Moses and learn from him, but our loyalty is to the one of whom he spoke, the one who took Moses' law and "filled it full". In other words, Jesus' lordship extends even over Moses. It is no longer Moses, but Jesus, who informs our conscience. It is *his* moral instruction that shapes our lives and defines true sanctification... Paul reasons from this very premise in 1 Cor. 9:20-21, where he argues that he is not bound by Moses; he is rather "under the law of *Christ*"... He is *not* obliged to Moses' law... he *is* obliged to the law of Christ. Again, Jesus stands above even Moses... This... is frequently fleshed out in the New Testament... For all the New Testament writers, Jesus has the highest priority, even in terms of moral and ethical instruction. We will not go back to Moses, for it is in Jesus that Moses is made "complete"... Divine law continues, but not in its Mosaic formulation. Christ supersedes Moses. This is no "destroying" of Moses, but rather his "fulfilling" (Matt. 5:17... Deut. 18:15-19). Christ is the one of whom Moses wrote (John 5:46), whose law would be absolute and the ultimate standard of judgement (Deut. 18:15-19). By no means are we left without law. Rather, Christ has taken morals a step higher, above Moses. From him we learn God's highest expression of holiness'. Ridderbos: 'This is not to say that the law has no further use... but outside of Christ the law has no claims upon the believers any longer; so far as both its mandatory character and its content go the law must be seen and judged entirely from the point of view of Christ (*cf.* Gal. 6:2; 1 Cor. 9:21)' (Witherington pp247,275; Zaspel pp158-159,162, emphasis his; Ridderbos p187). For the Anabaptist position on this, and their citation of various laws no longer applicable to believers, see chapter 6.

Objection 4: If believers are not under the law of Moses, why did James say that believers who keep 'the perfect law of liberty' will be blessed? and why did he say that believers will be judged by that law?

Just a reminder: 'Explicit references to Lev. 19:18 are lacking in Jewish literature before Paul... In contrast, Lev. 19:18 is the Pentateuchal passage most often cited in the New Testament... The stimulus to focus thus on Lev. 19:18 must therefore be peculiarly Christian and is best explained as deriving from Jesus himself' (Dunn p291). Witherington p383 agreed, but noted a Qumran reference.

Alderson was wrong to say 'the law of liberty' 'is nothing other than the ten commandments' (Alderson p5). What is more, in Jas. 2:8-13, we have a contrast between the law of liberty and the law of Moses. James, having referred to what he called 'the royal law according to the Scripture' (Jas. 2:8), which is Lev. 19:18 in the hands of Christ – Moo thought 'royal' 'is probably an allusion to Jesus' own teaching' (Moo: 'The Law' p217) – immediately moved to what he called 'the law' (Jas. 2:9,11), 'the whole law' (Jas. 2:10), making reference to some of the ten commandments. God, in the law of Moses, demanded absolute and perfect obedience to every command, with condemnation for one transgression. Turning to his readers, James said: 'So speak and so do as those who will be judged by the law of liberty' (Jas. 2:12); he did not say, as those who will be judged by 'the law', or by 'the law of Moses', or by '*this* law of liberty'. This is important. If he had used any of these phrases, James would in the context have been referring to the law of Moses. But by calling it '*the* law of liberty', he was distinguishing it from the law of Moses. He was making a contrast with the law of Moses. He was speaking of another law, the 'royal law', the fulfilment of Lev. 19:18 (Rom. 13:9; Gal. 5:14), which can be none other than 'the law of Christ' (Gal. 6:2), 'this rule' by which the Israel of God must walk (Gal. 6:16; Phil. 3:16), 'the law towards Christ' or 'Christ's law' (1 Cor. 9:21), 'the law of faith' (Rom. 3:27).

John Murray said of 'law' in Rom. 3:27, it could aptly be translated 'rule' (Murray: *Romans* Vol.1 pp122-123). In other words, 'the rule of faith' – 'the law of the Spirit of life in Christ Jesus' (Rom. 8:2), the gospel. *This* is the law by which believers must live, and by which they will be judged. Do the Reformed think they will be judged only by the ten commandments? Think about Matt. 5:21-22,27-30, for a start. Once again, we see that the Reformed system is less penetrating than the New Testament system of the law of Christ. George Wright: 'I regard the gospel as the perfect law of liberty which we are to look into and continue therein, and the sole and sufficient rule for the saints to walk by in serving God acceptably' (George Wright p241). And be judged by!

As a consequence, these verses, far from proving that the law of Moses is a perfect rule for believers, do the very opposite. They prove that the complete word, especially the gospel, the law of Christ, is 'the perfect law of liberty'. The law of Moses could never be called *that*. Freedom is never associated with the law of Moses, but with Christ: 'For freedom [he] has made us free' (Gal. 5:1, footnote). We have to 'stand fast... in the liberty by which Christ has made us free' (Gal. 5:1). 'Law' and 'freedom' are joined only by Christ. James 'associates ["the law that gives freedom"] closely with the gospel' (Moo: 'The Law' p217). 'If the Son makes you free, you shall be free indeed' (John 8:36). See also John 8:31-32; Rom. 6:18,22; 8:21; 1 Cor. 7:22; 2 Cor. 3:17; Gal. 4:31; 5:13; 1 Pet. 2:16.

Just in case it needs to be repeated, yet again: I am not rejecting the law when I say this. Nor am I saying the believer is law-less; how could I on such a passage? But although the law of Moses plays its part in the believer's life, it is not his perfect, his entire rule, and certainly not his rule of *liberty*. The Jew was under the law of Moses, the pedagogue, the custodian, the yoke which none (but Christ himself) could bear; the believer is under the law of Christ, that easy yoke and light burden which Christ enables his people to bear, that law which encompasses the entire word of God, and therefore includes and encapsulates the ten commandments and all the Mosaic law, but that law *as interpreted and applied by Christ and the apostles in the new covenant*.

Manton: 'I understand [the perfect law of liberty to be] the whole doctrine and word of God, and chiefly the gospel. The will of God in Scripture is called a law... [Ps. 1 and 119] where by law is understood the whole word; and the gospel is called... 'the law of faith' [Rom. 3:27]. Now this law is said to be perfect, because it is so... in itself, and they that look into it will see that there needs no other word to make the man of God perfect... The gospel is a law... [Rom. 8:2]... Look upon the gospel as a law and rule, according to which... your lives must be conformed: "Peace on them that walk according to this rule" [Gal. 6:16]; that is, the directions of the gospel... The gospel itself is a law, partly as it is a rule, partly because of the commanding prevailing power it has over the heart. So it is "the law of the Spirit of life"; so that they that are in Christ are not without law... [1 Cor. 9:21], "I am not without the law, but under the law to Christ"; that is, under the rule and direction of the moral law, as adopted and taken in as part of the gospel by Christ...'. See chapter 18 for more on this important qualification. Manton continued: 'The gospel... is a "law of liberty"'... It teaches the way to true liberty, and freedom from sin, wrath, death... The gospel is a doctrine of liberty and deliverance [John 8:36]... There is no state so free as that which we enjoy by the gospel... The bond of obedience that is laid upon us is indeed and in truth a perfect freedom... Duty is the greatest liberty... We do it upon free principles. Whatever we do, we do it as "the Lord's freemen" [1 Cor. 7:22] upon principles of love and thankfulness... [Rom. 12:1 and Tit. 2:11-12]. The motives of the gospel are mercy and grace; and the obedience of the gospel is an obedience performed out of gratitude or thankfulness. We have the assistance of a free Spirit... A free Spirit, because he makes us free, helps us serve God willingly and freely. There is spirit and life in the commandment... and that makes it a "perfect law of liberty". Of old, there was... no help to fulfil it' (Manton: *James* pp161-165; see also pp218-219).

In other words, as I have said, the law of liberty is the law of Christ. And this is the rule for believers – not the law of Moses. This is the law by which believers must live and by which they will be judged.

Robert Johnstone: 'The "law of liberty" is evidently... another name for the "word of truth", by which God regenerates, and the hearty acceptance of which constituted "the faith of our Lord Jesus Christ", and was the root of the religion professed by James's readers (Jas. 1:18,27; 2:1). But, no less evidently, while it is the gospel that is in his thoughts, it is *the gospel regarded specially in its sanctifying aspect*... More exactly, "the law of liberty" is the divine law considered as taken up into the grand redemptive system, which has for its purpose to make men spiritually like God, "holy and without blame before him in love" – the divine law, as those who are in Christ see it, exhibited under the gospel with new motives and in connection with new spiritual motives – the "old commandment, which we had from the beginning", and yet "new" in Christ'. See chapter 18 for more on this important qualification. Johnstone continued: 'The code of morals exhibited by God in "the word of truth" is for the Christian a binding law... He is "not without law to God, but under the law to Christ" (1 Cor. 9:21). And through this... the law is for him "the law of liberty"'... The divine law, as seen by the Christian, exhibits liberty, gives liberty, is liberty' (Johnstone: *James* pp117-118, emphasis mine).

Johnstone later said: 'Christians should remember continually their subjection to the great law... their being "under the law to Christ". We should have much before our minds and hearts the fact that to glorify God – the end for which we were made at the first, and for which we were created anew in Christ Jesus – is to keep his law; that "without holiness no man shall see the Lord"; that sincere and growing conformity to the divine law is the only satisfactory evidence of our having given ourselves up to be saved through Christ... The fact... that the law under which Christians are placed is the "law of liberty", should be much before us, as fitted to stimulate and sustain us in the narrow way of godliness... The comforts of the gospel... and the motives which it presents to holy obedience, ought to be often pondered by the child of God, that he may be spurred to ardour in the divine life, and thus experience increasingly the sense of liberty – the joyous buoyancy of spirit which we may have and should have in keeping God's law – that sweet constraint of the love of Christ which is perfect freedom' (Johnstone: *James* pp172-173). Nothing here of Calvin's third use of the law.

Objection 5: If believers are not under the law of Moses, why did Paul say that 'keeping the commandments of God is what matters' (1 Cor. 7:19)?

Witherington: 'The question must be raised – which commandments of God? The answer is those that are part of the law of Christ, not simply those found in the Mosaic law' (Witherington p370). See Kruse p124; Moo: 'The Law' p216.

In addition to the above, Bigg: *Pursuit* pp109-112; Brown: *Hebrews* p365; Guthrie p172.

CHAPTER 18: THE BELIEVER'S RULE: SEVEN OBJECTIONS
THE SEVENTH

The Israel and Judah in question

Dispensationalists think such prophecies as Jer. 31 refer to the blessing of national Israel at the end of the gospel age; they expect a general conversion of the Jews towards the end of this dispensation. In particular, they think Jeremiah was speaking of the covenant which God will make with the Jewish nation in those days. Take Decker: 'The parties of the new covenant are God and Israel... The covenant anticipates a reunited and restored Israel as a national entity... The covenant is not promised to any other group or nation. The Old Testament is unanimous in stating that the new covenant will be made with Israel... The church is not a party with whom the new covenant is made'. This, it goes without saying, begs the question, and one or two more! Israel, according to Decker, is the real beneficiary of the promise of the new covenant; he regarded 'the Gentiles more as onlookers than as participants in the covenant'. He came to the somewhat grudging conclusion 'that [although] only Israel is addressed in the Old Testament passages on the new covenant [this] does not mean that others are excluded... All that can be said is that the Old Testament speaks only of Israel's inclusion'. But what about the New Testament? Decker was also less than enthusiastic in his admission: 'It is difficult to avoid the conclusion that the book of Hebrews views the new covenant as having been ratified at the cross... It seems inescapable that this new, better covenant is relevant to the Christians whom the writer of Hebrews addressed'. Who wants to 'avoid' the conclusion? Again, the writer to the Hebrews addressed *all* Christians! And what about 'seems'? Decker found other New Testament evidence for the end of the old covenant with the work of Christ (Matt. 26:28; Mark 14:24; Luke 22:20; 1 Cor. 11:25; 2 Cor. 3:6-18) incontrovertible, but still feebly concluded: 'It suggests... that God's theocratic administrative covenant for the old era – the old or Mosaic covenant – has been superseded by a new arrangement'. It does not 'suggest' it; it categorically states it! Decker listed three dispensational views of the relationship between the church and the new covenant. He rightly dismissed Lewis Sperry Chafer's view that the new covenant for the church is different to the new covenant for Israel. He did the same with John Nelson Darby's view that the church has no relationship to the new covenant, and showed Darby was inconsistent and obscure. The best that Decker would allow is a measly: 'The church participates in some aspects of the new covenant... The majority view in dispensational circles today is that the church participates in some way in the new covenant, but there is considerable diversity in the explanations' (Decker pp293-302,330-331,431-454). See also Wells p21; Hoch pp61-62

As is well known, it is not only dispensationalists who believe in a massive awakening in national Israel. Consider the words of John Brown – certainly no dispensationalist – which may be taken as typical: 'It seems to me quite plain, that the words are a prophecy of that general conversion of the Jews to Christianity which we are warranted to look for from many Old Testament predictions, and from that express declaration of the apostle, that a period is coming when "all Israel shall be saved" [Rom. 11:26]' (Brown: *Hebrews* p372). This, of course, is not the only interpretation of Rom. 11:26. Allowing this for the moment, due weight must be given to the thrust of Brown's next remarks. He also said of this covenant with the Jews, which he believed would be made with them at the end of the age: It 'is substantially the same covenant which, ratified by the blood of Jesus' is during this gospel age, 'diffusing its blessings to' all believers (Brown: *Hebrews* p372). So much for the first view. If this is right, Jeremiah was prophesying of a covenant yet to be made with national Israel.

Now for some comments from the other side. I turn to Owen. Jeremiah's prophecy in the first instance concerned the nation of Israel, which Owen saw fulfilled in the preaching of the gospel to the Jews before it was taken to the Gentiles. We know this is what happened historically – as commanded by Christ (Luke 24:47-49; Acts 1:8), and as carried out by the apostles (Acts 3:26; 10:36; 13:26,46; Rom. 1:16; 2:9-10). And then to the Gentiles (Acts 10:47; 11:17-18; 13:46-49; Rom. 1:16; *etc.*). Owen himself cited Acts 2:39; 3:25-26 and 13:46. But the larger fulfilment of Jeremiah's prophecy of the new covenant, Owen argued, is to all believers – whether Jew or Gentile – throughout this entire gospel age: 'Hence alone it is that the promises of grace under the Old Testament are given unto the church under these names [that is, Israel and Judah], because they were types of them who should really and effectually be made partakers of them... These are the true Israel and Judah' (Owen: *Hebrews* Vol.3 Part 3 pp117-118; see also p139).

Gouge was of a similar mind to Owen; he also thought the reference is to the church: 'These two names, Israel, Judah, comprise... the whole church of God'. He dismissed the suggestion of 'some [who] refer this [prophecy] to the calling of the Jews. But this is not agreeable to the scope' of the inspired writer of the letter to the Hebrews, he declared; rather the inspired writer 'speaks of all God's [people]... who shall be under the new covenant, whether Jews or Gentiles'. Gouge cited Eph. 2:14-17 in support (Gouge pp560-561).

All this raises a very important point of biblical interpretation. Jeremiah spoke of Israel and Judah, but, said Owen and Gouge, the new-covenant interpretation of such a promise is to read it as a promise to the Israel of God, the church (Gal. 6:16; 1 Pet. 2:9-10). This is the way believers must interpret such prophecies. Is this right? Or, as others maintain, should we understand it as a promise to literal Israel? Leaving this for the moment, what of the other question – what law is it to which the prophet refers? How should we understand this aspect of his prophecy? Jeremiah prophesied about the law. To what law was he referring? The writer to the Hebrews quoted Jeremiah from the Septuagint; he spoke of 'laws' (Heb. 8:10; 10:16) not 'law' (Jer. 31:33). Merely noting the fact for now, what should we understand by 'law' in Jeremiah's prophecy? This is *the* question. Barcellos called it 'the issue at stake... This is a key text... the beginning point in a study of new-covenant theology... the place to start' (Barcellos pp15-16).

The law in question
As before, there are two main views, dividing in precisely the same way as over the first question. But although there is disagreement over this part of the prophecy, there is a measure of inconsistency; some want to regard the 'Israel and Judah' as spiritual Israel but keep the law as the law of Moses. See below. Some think Jeremiah was speaking of the law of Moses: 'The rabbis generally interpreted the passage in Jeremiah in reference to the old *torah*' (W.D.Davies p224). Many (most?) of the Reformed think Jeremiah was speaking of the ten commandments. Others think he was speaking of the law of Christ. Hoch: 'What *torah* will be/is written on the hearts of "Israel and Judah"? Is it the entirety of the Old Testament directives to Israel? All Pentateuchal legislation? The moral and civil commands of the old covenant? The moral commands of the old covenant? Basic, fundamental commands such as loving God and loving neighbour? Or is the term a synonym for God's will without any definite legal content?' (Hoch p58). Or is it something else?

Moo: 'If Jeremiah and Ezekiel are indeed referring to the Mosaic law,[1] there is no basis to confine the reference to only one part of the law (*e.g.*, the so-called "moral" law). Yet it is evident that the totality of the Mosaic law has not been re-instituted as an authoritative source [*sic*; rule?] of life in the new covenant – its laws pertaining to food, sacrifices, festivals and civic matters are not binding on Christians (Mark 7:19; Acts 10:9-16; Hebrews, *passim*). Those who argue, then, that the Mosaic law continues intact in the new covenant must recognise that it does not continue without variation and modification. The writing of the law in the heart may indeed [it does!] involve transformation of the actual

---

[1] As they were in their day. But the real question to be faced is, what is 'the law' in the *fulfilment* of the prophecies?

content of the law' (Moo: 'Galatians' pp28-29). Many Reformed teachers claim that 'the law' is 'the law', both in the prophecy and its fulfilment, yet blithely whittle this down to the ten commandments. Biblical warrant would be nice! Actually, it is essential. May we have it, please?

Chantry was convinced the prophecy was of the ten commandments, the so-called moral law (Chantry: *Righteous* p73), as was Malcolm Watts, who dismissed any suggestion he might be mistaken: 'Surely any one would *assume* that the law to which God is referring is the law he acknowledges throughout Scripture – his moral law' (Malcolm Watts p22, emphasis mine). Reader, this cavalier approach to Scripture will not do; Watts simply assumed he was right and took it for granted that 'the law' means the ten commandments. Manifestly, this is not always so. Indeed, rarely is it. Does the word 'law' always mean precisely the same thing? Is 'the law of faith' (Rom. 3:27) the ten commandments? Is 'the law of the Spirit of life in Christ Jesus' (Rom. 8:2) 'the moral law' of the Reformed? Is 'the law of liberty' (Jas. 2:12) the law of Moses? Is 'the law of Christ' (Gal. 6:2)? Could Jeremiah not have been prophesying of this last law? Must we *assume* the Spirit of God was speaking of the law of Moses? More – must we *assume* he was referring to only sixteen verses of Scripture? Above all, is it not possible that a prophecy of the *new* covenant might be concerned with something other than the law of the *old* covenant, the law of Moses?

Bayes saw the issue: 'What is the law which is written on the heart in the new covenant?', he asked, calling this 'the chief question' (Bayes p194). He did not seem to see any importance in the other question; namely, as to who the Israel and Judah are. Consequently, he missed a vital piece in the jig-saw, with far-reaching consequences, as I will show. 'A new "law"', he agreed, 'must supplant the old... There are hints [far too weak a word!] that [the writer to the Hebrews] is prepared to consider the new-covenant economy in Christ as a new law'. Bayes, while saying 'the law' in the new covenant is 'substantially the same in content as the Old Testament revelation', grappled with the 'newness of the new covenant', interpreting 'the law written upon the heart more broadly than simply God's moral requirements, as the self-revelation of God in his essential being, as the living voice of the eternal God'. It certainly *is* more broad than that! As Bayes pointed out, the letter to the Hebrews 'begins by describing the Son of God himself as that vital word (Heb. 1:2)... He fulfils in himself, with complete finality, the law in its entirety'. In other words, the law written on the heart is Christ. 'He is the law personified', Bayes continued. 'Christ is the law in its ultimate manifestation. The law written on the heart is nothing other than what Paul calls Christ dwelling in the heart by faith (Eph. 3:17)... He is the true law, the authentic revelation of God. Now he has come, and is the law in the hearts of his people'. 'Christ [is] the *torah* written upon the heart', God's 'saving self-revelation in Christ'. 'Christ, who is the law personified... becomes, under new-covenant arrangements, the law written on the heart of the believer' (Bayes pp191,197,199-200,206,208). In saying this, of course, Bayes was not a million miles away from saying that the law of which Jeremiah prophesied is the law of Christ. 'Christ in you' is what I call 'the ultimate point' in my setting out of the law of Christ. See chapter 16. I find Bayes' words significant. He wrote his book to establish the vital ongoing place of the ten commandments in the life of the believer as the perfect rule of sanctification, yet he could not bring himself to say the law written on the heart in the new covenant is the ten commandments! Which, of course, it is not. But in failing to say 'the law' in question is the ten commandments, Bayes was exposing the inadequacy of his case at the vital point.

Owen thought the law in the new covenant is the whole revelation of God: 'So the law of the Redeemer went forth from Zion', he said. He argued that 'the laws of God' in question are to be 'taken largely for the whole revelation of the mind and will of God... By what way or revelation soever God makes known himself and his will to us, requiring our obedience therein, it is all comprised in that expression of "his laws"'. Thus God promises in this new covenant, said Owen, 'the effectual operation of his Spirit in the renovation and saving illumination of our minds, whereby they are habitually made conformable to the whole law of God – that is, the rule and the law of our obedience in the new covenant – and enabled [to do] all acts and duties that are required of us'. Owen compared God's writing of the ten commandments on stone in the first covenant with his 'writing these laws now in our hearts, which he wrote before only in tables of stone'. I pause. Owen was not careful enough here. But he was not saying that God writes the same laws in both covenants. Not at all! He was contrasting the stone tablets with the heart. Owen was saying that in the new covenant, new laws are written in a new place. To let Owen continue: 'That is, he will effectually work that obedience in us which the law requires, for he "works in us both to will and to do of his good pleasure"'. Owen spoke of the 'two parts' of the work; 'namely, the removal out of the heart of whatever is contrary to the law of God, and the implanting of principles of obedience... Wherefore in this promise, the whole of our sanctification, in its beginning and progress, in its work upon our whole souls and all their faculties, is comprised' (Owen: *Hebrews* Vol.3 Part 3 pp118,149-151).

Gouge: 'By... laws are meant God's will made known to his people, which is called a law because it binds all to whom it is revealed unto obedience. A law is given to them, and necessity lies upon them to observe it. The plural number, laws, is used because the precepts and promises of God's covenant are many, but all binding as so many laws' (Gouge p576). Gouge also thought that 'this putting his laws into men's hearts, and writing them in their minds, have [*sic*] respect to their sanctification' (Gouge p704). However, he thought the law in the old and new covenants was (is) 'one and the same law' (Gouge p576). Similarly, Taylor: 'We read of a twofold law, but in substance the same: the law of God, and the law of Christ... The newness of [the latter]... stands not in any new matter and substance of doctrine' (Taylor p12). Oh? New covenant, but old law? Really? How does this fit in with the wineskins (Luke 5:36-38)?

Brown thought 'the laws' spoke of 'a revelation of [God's] will' (Brown: *Hebrews* p373). This is borne out by the apostolic command to believers: 'Receive with meekness the implanted [better than AV, engrafted] word' (Jas. 1:21). Implanted? God prepares the hearts of his people – like soil – and plants his word there, in order that it might grow and bear fruit to his praise. Note the 'firstfruits' (Jas. 1:18). Is this not the fulfilling of Jeremiah's prophecy? Manton thought so: 'It is God's promise (Jer. 31:33)', he said (Manton: *James* p150). Now, as I explained in the previous chapter, 'the word' here means the complete word of God. It cannot be limited to the old law, and certainly not confined to the ten commandments. It is the entire word of God, especially the gospel (see Manton: *James* pp119,151; Johnstone: *James* pp88,107), 'the word of truth' of the context (Jas. 1:18; see also 2 Cor. 6:7; Eph. 1:13; Col. 1:13; 2 Tim. 2:15). This is the law in question.

Barcellos, on the other hand, after making what he called 'a careful exegesis' of the Jeremiah passage, concluded that the law of Jeremiah's prophecy is the ten commandments (Barcellos pp16-24). I leave you, reader, to judge how far he succeeded. In my opinion, however, Barcellos did little more than beg the question. Naturally, Jeremiah spoke of God's law, not 'our law'; and, of course, in the prophet's day 'the law' was the *torah* – just as 'Israel and Judah' meant 'the nation of Israel'. But Barcellos' claim – that the fulfilment of Jeremiah's prophecy means 'the law' for the new-covenant people is the same as 'was set before the old-covenant people of God... something that was set before the fathers', that 'the law of God under the new covenant is referring to a law that was already written at the time of the writing of Jeremiah' – is the very thing to be proved. Barcellos made a root assumption, calling it 'the natural assumption of the text'; namely: 'If we allow antecedent theology to inform the writer [Jeremiah], the original audience [the old-covenant people], and all subsequent hearers, the only plausible answer to the question concerning the identity of the law is that it must be the same law God himself wrote previously' (Barcellos pp17-18). I draw your attention reader to 'all subsequent hearers'. If this is the right assumption then the issue is closed. Indeed, it was never opened! Nothing is gained, however, by *assuming* (echoes of Malcolm Watts – see above) that whatever 'the law' meant for Jeremiah and his readers it must mean for all subsequent readers, and consequently arguing 'the law' means the same today for new-covenant people as it meant in old-covenant days! The argument is circular. And is it the right assumption in the first place? Would Barcellos use the same argument in, say, Is. 53?

The truth is, Barcellos paid scant attention to the fact that Jeremiah was a *prophet*, devoting only a footnote to it: 'I realise that the prophecy looks forward in redemptive history, which might cause some to conclude that we must wait for subsequent revelation to define the law of the new covenant for us'. Too true! But the best Barcellos could say was: 'I agree with this, in part'. Why 'in part'? Even so, claimed Barcellos, 'the law' in question is the ten commandments: 'Heb. 8:10', for instance', 'in no way negates the exposition of Jer. 31:33 as referring to the decalogue' (Barcellos pp18-19). But Barcellos should have given far more weight than this to the fact that since Jeremiah was a prophet his words were a prophecy. It alters everything! Merely to assume that 'the law' has to be the same for 'all subsequent hearers' as in Jeremiah's day, is woefully inadequate. I notice Barcellos did not think it necessary to explain Jeremiah's use of Israel and Judah, and how we should understand the phrase in the new covenant. 'The new-covenant community', he simply stated, 'is a saved, regenerate community' (Barcellos p17). If he had been consistent in his argument, Barcellos would have said that Jeremiah and his original audience were thinking of national Israel and Judah, as should all subsequent readers of the prophecy; but he did not: 'The Christian [is] the citizen of the new covenant' (Barcellos pp38-40). On what basis, I wonder, does one part of the passage – 'Israel and Judah' – change its meaning according to prophetical principles, and the other – 'the law' – not?

Furthermore, as I have shown in chapter 1, 'the law' cannot be limited to the ten commandments, in any case. Barcellos saw this: 'The old covenant includes the whole Mosaic legislation, not merely the decalogue' (Barcellos p19). Again: '*Torah*... normally refers to the law revealed by God though Moses to Israel' (Barcellos p21). Quite! But he also saw where this would lead: 'Not reducing the *torah* to the decalogue produces the difficulty of answering the question why God would write temporary, ceremonial laws that point to Christ on the hearts of new-covenant people after Christ's work on the cross abrogated those very laws' (Barcellos p20). Just so! Barcellos, however, provided no answer to this pertinent question. He simply steamed ahead, reducing the *torah* to the ten commandments. This borders on blasphemy. If we are convinced that God's word says something, we dare not ignore it or water it down because we find it too difficult to cope with! Not surprisingly, when all is boiled down, Barcellos resorted to the usual double-think on the ten commandments. On the one hand he could assert: 'The basic, fundamental law of God under the new covenant is the decalogue' (Barcellos p20). Clear enough, you might think. But wait a moment! 'This in no way infers that the decalogue has the corner [that is, is the last word] on law in the new covenant... The decalogue contains the moral law, not exhausts it' (Barcellos p20). Oh? And, as a last resort: 'The change is not from one law to another, but from stone to hearts... It is not the ten commandments as old-covenant law that is being referred to, but as new-covenant law' (Barcellos p20). Under this system, how does one tell, reader, whether a command – which changes not an iota – is old covenant or new covenant? See chapter 6 for more on Reformed double-speak. Barcellos wrote his book to refute new-covenant theology. If this is the best...

Let us take Hebrews seriously! 'In Jeremiah, the *torah* is the law of Moses', Hoch admitted. Of course it is! 'But what is the *torah/nomos* that will be written on the heart according to Hebrews?' That is the question. 'It would be incongruous for the author of Hebrews to envisage the restitution of the Mosaic covenant in Heb. 8:10 and then proceed to call that covenant "old", "obsolete", and "ready to disappear" in Heb. 8:13!'. Having referred to 'the change of law' (Heb. 7:12) and the use of 'laws' instead of 'law', Hoch went on: 'It hardly seems possible, then, that the writer of Hebrews regarded the Mosaic law as [the law] written on the heart when he calls that [Mosaic] law "old", "obsolete", "ready to disappear" and "changed"'. Hoch concluded: 'The law written on the heart of the new-covenant believer is the law of Christ' (Hoch pp70-71,73; see also Geoff A.Adams pp87-94). Note the 'hardly seems possible'. It utterly impossible!

Kring quoted Philip Hughes who claimed 'it is the self-same law which was graven on tables of stone at Sinai that in this age of the new covenant is graven on the tables of the human heart'. Kring challenged this: 'In all honesty the exegesis of 2 Cor. 3 (see my chapters 11 and 15) compels us to ask: "But is he right?" Is this how we best understand Jeremiah's prophecy? If it is the "self-same law", then are seventh-day [keepers]... more consistent than [those] who worship on the first day of the week?'. I pause. Far too weak. Of course they are! Kring used the word 'Baptists', maybe reflecting the origin of his article as a paper. The point applies to all 'law men', whether they are Baptists, Presbyterians or whatever. To let Kring go on: 'If it is the "self-same law", then does Hughes feel that the form in which God gave his law at Sinai was its final form, and that Jesus contributed nothing new or deeper? Surely both the Sermon on the Mount and John 13:34 suggest otherwise' (Kring pp112-113). Suggest?

Similar comments apply to Bruce's view: 'In that oracle [Jer. 31:31-34] there is no substantial difference in content between the law which Israel failed to keep under the old covenant and the law which God undertakes hereafter to place within his people, writing it "upon their hearts". The difference lies between their once knowing the law as an external code and their knowing it henceforth as an inward principle. So for Paul there is no difference between the "just requirement of the law" which cannot be kept by those who live "according to the flesh" and the just requirement fulfilled in those who live "according to the Spirit". The difference [lies] in the fact that a new inward power [is] now imparted, enabling the believer to fulfil what he could not fulfil before. The will of God [has] not changed; but whereas formerly it was recorded on tablets of stone it [is] now engraved on human hearts, and inward impulsion [accomplishes] what external compulsion could not. So far as the written requirements of the law [are] concerned, Paul in his pre-Christian days had kept them punctiliously [Gal. 1:14; Phil. 3:6], but his keeping them all did not add up to doing the will of God from the heart. For the sum of the commandments [is] love [Rom. 13:8-10], and this [is] something which became possible to him only when the divine love was poured into his heart by the Spirit (Rom. 5:5; [1 Thess. 4:9]). The reference to the Spirit [in Rom. 8:1-4] should remind us that Paul's teaching here points to the fulfilment not only of Jeremiah's "new-covenant" oracle but also of the companion oracles in Ezek. 11:19ff and 36:25-27, where God promises to implant within his people a new heart and a new spirit – his own Spirit – enabling them to do his will effectively'.

But although he had started on the Reformed track, Bruce was inadvertently setting out the biblical objection to his case. The law written on the heart in the new covenant is not simply the old-covenant law. 'The righteous requirement of the law' (Rom. 8:4) is love, the fulfilment of the law; in other words, the law of Christ. See chapter 10 for the argument. Contrary to Bruce, there is a 'difference' between the old law and the new – and in the above paragraph he had actually begun to spell it out. He went on: 'It is to this new heart, "a heart of flesh" (Ezek. 11:19; 36:26), that Paul refers when he says that the message of the new age is written "with the Spirit of the living God, not on tablets of stone but on tablets which are hearts of flesh" (2 Cor. 3:3). A written law-code was an inadequate vehicle for communicating the will of God; the will of God was given that form only for a temporary purpose – to make quite clear to man the inability and sinfulness to which he was prone in the flesh – that is, in his creaturely weakness. Doing the will of God is not a matter of conformity to outward rules but of giving expression to inward love, such as the Spirit begets. Hence, says Paul, "the written code kills, but the Spirit gives life" (2 Cor. 3:6). The written code kills, because it declares the will of God without imparting the power to do it, and pronounces the death sentence on those who break it. The Spirit gives life, and with the life he imparts the inward power as well as the desire to do the will of God... The Spirit is holy in [two] respects – both as being the Spirit of God and as creating holiness in man. It is the Spirit who renews the minds of the people of God so that they not only approve but do his will – everything, that is, which is "good and acceptable and perfect" (Rom. 12:2). The holiness which the Spirit creates is nothing less than transformation into the likeness of Christ, who is the image of God; and this cannot be effected by external constraint: "Where the Spirit of the Lord is, there is freedom" (2 Cor. 3:17ff). The purpose of the law, that men should be holy as God is holy (Lev. 11:44ff; *etc.*), is thus... realised in the gospel [2 Cor. 7:1; 1 Thess. 4:7-8; 1 Pet. 1:13-25, for instance]... Only in the atmosphere of spiritual liberty can God's [revealed] will be properly obeyed and his law upheld... If [better, since] the law of the Spirit is the law of love, then it is identical with what Paul elsewhere calls "the law of Christ"... (Gal.. 6:2)... The law of love ["the law of Christ" (Matt. 22:40; Rom. 13:10; Gal. 5:14; 6:2)] is a different kind of law entirely [to] that which Paul describes as a yoke of slavery. Love is generated by an inner spontaneity and cannot be enforced by penal sanctions... So far as Paul is concerned, guidance for the church is provided by the law of love, not by the "law of commandments and ordinances" (Eph. 2:15)'. Contrary to the Lutheran view – see Bruce pp265,277; see, for instance, Rom. 14:15. I agree with Bruce to this extent: 'The law of love ["the law of Christ"] is a different kind of law entirely [to] that which Paul describes as a yoke of slavery'.

Bruce continued: 'The insistence on the law of love, instead of prudential rules and regulations, was felt by many of Paul's Christian contemporaries to come unrealistically near to encouraging moral indifferentism; and many Christians since his day have shared their sentiments. But, unlike Paul's contemporary critics, Christian moralists since Paul's day have tended to hold that, in insisting on prudential rules and regulations, they are following the implications of his teaching, if not his express judgements... But if they are right then Paul [at times] expresses himself very carelessly, to say the least. It is better to appreciate that Paul conforms no more to the conventions of religious people today than he conformed to the conventions of religious people around AD50; it is best to let Paul be Paul. And when we do that, we shall recognise in him the supreme libertarian, the great herald of Christian freedom, insisting that man in Christ has reached his spiritual majority and must no longer be confined to the leading-strings of infancy, but enjoy the birthright of the freeborn sons of God' (Bruce: *Paul* pp275-278).

Boiling it all down, Zaspel: 'The new-covenant believer is not under the old covenant but the new. It would be an odd thing indeed if "the words of the (old) covenant, the ten commandments" (Ex. 34:28) were made to be the new-covenant believer's rule of life. We would rather expect that for new-covenant believers, divine law would be codified in the new covenant' (Zaspel p155).

For a suggested link between Amos 9, Acts 15 and Gal. 2, see Witherington pp237-238. Of Heb. 12:22, the dispensationalist, Decker, admitted: 'Zion must be taken figuratively; it is the "heavenly Jerusalem", not the physical city in Palestine'. He noted the contrast between Israel and the church. Israel came historically to a physical mountain, while believers do not come 'to a physical mountain, but to Christ. The reference cannot be to the future arrival of Christians in heaven or the new Jerusalem, but must be a reference to their salvation. The phrases that follow describe the realities of the spiritual realm to which they have come'. He also admitted the new-covenant context (Heb. 12:24). But once again he was grudging: 'If these descriptions describe the present realities of the believer's position, then the context of the new-covenant mediatorship of Jesus in verse 24 would seem to be a present function of an inaugurated covenant rather than an eschatological role' (Decker pp453-454). There is no 'if' about it, and 'would seem' is woefully inadequate.

Eph. 3 – the mystery

Let Decker give the dispensationalist view: 'The church is a mystery and thus was not revealed in the Old Testament'. He cited Eph. 3:3 as proof. 'The significance of this passage', Decker argued, 'is that information about the church should not be expected in the Old Testament' (Decker p455).

This is wrong. A 'mystery' does not mean something hard to grasp; nor does it mean something vague, abstract or indefinite. A 'mystery', in its New Testament sense, is a precise technical term; it is something which cannot be known by man unless God reveals it to him, something beyond discovery by human effort or ability (*mustērion* in Arndt and Gingrich; Thayer; Vincent Vol.2 p902; Lloyd-Jones: *Unsearchable* pp32-35,40-41; Baynes pp116-117; W.D.Davies pp91-92, *etc.*).

Decker was mistaken on more than one count. First, the mystery, said Paul, is not the church, but the fact 'that the Gentiles should be fellow-heirs, of the same body, and partakers of [God's] promise in Christ through the gospel' (Eph. 3:6). Decker admitted as much. The mystery, he said, was God's 'eternal plan [which] included the formation of a group of believers drawn from both Jews and Gentiles following the coming of Christ' (Decker p455). Lloyd-Jones: 'The mystery... is not simply the fact that the Gentiles are to be saved, but that Gentile and Jew are to be together in the... church... The apostle's point is that the old distinction between Jew and Gentile is abolished once and for ever. He has already shown that in the second chapter, stating that "the middle wall of partition" has gone, that Christ has demolished it, and has made "one new man, so making peace". The old distinction has gone... Paul actually said, [the Gentiles are to be] "fellow-heirs, fellow-members of the body, fellow-partakers of the promise"... with the Jews. This refers to the new covenant that God had promised' (Lloyd-Jones: *Unsearchable* pp48-51). Allis: 'It is significant that Paul never uses the expression, "the mystery of the church". He does not tell us the church is a mystery. What he is concerned to tell us is, that something about the church is a mystery... The mystery is, that the Gentiles are to enjoy, and actually do enjoy, a status of complete equality with the Jews in the... church... It was a mystery in the sense that... it was not *fully* revealed in the Old Testament and was completely hidden from the carnal minded... But... it was not the church itself, but this doctrine regarding the church which was the mystery' (Allis pp92-93,95, emphasis mine).

In the second place, Paul did not say that the fact that Jews and Gentiles would form one body was totally unknown in the Old Testament. Certainly not! He said this mystery 'in other ages was not made known to the sons of men, *as it has now been revealed* by the Spirit to his holy apostles and prophets' (Eph. 3:5). As? The word is *hōs*, 'in the same manner as, just as, exactly like', 'in such a way as' (Thayer; Arndt and Gingrich). In other words, it had been made known before, but not to the same extent, not with the same clarity.

As Allis observed, 'the word "mystery" occurs twenty-nine times in the New Testament, most of which are in Paul's letters, six being in Ephesians'. Listing several of these 'mysteries' (Eph. 1:9; 6:19; Col. [1:27;] 2:2; 4:3; 2 Thess. 2:7; 1 Tim. 3:9,16), Allis noted a mystery 'does not necessarily imply... that it was *entirely* unknown. It might be known, yet still a mystery because not *fully* known' (Allis p90, emphasis mine). 'The words, "as it has now been revealed"', said Allis, 'definitely assert that it *was* previously known, *only not with same clearness and fullness*' (Allis pp94-95,97,107-108, emphasis mine).

Calvin: 'The words of Paul must not be understood to mean there had been no knowledge at all on these subjects... The prophets... though they spoke with the certainty of revelation, left the time and manner undetermined. They knew that some communication of the grace of God would be made to the Gentiles, but at what time, in what manner, and by what means it should be accomplished, they had no information whatever' (Calvin: *Commentaries* Vol.21 Part 1 p250).

Lloyd-Jones again: 'The apostle is not saying that it had never been revealed before. What he is saying is that it was not revealed before "as", "to the extent that", it is now revealed. It was there in embryo; it is now in full bloom and development. It was there in shadow as a suggestion; it is now fully revealed' (Lloyd-Jones: *Unsearchable* p47).

Baynes, likewise, was clear; Paul was saying: 'My meaning is not that it was altogether concealed, but it was not so revealed as now it is to the holy apostles and prophets'. As for the 'as now', Baynes said, 'since Christ we have [had] more fully opened the mystery of our salvation. The [former] revelation was a hiding of it in comparison with this we have obtained... We see that these times, since Christ, have... a fuller word revealing, and more clear word... These times have a more full inward illumination... so... [we have] a more full enlightening... a fuller apprehension' (Baynes pp121-125).

Other prophecies
Speaking of the prophecy of Zion in Isaiah 28:16, 'Behold, I lay in Zion a stone for a foundation, a tried stone, a precious cornerstone, a sure foundation; whoever believes will not act hastily', and the use the New Testament makes of it (Rom. 9:33; 1 Pet. 2:6), Fairbairn said: 'We regard it... as by much the most natural method to take word of the prophet there as a direct prediction of gospel times. The difficulty of finding a specific object of reference otherwise, is itself no small proof of the correctness of this view – some understanding it of the temple, some of the law, others of Zion, and others still again of Hezekiah. The prophet, we are persuaded, is looking above and beyond all these... It can be understood of nothing properly but Christ. And therefore we have no hesitation in considering the word as a direct prediction of gospel times' (Fairbairn: *Typology* Vol.1 p385; Fairbairn mistakenly cited 1 Pet. 2:7-8 instead of 2:6). As he later said, on Rom. 11:26: 'The old literal Zion, in the apostle's view, was now gone; its external framework was presently [that is, in AD70] to be laid in ruins: and the only Zion, in connection with which the Redeemer could henceforth come, was that Zion in which he now dwells, which is the same [as] the heavenly Jerusalem, the church of the New Testament' (Fairbairn: *Typology* Vol.1 p390). It is possible, of course, to read the prophecy as referring to Christ's first coming.

Paul applied Hos. 1:10 and 2:23 to the calling of the Gentiles (Rom. 9:24-25), yet Hosea 1:8-11 itself speaks only of the children of Israel. The context of Hos. 1 is the defection and judgement of Israel, and God's surprising mercy to them despite their departure from him. The same applies to Hos. 2:23. The word 'Gentiles' does not appear in Hosea, except in Hos. 8:8, and this has no connection whatsoever with their salvation. A literalist, an interpreter wedded to the old-covenant, Jewish, explanation, would never see – could never see – the calling of the Gentiles in Hosea. *But Paul did.* John Murray drew attention to the point: 'In Hosea [the words] refer to the tribes of Israel and not to the Gentile nations'. While Murray thought Paul used Hosea's words to speak of the 'parallel' for the Gentiles (Murray: *Romans* Vol.2 p38), this is not strong enough. Paul did not draw a parallel. Rather, rightly interpreting the verses, he showed us the way to read the prophets and their prophecies.

Fairbairn: Paul 'must have considered the prophecy as uttered respecting the... church of God... converted Gentiles' (Fairbairn: *Typology* Vol.1 pp388-389; Fairbairn completed the sentence with, 'not less than believing Jews'. But Paul applied the words to Gentiles – Jews did not come into it). Indeed he did! And in so doing, he gave us the definitive way to understand the Old Testament in this matter.

Moo got it right: 'We must conclude that this text reflects a hermeneutical supposition for which we find evidence' – what is more, we never find evidence to the contrary –

'elsewhere in Paul and in the New Testament [in general]: that Old Testament predictions of a renewed Israel find their fulfilment in the church'. The fact is, 'God's final revelation in Christ gives to him [Paul] a *new* hermeneutical key by which to interpret and apply the Old Testament' (Moo: *Romans* p613, emphasis mine). 'New' is the exact word; we are talking about the new covenant. See below for more on its 'newness'. Hos. 2:23 is applied by Peter in 1 Pet. 2:10 in the same way as Paul in Rom. 9:25-26, which 'suggests... that the text may have been a standard "proof-text" in early Christianity' (Moo: *Romans* p612). And Paul's key must be ours. Moo rightly discarded the usual ways of avoiding this. But when commenting on Rom. 10:20-21, he contradicted himself; Paul, he alleged, 'as he did with Hos. 1:10; 2:23 in Rom. 9:25-26... takes Old Testament texts that speak of Israel and applies them, on the principle of analogy, to the Gentiles'! On Isa. 65:1-2, Moo took what he called 'the majority view' and thought both verses were said of Israel (Moo: *Romans* p669); if so, once again we have an Old Testament promise of blessing for Israel (Isa. 65:1) fulfilled in the church. But if in fact Isa. 65:1 was about the Gentiles and Isa. 65:2 was about Israel, as I think (see Young Vol.3 pp501-503; Barnes: *Old* Vol.7 Part2 p408), no explanation of Paul's use of the passage is required.

Consider such passages as: Luke 24:27,44-47; John 1:45; Acts 3:18,24-25; 7:52; 8:30-35; 26:22-23 and 1 Pet. 1:9-12. See Hendriksen's list of suggested passages. Unless we see Christ in the Old Testament – both law and prophets – we shall never read it and them aright. See Hendriksen: *John* p109. 'Only when we see how all the Scriptures are centred in Christ... so that everything in the Old Testament points forward to him, and in the New Testament everything proceeds from him, will we be able to understand the Bible' (Hendriksen: *Luke* pp1065,1068).

Gal. 6:16, 'the Israel of God'
Richardson called the order in Gal. 6:16 'illogical', although he recognised it occurs in the Nineteenth Benediction in the liturgy of the synagogue, which he thought Paul might be using here. But having examined the points thoroughly, he concluded 'there is little help in explaining the structure of the sentence in Gal. 6:16' (Richardson pp76-81). I agree, and say no more upon it.

What of the 'and' in '*and* upon the Israel of God'? This phrase, in Witherington's words, is 'quite awkward' (Witherington p451). Richardson: 'It is difficult to account for "the Israel of God"' (Richardson p80). Dunn rightly saw how the Jewish emphasis in the context (see below) explains 'the otherwise puzzling and unique phrase' (Dunn p344). But I do not agree with his 'as also' for *kai*. For if, when Paul said '*and* the Israel of God', he was using 'and' as 'also', it would mean that Paul speaking of two distinct groups – on the one hand, those who were living according to Christ's rule, *and also*, on the other, the Israel of God. He was doing nothing of the sort! Even so, as to whether or not this involved the 'peace and mercy' and/or the third 'and', Richardson thought two groups (Richardson pp76-84). Dunn 'probably... preferred' two groups (Dunn p345). Witherington thought one group the 'far more likely view' (Witherington pp451-453). It is one group – the church.

Not only can I not accept that Gal. 6:16 teaches that Paul prayed for 'peace and mercy' both for believers and unbelievers, I am unable to see how it supports the view that Paul prayed for two sorts of believers – Gentile and Jewish. The idea that the people of God can be divided into Gentile believers and Jewish believers is foreign to Galatians, and is surely eliminated by Eph. 2:11-22. Paul never does such a thing. So this cannot be how we are to understand the phrase, 'and the Israel of God'. Witherington repeatedly pointed out that the law of Moses divided men whereas Christ unites, and how this is a vital part of Galatians (Witherington pp136-137,238,256,269,393,453). John Brown, in one of his rare slips, was even more way out: 'The apostle refers to two classes of persons; the first application refers to teachers of Christianity, and the second to private Christians' (Brown: *Galatians* p381).

Ironically, Brown criticised the views of others on 'the rule' as 'fantastic exegesis' (Brown: *Galatians* p381), a term which might well be applied to his 'two classes' here.

The fact is, Paul was not praying for two groups at all. The *kai* can be translated 'namely', 'even' or 'that is', and this is how it should be read here: 'Peace and mercy to all who follow this rule, even to the Israel of God' (NIV). See Thayer; Arndt and Gingrich. For instance, 'told everything, *namely* what had happened' (Matt. 8:33); 'lowly, *that is* sitting on a donkey' (Matt. 21:5); 'the hope, *namely* the resurrection' (Acts 23:6); 'God gives it a body as he pleases, *that is* to each seed its own body' (1 Cor. 15:38); 'Abraham... offered up Isaac, *that is* he who had received the promises offered up his only begotten son' (Heb. 11:17), *etc*. Above all, '*even* we have believed' (Gal. 2:16, NKJV, NASB, AV); that is, 'we who are Jews by nature and not sinners of the Gentiles... even we have believed in Christ Jesus, that we might be justified by faith in Christ and not by the works of the law'. See Ridderbos pp100-101. See chapter 18 for a similar discussion of the word in question, *kai*. Indeed, *kai* is sometimes best left untranslated. The upshot is, Paul prayed 'peace and mercy be upon them, [that is, namely, even] upon the Israel of God'. In other words, he desired peace and mercy upon all who walk according to Christ's law; that is, all believers. The Israel of God, therefore, is an all-encompassing term for all believers, for all – for 'as many as', whether Jews or Gentiles – for all who live according to Christ's law. See Lightfoot: *Galatians* p224; Moo: *Romans* p574.

For the name 'Israel', see Trench pp137-143; Moo: *Romans* pp560-561.

In the apostle's use of 'peace and mercy', unmistakeable Jewish overtones are evident once again. See Dunn pp343-344; Witherington p452; Lightfoot: *Galatians* p224.

And not the least aspect of the phrase's fascination lies in the fact that, according to Richardson, 'the Israel of God' is 'an almost impossible expression in Hebrew' (Richardson p80). Both 'law' and 'Israel' have been taken over and transformed in the change of covenants as Paul used the two Jewish words, so pregnant with meaning, to coin two new-covenant phrases, 'the law of Christ' and 'the Israel of God'. It is a classic demonstration of how 'Paul was quite capable of transferring language and titles applied to God's old-covenant people, Israel, to his new-covenant people, the church' (Moo: *Romans* p574). See Witherington p274. The law of Christ is the new law for the new people. 'As the Old Testament had its law of Moses, so the New Testament has its law of Christ' (Moo: 'The Law' p208).

The law of Moses gave way to the law of Christ (Gal. 6:2), and Israel after the flesh gave way to the Israel of God (Gal. 6:16). See Witherington p453. Lightfoot: 'The "Israel of God" is in implied contrast to the "Israel after the flesh" (1 Cor. 10:18)... It stands here not for the faithful converts from the circumcision alone, but for the spiritual Israel generally, the whole body of believers whether Jew or Gentile'. In short: 'On all those who shall guide their steps by this rule may peace and mercy abide; for they are the true Israel of God' (Lightfoot: *Galatians* pp224-225).

'For Paul it was God who was in Christ, and therefore the community constituted in him became for Paul the people of God, and "the life in the Spirit marked the church as being the true Israel of God in its eschatological manifestation (Gal. 6:15-16)". Paul saw in the emergence of the church that the Israel of God had entered upon a new phase in its history' (W.D.Davies pp74-75, quoting Dodd). 'The community gathered by Jesus was for him [Christ] the nucleus of a new Israel... The twelve disciples he chose corresponded to the twelve tribes of Israel. That this was so is substantiated by the two acts of prophetic symbolism which accompanied his last visit to Jerusalem, the triumphal entry, and the cleansing of the temple, and also by the third act of prophetic symbolism, the institution of the [Lord's supper] at the last supper. The "great refusal" of Jesus by Israel meant the death of the "old Israel", a doom is pronounced on the temple, the fig tree will no longer bear fruit. Nevertheless... a "new Israel" will be established, and in the [Lord's supper] the disciples are being treated as the nucleus of the "new Israel"... Paul's conception of the church as the new Israel has its roots in the teaching of Jesus' (Davies pp100-101). See also Davies pp75-76,85,102,105,113,115,201,208.

'The Israel of God'! Henry Alford struck the right note: 'The subject of the whole letter seems to have given rise to this expression. Not the Israel after the flesh... but the Israel of God' (Alford Vol.2 Part 1 p360). 'Peace and mercy be upon *them*'. For overall discussion, see Calvin: *Commentaries* Vol.21 Part 1 pp186-187; Hendriksen: *Galatians* pp246-247; Witherington pp451-453; Dunn pp343-346; Richardson pp74-84.

Diprose pp45-47 gave extracts from others both for and against the view I have put forward, but the strongest conclusion he could draw was only negative. I agree, of course, Gal. 6:16 'is insufficient grounds on which to base an innovative theological concept such as understanding the church to be the new and/or true Israel' (Diprose p47), but I for one do not do it. I can only refer you, reader, to the abundant biblical evidence I have cited. Gal. 6:16 is only one part of this. But it is a part! And it is all very well for Diprose to tell us what he felt we *cannot* deduce from the verse, but what *was* Paul saying?

Bayes did not discuss the question concerning 'Israel and Judah' in Jeremiah's prophecy. In passing, he used phrases like 'his people' or 'God's people' (Bayes pp200,202-206), 'the believer' (Bayes pp204-205,208), but offered no discussion of the point. But as I have shown, both parts of the prophecy – 'the law' and 'Israel and Judah' – are transformed by the epochal change of covenant. Bayes acknowledged 'Paul's equivalent terminology in Galatians [to that used in Hebrews] is to replace the law in epochal terms by the Spirit' (Bayes p208), and he seemed to assume that 'Israel' has become 'believers'. If he had tackled 'the Israel of God' (Gal. 6:16) – sadly, he did not – I have little doubt that the same principles of interpretation which took him from 'Israel after the flesh' to 'the Israel of God' would have affected his view of the law.

Richardson suggested that the 'Israel of God' are 'all those Israelites who are going to come to their senses and receive the good news of Christ'. He rejected the claim that 'the Israel of God' is the church (Richardson pp82-84). But he leant heavily upon a benediction used in the synagogues, (see, however, Witherington p452), and upon the punctuation of 'peace and mercy' (Richardson pp76-82). Furthermore, Richardson claimed that with the writing of the later letters of the New Testament, the idea that 'Israel' became 'the church' developed, and was complete by AD160 (Richardson pp117-206). I reject Richardson's view of the New Testament Scriptures. I see no contradiction between the earlier and later portions. And when Richardson opened his book by saying 'the word "Israel" is applied to the... church for the first time by Justin Martyr *c.* AD160' (Richardson p1), to my mind he was begging the question. I am convinced Paul used 'Israel' in this way in Gal. 6:16.

And all this has relevance for the law of Christ. W.D.Davies: 'By the Spirit, Christ, who [is] the new *torah*... dwell[s] in the hearts of Christians... The inwardness of the new covenant of Jeremiah's hope is achieved... through the indwelling Christ, the new *torah* "written in the heart". The law within [the believer] is Christ in him; the indwelling Christ has replaced the old *torah* written on tablets of stone and has become a *torah* written within' (Davies p226). I have omitted Davies' 'we are probably to understand...'.

Let the following bring this chapter to a close. John Brown: 'The general sentiment is... in becoming Christians, you have joined a holy and happy society, at the head of which is the Father of spirits, and next to him, Jesus, the captain of our salvation, and the whole family of redeemed men [and women], whether on earth or in heaven' (John Brown: *Hebrews* p651). And John Owen: 'The sum of the whole is that by the gospel we are called unto a participation of all the glory which was ascribed or promised unto the church under these names, in opposition to what the people received in and by the law at Mount Sinai... The means on our part whereby we come to this state and society, is by faith in Christ alone. Hereby we come to him; and coming to him, he makes us free citizens of the heavenly Jerusalem' (Owen: *Hebrews* Vol.4 Part 2 pp330,352). This is surely right. The context is the new covenant (Heb. 12:24). And *this* is the way to read the prophets.

In addition to the above, Edgar H.Andrews p329; Bennett: 'Primer' p34; Bolton pp144-147; Brown: *Hebrews* p373; *1 Peter* Vol.1 pp220-221,318-319,355-356,397-402,417-418; Vol.2 pp270-321; Bruce: *Paul* p265; Chamblin p182; W.D.Davies pp37,69; Curtis Evans pp305-325; Fairbairn: *Typology* Vol.2 pp165-166; Fee: *Empowering* pp812-816; Franck pp149-150; Gay: *Infant*; *Pastor*; Hendriksen: *John* p109; Hoch pp59,69-72,98; Lloyd-Jones: *Law* pp90-94,347; Philpot: 'Three' pp95-96; *Dead* pp23-26; Reymond: *Paul* pp489-491; Ridderbos pp100-101; Michael Thompson p7; George Wright p235.

CONCLUSION

Lewis: 'A man can't be always defending the truth; there must be time to feed on it' (Lewis: *Reflections* p646). And, having fed upon it – supremely, not 'it', but the person of Christ – there is a life to be spent in living it out.

Tozer: 'The work of a good book is to incite the reader to moral action, to turn his eyes towards God, and urge him forward. Beyond that it cannot go' (Tozer: *Divine* p15).

Even if I have failed to convince them, I hope I may have stimulated Reformed and evangelical advocates of the law to think again. Tozer: 'In spite of all our opportunity to know the truth, most of us are still slow to learn. The tendency to accept without question and follow without knowing "why" is very strong in us. For this reason, whatever the majority of Christians hold at any given time is sure to be accepted as true and right beyond a doubt. It is easier to imitate than originate; it is easier and, for the time being, safer, to fall into step without asking too many questions about where the parade is headed' (Tozer: *Root* pp72-73).

What makes the Reformed tick? Gary W.Evans culled some enlightening statements from two Reformed books – R.C.Sproul's *The Soul's Quest for God*, and D.James Kennedy's *How Do I Live for God?*. Please see the complete article for precise attribution. This is what such men teach: 'Our guidebook for this tour of transforming Bible precepts will be the Westminster Confession of Faith and the Westminster Larger and Shorter Catechisms'. 'One of the most important contributions John Calvin made to the Protestant Reformation was his explanation of the role the law plays in the life of a Christian'. 'The law informs Christians of the will of God'. The law is our source 'of spiritual light and guidance' and 'revelation of what is pleasing to God'. 'The easiest and best way to learn the will of God is by studying his law'. 'The law... reveals what pleases God'. The law 'is the Christian's life!' The law 'encourages a closer walk with God'. 'The law's 'purposes are God's grace to us... It helps us to live our new life'. 'The law directs and... binds the child of God'. 'The incitement of the law to obedience is a means of grace for the believer. The law now excites our souls to please our Saviour'. The law 'propels us along the pathway of obedience' (Gary Evans pp1-7).

Well, that's clear enough. The Confessions, the Catechisms, Calvin and his third use of the law, and the law itself – this is what makes such men tick! Really? How did the early Christians go on? We have seen what restricted use they made of the law. And, of course, they did not have the advantage of the Confessions and the Catechisms. So, I ask again, how ever did they cope?

And take the blurb from Peter Master's: *God's Rules for Holiness*: 'Taken at face value the ten commandments are binding on all people, and will guard the way to heaven. But the commandments are far greater than their surface meaning, as this book shows. They challenge us as Christians on a wide range of deeds and attitudes, providing positive virtues as goals. And they give immense help for staying close to the Lord in our walk and worship. The commandments are vital for godly living and for greater blessing, but we need to enter into the panoramic view they provide of the standards and goals for redeemed people'.

Begging a few questions there, I think. I wonder what Bible version such men read.

Let Calvin direct our attention to the proper focus of our attention: 'When we see that the whole sum of our salvation, and every single part of it, are comprehended in Christ, we must beware of deriving even the minutest portion of it from any other quarter. If we seek salvation, we are taught by the very name of Jesus that he possesses it; if we seek any other gifts of the Spirit, we shall find them in his unction; strength in his government; purity in his conception; indulgence in his nativity, in which he was made like us in all respects, in order that he might learn to sympathise with us: if we seek redemption, we shall find it in his passion; acquittal in his condemnation; remission of the curse in his cross; satisfaction in his sacrifice; purification in his blood; reconciliation in his descent to hell; mortification of the flesh in his sepulchre; newness of life in his resurrection; immortality also in his resurrection; the inheritance of a celestial kingdom in his entrance into heaven; protection, security, and the abundant supply of all blessings, in his kingdom; secure anticipation of judgment in the power of judging committed to him. In fine, since in him all kinds of blessings are treasured up, let us draw a full supply from him, and none from any other quarter. Those who, not satisfied with him alone, entertain various hopes from others, though they may continue to look to him chiefly, deviate from the right path by the simple fact, that some portion of their thought takes a different direction. No distrust of this description can arise when once the abundance of his blessings is properly known' (Calvin: *Institutes* Vol.1 p452).

I draw attention to these words: 'When we see that the whole sum of our salvation, and every single part of it, are comprehended in Christ, we must beware of deriving even the minutest portion of it from any other quarter... Since in him all kinds of blessings are treasured up, let us draw a full supply from him, and none from any other quarter'. In short and in particular, for sanctification, for its motive, spur, means and standard, let us draw all from Christ and from Christ alone. Let it be true for us that Christ is all!

Bolton pp144-147; W.D.Davies p69; Fee: *Empowering* pp812-816; Lloyd-Jones: *Law* pp90-94,347.

Source List

Adams, Brooks: *The Emancipation of Massachusetts: The Dream and the Reality*, Houghton Mifflin, Boston, Sentry edition 1962.

Adams, Geoff A.: 'The New Covenant of Jeremiah 31:31-37', *Reformation & Revival Journal*, editor John H.Armstrong, Reformation & Revival Ministries, Inc., Carol Stream, Vol.6, Number 3, Summer 1997.

Adams, James Truslow: *The Founding of New England*, Little, Brown and Company, Boston, 1939.

Adamson, J.H. and Folland, H.F.: *Sir Harry Vane: His Life and Times 1613-1662*, Bodley Head, London, 1973.

Alderson, Richard: 'The Place of the Law in the Christian's Life', *The Banner of Truth*, issue 277, October 1986.

Alford, Henry: *The New Testament for English Readers...*, Rivingtons, London, 1865.

Alleine, Joseph: *An Alarm to the Unconverted*, The Banner of Truth Trust, London, 1964.

Allis, Oswald T.: *Prophecy and the Church*, Baker Book House, Grand Rapids, 1947.

Andrews, Edgar H.: *Free in Christ: The Message of Galatians*, Evangelical Press, Darlington, 1996.

Andrews, J.N.: *History of the Sabbath and First Day of the Week*, Steam Press of the Seventh-Day Adventist Publishing Association, Battle Creek, Mich., 1873.

Anon.: *Golden Words: A Selection of Eloquent Extracts from the Writings of the Most Eminent Divines of the Fifteenth, Sixteenth and Seventeenth Centuries*, Ward, Lock and Tyler, London, 1863.

Aquinas, Thomas: *The Summa Theologica*, translated by the Fathers of the English Dominican Province, revised by Daniel J. Sullivan, William Benton, Encyclopaedia Britannica, Inc., by arrangement with Burns, Oates & Washbourne Ltd., London, and Benziger Brothers, Inc., New York, 1952.

Armstrong, John H. (ed.): *Reformation & Revival Journal*, Reformation & Revival Ministries, Inc., Carol Stream, Vol.6, Number 3, Summer 1997.

Arndt, William and Gingrich, F.Wilbur: *A Greek-English Lexicon of the New Testament and Other Early Christian Literature*, The University of Chicago Press, Chicago, Illinois, and The Syndics of the Cambridge University Press, London, 1957.

Articles of Faith of the Gospel Standard Aid and Poor Relief Societies, The Gospel Standard Societies, Harpenden.

Bainton, Roland H.: *The Reformation of the Sixteenth Century*, Hodder and Stoughton Limited, London, 1953.

Bainton, Roland H.: *Hunted Heretic: The Life and Death of Michael Servetus, 1511-1553*, The Beacon Press, Boston, 1960.

Baptist Praise and Worship, Oxford University Press, Oxford, 1991.

Barcellos, Richard C.: *In Defense of the Decalogue: A Critique of New-Covenant Theology*, Winepress Publishing, Enumclaw, 2001.

Barnes, Albert: *Notes on the Old Testament: Critical, Explanatory, and Practical*, Blackie and Son, London.

Barnes, Albert: *Notes on the New Testament: Explanatory and Practical*, Blackie and Son, London.

Barrett, C.K.: *Paul: An Introduction to His Thought*, Geoffrey Chapman, London, 1994.

Bayes, Jonathan F.: *The Weakness of the Law: God's Law and the Christian in New Testament Perspective*, Paternoster Press, Cumbria, 2000.

Bayly, Lewis: *The Practice of Piety: Directing a Christian How to Walk that He May Please God*, Soli Deo Gloria Publications, Morgan, a reprint of the London 1842 edition.

Baynes, Paul: *An Exposition of Ephesians Chapter 2:11 – 6:18*, Sovereign Grace Publishers, 1959.

Baxter, Richard: *The Autobiography of Richard Baxter*, J.M.Dent & Sons Ltd., London, 1931.

Beeke, Joel R.: The *Quest for Full Assurance: The Legacy of Calvin and his Successors*, The Banner of Truth Trust, Edinburgh, 1999.

Belcher, Richard P. and Martin, Anthony: *A Discussion of Seventeenth-Century Particular Baptist Confessions of Faith*, Crowne Publications, Inc., Southbridge, MA, 1990.

Bender, Harold S.: 'The Anabaptist Theology of Discipleship', *Radical Reformation Reader: Concern No.18*, 1971.

Bender, Harold S.: 'The Pacifism of the Sixteenth-Century Anabaptists', *Radical Reformation Reader: Concern No.18*, 1971.

Bengel, John Albert: *Gnomon of the New Testament*, T.& T.Clark, Edinburgh, 1869.

Bennett, Christopher: 'Law and the Christian Life: A primer on the current debate', *Foundations*, FIEC, No.43, Autumn 1999.

Bennett, Christopher: 'The Use of the Mosaic Law in the New Testament Church', Affinity Theological Study Conference: *The End of the Law?*, February, 2009.

Benton, John: *Coming to Faith in Christ*, The Banner of Truth Trust, Edinburgh, 1977.

Bercot, David W. (ed.): *A Dictionary of Early Christian Beliefs: A Reference Guide to More Than 700 Topics Discussed by the Early Church Fathers*, Hendrickson Publishers, Peabody, Massachusetts, 1998.

Berkhof, Louis: *Systematic Theology*, The Banner of Truth Trust, London, 1959.

Berridge, John: *Outlines of Sermons*, in *The Works of... John Berridge...*, edited by... Richard Whittingham, Old Paths Gospel Press, Choteau.

Berridge, John: *Observations on Passages of Scripture*, in *The Works of... John Berridge...*, edited by... Richard Whittingham, Old Paths Gospel Press, Choteau.

Berridge, John: *The Christian World Unmasked: Pray Come and Peep*, in *The Works of... John Berridge...*, edited by... Richard Whittingham, Old Paths Gospel Press, Choteau.

Berridge, John: *Sion's Songs or Hymns*, in *The Works of... John Berridge...*, edited by... Richard Whittingham, Old Paths Gospel Press, Choteau.

Bigg, Derek: *In Pursuit of Truth*, Dewcroft Publications, Haywards Heath, 2003.

Bigg, Derek: 'Fulfilling the Law', *Foundations*, FIEC, No.55, Spring 2006.

Blanchard, John: *Does God Believe in Atheists?*, Evangelical Press, Darlington, 2000.

Bolton, Samuel: *The True Bounds of Christian Freedom*, The Banner of Truth Trust, London, 1964.

Bonar, H.N.: *Hymns by Horatius Bonar. Selected and Arranged by his son*, Henry Frowde, London, 1904.

Booth, Abraham: *The Reign of Grace from its Rise to its Consummation*, Old Paths Gospel Press, Choteau.

Boston, Thomas: *Memoirs of... Thomas Boston*, The Banner of Truth Trust, Edinburgh, 1988.

Boston, Thomas: Notes in Edward Fisher: *The Marrow of Modern Divinity: in two parts. Part 1. The Covenant of Works and the Covenant of Grace. Part II. An Exposition of the Ten Commandments*, Still Waters Revival Books, Edmonton, Canada, reprint edition 1991.

Boston, Thomas: *The Beauties of Thomas Boston: A Selection of his Writings*, edited by Samuel M'Millan, Christian Focus Publications, Inverness, 1979.

Brainerd, David: *First Appendix to Mr. Brainerd's Journal...*, in *The Works of Jonathan Edwards, Revised and Corrected by Edward Hickman*, Vol.2, The Banner of Truth Trust, Edinburgh, 1974.

Bremer, Francis J.: *Congregational Communion: Clerical Friendship in the Anglo-American Puritan Community, 1610-1692*, Northeastern University Press, Boston, 1994.

Bromiley, G.W: *Thomas Cranmer: Theologian*, Lutterworth Press, London, 1956.

Brook, Benjamin: *The Lives of the Puritans*, Soli Deo Gloria Publications, Morgan, reprinted 1994.

Brooks, Thomas: *The Works of Thomas Brooks*, The Banner of Truth Trust, Edinburgh, 1980.

Brown, Archibald G.: 'Bill Sykes and "That Little Bit"', *The Banner of Truth*, Dec. 2011.

Brown, Colin (ed.): *The New International Dictionary of the New Testament* Vol.2, Regency Reference Library, Zondervan, Grand Rapids, 1986.

Brown, David: *The Epistle to the Romans...*, T.&T.Clark, Edinburgh.

Brown, John: *Discourses and Sayings of Our Lord Jesus Christ*, The Banner of Truth Trust, Edinburgh, 1990.

Brown, John: *An Exposition of the Epistle of Paul the Apostle to the Galatians*, The Sovereign Grace Book Club, Evansville, Indiana, 1957.

Brown, John: *An Exposition of Hebrews*, The Banner of Truth Trust, London, 1961.

Brown, John: *Expository Discourses on 1 Peter*, The Banner of Truth Trust, Edinburgh, 1975.

Bruce, F.F.: *The Epistle of Paul to the Romans...*, The Tyndale Press, London, 1963.

Bruce, F.F.: *The Apostolic Defence of the Gospel...*, Inter-Varsity Press, London, 1970.

Bruce, F.F.: *Paul and the Law of Moses*, The John Rylands University of Manchester, Manchester, 1975, reprinted from the *Bulletin of the John Rylands University Library of Manchester*, Vol.57, No.2, Spring 1975.

Bruce, F.F.: 'Christ Our Righteousness', *Jesus: Past, Present and Future: The Work of Christ*, I.V.P., Downers Grove, 1979.

Bruce, F.F.: *The Spreading Flame*, The Paternoster Press, London, 1958.

Bunyan, John: *A Vindication of Gospel Truths Opened According to the Scriptures*, in *The Entire Works of John Bunyan*, edited by Henry Stebbing, John Hirst, London, 1862.

Bunyan, John: *Of The Law and A Christian*, in *The Entire Works of John Bunyan*, edited by Henry Stebbing, John Hirst, London, 1862.

Bunyan, John: *The Doctrine of the Law and Grace Unfolded; or, A Discourse Touching the Law and Grace*, in *The Entire Works of John Bunyan*, edited by Henry Stebbing, John Hirst, London, 1862.

Burgess, Anthony: *Vindiciae Legis*, London, 1646, Ernest Kevan: *The Grace of Law: A Study in Puritan Theology*, The Carey Kingsgate Press, London, 1964.

Burroughs, Jeremiah: *The Saints' Treasury*, Soli Deo Gloria Publications, Ligonier, PA, 1991.

Calvin, John: *Institutes of the Christian Religion*, A New Translation by Henry Beveridge, James Clarke & Co., Limited, London, 1957.

Calvin, John: *Calvin's Commentaries*, Baker Book House, Grand Rapids, 1979.

Calvin, John: *Treatises Against the Anabaptists and Against the Libertines: Translation, Introduction, and Notes*, Benjamin Wirt Farley, Editor and Translator, Baker Book House, Grand Rapids, 1982.

Calvin, John: *Sermons on the Epistle to the Ephesians*, The Banner of Truth Trust, Edinburgh, reprinted 1975.

Calvin, John: 'Appendix on the Justification Controversy', *A Reformation Debate: John Calvin and Jacopo Sadoleto*, John C.Olin, Baker Book House, Grand Rapids, Ninth Printing 1991.

Calvin, John: *Calvin's Calvinism: Treatises on the Eternal Predestination of God & The Secret Providence of God*, translated by Henry Cole, Reformed Free Publishing Association, Grand Rapids.

Campbell, Iain D.: 'The Threefold Division of the Mosaic Law', Affinity Theological Study Conference: *The End of the Law?*, February, 2009.

Campbell, K.M.: 'The Antinomian Controversies of the 17th Century', a paper read at The Westminster Conference, 1974: *Living the Christian Life*, The Westminster Conference.

Carson, D.A.: *Matthew 13-28*, Zondervan, Grand Rapids, 1995.

Chamblin, Knox: 'The Law of Moses and the Law of Christ', *Continuity and Discontinuity: Perspectives on the Relationship between the Old and New Testaments*, John S.Feinberg (editor), Crossway Books, Westchester, 1988.

Chantry, Walter J.: *The Covenants – Of Works and Of Grace.*

Chantry, Walter J.: *God's Righteous Kingdom: Focussing on the Law's Connection with the Gospel*, The Banner of Truth Trust, Edinburgh, 1980.

Chantry, Walter: *Call the Sabbath a Delight*, The Banner of Truth Trust, Edinburgh, 1991.

Christian Hymns (Old), Evangelical Movement of Wales, Bryntirion, 1988.

Clarkson, David: *Of Faith*, in *The Works of David Clarkson*, Vol.1, The Banner of Truth Trust, Edinburgh, 1988.

Cleveland, Christopher: *Thomism in John Owen*, Ashgate, Farnham, 2013.

Clifford, Alan C.: *Atonement and Justification: English Evangelical Theology 1640-1790. An Evaluation*, Clarendon Press, Oxford, 1990.

Clifford, Alan C.: *The Good Doctor: Philip Doddridge of Northampton – A Tercentenary Tribute*, Charenton Reformed Publishing, Norwich, 2002.

Cockrell, H.: 'Our Relationship to the Law', *The Harvester*, Vol.L No.8, August 1971.

Cockrell, H.: 'Law and Grace – Contradictions', *The Harvester*, Vol.L No.9, September 1971.

Cohn, Norman: *The Pursuit of the Millennium: Revolutionary Millenarians and Mystical Anarchists of the Middle Ages*, Paladin, 1972.

Cramp, J.M.: *Baptist History: From the Foundation of the Christian Church to the Present Time*, Elliot Stock, London, 1875.

Crisp, Tobias: *Christ Alone Exalted in the Perfection and Encouragement of the Saints, Notwithstanding Sins and Trials; being the Complete Works of Tobias Crisp*, edited by John Gill, Old Paths Gospel Press, Choteau.

Crisp, Tobias: *The Sermons of Tobias Crisp with John Gill's Notes: Tobias Crisp Series: Issues 1 &2*, The Christian Bookshop, Ossett, 1995.

Cullmann, Oscar: *Salvation in History*, SCM Press Ltd., London, 1967.

Cunningham, William: *Historical Theology: A Review of the Principal Doctrinal Discussions in the Christian Church since the Apostolic Age*, The Banner of Truth Trust, Edinburgh, 1994.

Dabney, R.L.: *Systematic Theology*, The Banner of Truth Trust, Edinburgh, 1985.

Daniel, Curt D.: *Hyper-Calvinism and John Gill*, an unpublished Ph.D. thesis, University of Edinburgh, 1983.

Daniel, Curt: 'John Gill and Calvinistic Antinomianism', *The Life and Thought of John Gill (1697-1771): A Tercentennial Appreciation*, edited by Michael A.G.Haykin, Brill, Leiden, 1997.

Davies, Horton: *Worship and Theology in England...*, Book 1, William B.Eerdmans, Grand Rapids, 1996.

Davies, W.D.: *Paul and Rabbinic Judaism: Some Rabbinic Elements in Pauline Theology*, S.P.C.K., London, third edition 1970.

Decker, Rodney J.: *The Church's Relationship to the New Covenant*, Bibliotheca Sacra, Dallas Theological Seminary, July-September 1995 and October-December 1995.

Denck, John: *Whether God is the Cause of Evil* (1526), in *Spiritual and Anabaptist Writers: Documents Illustrative of the Radical Reformation*, edited by George Huntston Williams, SCM Press Ltd., London, 1957.

Denney, J: 'Law (In New Testament)', in (ed.) Hastings, James: *A Dictionary Of The Bible...*, T. & T. Clark, Edinburgh, 1900.

Dickens, A.G.: *The English Reformation*, B.T.Batsford Ltd., London, 1964.

Diprose, Ronald E.: *Israel in the Development of Christian Thought*, Instituto Biblico Evangelico Italiano, Rome, 2000.

Dix, Kenneth: *Strict and Particular: English Strict and Particular Baptists in the Nineteenth Century*, The Baptist Historical Society for The Strict Baptist Historical Society, Didcot, 2001.

Douglas, J.D.(general editor): *The New International Dictionary of the Christian Church*, The Paternoster Press, Exeter, 1974.

Duffield, Gervase E.: 'The Growth of Calvin's Institutes', The Puritan and Reformed Studies Conference, 1964: *Able Ministers of the New Testament*, Clonmel Evangelical Bookroom, Clonmel, 1992.

Dumbrell, W.J.: 'Law and Grace: The Nature of the Contrast in John 1:17', *Evangelical Quarterly*, Vol.LVIII No.1, January 1986.

Dunn, James D.G.: *The Epistle to the Galatians*, A & C Black, London, 1993.

Durant, Will: *The Reformation: A History of European Civilisation from Wyclif to Calvin: 1300-1564*, Simon and Schuster, New York, 1957.

Dyck, Cornelius J.: *Spiritual Life in Anabaptism*, Herald Press, Scottdale, 1995.

Eaton, Michael: *Living Under Grace: Preaching Through Romans 6:1 – 7:25*, Nelson Word Ltd., Milton Keynes, 1994.

Eaton, Michael A.: *A Theology of Encouragement*, Paternoster Press, Carlisle, 1995.

Eaton, Michael A.: *Applying God's Law*, OM Publishing, Carlisle, 1999.

Edwards, Brian H.: *Not Under Law*, Day One Publications, Bromley, 1994.

Edwards, Jonathan: *Diary*, in *The Works of Jonathan Edwards, Revised and Corrected by Edward Hickman*, Vol.1, The Banner of Truth Trust, Edinburgh, 1974.

Edwards, Jonathan: *Sermons XIII-XV: The Perpetuity and Change of the Sabbath*, in *III. Fifteen Sermons on Various Subjects*, in *The Works of Jonathan Edwards, Revised and Corrected by Edward Hickman*, Vol.2, The Banner of Truth Trust, Edinburgh, 1974.

Edwards, Jonathan: *Life and Diary of... David Brainerd*, in *The Works of Jonathan Edwards, Revised and Corrected by Edward Hickman*, Vol.2, The Banner of Truth Trust, Edinburgh, 1974.

Ella, George M.: *John Gill and the Cause of God and Truth*, Go Publications, Eggleston, 1995.

Ella, George M.: *Law & Gospel in the Theology of Andrew Fuller*, Go Publications, Eggleston, 1996.

Ella, George M.: *James Hervey: Preacher of Righteousness*, Go Publications, Eggleston, 1997.

Ella, George M.: *John Gill and Justification from Eternity: A Tercentenary Appreciation 1697-1997*, Go Publications, Eggleston, 1998.

Ella, George M.: *Mountain Movers*, Go Publications, Eggleston, 1999.

Engelsma, David J.: *The Covenant of God and the Children of Believers*, Protestant Reformed Church, South Holland, Illinois, third printing, 1993.

Erikson, Kai T.: *Wayward Puritans: A Study in the Sociology of Deviance*, John Wiley & Sons, Inc., New York, 1966.

Estep, William R.: *The Anabaptist Story*, William B.Eerdmans Publishing Company, Grand Rapids, revised edition 1975.

Evans, Curtis J.: 'The Role of the Moral Law in Thomas Shepard's Doctrine of the Sabbath', *The Westminster Theological Journal*, Vol.63, No 2, Fall 2001, Westminster Theological Seminary, Philadelphia.

Evans, Gary W.: 'Spiritual Deviations from Reformation to Regression', *Searching Together*, Spring 2001.

Fairbairn, Patrick: *The Revelation of Law in Scripture*, Alpha Publications, Indiana, 1979.

Fairbairn, Patrick: *The Typology of Scripture Viewed in Connection With The Whole Series of... The Divine Dispensations*, Evangelical Press, Welwyn, 1975.

Fee, Gordon D.: *The First Epistle to the Corinthians*, in *The New International Commentary on the New Testament*, William B.Eerdmans Publishing Company, Grand Rapids, reprinted 1991.

Fee, Gordon D.: *God's Empowering Presence: The Holy Spirit in the Letters of Paul*, Hendrickson Publishers, Peabody, Massachusetts, 1994.

Fee, Gordon D.: *1 & 2 Timothy, Titus*, Hendrickson Publishers, Peabody, Massachusetts, 1988.

Feinberg, Paul D.: 'Hermeneutics of Discontinuity', *Continuity and Discontinuity: Perspectives on the Relationship between the Old and New Testaments*, John S.Feinberg (editor), Crossway Books, Westchester, 1988.

Fisher, Edward: *The Marrow of Modern Divinity: in two parts. Part 1. The Covenant of Works and the Covenant of Grace. Part II. An Exposition of the Ten Commandments*, with notes by Thomas Boston, Still Waters Revival Books, Edmonton, Canada, reprint edition 1991.

Flavel, John: *The Method of Grace in The Gospel Redemption*, in *Works Vol.2*, The Banner of Truth Trust, Edinburgh, 1968.

Franck, Sebastian: *A Letter to John Campanus* (1531), in *Spiritual and Anabaptist Writers: Documents Illustrative of the Radical Reformation*, edited by George Huntston Williams, SCM Press Ltd., London, 1957.

Friesen, Abraham: *Erasmus, the Anabaptists, and the Great Commission*, William B.Eerdmans Publishing Company, Grand Rapids, 1998.

French, Allen: *Charles I and the Puritan Upheaval: A Study of the Causes of the Great Migration*, George Allen & Unwin Ltd., London, 1955.

Fuller, Andrew: *Dialogues and Letters Between Crispus and Gaius*, in *The Complete Works of... Andrew Fuller, With a Memoir of his Life*, edited by Andrew Gunton Fuller, Henry G.Bohn, London, 1866.

Fuller, Andrew: *Antinomianism Contrasted with the Religion Taught and Exemplified in the Holy Scriptures*, in *The Complete Works of... Andrew Fuller, With a Memoir of his Life*, edited by Andrew Gunton Fuller, Henry G.Bohn, London, 1866.

Fuller, Andrew: *The Moral Law the Rule of Conduct to Believers* in *Miscellaneous Tracts, Essays, Letters &c.*, in *The Complete Works of... Andrew Fuller, With a Memoir of his Life*, edited by Andrew Gunton Fuller, Henry G.Bohn, London, 1866.

Fuller, Andrew: *The Gospel Worthy of All Acceptation, or, The Duty of Sinners to Believe in Jesus Christ...*, in *The Complete Works of... Andrew Fuller, With a Memoir of his Life*, edited by Andrew Gunton Fuller, Henry G.Bohn, London, 1866.

Fuller, Daniel P.: *Gospel and Law: Contrast or Continuum?...*, William B.Eerdmans Publishing Company, Grand Rapids, 1980.

Gadsby, William: *The Gospel the Believer's Rule of Conduct, being A Few Remarks upon a Letter Written By Gaius...*, in *The Works of the Late Mr William Gadsby, Manchester, in Two Volumes*, Vol.1, London, 1851, the 1870 edition.

Gadsby, William: *The Present State of Religion; or, What are the People Miscalled Antinomians?...*, in *The Works of the Late Mr William Gadsby, Manchester, in Two Volumes*, Vol.1, London, 1851, the 1870 edition.

Gadsby, William: *The Perfect Law of Liberty; or, The Glory of God Revealed in the Gospel*, in *The Works of the Late Mr William Gadsby, Manchester, in Two Volumes*, Vol.1, London, 1851, the 1870 edition.

Gadsby, William: *Sermons by William Gadsby 1773-1844 with a short biography by B.A.Ramsbottom*, Gospel Standard Trust Publications, Harpenden, 1991.

Gadsby, William: *A Selection of Hymns for Public Worship,* C.J.Farncombe & Sons, Ltd., London, 1924.

Gay, David: *Battle for the Church*, Brachus, Lowestoft, 1997.

Gay, David H.J.: *Particular Redemption and the Free Offer*, Brachus, Biggleswade, 2008.

Gay, David H.J.: *Infant Baptism Tested*, Brachus, Biggleswade, 2009.

Gay, David H.J.: *Baptist Sacramentalism: A Warning to Baptists*, Brachus, Biggleswade, 2011.

Gay, David H.J.: *The Priesthood of All Believers*, Brachus, Biggleswade, 2011.

Gay, David H.J.: *Battle for the Church*, second edition, Brachus, Biggleswade, 2011.

George, Timothy: 'The Spirituality of the Radical Reformation', *Christian Spirituality: High Middle Ages and Reformation*, edited by Jill Raitt in collaboration with Bernard McGinn and John Meyendorff, SCM Press Ltd., London, 1996.

Gill, John: *A Complete Body of Doctrinal and Practical Divinity...*, W.Winterbotham, London, 1796.

Gill, John: *The Cause of God and Truth*, W.H.Collingridge, London, 1855.

Gill, John: *Gill's Commentary*, Baker Book House, Grand Rapids, 1980.

Gill, John: *Sermons and Tracts*, Old Paths Gospel Press, Choteau, 1997.

Good, Kenneth H.: *Are Baptists Reformed?*, Regular Baptist Heritage Fellowship, Lorain, Ohio, 1986.

Goodwin, Thomas: *A Discourse of the Glory of the Gospel*, in *The Works of Thomas Goodwin*, Vol.4, James Nichol, Edinburgh, 1862.

Gospel Hymns, The Strict and Particular Baptist Society, Robert Stockwell, London, 1915.

Gouge, William: *Commentary on Hebrews*, Kregel Publications, Grand Rapids, 1980.

Govett, R.: *Is The Law The Christian's Rule Of Life?*, Fletcher and Son, Norwich, Third edition, 1874.

Grebel, Conrad (and Friends): *Letters to Thomas Muntzer* (1524), in *Spiritual and Anabaptist Writers: Documents Illustrative of the Radical Reformation*, edited by George Huntston Williams, SCM Press Ltd., London, 1957.

Guthrie, Donald: *The Letter to the Hebrews: An Introduction and Commentary*, Inter-Varsity Press, Leicester, 1983.

Guthrie, William: *The Christian's Great Interest*, Publications Committee of the Free Presbyterian Church of Scotland, Glasgow, 1952.

Haldane, Robert: *Exposition of the Epistle to the Romans*, The Banner of Truth Trust, London, 1959.

Haldane, Robert: *Sanctification of the Sabbath*, in his *Exposition of the Epistle to the Romans*, The Banner of Truth Trust, London, 1959.

Harris, J.L.: *Christian Witness*, Plymouth, January 1835.

Hart, Colin: Foreword, Mackay, John L.: *The Moral Law: Its place in Scripture and its relevance today*, The Christian Institute, Newcastle upon Tyne, reprinted 2010.

Hart, Joseph: *Hart's Hymns*, Old Paths Gospel Press, Choteau, 1965.

Haykin, Michael A.G.: *Kiffin, Knollys and Keach – Rediscovering Our English Baptist Heritage*, Reformation Today Trust, Leeds, 1996.

Haynes, Carlyle B.: *The Attempt To Change God's Holy Day... From Sabbath to Sunday*, Review and Herald Publishing Association, Hagerstown, Maryland, 1928.

Helm, Paul: *Calvin and the Calvinists*, The Banner of Truth Trust, Edinburgh, 1982.

Helm, Paul: 'The Place of the Mosaic Law in Society Today', Affinity Theological Study Conference: *The End of the Law?*, February, 2009.

Hendriksen, William: *The Gospel of Matthew*, The Banner of Truth Trust, Edinburgh, 1974.

Hendriksen, William: *The Gospel of Luke*, The Banner of Truth Trust, Edinburgh, 1979.

Hendriksen, William: *A Commentary on the Gospel of John*, The Banner of Truth Trust, London, 1959.

Hendriksen, William: *Galatians*, The Banner of Truth Trust, London, 1969, reprinted 1974.

Hendriksen, William: *Ephesians*, The Banner of Truth Trust, Edinburgh, 1972.

Hendriksen, William: *A Commentary on the Epistle to the Philippians*, The Banner of Truth Trust, London, 1963.

Hendriksen, William: *Commentary on Colossians and Philemon*, The Banner of Truth Trust, Edinburgh, reprinted 1974.

Hendriksen, William: *A Commentary on I and II Thessalonians*, The Banner of Truth Trust, London, 1972.

Hendriksen, William: *A Commentary on I and II Timothy and Titus*, The Banner of Truth Trust, London, 1959.

Henry, Matthew: *An Exposition of the Old and New Testament*, James Nisbet & Co., Limited, London.

Hessey, James Augustus: *Sunday. Its Origin, History, and Present Obligation*, (Bampton Lectures 1860), John Murray, London, 1866.

Hill, Christopher: *The World Turned Upside Down: Radical Ideas during the English Revolution*, Penguin Books, London, reprinted 1991.

Hill, Christopher: 'Quakers and the English Revolution', *New Light on George Fox (1624-1691): A Collection of Essays*, edited by Michael Mullett, William Sessions Limited, York, 1993(?).

Hill, Christopher: *The Experience of Defeat: Milton and Some Contemporaries*, Bookmarks, London, 1994.

Hill, Christopher: *Liberty Against The Law: Some Seventeenth-Century Controversies*, Allen Lane: The Penguin Press, London, 1996.

Hill, Christopher: 'Freethinking and Libertinism', Christopher Hill: *England's Turning Point: Essays on 17th Century English History*, Bookmarks, London, 1998.

Hoch, Carl B., Jr.: 'The New Covenant: Its Problems, Certainties and Some Proposals', *Reformation & Revival Journal*, editor John H.Armstrong, Reformation & Revival Ministries, Inc., Carol Stream, Vol.6, Number 3, Summer 1997.

Hodge, A.A.: *Outlines of Theology*, The Banner of Truth Trust, London, 1972.

Hodge, Charles: *A Commentary on Romans*, The Banner of Truth Trust, London, 1972.

Hodge, Charles: *A Commentary on the Epistle to the Ephesians*, The Banner of Truth Trust, London, 1964.

Hoekema, Anthony A.: *Created in God's Image*, William B.Eerdmans Publishing Company, Grand Rapids, 1986.

Hofmann, Melchior: *The Ordinance of God* (1530), in *Spiritual and Anabaptist Writers: Documents Illustrative of the Radical Reformation*, edited by George Huntston Williams, SCM Press Ltd., London, 1957.

Hong, In-Gyu: 'Being "Under the Law" in Galatians', *Evangelical Review of Theology*, Paternoster, Nottingham, 2002.

Horn, Robert M.: 'Thomas Hooker – The Soul's Preparation for Christ', The Westminster Conference, 1976: *The Puritan Experiment in the New World*, The Westminster Conference.

Horton, Michael: 'Law and Gospel: Contrast or Continuity', Affinity Theological Study Conference: *The End of the Law?*, February, 2009.

Howe, Daniel Wait: *The Puritan Republic of Massachusetts Bay in New England*, The Bowen-Merrill Company, Indianapolis, 1899.

Hubmaier, Balthasar: *On Free Will* (1527), in *Spiritual and Anabaptist Writers: Documents Illustrative of the Radical Reformation*, edited by George Huntston Williams, SCM Press Ltd., London, 1957.

Hubner, Hans: *Law in Paul's Thought: A Contribution to the Development of Pauline Theology*, T.&T.Clark, Edinburgh, 1986.

Hughes, Philip: *A Popular History of the Reformation*, Hollis & Carter, London, 1957.

Hulse, Erroll: *The Restoration of Israel,* Henry E.Walter Ltd., Worthing, 1968.

Hulse, Erroll: *Sunday*, a tract published by *Reformation Today*, Haywards Heath.

Hulse, Erroll: *The Believer's Experience*, Carey Publications, Haywards Heath.

Hulse, Erroll: 'The 1689 Confession – Its History and Role Today', Paul Clarke and others: *Our Baptist Heritage*, Reformation Today Trust, Leeds, 1993.

Hulse, Erroll: 'What is Covenant Theology?', *Reformation Today*, Leeds, 1980.

Hulse, Erroll: *The Puritans*, Evangelical Press, Darlington, 2000.

Hutcheson, George: *The Gospel of John*, The Banner of Truth Trust, London, 1972.

Jackson, Douglas MacG.,: *The Sanctity of Life*, The Tyndale Press for the Christian Medical Fellowship, London, 1962.

Johnstone, Robert: *Lectures on the Epistle to the Philippians*, Klock & Klock, Minneapolis, 1977.

Johnstone, Robert: *A Commentary on James*, The Banner of Truth Trust, Edinburgh, 1977.

Karlberg, Mark W.: 'Paul, the Old Testament and Judaism: A Review Article', *Foundations*, FIEC, No.43, Autumn 1999.

Kautz, Jakob: *Seven Theses*, edited by Manfred Krebs, 1951.

Kendall, R.T.: *Calvin and English Calvinism to 1649*, Paternoster Press, 1997.

Kennedy, D.James: *How Do I Live for God?*, Fleming H.Revell, Grand Rapids, 1995.

Kent, Homer A.: *The Pastoral Epistles. Studies in I and II Timothy and Titus*, Moody Press, Chicago, Tenth Printing, 1978.

Kevan, Ernest: *The Law of God in Christian Experience: A Study in the Epistle to the Galatians*, Pickering and Inglis Ltd., London, 1955.

Kevan, Ernest: *The Evangelical Doctrine of Law*, The Tyndale Press, London, 1956.

Kevan, Ernest: *The Grace of Law: A Study in Puritan Theology*, The Carey Kingsgate Press, London, 1964.

Kevan, Ernest: *Moral Law*, Sovereign Grace Publishers, Grand Rapids, 1971.

Kingdon, David: 'Church Discipline Among the Anabaptists', *The Way Ahead*, the Carey Conference, 1975.

Klassen, Walter: 'Anabaptist Studies', *Radical Reformation Reader: Concern No.18*, 1971.

Klassen, Walter: 'Radical Reformation', *Radical Reformation Reader: Concern No.18*, 1971.

Klassen, Walter: *Anabaptism: Neither Catholic Nor Protestant*, Conrad Press, 1973.

Kring, Stephen: 'The Superior Covenant', *Reformation & Revival Journal*, editor John H.Armstrong, Reformation & Revival Ministries, Inc., Carol Stream, Vol.6, Number 3, Summer 1997.

Kruse, Colin G.: *Paul, The Law and Justification*, Hendrickson Publishers, Peabody, Massachusetts, 1997.

Laicus: *Romans VII: What Does It Teach?*, S.W.Partridge & Co., London, 1875.

Latourette, Kenneth Scott: *A History of Christianity*, HarperSanFrancisco, 1975.

Lee, N.: *The Sabbath in the Bible*, LDOS, London.

Letham, Robert: 'The Concept of Covenant in the History of Theology', *Affinity Theological Study Conference: The End of the Law?*, February, 2009.

Levy, Leonard W. and Young, Alfred: Foreword, *Puritan Political Ideas 1558-1794*, edited by Edmund S. Morgan, The Bobbs-Merrill Company, Inc., Indianapolis, 1965.

Lewis, C.S.: *Mere Christianity*, in *Selected Books*, HarperCollins, London, 1999.

Lewis, C.S.: *Reflections on the Psalms*, in *Selected Books*, HarperCollins, London, 1999.

Lightfoot, J.B.: *...Paul's Epistle to the Galatians: A Revised Text with Introduction, Notes, and Dissertations*, Macmillan and Co., London, 1890.

Lightfoot, J.B.: *...Paul's Epistle to the Philippians: A Revised Text with Introduction, Notes, and Dissertations*, Macmillan and Co., London, 1891.

Liversidge, J.H.: *Progress: A Study in Christian Living*, Japan Evangelistic Band, London, 1973.

Lloyd-Jones, D.Martyn: *Studies in the Sermon on the Mount*, Inter-Varsity Fellowship, London, 1960.

Lloyd-Jones, D.Martyn: *Romans: An Exposition of Chapter 1. The Gospel of God*, The Banner of Truth Trust, Edinburgh, 1985.

Lloyd-Jones, D.Martyn: *Romans: An Exposition of Chapters 2:1 – 3:20. The Righteous Judgement of God*, The Banner of Truth Trust, Edinburgh, 1972.

Lloyd-Jones, D.Martyn: *Romans: An Exposition of Chapters 3:20 – 4:25. Atonement and Justification*, The Banner of Truth Trust, London, 1971.

Lloyd-Jones, D.Martyn: *Romans: An Exposition of Chapter 5. Assurance*, The Banner of Truth Trust, London, 1971.

Lloyd-Jones, D.Martyn: *Romans: An Exposition of Chapter 6. The New Man*, The Banner of Truth Trust, Edinburgh, 1972.

Lloyd-Jones, D.Martyn: *Romans: An Exposition of Chapters 7:1 – 8:4. The Law: Its Function and Limits*, The Banner of Truth Trust, Edinburgh, 1973.

Lloyd-Jones, D.Martyn: *Romans: An Exposition of Chapter 8:5-17. The Sons of God*, The Banner of Truth Trust, Edinburgh, 1974.

Lloyd-Jones, D.Martyn: *Romans: An Exposition of Chapter 8:17-39. The Final Perseverance of the Saints*, The Banner of Truth Trust, Edinburgh, 1975.

Lloyd-Jones, D.Martyn: *God's Way of Reconciliation: Studies in Ephesians 2*, Evangelical Press, London, 1972.

Lloyd-Jones, D.Martyn: *The Unsearchable Riches of Christ: An Exposition of Ephesians 3:1 to 21*, The Banner of Truth Trust, Edinburgh, 1979.

Lloyd-Jones, D.Martyn: *Life in the Spirit*, Kingsway Publications Ltd., Eastbourne, 1996.

Lloyd-Jones, D.M.: *The Puritans: The Origins and Successors: Addresses delivered at The Puritan and Westminster Conferences 1959-1978*, The Banner of Truth Trust, Edinburgh, 1991.

Lloyd-Jones, D.Martyn: *Expository Sermons on 2 Peter*, The Banner of Truth Trust, Edinburgh, 1983.

Longenecker, Richard N.: 'The Pedagogical Nature of the Law in Galatians 3:19 – 4:7', *The Journal of the Evangelical Theological Society*, March 1982, (etsjets.org).

Lumpkin, William L.: *Baptist Confessions of Faith*, Judson Press, Valley Forge, revised edition 1969.

Luther, Martin: *A Commentary on... Paul's Epistle to the Galatians*, James Clarke and Co., Ltd., London, reprinted 1961.

Machen, J.Gresham: *Machen's Notes on Galatians: Notes on Biblical Exposition and Other Aids to the Interpretation of the Epistle to the Galatians From the Writings of J.Gresham Machen*, John H.Skilton (ed.), Presbyterian and Reformed Publishing Co., New Jersey, 1977.

Mackay, John L.: *The Moral Law: Its place in Scripture and its relevance today*, The Christian Institute, Newcastle upon Tyne, reprinted 2010.

Macleod, Donald: 'Luther and Calvin on the Place of the Law', The Westminster Conference, 1974: *Living the Christian Life*, The Westminster Conference.

Macleod, Donald: 'God or god? Arianism, Ancient and Modern', *The Evangelical Quarterly*, April-June, 1996.

Macleod, John: *Scottish Theology in Relation to Church History since the Reformation*, The Banner of Truth Trust, Edinburgh, 1974.

Manton, Thomas: *Sermons Upon John XVII*, Sovereign Grace Publishers, Wilmington, 1972.

Manton, Thomas: *An Exposition on the Epistle of James*, The Banner of Truth Trust, London, 1962.

Marbury, Edward: *Obadiah and Habakkuk*, Klock & Klock, Minneapolis, 1979.

Masters, Peter: 'Privilege Of The Help Of The Holy Spirit', *Sword and Trowel*, issue number 1, The Metropolitan Tabernacle, London, 2011.

Mather, Cotton: *The Great Works of Christ in America: Magnalia Christi Americana*, The Banner of Truth Trust, Edinburgh, 1979.

McClain, Alva J.: *Law And Grace: A Study of New Testament Concepts as They Relate to the Christian Life*, Moody Press, Chicago, 1967.

M'Cheyne, Robert Murray: *Sermons of Robert Murray M'Cheyne*, The Banner of Truth Trust, London, 1961.

Miller, Perry: *The New England Mind: From Colony to Province*, Beacon Press, Boston, 1961.

Moo, Douglas J.: 'The Law of Moses or the Law of Christ', *Continuity and Discontinuity: Perspectives on the Relationship between the Old and New Testaments*, John S.Feinberg (editor), Crossway Books, Westchester, 1988.

Moo, Douglas J.: *The Epistle to the Romans*, William B.Eerdmans Publishing Company, Grand Rapids, 1996.

Moo, Douglas J.: 'The Covenants and the Mosaic Law: The View from Galatians', Affinity Theological Study Conference: *The End of the Law?*, February, 2009.

Morden, Peter: *John Bunyan: The People's Pilgrim*, CWR, Farnham, 2013.

Morgan, Edmund S.: *The Puritan Dilemma. The Story of John Winthrop*, Little, Brown and Company, Boston, 1958.

Morgan, Edmund S.: *Visible Saints: The History of a Puritan Idea*, Cornell University Press, Ithaca, 1963.

Morris, Leon: *The First Epistle of Paul to the Corinthians: An Introduction and Commentary*, The Tyndale Press, London, 1963.

Mosheim, John Lawrence: *An Ecclesiastical History...*, Thomas Tegg and Son, London, 1838.

Murray, Iain H.: *The Life of Arthur W.Pink: His Life and Thought*, The Banner of Truth Trust, Edinburgh, 1981.

Murray, Iain H.: *D.Martyn Lloyd-Jones: The Fight of Faith 1939-1981*, The Banner of Truth Trust, Edinburgh, 1990.

Murray, John: *The Sanctity of the Moral Law*, in *Collected Writings of John Murray, Volume 1: The Claims of Truth*, The Banner of Truth Trust, Edinburgh, 1976.

Murray, John: *The Adamic Administration*, in *Collected Writings of John Murray, Volume 2: Systematic Theology*, The Banner of Truth Trust, Edinburgh, 1977.

Murray, John: *The Epistle to the Romans...*, Two Volumes in One, Marshall Morgan and Scott, London, 1974.

Murray, Stuart: *Biblical Interpretation in the Anabaptist Tradition*, Pandora Press, Kitchener, Ontario, 2000.

Naylor, Peter: *Picking up a Pin for the Lord: English Particular Baptists from 1688 to the Early Nineteenth Century*, Grace Publications, London, 1992.

Nelson, P.G.: 'Christian Morality: Jesus' teaching on the Law', *Themelios*, October 2006.

Nettles, Thomas J.: *By His Grace And For His Glory: A Historical, Theological, and Practical Study of the Doctrines of Grace in Baptist Life*, Baker Book House, Grand Rapids, 1990.

Source List

New Focus, Go Publications, Eggleston, August/September 1999, Vol.4 No.2.

Newton, Benjamin Wills: *The First and Second Chapters of the Epistle to the Romans Considered...*, Sovereign Grace Advent Testimony Movement, London.

Nuttall, Geoffrey F.: 'Introduction: George Fox and his Journal', *The Journal of George Fox*, a revised edition by John L.Nickalls, Religious Society of Friends, London, reprinted 1986.

Oliver, Robert William: 'The Emergence of a Strict and Particular Baptist Community among the English Calvinistic Baptists 1770-1850', an unpublished PhD. thesis, London Bible College, 1986.

Onions, C.T., reviser and editor: *The Shorter Oxford Dictionary on Historical Principles*, Guild Publishing, London, reprinted 1988.

Owen, John: *The Doctrine of Justification by Faith...*, in *The Works of John Owen*, Vol.1, edited by William H.Goold, The Banner of Truth Trust, London, 1967.

Owen, John: *A Discourse Concerning the Holy Spirit*, in *The Works of John Owen*, Vol.3, edited by William H.Goold, The Banner of Truth Trust, London, 1966.

Owen, John: *An Exposition Upon Psalm 130*, in *The Works of John Owen*, Vol.6, edited by William H.Goold, The Banner of Truth Trust, London, 1966.

Owen, John: *A Treatise of the Dominion of Sin and Grace; Wherein Sin's Reign is Discovered... How the Law Supports it; How Grace Delivers from it...*, in *The Works of John Owen*, Vol.7, edited by William H.Goold, The Banner of Truth Trust, London, 1965.

Owen, John: *Indices...*, in *The Works of John Owen*, Vol.16, edited by William H.Goold, The Banner of Truth Trust, London, 1968.

Owen, John: *An Exposition of Hebrews*, 7 Volumes in 4, Vol.3, Sovereign Grace Publishers, Evansville 13, Indiana, 1960.

Owen, John: *Exercitations Concerning the Name, Original, Nature, Use, and Continuance of a Day of Sacred Rest, Wherein the Original of the Sabbath from the Foundation of the World, the Morality of the Fourth Commandment, with the Change of the Seventh Day, are Inquired into; together with an Assertion of the Divine Institution of the Lord's Day, and Practical Directions for its Due Observance*, 1671.

Packer, J.I.: 'The Puritan View of Preaching the Gospel', The Puritan and Reformed Studies Conference, December 1959, *How Shall They Hear?*, London, 1960.

Packer, J.I.: *Our Lord's Understanding of the Law of God*, The Campbell Morgan Lecture, 1962, Westminster Chapel.

Packer, J.I.: *Among God's Giants: Aspects of Puritan Christianity*, Kingsway Publications, Eastbourne, 1991.

Parnham, David: 'Motions of Law and Grace: The Puritan in the Antinomian', *Westminster Theological Journal*, Spring, 2008.

Payne, Ernest A.: *The Fellowship of Believers. Baptist Thought and Practice Yesterday and Today*, The Carey Kingsgate Press, London, 1952.

Pettit, Norman: *The Heart Prepared: Grace and Conversion in Puritan Spiritual Life*, Yale University Press, New Haven and London, 1966.

Philpot, J.C.: Three letters to 'a minister in Scotland' under Romans 7:4, *The Gospel Standard*, February 1, March 1 and May 1, 1861. Republished as Philpot, J.C.: *Dead to the Law: A Series of Letters on the Believer's relationship to the Law*, The Huntingtonian Press, Southampton, March 2000.

Philpot, J.C: *Meditations on Matters of Christian Faith and Experience*, First Series, J.Gadsby, London, 1875(?).

Philips, Dietrich: *The Church of God* (c.1560), in *Spiritual and Anabaptist Writers: Documents Illustrative of the Radical Reformation*, edited by George Huntston Williams, SCM Press Ltd., London, 1957.

Pink, A.W.: *Exposition of the Gospel of John*, Zondervan, Grand Rapids, 1968.

Pink, Arthur W.: *The Law and the Saint*, Evangelical Press, Welwyn.

Pink, Arthur W.: *An Exposition of the Sermon on the Mount*, Baker Book House, Grand Rapids, 1974.

Pipa, Joseph A.: *The Lord's Day*, Christian Focus, Fearn, 1997.

Plumer, William S.: *Commentary on Romans*, Kregel Publications, Grand Rapids, 1971.

Plumer, William S.: *Commentary on the Epistle of Paul, the Apostle, to the Hebrews*, Baker Book House, Grand Rapids, reprinted 1980.

Poole, Matthew: *A Commentary on the Holy Bible*, Vol.3, The Banner of Truth Trust, Edinburgh, reprinted 1975.

Psalms and Hymns and Spiritual Songs, Selected 1978, Believers Bookshelf Inc., Sunbury, Pa., 1987.

Rainsford, M.: *Lectures on... John XVII*, John Hoby, London.

Reformation & Revival Journal, editor John H.Armstrong, Reformation & Revival Ministries, Inc., Carol Stream, Vol.6, Number 3, Summer 1997.

Reformation Today, Leeds, March-April 2012.

Reisinger, John G.: *The Law/Grace Controversy*, A Prothumian Booklet (Acts 17:11), 1982.

Reisinger, John G.: *Tablets of Stone*, Crown Publications, Inc., Southbridge, Massachusetts, 1989.

Reisinger, John G.: 'An Open Letter to Dr R.C.Sproul', *Sound of Grace*, Frederick, Vol.9 number 4, February 2003.

Reymond, Robert L.: *Paul, Missionary Theologian: A Survey of his Missionary Labours and Theology*, Christian Focus Publications, Fearn, 2000.

Reymond, Robert L.: *Contending for the Faith...*, Mentor, Fearn, 2005.

Richardson, Peter: *Israel in the Apostolic Church*, The University Press, Cambridge, 1969.

Ridderbos, Herman N.: *The Epistle of Paul to the Churches of Galatia: The English Text with Introduction, Exposition and Notes*, Wm.B.Eerdmans Publishing Co., Grand Rapids, reprinted 1981.

Roberts, Maurice: 'Three Forms of Law', *The Banner of Truth*, December 2006.

Robertson, O.Palmer: 'Hermeneutics of Continuity', *Continuity and Discontinuity: Perspectives on the Relationship between the Old and New Testaments*, John S.Feinberg (editor), Crossway Books, Westchester, 1988.

Ruether, Rosemary Radford & Keller, Rosemary Skinner (General Editors): *Women & Religion in America*, Volume 2, *The Colonial and Revolutionary Periods. A Documentary History*, Harper & Row, San Francisco, 1983.

Rushdooney, Rousas John: *The Institutes of Biblical Law*, The Presbyterian and Reformed Publishing Company, 1973.

Ryle, J.C.: *Expository Thoughts on the Gospels: Luke*, James Clarke & Co. Ltd., London, 1956.

Ryle, J.C.: *Expository Thoughts on the Gospels: John*, The Banner of Truth Trust, Edinburgh, 1987.

Sanday, William and Headlam, Arthur: *A Critical and Exegetical Commentary on the Epistle to the Romans*, T.&T.Clark, Edinburgh, fourth edition 1900.

Sattler, Michael: *Concerning the Satisfaction of Christ*, introduced and translated by J.C.Wenger: *Mennonite Quarterly Review*, XX, 1946.

Schaff, Philip: *History of the Christian* Church, Hendrickson, Peabody, Massachusetts, 1996.

Schreiner, Thomas R.: *40 Questions About Christians and Biblical Law*, Kregel, Grand Rapids, 2010.

Sears, Septimus: 'Sermons by the Editor', number LXXXVIII on John 6:45, 'Divine Teaching and Its Results', *The Sower*, May 1877.

Sell, Alan P.F.: *The Great Debate*, H.E.Walter Ltd., Worthing, 1982.

Servetus, Michael: *Thirty Letters to Calvin...*, translated by Hoffman, Christopher and Hiller, Marian, The Edwin Mellen Press, Lampeter, 2010.

Shaw, Robert: *The Reformed Faith: An Exposition of the Westminster Confession of Faith*, Christian Focus Publications, Inverness, reprinted 1974.

Shepard, Thomas: *The Church Membership of Children*, Iain Murray: *The Reformation of the Church: A Collection of Reformed and Puritan Documents on Church Issues*, selected with introductory notes, The Banner of Truth Trust, London, 1965.

Sibbes, Richard: *The Bruised Reed and Smoking Flax*, in *Works of Richard Sibbes*, Vol.1, The Banner of Truth Trust, Edinburgh, 1973.

Sibbes, Richard: *The Ungodly's Misery*, in *Works of Richard Sibbes*, Vol.1, The Banner of Truth Trust, Edinburgh, 1973.

Sibbes, Richard: *The Excellency of the Gospel Above the Law*, in *Works of Richard Sibbes*, Vol.4, The Banner of Truth Trust, Edinburgh, 1983.

Sibbes, Richard: *Lydia's Conversion*, in *Works of Richard Sibbes*, Vol.6, The Banner of Truth Trust, Edinburgh, 1983.

Silva, Moisés: *Explorations in Exegetical Methods: Galatians as a Test Case*, Baker Books, Michigan, 1996.

Simon, Edith: *Luther Alive: Martin Luther and the Making of the Reformation*, Hodder and Stoughton, London.

Simons, Menno: *"Confession" and the New Birth: The New Birth and Who They Are Who Have the Promise*, translated and edited by Irvin B.Horst, Lancaster Mennonite Historical Society, Lancaster, PA, 1996.

Snyder, Arnold: *The (Not-So) 'Simple Confession' of the Late Sixteenth-Century Swiss Brethren. Part II: The Evolution of Separatist Anabaptism*, Mennonite Quarterly Review, January 2000, LXXIV Number One.

Sproul, R.C.: *The Soul's Quest for God*, Tyndale House, Wheaton, 1992.

Spurgeon, C.H.: *New Park Street Pulpit...*, Vol.1, The Banner of Truth Trust, London, 1963.

Spurgeon, C.H.: *New Park Street Pulpit...*, Vol.2, The Banner of Truth Trust, London, 1963.

Spurgeon, C.H.: *New Park Street Pulpit...*, Vol.3, The Banner of Truth Trust, London, 1964.

Spurgeon, C.H.: *The New Park Street Pulpit...*, Vol.6, The Banner of Truth Trust, London, 1964.

Spurgeon, C.H.: *The Metropolitan Tabernacle Pulpit...*, Vol.9, Passmore and Alabaster, London, 1864.

Spurgeon, C.H.: *The Metropolitan Tabernacle Pulpit...*, Vol.12, Passmore and Alabaster, London, 1867.

Spurgeon, C.H.: *The Metropolitan Tabernacle Pulpit...*, Vol.15, Passmore and Alabaster, London, 1870.

Spurgeon, C.H.: *The Metropolitan Tabernacle Pulpit...*, Vol.20, Passmore and Alabaster, London, 1875.

Spurgeon, C.H.: *The Metropolitan Tabernacle Pulpit...*, Vol.28, The Banner of Truth Trust, London, 1971.

Spurgeon, C.H.: *The Metropolitan Tabernacle Pulpit...*, Vol.32, The Banner of Truth Trust, London, 1969.

Spurgeon, C.H.: *The Metropolitan Tabernacle Pulpit...*, Vol.33, The Banner of Truth Trust, London, 1969.

Spurgeon, C.H.: *The Metropolitan Tabernacle Pulpit...*, Vol.34, Passmore and Alabaster, London, 1889.

Spurgeon, C.H.: *The Metropolitan Tabernacle Pulpit...*, Vol.35, The Banner of Truth Trust, London, 1970.

Spurgeon, C.H.: *Commenting & Commentaries*, The Banner of Truth Trust, London, 1969.

Spurgeon, C.H.: *Lectures to my Students*, Second Series, Passmore and Alabaster, London, 1885.

Steele, Anne: *Hymns*, Gospel Standard Trust, London, 1967.

Stott, John R.W.: *The Letters of John: An Introduction and Commentary*, Inter-Varsity Press, Leicester, 1995.

Stout, Harry S.: *The New England Soul: Preaching and Religious Culture in Colonial New England*, Oxford University Press, 1986.

Strickland, Don: 'E.F.Kevan, Samuel Petto and Covenant Theology', *Reformation Today*, No.137, Jan-Feb 1994.

Taylor, Thomas: *An Exposition of Titus*, Christian Classics, Grand Rapids, first published in London, 1658.

Tasker, R.V.G.: *The Gospel according to... John*, The Tyndale Press, London, 1961.

Thackway, John P.: 'The Ten Commandments – Rome and Us: 1', *Bible League Quarterly*, number 407, October- December 2001.

Thayer, Joseph Henry: *A Greek-English Lexicon of the New Testament*, Baker Book House, Grand Rapids, Ninth Printing 1991.

The Answer of the Assembly of Divines to the Reasons of the Dissenting Brethren, 1648, Ronald E.Diprose: *Israel in the Development of Christian Thought*, Instituto Biblico Evangelico Italiano, Rome, 2000.

The Baptist Confession of Faith of 1689.

The Mennonite Encyclopaedia Vol.4.

The New International Dictionary of the Christian Church, J.D.Douglas (general editor), The Paternoster Press, Exeter, 1974.

The Westminster Confession of Faith, The Publications Committee of the Free Presbyterian Church of Scotland, 1967.

The Westminster Larger Catechism, The Publications Committee of the Free Presbyterian Church of Scotland, 1967.

The Westminster Shorter Catechism, The Publications Committee of the Free Presbyterian Church of Scotland, 1967.

Thielman, Frank: *The Law and the New Testament: The Question of Continuity*, The Crossroad Publishing Company, New York, 1999.

Thomas, Geoffrey: 'Becoming a Christian – Covenant Theology: A Historical Survey', The Westminster Conference, 1972: *Becoming a Christian*, The Westminster Conference.

Thompson, Ian H.: *Chiasmus in the Pauline Letters*, Sheffield Academic Press, Sheffield, 1995.

Thompson, Michael B.: *The New Perspective on Paul*, Grove Books Limited, Cambridge, 2002.

Tow, Timothy: *The Law of Moses and of Jesus*, Christian Life Publishers, Singapore, 1986.

Tozer, A.W.: *The Divine Conquest*, Oliphants, London, 1964.

Tozer, A.W.: *The Root of the Righteous*, OM Publishing, Carlisle, 1996.

Traill, Robert: *A Vindication of the Protestant Doctrine concerning Justification, and of its Preachers and Professors, from the Unjust Charge of Antinomianism...*, in *Select Practical Writings of Robert Traill*, The Assembly's Committee, Edinburgh, 1845.

Trench, Richard Chenevix: *Synonyms of the New Testament*, Macmillan and Co., London, ninth edition, improved, 1880.

Tyndale, William: *A Prologue Upon the Epistle of... Paul to the Romans*, in *Writings of... William Tindal, Translator of the Scripture, and Martyr, AD 1536*, originally published by The Religious Tract Society, London, Focus Christian Ministries Trust, Lewes, 1986.

VanGemeren, Willem: 'Systems of Continuity', *Continuity and Discontinuity: Perspectives on the Relationship between the Old and New Testaments*, John S.Feinberg (editor), Crossway Books, Westchester, 1988.

Verduin, Leonard: *The Reformers and Their Stepchildren*, The Paternoster Press, Exeter, 1964.

Verduin, Leonard: *The Anatomy of a Hybrid: A Study in Church-State Relationships*, The Christian Harmony Publishers, Sarasota, 1992.

Vincent, M.R.: *Word Studies in the New Testament*, Macdonald Publishing Company, Florida.

Wakefield, Gordon: 'Puritans and Methodists', Peter Cornwell (ed.): *Prejudice in Religion: Can we move beyond it?*, Geoffrey Chapman, London, 1997.

Walker, Williston: *A History of the Christian Church*, T.&T.Clark, Edinburgh, 1959.

Watson, Thomas: *The Ten Commandments*, The Banner of Truth Trust, London, 1959.

Watts, Malcolm: 'The Permanence and Glory of the Moral Law', *Sword and Trowel*, 1993 No.3, The Metropolitan Tabernacle, London.

Watts, Michael R.: *The Dissenters*, Clarendon Press, Oxford, 1978.

We Believe: Strict Baptist Affirmation of Faith 1966, second edition 1973.

Wells, Tom: 'What is This Thing called the New Covenant?', *Reformation & Revival Journal*, editor John H.Armstrong, Reformation & Revival Ministries, Inc., Carol Stream, Vol.6, Number 3, Summer 1997.

Wendel, Francois: *Calvin: The Origins and Development of his Religious Thought*, Collins, London, 1963.

Wenger, John C.: 'Biblicism of the Anabaptists', *The Recovery of the Anabaptist Vision*, Editor Guy F.Horschberger, Herald Press, Scottdale, 1957.

Wesson, John: 'Sunday, Puzzling Sunday', *Christian Graduate*, IVF, London, September 1973.

Westerholm, Stephen: *Perspectives Old and New on Paul: The 'Lutheran' Paul and His Critics*, Wm.B.Eerdmans Publishing Co., Grand Rapids, 2004.

White, B.R.: *The English Baptists of the 17th Century*, The Baptist Historical Society, London, 1983.

Whitefield, George: *Sermons on Important Subjects by... George Whitefield*, Thomas Tegg & Son, London, 1838.

Whitefield, George: *Select Sermons of George Whitefield*, The Banner of Truth Trust, London, 1959.

Whittingham, Richard: *The Works of... John Berridge...*, Simpkin, Marshall, and Company; and Frazer, Potton, 1838, can be seen in Google Books.

Williams, George Huntston: *Spiritual and Anabaptist Writers: Documents Illustrative of the Radical Reformation*, SCM Press Ltd., London, 1957.

Williams, George Huntston: *The Radical Reformation*, Weidenfeld and Nicolson, London, 1962.

Witherington III, Ben: *Grace in Galatia: A Commentary on... Paul's Letter to the Galatians*, T.&T.Clark, Edinburgh, 1998.

Wright, George: *Memorials of George Wright, for forty-eight years pastor of the Baptist church at Beccles*, compiled by Samuel K.Bland, Elliot Stock, London, 1875.

Wright, N.T.: *The Climax of the Covenant: Christ and Law in Pauline Theology*, Fortress Press, Minneapolis, 1993.

Yoder, John Howard: 'The Recovery of the Anabaptist Vision', *Radical Reformation Reader: Concern No.18*, 1971.

Young, Edward J.: *The Book of Isaiah*, The English Text, with Introduction, Exposition, and Notes, William B.Eerdmans Publishing Company, Grand Rapids, 1977.

Zaspel, Fred G.: 'Divine Law: A New-Covenant Perspective', *Reformation & Revival Journal*, editor John H.Armstrong, Reformation & Revival Ministries, Inc., Carol Stream, Vol.6, Number 3, Summer 1997.

Zens, Jon: 'Is There a Covenant of Grace?' & 'Crucial Thoughts on "Law" in the New Covenant', *Searching Together*, St. Croix Falls, Part 1 p3. (These two articles originally appeared in *Baptist Reformation Review*, 6:3, 1977; 7:1, 1978).

Zens, Jon: *Studies in Theology and Ethics*, BREM, INC.,1981.

Zins, Robert M.: *On the Edge of Apostasy: The Evangelical Romance with Rome*, White Horse Publications, Huntsville, Alabama, 1998.

Printed in Great Britain
by Amazon